FRAN

BUS

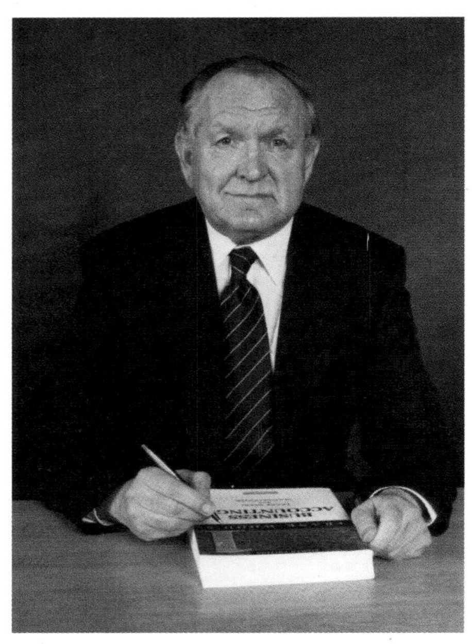

Frank Wood

1926–2000

# FRANK WOOD'S BUSINESS ACCOUNTING 2

THIRTEENTH EDITION

**ALAN SANGSTER** BA, MSc, PhD, Cert TESOL, CA

Formerly authored by Frank Wood BSc (Econ), FCA

PEARSON

Harlow, England • London • New York • Boston • San Francisco • Toronto • Sydney • Auckland • Singapore • Hong Kong
Tokyo • Seoul • Taipei • New Delhi • Cape Town • São Paulo • Mexico City • Madrid • Amsterdam • Munich • Paris • Milan

**Pearson Education Limited**

Edinburgh Gate
Harlow CM20 2JE
United Kingdom
Tel: +44 (0)1279 623623
Web: www.pearson.com/uk

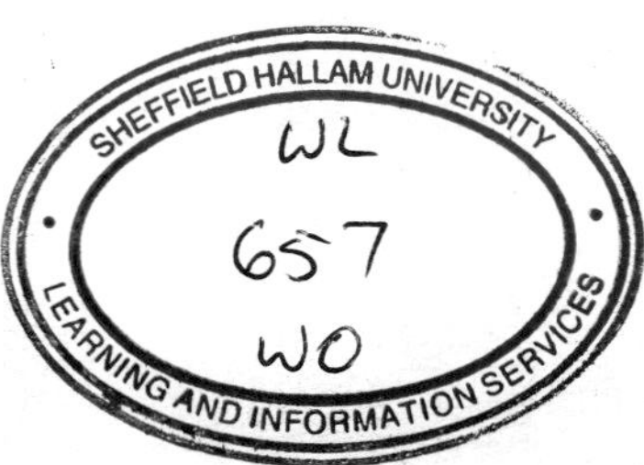


First edition published 1967
Second edition published under the Longman imprint in 1972
Third edition published 1979
Fourth edition published 1984
Fifth edition published 1989
Sixth edition published 1993
Seventh edition published 1996
Eighth edition published under the Financial Times Pitman Publishing imprint in 1999
Ninth edition published 2002
Tenth edition published 2005
Revised tenth edition published 2007
Eleventh edition published 2008
Twelfth edition published 2012
**Thirteenth edition published 2016 (print and electronic)**



ISBN: 978-1-292-08505-0 (print)
978-1-292-08510-4 (PDF)
978-1-292-08507-4 (eText)
978-1-292-08508-1 (ePub)

**British Library Cataloguing-in-Publication Data**
A catalogue record for the print edition is available from the British Library

**Library of Congress Cataloging-in-Publication Data**
A catalog record for the print edition is available from the Library of Congress

10 9 8 7 6 5 4 3 2 1
19 18 17 16 15

Front cover image: Getty Images

Print edition typeset in 9.5/11.5pt Sabon LT Pro by 71
Printed and bound by L.E.G.O. S.p.A., Italy

NOTE THAT ANY PAGE CROSS REFERENCES REFER TO THE PRINT EDITION

# Contents

## part 10 Planning, control and decision-making



## Appendices



## Supporting resources

Visit www.pearsoned.co.uk/Wood to find valuable online resources

**For instructors**

- Complete Solutions Manual for answers within the book
- PowerPoint slides that can be downloaded and used for presentations

# Dedication

For Aparecida who thinks this is what it is not and not what it is.

# Notes for teachers and lecturers

This textbook has been written so that a very thorough introduction to accounting is covered in two volumes. The split into two volumes is made in recognition of the fact that many students new to accounting will find all that they require in *Frank Wood's Business Accounting 1*.

This second volume completes the coverage of the financial accounting and management accounting parts of many examinations in accounting and should be suitable for anyone studying intermediate and final level financial accounting or anyone studying management accounting at introductory and intermediate levels on courses at school, college, or university; or studying for qualifications from the LCCI, Association of Accounting Technicians, the Institute of Secretaries and Administrators; or for qualifications of any of the six UK and Irish Chartered Accountancy bodies.

As examination syllabuses are constantly being revised, it would not make sense to be too specific as to which chapters would be needed by students taking each of the various examinations. However, **Financial Accounting and Financial Reporting are covered in Chapters 1–39 and Management Accounting is covered in Chapters 40–51**.

While management accounting has evolved to a point where changes in practice are limited, and the double entry method of bookkeeping and the fundamentals of financial accounting have long been established, the same is not true of financial reporting. Far from being the never-changing subject many perceive it to be, it is in a constant state of change. The current major ongoing change, begun in 2005 and still ongoing, is the switch from domestic accounting rules to international rules. Specifically, the rules that had been developed in the UK since 1970, known as Statements of Standard Accounting Practice (SSAPs) and Financial Reporting Standards (FRSs), are being phased out. In their place most businesses are now using International GAAP, i.e. International Financial Reporting Standards (IFRSs) and International Accounting Standards (IASs).

Some small and medium-sized businesses continue to use UK standards. These were consolidated and revised in 2013 and 2014 and now have simpler requirements more in keeping (in terms of length and detail, but not in substance) with those issued under International GAAP. It now seems only a matter of time before all businesses will be using International GAAP.

A number of changes have been made in this new edition, some topics have moved within the book, some new ones have been added, and all the content has been updated. Major changes include:

- The term 'Income statement' has been replaced throughout with, 'Statement of profit or loss'. This is in line with the IFRS. The change was requested by a number of users of the book who felt it more appropriate, not simply because it was recommended by the IASB, but because it reflected more accurately the content of the statement.
- Chapter 2 has been retitled *Purchases by instalments* to better reflect its contents.
- Chapter 11 has been renamed *Accounting standards, related documents and accounting ethics*. It has been updated to incorporate international standards in issue in February 2015 and a new section, 11.49, *Professional ethics*, has been added in response to requests that students be made aware of this aspect of accountancy practice.
- Chapter 12, *The financial statements of limited companies: statements of profit or loss, related statements and notes*, now includes a new Section 12.2 which contains what was previously in Sections 19 and 21 of Chapter 29, *Accounting theory*.

- Chapter 26 has been extensively revised and retitled *Standards covering subsidiaries, associates and joint arrangements* following changes introduced by recent changes to IAS 27, *Separate financial statements.*
- Chapter 27, *Interest, annuities, and leasing*, was previously Chapter 45.
- Chapter 29 (was Chapter 28) has been retitled *Interpretation of financial information* and Section 29.8 has been added on ***Earnings Management***. This was added in response to requests to provide students with some understanding of what is actually done by organisations to portray the financial performance and financial position they wish to show rather than the one that simply presents a true and fair view.
- **Chapter 30, *Theories of accounting-related choice,* is new** and has been added at the request of some reviewers who wished to be able to take their students beyond the interpretation of financial information presented in Chapter 29. **This new chapter presents many of the theories typically included in courses on Accounting Theory.** These theories describe, explain, and predict accounting-related choices made by companies, managers, investors, groups of stakeholders, and regulators. In addition, social judgement theories are introduced that explain how some accounting-related decisions are taken.
- Chapter 31 (previously Chapter 29) has been retitled *Theories of accounting practice* to better reflect its focus upon theories that underpin accounting practice. Two sections from Part III (Objectives of financial statements), Sections 19 and 21, have been moved to Chapter 12. The remaining section in Part III has been deleted as its topic is covered elsewhere.
- Chapter 33 (previously Chapter 31) has been completely rewritten. It now also includes **integrated reporting** and has been retitled *Social and environmental reporting and integrated reporting.*
- Chapter 34 (previously Chapter 32), *Corporate governance*, has been extensively rewritten to incorporate recent legislation and updates of the relevant Codes.
- Part 10 has been moved to become Part 6 with Chapters 48 (*The supply chain and enterprise resource planning systems*), 49 (*E-commerce and accounting*), and 50 (*Forensic accounting*) becoming Chapters 37, 38, and 39, respectively.
- Chapter 38 (previously 49), *E-commerce and accounting,* has been updated to reflect current trends.
- Chapter 39 (previously 50), *Forensic accounting,* has been extensively revised.
- The *Notes for Students* on the next page have been updated.
- Over 120 new questions have been included in this edition.

As previously:

1 Each chapter:
   (*a*) starts with *Learning Objectives;*
   (*b*) uses colour, especially blue, to enhance readability and bring out key points in the text;
   (*c*) contains *Activities* designed to broaden and reinforce students' understanding of the concepts being covered and, in some cases, to introduce new concepts in such a way that they do not come as a surprise when introduced formally later in the book;
   (*d*) ends with *Learning Outcomes* that can be mapped back to the Learning Objectives, so reinforcing the major topics and concepts covered in the chapter;
   (*e*) contains answers to all the Activities immediately after the Learning Outcomes.

2 The book has an alphabetical Glossary (in Appendix 3) of all the significant terms introduced, including those added for the first time in this edition. Each entry is referenced back to the chapter in which it appeared.

3 A set of Notes for Students is presented on the next page. This covers how to use this book, how to tackle the end-of-chapter Review Questions, and how to study for and sit examinations. It should be read by students before they start working through the main text.

I hope that you find these changes helpful and appropriate and would welcome comments on these and on any other changes you feel ought to be made in future editions. You can contact me by email at **a.j.a.sangster@btinternet.com** or by letter via the publishers.

Three chapters from the *eighth* edition (3, *Container accounts;* 17, *Value added statements;* and 18, *Investment accounts*) can be found on this book's website.

A *Solutions Manual* giving suggested solutions to those questions with the suffix A in the book (e.g. 5.8A) is available to teachers and lecturers adopting this book on their course. They can download them from the lecturers' section of the website for *Frank Wood's Business Accounting 1* and *Frank Wood's Business Accounting 2* at **www.pearsoned.co.uk/Wood.**

Finally, I would like to thank all those teachers and lecturers who contacted me offering advice as to the changes they would like to see incorporated in this edition. A special mention should go, in particular, to Christopher Foo for all his advice and contributions over the past decade.

*Alan Sangster*

# Notes for students

This textbook presents your topics in what has been found to be the most appropriate sequencing of topics as you build upon the foundations of accounting knowledge that you developed when you studied *Frank Wood's Business Accounting 1*. You will find that a number of features of the book, properly used, will enhance your understanding and extend your ability to cope with what will possibly appear, at first, to be a mystifying array of rules and procedures.

While much, but by no means all, of what follows was in *Frank Wood's Business Accounting 1,* all of the advice given to you in that book will apply to you throughout your studies of accounting, whatever the level. I therefore offer no apologies for repeating some of it here along with some new advice appropriate to the level of *Frank Wood's Business Accounting 2.*

In order to make best use of this resource, you should consider the following as being a proven path to success:

- At the start of each chapter, **read the Learning Objectives**. Then, while you work through the material, try to detect when you have achieved each of these objectives.
- At the end of each chapter **check what you have learnt against the Learning Outcomes** that follow the main text.
- If you find that you cannot say 'yes, I have achieved this' to any of the Learning Outcomes, look back through the chapter and reread the topic you have not yet learnt.
- **Learn the meaning of each new term as it appears.** Do not leave learning what terms mean until you are revising for an exam. Accounting is best learnt as a series of building blocks. If you don't remember what terms mean, your knowledge and ability to 'do' accounting will be very seriously undermined, in much the same way as a wall built without mortar is likely to collapse the first time someone leans against it.
- **Attempt each of the Activities in the book *at the point at which they appear* .** This is ***very*** important. They will reinforce your learning and help set in context some of the material that may otherwise appear very artificial and distant from the world you live in. The answers are at the end of each chapter. **Do not look at the answers before you attempt the questions; you'll just be cheating yourself.** Once you have answered one, check your answer against the one in the book and be sure you understand it before moving on.
- Above all, remember that accounting is a vehicle for providing financial information in a form that assists decision-making. Work hard at presenting your work as neatly as possible and remember that pictures (in this case, financial figures) only carry half the message. When you are asked for them, words of explanation and insight are essential in order to make an examiner appreciate what you know and that you actually understand what the figures mean.

There are two subjects we would like you to consider very carefully: making best use of the end-of-chapter Review Questions and your examination technique.

## Review questions: the best approach

As I did in *Business Accounting 1,* I have set Review Questions at the end of most chapters for you to gauge how well you understand and can apply what you have learnt. **If you simply read the chapters without attempting these questions, you will not pass your examinations.** You should first of all attempt each question for which there is an answer at the back of the book. Then check it fully against the answer.

**Do not simply compare the question with the answer and tick off the bits of the answer against the relevant part of the question.** Doing so is no substitute for attempting to answer the question. No one ever learnt to do accounting properly that way. It is tempting to save time in so doing, but you will regret it eventually.

## Need for practice

Try to find the time to answer as many Review Questions as possible. This is why:

1 Even though you may think you understand the text, when you come to answer the questions you may find you don't. The true test of understanding is whether or not you can tackle the questions competently.
2 It is often said that practice makes perfect. If you don't practise doing accounting questions you will almost certainly not become good at accounting.
3 You need to be able to answer questions quickly: many fail accounting exams because they run out of time. A lot is expected from you in an accounting exam in a very short time because examining boards believe, and have always believed, that an adequately prepared student will be able to work quickly on the problems set. By an 'adequately prepared' student, they mean a student who not only has the knowledge, but has been trained to work quickly and at the same time maintain accuracy and neatness.
4 Speed itself is not enough; **you also have to be neat and tidy,** and follow all the proper practices and procedures while working at speed. Fast, correct, but really scruffy and unreadable work can cause you to fail the exam. Why is this so? At this level the accounting examiner is mainly concerned about your practical ability in the subject. Accounting is a practical subject, and your practical competence is about to be tested. The examiner will therefore expect the answers to be neat and well set out. Untidy work with figures spread over the page in a haphazard way, badly written figures, and columns of figures in which the vertical columns are not set down in straight lines will be penalised and can easily mean the difference between a pass and a fail.
5 Appropriate presentation of information is important. Learn how to present the various financial statements you may need to produce in an examination. Examiners expect to see the items in statements of profit or loss, statements of financial position and statements of cash flow in the correct order and will probably deduct marks if they aren't. Practise by writing down examples of these statements without any numbers until you always get the layout correct. One exam trick most students overlook is that the layout of a financial statement is often included in an examination paper as part of one question yet another question asks you to produce an answer using the format of that financial statement. **The one you need to produce will contain different numbers but the general layout should be very similar.**

### Need for headings

Your work should not only be neat, it should be well presented. **Headings should always be given, and any dates needed should be inserted.** The test you should apply is to imagine that you are a partner in a firm of professional accountants and have taken a holiday for a few weeks. During that time your assistants have completed all sorts of work including reports, drafting final accounts, various forms of other computations and so on. All of this work is waiting for you when you return. When you return you look at each item in the pile awaiting your attention.

Suppose the first one looks like a statement of financial position as at 31 December in respect of one of your clients. When you looked at it you could see that it was a statement of financial position, but you didn't know for which client, neither did you know which year it was for. Would you be annoyed with your assistant who prepared it? Of course you would. So in an exam why should the examiner give you high marks if you prepare a statement of financial position answer without the date or the name of the business or the fact that it is a statement of financial position written clearly across the top? If proper headings are not given, you may lose a lot of marks. **Don't wait until your examination to do this.** You also need to take similar care with sub-totals and sub-headings that need to be shown, such as those for non-current assets or for current liabilities.

## The examiner

When answering an examination question, think about what you would say if you were employing an accounts assistant who gave you a sheet of paper with accounting entries written in the same style as your own efforts in answering the exam question.

Anyone who works in accounting knows well that untidy work leads to unnecessary errors. This is why examiners penalise unclear, untidy, poorly presented work. Examiners want to ensure that you are not going to mess up the work of an accounting department. Even today, accountants still write down many things on paper, so don't imagine that examiners will overlook such messy work just because most accounting is now done using a computer.

Imagine going to the savings bank and the manager says to you: 'We don't know whether you've got £5 in the account or £5,000. You see, the work of our clerks is so untidy that we can never sort out exactly how much is in anybody's account.' We would guess that you would not want to put a lot of money into an account at that bank. How would you feel if someone took you to court for not paying a debt of £100 when in fact you owed them nothing? This sort of thing would happen all the time if we simply allowed people to keep untidy accounts. The examiner is there to ensure that the person to whom they award a pass will be worthy of it, and will not continually mess up the work of any firm at which they may work in the future.

If you want to pass your accounting exam, and your work is untidy, what can you do about it? Well, the answer is simple enough: start right now to be neat and tidy in your work. I did. My writing was so bad that my accounting teacher at school told me to print everything in capital letters. I thought he was mad, but my marks improved immediately, and so did my handwriting and my overall neatness in preparing answers. **Start being neat now. You cannot suddenly become neat in an examination.**

## The structure of the questions

The review questions in each chapter generally start with the easiest and then get gradually more difficult. Some are very difficult and time-consuming. If all the questions were easy, the shock of meeting more complicated questions for the first time in an examination could lead you to fail it. By giving you a mixture of straightforward and complicated questions, you will learn how to deal with the complex issues before meeting them in an exam. It's in your best interests not to ignore review questions you find hard. Put in the effort, the practice will increase your knowledge and understanding, and your performance in the exam will improve as a result.

## The answers

At the back of the book, you will find answers to approximately half of the Review Questions. The answers to the other Review Questions (indicated by the letter 'A' after the question number) are only available to you from your teacher or lecturer. Don't worry if you are studying this subject on your own. There are still more than sufficient Review Questions with answers in this book to ensure you know and understand the material you are learning.

## Examination technique

If you were completely devoid of examination technique, you would probably not have advanced to this stage of your accounting studies. A lot of what follows was written in *Frank Wood's Business Accounting 1*. Don't avoid reading it just because you read it when you were studying the material in that book.

In your first accounting examination you were competing with people who had probably never sat an accounting examination before. A lot of them will not get past Stage 1. In Stage 2 you are competing against people who have already proved they have a certain degree of competence in the subject. You might have got away with a certain amount of poor examination technique at Stage 1, but that will not be as easy at Stage 2.

I'll concentrate here on the main deficiencies noted by examiners. These never change.

### Failing to read the question carefully

A large number of students do not answer the questions that they are asked by the examiner. This happens because they have not read the question properly. They answer what they think the examiner wants, not what the examiner is asking for.

Taking a simple example, suppose the examiner sets the following question: 'Describe the use of accounting ratios in assessing the performance of businesses.'

A lot of students will immediately start to describe how to calculate various accounting ratios. Marks which will be obtained – NIL. The question asked for the *use* of accounting ratios, not *how to calculate* them.

Many other students will have concentrated on the word *use*. They will then write their answer based on comparing this year's accounting ratios in a business with those of last year. They may well even mention trends in ratios and that will earn them some extra marks. If they, however, restrict their discussion to comparing ratios of a business for one year compared with other years, they cannot get top marks, no matter how well they have written their answers. They have failed to think carefully enough about what they are being asked: businesses, not a business.

The examiner did not restrict them to only looking internally, so the best answer would be one that looks both internally *and* externally, by mentioning comparison of the ratios of the business with those of its competitors and with the rest of the industry in which it operates. The examiner will have set aside marks for mentioning these external comparisons. Failing to mention them will be guaranteed to lose marks.

**So, (a) *read* the question carefully, (b) *underline* the *key* words to get to the meaning of the question, (c) *think carefully* about how comprehensive your answer should be.**

Be careful also not to make the opposite mistake: *don't* go beyond what is asked in the question. In this example, the question is asking about the *use* of *accounting* ratios, *not* the use of *all types* of ratios. Besides accounting ratios there are marketing ratios – e.g. size of share of market, how long it takes to supply orders, ratios of defective goods, etc. The question does not ask for these. If you give them, you will not get any extra marks, no matter how well you do so.

### Poor time management

Using time well to gain the highest possible marks is essential. Examiners constantly report that students are very poor in this aspect of tackling an examination. How, then, can you avoid the usual pitfalls?

First of all, **read the *rubric* carefully**. This is the instructions at the top of the paper. For example, 'Attempt four questions only: the three questions in Section A and one from Section B. Begin each answer on a separate page.'

There are four instructions in this rubric, but some students won't notice. Some, for example, will try to answer more than one question from Section B. If you tackle two questions from Section B, you will get marks for only one of your answers. Few examiners will mark both and then give you the marks for your highest marked answer. Many will simply mark the first of the optional questions answered and ignore the next, unnecessary, answer. As a result, your best answer may not gain any marks.

Having been told to do so, if you don't **start each answer on a new page**, you'll only annoy the examiner, which is the last thing you should do. It is your job to make the examiner's work as easy as possible. Examiners are only human, and it would be surprising if their annoyance did not result in its influencing the marking of your paper.

Whatever the rubric, you really *must* attempt each and every question you are required to answer according to what is said in the rubric. If you have to answer five questions then you must avoid attempting only four questions. You won't get the extra marks for the question you did not attempt added to your total. They will be lost, permanently.

Students often feel that they would be better spending their time getting four good answers instead of five answers, some of which have not been finished. In accounting examinations this is not true:

1 Accounting examiners use positive marking. This means that if you have done 80 per cent of an answer worth 20 marks in total, and you have got it absolutely correct, then you get 80% of 20 = 16 marks.
2 **The first marks in a question are the easiest marks to obtain.** It is easier to get the first 10 marks out of 20 than it is to get the second 10 marks. By attempting all the questions you have to answer, you ensure that you get the easiest marks on every question. Any questions you finish will raise your mark even higher but **do not finish answering a question if it means you do not attempt to answer a question you were required to answer.**

To ensure that you tackle (not necessarily finish) each question you should **mark the number of minutes to be allowed by *yourself* for each question.** Thus, a 20-mark question in a 100-mark exam should be given 20 per cent of the time. Twenty per cent of 2 hours = 24 minutes. When 24 minutes have passed, *stop answering the question* unless it is the last question to be attempted, and go on to the next question.

If you don't know the answer, or part of an answer, you should guess. You don't lose marks for guessing and, if you guess correctly, you get the marks. Intuition will often give the correct answer. If you don't guess on part of a computational question you will often be unable to go on to the remainder of the question which you can answer.

## Workings

You may wonder why this is under a separate heading. I cannot emphasise enough how important it is that you should:

(*a*) submit all your workings; and
(*b*) ensure that your workings are set out in a way that the examiner can easily follow.

A very high percentage of candidates in an examination are near the pass mark, within either a few percentage points above it or below it. If you are one of them and, as we have said, there are a lot of you in the same position, handing in workings which can be understood by the examiner will often make the difference between a pass and a fail. Conversely, no workings, or completely messy and unclear workings, may result in your failing an examination you should have passed.

This last point is important. Some students think that putting down a set of random notes and calling them 'workings' will gain marks. It won't. **Examiners won't waste time searching through random notes for something relevant.** Treat your workings as if they, themselves, are part of your answer. **Insert titles and headings to indicate what each item in your workings is for.**

## Tackle the easiest questions first

**Never start your examination by tackling a difficult question.** You must be able to settle down properly and not let your nerves get out of control. Starting off on the easiest question is the best way to enable you to get off to a good start. Much more about this was written in *Frank Wood's Business Accounting 1*.

## State your assumptions

Sometimes a question is ambiguous. Examiners try to prevent this from happening, but it does happen despite all the care taken to prevent it. Questions also do, sometimes, contain errors.

In both of these cases, in your answer, you must point out the ambiguity/error. You should then make an assumption, based on what you thought the examiner meant, and carry on with your answer. **You must state what your assumption is.** Try to make your assumption as sensible as possible. The examiner will then mark your answer accordingly. If you make a ridiculous assumption, it is unlikely that you will be given any marks for that part of your answer. Don't be sarcastic in your comments or complain about inefficiency – there are other times and places for that.

## Answering easy questions

### The problem

Unlike computational answers, you will not know whether your written narrative answers are good enough until you receive your examination result. In addition, written questions lack the certainty and precision of accounting problems and it is often difficult to decide what the examiner requires of you. For this reason, having a sound exam technique is essential, along with precise knowledge of relevant laws and accounting regulations, such as IFRSs.

There are several major aspects to success in written papers. *Plan* your answer, answer the question *as set*, pay attention to good *layout*, and explain in clear and simple terms what you are doing. Remember you can only be marked on what you write down. You have no opportunity to explain any ambiguity in your answers and if what you write is unclear you will *not* get the benefit of the doubt.

### Plan

First read the question and note down the key *verb* within it, i.e. your instructions; this may be to discuss, explain, advise, set out, list, draft an audit programme, write a letter, etc.

If the question requires a discussion or an explanation, it should be written in proper paragraph form. Each paragraph should be self-contained and explain the point it makes. Sentences should be short and to the point. **The ideal length for a paragraph is three short sentences, with four as a maximum.** Over four and you are probably making more than one point and should have gone into two paragraphs.

Plan how many points you are going to make and what the answer is. This is essential as otherwise your answer will 'drift' as you struggle to arrive at a conclusion. The plan should consist of arrows connecting points to each other so that the answer will flow and be logical. The plan need not be too extensive; it is silly to waste time on a 'mini-answer'. It should consist of the *headings* you are going to use. Putting these into a bullet point list can be useful in organising your answer.

### Layout

Whenever examiners meet to discuss results, or write down their commentary on students' performance, they all agree on the importance of good layout; yet students generally tend to take no notice. The range of marks between good papers and poor papers tends to be quite small. Anything you can do to put the examiner on your side will pay off in those few extra marks.

The main areas for good layout are:

1 *Tabulate* in numbered points, unless you are writing an essay-type question (as explained above).
2 Leave a blank line between each point or paragraph.
3 Use headings whenever possible to indicate what major point or series of points you are about to make. Make it easy for the examiner to read your work and follow what you are doing. A solid mass of material is difficult to read, provides no respite for the eye and shows a lack of discipline.
4 Take care with your *language*. Be objective and avoid the use of the words 'I' or 'we' at too frequent intervals. Be direct and concise, say what you mean, do not use pompous terminology, and make sure that any technical words are used with their correct meaning.

   Short sentences are far more effective and punchy than long ones. An evaluation of an internal control system could well start with a series of *verbs*. Good ones are: test, examine, inspect, calculate, reconcile, compare, summarise, enquire, investigate. These key words will help you to construct answers to these types of questions that are much more direct and to the point. If you start with them you are bound to avoid falling into the trap of being long-winded, or of padding out your answer. You only have a limited time and everything you write down *must* earn you marks.
5 *Think* while you are writing out your answer to make sure you are answering the question *as set*. Keep on reading the instructions and make sure you are following them. Use the question to help you to get the answer and, while this should be tackled at the planning stage, it is always possible that inspiration will strike while you are writing out your answer. In this case, note down the point beside your plan, otherwise you might forget it and that can cause frustration. What you say should be relevant, but if you are in doubt about the relevance but sure about the accuracy – include it in your answer. You cannot lose and it may be one of the key points the examiner was looking for.

## Key points

**Do try to find a couple of key points to each question.** These are points which you feel are vital to answer the question. You may well be right, and anyway, noting them down after you have read the question carefully can help to give your answer much needed direction.

## Practice

You will need to practise these routines. Written answers need more practice than computational ones. Attempt a question. Write out the answer as you would in the examination. Compare it with the suggested answers.

**Write at the foot of your answer what you left out and what you got wrong.** Learn from the answers and from the work you do, so that when you see a similar question you will produce a better answer.

## Time pressure

If you experience a lot of time pressure as you write your answers, don't worry: this is a good sign.

In the examination, spread your time sensibly. **Start with the questions you like the most** and, if you have to go slightly over the time you allotted for those, do so, but not by very much! End with the question you think you cannot answer or will be hardest to answer, **but give yourself time to have a reasonable go at it.**

If a narrative question is included in a computational paper, do not spend more than the allocated time on it but *do spend that time answering it.* **Examiners pay great attention to the written parts of computational papers – they often carry more marks than the computation part, so do not treat those parts as if they don't matter.**

All this sounds formidable. It is. Exams require skill, application and, above all, confidence. Practice makes perfect and once the skill is acquired then, like riding a bicycle, it will not be for-gotten. Take pride in your work and be critical of your own efforts, but do not imagine your answers have to be perfect to pass an exam. Suggested answers you may have seen that were provided by examiners tend to be quite long because examiners do not wish to reveal any signs of weakness or ignorance about the subjects of which they are considered to be experts.

Go for the main points and make them well. That is the secret of success.

## Summary

**Remember:**

1. **Read the rubric, i.e. the instructions.**
2. **Plan your time before you start.**
3. **Tackle the easiest questions first.**
4. **Finish off answering each question when your time allocation for the question is up.**
5. **Hand in and label all your workings.**
6. **Do remember to be neat, also include all proper headings, dates, sub-totals, etc. A lot of marks can be lost if you don't.**
7. **Only answer as many questions as you are asked to tackle by the examiner. Extra answers will not normally be marked.**
8. **Underline the *key* words in each question to ensure that you answer the question set, and not the question you wrongly take it to be.**
9. **Never write out the text of essay questions.**

Good luck with your exam. I hope you get the rewards you deserve!

*Alan Sangster*

# The Last Lecture

*Our course is run, our harvest garnered in,*
*And taking stock of what we have, we note how life,*
*This strange, mysterious life which now we hold and now*
*eludes our grasp,*
*Is governed still by natural law, and its events*
*Tread on each other's heels, each one compelled to follow*
*where the first has led.*
*Noting all this, and judging by the past,*
*We form our plans, until we know at last*
*The treasure in the future's lap.*

*The man, the plant, the beast, must all obey this law,*
*Since in the early dawn of this old world*
*The law was given, and the stuff was made*
*Which still alone can hold the breath of life:*
*Whereby we know that grass and man are kin,*
*The bond a common substance which within*
*Controls their growth.*

*Can we know all? Nay, but the major part*
*Of all that is must still elude our grasp,*
*For life transcends itself, and slowly noting what it is,*
*Gathers but fragments from the stream of time.*
*Thus what we teach is only partly true.*
*Not knowing all, we act as if we knew,*
*Compelled to act or die.*

*Yet as we grow in wisdom and in skill*
*The upward path is steeper and each step*
*Comes higher unto heaven, piercing the clouds*
*Which heretofore have hid the stars from view.*
*The new-gained knowledge seems to fill the air,*
*It seems to us the soul of truth is there.*
*Our quest is won.*

*Bold climber, all that thou hast won*
*Lies still in shadow of the peaks above;*
*Yet in the morning hours the sun*
*Rewards thy work of love,*
*Resting a moment on thy lesser height,*
*Piercing the vault with rays too bright to face,*
*Strengthens thy soul and gives thee ample might*
*To serve thy human race.*

Theodore Dru Allison Cockerell (1866–1948)
*Zoölogy: A Textbook for Colleges and Universities*, Yonkers-on-Hudson, NY: World Book Company, 1920, pp. 538–539

# Acknowledgements

We are very grateful to teachers of accounting in many schools, colleges of further education and universities whose generous advice has contributed to the development of this new edition. We wish to thank, in particular:

Elayne Taylor, University of Dundee
Mohammed Fadzil Bin Dawood, Millennia Institute
Dr Shenba Kanagasabapathy, HELP University
Stephen Hicks, Keele University
Stephen McNamee, University of Ulster
Theresa Choi, Community College of City University, Hong Kong
Vivienne Prudden, FCA, MProf, BA, PGCLT, Southampton Solent University
Waseem Mirza, Bahrain Institute of Banking and Finance

Most of all, thank you Christopher Foo for your interest, concern and help – your efforts are all greatly appreciated.

All answers to questions are the authors' own work and have not been supplied by any of the examining bodies.

We are grateful to the following for permission to reproduce copyright material:

### Text

Exhibit 11.1 adapted from *Accounting Standards Board Statement of Principles 1999*, Accounting Standards Board Ltd (1991, 1999), © Accounting Standards Board (ASB). Adapted and reproduced with the kind permission of the Financial Reporting Council. All rights reserved. For further information please visit www.frc.org.uk/asb or call +44 (0)20 7492 2300.

Exhibit 33.1 The PwC Integrated reporting model; Exhibit 33.2 Information areas and their interdependencies in an *Integrated Report:* PricewaterhouseCoopers.

### Photos

**Getty Images:** front cover image; **Image Store:** pp. 1, 47, 57, 277, 397, 459, 545, 567, 627, 671, 713

In some instances we have been unable to trace the owners of copyright material, and we would appreciate any information that would enable us to do so.

part 1

# SPECIAL ACCOUNTS

## Introduction

**The first two chapters of this part are concerned with two items that are treated in a similar way, irrespective of the form of business involved. The third deals with something the treatment of which may vary.**

chapter 1

# Accounting for branches

## Learning objectives

**After you have studied this chapter, you should be able to:**

- explain two methods of recording the entries relating to branches
- describe how double column statements of profit or loss can be used in order to monitor any unexpected losses
- explain the difference between using a memoranda columns approach and an integrated inventory monitoring system for inventory control
- explain the issues relating to maintaining branch accounts for foreign branches

## Introduction

In this chapter, you'll learn about two methods of recording branch transactions and of the issues that arise when items are in transit between branches. You'll also learn about how to record the entries in the books when branches are located in different countries.

## 1.1 Background

Branch accounting was the genesis for accounting as we know it today. Merchants in thirteenth-century Europe were able to move along the trade routes established in the Crusades, and their knowledge of what lay where had developed well beyond knowing simply what existed within a few days' walk of their homes. The more adventurous merchants started travelling further afield, some to fairs in other towns, districts, and even countries. There they would sell their own products and buy or barter the products of others to take home and sell to their fellow townsfolk.

In time, this grew to the point where a merchant had simply too many opportunities and too much to do. Agencies were formed in other towns and countries, and employees were engaged to do the travelling while the merchants stayed home. Some of those merchants were so successful that they became 'merchant princes' with power, wealth and authority to rival the aristocracy. Nowhere was this more so than in what is now the northern part of Italy. From Naples to Milan and Genoa in the west, and Perugia to Venice in the east, merchants' businesses became increasingly large.

A method had to be found for merchants to record and monitor the activities of their salesmen and their branches. The result is what we now know as 'joint venture accounting' (see *Frank Wood's Business Accounting 1*) and 'branch accounting', the topic of this chapter.

## 1.2 Accounting records and branches

There are two commonly used methods for recording transactions for branches of an organisation:

(*a*) the headquarters (or 'head office') keeps all the accounting records; or
(*b*) each branch has its own full accounting system.

It is easier to understand accounting for branches if these two methods are dealt with separately. The first is shown in Sections 1.3–1.8; and the second in Sections 1.9–1.13. Sections 1.12 and 1.13 may also apply to the first method.

## 1.3 If headquarters maintains all the accounting records

The ledgers are used for three main purposes:

(*a*) to record transactions showing changes in assets, liabilities and capital;
(*b*) to ascertain the profitability of each branch; and
(*c*) to enable checks to be made that might indicate whether anyone at the branches is stealing goods or cash.

**This third purpose is very important for businesses that have many branches.** The people who manage or work in these branches may be receiving and paying out large sums of money. In addition, they may be handling large amounts of goods. The branches may be a considerable distance away from the head office, the headquarters of the business. Being at a distance from control can be tempting to some people for whom distance equates to freedom to do what they wish. Some may think that this includes being able to steal things without being caught.

## 1.4 Methods for checking inventory and cash

If a business with just a few branches sells only very expensive cars, it would be easy to check on purchases and sales of the cars. The number of cars sold would be relatively small. Checking that cars or money have not been stolen would be easy. However, a business with branches selling many thousands of cheap items could not be checked so easily. To maintain a check on each carton of salt or bag of flour sold would be almost impossible. Even if it could be done, such checks would cost much more than they could possibly save.

One solution to this problem is to record all transactions at the branch in terms of selling prices. For each accounting period, it should then be possible to check whether the closing inventory is as it should be. For a small branch, you may be given the following figures:

| | £ |
|---|---|
| Inventory at 1 January – at selling price | 5,000 |
| January – Goods sent to the branch by the head office – at selling price | 20,000 |
| January – Sales by the branch – obviously at selling price | 18,000 |

The calculation of the closing inventory is:

| | £ |
|---|---|
| Opening inventory (selling price) | 5,000 |
| *Add* Goods sent to the branch (selling price) | 20,000 |
| Goods which the branch had available for sale (selling price) | 25,000 |
| *Less* Goods sold (selling price) | (18,000) |
| Closing inventory should be (selling price) | 7,000 |

## 1.5 Allowances for deficiencies

In every business there will be:

(*a*) wastage of goods for some reason – goods may be damaged or broken, or they may be kept too long and become unsaleable;
(*b*) stealing by customers, especially in a retail business;
(*c*) thefts by employees.

No one can be certain how much inventory is wasted or stolen during a period. Only experience will enable a good estimate to be made of these losses.

## 1.6 The double column system

At regular intervals, at least once a year but usually more frequently now that accounting for branches is virtually always computerised, headquarters prepares a special type of trading account for each branch. The trading account can be shown in a form similar to a 'T-account' but with two columns on each side, as shown in Exhibit 1.1.

The right-hand column on the left side shows goods sent to the branch or held in inventory at cost price, i.e. the normal basis for any business. The other columns show all trading account items at selling price. This allows deficiencies in trading to be compared with the normal allowance for wastages, etc. of the business.

When such a system is in place, it is easy for head office to tell if the branch is operating as expected; and, of course, easy for the branch itself to assess its own operations against the norms for the business.

### Exhibit 1.1

**Branch Trading Account for the year ending 31.12.2015**

| | *At selling price* | | | *At selling price* | |
|---|---|---|---|---|---|
| | £ | £ | | £ | £ |
| Inventory 1 Jan 2015 | 1,600 | 1,200 | Sales | 7,428 | 7,428 |
| Goods from head office | 8,000 | 6,000 | Deficiency (difference) | 172 | |
| | 9,600 | 7,200 | | | |
| *Less* Inventory 31 Dec 2015 | 2,000 | 1,500 | | | |
| | 7,600 | 5,700 | | | |
| Gross profit c/d | | 1,728 | | | |
| | 7,600 | 7,428 | | 7,600 | 7,428 |
| | | | Gross profit b/d | | 1,728 |

Exhibit 1.1 is drafted from the following details for a business which sells goods at a uniform mark-up of $33\frac{1}{3}$% on cost price:

| | £ |
|---|---|
| Inventory 1 Jan 2015 (at cost) | 1,200 |
| Goods sent to the branch during the year (at cost) | 6,000 |
| Sales (selling price) | 7,428 |
| Inventory 31 Dec 2015 (at cost) | 1,500 |

Allowances for wastage, etc., 1% of sales.

As the actual deficiency of £172 exceeds the amount expected, i.e. 1% of £7,428 = £74, an investigation will be made.

**This method is suitable where all the sales are for cash, there being no sales on credit, or when debtors make their payments to the branch where the sale took place.**

Why should it make any difference if debtors make payment to a branch other than the one where the sale took place?

## 1.7 The inventory and accounts receivable system

Further adjustments are needed when there are credit sales as well as cash sales. There are two ways of making the entries. These are:

(*a*) using memoranda columns *only* to keep a check on inventory;
(*b*) integrating inventory control into the double entry system. This is often called an 'integrated method'.

Under both these approaches, information is kept relating to inventory and debtors.

Using the following data, Exhibit 1.2 shows the records in the head office books when (a), the memoranda method, is used. Exhibit 1.3 shows (b) the records when the integrated method is used.

*Data*: A branch sells all its goods at a uniform mark-up of 50% on cost price. Credit customers are to pay their accounts directly to the head office.

| | | £ |
|---|---|---|
| First day of the period: | | |
| Inventory (at cost) | (A) | 2,000 |
| Accounts receivable | (B) | 400 |
| During the period: | | |
| Goods sent to the branch (at cost) | (C) | 7,000 |
| Sales – cash | (D) | 6,000 |
| Sales – credit | (E) | 4,800 |
| Cash remitted by debtors to head office | (F) | 4,500 |
| At the close of the last day of the period: | | |
| Inventory (at cost) | (G) | 1,800 |
| Accounts receivable | (H) | 700 |

***Note*: The letters A to H beside the figures have been inserted to identify the entries in Exhibits 1.2 and 1.3.**

### (a) Memoranda columns method

**Exhibit 1.2**

**Branch Inventory**

| | | *Selling price (memo only)* | | | | *Selling price (memo only)* | |
|---|---|---|---|---|---|---|---|
| | | £ | £ | | | £ | £ |
| Inventory b/d | (A) | 3,000 | 2,000 | Sales: Cash | (D) | 6,000 | 6,000 |
| Goods sent | (C) | 10,500 | 7,000 | Credit | (E) | 4,800 | 4,800 |
| Gross profit to profit and loss | | | 3,600 | Inventory c/d | (G) | 2,700 | 1,800 |
| | | 13,500 | 12,600 | | | 13,500 | 12,600 |
| Inventory b/d | (G) | 2,700 | 1,800 | | | | |

**Branch Accounts Receivable**

| | | £ | | | £ |
|---|---|---|---|---|---|
| Balances b/d | (B) | 400 | Cash | (F) | 4,500 |
| Branch inventory | (E) | 4,800 | Balance c/d | (H) | 700 |
| | | 5,200 | | | 5,200 |
| Balance b/d | | 700 | | | |

**Goods Sent to Branches**

| | £ | | | £ |
|---|---|---|---|---|
| Headquarters trading | 7,000 | Branch inventory | (C) | 7,000 |

**Cash Book**

| | | £ | |
|---|---|---|---|
| Branch inventory – cash sales | (D) | 6,000 | |
| Branch accounts receivable | (E) | 4,500 | |

The branch inventory account is similar to the branch trading account you saw in Exhibit 1.1. However, in addition a branch accounts receivable account is in use.

The balance of the goods sent to the branch account is shown as being transferred to the headquarters trading account at cost. This figure is deducted from the purchases in the headquarters trading account, so that goods bought for the branch can be disregarded when the gross profit earned by the business is calculated.

## (b) The integrated method

The integrated method introduces the idea that gross profit can be calculated by reference to profit margins. It relies upon all selling prices being set strictly on the basis of the profit margins adopted by the business. For example, assume that a travelling salesman sells all his goods at cost price plus 25%. At the start of a week he has £80 of goods at cost, he buys goods costing £800, he sells goods for £900 (selling price) and he has goods at the end of the week which have cost him £160. A trading account based on this data is shown below.

**Trading**

| | £ | | £ |
|---|---|---|---|
| Inventory b/d | 80 | Sales | 900 |
| Purchases | 800 | Inventory c/d | 160 |
| Gross profit c/d | 180 | | |
| | 1,060 | | 1,060 |
| | | Gross profit b/d | 180 |

This could be shown as an extract from the statement of profit or loss or could be presented as:

| | £ |
|---|---|
| Profit made when opening inventory is sold | 20 |
| Profit made when purchases are sold | 200 |
| Profit made when all goods are sold | 220 |
| But he still has left unsold goods (cost £160) on which the profit still has to be realised | (40) |
| Therefore profit realised | 180 |

This could be expressed in account form as:

**Salesman's Profit Adjustment**

| | £ | | £ |
|---|---|---|---|
| Gross profit realised | 180 | Unrealised profit b/d | 20 |
| Unrealised profit c/d | 40 | Unrealised profit when goods were bought | 200 |
| | 220 | | 220 |

The integrated system uses an adjustment account because goods sent to the branch are shown at cost price in a 'goods sent to branch account'. (This is the same as under the memoranda column method.) In the branch inventory account, these goods are shown at selling price. Obviously, if one entry is made at cost price and the other at selling price, the accounts would not balance. As the integrated method does not use memoranda columns, to correct this an extra account called a 'branch adjustment account' is opened. As with the salesman's profit adjustment account shown above, the entries in this account are in respect of the profit content *only* of goods.

The branch inventory account acts as a check upon inventory deficiencies. The branch adjustment account shows the amount of gross profit realised (i.e. earned) and unrealised during the period.

Exhibit 1.3 shows the ledger accounts needed for the integrated system from the same information given on p. 6 that was used to complete Exhibit 1.2. (For simplicity, there is no deficiency in the inventory in this example.)

### Exhibit 1.3

**Branch Inventory (Selling Price)**

| | | £ | | | £ |
|---|---|---|---|---|---|
| Balance b/d | (A) | 3,000 | Sales: Cash | (D) | 6,000 |
| Goods sent to branch | (C) | 10,500 | Credit | (E) | 4,800 |
| | | | Balance c/d | (G) | 2,700 |
| | | 13,500 | | | 13,500 |
| Balance b/d | (G) | 2,700 | | | |

**Branch Accounts Receivable (Selling Price)**

| | | £ | | | £ |
|---|---|---|---|---|---|
| Balances b/d | (B) | 400 | Cash | (F) | 4,500 |
| Branch inventory | (E) | 4,800 | Balances c/d | (H) | 700 |
| | | 5,200 | | | 5,200 |
| Balances b/d | (H) | 700 | | | |

**Goods Sent to Branch (Cost Price)**

| | | £ | | | £ |
|---|---|---|---|---|---|
| Headquarters trading | | 7,000 | Branch inventory | (C) | 7,000 |

**Branch Adjustment (Profit Content)**

| | | £ | | | £ |
|---|---|---|---|---|---|
| Gross profit to profit and loss | | 3,600 | Unrealised profit b/d | (A) | 1,000 |
| Unrealised profit c/d | (G) | 900 | Branch inventory – goods sent | (C) | 3,500 |
| | | 4,500 | | | 4,500 |
| | | | Unrealised profit b/d | (G) | 900 |

The opening and closing inventories are shown in the branch inventory account at selling price. However, the statement of financial position should show the inventory at cost price. The previous statement of financial position should therefore have shown inventory at a cost of £2,000. This is achieved by having a compensating £1,000 credit balance brought forward in the branch adjustment account so that the debit balance of £3,000 in the branch inventory account is offset by that £1,000, leaving a balance of £2,000 to be shown in the statement of financial position. Similarly, at the close of the period the statement of financial position will show inventory at £1,800 (branch inventory debit balance £2,700 *less* branch adjustment credit balance £900).

Compare the entries in the branch adjustment account to the differences between the memoranda and 'real' column figure in the branch account shown in Exhibit 1.2. You should be able to see how both methods show the same information, one (the *memoranda columns method*) using gross amounts as the basis for presentation while the other (the *integrated method*) presents the gross profits as separate amounts.

## 1.8 The inventory and accounts receivable integrated method – further points

### Returns

Goods may be returned:

(*a*) from the branch inventory to the head office;
(*b*) from customers of the branch to the branch inventory;
(*c*) from customers of the branch to the headquarters of the business.

Exhibit 1.4 shows the entries when all the returns were by debtors (i.e. the original sales were credit sales).

### Exhibit 1.4

To examine the entries needed, suppose a business sells goods at cost plus 25% profit, and goods sold at the following prices were returned: (*a*) £90, (*b*) £150, (*c*) £30. The entries needed are:

**Branch Inventory (Selling Price)**

| | | £ | | | £ |
|---|---|---|---|---|---|
| Returns from debtors | (*b*) | 150 | Returns to headquarters | (*a*) | 90 |

**Branch Adjustment (Profit)**

| | | £ | | | |
|---|---|---|---|---|---|
| Returns from branch | (*a*) | 18 | | | |
| Returns from debtors | (*c*) | 6 | | | |

**Goods Sent to Branch (Cost Price)**

| | | £ | | | |
|---|---|---|---|---|---|
| Returns from branch | (*a*) | 72 | | | |
| Returns from debtors | (*c*) | 24 | | | |

**Branch Accounts Receivable (Selling Price)**

| | | | | | £ |
|---|---|---|---|---|---|
| | | | Returns to branch | (*b*) | 150 |
| | | | Returns to headquarters | (*c*) | 30 |

Entries (*b*), both being in accounts shown at selling price, were two in number, i.e. £150 *Dr* and £150 *Cr*; entries (a) and (c) each needed entries in three accounts, (a) being £90 *Cr* and £18 *Dr* and £72 *Dr*, (c) being £30 *Cr* and £24 *Dr* and £6 *Dr*.

## 1.9 If each branch maintains full accounting records

Branches rarely maintain full accounting records. When they do, it is usually in a business with just a few branches, and is normally done only when a branch is large enough to justify employing its own accounting staff.

A branch cannot operate on its own without resources, and it is the business as a whole which provides these in the first instance. It will want to know how much money it has invested in each branch, and from this arises the concept of branch and headquarters current accounts. The relationship between the branch and the headquarters is seen as that of a debtor/creditor. The current account shows the branch as a debtor in the headquarters records, while the headquarters is shown as a creditor in the branch records. (This is similar to what you learnt about joint venture accounting in *Business Accounting 1*.)

The current accounts are used for transactions concerned with supplying resources to the branch or in taking back resources. For such transactions, full double entry records are needed, both in the branch records and in the headquarters records: each item is recorded twice in each set of records. Some transactions, however, will concern the branch only, and these will merely need two entries in the branch records and none in the headquarters records. Exhibit 1.5 shows several transactions and the records needed.

### Exhibit 1.5

A company with its headquarters in London opened a branch in Manchester. The following transactions took place in the first month:

(A) Opened a bank account at Manchester by transferring £10,000 from the London bank account.
(B) Bought premises in Manchester, paying by cheque drawn on the London bank account, £50,000.
(C) Manchester bought a motor van, paying £6,000 from its own bank account.
(D) Manchester bought fixtures on credit from A B Equipment Ltd, £2,900.
(E) London supplied a machine valued at £2,500 from its own machinery.
(F) Manchester bought goods from suppliers, paying by cheque on its own account, £2,700.
(G) Manchester's cash sales banked immediately in its own bank account, £30,000.
(H) Goods invoiced at cost to Manchester during the month by London (no cash or cheques being paid specifically for these goods by Manchester), £28,000.
(I) A cheque is paid to London by Manchester as a return of funds, £18,000.
(J) Goods returned to London by Manchester – at cost price, £1,000.

The exact dates have been omitted. You will see later that complications arise because of differences in the timing of transactions for the two locations. For example, a cheque sent on one day will arrive on another day. Each transaction has been identified by a capital letter. The relevant letter will be shown against each entry in the accounts.

**Headquarters Records (in London)**

*Manchester Branch Current Account*

| | | £ | | | £ |
|---|---|---|---|---|---|
| Bank | (A) | 10,000 | Bank | (I) | 18,000 |
| Bank – premises | (B) | 50,000 | Returns from Branch | (J) | 1,000 |
| Machinery | (E) | 2,500 | | | |
| Goods sent to Branch | (H) | 28,000 | | | |

*Bank*

| | | £ | | | £ |
|---|---|---|---|---|---|
| Manchester Branch | (I) | 18,000 | Manchester Branch | (A) | 10,000 |
| | | | Manchester premises | (B) | 50,000 |

*Machinery*

| | | £ | | | £ |
|---|---|---|---|---|---|
| | | | Manchester Branch | (E) | 2,500 |

*Goods Sent to Branch*

| | | £ | | | £ |
|---|---|---|---|---|---|
| Returns from Branch | (J) | 1,000 | Manchester Branch | (H) | 28,000 |

**Branch Records (in Manchester)**

*Headquarters Current Account*

| | | £ | | | £ |
|---|---|---|---|---|---|
| Bank | (I) | 18,000 | Bank | (A) | 10,000 |
| Returns | (J) | 1,000 | Premises | (B) | 50,000 |
| | | | Machinery | (E) | 2,500 |
| | | | Headquarters current: Goods | (H) | 28,000 |

*Bank*

| | | £ | | | £ |
|---|---|---|---|---|---|
| Headquarters current | (A) | 10,000 | Motor van | (C) | 6,000 |
| Cash sales | (G) | 30,000 | Purchases | (F) | 2,700 |
| | | | Headquarters current | (I) | 18,000 |

*Premises*

| | | £ | | | |
|---|---|---|---|---|---|
| Headquarters current | (B) | 50,000 | | | |

*Motor Van*

| | | £ | | | |
|---|---|---|---|---|---|
| Bank | (C) | 6,000 | | | |

*Fixtures*

| | | £ | | | |
|---|---|---|---|---|---|
| A B Equipment Ltd | (D) | 2,900 | | | |

*A B Equipment Ltd*

| | | | | | £ |
|---|---|---|---|---|---|
| | | | Fixtures | (D) | 2,900 |

*Machinery*

| | | £ | | | |
|---|---|---|---|---|---|
| Headquarters current | (E) | 2,500 | | | |

*Purchases*

| | | £ | | | |
|---|---|---|---|---|---|
| Bank | (F) | 2,700 | | | |

→

*Sales*

| | | | | | |
|---|---|---|---|---|---|
| | | | | | £ |
| | | | Bank | (G) | 30,000 |

*Goods from Headquarters*

| | | | | | |
|---|---|---|---|---|---|
| | | £ | | | £ |
| Headquarters current | (H) | 28,000 | Headquarters current: Returns | (J) | 1,000 |

***Note***: **It can be seen that items C, D, F and G are entered only in the Manchester records. This is because these items are purely internal transactions and are not concerned with resources flowing between London and Manchester.**

## 1.10 Profit or loss and current accounts

The profit or loss earned by the branch does not belong to the branch. It belongs to the business and, therefore, must be shown as such. The headquarters represents the central authority of the business and profit of the branch should be credited to the Headquarters Current Account, any loss being debited.

The branch will therefore maintain its own trading account and its own profit and loss account (T-accounts). After agreement with headquarters the net profit will then be transferred to the credit of the Headquarters Current Account. The head office will then debit the Branch Current Account in its own records and credit its own profit and loss account. Taking the net profit earned in Exhibit 1.5 as £7,000, the two accounts in the two sets of books would be:

**Headquarters Records (in London)**

*Profit and Loss*

| | | | |
|---|---|---|---|
| | | | £ |
| | | Net profit earned by the Manchester Branch | 7,000 |

*Manchester Branch Current Account*

| | | | |
|---|---|---|---|
| | £ | | £ |
| Bank | 10,000 | Bank | 18,000 |
| Bank: Premises | 50,000 | Returns from Branch | 1,000 |
| Machinery | 2,500 | | |
| Goods sent to Branch | 28,000 | | |
| Headquarters profit and loss: Net profit | 7,000 | Balance c/d | 78,500 |
| | 97,500 | | 97,500 |
| Balance b/d | 78,500 | | |

**Branch Records (in Manchester)**

*Manchester Profit and Loss*

| | | | |
|---|---|---|---|
| | £ | | |
| Headquarters current: Net profit | 7,000 | | |

*Headquarters Current Account*

| | £ | | £ |
|---|---|---|---|
| Returns to Headquarters | 1,000 | Bank | 10,000 |
| Bank | 18,000 | Premises | 50,000 |
| | | Machinery | 2,500 |
| | | Goods from Headquarters | 28,000 |
| Balance c/d | 78,500 | Profit and loss | 7,000 |
| | 97,500 | | 97,500 |
| | | Balance b/d | 78,500 |

The statement of profit or loss for the business can then be prepared.

## 1.11 The combined statement of financial position

After the company's statement of profit or loss has been prepared, a company statement of financial position can be done. The branch sends its trial balance to headquarters which adds the assets and liabilities of the branch to those in the headquarters trial balance.

In the trial balances, the Headquarters Current Account will be a debit balance while the Branch Current Account will be a credit balance, e.g. the figures of £78,500 in the London books and Manchester books. These cancel each other out and are not shown in the combined statement of financial position. This is the correct treatment, as the two balances do not represent assets or liabilities of the business.

**Activity 1.2** If the current account balances do not represent assets or liabilities, what do they represent?

## 1.12 Items in transit

Earlier in this chapter, it was mentioned that the timing of transactions could raise complications. These are similar to those that give rise to the need for bank reconciliations, which you learnt about in *Business Accounting 1*. Obviously, a cheque sent by post by a Manchester branch would probably arrive in London the next day, while goods sent from London to Manchester, or returned from Manchester to London, could arrive on the same day or anything up to several days later.

Both headquarters and the branch will have entered the transactions at the dates of remittance or receipt and, as the remittance from one place will occur on one day and the receipt may occur at the other place on another day, items which are in transit at the end of a financial period may not be recorded in both sets of books. That is, the two sets of books will not contain identical figures and the balances on the current accounts will not be equal to one another.

Not surprisingly, they must be adjusted to agree at the correct amount, so that they cancel out when the combined statement of financial position is prepared. As the two sets of records contain some figures which are different from each other, they must somehow be reconciled so that the balances carried down are the same.

When preparing a bank reconciliation, permanent adjustments are made to the bank account balance recorded in the books. In contrast, when dealing with reconciliations of branch and headquarters current accounts, adjustments are made that are then carried down as balances to the next period. Which set of figures is to be altered? The amendments are all made in the headquarters' books. Otherwise, when several branches are involved, things could get very confusing indeed.

Exhibit 1.6 is for a second month of the business shown in Exhibit 1.5. However, whereas there were no items in transit at the end of the first month, this is not the case at the end of the second month.

## Exhibit 1.6

| | £ |
|---|---|
| *Headquarters' records (showing current accounts only)* | |
| Goods sent to Branch | 37,000 |
| Cheques received from Branch | 29,500 |
| Returns received from Branch | 4,400 |
| *Branch records* | |
| Goods received from Headquarters | 35,000 |
| Cheques sent to Headquarters | 30,300 |
| Returns sent to Headquarters | 5,000 |

The net profit shown by the profit and loss account of the branch is £8,000.

**Branch Records (in Manchester)**
*Headquarters Current Account*

| | £ | | £ |
|---|---|---|---|
| Bank | 30,300 | Balance b/d | 78,500 |
| Returns to Headquarters | 5,000 | Goods from Headquarters | 35,000 |
| Balance c/d | 86,200 | Net profit | 8,000 |
| | 121,500 | | 121,500 |
| | | Balance b/d | 86,200 |

**Headquarters Records (in London)**
*Manchester Branch Current Account*

| | | £ | | | £ |
|---|---|---|---|---|---|
| Balance b/d | | 78,500 | Bank | (B) | 29,500 |
| Goods sent to Branch | (A) | 37,000 | Returns received | (C) | 4,400 |
| Net profit | | 8,000 | | | |

At this point, the following items are found to be in transit at the end of the period (these should be confirmed to ensure that they are not merely errors in accounting records):

(A) Goods sent to the branch amounting to £2,000 (£37,000 – £35,000).
(B) Cheques sent by the branch amounting to £800 (£30,300 – £29,500).
(C) Returns from the branch amounting to £600 (£5,000 – £4,400).

- (A) needs amending to £35,000. This is done by crediting the account with £2,000.
- (B) needs amending to £30,300. This is done by crediting the account with £800.
- (C) needs amending to £5,000. This is done by crediting the account with £600.

As these are items in transit, they need to be carried down as balances into the next period. The branch current account will now be completed.

It may appear at first sight to be rather strange that all the items in transit are shown as debit balances. However, it must be appreciated that goods (including returns) and money in transit are assets of the business at the end of a financial period. That they are in transit does not alter the fact that they belong to the business. Assets are always shown as debit balances and there is no reason why it should be different just because they have not reached their destination on a certain date.

*Manchester Branch Current Account*

| | £ | | £ |
|---|---|---|---|
| Balance b/d | 78,500 | Bank | 29,500 |
| Goods sent to branch | 37,000 | Returns received | 4,400 |
| Net profit | 8,000 | Goods in transit c/d | 2,000 |
| | | Cheques in transit c/d | 800 |
| | | Returns in transit c/d | 600 |
| | | Balance c/d | 86,200 |
| | 123,500 | | 123,500 |
| Balance b/d | 86,200 | | |
| Goods in transit b/d | 2,000 | | |
| Cheques in transit b/d | 800 | | |
| Returns in transit b/d | 600 | | |

All of these four balances are shown in the trial balance. When the combined statement of financial position is being prepared the balance of the two current accounts (in this case £86,200) will cancel out as it is a debit balance in one trial balance and a credit balance in the other. The goods in transit £2,000, and the returns in transit, £600, both being goods, are added to the inventory in the statement of financial position. This is because at the end of the second month, inventory is made up of the following items:

| | £ |
|---|---|
| Inventory at London | |
| *Add* Inventory at Manchester | |
| *Add* Inventory in transit (£2,000 + £600) | 2,600 |
| Total inventory | |

Similarly, the balance for cheques or remittances in transit is added to the bank balances at London and Manchester:

| | £ |
|---|---|
| Bank balance at London | |
| *Add* Bank balance in Manchester | |
| *Add* Remittances in transit | 800 |

This is rather like a man who has £14 in one pocket and £3 in another. He takes a £5 note from the pocket containing the larger amount and is transferring it to his other pocket when someone asks him to stay perfectly still and calculate the total cash in his possession. He therefore has:

| | £ |
|---|---|
| Pocket 1 (£14 − £5) | 9 |
| Pocket 2 | 3 |
| Cash in transit | 5 |
| | 17 |

## 1.13 Items in transit and the statement of financial position

Using the figures already given in Exhibit 1.6, but adding some further information, trial balances for the London headquarters and the Manchester branch are shown in Exhibit 1.7 after the statement of profit or loss of the business has been prepared for the second month, and trial balances for both headquarters and the branch have been drawn up.

**Exhibit 1.7**

**Trial Balances as at end of month 2**

| | London Headquarters Dr | London Headquarters Cr | Manchester Branch Dr | Manchester Branch Cr |
|---|---|---|---|---|
| | £ | £ | £ | £ |
| Premises | 100,000 | | 50,000 | |
| Machinery | 20,000 | | 2,500 | |
| Fixtures | 31,000 | | 2,900 | |
| Motor vans | 15,000 | | 6,000 | |
| Closing inventory | 38,000 | | 7,000 | |
| Accounts receivable | 11,000 | | 8,000 | |
| Bank | 122,000 | | 21,600 | |
| Headquarters Current Account | | | | 86,200 |
| Branch Current Account | 86,200 | | | |
| Goods in transit | 2,000 | | | |
| Cheques in transit | 800 | | | |
| Returns in transit | 600 | | | |
| Accounts payable | | 13,000 | | 11,800 |
| Capital account as at start of month 1 | | 378,600 | | |
| Net profit for the two months from the statement of profit or loss (Branch £15,000 + Head Office £20,000) | | 35,000 | | |
| | 426,600 | 426,600 | 98,000 | 98,000 |

The combined statement of financial position can now be drawn up.

**Statement of Financial Position as at end of month 2**

| | £ | £ |
|---|---|---|
| *Non-current assets* | | |
| Premises | | 150,000 |
| Machinery | | 22,500 |
| Fixtures | | 33,900 |
| Motor vans | | 21,000 |
| | | 227,400 |
| *Current assets* | | |
| Inventory (Note 1) | 47,600 | |
| Accounts receivable (Note 2) | 19,000 | |
| Bank | 144,400 | 211,000 |
| Total assets | | 438,400 |
| *Less Current liabilities* | | |
| Accounts payable | | (24,800) |
| Net assets | | 413,600 |
| *Capital* | | |
| Opening balance | | 378,600 |
| *Add* Net profit: | | |
| London | 20,000 | |
| Manchester | 15,000 | 35,000 |
| | | 413,600 |

*Notes:*

| | | £ |
|---|---|---|
| (1) Inventory: | London | 38,000 |
| | Manchester | 7,000 |
| | In transit (£2,000 + £600) | 2,600 |
| | | 47,600 |

| | | £ |
|---|---|---|
| (2) Bank: | London | 122,000 |
| | Manchester | 21,600 |
| | In transit | 800 |
| | | 144,400 |

## 1.14 Foreign branch accounts

The treatment of the accounts of foreign branches is subject to only one exception from that of branches in your own country. This is concerned with the fact that when the trial balance is drawn up by the branch then this will be stated in a foreign currency. To amalgamate these figures with your own country's figures will mean that the foreign branch figures will have to be translated into your currency.

There are rules for general guidance as to how this can be done. These are given in IAS 21 *The effects of changes in foreign exchange rates*. These are the ones which will be shown. (Before you read further you should check whether or not this topic is part of your examination requirements.)

The amount of a particular currency which one can obtain for another currency is known as the exchange rate. Taking an imaginary country with a currency called *chips*, there might be a general agreement that the exchange rate should stay about 5 chips to £1. At certain times the exchange rate will exactly equal that figure, but due to all sorts of economic reasons it may well be 5.02 chips to £1 on one day and 4.97 chips to £1 several days later. In addition, some years ago there may have been an act of devaluation by one of the countries involved; the exchange rate could then have been 3 chips to £1. To understand more about exchange rates, devaluation and revaluation of currencies, you may wish to consult a relevant economics textbook.

All items in the trial balance should *not* be converted to your currency on the basis of the exchange rate ruling at the date of the trial balance. The rules in IAS 21 have been devised in an attempt to bring about conversion into your currency so as not to distort reported trading results.

## 1.15 IAS 21 The effects of changes in foreign exchange rates

IAS 21 states how transactions in a foreign currency and foreign operations should be included in the financial statements. Transactions denominated in a foreign currency should be translated at the exchange rate on the date of the transaction. At the date of the statement of financial position:

- foreign currency monetary items are translated at the 'closing rate' (i.e. the exchange rate on the date of the statement of financial position);
- non-monetary items measured at historical cost in a foreign currency are translated using the exchange rate at the date of the transaction;
- non-monetary items measured at fair value in a foreign currency are translated using the exchange rate at the date when the fair value was determined.

Exchange-rate differences arising on the settlement of monetary items or on translating monetary items at rates that differ from those at initial recognition are generally recognised in profit or loss.

When a foreign operation (e.g. a subsidiary located in Spain when the parent company is located in the UK) is translated so as to include it in the group's financial statements: assets and liabilities are translated at the closing rate; income and expenditure are translated at the exchange rates on the dates of the transactions. All resulting exchange differences are recognised as a separate component of equity (i.e. they are not included in profit or loss). However, when disposed of, all exchange differences that had been deferred in the separate component of equity are recognised in profit or loss. An example is shown in Exhibit 1.8.

### Exhibit 1.8

An example of the conversion of a trial balance into UK currency is now shown. The branch is in Flavia, and the unit of currency is the Flavian dollar. The exchange rates needed are:

(*a*) On 1 January 2010, 10 dollars = £1
(*b*) On 1 January 2012, 11 dollars = £1
(*c*) On 1 January 2015, 17 dollars = £1
(*d*) On 31 December 2015, 15 dollars = £1
(e) If no further information were given the average rate for 2015 would have to be taken as (*c*) + (*d*) ÷ 2, i.e. 16 dollars = £1. This is not an advisable procedure in practice; the fact that the average has been calculated from only two readings could mean that the average calculated might be far different from a more accurate one calculated from a larger number of readings.

**Trial Balance as at 31 December 2015**

| | *Dr (F$)* | *Cr (F$)* | *Exchange Rates* | *Dr (£)* | *Cr (£)* |
|---|---|---|---|---|---|
| Non-current assets: | | | | | |
| Bought 1 Jan 2010 | 10,000 | | 10 = £1 | 1,000 | |
| Bought 1 Jan 2012 | 8,800 | | 11 = £1 | 800 | |
| Inventory 1 Jan 2015 | 6,800 | | 17 = £1 | 400 | |
| Expense accounts | 8,000 | | 16 = £1 | 500 | |
| Sales | | 32,000 | 16 = £1 | | 2,000 |
| Goods from Headquarters | 21,900 | | £ per account in Headquarters' books | 1,490 | |
| Headquarters current account | | 43,000 | £ per account in Headquarters' books | | 3,380 |
| Accounts receivable | 9,000 | | 15 = £1 | 600 | |
| Accounts payable | | 4,500 | 15 = £1 | | 300 |
| Bank | 15,000 | | 15 = £1 | 1,000 | |
| | 79,500 | 79,500 | | 5,790 | 5,680 |
| **Difference on exchange account** | | | | | 110 |
| | | | | 5,790 | 5,790 |

The value of the inventory at 31 December 2015 is 12,000 Flavian dollars. When the trading account is drawn up, this is converted at F$15 = £1, i.e. £800.

**Note: Don't forget that either the term 'head office' or the term 'headquarters' (or 'HQ') may be used by examiners.**

## Learning outcomes

**You should now have learnt:**

**1** There are two main methods used to record transactions of the branches of an organisation:
   (*a*) all accounting records are kept by headquarters;
   (*b*) each branch has its own full accounting system.

**2** When all sales are for cash a double column trading account can be used in order to monitor any unexpected losses.

**3** When some sales are on credit, either memoranda columns can be used in the branch inventory account in order to monitor inventory or inventory control can be integrated into the double entry system.

**4** Foreign branch figures need to be translated using the principles set down in IAS 21 *The effects of changes in foreign exchange rates.*

## Answers to activities

1.1 When a second branch or head office is also involved in receiving payments from debtors of another branch, the focus of control shifts from being purely connected with one branch. More sophisticated methods of recording the transaction data are therefore required.

1.2 They are merely a measure of the resources at the branch. The underlying assets and liabilities they represent are already included in the statement of financial position.

## Review questions

**1.1** F Gibb Ltd has a branch in Stirling at which a full set of books is kept. At the end of the year the following summary is compiled of the transactions between the branch and headquarters as recorded in the latter's books:

| | |
|---|---:|
| Balance due from branch 1 April | 181,440 |
| Cash received from branch | 270,000 |
| Goods supplied to branch | 208,440 |
| Goods returned by branch | 3,600 |
| Expenses paid on behalf of branch | 33,000 |

At 30 September the branch profit and loss account showed a net profit of £120,000 for the six months.

(*a*) Show the above items as they would appear in the ledger of the head office.
(*b*) How can any resulting balance from these figures be proved, and what does it indicate?

**1.2** J Micheil Ltd, whose head office is in Cumbernauld, operates a branch in Lincoln. All goods are purchased by head office and invoiced to and sold by the branch at cost plus 60%.

Other than a sales ledger kept in Lincoln, all transactions are recorded in the books in Cumbernauld.

The following particulars are given of the transactions at the branch during the year ended 30 June 2016.

| | |
|---|---:|
| Inventory on hand, 1 July 2015, at invoice price | 80,320 |
| Accounts receivable on 1 July 2015 | 35,514 |
| Inventory on hand, 30 June 2016, at invoice price | 71,120 |
| Goods sent from Bristol during the year at invoice price | 446,400 |
| Credit sales | 387,000 |
| Cash sales | 21,600 |
| Returns to head office at invoice price | 18,000 |
| Invoice value of goods stolen | 10,800 |
| Bad debts written off | 1,332 |
| Cash from debtors | 403,200 |
| Normal loss at invoice price due to wastage | 1,800 |
| Cash discount allowed to debtors | 3,852 |

→

**You are required to** write up the branch inventory account and branch total accounts receivable account for the year ended 30 June 2016, as they would appear in the head office books, showing clearly any abnormal wastage.

**1.3** RST Limited is a family-controlled company which operates a chain of retail outlets specialising in motor spares and accessories.

Branch inventory is purchased by a centralised purchasing function in order to obtain the best terms from suppliers.

A 10% handling charge is applied by headquarters to the cost of the purchases, and branches are expected to add 25% to the resulting figure to arrive at normal selling prices, although branch managers are authorised to reduce normal prices in special situations. The effect of such reductions must be notified to headquarters.

On 1 April 2016, a new branch was established at Derham. The following details have been recorded for the year ended 31 March 2017:

| | £ |
|---|---|
| Purchase cost to head office of inventory transferred to Derham | 82,400 |
| Derham branch sales: cash | 89,940 |
| credit | 1,870 |
| Inventory transferred from Derham to other branches, at normal selling prices | 3,300 |
| Authorised reductions from normal selling prices during the year | 2,250 |

All records in respect of branch activities are maintained at head office, and the branch profit margin is dealt with through a branch inventory adjustment account.

**Required:**

(*a*) Prepare:

(*i*) the branch inventory account (maintained at branch selling prices);

(*ii*) the branch inventory adjustment account.

The *book inventory* should be taken for this part of the question.

(*b*) List four of the possible reasons for the inventory difference revealed when a physical stock-taking at the Derham branch on 31 March 2017 showed inventory valued at selling prices amounting to £14,850.

(*c*) State which of the following is the figure to be included in RST Limited's statement of financial position at 31 March 2017, for Derham branch inventory:

(*i*) £11,138

(*ii*) £11,880

(*iii*) £10,800

(*iv*) None of these.

Justify your choice with appropriate calculations.

(*Chartered Institute of Management Accountants*)

**1.4A** Paper Products has a head office in London and a branch in Bristol. The following information has been extracted from the head office books of account as at 31 March 2016:

**Information relating to the branch**

| *Balances* | *Opening* | | *Closing* |
|---|---|---|---|
| | *£000* | | *£000* |
| Branch bank account (positive balance) | 3 | | 12 |
| Branch accounts receivable | 66 | | 81 |
| Branch inventory (at transfer price) | 75 | | 90 |
| *Transactions during the year* | | *£000* | |
| Bad debts written off | | 15 | |
| Branch general expenses (paid from bank branch account) | | 42 | |
| Cash received from credit customers and banked | | 390 | |
| Cash sales banked | | 120 | |
| Cash transferred from branch to head office bank account | | 459 | |
| Credit sales | | 437 | |
| Discounts allowed to credit customers | | 9 | |
| Goods returned by credit customers | | 8 | |
| Goods returned from branch (at transfer price from head office) | | | 30 |
| Goods sent to branch (at transfer price from head office) | | | 600 |

**Information relating to head office**

| *Balances* | *Opening* | | *Closing* |
|---|---|---|---|
| | *£000* | | *£000* |
| Inventory | 180 | | 220 |
| *Transactions during the year* | | *£000* | |
| Bad debts written off | | 24 | |
| Cash sales | | 1,500 | |
| Credit sales | | 2,000 | |
| Discounts allowed to credit customers | | 29 | |
| General expenses | | 410 | |
| Goods returned by credit customers | | 40 | |
| Purchases | | 2,780 | |

*Additional information*:

1 Most of the accounting records relating to the branch are kept by the head office in its own books of account.

2 All purchases are made by the head office, and goods are invoiced to the branch at selling price, that is, at cost price plus 50%.

**Required:**

(*a*) Write up the following ledger accounts for the year to 31 March 2016, being careful to bring down any balances as at that date:
- (i) branch inventory account;
- (*ii*) goods sent to branch account;
- (*iii*) branch inventory adjustment account;
- (*iv*) branch accounts receivable account; and
- (*v*) branch bank account.

(*b*) Compile Paper Products' statement of profit or loss for the year ending 31 March 2016. Author's note

(*c*) Examine briefly the merits and demerits of Paper Products' method of branch bookkeeping including comments on the significance of the 'balancing figure' in the branch inventory account.

(*Association of Accounting Technicians*)

***Author's note***: **Part (b) should show a column for head office, a column for the branch, and a column for the total.**

**1.5** Packer and Stringer were in partnership as retail traders sharing profits and losses: Packer $^3/_4$, Stringer $^1/_4$. The partners were credited annually with interest at the rate of 6% per annum on their fixed capitals; no interest was charged on their drawings.

Stringer was responsible for the buying department of the business. Packer managed the head office and Paper was employed as the branch manager. Packer and Paper were each entitled to a commission of 10% of the net profits (after charging such commission) of the shop managed by him.

All goods were purchased by head office and goods sent to the branch were invoiced at cost.

The following was the trial balance as on 31 December 2017.

| | *Head Office Books* | | *Branch Books* | |
|---|---|---|---|---|
| | *Dr* | *Cr* | *Dr* | *Cr* |
| | £ | £ | £ | £ |
| Drawings accounts and fixed capital accounts: Packer | 2,500 | 14,000 | | |
| Stringer | 1,200 | 4,000 | | |
| Furniture and fittings, at cost | 1,500 | | 1,100 | |
| Furniture and fittings, provision for depreciation as at 31 December 2016 | | 500 | | 350 |
| Inventory on 31 December 2016 | 13,000 | | 4,400 | |
| Purchases | 37,000 | | | |
| Goods sent to branches | | 18,000 | 17,200 | |
| Sales | | 39,000 | | 26,000 |
| Allowance for doubtful debts | | 600 | | 200 |
| Branch and head office current accounts | 6,800 | | | 3,600 |
| Salaries and wages | 4,500 | | 3,200 | |
| Paper, on account of commission | | | 240 | |
| Carriage and travelling expenses | 2,200 | | 960 | |
| Administrative expenses | 2,400 | | | |
| Trade and general expenses | 3,200 | | 1,800 | |
| Sundry accounts receivable | 7,000 | | 3,000 | |
| Sundry accounts payable | | 5,800 | | 400 |
| Bank balances | 600 | | | 1,350 |
| | 81,900 | 81,900 | 31,900 | 31,900 |

You are given the following additional information:

(*a*) Inventory on 31 December 2017 amounted to: head office £14,440, branch £6,570.

(*b*) Administrative expenses are to be apportioned between head office and the branch in proportion to sales.

(*c*) Depreciation is to be provided on furniture and fittings at 10% of cost.

(*d*) The allowance for doubtful debts is to be increased by £50 in respect of head office accounts receivable and decreased by £20 in the case of those of the branch.

(*e*) On 31 December 2017 cash amounting to £2,400, in transit from the branch to head office, had been recorded in the branch books but not in those of head office; and on that date goods invoiced at £800, in transit from head office to the branch, had been recorded in the head office books but not in the branch books.

Any adjustments necessary are to be made in the head office books.

**You are required to:**

(*a*) prepare statements of profit or loss and the appropriation account for the year ending 31 December 2017, showing the net profit of the head office and branch respectively;

(*b*) prepare the statement of financial position as on that date; and

(*c*) show the closing entries in the branch current accounts giving the make-up of the closing balance.

Income tax is to be ignored.

(*Institute of Chartered Accountants*)

**1.6A** LR, a trader, commenced business on 1 January 2016, with a head office and one branch.

All goods were purchased by the head office and goods sent to the branch were invoiced at a fixed selling price of 25% above cost. All sales, both by the head office and the branch, were made at the fixed selling price.

The following trial balance was extracted from the books at the head office at 31 December 2016.

**Trial Balance**

| | £ | £ |
|---|---|---|
| Capital | | 52,000 |
| Drawings | 1,740 | |
| Purchases | 123,380 | |
| Sales | | 83,550 |
| Goods sent to branch (at selling price) | | 56,250 |
| Branch current account | 24,550 | |
| Non-current assets | 33,000 | |
| Accounts receivable and accounts payable | 7,980 | 11,060 |
| General expenses | 8,470 | |
| Balance at bank | 3,740 | |
| | 202,860 | 202,860 |

No entries had been made in the head office books for cash in transit from the branch to head office at 31 December 2016, £1,000.

When the balances shown below were extracted from the branch books at 31 December 2016, no entries had been made in the books of the branch for goods in transit on that date from head office to branch, £920 (selling price).

In addition to the balances which can be deduced from the information given above, the following balances appeared in the branch books on 31 December 2016.

| | £ |
|---|---|
| Non-current assets | 6,000 |
| General expenses | 6,070 |
| Accounts receivable | 7,040 |
| Accounts payable (excluding head office) | 1,630 |
| Sales | 51,700 |
| Balance at bank | 1,520 |

When inventory was taken on 31 December 2016, it was found that there was no shortage at the head office, but at the branch there were shortages amounting to £300, at selling price.

**You are required to**: prepare statements of profit or loss (*a*) for head office and (*b*) for the branch, as they would have appeared if goods sent to the branch had been invoiced at cost, and a statement of financial position of the whole business as on 31 December 2016.

Head office and branch inventories are to be valued at cost.

Ignore depreciation of non-current assets.

(*Institute of Chartered Secretaries and Administrators*)

→

**1.7** Nion is a retail goods outlet operating from a head office in London and a branch in Brighton. The following trial balances have been extracted from the books of account as at 31 October 2018.

| | *Head Office Books* | | *Branch Books* | |
|---|---|---|---|---|
| | *Dr* | *Cr* | *Dr* | *Cr* |
| | £ | £ | £ | £ |
| Drawings | 40,000 | | | |
| Non-current assets: at cost | 350,000 | | 100,000 | |
| accumulated depreciation (at 1 November 2017) | | 140,000 | | 30,000 |
| Inventory (at 1 November 2017) | 8,000 | | 20,000 | |
| Provision for unrealised profit | | 4,000 | | |
| Purchases | 914,000 | | | |
| Goods sent to branch at invoiced value | | 380,000 | 375,000 | |
| Sales | | 850,000 | | 437,000 |
| Allowance for doubtful debts | | 9,000 | | 2,500 |
| Head office/branch current accounts | 175,000 | | | 120,000 |
| Distribution expenses | 80,500 | | 5,000 | |
| Administrative expenses | 200,000 | | 16,500 | |
| Trade accounts receivable | 60,000 | | 60,000 | |
| Trade accounts payable | | 50,000 | | |
| Cash and bank balances | 15,500 | | 13,000 | |
| Capital | | 410,000 | | |
| | £1,843,000 | £1,843,000 | £589,500 | £589,500 |

*Additional information*:

1 All goods are purchased by the head office. Those goods sent to the branch are invoiced at cost plus 25%.

2 Inventories were valued at 31 October 2018 as being at head office, £12,000; and at the branch, £15,000 at their invoiced price.

3 Depreciation is to be provided for the year on the non-current assets at a rate of 10% on the historic cost.

4 The allowance for doubtful debts is to be maintained at a rate of 5% of outstanding trade debtors as at the end of the financial year.

5 As at 31 October 2018, there was £50,000 cash in transit from the branch to the head office; this cash was received in London on 3 November 2018. There was also £5,000 of goods in transit at invoice price from the head office to the branch; the branch received these goods on 10 November 2018.

**Required:**

Prepare in adjacent columns: (*a*) the head office, and (*b*) the branch statements of profit or loss for the year ending 31 October 2018; and a **combined** statement of financial position for Nion as at that date.

*Notes*:

(*i*) a combined statement of profit or loss is NOT required; and

(*ii*) separate statements of financial position for the head office and the branch are also NOT required.

(*Association of Accounting Technicians*)

**1.8A** Star Stores has its head office and main store in Crewe, and a branch store in Leek. All goods are purchased by the head office. Goods are invoiced to the branch at cost price plus a profit loading of 20%. The following trial balances have been extracted from the books of account of both the head office and the branch as at 31 December 2016:

| | *Head Office* | *Books* | *Branch* | *Books* |
|---|---|---|---|---|
| | *Dr* | *Cr* | *Dr* | *Cr* |
| | *£000* | *£000* | *£000* | *£000* |
| Administrative expenses | 380 | | 30 | |
| Distribution costs | 157 | | 172 | |
| Capital (at 1 January 2016) | | 550 | | |
| Cash and bank | 25 | | 2 | |
| Accounts payable and accruals | | 176 | | 20 |
| Current accounts | 255 | | | 180 |
| Accounts receivable and prepayments | 130 | | 76 | |
| Motor vehicles: | | | | |
| at cost | 470 | | 230 | |
| accumulated depreciation at 31 December 2016 | | 280 | | 120 |
| Plant and equipment: | | | | |
| at cost | 250 | | 80 | |
| accumulated depreciation at 31 December 2016 | | 120 | | 30 |
| Proprietor's drawings during the year | 64 | | | |
| Provision for unrealised profit on branch inventory at 1 January 2016 | | 5 | | |
| Purchases | 880 | | | |
| Sales | | 1,200 | | 570 |
| Inventory at cost/invoiced amount at 1 January 2016 | 80 | | 30 | |
| Transfer of goods to the branch/from the head office | | 360 | 300 | |
| | £2,691 | £2,691 | £920 | £920 |

*Additional information*:

1 The inventories in hand at 31 December 2016 were estimated to be as follows:

| | *£000* |
|---|---|
| At head office (at cost) | 100 |
| At the branch (at invoiced price) | 48 |

In addition, £60,000 of inventory at invoiced price had been despatched to the branch on 28 December 2016. These goods had not been received by the branch until 5 January 2017 and so they had not been included in the branch books of account.

2 On 31 December 2016, the branch had transferred £15,000 of cash to the head office bank, but this was not received in Crewe until 2 January 2017.

**Required:**

(*a*) Prepare in adjacent columns: (*i*) the head office, and (*ii*) the branch trading accounts and profit and loss accounts for the year ending 31 December 2016 (*note*: a combined statement of profit or loss is NOT required); and

(*b*) Prepare Star Stores' statement of financial position as at 31 December 2016 (*note*: separate statements of financial position for the head office and the branch are NOT required).

*(Association of Accounting Technicians)*

**1.9** EG Company Limited, a manufacturing business, exports some of its products through an overseas branch whose currency is 'florins', which carries out the final assembly operations before selling the goods.

The trial balances of the head office and branch at 30 June 2018 were:

| | *Head Office* | | *Branch* | |
|---|---|---|---|---|
| | £ | £ | Fl. | Fl. |
| Freehold buildings at cost | 14,000 | | 63,000 | |
| Accounts receivable and accounts payable | 8,900 | 9,500 | 36,000 | 1,560 |
| Sales | | 104,000 | | 432,000 |
| Authorised and issued capital | | 40,000 | | |
| Components sent to branch | | 35,000 | | |
| Head office/branch accounts | 60,100 | | | 504,260 |
| Branch cost of sales | | | 360,000 | |
| Depreciation provision, machinery | | 1,500 | | 56,700 |
| Head office cost of sales (including goods to branch) | 59,000 | | | |
| Administration costs | 15,200 | | 18,000 | |
| Inventory at 30 June 2018 | 28,900 | | 11,520 | |
| Retained profits | | 2,000 | | |
| Machinery at cost | 6,000 | | 126,000 | |
| Remittances | | 28,000 | 272,000 | |
| Balance at bank | 4,600 | | 79,200 | |
| Selling and distribution costs | 23,300 | | 28,800 | |
| | 220,000 | 220,000 | 994,520 | 994,520 |

The following adjustments are to be made:

1. The cost of sales figures include a depreciation charge of 10% per annum on cost for machinery.
2. A provision of £300 for unrealised profit in branch inventory is to be made.
3. On 26 June 2018 the branch remitted 16,000 Fl.; these were received by the head office on 4 July and realised £1,990.
4. During May a branch customer in error paid the head office for goods supplied. The amount due was 320 Fl. which realised £36. It has been correctly dealt with by head office but not yet entered in the branch books.
5. A provision has to be made for a commission of 5% of the net profit of the branch after charging such commission, which is due to the branch manager.

The rates of exchange were:

| | |
|---|---|
| At 1 July 2017 | 10 Fl. = £1 |
| At 30 June 2018 | 8 Fl. = £1 |
| Average for the year | 9 Fl. = £1 |
| On purchase of buildings and machinery | 7 Fl. = £1 |

**You are required to prepare, for internal use:**

(*a*) detailed operating accounts for the year ended 30 June 2018; Author's note

(*b*) combined head office and branch statement of financial position as at 30 June 2018;

(*c*) the branch account in the head office books, in both sterling and currency, the opening balance on 1 July 2017 being £25,136 (189,260 Fl.).

Taxation is to be ignored.

(*Chartered Institute of Management Accountants*)

***Author's note***: **The question is looking for a statement of profit or loss for both the branch and head office showing overall net profit.**

**1.10** OTL Ltd commenced business on 1 January 2017. The head office is in London and there is a branch in Highland. The currency of Highland is the crown.

The following are the trial balances of the head office and the Highland branch as at 31 December 2017:

| | *Head Office* | | *Highland Branch* | |
|---|---|---|---|---|
| | £ | £ | *Crowns* | *Crowns* |
| Branch account | 65,280 | | | |
| Balances at bank | 10,560 | | 66,000 | |
| Accounts payable | | 21,120 | | 92,400 |
| Accounts receivable | 18,480 | | 158,400 | |
| Non-current assets (purchased 1 January 2017) | 39,600 | | 145,200 | |
| Head office account | | | | 316,800 |
| Profit and loss account (net profit for year) | | 52,800 | | 79,200 |
| Issued share capital | | 86,400 | | |
| Inventory | 26,400 | | 118,800 | |
| | 160,320 | 160,320 | 488,400 | 488,400 |

The trial balance of the head office was prepared before any entries had been made in respect of any profits or losses of the branch.

Remittances from head office to branch and from branch to head office were recorded in the books at the actual amounts paid and received.

The rates of exchange were:

| | |
|---|---|
| On 1 January 2017 | 5 crowns = £1 |
| Average rate for year 2017 | 4.4 crowns = £1 |
| On 31 December 2017 | 4 crowns = £1 |

**Required:**

(*a*) The trial balance of the Highland branch as at 31 December 2017, in sterling.

(*b*) The closing entries, as at 31 December 2017, in the branch account in the books of the head office.

(*c*) A summary of the statement of financial position of OTL Ltd as at 31 December 2017.

Ignore depreciation of fixed assets.

Ignore taxation.

(*Institute of Chartered Secretaries and Administrators*)

**1.11A** Home Ltd is incorporated in the UK and rents mobile homes to holidaymakers in this country and in Carea. The company has a head office in London and a branch in Carea where the local currency is 'Mics'. The following balances are extracted from the books of the head office and its 'self-accounting' branch at 31 December 2017.

| | *Head Office* | *Branch* |
|---|---|---|
| | £ | *Mics* |
| Debit balances | | |
| Non-current assets at cost | 450,000 | 900,000 |
| Accounts receivable and cash | 17,600 | 36,000 |
| Operating costs | 103,700 | 225,000 |
| Branch current account | 42,600 | |
| | 613,900 | 1,161,000 |
| Credit balances | | |
| Share capital | 200,000 | – |
| Retained profit, 1 January 2017 | 110,800 | – |
| Sales revenue | 186,300 | 480,000 |
| Accounts payable | 9,700 | 25,000 |
| Head office current account | – | 420,000 |
| Accumulated depreciation | 107,100 | 236,000 |
| | 613,900 | 1,161,000 |

→

The following information is provided regarding exchange rates, some of which is relevant.

The non-current assets of the branch were acquired when there were 8 Mics to the £. Exchange rates ruling during 2017 were:

| | *Mics to the £* |
|---|---|
| 1 January | 6 |
| Average | 5 |
| 31 December | 4 |

There are no cash or goods in transit between head office and branch at the year end.

**Required:**
The final accounts of Home Ltd for 2017. The accounts should be expressed in £s sterling and, for this purpose, the conversion of Mics should be made in accordance with IAS 21 *The effects of changes in foreign exchange rates.*

(*Institute of Chartered Secretaries and Administrators*)

# chapter 2 Purchases by instalments

## Learning objectives

**After you have studied this chapter, you should be able to:**

- explain the term 'hire purchase'
- explain what distinguishes hire purchase from outright purchase
- explain what distinguishes hire purchase from a lease
- record the entries relating to hire purchase transactions

## Introduction

In this chapter you'll learn about the nature of hire purchase; of the difference to the cost to the buyer of paying the same amount each period as compared with paying a variable amount linked to the outstanding amount owed; and the accounting treatment and entries required when hire purchase transactions occur. You will also be introduced to leases and to the differences between leases and hire purchase agreements.

## 2.1 Nature of hire purchase

Hire purchase (also known as 'rent-to-own' or 'instalment plan purchase') is a way of buying assets that avoids the need to pay in full either at the time of purchase or very soon thereafter. When using a hire purchase contract, the buyer is renting (or leasing) the item being purchased. Ownership does not pass to the purchaser until the full amount of the contract is paid.

The essential differences between a hire purchase and a 'normal' purchase are therefore:

1 The asset does not belong to the purchaser when it is received from the supplier. Instead it belongs to the supplier providing the hire purchase.
2 The purchaser will pay for the item by instalments over a period of time. This may be for as long as two or three years, or even longer.
3 The asset does not legally belong to the purchaser until two things happen:
   (*a*) the final instalment is paid; and
   (*b*) the purchaser agrees to a legal option to buy the asset; and, not surprisingly,
4 The cost to the buyer will be higher than it would have been had the item been paid for at the time of purchase. The extra money paid is interest.

Anyone who buys something using hire purchase can stop paying the instalments at any time. The item purchased must then be returned to the seller. If this happens, the buyer is not entitled to a refund of any of the instalments already paid.

If the purchaser is unable to continue paying the instalments, the seller normally repossesses the asset and keeps all the instalments already paid.

Activity 2.1

Why do you think organisations purchase assets on hire purchase?

## 2.2 Law of hire purchase

The Hire Purchase Act 1964 governs all hire purchase transactions in the UK.

## 2.3 Interest payable on hire purchase

Each payment made on a hire purchase contract consists of two things:

1 **Capital.** Paying off some of the amount owing for the cash price of the asset.
2 **Interest.** Paying off some of the interest that has accrued since the start of the agreement.

The total payment (1) + (2) made for each instalment may be the same, or may differ. Normally, however, the same amount in total is paid each time an instalment is due.

### Exhibit 2.1 Unequal instalments

1 A high-spec laptop is bought from A King at the start of Year 1. Cash price is £2,000.
2 Hire purchase price is £2,300.
3 Payable in two annual instalments at the end of each year. Each instalment to be £1,000 plus interest accrued for that year.
4 Rate of interest is 10% per annum.

| | | | £ |
|---|---|---|---|
| Year 1: | Cash price | (A) | 2,000 |
| | *Add* Interest 10% of (A) £2,000 | | 200 |
| | | | 2,200 |
| | *Less* Instalment paid | | (1,200) |
| | Owing at end of Year 1 | (B) | 1,000 |
| Year 2: | *Add* Interest 10% of (B) £1,000 | | 100 |
| | | | 1,100 |
| | *Less* Instalment paid | | (1,100) |
| | Owing at end of Year 2 | | – |

### Exhibit 2.2 Equal instalments

The facts are the same as in Exhibit 2.1, except that each instalment is £1,152. (Each interest payment is rounded down to the nearest £.)

| | | | £ |
|---|---|---|---|
| Year 1: | Cash price | (A) | 2,000 |
| | *Add* Interest 10% of (A) £2,000 | | 200 |
| | | | 2,200 |
| | *Less* Instalment paid | | (1,152) |
| | Owing at end of Year 1 | (B) | 1,048 |
| Year 2: | *Add* Interest 10% of (B) £1,048 | | 104 |
| | | | 1,152 |
| | *Less* Instalment paid | | (1,152) |
| | Owing at end of Year 2 | | – |

*Note*: The interest for Year 1 is the same for both the equal and the unequal instalments (in Exhibits 2.1 and 2.2), as the whole of the cash price is owed in both cases for a full year.

Why is the amount paid in Year 2 in Exhibit 2.2 different from the amount paid in Year 2 in Exhibit 2.1?

***Note*: In this example, no payment was made until 12 months after the transaction occurred. Often, the first instalment is paid at the time of the transaction; if so, it is a repayment of capital. The difference shown between unequal instalments and equal instalments would still be similar to those shown in Exhibit 2.1 because some of the amount due includes interest and interest due depends upon how it is calculated.**

## 2.4 Accounting for hire purchase

Accounting treats assets bought on hire purchase as though they belonged immediately to the purchaser.

This is because businesses normally buy assets on hire purchase with the intention of paying all the instalments, so that the asset finally will belong to them. As they mean to keep the asset and legally own it after the final payment, accounting treats it as though legal ownership occurred on purchase.

This is an illustration of the use of the 'substance over form' concept. Legally the purchaser does not yet own the asset (form) yet it does own it from an economic perspective (substance).

The total purchase price is split into two parts for the financial statements:

1 **Cash price.** This is the amount to be debited to the non-current asset account.
2 **Interest.** This is an expense of borrowing money and is charged to an expense account, i.e. hire purchase interest account.

**As interest accrues over time, each period should be charged only with the interest accrued for that period.** This is shown in Exhibit 2.3:

**Exhibit 2.3**

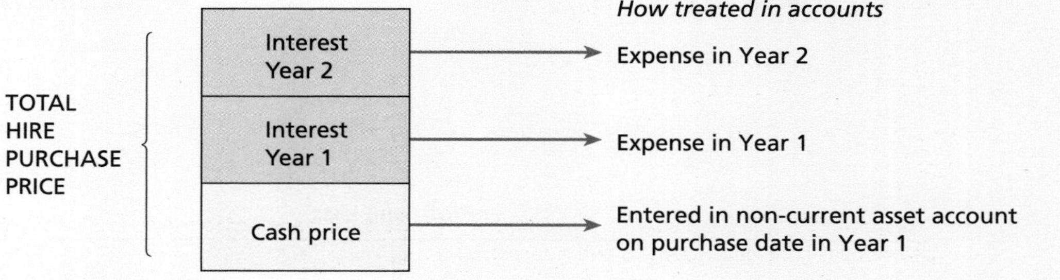


## 2.5 Illustrations of purchaser's accounts

The double entry needed is:

| | |
|---|---|
| (A) Cash price: | Debit non-current asset<br>Credit supplier |
| (B) Hire purchase interest (for each period's interest): | Debit hire purchase interest<br>Credit supplier |
| (C) Hire purchase instalments: | Debit supplier<br>Credit bank |
| (D) Charge interest to profit and loss: | Debit profit and loss<br>Credit hire purchase interest |

Let's look at the ledger accounts which would have been used to enter the facts as in Exhibit 2.1. (For simplicity, depreciation has been omitted from the example.) Letters entered against the entries refer to the double entries given above.

**Laptop**

| | | | | £ | | | | | £ |
|---|---|---|---|---|---|---|---|---|---|
| Year 1 | | | | | | | | | |
| Jan | 1 | A King | (A) | 2,000 | | | | | |

**Hire Purchase Interest**

| | | | | £ | | | | | £ |
|---|---|---|---|---|---|---|---|---|---|
| Year 1 | | | | | Year 1 | | | | |
| Dec | 31 | A King | (B) | 200 | Dec | 31 | Profit and loss | (D) | 200 |
| Year 2 | | | | | Year 2 | | | | |
| Dec | 31 | A King | (B) | 100 | Dec | 31 | Profit and loss | (D) | 100 |

**A King**

| | | | | £ | | | | | £ |
|---|---|---|---|---|---|---|---|---|---|
| Year 1 | | | | | Year 1 | | | | |
| Dec | 31 | Bank | (C) | 1,200 | Jan | 1 | Laptop | (A) | 2,000 |
| | 31 | Balance c/d | | 1,000 | Dec | 31 | HP interest | (B) | 200 |
| | | | | 2,200 | | | | | 2,200 |
| Year 2 | | | | | Year 2 | | | | |
| Dec | 31 | Bank | (C) | 1,100 | Jan | 1 | Balance b/d | | 1,000 |
| | | | | | Dec | 31 | HP interest | (B) | 100 |
| | | | | 1,100 | | | | | 1,100 |

**Bank**

| | | | | £ | | | | | £ |
|---|---|---|---|---|---|---|---|---|---|
| | | | | | Year 1 | | | | |
| | | | | | Dec | 31 | A King | (C) | 1,200 |
| | | | | | Year 2 | | | | |
| | | | | | Dec | 31 | A King | (C) | 1,100 |

**Profit and Loss**

| | | | | £ | | | | | £ |
|---|---|---|---|---|---|---|---|---|---|
| Year 1 | | | | | | | | | |
| Dec | 31 | HP interest | (D) | 200 | | | | | |
| Year 2 | | | | | | | | | |
| Dec | 31 | HP interest | (D) | 100 | | | | | |

## 2.6 Depreciation and assets bought on hire purchase

Depreciation is based on the cash price. Hire purchase interest is an expense in the statement of profit or loss and so does not enter depreciation calculations. Only the initial (cash) price of the non-current asset is depreciated.

## 2.7 Statements of financial position and assets bought on hire purchase

In the statement of financial position for a sole proprietor or a partnership, purchases on hire purchase of non-current assets can be shown as follows:

| | £ | £ |
|---|---|---|
| *Non-current assets* | | |
| Machinery at cost[(1)] | | 20,000 |
| *Less* Owing on hire purchase[(2)] | 6,000 | |
| Depreciation to date | 10,000 | |
| | | (16,000) |
| | | 4,000 |

*Notes*

(1) This is the cash price of the machinery.

(2) This is the amount of the original cash price still unpaid.

Returning to Exhibit 2.1, if the laptop had been depreciated using the straight-line method at 25%, the statement of financial position entries would have been:

**Statement of Financial Position (End of Year 1)**

| | £ | £ |
|---|---|---|
| *Non-current assets* | | |
| Laptop at cost | | 2,000 |
| *Less* Owing on hire purchase* | 1,000 | |
| Depreciation to date | 500 | |
| | | (1,500) |
| | | 500 |

*This is the balance of A King's account and does not include interest.

**Statement of Financial Position (End of Year 2)**

| | £ | £ |
|---|---|---|
| *Non-current assets* | | |
| Laptop at cost | | 2,000 |
| *Less* Depreciation to date | | (1,000) |
| | | 1,000 |

*Note*: At the end of Year 2 there was nothing owing to A King for hire purchase.

However, in company statements of financial position this is *not* allowed. The Companies Acts do not permit an amount owing on a hire purchase contract to be deducted from the value of the asset in the statement of financial position. Netting-off of assets and liabilities other than when the same entity is involved (as in, for example, the case where the same business is a debtor and a creditor) is not permitted.

In a company's statement of financial position, the entries relating to Exhibit 2.1 would be:

**Statement of Financial Position (End of Year 1)**

| | £ | £ |
|---|---|---|
| *Non-current assets* | | |
| Laptop at cost | | 2,000 |
| *Less* Depreciation to date | | (500) |
| | | 1,500 |
| *Liabilities* | | |
| Accounts payable (Owing on hire purchase)* | | 1,000 |

*This is the balance of A King's account and does not include interest.

**Statement of Financial Position (End of Year 2)**

| | £ |
|---|---|
| *Non-current assets* | |
| Laptop at cost | 2,000 |
| *Less* Depreciation to date | (1,000) |
| | 1,000 |

## 2.8 A fully worked example

Exhibit 2.4 illustrates hire purchase more fully. It covers three years of hire purchase and shows the statement of financial position figures that would appear if sole traders and partnerships adopted the first approach shown in Section 2.7. We'll also be using this example in Sections 2.9 and 2.10.

### Exhibit 2.4

1 A machine is bought by K Thomas for £3,618 on hire purchase from Suppliers Ltd on 1 January 2016.
2 It is paid for by three instalments of £1,206 on 31 December of 2016, 2017 and 2018.
3 The cash price is £3,000.
4 Rate of interest is 10% per annum on the balance outstanding at the start of the year.
5 Straight-line depreciation of 20% per annum is to be provided.

***Note***: **The letters (A) to (F) refer to the description of entries following the account.**

**Machinery**

| | | | | £ | | | | | |
|---|---|---|---|---|---|---|---|---|---|
| 2016 | | | | | | | | | |
| Jan | 1 | Suppliers Ltd | (A) | 3,000 | | | | | |

**Suppliers Ltd**

| | | | | £ | | | | | £ |
|---|---|---|---|---|---|---|---|---|---|
| 2016 | | | | | 2016 | | | | |
| Dec | 31 | Bank | (B) | 1,206 | Jan | 1 | Machinery | (A) | 3,000 |
| | 31 | Balance c/d | (D) | 2,094 | Dec | 31 | HP interest | (C) | 300 |
| | | | | 3,300 | | | | | 3,300 |
| 2017 | | | | | 2017 | | | | |
| Dec | 31 | Bank | (B) | 1,206 | Jan | 1 | Balance b/d | (D) | 2,094 |
| | 31 | Balance c/d | (D) | 1,097 | Dec | 31 | HP interest | (C) | 209 |
| | | | | 2,303 | | | | | 2,303 |
| 2018 | | | | | 2018 | | | | |
| Dec | 31 | Bank | (B) | 1,206 | Jan | 1 | Balance b/d | (D) | 1,097 |
| | | | | | Dec | 31 | HP interest | (C) | 109 |
| | | | | 1,206 | | | | | 1,206 |

**Hire Purchase Interest**

| | | | | £ | | | | | £ |
|---|---|---|---|---|---|---|---|---|---|
| 2016 | | | | | 2016 | | | | |
| Dec | 31 | Suppliers Ltd | (C) | 300 | Dec | 31 | Profit and loss | (E) | 300 |
| 2017 | | | | | 2017 | | | | |
| Dec | 31 | Suppliers Ltd | (C) | 209 | Dec | 31 | Profit and loss | (E) | 209 |
| 2018 | | | | | 2018 | | | | |
| Dec | 31 | Suppliers Ltd | (C) | 109 | Dec | 31 | Profit and loss | (E) | 109 |

**Provision for Depreciation: Machinery**

| | | | | | | | | | £ |
|---|---|---|---|---|---|---|---|---|---|
| | | | | | 2016 | | | | |
| | | | | | Dec | 31 | Profit and loss | (F) | 600 |
| | | | | | 2017 | | | | |
| | | | | | Dec | 31 | Profit and loss | (F) | 600 |
| | | | | | 2018 | | | | |
| | | | | | Dec | 31 | Profit and loss | (F) | 600 |

**Statements of Financial Position as at 31 December**

| | | £ | £ | £ |
|---|---|---|---|---|
| 2016 | Machinery (at cost) | | 3,000 | |
| | *Less* Depreciation | 600 | | |
| | Owing on hire purchase agreement | 2,094 | | |
| | | | (2,694) | |
| | | | | 306 |
| 2017 | Machinery (at cost) | | 3,000 | |
| | *Less* Depreciation to date | 1,200 | | |
| | Owing on hire purchase agreement | 1,097 | | |
| | | | (2,297) | |
| | | | | 703 |
| 2018 | Machinery (at cost) | | 3,000 | |
| | *Less* Depreciation to date | | (1,800) | |
| | | | | 1,200 |

*Description of entries:*

(A) When the asset is acquired the cash price is debited to the asset account and the credit is in the supplier's account.
(B) The instalments paid are credited to the bank account and debited to the supplier's account.
(C) The interest is credited to the supplier's account for each period as it accrues, and it is debited to the expense account, later to be transferred to the profit and loss account for the period (E).
(D) The balance carried down each year is the amount of the cash price still owing.
(E) Depreciation provisions are calculated on the full cash price, as the depreciation of an asset is in no way affected by whether or not it has been fully paid for.

In the case of a company, the statement of financial position entries consist of balance (A), the cash price, *less* balance (F), the amount of the cash price apportioned as depreciation. Balance (D), the amount of the cash price still owing at each date of the statement of financial position, is shown separately under accounts payable.

## 2.9 The seller's books: apportionment of profits

There are many ways of incorporating sales on hire purchase in the financial statements. The method used should be the one most suitable for the business.

The total profit for the seller of goods on hire purchase breaks down as follows:

| | £ |
|---|---|
| Profit on item sold: Cash price *less* cost | xxx |
| Income made from interest charged | xxx |
| | xxx |

In Exhibit 2.4, Suppliers Ltd sold a machine to K Thomas. Assume that the machine cost Suppliers Ltd £2,100. The total profit upon the final instalment being paid is found as follows:

| | | £ | £ |
|---|---|---|---|
| Profit on sale of machine: | Cash price | 3,000 | |
| | Cost | (2,100) | |
| | | | 900 |
| Income earned by charging interest: | 2016 | 300 | |
| | 2017 | 209 | |
| | 2018 | 109 | |
| | | | 618 |
| Total profit over three years | | | 1,518 |

### Apportionment of profit on sale

There are two main methods for allocating the profit on sale (£900) between the years of the agreement. (This profit does *not* include the hire purchase interest.)

1 It is considered profit in the period in which it was first sold to the purchaser. In this case all the £900 would be shown as profit for 2016.
2 The profit is divided among the three years. In this case, the following formula is used to find the amount of interest to be recognised as profit each year:

$$\frac{\text{Cash received in period}}{\text{Total cash to be received}} \times \text{Profit}$$

In this case the profits will be shown as:

$$2016 \quad \frac{£1{,}206}{£1{,}206 \times 3} \times £900 = \frac{1}{3} \times £900 = £300$$

$$2017 \quad \frac{£1{,}206}{£1{,}206 \times 3} \times £900 = \frac{1}{3} \times £900 = £300$$

$$2018 \quad \frac{£1{,}206}{£1{,}206 \times 3} \times £900 = \frac{1}{3} \times £900 = £300$$

| | |
|---|---|
| Total profit on sale for three years | £900 |

**This case shows equal profits because equal instalments were paid each year. Unequal payments would result in unequal profits.**

### Apportionment of interest to profit and loss

The interest accrued for each period should be taken into profit calculations. As the amount owed decreases, so does the interest:

| | £ |
|---|---|
| 2016 | 300 |
| 2017 | 209 |
| 2018 | 109 |
| Total interest for the three years | 618 |

## 2.10 The seller's books: accounts needed

We can now look at Exhibit 2.5, taking the details from Exhibit 2.4 as it would appear in the seller's books. Items (A) to (C) have already been shown in Exhibit 2.4:

**Exhibit 2.5**

(A) The machine was sold on 1 January 2016 to K Thomas on hire purchase terms. Cash price was £3,000 plus hire purchase interest.
(B) Hire purchase interest was at a rate of 10% per annum.
(C) There are to be three instalments of £1,206 each, receivable on 31 December of 2016, 2017 and 2018. These were paid by K Thomas on the correct dates.
(D) This was the only hire purchase sale during the three years.
(E) The profit on the cash price is to be shown as profits for 2016, the year in which the sale was made.
(F) The cost of the machine to Suppliers Ltd was £2,100.

**Hire Purchase Sales**

| | | | | £ | | | | | £ |
|---|---|---|---|---|---|---|---|---|---|
| 2016 | | | | | 2016 | | | | |
| Dec | 31 | Trading | | 3,000 | Jan | 1 | K Thomas | (A) | 3,000 |

**K Thomas**

| | | | | £ | | | | | £ |
|---|---|---|---|---|---|---|---|---|---|
| 2016 | | | | | 2016 | | | | |
| Jan | 1 | Sales | (A) | 3,000 | Dec | 31 | Bank | (C) | 1,206 |
| Dec | 31 | HP interest | (B) | 300 | Dec | 31 | Balance c/d | | 2,094 |
| | | | | 3,300 | | | | | 3,300 |
| 2017 | | | | | 2017 | | | | |
| Jan | 1 | Balance b/d | | 2,094 | Dec | 31 | Bank | (C) | 1,206 |
| Dec | 31 | HP interest | (B) | 209 | Dec | 31 | Balance c/d | | 1,097 |
| | | | | 2,303 | | | | | 2,303 |
| 2018 | | | | | 2018 | | | | |
| Jan | 1 | Balance b/d | | 1,097 | Dec | 31 | Bank | (C) | 1,206 |
| Dec | 31 | HP interest | (B) | 109 | | | | | |
| | | | | 1,206 | | | | | 1,206 |

**Hire Purchase Interest**

| | | | | £ | | | | | £ |
|---|---|---|---|---|---|---|---|---|---|
| 2016 | | | | | 2016 | | | | |
| Dec | 31 | HP trading | | 300 | Dec | 31 | K Thomas | (B) | 300 |
| 2017 | | | | | 2017 | | | | |
| Dec | 31 | HP trading | | 209 | Dec | 31 | K Thomas | (B) | 209 |
| 2018 | | | | | 2018 | | | | |
| Dec | 31 | HP trading | | 109 | Dec | 31 | K Thomas | (B) | 109 |

**Hire Purchase Goods**

| | | | | £ | | | | | £ |
|---|---|---|---|---|---|---|---|---|---|
| 2016 | | | | | 2016 | | | | |
| Jan | 1 | Bank | (F) | 2,100 | Dec | 31 | HP trading | | 2,100 |

**Bank**

| | | | | £ | | | | | £ |
|---|---|---|---|---|---|---|---|---|---|
| 2016 | | | | | 2016 | | | | |
| Dec | 31 | K Thomas | (C) | 1,206 | Jan | 1 | HP goods | (F) | 2,100 |
| 2017 | | | | | | | | | |
| Dec | 31 | K Thomas | (C) | 1,206 | | | | | |
| 2018 | | | | | | | | | |
| Dec | 31 | K Thomas | (C) | 1,206 | | | | | |

**Hire Purchase Trading**

| | | | | £ | | | | | £ |
|---|---|---|---|---|---|---|---|---|---|
| 2016 | | | | | 2016 | | | | |
| Dec | 31 | HP goods | | 2,100 | Dec | 31 | HP sales | | 3,000 |
| | | Gross profit | | 1,200 | | | HP interest | | 300 |
| | | | | 3,300 | | | | | 3,300 |
| 2017 | | | | | 2017 | | | | |
| Dec | 31 | Gross profit | | 209 | Dec | 31 | HP interest | | 209 |
| 2018 | | | | | 2018 | | | | |
| Dec | 31 | Gross profit | | 109 | Dec | 31 | HP interest | | 109 |

In Exhibit 2.5 all the profit was taken as being earned in 2016 other than the interest allocated to 2017 and 2018. If we decided to take the profit as being earned when the instalments are received, then the only account which would be altered would be the trading account plus one other: the hire purchase profit deferred account. All the other accounts would be exactly the same as in Exhibit 2.5.

The amendments needed are shown as Exhibit 2.6:

**Exhibit 2.6**

**Hire Purchase Trading**

| | | | | £ | | | | | £ |
|---|---|---|---|---|---|---|---|---|---|
| 2016 | | | | | 2016 | | | | |
| Dec | 31 | HP goods | | 2,100 | Dec | 31 | HP sales | | 3,000 |
| | | HP profit deferred | (G) | 600 | | | HP interest | | 300 |
| | | Gross profit | | 600 | | | | | |
| | | | | 3,300 | | | | | 3,300 |
| 2017 | | | | | 2017 | | | | |
| Dec | 31 | Gross profit | | 509 | Dec | 31 | HP profit deferred | (H) | 300 |
| | | | | | | | HP interest | | 209 |
| | | | | 509 | | | | | 509 |
| 2018 | | | | | 2018 | | | | |
| Dec | 31 | Gross profit | | 409 | Dec | 31 | HP profit deferred | (H) | 300 |
| | | | | | | | HP interest | | 109 |
| | | | | 409 | | | | | 409 |

**Hire Purchase Profit Deferred**

| | | | | £ | | | | | £ |
|---|---|---|---|---|---|---|---|---|---|
| 2016 | | | | | 2016 | | | | |
| Dec | 31 | Balance c/d | | 600 | Dec | 31 | HP trading | (G) | 600 |
| 2017 | | | | | 2017 | | | | |
| Dec | 31 | HP trading | | 300 | Jan | 1 | Balance b/d | | 600 |
| | | Balance c/d | | 300 | | | | | |
| | | | | 600 | | | | | 600 |
| 2018 | | | | | 2018 | | | | |
| Dec | 31 | HP trading | (H) | 300 | Jan | 1 | Balance b/d | | 300 |

The double entry needed was:

(G) In year of sale: Debit hire purchase trading account with profits carried to future years
Credit hire purchase profit deferred

(H) In following years: Debit hire purchase profit deferred with profits earned in each year
Credit hire purchase trading account

***Note*: The entries for hire purchase interest have not changed.**

## 2.11 Repossessions

When customers stop paying their instalments before they should, the goods can be taken away from them. This is called *repossession*. The amounts already paid by the customers will be kept by the seller.

The repossessed items should be entered in the books of the seller, as they are now back in inventory, but they will be valued as used goods.

Exhibit 2.7 shows the entries that must be made in the hire purchase trading account:

1 On 1 January 2017 we buy 15 electronic agendas for £300 each.
2 On 1 January 2017 we sell 12 of them for a cash price of £480 plus £120 interest to be paid = £600 total.
3 24 monthly instalments are to be paid of £25 each = £600.
4 Because of the difficulties of apportioning interest, each instalment is taken to include £5 interest, i.e. 24 × £5 = £120 interest.
5 On 1 November 2017, after 10 instalments have been received, a customer who bought two of the agendas cannot pay any more instalments. Both of them are returned by him. We do not have to repay the instalments paid by him.
6 The two agendas returned are valued at £140 each. Also in inventory on 31 December 2017 are three of the agendas bought on 1 January 2017 for £300 each and still valued at that amount.
7 Profit is to be calculated based on the number of instalments paid.

## Exhibit 2.7

**Hire Purchase Trading**

| 2017 | | £ | 2017 | | £ |
|---|---|---|---|---|---|
| Purchases | (*a*) | 4,500 | Sales at cash price | (*b*) | 4,800 |
| HP profit deferred | (*f*) | 900 | HP interest | (*c*) | 600 |
| Gross profit | (*g*) | 1,680 | Instalments received on repossessions | (*d*) | 500 |
| | | | Inventory | (*e*) | 1,180 |
| | | 7,080 | | | 7,080 |

*Notes*

Calculations are made as follows:

(*a*) 15 × £300 each = £4,500.
(*b*) 10 were sold (and not returned) at cash price of £480 each.
(*c*) Interest on 10 sold (and not returned) × £5 × 12 months = £600.
(*d*) 10 instalments paid (including interest) on two agendas = 10 × £25 × 2 = £500.

| | | £ |
|---|---|---|
| (*e*) Inventory = new items 3 × £300 | = | 900 |
| repossessed items 2 × £140 | = | 280 |
| | | 1,180 |

| | | £ |
|---|---|---|
| (*f*) Profit per agenda = cash price £480 − cost £300 | = | 180 |
| To be paid: 12 instalments out of 24 = ½ profit | = | 90 |
| Number sold and not returned, 10 × £90 | = | 900 |

| (*g*) Gross profit can be checked: | | | | | |
|---|---|---|---|---|---|
| Earned to date 10 × £90 | | | | = | 900 |
| Interest earned to date £5 × 10 × 12 months | | | | = | 600 |
| Profit on repossessions: | | | £ | | |
| Instalments received | | | 500 | | |
| *Less* Loss of value on repossessions | £ | | | | |
| Cost 2 × £300 | 600 | | | | |
| Value taken back | (280) | = | (320) | | |
| | | | | | 180 |
| | | | | | 1,680 |

## 2.12 IAS 17 Leases

Leasing and hire purchase contracts are means by which organisations acquire the right to use (lease) or purchase (hire purchase) non-current assets. In the UK there is normally no provision in a lease contract for legal title to the leased asset to pass to the lessee during the term of a lease. However, under a **hire purchase agreement** the hirer may acquire legal title by exercising an option to purchase the asset upon fulfilment of certain conditions (normally the payment of an agreed number of instalments).

Lessors fall into three broad categories: (i) companies, including banks and finance houses, which provide finance under lease contracts to enable a single customer to acquire the use of an asset for the greater part of its useful life; (ii) businesses which rent out assets for varying periods of time probably to more than one customer; or, (iii) manufacturers or dealer lessors (such as car salerooms) which use leasing as a means of marketing their products, which may involve leasing a product to one customer or to several customers.

As a lessor and lessee are both parties to the same transaction it is appropriate that the same definitions should be used and the accounting treatment recommended should ideally be complementary. However, because the pattern of cash flows and the taxation consequences will be different, the recorded balances in both sets of financial statements will also be different.

There are two types of leases: finance leases and operating leases. The distinction between a finance lease and an operating lease will usually be evident from the contract between the lessor and the lessee. A lease is classified as a finance lease if it transfers substantially all the risks and rewards incidental to ownership. If it does not, it is an operating lease.

A **finance lease** usually involves repayment to a lessor by a lessee of the full cost of the asset together with a return on the finance provided by the lessor. As such, a lease of this type is normally non-cancellable or cancellable only under certain conditions, and the lessee enjoys substantially all the risks and rewards associated with the ownership of an asset, other than the legal title. A finance lease is, therefore, very similar to a hire purchase agreement.

An **operating lease** involves the lessee paying a rental for the hire of an asset for a period of time which is normally substantially less than its useful economic life. The lessor retains the risks and rewards of ownership of an asset in an operating lease and normally assumes responsibility for repairs, maintenance and insurance.

IAS 17 requires that a finance lease should be accounted for by the lessee as if it were the purchase of the proprietory rights in an asset with simultaneous recognition of the obligation to make future payments, in the same way that a hire purchase is normally accounted for.

Under an operating lease, only the rental will be taken into account by the lessee. The asset involved does not appear in the statement of financial position of the lessee. A lease of land and buildings should be split into two separate leases, one for land and one for buildings. Leases of land should normally be treated as operating leases unless title to the land is expected to pass to the lessee at the end of the lease term. The standard recognises that the substance of the transaction rather than its legal form should govern the accounting treatment.

These have been the rules applied to leases for a long time. The IASB has issued two exposure drafts proposing changes to this standard, the most recent in 2013. The proposed standard will require that lessees recognise all but insignificant leased items as assets. This will end the distinction between operating and finance leases. All leases will be finance leases. The revised standard is expected to be issued during the second half of 2015.

## Learning outcomes

**You should now have learnt:**

**1** Hire purchase is a means of buying assets where:

(*a*) the asset does not belong to the purchaser until the final instalment is paid *and* the purchaser agrees to a legal option to buy the asset; *but*

(*b*) for accounting purposes, the asset is treated immediately as if it belongs to the purchaser.

**2** Each payment made on a hire purchase contract is part interest and part payment of the cash price of the asset.

**3** How to record the various entries relating to hire purchase.

**4** How to treat hire purchase transactions in the hire purchase trading account, the statement of profit or loss, and the statement of financial position.

**5** The difference between hire purchase and leasing.

**6** The difference between a finance lease and an operating lease as defined by IAS 17 *Leases.*

## Answers to activities

2.1 An organisation may have a shortage of cash, or may prefer to use its cash for other purposes. It may not wish to keep the asset permanently and may buy it on hire purchase so that after a couple of years it can stop paying the instalments. Sometimes, hire purchase is offered at zero interest so it is actually cheaper to purchase an item on hire purchase (because interest can be earned by the buyer on the amount not yet paid).

2.2 Because £48 less was paid in Exhibit 2.2 at the end of Year 1. Interest was charged at 10% on that £48, resulting in an additional £4 having to be paid in Year 2 as well as the £48 that was not paid in Year 1. Overall, this meant that the Year 2 payment in Exhibit 2.2 was £52 greater than in Exhibit 2.1. However, over the two years, the difference in cost to the buyer was the £4 interest that arose as a result of the first-year payment having been slightly lower in Exhibit 2.2.

## Review questions

**2.1** A large bakery scrapped all its equipment and replaced it with new equipment purchased on hire purchase over a period of three years, paying £9,980 on 1 January 2016, and further annual payments of £40,400 due on 31 December 2016, 2017 and 2018.

The cash price of the equipment was £120,000 and the vendor company charged interest at 5% per annum on outstanding balances.

Show the appropriate ledger accounts in the purchaser's books for the three years and how the items would appear in the statement of financial position at 31 December 2016; depreciation at 10% per annum straight line is to be charged and interest calculated to the nearest £.

**2.2A** On 1 January 2015 J McFarlane bought a computer (cash price £2,092) from Pear Ltd on the following hire purchase terms. McFarlane was to make an immediate payment of £600 and three annual payments of £600 on 31 December in each year. The rate of interest chargeable is 10% per annum on the balance at the start of the year.

→

J McFarlane depreciates this computer by 40% reducing balance each year.

(*a*) Make the entries relating to this computer in McFarlane's ledger for the years 2015, 2016 and 2017. (All calculations are to be made to the nearest £.)

(*b*) Show how the item 'computer' would appear in the statement of financial position as at 31 December 2015.

**2.3** Bulwell Aggregates Ltd wish to expand their transport fleet and have purchased three heavy lorries with a list price of £18,000 each. Robert Bulwell has negotiated hire purchase finance to fund this expansion, and the company has entered into a hire purchase agreement with Granby Garages plc on 1 January 2015. The agreement states that Bulwell Aggregates will pay a deposit of £9,000 on 1 January 2015, and two annual instalments of £24,000 on 31 December 2015 and 2016 and a final instalment of £20,391 on 31 December 2017.

Interest is to be calculated at 25% on the balance outstanding on 1 January each year and paid on 31 December each year.

The depreciation policy of Bulwell Aggregates Ltd is to write off the vehicles over a four-year period using the straight line method and assuming a scrap value of £1,333 for each vehicle at the end of its useful life.

The cost of the vehicles to Granby Garages is £14,400 each.

**Required:**

(*a*) Account for the above transactions in the books of Bulwell Aggregates Ltd, showing the entries in the statement of profit or loss and statement of financial position for the years 2015, 2016, 2017 and 2018.

(*b*) Account for the above transactions in the books of Granby Garages plc, showing the entries in the hire purchase trading account for the years 2015, 2016, 2017. This is the only hire purchase transaction undertaken by this company.

Calculations to the nearest £.

(*Association of Accounting Technicians*)

**2.4A** D Lane purchased two cars for his business under hire purchase agreements:

| | | |
|---|---|---|
| Registration number | DL 1 | DL 2 |
| Date of purchase | 31 July 2016 | 30 November 2016 |
| Cash price | £27,000 | £36,000 |
| Deposit | £4,680 | £7,200 |
| Interest (deemed to accrue evenly over the period of the agreement) | £2,880 | £3,600 |

Both agreements provided for payment to be made in 24 monthly instalments commencing on the last day of the month following purchase.

On 1 September 2017, vehicle DL 1 was involved in a crash and was declared a write-off. In full settlement on 20 September 2017:

(*a*) the motor insurers paid out £18,750; and

(*b*) the hire purchase company accepted £10,700 for the termination of the agreement.

The firm prepares its financial statements to 31 December and provides depreciation on a straight line basis at a rate of 25% per annum for motor vehicles, apportioned as from the date of purchase and up to the date of disposal.

All instalments were paid on the due dates.

The remaining balance on the hire purchase company account in respect of vehicle DL 1 is to be written off.

**Required:**

Record these transactions in the following accounts, carrying down the balances as on 31 December 2016 and 31 December 2017:

(*a*) Motor vehicles
(*b*) Depreciation
(*c*) Hire purchase company
(*d*) Assets disposal.

**2.5** On 31 March 2014, D Biggs, who prepares his financial statements to 31 March, bought a lorry on hire purchase from Truck Fleet Ltd. The cash price of the lorry was £61,620. Under the terms of the hire purchase agreement, Biggs paid a deposit of £20,000 on 31 March 2014, and two instalments of £23,981 on 31 March 2015 and 2016. The hire vendor charged interest at 10% per annum on the balance outstanding on 1 April each year. All payments were made on the due dates.

Biggs maintained the motor lorry account at cost and accumulated the annual provision for depreciation, at 40% on the reducing balance method, in a separate account. A full year's depreciation is charged in the year of purchase, irrespective of the date acquired.

**Required:**

(*a*) Prepare the following accounts as they would appear in the ledger of D Biggs for the period of the contract:
  (*i*) Truck Fleet Ltd
  (*ii*) Motor lorry on hire purchase
  (*iii*) Provision for depreciation of motor lorry
  (*iv*) Hire purchase interest payable.

(*b*) Show how the above matters would appear in the statement of financial position of D Biggs at 31 March 2015.

Truck Fleet Ltd prepares its financial statements to 31 March, on which date it charges D Biggs with the interest due.

Make calculations to the nearest £.

**2.6** J Tocher started business on 1 April 2016 selling one model of digital cameras on hire purchase. During the year to 31 March 2017 he purchased 2,000 cameras at a uniform price of £110 and sold 1,900 cameras at a total selling price under hire purchase agreements of £165 per camera, payable by an initial deposit of £45 and 10 quarterly instalments of £12.

The following trial balance was extracted from Tocher's books as at 31 March 2017.

| | £ | £ |
|---|---:|---:|
| Capital | | 175,926 |
| Drawings | 40,000 | |
| Non-current assets | 9,500 | |
| Purchases | 220,000 | |
| Cash collected from customers | | 131,100 |
| Rent, business rates and insurance | 5,000 | |
| Wages | 27,000 | |
| General expenses | 5,100 | |
| Balance at bank | 13,026 | |
| Sundry trade accounts payable | | 12,600 |
| | 319,626 | 319,626 |

The personal accounts of customers are memorandum records (i.e. they are not part of the double entry system).

Tocher prepares his financial statements on the basis of taking credit for profit (including interest) in proportion to cash collected from customers.

Prepare Tocher's hire purchase statement of profit or loss for the year ending 31 March 2017 and a statement of financial position as at that date.

Ignore depreciation of non-current assets.

**2.7** RJ commenced business on 1 January 2018. He sells refrigerators, all of one standard type, on hire purchase terms. The total amount, including interest, payable for each refrigerator is £300. Customers are required to pay an initial deposit of £60, followed by eight quarterly instalments of £30 each. The cost of each refrigerator to RJ is £200.

The following trial balance was extracted from RJ's books as on 31 December 2018.

**Trial Balance**

| | £ | £ |
|---|---|---|
| Capital | | 100,000 |
| Non-current assets | 10,000 | |
| Drawings | 4,000 | |
| Bank overdraft | | 19,600 |
| Creditors | | 16,600 |
| Purchases | 180,000 | |
| Cash collected from customers | | 76,500 |
| Bank interest | 400 | |
| Wages and salaries | 12,800 | |
| General expenses | 5,500 | |
| | £212,700 | £212,700 |

850 machines were sold on hire purchase terms during 2018.

The annual accounts are prepared on the basis of taking credit for profit (including interest) in proportion to the cash collected from customers.

**You are required to** prepare the hire purchase trading account and statement of profit or loss for the year 2018 and statement of financial position as on 31 December 2018.

Ignore depreciation of non-current assets.

Show your calculations.

*(Institute of Chartered Secretaries and Administrators)*

**2.8A** Object Limited is a retail outlet selling word processing equipment both for cash and on hire purchase terms. The following information has been extracted from the books of account as at 31 August 2016:

| | *Dr* £ | *Cr* £ |
|---|---|---|
| Authorised, issued and fully paid share capital (ordinary shares of £1 each) | | 75,000 |
| Administration and shop expenses | 130,000 | |
| Cash at bank and in hand | 6,208 | |
| Cash received from hire purchase customers | | 315,468 |
| Cash sales | | 71,000 |
| Depreciation of premises and equipment (at 1 September 2015) | | 45,000 |
| Hire purchase accounts receivable (at 1 September 2015) | 2,268 | |
| Premises and equipment at cost | 100,000 | |
| Retained profits (at 1 September 2015) | | 8,000 |
| Provision for unrealised profit (at 1 September 2015) | | 1,008 |
| Purchases | 342,000 | |
| Inventory (at 1 September 2015) | 15,000 | |
| Trade accounts payable | | 80,000 |
| | 595,476 | 595,476 |

*Additional information:*

1 The company's policy is to take credit for gross profit (including interest) for hire purchase sales in proportion to the instalments collected. It does this by raising a provision against the profit included in hire purchase accounts receivables not yet due.

2 The cash selling price is fixed at 50% and the hire purchase selling price at 80% above the cost of goods purchased.
3 The hire purchase contract requires an initial deposit of 20% of the hire purchase selling price, the balance to be paid in four equal instalments at quarterly intervals. The first instalment is due three months after the agreement is signed.
4 Hire purchase sales for the year amounted to £540,000 (including interest).
5 In February 2016 the company repossessed some goods which had been sold earlier in the year. These goods had been purchased for £3,000, and the unpaid instalments on them amounted to £3,240. They were then taken back into inventory at a value of £2,500. Later on in the year they were sold on cash terms for £3,500.
6 Depreciation is charged on premises and equipment at a rate of 15% per annum on cost.

**Required:**
Prepare Object Limited's statement of profit or loss for the year ending 31 August 2016, and a statement of financial position as at that date.

Your workings should be submitted.

*(Association of Accounting Technicians)*

**2.9A** On 1 January 2016, F Limited commenced business selling goods on hire purchase. Under the terms of the agreements, an initial deposit of 20% is payable on delivery, followed by four equal quarterly instalments, the first being due three months after the date of sale. During the year sales were made as follows:

| | *Cost price* | *HP sales price* |
|---|---|---|
| | £ | £ |
| 10 January | 150 | 225 |
| 8 March | 350 | 525 |
| 12 May | 90 | 135 |
| 6 July | 200 | 300 |
| 20 September | 70 | 105 |
| 15 October | 190 | 285 |
| 21 November | 160 | 240 |

The goods sold in July were returned in September and eventually sold in November for £187 cash. All other instalments are paid on the due dates.

It may be assumed that:

(*a*) gross profit and interest are credited to profit and loss in the proportion that deposits and instalments received bear to hire purchase price; or
(*b*) the cost is deemed to be paid in full before any credit is taken for gross profit and interest.

You are to prepare for the first year of trading, an extract of the hire purchase statement of profit or loss showing gross profit compiled firstly on assumption (*a*) and secondly on assumption (*b*) and give the relevant statement of financial position entries under each assumption.

Workings should be clearly shown.

**2.10A** On 1 January 2016, Carver bought a machine costing £20,000 on hire purchase. He paid a deposit of £6,000 on 1 January 2016 and he also agreed to pay two annual instalments of £5,828 on 31 December in each year, and a final instalment of £5,831 on 31 December 2018.

The implied rate of interest in the agreement was 12%. This rate of interest is to be applied to the amount outstanding in the hire purchase loan account as at the beginning of the year.

The machine is to be depreciated on a straight line basis over five years on the assumption that the machine will have no residual value at the end of that time.

→

**Required:**

(*a*) Write up the following accounts for each of the three years to 31 December 2016, 2017 and 2018 respectively:
  (*i*) machine account;
  (*ii*) accumulated depreciation on machine account; and
  (*iii*) hire purchase loan account.

(*b*) Show the statement of financial position extracts for the year as at 31 December 2016, 2017 and 2018 respectively for the following items:
  (*i*) machine at cost;
  (*ii*) accumulated depreciation on the machine;
  (*iii*) non-current liabilities: obligations under hire purchase contract; and
  (*iv*) current liabilities: obligations under hire purchase contract.

(*Association of Accounting Technicians*)

**2.11** Dundas Limited purchased a machine under a hire purchase agreement on 1 January 2015. The agreement provided for an immediate payment of £2,000, followed by five equal instalments of £3,056, each instalment to be paid on 30 June and 31 December respectively.

The cash price of the machine was £10,000. Dundas estimated that it would have a useful economic life of five years, and its residual value would then be £1,000.

In apportioning interest to respective accounting periods, the company uses the 'sum of digits'[Author's note] method.

**Required:**

(*a*) Write up the following ledger accounts for each of the three years to 31 December 2015, 2016 and 2017 respectively:
  (*i*) machine hire purchase loan account; and
  (*ii*) machine hire purchase interest account.

(*b*) Show the following statement of financial position extracts relating to the machine as at 31 December 2015, 2016 and 2017 respectively:
  (*i*) non-current assets: machine at net book value;
  (*ii*) current liabilities: accounts payable – obligation under hire purchase contract; and
  (*iii*) non-current liabilities: accounts payable – obligation under hire purchase contract.

***Author's note – sum of digits***

**This is very similar to the 'rule of 78', which is explained in Section 27.12. It is explained in detail in Section 26.12 of the thirteenth edition of *Frank Wood's Business Accounting 1*. In brief, if a machine is expected to last four years, you write off the cost by weighting year 1 as 4, year 2 as 3, year 3 as 2 and year 4 as 1. The total of these weights is used as the denominator. Thus, year 1 depreciation would be 4/10 of the amount to be written off; year 2 would be 3/10, year 3 would be 2/10 and year 4 would be 1/10.**

(*Association of Accounting Technicians*)

chapter 3

# Contract accounts

## Learning objectives

**After you have studied this chapter, you should be able to:**

- describe the factors that are involved in accounting for contracts
- describe how accounting records of contracts are maintained
- explain the need to apply prudence when assessing profit or loss on a contract that is still in progress
- describe some of the requirements of IAS 11 and IAS 18 relating to long-term contracts

## Introduction

In this chapter you'll learn how to record revenues and expenditures arising on contracts in contract accounts and how to estimate profits and losses on long-term contracts so that appropriate entries may be included in the financial statements for internal use.

## 3.1 Financial statements and the business cycle

The span of production differs between businesses, and some fit into the normal pattern of annual financial statements more easily than others. A farmer's financial statements are usually admirably suited to the yearly pattern, as the goods they produce are in accordance with the seasons, and therefore repeat themselves annually. With a firm whose production span is a day or two, the annual financial statements are also quite suitable.

On the other hand, there are businesses whose work does not fit neatly with a financial year's calculation of profits. Assume that a firm of contractors has only one contract in progress, the construction of a large oil refinery complex which is expected to take five years to complete. Until it is completed, the actual profit or loss on the contract cannot be accurately stated – too many things could happen that would affect the final profit or loss over the five years of the contract. However, if the company was formed solely for the purpose of undertaking this contract, the shareholders would not want to wait for five years before the profit could be calculated and dividends paid. As a result, an attempt must be made to calculate profits earned to date at the end of each financial year. Some companies will have more than one contract under way at a time, each at a different stage, in which case the profit earned to date on each contract must be calculated.

## 3.2 Contract accounts

When a company starts a long-term contract, an account is opened for it. It is, in fact, a form of trading account. As an example, if a company has a contract to construct a new college building, it may be called 'Contract 71', in which case an account for Contract 71 would be opened. All expenditure traceable to the contract is charged to the account. This is far easier than apportioning expenses to specific products manufactured in a factory, as any expenditure on the contract site will be expenses of the contract, e.g. wages for the manual workers, rental of telephone lines, hire of machinery, wages for the timekeepers, clerks.

**Activity 3.1**

As each contract has or will have a unique flow of revenue, it makes sound business sense to know the profit or loss it generates. Hence the use of individual contract accounts. When financial statements are produced that include long-term contracts (those that extend into future accounting periods), which fundamental accounting concept is adhered to by maintaining a separate contract account for each contract?

## 3.3 Certification of work done

When a building is being constructed, the contractor is paid on the basis of architects' certificates. In the case of an engineering contract, it is on the basis of an engineer's certificate. The architect, or engineer, will visit the site at regular intervals and will issue a certificate stating his or her estimate of the value of the work done, in terms of the total contract price (the sale price of the whole contract). For example, a certificate may be issued for £90,000 which represents the proportion of the total contract amount which he or she believes has been completed.

Normally, the terms governing the contract will contain a clause concerning 'retention money'. This is the amount, usually stated as a percentage, which will be retained, i.e. held back, in case the contract is not completed by a stated date, or in case there are claims made for faulty workmanship, etc. A 10% retention in this case would lead to £81,000 being payable by the organisation for which the contract was being performed.

## 3.4 Allocation of overheads

Any administration overhead expenses that are not directly traceable to individual contract sites may be split between the contracts using an appropriate base, such as the overall contract amount or the labour cost to date. Of course, if there were only one contract then all the overhead expenses would quite rightly be chargeable against it. On the other hand, if there are 20 contracts, any apportionment will be arbitrary. No one can perfectly apportion the administration overhead expenses of, for example, the managing director's salary, the cost of advertising to give the business the right 'image', or the costs of running the accounting system for the whole company, and these are only a few of such difficult-to-apportion expenses.

Similar to the effects of apportioning overheads in departmental accounts, as covered in Chapter 38 of *Frank Wood's Business Accounting 1,* the allocation of overheads to individual contracts may sometimes produce misleading results. It is, therefore, far better for the administrative overhead expenses which are obviously not chargeable to a contract to be omitted from the contract accounts. The surplus left on each contract account would, therefore, represent the 'contribution' of each contract to administrative overhead expenses and, thus, to profit.

Let's look at a worked example.

## 3.5 A worked example of a contract account

In many cases, contracts will start and finish in the same financial period. In such cases, there is no need to estimate profits and losses at the period end. However, when a contract extends into one or more periods after it started, it is known as a 'long-term contract' and an appropriate estimate of profits or losses must be made so that appropriate entries can be made in the financial statements. In Exhibit 3.1, Contract 44 extends into a second accounting period.

This example shows how profit or loss may be calculated for inclusion in financial statements prepared for internal purposes. As you will later learn, when financial statements are prepared for publication, a more complex approach to the calculation of profit or loss must be used.

### Exhibit 3.1

Contract 44 is for a school which is being built for the Blankshire County Council. By the end of the construction company's financial year, the following items have been charged to the contract account:

**Contract 44**

| | £ |
|---|---|
| Wages – labour on site | 50,000 |
| Wages – foreman and clerks on the site | 32,000 |
| Materials | 40,000 |
| Subcontractors on the site | 9,000 |
| Other site expenses | 3,000 |
| Hire of special machinery | 2,000 |
| Plant bought for the contract | 20,000 |

The entries concerning expenditure traceable direct to the contract are relatively simple. These are charged to the contract account. These can be seen in the contract account shown below.

Architects' certificates have been received during the year amounting to £147,000. It is assumed that the certificates relate to all work done up to the year end. A retention of 10% is to be made, and the Blankshire County Council has paid £132,300 so far. The £147,000 has been credited to a holding account called an architects' certificates account and debited to the Blankshire County Council account.

The total of the Architects' Certificates Account now needs to be transferred to the Contract 44 account. It is, after all, the 'sale' price of the work done so far, and the contract account is a type of trading account. The £132,300 received has been debited to the bank and credited to the Blankshire County Council account, which now shows a balance of £14,700 representing the retention money.

The cost of the materials on the site at the end of the period is not included in the value of the architects' certificates and is, therefore, carried forward to the next period at cost. The value of the plant at the end of the year is also carried forward. In this case the value of the cost of the plant not yet used is £14,000. This means that £20,000 has been debited for the plant and £14,000 credited thus, effectively, charging £6,000 for depreciation. Assume that the unused materials cost £8,000.

The Contract 44 account will appear as follows:

**Contract 44**

| | £ | | £ |
|---|---|---|---|
| Wages – labour on site | 50,000 | Architects' certificates | 147,000 |
| Wages – foreman and clerks on the site | 32,000 | Unused materials c/d | 8,000 |
| Materials | 40,000 | Value of plant c/d | 14,000 |
| Subcontractors on the site | 8,000 | | |
| Other site expenses | 3,000 | | |
| Hire of special machinery | 2,000 | | |
| Plant bought for the contract | 20,000 | | |

Activity 3.2 What is the profit to date on Contract 44?

## 3.6 Profit estimation

In order to estimate the profit or loss on Contract 44, more information is needed beyond the values shown in the contract account. The contract is only part-completed, and costly snags may crop up which would dissipate any potential profit earned, or problems may have developed already, such as subsidence, which have remained unnoticed as yet. It is not possible to identify all known factors of this type. To minimise the risk of profits being overstated or losses understated, the concept of prudence is applied and the profit is reduced according to an 'appropriate' modifier.

A custom developed over many years of multiplying the profit shown on the contract account by two-thirds and then multiplying the result by the proportion of **work certified** for which cash had been received. **While the current, and far more complex, IAS 11 and IAS 18 rules must be adopted in practice when preparing financial statements for publication, the previous, simpler approach is an excellent example of the prudence concept and is still used in examinations. You will, therefore, need to learn how to apply it.**

It is relatively straightforward to apply, as shown in the following example:

$$\text{Apparent profit} \times \frac{2}{3} \times \frac{\text{Cash received}}{\text{Work certified}} = \text{Amount available for dividends, etc.}$$

For example, the apparent profit earned to date on Contract 44 is £14,000 (*see* Activity 3.2):

$$£14{,}000 \times \frac{2}{3} \times \frac{132{,}300}{147{,}000} = £8{,}400.$$

On the basis of the £8,400 profit calculated above, the Contract 44 account can now be completed.

**Contract 44**

| | £ | | £ |
|---|---|---|---|
| Wages – labour on site | 50,000 | Architects' certificates | 147,000 |
| Wages – foreman and clerks on the site | 32,000 | Unused materials c/d | 8,000 |
| Materials | 40,000 | Value of plant c/d | 14,000 |
| Subcontractors on the site | 8,000 | | |
| Other site expenses | 3,000 | | |
| Hire of special machinery | 2,000 | | |
| Plant bought for the contract | 20,000 | | |
| Profit to profit and loss | 8,400 | | |
| Reserve **(the part of the apparent profit not yet recognised as earned)** c/d | 5,600 | | |
| | 169,000 | | 169,000 |
| Unused materials b/d | 8,000 | Reserve b/d | 5,600 |
| Value of plant b/d | 14,000 | | |

**Profit and Loss**

| | *Profit from contracts* | £ |
|---|---|---|
| | Contract 43 | ? |
| | Contract 44 | 8,400 |
| | Contract 45 | ? |

## 3.7 Anticipated losses

In the above case, there was an apparent profit earned to date of £14,000 but we only recognise £8,400 in the financial statements. If instead of revealing such a profit, the contract account had shown a loss, *all* the loss would be recognised *now*. Thus, if the loss were £9,000, that would be the amount transferred to profit and loss. This is in accordance with the concept of prudence.

As is the case with valuation of inventory, it is not always the case that an engineer or architect will certify the work done on the last day of the financial year. He or she may call several days before or after the year end. The cost of any work done but not certified at the year end is carried down at cost as a balance to the next period when certification will take place.

So far, we have considered how the various figures to be included in the financial statements prepared for internal use may be calculated. When financial statements are prepared for external use, i.e. for publication, the more complex IAS 11/IAS 18 approach must be adopted.

**You may not need to know the current accounting standard rules relating to long-term contracts. It depends upon which examinations you are studying for.** If you do, Section 3.8 provides an introduction to the rules contained in IAS 11 (*Construction contracts*) and IAS 18 (*Revenue*) but you may need to consult the relevant international accounting standards or a more advanced textbook on the subject before tackling your examinations.

## 3.8 Long-term contracts and accounting standards

Long-term contracts should be assessed on a contract-by-contract basis. They should be reflected in profit and loss by recording turnover and related costs as contract activity progresses. Turnover should be ascertained in a manner appropriate to the stage of completion of the contract, the business and the industry in which it operates. Where the outcome of a contract can be assessed with reasonable accuracy, profit should be recognised (so far as prudence permits) as the difference between recognised turnover and related costs. Any foreseeable losses identified should be immediately recognised.

The amount of long-term contracts, at costs incurred, net of amounts transferred to cost of sales, after deducting foreseeable losses and payments on account not matched with turnover, should be classified as 'long-term contract balances' and disclosed separately within the statement of financial position heading of 'inventory'. The statement of financial position note should disclose separately the balances of 'net cost less foreseeable losses' and 'applicable payments on account'.

### Profit recognition

There are two definitions relevant to any consideration of long-term contracts: those of 'attributable profit' and 'foreseeable losses'.

*Attributable profit* is that part of total profit currently estimated to arise over the duration of the contract, after allowing for estimated remedial and maintenance costs and increases in costs (so far as not recoverable under the terms of the contract), that fairly reflects the profit attributable to that part of the work performed at the accounting date. There can be no attributable profit until the outcome of the contract can be assessed with reasonable certainty.

*Foreseeable losses* are those losses estimated to arise over the duration of the contract, after allowing for estimated remedial and maintenance costs and increases in costs (so far as not recoverable under the terms of the contract), *whether or not* work has commenced, and irrespective of both the proportion of work completed and profits expected on other contracts.

A contract's outcome must be capable of being assessed with reasonable certainty before any profit should be recognised. This leaves it entirely to individual judgement as to when to start recognising profit on a long-term contract. One company may recognise profit after the first six months, while another may wait until a year has passed. As a result, inter-company comparability is impaired. However, the standards do assist in intracompany comparison from one year to the next as they require consistent application of the method of ascertaining attributable profit both within the business, and from year to year.

Clearly, future costs must be estimated in arriving at a figure for attributable profit or foreseeable losses. Unfortunately, no two people are likely to arrive independently at exactly the same amount. Thus, the profits or losses recognised are likely to vary considerably from one company to another and intercompany comparability is further impaired.

## Turnover valuation

Turnover should be ascertained in a manner suitable to the industry and the specific contracts concerned. The valuation of work carried out may be used to derive a value for turnover and profit then calculated; or profit should be regarded as earned in relation to the *amount* of work performed to date. These two approaches often produce different results, but the profit recognised needs to reflect the proportion of the work carried out and to take into account any known inequalities of profitability in the various stages of a contract. Consequently, when there is a work-certified value, this should be used as the turnover value and the costs incurred in achieving that turnover charged to cost of sales.

Where no work-certified figure exists, costs to date as a proportion of total expected costs should be applied to the contract value in order to determine the figure for turnover. Where the work-certified value is not available for all work completed, a combination of the two approaches would be appropriate. One further point regarding turnover concerns settlements of claims against the purchaser arising from circumstances not foreseen in the contract: these should only be incorporated when there is sufficient evidence that payment will be received.

## Complexity

The standards relevant to this topic are extremely complex and it is beyond the scope of this book, where this topic is being introduced rather than developed in detail, to extend coverage to the level of complexity that would be required in order to cover the rules adequately.

From the perspective of the review questions that follow at the end of this chapter, apart from question 3.5A, *unless otherwise indicated in the question,* you should apply the two-thirds rule of thumb given above. Doing so will develop an awareness of the complexity of contract accounts without the added complexity of applying the IAS 11 and IAS 18 rules. By adopting this approach, you will be well placed to progress to an understanding of the rules in these accounting standards. The answer to question 3.5A is based on the IAS 11 and IAS 18 rules, and is provided for the benefit of anyone who chooses to study those rules.

**A new standard, IFRS 15 (*Revenue from contracts with customers*), is due to come into force on 1 January 2018, at which point it will replace IAS 11 and IAS 18.**

## Learning outcomes

**You should now have learnt:**

1. That a separate contract account should be opened in respect of every contract.
2. That profits or losses on each uncompleted contract must be estimated at the end of each accounting period.
3. That losses should be written off immediately they are identified.
4. That an appropriate amount of any profit should be included in the financial statements.
5. Some of the definitions and requirements of IAS 11 (*Construction contracts*) and IAS 18 (*Revenue*) relating to long-term contracts.
6. That the rule of thumb profit/loss ascertainment approach adopted in this chapter is necessarily simplified in order to ensure the topic is well understood; IAS 11 and IAS 18 should be consulted for the definitive approach to adopt when preparing financial statements.

## Answers to activities

3.1 While it is ongoing, each contract represents an asset or liability. The separate determination concept – see Chapter 10 in *Frank Wood's Business Accounting 1* – requires that the amount of each individual asset or liability be determined separately from all other assets and liabilities. Maintaining a separate contract account for each contract enables compliance with this fundamental accounting concept.

3.2 The difference between the two sides (Credit side £169,000; Debit side £155,000) is £14,000. At this stage, as the contract is incomplete, the £14,000 simply reflects the excess of potential revenue over expenditure to date on the contract. It does not necessarily mean that the contract will ultimately result in a profit and it certainly does not mean that there is a profit to date on the contract of £14,000 – the inventory of materials, for example, would need to be sold for precisely the amount shown and the plant disposed of at the amount it is valued at, neither of which is particularly likely.

## Review questions

**3.1** The financial statements of Banaghan Ltd are made up to 31 March in each year. Work on Contract 32 started on 1 July 2016 and completed on 31 January 2018. The total contract price was £1,200,000 but a penalty of £120,000 was suffered for failure to complete by 31 December 2017.

The following is a summary of receipts and payments relating to the contract:

| | *Year to 31 March* | |
|---|---|---|
| | *2017* | *2018* |
| Payments | | |
| Materials | 163,200 | 214,400 |
| Wages | 182,400 | 291,200 |
| Direct expenses | 12,800 | 19,200 |
| Purchases of plant on 1 July 2016 | 76,800 | – |
| Receipts | | |
| Contract price (*less* penalty) | 360,000 | 816,000 |
| Sale, on 31 January 2018, of all plant purchased on 1 July 2016 | – | 4,800 |

The amount received from the customer in 2017 represented the contract price of all work certified in that financial year less 10% retention money.

When the financial statements to 31 March 2017 were prepared, it was estimated that the contract would be completed on 31 December 2017, and that the market value of the plant would be £4,800,000 on that date. It was estimated that further expenditure on the contract would be £515,200.

For the purposes of the financial statements, depreciation of plant is calculated, in the case of uncompleted contracts, by reference to the expected market value of the plant on the date when the contract is expected to be completed, and is allocated between accounting periods by the straight line method.

Credit is taken, in the financial statements, for such a part of the estimated total profit, on each uncompleted contract, as corresponds to the proportion between the contract price of the work certified and the total contract price.

**Required:**
Prepare a summary of the account for Contract 32, showing the amounts transferred to profit and loss at 31 March 2017 and 31 March 2018.

**3.2** Stannard and Sykes Ltd are contractors for the construction of a pier for the Seafront Development Corporation. The value of the contract is £300,000, and payment is by engineer's certificate subject to a retention of 10% of the amount certified; this is to be held by the Seafront Development Corporation for six months after the completion of the contract.

The following information is extracted from the records of Stannard and Sykes Ltd.

| | £ |
|---|---:|
| Wages on site | 41,260 |
| Materials delivered to site by supplier | 58,966 |
| Materials delivered to site from store | 10,180 |
| Hire of plant | 21,030 |
| Expenses charged to contract | 3,065 |
| Overheads charged to contract | 8,330 |
| Materials on site at 30 November 2018 | 11,660 |
| Work certified | 150,000 |
| Payment received | 135,000 |
| Work in progress at cost (not the subject of a certificate to date) | 12,613 |
| Wages accrued to 30 November 2018 | 2,826 |

**Required:**
Prepare the Pier Contract Account to 30 November 2018, and suggest a method by which profit could be prudently estimated.

*(Association of Chartered Certified Accountants)*

**3.3A** Cantilever Ltd was awarded a contract to build an office block in London and work commenced at the site on 1 May 2017.

During the period to 28 February 2018, the expenditure on the contract was as follows:

| | £ |
|---|---:|
| Materials issued from stores | 9,411 |
| Materials purchased | 28,070 |
| Direct expenses | 6,149 |
| Wages | 18,493 |
| Charge made by the company for administration expenses | 2,146 |
| Plant and machinery purchased on 1 May 2017, for use at site | 12,180 |

On 28 February 2018, the materials at the site amounted to £2,164 and there were amounts outstanding for wages £366 and direct expenses £49.

Cantilever Ltd has received on account the sum of £64,170 which represents the amount of Certificate No. 1 issued by the architects in respect of work completed to 28 February 2018, after deducting 10% retention money.

The following relevant information is also available:

(*a*) the plant and machinery have an effective life of five years, with no residual value; and
(*b*) the company only takes credit for two-thirds of the profit on work certified.

**Required:**
(*a*) prepare a contract account for the period to 28 February 2018; and
(*b*) show your calculation of the profit to be taken to profit and loss in respect of the work covered by Certificate No. 1.

(*Institute of Chartered Accountants*)

**3.4A** You are required to prepare the contract account for the year ended 31 December 2017, and show the calculation of the sum to be credited to profit and loss for that year.

On 1 April 2017 MN Ltd commenced work on a contract which was to be completed by 30 June 2018 at an agreed price of £520,000.

MN Ltd's financial year ended on 31 December 2017, and on that day expenditure on the contract totalled £263,000 made up as under:

| | £ |
|---|---|
| Plant | 30,000 |
| Materials | 124,000 |
| Wages | 95,000 |
| Sundry expenses | 5,000 |
| Head office charges | 9,000 |
| | 263,000 |

Cash totalling £195,000 had been received by 31 December 2017 representing 75% of the work certified as completed on that date, but in addition, work costing £30,000 had been completed but not certified.

A sum of £9,000 had been obtained on the sale of materials which had cost £8,000 but which had been found unsuitable. On 31 December 2017 unused materials on site had cost £10,000 and the plant was valued at £20,000.

To complete the contract by 30 June 2018 it was estimated that:

(*a*) the following additional expenditures would be incurred:

| | £ |
|---|---|
| Wages | 64,000 |
| Materials | 74,400 |
| Sundry expenses | 9,000 |

(*b*) further plant costing £25,000 would be required;
(*c*) the residual value of all plant used on the contract at 30 June 2018 would be £15,000;
(*d*) head office charges to the contract would be at the same annual rate plus 10%.

It was estimated that the contract would be completed on time but that a contingency provision of £15,000 should be made. From this estimate and the expenditure already incurred, it was decided to estimate the total profit that would be made on the contract and to take to profit and loss, for the year ending 31 December 2017, that proportion of the total profit relating to the work actually certified to that date.

(*Chartered Institute of Management Accountants*)

***Note*: The next question requires the application of the rules contained in IAS 11 and IAS 18.** →

**3.5A** *General information on the Lytax group of companies:*

Lytax Ltd is a company in the building construction industry.

It has three regional offices, North Borders, Midlands and South Downs, which are constituted as separate units for accounting purposes.

On 25 May 2017 Lytax Ltd acquired 90% of the ordinary share capital of Ceprem Ltd, a company which manufactures building materials.

Lytax Ltd has for three years held 15% of the ordinary share capital of Bleco plc. This company carries out specialist research and development activities into building and construction materials, technology and techniques. It then sells the results of these activities to other companies.

*Details of long-term contract work undertaken by Lytax Ltd:*

At 31 October 2017, Lytax Ltd was engaged in various contracts including five long-term contracts, details of which are given below:

| | *1* | *2* | *3* | *4* | *5* |
|---|---|---|---|---|---|
| | *£000* | *£000* | *£000* | *£000* | *£000* |
| Contract price | 1,100 | 950 | 1,400 | 1,300 | 1,200 |
| *At 31 October 2017:* | | | | | |
| Cumulative costs incurred | 664 | 535 | 810 | 640 | 1,070 |
| Estimated further costs to completion | 106 | 75 | 680 | 800 | 165 |
| Estimated cost of post-completion guarantee/rectification work | 30 | 10 | 45 | 20 | 5 |
| Cumulative costs incurred transferred to cost of sales | 580 | 470 | 646 | 525 | 900 |
| *Progress payments* | | | | | |
| Cumulative receipts | 615 | 680 | 615 | 385 | 722 |
| Invoiced: | | | | | |
| Awaiting receipt | 60 | 40 | 25 | 200 | 34 |
| Retained by contractee | 75 | 80 | 60 | 65 | 84 |

It is not expected that any contractees will default on their payments.

Up to 31 October 2016, the following amounts had been included in the turnover and cost of sales figures:

| | *1* | *2* | *3* | *4* | *5* |
|---|---|---|---|---|---|
| | *£000* | *£000* | *£000* | *£000* | *£000* |
| Cumulative turnover | 560 | 340 | 517 | 400 | 610 |
| Cumulative costs incurred transferred to cost of sales | 460 | 245 | 517 | 400 | 610 |
| Foreseeable loss transferred to cost of sales | – | – | – | 70 | – |

It is the accounting policy of Lytax Ltd to arrive at contract turnover by adjusting contract cost of sales (including foreseeable losses) by the amount of contract profit or loss to be regarded as recognised, separately for each contract.

**Required:**

(*a*) Calculate the amounts to be included within the turnover and cost of sales figures of the statement of profit or loss of Lytax Ltd for the year ending 31 October 2017, in respect of the long-term contracts.

(*b*) Prepare extracts from the statement of financial position of Lytax Ltd at 31 October 2017 incorporating the financial effects of the long-term contracts.

**Your answer should comply with the requirements of IAS 11 (Contract accounts) and IAS 18 (Revenue) and should include any supporting notes required by those standards.**

Workings for individual contracts which build up to the total for each item must be shown.

All calculations should be made to the nearest £1,000.

(*Association of Chartered Certified Accountants*)

part 2

# COMPANIES

## Introduction

**This part is concerned with the accounts and financial statements of limited companies. It considers how various accounting transactions should be entered in the books and how the financial statements should be presented, including the requirements of the Companies Acts and of accounting standards.**

chapter 4

# Limited companies: general background

## Learning objectives

**After you have studied this chapter, you should be able to:**

- explain the legal nature of limited companies
- explain the importance of the concept of limited liability
- describe the statutory framework governing limited companies
- describe some of the major characteristics of limited companies
- explain the difference between the Memorandum of Association and the Articles of Association

## Introduction

In this chapter, you'll learn about the legislation that governs how companies are formed and lays out the rules within which companies operate in the UK. You'll learn about the importance of limited liability and of the relationship between companies, their shares and the stock exchange.

## 4.1 Preliminary study

An introduction was made to the financial statements of limited companies in *Frank Wood's Business Accounting 1*. It was intended to show some of the basic outlines of the financial statements of limited companies to those people who would be finishing their studies of accounting with the completion of *Business Accounting 1*. This volume now carries the study of limited companies accounting to a more advanced stage.

## 4.2 The Companies Acts

The Act of Parliament governing limited companies in the UK is the Companies Act 2006. In this book, we cannot deal with many of the complicated issues arising from the Companies Act. These are better left until readers have reached a more advanced stage in their studies.

The Companies Act is the descendant of modern limited liability company legislation which can be traced back to the passing of the Companies Act 1862. This Act was a triumph for the development of the limited liability principle which had been severely restricted since the 'Bubble Act' of 1720, which was introduced to address a multitude of spectacular frauds perpetrated behind the cloak of limited liability. Not until 1862 was prejudice against the principle of limited liability overcome, and the way paved for the general use of the limited liability principle which is now commonplace. Company law consists of the Companies Act 2006, together with a considerable body of case law which has been built up over the years. Apart from companies that have been formed since the first Companies Act came into force in 1862, there are companies dating from earlier times which were either incorporated by Royal Charter, such as the Hudson's Bay Company, or by special Acts of Parliament. While such companies may have been subject to different rules at the time of their formation, they are subject to the same Companies Act as all other companies so far as their financial reporting is concerned.

## 4.3 Changes in company law

Company law has changed considerably since the mid-1960s. This has been brought about largely because of the obligation to observe the company law directives issued by the Council of European Communities, i.e. the EU. Such changes have not completely eliminated the differences in company law throughout the European Union, but they have considerably reduced such differences and have provided a set of minimum common standards to be observed.

The 1985 and 1989 Companies Acts laid down detailed rules of the format of the financial statements of limited companies. These were based on the formats contained in the Fourth Directive of the Council of European Communities. Companies reporting under International GAAP must follow the requirements contained within the international accounting standards. They must also, where appropriate (see, for example, Section 12.8), comply with the requirements of the Companies Act.

Banks and insurance companies do not come under the same legislation as that which applies to other companies. A separate part of the 1989 Act deals with banks, while insurance companies are the subject of a special directive.

## 4.4 Other forms of company

The Companies Acts also cover companies with unlimited liability, of which there are very few. They also cover companies limited by guarantee, which may or may not have share capital, though the Companies Act 1985 prohibited the future formation of such companies unless they do have share capital.

The Companies (Audit, Investigations and Community Enterprise) Act 2004 established another form of company: a community interest company. Companies with or without share capital can become community interest companies, including companies limited by guarantee. A community interest company cannot issue share capital but can issue interest-bearing preference shares – it can then pay dividends up to a fixed percentage above the base rate of interest.

These types of limited company and chartered companies are relatively unimportant, so any future reference in this book to 'a limited company' or 'a company' will be concerned with limited liability companies.

## 4.5 Separate legal entity

The outstanding feature of a **limited company** is that, no matter how many individuals have bought shares in it, it is treated in its dealings with the outside world as if it were a person in its own right: it is said to be a separate 'legal entity'. A prime example of its identity as a separate legal entity is that it may sue other business entities, people – even its own shareholders – or, in turn, be sued by them.

Just as the law can create this separate legal person, it can also eliminate it, but only by using the proper legal procedures. The identity of the shareholders in a large company may change daily as shares are bought and sold by different people, but this, itself, has no immediate impact upon the existence or nature of the company.

On the other hand, a small private company may have the same shareholders from the day it is incorporated (when it legally came into being), until the date when liquidation is completed (the cessation of the company, often known also as 'winding up' or 'being wound up').

Why would it be advantageous for a company to be able to sue other business entities, rather than for the directors or an employee to do so?

The legal formalities by which a company comes into existence can be found in any textbook on company law. It is not the purpose of this book to discuss company law in any great detail; this is far better left to a later stage of your studies. As companies must, however, comply with the law, the essential company law concerning accounting matters will be dealt with in this book as far as is necessary.

What is important is that the basic principles connected with company financial statements can be seen in operation. So that you are not unduly confused, points which rarely occur, or on which the legal arguments are extremely involved and may not yet have been finally settled, will be left out completely or merely mentioned in passing. This means that some generalisations made in this book will need to be expanded upon when your accounting studies reach a more advanced stage.

## 4.6 Memorandum and Articles of Association and company registration

### Memorandum of Association

A **Memorandum of Association** is a memorandum stating that the subscribers wish to form a company under the Companies Act and agree to become members of the company and, in the case of a company that is to have a share capital, to take at least one share each.

### Articles of Association

A company must have **Articles of Association** prescribing regulations for the company. Unless it is a company to which default model Articles apply (i.e. Articles prescribed for a company of that description as in force at the date on which the company is registered), it must register Articles of Association which must be contained in a single document, and be divided into paragraphs numbered consecutively.

### Default application of model Articles

On the formation of a limited company, if Articles are not registered or, if Articles are registered, in so far as they do not exclude or modify the relevant model Articles, the relevant model Articles (so far as applicable) form part of the company's Articles in the same manner and to the same extent as if Articles in the form of those Articles had been duly registered.

### Company registration

The Memorandum of Association must be delivered to the registrar together with an application for registration of the company, the documents required by this section and a statement of compliance.

The application for registration must state:

(*a*) the company's proposed name;
(*b*) whether the company's registered office is to be situated in England and Wales (or in Wales), in Scotland or in Northern Ireland;
(*c*) whether the liability of the members of the company is to be limited, and if so whether it is to be limited by shares or by guarantee;
(*d*) whether the company is to be a private or a public company;
(*e*) in the case of a company that is to have a share capital, a statement of capital and initial shareholdings;
(*f*) in the case of a company that is to be limited by guarantee, a statement of guarantee;
(*g*) a statement of the company's proposed officers.

The application must also contain a statement of the intended address of the company's registered office; and a copy of any proposed Articles of Association (to the extent that these are not supplied by the default application of model Articles).

### Statement of capital and initial shareholdings

The statement of capital and initial shareholdings required to be delivered in the case of a company that is to have a share capital must state:

(*a*) the total number of shares of the company to be taken on formation by the subscribers to the Memorandum of Association;
(*b*) the aggregate nominal value of those shares;
(*c*) for each class of shares:

- prescribed particulars of the rights attached to the shares;
- the total number of shares of that class;
- the aggregate nominal value of shares of that class;
- the amount to be paid up and the amount (if any) to be unpaid on each share (whether on account of the nominal value of the share or by way of premium).

It must contain such information as may be prescribed for the purpose of identifying the subscribers to the Memorandum of Association.

It must state, with respect to each subscriber to the Memorandum, the number, nominal value (of each share) and class of shares to be taken by him on formation, and the amount to be paid up and the amount (if any) to be unpaid on each share (whether on account of the nominal value of the share or by way of premium).

Where a subscriber to the Memorandum is to take shares of more than one class, the information is required for each class.

## 4.7 Limited liability

The principle of limited liability underlying item (*c*) in the registration list has been of great importance in industry and commerce. Without it, it is inconceivable that large business units, such as GlaxoSmithKline plc or Marks & Spencer plc, could have existed. The investor in a limited company, i.e. someone who owns shares in the company, is a shareholder. The most he or she can lose is the money paid for the shares although, where they are only partly paid, the shareholder is also liable for the unpaid part. With public companies, whose shares are traded on a stock exchange, shares can be sold easily whenever a shareholder wishes. Selling shares in a private company is normally far more difficult.

Why is it unlikely that many large companies could have existed if limited liability did not exist?

## 4.8 Classes of shares

The main types or classes of shares are *ordinary shares* and *preference shares*. Unless otherwise stated, preference shares are assumed to be of the cumulative variety – see *Business Accounting 1*.

There is also a variety of other shares. The rights attaching to these shares are purely dependent upon the skill and ingenuity of the person who prepares the company's registration. An entirely new type of share may be created provided it does not contravene the law.

The shares which carry the right to the whole of the profits remaining after dividends have been paid on any preference shares (and any other fixed dividend shares) are often known as 'equity share capital' or as '*equities*'.

## 4.9 Distributable profits

The calculation of dividends from profits available for distribution was described in *Business Accounting 1*. Clearly, in order to do this, there needs to be some way of knowing what the amount of *distributable profits* is.

A company's realised profits and losses are '*those profits and losses which are treated as realised in the financial statements, in accordance with principles generally accepted with respect to the determination of realised profits and losses for accounting purposes at the time when those accounts are prepared*'. In accounting, the realisation concept recognises profit or loss at the point when a contract is made in the market to buy or sell assets. The definition of realised profits and realised losses also applies for the purpose of calculating a company's distributable profits.

## 4.10 A company's constitution

A company's constitution comprises the regulations contained in the Articles of Association and any resolutions or agreements passed subsequently by the company. Among those regulated are those governing the rights and duties of the directors. Any such regulations are of the utmost importance when it is realised that the legal owners of the business, the shareholders, have entrusted the running of the company to the directors.

The shareholders' rights are largely limited to attending meetings, such as the annual general meeting, where they have the right to vote. However, some shares do not carry voting rights and the holders of these shares may attend but not vote at such meetings.

The Companies Acts make the keeping of proper sets of accounting records and the preparation of Final Accounts (financial statements) compulsory for every company. In addition, the financial statements for large companies must be audited, this being quite different from the situation in a partnership or a sole proprietor's business where an audit is not compulsory.

Companies with limited liability, whether they are private or public companies, have to send a copy of their Final Accounts (i.e. their financial statements), drawn up in a prescribed manner, to the Registrar of Companies. Public companies must submit them within six months of their financial year end; private companies within nine months of their financial year end.

**Look at Chapters 12–14 for the accounting requirements of the Companies Acts.**

## 4.11 Public companies and the stock exchange

Dealings in the shares of most public companies are conducted on one or other of the recognised stock exchanges. The shares of private companies cannot be bought or sold on any stock exchange, as this would contravene the requirements for the company being recognised as a 'private' company.

The only entry made in a company's books when a shareholder sells all, or some, of his shares to someone else, is to record the change of identity of the shareholders. The price at which the shares were sold on the stock exchange is not entered into the company's books.

**Although no accounting entries are made, the price of the shares on the stock exchange does have repercussions upon the financial policy of the company.**

Why?

Stock exchanges are the 'second-hand markets' for company shares. Companies do not actually sell (normally called '*issue*') their shares in a stock exchange. Companies issue new shares directly to the people who make application to them for the shares at the time when they have shares available for issue. Shares of a public company sold and bought on stock exchanges are passing from one shareholder to another person who will then become a shareholder. So far as the company is concerned, the number of shares in issue is unchanged.

## 4.12 Stocks and shares

Later in this book you will learn about the procedure whereby the shares of a company may be made into *stock*. Thus 500 ordinary shares of £1 each may be made into £500 stock. The dividends paid on the shares or the stock would be the same, and the voting powers would also be the same. Apart from administrative convenience there is really no difference between shares and stock.

### Learning outcomes

**You should now have learnt:**

1. Limited companies are governed by the Companies Acts and EU directives.
2. Limited companies are each a separate legal entity.
3. Each company is governed by its constitution which, initially, is contained in its Articles of Association.
4. What is meant by 'limited liability'.
5. Investors in limited companies can only lose the amount they paid (plus any amount still unpaid if the shares are only part-paid) when they acquired their investment in the company, i.e. they have 'limited liability'.

## Answers to activities

4.1 If a director sued another business entity on behalf of a company, the director would be liable for any legal costs incurred were the case unsuccessful. Perhaps more meaningfully, if companies could not be sued, directors and employees could be exposed to the risk of being sued for actions taken by the company, even when they were not personally involved in what had occurred. In effect, granting companies a legal identity separate from their owners makes it possible to operate limited liability effectively.

4.2 Without limited liability, investors would be very unwilling to buy shares in companies. They would fear that they may lose everything they owned if the company failed. Companies would, therefore, find it very difficult to raise funds other than from banks and other financial institutions. Such funds would carry interest costs that would have to be paid irrespective of how well the companies were doing. In the early years of a new business, it can take quite a long time to become profitable and the reliance upon loan funding would increase the possibility that the company will fail. As a result, in an economic environment where there was no limited liability, the investors in the failed company could lose everything they own. It is unlikely that many would be willing to take this risk. Hence, it is unlikely that many large companies would exist were it not for limited liability.

4.3 If some new shares are to be issued, the price they are to be issued at will be largely dependent on the stock exchange valuation. If another business is to be taken over by the company, part of the purchase price being paid using some of the company's shares, then the stock exchange value will also affect the value placed upon the shares being given. A takeover bid from another business may well be caused because the stock exchange value of the shares has made a takeover seem worthwhile.

chapter 5

# The issue of shares and loan notes

## Learning objectives

**After you have studied this chapter, you should be able to:**

- explain the terminology relating to the issue of shares and loan notes
- describe the steps in the process of issuing of shares and loan notes
- record the accounting entries relating to the issue of shares and loan notes
- make the necessary entries in the ledger accounts when shares are forfeited

## Introduction

In this chapter, you'll learn about the alternatives available to companies when they wish to issue shares and of the various entries to be made in the ledger accounts. You'll learn about how to record the issue of shares at a price greater than their nominal value and how to record the issue of shares to existing shareholders, rather than to non-shareholders wishing to purchase them. You will also learn about the difference in accounting entries made when loan notes (a form of loan capital), rather than shares, are issued.

## 5.1 The issue of shares

The cost of issuing shares can be very high. As a result, the number of shares issued must be sufficient to ensure the cost of doing so is relatively insignificant compared to the amounts received.

When shares are issued, they may be payable, either (*a*) immediately on application, or (*b*) by instalments. Issues of shares may take place on the following terms connected with the price of the shares:

1 Shares issued at par. This would mean that a share of £1 nominal value would be issued for £1 each.
2 Shares issued at a premium. In this case a share of £1 nominal value would be issued for more than £1 each, say for £3 each.

***Note*: At one time, shares could be issued at a discount. Thus, shares each of £5 nominal value might have been issued for £3 each. However, this was expressly forbidden in the Companies Act 1980.**

Why do you think companies may wish to issue shares at a discount and how do you think companies avoid being in this position?

## 5.2 Share premiums and discounts

This will all seem rather strange at first. How can a share with a nominal value of 10p, which states that value on the face of it, be issued for £3, and who would be foolish enough to buy it? The reasons for this apparently strange state of affairs stem from the Companies Act requirement that the share capital accounts always show shares at their nominal value, irrespective of how much the shares are worth or how much they were issued for. To illustrate this, the progress of two companies, A Ltd and B Ltd, can be looked at. Both started in business on 1 January 2013 and issued 1 million ordinary shares each of 10p nominal value at par. Ignoring any issue expenses, each of the statements of financial position on that date would be identical:

**Statements of Financial Position as at 1 January 2013**

| | £ |
|---|---|
| Bank | 100,000 |
| Capital | 100,000 |

Five years later, on 31 December 2017, the statements of financial position show that the companies have fared quite differently. It is to be assumed here, for purposes of illustration, that the statement of financial position values and any other interpretation of values happen to be identical.

A Ltd needs £100,000 more capital, and this is to be met by issuing more ordinary shares. Suppose that another 1 million ordinary shares of 10p nominal value each are issued at par. Column (*a*) in Exhibit 5.1 shows the statement of financial position before the issue, and column (*b*) shows the statement of financial position after the issue has taken place.

### Exhibit 5.1

**A Ltd Statements of Financial Position (Solution 1) as at 31 December 2017**

| | (*a*) | (*b*) |
|---|---|---|
| | £ | £ |
| Non-current and current assets (other than bank) | 225,000 | 225,000 |
| Bank | 25,000 | 125,000 |
| | 250,000 | 350,000 |
| Equity | | |
| Ordinary share capital | 100,000 | 200,000 |
| Retained profits | 150,000 | 150,000 |
| | 250,000 | 350,000 |

### Share premiums

Now the effect of what has happened can be appreciated. Before the new issue there were 1 million shares. As there were £250,000 of assets and no liabilities, each share was worth 25p. After the issue, there are 2 million shares and £350,000 of assets, so each share is now worth 17.5p. This would be extremely disconcerting to the original shareholders who have seen the value of each of their shares fall by 30% (7.5p).

On the other hand, the new shareholder who has just bought shares for 10p each saw them rise in value immediately by 75% to be worth 17.5p each. Only in one specific case would this be fair, and that is where each original shareholder buys an equivalent number of new shares.

What is required is a price which is equitable as far as the interests of the old shareholders are concerned, and yet will attract sufficient applications to provide the capital required. As in this case the statement of financial position value and the real value are the same, the answer is that each old share was worth 25p and therefore each new share should be issued at a price of 25p. If this were done, the statements of financial position would become as shown in Exhibit 5.2:

**Exhibit 5.2**

**A Ltd Statements of Financial Position (Solution 2) as at 31 December 2017**

| | (a) | (b) |
|---|---|---|
| | £ | £ |
| Non-current and current assets (other than bank) | 225,000 | 225,000 |
| Bank | 25,000 | 275,000 |
| | 250,000 | 500,000 |
| Equity | | |
| Ordinary share capital (at nominal value) | 100,000 | 200,000 |
| Share premium (*see* note below) | – | 150,000 |
| Retained profits | 150,000 | 150,000 |
| | 250,000 | 500,000 |

Thus in (*a*) above, 1 million shares own between them £250,000 of assets = 25 p each, while in (*b*) 2 million shares are shown as owning £500,000 of assets = 25p each. Both the old and new shareholders are therefore satisfied with the bargain that has been made.

***Note*: The share premium shown on the capital side of the statement of financial position is needed because the statement of financial position would not balance without it.** If shares are stated at nominal value but issued at another price, the actual amount received increases the bank balance, but the share capital is increased by a different figure. The share premium therefore represents the excess of the cash received over the nominal value of the shares issued.

## Share discount

The other company, B Ltd, has not fared so well. It has, in fact, lost money. The accumulated losses are reflected in a debit balance on the profit and loss account as shown below in column (*c*) of Exhibit 5.3. There are £80,000 of assets to represent the shareholders' stake in the firm of 1 million shares, i.e. each share is worth 8p. If more capital was needed, 1 million more shares could be issued. From the action taken in the previous case it will now be obvious that each new share of 10p nominal value would be issued for its real value of 8p each, were it permitted. The statements of financial position would appear:

**Exhibit 5.3**

**B Ltd Statements of Financial Position (correct solution) as at 31 December 2017**

| | (c) | (d) |
|---|---|---|
| Non-current and current assets (other than bank) | 55,000 | 55,000 |
| Bank | 25,000 | 105,000 |
| | 80,000 | 160,000 |
| Equity | | |
| Ordinary share capital | 100,000 | 200,000 |
| Discounts on shares (*see* below) | | (20,000) |
| Retained profits – debit balance | (20,000) | (20,000) |
| | 80,000 | 160,000 |

Although shares cannot now be issued at a discount, some companies still exist which issued shares at a discount before 1980. In these cases, a separate heading will have to be inserted in the statement of financial position for the discount.

***Note*: Once again, as the share capital is shown at nominal value but the shares are issued at a different figure, the discount on the shares issued must be shown in order that the statement of financial position balances.** **Share discount** is, of course, a balancing figure needed because the entries already made for an increase in the ordinary share capital and the increase in the bank balance have been at different figures. The figure for discounts on shares therefore rectifies the double entry 'imbalance'.

A statement of financial position is a historical view of the past based on records made according to the company's interpretation and use of accounting concepts and conventions. When shares are being issued it is not the view of the past that is important, but the view of the future. Therefore the actual premiums on shares being issued are a matter not merely of statement of financial position values, but of the issuing company's view of the future and its estimate of how the investing public will react to the price at which the shares are being offered.

**It is to be noted that there are *no* restrictions on issuing shares at par or at a premium.** Let's now look at the double entries that need to be made when shares are issued. First we'll consider the case where the full amount is due in one payment made at the time of issue.

## 5.3 Shares payable in full on application

The issue of shares in illustrations (1) and (2) which follow are based on the statements of financial position that have just been considered. First, let's look at the entries when shares are issued at their par value.

### 1 Shares issued at par

One million ordinary shares with a nominal value of 10p each are to be issued. Applications, together with the necessary money, are received for exactly 1 million shares. The shares are then allotted to the applicants.

**Bank**

| | | | | | |
|---|---|---|---|---|---|
| | | £ | | | |
| Ordinary share applicants | (A) | 100,000 | | | |

**Ordinary Share Applicants**

| | | | | | |
|---|---|---|---|---|---|
| | | £ | | | £ |
| Ordinary share capital | (B) | 100,000 | Bank | (A) | 100,000 |

**Ordinary Share Capital**

| | | | | | |
|---|---|---|---|---|---|
| | | | | | £ |
| | | | Ordinary share applicants | (B) | 100,000 |

It may appear that the ordinary share applicants account is unnecessary, and that the only entries needed are a debit in the bank account and a credit in the ordinary share capital account. However, applicants do not always become shareholders; this is shown later. The applicant must make an offer for the shares being issued, accompanied by the necessary money: this is the application. After the applications have been vetted, the allotments of shares are made by the company. This represents the acceptance of the offer by the company and it is at this point that the applicant becomes a shareholder. Therefore (A) represents the offer by the applicant while (B) is the acceptance by the company. **No entry must be made in the share capital account until (B) happens,**

**for it is not until that point that the share capital is in existence.** The share applicants account is an intermediary account pending allotments being made.

Now let's look at the entries to be made when the shares are issued at more than their par value.

## 2 Shares issued at a premium

One million ordinary shares with a nominal value of 10p each are to be issued for 25p each (*see* Exhibit 5.2 A Ltd previously). Thus a premium of 15p per share has been charged. Applications and the money are received for exactly 1 million shares.

**Bank**

| | | £ | | | £ |
|---|---|---|---|---|---|
| Balance b/d | | 25,000 | | | |
| Ordinary share applicants | | 250,000 | | | |

**Ordinary Share Applicants**

| | | £ | | | £ |
|---|---|---|---|---|---|
| Ordinary share capital | (A) | 100,000 | Bank | | 250,000 |
| Share premium | (B) | 150,000 | | | |
| | | 250,000 | | | 250,000 |

**Share Premium**

| | | | | | £ |
|---|---|---|---|---|---|
| | | | Ordinary share applicants | (B) | 150,000 |

**Ordinary Share Capital (A Ltd)**

| | | | | | £ |
|---|---|---|---|---|---|
| | | | Balance b/d | | 100,000 |
| | | | Ordinary share applicants | (A) | 100,000 |

***Note*: (A) is shown as £100,000 because the share capital is shown at nominal value, not total issued value. The £150,000 share premiums (B) therefore must be credited to a share premium account to preserve double entry balancing.**

Let's now look at the entries to be made when the number of shares applied for is not equal to the number of shares on offer.

## 3 Oversubscription and undersubscription for shares

When a company invites investors to apply for its shares it is obviously rare indeed if applications for shares equal exactly the number of shares to be issued. Where more shares are applied for than are available for issue, then the issue is said to be *oversubscribed*. Where fewer shares are applied for than are available for issue, then the issue has been *undersubscribed*.

With a new company, an amount is set in advance as being the minimum necessary to carry on any further with the running of the company. If the applications are less than the minimum stated, then the application monies are returned to the senders. This does not apply to an established company.

If 1 million shares of 10p each are available for issue, but only 875,000 shares are applied for, then only 875,000 shares will be issued. The accounting entries will be in respect of 875,000 shares, no entries being needed for the 125,000 shares not applied for, as they do not represent a transaction.

The opposite occurs when shares are oversubscribed. In this case, rationing is applied so that the issue is restricted to the shares available for issue. The process of selecting which applicants will get how many shares depends on the policy of the company. Some, for example, prefer to have large shareholders because this leads to lower administrative costs.

You can see why by considering the cost of calling a meeting of two companies each with 200,000 shares. H Ltd has 20 shareholders with an average holding of 10,000 shares. J Ltd has 1,000 shareholders with an average holding of 200 shares. They all have to be notified by post and given various documents including a set of the financial statements. The cost of printing and sending these is less for H Ltd with 20 shareholders than for J Ltd with 1,000 shareholders. This is only one example of the costs involved, but it will also apply with equal force to many items connected with the shares. Conversely, the directors may prefer to have more shareholders with smaller holdings, one reason being that it decreases the amount of voting power in any one individual's hands.

The actual process of rationing the shares is straightforward once a policy is in place. It may consist of scaling down applications, of drawing lots or some other chance selection, but it will eventually bring the number of shares to be issued down to the number of shares available. Excess application monies received will then be refunded by the company.

An issue of shares where 1 million ordinary shares of 10p nominal value each are to be issued at par payable in full but 1.55 million shares are applied for, will be recorded as follows:

**Bank**

| | £ | | £ |
|---|---|---|---|
| Ordinary share applicants | 155,000 | Ordinary share applicants (refunds) | 55,000 |

**Ordinary Share Applicants**

| | £ | | £ |
|---|---|---|---|
| Bank | 55,000 | Bank | 155,000 |
| Ordinary share capital | 100,000 | | |
| | 155,000 | | 155,000 |

**Ordinary Share Capital**

| | | | £ |
|---|---|---|---|
| | | Ordinary share applicants | 100,000 |

Let's now look at the entries to be made when payment for shares purchased is to be made in instalments.

## 5.4 Issue of shares payable by instalments

The shares considered so far have all been issued as paid in full on application. Conversely, many issues are made which require payment by instalments. These are probably more common with public companies than with private companies. It should be noted that a public company is now not allowed to allot a share (i.e. pass ownership to the subscriber) unless a sum equal to at least one-quarter of its nominal value plus the whole of any premium has been paid on it. When the premium is large compared to the nominal value, this clearly affects the manner in which the instalments are divided.

The various stages, after the initial invitation has been made to the public to buy shares by means of advertisements (if it is a public company), etc., are as follows:

(A) Applications are received together with the application monies.
(B) The applications are vetted and the shares allotted, letters of allotment being sent out.

(C) The excess application monies from wholly unsuccessful applicants, or, where the application monies received exceed both the application and allotment monies required, from wholly and partly unsuccessful applicants, are returned to them. Usually, if a person has been partly unsuccessful, his excess application monies are held by the company and will reduce the amount needed to be paid by him on allotment.
(D) Allotment monies are received.
(E) The next instalment, known as the first call, is requested.
(F) The monies are received from the first call.
(G) The next instalment, known as the second call, is requested.
(H) The monies are received from the second call.

This carries on until the full number of calls have been made, although there is not usually a large number of calls to be made in an issue.

The reasons for the payments by instalments become obvious if it is realised that a company will not necessarily require the immediate use of all the money to be raised by the issue. Suppose a new company is to be formed: it is to buy land, erect a factory, equip it with machinery and then go into production. This might take two years altogether. Suppose the total sum needed was £1 million, required as follows:

**Ordinary Share Capital**

| | £ |
|---|---|
| Cost of land, payable within 1 month | 300,000 |
| Cost of buildings, payable in 1 year's time | 200,000 |
| Cost of machinery, payable in 18 months' time | 200,000 |
| Working capital required in 2 years' time | 300,000 |
| | 1,000,000 |

A decision may be made to match the timing of the payment of the instalments of the share issue to the timing of the requirement for funding. If so, the share issue may be on the following terms:

| | *Per cent* |
|---|---|
| Application money per share, payable immediately | 10 |
| Allotment money per share, payable within 1 month | 20 |
| First call, money payable in 12 months' time | 20 |
| Second call, money payable in 18 months' time | 20 |
| Third call, money payable in 24 months' time | 30 |
| | 100 |

The entries made in the share capital account should equal the amount of money requested to that point in time. However, instead of one share applicants account, there are usually several accounts each representing one of the instalments. For this purpose application and allotment are usually joined together in one account, the *application and allotment account*. This cuts out the need for transfers where excess *application monies* are held over and set off against allotment monies needed. That is, instead of refunding excess application monies, they are retained and used to meet subsequent instalments.

When allotment is made, and not until then, an entry of £300,000 (10% + 20%) would be made in the share capital account. On the first call, an entry of £200,000 would be made in the share capital account; likewise £200,000 on the second call and £300,000 on the third call. The share capital account will therefore contain not the monies received, but the amount of money requested. Exhibit 5.4 now shows an example of a share issue with payments by instalments.

**Exhibit 5.4**

A company is issuing 100,000 7% preference shares of £1 each, payable 10% on application, 20% on allotment, 40% on the first call and 30% on the second call. Applications are received for 155,000 shares. A refund of the money is made in respect of 5,000 shares while, for the remaining 150,000 applied for, an allotment is to be made on the basis of two shares for every three applied for (assume that this will not involve any fractions of shares). The excess application monies are set off against the allotment monies asked for. The remaining requested instalments are all paid in full. The letters by the side of each entry refer to the various stages outlined earlier.

**Bank**

| | | £ | | | £ |
|---|---|---|---|---|---|
| Application and allotment: | | | Application and allotment refund (C) | | 500 |
| Application monies | (A) | 15,500 | | | |
| Allotment monies | | | | | |
| (£100,000 × 20% *less* excess | | | | | |
| application monies £5,000) | (D) | 15,000 | | | |
| First call | (F) | 40,000 | | | |
| Second call | (H) | 30,000 | | | |

**Application and Allotment**

| | | £ | | | £ |
|---|---|---|---|---|---|
| Bank – refund of application monies | (C) | 500 | Bank | (A) | 15,500 |
| Preference share capital | (B) | 30,000 | Bank | (D) | 15,000 |
| | | 30,500 | | | 30,500 |

**First Call**

| | | £ | | | £ |
|---|---|---|---|---|---|
| Preference share capital | (E) | 40,000 | Bank | (F) | 40,000 |

**Second Call**

| | | £ | | | £ |
|---|---|---|---|---|---|
| Preference share capital | (G) | 30,000 | Bank | (H) | 30,000 |

**7% Preference Share Capital**

| | | £ | | | £ |
|---|---|---|---|---|---|
| Balance c/d | | 100,000 | Application and allotment | (B) | 30,000 |
| | | | First call | (E) | 40,000 |
| | | | Second call | (G) | 30,000 |
| | | 100,000 | | | 100,000 |
| | | | Balance b/d | | 100,000 |

**If more than one type of share is being issued at the same time, e.g. preference shares and ordinary shares, then separate share capital accounts and separate application and allotment accounts and call accounts should be opened.**

Now let's look at the entries to be made when a purchaser of the shares fails to pay the instalments due.

## 5.5 Forfeited shares

Sometimes, some shareholders fail to pay the calls requested. If drawn up with care, the Articles of Association of the company will provide that the defaulting shareholder forfeits the shares allocated. In this case, the shares will be cancelled. The instalments already paid by the shareholder will be forfeited and retained by the company.

After the forfeiture, the company may or may not choose to reissue the shares (though, in some cases, there may be a provision in the Articles of Association which prevents their reissue). There are regulations governing the prices at which such shares can be reissued. The amount received on reissue plus the amount received from the original shareholder should at least equal (*a*) the called-up value where the shares are not fully called up, or (*b*) the nominal value where the full amount has been called up. Any premium previously paid is disregarded in determining the minimum reissue price.

### Exhibit 5.5

Take the same information as that contained in Exhibit 5.4, but, instead of all the calls being paid in full, Allen, the holder of 10,000 shares, fails to pay the first and second calls. He had already paid the application and allotment monies on the required dates. The directors conform to the provisions of the Articles of Association and (A) Allen is forced to suffer the forfeiture of his shares; (B) the amount still outstanding from Allen will be written off; (C) the directors then reissue the shares at 75% of nominal value to J Dougan; (D) Dougan pays for the shares.

**First Call**

| | | £ | | | £ |
|---|---|---|---|---|---|
| Preference share capital | | 40,000 | Bank | | 36,000 |
| | | | Forfeited shares | (B) | 4,000 |
| | | 40,000 | | | 40,000 |

**Second Call**

| | | £ | | | £ |
|---|---|---|---|---|---|
| Preference share capital | | 30,000 | Bank | | 27,000 |
| | | | Forfeited shares | (B) | 3,000 |
| | | 30,000 | | | 30,000 |

**7% Preference Share Capital**

| | | £ | | | £ |
|---|---|---|---|---|---|
| Forfeited shares | (A) | 10,000 | Application and allotment | | 30,000 |
| Balance c/d | | 90,000 | First call | | 40,000 |
| | | | Second call | | 30,000 |
| | | 100,000 | | | 100,000 |
| Balance c/d | | 100,000 | Balance b/d | | 90,000 |
| | | | J. Dougan | (C) | 10,000 |
| | | 100,000 | | | 100,000 |
| | | | Balance b/d | | 100,000 |

**Forfeited Shares**

| | | | | | |
|---|---|---|---|---|---|
| | | £ | | | £ |
| First call | (B) | 4,000 | Preference share capital | (A) | 10,000 |
| Second call | (B) | 3,000 | | | |
| Balance c/d | | 3,000 | | | |
| | | 10,000 | | | 10,000 |
| J Dougan* | | 2,500 | Balance b/d | | 3,000 |
| Balance c/d | | 500 | | | |
| | | 3,000 | | | 3,000 |
| | | | Balance b/d | | 500 |

**Bank**

| | | | | | |
|---|---|---|---|---|---|
| | | £ | | | |
| First call (£90,000 × 40%) | | 36,000 | | | |
| Second call (£90,000 × 30%) | | 27,000 | | | |
| J Dougan | (D) | 7,500 | | | |

**J Dougan**

| | | | | | |
|---|---|---|---|---|---|
| | | £ | | | £ |
| Preference share capital | | 10,000 | Bank | (D) | 7,500 |
| | | | Forfeited shares (discount on reissue)* | | 2,500 |
| | | 10,000 | | | 10,000 |

***The transfer of £2,500 from the forfeited shares account to J Dougan's account is needed because the reissue was entered in the preference share capital account and Dougan's account at nominal value, i.e. following standard practice by which a share capital account is concerned with nominal values. But Dougan was not required to pay the full nominal price. Therefore the transfer of £2,500 is needed to close his account.**

Why do you think companies make new share issues?
[Note: these are not the same as the shares issued when a company is first formed.]

The balance of £500 on the forfeited shares account can be seen to be: cash received from original shareholder on application and allotment £3,000 + from Dougan £7,500 = £10,500. This is £500 over the nominal value so the £500 appears as an extra credit balance. This could be transferred to a profit on reissue of forfeited shares account, but it would be pointless for small amounts. More normally it would be transferred to the credit of a share premium account.

Having looked at what is done when payments are not made, let's consider the treatment of payments being received early or received late.

## 5.6 Calls in advance and in arrear and the statement of financial position

At the date of the statement of financial position some shareholders will not have paid all the calls made. These are collectively known as *calls in arrear*. On the other hand, some shareholders may have paid amounts in respect of calls not made by the date of the statement of financial position. These are *calls in advance*.

So far, we have looked at the issue of shares to anyone, whether or not they are existing shareholders. Now, let's look at what happens when a company wishes to offer shares for sale to existing shareholders.

## 5.7 Rights issues

The costs of making a new issue of shares can be quite high. One way to reduce the costs of raising new long-term capital in the form of issuing shares is to do so in the form of a **rights issue**. To do this, the company contacts the existing shareholders, and informs them of the number of shares which each one of them is entitled to buy of the new issue. In most cases, shareholders are allowed to renounce their rights to the new shares in favour of someone else to whom they sell the right to purchase the shares.

A rights issue is usually pitched at a price which enables the rights to be sold. If any shareholders do not either buy the shares or transfer their rights, the directors have the power to dispose of the shares not taken up by issuing them in some other way. Alternatively, they may choose not to issue them.

So far in this chapter, we have looked at the issue of shares. Companies may also raise funds by issuing long-term loams. These are called *loan notes*.

## 5.8 Loan notes

A **loan note** is a certificate acknowledging a loan to a company. It is usually issued under the company's seal (i.e. is an official document issued by the company, similar to a share certificate) and bears a fixed rate of interest (similar to preference shares). However, unlike shares, which normally depend on profits out of which to appropriate dividends, interest on loan notes is payable whether or not profits are made.

A loan note may be *redeemable*, i.e. repayable at or by a specified date. Conversely it may be irredeemable, redemption taking place only when the company is eventually liquidated, or in a case such as when the loan-note interest is not paid within a given time limit.

People lending money to companies in the form of loan notes will obviously be interested in how safe their investment will be. In the case of some loan notes, the loan-note holders are given the legal right that on certain happenings they will be able to take control of specific assets, or of the whole of the assets. They can then sell the assets and recoup the amount due under their loan notes, or deal with the assets in ways specified in the deed under which the loan notes were issued. Such loan notes are known as being secured against the assets, the term *mortgage loan notes* often being used. Other loan notes carry no prior right to control the assets under any circumstances. These are known as *simple* or *naked loan notes*.

Under UK GAAP, loan notes are called 'debentures'. You, therefore, may see some UK companies with items in the statement of financial position called 'debentures' or 'mortgage debentures', and may read in the financial press and in textbooks of 'simple debentures' and 'naked debentures'. In all cases, these are the same as the equivalent form of loan note.

**Activity 5.3**

Why do you think companies issue loan notes rather than making a new share issue?

## 5.9 The issue of loan notes

The entries for the issue of loan notes are similar to those for shares but, nowadays, they are normally issued at their nominal value. If the term 'loan note' is substituted for 'share capital' in the T-accounts you saw earlier in this chapter, the entries in the ledger accounts would be identical.

## 5.10 Shares of no par value

You should now realise that a fixed par value for a share can be very confusing. For anyone who has not studied accounting, it may come as a shock to find that a share with a par value of £1 might have been issued for £5. If the share is dealt on the Stock Exchange, they might find a £1 share selling at £10 or even £20 or, equally well, it may sell for only 10p.

Another problem with the use of a par value is that it can give people entirely the wrong impression of the amount of dividend paid. If a low par value is used, the dividend (which is declared as a percentage of the par value) can look excessive when it really isn't.

### Exhibit 5.6

Jones bought a share 40 years ago for £1. At the time, he was satisfied with a return of 5% on his money. With a 5% dividend he could buy a certain amount of goods which will be called *x*. Now, 40 years later, to buy that same amount of goods, he would need, say, 20 times as much money. Where previously £5 would have bought *x*, now he would need £100. To keep the dividend at the same level of purchasing power, he would need a dividend now of 100%, as compared with the 5% dividend of 40 years ago.

In many countries, including the USA and Canada, no par value is attached to shares being issued. **Shares at no par value** are issued at whatever price is suitable at the time, and the money received is credited to a share capital account.

Why do you think companies are not allowed to issue shares at no par value in the UK?

### Learning outcomes

**You should now have learnt:**

**1** Shares may be issued either:
  (*a*) at par, or nominal value – i.e. a £1 ordinary share would be issued in exchange for payment of £1, or
  (*b*) at a premium, i.e. if a £1 ordinary share were issued at a premium of 25p, it would cost the buyer £1.25 (and the 25p would be put into the issuing company's *share premium* account).

**2** How to make the accounting entries when shares are issued.

**3** How to make the accounting entries when shares are forfeited.

**4** How to make the accounting entries when loan notes are issued.

**5** The accounting entries made on the issue of loan notes are identical to the accounting entries made on the issue of shares, though, obviously, loan-note ledger accounts are used rather than share-capital ledger accounts.

## Answers to activities

5.1 If a company is not performing very well and its share price has fallen below its nominal value, it would find it very difficult to issue shares at par or above. Hence, it may wish to issue shares at a discount. As companies are prohibited from doing so, it is common nowadays for shares to be given very low nominal values and then issued, in the first instance, at a price considerably in excess of their nominal value. This makes the likelihood of companies ever being in a position where they would wish to issue shares at a discount extremely rare. In effect, by adopting very low nominal values, companies make the restriction on their being able to issue shares at a discount irrelevant.

5.2 Nowadays, companies often make new share issues in order to obtain funds or in order to use the new shares to purchase another business entity.

5.3 Issuing shares may not be appropriate because the current share price is low and it is felt that issuing new shares at this time will enable investors to buy into the company too cheaply, with the result that when the share price rises, the new investors will make substantial profits on their investment. A company may prefer to wait until the share price is higher before selling new shares. It may also be the case that the share price is low because investors do not feel that the company is a good investment at present. Selling new shares may be difficult. Loan notes do not involve transference of rights of ownership. Buyers of loan notes receive interest, rather than a share of profit. If the company feels its profits are going to grow, it may prefer to issue loan notes so that existing shareholders receive the maximum long-term benefit of their investment in the company. That is, their share of future profits is not diluted by the issue of new shares.

5.4 When shares are issued at a premium, the excess above the nominal value is put into a reserve (the share premium account). Such a reserve can, in certain circumstances, be distributed or utilised. Doing so has no effect upon the share capital account. If shares are issued with no nominal value, share capital in the statement of financial position would represent the total amount received by a company when it issued shares. The share premium account would no longer be readily identifiable. In fact, it would not and could not exist (as no notion of par value would exist). By requiring shares to have a nominal value, additional flexibility is granted to the company in how it uses the funds received when it issues shares.

## Review questions

**5.1** Jonny Ltd has a nominal share capital of £600,000 comprising 600,000 ordinary shares of £1 each. The whole of the capital was issued at par on the following terms:

| | *Per share* |
|---|---|
| Payable on application | 10p |
| Payable on allotment | 25p |
| First call | 35p |
| Second call | 30p |

Applications were received for 1 million shares and it was decided to allot the shares on the basis of three for every five for which applications had been made. The balance of application monies was applied to the allotment, no cash being refunded. The balance of allotment monies was paid by the members.

The calls were made and paid in full by the members, with the exception of one who failed to pay the first and second calls on the 5,000 shares allotted to her. A resolution was passed by the directors to forfeit the shares. The forfeited shares were later issued to E Kershaw at 90p each.

Show the ledger accounts recording all the above transactions, and the relevant extracts from a statement of financial position after all the transactions had been completed.

**5.2** Easy Heart Ltd has an authorised capital of £800,000 comprising ordinary shares of £1 each. The shares were issued at par, payments being made as follows:

| | *Per share* |
|---|---|
| Payable on application | 20p |
| Payable on allotment | 28p |
| First call | 27p |
| Second call | 25p |

Applications were received for 1.08 million shares. It was decided to refund application monies on 80,000 shares and to allot the shares on the basis of four for every five applied for. The £40,000 excess application monies sent by the applicants whose applications were successful are not to be refunded but are to be held and so reduce the amount payable on allotment.

The calls were made and paid in full with the exception of two members holding a combined total of 5,000 shares who paid neither the first nor the second call and another member who did not pay the second call on 2,000 shares. The shares were forfeited and reissued to H Vipond at a price of 80p per share.

You are to draft the ledger accounts to record the transactions.

**5.3** The authorised and issued share capital of Cosy Fires Ltd was £75,000 divided into 75,000 ordinary shares of £1 each, fully paid. On 2 January 2017, the authorised capital was increased by a further 85,000 ordinary shares of £1 each to £160,000. On the same date 40,000 ordinary shares of £1 each were offered to the public at £1.25 per share payable as to £0.60 on application (including the premium), £0.35 on allotment and £0.30 on 6 April 2017.

The lists were closed on 10 January 2017. By that date, applications for 65,000 shares had been received. Applications for 5,000 shares received no allotment and the cash paid in respect of such shares was returned. All shares were then allocated to the remaining applicants pro rata to their original applications, the balance of the monies received on applications was applied to the amounts due on allotment.

The balances due on allotment were received on 31 January 2017, with the exception of one allottee of 500 shares and these were declared forfeited on 4 April 2017. These shares were reissued as fully paid on 2 May 2017, at £1.10 per share. The call due on 6 April 2017 was duly paid by the other shareholders.

**You are required:**

(*a*) to record the above-mentioned transactions in the appropriate ledger accounts; and

(*b*) to show how the balances on such accounts should appear in the company's statement of financial position as at 31 May 2017.

(*Association of Chartered Certified Accountants*)

**5.4A** During the year to 30 September 2017, Kammer plc made a new offer of shares. The details of the offer were as follows:

**1** 100,000 ordinary shares of £1 each were issued payable in instalments as follows:

| | *Per share* |
|---|---|
| | £ |
| On application at 1 November 2016 | 0.65 |
| On allotment (including the share premium of £0.50 per share) on 1 December 2017 | 0.55 |
| On first and final call on 1 June 2016 | 0.30 |
| | £1.50 |

**2** Applications for 200,000 shares were received, and it was decided to deal with them as follows:

(*a*) to return cheques for 75,000 shares;

(*b*) to accept in full applications for 25,000 shares; and

(*c*) to allot the remaining shares on the basis of three shares for every four shares applied for.

**3** On the first and final call, one applicant who had been allotted 5,000 shares failed to pay the due amount, and his shares were duly declared forfeited. They were then reissued to Amber Ltd on 1 September 2017 at a price of £0.80 per share fully paid.

*Note*: Kammer's issued share capital on 1 October 2016 consisted of 500,000 ordinary shares of £1 each.

**Required:**
Record the above transactions in the following ledger accounts:

(*a*) ordinary share capital;
(*b*) share premium;
(*c*) application and allotment;
(*d*) first and final call;
(*e*) forfeited shares; and
(*f*) Amber Ltd's account.

(*Association of Accounting Technicians*)

**5.5** M Limited has an authorised share capital of £1,500,000 divided into 1,500,000 ordinary shares of £1 each. The issued share capital at 31 March 2017 was £500,000 which was fully paid, and had been issued at par. On 1 April 2017, the directors, in accordance with the company's Articles, decided to increase the share capital of the company by offering a further 500,000 ordinary shares of £1 each at a price of £1.60 per share, payable as follows:

| | |
|---|---|
| On application, including the premium | £0.85 per share |
| On allotment | £0.25 per share |
| On first and final call on 3 August 2017 | £0.50 per share |

On 13 April 2017, applications had been received for 750,000 shares and it was decided to allot the shares to applicants for 625,000 shares, on the basis of four shares for every five shares for which applications had been received. The balance of the money received on application was to be applied to the amounts due on allotment. The shares were allotted on 1 May 2017, the unsuccessful applicants being repaid their cash on this date. The balance of the allotment money was received in full by 15 May 2017.

With the exception of one member who failed to pay the call on the 5,000 shares allotted to him, the remainder of the call was paid in full within two weeks of the call being made.

The directors resolved to forfeit these shares on 1 September 2017, after giving the required notice. The forfeited shares were reissued on 30 September 2017 to another member at £0.90 per share.

**You are required to** write up the ledger accounts necessary to record these transactions in the books of M Limited.

(*Chartered Institute of Management Accountants*)

**5.6A** Applications were invited by the directors of Grobigg Ltd for 150,000 of its £1 ordinary shares at £1.15 per share payable as follows:

| | *Per share* |
|---|---|
| On application on 1 April 2018 | £0.75 |
| On allotment on 30 April 2018 (including the premium of £0.15 per share) | £0.20 |
| On first and final call on 31 May 2018 | £0.20 |

Applications were received for 180,000 shares and it was decided to deal with these as follows:

**1** To refuse allotment to applicants for 8,000 shares.
**2** To give full allotment to applicants for 22,000 shares.
**3** To allot the remainder of the available shares pro rata among the other applicants.
**4** To utilise the surplus received on applications in part payment of amounts due on allotment.

An applicant, to whom 400 shares had been allotted, failed to pay the amount due on the first and final call and his shares were declared forfeit on 31 July 2018. These shares were reissued on 3 September 2018 as fully paid at £0.90 per share.

Show how the transactions would be recorded in the company's books.

(*Association of Chartered Certified Accountants*)

chapter 6

# Companies purchasing and redeeming their own shares and loan notes

## Learning objectives

**After you have studied this chapter, you should be able to:**

- explain, in the context of shares and loan notes, the difference between the terms 'purchasing' and 'redeeming'
- describe the alternative ways in which a company may purchase or redeem its own shares and loan notes
- explain the difference between the purchase/redemption opportunities available to private companies, and those available to other companies
- record the accounting entries relating to the purchase and the redemption of shares and loan notes

## Introduction

In this chapter, you'll learn the difference between the terms 'redemption' and 'purchase' of a company's own shares and loan notes and the rules relating to companies that do either of these things. You will learn how to record such activities in the ledger accounts and of the effects of such activities upon the statement of financial position.

## 6.1 Purchasing and redeeming own shares

In the context of shares and loan notes, to all intents and purposes, the words 'purchasing' and 'redeeming' may appear to be identical and interchangeable. They both involve an outflow of cash incurred by a company in getting back its own shares so that it may then cancel them. However, legally, 'redeeming' means the buying back of shares which were originally issued as 'redeemable shares'. That is, the company stated when they were issued that they would or could be bought back at some time in the future by the company. The actual terms of the redemption are declared at the time when the shares are issued. In contrast, when shares issued are not stated to be redeemable, if they are subsequently bought back by the company, the company is said to be 'purchasing' its own shares rather than 'redeeming' them.

Since 1981, if authorised by its Articles of Association, a company may:

(*a*) issue redeemable shares of any class (preference, ordinary, etc.). Redeemable shares include those that are to be redeemed on a particular date as well as those that are merely liable to be redeemed at the discretion of the shareholder or of the company. There is an important proviso that a company can only issue redeemable shares if it has in issue shares that are *not* redeemable. Without this restriction, a company could issue only redeemable shares, then later redeem all of its shares, and thus finish up without any shareholders;

(*b*) 'purchase' its own shares (i.e. shares that were not issued as being redeemable shares). Again, the company must, *after* the purchase, have other shares in issue at least some of which are not redeemable. This again prevents a company redeeming its whole share capital and thus ceasing to have any shareholders.

Why do you think the rules concerning purchase and redemption were changed in 1981?

## 6.2 Advantages to companies of being able to purchase and redeem their own shares

There are many advantages to a company arising from its being able to buy back its own shares. For public companies, the main advantage is that those with surplus cash resources can return some of this surplus cash back to their shareholders by buying back some of their own shares, rather than being pressurised to use such cash in other, less economic ways.

However, the greatest advantages are for private companies and relate to overcoming problems which occur when shareholders cannot sell their shares on the 'open market'. This means that:

1 They can help shareholders who have difficulties in selling their shares to realise their investment when needed.
2 People will be more willing to buy shares from private companies. The fear of not being able to dispose of them previously led to finance being relatively difficult for private companies to obtain from people other than the original main proprietors of the company.
3 In many 'family' companies, cash is needed to pay for taxes on the death of a shareholder.
4 Shareholders with grievances against the company can be bought out, thus contributing to the more efficient management of the company.
5 Family-owned companies are helped in their desire to keep control of the company when a family shareholder with a large number of shares dies or retires.
6 As with public companies, private companies can return unwanted cash resources to their shareholders.
7 For both private companies, and for public companies whose shares are not listed on a stock exchange, it may help boost share schemes for employees, as the employees would know that they could dispose of the shares fairly easily.

## 6.3 Accounting entries

The accounting entries for the purchase and the redemption of shares are exactly the same, except that the word 'redeemable' will appear as the first word in the title of the ledger accounts for shares that are redeemable. The figures to be entered will naturally be affected by the *terms* under which shares are redeemed or purchased, but the *location* of the debits and credits to be made will be the same.

You will understand better the rather complicated entries needed if you realise that protection of the creditor was uppermost in the minds of Parliament when, for the first time, it permitted companies to purchase their own shares in the 1981 Companies Act. The general idea is that *capital* should not be returned to the shareholders, except under certain circumstances. If capital is returned to the shareholders, thus reducing the cash and bank balances, then the creditors could lose out badly if there was not then sufficient cash/bank balances to pay their claims. Thus the shareholders, seeing that things were not progressing too well in the company, could get their money out, leaving the creditors with nothing.

There are dividends which can quite legitimately be paid to the shareholders out of distributable profits but, in order to prevent shareholders withdrawing all their capital, included under the general heading of 'capital' are reserves which *cannot* be used for the payment of cash dividends.

There are exceptions to this, namely the reduction of capital by public companies (*see* Chapter 10) and the special powers of a private company to purchase or redeem its own shares out of capital (which you will learn about later in this chapter). However, apart from these special cases, company law regulations are intended to ensure that capital does not decrease when shares are redeemed or purchased. This is what lies behind the accounting entries we'll now consider.

The safeguards for the protection of capital contained in the Companies Acts are summarised in the next six sections.

## 6.4 Rules for redemption or purchase

In *all* cases, shares can only be redeemed or purchased when they are fully paid.

Why do you think shares need to be fully paid before they can be redeemed or purchased?

A company may redeem its redeemable shares by either:

(*a*) Issuing new shares to provide funds for the redemption; or,
(*b*) Through use of a capital redemption reserve; or,
(*c*) By a combination of (*a*) and (*b*).

## 6.5 Nominal value

In respect of the *nominal value* of shares redeemed or purchased, either (*a*) there must be a new issue of shares to provide the funds for redemption or purchase or (*b*) sufficient distributable profits must be available (i.e. a large enough credit balance on the appropriation account) which could be diverted from being used up as dividends to being treated as used up for the purpose of redeeming or purchasing the shares.

Therefore, when shares are redeemed or purchased other than by using the proceeds of a new share issue, the amount of distributable profits treated as being used up to redeem or purchase the *nominal* value of the shares redeemed or purchased is debited to the appropriation account and credited to a **capital redemption reserve**. (Previously, this was called a 'capital redemption reserve fund'.)

Thus, the old share capital amount is equal to the total of the new share capital *plus* the capital redemption reserve. The capital redemption reserve is a 'non-distributable' reserve. It *cannot* be transferred back to the credit of the appropriation account, and so increase the profits available for distribution as cash dividends. The process of diverting profits from being usable for dividends means that the non-payment of the dividends leaves more cash in the company against which creditors could claim if necessary.

***Note*: In all the examples that follow, as the entries are the same, no attempt is made to indicate whether or not the shares being redeemed/purchased are redeemable shares. In a real company, the titles of the accounts would indicate which shares were redeemable.**

In Exhibit 6.1, journal entries are shown first, followed by the changes in the statement of financial position amounts.

***Note*: In all these examples, the amounts involved are kept small so that you can follow more easily the entries and changes that arise.**

## Exhibit 6.1

£2,000 preference shares are redeemed/purchased at par. In order to do so, a new issue is to be made of £2,000 ordinary £1 shares at par. The journal entries are:

| | | *Dr* | *Cr* |
|---|---|---|---|
| | | £ | £ |
| (A1) | Bank | 2,000 | |
| (A2) | Ordinary share applicants | | 2,000 |
| | Cash received from applicants | | |
| (B1) | Ordinary share applicants | 2,000 | |
| (B2) | Ordinary share capital | | 2,000 |
| | Ordinary shares allotted | | |
| (C1) | Preference share capital | 2,000 | |
| (C2) | Preference share purchase* | | 2,000 |
| | Shares to be redeemed/purchased | | |
| (D1) | Preference share purchase* | 2,000 | |
| (D2) | Bank | | 2,000 |
| | Payment made to redeem/purchase shares | | |

***To make it easier to follow, all these examples refer only to the redemption of preference shares. The process is identical whatever the type of shares being redeemed or purchased, only the names of the accounts to be used are different. When ordinary shares are redeemed, they are transferred to a 'share redemption account'. If they are purchased, a 'share purchase account' is used instead of a 'preference share purchase account'.**

| | *Balances before* | *Effect* | | | | *Balances after* |
|---|---|---|---|---|---|---|
| | | | *Dr* | | *Cr* | |
| | £ | | £ | | £ | £ |
| Net assets (except bank) | 7,500 | | | | | 7,500 |
| Bank | 2,500 | (A1) | 2,000 | (D2) | 2,000 | 2,500 |
| | 10,000 | | | | | 10,000 |
| Ordinary share capital | 5,000 | | | (B2) | 2,000 | 7,000 |
| Ordinary share applicants | – | (B1) | 2,000 | (A2) | 2,000 | – |
| Preference share capital | 2,000 | (C1) | 2,000 | | | – |
| Preference share purchase | – | (D1) | 2,000 | (C2) | 2,000 | – |
| Total 'capitals'* | 7,000 | | | | | 7,000 |
| Retained profits | 3,000 | | | | | 3,000 |
| | 10,000 | | | | | 10,000 |

***Total 'capitals' remain the same as the preference share capital has been replaced with additional ordinary capital.**

Exhibit 6.2 shows the journal entries and the changes to the statement of financial position amounts when reserves are used to redeem or purchase shares.

## Exhibit 6.2

£2,000 preference shares are redeemed/purchased at par, with no new issue of shares to provide funds for the purpose. Therefore an amount equal to the nominal value of the shares redeemed *must* be transferred from retained profits to a capital redemption reserve.

| | | *Dr* | *Cr* |
|---|---|---|---|
| | | £ | £ |
| (A1) | Preference share capital | 2,000 | |
| (A2) | Preference share purchase | | 2,000 |
| | Shares to be redeemed/purchased | | |
| (B1) | Preference share purchase | 2,000 | |
| (B2) | Bank | | 2,000 |
| | Cash paid as purchase/redemption | | |
| (C1) | Retained profits | 2,000 | |
| (C2) | Capital redemption reserve | | 2,000 |
| | Transfer to reserve on redemption of shares | | |

| | *Balances before* | *Effect* | | | | *Balances after* |
|---|---|---|---|---|---|---|
| | | | *Dr* | | *Cr* | |
| | £ | | £ | | £ | £ |
| Net assets (except bank) | 7,500 | | | | | 7,500 |
| Bank | 2,500 | | | (B2) | 2,000 | 500 |
| | 10,000 | | | | | 8,000 |
| Ordinary share capital | 5,000 | | | | | 5,000 |
| Preference share capital | 2,000 | (A1) | 2,000 | | | – |
| Preference share purchase | – | (B1) | 2,000 | (A2) | 2,000 | – |
| Capital redemption reserve | – | | | (C2) | 2,000 | 2,000 |
| Total 'capitals'* | 7,000 | | | | | 7,000 |
| Retained profits | 3,000 | (C1) | 2,000 | | | 1,000 |
| | 10,000 | | | | | 8,000 |

***The total 'capitals' (i.e. share capital + non-distributable reserves) remain the same at £7,000.**

Exhibit 6.3 shows the journal entries and the changes to the statement of financial position amounts when both the Exhibit 6.1 and Exhibit 6.2 approaches are used.

## Exhibit 6.3

£2,000 preference shares are redeemed/purchased at par, being £1,200 from issue of ordinary shares at par and partly by using retained profits.

| | | *Dr* | *Cr* |
|---|---|---|---|
| | | £ | £ |
| (A1) | Bank | 1,200 | |
| (A2) | Ordinary share applicants | | 1,200 |
| | Cash received from applicants | | |
| (B1) | Ordinary share applicants | 1,200 | |
| (B2) | Ordinary share capital | | 1,200 |
| | Ordinary shares allotted | | |
| (C1) | Retained profits | 800 | |
| (C2) | Capital redemption reserve | | 800 |
| | Part of redemption/purchase not covered by new issue | | |
| (D1) | Preference share capital | 2,000 | |
| (D2) | Preference share purchase | | 2,000 |
| | Shares being redeemed/purchased | | |
| (E1) | Preference share purchase | 2,000 | |
| (E2) | Bank | | 2,000 |
| | Payment made for redemption/purchase | | |

→

→

| | Balances before £ | | Effect Dr £ | | Cr £ | Balances after £ |
|---|---|---|---|---|---|---|
| Net assets (except bank) | 7,500 | | | | | 7,500 |
| Bank | 2,500 | (A1) | 1,200 | (E2) | 2,000 | 1,700 |
| | 10,000 | | | | | 9,200 |
| Ordinary share capital | 5,000 | | | (B2) | 1,200 | 6,200 |
| Ordinary share applicants | – | (B1) | 1,200 | (A2) | 1,200 | – |
| Preference share capital | 2,000 | (D1) | 2,000 | | | – |
| Preference share purchase | – | (E1) | 2,000 | (D2) | 2,000 | – |
| Capital redemption reserve | – | | | (C2) | 800 | 800 |
| Total 'capitals'* | 7,000 | | | | | 7,000 |
| Retained profits | 3,000 | (C1) | 800 | | | 2,200 |
| | 10,000 | | | | | 9,200 |

*Total 'capitals' remain the same.

## 6.6 Premiums

When shares are being redeemed/purchased at a premium that were *not* originally issued at a premium, then an amount equal to the premium *must* be transferred from retained profits to the credit of the share purchase/redemption account. As before, this is required so as to maintain total capitals by diverting profits from being distributable to being part of the non-distributable capital.

### Exhibit 6.4

£2,000 preference shares which were originally issued at par are redeemed/purchased at a premium of 20%. There is no new issue of shares for the purpose. The ordinary shares were issued at a premium, thus the reason for the share premium account being in existence. However, as it is *not* the ordinary shares which are being redeemed, the share premium *cannot* be used to source the premium paid on the redemption/purchase.

| | | Dr £ | Cr £ |
|---|---|---|---|
| (A1) | Preference share capital | 2,000 | |
| (A2) | Preference share purchase | | 2,000 |
| | Shares being redeemed/purchased | | |
| (B1) | Retained profits | 400 | |
| (B2) | Preference share purchase | | 400 |
| | Premium on purchase/redemption of shares *not* previously issued at premium | | |
| (C1) | Retained profits | 2,000 | |
| (C2) | Capital redemption reserve | | 2,000 |
| | Transfer because shares redeemed/purchased out of distributable profits | | |
| (D1) | Preference share purchase | 2,400 | |
| (D2) | Bank | | 2,400 |
| | Payment on purchase/redemption | | |

| | Balances before | Effect | | | | Balances after |
|---|---|---|---|---|---|---|
| | | | Dr | | Cr | |
| | £ | | £ | | £ | £ |
| Net assets (except bank) | 7,500 | | | | | 7,500 |
| Bank | 2,500 | | | (D2) | 2,400 | 100 |
| | 10,000 | | | | | 7,600 |
| Ordinary share capital | 4,500 | | | | | 4,500 |
| Preference share capital | 2,000 | (A1) | 2,000 | | | – |
| Preference share purchase | – | (D1) | 2,400 | (A2) | 2,000 | |
| | | | | (B2) | 400 | – |
| Capital redemption reserve | – | | | (C2) | 2,000 | 2,000 |
| Share premium | 500 | | | | | 500 |
| Total 'capitals'* | 7,000 | | | | | 7,000 |
| Retained profits | 3,000 | (C1) | 2,000 | | | |
| | | (B1) | 400 | | | 600 |
| | 10,000 | | | | | 7,600 |

***Once again, the total 'capitals' remain the same.**

When shares are being redeemed or purchased at a premium, *and* they were originally issued at a premium, *and* a new issue of shares is being made for the purpose, then the share premium account *can* have an amount calculated as follows transferred to the credit of the share purchase/redemption account. This is shown as (E) below.

**Share Premium Account**

| | | | £ |
|---|---|---|---|
| Balance before new issue | (A) | | xxx |
| *Add* Premium on new issue | (B) | | xxx |
| Balance after new issue | (C) | | xxx |
| Amount that *may* be transferred is the lesser of: | | | |
| Premiums that were received when it first issued the shares now being redeemed/purchased | (D) | xxx | |
| *or* | | | |
| Balance after new issue (C) above | | xxx | |
| Transfer from share premium to share purchase/redemption (the lesser of D and C) | (E) | | (xxx) |
| New balance for statement of financial position (could be nil) | | | xxx |

Where the amount being deducted (E) is *less* than the premium paid on the *current* redemption or purchase, then an amount equivalent to the difference must be transferred from the debit of the retained profits to the credit of the share purchase/redemption account. (An example of this is shown below in Exhibit 6.5.) This again diverts the appropriate amount of profits away from being distributable.

***Note*: If no premium was charged when the shares being redeemed were issued, *all* the premium paid over par upon redemption *must* be charged to retained profits.**

## Exhibit 6.5

£2,000 preference shares of three companies which were originally issued at a premium of 20% are now purchased/redeemed at a premium of 25%. The changes to the share premium account are shown below for the three companies.

- Company 1 issues 2,400 ordinary £1 shares at par.
- Company 2 issues 2,000 ordinary £1 shares at 20% premium.
- Company 3 issues 1,600 ordinary £1 shares at 50% premium.

**Share Premium Account**

| | | *Company 1* | *Company 2* | *Company 3* |
|---|---|---|---|---|
| | | £ | £ | £ |
| Balance before new issue | (A) | 150[Note (a)] | 400 | 400 |
| Premium on new issue | | ___ | 400 | 800 (B) |
| Balance after new issue | (C) | 150 | 800 | 1,200 |
| Amount transferable to share purchase/ redemption is therefore the lower of (C) or original premium on issue (£400) | | (150)[Note (b)] | (400)[Note (b)] | (400)[Note (b)] |
| New balance for statement of financial position | | – | 400 | 800 |

***Note*** **(*a*): In Company 1 it is assumed that, of the original £400 premium, the sum of £250 had been used to issue bonus shares (*see* Chapter 10).**

***Note*** **(*b*): As these figures are less than the premium of £500 *now* being paid, the differences (Company 1 £350; Companies 2 and 3 £100 each) must be transferred from retained profits to the preference share/purchase redemption account.**

***Journal entries*:**

| | *Company 1* | | *Company 2* | | *Company 3* | |
|---|---|---|---|---|---|---|
| | *Dr* | *Cr* | *Dr* | *Cr* | *Dr* | *Cr* |
| | £ | £ | £ | £ | £ | £ |
| (A1) Bank | 2,400 | | 2,400 | | 2,400 | |
| (A2) Ordinary share applicants | | 2,400 | | 2,400 | | 2,400 |
| Cash received from applicants | | | | | | |
| (B1) Ordinary share applicants | 2,400 | | 2,400 | | 2,400 | |
| (B2) Ordinary share capital | | 2,400 | | 2,000 | | 1,600 |
| (B3) Share premium | | – | | 400 | | 800 |
| Ordinary shares allotted | | | | | | |
| (C1) Preference share capital | 2,000 | | 2,000 | | 2,000 | |
| (C2) Preference share purchase | | 2,000 | | 2,000 | | 2,000 |
| Shares being redeemed/purchased | | | | | | |
| (D1) Share premium account | 150 | | 400 | | 400 | |
| (D2) Preference share purchase | | 150 | | 400 | | 400 |
| Amount of share premium account used for redemption/purchase | | | | | | |
| (E1) Retained profits | 350 | | 100 | | 100 | |
| (E2) Preference share purchase | | 350 | | 100 | | 100 |
| Excess of premium payable over amount of share premium account usable for the purpose | | | | | | |
| (F1) Preference share purchase | 2,500 | | 2,500 | | 2,500 | |
| (F2) Bank | | 2,500 | | 2,500 | | 2,500 |
| Amount paid on redemption/purchase | | | | | | |

## Exhibit 6.6

The following statements of financial position for the three companies in Exhibit 6.5 are given *before* the purchase/redemption. The statements of financial position are then shown *after* purchase/redemption.

**Statements of Financial Position (*before* redemption/purchase)**

| | *Company 1* | *Company 2* | *Company 3* |
|---|---|---|---|
| | £ | £ | £ |
| Net assets (except bank) | 7,500 | 7,500 | 7,500 |
| Bank | 2,500 | 2,500 | 2,500 |
| | 10,000 | 10,000 | 10,000 |
| Ordinary share capital | 4,850 | 4,600 | 4,600 |
| Preference share capital | 2,000 | 2,000 | 2,000 |
| Share premium | 150 | 400 | 400 |
| | 7,000 | 7,000 | 7,000 |
| Retained profits | 3,000 | 3,000 | 3,000 |
| | 10,000 | 10,000 | 10,000 |

**Statements of Financial Position (*after* redemption/purchase)**

| | *Company 1* | *Company 2* | *Company 3* |
|---|---|---|---|
| | £ | £ | £ |
| Net assets (except bank) | 7,500 | 7,500 | 7,500 |
| Bank | 2,400 | 2,400 | 2,400 |
| | 9,900 | 9,900 | 9,900 |
| Ordinary share capital | 7,250 | 6,600 | 6,200 |
| Share premium | – | 400 | 800 |
| | 7,250 | 7,000 | 7,000 |
| Retained profits | 2,650 | 2,900 | 2,900 |
| | 9,900 | 9,900 | 9,900 |

**The following scenarios each contain a different share redemption situation. Prepare the appropriate journal entries and explain what you have done in each case:**

**Scenario 1**
A company redeemed its 200,000 6% preference share capital of £1 each at a premium of £0.10. Originally these shares were issued at a premium of £0.05 per share. There was no issue of new shares to finance the redemption.

**Scenario 2**
100,000 8% preference shares of £0.75 each were redeemed at a premium of £0.10 per share. These shares were originally issued at par. To finance the redemption, the company issued 150,000 ordinary shares of £1 each at a premium of £0.25 per share.

**Scenario 3**
A company redeemed its 180,000 8% £1 preference share capital at a premium of £0.15 per share. In order to do so, it issued an equal number of 6% £0.50 preference shares at par. The shares being redeemed were originally issued at a premium of £0.25 and the balance on the share premium account is £30,000.

**Scenario 4**
A company issued 100,000 6% £1 preference shares at a premium of £0.16 per share in order to finance the redemption of 200,000 8% preference shares of £0.50 each at a premium of £0.15 per share. These shares were originally issued at a premium of £0.10 per share, which was utilised to issue bonus shares to the ordinary shareholders. There is no balance in the share premium account.

**Scenario 5**
A company, which had issued 100,000 8% preference share capital of £1 at par, redeemed the shares at a premium of £0.15 per share. To finance the redemption, the company issued 100,000 6% preference shares of £0.50 each at £1.15.

## 6.7 Private companies: redemption or purchase of shares out of capital

The Companies Act 1981 introduced a new power for a *private* company to redeem/purchase its own shares where *either* it has insufficient distributable profits for the purpose *or* it cannot raise the amount required by a new issue. Previously it would have had to apply to the court for *capital reduction* (which you will learn about in Chapter 10). The 1981 legislation made it far easier to achieve the same objectives, in terms of both time and expense.

The full details of the various matters which must be dealt with by private companies who pursue this option are beyond the scope of this book. If you wish to go into this topic in greater detail, you will need to consult a book on company law. For our purposes, a very brief outline is as follows:

1 The private company must be authorised to redeem or purchase its own shares out of capital by its Articles of Association.
2 *Permissible capital payment* is the amount by which the price of redemption or purchase exceeds the aggregate of (*a*) the company's distributable profits and (*b*) the proceeds of any new issue. This means that a private company must use its available profits and any share proceeds before making a payment out of capital. (This is dealt with in greater detail in the next section.)
3 Directors must certify that, after the permissible capital payment, the company will be able to carry on as a going concern during the next twelve months, and be able to pay its debts immediately after the payment and also during the next twelve months.
4 The company's auditors make a satisfactory report.

**Activity 6.4** Why do you think the rules are less restrictive for private companies?

## 6.8 Permissible capital payments

1 Where the permissible capital payment is *less* than the nominal value of shares redeemed/purchased, the amount of the difference *shall* be transferred to the capital redemption reserve from retained profits or other undistributed profits (such as a repairs reserve).
2 Where the permissible capital payment is *greater* than the nominal value of shares redeemed/purchased, *any* non-distributable reserves (e.g. share premium account, capital redemption reserve, revaluation reserve, etc.) or fully paid share capital can be reduced by the excess.

This can be illustrated by taking two companies, R and S, with similar account balances *before* the purchase/redemption, which are redeeming their shares on different terms:

***Note***: **To ensure maximum clarity, the values used have been kept unrealistically low.**

## Exhibit 6.7

| | Before | | Dr | | Cr | After |
|---|---|---|---|---|---|---|
| **Company R** | £ | | £ | | £ | £ |
| Net assets (except bank) | 2,500 | | | | | 2,500 |
| Bank | 7,500 | | | (B2) | 4,000 | 3,500 |
| | 10,000 | | | | | 6,000 |
| Ordinary shares | 1,000 | | | | | 1,000 |
| Preference shares | 4,000 | (A1) | 4,000 | | | – |
| Non-distributable reserves | 2,000 | | | | | 2,000 |
| Capital redemption reserve | | | | (C2) | 3,000 | 3,000 |
| Preference share purchase | – | (B1) | 4,000 | (A2) | 4,000 | |
| | 7,000 | | | | | |
| Retained profits | 3,000 | (C1) | 3,000 | | | |
| | 10,000 | | | | | 6,000 |

The preference shares were redeemed at par, £4,000. No new issue was made.
(A1) and (A2) represent transfer of shares redeemed/purchased.
(B1) and (B2) represent payment to shareholders.

| | |
|---|---|
| Therefore pay | 4,000 |
| *Less* Retained profits | 3,000 |
| Permissible capital payment | 1,000 |
| Nominal amount of shares redeemed/purchased | 4,000 |
| *Less* Permissible capital payment | 1,000 |
| *Deficiency* to transfer to capital redemption reserve (C1 and C2) | 3,000 |

| The steps taken were: | Dr | Cr |
|---|---|---|
| (A1) Preference shares | 4,000 | |
| (A2) Preference share purchase | | 4,000 |
| (B1) Preference share purchase | 4,000 | |
| (B2) Bank | | 4,000 |
| (C1) Retained profits | 3,000 | |
| (C2) Capital redemption reserve | | 3,000 |

| | Before | | Dr | | Cr | After |
|---|---|---|---|---|---|---|
| **Company S** | £ | | £ | | £ | £ |
| Net assets (except bank) | 2,500 | | | | | 2,500 |
| Bank | 7,500 | | | (D2) | 7,200 | 300 |
| | 10,000 | | | | | 2,800 |
| Ordinary share capital | 1,000 | | | | | 1,000 |
| Preference shares | 4,000 | (A1) | 4,000 | | | – |
| Non-distributable reserves | 2,000 | (C1) | 200 | | | 1,800 |
| Capital redemption reserve | – | | | | | – |
| Preference share purchase | | (D1) | 7,200 | (A2) | 4,000 | |
| | | | | (B2) | 3,000 | |
| | | | | (C2) | 200 | |
| | 7,000 | | | | | 2,800 |
| Retained profits | 3,000 | (B1) | 3,000 | | | – |
| | 10,000 | | | | | 2,800 |

→

→ The preference shares were redeemed/purchased at a premium of 80%. No new issue was made.

(A1) and (A2) represent shares redeemed/purchased.
(B1) and (B2) are transfers to redemption/purchase account of part of source of funds.
(D1) and (D2) are payment to shareholders.

| | |
|---|---|
| Therefore pay | 7,200 |
| *Less* Retained profits | (3,000) |
| Permissible capital payment | 4,200 |
| Permissible capital payment | 4,200 |
| *Less* Nominal amount redeemed/purchased | (4,000) |
| *Excess* from *any* non-distributable reserves (or capital) (C1 and C2) | 200 |

| The steps taken were: | *Dr* | *Cr* |
|---|---|---|
| (A1) Preference shares | 4,000 | |
| (A2) Preference share purchase | | 4,000 |
| (B1) Retained profits | 3,000 | |
| (B2) Preference share purchase | | 3,000 |
| (C1) Non-distributable reserves | 200 | |
| (C2) Preference share purchase | | 200 |
| (D1) Preference share purchase | 7,200 | |
| (D2) Bank | | 7,200 |

## 6.9 Cancellation of shares purchased/redeemed

All shares purchased/redeemed must be cancelled immediately. They cannot be kept by the company and later traded.

## 6.10 Redemption of loan notes

Unless they are stated to be irredeemable, loan notes are redeemed according to the terms of the issue. The necessary funds to finance the redemption may be from:

(*a*) an issue of shares or loan notes;
(*b*) the resources of the company.

As (*a*) resembles the redemption of redeemable preference shares, you won't be surprised to learn that no transfer of profits from retained profits to a reserve account is needed. However, when financed as in (*b*), it is good accounting practice, although not legally necessary, to divert profits from being used as dividends by transferring an amount equal to the nominal value redeemed from retained profits to the credit of a reserve account.

Redemption may be done in one of three ways:

(*a*) by annual transfers out of profits;
(*b*) by purchase in the open market when the price is favourable, i.e. when it is less than the price which will have to be paid if the company waits until the last date by which redemption has to be carried out;
(*c*) in a lump sum to be provided by the accumulation of a *sinking fund*.

These three approaches can now be examined in more detail.

## 1 Redeemed by transfers out of profits

### [a] When loan notes are redeemed at a premium

In this case, the source of the funds with which the premium is paid should be taken to be (i) the share premium account, or if this does not exist, or the premium paid is in excess of the balance on the share premium account, then any part not covered by a share premium account is deemed to come from (ii) retained profits. Exhibit 6.8 shows the effect on a statement of financial position where there is no share premium account, while Exhibit 6.9 illustrates the case when a share premium account is in existence with a balance large enough to source the premium.

### Exhibit 6.8

Starting with the *before* statement of financial position, £400 of the loan notes are redeemed at a premium of 20%, i.e. £80.

***Note*: As before, the values involved have been kept unrealistically low for greater clarity.**

**Statements of Financial Position**

| | *Before* | *+ or −* | *After* |
|---|---|---|---|
| | £ | £ | £ |
| Other assets | 12,900 | | 12,900 |
| Bank | 3,400 | −480 (A) | 2,920 |
| | 16,300 | | 15,820 |
| Loan notes | (2,000) | −400 (A) | (1,600) |
| | 14,300 | | 14,220 |
| Share capital | 10,000 | | 10,000 |
| Loan note redemption reserve | – | +400 (B) | 400 |
| Retained profits | 4,300 | −400 (B) | |
| | | −80 (A) | 3,820 |
| | 14,300 | | 14,220 |

### Exhibit 6.9

Starting with the *before* statement of financial position, £400 of the loan notes are redeemed at a premium of 20%, i.e. £80.

**Statements of Financial Position**

| | *Before* | *+ or −* | *After* |
|---|---|---|---|
| | £ | £ | £ |
| Other assets | 13,500 | | 13,500 |
| Bank | 3,400 | −480 (A) | 2,920 |
| | 16,900 | | 16,420 |
| Loan notes | (2,000) | −400 (A) | (1,600) |
| | 14,900 | | 14,820 |
| Share capital | 10,000 | | 10,000 |
| Share premium | 600 | −80 (A) | 520 |
| Loan note redemption reserve | – | +400 (B) | 400 |
| Retained profits | 4,300 | −400 (B) | 3,900 |
| | 14,900 | | 14,820 |

In both Exhibits 6.8 and 6.9 the balance on the loan-note redemption reserve account is increased by the nominal value of the loan notes redeemed each year. Any element of the redemption sourced by the share premium account is entered as a debit to that account and is not included in the loan note redemption reserve.

When the whole issue of loan notes has been redeemed, the balance on the loan-note redemption reserve account is transferred to the credit of a general reserve account. It is, after all, an accumulation of undistributed profits.

### [b] When loan notes are redeemed but originally issued at a discount

The discount on issue was given in order to attract investors to buy the loan notes and is, therefore, as much a cost of borrowing as is loan-note interest. The discount therefore needs to be written off during the life of the loan notes. It might be more rational to write it off to profit or loss, but accounting custom, as permitted by law, would first of all write it off against any share premium account and, secondly, against the retained profits.

The amounts written off over the life of the loan notes are:

(*a*) equal annual amounts over the life of the loan notes; or
(*b*) in proportion to the loan-note debt outstanding at the start of each year. Exhibit 6.10 shows such a situation.

**Exhibit 6.10**

£30,000 loan notes are issued at a discount of 5%. They are repayable at par over five years at the rate of £6,000 per annum.

| *Year* | *Outstanding at start of each year* | *Proportion written off* | | *Amount* |
|---|---|---|---|---|
| | £ | | | £ |
| 1 | 30,000 | $^{30}/_{90} \times$ £1,500 | = | 500 |
| 2 | 24,000 | $^{24}/_{90} \times$ £1,500 | = | 400 |
| 3 | 18,000 | $^{18}/_{90} \times$ £1,500 | = | 300 |
| 4 | 12,000 | $^{12}/_{90} \times$ £1,500 | = | 200 |
| 5 | 6,000 | $^{6}/_{90} \times$ £1,500 | = | 100 |
| | 90,000 | | | 1,500 |

## 2 Redemption of loan notes by purchase in the open market

A sum equal to the cash actually paid on redemption is transferred from retained profits to the loan-note redemption reserve account. The sum actually paid will have been credited to the bank account and debited to the loan notes account.

Any discount (or profit) on purchase will be transferred to a reserve account. Any premium (or loss) on purchase will be deemed to come out of such a reserve account, or if no such account exists or if it is insufficient, then it will be deemed to come out of the share premium account. Failing the existence of these accounts any loss must come out of retained profits. It may seem that purchase would not be a good idea if the loan notes had to be redeemed at a premium. However, it would still be advantageous if the premium paid was not as high as the premium to be paid if the final date for redemption was awaited.

## 3 Redemption of loan notes sourced from a sinking fund

Where loan notes are issued which are redeemable (which most are) consideration should be given to the availability of cash funds at the time.

This method involves the investment of cash outside the business. The aim is to make a regular investment of money which, together with the accumulated interest or dividends, is sufficient to finance the redemption of the loan notes at the requisite time.

As each period's interest (or dividend) from the investment is received, it is immediately reinvested to earn more interest. In addition, an equal amount is invested each period.

If, for example, the money is to be invested at 5% per annum, and the loan note is £500 to be redeemed in five years' time, how much should be invested each year? If £100 were invested at the start of each year for five years, the interest earned would mean that more than £500 was set aside by the end of the five-year period. Therefore, an amount less than £100 per annum is needed. The exact amount can be calculated by the use of the compound interest formula. Chapter 45 illustrates how the amount needed can be calculated. As these calculations are left until later in this book, a summarised set of tables is shown below in Exhibit 6.11.

**Exhibit 6.11**

**Annual Sinking Fund Instalments to Provide £1**

| *Years* | *3%* | *3½%* | *4%* | *4½%* | *5%* |
|---|---|---|---|---|---|
| 3 | 0.323530 | 0.321933 | 0.320348 | 0.318773 | 0.317208 |
| 4 | 0.239028 | 0.237251 | 0.235490 | 0.233744 | 0.232012 |
| 5 | 0.188354 | 0.186481 | 0.184627 | 0.182792 | 0.180975 |
| 6 | 0.154597 | 0.152668 | 0.150761 | 0.148878 | 0.147017 |
| 7 | 0.130506 | 0.128544 | 0.126609 | 0.124701 | 0.122819 |
| 8 | 0.112456 | 0.110476 | 0.108527 | 0.106609 | 0.104721 |
| 9 | 0.098433 | 0.096446 | 0.094493 | 0.092574 | 0.090690 |
| 10 | 0.087230 | 0.085241 | 0.083291 | 0.081378 | 0.079504 |

The table gives the amount required to provide £1 at the end of the relevant number of years at a given rate of interest. To provide £1,000 multiply the amount shown in the table by 1,000; to provide for £4,986 multiply by 4,986; and so on.

Now, let's look at the double entries required when a **sinking fund** is being used.

## 6.11 Double entries for a sinking fund

When the annual instalment has been found, the double entry needed each year is:

1 Annual instalment:
   *Dr* Retained profits (*or* profit and loss appropriation – *see* note)
      *Cr* Loan-note redemption reserve
2 Investment of first instalment:
   *Dr* Loan-note sinking fund investment
      *Cr* Bank
3 Interest/dividends on sinking fund investment:
   *Dr* Bank
      *Cr* Loan-note redemption reserve
4 Investment of second and later instalments (these consist of equal annual instalment plus interest/dividend just received):
   *Dr* Loan-note sinking fund investment
      *Cr* Bank

***Note*: In all the examples so far we have made transfers from retained profits; these will normally be shown in the statement of changes in equity. While it is understandable that many books state that the debit of these entries is made to the profit and loss appropriation account, the correct**

**account to debit is retained profits – this has been custom and practice for many years. However, under International GAAP, while this account (the profit and loss appropriation account) may exist it does not have a place in published financial statements. Nevertheless, many companies do have a profit and loss appropriation account in their ledger and many examiners expect use of the profit and loss appropriation account for the entries. Consequently, in Exhibit 6.12, we will show the entries to that account.**

## Exhibit 6.12

Loan notes of £10,000 are issued on 1 January 2014. They are redeemable five years later on 31 December 2018 on identical terms (i.e. £10,000). The company therefore decides to set aside an equal annual amount which, at an interest rate of 5%, will provide £10,000 on 31 December 2018. According to the table in Exhibit 6.11, £0.180975 invested annually at 5% will provide £1 in five years' time. Therefore, £0.180975 × 10,000 will be needed annually = £1,809.75

***Note*: Each double entry is shown by the letters in brackets. The letters represent the sequence in which the entries would be made.**

**Profit and Loss Appropriation**

| | | £ | | | £ |
|---|---|---|---|---|---|
| 2014 Loan-notes redemption reserve | (B) | 1,809.75 | | | |
| 2015 Loan-notes redemption reserve | (E) | 1,809.75 | | | |
| 2016 Loan-notes redemption reserve | (H) | 1,809.75 | | | |
| 2017 Loan-notes redemption reserve | (K) | 1,809.75 | | | |
| 2018 Loan-notes redemption reserve | (N) | 1,809.75 | 2018 Loan-notes redemption reserve | (R) | 10,000 |

**Loan-notes Redemption Reserve**

| | | £ | | | £ |
|---|---|---|---|---|---|
| 2014 | | | 2014 | | |
| Dec 31 Balance c/d | | 1,809.75 | Dec 31 Profit and loss appropriation | (B) | 1,809.75 |
| 2015 | | | 2015 | | |
| Dec 31 Balance c/d | | 3,709.99 | Jan 1 Balance b/d | | 1,809.75 |
| | | | Dec 31 Bank interest | | |
| | | | (5% of £1,809.75) | (D) | 90.49 |
| | | | Dec 31 Profit and loss appropriation | (E) | 1,809.75 |
| | | 3,709.99 | | | 3,709.99 |
| 2016 | | | 2016 | | |
| Dec 31 Balance c/d | | 5,705.23 | Jan 1 Balance b/d | | 3,709.99 |
| | | | Dec 31 Bank interest | | |
| | | | (5% of £3,709.99) | (G) | 185.49 |
| | | | Dec 31 Profit and loss appropriation | (H) | 1,809.75 |
| | | 5,705.23 | | | 5,705.23 |
| 2017 | | | 2017 | | |
| Dec 31 Balance c/d | | 7,800.24 | Jan 1 Balance b/d | | 5,705.23 |
| | | | Dec 31 Bank interest | | |
| | | | (5% of £5,705.23) | (J) | 285.26 |
| | | | Dec 31 Profit and loss appropriation | (K) | 1,809.75 |
| | | 7,800.24 | | | 7,800.24 |
| 2018 | | | 2018 | | |
| Dec 31 Profit and loss appropriation | | | Jan 1 Balance b/d | | 7,800.24 |
| (reserve no longer | | | Dec 31 Bank interest | | |
| required) | (R) | 10,000.00 | (5% of £7,800.24) | (M) | 390.01 |
| | | | Dec 31 Profit and loss appropriation | (N) | 1,809.75 |
| | | 10,000.00 | | | 10,000.00 |

**Loan-notes Sinking Fund Investment**

| | | | £ | | | | £ |
|---|---|---|---|---|---|---|---|
| 2014 | | | | | | | |
| Dec 31 | Bank | (C) | 1,809.75 | | | | |
| 2015 | | | | | | | |
| Dec 31 | Bank[Note (a)] | (F) | 1,900.24 | | | | |
| 2016 | | | | | | | |
| Dec 31 | Bank[Note (b)] | (I) | 1,995.24 | | | | |
| 2017 | | | | | | | |
| Dec 31 | Bank[Note (c)] | (L) | 2,095.01 | | | | |
| 2018 | | | | 2018 | | | |
| Dec 31 | Bank[Note (d)] | (O) | 2,199.76 | Dec 31 | Bank | (P) | 10,000.00 |
| | | | 10,000.00 | | | | 10,000.00 |

*Notes:*

| *Cash invested* | *(a)* | *(b)* | *(c)* | *(d)* |
|---|---|---|---|---|
| | £ | £ | £ | £ |
| The yearly instalment | 1,809.75 | 1,809.75 | 1,809.75 | 1,809.75 |
| *Add* Interest received on sinking fund balance | 90.49 | 185.49 | 285.26 | 390.01 |
| | 1,900.24 | 1,995.24 | 2,095.01 | 2,199.76 |

**Bank (extracts)**

| | | | £ | | | | £ |
|---|---|---|---|---|---|---|---|
| 2014 | | | | 2014 | | | |
| Jan 1 | Loan notes (issued) | (A) | 10,000.00 | Dec 31 | Loan-notes sinking fund investment | (C) | 1,809.75 |
| 2015 | | | | 2015 | | | |
| Dec 31 | Loan-notes redemption reserve (interest on investment) | (C) | 90.49 | Dec 31 | Loan-notes sinking fund investment | (F) | 1,900.24 |
| 2016 | | | | 2016 | | | |
| Dec 31 | Loan-notes redemption reserve (interest on investment) | (G) | 185.49 | Dec 31 | Loan-notes sinking fund investment | (I) | 1,995.24 |
| 2017 | | | | 2017 | | | |
| Dec 31 | Loan-notes redemption reserve (interest on investment) | (J) | 285.26 | Dec 31 | Loan-notes sinking fund investment | (L) | 2,095.01 |
| 2018 | | | | 2018 | | | |
| Dec 31 | Loan-notes redemption reserve (interest on investment) | (M) | 390.01 | Dec 31 | Loan-notes sinking fund | (O) | 2,199.76 |
| 31 | Loan-notes sinking fund | (P) | 10,000.00 | 31 | Loan-notes (redemption) | (Q) | 10,000.00 |

**Loan notes**

| | | | £ | | | | £ |
|---|---|---|---|---|---|---|---|
| 2018 | | | | 2014 | | | |
| Dec 31 | Bank (redemption) | (Q) | 10,000.00 | Jan 1 | Bank | (A) | 10,000.00 |

The final payment into the sinking fund of £2,199.76 would probably not physically happen unless it was a condition of the investment that a fifth deposit was made before the amount invested could be withdrawn. (There is no point in paying money out of the bank account into the sinking fund and then, on the same day, withdrawing it from the sinking fund and redepositing it in the bank account.) The entries are presented in this way so as to make it clear that the entire £10,000 has been set aside over the five years. If no transfer was shown (of the £2,199.76), the balance on the sinking fund would be £7,800.24 and this amount would be transferred to the bank account. The amount available in the bank account would still be £10,000.

Sometimes loan notes bought in the open market are not cancelled, but are kept 'alive' and are treated as investments of the sinking fund. The annual appropriation of profits is credited to the sinking fund account, while the amount expended on the purchase of the loan notes is debited to the sinking fund investment account. Interest on such loan notes is debited to profit and loss and credited to the sinking fund account. Thus the interest, so far as the sinking fund account is concerned, is treated in the same fashion as if it was cash actually received by the business from an outside investment. The sum expended on investments will then be equal to the annual appropriation + the interest on investments actually received + the interest on loan notes kept in hand.

## 6.12 Convertible loan stock

Particularly in periods of high inflation, but at other times too, the attraction to lenders to provide funds at reasonable rates of interest is much reduced as they stand to lose significantly on the real value of the funds lent, since the repayment of the loan is normally fixed at its original cash value. One way of attracting lenders is to give them the right to convert their loan into shares. The right can usually be exercised at a given rate of conversion from loan to shares, once a year over a stated length of time. The value of the conversion right will depend on the performance of the shares in the market. If the shares increase in value significantly, the conversion value will increase and attract the lender to opt into shares. If the shares do badly, the lender can retain the loan stock with its higher levels of security.

The accounting entries are the same as those described in Section 6.10 for the redemption of loan notes. The value of the shares issued to meet the redemption will be fixed under the terms of the original agreement by reference to their market prices at specified dates.

## Learning outcomes

**You should now have learnt:**

1. The difference between the terms 'redemption' and 'purchase' in the context of shares and loan notes.
2. How to make the accounting entries relating to the redemption or purchase by a company of its own shares.
3. That the accounting entries made on the redemption by a company of its own shares are the same as when it purchases its own shares, except that the word 'redeemable' will appear as the first word in the title of the accounts for shares that are redeemed.
4. That in order to protect creditors, companies *must* still have irredeemable shares in issue after undertaking any purchase or redemption of its own shares.
5. That a company cannot redeem or purchase its own shares unless they are fully paid.
6. That the rules on reserves to use when purchasing or issuing their own shares at a premium are less strict for private companies.
7. How to make the accounting entries relating to the redemption or purchase by a company of its own loan notes.
8. That loan notes are redeemed according to the terms of their issue.

## Answers to activities

6.1 Apart from moving into line with the rest of Europe, the restriction that remained (of having one member, i.e. shareholder) minimised the risk of abuse of creditors, which was the main reason for having the rule preventing purchase and redemption in the first place.

6.2 If this occurred, it would suggest that the company issued them only to have free use of the funds they realised for a short time. In effect, they were simply a form of interest-free loan. By requiring that shares be fully paid before being redeemed or purchased back by the company, the possibility that companies would engage in this form of sharp practice is minimised.

6.3 **Scenario 1**
A company redeemed its 200,000 6% preference share capital of £1 each at a premium of £0.10. Originally these shares were issued at a premium of £0.05 per share. There was no issue of new shares to finance the redemption.

| | | Debit | Credit |
|---|---|---|---|
| 6% preference share capital | (200,000 × £1) | 200,000 | |
| Retained profits | (200,000 × £0.10) | 20,000 | |
| Bank | (200,000 × £1.10) | | 220,000 |
| Retained profits | | 200,000 | |
| Capital redemption reserve | | | 200,000 |

Although the preference shares being redeemed were originally issued at a premium, the redemption is not being financed by an issue of new shares. The entire redemption premium is, therefore, charged to retained profits. A capital redemption reserve must be created equal to the nominal value of the share capital redeemed.

**Scenario 2**
100,000 8% preference shares of £0.75 each were redeemed at a premium of £0.10 per share. These shares were originally issued at par. To finance the redemption, the company issued 150,000 ordinary shares of £1 each at a premium of £0.25 per share.

| | | Debit | Credit |
|---|---|---|---|
| Bank (150,000 × £1.25) | | 187,500 | |
| Ordinary share capital | (150,000 × £1.00) | | 150,000 |
| Share premium | (150,000 × £0.25) | | 37,500 |
| 8% preference share capital | (100,000 × £0.75) | 75,000 | |
| Retained profits | (100,000 × £0.10) | 10,000 | |
| Bank | (100,000 × £0.85) | | 85,000 |

Since the redemption is financed by an issue of new shares and the funds received are greater than the nominal value of the share capital redeemed, no capital redemption reserve is created.
As the shares being redeemed at a premium were originally issued at par, the redemption premium is charged to retained profits.

**Scenario 3**
A company redeemed its 180,000 8% £1 preference share capital at a premium of £0.15 per share. In order to do so, it issued an equal number of 6% £0.50 preference shares at par. The shares being redeemed were originally issued at a premium of £0.25 and balance on the share premium account is £30,000.

| | | Debit | Credit |
|---|---|---|---|
| Bank (180,000 × £0.50) | | 90,000 | |
| 6% preference share capital | (180,000 × £0.50) | | 90,000 |
| 8% preference share capital | (180,000 × £1.00) | 180,000 | |
| Share premium | (180,000 × £0.15) | 27,000 | |
| Bank | (180,000 × £1.15) | | 207,000 |
| Retained profits | (180,000 − 90,000) | 90,000 | |
| Capital redemption reserve | | | 90,000 |

The redemption is being financed partly by the new share issue. As the funds received from the share issue are less than the nominal value of the shares being redeemed, a capital redemption reserve for the difference is created.

Since the redemption premium of £27,000 (180,000 × £0.15) is less than the amount of the share premium received when they were issued, i.e. £45,000 (180,000 × £0.25), and there exist sufficient funds in the share premium account to cover the premium being paid, the entire redemption premium is charged to the share premium account.

**Scenario 4**

A company issued 100,000 6% £1 preference shares at a premium of £0.16 per share in order to finance the redemption of 200,000 8% preference shares of £0.50 each at a premium of £0.15 per share. These shares were originally issued at a premium of £0.10 per share, which was utilised to issue bonus shares to the ordinary shareholders. There is no balance in the share premium account.

| | | Debit | Credit |
|---|---|---|---|
| Bank (100,000 × £1.16) | | 116,000 | |
| 6% preference share capital | (100,000 × £1.00) | | 100,000 |
| Share premium | (100,000 × £0.15) | | 16,000 |
| 8% preference share capital | (200,000 × £0.50) | 100,000 | |
| Share premium | | 16,000 | |
| Retained profits | | 14,000 | |
| Bank | (200,000 × £0.65) | | 130,000 |

Since the redemption is financed by an issue of new shares and the funds received are greater than the nominal value of the share capital redeemed, no capital redemption reserve is created.

The shares being redeemed were originally issued at a premium of £20,000 (200,000 × £0.10) and are now being redeemed at a premium of £30,000 (200,000 × £0.15). The amount of the original premium of £20,000 could be charged to the share premium account but it had a zero balance before the issue of the new shares and now only has a balance of £16,000. The £14,000 balance of the £30,000 redemption premium is charged to retained profits.

**Scenario 5**

A company, which had issued 100,000 8% preference share capital of £1 at par, redeemed the shares at a premium of £0.15 per share. To finance the redemption, the company issued 100,000 6% preference shares of £0.50 each at £1.15.

| | Debit | Credit |
|---|---|---|
| Bank | 115,000 | |
| 6% preference share capital | | 50,000 |
| Share premium | | 65,000 |
| 8% preference share capital | 100,000 | |
| Retained profits | 15,000 | |
| Bank | | 115,000 |

Since the redemption is financed by an issue of new shares and the funds received are greater than the nominal value of the share capital redeemed, no capital redemption reserve is created.

The shares being redeemed at a premium were originally issued at a premium of par, therefore, the redemption premium is charged to retained profits.

6.4 Private companies are much smaller than public ones. Their shares are often held by a far smaller group of shareholders, often all known to each other. There is not, therefore, the same need to protect shareholders, but there is often a greater need to assist shareholders wishing to reduce their shareholdings. Private companies also tend to have far smaller and less extensive groups of creditors in need of protection. If you refer back to the advantages listed in Section 6.2, you can see why it is important that private companies have greater flexibility in this respect than public ones.

## Review questions

**6.1** Exercises (*a*) to (*e*) are based on the following statement of financial position.

**E Whitelock Ltd**
**Statement of Financial Position**

| | £ |
|---|---|
| Net assets (except bank) | 32,000 |
| Bank | 20,800 |
| | 52,800 |
| Preference share capital | 8,000 |
| Ordinary share capital | 24,000 |
| Share premium | 3,200 |
| | 35,200 |
| Retained profits | 17,600 |
| | 52,800 |

Note also that each of exercises (*a*) to (*e*) is independent of any other. The exercises are not cumulative.

**Required:**

(*a*) E Whitelock Ltd redeems £8,000 preference shares at par, a new issue of £8,000 ordinary shares at par being made for the purpose. Show the statement of financial position after completion of these transactions. Workings are to be shown as journal entries.

(*b*) E Whitelock Ltd redeems £8,000 preference shares at par, with no new issue of shares to provide funds. Show the statement of financial position after completing the transaction. Workings: show journal entries.

(*c*) E Whitelock Ltd redeems £8,000 preference shares at par. To help finance this an issue of £2,400 ordinary shares at par is effected. Show the statement of financial position after these transactions have been completed; also show the necessary journal entries.

(*d*) E Whitelock Ltd redeems £8,000 preference shares at a premium of 20%. There is no new issue of shares for the purpose. In this question the share premium account is taken as being from the issue of ordinary shares some years ago. Show the statement of financial position after these transactions have been completed, and the supporting journal entries.

(*e*) E Whitelock Ltd redeems £8,000 preference shares at a premium of 30%. There is an issue of £10,400 ordinary shares at par for the purpose. The preference shares had originally been issued at a premium of 25%. Show the statement of financial position after these transactions have been completed, and also the supporting journal entries. →

**6.2A** Exercises (*a*) to (*e*) are based on the following statement of financial position.

**A Rooney Ltd**
**Statement of Financial Position**

| | £ |
|---|---|
| Net assets (except bank) | 31,000 |
| Bank | 16,000 |
| | 47,000 |
| Preference share capital | 8,000 |
| Ordinary share capital | 20,000 |
| Share premium | 4,000 |
| | 32,000 |
| Retained profits | 15,000 |
| | 47,000 |

Note also that exercises (*a*) to (*e*) are independent of each other. They are not cumulative.

**Required:**

(*a*) A Rooney Ltd purchases £10,000 of its own ordinary share capital at par. To help finance this £7,000 preference shares are issued at par. Show the necessary journal entries and the statement of financial position after the transactions have been completed.

(*b*) A Rooney Ltd purchases £12,000 of its own ordinary shares at a premium of 20%. No new issue of shares is made for the purpose. It is assumed that the share premium account is in respect of the issue of preference shares some years before. Show the statement of financial position after the transactions have been completed, and also the supporting journal entries.

(*c*) A Rooney Ltd purchases all the preference share capital at par. These shares were not originally redeemable preference shares. There is no new issue of shares to provide funds. Show the requisite journal entries, and the closing statement of financial position when the transaction has been completed.

(*d*) A Rooney Ltd purchases £12,000 of its own ordinary shares at par, a new issue of £12,000 preference shares at par being made for the purpose. Show the journal entries needed and the statement of financial position after completing these transactions.

(*e*) A Rooney Ltd purchases £6,000 ordinary shares at a premium of 50%. They had originally been issued at a premium of 20%. There is an issue of £10,000 preference shares at par for the purpose. Show the amended statement of financial position, together with the journal entries.

**6.3** A company's statement of financial position appears as follows:

| | £ |
|---|---|
| Net assets (except bank) | 40,000 |
| Bank | 41,600 |
| | 81,600 |
| Preference share capital | 16,000 |
| Ordinary share capital | 32,000 |
| Non-distributable reserves | 19,200 |
| | 67,200 |
| Retained profits | 14,400 |
| | 81,600 |

**Required:**

(*a*) If £19,200 of the ordinary shares were purchased at par, there being no new issue of shares for the purpose, show the journal entries to record the transactions and the amended statement of financial position.

(*b*) If, instead of (*a*), £19,200 ordinary shares were purchased at a premium of 80%, there being no new issue of shares for the purpose, show the journal entries to record the transactions and the amended statement of financial position.

**6.4A** Loan notes of £48,000 are issued on 1 January 2017. Redemption is to take place, on equal terms, four years later. The company decides to put aside an equal amount to be invested at 6% which will provide £48,000 on maturity. Tables show that £0.22857142 invested annually will produce £1 in four years' time.

**You are required to show:**

(*a*) loan-note redemption reserve account
(*b*) loan-note sinking fund investment account
(*c*) loan-notes account
(*d*) retained profits account extracts.

**6.5** Some years ago M plc had issued £375,000 of 10% loan notes 2016/2020 at par. The terms of the issue allow the company the right to repurchase these loan notes for cancellation at or below par, with an option to redeem, at a premium of 1%, on 30 September 2016. To exercise this option the company must give three months' notice, which it duly did on 30 June 2016, indicating its intention to redeem all the loan notes outstanding at 30 September 2016.

M plc had established a sinking fund designed to accumulate the sum of £378,750 by 30 September 2016 and had appropriated profits annually and invested these, together with the interest from such investments and the profits made on any realisations from time to time. A special No. 2 bank account was established specifically to deal with the receipts and payments relating to the loan notes and the sinking fund.

By 30 June 2016 annual contributions amounting to £334,485, together with the interest on the sinking fund investments of £39,480, had all been invested except for £2,475 which remained in the No. 2 bank account at that date.

The only investments sold, prior to 30 June 2016, had cost £144,915 and realised £147,243. This was used to repurchase loan notes with a par value of £150,000.

Transactions occurring between 1 July and 30 September 2016 were:

(*i*) interest received on the sinking fund investments:
  7 July £1,756
  13 September £1,455
(*ii*) proceeds from the sale of investments:
  2 August £73,215 (book value was £69,322)
  25 September £160,238 (remaining investments)
(*iii*) redemption of all the loan notes, on 30 September, with the exception of £15,000 held by B Limited. The company had received notice of a garnishee order.*
(*iv*) M plc deposited with the W Bank plc the sum of £15,150 on 30 September 2016.

You are to ignore loan-note interest and income tax.

**You are required,** from the information given above, to prepare the ledger accounts (including the No. 2 bank account) in the books of M plc for the period 30 June to 30 September 2016, showing the transfer of the final balances to the appropriate accounts.

**Note – Garnishee order*
This order, issued by the court, instructs M plc not to release the money owing to B Limited until directed by the court to do so.

(*Chartered Institute of Management Accountants*)

→

→ **6.6A** The following information relates to White Rabbit Trading plc:

**Summarised Statement of Financial Position as at 31 January 2017**

| | £000 |
|---|---|
| *Non-current assets* | 2,400 |
| *Investments* | 120 |
| *Current assets* | 1,880 |
| | 4,400 |
| 8% loan notes (2017/2020) | (400) |
| Equity | 4,000 |
| *Capital and reserves* | |
| Ordinary shares of 50p each fully paid | 2,000 |
| Redeemable shares of £1 each (2017/2021) | 500 |
| Share premium | 200 |
| Revaluation surplus | 400 |
| Retained profits | 900 |
| | 4,000 |

On 1 February 2017 the company closed the list of applications for 400,000 ordinary shares at a premium of 50p. The shares were to be paid for as follows: 60p on application, 25p on allotment and 15p on the first and final call, which was to be made on 1 May 2017. A total of £1,320,000 was received, the shares were allotted and £1,032,000 was returned to unsuccessful applicants. The call money was received by 31 May from all shareholders, with the exception of two shareholders, one of whom had been allotted 500 shares. The other subscriber for 100 shares still owed £25 for allotment in addition to the call money. Eventually both lots of shares were forfeited and reissued to an existing shareholder for a payment of £500 which was duly received.

At a board meeting on 15 February 2017 the directors decided to make a fresh issue of 500,000 £1 redeemable shares at a premium of 60p, and to redeem all of the existing redeemable shares at a premium of 40p. The shares had originally been issued for £1.20 each. All monies due on application were duly received by 31 March 2017, and the redemption took place on 6 April 2017.

In January 2015 White Rabbit Trading plc had purchased, for cash, 80,000 25p ordinary shares in March Hares Ltd for £25,000, and this is included in investments on the statement of financial position at 31 January 2017. On 1 April 2017 the company purchased 400,000 out of a total issue of 500,000 25p ordinary shares in March Hares Ltd, by exchanging 200,000 of its own ordinary shares.

The 8% loan notes were redeemed on 15 May 2017 at a 10% premium, and on the same date £500,000 7% loan notes (2020/2023) were issued at a discount of 5%.

**Required:**
Show the full journal entries to record the above events, including cash/bank transactions, in the books of White Rabbit Trading plc.

(*Association of Chartered Certified Accountants*)

**6.7** During the year to 30 September 2016, Popham plc issued 100,000 £1 ordinary shares. The terms of the offer were as follows:

| 2016 | | £ |
|---|---|---|
| 31 March | on application | 0.30 (including the premium) |
| 30 April | on allotment | 0.70 |
| 30 June | first and final call | 0.20 |

Applications were received for 200,000 shares. The directors decided to allot the shares on the basis of one for every two shares applied for and apply the excess application money received against the amount due on allotment.

All amounts due on application and allotment were received on the due dates, with the exception of one shareholder who had been allotted 10,000 shares, and who defaulted on the first and final call. These shares were forfeited on 31 July 2016, and reissued on 31 August 2016 at a price of £1.10 per share.

**Required:**
Write up the above details in the books of account of Popham plc using the following ledger accounts:
(*i*) application and allotment
(*ii*) first and final call
(*iii*) investment – own shares.

(*Association of Accounting Technicians*)

**6.8A** Alas plc has an authorised share capital of 150,000 ordinary shares of £10 each. Upon incorporation, 50,000 shares were issued and fully paid. The company has decided to issue another 50,000 shares, the details of which are as follows:

| | *Per share* |
|---|---|
| Upon: | £ |
| Application | 3 |
| Allotment (including a premium of £5) | 8 |
| First call | 2 |
| Final call | 2 |
| | 15 |

*Additional information*:
1 Applications were received for 85,000 shares out of which 10,000 shares were rejected, the cash being returned immediately to the applicants. The remaining applicants were allotted two shares for every three shares applied for, and the surplus application money was carried forward to the allotment stage.
2 The total amount due on allotment was duly received.
3 All cash due at the first call was received, but the final call resulted in 5,000 shares being forfeited. These shares were subsequently reissued at a price of £13 per share.

**Required:**
Compile the following ledger accounts:
(*a*) ordinary share capital
(*b*) ordinary share applications
(*c*) ordinary share allotment
(*d*) share premium
(*e*) ordinary share first call
(*f*) ordinary share final call
(*g*) investments – own shares (originally known as the forfeited shares account).

**6.9** The following information relates to Grigg plc:
1 On 1 April 2018 the company had £100,000 10% loan notes in issue. The interest on these loan notes is paid on 30 September and 31 March.
2 The loan note redemption fund balance (relating to the redemption of these loan notes) at 1 April 2018 was £20,000. This fund is being built up by annual appropriations of £2,000. The annual appropriation (along with any dividends or interest on the investments) is invested on 31 March.
3 Loan note redemption fund investments can be realised at any time in order to purchase loan notes in the open market either at or below par value. Such loan notes are then cancelled.
4 On 31 December 2018 £10,000 of investments were sold for £11,400 and the proceeds were used to purchase loan notes with a par value of £12,000.
5 Dividends and interest on redemption fund investments during the year to 31 March 2019 amounted to £1,600.
6 The cost of dealing with the above matters and any taxation effects may be ignored.

**Required:**
Write up the following ledger accounts for the year to 31 March 2019:
(*a*) 10% loan notes
(*b*) loan note redemption fund
(*c*) loan note redemption fund investments
(*d*) loan note redemption
(*e*) loan note interest.

*Note*: The loan note redemption fund is sometimes known as a sinking fund.

chapter

# 7 Limited companies taking over other businesses

## Learning objectives

**After you have studied this chapter, you should be able to:**

- explain how goodwill may arise on the purchase of a business
- explain the difference between goodwill and gain on a bargain purchase
- record the accounting entries relating to a limited company taking over another business
- describe the difference in the accounting treatment of takeovers by limited companies of sole proprietors, partnerships and limited companies
- describe the two methods whereby a limited company may take over another limited company
- deal with pre-incorporation profits and losses
- deal with formation expenses

## Introduction

In this chapter, you'll learn about goodwill and gain on a bargain purchase and you will learn how to record the purchase of a business in the books of the purchaser using a variety of methods of paying for the purchase. You will also learn about how to deal with pre-incorporation losses and profits and formation expenses.

## 7.1 Background

From time to time, limited companies take over other businesses. The purchase may be: (i) in cash; (ii) by giving the company's shares to the sellers; (iii) by giving the company's loan notes; or (iv) by any combination of the three.

Never be mistaken into thinking that because the assets bought are shown in the selling entity's books at one value, the purchasing company must record the assets taken over in its own books at the same value. The values shown in the purchasing company's books are those values at which the company is buying the assets (known as their 'fair' values), such values being frequently quite different from those shown in the selling firm's books.

For example, the selling entity may have bought premises many years earlier for £100,000 which are now worth £250,000. The company buying the premises will obviously have to pay £250,000 for the premises and it is this value that is recorded in the buying company's books. Alternatively, if its value has fallen, the value at which it is recorded in the buying company's books would be less than that shown in the selling entity's books.

The recording of the transactions is the simple part. The negotiations that take place before agreement is reached, and the various strategies undertaken by the various parties, are a study in themselves. The accounting entries are, in effect, the tip of the iceberg, i.e. that part of the whole affair which is seen by the eventual reader of the financial statements.

Where the total purchase consideration exceeds the total value of the identifiable assets as recorded in the ledger of the purchasing company, the excess is the *goodwill*, and is entered as a debit in a goodwill account in the purchasing company's books.

Should the total purchase consideration be less than the values of the identifiable assets recorded in the purchasing company's ledger, the difference is known as *gain on a bargain purchase* and is entered as a credit in a gain on a bargain purchase account. ***Note*: The goodwill amount is shown in the assets section of the statement of financial position. Any gain on a bargain purchase must be eliminated immediately, normally by recognising the gain in the statement of profit or loss.**

**Activity 7.1**

Why do you think the amount paid for a business may be different from the total value of its net assets as shown in its financial statements?

Let's now look at how business takeovers are recorded in the accounting records of the purchaser.

## 7.2 Taking over a sole proprietor

We'll start with the takeover of the simplest sort of business unit, that of a sole proprietor (Exhibit 7.1). Some of the statements of financial position shown will be deliberately simplified so that the principles involved are not hidden behind a mass of complicated calculations.

### Exhibit 7.1

Earl Ltd is to buy the business of M Kearney. The purchase consideration is to be £60,000 cash, the company placing the following values on the assets taken over – machinery £30,000; inventory £10,000. The goodwill must therefore be £20,000, because the total price of £60,000 exceeds the sum of the values of the machinery £30,000 and inventory £10,000 by £20,000. The company's statements of financial position before and after the takeover are shown below:

**M Kearney**
**Statements of Financial Position**

| | £ |
|---|---|
| Machinery | 30,000 |
| Inventory | 10,000 |
| | 40,000 |
| Capital | 40,000 |

**Earl Ltd**
**Statements of Financial Position**

| | *Before* | *+ or –* | *After* |
|---|---|---|---|
| | £ | £ | £ |
| Goodwill | | +20,000 | 20,000 |
| Machinery | 110,000 | +30,000 | 140,000 |
| Inventory | 50,000 | +10,000 | 60,000 |
| Bank | 90,000 | −60,000 | 30,000 |
| | 250,000 | | 250,000 |
| Share capital | 200,000 | | 200,000 |
| Retained profits | 50,000 | | 50,000 |
| | 250,000 | | 250,000 |

If shares had been issued to Kearney instead of cash, the new statement of financial position of Earl Ltd would be as above except that bank would be £90,000 and share capital would be £260,000, as shown in Exhibit 7.2:

### Exhibit 7.2

**Earl Ltd**
**Statements of Financial Position**

| | *Before* | *+ or –* | *After* |
|---|---|---|---|
| | £ | £ | £ |
| Goodwill | | +20,000 | 20,000 |
| Machinery | 110,000 | +30,000 | 140,000 |
| Inventory | 50,000 | +10,000 | 60,000 |
| Bank | 90,000 | | 90,000 |
| | 250,000 | | 310,000 |
| Share capital | 200,000 | +60,000 | 260,000 |
| Retained profits | 50,000 | | 50,000 |
| | 250,000 | | 310,000 |

### Exhibit 7.3

If the purchase had been made by issuing 50,000 shares of £1 each at a premium of 50%, then the total consideration would have been worth £75,000 which, if the assets of £40,000 are deducted, leaves goodwill of £35,000. The statements of financial position would then be:

**Earl Ltd**
**Statements of Financial Position**

| | *Before* | *+ or –* | *After* |
|---|---|---|---|
| | £ | £ | £ |
| Goodwill | | +35,000 | 35,000 |
| Machinery | 110,000 | +30,000 | 140,000 |
| Inventory | 50,000 | +10,000 | 60,000 |
| Bank | 90,000 | | 90,000 |
| | 250,000 | | 325,000 |
| Share capital | 200,000 | +50,000 | 250,000 |
| Share premium | | +25,000 | 25,000 |
| Retained profits | 50,000 | | 50,000 |
| | 250,000 | | 325,000 |

You should now realise just how straightforward the statement of financial position changes are. You simply adjust the statement of financial position for the assets (and liabilities) acquired and for the items used in order to complete the purchase. Whatever the difference is between the two parts of the statement of financial position, must be the goodwill.

In each of Exhibits 7.1 to 7.4 it has been assumed that all transactions were started and completed at the same time. In reality, an intermediary account would first be created but then closed when the purchase consideration was handed over.

Taking Exhibit 7.3 as an example, a credit entry will be made in the share capital account and another in the share premium account, plus debit entries in the goodwill, machinery and inventory accounts. Think about this. Shares cannot be issued to goodwill, machinery or inventory. They have, in fact, been issued to M Kearney. This means that there should have been an account for M Kearney involved in the double entries, but the balance on it was cancelled when the purchase was completed. The actual accounts used for Exhibit 7.3 in the books of Earl Ltd were:

**Share Premium**

| | | | |
|---|---|---|---|
| | | | £ |
| | | M Kearney | 25,000 |

**Share Capital**

| | | | |
|---|---|---|---|
| | £ | | £ |
| Balance c/d | 250,000 | Balance b/d | 200,000 |
| | | M Kearney | 50,000 |
| | 250,000 | | 250,000 |
| | | Balance b/d | 250,000 |

**Retained Profits**

| | | | |
|---|---|---|---|
| | | | £ |
| | | Balance b/d | 50,000 |

**Goodwill**

| | | | |
|---|---|---|---|
| | £ | | |
| M Kearney | 35,000 | | |

**Machinery**

| | | | |
|---|---|---|---|
| | £ | | £ |
| Balance b/d | 110,000 | Balance c/d | 140,000 |
| M Kearney | 30,000 | | |
| | 140,000 | | 140,000 |
| Balance b/d | 140,000 | | |

**Inventory**

| | | | |
|---|---|---|---|
| | £ | | £ |
| Balance b/d | 50,000 | Balance c/d | 60,000 |
| M Kearney | 10,000 | | |
| | 60,000 | | 60,000 |
| Balance b/d | 60,000 | | |

***Note*: The £10,000 may have been entered in the purchases account. However, Kearney's £10,000 inventory obviously increased the actual amount of inventory held after the takeover of Kearney's business.**

**Bank**

| | | | |
|---|---|---|---|
| | £ | | |
| Balance b/d | 90,000 | | |

**M Kearney**

| | | | |
|---|---|---|---|
| | £ | | £ |
| Consideration passing: | | Assets taken over: | |
| Share capital | 50,000 | Goodwill | 35,000 |
| Share premium | 25,000 | Machinery | 30,000 |
| | | Inventory | 10,000 |
| | 75,000 | | 75,000 |

Some accountants use a business purchase account instead of an account in the name of the owner.

Sometimes the company taking over the business of a sole proprietor pays for the assets and takes over the accounts payable of the business acquired. Take the case of a sole proprietor with assets valued at premises £50,000 and inventory of £40,000. To gain control of these assets, a company is to pay the sole proprietor £110,000 in cash. In addition, the company will pay off the accounts payable £10,000. Goodwill is, therefore, £30,000:

| | £ | £ |
|---|---|---|
| *Paid by the company to gain control of the sole proprietor's assets*: | | |
| Cash to the sole proprietor | | 110,000 |
| Cash to the sole proprietor's creditors | | 10,000 |
| | | 120,000 |
| The company receives assets: | | |
| Premises | 50,000 | |
| Inventory | 40,000 | |
| | | (90,000) |
| Excess paid for goodwill | | 30,000 |

**Exhibit 7.4**

If the purchase had been made by the issue of 10,000 shares of £1 each at a premium of 40%, £30,000 worth of 7% loan notes at par and £40,000 in cash, the total purchase consideration would be ordinary shares valued at £14,000, loan notes valued at £30,000 and £40,000 in cash, making a total of £84,000. The assets are valued at £40,000, so the goodwill must be £44,000. The statements of financial position would be:

**Earl Ltd**
**Statements of Financial Position**

| | *Before* | *+ or −* | *After* |
|---|---|---|---|
| | £ | £ | £ |
| Goodwill | | +44,000 | 44,000 |
| Machinery | 110,000 | +30,000 | 140,000 |
| Inventory | 50,000 | +10,000 | 60,000 |
| Bank | 90,000 | −40,000 | 50,000 |
| | 250,000 | | 294,000 |
| *Less* Loan notes | – | +30,000 | (30,000) |
| | 250,000 | | 264,000 |
| Share capital | 200,000 | +10,000 | 210,000 |
| Share premium | | +4,000 | 4,000 |
| Retained profits | 50,000 | | 50,000 |
| | 250,000 | | 264,000 |

## 7.3 Taking over a partnership

The entries are virtually the same as those made when taking over a sole proprietor. The main difference is the distribution of the purchase consideration. In the case of a sole proprietor, the sole proprietor gets all of it. In a partnership, it has to be divided between the partners.

This means that a partnership realisation account will have to be drawn up to calculate the profit or loss on sale of the partnership business which is attributable to each partner. The profit or loss on sale will then be shared between the partners in their profit/loss-sharing ratios.

The double entry needed *in the partnership books* is:

(A) Transfer assets being disposed of to the realisation account:
*Dr* Realisation
*Cr* Assets (various)

(B) Transfer liabilities being disposed of to the realisation account:
*Dr* Liabilities (various)
*Cr* Realisation
(C) Enter purchase price:
*Dr* Limited company (purchaser)
*Cr* Realisation
(D) If profit on sale:
*Dr* Realisation
*Cr* Partners' capitals (profit-sharing ratio)
(E) If loss on sale:
*Dr* Partners' capitals (profit-sharing ratio)
*Cr* Realisation
(F) Receipt purchase price:
*Dr* Cash
*Dr* Shares (if any) in limited company
*Dr* Loan notes (if any) in limited company
*Cr* Limited company (purchaser)
(G) Final settlement with partners:
*Dr* Partners' capital and current accounts
*Cr* Cash
*Cr* Shares (if any) in limited company
*Cr* Loan notes (if any) in limited company

Exhibit 7.5 shows how this is done:

## Exhibit 7.5

Kay and Lee were in partnership, sharing profits and losses in the ratio 2:1 respectively. The following was their statement of financial position as at 31 December 2017.

**Kay and Lee**
**Statement of Financial Position as at 31 December 2017**

| | £ | £ |
|---|---|---|
| *Non-current assets* | | |
| Buildings | | 300,000 |
| Motor vehicles | | 150,000 |
| | | 450,000 |
| *Current assets* | | |
| Inventory | 80,000 | |
| Accounts receivable | 60,000 | |
| Bank | 10,000 | |
| | | 150,000 |
| Total assets | | 600,000 |
| *Current liabilities* | | |
| Accounts payable | | (50,000) |
| Net assets | | 550,000 |
| *Capital accounts*: Kay | 320,000 | |
| Lee | 160,000 | |
| | | 480,000 |
| *Current accounts*: Kay | 30,000 | |
| Lee | 40,000 | |
| | | 70,000 |
| | | 550,000 |

→

On 1 January 2018, Cayley Ltd took over the assets, other than bank. The purchase price is £800,000, payable by £600,000 in £1 shares in Cayley Ltd at par, plus £200,000 cash. Kay and Lee will pay off their own creditors. Shares are to be divided between the partners in their profit-sharing ratio.

First, let's look at the closing entries in the accounts of Kay and Lee. The only asset account shown will be the bank account. The individual accounts payable accounts are also not shown. The letters in brackets refer to the description of the double entry already given.

**Books of Kay and Lee**

*Realisation*

| | | | £ | | | £ |
|---|---|---|---|---|---|---|
| *Assets taken over*: | | | | Cayley Ltd | (C) | 800,000 |
| Buildings | (A) | | 300,000 | | | |
| Motor vehicles | (A) | | 150,000 | | | |
| Inventory | (A) | | 80,000 | | | |
| Accounts receivable | (A) | | 60,000 | | | |
| *Profit on realisation*: | | | | | | |
| Kay $^2/_3$ | (D) | 140,000 | | | | |
| Lee $^1/_3$ | (D) | 70,000 | 210,000 | | | |
| | | | 800,000 | | | 800,000 |

*Cayley Ltd*

| | | £ | | | £ |
|---|---|---|---|---|---|
| Realisation: sale price | (C) | 800,000 | Bank | (F) | 200,000 |
| | | | Shares in Cayley Ltd | (F) | 600,000 |
| | | 800,000 | | | 800,000 |

*Shares in Cayley Ltd*

| | | £ | | | £ |
|---|---|---|---|---|---|
| Cayley Ltd | (F) | 600,000 | Capital accounts: | Kay (G) | 400,000 |
| | | | | Lee (G) | 200,000 |
| | | 600,000 | | | 600,000 |

*Capital Accounts*

| | | Kay | Lee | | | Kay | Lee |
|---|---|---|---|---|---|---|---|
| | | £ | £ | | | £ | £ |
| Shares in Cayley | (G) | 400,000 | 200,000 | Balances b/d | | 320,000 | 160,000 |
| Bank | (G) | 60,000 | 30,000 | Realisation (profit) | (D) | 140,000 | 70,000 |
| | | 460,000 | 230,000 | | | 460,000 | 230,000 |

*Current Accounts*

| | | Kay | Lee | | Kay | Lee |
|---|---|---|---|---|---|---|
| | | £ | £ | | £ | £ |
| Bank | (G) | 30,000 | 40,000 | Balances b/d | 30,000 | 40,000 |

*Bank*

| | | £ | | | £ |
|---|---|---|---|---|---|
| Bank b/d | | 10,000 | Accounts payable | | 50,000 |
| Cayley Ltd | (F) | 200,000 | Capital accounts: | Kay | 60,000 |
| | | | | Lee | 30,000 |
| | | | Current accounts: | Kay | 30,000 |
| | | | | Lee | 40,000 |
| | | 210,000 | | | 210,000 |

***Note*: It would have been possible to transfer the balances of the current accounts to the capital accounts before settlement.**

Assuming that Cayley values the buildings at £410,000 and the inventory at £70,000, its statement of financial position at 1 January 2018 would appear as in (B) below. The items shown under (A) were the balances before the takeover.

**Statement(s) of Financial Position**

| | (A) *Before* | + | – | (B) *After* |
|---|---|---|---|---|
| | £ | £ | £ | £ |
| Goodwill | | 110,000 | | 110,000 |
| Buildings | 500,000 | 410,000 | | 910,000 |
| Motor vehicles | 250,000 | 150,000 | | 400,000 |
| Inventory | 280,000 | 70,000 | | 350,000 |
| Accounts receivable | 170,000 | 60,000 | | 230,000 |
| Bank | 300,000 | | | 100,000 |
| Total assets | 1,500,000 | | | 2,100,000 |
| Accounts payable | (100,000) | | | (100,000) |
| Net assets | 1,400,000 | 800,000 | 200,000 | 2,000,000 |
| Share capital (£1 shares) | 1,000,000 | 600,000 | | 1,600,000 |
| Retained profits | 400,000 | | | 400,000 |
| | 1,400,000 | 600,000 | | 2,000,000 |

## 7.4 The takeover of one company by another

There are two methods by which one company may take over another:

1 Buying all the assets of the other company with cash, shares or loan notes. The selling company may afterwards be wound up: the liquidators may distribute the purchasing company's shares and loan notes among the shareholders of the selling company, or the shares and loan notes of the buying company may be sold and the cash distributed instead.
2 Giving its own shares and loan notes in exchange for the shares and loan notes of the selling company's share and loan-note holders.

The two methods are shown in Exhibit 7.6:

### Exhibit 7.6

The following are the statements of financial position of three companies as at the same date.

**Statements of Financial Position**

| | *R Ltd* | *S Ltd* | *T Ltd* |
|---|---|---|---|
| | £ | £ | £ |
| Buildings | 130,000 | – | 10,000 |
| Machinery | 40,000 | 20,000 | 10,000 |
| Inventory | 30,000 | 10,000 | 20,000 |
| Accounts receivable | 20,000 | 10,000 | 30,000 |
| Bank | 10,000 | 20,000 | 30,000 |
| Total assets | 230,000 | 60,000 | 100,000 |
| Current liabilities | (30,000) | (20,000) | (10,000) |
| Net assets | 200,000 | 40,000 | 90,000 |
| Share capital (£1 shares) | 180,000 | 30,000 | 50,000 |
| Retained profits | 20,000 | 10,000 | 40,000 |
| | 200,000 | 40,000 | 90,000 |

→

→

R takes over S by exchanging with the shareholders of S two shares in R at a premium of 10% for every share they hold in S.

R takes over T by buying all the assets of T, the purchase consideration being 120,000 £1 shares in R at a premium of 10%, and R will pay off T's accounts payable. R values T's assets at buildings £20,000; machinery £6,000; inventory £14,000; accounts receivable £25,000; and the bank is £30,000, a total of £95,000.

R's deal with the shareholders of S means that R now has complete control of S Ltd, so that S Ltd becomes what is known as a subsidiary of R Ltd, and will be shown as an investment in R's statement of financial position.

On the other hand, the deal with T has resulted in the ownership of the assets resting with R. These must therefore be added to R's assets in its own statement of financial position. As R has given 120,000 £1 shares at a premium of 10% plus taking over the responsibility for accounts payable of £10,000, the total purchase consideration for the assets taken over is £120,000 + £12,000 (10% of £120,000) + £10,000 = £142,000. Identifiable assets as already stated are valued at £95,000, therefore the goodwill is £142,000 − £95,000 = £47,000.

The distinction between the acquisition of the two businesses can be seen to be a rather fine one. With S, the shares are taken over, the possession of these in turn giving rise to the ownership of the assets. In the books of R this is regarded as an investment. With T, the actual assets and liabilities are taken over so that the assets now directly belong to R. In the books of R this is therefore regarded as the acquisition of additional assets and liabilities and not as an investment (using the meaning of 'investment' which is used in the statements of financial position of companies). The statement of financial position of R Ltd therefore becomes:

**R Ltd**
**Statement of Financial Position**

| | *Before* | | *+ or −* | *After* |
|---|---|---|---|---|
| | £ | | £ | £ |
| Goodwill | | +(T) | 47,000 | 47,000 |
| Buildings | 130,000 | +(T) | 20,000 | 150,000 |
| Machinery | 40,000 | +(T) | 6,000 | 46,000 |
| Investment in S at cost | | +(S) | 66,000 | 66,000 |
| Inventory | 30,000 | +(T) | 14,000 | 44,000 |
| Accounts receivable | 20,000 | +(T) | 25,000 | 45,000 |
| Bank | 10,000 | +(T) | 30,000 | 40,000 |
| | 230,000 | | | 438,000 |
| *Less* Current liabilities | (30,000) | +(T) | 10,000 | (40,000) |
| | 200,000 | | | 398,000 |
| Share capital | 180,000 | +(S) | 60,000 | |
| | | +(T) | 120,000 | = 360,000 |
| Share premium | | +(S) | 6,000 | |
| | | +(T) | 12,000 | = 18,000 |
| Retained profits | 20,000 | | | 20,000 |
| | 200,000 | | | 398,000 |

**Note: No entry is necessary in the books of S Ltd, as it is merely the identity of the shareholders that has changed. This would be duly recorded in the register of members, but this is not part of the double entry accounting system. As you will see, later, when group financial statements are prepared, the assets and liabilities of S are added to those of R and the goodwill at the time of R's acquisition of S (of £26,000) is also shown on the group statement of financial position.**

If, however, T Ltd is now liquidated, then a realisation account must be drawn up and the distribution of the shares (or cash if the shares are sold) to the shareholders of T Ltd must be shown. Such accounts would appear as follows:

**Books of T Ltd**

*Realisation*

| | £ | | £ |
|---|---|---|---|
| Book values of assets disposed of: | | R Ltd: Total purchase consideration | 142,000 |
| Buildings | 10,000 | | |
| Machinery | 10,000 | | |
| Inventory | 20,000 | | |
| Accounts receivable | 30,000 | | |
| Bank | 30,000 | | |
| Profit on realisation transferred to sundry shareholders | 42,000 | | |
| | 142,000 | | 142,000 |

*Share Capital*

| | £ | | £ |
|---|---|---|---|
| Sundry shareholders | 50,000 | Balance b/d | 50,000 |

*Retained Profits*

| | £ | | £ |
|---|---|---|---|
| Sundry shareholders | 40,000 | Balance b/d | 40,000 |

*Accounts Payable*

| | £ | | £ |
|---|---|---|---|
| R Ltd – taken over | 10,000 | Balance b/d | 10,000 |

*R Ltd*

| | £ | | £ |
|---|---|---|---|
| Realisation: | | Accounts payable | 10,000 |
| Total consideration | 142,000 | Sundry shareholders: 120,000 £1 shares received at premium of 10% | 132,000 |
| | 142,000 | | 142,000 |

*Sundry Shareholders*

| | £ | | £ |
|---|---|---|---|
| R Ltd: 120,000 £1 shares at premium of 10% | 132,000 | Share capital | 50,000 |
| | | Retained profits | 40,000 |
| | | Realisation (profit) | 42,000 |
| | 132,000 | | 132,000 |

It can be seen that the items possessed by the sundry shareholders have been transferred to an account in their name. These are (*a*) the share capital which obviously belongs to them, (*b*) the retained profits built up by withholding cash dividends from the shareholders, and (*c*) the profit on realisation which they, as owners of the business, are entitled to take. As there were 50,000 shares in T Ltd, and 120,000 shares have been given by R Ltd, then each holder of five shares in T Ltd will now be given 12 shares in R Ltd to complete the liquidation of the company.

## 7.5 The exchange of loan notes

Sometimes loan notes in the company taking over are given in exchange for loan notes of the company being taken over. This may be simply on the basis of a £1 loan note in Company A for each £1 loan note in Company B. However, when the exchange is in terms of one or both sets of loan notes being at a discount or at a premium, it becomes more complex. This form of exchange may occur because:

1 There is a desire to persuade the holders of loan notes in Company B to give up their loan notes but they need some form of inducement, such as letting them have A's loan notes at a discount, even though they may well be worth their par value.
2 There may be a difference between the interest rates of the two loan notes. For instance, a person with a £100 7% loan note would not normally gladly part with it in exchange for a £100 6% loan note in another company. The first loan note gives the investor £7 a year interest, the second one only £6 per year. Thus, the loan note in the second company may be issued at a discount so that holders who switch to it continue to receive £7 a year for each £100 they originally invested. As the amount of interest is only one factor – others include the certainty of the loan-note holder regaining his/her money if the business had to close down – the precise terms of the exchange cannot be based merely on arithmetical calculations of interest rates, but it is one of the measures taken when negotiating the exchange of loan notes and is the most obvious.

**Exhibit 7.7**

1 D Ltd is to give the necessary loan notes at a discount of 10% required to redeem £9,000 loan notes in J Ltd at a premium of 5%. The problem here is to find exactly what amount of loan notes must be given by D Ltd.

$$\text{Total nominal value of loan notes to be redeemed (exchanged)} \times \frac{\text{Redeemable value of each £100 loan note of J Ltd}}{\text{Issue value of each £100 loan note of D Ltd}}$$

$$= \text{Total nominal value of D Ltd to be issued}$$

$$= £9,000 \times \frac{105}{90}$$

$$= £10,500$$

Thus, to satisfy the agreement, loan notes of D Ltd of a total nominal value of £10,500 are issued at a discount of 10% to the loan-note holder of J Ltd.

2 H Ltd is to give the necessary loan notes at par to redeem £5,000 loan notes in M Ltd at a premium of 4%.

$$£5,000 \times \frac{104}{100} = \text{Loan notes of £5,200 nominal value are given by H Ltd at par}$$

3 I Ltd is to give the necessary amount of 5% loan notes at par to redeem £20,000 loan notes of 6% of K Ltd.

$$£20,000 \times 6\% = £1,200 \text{ Interest per year}$$

$$\therefore \frac{£1,200}{0.05} = \text{£24,000 loan notes of 5\% must be issued by I Ltd in exchange for the £20,000 loan notes of 6\% in K Ltd}$$

Now, let's move on to a look at something that often happens when a company is first formed – profits or losses have been earned prior to incorporation.

## 7.6 The treatment of profits (or losses) prior to incorporation

Quite frequently, companies are formed after a business has been in existence for some time and profits or losses have been earned. For example, it could be that two people enter into business and start trading with the intention of running the business as a limited company. However, it takes more than a few days to attend to all the necessary formalities before the company can be incorporated. The actual time taken depends on the speed with which the formation is pushed through and the resolution of any problems which arise.

When a company is incorporated, it may enter into a contract whereby it adopts all the transactions retrospectively to the date that the business had started trading. This means that the company accepts all the benefits and disadvantages which have flowed from the transactions which have occurred. The example used was that of a new business. It could have been an old, established business that was taken over from a date predating incorporation of the company.

**Legally, a company cannot earn profits before it comes into existence (i.e. incorporated).** Therefore, to decide what action to take, profits must be calculated. Any such profits are of a capital nature and must be transferred to a capital reserve account, normally titled *Pre-incorporation Profit Account* or *Profit Prior to Incorporation Account*. That this should be done is obvious if you realise that, even though the actual date from which the transactions have been adopted falls before the date of incorporation, the price at which the business was taken over was influenced by the values of the net assets of the business at the date when the company was incorporated.

Let's consider an example. Suppose that Doolin and Kershaw start a business on 1 January 2016 with £1,000 capital, and very shortly afterwards Davie and Parker become involved and the four of them form a company in which they will all become directors – Davie and Parker to start active work when the company is incorporated.

The company is incorporated on 1 May 2016 and the original owners of the business, Doolin and Kershaw, are to be given shares in the new company to compensate them for handing over the business. If they knew that the original £1,000 assets have grown to net assets of £6,000, then they would not part with the business to the company for £1,000. Ignoring goodwill, they would want £6,000 of shares. Conversely, if the net assets have shrunk to £400, would Davie and Parker be happy to see £1,000 of shares handed over? This means that the price at which the business is taken over is dependent on the expected value at the date of the company incorporation, and that value clearly includes profits or losses earned to that date.

In the case where net assets have increased to £6,000, the £5,000 difference is made up of profits. If these profits could be distributed as dividends, the capital payment of £6,000 in shares is being partly used for dividend purposes. This is inappropriate and is in direct contradiction to the normal accounting practice of keeping capital intact. The £5,000 profits, therefore, must be regarded as not being available for dividends. They are a capital reserve.

Although **pre-incorporation profit** cannot be regarded as free for use as dividends, any **pre-incorporation loss** can be used to restrict the dividends which could be paid out of the profits made after incorporation. This is an example of application of the prudence concept and, if the price paid on takeover was higher than was justified by the net worth of the business at that time, and it was discovered later that a pre-incorporation loss had been made, then the restriction of dividends leads to the capital lost being replaced by assets held back within the business.

It is possible for the profits up to the date of incorporation to be calculated separately from those earned after incorporation. (This is invariably the case in examination questions.) However, the cost of doing so may not be worthwhile incurring when there is no legal requirement to do so.

Therefore, when the financial statements for the full financial year are prepared, they will consist of profits pre- and post-incorporation. The financial statements must, therefore, be split to reveal the two sets of profit (or loss), so that distinction can be made between those profits usable, and those not usable, for dividend purposes. There is no hard-and-fast rule as to how this is done. Known facts must prevail and, where an arbitrary apportionment must be made, it should meet the test of common sense. Exhibit 7.8 shows an attempt to determine the amount of pre- and post-incorporation profits.

## Exhibit 7.8

Slack and King are partners. Their business was taken over as from 1 January 2017 by Monk Ltd which was incorporated on 1 April 2017. It was agreed that all profits made from 1 January 2017 should belong to the company, and that Slack and King are entitled to interest on the purchase price from 1 January to the date of payment.

The purchase price was paid on 30 April 2017, including £1,600 interest. A statement of profit or loss is drawn up for the year ending 31 December 2013. This is shown as column (X). This is then split into pre-incorporation, shown as column (Y), and post-incorporation as column (Z). The methods used to apportion the particular items are shown after the statement of profit or loss, the letters (A) to (I) against the items being references to notes below the statement of profit or loss.

**These methods of apportionment must *not* be used in all cases for similar expenses. They are only an indication of different methods of apportionment. The facts and the peculiarities of each business must be taken into account, and no method should be adopted simply because it was used before.**

Assume for this example that all calendar months are of equal length.

**Monk Ltd**
**Statement of Profit or Loss (extract) for the year ending 31 December 2017**

| | | *(X)* *Full year* | | *(Y)* *Pre-incorporation* | | *(Z)* *After* | |
|---|---|---|---|---|---|---|---|
| | | £ | £ | £ | £ | £ | £ |
| Gross profit | (A) | | 38,000 | | 8,000 | | 30,000 |
| *Less* | | | | | | | |
| Partnership salaries | (B) | 1,000 | | 1,000 | | | |
| Employees' remuneration | (C) | 12,000 | | 3,000 | | 9,000 | |
| General expenses | (C) | 800 | | 200 | | 600 | |
| Commission on sales | (D) | 1,700 | | 200 | | 1,500 | |
| Distribution expenses | (E) | 1,900 | | 400 | | 1,500 | |
| Bad debts | (F) | 100 | | 20 | | 80 | |
| Bank overdraft interest | (G) | 200 | | | | 200 | |
| Directors' remuneration | (H) | 5,000 | | | | 5,000 | |
| Directors' expenses | (H) | 400 | | | | 400 | |
| Loan-note interest | (H) | 500 | | | | 500 | |
| Depreciation | (C) | 1,000 | | 250 | | 750 | |
| Interest paid to vendors | (I) | 1,600 | | 1,200 | | 400 | |
| | | | (26,200) | | (6,270) | | (19,930) |
| Net profit | | | 11,800 | | | | |
| Transferred to capital reserves | | | | | 1,730 | | |
| Retained profits carried forward | | | | | | | 10,070 |

*Notes:*

(A) For the three months to 31 March sales amounted to £40,000, and for the remaining nine months they were £150,000. Gross profit is at a uniform rate of 20% of selling price throughout the year. Therefore the gross profit is apportioned (Y) 20% of £40,000 = £8,000, and (Z) 20% of £150,000 = £30,000.

(B) The partnership salaries of the vendors, Slack and King, obviously belong to (Y), because that is the period of the partnership.

(C) These expenses, in this particular case, have accrued evenly throughout the year and are therefore split on the time basis of (Y) three-twelfths, (Z) nine-twelfths.

(D) Commission to the sales force was paid at the rate of $^1/_2$% on sales up to 31 March, and 1% thereafter. The commission figure is split:

| | |
|---|---|
| (Y) $^1/_2$% of £40,000 = | 200 |
| (Z) 1% of £150,000 = | 1,500 |
| | 1,700 |

(E) In this particular case (but not always true in every case) the distribution expenses have varied directly with the value of sales. They are therefore split:

$$(Y)\frac{\text{Y sales}}{\text{Total sales}} \times \text{Expenses} = \frac{40,000}{190,000} \times £1,900 = \frac{4}{19} \times £1,900 = £400$$

$$(Z)\frac{\text{Z sales}}{\text{Total sales}} \times \text{Expenses} = \frac{150,000}{190,000} \times £1,900 = \frac{15}{19} \times £1,900 = £1,500$$

(F) There were two bad debts:
 (*i*) in respect of a sale in January, the debtor dying penniless in March, £20;
 (*ii*) in respect of a sale in June, the debtor being declared bankrupt in December, £80.

(G) The bank account was never overdrawn until June, so that the interest charged must be for period (Z).

(H) Only in companies are such expenses as directors' salaries, directors' expenses and loan-note interest to be found. These must naturally be shown in period (Z).

(I) The interest paid to the vendors was due to the fact that the company was receiving all the benefits from 1 January but did not in fact pay any cash for the business until 30 April. This is therefore, in effect, loan interest which should be spread over the period it was borrowed, i.e. three months to (Y) and one month to (Z).

## 7.7 The treatment of formation expenses

These are also known as preliminary expenses. They may be written off immediately to profit or loss or capitalised and amortised over an appropriate period. Normally, they would be written off.

### Learning outcomes

**You should now have learnt:**

1. Why goodwill may arise when a business is taken over.
2. The difference between goodwill and gain on a bargain purchase.
3. The basic accounting entries are the same whether a limited company takes over a sole proprietor or a partnership.
4. Limited companies may take over other limited companies either:
   (*a*) by buying all the assets of the other company; or
   (*b*) by giving its own shares and loan notes in exchange for the shares and loan notes of the company being taken over.
5. How to record pre-incorporation losses and profits.
6. That pre-incorporation profits are not available for distribution.
7. The alternative treatments of formation expenses.

### Answer to activity

7.1 Apart from the obvious difference that may arise between the net book value of an individual asset and its fair value (i.e. its true worth), such as in the example of the property given in the text, when a business is sold, the purchaser may have to pay extra to cover the value of intangible assets that do not appear in the statement of financial position. Examples would include the reputation and customer base of the business being purchased, neither of which can appear in a statement of financial position.

It is also possible that less may be paid than the net worth of a business because some assets may be considered as not being worth the amounts shown in the financial statements – it may be considered, for example, that accounts receivable are likely to be overvalued or that individual assets are worth less to the purchaser than the values shown in the financial statements.

Of course, buyers generally try to pay as little as possible for a business. If a seller is very keen to sell, a price may be agreed that is below the net worth as shown in the statement of financial position, even though that value is correct. It all depends on how the transaction is negotiated by the purchaser and the seller.

## Review questions

**7.1** The Club Ltd was incorporated on 15 May 2017 and took over the business of Poker Ltd on 1 June 2017. It was agreed that all profits made from 1 June should belong to The Club Ltd and that the vendors should be entitled to interest on the purchase price from 1 June to the date of payment. The purchase price was paid on 31 October 2017 including £6,600 interest.

The following is the statement of profit or loss extract for the year ending 31 May 2018:

| | £ | £ | £ |
|---|---|---|---|
| Gross profit | | | 224,000 |
| *Less* Expenses | | | |
| Salary to vendor of Poker Ltd | | 13,560 | |
| Wages and general expenses | | 69,120 | |
| Rent | | 6,880 | |
| Distribution expenses | | 13,440 | |
| Commission on sales | | 5,600 | |
| Bad debts | | 2,512 | |
| Interest paid to vendors | | 13,200 | |
| Directors' remuneration | | 32,000 | |
| Directors' expenses | | 4,120 | |
| Depreciation | | | |
| Vans | 15,200 | | |
| Machinery | 4,600 | | |
| | | 19,800 | |
| Bank interest | | 1,344 | (181,576) |
| Net profit | | | 42,424 |

You are given the following information:

1 Sales amounted to £160,000 for the three months to 31 August 2017 and £400,000 for the nine months to 31 May 2018. Gross profit is at a uniform rate of 40% of selling price throughout the year, and commission at a rate of 1% is paid on all sales.
2 A salary of £13,560 was paid to the vendor of Poker Ltd for her assistance in running the business up to 31 August 2017.
3 The bad debts written off are:
   (*a*) a debt of £832 taken over from the vendors;
   (*b*) a debt of £1,680 in respect of goods sold in November 2017.
4 On 1 June 2017, four vans were bought for £56,000 and machinery for £40,000. On 1 August 2017 another two vans were bought for £24,000 and on 1 March 2018, another machine was added for £24,000. Depreciation has been written off vans at 20% per annum, and machinery at 10% per annum. Depreciation is written off for each month in which an asset is owned.
5 Wages and general expenses and rent all accrued at an even rate throughout the year.
6 The bank granted an overdraft facility in September 2017.

Assuming all calendar months are of equal length:

(*a*) set out the statement of profit or loss in columnar form, so as to distinguish between the period prior to the company's incorporation and the period after incorporation;
(*b*) state how you would deal with the profit prior to incorporation;
(*c*) state how you would deal with the results prior to incorporation if they had turned out to be a net loss.

**7.2** On 30 June 2017 Jones and Sons Ltd acquired all the assets, except the investments, of Spade Ltd. The following are the summaries of the statements of profit or loss of Spade Ltd for the years ending 30 June 2015, 2016 and 2017:

| | *2015* | *2016* | *2017* | | *2015* | *2016* | *2017* |
|---|---|---|---|---|---|---|---|
| Motor expenses | 15,040 | 15,840 | 16,480 | Gross profit | 236,680 | 285,120 | 283,840 |
| Management salaries | 51,200 | 56,000 | 57,600 | Investment income | 3,360 | 4,640 | 6,720 |
| Depreciation of plant and machinery | 19,200 | 15,360 | 12,288 | Rents received | 12,480 | 5,280 | – |
| Overdraft interest | 704 | 1,792 | 2,176 | Profit on sale of property | – | 37,120 | – |
| Wrapping expenses | 8,016 | 9,168 | 9,792 | | | | |
| Preliminary expenses written off | | 7,040 | | | | | |
| Net profit | 185,360 | 226,960 | 192,224 | | | | |
| | 279,520 | 332,160 | 290,560 | | 279,520 | 332,160 | 290,560 |

The purchase price is to be the amount on which an estimated maintainable profit would represent a return of 20% per annum.

The maintainable profit is to be taken as the average of the profits of the three years 2015, 2016 and 2017, after making any necessary adjustments.

You are given the following information:

(*a*) The cost of the plant and machinery was £96,000. It has been agreed that depreciation should have been written off at the rate of 10% per annum using the straight line method.
(*b*) A new type of wrapping material means that wrapping expenses will be halved in future.
(*c*) By switching to a contract supply basis on motor fuel and motor repairs, it is estimated that motor expenses will fall by 25% in future.
(*d*) Inventory treated as valueless at 30 June 2014 was sold for £7,520 in 2016.
(*e*) The working capital of the new company is sound and it is felt that there will be no need for a bank overdraft in the foreseeable future.
(*f*) Management salaries have been inadequate and will have to be increased by £56,000 a year in future.

**You are required to** set out your calculation of the purchase price. All workings must be shown. In fact, your managing director, who is not an accountant, should be able to decipher how the price was calculated.

**7.3** CJK Ltd was incorporated on 15 December 2016 with an authorised capital of 200,000 ordinary shares of £0.20 each to acquire as at 31 December 2016 the business of CK, a sole proprietor, and RP Ltd, a company.

From the following information you are required to prepare:

(*a*) the realisation and capital accounts in the books of CK and RP Ltd showing the winding up of these two concerns;
(*b*) the journal entries to open the books of CJK Ltd, including cash transactions and the raising of finance;
(*c*) the statement of financial position of CJK Ltd after the transactions have been completed.

The statement of financial position of CK as at 31 December 2016 is as follows:

**Statement of Financial Position**

| | £ |
|---|---|
| Freehold premises | 8,000 |
| Plant | 4,000 |
| Inventory | 2,000 |
| Accounts receivable | 5,000 |
| Cash | 200 |
| Total assets | 19,200 |
| Accounts payable | (3,200) |
| Net assets | 16,000 |
| Equity | 16,000 |

The assets (excluding cash) and the liabilities were taken over at the following values: freehold premises £10,000; plant £3,500; inventory £2,000; accounts receivable £5,000 less an allowance for doubtful debts of £300; goodwill £7,000; accounts payable £3,200 less a discount provision of £150. The purchase consideration, based on these values, was settled by the issue of shares at par.

The statement of financial position of RP Ltd as at 31 December 2016 is as follows:

**Statement of Financial Position**

| | £ | £ |
|---|---|---|
| Freehold premises | | 4,500 |
| Plant | | 2,000 |
| Inventory | | 1,600 |
| Accounts receivable | | 3,400 |
| Total assets | | 11,500 |
| Current liabilities | 1,500 | |
| Accounts payable | 3,500 | |
| Bank overdraft | | (5,000) |
| | | 6,500 |
| Equity | | |
| 10,000 shares of £0.40 each | | 4,000 |
| Retained profits | | 2,500 |
| | | 6,500 |

The assets and liabilities were taken over at book value with the exception of the freehold premises which were revalued at £5,500. The purchase consideration was a cash payment of £1 and three shares in CJK Ltd at par in exchange for every two shares in RP Ltd.

Additional working capital and the funds required to complete the purchase of RP Ltd were provided by the issue for cash of:

(*i*) 10,000 shares at a premium of £0.30 per share;
(*ii*) £8,000 7% loan notes at 98.

The expenses of incorporating CJK Ltd were paid, amounting to £1,200.

(*Chartered Institute of Management Accountants*)

**7.4A** The statement of financial position of Hubble Ltd as at 31 May 2017 is shown below.

**Hubble Ltd**

| | £ | £ |
|---|---|---|
| *Non-current assets* | | |
| Freehold premises at cost | | 375,000 |
| Plant and machinery at cost | | |
| *Less* Depreciation £48,765 | | 101,235 |
| Motor vehicles at cost | | |
| *Less* Depreciation £1,695 | | 6,775 |
| | | 483,010 |
| *Current assets* | | |
| Inventory | 102,550 | |
| Accounts receivable | 96,340 | |
| Cash in hand | 105 | |
| | | 198,995 |
| Total assets | | 682,005 |
| *Current liabilities* | | |
| Trade accounts payable | 63,200 | |
| Bank overdraft | 38,175 | |
| Net assets | | 101,375 |
| Equity | | 580,630 |
| Authorised share capital 650,000 ordinary shares of £1 each | 650,000 | |
| Issued share capital 400,000 ordinary shares of £1 each fully paid | | 400,000 |
| Retained profits | | 180,630 |
| | | 580,630 |

Hubble Ltd agreed to purchase at this date the freehold premises, plant and machinery and inventory of A Bubble at agreed valuations of £100,000, £10,000, and £55,000, respectively. The purchase price was to be settled fully by the issue to Bubble of 120,000 ordinary shares of £1 each in Hubble Ltd, and a cash payment to Bubble of £25,000. Bubble was to collect his debts and to pay his creditors.

Hubble Ltd sold one of its own premises prior to taking over Bubble for £75,000 (cost £55,000) and revalued the remainder at £400,000 (excluding those acquired from Bubble).

**You are required to**:

(*a*) show the journal entries, including cash items, in the books of Hubble Ltd to give effect to the above transactions; and

(*b*) show the statement of financial position of Hubble Ltd after completing them.

(*Association of Chartered Certified Accountants*)

**7.5A** From the following information you are required to prepare a statement apportioning the retained profit between the pre-incorporation and post-incorporation periods, showing the basis of apportionment:

VU Limited was incorporated on 1 July 2016 with an authorised share capital of 60,000 ordinary shares of £1 each, to take over the business of L and Sons as from 1 April 2016.

The purchase consideration was agreed at £50,000 for the net tangible assets taken over, plus a further £6,000 for goodwill.

Payment was satisfied by the issue of £30,000 8% loan notes and 26,000 ordinary shares both at par, on 1 August 2016. Interest at 10% per annum on the purchase consideration was paid up to this date.

The company raised a further £20,000 on 1 August 2016 by the issue of ordinary shares at a premium of £0.25 per share.

The abridged statement of profit or loss for the year ending 31 March 2017 was as follows:

| | £ | £ |
|---|---|---|
| Sales: | | |
| 1 April 2016 to 30 June 2016 | 30,000 | |
| 1 July 2016 to 31 March 2017 | 95,000 | |
| | | 125,000 |
| Cost of sales for the year | 80,000 | |
| Depreciation | 2,220 | |
| Directors' fees | 500 | |
| Administration salaries and expenses | 8,840 | |
| Sales commission | 4,375 | |
| Goodwill impaired written off | 1,000 | |
| Interest on purchase consideration, gross | 1,867 | |
| Distribution costs (60% variable) | 6,250 | |
| Preliminary expenses written off | 1,650 | |
| Loan note interest, gross | 1,600 | |
| Dividend paid on ordinary shares | 7,560 | |
| | | 115,862 |
| Retained profits carried forward | | 9,138 |

The company sells one product only, of which the unit selling price has remained constant during the year, but due to improved buying the unit cost of sales was reduced by 10% in the post-incorporation period as compared with the pre-incorporation period.

Taxation is to be ignored.

(*Chartered Institute of Management Accountants [part (a) of question only]*)

**7.6A** Rowlock Ltd was incorporated on 1 October 2015 to acquire Rowlock's mail order business, with effect from 1 June 2015.

The purchase consideration was agreed at £35,000 to be satisfied by the issue on 1 December 2015 to Rowlock or his nominee of 20,000 ordinary shares of £1 each, fully paid, and £15,000 7% loan notes.

The entries relating to the transfer were not made in the books which were carried on without a break until 31 May 2016.

On 31 May 2016 the trial balance extracted from the books is:

| | £ | £ |
|---|---:|---:|
| Sales | | 52,185 |
| Purchases | 38,829 | |
| Wrapping | 840 | |
| Postage | 441 | |
| Warehouse rent and rates | 921 | |
| Packing expenses | 1,890 | |
| Office expenses | 627 | |
| Inventory on 31 May 2015 | 5,261 | |
| Director's salary | 1,000 | |
| Loan note interest (gross) | 525 | |
| Non-current assets | 25,000 | |
| Current assets (other than inventory) | 9,745 | |
| Current liabilities | | 4,162 |
| Formation expenses | 218 | |
| Capital account – Rowlock, 31 May 2015 | | 29,450 |
| Drawings account – Rowlock, 31 May 2015 | 500 | |
| | 85,797 | 85,797 |

You also ascertain the following:

1 Inventory on 31 May 2016 amounted to £4,946.
2 The average monthly sales for June, July and August were one-half of those for the remaining months of the year. The gross profit margin was constant throughout the year.
3 Wrapping, postage and packing expenses varied in direct proportion to sales, whilst office expenses were constant each month.
4 Formation expenses are to be written off.

**You are required to** prepare the statement of profit or loss for the year ending 31 May 2016 apportioned between the periods before and after incorporation, and the statement of financial position as at that date.

(*Chartered Institute of Management Accountants*)

chapter

# 8 Taxation in company financial statements

## Learning objectives

**After you have studied this chapter, you should be able to:**

- explain why profit per the statement of profit or loss is normally different from assessable profit for corporation tax calculations
- explain how income tax on interest affects companies and individuals
- describe how the 'imputation system' operates
- describe how and why deferred tax is relevant to capital allowances

## Introduction

In this chapter, you'll learn that in the UK depreciation is not allowed as an expense for tax purposes and that something called a 'capital allowance' is granted instead. You'll also learn that the result of replacing depreciation with capital allowances when calculating tax is that taxable profit is very rarely the same amount as the figure shown for net profit in the financial statements. You'll learn how to apportion taxable profit across two tax periods, when corporation tax is payable, and the differences between the UK tax system for companies compared with the one that operates for sole proprietors and partnerships. Finally, you will learn about deferred tax and how it is calculated and applied to avoid financial statements being misleading in the way they present future tax liabilities in the statement of financial position.

## 8.1 Background

This chapter is concerned with the entries made in the financial statements of companies in respect of taxation. It is not concerned with the actual calculation of the taxes as tax legislation is extremely complex and contains too many exceptions to the general rules applicable to companies for us to attempt to cover the entire subject in this book. It should be appreciated, therefore, that although the rules described in this chapter apply to the great majority of UK companies, there are many for which more complex tax rules will apply.

Taxation that affects UK companies can be split between:

1 Value added tax (VAT). This was covered in *Frank Wood's Business Accounting 1*.
2 Direct taxes, payable to Revenue and Customs, the government department responsible for the calculation and collection of the taxes. For a company, the relevant taxes are corporation tax and income tax. IAS 12 *Income taxes* deals with the treatment of taxation in company financial statements and will be adhered to in this chapter.

## 8.2 Limited companies: corporation tax and income tax

The principal tax paid by limited companies is **corporation tax**. Legally, it is an appropriation of profits, *not* an expense. Taxation is the last deduction shown in the statement of profit or loss and appears after the line showing profit for the year before taxation.

A company's profits are assessable to corporation tax. But corporation tax is assessable on the profit calculated *after certain adjustments have been made* to the net profit. These adjustments are not made in the financial statements. They are done quite separately from the drafting of financial statements and are not entered in the accounting books of the company.

Let's look at an example of one of these adjustments. Suppose that K Ltd has the following net profit:

**K Ltd Statement of Profit or Loss for the year ending 31 March 2015**

| | £ | £ |
|---|---|---|
| Gross profit | | 100,000 |
| *Less* General expenses | 25,000 | |
| Depreciation of machinery | 20,000 | |
| | | (45,000) |
| Net profit | | 55,000 |

The depreciation provision for machinery is the accounting figure used for the financial statements. It must be reversed when calculating the taxable profit and replaced by another deduction, *capital allowances*. These are the Revenue and Customs' equivalent of depreciation and are calculated by rules which usually vary at one point or another from the methods applied by companies in determining their depreciation provisions. As a result, taxable profit assessed in any year is normally not the same as the net profit for that year as shown in the statement of profit or loss.

Why do you think the rules for capital allowances are different from the rules for depreciation?

In the case of K Ltd, assume that the capital allowances amount to £27,000 and that the rate of corporation tax is 40% on assessable profits. The calculation of the corporation tax liability would be:

| | £ |
|---|---|
| Net profit per the financial statements | 55,000 |
| *Add* Depreciation provision not allowed as a deduction for corporation tax purposes | 20,000 |
| | 75,000 |
| *Less* Capital allowances | (27,000) |
| Adjusted profits assessable to corporation tax | 48,000 |

At a corporation tax rate of 40%, the corporation tax liability will be £48,000 × 40% = £19,200.

In this example, taxable profits were higher than the net profit. Yet, over the life of a non-current asset, the amount of profit assessed in total for tax will always equal the total net profit for that period. Why?

As you might imagine, it is usually impossible to calculate the corporation tax payable by a company directly from its net profit. In fact, in addition to depreciation, other items in the financial statements often also need to be adjusted to find the assessable profits for corporation tax purposes.

## 8.3 The rate of corporation tax

The rate of corporation tax covering the period from 1 April to 31 March of the following year is fixed by the Chancellor of the Exchequer in the Budget, presented to Parliament each year. This rate is applied to the assessable profits of companies earned during this period. A company which has a financial year end other than 31 March spans two tax years, and apportions its taxable profits across the two periods.

Let's look at an example of this in Exhibit 8.1.

### Exhibit 8.1

Company T Ltd: adjusted profits for the year ended 31 December 2015 = £160,000.

*Rates of corporation tax*:
For the tax year ended 31.3.2015, 45%.
For the tax year ended 31.3.2016, 40%.

| | £ |
|---|---|
| 3 months' profit 1.1.2015 to 31.3.2015 | |
| 3/12 months × £160,000 = £40,000 × 45% | 18,000 |
| 9 months' profit 1.4.2015 to 31.12.2015 | |
| 9/12 months × £160,000 = £120,000 × 40% | 48,000 |
| Corporation tax payable on adjusted profits for the year ended 31 December 2015 | 66,000 |

## 8.4 Corporation tax – when payable

All companies have a payment date of nine months after the end of their accounting period. For the rest of this chapter, although companies with relatively small profits can pay tax at a lower rate than companies with greater profits, unless mentioned otherwise corporation tax will be assumed to be 40%.

## 8.5 Income tax

You've just learnt that companies pay corporation tax, not income tax. In the case of a sole proprietor, income tax is not directly connected with the business, as the individual *not* the business is liable to pay tax on the profits earned. Calculation of the tax due depends on many factors including, for example, whether the sole proprietor has other taxable income. The income tax paid by a sole proprietor should be treated as drawings if paid from the business bank account.

**Activity 8.3**

If a sole proprietor has the same net profit each year as is earned by a small company, all other things being equal, which business will show the greater retained profits if:

(*a*) the sole proprietor pays income tax out of the business bank account;
(*b*) the sole proprietor pays income tax out of a personal bank account and does not draw any extra funds out of the business to cover the payment.

Why are these two answers different?

The income tax charged upon a partnership is also subject to the personal situation of the partners. The actual apportionment of the tax between the partners must be performed by some-one who has access to the personal tax computations. It is *not* apportioned in the partners' profit-sharing ratios but on the basis of how much income tax each partner was required to pay. When the apportionment has been made, each partner should have the relevant amount debited to his drawings account. Remember, neither sole proprietors nor partnerships are liable to corporation tax and income tax does not appear in their statements of profit or loss.

In contrast, income tax does appear in the accounts of companies. When a company pays dividends or pays charges such as loan-note interest, it deducts income tax from the amount paid. This figure of income tax is then payable by the company to the Revenue and Customs. In effect, the company is acting as a tax collector on behalf of Revenue and Customs, similar to the position a company is in regarding VAT.

Let's look at an example. Suppose a company has a thousand different holders of loan notes. It is far easier for Revenue and Customs if the company pays only the net amount (i.e. the amount of interest less income tax) due to each holder and then pays the income tax deducted, in one figure, to the Revenue and Customs. This saves the Revenue and Customs having to trace a thousand loan-note holders and then collect the money from them. It obviously cuts down on the bad debts that Revenue and Customs might suffer, and makes it more difficult to evade the payment of income tax, plus it makes it cheaper for Revenue and Customs to administer the system. This system is similar to the way PAYE on wages or salaries is operated, something you learnt about in *Frank Wood's Business Accounting 1*.

*For clarity, throughout the rest of this chapter it will be assumed that the basic rate of income tax is 25%*. The real rate will obviously differ from time to time. In addition, when someone has a relatively high or low income, the rate of income tax they pay may be higher or lower than 25%. However, even though individual loan-note holders may have to pay income tax at higher rates, or indeed pay lower rates or no income tax at all, companies deduct income tax at the basic rate.

Thus, if a company has issued £100,000 of 8% loan notes, cheques amounting to a total of £6,000 (8% of £100,000 = £8,000 less 25% income tax, £2,000 = £6,000) will be paid to the loan-note holders. A cheque for £2,000 will then be paid to the Revenue and Customs by the company.

Let's consider some possible scenarios relating to this company's loan-note holders (Exhibit 8.2).

## Exhibit 8.2

If loan-note holder AB pays income tax at the rate of 25%, and he received £75 net (i.e. £100 gross less income tax £25), on his loan note of £1,250, then he has already suffered his rightful income tax by deduction at source. He will not get a further bill from Revenue and Customs for the £25 tax. The company has already paid the £25 income tax he owed as part of the total income tax cheque it paid of £2,000.

On the other hand, loan-note holder CD is not liable to income tax because his income is low. He also has a loan note of £1,250 and so also receives a cheque for interest of £75. As he is not liable to income tax, but £25 of his money has been included in the total cheque paid by the company to Revenue and Customs of £2,000, he will be able to claim a refund of £25 from Revenue and Customs. Such a claim is made direct to Revenue and Customs, not to the company.

A third loan-note holder EF pays tax at a rate of 40% on his income. If he also has a loan note of £1,250, the company will pay a cheque to him of £75. But he is really liable to pay tax of £40, not £25. As £25 income tax has been taken from him and handed over by the company in the total cheque of £2,000 income tax paid to Revenue and Customs, the Revenue and Customs will send an extra demand to him for income tax of £15. Once again, the company has nothing to do with this extra demand.

## 8.6 Income tax on interest

Of course, a company may well have bought loan notes or may own royalties, for example, in another company. This may mean that the company not only pays charges, such as loan-note interest, but also receives similar items from other companies. The company will receive such items net after income tax has been deducted. When the company both receives and pays such items, it may set off the tax already suffered by it from such interest etc. received against the tax collected by it from its own charges, and pay the resultant net figure of income tax to Revenue and Customs. Again, this is similar to the treatment of VAT.

The figures of charges to be shown as being paid or received by the company in the company's own statement of profit or loss are the gross charges, i.e. the same as they would have been if income tax had never been invented. Exhibit 8.3 illustrates this:

### Exhibit 8.3

RST Ltd has 7% loan notes amounting to £100,000 and has bought a £40,000 loan note of 10% in a private company, XYZ Ltd. During the year, cheques amounting to £5,250 (£7,000 less 25%) have been paid to loan-note holders by RST, and a cheque for £3,000 (£4,000 less 25%) has been received from XYZ Ltd. Instead of paying over the £1,750 income tax deducted on payment of loan-note interest, RST Ltd waits until the cheque is received from XYZ Ltd and then pays a cheque for £750 (£1,750 collected less £1,000 already suffered by deduction by XYZ Ltd) to Revenue and Customs in settlement.

**Loan-note Interest Payable**

| | £ | | £ |
|---|---|---|---|
| Cash | 5,250 | Profit and loss | 7,000 |
| Income tax | 1,750 | | |
| | 7,000 | | 7,000 |

**Loan-note Interest Receivable**

| | £ | | £ |
|---|---|---|---|
| Profit and loss | 4,000 | Cash | 3,000 |
| | | Income tax | 1,000 |
| | 4,000 | | 4,000 |

**Income Tax**

| | £ | | £ |
|---|---|---|---|
| Unquoted investment income | 1,000 | Loan-note interest payable | 1,750 |
| Cash | 750 | | |
| | 1,750 | | 1,750 |

It may well have been the case that although the income tax had been deducted at source from both the payment out of the company and the amount received, no cash has been paid specifically to Revenue and Customs by the company by the date of the statement of financial position. In this case, the balance of £750 owing to Revenue and Customs will be carried down as a credit balance and will be shown under current liabilities in the statement of financial position.

## 8.7 IAS 12 (*Income taxes*) and current tax

The international accounting standard relevant to this topic is IAS 12. It requires:

- current tax to be shown separately on the statement of financial position;
- tax on items charged or credited to equity to be treated in the same way;
- tax on discontinued operations to be disclosed.

The standard is covered in more detail in Chapter 11.

## 8.8 Deferred taxation

It was pointed out earlier in the chapter that *profits according to the financial statements* and *profits on which tax is payable* are often different. The main reasons for this are as follows:

1 The figure of depreciation shown in the statement of profit or loss may be different from Revenue and Customs' figure for 'capital allowances', which is *their* way of calculating allowances for depreciation.
2 Some items of expense charged in the statement of profit or loss will not be allowed by Revenue and Customs as expenses. Examples are political donations, fines for illegal acts and expenses for entertaining UK customers.

### Timing differences

In the case of capital allowances under (**1**) above, as you learnt in Activity 8.2, the amount of 'depreciation' charged for an asset over the years will eventually equal the amount allowed by Revenue and Customs as 'capital allowances'. Where the difference lies is in the periods when these items will be taken into account.

For instance, take an asset which cost £4,800 and will be sold after three years for £2,025. The depreciation rate is 33⅓% straight line. Revenue and Customs capital allowances are 25% reducing balance.

| *Years ended 5 April** | *2016* | *2017* | *2018* | *Overall* |
|---|---|---|---|---|
| | £ | £ | £ | £ |
| Depreciation | 925 | 925 | 925 | 2,775 |
| Capital allowances | 1,200 | 900 | 675 | 2,775 |
| Timing differences | +275 | −25 | −250 | nil |

***The Revenue and Customs tax year actually ends on 5 April, not 31 March, though 31 March is used for companies.**

**Activity 8.4** Why do you think the depreciation is £925 per year?

Thus, over the economic life of the asset, the same amount was deducted from profit for depreciation as was allowed as a deduction in the form of capital allowances.

What about retained profits, are they the same too? If profits for each year after depreciation were £1,000:

| *Years ended 5 April* | *2016* | *2017* | *2018* | *Overall* |
|---|---|---|---|---|
| | £ | £ | £ | £ |
| Profits after depreciation | 1,000 | 1,000 | 1,000 | 3,000 |
| Profits for tax purposes | 725 | 1,025 | 1,250 | 3,000 |
| Differences | −270 | +25 | +250 | nil |

As you can see, profits have in fact remained the same overall at £1,000. It is the difference in the timing of the deduction of capital allowances compared to that for depreciation which causes there to be different taxable profit figures each year compared to the net profit figures. These are known as 'timing differences'. Taking the point of view that profits of £1,000 per year give a more sensible picture than the £725, £1,025 and £1,250 in the Revenue and Customs calculations, the company's way of depreciating is probably more appropriate for individual companies than the Revenue and Customs method which does not vary between companies.

You may well be wondering if it matters what amount is deducted for depreciation. Analysts and potential investors and shareholders themselves place a great reliance on something called '*earnings per share after tax*'. Suppose that corporation tax was 40% for each of the three years and that there were 1 million shares. This would give the following figures:

*Tax based on net profit, i.e. the company's calculations*:

| | *2016* | *2017* | *2018* |
|---|---|---|---|
| | £000 | £000 | £000 |
| Profit per financial statements before taxation | 1,000 | 1,000 | 1,000 |
| *Less* Corporation tax (40%) | (400) | (400) | (400) |
| Profit after tax | 600 | 600 | 600 |
| Earnings per share = Profit after tax ÷ 1 million = | 60p | 60p | 60p |

*Tax based on Revenue and Customs calculations*:

| | *2016* | *2017* | *2018* |
|---|---|---|---|
| | £000 | £000 | £000 |
| Profit per financial statements before tax | 1,000 | 1,000 | 1,000 |
| *Less* Corporation tax: | | | |
| 40% of £725 | (290) | | |
| 40% of £1,025 | | (410) | |
| 40% of £1,250 | | | (500) |
| Profit after tax | 710 | 590 | 500 |
| Earnings per share = Profit after tax ÷ 1 million = | 71p | 59p | 50p |

In truth, all of the years have been equally profitable – this is shown by the company's calculation of 60p earnings per share each year. On the other hand, if no adjustment is made, the financial statements when based on actual tax paid would show 71p, 59p and 50p. This could confuse shareholders and would-be shareholders.

In order not to distort the picture given by financial statements, the concept of **deferred taxation** was brought in by accountants. IAS 12 (*Income taxes*) sets down the rules to apply.

It requires that deferred tax is provided on timing differences relating to:

- capital allowances and depreciation;
- accruals for pension costs and other post-retirement benefits;
- the elimination of unrealised intra-group profits;
- unrelieved tax losses;
- annual revaluations of assets where changes in fair value are taken to profit and loss;
- other short-term timing differences.

The double entry is as follows:

1 In the years when taxation is lower than it would be on comparable accounting profits, e.g. £40 on £200 net profit instead of £80:

*Dr* Profit and loss
*Cr* Deferred taxation account

with the amount of taxation understated.

Capital allowances, etc. have reduced taxable profit this year but at some point in the future, the reverse will occur.

2 In the years when taxation is higher than it would be on comparable accounting profits, e.g. £100 on £200 net profit instead of £80:

*Dr* Deferred taxation account
*Cr* Profit and loss

with the amount of taxation overstated.

By making these adjustments, a 'fair' amount of tax has either been set aside or paid each year. As a result, when the timing differences reverse, the retained profits will neither suddenly fall nor suddenly rise.

Let's now look at how the statement of profit or loss and the T-accounts for corporation tax and for deferred taxation would have been drawn up in the last example. We shall use the wording which applies to published company financial statements. As a result, instead of 'Profit per financial statements before taxation', we shall use 'Profit before taxation' (Exhibit 8.4).

## Exhibit 8.4

**Statement of Profit or Loss (extract) for the years ending 5 April**

| | *2016* | | *2017* | | *2018* | |
|---|---|---|---|---|---|---|
| | £000 | £000 | £000 | £000 | £000 | £000 |
| Profit before taxation | | 1,000 | | 1,000 | | 1,000 |
| Taxation | | | | | | |
| Corporation tax | 290 | | 410 | | 500 | |
| Deferred taxation | 110 | (400) | (10) | (400) | (100) | (400) |
| Profit for the year | | 600 | | 600 | | 600 |

For stakeholders, such as shareholders, stock exchange analysts, and would-be shareholders, the profit after taxation figures on which earnings per share (EPS) would be calculated is £600,000 in each of the three years. The timing difference distortion has thus been eliminated by inclusion of the deferred tax adjustments.

Assuming that corporation tax is payable on 1 January following each accounting year end, the ledger accounts for corporation tax and deferred tax would be as follows:

**Corporation Tax**

| | | | £000 | | | | £000 |
|---|---|---|---|---|---|---|---|
| 2016 | | | | 2016 | | | |
| Apr | 5 | Balance c/d | 290 | Apr | 5 | Profit and loss[Note] | 290 |
| | | | 290 | | | | 290 |
| 2017 | | | | 2016 | | | |
| Jan | 1 | Bank | 290 | Apr | 6 | Balance b/d | 290 |
| | | | | 2017 | | | |
| Apr | 5 | Balance c/d | 410 | Apr | 5 | Profit and loss | 410 |
| | | | 700 | | | | 700 |
| 2018 | | | | 2017 | | | |
| Jan | 1 | Bank | 410 | Apr | 6 | Balance b/d | 410 |
| | | | | 2018 | | | |
| Apr | 5 | Balance c/d | 500 | Apr | 5 | Profit and loss | 500 |
| | | | 910 | | | | 910 |
| | | | | 2018 | | | |
| | | | | Apr | 6 | Balance b/d | 500 |

**Deferred Taxation**

| | | £000 | | | £000 |
|---|---|---|---|---|---|
| 2016 | | | 2016 | | |
| Apr 5 | Balance c/d | 110 | Apr 5 | Profit and loss[Note] | 110 |
| | | 110 | | | 110 |
| 2017 | | | 2016 | | |
| Apr 5 | Profit and loss | 10 | Apr 6 | Balance b/d | 110 |
| 5 | Balance c/d | 100 | | | |
| | | 110 | | | 110 |
| 2018 | | | 2017 | | |
| Apr 5 | Profit and loss | 100 | Apr 6 | Balance b/d | 100 |
| | | 100 | | | 100 |

The statements of financial position would appear:

| | *2016* | *2017* | *2018* |
|---|---|---|---|
| *Creditors:* | £000 | £000 | £000 |
| Corporation tax | 290 | 410 | 500 |
| *Provisions:* | | | |
| Deferred taxation | 110 | 100 | – |

***Note*: The double entry is to the T-account for profit and loss. Detail from that account is then entered in the statement of profit or loss.**

## Permanent differences

No adjustments are made to the accounting profit for differences between it and the taxable profit that arise because of non-tax-deductible items, such as political donations, and some entertaining expenses.

## A fully worked example

Exhibit 8.5 shows the ledger accounts in which tax will be involved for the first year of a new company, Harlow Ltd. Exhibit 8.6 shows the second year of that company. **This should help make your understanding of this topic clearer – to consider just one year very often leaves many unanswered questions.**

### Exhibit 8.5

Harlow Ltd has just finished its first year of trading on 31 December 2017. Corporation tax throughout was 35%, and income tax was 25%. You are given the following information:

(A) Net trading profit for the year was £165,000, before adjustment for loan-note interest.
(B) Loan-note interest (net) of £12,000 was paid on 31 December 2017 and (C) the income tax deducted was paid on the same date.
(D) An ordinary interim dividend of 10% on the 210,000 £1 ordinary shares was paid on 1 July 2017.
(E) A proposed final ordinary dividend of 25% for the year is to be accrued.[Note]
(F) Depreciation of £12,000 has been charged before arriving at net trading profit. Capital allowances of £37,000 have been approved by Revenue and Customs. Account for timing differences.
(G) Corporation tax on the first year's trading is expected to be £38,500.

**You are required to:**
(*a*) show double entry accounts (other than bank) to record the above;
(*b*) prepare extracts from the statement of profit or loss and statement of financial position.

***Note*: Dividends proposed do not appear in financial statements, nor are they accrued. They should appear only as a note to the financial statements.**

**Loan-note Interest**

| 2017 | | | £ | 2017 | | £ |
|---|---|---|---|---|---|---|
| Dec 31 | Bank | (B) | 12,000 | Dec 31 | Profit and loss | 16,000 |
| 31 | Income tax | (C) | 4,000 | | | |
| | | | 16,000 | | | 16,000 |

**Income Tax**

| 2017 | | | £ | 2017 | | | £ |
|---|---|---|---|---|---|---|---|
| Dec 31 | Bank | (C) | 4,000 | Dec 31 | Loan-note interest | (C) | 4,000 |

**Ordinary Dividends**

| 2017 | | | £ | 2017 | | £ |
|---|---|---|---|---|---|---|
| Jul 1 | Bank | (D) | 21,000 | Dec 31 | Retained profits* | 21,000 |

***This does not appear in the statement of profit or loss. It is shown in the Statement of Changes in Equity (see Section 12.11).**

**Deferred Taxation**

| 2017 | | £ | 2017 | | | £ |
|---|---|---|---|---|---|---|
| Dec 31 | Balance c/d | 8,750 | Dec 31 | Profit and loss* | (F) | 8,750 |

***(F) allowed £37,000 but only charged £12,000 = £25,000 × 35% corporation tax deferred = £8,750.**

**Corporation Tax**

| 2017 | | £ | 2017 | | | £ |
|---|---|---|---|---|---|---|
| Dec 31 | Balance c/d | 38,500 | Dec 31 | Profit and loss | (G) | 38,500 |

**Statement of Profit or Loss (extracts) for the year ending 31 December 2017**

| | | £ | £ |
|---|---|---|---|
| Net trading profit | (A) | | 165,000 |
| *Less* Loan-note interest | (B) | | 16,000 |
| Profit before taxation | | | 149,000 |
| Corporation tax | (G) | 38,500 | |
| Deferred taxation | (F) | 8,750 | |
| | | | (47,250) |
| Profit for the year | | | 101,750 |

**Statement of Financial Position (extracts) as at 31 December 2017**

| | £ |
|---|---|
| *Current liabilities* | |
| Corporation tax | 38,500 |
| *Non-current liabilities* | |
| Deferred tax | 8,750 |

## Exhibit 8.6

Harlow Ltd, as per Exhibit 8.5, has now finished its second year of trading. From 2017 there will be two ledger account balances to be brought forward from Exhibit 8.5. These accounts are:

| | | | |
|---|---|---|---|
| Deferred taxation | (A) | *Cr* | £8,750 |
| Corporation tax | (B) | *Cr* | £38,500 |

You are given the following information:

(D) The proposed ordinary dividend £52,500 was paid on 1 March 2018.
(E) Corporation tax remains at 35% and income tax remains at 25%.
(F) Shares had been bought in STU Ltd and a dividend of £1,500 was received on 31 August 2018.
(G) An interim dividend of 15% on the 210,000 £1 ordinary shares was paid on 1 July 2018.
(H) Loan notes had been bought in RRR Ltd and interest (net) of £4,500 was received on 30 December 2018.
(I) Harlow Ltd paid its own loan-note interest (net) of £12,000 on 31 December 2018, and (I) the income tax account (net) was paid on the same date.
(J) The corporation tax due for 2017 was paid on 30 September 2018.
(K) A final ordinary dividend for the year of 30% was proposed. This will be paid in March 2019.
(L) Corporation tax for the year ended 31 December 2018 is expected to be £41,300.
(M) Depreciation of £28,000 has been charged in the accounts, while capital allowances amounted to £22,000.
(N) Net trading profit after deducting depreciation but before adjusting for the above was £178,000.

**To record these items, we open a tax on profit on ordinary activities account and transfer tax items to it. After all entries have been made, the balance on the account is transferred to the profit and loss.**

**Ordinary Dividends**

| 2018 | | | | £ | 2018 | | | | £ |
|---|---|---|---|---|---|---|---|---|---|
| Mar | 1 | Bank | (C) | 52,500 | Dec | 31 | Profit and loss | | 84,000 |
| Jul | 1 | Bank interim | (F) | 31,500 | | | | | |
| | | | | 84,000 | | | | | 84,000 |

**Investment Income**

| 2018 | | | | £ | 2018 | | | | £ |
|---|---|---|---|---|---|---|---|---|---|
| Dec | 31 | Profit and loss | | 1,500 | Aug | 31 | Bank | (E) | 1,500 |
| | | | | 1,500 | | | | | 1,500 |

**Loan-note Interest Payable**

| 2018 | | | | £ | 2018 | | | | £ |
|---|---|---|---|---|---|---|---|---|---|
| Dec | 31 | Bank | (H) | 12,000 | Dec | 31 | Profit and loss | | 16,000 |
| | 31 | Income tax | | 4,000 | | | | | |
| | | | | 16,000 | | | | | 16,000 |

**Loan-note Interest Receivable**

| 2018 | | | | £ | 2018 | | | | £ |
|---|---|---|---|---|---|---|---|---|---|
| Dec | 31 | Profit and loss | | 6,000 | Dec | 30 | Bank | (G) | 4,500 |
| | | | | | | 30 | Income tax | | 1,500 |
| | | | | 6,000 | | | | | 6,000 |

→

→

**Income Tax**

| 2018 | | | | £ | 2018 | | | | £ |
|---|---|---|---|---|---|---|---|---|---|
| Dec | 30 | Loan-note interest receivable | | 1,500 | Dec | 31 | Loan-note interest payable | | 4,000 |
| | 31 | Bank | (I) | 2,500 | | | | | |
| | | | | 4,000 | | | | | 4,000 |

**Deferred Taxation**

| 2018 | | | | £ | 2018 | | | | £ |
|---|---|---|---|---|---|---|---|---|---|
| Dec | 31 | Tax on profit on ordinary activities (6,000 × 35%) | (M) | 2,100 | Jan | 1 | Balance b/d | (A) | 8,750 |
| | 31 | Balance c/d | | 6,650 | | | | | |
| | | | | 8,750 | | | | | 8,750 |

**Corporation Tax**

| 2018 | | | | £ | 2018 | | | | £ |
|---|---|---|---|---|---|---|---|---|---|
| Sep | 30 | Bank | (J) | 38,500 | Jan | 1 | Balance b/d | (B) | 38,500 |
| Dec | 31 | Accrued c/d | | 41,300 | Dec | 31 | Tax on profit on ordinary activities | (L) | 41,300 |
| | | | | 79,800 | | | | | 79,800 |

**Tax on Profit on Ordinary Activities**

| 2018 | | | | £ | 2018 | | | | £ |
|---|---|---|---|---|---|---|---|---|---|
| Dec | 31 | Corporation tax | (L) | 41,300 | Dec | 31 | Deferred taxation | (M) | 2,100 |
| | | | | | | 31 | Profit and loss | | 39,200 |
| | | | | 41,300 | | | | | 41,300 |

**Statement of Profit or Loss (extract) for the year ending 31 December 2018**

| | | £ | £ |
|---|---|---|---|
| Net trading profit | (O) | | 178,000 |
| *Add* Loan-note interest received | | 6,000 | |
| Investment income | | 1,500 | |
| | | | 7,500 |
| | | | 185,500 |
| *Less* Loan-note interest payable | | | (16,000) |
| Profit before taxation | | | 169,500 |
| Taxation | | | (39,200) |
| Profit for the year | | | 129,700 |

**Statement of Financial Position (extracts) as at 31 December 2018**

| | £ |
|---|---|
| *Current liabilities* | |
| Corporation tax | 41,300 |
| *Non-current liabilities* | |
| Deferred tax | 6,650 |

## Learning outcomes

**You should now have learnt:**

1. Depreciation is not allowed as an expense when calculating tax liability.
2. Capital allowances are the equivalent of depreciation that the government allows to be deducted when calculating tax liability.
3. The profit shown in the financial statements is normally different from assessable profit for corporation tax calculations.
4. Deferred tax eliminates the differences that arise as a result of depreciation being replaced by capital allowances when calculating corporation tax payable.
5. IAS 12 *Income taxes* regulates the calculation of the figure for deferred tax that appears in the statement of financial position.

## Answers to activities

8.1 To answer this question, you need to consider why each of these rules is in place. Depreciation is governed by IAS 16 *Property, plant and equipment* (see Chapter 11). It is calculated so as to reflect the reduction in economic value of an asset over an accounting period. In other words, it is intended to give a true and fair view of the true remaining value of an asset, subject to the effect of the basis upon which the base value of the asset has been derived. For example, if historical cost is the base, the remaining amount after depreciation has been deducted represents that proportion of the original value of the asset that remains at the date of the statement of financial position.

Capital allowances are the government's assessment of how much of the historical cost of an asset can legitimately be treated as an expense in a given year. In most cases, the rate and method of calculation selected bear little relation to either the actual expected economic life of an individual asset or to the extent to which use of an asset has reduced its future economic life.

In some cases, capital allowances are intended to encourage successful business by enabling taxable profits to be reduced significantly in one year so that tax is lower than it would otherwise be. For example, capital allowances of 100% may be permitted for any company operating in economically depressed parts of the UK. The motivation for capital allowances is, therefore, very different from the principles underlying depreciation provisions.

8.2 Capital allowances are allowed as a deduction against profit over the life of a non-current asset, as is depreciation. Thus, although in any particular period the amount of capital allowance is usually different from the depreciation charged in the statement of profit or loss, by the end of the life of a non-current asset, the amount granted in capital allowances will be the same as the total amount of depreciation charged.

8.3 (a) Both businesses will have the same amount of accumulated profits.
(b) The sole proprietor's business will have a greater amount of accumulated profits. It will, therefore, appear more successful than the company, even though both businesses are making the same annual profits. In fact, because the sole proprietor will have more assets in the business than the company (due to the fact that less cash has been paid out), it can be argued that it is the company that is the more successful business.

The answers are different because the sole proprietor has chosen to accept a lower level of net annual income than the owners of the company.

8.4 You will either have found this question simple, straightforward and obvious, or you will have struggled to find the answer. Whichever position you were in, it is important that you remember this question whenever you are thinking about depreciation and/or about deferred tax. The answer is that depreciation is based on the difference between cost and the estimated disposal value of the asset. This asset cost £4,800. It is to be used for three years and its disposal value is estimated at £2,025. The amount to be depreciated over the three years is, therefore, £2,775. At $33\frac{1}{3}$% per annum straight-line, the annual depreciation charge is £925.

## Review questions

***Note***: **Questions 8.5 and 8.6 will be sufficient for those taking examinations with little tax content.**

**8.1** Frank Jon Ltd has just finished its first year of trading to 31 December 2016. Corporation tax throughout was 40% and income tax 20%. You are given the following information:

(*i*) Net trading profit, after adjustment for (*ii*) but before other adjustments, was £390,000.
(*ii*) Depreciation of £70,000 was charged. Capital allowances were £110,000.
(*iii*) An interim dividend of 4% on 0.8 million £1 ordinary shares was paid on 1 July 2016.
(*iv*) Loan-note interest of £14,000 (net) was paid on 31 December 2016.
(*v*) Income tax deducted from loan-note interest was paid on 31 January 2017.
(*vi*) A final dividend of 6% was proposed for the year.
(*vii*) Corporation tax for the year was estimated to be £145,000.

**You are required to:**
(*a*) draw up the double entry accounts recording the above (except bank);
(*b*) show the relevant extracts from the statement of profit or loss and the statement of financial position.

***Note***: **Question 8.2A is concerned with the second year of trading for Frank Jon Ltd.**

**8.2A** Frank Jon Ltd has just finished its second year of trading to 31 December 2017. Balances from Question 8.1 need to be brought forward into this question. Tax rates are the same as for 2016.

The following information is available:

(*i*) The proposed final dividend for 2016 (*see* Review Question 8.1) was paid on 31 January 2017.
(*ii*) Shares in Dagda Ltd were bought on 1 January 2017. A dividend of £4,200 was received on 30 September 2017.
(*iii*) Loan notes in Dagda Ltd were bought on 1 July 2017. Loan-note interest of £8,400 (net) was received on 31 December 2017.
(*iv*) Loan-note interest of £14,000 (net) was paid by Frank Jon Ltd on 31 December 2017.
(*v*) Income tax owing to the Revenue and Customs for 2017 was not paid until 2018. The 2016 income tax was paid on 30 January 2017.
(*vi*) An interim dividend of 5% on 0.8 million £1 ordinary shares was paid on 10 July 2017.
(*vii*) A final dividend of 9% was proposed for the year.
(*viii*) Depreciation of £90,000 was charged. Capital allowances were £120,000.
(*ix*) Net trading profit (before taking into account (*ii*), (*iii*), and (*iv*)) was £540,000.
(*x*) The corporation tax due for 2016 was paid on 1 October 2017. Corporation tax for the year to 31 December 2017 is expected to be £160,000.

**You are required to:**
(*a*) Draw up the double entry accounts recording the above (except bank).
(*b*) Show the relevant extracts from the statement of profit or loss for the year and statement of financial position at the year end.

***Note***: **Question 8.3 is in the style of a typical professional accounting body's examination question. It is not easy. Remember to bring forward the balances from the previous year, some of which will often have to be deduced. The letters (A) to (L) against the information will make it easier for you to check your answer against the one at the back of the book.**

**To answer questions of this type, first prepare all the T-accounts.**

**8.3** Corporation tax for the tax years 2014, 2015, and 2016 was 40% and income tax for each year was 20%.

(A) Tilt Ltd's draft statement of profit or loss for the year ending 31 December 2015 shows a net trading profit from operations of £600,000. This figure is before taking into account (B) and (C1) and (C2).
(B) Loan-note interest paid on 5 December 2015 (gross) was £100,000. Ignore accruals.
($C_1$) Fixed rate interest received is £60,000 (net). Date received is 9 November 2015. Ignore accruals.
($C_2$) A dividend of £1,000 was received from Diamond Ltd on 1 October.
(D) Depreciation was £90,000. This compares with £130,000 capital allowances given by Revenue and Customs. There is to be full provision for all timing differences for 2015.
(E) The income tax bill (net) in respect of (B) and (C1) was paid on 19 December 2015.
(F) Preference dividend paid on 6 July 2015 £16,000.
(G) Ordinary interim dividend paid 8 August 2015 £90,000.
(H) Proposed final ordinary dividend for 2015 (paid in 2016) was £150,000.
(I) Proposed final ordinary dividend for 2014 (paid 10 March 2015) was £120,000.
(J) There was a credit balance on the deferred taxation account at 31 December 2014 of £85,000.
(K) Tax for 2014 had been provided for at £140,000 but was finally agreed at £136,000 (paid on 6 October 2015).
(L) Corporation tax for 2015 is estimated to be £170,000.

**You are required to** enter up the following accounts for the year ended 31 December 2015 for Tilt Ltd: Deferred tax; Income tax; Interest receivable; Loan-note interest; Investment income; Corporation tax; Preference dividends; Ordinary dividends; Statement of profit or loss extract. Also prepare the relevant statement of financial position extracts as at 31 December 2015.

**8.4** Joytan Ltd has a trading profit, before dealing with any of the undermentioned items, for the year ended 31 December 2017 of £500,000. Prepare the statement of profit or loss for the year.

(*a*) The standard rate of income tax is 25%.
(*b*) Joytan Ltd has bought £100,000 of 8% loan notes in another company. Joytan Ltd receives its interest, less income tax, for the year on 6 November 2017.
(*c*) Joytan has issued £300,000 of 10% loan notes, and pays interest, less income tax, for the year on 22 December 2017.
(*d*) No cheque has been paid to Revenue and Customs for income tax.
(*e*) Joytan Ltd has a liability for corporation tax, based on the year's profits for 2017, of £210,000.
(*f*) Joytan Ltd owns 90,000 ordinary shares of £1 each in Plax Ltd, and receives a cheque for the dividend of 15% in October 2017. Plax Ltd is neither a subsidiary company nor a related company of Joytan Ltd.
(*g*) Joytan Ltd proposed a dividend of 9% on its 500,000 ordinary shares of £1 each, payable out of the profits for 2017.
(*h*) Transfer £50,000 to general reserve.
(*i*) Unappropriated profits brought forward from last year amounted to £122,000.

**8.5** Sunset Ltd has an operating profit for the year ended 31 December 2016, before dealing with the following items, of £150,000. Complete the statement of profit or loss.

(*a*) The standard rate of income tax is 25%.
(*b*) Sunset Ltd had issued £50,000 of 6% loan notes. It paid the interest for the year, less income tax, on 31 December 2016.
(*c*) Sunset Ltd owns £20,000 of 5% loan notes in another company. It received a year's interest, less income tax, on 27 December 2016.
(*d*) No cheque has been paid to Revenue and Customs for income tax.
(*e*) Sunset Ltd has 30,000 ordinary shares of £1 each in Moonshine Ltd. Moonshine Ltd paid a dividend to Sunset Ltd of 12% on 24 November 2016. Moonshine Ltd is a 'related company' of Sunset Ltd.

→

(*f*) Sunset Ltd had a liability for corporation tax, based on profits for 2016, of £54,000.
(*g*) Sunset proposed a dividend of 10% on its 200,000 ordinary shares of £1 each, out of the profits for 2016.
(*h*) Transfer £10,000 to general reserve.
(*i*) Retained profits brought forward from last year amounted to £22,480.

**8.6** The following information relates to Kemp plc for the year to 31 March 2016:

| | | £m |
|---|---|---|
| **1** | Dividends | |
| | Proposed final ordinary dividend for the year to 31 March 2015 paid on 31 August 2015 | 28 |
| | Interim ordinary dividend paid on 31 December 2015 | 12 |
| | Proposed final ordinary dividend for the year 31 March 2016 to be paid on 31 July 2016 | 36 |
| **2** | Deferred taxation account | |
| | Credit balance at 1 April 2015 | 3 |
| | During the year to 31 March 2016 a transfer of £5 million was made from profit and loss to the deferred taxation account. | |
| **3** | Tax rates | |
| | Corporation tax 35% | |
| | Income tax 25% | |

**Required:**
Write up the following accounts for the year to 31 March 2016, being careful to insert the appropriate date for each entry and to bring down the balances as at 31 March 2016:

(i) ordinary dividends;
(ii) deferred taxation.

(*Association of Accounting Technicians*)

**8.7A** The following figures appeared in W Ltd's statement of financial position at 31 March 2017:

| | |
|---|---|
| Current liability – corporation tax | £600,000 |
| Deferred taxation | £300,000 |

During the year ended 31 March 2018, W Ltd made a payment of £520,000 to Revenue and Customs in settlement of the company's corporation tax for the year ended 31 March 2017. Dividend payments totalling £60,000 were made during the year ended 31 March 2017 and a further dividend of £200,000 had been proposed at the year end.

Two dividend payments were made during the year ended 31 March 2018. A payment of £200,000 was made for the final dividend for the year ended 31 March 2017. An interim dividend of £40,000 was paid for the year ended 31 March 2018. These payments were made in May 2017 and September 2017 respectively. The directors have provided a final dividend of £240,000 for the year ended 31 March 2018.

W Ltd received a dividend of £12,000 from a UK quoted company. This was received in August 2017.

W Ltd's tax advisers believe that corporation tax of £740,000 will be charged on the company's profits for the year ended 31 March 2018. This amount is net of the tax relief of £104,000 which should be granted in respect of the exceptional loss which the company incurred during the year. It has been assumed that corporation tax will be charged at a rate of 35%. The basic rate of income tax was 25%.

It has been decided that the provision for deferred tax should be increased by £20,000. No provision is to be made in respect of timing differences of £400,000.

**You are required:**

(*a*) to prepare the note which will support the figure for the provision for corporation tax in W Ltd's published statement of profit or loss for the year ended 31 March 2018;

(*b*) to calculate the liability for corporation tax which will appear in W Ltd's published statement of financial position at 31 March 2018;

(*c*) to prepare the deferred tax note which will support the figure for the liability which will appear in W Ltd's published statement of financial position at 31 March 2018.

(*Chartered Institute of Management Accountants*)

chapter 9

# Provisions, reserves and liabilities

## Learning objectives

**After you have studied this chapter, you should be able to:**

- explain the difference between a provision and a liability
- explain the difference between revenue reserves and capital reserves
- describe how capital reserves may be used
- describe what normally comprises distributable profits

## Introduction

In this chapter, you'll learn about the difference between provisions and liabilities and about the difference between revenue reserves and capital reserves. You will also learn about some of the restrictions on the use of reserves and learn more about what is meant by 'distributable profit'.

## 9.1 Provisions

A **provision** is an amount written off or retained in order to provide for renewals of, or diminution in, value of assets, or retained to provide for any known liability of which the amount cannot be determined with 'substantial' accuracy. This therefore covers such items as *provisions for depreciation* and *allowances for doubtful debts*. A *liability* is an amount owing which can be determined with substantial accuracy.

Sometimes, therefore, the difference between a provision and a liability hinges around what is meant by 'substantial' accuracy. Rent owing at the end of a financial year would normally be known with precision, so would obviously be a liability. Legal charges for a court case which has been heard, but for which the lawyers have not yet submitted their bill, would be a provision.

**Chapter 12 clarifies the need for the distinction between liabilities and provisions when the requirements regarding disclosures in the financial statements are examined.**

## 9.2 Revenue reserves

A **revenue reserve** is an account to which an amount has been voluntarily transferred from retained profits to an appropriate *reserve account*. The reserve may be for some particular purpose, such as a *foreign exchange reserve account* created just in case the business should ever meet a situation where it would suffer loss because of foreign currency exchange rate movements; or it could be a *general reserve account* that could be used for any purpose.

See Section 9.3 for a further look at general reserves.

Such transfers are an indication to the shareholders that it would be unwise at the time of the transfer to pay out all the available profits as dividends. The resources represented by this part of the profits should be retained, at least for the time being. Revenue reserves can be called upon in future years to help swell the profits available for dividend purposes.

Why do you think special revenue reserves are used, rather than simply leaving everything in retained profits (which is, itself, a revenue reserve)?

## 9.3 General reserve

A general reserve is one that can be used for any purpose. For example, it may be needed because of the effect of inflation: assume a company needs £4,000 working capital in 2014 and that the volume of trade remains the same for the next three years but that during that time, the general level of prices increases by 25%: the working capital requirement will now be £5,000. If all the profits are distributed, the company will still have only £4,000 working capital which cannot possibly finance the same volume of trade as it did in 2014. Transferring annual amounts of profits to a general reserve instead of paying them out as dividends is one way to help overcome this problem.

In terms of the amount of working capital, what is the difference between doing this and leaving the amount transferred in retained profits?

On the other hand, it may just be the conservatism convention asserting itself, with a philosophy of 'better safe than sorry'; in this case to restrict dividends because the funds they would withdraw from the business may be needed in future. This is sometimes overdone, with the result that a business has excessive amounts of liquid funds being inefficiently used when, if they were paid out to the shareholders, who are, after all, the owners of the business, the shareholders could put the funds to better use themselves.

This then leaves the question of the balance of retained profits. If it is a credit balance, is it a revenue reserve? Yes. If profits are not distributed by way of dividend, they are revenue reserves until such time as they are converted into share capital or transferred to other reserves.

## 9.4 Capital reserves

A **capital reserve** is a reserve which is *not* available for cash dividends. Most capital reserves can never be utilised for cash dividend purposes – notice the use of the word 'cash', as it will be seen later that bonus shares may be issued as a 'non-cash' dividend.

Let's look at the ways in which capital reserves are created.

### Capital reserves created in accordance with the Companies Acts

The Companies Acts state that the following are capital reserves and can never be utilised for the declaration of dividends payable in cash:

1 Capital redemption reserve – *see* Chapter 6.
2 Share premium account – *see* Chapter 5.
3 Revaluation reserve – where an asset has been revalued, an increase is shown by a debit in the requisite asset account and a credit to a revaluation reserve account. The recording of a reduction in value is shown by a credit in the asset account and a debit in the revaluation reserve account.

### Capital reserves created by case law

Distributable profits as defined by the Companies Acts have been described earlier in this book. The definition includes the words 'in accordance with principles generally accepted'. As accounting develops and changes there will obviously be changes made in the 'principles generally accepted'.

Quite a few legal cases have established exactly whether an item represents a distributable profit and, therefore, is available for cash dividend purposes. Where it is not, the item that is not distributable should be transferred to a capital reserve account. These cases will be studied at the more advanced stages of accounting, so will not be dealt with here.

## 9.5 Using capital reserves

These can only be used in accordance with the Companies Acts. The following description of the actions which can be taken assumes that the Articles of Association (*see* Chapter 4) contain no provisions to prohibit such actions.

### Capital redemption reserve (for creation *see* Chapter 6)

1 To be applied in paying up unissued shares of the company as fully paid shares. These are commonly called bonus shares, and are dealt with in Chapter 10.
2 Can be reduced only in the manner as to reduction of share capital (*see* Chapter 10).
3 Can be reduced, in the case of a private company, where the permissible capital payment is greater than the nominal value of shares redeemed/purchased (*see* Chapter 6).

### Share premium account (for creation *see* Chapter 5)

1 The same provision referring to bonus shares as exists with the capital redemption reserve.
2 Writing off expenses and commission paid on the issue of shares that gave rise to the share premium used for this purpose.
3 Providing any premium payable on redemption or purchases of shares or loan notes.

### Revaluation reserve

Where the directors are of the opinion that any amount standing to the credit of the revaluation reserve is no longer necessary then the reserve must be reduced accordingly. An instance of this would be where an increase in the value of an asset had been credited to the revaluation account, and there had subsequently been a fall in the value of that asset.

The revaluation reserve may also be reduced where the permissible capital payment exceeds the nominal value of the shares redeemed/purchased.

### Profits prior to incorporation (for creation *see* Chapter 7)

These can be used for the issuing of bonus shares, paying up partly paid shares, or alternatively they may be used to write down goodwill or some such similar asset.

### Created by case law

These can be used in the issue of bonus shares or in the paying up of partly paid shares.

## 9.6 Distributable profits

Distributable profits have already been defined. Accounting standards will apply unless they come into conflict with the Companies Acts themselves.

Normally the revenue reserves, including any retained profits, would equal distributable profit.

### Distributions in kind

Where a company makes a non-cash distribution, for example by giving an investment, and that item (i.e. in this case the investment) has been revalued, it could generally be said that part of the distribution was unrealised profit locked into investment. However, the Companies Acts allow this because the 'unrealised' profit is 'realised' by the distribution (from the company's viewpoint, anyway).

## 9.7 Distributions and auditors' reports

Distributions cannot be made if the auditor's report is qualified, with one exception. The exception is that if the amount involved is *not* material and the auditor agrees to this fact, then distribution of an item can take place.

If a distribution is unlawfully made, any member knowing it to be so could be made to repay it. If the company could not recover such distributions then legal proceedings could be taken against the directors.

### Learning outcomes

**You should now have learnt:**

1. Provisions involve uncertainty over the precise amount involved, it being impossible to determine the amount with 'substantial' accuracy.
2. Liabilities can be determined with 'substantial' accuracy.
3. That there are two main categories of reserves:
   (*a*) revenue reserves (can be freely distributed);
   (*b*) capital reserves (subject to restrictions on their distribution).
4. That there is often no need to transfer amounts from retained profits into a revenue reserve. However, doing so does signal the likelihood of some future event and so could improve the true and fair view of the financial statements.
5. Some of the uses that can be made of capital reserves.
6. What distributable profits normally comprise.

## Answers to activities

9.1 There is no simple answer to this question. Reserves of this type were fairly common some years ago, mainly because they signalled that the business was being prudent and preparing to meet some future expense. Some people might suggest that some transfers of this type were made so as to retain cash in the business and thus avoid the interest costs of borrowing funds. (Funds already held by a business are the cheapest form of finance available.) It could be argued that transferring reserves from the profit and loss account to a repairs reserve, for example, stops shareholders complaining that they have not received a high enough dividend, thus enabling the company to use its cash resources for other purposes.

However, nowadays, investors are more sophisticated than in the past and they are unlikely to be confused by such a transfer between reserves. That is, the fact that reserves had been transferred into a repairs reserve would not prevent investors from complaining that they had not received a high enough dividend. Also, nowadays, they would both wish to know why the transfer had taken place *and* expect it to be used for the purpose indicated.

In reality, it matters not a bit whether businesses make reserve transfers of this type. They may feel it is more informative to do so, but there is no need for such transfers to occur.

9.2 There is no difference. The cash has not been paid out so, in both cases, working capital increases accordingly. Transferring the amount from retained profits to a general reserve simply indicates that some funds are being retained for an undefined purpose.

## Review question

**9.1** An extract from the draft financial statements of Either Ltd at 30 November 2018 shows the following figures before allowing for any dividend which might be proposed:

| | *£000* |
|---|---|
| Ordinary shares of £1 each | 400 |
| 6% preference shares of £1 each | 150 |
| Capital redemption reserve | 300 |
| Revaluation reserve | 125 |
| General reserve | 80 |
| Retained profits | 13 |
| | 1,068 |
| Profit before taxation for the year | 302 |
| Taxation | 145 |
| | 157 |

*Additional information*:

(*i*) The revaluation reserve consists of an increase in the value of freehold property following a valuation in 2016. The property concerned was one of three freehold properties owned by the company and was subsequently sold at the revalued amount.

(*ii*) It has been found that a number of inventory items have been included at cost price, but were being sold after the date of the statement of financial position at prices well below cost. To allow for this, inventory at 30 November 2018 would need to be reduced by £35,000.

(*iii*) Provision for directors' remuneration should be made in the sum of £43,000.

(*iv*) Included on the statement of financial position is £250,000 of research and development expenditure carried forward.

(*v*) No dividends have yet been paid on either ordinary or preference shares for the year to 30 November 2018, but the directors wish to pay the maximum permissible dividends for the year.

(*vi*) Since the draft financial statements were produced it has been reported that a major customer of Either Ltd has gone into liquidation and is unlikely to be able to pay more than 50p in the £ to its creditors. At 30 November 2018 this customer owed £60,000 and this has since risen to £180,000.

(*vii*) It has been decided that the depreciation rates for plant and machinery are too low but the effect of the new rates has not been taken into account in constructing the draft financial statements. The following information is available:

| Plant and machinery | | £ |
|---|---|---|
| Purchases at the commencement of the business on 1 December 2014 at cost | | 100,000 |
| Later purchases were: | 1 June 2016 | 25,000 |
| | 29 February 2017 | 28,000 |
| | 31 May 2017 | 45,000 |
| | 1 December 2017 | 50,000 |

In the draft financial statements depreciation has been charged at the rate of 25% using the reducing balance method and charging a full year's depreciation in the year of purchase. It has been decided to change to the straight line method using the same percentage but charging only an appropriate portion of the depreciation in the year of purchase. There have been no sales of plant and machinery during the period.

**Required:**

(*a*) Calculate the maximum amount which the directors of Either Ltd may propose as a dividend to be paid to the ordinary shareholders whilst observing the requirements of the Companies Acts. Show all workings and state any assumptions made.

(*b*) Outline and discuss any differences which might have been made to your answer to (*a*) if the company were a public limited company.

For the purposes of this question you may take it that corporation tax is levied at the rate of 50%.

(*Association of Chartered Certified Accountants*)

chapter 10

# The increase and reduction of the share capital of limited companies

## Learning objectives

**After you have studied this chapter, you should be able to:**

- explain the various ways in which a limited company may alter its share capital
- describe the difference between a bonus issue and a rights issue of shares
- explain why a company may introduce a scheme for the reduction of its capital
- describe the effect upon the statement of financial position of bonus issues, rights issues and schemes for the reduction of capital

## Introduction

Sometimes companies need to alter their issued share capital. In this chapter, you'll learn about the alternatives available. You'll learn about the difference between scrip issues and rights issues and how to record the appropriate ledger account entries when either occurs. You will also learn that the nominal value of share capital can be reduced, and how to do so.

## 10.1 Alteration of capital

A limited company may, if authorised by its Articles, and if the correct legal formalities are observed, alter its share capital in any of the following ways:

1. Increase its share capital by issuing new shares, e.g. increase authorised share capital from £500,000 to £1 million and then issue more shares.
2. Consolidate and divide all or any of its share capital into shares of a larger nominal value than its existing shares, for instance convert 500,000 ordinary shares of £1 each into 100,000 ordinary shares of £5 each.
3. Subdivide all, or any, of its shares into shares of smaller denominations, e.g. convert 1 million ordinary shares of £1 each into 2 million ordinary shares of £0.50 each, or 4 million ordinary shares of 25p each.
4. Cancel shares which have not been taken up. This is known as 'diminution of capital', and is not to be confused with 'reduction of capital', described later in the chapter. Thus, a company with an authorised share capital of £200,000 and an issued share capital of £175,000 can alter its share capital to authorised share capital of £175,000 and issued share capital of £175,000.
5. Redenominate shares from a fixed nominal value in one currency (e.g. £) to a fixed nominal value in another currency (e.g. €).

Why do you think a company would wish to change its share capital?

## 10.2 Bonus shares

**Bonus shares** are shares issued to existing shareholders free of charge. An alternative name often used is *scrip issue*.

If the Articles give the power, and the requisite legal formalities are observed, the following may be applied in the issuing of bonus shares:

1 the retained profits;
2 any other revenue reserve;
3 any capital reserve, e.g. share premium.

This is thus all of the reserves.

The reason why this should ever be needed can be illustrated by taking the somewhat exaggerated example shown in Exhibit 10.1:

### Exhibit 10.1

When Better Price Ltd started in business 50 years ago, it issued 10,000 ordinary shares of £1 each and deposited £10,000 in the bank. The company has constantly retained a proportion of its profits to finance its operations, thus diverting them from being used for cash dividend purposes. This has preserved an appropriate level of working capital.

The firm's statement of financial position as at 31 December 2017 is shown as:

**Better Price Ltd**
**Statement of Financial Position as at 31 December 2017**
(before bonus shares are issued)

| | £ |
|---|---:|
| Non-current assets | 150,000 |
| Current assets | 220,000 |
| Total assets | 370,000 |
| Current liabilities | (70,000) |
| Net assets | 300,000 |
| Share capital | 10,000 |
| Reserves (including retained profits) | 290,000 |
| | 300,000 |

If an annual profit of £45,000 was being earned (i.e. 15% on capital employed) and £10,000 were paid annually as cash dividends, then the dividend declared each year would be 100% (i.e. a dividend of £10,000 on shares with a nominal value of £10,000).

It is obvious that the dividends and the share capital are out of step with one another. Employees and trade unions could start complaining due to a lack of accounting knowledge (or even misuse of it) because they believe that the company is making unduly excessive profits. Customers may also be deluded into thinking that they are being charged excessive prices. Even though this could be demonstrated not to be true because of the prices charged by competitors, they may still have the feeling that they are somehow being duped.

In fact, an efficient company in this industry may only be achieving 'average' rewards for the risks it has taken if it is making a profit of 15% on capital employed. The figure of 100% for the dividend is due to the very misleading convention in accounting in the UK of calculating dividends in relationship to the nominal amount of the share capital, rather than the capital employed. →

If it is felt that £80,000 of the reserves could not be used for dividend purposes, due to the fact that the net assets should remain at a minimum of £90,000, made up of non-current assets of £80,000 and working capital of £10,000, then besides the £10,000 share capital which cannot be returned to the shareholders there are also £80,000 of reserves which cannot be rationally returned to them. Instead of this £80,000 being called reserves, it might as well be called capital, as it is needed by the business on a permanent basis.

To remedy this position, as well as some other less obvious needs, the concept of bonus shares was developed. The reserves are made non-returnable to the shareholders by being converted into share capital. Each holder of one ordinary share of £1 each will receive eight bonus shares (in the shape of eight ordinary shares) of £1 each. The statement of financial position, if the bonus shares had been issued immediately, would be:

**Better Price Ltd**
**Statement of Financial Position as at 31 December 2017**
(after bonus shares are issued)

| | £ |
|---|---|
| Non-current assets | 150,000 |
| Current assets | 220,000 |
| Total assets | 370,000 |
| Current liabilities | (70,000) |
| Net assets | 300,000 |
| Share capital (£10,000 + £80,000) | 90,000 |
| Reserves (£290,000 − £80,000) | 210,000 |
| | 300,000 |

When the annual dividends of £10,000 are declared in the future, they will represent:

$$\frac{£10,000}{£90,000} \times \frac{100}{1} = \text{a dividend of } 11.1\%$$

This will cause fewer problems in the minds of employees, trade unions and customers.

Of course the issue of bonus shares may be seen by any of the interested parties to be some form of excessive generosity on the part of the company. To give eight shares of £1 each free for one previously owned may be seen as unfair by employees and their trade unions. In fact, the shareholders have gained nothing. Before the bonus issue there were 10,000 shareholders who owned between them £300,000 of net assets. Therefore, assuming for this purpose that the book 'value' is the same as any other 'value', each share was worth £30. After the bonus issue, each shareholder has nine shares for every one share held before. If a shareholder had owned one share only, he now owns nine shares. He is therefore, the owner of 9/90,000 of the company. The 'value' of the net assets is £300,000, and he owns 9/90,000 of them, so his shares are worth £30. This is exactly the same 'value' as that applying before the bonus issue was made.

It would be useful, in addition, to refer to other matters for comparison. Anyone who had owned a £1 share 50 years ago, then worth £1, would now have nine £1 shares. A new house of a certain type 50 years ago might have cost £*x*; it may now cost £9*x*. Price inflation affects different items in different ways. The cost of a bottle of beer may now be *y* times greater than it was 50 years ago, a loaf of bread may cost *z* times more, and so on. But, at least the shareholders now have some tangible increase in the nominal value of their investment. Of course, the company has brought a lot of trouble on itself by waiting so many years to capitalise its reserves. It should have been done in several stages over the years.

This is a very simplified example, but it is a situation many companies have had to face. There is, also, no doubt that a misunderstanding of accounting and financial matters has caused a great deal of unnecessary friction in the past and will probably still do so in the future. Yet another very common misunderstanding is the assumption that the asset statement of financial position values equal the amount they could be sold for. Thus, a profit of £100,000 when the book value of the net assets is £200,000 may appear to be excessive yet, if the realisable value of the net assets were used, the net worth of the company may be £2 million, making a profit of £100,000 appear perhaps a little low, rather than appearing excessive.

The accounting entries when bonus shares are issued are to debit the reserve accounts utilised, and to credit a bonus account. The shares are then issued and the entry required to record this is to credit the share capital account and to debit the bonus account. The journal entries in our example would be:

**The Journal**

| | *Dr* | *Cr* |
|---|---|---|
| | £ | £ |
| Reserve account(s) (show each account separately) | 80,000 | |
| Bonus account | | 80,000 |
| *Transfer of an amount equal to the bonus payable in fully paid shares* | | |
| Bonus account | 80,000 | |
| Share capital account | | 80,000 |
| *Allotment and issue of 80,000 shares of £1 each, in satisfaction of the bonus declared* | | |

## 10.3 Rights issue

You learnt in Chapter 5 that a company can also increase its issued share capital by making a *rights issue*. This is the issue of shares to existing shareholders at a price lower than the ruling market price of the shares. You will remember that the price is lower so as to compensate for the reduction in value of shares held previously.

The price at which the shares of a profitable company are quoted on the Stock Exchange is usually higher than the nominal value of the shares. For instance, the market price of the shares of a company might be quoted at £2.50 while the nominal value per share is only £1.00. If the company has 800,000 shares of £1 each and declares a rights issue of one for every eight held at a price of £1.50 per share, it is obvious that it will be cheaper for the existing shareholders to buy the rights issue at this price instead of buying the same shares in the open market for £2.50 per share. Assume that all the rights issue were taken up, then the number of shares taken up will be 100,000 (i.e. 800,000 ÷ 8), and the amount paid for them will be £150,000. The journal entries will be:

**The Journal**

| | *Dr* | *Cr* |
|---|---|---|
| | £ | £ |
| Cash | 150,000 | |
| Share capital | | 100,000 |
| Share premium | | 50,000 |
| Being the rights issue of one for every eight shares held at a price of £1.50 nominal value being £1.00 | | |

As the nominal value of each share is £1.00 while £1.50 was paid, the extra 50p constitutes a share premium to the company.

Notice also that the market value of the shares will be reduced or 'diluted' by the rights issue, as was the case for bonus shares. Before the rights issue there were 800,000 shares at a price of £2.50, giving a market capitalisation of £2 million. After the rights issue there are 900,000 shares and the assets have increased by £150,000. The market value may now be £2.39 [(£2 million + £150,000)/900,000], although the precise market price after the rights issue will be influenced by the information given surrounding the sale about the future prospects of the company and may not be exactly the £2.39 calculated above.

## 10.4 Reduction of capital

### Where capital is not represented by assets

Any scheme for the reduction of capital needs to go through legal formalities via the shareholders and other interested parties, and must receive the consent of the court.

Capital reduction means that the share capital – all of it if there is only one class such as ordinary shares, or all or part of it if there is more than one class of shares – has been subjected to a lessening of its nominal value, or of the called-up part of the nominal value. Thus:

(*a*) a £4 share might be converted into a £3 share;
(*b*) a £5 share might be converted into a £1 share;
(*c*) a £3 share, £2 called up, might be converted into a £1 share fully paid up;
(*d*) a £5 share, £3 called up, might be converted into a £3 share £1 called up;

plus any other variations.

Why should such action be necessary? The reasons are rather like the issue of bonus shares in reverse. However, in this case, the share capital has fallen out of line with the assets, in that the share capital is not fully represented by assets. For example, Robert Ltd may have a statement of financial position as follows:

**Robert Ltd**
**Statement of Financial Position as at 31 December 2017**

| | £ |
|---|---|
| Net assets | 300,000 |
| Equity | |
| 100,000 ordinary shares of £5 each, fully paid | 500,000 |
| *Less* Retained profits (debit balance) | (200,000) |
| | 300,000 |

The net assets are shown at £300,000, and it is felt that the book value represents a true and fair view of their actual value. The company will almost certainly be precluded from paying dividends until the debit balance of retained profits has been eradicated and replaced with a credit balance. If profits remaining after taxation are now running at the rate of £30,000 per annum, it will be seven years before a dividend can be paid. One reason for buying shares is to provide income (although there may well enter another reason, such as capital appreciation). Consequently, the denial of income to the shareholders for this period of time could seriously affect the company.

A solution would be to cancel, i.e. reduce, the capital which was no longer represented by assets. In this case, £200,000 of the share capital can lay no claim to any assets. The share capital should therefore be reduced by £200,000. This is done by converting the shares into £3 shares fully paid instead of £5 shares. The statement of financial position would become:

**Robert Ltd**
**Statement of Financial Position as at 31 December 2017**

| | £ |
|---|---|
| Net assets | 300,000 |
| | 300,000 |
| Ordinary share capital | 300,000 |
| | 300,000 |

Now that there is no debit balance of retained profits, the £30,000 available profit next year can be distributed as dividends.

Of course, the Robert Ltd example has been simplified to make what is being explained easier to understand. Often, both preference and ordinary shareholders are involved. Sometimes, loan-note holders as well. Even creditors occasionally sacrifice part of the amount owing to them, the idea being that the increase in working capital so generated will help the business to achieve prosperity, in which case the creditors hope to once again enjoy the profitable contact that they used to have with the company.

Capital reduction schemes are matters for negotiation between the various interested parties. For instance, preference shareholders may be quite content for the nominal value of their shares to be reduced if the rate of interest they receive is increased accordingly. As with any negotiation, the various parties will put forward their points of view and discussions will take place until a compromise solution is arrived at. When the court's sanction has been obtained, the accounting entries are:

1 For amounts written off assets:
*Dr* Capital reduction account
*Cr* Various asset accounts

2 For reduction in liabilities (e.g. creditors):
*Dr* Liability accounts
*Cr* Capital reduction account

3 The reduction in the share capital:
*Dr* Share capital accounts (each type)
*Cr* Capital reduction account

4 If a credit balance now exists on the capital reduction account:
*Dr* Capital reduction account (to close)
*Cr* Capital reserve

It is unlikely that there would ever be a debit balance on the capital reduction account, as the court would rarely agree to any scheme which would bring this about.

Capital reduction schemes for private companies are used less frequently now than previously, thanks to companies having been granted the right to purchase their own shares.

## Where some of the assets are no longer needed

Where some of the assets are no longer needed, probably due to a contraction in a company's activities, it may find itself with a surplus of liquid assets. Subject to the legal formalities being observed, in this case the reduction of capital is effected by returning cash to the shareholders, i.e.:

1 *Dr* Share capital account (with amount returnable)
*Cr* Sundry shareholders

2 *Dr* Sundry shareholders
*Cr* Bank (amount actually paid)

Such a scheme could be objected to by the creditors if it affected their interests.

## Learning outcomes

**You should now have learnt:**

1 That a limited company may alter its share capital if it is authorised to do so by its Articles of Association.

2 Alterations to share capital can be made by a limited company:
   (*a*) issuing new shares;
   (*b*) consolidating all or any of its share capital into shares of a higher nominal value;
   (*c*) subdividing all or any of its share capital into shares of a lower nominal value;
   (*d*) cancelling shares that have not been 'taken up' – the difference between the 'authorised share capital' and the 'issued share capital';
   (*e*) redenominating shares into a different currency.

3 Some reasons why companies change their share capital.

4 That where share capital is overvalued in relation to assets, a capital reduction scheme may be adopted in order to bring the share capital into line with the underlying asset value of the business as reported in the statement of financial position.

## Answer to activity

10.1 As you will see later in this chapter, there are many possible reasons. It may be that the nominal value of the share capital is significantly understated compared with current earnings. An increase in nominal share capital would help redress this imbalance and make things like earnings per share more intuitively meaningful. Alternatively, it may be that large reserves have been built up and the company wishes to increase the amount of its share capital by converting the reserves into shares. Another possibility is that the share price has risen significantly since the shares were first quoted on the Stock Exchange and it now appears unreasonably high relative to comparable shares. By splitting each share into a number of shares of a lower nominal value, the share price can be brought back to an appropriate level. Don't forget, companies can both increase and reduce the nominal value of their share capital.

## Review questions

**10.1** The Merton Manufacturing Co Ltd has been in business for many years making fitted furniture and chairs. During 2017 and 2018 substantial losses have been sustained on the manufacture of chairs and the directors have decided to concentrate on the fitted furniture side of the business which is expected to produce a profit of at least £22,500 per annum before interest charges and taxation. A capital reduction scheme has been proposed under which:

(*i*) a new ordinary share of 50p nominal value will be created;
(*ii*) the £1 ordinary shares will be written off and the shareholders will be offered one new ordinary share for every six old shares held;
(*iii*) the £1 6% redeemable preference shares will be cancelled and the holders will be offered for every three existing preference shares one new ordinary share;
(*iv*) the existing 11½% loan note will be exchanged for a new loan note yielding 8% at a rate of two old loan notes for three new loan notes. In addition, existing loan-note holders will be offered one new ordinary share for every £4 of the old loan note held;

(*v*) existing reserves will be written off;
(*vi*) goodwill is totally impaired and to be written off;
(*vii*) any remaining balance of write-off which is necessary is to be achieved by writing down plant and equipment; and
(*viii*) existing ordinary shareholders will be invited to subscribe for two fully paid new ordinary shares at par for every three old shares held.

The statement of financial position of the Merton Manufacturing Co Ltd immediately prior to the capital reduction is as follows:

| | £ | £ |
|---|---|---|
| *Non-current intangible assets* | | |
| Goodwill | | 50,000 |
| *Non-current tangible assets* | | |
| Freehold land and buildings at cost | | 95,000 |
| Plant and equipment at cost | 275,000 | |
| *Less* Depreciation to date | (89,500) | |
| | | 185,500 |
| | | 330,500 |
| *Current assets* | | |
| Inventory | 25,000 | |
| Accounts receivable | 50,000 | |
| | | 75,000 |
| Total assets | | 405,500 |
| *Current liabilities* | | |
| Accounts payable | 63,500 | |
| Bank overdraft | 15,850 | |
| | 79,350 | |
| *Non-current liabilities* | | |
| 11½% loan note, secured on the freehold land and buildings | 100,000 | |
| Total liabilities | | 179,350 |
| Net assets | | 226,150 |
| *Equity* | | |
| £1 ordinary shares fully paid | | 90,000 |
| 6% £1 redeemable preference shares fully paid | | 150,000 |
| Share premium account | | 25,000 |
| Retained profits | | (38,850) |
| | | 226,150 |

On liquidation, freehold land and buildings are expected to produce £120,000; plant and equipment £40,000; inventory £15,000; and accounts receivable £45,000. Goodwill has no value.

There are no termination costs associated with ceasing the manufacture of chairs.

**Required:**

(*a*) Assuming that the necessary approval is obtained and that the new share issue is successful, produce a statement of financial position of the company showing the position immediately after the scheme has been put into effect.
(*b*) Show the effect of the scheme on the expected earnings of the old shareholders.
(*c*) Indicate the points which a preference shareholder should take into account before voting on the scheme.

Corporation tax may be taken at $33^1/_3$%.

(*Association of Chartered Certified Accountants*)

**10.2** Deflation Ltd, which had experienced trading difficulties, decided to reorganise its finances. On 31 December 2016 a final trial balance extracted from the books showed the following position:

| | | £ | £ |
|---|---|---|---|
| Share capital, authorised and issued: | | | |
| 150,000 6% cumulative preference shares of £1 each | | | 150,000 |
| 200,000 ordinary shares of £1 each | | | 200,000 |
| Share premium account | | | 40,000 |
| Retained profits | | 114,375 | |
| Preliminary expenses | | 7,250 | |
| Goodwill (at cost) | | 55,000 | |
| Trade accounts payable | | | 43,500 |
| Accounts receivable | | 31,200 | |
| Bank overdraft | | | 51,000 |
| Leasehold property | (at cost) | 80,000 | |
| | (provision for depreciation) | | 30,000 |
| Plant and machinery | (at cost) | 210,000 | |
| | (provision for depreciation) | | 62,500 |
| Inventory | | 79,175 | |
| | | 577,000 | 577,000 |

Approval of the Court was obtained for the following scheme for reduction of capital:

1 The preference shares to be reduced to £0.75 per share.
2 The ordinary shares to be reduced to £0.125 per share.
3 One £0.125 ordinary share to be issued for each £1 of gross preference dividend arrears; the preference dividend had not been paid for three years.
4 The balance on the share premium account to be utilised.
5 Plant and machinery to be written down to £75,000.
6 The retained profits, and all intangible assets, to be written off.

At the same time as the resolution to reduce capital was passed, another resolution was approved restoring the total authorised capital to £350,000, consisting of 150,000 6% cumulative preference shares of £0.75 each and the balance in ordinary shares of £0.125 each. As soon as the above resolutions had been passed, 500,000 ordinary shares were issued at par, for cash, payable in full upon application.

**You are required:**

(*a*) to show the journal entries necessary to record the above transactions in the company's books; and

(*b*) to prepare a statement of financial position of the company, after completion of the scheme.

(*Institute of Chartered Accountants*)

**10.3** On 31 March 2016, the following was the statement of financial position of Greenmantle Ltd:

**Statement of Financial Position**

| | £ | £ |
|---|---|---|
| *Non-current assets* | | |
| Goodwill and trade marks as valued | 896,000 | |
| Plant and machinery (at cost *less* depreciation) | 1,024,000 | |
| Furniture and fittings (at cost *less* depreciation) | 26,880 | 1,946,880 |
| *Current assets* | | |
| Inventory | 608,640 | |
| Sundry accounts receivable | 238,720 | |
| Cash | 960 | |
| | | 848,320 |
| Total assets | | 2,795,200 |
| *Current liabilities* | | |
| Sundry accounts payable | 106,240 | |
| Bank overdraft | 142,080 | |
| | | (248,320) |
| Net assets | | 2,546,880 |
| Equity | | |
| *Authorised capital* | | |
| 640,000 6% preference shares of £1 each | 640,000 | |
| 9.6 million ordinary shares of 50p each | 4,800,000 | |
| | 5,440,000 | |
| *Issued and fully paid capital* | | |
| 320,000 6% preference shares of £1 each | | 320,000 |
| 5.6 million ordinary shares of 50p each | | 2,800,000 |
| | | 3,120,000 |
| Capital reserve | 192,000 | |
| *Less*: Retained profits | (765,120) | (573,120) |
| | | 2,546,880 |

The following scheme of capital reduction was sanctioned by the Court and agreed by the shareholders:

(*a*) Preference shares were to be reduced to 80p each.
(*b*) Ordinary shares were to be reduced to 25p each.
(*c*) The capital reserve was to be eliminated.
(*d*) The reduced shares of both classes were to be consolidated into new ordinary shares of £1 each.
(*e*) An issue of £960,000 5% loan notes at par was to be made to provide fresh working capital.
(*f*) The sum written-off the issued capital of the company and the capital reserve to be used to write off the debit balance of retained profit and to reduce non-current assets by the following amounts:

| | |
|---|---|
| Goodwill and trade marks | £800,000 |
| Plant and machinery | £76,800 |
| Furniture and fittings | £14,080 |

(*g*) The bank overdraft was to be paid off out of the proceeds of the loan notes which were duly issued and paid in full.

A further resolution was passed to reduce the authorised capital of the company to 5,600,000 ordinary shares of £1 each.

**Required:**
Prepare journal entries (cash transactions to be journalised) to give effect to the above scheme and draw up the statement of financial position of the company after completion of the scheme.

**10.4A** The statement of financial position of Tatters Ltd on 31 December 2015 was as follows:

**Statement of Financial Position**

| | £ | £ |
|---|---|---|
| Goodwill | | 50,000 |
| *Non-current assets* | | 190,000 |
| | | 240,000 |
| *Current assets* | | |
| Inventory | 21,000 | |
| Work in progress | 3,000 | |
| Accounts receivable | 25,000 | |
| Bank | 18,000 | |
| | | 67,000 |
| *Capital expenses* | | |
| Formation expenses | | 3,000 |
| Total assets | | 310,000 |
| Current liabilities: accounts payable | 30,000 | |
| Non-current liabilities: 5% loan notes | 60,000 | |
| Total liabilities | | (90,000) |
| | | 220,000 |
| *Equity* | | |
| Issued share capital | | |
| 200,000 ordinary shares of £1 each | | 200,000 |
| 100,000 4% cumulative preference shares of £1 each | | 100,000 |
| | | 300,000 |
| Retained profits | | (80,000) |
| | | 220,000 |

The dividend on the preference shares is £12,000 in arrears. A scheme of reconstruction was accepted by all parties and was completed on 1 January 2016.

A new company was formed, Rags Ltd, with an authorised share capital of £250,000, consisting of 250,000 ordinary shares of £1 each. This company took over all the assets of Tatters Ltd. The purchase consideration was satisfied partly in cash and partly by the issue, at par, of shares and 6% loan notes by the new company in accordance with the following arrangements:

1 The creditors of the old company received, in settlement of each £10 due to them, £6 in cash and four fully paid ordinary shares in the new company.
2 The holders of preference shares in the old company received nine fully paid ordinary shares in the new company to every ten preference shares in the old company and four fully paid ordinary shares in the new company for every £5 of arrears of dividend.
3 The ordinary shareholders in the old company received one fully paid share in the new company for every four ordinary shares in the old company.
4 The holders of 5% loan notes in the old company received £50 in cash and £50 of 6% loan notes issued at par for every £100 loan notes held in the old company.
5 The balance of the authorised capital of the new company was issued at par for cash and was fully paid on 1 January 2016.
6 Goodwill was eliminated, the inventory was valued at £15,000 and the other current assets were brought into the new company's books at the amounts at which they appeared in the old company's statement of financial position. The balance of the purchase consideration represented the agreed value of the non-current assets.

**You are required to show:**

(*a*) the closing entries in the realisation account and the sundry shareholders account in the books of Tatters Ltd;

(*b*) your calculation of:
  (*i*) the purchase consideration for the assets, and
  (*ii*) the agreed value of the non-current assets;
(*c*) the summarised statement of financial position of Rags Ltd as on 1 January 2016.

**10.5A** The ledger balances of Timely Ltd at 31 March 2018 were as follows:

| | £ |
|---|---|
| Freehold premises | 162,000 |
| Plant | 540,000 |
| Inventory | 147,600 |
| Accounts receivable | 172,800 |
| Development expenditure* | 198,000 |
| Cash at bank | 19,800 |
| Retained profits (debit balance) | 217,800 |
| 450,000 8% preference shares of £1 each | 450,000 |
| 900,000 ordinary shares of £1 each | 900,000 |
| Accounts payable | 108,000 |

A capital reduction scheme has been sanctioned under which the 450,000 preference shares are to be reduced to 60p each, fully paid; and the 900,000 ordinary shares are to be reduced to 25p each, fully paid.

Development expenditure and the debit balance of retained profits are to be written off, the balance remaining being used to reduce the book value of the plant.

**Required:**
Prepare the journal entries recording the reduction scheme and the statement of financial position as it would appear immediately after the reduction. Narrations are not required in connection with journal entries.

*** Note: Development expenditure is a non-current asset (*See* Chapter 11).**

chapter 11

# Accounting standards, related documents and accounting ethics

## Learning objectives

**After you have studied this chapter, you should be able to:**

- explain the measures being taken by the International Accounting Standards Board to develop a framework for the preparation and presentation of financial statements
- describe the full range of international accounting standards currently in issue and their aims and objectives
- describe what fundamental ethical principles an accountant must follow

## Introduction

In this chapter, you'll learn about the background to the formation of the International Accounting Standards Board and about the range of international accounting standards and international financial reporting standards currently in force; and you will be introduced to the fundamental ethical principles all accountants must follow.

## 11.1 Why do we need accounting standards?

Accounting is used in every kind of business and organisation from large multinational organisations to your local shop, from sole proprietors to companies. It can cover an unlimited range of activities as different as breweries, charities, churches, dentists, doctors, lawyers, mines, oil wells, betting shops, banks, cinemas, circuses, undertakers, farms, waste disposal, deep-sea diving, airlines, estate agents and so on.

Let's assume that you have received a copy of the published financial statements of a company. You want to be sure that you can rely on the methods it selected to calculate its revenues, expenditures and statement of financial position values. Without this assurance you would not be able to have any faith at all in the figures, and could not sensibly take any decision concerning your relationship with the company.

It is the same for all investors. People invest in organisations of all types and they would all like to have faith and trust in the figures reported in their financial statements. But this diversity of type of business, and also of size, means that, while general principles can be laid down, detailed regulations that it would make sense to apply to one company would be wholly inappropriate for another company. It is, quite simply, impossible to provide 100% assurance of the validity of the financial statements of every conceivable organisation through the creation of a single set of rules and procedures. There has to be some flexibility within the rules laid down.

If it isn't feasible to produce a set of all-encompassing regulations, why bother with rules at all? To understand why there was a move to regulation, we need to look back to what happened in the 1960s.

## 11.2 The background in the UK

In the late 1960s there was a general outcry that the methods used by different businesses were showing vastly different profits on similar data. In the UK, a controversy had arisen following the takeover of AEI Ltd by GEC Ltd. In fighting the takeover bid made by GEC, the AEI directors had produced a forecast, in the tenth month of their financial year, that the profit before tax for the year would be £10 million. After the takeover, the financial statements of AEI for that same year showed a loss of £4.5 million. The difference was attributed to there being £5 million of 'matters substantially of fact' and £9.5 million of 'adjustments which remain matters substantially of judgement'.

The financial pages of the national press started demanding action, calling for the accounting profession to lay down consistent principles for businesses to follow.

In December 1969, the Institute of Chartered Accountants in England and Wales issued a *Statement of Intent on Accounting Standards in the 1970s*. The Institute set up the Accounting Standards Steering Committee in 1970. Over the following six years, it was joined by the five other UK and Irish accountancy bodies and, in 1976, the committee became the Accounting Standards Committee (ASC). The six accountancy bodies formed the Consultative Committee of Accountancy Bodies (CCAB).

Prior to the issue of any accounting standard by the ASC, a great deal of preparatory work was done and an exposure draft (ED) was issued and sent for comment to those with a special interest in the topic. The journals of the CCAB (i.e. the official magazines of each of the six accountancy bodies) also gave full details of the exposure drafts. After the period allowed for consultation ended, if it was seen to be desirable an accounting standard on the topic was issued. The standards issued by the ASC were called Statements of Standard Accounting Practice (SSAPs).

Because the ASC had to obtain approval from its six professional accountancy body members, it did not appear to be as decisive and independent as was desired. In 1990, a new body, the Accounting Standards Board (ASB), took over the functions of the ASC. The ASB was more independent of the accounting bodies and could issue its recommendations, known as financial reporting standards (FRSs), without approval from any other body. The ASB adopted the SSAPs in force and began to phase them out. As with the ASC, the ASB issued exposure drafts – FREDs – on which comments were invited prior to the issue of a new standard.

In 1997, the ASB issued a third category of standard – the Financial Reporting Standard for Smaller Entities (FRSSE). SSAPs and FRSs had generally been developed with the larger company in mind. The FRSSE was the ASB's response to the view that smaller companies should not have to apply all the cumbersome rules contained in the SSAPs and FRSs. It was, in effect, a collection of some of the rules from virtually all the other accounting standards. Small companies could choose whether or not to apply the FRSSE or continue to apply all the other accounting standards.

In addition to the FRSs and the FRSSE, the ASB also issued Urgent Issues Task Force Abstracts (UITFs). These were issued in response to an urgent need to regulate something pending the issue of a new or amended FRS. They had the same status as an FRS but, due to the perceived urgent need for them to be issued, no exposure drafts were issued before they were released.

While there is no general law compelling observation of the standards, accounting standards have had statutory recognition since the Companies Act 1989. As a result, apart from entities exempted from certain standards or sections within standards – SSAPs 13 (*Research and development*) and 25 (*Segmental reporting*), and FRS 1 (*Cash flow statements*), for example, all contained exemption clauses based on company size – accounting standards must be complied with by all entities that are reporting under UK GAAP when preparing financial statements intended to present a 'true and fair view'. The Companies Acts state that failure to comply with the requirements of an accounting standard must be explained in the financial statements.

Historically, the main method of ensuring compliance with the standards by their members has always been through each professional accountancy body's own disciplinary procedures against their members.

The ASB felt this was insufficient – such measures only seek to control individual accountants, not the organisations they work for. As a result, it created a Review Panel with power to prosecute companies under civil law where their financial statements contain a major breach of the standards.

In 2005, most companies whose shares were quoted on the London Stock Exchange were required to switch to International Accounting Standards, and other entities could do so if they wished. In 2007, this was extended to companies listed on the Alternative Investment Market (AIM). All other companies were given the option of doing so and, by 2010, many had switched voluntarily to International GAAP. Among those that had not switched to International GAAP, many had changed from UK GAAP terminology in their financial statements (such as 'stock' and 'Profit and Loss Account') to International GAAP terminology (such as 'inventory' and 'statement of profit or loss').

The usefulness of UK accounting standards was clearly on the wane. Consequently, in 2010 the ASB published an exposure draft on the future of financial reporting in the UK and Republic of Ireland. It proposed a revised **Conceptual Framework** aimed at balancing the needs of preparers and users of financial statements – *see* Section 11.4 – and sought to simplify UK standards into a concise, coherent and updated form.

In 2012 the Financial Reporting Council (FRC) took over the work of the ASB. It very quickly replaced almost all extant standards, initially with three Financial Reporting Standards:

- FRS 100 *Application of Financial Reporting Requirements* (issued November 2012; amended July 2014);
- FRS 101 *Reduced Disclosure Framework* (issued November 2012; amended July 2014);
- FRS 102 *The Financial Reporting Standard applicable in the UK and Republic of Ireland* (issued March 2013);

In March 2014, it issued a fourth, FRS 103 *Insurance Contracts.*

The smallest companies continue to use the simplified version of UK standards, *Financial Reporting Standard for Smaller Entities,* known as the FRSSE. An updated version of the FRSSE was issued in July 2013.

The ASB and now the FRC have been at pains to ensure that most of the provisions of the relevant international standards are incorporated into the standards in issue, so making transition to IFRS relatively straightforward.

You can find out more about the work of the FRC and the standards currently in issue at its website (**https://www.frc.org.uk/Our-Work/Codes-Standards/Accounting-and-Reporting-Policy/Accounting-Standards-and-Statements-issued-by-the/Standards-in-Issue.aspx**).

Why do you think many UK and Irish companies are switching voluntarily to international accounting standards?

This book deals in outline with all international accounting standards issued and still in force up to May 2015. It does not deal with all the many detailed points contained in the standards and exposure drafts. It would be a far larger book if this was attempted. You will find similar details and coverage of UK GAAP in *Frank Wood's Business Accounting UK GAAP*. Students at the later stages of their professional examinations will need to get full copies of all standards and study them thoroughly. There are many web-based resources which provide the latest details on international standards. For example, **www.iasplus.com** contains summaries of all extant international standards.

The remainder of this chapter deals with all the current international accounting standards and related documents which are not covered in detail elsewhere in this book.

The next section presents an overview of the history of international accounting standards.

## 11.3 International accounting standards

The Accounting Standards Board issues accounting standards for adoption in the UK and Ireland. Other countries also have their own accounting standards boards – for example, the FASB (Financial Accounting Standards Board) operates in the USA and Australia has the AASB (Australian Accounting Standards Board). However, many smaller countries could not justify the creation of their own accounting standards but needed some form of regulation over the financial statements produced. This led, in 1973, to the setting up of the International Accounting Standards Committee (IASC). The IASC was replaced in 2001 by the International Accounting Standards Board (IASB). At that time, like the ASB, the IASB adopted all the International Accounting Standards (IASs) that the IASC had issued. All new standards issued by the IASB are called International Financial Reporting Standards (IFRSs).

The work of the IASB is overseen by 22 trustees, six from Europe, six from North America, six from Asia / Oceania, one from Africa, one from South America, and two from the rest of the world. The IASB has 14 full-time members. Its members are appointed by the Trustees and must also reflect an appropriate balance of auditors, financial statement preparers, users of financial statements and academics, and have a broad geographical spread.

When the IASC was founded, it had no formal authority and the IASs were entirely voluntary and initially intended for use in countries that did not have their own accounting standards or those which had considerable logistical difficulty in establishing and maintaining the infrastructure necessary to sustain a national accounting standards board.

Apart from providing standards for use in countries that do not issue their own accounting standards, the need today for the IASB is mainly due to:

1 The considerable growth in international investment, which means it is desirable to have similar methods the world over so that investment decisions are based on more compatible information.
2 The growth in multinational firms which have to produce financial statements covering a large number of countries. Standardisation between countries makes the accounting work easier, and reduces costs.
3 It is desirable that the activities and efforts of the various national standard-setting bodies be harmonised.

Currently (May 2015) there are 28 IASs, 15 IFRSs, and one IFRS for small and medium-sized entities (SMEs) in use, plus two IFRSs due to come into force in 2016 and 2017.

Let's look at the principles that underpin accounting standards.

## 11.4 *The Framework for the Preparation and Presentation of Financial Statements*

A conceptual framework outlines the underlying principles that underpin a set of pronouncements. It provides a set of assumptions that are consistent across all such pronouncements and avoids any contradictions in fundamental concepts being applied. However, in accounting, no conceptual framework existed in a complete form until 1989, when the IASC issued *The Framework for the Preparation and Presentation of Financial Statements* and neither the ASC/ASB nor the FASB ever issued a complete conceptual framework.

As a result, there are many contradictions and differences in definition or meaning across the standards each of these bodies has issued. Recognising this defect in the standard setting process, the IASB and the FASB agreed in 2004 to embark on a project to develop a new conceptual framework, but the project was terminated in 2010 without a new conceptual framework being completed. In 2012, the IASB returned to the project and is currently working alone on developing a new conceptual framework. An exposure draft is likely to be issued in 2015.

The current conceptual framework is split into seven main sections:

1 the objective of financial statements;
2 underlying assumptions;
3 qualitative characteristics of financial statements;
4 the elements of financial statements;
5 recognition of the elements of financial statements;
6 measurement of the elements of financial statements;
7 concepts of capital and capital maintenance.

## 1 The objective of financial statements

The objective of financial statements is to provide information about the financial position, performance and changes in financial position of an entity that is useful to a wide range of users in making economic decisions.

## 2 Underlying assumptions

In order to meet their objectives, financial statements are prepared on the accrual basis of accounting and on the assumption that an entity is a going concern and will continue in operation for the foreseeable future.

## 3 Qualitative characteristics of financial statements

Qualitative characteristics are the attributes that make the information provided in financial statements useful to users. The four principal qualitative characteristics are *understandability*, *relevance*, *reliability* and *comparability*.

### Understandability

An essential quality of the information provided in financial statements is that it is readily understandable by users. Information about complex matters that should be included because of its relevance to the economic decision-making needs of users should not be excluded merely because it may be too difficult for certain users to understand.

### Relevance

To be useful, information must be relevant to the decision-making needs of users. Information is relevant when it influences the economic decisions of users by helping them evaluate past, present or future events or confirming, or correcting, their past evaluations. Other aspects of information must be considered when considering the relevance of information:

(*i*) **Materiality** is crucial to relevance: information is material if its omission or misstatement could influence the economic decisions of users taken on the basis of the financial statements. It depends on the size of the item or error judged in the particular circumstances of its omission or misstatement. Thus, materiality provides a threshold or cut-off point rather than being a primary qualitative characteristic which information must have if it is to be useful.

(*ii*) **Reliability** exists when information is free from material error and bias and can be depended upon by users to represent faithfully that which it either purports to represent or could reasonably be expected to represent.

(*iii*) **Faithful representation** exists when information represents faithfully the transactions and other events it either purports to represent or could reasonably be expected to represent.

(*iv*) **Substance over form** must be applied, in that transactions and other events that information purports to represent must be accounted for and presented in accordance with their substance and economic reality and not merely their legal form.

(*v*) **Neutrality**, i.e. a lack of bias, must be a characteristic of the information presented. Much of the information presented in financial statements is determined by the person preparing those statements. This often entails taking decisions concerning what to include and what to exclude – for example, what allowance to make for doubtful debts. Any such accounting estimates must be neutral, neither understated nor overstated.

(*vi*) **Prudence** is related to neutrality. Prudence is the inclusion of a degree of caution in the exercise of the judgements needed in making the estimates required under conditions of uncertainty, such that assets or income are not overstated and liabilities or expenses are not understated.

(*vii*) **Completeness** of the information in financial statements must be achieved within the bounds of materiality and cost if that information is to be reliable. An omission can cause information to be false or misleading and thus unreliable and deficient in terms of its relevance.

### Comparability

To enable users to identify trends in its financial position and performance, the measurement and display of the financial effect of like transactions and other events must be carried out in a consistent way throughout an entity and over time. To this end, financial statements must also show corresponding information for the preceding period.

### Constraints on relevant and reliable information

There are four such constraints:

(*a*) **Timeliness**: if there is undue delay in the reporting of information it may lose its relevance but information presented too soon may be too uncertain to be reliable. In achieving a balance between relevance and reliability, the overriding consideration is how best to satisfy the economic decision-making needs of users.

(*b*) **Balance between benefit and cost**: the benefits derived from information should exceed the cost of providing it. This constraint is pervasive throughout accounting and is often raised as an issue to consider before embarking upon obtaining information that is difficult to obtain.

(*c*) **Balance between qualitative characteristics**: in practice, a trade-off between qualitative characteristics is often necessary. Any such trade-off should meet the objective of financial statements.

(*d*) **True and fair view/fair presentation**: the application of the principal qualitative characteristics and of appropriate accounting standards normally results in financial statements that convey what is generally understood as a true and fair view of, or as presenting fairly, such information.

A useful diagram (Exhibit 11.1) illustrating the qualitative characteristics of accounting information was included by the ASB in an early draft of its equivalent of the IASB Principles (upon which it was based):

Have a look at Exhibit 11.1: why do you think there is such an emphasis on the qualitative aspects of information in the *Framework for the Preparation and Presentation of Financial Statements*?

## Exhibit 11.1 The qualitative characteristics of accounting information

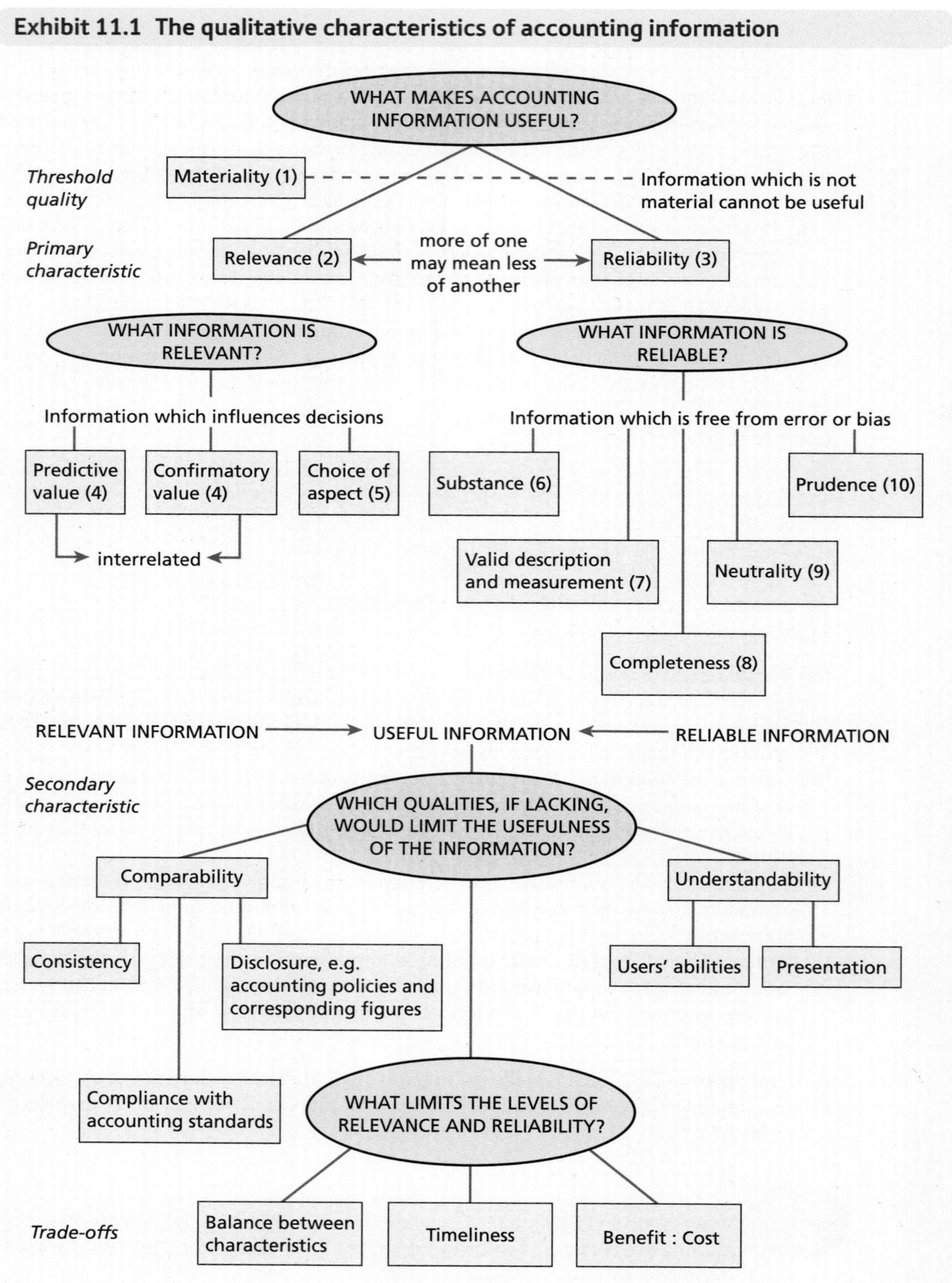


*Source*: Adapted from Accounting Standards Board Ltd (1991, 1999), *Accounting Standards Board Statement of Principles 1999*. 

## 4 The elements of financial statements

The elements of financial statements are the broad classes into which the financial effects of transactions and other events are grouped (according to their economic characteristics) in financial statements. The elements directly related to the measurement of financial position in the statement of financial position are assets, liabilities and equity. The elements directly related to the measurement of performance in the statement of profit or loss are income and expenses.

## 5 Recognition of the elements of financial statements

Recognition is the process of incorporating in the statement of financial position or statement of profit or loss an item that meets the definition of an element and satisfies the following criteria for recognition:

- it is probable that any future economic benefit associated with the item will flow to or from the entity; and
- it has a cost or value that can be measured with reliability.

Recognition involves the depiction of the item in words and by a monetary amount and the inclusion of that amount in the statement of financial position or statement of profit or loss totals. Items that satisfy the recognition criteria must be recognised in the statement of financial position or statement of profit or loss. Failure to do so is not rectified by disclosure of the accounting policies used or by notes or explanatory material.

## 6 Measurement of the elements of financial statements

Measurement is the process of determining the monetary amounts at which the elements of the financial statements are to be recognised and carried in the statement of financial position and statement of profit or loss. The most commonly adopted measurement basis is historical cost, with other bases being adopted where appropriate – for example, the valuing of inventories at the lower of cost and net realisable value.

## 7 Concepts of capital and capital maintenance

### Concepts of capital

Under a *financial concept of capital* (which is the one adopted by most entities), capital is synonymous with the net assets or equity of the entity. Under a *physical concept of capital*, such as operating capability, capital is regarded as the productive capacity of the entity based on, for example, units of output per day. The selection of the appropriate concept of capital by an entity should be based on the needs of the users of its financial statements.

(*a*) When would it be appropriate for an entity to adopt a financial concept of capital?
(*b*) When would it be appropriate for an entity to adopt a physical concept of capital?

### Concepts of capital maintenance

These provide the link between the concepts of capital and the concepts of profit by providing the point of reference by which profit is measured. Only inflows of assets in excess of amounts needed to maintain capital may be regarded as profit and therefore as a return on capital. Hence, profit or loss is the residual amount that remains after expenses have been deducted from income.

The two concepts of capital give rise to two concepts of capital maintenance:

(*a*) *Financial capital maintenance*: a profit is earned only if the financial amount of the net assets at the end of the period exceeds the financial amount of net assets at the beginning of the period, after excluding any distributions to, and contributions from, owners during the period.
(*b*) *Physical capital maintenance*: a profit is earned only if the physical productive capacity (or operating capability) of the entity (or the resources or funds needed to achieve that capacity) at the end of the period exceeds the physical productive capacity at the beginning of the period, after excluding any distributions to, and contributions from, owners during the period.

We'll now look at each of the current international accounting standards, in number order. However, because it underpins every other international accounting standard, we'll start by looking at IAS 8 (*Accounting policies, changes in accounting estimates and errors*).

## 11.5 IAS 8 Accounting policies, changes in accounting estimates and errors

Users of financial statements issued by organisations want to analyse and evaluate the figures contained within them. They cannot do this effectively unless they know which accounting policies have been used when preparing such statements.

### Accounting policies

These are defined in IAS 8 as:

> *the specific principles, bases, conventions, rules and practices applied by an entity in preparing and presenting financial statements.*

In other words, accounting policies define the processes whereby relevant and reliable information about the transactions, other events and conditions to which they apply are reflected in the financial statements. The accounting policies selected should enable the financial statements to give a true and fair view.

When selecting an accounting policy, its appropriateness should be considered in the context of producing information that is:

(*a*) relevant to the economic decision-making needs of users; and
(*b*) reliable, in that the financial statements:

  (*i*) represent faithfully the financial position, financial performance and cash flows of the entity;
  (*ii*) reflect the economic substance of transactions, other events and conditions, and not merely the legal form;
  (*iii*) are neutral, i.e. free from bias;
  (*iv*) are prudent;
  (*v*) are complete in all material aspects.

### Changes in estimates

The use of estimates is an essential part of the preparation of financial statements and does not undermine their reliability. Business is full of uncertainty and many items in financial statements must be estimated. Making an estimate involves judgements based on the latest available, reliable information. For example, estimates may be required of:

(*a*) doubtful debts;
(*b*) obsolescence of inventory;

(*c*) the fair value of financial assets or financial liabilities;
(*d*) the useful lives of, or expected pattern of consumption of the future economic benefits embodied in, depreciable assets; and
(*e*) warranty obligations.

An estimate may need to be revised if changes occur in the circumstances upon which it was based or as a result of new information or more experience. By its nature, the revision of an estimate does not relate to prior periods and is not the correction of an error.

A change in the measurement basis applied is a change in an accounting policy, and is not a change in an accounting estimate. When it is difficult to distinguish a change in an accounting policy from a change in an accounting estimate, the change is treated as a change in an accounting estimate.

The effect of a change in an accounting estimate is recognised by including it in profit or loss in:

(*i*) the period of the change, if the change affects that period only; or
(*ii*) the period of the change and future periods, if the change affects both.

### Errors

Errors can arise in respect of the recognition, measurement, presentation or disclosure of elements of financial statements. Financial statements do not comply with accounting standards if they contain errors made intentionally to achieve a particular presentation of an entity's financial position, financial performance or cash flows. Errors are sometimes not discovered until a subsequent period. When an error is found in a subsequent period, the error must be corrected in the comparative information presented in the financial statements for that subsequent period.

Corrections of errors are *not* changes in accounting estimates. Accounting estimates are approximations that may need revision as additional information becomes known. For example, the gain or loss recognised on the outcome of a contingency is not the correction of an error.

## 11.6 IAS 1 Presentation of financial statements

IAS 1 prescribes the basis for presentation of general purpose financial statements to ensure comparability both with the entity's financial statements of previous periods and with the financial statements of other entities. It sets out the overall requirements for the presentation of financial statements, guidelines for their structure and minimum requirements for their content.

### Purpose of financial statements

The standard states that:

> *financial statements are a structured representation of the financial position and financial performance of an entity. The objective of financial statements is to provide information about the financial position, financial performance and cash flows of an entity that is useful to a wide range of users in making economic decisions. Financial statements also show the results of the management's stewardship of the resources entrusted to it. To meet this objective, financial statements provide information about an entity's:*
>
> (*a*) *assets;*
> (*b*) *liabilities;*

(*c*) *equity;*
(*d*) *income and expenses, including gains and losses;*
(*e*) *contributions by and distributions to owners in their capacity as owners; and*
(*f*) *cash flows.*

*This information, along with other information in the notes, assists users of financial statements in predicting the entity's future cash flows and, in particular, their timing and certainty.*

## A complete set of financial statements

There are seven components to a complete set of financial statements that entities can produce (six, if the statement of profit or loss information is included within the statement of comprehensive income), all of which must be given equal prominence:

(*a*) A *statement of financial position* as at the end of the period.
(*b*) A *statement of profit or loss* (if shown separately from the statement of comprehensive income) which should show *as a minimum* line items for:
  **1** revenue;
  **2** finance costs;
  **3** share of the profit or loss of associates and joint ventures accounted for using the equity method;
  **4** tax expense;
  **5** a single amount comprising the total of:
    (*i*) the post-tax profit or loss of discontinued operations; and
    (*ii*) the post-tax gain or loss recognised on the measurement to fair value less costs to sell or on the disposal of the assets or disposal group(s) constituting the discontinued operation;
  **6** profit or loss.
(*c*) A *statement of comprehensive income* which, if no separate statement of profit or loss is prepared, includes the items that would otherwise appear in the statement of profit or loss plus:
  **6** the profit or loss (as shown in the statement of profit or loss);
  **7** each component of other comprehensive income (i.e. items of income and expense that are not recognised in profit and loss) classified by nature. These include:
  - changes in revaluation surplus (IAS 16 *Property, plant and equipment* and IAS 38 *Intangible assets*);
  - actuarial gains and losses on defined benefit plans recognised in accordance with paragraph 93A of IAS 19 (*Employee benefits*);
  - gains and losses arising from translating the financial statements of a foreign operation (IAS 21 *Effects of changes in foreign exchange rates*);
  - gains and losses on remeasuring available-for-sale financial assets (IAS 39 *Financial instruments: recognition and measurement*);
  - the effective portion of gains and losses on hedging instruments in a cash flow hedge (IAS 39);

  **8** share of the other comprehensive income of associates and joint ventures accounted for using the equity method; and
  **9** total comprehensive income.

If no statement of profit or loss is prepared, the statement of comprehensive income must contain *as a minimum* all nine items listed above.

(*d*) *A statement of changes in equity.*
(*e*) *A statement of cash flows.*
(*f*) *Notes,* comprising a summary of significant accounting policies and other explanatory information. As a minimum, the notes must include information about:

- accounting policies followed;
- the judgements that management has made in the process of applying the entity's accounting policies that have the most significant effect on the amounts recognised in the financial statements; and
- the key assumptions concerning the future, and other key sources of estimation uncertainty, that have a significant risk of causing a material adjustment to the carrying amounts of assets and liabilities within the next financial year.

Preparation of the seventh component to a complete set of financial statements obviously depends upon circumstances and is unlikely to be prepared very frequently:

(*g*) A *statement of financial position* as at the beginning of the earliest comparative period when an entity applies an accounting policy retrospectively or makes a retrospective restatement of items in its financial statements, or when it reclassifies items in its financial statements.

## The statement of financial position

IAS 1 does not prescribe the order or format in which items are presented. However, *as a minimum* the statement of financial position should include the following line items:

(*a*) property, plant and equipment;
(*b*) investment property;
(*c*) intangible assets;
(*d*) financial assets (excluding amounts shown under (*e*), (*h*) and (*i*));
(*e*) investments accounted for using the equity method;
(*f*) biological assets;
(*g*) inventories;
(*h*) trade and other receivables;
(*i*) cash and cash equivalents;
(*j*) the total of assets classified as held for sale and assets included in disposal groups classified as held for sale in accordance with IFRS 5 *Non-current assets held for sale and discontinued operations;*
(*k*) trade and other payables;
(*l*) provisions;
(*m*) financial liabilities (excluding amounts shown under (*k*) and (*l*));
(*n*) liabilities and assets for current tax, as defined in IAS 12 *Income taxes;*
(*o*) deferred tax liabilities and deferred tax assets, as defined in IAS 12;
(*p*) liabilities included in disposal groups classified as held for sale in accordance with IFRS 5;
(*q*) non-controlling interest, presented within equity; and
(*r*) issued capital and reserves attributable to owners of the parent.

## The statement of changes in equity

This statement must show the following four items:

(*i*) total comprehensive income for the period, showing separately the total amounts attributable to owners of the parent and to non-controlling interest;
(*ii*) for each component of equity, the effects of retrospective application or retrospective restatement recognised in accordance with IAS 8 (*Accounting policies*);
(*iii*) the amounts of transactions with owners in their capacity as owners, showing separately contributions by and distributions to owners; and
(*iv*) for each component of equity, a reconciliation between the carrying amount at the beginning and the end of the period, separately disclosing each change.

In addition, the amount of dividends recognised as distributions to owners during the period and the related amount per share must be shown, either in the statement or as a note.

### The titles of financial statements

Entities are permitted to use whatever title they wish for each financial statement, so long as it is clear what the statements are presenting.

### Comparative information

Two versions of each financial statement must be prepared, one for the current period and one for the preceding period. This is usually done by including additional columns in the financial statements for the preceding period amounts.

## 11.7 IAS 2 Inventories

Due to the many varying kinds of businesses and conditions in companies, there simply cannot be one system of valuation for inventories. All that the standard can do is to narrow down the different methods that could be used.

### Inventories

Inventories should be stated at the total of the lower of cost and net realisable value. The same cost formula must be used for all inventory of a similar nature and use to the entity. Profit should not be recognised in advance, but immediate account should be made for anticipated losses.

In the statement of financial position (or in the notes), stocks should be sub-classified so as to indicate the amounts held in each of the main categories: raw materials and consumables; work in progress; finished goods and goods for resale; and payments on account.

*Net realisable value* consists of the expected selling price less any expenses necessary to sell the product. This may be below cost because of obsolescence, deterioration or falling selling prices. Replacement cost may be used if it is the best available measure of net realisable value.

**Cost** is defined as: *'all costs of purchase, conversion and other costs incurred in bringing the inventories to their present location and condition'*.

*Cost of purchase* comprises purchase price including import duties and other irrecoverable taxes, transport and handling costs and any other directly attributable costs, less trade discounts, rebates and subsidies.

*Cost of conversion* comprises:

(*a*) costs which are specifically attributable to units of production, i.e. direct labour, direct expenses and subcontracted work;
(*b*) systematically allocated fixed and variable production overheads.

*Other costs* comprise any other expenditure attributable to bringing the product or service to its present location and condition.

*Fixed production overheads* are allocated on the basis of the normal capacity of the production facilities expected to be achieved on average over a number of periods under normal circumstances. Obviously, neither selling nor administrative overheads should be included in cost.

Notice that abnormal costs should not be included, as they should not have the effect of increasing inventory valuation; and neither should storage costs.

The last in, first out (LIFO) method should not be used for valuation of inventory, as it does not provide an up-to-date valuation.

The financial statements should disclose:

(*a*) the accounting policies adopted in measuring inventories, including the cost formula used;
(*b*) the total carrying amount of inventories and the carrying amount in classifications appropriate to the entity;
(*c*) the carrying amount of inventories carried at fair value less costs to sell;
(*d*) the amount of inventories recognised as an expense during the period;
(*e*) the amount of any write-down of inventories recognised as an expense in the period;
(*f*) the amount of any reversal of any write-down that is recognised as a reduction in the amount of inventories recognised as expense in the period;
(*g*) the circumstances or events that led to the reversal of a write-down of inventories; and
(*h*) the carrying amount of inventories pledged as security for liabilities.

Information about the carrying amounts held in different classifications of inventories and the extent of the changes in these assets is useful to financial statement users. Common classifications of inventories are merchandise, production supplies, materials, work in progress and finished goods. The inventories of a service provider may be described as work in progress.

## 11.8 IAS 7 Statement of cash flows

This accounting standard is covered in Chapter 15.

## 11.9 IAS 8 Accounting policies, changes in accounting estimates and errors

This accounting standard was covered in Section 11.5.

## 11.10 IAS 10 Events after the reporting period

Obviously, any event which occurred during a financial period will be taken into account when the financial statements were prepared. Generally, once financial statements have been approved and authorised for issue, it becomes impossible to alter them. However, during the period between the date of the statement of financial position and the date when the financial statements are authorised for issue, events may arise which throw some light upon the valuation of assets or amounts of liabilities in those financial statements. IAS 10 directs its attention to such events during this period.

To clarify the period involved, entities must report the date on which their financial statements were authorised for issue. For companies, this *is not* the date when they are presented to the shareholders at the AGM. Rather, it is the date on which the directors authorised the financial statements to be issued.

Two terms are of particular importance in applying the requirements of IAS 10: 'adjusting events' and 'non-adjusting events'.

### Adjusting events

These are events which provide evidence of conditions that existed at the date of the statement of financial position for which the entity shall adjust the amounts recognised in its financial statements or recognise items that were not previously recognised. Examples include:

- The settlement after the date of the statement of financial position of a court case that confirms the liability of the entity at the date of the statement of financial position.
- The discovery after the date of the statement of financial position of errors or frauds which show that the financial statements were incorrect.
- Information received after the date of the statement of financial position that indicates that the value of an asset was impaired (i.e. less than previously believed) at the date of the statement of financial position. This could arise in many ways, for example:
  (*a*) **Non-current assets.** The subsequent determination of the purchase price or of the proceeds of sale of assets purchased or sold before the year end.
  (*b*) **Property.** A valuation which provides evidence of a permanent diminution in value.
  (*c*) **Investments.** The receipt of a copy of the financial statements or other information in respect of an unlisted company which provides evidence of a permanent diminution in the value of a long-term investment.
  (*d*) **Inventories of raw materials, goods for resale and work in progress:**
    (*i*) the receipt of proceeds of sales after the date of the statement of financial position or other evidence concerning the net realisable value of inventory;
    (*ii*) the receipt of evidence that the previous estimate of accrued profit on a long-term contract was materially inaccurate.
  (*e*) **Debtors.** The renegotiation of amounts owing by debtors, or the insolvency of a debtor.

## Non-adjusting events

These are events which arise after the date of the statement of financial position and concern conditions which did not exist at that time. Consequently they do not result in changes in amounts in financial statements. They may, however, be of such materiality that their disclosure is required by way of notes to ensure that the financial statements are not misleading. Such disclosure should describe the nature of the event and an estimate of its financial effect (or a statement that it is not possible to do so).

Examples of non-adjusting events given in IAS 10 which may require disclosure include:

- a decline in market value of investments between the date of the statement of financial position and the date when the financial statements are authorised for issue;
- a major business combination after the date of the statement of financial position or disposing of a major subsidiary;
- announcing a plan to discontinue an operation, disposing of assets or settling liabilities attributable to a discontinuing operation or entering into binding agreements to sell such assets or settle such liabilities;
- major purchases and disposals of assets, or expropriation of major assets by government;
- the destruction of a major production plant by a fire after the date of the statement of financial position;
- announcing, or commencing the implementation of, a major restructuring;
- major ordinary share transactions and potential ordinary share transactions after the date of the statement of financial position;
- abnormally large changes after the date of the statement of financial position in asset prices or foreign exchange rates;
- changes in tax rates or tax laws enacted or announced after the date of the statement of financial position that have a significant effect on current and deferred tax assets and liabilities;
- entering into significant commitments or contingent liabilities, for example by issuing significant guarantees;
- commencing major litigation arising solely out of events that occurred after the date of the statement of financial position.

The standard makes it clear that dividends proposed or declared after the date of the statement of financial position are not to be treated as a liability in the statement of financial position. Rather they are to be disclosed in a note to the financial statements.

## 11.11 IAS 11 Construction contracts

This standard will be replaced on 1 January 2017 by IFRS 15 (*Revenue from contracts with customers*). Chapter 3 deals with this topic.

## 11.12 IAS 12 Income taxes

The standard prescribes the treatment of tax on income in the financial statements. It distinguishes between two categories of tax:

1. **Current tax.** This refers to the amount of tax payable on taxable profits for the period. Income tax payable for current and prior periods is recognised as a liability. Income tax refundable is recognised as an asset.
2. **Deferred tax.** This relates to the difference between the carrying amount of assets and liabilities in the statement of financial position and the tax base (i.e. the amount that will be deductible for tax purposes against any taxable economic benefits that will flow to an entity when it recovers the carrying amount) of those assets and liabilities.

For example, a machine cost £15,000 and has a carrying amount of £10,000. Tax depreciation in the form of capital allowances, to date, is £9,000. The tax rate is 25%. The tax base is £6,000 (i.e. cost minus tax depreciation = £15,000 − £9,000). To recover the carrying amount (of £10,000), the entity must earn that amount, i.e. £10,000, but will only be able to deduct additional tax depreciation of £6,000 (= the tax base or the so far unclaimed element of the original cost). The entity must recognise the deferred tax liability of £10,000 (i.e. £10,000 − £6,000 = £4,000 @ 25%).

A deferred tax liability must be recognised in full. A deferred tax asset is recognised only to the extent that it is probable that a tax benefit will be realised in the future.

Deferred tax is measured at the tax rate expected to apply when it is realised (asset) or settled (liability).

Deferred tax is a non-current item in the statement of financial position.

Both the taxation charge for the current period and the deferred tax charged to the current period are shown on the face of the statement of profit or loss.

## 11.13 IAS 16 Property, plant and equipment

This IAS applies to all tangible non-current assets except investment properties, biological assets related to agricultural activity (IAS 41), exploration and evaluation assets (IFRS 6), and non-current assets held for sale (IFRS 5).

The standard provides a number of definitions:

*Carrying amount*: the amount at which an asset is recognised after deducting any accumulated depreciation and accumulated impairment losses.

*Cost*: the amount of cash or cash equivalents paid or the fair value of the other consideration given to acquire an asset at the time of its acquisition or construction or, where applicable, the amount attributed to that asset when initially recognised in accordance with the specific requirements of other IFRSs. Cost includes amounts incurred subsequently to add to, replace part of, or service an asset.

*Depreciable amount*: the cost of an asset, or other amount substituted for cost, less its residual value.

*Depreciation*: the systematic allocation of the depreciable amount of an asset over its useful life.

*Entity-specific value*: the present value of the cash flows an entity expects to arise from the continuing use of an asset and from its disposal at the end of its useful life or expects to incur when settling a liability.

*Fair value*: the amount for which an asset could be exchanged between knowledgeable, willing parties in an arm's-length transaction.

*An impairment loss*: the amount by which the carrying amount of an asset exceeds its recoverable amount.

*Property, plant and equipment*: tangible items that: (*i*) are held for use in the production or supply of goods or services, for rental to others, or for administrative purposes; and (*ii*) are expected to be used during more than one period.

*Recoverable amount*: the higher of an asset's net selling price and its value in use.

The *residual value* of an asset: the estimated amount that an entity would *currently* obtain from disposal of the asset, after deducting the estimated costs of disposal, if the asset were already of the age and in the condition expected at the end of its useful life.

*Useful life* is:

(*a*) the period over which an asset is expected to be available for use by an entity; or
(*b*) the number of production or similar units expected to be obtained from the asset by an entity.

Depreciation should be provided in respect of all tangible non-current assets which have a finite useful life other than those excluded by other IASs and IFRSs. It should be provided by allocating the cost (or revalued amount) less net realisable value over the periods expected to benefit from the use of the asset being depreciated. Depreciation begins when an asset is available for use. No depreciation method is prescribed, but the method selected should be that which produces the most appropriate allocation of depreciation to each period in relation to the benefit being received in that period through use of the asset. In doing so, it should reflect the pattern in which the asset's future economic benefits are expected to be consumed by the entity. The depreciation should be recognised in profit or loss, not against reserves.

When the useful life of an asset is longer than 50 years, no depreciation need be charged.

Useful lives and residual values should be reviewed at least at the end of each reporting period. If expectations differ from previous estimates, the changes are accounted for as changes in accounting estimates in accordance with IAS 8 (*Accounting policies, changes in accounting estimates and errors*).

The depreciation method may be changed only if there is a change in the expected pattern of consumption of those future economic benefits embodied in the asset, i.e. only when to do so will give a fairer presentation of the results and of the financial position. A change in depreciation method does not constitute a change in accounting policy. Where a change of method occurs, the effect, if material, should be shown as a note attached to the financial statements, as required by IAS 8.

## Asset measurement after recognition

An entity shall choose either the cost model or the revaluation model as its accounting policy and shall apply that policy to an entire class of property, plant and equipment.

### Cost model

After recognition as an asset, an item of property, plant and equipment shall be carried at its cost less any accumulated depreciation and any accumulated impairment losses.

### Revaluation model

After recognition as an asset, an item of property, plant and equipment whose fair value can be measured reliably shall be carried at a revalued amount, being its fair value at the date of the revaluation less any subsequent accumulated depreciation and subsequent accumulated impairment losses. Revaluations shall be made with sufficient regularity to ensure that the carrying amount does not differ materially from that which would be determined using fair value at the date of the statement of financial position.

The fair value of land and buildings is usually determined from market-based evidence by appraisal that is normally undertaken by professionally qualified valuers. The fair value of items of plant and equipment is usually their market value determined by appraisal.

If an item of property, plant and equipment is revalued, the entire class of property, plant and equipment to which that asset belongs must be revalued.

If an asset's carrying amount is increased as a result of a revaluation, the increase shall be credited directly to equity under the heading of revaluation surplus. However, the increase shall be recognised in profit or loss to the extent that it reverses a revaluation decrease of the same asset previously recognised in profit or loss.

If an asset's carrying amount is decreased as a result of a revaluation, the decrease shall be recognised in profit or loss. However, the decrease shall be debited directly to equity under the heading of revaluation surplus to the extent of any credit balance existing in the revaluation surplus in respect of that asset.

### Land and buildings

Land and buildings are separable assets and are accounted for separately, even when they are acquired together. With some exceptions, such as quarries and sites used for landfill, land has an unlimited useful life and therefore is not depreciated. Buildings have a limited useful life and therefore are depreciable assets. An increase in the value of the land on which a building stands does not affect the determination of the depreciable amount of the building.

### Disclosure

The financial statements shall disclose, for each class of property, plant and equipment:

(*a*) the measurement bases used for determining the gross carrying amount;
(*b*) the depreciation methods used;
(*c*) the useful lives or the depreciation rates used;
(*d*) the gross carrying amount and the accumulated depreciation (aggregated with accumulated impairment losses) at the beginning and end of the period; and
(*e*) a reconciliation of the carrying amount at the beginning and end of the period showing:
  (*i*) additions;
  (*ii*) assets classified as held for sale or included in a disposal group classified as held for sale in accordance with IFRS 5 and other disposals;
  (*iii*) acquisitions through business combinations;
(*f*) increases or decreases resulting from revaluations and from impairment losses recognised or reversed directly in equity in accordance with IAS 36;
(*g*) impairment losses recognised in profit or loss in accordance with IAS 36;
(*h*) impairment losses reversed in profit or loss in accordance with IAS 36;
(*i*) depreciation;
(*j*) the net exchange differences arising on the translation of the financial statements from the functional currency into a different presentation currency, including the translation of a foreign operation into the presentation currency of the reporting entity; and
(*k*) other changes.

## 11.14 IAS 17 Leases

Details of IAS 17 are given in Chapter 2.

## 11.15 IAS 18 Revenue

Revenue is measured at the fair value of the consideration received or receivable. Revenue from sale of goods is recognised when:

(*a*) significant risks and rewards of ownership are transferred to the buyer;
(*b*) the seller has no continuing managerial involvement or control over the goods;
(*c*) the amount of revenue can be measured reliably;
(*d*) it is probable that economic benefits will flow to the seller (i.e. the seller will be paid);
(*e*) the costs of the transaction can be measured reliably.

Revenue from services is recognised when (*c*), (*d*) and (*e*) are satisfied plus the stage of completion of the transaction can be measured reliably. If the outcome cannot be measured reliably, revenue can only be recognised to the extent that the expenditures recognised are recoverable.

## 11.16 IAS 19 Employee benefits

This standard prescribes how to account for and how to disclose employee benefits. There are four categories of employee benefit:

(*i*) short-term employee benefits, such as wages, salaries, National Insurance contributions, paid annual leave, paid sick leave, profit-sharing, bonuses, medical care, cars, housing, and free goods or services. These must be recognised when the employee has performed the work for which the benefit is to be paid;
(*ii*) post-employment benefits, e.g. pensions;
(*iii*) other long-term employee benefits, such as long-service leave or sabbatical leave, long-term disability benefits;
(*iv*) termination benefits.

Categories (*ii*), (*iii*) and (*iv*) have more complex rules for recognition that lie outside the scope of this book. Students wishing to find out more on this topic should consult IAS 19.

## 11.17 IAS 20 Accounting for government grants and disclosure of government assistance

Many different types of grant are or have been obtainable from government departments. Where these relate to revenue expenditure, e.g. subsidies on wages, they should be credited to revenue in the period when the revenue is incurred. The principle is that the grants should be recognised in profit and loss so as to match the expenditure to which they are intended to contribute. This is done either by including such grants as 'other income' or by deducting them from the related expenditure.

Where there are grants relating to capital expenditure, they should be recognised as income over the periods necessary to match them with the related costs which they are intended to compensate, on a systematic basis. This is achieved by treating the amount of the grant as a deferred income, a portion of which is credited to profit and loss annually, over the life of the asset, on a basis consistent with depreciation. The amount of the deferred credit should, if material, be shown separately. It should not be shown as part of shareholders' funds.

The same effect as treating the grant as deferred income could be achieved by crediting the grant to the asset account and depreciating only the net balance of the cost of the asset over its lifetime (depreciation is thus reduced by the grant). However, while this is permitted under IAS 20, it is prohibited by the Companies Act.

## 11.18 IAS 21 The effects of changes in foreign exchange rates

This standard is discussed in Chapter 1, Section 1.14.

## 11.19 IAS 23 Borrowing costs

Borrowing costs comprise interest and other costs incurred on funds borrowed. Borrowing costs are recognised as an expense when incurred. However, borrowing costs that are directly attributable to the acquisition, construction or production of a 'qualifying asset' (i.e. an asset that necessarily takes a substantial period of time to get ready for its intended use or sale) may be capitalised.

## 11.20 IAS 24 Related party disclosures

This standard prescribes the disclosures to be made when related parties exist or when transactions have occurred and/or balances exist with related parties. A related party transaction is a transfer of resources, services, or obligations between related parties, whether or not a price is charged.

A party is related to an entity if:

(*a*) directly, or indirectly through one or more intermediaries, the party:
- (*i*) controls, is controlled by, or is under common control with, the entity (this includes parents, subsidiaries and fellow subsidiaries);
- (*ii*) has an interest in the entity that gives it significant influence over the entity; or
- (*iii*) has joint control over the entity;

(*b*) the party is an associate (as defined in IAS 28 *Investments in associates*) of the entity;

(*c*) the party is a joint venture in which the entity is a venturer (see IFRS 11 *Joint arrangements* and IFRS 12 *Disclosure of interests in other entities*);

(*d*) the party is a member of the key management personnel of the entity or its parent;

(*e*) the party is a close member of the family of any individual referred to in (*a*) or (*d*);

(*f*) the party is an entity that is controlled, jointly controlled or significantly influenced by, or for which significant voting power in such entity resides with, directly or indirectly, any individual referred to in (*d*) or (*e*);

(*g*) the party is a post-employment benefit plan for the benefit of employees of the entity, or of any entity that is a related party of the entity; or

(*h*) the entity, or any member of a group of which it is a part, provides key management personnel services to the reporting entity or to the parent of the reporting entity

## 11.21 IAS 26 Accounting and reporting by retirement benefit plans

This standard specifies the disclosures to make in the financial statements of retirement benefit plans. A retirement benefit plan is an arrangement where an entity provides benefits for employees on or after termination of service (e.g. after they retire). There are two types:

- **Defined contribution plans** – amounts to be paid as retirement benefits are determined by contributions to a fund plus the earnings from the investment of the fund. In this case, the financial statements should contain a statement of net assets available for benefits and a description of the funding policy.
- **Defined benefit plans** – amounts to be paid as retirement benefits are determined by a formula usually based on employee earnings and/or years of service. In this case, the financial statements should contain either:

(*a*) a statement that shows:
  (*i*) the net assets available for benefits;
  (*ii*) the actuarial present value of promised retirement benefits, distinguishing between vested benefits and non-vested benefits; and
  (*iii*) the resulting excess or deficit; or
(*b*) a statement of net assets available for benefits including either:
  (*i*) a note disclosing the actuarial present value of promised retirement benefits, distinguishing between vested benefits and non-vested benefits; or
  (*ii*) a reference to this information in an accompanying actuarial report.

If an actuarial valuation has not been prepared at the date of the financial statements, the most recent valuation shall be used as a base and the date of the valuation disclosed.

## 11.22 IAS 27 Consolidated and separate financial statements

This standard is discussed in Chapter 26.

## 11.23 IAS 28 Investments in associates

This standard is discussed in Chapter 26.

## 11.24 IAS 29 Financial reporting in hyperinflationary economies

The results of an entity whose functional currency is the currency of a hyperinflationary economy must be restated in terms of the measuring unit current at the date of the statement of financial position (i.e. the currency value at that date) before being translated into a different presentation currency. Comparative figures for prior periods are also restated into the measuring unit at the current date of the statement of financial position. Statement of financial position amounts not already expressed in terms of the measuring unit current at the date of the statement of financial position are restated by applying a general price index. Any gain or loss as a result of the net monetary position must be included in net income and separately disclosed.

## 11.25 IAS 32 Financial instruments: disclosure and presentation

A financial instrument is any contract that gives rise to a financial asset of one entity and a financial liability or equity instrument of another entity. Each financial instrument must be classified as either a financial liability or as an equity instrument. It is an equity instrument if, and only if, both the following conditions are met:

1 The instrument includes no contractual obligation:
  (*a*) to deliver cash or another financial asset to another entity; or
  (*b*) to exchange financial assets or financial liabilities with another entity under conditions that are potentially unfavourable to the issuer.
2 If the instrument will or may be settled in the issuer's own equity instruments, it is:
  (*a*) a non-derivative that includes no contractual obligation for the issuer to deliver a variable number of its own equity instruments; or

(*b*) a derivative that will be settled by the issuer exchanging a fixed amount of cash or another financial asset for a fixed number of its own equity instruments. For this purpose, the issuer's own equity instruments do not include instruments that are themselves contracts for the future receipt or delivery of the issuer's own equity instruments.

If it does not meet these conditions, it is a financial liability.

An example of a type of financial instrument that you have encountered many times in *Frank Wood's Business Accounting* 1 and 2 is preference shares. They may be either financial liabilities or equity instruments. If they are not redeemable and dividends are at the discretion of the issuer, they are equity instruments and are included in equity in the statement of financial position. In contrast, where they are redeemable for fixed or determinable amounts at a fixed or determinable future date, or where the holder has the option to redeem them, they are classified as a financial liability and included in liabilities in the statement of financial position. This issue is currently under review by the IASB.

## 11.26 IAS 33 Earnings per share

The objective of earnings per share (EPS) information is to provide a measure of the interests of each ordinary share of a parent entity in the performance of the entity over the reporting period. Basic earnings per share is a widely used stock market measure. The standard tries to bring about a consistent method to aid comparability and reduce misunderstandings.

Under IAS 33, entities must calculate basic earnings per share amounts for profit or loss attributable to ordinary equity holders of the parent entity and, if presented, profit or loss from continuing operations attributable to those equity holders. Basic earnings per share is calculated by dividing profit or loss attributable to ordinary equity holders of the parent entity (the numerator) by the weighted average number of ordinary shares outstanding (the denominator) during the period.

When there are potential ordinary shares (for example if share options are exercised) they are treated as dilutive when, and only when, their conversion to ordinary shares would decrease earnings per share or increase loss per share from continuing operations. When there are dilutive ordinary shares, a diluted earnings per share must also be calculated.

On the face of the statement of profit or loss, entities must present basic and, where applicable, diluted earnings per share for profit or loss from continuing operations attributable to the ordinary equity holders of the parent entity and for profit or loss attributable to the ordinary equity holders of the parent entity for the period for each class of ordinary shares that has a different right to share in profit for the period. Basic and diluted earnings per share must be presented with equal prominence for all periods presented.

The standard prescribes how to adjust the average number of shares when events occur to change the number of ordinary shares, such as bonus issues, share splits, and share consolidations. Students taking examinations which cover IAS 33 in detail should read the actual standard.

| Basic EPS is calculated as follows: | £ | £ |
|---|---|---|
| Profit on continuing activities after taxation | | XXX |
| *Less*: Non-controlling interest (see chapters on group financial statements)[Note] | XXX | |
| Preference dividends | XXX | |
| | | (XXX) |
| Profit available to equity shareholders | | XXX |

$$\text{EPS} = \frac{\text{Profit available to equity shareholders}}{\text{Number of ordinary shares}} = \text{EPS in pence}$$

***Note*: You will see later that non-controlling interests exist only where the entity controls another entity which is partly owned by outsiders.**

## 11.27 IAS 34 Interim financial reporting

Companies listed on the Stock Exchange are required to produce half-year interim reports. The Listing Rules stipulate the minimum requirements for the report. IAS 34 also defines the minimum requirements, and entities must comply with them, whether or not they are subject to the Listing Rules.

Among the requirements are:

- comparative amounts for the statement of financial position at the end of the previous full financial year must be disclosed;
- quarterly interim reports must contain figures (except for the statement of financial position) for the cumulative period to date and for the corresponding period of the preceding year;
- minimum content of an interim financial report is a condensed statement of financial position, condensed statement of profit or loss, condensed statement of cash flows, condensed statement of changes in equity, plus notes;
- notes in interim reports are primarily an explanation of the events and changes that are significant to an understanding of the changes in financial position and performance of the entity since the last reporting date;
- accounting policies should be consistent with those applied in the annual financial statements unless a change in accounting policy is to be made in the next annual report, in which case the new accounting policy can be adopted in the interim report;
- basic and diluted earnings per share must be presented on the face of the statement of profit or loss;
- consolidated interim financial statements must be produced if the last annual report was prepared on a consolidated basis.

## 11.28 IAS 36 Impairment of assets

This standard prescribes the procedures to be applied by an entity to ensure that its assets are carried at no more than their recoverable amount. An asset is carried at more than its recoverable amount if its 'carrying amount' exceeds the amount to be recovered through use or sale of the asset. (*Carrying amount* is the amount at which an asset is recognised after deducting any accumulated depreciation and accumulated impairment losses thereon.) If this is the case, the asset is described as impaired and IAS 36 requires the entity to recognise an impairment loss. The standard also specifies when an entity should reverse an impairment loss and the disclosures to make.

Other standards applicable to some types of assets contain requirements for recognising and measuring certain assets. As a result, IAS 36 does not apply to:

(*a*) inventories (IAS 2 *Inventories*);
(*b*) assets arising from construction contracts (IAS 11 *Construction contracts*);
(*c*) deferred tax assets (IAS 12 *Income taxes*);
(*d*) assets arising from employee benefits (IAS 19 *Employee benefits*);
(*e*) assets classified as held for sale (or included in a disposal group that is classified as held for sale) (IFRS 5 *Non-current assets held for sale and discontinued operations*);
(*f*) financial assets that are within the scope of IAS 39 *Financial instruments: recognition and measurement;*
(*g*) investment property that is measured at fair value (IAS 40 *Investment property*);
(*h*) biological assets related to agricultural activity that are measured at fair value less estimated point-of-sale costs (IAS 41 *Agriculture*);
(*i*) deferred acquisition costs, and intangible assets, arising from an insurer's contractual rights under insurance contracts within the scope of IFRS 4 (*Insurance contracts*).

IAS 36 applies to financial assets classified as:

- subsidiaries, as defined in IAS 27 (*Consolidated and separate financial statements*);
- associates, as defined in IAS 28 (*Investments in associates*); and
- joint ventures, as defined in IFRS II *(Joint arrangements)*

and to assets that are carried at revalued amount (i.e. fair value) in accordance with other standards (e.g. the revaluation model in IAS 16 *Property, plant and equipment*).

Identifying whether a revalued asset may be impaired depends on the basis used to determine fair value:

(*a*) if the asset's fair value is its market value, the only difference between the asset's fair value and its fair value less costs to sell is the cost of disposal:
  (*i*) if the disposal costs are negligible, the recoverable amount of the revalued asset is necessarily close to, or greater than, its revalued amount (i.e. fair value). In this case, it is unlikely that the revalued asset is impaired and the recoverable amount need not be estimated.
  (*ii*) if the disposal costs are not negligible, the fair value less costs to sell of the revalued asset is necessarily less than its fair value. Therefore, the revalued asset will be impaired if its value in use is less than its revalued amount (i.e. fair value). In this case, after the revaluation requirements have been applied, an entity applies IAS 36 to determine whether the asset may be impaired.

(*b*) if the asset's fair value is determined on a basis other than its market value, its revalued amount (i.e. fair value) may be greater or lower than its recoverable amount. Hence, after the revaluation requirements have been applied, an entity applies IAS 36 to determine whether the asset may be impaired.

## Impairment review

Entities must assess at each reporting date whether there is any indication that an asset may be impaired. If there is, the recoverable amount of the asset must be estimated. Irrespective of whether there is any indication of impairment, entities must also:

(*a*) test goodwill acquired in a business combination for impairment annually; and

(*b*) annually test intangible assets with indefinite useful lives and intangible assets not yet available for use for impairment by comparing their carrying amounts with their recoverable amounts. This impairment test may be performed at any time during an annual period, provided it is performed at the same time every year. Different intangible assets may be tested for impairment at different times. If an intangible asset was initially recognised during a period, it must be tested for impairment before the end of that period.

In assessing whether there is any indication that an asset may be impaired, entities should consider *at least* the following indicators of impairment:

(*i*) During the period, has an asset's market value declined significantly more than would be expected as a result of the passage of time or normal use?

(*ii*) Have significant changes with an adverse effect on the entity occurred during the period, or take place in the near future, in the technological, market, economic or legal environment in which the entity operates or in the market to which an asset is dedicated?

(*iii*) Have market interest rates or other market rates of return on investments increased during the period, and are those increases likely to affect the discount rate used in calculating an asset's value in use and decrease the asset's recoverable amount materially?

(*iv*) Is the carrying amount of the net assets of the entity more than its market capitalisation?

(*v*) Is evidence available of obsolescence or physical damage of an asset?

(*vi*) Have significant changes with an adverse effect on the entity taken place during the period, or are expected to take place in the near future, in the extent to which, or manner in which, an asset is used or is expected to be used? (These changes include the asset becoming idle, plans to discontinue or restructure the operation to which an asset belongs, plans to dispose of an asset before the previously expected date, and reassessing the useful life of an asset as finite rather than indefinite.)

(*vii*) Is evidence available from internal reporting that indicates that the economic performance of an asset is, or will be, worse than expected?

## Recognition of impairment losses

The carrying amount of the asset must be reduced to its recoverable amount if, and only if, the recoverable amount of an asset is less than its carrying amount. *That reduction is an impairment loss.*

*Non-revalued assets* – an impairment loss on a non-revalued asset is recognised in profit or loss.

*Revalued assets* – an impairment loss on a revalued asset is recognised directly against any revaluation surplus for the asset to the extent that the impairment loss does not exceed the amount in the revaluation surplus for that same asset.

When the amount estimated for an impairment loss is greater than the carrying amount of the asset to which it relates, an entity shall recognise a liability if, and only if, required by another standard.

After the recognition of an impairment loss, the depreciation or amortisation charge for the asset must be adjusted in future periods to allocate the asset's revised carrying amount, less any residual value, on a systematic basis over its remaining useful life.

## Goodwill

### Allocating goodwill to cash-generating units

A *cash-generating unit* is 'the smallest identifiable group of assets that generates cash inflows that are largely independent of the cash inflows from other assets or groups of assets'. For the purposes of impairment review, goodwill acquired in a business combination is allocated to each of the acquirer's cash-generating units, or groups of cash-generating units expected to benefit from the combination, irrespective of whether other assets or liabilities of the acquiree are assigned to those units or groups of units. Each unit or group of units to which the goodwill is allocated must:

(*i*) represent the lowest level within the entity at which the goodwill is monitored for internal management purposes; and

(*ii*) not be larger than an operating segment determined in accordance with IFRS 8 *Operating segments.*

A cash-generating unit to which goodwill has been allocated must be tested for impairment both annually and whenever there is an 'indication that the unit may be impaired, by comparing the carrying amount of the unit, including the goodwill, with the recoverable amount of the unit. If the carrying amount of the unit exceeds the recoverable amount of the unit, the entity must recognise the impairment loss by allocating it to reduce the carrying amount of the assets of the unit (group of units) in the order:

(*a*) to reduce the carrying amount of any goodwill allocated to the cash-generating unit (group of units);

(*b*) to the other assets of the unit (group of units) pro rata on the basis of the carrying amount of each asset in the unit (group of units).

In doing so, the carrying amount of an asset must not be reduced below the highest of:

- its fair value less costs to sell;
- its value in use; and
- zero.

The amount of the impairment loss that would otherwise have been allocated to the asset shall be allocated pro rata to the other assets of the unit or group of units.

### Reversing an impairment loss for goodwill

An impairment loss recognised for goodwill cannot be reversed, as it is likely to be an increase in internally generated goodwill which IAS 38 (*Intangible assets*) prohibits from recognition.

### Reversing an impairment loss of assets other than goodwill

If it appears that an impairment loss recognised for an asset other than goodwill may no longer exist or may have decreased, this may indicate that the remaining useful life, the depreciation (or amortisation) method or the residual value may need to be reviewed and adjusted in accordance with the standard applicable to the asset, even if this means that no impairment loss is reversed for the asset. When this is not the case, an impairment loss recognised in prior periods for an asset other than goodwill is reversed if, and only if, there has been a change in the estimates used to determine the asset's recoverable amount since the last impairment loss was recognised. If so, the carrying amount of the asset must be increased to its recoverable amount. *That increase is a reversal of an impairment loss.*

However, the increased carrying amount of an asset other than goodwill attributable to a reversal of an impairment loss cannot exceed the carrying amount that would have been determined (net of amortisation or depreciation) had no impairment loss been recognised for the asset in prior years. *When it does, the excess is a revaluation.*

A reversal of an impairment loss for an asset other than goodwill is recognised immediately in profit or loss. However, if the asset is carried at a revalued amount it is treated as a revaluation increase and credited directly to equity under the heading revaluation surplus *unless* the impairment loss was previously recognised in profit or loss, in which case a reversal of that impairment loss is also recognised in profit or loss.

### Reversal of an impairment loss for cash-generating units

Reversals of this type must be allocated to the assets of the unit, except for goodwill, pro rata with the carrying amounts of those assets. These increases in carrying amounts are treated in the same way as reversals of impairment losses for individual assets. The carrying amount of an asset cannot be increased above the lower of:

(*i*) its recoverable amount; and
(*ii*) the carrying amount that would have been determined (net of amortisation or depreciation) had no impairment loss been recognised for the asset in prior periods.

Any excess reversal that would otherwise have been allocated to that asset must be allocated pro rata to the other assets of the unit, except for goodwill.

## 11.29 IAS 37 Provisions, contingent liabilities and contingent assets

IAS 37 defines a provision as: '*a liability that is of uncertain timing or amount*'.

A provision should be recognised only when it is probable that a transfer of economic benefits will have to occur and a reasonable estimate can be made of the amount involved.

A contingent liability is:

*either a possible obligation arising from past events whose existence will be confirmed only by the occurrence of one or more uncertain future events not wholly within the entity's control; or a present obligation that arises from past events but is not recognised because it is not probable that a transfer of economic benefits will be required to settle the obligation or because the amount of the obligation cannot be measured with sufficient reliability.*

A contingent asset is:

*a possible asset arising from past events whose existence will be confirmed only by the occurrence of one or more uncertain events not wholly within the entity's control.*

Neither contingent liabilities nor contingent assets should be recognised. Contingent liabilities should be disclosed unless the possibility of an outflow of resources embodying economic benefits is remote. Contingent assets should only be disclosed where an inflow of economic benefits is probable.

## 11.30 IAS 38 Intangible assets

Entities frequently expend resources, or incur liabilities, on the acquisition, development, maintenance or enhancement of intangible resources. An *intangible asset* is an identifiable non-monetary asset without physical substance, such as the results of expenditure on advertising and on training; and research and development activities. As with all assets, an intangible asset must be identifiable, the entity must have control over it, and future economic benefits must be expected to flow to the entity as a result of its existence. An intangible asset will be recognised if, and only if, it is probable that the expected future economic benefits that are attributable to the asset will flow to the entity and the cost of the asset can be measured reliably.

For example, an intangible asset held under a finance lease (*see* Chapter 2) is accounted for using the rules of this standard, as are rights under licensing agreements for items such as motion picture films, video recordings, plays, manuscripts, patents and copyrights.

The accounting treatment of some intangible assets is dealt with in other standards and is not subject to the rules of IAS 38. These intangible assets include:

- intangible assets held by an entity for sale in the ordinary course of business (IAS 2 *Inventories* and IAS 11 *Construction contracts*);
- deferred tax assets (IAS 12 *Income taxes*);
- leases that are within the scope of IAS 17 *Leases;*
- assets arising from employee benefits (IAS 19 *Employee benefits*);
- financial assets as defined in IAS 32 *Financial instruments: disclosure and presentation,* the recognition and measurement of some of which are covered by IAS 27 *Consolidated and separate financial statements,* IAS 28 *Investments in associates,* and IFRS 11 *Joint arrangements;*
- goodwill acquired in a business combination (IFRS 3 *Business combinations*);
- deferred acquisition costs, and intangible assets, arising from an insurer's contractual rights under insurance contracts within the scope of IFRS 4 *Insurance contracts.* IFRS 4 sets out specific disclosure requirements for those deferred acquisition costs but not for those intangible assets. Therefore, the disclosure requirements in this standard apply to those intangible assets;
- non-current intangible assets classified as held for sale (or included in a disposal group that is classified as held for sale) in accordance with IFRS 5 *Non-current assets held for sale and discontinued operations;*
- the recognition and measurement of exploration and evaluation assets (IFRS 6 *Exploration for and evaluation of mineral resources*).

Also excluded from the scope of IAS 38 is expenditure on the development and extraction of minerals, oil, natural gas and similar non-regenerative resources.

One form of asset that has caused considerable problems over the years is expenditure on research and development.

## Research and development

Research and development activities involve the development of knowledge. Therefore, although these activities may result in an asset with physical substance (e.g. a prototype), the physical element of the asset is secondary to its intangible component – the knowledge embodied within it.

***Research*** is original and planned investigation undertaken with the prospect of gaining new scientific or technical knowledge and understanding. No intangible asset arising from research (or from the research phase of an internal project) shall be recognised. Expenditure on research (or on the research phase of an internal project) shall be recognised as an expense when it is incurred.

***Development*** is the application of research findings or other knowledge to a plan or design for the production of new or substantially improved materials, devices, products, processes, systems or services before the start of commercial production or use. An intangible asset arising from development (or from the development phase of an internal project) shall be recognised if, and only if, an entity can demonstrate all of the following:

(*i*) the technical feasibility of completing the intangible asset so that it will be available for use or sale;
(*ii*) its intention to complete the intangible asset and use or sell it;
(*iii*) its ability to use or sell the intangible asset;
(*iv*) how the intangible asset will generate probable future economic benefits. Among other things, the entity can demonstrate the existence of a market for the output of the intangible asset or the intangible asset itself or, if it is to be used internally, the usefulness of the intangible asset;
(*v*) the availability of adequate technical, financial and other resources to complete the development and to use or sell the intangible asset;
(*vi*) its ability to measure reliably the expenditure attributable to the intangible asset during its development.

Apart from defining what can be considered to be an intangible asset, IAS 38 also specifies how to measure that carrying amount of intangible assets and states the specified disclosures to be made about intangible assets in the financial statements.

## Measurement

As with all assets, intangible assets are initially measured at cost comprising:

(*a*) purchase price, including import duties and non-refundable purchase taxes, after deducting trade discounts and rebates; and
(*b*) any directly attributable cost of preparing the asset for its intended use, for example costs of employee benefits (as defined in IAS 19) arising directly from bringing the asset to its working condition; professional fees arising directly from bringing the asset to its working condition; and costs of testing whether the asset is functioning properly.

Expenditures that are not part of the cost of an intangible asset include:

(*i*) costs of introducing a new product or service (including costs of advertising and promotional activities);
(*ii*) costs of conducting business in a new location or with a new class of customer (including costs of staff training); and
(*iii*) administration and other general overhead costs.

Different treatments are adopted depending upon whether an intangible asset has a finite or an indefinite useful life.

## Intangible assets with finite useful lives

As with tangible non-current assets, the depreciable amount of an intangible asset with a finite useful life must be allocated on a systematic basis over its useful life. Amortisation begins when the asset is available for use, i.e. when it is in the location and condition necessary for it to be capable of operating in the manner intended by management. Amortisation ceases at the earlier of the date that the asset is classified as held for sale (or included in a disposal group that is classified as held for sale) in accordance with IFRS 5 and the date that the asset is derecognised.

The amortisation method used must reflect the pattern in which the asset's future economic benefits are expected to be consumed by the entity. If that pattern cannot be determined reliably, the straight line method shall be used.

The amortisation charge for each period is recognised in profit or loss unless IAS 38 *or another standard* permits or requires it to be included in the carrying amount of another asset. For example, the amortisation of intangible assets used in a production process is included in the carrying amount of inventories (see IAS 2 *Inventories*).

A variety of amortisation methods can be used to allocate the depreciable amount of an asset on a systematic basis over its useful life, including straight line, reducing balance, and unit of production. The method used is selected on the basis of the expected pattern of consumption of the expected future economic benefits embodied in the asset and is applied consistently from period to period, unless there is a change in the expected pattern of consumption of those future economic benefits. There is rarely, if ever, persuasive evidence to support an amortisation method for intangible assets with finite useful lives that results in a lower amount of accumulated amortisation than under the straight line method, such as would occur if an inverted version of the reducing balance method were used.

The amortisation period and the amortisation method for an intangible asset with a finite useful life must be reviewed at least at each financial year-end. If the expected useful life of the asset is different from previous estimates, the amortisation period must be changed accordingly. If there has been a change in the expected pattern of consumption of the future economic benefits embodied in the asset, the amortisation method should be changed to reflect the changed pattern. Such changes are treated as changes in accounting estimates in accordance with IAS 8.

## Intangible assets with indefinite useful lives

If an intangible asset is assessed as having an indefinite useful life, the carrying amount of that asset and the reasons supporting the indefinite useful life assessment must be disclosed. Such an asset should not be amortised *but* its useful life should be reviewed each reporting period to determine whether events and circumstance continue to support an indefinite useful life assessment for that asset. If they do not, the change in the useful life assessment from indefinite to finite should be accounted for as a change in accounting estimates in accordance with IAS 8.

## Impairment review of intangible assets

In accordance with IAS 36, an entity is required to test an intangible asset with an indefinite useful life for impairment by comparing its recoverable amount with its carrying amount:

(*a*) annually; and
(*b*) whenever there is an indication that the intangible asset may be impaired.

## Retirements and disposals

An intangible asset is derecognised on disposal, or when no future economic benefits are expected from its use or disposal. The gain or loss arising from the derecognition of an intangible asset is determined as the difference between the net disposal proceeds, if any, and the carrying amount of the asset. It is recognised in profit or loss when the asset is derecognised (unless IAS 17 requires otherwise on a sale and leaseback). Gains are *not* classified as revenue.

Amortisation of an intangible asset with a finite useful life does not cease when the intangible asset is no longer used, unless the asset has been fully depreciated or is classified as held for sale (or included in a disposal group that is classified as held for sale) as under IFRS 5.

## Disclosure

An entity must disclose the following for each class of intangible assets, distinguishing between internally generated intangible assets and other intangible assets:

(*a*) whether the useful lives are indefinite or finite and, if finite, the useful lives or the amortisation rates used;
(*b*) the amortisation methods used for intangible assets with finite useful lives;
(*c*) the gross carrying amount and any accumulated amortisation (aggregated with accumulated impairment losses) at the beginning and end of the period;
(*d*) the line item(s) of the statement of profit or loss in which any amortisation of intangible assets is included;
(*e*) a reconciliation of the carrying amount at the beginning and end of the period showing:
  (*i*) additions, indicating separately those from internal development, those acquired separately, and those acquired through business combinations;
  (*ii*) assets classified as held for sale or included in a disposal group classified as held for sale in accordance with IFRS 5 and other disposals;
  (*iii*) increases or decreases during the period resulting from revaluations and from impairment losses recognised or reversed directly in equity in accordance with IAS 36;
  (*iv*) impairment losses recognised in profit or loss during the period in accordance with IAS 36;
  (*v*) impairment losses reversed in profit or loss during the period in accordance with IAS 36;
  (*vi*) any amortisation recognised during the period;
  (*vii*) net exchange differences arising on the translation of the financial statements into the presentation currency, and on the translation of a foreign operation into the presentation currency of the entity; and
  (*viii*) other changes in the carrying amount during the period.

Entities must also disclose:

- for intangible assets assessed as having an indefinite useful life, the carrying amount of each asset and the reasons supporting the assessment of an indefinite useful life including a description of the factors that played a significant role in determining that the asset has an indefinite useful life;
- a description, the carrying amount and remaining amortisation period of any individual intangible asset that is material to the entity's financial statements;
- for intangible assets acquired by way of a government grant and initially recognised at fair value:
  - the fair value initially recognised for these assets;
  - their carrying amount; and
  - whether they are measured after recognition under the cost model or the revaluation model;
- the existence and carrying amounts of intangible assets whose title is restricted and the carrying amounts of intangible assets pledged as security for liabilities;
- the amount of contractual commitments for the acquisition of intangible assets.

### Intangible assets measured after recognition using the revaluation model

If intangible assets are accounted for at revalued amounts, an entity shall disclose the following:

- by class of intangible assets:
  - the effective date of the revaluation;
  - the carrying amount of revalued intangible assets; and
  - the carrying amount that would have been recognised had the revalued class of intangible assets been measured after recognition;
- the amount of the revaluation surplus that relates to intangible assets at the beginning and end of the period, indicating the changes during the period and any restrictions on the distribution of the balance to shareholders; and
- the methods and significant assumptions applied in estimating the assets' fair values.

### Research and development expenditure

The aggregate amount of research and development expenditure recognised as an expense during the period must be disclosed.

### Other information that may be disclosed

Entities are encouraged to disclose the following information:

(*a*) a description of any fully amortised intangible asset that is still in use; and
(*b*) a brief description of significant intangible assets controlled by the entity but not recognised as assets because they did not meet the recognition criteria in this standard or because they were acquired or generated before the version of IAS 38 (*Intangible assets*) issued in 1998 (which this version replaced in 2004) was effective.

## 11.31 IAS 39 Financial instruments: recognition and measurement

The definition of a financial instrument is extremely wide and includes cash, debt, and equity investments, loans, trade receivable and payables, certain provisions, and derivatives. IAS 39 covers the recognition, measurement and derecognition of financial instruments, along with rules on hedge accounting (relating to attempts to offset risk). IAS 39 is possibly the most complex of all standards and is beyond the scope of this book. The classification and measurement provisions of the standard will be replaced by IFRS 9.

## 11.32 IAS 40 Investment property

Investment property is property (land or a building – or part of a building – or both) held (by the owner or by the lessee under a finance lease) to earn rentals or for capital appreciation or both, rather than for:

(*a*) use in the production or supply of goods or services or for administrative purposes; or
(*b*) sale in the ordinary course of business. Investment property is initially recognised at cost. A decision must then be made as to which of two methods are to be adopted thereafter:

  - Cost less accumulated depreciation and any accumulated impairment losses, as per IAS 16 (*Property, plant and equipment*); or
  - Fair value, i.e. the price at which the property could be exchanged between knowledgeable, willing parties in an arm's length transaction. Movements in fair value are recognised immediately in profit or loss.

All investment properties of an entity must be accounted for on the same basis and the method adopted must be disclosed.

A change from one method to the other is made only if the change results in a more appropriate presentation. Whereas under the revaluation model, increases in carrying amount above a cost-based measure are recognised as revaluation surplus, under the fair value model all changes in fair value are recognised in profit or loss. Investment properties held under an operating lease must be accounted for by the lessee using the fair value model.

Students often overlook the fact that investment property can be land. The standard offers the following examples of investment property:

- land held for long-term capital appreciation rather than for short-term sale in the ordinary course of business;
- land held for a currently undetermined future use (if an entity has not determined that it will use the land as owner-occupied property or for short-term sale in the ordinary course of business, the land is regarded as held for capital appreciation);
- a building owned by the entity (or held by the entity under a finance lease) and leased out under one or more operating leases;
- a building that is vacant but is held to be leased out under one or more operating leases.

Gains or losses arising from the retirement or disposal of investment property are equal to the difference between the net disposal proceeds and the carrying amount of the asset and are recognised in profit or loss (unless IAS 17 requires otherwise on a sale and leaseback) in the period of the retirement or disposal.

## 11.33 IAS 41 Agriculture

IAS 41 prescribes the accounting treatment, financial statement presentation, and disclosures related to agricultural activity, a matter not covered in other standards. Agricultural activity is the '*management by an entity of the biological transformation of living animals or plants (biological assets) for sale, into agricultural produce, or into additional biological assets*'. IAS 41 is applied to agricultural produce (i.e. the harvested product of the entity's biological assets) only at the point of harvest. Thereafter, IAS 2 *Inventories* or another applicable standard is applied. The standard does not apply to:

(*a*) land related to agricultural activity (see IAS 16 *Property, plant and equipment* and IAS 40 *Investment property*); and
(*b*) intangible assets related to agricultural activity (see IAS 38 *Intangible assets*).

Agricultural produce harvested from an entity's biological assets is measured at its fair value less estimated point-of-sale costs at the point of harvest. Gains or losses arising on initial recognition at fair value less point-of-sale costs and from a change in fair value less point-of-sale costs is included in profit or loss. Unconditional government grants related to biological assets are recognised as income when the grant becomes receivable. Conditional government grants are not recognised until the conditions attaching to them are met.

## 11.34 IFRS 1 The first-time adoption of international reporting standards

IFRS 1 applies to entities the first time they switch to International GAAP. Entities must comply with each IFRS effective at the reporting date of their first IFRS financial statements. The main requirement is that in the opening IFRS statement of financial position it prepares as a starting point for its accounting under IFRSs, an entity must:

(*i*) recognise all assets and liabilities whose recognition is required by IFRSs;
(*ii*) not recognise items as assets or liabilities if IFRSs do not permit such recognition;
(*iii*) reclassify items that it recognised under previous GAAP as one type of asset, liability or component of equity, but are a different type of asset, liability or component of equity under IFRSs; and
(*iv*) apply IFRSs in measuring all recognised assets and liabilities.

The IFRS gives limited exemptions from these requirements in specified areas where the cost of complying with them would be likely to exceed the benefits to users of financial statements. The IFRS also prohibits retrospective application of IFRSs in some areas, particularly where retrospective application would require judgements by management about past conditions after the outcome of a particular transaction is already known.

The IFRS requires disclosures that explain how the transition from previous GAAP to IFRSs affected the entity's reported financial position, financial performance and cash flows.

## 11.35 IFRS 2 Share-based payment

Under IFRS 2, share-based payments must be recognised as an expense, measured at fair value which should be based on market prices and should take into account the terms and conditions upon which the instruments were granted. The standard gives the accounting treatment to be adopted and disclosures to be made by entities making such payments.

IFRS 2 identifies three types of share-based payment transaction:

(*a*) equity-settled share-based payment transactions. These are transactions in which the entity receives goods or services as consideration for equity instruments of the entity;
(*b*) cash-settled share-based payment transactions. These are transactions in which the entity acquires goods or services by incurring liabilities to the supplier of those goods or services for amounts that are based on the price (or value) of the entity's equity instruments;
(*c*) transactions in which the entity receives or acquires goods or services and the terms of the arrangement provide one or other of the parties to the transaction with a choice as to whether the transaction is settled in cash or by issuing equity instruments.

Examples of share-based payments include:

(*a*) all types of executive share option and share purchase plans and employee share option and share purchase schemes, including Save-As-You-Earn (SAYE) plans and similar arrangements;
(*b*) arrangements such as share appreciation rights, where a cash payment is made, the amount of which depends on the share price; and
(*c*) transactions with suppliers of goods or non-employee services that involve share-based payments being made in exchange for those goods or services.

## 11.36 IFRS 3 Business combinations

This standard is covered in Chapter 25. Among the topics it deals with is goodwill. Purchased goodwill should be capitalised. It must not be amortised but should be checked for impairment annually. Any impairment should be written off to profit or loss and cannot be reinstated. Gain from a bargain purchase must be eliminated immediately by reviewing and amending the fair values of the net assets acquired and, if necessary, recognising the gain in profit or loss.

## 11.37 IFRS 4 Insurance contracts

IFRS 4 applies to all insurance contracts (including reinsurance contracts) that an entity issues and to reinsurance contracts that it holds, except for specified contracts covered by other IFRSs. It does not apply to other assets and liabilities of an insurer, such as financial assets and financial liabilities within the scope of IAS 39 *Financial instruments: recognition and measurement*. Furthermore, it does not address accounting by policyholders.

This IFRS does not address other aspects of accounting by insurers, such as accounting for financial assets held by insurers and financial liabilities issued by insurers (IAS 32 *Financial instruments: presentation,* IAS 39 *Financial instruments: recognition and measurement* and IFRS 7 *Financial instruments: disclosures*).

An entity shall not apply this IFRS to:

(*a*) product warranties issued directly by a manufacturer, dealer or retailer (IAS 18 *Revenue* and IAS 37 *Provisions, contingent liabilities and contingent assets*);
(*b*) employers' assets and liabilities under employee benefit plans (IAS 19 *Employee benefits* and IFRS 2 *Share-based payment*) and retirement benefit obligations reported by defined benefit retirement plans (IAS 26 *Accounting and reporting by retirement benefit plans*);
(*c*) contractual rights or contractual obligations that are contingent on the future use of, or right to use, a non-financial item (for example, some licence fees, royalties, contingent lease payments and similar items), as well as a lessee's residual value guarantee embedded in a finance lease (IAS 17 *Leases,* IAS 18 *Revenue* and IAS 38 *Intangible assets*);
(*d*) financial guarantee contracts unless the issuer has previously asserted explicitly that it regards such contracts as insurance contracts and has used accounting applicable to insurance contracts, in which case the issuer may elect to apply either IAS 39, IAS 32 and IFRS 7 or this standard to such financial guarantee contracts. The issuer may make that election contract by contract, but the election for each contract is irrevocable;
(*e*) contingent consideration payable or receivable in a business combination (IFRS 3 *Business combinations*);
(*f*) direct insurance contracts that the entity holds (i.e. direct insurance contracts in which the entity is the *policyholder*). However, a *cedant* shall apply this IFRS to reinsurance contracts that it holds.

An insurer may change its accounting policies for insurance contracts if, and only if, the change makes the financial statements more relevant to the economic decision-making needs of users and no less reliable, or more reliable and no less relevant to those needs. An insurer shall judge relevance and reliability by the criteria in IAS 8 (*Accounting policies, changes in accounting estimates and errors*).

The IFRS specifies the financial reporting for *insurance contracts* by any entity that issues such contracts (described in this IFRS as an *insurer*) and requires:

(*i*) limited improvements to accounting by insurers for insurance contracts;
(*ii*) disclosure that identifies and explains the amounts in an insurer's financial statements arising from insurance contracts and helps users of those financial statements understand the amount, timing and uncertainty of future cash flows from insurance contracts.

## 11.38 IFRS 5 Non-current assets held for sale and discontinued operations

Non-current assets are assets that include amounts expected to be recovered more than 12 months after the date of the statement of financial position. IFRS 5 requires that a non-current asset (or disposal group) be classified as held for sale if its carrying amount will be recovered principally through a sale transaction rather than through continuing use. Assets or disposal groups that are classified as held for sale are carried at the lower of carrying amount and fair value less costs to sell, are not depreciated, are presented separately on the statement of financial position, and their results are disclosed separately in the statement of profit or loss.

A 'component of an entity' comprises operations and cash flows that can be clearly distinguished, operationally and for financial reporting purposes, from the rest of the entity, i.e. a cash-generating unit or a group of cash-generating units. A 'discontinued operation' is a component of an entity that either has been disposed of, or is classified as held for sale, and:

- represents a separate major line of business or geographical area of operations;
- is part of a single coordinated plan to dispose of a separate major line of business or geographical area of operations; or
- is a subsidiary acquired exclusively with a view to resale.

The results of discontinued operations are shown separately on the face of the statement of profit or loss in the form of a single line comprising the total of (*a*) the post-tax profit/loss from discontinued operations, plus (*b*) the post-tax gain/loss recognised in the measurement of the fair value less costs to sell or on the disposal of the assets of the discontinued operations.

Sometimes an entity disposes of a group of assets, possibly with some directly associated liabilities, in a single transaction. Such a disposal group may be a group of *cash-generating units,* a single cash-generating unit, or part of a cash-generating unit. The disposal group may include any assets and any liabilities of the entity, including current assets, current liabilities and assets excluded from the measurement requirements of IFRS 5. If a non-current asset within the scope of the measurement requirements of IFRS 5 is part of a disposal group, the measurement requirements of IFRS 5 apply to the group as a whole, so that the group is measured at the lower of its carrying amount and fair value less costs to sell.

The classification and presentation requirements of this IFRS apply to all recognised non-current assets and to all *disposal groups* of an entity. The measurement requirements of IFRS 5 apply to all recognised non-current assets and disposal groups except:

- deferred tax assets (IAS 12 *Income taxes*);
- assets arising from employee benefits (IAS 19 *Employee benefits*);
- financial assets within the scope of IAS 39 *Financial instruments: recognition and measurement;*
- non-current assets that are accounted for in accordance with the fair value model in IAS 40 *Investment property;*
- non-current assets that are measured at fair value less estimated point-of-sale costs in accordance with IAS 41 *Agriculture;*
- contractual rights under insurance contracts as defined in IFRS 4 *Insurance contracts.*

Assets classified as non-current in accordance with IAS 1 (*Presentation of financial statements*) should not be reclassified as *current assets* until they meet the criteria to be classified as held for sale in accordance with IFRS 5. Assets of a class that an entity would normally regard as non-current that are acquired exclusively with a view to resale shall not be classified as current unless they meet the criteria to be classified as held for sale in accordance with IFRS 5.

An entity must present and disclose information that enables users of the financial statements to evaluate the financial effects of discontinued operations and disposals of non-current assets (or disposal groups).

## 11.39 IFRS 6 Exploration for and evaluation of mineral resources

IFRS 6 specifies the financial reporting for the exploration for and evaluation of mineral resources. The IFRS requires exploration and evaluation assets to be measured at cost and requires entities that recognise exploration and evaluation assets to assess such assets for impairment and measure any impairment in accordance with IAS 36 *Impairment of assets.* It also requires the disclosures that identify and explain the amounts in the entity's financial statements arising from the exploration for and evaluation of mineral resources and help users of those financial statements understand the amount, timing and certainty of future cash flows from any exploration and evaluation assets recognised.

The IFRS:

(*a*) permits an entity to develop an accounting policy for exploration and evaluation assets without specifically considering the requirements of paragraphs 11 and 12 of IAS 8 *Accounting policies, changes in accounting estimates and errors*. Thus, an entity adopting IFRS 6 may continue to use the accounting policies applied immediately before adopting the IFRS. This includes continuing to use recognition and measurement practices that are part of those accounting policies;

(*b*) requires entities recognising exploration and evaluation assets to perform an impairment test on those assets when facts and circumstances suggest that the carrying amount of the assets may exceed their recoverable amount;

(*c*) varies the recognition of impairment from that in IAS 36 but measures the impairment in accordance with IAS 36 once the impairment is identified.

Entities must apply IFRS 6 to exploration and evaluation expenditures that they incur. However, the IFRS does not address other aspects of accounting by entities engaged in the exploration for and evaluation of mineral resources.

Entities must not apply the IFRS to expenditures incurred:

(*i*) before the exploration for and evaluation of mineral resources, such as expenditures incurred before the entity has obtained the legal rights to explore a specific area; or

(*ii*) after the technical feasibility and commercial viability of extracting a mineral resource are demonstrable.

Entities must determine an accounting policy specifying which expenditures are recognised as exploration and evaluation assets and apply the policy consistently. In making this determination, entities must consider the degree to which the expenditure can be associated with finding specific mineral resources.

Examples of expenditures that might be included in the initial measurement of exploration and evaluation assets include:

- acquisition of rights to explore;
- topographical, geological, geochemical and geophysical studies;
- exploratory drilling;
- trenching;
- sampling; and
- activities in relation to evaluating the technical feasibility and commercial viability of extracting a mineral resource.

Expenditures related to the development of mineral resources are not exploration and evaluation assets. The *Framework* and IAS 38 (*Intangible assets*) provide guidance on the recognition of assets arising from development.

In accordance with IAS 37 (*Provisions, contingent liabilities and contingent assets*) an entity recognises any obligations for removal and restoration that are incurred during a particular period as a consequence of having undertaken the exploration for and evaluation of mineral resources.

After recognition, an entity must apply either the cost model or the revaluation model to the exploration and evaluation assets. If the revaluation model is applied (either the model in IAS 16 *Property, plant and equipment* or the model in IAS 38), it must be consistent with the classification of the assets.

An entity may change its accounting policies for exploration and evaluation expenditures if the change makes the financial statements more relevant to the economic decision-making needs of users and no less reliable, or more reliable and no less relevant to those needs. An entity must judge relevance and reliability using the criteria in IAS 8.

### Classification of exploration and evaluation assets

An entity must classify exploration and evaluation assets as tangible or intangible according to the nature of the assets acquired and apply the classification consistently.

Some exploration and evaluation assets are treated as intangible (e.g. drilling rights). Others are tangible (e.g. vehicles and drilling rigs). To the extent that a tangible asset is consumed in developing an intangible asset, the amount reflecting that consumption is part of the cost of the intangible asset. However, using a tangible asset to develop an intangible asset does not change a tangible asset into an intangible asset.

### Reclassification of exploration and evaluation assets

When the technical feasibility and commercial viability of extracting a mineral resource are demonstrable, an asset previously classified as an exploration and evaluation asset loses its classification. Exploration and evaluation assets must be assessed for impairment, and any impairment loss recognised, before reclassification.

Exploration and evaluation assets should be assessed for impairment when facts and circumstances suggest that the carrying amount of an exploration and evaluation asset may exceed its recoverable amount. When facts and circumstances confirm that this is the case, an entity must measure, present and disclose any resulting impairment loss in accordance with IAS 36.

### Disclosure

Entities must disclose:

(*a*) their accounting policies for exploration and evaluation expenditures including the recognition of exploration and evaluation assets;
(*b*) the amounts of assets, liabilities, income and expense and operating and investing cash flows arising from the exploration for and evaluation of mineral resources.

In doing so, entities should treat exploration and evaluation assets as a separate class of assets and make the disclosures required by either IAS 16 or IAS 38 consistent with how the assets are classified.

## 11.40 IFRS 7 Financial instruments: disclosures

IFRS 7 complements the principles for recognising, measuring and presenting financial assets and financial liabilities in IAS 32 (*Financial instruments: disclosure and presentation*) and IAS 39 (*Financial instruments: recognition and measurement*). It regulates the disclosures that must be made in the financial statements of entities with financial instruments. These disclosures are intended to enable users to evaluate:

(*i*) the significance of financial instruments for the entity's financial position and performance; and
(*ii*) the nature and extent of risks arising from financial instruments to which the entity is exposed during the period and at the reporting date, and how the entity manages those risks.

As with IAS 39, IFRS 7 is beyond the scope of this book.

## 11.41 IFRS 8 Operating segments

IFRS 8 requires an entity to disclose information that enables users of its financial statements to evaluate the nature and financial effects of the business activities in which it engages and the economic environments in which it operates. In order to do so, the financial and descriptive information reported under the standard must be allocated across appropriate segments of the business called 'operating segments'. An operating segment is a component of an entity that engages in business activities from which it may earn revenues and incur expenses and about which separate financial information is available that is evaluated regularly by the chief operating decision-maker in deciding how to allocate resources and in assessing performance.

An entity must report separately information about each operating segment that meets any of the following quantitative thresholds:

(*i*) its reported revenue, including both sales to external customers and inter-segment sales or transfers, is 10% or more of the combined revenue, internal and external, of all operating segments;
(*ii*) the absolute amount of its reported profit or loss is 10% or more of the greater, in absolute amount, of (*a*) the combined reported profit of all operating segments that did not report a loss, and (*b*) the combined reported loss of all operating segments that reported a loss.
(*iii*) its assets are 10% or more of the combined assets of all operating segments.

Operating segments that do not meet any of the quantitative thresholds may be separately disclosed if management believes that information about the segment would be useful to users of the financial statements.

Operating segments that have similar economic characteristics can be aggregated and reported as one segment. When operating segments are considered to be too immaterial to be reported separately, they are combined and reported in an 'all other segments' category. The segments that remain after any aggregation are known as 'reportable segments'. It is these segments that the standard requires entities to report upon in both their annual financial statements and interim financial reports. IFRS 8 also sets out requirements for related disclosures about products and services, geographical areas and major customers.

The IFRS requires an entity to report operating segment profit or loss and segment assets, segment liabilities, and particular income and expense items if they are regularly provided to the chief operating decision-maker. It requires reconciliations of total reportable segment revenues, total profit or loss, total assets, liabilities and other amounts disclosed for reportable segments to corresponding amounts in the entity's financial statements.

Information must also be reported concerning the revenues derived from its products or services (or groups of similar products and services), about the countries in which it earns revenues and holds assets, and about major customers. However, the IFRS does not require an entity to report information that is not prepared for internal use if the necessary information is not available and the cost to develop it would be excessive.

The IFRS also requires an entity to give descriptive information about the way the operating segments were determined, the products and services provided by the segments, differences between the measurements used in reporting segment information and those used in the entity's financial statements, and changes in the measurement of segment amounts from period to period.

Unlike other IFRSs, IFRS 8 only applies to separate or consolidated financial statements of entities listed or seeking listing on a stock exchange for its debt or equity instruments. However, if a financial report contains both the consolidated financial statements of a parent that is within the scope of IFRS 8 as well as the parent's separate financial statements, segment information is required only in the consolidated financial statements.

Entities must also disclose the following general information:

(*i*) the factors used to identify the entity's reportable segments, including the basis of organisation (e.g. whether management has chosen to organise the entity around differences in products and services, geographical areas, regulatory environments, or a combination of factors and whether operating segments have been aggregated); and

(*ii*) the types of products and services from which each reportable segment derives its revenues.

## 11.42 IFRS 9 Financial instruments

This accounting standard was issued in 2009 in the first stage of a move to replace IAS 39 (*Financial instruments: recognition and measurement*). It became compulsory on 1 January 2015.

Under IFRS 9, all financial instruments are initially measured at fair value, normally at transaction cost. Some previously acquired financial assets that involve debt (i.e. loan notes) may be measured at amortised cost and must have been measured in that way at the time they were initially recognised. All equity financial instruments are measured at fair value in the statement of financial position. Gains or losses on valuation are normally taken to profit or loss.

## 11.43 IFRS 10 Consolidated financial statements

This standard establishes how consolidated financial statements should be presented and defines the principle of 'control'.

## 11.44 IFRS 11 Joint arrangements

This standard is covered in Section 26.7.

## 11.45 IFRS 12 Disclosure of interests in other entities

The standard requires entities to disclose information so that users of its financial statements can assess the nature of and the risks entailed in its interests in other entities, such as subsidiaries, joint arrangements, associates and unconsolidated entities. It is covered in Section 26.8.

## 11.46 IFRS 13 Fair value measurement

This standard replaces the variety of definitions of 'fair value' contained in other IASs and IFRSs into one single definition: 'the price that would be received to sell an asset or paid to transfer a liability in an orderly transaction between market participants at the measurement date'.

## 11.47 IFRS for small and medium-sized entities

This standard is for use by entities whose shares or debt instruments are not publicly traded and which are typically of a size which local legislation or regulation would consider 'small' or 'medium-sized' rather than 'large'. In the UK, the same entities which were eligible to adopt the UK GAAP financial reporting standard for small-sized entities would be eligible to adopt this IFRS.

The standard contains simplified versions of the extant accounting standards, so reducing the volume of accounting requirements compared to entities reporting under the full set of IASs and IFRSs.

## 11.48 Other IFRSs not effective until 2016 and 2018

Two new IFRSs have been issued but are not yet compulsory, though they may be adopted before the effective date if an entity wishes to do so:

- IFRS 14 *Regulatory deferral accounts*. This standard relates to first-time adopters of IFRS. It permits them to continue to account for balances on regulatory deferral accounts in the same way that they did under the version of GAAP they used before they adopted IFRS. Regulatory deferral accounts are defined as, *'The balance of any expense (or income) account that would not be recognised as an asset or a liability in accordance with other Standards, but that qualifies for deferral because it is included, or is expected to be included, by the rate regulator in establishing the rate(s) that can be charged to customers.'* IFRS 14 comes into effect on 1 January 2016.
- IFRS 15 *Revenue from contracts with customers*. The standard specifies how and when revenue should be recognised and that it should be recognised at the amount the entity expects to receive in exchange for goods or services. IFRS 15 comes into effect on 1 January 2018.

Information on the latest developments in international standards can be found at the IASB website: **www.iasb.org**

## 11.49 Professional ethics

It is now recognised that accountants have a professional responsibility to be 'ethical'. This is a relatively new development. For many years, ethics were an informal element of the training of accountants. However, an apparently never-ending stream of high-profile financial scandals since the 1960s has threatened the reputation of the accounting profession. As a result, the informal approach to ethics has been formalised in an attempt to stop such events occurring.

It is for this reason that some accountancy bodies now include a separate ethics course in their training. Others have embedded ethics into some of their courses and examinations. But what does it mean to be 'ethical'?

Being ethical involves showing integrity, fairness, respect and openness in behaviour and attitude in all situations. Members of all professions have a responsibility to society because they have the specialist knowledge and expertise to deal with certain situations in a more informed way than those who are not so qualified. For accountants, their professional ethics are not just concerned with how an accountant should be in the workplace, they also relate to how accountants should behave in all aspects of their public life.

Ethics apply not only to what an accountant does, and to his or her interaction with those who are not accountants; ethics also apply to how accountants conduct themselves with each other and with those aspiring to be accountants. Managers and trainers of accountants have an ethical responsibility to present themselves as respectful, honest, and trustworthy; and to ensure that their accounting trainees embrace those same values.

The International Federation of Accountants is the world umbrella body for professional accountancy bodies. It has over 175 membership bodies and associate bodies in 130 countries, representing more than 2.5 million accountants in public practice, education, government service, industry, and commerce. Its 2014 *Code of Ethics for Professional Accountants* forms the basis for many of the ethical codes applied by its member bodies. The IFAC Code is available at **http://web.ifac.org/publications/international-ethics-standards-board-for-accountants/code-of-ethics**

In the IFAC Code, it is stated that a professional accountant must comply with the following fundamental principles:

(*a*) *Integrity* – to be straightforward and honest in all professional and business relationships.
(*b*) *Objectivity* – to not allow bias, conflict of interest or undue influence of others to override professional or business judgements.

(*c*) *Professional competence and due care* – to maintain professional knowledge and skill at the level required to ensure that a client or employer receives competent professional services based on current developments in practice, legislation and techniques and acts diligently and in accordance with applicable technical and professional standards.

(*a*) *Confidentiality* – to respect the confidentiality of information acquired as a result of professional and business relationships and, therefore, not disclose any such information to third parties without proper and specific authority, unless there is a legal or professional right or duty to disclose, or use the information for the personal advantage of the professional accountant or third parties.

(*b*) *Professional behaviour* – to comply with relevant laws and regulations and avoid any action that discredits the profession.

To supplement their ethical codes, accountancy bodies worldwide operate their own disciplinary code which establishes what steps may be taken should a member act unethically. These disciplinary codes are designed to protect non-accountants and to maintain the reputation of the profession and the demand for its services. Accountants found guilty of unethical behaviour risk the possibility of fines or even expulsion from their professional body.

Do you think that such a system of self-regulation is appropriate?

## Learning outcomes

**You should now have learnt:**

1. That accounting standards have statutory recognition and must, therefore, be complied with when preparing financial statements intended to present a true and fair view.
2. That the *Framework for the Preparation and Presentation of Financial Statements* provides details of the concepts that underpin accounting standards.
3. That as of May 2015, there were 44 international accounting standards (28 IASs, 15 JFRSs, and one IFRS for SMEs), plus two IFRSs due to come into force in 2016 and 2017.
4. About the main requirements of a range of accounting standards.
5. About the fundamental ethical principles that accountants must follow.

## Answers to activities

11.1 Apart from the legal requirement that certain companies switch to international standards, international accounting standards are becoming increasingly adopted across the world. At the same time, there is an increasing internationalisation of business and a need for greater international uniformity in the regulations underpinning the preparation of company financial statements, particularly for multinational companies.

11.2 Most non-accountants assume that the information in financial statements is accurate, correct and free of bias. They believe this to be the case because they assume that all such information is based on firm facts – for example, that what something cost is shown in the invoice and confirmed by the amount paid for it as shown in the bank statement. They do not realise that many of the figures shown are based on estimates and subject to the subjective interpretation of a situation by the person preparing the financial statements. They are unaware that accountants have many choices to make, so much so that it is unlikely that two accountants would ever produce identical financial statements for any but the smallest of organisations.

By placing an emphasis on the qualitative aspects of information, the *Statement of Principles* seeks to restrict diversity in the range of options open to the preparers of financial statements and so guide them towards a more uniform interpretation of the options available to them, thereby increasing the level of faith that users of those statements may have in the information they contain.

11.3 (From the *Framework*, paragraph 103) A financial concept of capital should be adopted if the users of financial statements are primarily concerned with the maintenance of nominal invested capital or the purchasing power of invested capital. If, however, the main concern of users is with the operating capability of the entity, a physical concept of capital should be used. The concept chosen indicates the goal to be attained in determining profit, even though there may be some measurement difficulties in making the concept operational.

11.4 As with all professions, enforcement of a code of ethics in a manner which encourages outsiders to believe that accountancy bodies are serious on this issue is not simply a case of having a disciplinary code. Outsiders can be very sceptical about self-regulation, especially if accountants found guilty of unethical conduct are let off with a warning or a minor fine. This is a difficult situation to address: non-accountants lack the technical knowledge and expertise to interpret accounting practice and so are incapable of truly understanding many of the situations that may arise. Finding something more appropriate is difficult, if not impossible.

## Review questions

**11.1** In preparing its accounts for the year to 31 May 2017, Whiting plc had been faced with a number of accounting problems, the details of which were as follows:

(*i*) The company had closed down its entire American operations which represented a significant part of Whiting plc's business.
(*ii*) The corporation tax for the year to 31 May 2016 had been over-provided by £5,000.
(*iii*) Land and buildings had been revalued at an amount well in excess of the historic cost (note: the current value is to be adjusted in the financial statements).
(*iv*) A trade debtor had gone into liquidation owing Whiting plc an amount equivalent to 20% of Whiting's turnover for the year. It is highly unlikely that any of this debt will ever be repaid.
(*v*) During the year, the company changed its method of valuing inventory. If the same method had been adopted in the previous year, the profits for that year would have been considerably less than had previously been reported.

**Required:**
Being careful to give your reasons, explain how each of the above matters should be treated in the financial statements of Whiting plc for the year to 31 May 2017 if the company follows the requirements of IAS 1 and IFRS 5.

(*Association of Accounting Technicians*)

**11.2** The directors are preparing the published accounts of Dorman plc for the year to 31 October 2018. The following information is provided for certain of the items which are to be included in the final accounts.

(*i*) *Inventories of raw material, monolite*:

| | £ |
|---|---|
| Cost | 26,500 |
| Replacement cost | 48,100 |

(*ii*) *Inventory of finished goods*:

| | *Paramite* | *Paraton* |
|---|---|---|
| | £ | £ |
| Direct costs | 72,600 | 10,200 |
| Proportion of fixed factory overhead | 15,300 | 4,600 |
| Proportion of selling expenses | 6,870 | 1,800 |
| Net realisable value | 123,500 | 9,520 |

→

(*iii*) *Plant and machinery.* An item of plant was shown in the 2017 accounts at a net book value of £90,000 (£160,000 cost less accumulated depreciation £70,000). The plant was purchased on 1 November 2015 and has been depreciated at 25% reducing balance. The directors now consider the straight line basis to be more appropriate: they have estimated that at 1 November 2017 the plant had a remaining useful life of six years and will possess zero residual value at the end of that period.

(*iv*) *Freehold property.* The company purchased a freehold property for £250,000 11 years ago, and it is estimated that the land element was worth £50,000 at that date.

The company has never charged depreciation on the property but the directors now feel that it should have done so; the building is expected to have a total useful life of 40 years.

(*v*) *Research expenditure* incurred in an attempt to discover a substitute for raw materials currently purchased from a politically sensitive area of the world amounted to £17,500 during the year.

(*vi*) *Development expenditure* on Tercil, which is nearly ready for production, amounted to £30,000. Demand for Tercil is expected significantly to exceed supply for at least the next four years.

(*vii*) *Accident.* On 1 December 2018 there was a fire in the warehouse which damaged inventory, other than the items referred to in (*i*) and (*ii*) above. The book value of the damaged inventory was £92,000. The company has discovered that it was underinsured and only expects to recover £71,000 from the insurers.

(*viii*) *Investments.* Dorman purchased 30,000 ordinary shares in Lilleshall Ltd on 1 November 2017 for £96,000, and immediately succeeded in appointing two of its directors to Lilleshall's board. The issued share capital of Lilleshall consists of 100,000 ordinary shares of £1 each. The profits of Lilleshall for the year to 31 October 2018 amounted to £40,000. (Ignore taxation.)

**Required:**

Explain how each of the above items should be dealt with in the published financial statements of Dorman plc.

(*Institute of Chartered Secretaries and Administrators*)

**11.3A** In preparing the published financial statements of a company, briefly state the significant accounting/disclosure requirements you would have in mind in ensuring that the financial statements comply with best accounting practice as embodied in accounting standards and the Companies Act 2006 concerning:

(*a*) Value added tax.
(*b*) Earnings per share.
(*c*) The disclosure requirements of each major class of depreciable assets.
(*d*) Research expenditure.
(*e*) Capital-based grants relating to fixed assets.
(*f*) Goodwill on consolidation.
(*g*) The disclosure requirements relating to generally accepted fundamental accounting concepts.
(*h*) The accounts of a subsidiary undertaking having similar activities to that of the parent undertaking.

(*Association of Accounting Technicians*)

**11.4A** Oldfield Enterprises Limited was formed on 1 January 2018 to manufacture and sell a new type of lawn mower. The bookkeeping staff of the company have produced monthly figures for the first 10 months to 31 October 2018 and from these figures together with estimates for the remaining two months, Barry Lamb, the managing director, has drawn up a forecast profit and loss account for the year to 31 December 2018 and a statement of financial position as at that date.

These statements together with the notes are submitted to the board for comment. During the board meeting discussion centres on the treatment given to the various assets. The various opinions are summarised by Barry Lamb who brings them, with the draft accounts, to you as the company's financial adviser.

**Oldfield Enterprises Ltd**
**Draft Statement of Profit or Loss (extract) for the year ending 31 December 2018**

| | £000 | £000 |
|---|---|---|
| Revenue | | 3,000 |
| Cost of sales | | 1,750 |
| Gross profit | | 1,250 |
| Administration overheads | 350 | |
| Selling and distribution overheads | 530 | |
| | | 880 |
| Net profit before taxation | | 370 |

**Draft Statement of Financial Position at 31 December 2018**

| *Non-current assets – tangible* | Cost<br>£000 | Depreciation and amortisation<br>£000 | Net<br>£000 |
|---|---|---|---|
| Leasehold land and buildings | 375 | 125 | 250 |
| Freehold land and buildings | 350 | – | 350 |
| Plant and machinery | 1,312 | 197 | 1,115 |
| | 2,037 | 322 | 1,715 |
| *Non-current assets – intangible* | | | |
| Research and development | | | 375 |
| *Current assets* | | | |
| Inventory | | 375 | |
| Accounts receivable | | 780 | |
| | | | 1,155 |
| Total assets | | | 3,245 |
| *Current liabilities* | | | |
| Accounts payable | | 250 | |
| Bank overdraft | | 125 | |
| | | | 375 |
| Net assets | | | 2,870 |
| *Equity* | | | |
| Share capital | | | 2,500 |
| Retained profits | | | 370 |
| | | | 2,870 |

*Notes*:

(*a*) Administration overheads include £50,000 written off research and development.

(*b*) The lease is for 15 years and cost £75,000. Buildings have been put up on the leasehold land at a cost of £300,000. Plant and machinery has been depreciated at 15%. Both depreciation and amortisation are included in cost of sales.

*Opinions put forward*

*Leasehold land and buildings*:

The works director thinks that although the lease provides for a rent review after three years the buildings have a 50-year life. The buildings should therefore be depreciated over 50 years and the cost of the lease should be amortised over the period of the lease.

The managing director thinks that because of the rent review clause the whole of the cost should be depreciated over three years.

The sales director thinks it is a good idea to charge as much as the profits will allow in order to reduce the tax bill.

→ *Freehold land and buildings*:
The works director thinks that as the value of the property is going up with inflation no depreciation is necessary.

The sales director's opinion is the same as for leasehold property.

The managing director states that he has heard that if a property is always kept in good repair no depreciation is necessary. This should apply in the case of his company.

*Plant and machinery*:
The managing director agrees with the 15% for depreciation and proposes to use the reducing balance method.

The works director wants to charge 25% straight line.

*Research and development*:
The total spent in the year will be £425,000. Of this £250,000 is for research into the cutting characteristics of different types of grass, £100,000 is for the development of an improved drive system for lawn mowers and £75,000 is for market research to determine the ideal lawn mower characteristics for the average garden.

The managing director thinks that a small amount should be charged as an expense each year.

The works director wants to write off all the market research and 'all this nonsense of the cutting characteristics of grass'.

The sales director thinks that, as the company has only just started, all research and development expenditure relates to future sales so all this year's expenditure should be carried forward.

*Inventory*:
Both the managing director and the works director are of the opinion that inventory should be shown at prime cost.

The sales director's view is that inventory should be shown at sales price as the inventory is virtually all sold within a very short period.

**Required:**

(*a*) You are asked to comment on each opinion stating what factors should be taken into account to determine suitable depreciation and write-off amounts.

(*b*) Indicate what amounts should, in your opinion, be charged to profit or loss and show the adjusted profit produced by your recommendations, stating clearly any assumptions you may make.

(*Association of Chartered Certified Accountants*)

**11.5** The accountant of Hook, Line and Sinker, a partnership of seven people, has asked your advice in dealing with the following items in the partnership accounts for the year to 31 May 2017.

(*a*) (*i*) Included in invoices prepared and dated in June 2017 were £60,000 of goods despatched during the second half of May 2017.

(*ii*) Inventory of components at 31 May 2017 includes parts no longer used in production. These components originally cost £50,000 but have been written down for purposes of the accounts to £25,000. Scrap value of these items is estimated to be £1,000. Another user has expressed interest in buying these parts for £40,000.

(*b*) After May 2017 a customer who accounts for 50% of Hook, Line and Sinker sales suffered a serious fire which has disrupted his organisation. Payments for supplies are becoming slow and Hook, Line and Sinker sales for the current year are likely to be substantially lower than previously. This customer owed £80,000 to Hook, Line and Sinker at 31 May 2017.

(*c*) During the year to 31 May, Hook, Line and Sinker commenced a new advertising campaign using television and expensive magazine advertising for the first time. Sales during the year were not much higher than previous years as the partners consider that the effects of advertising will be seen in future years.

Expenditure on advertising during the year is made up of:

| | £ |
|---|---|
| Television | 50,000 |
| Advertisements in magazines | 60,000 |
| Advertisements in local papers | 25,000 |

All the expenditure has been treated as expense in the accounts but the partners wish to carry forward three-quarters of the television and magazine costs as it is expected that this cost will benefit future years' profits and because this year's profits will compare unfavourably with previous years if all the expenditure is charged in the accounts.

(*d*) Three projects for the construction of sinkers have the following cost and revenue characteristics:

| | *Project A* | *Project B* | *Project C* |
|---|---|---|---|
| Degree of completion | *75%* | *50%* | *15%* |
| | £ | £ | £ |
| Direct costs to date | 30,000 | 25,000 | 6,000 |
| Sales price of complete project | 55,000 | 50,000 | 57,500 |
| Overheads allocated to date | 4,000 | 2,000 | 500 |
| Costs to complete – Direct | 10,000 | 25,000 | 40,000 |
| – Overheads | 2,000 | 2,000 | 3,000 |

No profits or losses have been included in the accounts.

(e) After considerable discussion with management, the sales of a newly developed special purpose hook have been given the following probabilities:

*First year of production*

| *Sales* | *Probability* |
|---|---|
| £ | |
| 15,000 | 0.2 |
| 30,000 | 0.5 |
| 40,000 | 0.3 |

*Second year of production*

| *Increase over first year* | *Probability* |
|---|---|
| £ | |
| 10,000 | 0.1 |
| 20,000 | 0.5 |
| 30,000 | 0.4 |

Second-year sales may be assumed independent of first-year levels.
Cost–volume–profit analysis shows that the breakeven point is £50,000.

Production of the special purpose hook started prior to the end of the accounting year and inventory of the finished product is included at cost amounting to £20,000. It has been decided that if there is less than 0.7 probability of breakeven being reached in the second year then inventory should be written down by 25%.

(*f*) During the year it was discovered that some inventory sheets had been omitted from the calculations at the previous year end. The effect is that opening inventory for the current year, shown as £35,000, should be £42,000. No adjustment has yet been made.

**Required:**
Discuss the treatment of each item with reference to relevant accounting standards and accounting concepts and conventions. Recommend the appropriate treatment for each item showing the profit effect of each recommendation made.

(*Association of Chartered Certified Accountants*)

**11.6** The chief accountant of Uncertain Ltd is not sure of the appropriate accounting treatment for a number of events occurring during the year 2016/17.

(*i*) A significant number of employees have been made redundant, giving rise to redundancy payments of £100,000 which have been included in manufacturing cost of sales.

(*ii*) One of Uncertain Ltd's three factories has been closed down. Closure costs amounted to £575,000. This amount has been deducted from reserves in the statement of financial position.

(*iii*) The directors have changed the basis of charging depreciation on delivery vehicles. The difference between the old and new methods amounts to £258,800. This has been treated as a charge in accounting policy and the comparative figures have been adjusted accordingly.

(*iv*) During October 2016 a fire occurred in one of the remaining factories belonging to Uncertain Ltd and caused an estimated £350,000 of additional expenses. This amount has been included in manufacturing cost of sales.

(*v*) It was discovered on 31 October 2017 that a customer was unable to pay his debt to the company of £125,000. The £125,000 was made up of sales in the period July to September 2017. No adjustment has been made in the draft accounts for this item.

**Uncertain Ltd**
**Draft Statement of Profit or Loss for the year ending 30 September 2017**

| | £ | £ |
|---|---|---|
| Revenue | | 5,450,490 |
| Manufacturing cost of sales | | 3,284,500 |
| Gross profit | | 2,165,990 |
| Administration expenses | 785,420 | |
| Selling expenses | 629,800 | |
| | | (1,415,220) |
| | | 750,770 |
| Corporation tax (50%) | | (375,385) |
| Profit for the period | | 375,385 |

**Required:**

(*a*) Write a report to the chief accountant of Uncertain Ltd with suggestions for appropriate treatment for each of the items (*i*) to (*v*), with explanations for your proposals.

(*b*) Amend the draft statement of profit or loss to take account of your proposals.

(*Association of Chartered Certified Accountants*)

**11.7** With reference to IAS 10 *Events after the reporting period* and IAS 37 *Provisions, contingent liabilities and contingent assets*:

(*a*) define the following terms:
- (*i*) events after the reporting period
- (*ii*) adjusting events
- (*iii*) non-adjusting events
- (*iv*) contingent asset/liability;

(*b*) give FOUR examples of adjusting events, and FOUR examples of non-adjusting events; and

(*c*) state how
- (*i*) a material contingent liability, and
- (*ii*) material contingent assets should be accounted for in financial statements.

chapter 12

# The financial statements of limited companies: statements of profit or loss, related statements and notes

## Learning objectives

**After you have studied this chapter, you should be able to:**

- state for which of the various user groups of financial statements the statements are principally prepared
- explain how to present financial information under International GAAP in a statement of profit or loss, statement of comprehensive income, and statement of changes in equity
- describe the differences between the format of the statement of profit or loss for publication and the format generally adopted for internal use
- state how the Companies Act 2006 defines company size

## Introduction

In this chapter, you'll learn about the way in which international accounting standards and, in particular, IAS 1 (*Presentation of financial statements*) govern the presentation of information relating to income and changes in equity for a period in published company financial statements.

## 12.1 Background

When a company draws up its own financial statements, purely for internal use by directors and the management, it can adopt any format it wishes. It can, for example, switch the order of items in the statement of financial position, combine items that are never combined when official formats are used, and use its own terminology in place of normal accounting terminology. There are no rules which must be followed when preparing accounting information for internal use. Drawing up a statement of profit or loss and statement of financial position for a company's own use is not, therefore, necessarily the same as drawing up such financial statements for other purposes.

If an organisation wishes to charge something in the trading account that, in theory, ought to be charged to profit and loss, there is nothing to prevent it from doing so. On the other hand, students sitting an exam and accountants preparing financial statements for publication must base their work on accounting theory and accounting rules and regulations, *not* on the internal reporting practices of an organisation.

When it comes to publication of financial statements for external use, there are many different groups of users who will be interested in what they contain. These users are known as '**stakeholders**' – they have an interest in the company and what it is doing.

## 12.2 Users of financial statements

The main users of published financial statements of large companies and the main reasons they require the financial statements are:

1. **Shareholders of the company,** both existing and potential, who will want to know how effectively the directors are performing their stewardship function. They will use the financial statements as a base for decisions to dispose of some or all of their shares, or to buy some.
2. **The loan-creditor group.** This consists of existing and potential loan-note holders, and providers of short-term secured funds. They will want to ensure that interest payments will be made promptly and capital repayments will be made as agreed. Holders of loan notes, whether redeemable or irredeemable, will also want to be able to assess how easily they may dispose of their loan notes, should they so wish.
3. **Employee groups,** including existing, potential and past employees. These can include trade unions whose members are employees. Past employees will be mainly concerned with ensuring that any pensions, etc., paid by the company are maintained. Present employees will be interested in ensuring that the company is able to keep on operating, so maintaining their jobs and paying them acceptable wages, and that any pension contributions are maintained. In addition, they may want to ensure that the company is being fair to them, so that they get a reasonable share of the profits accruing to the firm from their efforts. Trade unions will be upholding the interests of their members, and will possibly use the financial statements in wage and pension negotiations. Potential employees will be interested in assessing whether or not it would be worth seeking employment with the company.
4. **Bankers.** Where the bank has not given a loan or granted an overdraft, there will be no great need to see the financial statements. Where money is owed to the banks, they will want to ensure that payments of interest will be made when due, and that the firm will be able to repay the loan or overdraft at the correct time.
5. **The business contact group.** This includes creditors and suppliers, who will want to know whether or not they will continue to be paid, and the prospects for a profitable future association. Customers are included, since they will want to know whether or not the company is a secure source of supply. Business rivals in this group will be trying to assess their own position compared with the firm. Potential takeover bidders, or those interested in a merger, will want to assess the desirability of any such move.
6. **Analysts and advisers.** These will need information for their clients or their readers. Financial journalists need information for their readers. Stockbrokers need it to advise investors. Credit agencies want it to be able to advise present and possible suppliers of goods and services to the company as to its creditworthiness.
7. **Revenue and Customs** will need the financial statements to assess the tax payable by the company.

8 **Other official agencies.** Various organisations concerned with the supervision of industry and commerce may want the financial statements for their purposes.
9 **Management.** In addition to the internally produced management accounts, the management is also vitally concerned with any published financial statements. It has to consider the effect of such published financial statements on the world at large.
10 **The public.** This consists of groups such as ratepayers, taxpayers, political parties, pressure groups and consumers. The needs of these parties will vary accordingly.

To meet the different and contrasting needs of all these different groups of stakeholders, a company's statement of profit or loss and statement of financial position produced for external publication would be a *very* multi-purpose document. To date, it has not been possible to produce such a multi-dimensional document. Instead, the focus is currently primarily upon producing information for shareholders (present and potential) and creditors.

When necessary, companies do produce special reports for certain groups of users. For example, banks usually wish to see a forecast of future cash flows, profits, and financial position before granting a loan or overdraft. HM Revenue & Customs will often require various analyses in order to agree the tax position. Some companies produce special reports for the use of their employees. In total, such extra reports represent only a fraction of the specially focused reports that could be issued.

The main reason that multiple additional reports are not produced, apart from a desire not to reveal too much of a company's business practices to its competitors, is cost. It would be extremely costly and time-consuming to produce reports tailored to every identifiable stakeholder group. Until such time as it may be cost-effective to produce a greater range of financial reports tailored to specific individual stakeholder groups, it is unlikely that companies will go further than they currently do to meet the needs of those stakeholders for whom, as with banks and HM Revenue & Customs, they have little choice but to provide the information they request.

Not only is the multi-purpose annual report published by companies unable to satisfy all the information needs of their users, it almost certainly does not fully satisfy *all* the needs of any one user group, even though in doing so companies must comply with the legal requirements of the Companies Act and the requirements of GAAP (e.g. IASs and IFRSs).

Published financial statements are, therefore, a compromise between the requirements of users and the maintenance of accounting concepts, subject to the overriding scrutiny of the auditor. Judgement has a major impact on the information presented. As a result if, for example, two companies operating in the same industry and in the same locations had *identical* share capitals, liabilities, numbers of employees, assets, turnover, costs, transactions, and so on, the published financial statements of the two companies *would not be identical.* Differences would arise for a number of reasons. For example, depreciation methods and policies may vary, as may inventory valuation assessments, allowances for doubtful debts, figures for revaluation of properties, accrual and prepayment adjustments, etc. There will also be other more subtle distinctions, many of which you will come across in the later stages of your studies.

**Of these 10 user groups, it is the first (shareholders) and second (creditors) who take precedence in the development of accounting standards and other pronouncements relating to financial statements for external use.**

Prior to 1981, UK companies had considerable freedom in how and what information was presented, but when financial statements are prepared under International GAAP for publication, i.e. when the financial statements are to be sent to the shareholders or to the Registrar of

Companies, the information to be shown and the information to prepare are laid down in IASs and IFRSs and in the *Framework for the Preparation and Presentation of Financial Statements*.

What do you think the advantages of companies having to follow set rules in this case may be?

A statement of comprehensive income must be prepared under International GAAP. This statement may incorporate the statement of profit or loss, or simply contain items not included in the statement of profit or loss. As custom in the UK has always been to prepare a statement of profit or loss, we'll adopt that approach and discuss the statement of comprehensive income in Section 12.10.

## 12.3 Financial statement formats

International GAAP permits two approaches for presentation of items in the statement of profit or loss: by function or by nature. In the UK, there is little difference in the presentation of information in the statement of profit or loss under International GAAP compared with UK GAAP. So far as the statement of financial position is concerned, the difference is far greater. Under International GAAP, in the statement of financial position assets are presented together in the order non-current then current (or in order of liquidity) and liabilities are then presented typically in the order current then non-current. Finally, there is a section for equity. Alternatively, equity may precede non-current and current liabilities.

We are going to approach this topic, first, by presenting you with a statement of profit or loss produced for use within a company (an 'internal' statement of profit or loss) which can easily be adapted to cover publication requirements under International GAAP. (We will deal with statements of financial position in Chapter 13.)

Despite freedom to do otherwise, most companies base the format of their internal financial statements on those required for published financial statements.

The reason for taking this approach ought to be fairly obvious. What do you think it is?

All companies, even the smallest, that adopt International GAAP must produce financial statements for their shareholders that adhere to its requirements. 'Small' and 'medium-sized' companies can, however, file summarised financial statements with the Registrar of Companies, but they must still prepare a full set of financial statements for their shareholders. In addition, listed companies may send their shareholders summary financial statements in place of the full version, but each shareholder has the right to request a full version, and many do.

The Companies Act 2006 definition of 'small' and 'medium-sized' companies is that, for the financial year in question and the previous year, the company is defined as 'small' or 'medium-sized' if it lies within the limits of at least two of the following three criteria:

| | *Small* | *Medium-sized* |
|---|---|---|
| Turnover not more than | £6.5 million | £25.9 million |
| Statement of financial position total not more than | £3.26 million | £12.9 million |
| Employees not more than | 50 | 250 |

## 12.4 Items to be presented on the face of the statement of profit or loss for publication

The following is the minimum information that must be shown on the face of the statement of profit or loss:

1 Revenue.
2 Finance costs.
3 Share of the profits or losses of associates and joint ventures accounted for using the equity method (*see* Chapter 26).
4 Taxation expenses.
5 Post-tax profit or loss of discontinued operations plus the post-tax gain or loss recognised on the measurements to fair value less cost to sell off the assets or disposal groups constituting the discontinued operation.
6 Profit or loss for the period.

An analysis of total expenses must be shown either on the face of the statement of profit or loss or in the notes on the basis of either the nature or function of the expenses (*see* Section 12.7).

Earnings per share must be shown at the foot of the statement (*see* Section 11.26).

Additional items can be shown when it is relevant to an understanding of the company's financial performance. (It is this flexibility that results in there being little difference between a statement of profit or loss prepared under International GAAP and one prepared under UK GAAP.)

In addition, in the case of consolidated statements of profit or loss, profit or loss for the period should be shown as allocated between non-controlling interests and equity holders. For example, if profit for the period were £165,000 and there was a 10% non-controlling interest in the group, lines would be inserted below the profit for the period line as follows:

| Attributable to: | £ |
|---|---|
| Owners of the parent | 148,500 |
| Non-controlling interest | 16,500 |
| | 165,000 |

## 12.5 Statement of profit or loss for internal use

Exhibit 12.1 shows a statement of profit or loss drawn up for internal use. As mentioned earlier, there are no statutory rules concerning how financial statements are prepared for internal use. However, as you learnt in Activity 12.2, if the internal financial statements were drawn up in a completely different fashion from those needed for publication, quite a lot of work might be needed in order to reassemble the figures into a statement of profit or loss for publication.

## Exhibit 12.1 Statement of profit or loss for internal use

**Block plc**
**Statement of Profit or Loss for the year ending 31 December 2016**

| | £000 | £000 | £000 |
|---|---|---|---|
| Revenue | | | 800 |
| *Less* Cost of sales: | | | |
| Inventory 1 January 2016 | | 100 | |
| *Add* Purchases | | 525 | |
| | | 625 | |
| *Less* Inventory 31 December 2016 | | (125) | |
| | | | (500) |
| Gross profit | | | 300 |
| Distribution costs | | | |
| Salaries and wages | 30 | | |
| Motor vehicle costs: Distribution | 20 | | |
| General distribution expenses | 5 | | |
| Depreciation: Motors | 3 | | |
| Machinery | 2 | | |
| | | 60 | |
| Administrative expenses | | | |
| Salaries and wages | 25 | | |
| Motor vehicle costs: Administration | 2 | | |
| General administration expenses | 7 | | |
| Auditors' remuneration | 2 | | |
| Depreciation: Motors | 3 | | |
| Machinery | 1 | | |
| | | 40 | |
| | | | (100) |
| | | | 200 |
| Other operating income | | | 30 |
| Operating profit | | | 230 |
| Finance income | | | |
| Income from shares in group entities | | 20 | |
| Income from associates and joint ventures | | 10 | |
| Income from shares from non-related companies | | 5 | |
| Other interest receivable | | 15 | |
| | | | 50 |
| | | | 280 |
| Finance costs | | | |
| Amounts written off investments | | 4 | |
| Interest payable | | | |
| Loans repayable within five years | 10 | | |
| Loans repayable in ten years | 6 | | |
| | | 16 | |
| | | | (20) |
| Profit before taxation | | | 260 |
| Taxation | | | (95) |
| Profit for the year | | | 165 |
| Retained profits brought forward from last year | | | 60 |
| | | | 225 |
| Transfer to general reserve | | 40 | |
| Ordinary dividend paid | | 100 | |
| | | | (140) |
| Retained profits carried forward to next year | | | 85 |

In Exhibit 12.1, the internal statement of profit or loss has been prepared using a format which makes it easy to get the figures for the published statement of profit or loss. Examination questions on this topic sometimes ask for both (*a*) internal and (*b*) published financial statements. You should find things are easier if the internal and published financial statements follow a similar format.

## 12.6 Statement of profit or loss for publication

Exhibit 12.2 redrafts Exhibit 12.1 into a form suitable for publication under International GAAP. You will see that one difference between the two exhibits is that the detail between each entry has been removed. Such detail could, of course, be included as notes to the published financial statement. The other main difference is that none of the lines after the profit for the year line appear in a statement of profit or loss for publication.

### Exhibit 12.2 Statement of profit or loss for publication complying with International GAAP

**Block plc**
**Statement of Profit or Loss for the year ending 31 December 2016**

| | | £000 | £000 |
|---|---|---|---|
| Revenue | | | 800 |
| Cost of sales | | | (500) |
| Gross profit | | | 300 |
| Distribution costs | | 60 | |
| Administrative expenses | | 40 | |
| | | | (100) |
| | | | 200 |
| Other operating income | | | 30 |
| Operating profit | | | 230 |
| Finance income | | | |
| Income from shares in group entities | | 20 | |
| Income from associates and joint ventures | | 10 | |
| Income from other non-current asset investments | | 5 | |
| Other interest receivable and similar income | | 15 | |
| | | | 50 |
| | | | 280 |
| Finance costs | | | |
| Amounts written off investments | | 4 | |
| Interest payable | | 16 | |
| | | | (20) |
| Profit before taxation | | | 260 |
| Taxation | | | (95) |
| Profit for the year | | | 165 |
| Attributable to: | £000 | | |
| Owners of the parent | 148.5 | | |
| Non-controlling interest | 16.5 | | |
| | 165.0 | | |
| Earnings per share 25p | | | |

***Note*: Appropriations of profits, such as dividend payments, should be shown either in the notes or in the separate statement of changes in equity.**

When internal financial statements are prepared in the format shown in Exhibit 12.1, they could be published just as they are but without the lines after 'profit for the year'. International GAAP does not force companies to publish financial statements as detailed as the one shown in

Exhibit 12.1. Rather, it states the *minimum* information that must be disclosed. A company can show more than the minimum if it wants to, but companies usually prefer to do so in notes to the financial statement, or, as noted above, in a separate statement.

**Activity 12.3** Why would most companies *not* want to publish detailed financial statements?

## 12.7 Classification of expenses by nature or function

The items on the face of the statement of profit or loss below revenue should be analysed using a classification based on either their nature or their function. This should be done either on the face of the statement of profit or loss (which is encouraged by IAS 1) or in the notes. Traditionally, this is done by function showing, for example:

(*a*) cost of sales
(*b*) gross profit
(*c*) other income
(*d*) distribution costs
(*e*) administration expenses
(*f*) other expenses.

This is the approach that was taken in Exhibit 12.2. This information should include depreciation and amortisation expenses and employee benefit costs (i.e. pension costs).

When analysed using a classification by nature, the analysis may comprise:

(*a*) other income
(*b*) changes in inventory of finished goods and work in progress
(*c*) raw materials and consumables used
(*d*) employee benefit costs
(*e*) depreciation and amortisation expense
(*f*) other expenses.

## 12.8 Other disclosure required in the notes

The list of possible items is lengthy and beyond the scope of this book. However, those most commonly encountered at this level include:

- research and development expenditure recognised as an expense during the period;
- foreign-exchange differences recognised in profit or loss;
- impairment losses and reversal of impairment losses recognised during the period for each class of asset;
- the amount of intangible asset amortisation for each class of intangible asset recognised during the period, plus where it is included in the statement of profit or loss;
- income, expenses, gains, and losses resulting from financial assets and financial liabilities;
- the major components of the taxation expense;
- the amount of each significant category of revenue recognised during the period including:
  (*i*) sale of goods
  (*ii*) rendering of services
  (*iii*) interest
  (*iv*) royalties
  (*v*) dividends;
- the nature and amount of any change in accounting estimate that has an effect in the current or a future period.

For UK companies, the Companies Act requires further disclosure in the notes of:

1 Interest on bank loans, overdrafts and other loans:
   (*a*) repayable within five years from the end of the accounting period;
   (*b*) finally repayable after five years from the end of the accounting period.
2 Amounts set aside for redemption of share capital and for redemption of loans.
3 Rents from land, if material.
4 Costs of hire of plant and machinery.
5 Auditors' remuneration, including expenses.

There is also more information required to be disclosed in the notes by a number of accounting standards. These were mainly covered in Chapter 11, and some are covered in Chapters 13–26.

## 12.9 Allocation of expenses

It will be obvious under which heading most expenses will be shown, whether they are:

(*a*) cost of sales;
(*b*) distribution costs; or
(*c*) administrative expenses.

However, as these terms are not defined, some items are not so easy to allocate with certainty. Some companies may choose one heading for a particular item, while others will choose another. For example:

1 **Discounts received.** These are for prompt payment of amounts owing by us. Where they are for payments to suppliers of goods they could be regarded either as a reduction in the cost of goods or, alternatively, as a financial recompense, i.e. the reward for paying money on time. If regarded in the first way they would be deducted from cost of sales, whereas the alternative approach would be to deduct them from administrative expenses. However, these discounts are also deducted when paying bills in respect of distribution costs or administrative expenses, and it would also be necessary to deduct from these headings if the cost of sales deduction approach is used. As this raises complications in the original recording of discounts received, it would be more suitable in this book if all cash discounts received are deducted in arriving at the figure of administrative expenses.
2 **Discounts allowed.** To be consistent in dealing with discounts, this should be included in administrative expenses.
3 **Bad debts.** These could be regarded as an expense connected with sales: after all, they are sales which are not paid for. The other point of view is that for a debt to become bad, at least part of the blame must be through the administrative procedures for checking customer creditworthiness having been inadequate. In this book, bad debts will be treated as being part of administrative expenses.

## 12.10 Statement of comprehensive income

As mentioned in Section 12.2, under IAS 1 the statement of profit or loss may be shown either as a separate primary financial statement or as part of a primary statement called a statement of comprehensive income. When a separate statement of profit or loss is prepared, the statement of comprehensive income comprises:

(*a*) profit or loss for the period (as shown in the statement of profit or loss);
(*b*) each component of other comprehensive income classified by nature;
(*c*) share of the other comprehensive income of associates and joint ventures accounted for using the equity method (*see* Chapter 26);
(*d*) total comprehensive income;

## Exhibit 12.3 An example of a statement of comprehensive income

**Block plc**
**Statement of Comprehensive Income for the year ending 31 December 2016**

| | | *£000* | *£000* |
|---|---|---|---|
| Revenue | | | 800 |
| Cost of sales | | | (500) |
| Gross profit | | | 300 |
| Distribution costs | | 60 | |
| Administrative expenses | | 40 | |
| | | | (100) |
| | | | 200 |
| Other operating income | | | 30 |
| Operating profit | | | 230 |
| Finance income: | | | |
| Income from shares in group entities | | 20 | |
| Income from interest in associates and joint ventures | | 10 | |
| Income from non-current asset investments | | 5 | |
| Other interest receivable and similar income | | 15 | |
| | | | 50 |
| | | | 280 |
| Finance costs: | | | |
| Amount written off investments | | 4 | |
| Interest payable | | 16 | |
| | | | (20) |
| Profit before taxation | | | 260 |
| Taxation | | | (95) |
| Profit for the year | | | 165 |
| Other comprehensive income: | | | |
| Changes in revaluation surplus | | 20 | |
| Actuarial loss on defined benefit plans | | (30) | |
| Gains from translation of financial statements of foreign operations | | 15 | |
| Losses from remeasuring available-for-sale financial assets | | (25) | |
| Gains on hedging instruments | | 5 | |
| | | | (15) |
| Total comprehensive income | | | 150 |
| Profit attributable to: | *£000* | | |
| Owners of the parent | 148.5 | | |
| Non-controlling interest | 16.5 | | |
| | 165.0 | | |
| Total comprehensive income attributable to: | | | |
| Owners of the parent | 135 | | |
| Non-controlling interest | 15 | | |
| | 150 | | |
| Earnings per share 25p | | | |

***Note*: Taxation on each item of other comprehensive income would be shown as a note. (The figures shown above are net of taxation.)**

and in the notes the total comprehensive income for the period is disclosed attributable to (*i*) non-controlling interests; and (*ii*) owners of the parent.

The items disclosed may be shown either net of taxation or before tax with a separate line showing the taxation amount. If the net approach is adopted, the tax on each item must be shown separately in a note.

Other comprehensive income comprises items of income and expense (including reclassification adjustments, i.e. the amounts reclassified to profit or loss in the current period that were recognised in other comprehensive income in the current or previous periods) that are not recognised in profit or loss such as:

(*a*) changes in revaluation surplus (see IAS 16 and IAS 38);
(*b*) actuarial gains and losses on defined benefit (pension) plans (see IAS 19);
(*c*) gains and losses arising from the translation of the financial statements of foreign operations (see IAS 21);
(*d*) gains and losses arising from remeasuring available-for-sale financial assets (see IAS 39);
(*e*) the effective portion of gains and losses on hedging instruments in a cash flow hedge (see IAS 39).

Total comprehensive income (i.e. that shown in the statement of profit or loss plus other comprehensive income) represents the change in equity during a period resulting from transactions and other events, other than those changes resulting from transactions with owners in their capacity as owners.

Exhibit 12.3 shows a statement of comprehensive income which includes the information that could have been shown separately in a statement of profit or loss. The statement of profit or loss shown previously in Exhibit 12.2 forms the first part.

## 12.11 Other statements and notes required by IAS 1

Three further primary statements are required by IAS 1:

### 1 Statement of changes in equity

This statement should disclose:

(*a*) profit or loss for the period;
(*b*) each item of income or expense for the period that is recognised directly in equity and the total of such items (e.g. revaluation of non-current assets and currency translation differences);
(*c*) total income and expense for the period (i.e. (*a*) plus (*b*)) showing separately between that part attributable to parent equity holders and to non-controlling interests;
(*d*) the effects of changes in accounting policies and correction of errors for each component of equity;
(*e*) transactions with equity holders:
  (*i*) issues of share capital;
  (*ii*) purchase of own shares;
  (*iii*) contracts that will be settled by the entity receiving or delivering a fixed number of its own equity instruments in exchange for a fixed amount of cash or another financial asset;
(*f*) transaction costs relating to the issue of share capital deducted from shareholders' equity;
(*g*) dividends and other distributions to owners;
(*h*) a reconciliation between the opening and closing amount for the following:
  (*i*) each class of share capital;
  (*ii*) share premium;
  (*iii*) own shares (treasury shares);
  (*iv*) each reserve including revaluation reserves; hedging reserves; foreign exchange translation reserves; current or deferred tax on items taken directly to or transferred from equity; equity-settled share-based payment transactions;
  (*v*) retained earnings;
(*i*) the equity conversion element of convertible debt.

As an alternative, a statement of recognised income and expense may be prepared. It comprises items (*a*) to (*d*). Items (*e*) to (*i*) must then be disclosed in the notes.

A large number of disclosures must also be made, including the number of each class of share authorised and issued and its par value.

Exhibit 12.4 presents an example of a statement of changes in equity:

**Exhibit 12.4 An example of a statement of changes in equity**

**Attributable to Equity Holders of the Company**

| | *Share capital* | *Share premium* | *Other reserves* | *Retained earnings* | *Total* | *Non-controlling interest* | *Total equity* |
|---|---|---|---|---|---|---|---|
| Balance at 1.1.2018 | 50,000 | 30,000 | 10,000 | 140,000 | 230,000 | 1,000 | 231,000 |
| Cash flow hedges, net of tax | | | (5) | | (5) | | (5) |
| Currency translation differences | | | (90) | | (90) | (20) | (110) |
| Net expense recognised directly into equity | | | (95) | | (95) | (20) | (115) |
| Profit for the year | | | | 45,000 | 45,000 | 4,000 | 49,000 |
| Total recognised income and expense for 2018 | | | (95) | 45,000 | 44,905 | 3,980 | 48,885 |
| Proceeds from shares issued | 10,000 | 20,000 | | | 30,000 | | 30,000 |
| Dividend relating to 2017 | | | | (32,000) | (32,000) | (700) | (32,700) |
| | 10,000 | 20,000 | | (32,000) | (2,000) | (700) | (2,700) |
| Balance at 31.12.2018 | 60,000 | 50,000 | 9,905 | 153,000 | 272,905 | 4,280 | 277,185 |

## 2 Statement of financial position

This topic is covered in Chapter 13.

## 3 Statement of cash flows

This topic is covered in Chapter 15.

## Learning outcomes

**You should now have learnt:**

1. A wide range of user groups require accounting information for a variety of reasons, resulting in it being impossible to satisfy all user groups with one set of financial statements.
2. Financial statements for external use are prepared primarily to meet the decision-making needs of shareholders (present and potential) and creditors.
3. How to present financial information under International GAAP in statements of profit or loss, statements of comprehensive income, and statements of changes in equity.
4. There are prescribed formats for the preparation of published financial statements.
5. Financial statements prepared for internal use need not comply with these formats but are often based upon them.
6. How the Companies Act 2006 defines company size.

## Answers to activities

12.1 Combined with the regulations enshrined in accounting standards that govern how data will be processed and selected for inclusion as information in the financial statements, the standardisation brought about by the Companies Act 1981 makes meaningful comparison between the financial statements of different companies feasible.

12.2 For the same reason that many small companies use the percentage rates provided by the tax rules relating to capital allowances when setting their depreciation rates – it saves them redoing the calculation – many small companies use the format for publication as the basis for their intermal financial statements, adding more detail when they feel it is appropriate to do so.

12.3 Because doing so may give their competitors information which would lead to the company losing some of its competitive advantage.

# Review questions

**12.1** From the following selected balances of Royal Oak plc as at 31 March 2018 draw up (*i*) a detailed statement of profit or loss for internal use, and (*ii*) a statement of profit or loss for publication.

| | £000s |
|---|---|
| Retained profits as at 31 March 2017 | 408 |
| Inventory 1 April 2017 | 336 |
| Purchases | 5,848 |
| Revenue | 9,824 |
| Returns inwards | 432 |
| Returns outwards | 148 |
| Carriage inwards | 56 |
| Wages and salaries (*see* Note (*b*)) | 544 |
| Rent and business rates (*see* Note (*c*)) | 60 |
| General distribution expenses | 112 |
| General administrative expenses | 96 |
| Discounts allowed | 144 |
| Bad debts | 20 |
| Loan-note interest | 48 |
| Motor expenses (*see* Note (*d*)) | 54 |
| Interest received on bank deposit | 24 |
| Income from associates and joint ventures | 12 |
| Motor vehicles at cost: Administrative | 216 |
| Distribution | 368 |
| Equipment at cost: Administrative | 60 |
| Distribution | 40 |
| Royalties receivable | 20 |
| Dividends paid | 420 |

*Notes:*

(*a*) Inventory at 31 March 2018 £408,000.
(*b*) Wages and salaries are to be apportioned: distribution costs $^1/_4$, administrative expenses $^3/_4$.
(*c*) Rent and business rates are to be apportioned: distribution costs 60%, administrative expenses 40%.
(*d*) Apportion motor expenses in the proportions 2:3 between distribution costs and administrative expenses.
(*e*) Depreciate motor vehicles 25% and equipment 10% on cost.
(*f*) Accrue auditors' remuneration of £44,000.
(*g*) Accrue corporation tax for the year on ordinary activity profits £1,456,000.
(*h*) A sum of £60,000 is to be transferred to general reserve.

→

**12.2** From the following selected balances of District plc as at 31 December 2018, prepare (*i*) a detailed statement of profit or loss for the year ending 31 December 2018 for internal use and (*ii*) a statement of profit or loss for the same period for publication.

| | £000s |
|---|---:|
| Inventory 1 January 2018 | 504 |
| Revenue | 6,696 |
| Purchases | 4,104 |
| Carriage inwards | 29 |
| Returns inwards | 32 |
| Returns outwards | 18 |
| Discounts allowed | 40 |
| Discounts received | 50 |
| Wages (putting goods into saleable condition) | 317 |
| Salaries and wages: Sales and distribution staff | 223 |
| Salaries and wages: Administrative staff | 266 |
| Motor expenses (*see* Note (*c*)) | 88 |
| Rent and business rates (*see* Note (*d*)) | 110 |
| Investments in associates (market value £148,000) | 360 |
| Income from associates | 18 |
| General distribution expenses | 43 |
| General administrative expenses | 22 |
| Bad debts | 7 |
| Interest from government securities | 11 |
| Haulage costs: Distribution | 14 |
| Loan-note interest payable | 7 |
| Retained profits 31 December 2017 | 338 |
| Motor vehicles at cost: Distribution and sales | 240 |
| Administrative | 92 |
| Plant and machinery at cost: Distribution and sales | 180 |
| Administrative | 120 |
| Production | 200 |
| Directors' remuneration | 130 |
| Dividends paid | 216 |

*Notes:*

(*a*) The production department puts goods bought into a saleable condition.
(*b*) Inventory at 31 December 2018 £576,000.
(*c*) Apportion motor expenses: distribution $^3/_4$, administrative $^1/_4$.
(*d*) Apportion rent and business rates: distribution 40%, administrative 60%.
(*e*) Write £94,000 off the value of investments in undertakings in which the company has a participating interest.
(*f*) Depreciate motor vehicles 25% on cost, plant and machinery 15% on cost.
(*g*) Accrue auditors' remuneration £50,000.
(*h*) Accrue corporation tax on ordinary activity profits £374,000.
(*i*) A sum of £90,000 is to be transferred to loan-note redemption reserve.

**12.3** The following information has been extracted from the books of account of Rufford plc for the year to 31 March 2016:

| | *Dr* | *Cr* |
|---|---|---|
| | *£000* | *£000* |
| Administration expenses | 97 | |
| Deferred taxation | | 24 |
| Depreciation on office machinery (for the year to 31 March 2016) | 8 | |
| Depreciation on delivery vans (for the year to 31 March 2016) | 19 | |
| Distribution costs | 33 | |
| Dividends received (from a UK listed company on 31 July 2015) | | 14 |
| Factory closure expenses (closed on 1 April 2015) | 12 | |
| Interest payable on bank overdraft (repayable within five years) | 6 | |
| Interim dividend (paid on 30 September 2015) | 21 | |
| Interest receivable | | 25 |
| Purchases | 401 | |
| Retained profit at 31 March 2015 | | 160 |
| Revenue (net of VAT) | | 642 |
| Inventory at 1 April 2015 | 60 | |

*Additional information:*

1 Administrative expenses include the following items:

| | *£000* |
|---|---|
| Auditors' remuneration | 20 |
| Directors' emoluments | 45 |
| Travelling expenses | 1 |
| Research expenditure | 11 |
| Hire of plant and machinery | 12 |

2 It is assumed that the following tax rates are applicable for the year to 31 March 2016:

| | |
|---|---|
| Corporation tax | 50% |
| Income tax | 30% |

3 There was an overprovision for corporation tax of £3,000 relating to the year to 31 March 2015.

4 Corporation tax payable for the year to 31 March 2016 (based on the profits for that year) is estimated to be £38,000. The company, in addition, intends to transfer a further £9,000 to its deferred taxation account.

5 A final dividend of £42,000 for the year to 31 March 2016 is expected to be paid on 2 June 2016.

6 Inventory at 31 March 2016 was valued at £71,000.

7 As a result of a change in accounting policy, a prior period charge of £15,000 (net of tax) is to be made.

8 The company's share capital consists of 420,000 ordinary shares of £1 each. There are no preference shares, and no change had been made to the company's issued share capital for some years.

**Required:**

(*a*) In so far as the information permits, prepare the company's published statement of profit or loss for the year to 31 March 2016 in the vertical format in accordance with the relevant accounting standards.
(NB: A statement of the company's accounting policies is not required.)

(*b*) Prepare statement of financial position extracts in order to illustrate the balances still remaining in the following accounts at 31 March 2016:
(*i*) corporation tax;
(*ii*) proposed dividend; and
(*iii*) deferred taxation.
(NB: A detailed statement of financial position is not required.)

(*Association of Accounting Technicians*)

→

**12.4A** From the following balances in the books of Breaker plc you are to draw up (*i*) a detailed statement of profit or loss for the year ending 31 March 2017 for internal use, and (*ii*) a statement of profit or loss for publication:

| | £ |
|---|---|
| Plant and machinery, at cost (*see* Note (*c*)) | 105,000 |
| Bank interest receivable | 3,000 |
| Discounts allowed | 7,000 |
| Discounts received | 6,000 |
| Hire of motor vehicles: Sales and distribution | 14,000 |
| Hire of motor vehicles: Administrative | 5,000 |
| Licence fees receivable | 13,000 |
| General distribution expenses | 26,000 |
| General administrative expenses | 19,000 |
| Wages and salaries: Sales and distribution | 177,000 |
| Administrative | 98,000 |
| Directors' remuneration | 41,000 |
| Motor expenses (*see* Note (*e*)) | 11,000 |
| Ordinary dividend paid | 80,000 |
| Inventory 31 March 2016 | 208,000 |
| Revenue | 1,450,000 |
| Purchases | 700,000 |
| Returns outwards | 22,000 |
| Returns inwards | 29,000 |
| Retained profits as at 31 March 2016 | 88,000 |

*Notes*:

(*a*) Inventory at 31 March 2017 £230,000.
(*b*) Accrue auditor's remuneration £8,000.
(*c*) Of the plant and machinery, £70,000 is distributive in nature, while £35,000 is for administration.
(*d*) Depreciate plant and machinery 25% on cost.
(*e*) Of the motor expenses, $^4/_5$ are for sales and distribution and $^1/_5$ for administration.
(*f*) Corporation tax on ordinary profits is estimated at £143,000.
(*g*) A sum of £25,000 is to be transferred to general reserve.

**12.5A** The following balances have been extracted from the books of Mitchell plc on 31 July 2016. From them draw up (*i*) a detailed statement of profit or loss for internal use, for the year ending 31 July 2016, also (*ii*) a statement of profit or loss for publication for the year to that date.

| | £ |
|---|---:|
| Purchases | 1,310,000 |
| Revenue | 1,790,000 |
| Returns inwards | 29,000 |
| Returns outwards | 57,000 |
| Carriage inwards | 10,000 |
| Wages – productive | 109,000 |
| Discounts allowed | 11,000 |
| Discounts received | 15,000 |
| Inventory 31 July 2015 | 317,000 |
| Wages and salaries: Sales and distribution | 41,000 |
| Wages and salaries: Administrative | 62,000 |
| Motor expenses: Sales and distribution | 26,000 |
| Motor expenses: Administrative | 8,000 |
| General distribution expenses | 7,000 |
| General administrative expenses | 6,000 |
| Rent and business rates (*see* Note (*c*)) | 17,000 |
| Directors' remuneration | 35,000 |
| Retained profits 31 July 2015 | 141,000 |
| Advertising | 19,000 |
| Bad debts | 3,000 |
| Hire of plant and machinery (*see* Note (*b*)) | 14,000 |
| Motor vehicles at cost: Sales and distribution | 45,000 |
| Administrative | 18,000 |
| Plant and machinery: Distribution | 13,000 |
| Loan-note interest payable | 7,000 |
| Income from shares in group entities | 8,000 |
| Income from associates and joint ventures | 5,000 |
| Preference dividend paid | 20,000 |
| Profit on disposal of investments | 14,000 |
| Tax on profit on disposal of investments | 3,000 |
| Ordinary dividend paid | 110,000 |

*Notes:*

(*a*) Inventory at 31 July 2016 £303,000.
(*b*) The hire of plant and machinery is to be apportioned: productive £12,000, administrative £2,000.
(*c*) Rent and business rates to be apportioned: distribution $^3/_4$, administrative $^1/_4$.
(*d*) Motors are to be depreciated at 33 $^1/_3$% on cost; plant and machinery to be depreciated at 10% on cost.
(*e*) Auditors' remuneration of £15,000 to be accrued.
(*f*) Corporation tax on profit from ordinary activities for the year is estimated at £29,000, excluding tax on disposal of investments.
(*g*) Transfer £50,000 to general reserve.

→

**12.6A** Bunker plc is a trading company; it does not carry out *any* manufacturing operations. The following information has been extracted from the books of account for the year to 31 March 2017:

| | | *£000* |
|---|---|---|
| Auditors' remuneration | | 30 |
| Corporation tax: | based on the accounting profit for the year to 31 March 2017 | 7,200 |
| | overprovision for the year to 31 March 2016 | 200 |
| | United Kingdom corporation tax relief on overseas operations: closure costs | 30 |
| Delivery expenses | | 1,200 |
| Dividends: | final (proposed – to be paid 1 August 2017) | 200 |
| | interim (paid on 1 October 2016) | 100 |
| Non-current assets at cost: | | |
| Delivery vans | | 200 |
| Office cars | | 40 |
| Stores plant and equipment | | 5,000 |
| Investment income (amount received from listed companies) | | 1,600 |
| Office expenses | | 800 |
| Overseas operations: closure costs of entire operations on 1 April 2016 | | 350 |
| Purchases (net of value added tax) | | 24,000 |
| Revenue (net of value added tax) | | 35,000 |
| Inventory at cost: | | |
| at 1 April 2016 | | 5,000 |
| at 31 March 2017 | | 6,000 |
| Storeroom costs | | 1,000 |
| Wages and salaries: | | |
| Delivery staff | | 700 |
| Directors' emoluments | | 300 |
| Office staff | | 100 |
| Storeroom staff | | 400 |

*Additional information:*

1 Depreciation policy:
Depreciation is provided at the following annual rates on a straight line basis: delivery vans 20%; office cars 7.5%; stores plant and equipment 10%.
2 The following taxation rates may be assumed:
corporation tax 35%; income tax 25%; value added tax 15%.
3 The investment income arises from investments held in non-current asset investments.
4 It has been decided to transfer an amount of £150,000 to the deferred taxation account.
5 There were 1,000,000 ordinary shares of £1 each in issue during the year to 31 March 2017. There were no preference shares in issue.

**Required:**
In so far as the information permits, prepare Bunker plc's published statement of profit or loss for the year ending 31 March 2017 in accordance with the minimum requirements of the related accounting standards.

***Note*: A statement of accounting policies is NOT required, but where appropriate, other formal notes SHOULD be attached to your statement of profit or loss. Detailed workings should also be submitted with your answer.**

(*Association of Accounting Technicians*)

chapter 13

# The financial statements of limited companies: statements of financial position

## Learning objectives

**After you have studied this chapter, you should be able to:**

- describe commonly used formats that may be used when preparing statements of financial position for external reporting purposes
- describe the differences between the formats used for publication and formats generally adopted for internal use
- describe the exemption of some 'small' companies from having their financial statements audited
- describe the exemptions available to small and medium-sized companies in respect of filing modified financial statements
- describe the option available to public limited companies to send members a summary financial statement

## Introduction

In this chapter, you'll learn about the format of statements of financial position prepared for publication under International GAAP. You will also be reminded of the fundamental accounting concepts that you covered in *Business Accounting 1* and introduced to the rules relating to the preparation of modified financial statements for small and medium-sized companies.

## 13.1 The title 'statement of financial position'

'Statement of financial position' is the name used nowadays under International GAAP for what used to be called a 'balance sheet'. It is not wrong to use the term 'balance sheet' – IAS 1 states that any title can be used for the statement of financial position so long as it does not mislead the users of the statement. However, unless you are told otherwise, 'statement of financial position' is the term you should use. **Beware, however, that your examiners may use the term 'balance sheet'. If they do, you should do so as well.**

## 13.2 Statement of financial position contents

A statement of financial position presents a summary of the financial position of an entity at a point in time. Companies prepare statements of financial position for publication at the end of each financial year (i.e. at the end of each 12-month period in which they operate). They must also prepare six-monthly interim statements of financial position if listed on a stock exchange.

A company is generally free to use its judgement concerning how to present the information in its statement of financial position and what to include in it and what to include in the notes that accompany it. However, at a minimum, it must present the following on the face of the statement of financial position:

- Assets
  - Non-current
    - (*a*) property, plant and equipment;
    - (*b*) investment property;
    - (*c*) intangible assets (*see* Section 13.4);
    - (*d*) financial assets (*see* Section 13.6);
    - (*e*) investments accounted for using the equity method;
    - (*f*) biological assets;
    - (*g*) deferred tax assets (*see* IAS 12, Chapter 11);
  - Current
    - (*h*) inventories;
    - (*i*) current tax assets (*see* IAS 12, Chapter 11);
    - (*j*) trade and other receivables;
    - (*k*) cash and cash equivalents (*see* Section 13.5);
  - Other
    - (*l*) (the total of) assets classified as held for sale and assets included in disposal groups classified as held for sale (*see* IFRS 5, Chapter 11).
- Liabilities
  - (*a*) trade and other payables;
  - (*b*) provisions;
  - (*c*) financial liabilities (excluding amounts included in (*a*) and (*b*));
  - (*d*) liabilities for current tax (*see* IAS 12, Chapter 11);
  - (*e*) deferred tax liabilities (*see* IAS 12, Chapter 11);
  - (*f*) liabilities included in disposal groups classified as held for sale (*see* IFRS, Chapter 11).
- Equity
  - (*a*) issued capital (*see* Section 13.3);
  - (*b*) reserves attributable to owners of the parent;
  - (*c*) non-controlling interest.

The standard does not prescribe the order or format in which the items are presented. However, a company should normally group assets and liabilities on a current and non-current basis, using 12 months after the reporting period to distinguish between the two categories.

**Activity 13.1** Why does the above list not split the liabilities into non-current and current?

## 13.3 Statement of financial position disclosure

Companies can show as much detail as they wish on the face of the statement of financial position. However, single-line entries are typically used for each of the items listed in Section 13.2, and the detail is shown in the notes.

Subject to materiality, the disclosure would, for example, disaggregate the line entry for:

(*a*) property, plant and equipment;
(*b*) receivables into trade receivables, receivables from related parties, prepayments, and other amounts;
(*c*) inventories into sub-categories such as finished goods, raw materials, and work in progress;
(*d*) provisions into provisions for employee benefits and other provisions;
(*e*) equity capital into various classes of equity and separating share premium from other reserves.

For each class of share capital, the following must be disclosed:

(*i*) the number of shares authorised;
(*ii*) the number of shares issued and fully paid;
(*iii*) the number of shares issued but not fully paid;
(*iv*) the par (or nominal) value per share;
(*v*) a reconciliation between the opening and closing number of shares in issue;
(*vi*) any rights, preferences, and restrictions, including restrictions on the distribution of dividends and the repayment of capital;
(*vii*) shares in the entity held by the entity or by its subsidiaries or associates;
(*viii*) shares reserved for issue under options and contracts for the sale of shares, including terms and amounts.

For each reserve, the nature and purpose must be disclosed.

## 13.4 Goodwill

Goodwill is included in intangible assets and is tested annually for impairment. Any impairment identified should be charged to profit or loss and cannot be reversed. Goodwill is not amortised (depreciated). Internally generated goodwill is never recognised. When the calculation results in a negative value, it is known as **a gain from a bargain purchase** and eliminated immediately as a gain in profit or loss.

## 13.5 Cash equivalents

These are short-term investments that are readily convertible to a known amount of cash within a short period from the date of acquisition. The maximum qualifying period is generally taken to be three months.

## 13.6 Financial assets

These comprise cash; a contractual right to receive cash or another financial asset; a contractual right to exchange financial assets or liabilities with another entity; or an equity instrument of another entity.

Such assets fall into one of four categories:

(*a*) held at fair value through profit or loss – i.e. financial assets acquired to generate a short-term profit (these assets are carried at fair value with gains or losses reported in income);
(*b*) held to maturity (these assets are carried at amortised cost);
(*c*) loans and receivables (the assets are carried at amortised cost);
(*d*) available for sale (these assets are carried at fair value with gains or losses reported in equity).

## 13.7 Dividends proposed

Dividends proposed and unpaid at the period end are *not* liabilities and do not appear either on the face of the statement of financial position or in the notes to the statement of financial position. They are disclosed in the notes to the statement of profit or loss.

## 13.8 Interest accrued on loan notes

Such interest which is unpaid at the period end is a current liability and appears on the face of the statement of financial position.

## 13.9 Fundamental accounting principles

The qualitative characteristics of financial statements as contained in *The Framework* (see Section 11.4) have, effectively, replaced the six principles shown below as the list of principles to be applied under International GAAP. However, as a statement of the basic principles to observe under European law, the six fundamental accounting principles listed below serve as a useful summary of the requirements of *The Framework*.

The following accounting principles (or 'valuation rules' as they are called in the Fourth Directive of the EU) must be followed when preparing company financial statements:

1 A company is presumed to be a going concern.
2 Accounting policies must be applied consistently from year to year.
3 The neutrality concept must be followed. ('Prudence' was the term used in the Fourth Directive. It has a slightly different meaning and may still be mentioned, especially in examinations.)
4 The accruals concept must be observed.
5 Each component item of assets and liabilities must be valued separately. As an instance of this, if a company has five different types of inventory, each type must be valued separately at the lower of cost and net realisable value, rather than be valued on an aggregate basis.
6 Amounts in respect of items representing assets or income may *not* be set off against items representing liabilities or expenditure. Thus an amount owing on a hire purchase contract cannot be deducted from the value of the asset in the statement of financial position.

## 13.10 True and fair view

If complying with the requirements of International GAAP would cause the financial statements not to be 'true and fair' then the directors must set aside such requirements. This is unlikely to arise and should not be done without real justification.

## 13.11 Layout of the statement of financial position for internal use

As mentioned in Section 13.2, companies have considerable freedom in how they present information in their statement of financial position. Statements of financial position for internal use (Exhibit 13.1) are typically far more detailed than those prepared for publication and are normally in a form similar to those shown in Chapter 45 of *Business Accounting 1*:

## Exhibit 13.1 A statement of financial position for internal use

**Statement of Financial Position as at 31 December 2018**

| | *Cost (£)* | *Depreciation to date (£)* | | *Net book value (£)* |
|---|---|---|---|---|
| Non-current assets | | | | |
| Goodwill[Note] | 255,000 | 30,000 | | 225,000 |
| Buildings | 1,050,000 | 110,000 | | 940,000 |
| Equipment | 120,000 | 36,000 | | 84,000 |
| Motor vehicles | 172,000 | 69,600 | | 102,400 |
| | 1,597,000 | 245,600 | | 1,351,400 |
| Current assets | | | | |
| Inventory | | 91,413 | | |
| Accounts receivable | | 186,100 | | |
| Bank | | 8,390 | | |
| | | | | 285,903 |
| Total assets | | | | 1,637,303 |
| Current liabilities | | | | |
| Accounts payable | | 113,700 | | |
| Loan-note interest accrued | | 15,000 | | |
| Taxation | | 50,000 | | |
| | | 178,700 | | |
| Non-current liabilities | | | | |
| 10% loan notes | | 300,000 | | |
| Total liabilities | | | | (478,700) |
| Net assets | | | | 1,158,603 |
| Equity | | | | |
| Share capital | | | Authorised | Issued |
| Preference shares | | | 200,000 | 200,000 |
| Ordinary shares | | | 1,000,000 | 700,000 |
| | | | 1,200,000 | 900,000 |
| Reserves | | | | |
| Share premium | | | 100,000 | |
| General reserve | | | 60,000 | |
| Retained profits | | | 98,603 | |
| | | | | 258,603 |
| Total equity | | | | 1,158,603 |

***Note*: The presentation of goodwill is contrary to that required by International GAAP. This is permissible for statements of financial position prepared for internal use. As you will see in Exhibit 13.2, in a statement of financial position prepared for publication, the treatment must comply with International GAAP.**

Why do you think companies might ignore the requirements of International GAAP in this case?

## 13.12 Layout of the statement of financial position for publication under International GAAP

Exhibit 13.2 shows the same information as Exhibit 13.1 but in a form that complies with International GAAP.

### Exhibit 13.2 A statement of financial position for publication

**Statement of Financial Position as at 31 December 2018**

| | £ | £ |
|---|---|---|
| Non-current assets | | |
| Property, plant and equipment | | 1,126,400 |
| Intangible assets | | 225,000 |
| | | 1,351,400 |
| Current assets | | |
| Inventory | 91,413 | |
| Trade and other receivables | 186,100 | |
| Cash and cash equivalents | 8,390 | |
| | | 285,903 |
| Total assets | | 1,637,303 |
| Current liabilities | | |
| Trade and other payables | 113,700 | |
| Financial liabilities | 15,000 | |
| Liability for current tax | 50,000 | |
| | 178,700 | |
| Non-current liabilities | | |
| Financial liabilities | 300,000 | |
| Total liabilities | | (478,700) |
| Net assets | | 1,158,603 |
| Equity | | |
| Issued capital | | 900,000 |
| Reserves | | 258,603 |
| Total equity | | 1,158,603 |

*Notes*: 1 This is the minimum presentation required. All detail for each line will appear as a note to the statement of financial position.

2 The IAS terminology for the lines has been used. This is less informative. For example, rather than stating on the face of the statement that the non-current financial liabilities were 10% Loan Notes, this detail would only appear in the notes to the financial statement. Exhibit 13.3 shows the same information as Exhibit 13.2 but with more informative line descriptors. Such presentation is equally permissible under International GAAP.

**Exhibit 13.3 A statement of financial position for publication using alternative line descriptors**

**Statement of Financial Position as at 31 December 2018**

| | £ | £ |
|---|---|---|
| Non-current assets | | |
| Property, plant and equipment | | 1,126,400 |
| Goodwill | | 225,000 |
| | | 1,351,400 |
| Current assets | | |
| Inventory | 91,413 | |
| Accounts receivable | 186,100 | |
| Bank | 8,390 | |
| | | 285,903 |
| Total assets | | 1,637,303 |
| Current liabilities | | |
| Accounts payable | 113,700 | |
| Loan-note interest accrued | 15,000 | |
| Taxation | 50,000 | |
| | 178,700 | |
| Non-current liabilities | | |
| 10% loan notes | 300,000 | |
| Total liabilities | | (478,700) |
| Net assets | | 1,158,603 |
| Equity | | |
| Share capital | | 900,000 |
| Reserves | | 258,603 |
| Total equity | | 1,158,603 |

***Note*: This layout is probably more appropriate at your stage of studies. Do not forget to include notes expanding the detail where appropriate – in this case, notes would be needed for property, plant and equipment; share capital; and reserves. You are free, however, simply to replace these single-line items with the expanded details on the face of the statement of financial position. Unless otherwise indicated, examiners would need to award full marks for either approach, i.e. detailed presentation on the face of the statement, or single-line entries plus relevant expanding notes.**

## 13.13 Small and medium-sized company reporting requirements

In the UK, small and medium-sized companies do not have to file a full set of financial statements with the Registrar of Companies. If they wish, they can send a full set of financial statements, but what they *have* to file is a minimum set of 'modified financial statements'. They still have to send a full set to their own shareholders who request them – the modified financial statements refer only to those filed with the Registrar.

In addition, there is no audit requirement for small companies with a turnover of not more than £5.6 million and a statement of financial position total of not more than £2.8 million, unless 10% or more of shareholders sign a formal notice requesting an audit and lodge this at the registered office. For medium-sized companies, the limits are £22.8 million and £11.4 million respectively.

Why do you think these small and medium-sized companies are exempted from having their financial statements audited?

## 13.14 Modified financial statements of small companies

1 Neither a statement of profit or loss nor a directors' report has to be filed with the Registrar.
2 A statement of financial position has to be filed.

## 13.15 Modified financial statements of medium-sized companies

1 The statement of profit or loss can begin with the figure of gross profit or loss.
2 The analyses of revenue and profit normally required as notes to the financial statements need not be given.
3 The statement of financial position must be filed.

***Note*: Illustrative examples of published company financial statements including notes required are at the end of Chapter 14.**

## 13.16 Summary financial statements

A public limited company (plc) may send a summary financial statement to members in place of the full statements, but any member who requests the full statements must be sent them. The summary statement must:

(*a*) state that it is only a summary of information in the company's financial statements and the directors' report;
(*b*) contain a statement by the company's auditors of their opinion as to whether the summary financial statement is consistent with those financial statements and that report and complies with the requirements of the section in the Companies Act (CA 2006, Section 427 (unquoted company) or 428 (quoted company)) that permits the distribution of this summary financial statement and the regulations made under it;
(*c*) state whether the auditors' report on the financial statements was unqualified or qualified, and if it was qualified set out the report in full together with any further material needed to understand the qualification;
(*d*) state whether the auditors' report on the annual accounts contained a statement under either:
  (*i*) CA 2006 Section 498(2)(a) or (b) – accounting records or returns inadequate or financial statements not agreeing with records or returns; or
  (*ii*) CA 2006 Section 498(3) – failure to obtain necessary information and explanations and, if so, set out the statement in full.

**Activity 13.4**

Why do you think companies are allowed to send their shareholders summary financial statements rather than the full statements?

## 13.17 Website publication

A quoted company (i.e. one whose shares are listed on a stock exchange) must make its annual accounts and reports available on a website.

### Learning outcomes

You should now have learnt:

1. There are minimum requirements for the preparation of published statements of financial position.
2. Statements of financial position for internal use need not comply with these requirements.
3. Accounting standards must be complied with when preparing financial statements intended to present a true and fair view.
4. Some small companies are exempted from having their financial statements audited.
5. Small and medium-sized companies may file modified financial statements with the Registrar if they wish.
6. Public limited companies may send a summary financial statement to members in place of the full statements, but any member who requests the full statements must be sent them.

### Answers to activities

13.1 Some of the liabilities, for example financial liabilities, may be either current (e.g. interest accrued) or non-current (e.g. loan notes).

13.2 When a statement of financial position is prepared for internal use, it is the company's management that will use it. They may wish to know, for example, how much of goodwill has been impaired and that information is easier to see on the face of the statement of financial position rather than by comparing the current statement of financial position with the one prepared when the goodwill was first recognised.

13.3 Having financial statements audited is estimated as costing an average of £1,400 for small companies and £3,800 for medium-sized ones. While this appears a small amount of money, it can be relatively expensive for SMEs, particularly when they are newly formed and are making little or no profit. Not surprisingly, over 60% of small companies are not audited. However, although this is a good reason for such companies not incurring the expense of having an audit, as the sole reason for not having an audit it goes against the principles upon which the need for an audit was based. A far more realistic explanation is that errors and misleading items in the financial statements of small companies have far less of an impact than in the case of larger organisations and, on a purely cost/benefit basis, it is unlikely that the costs of having an audit will be sufficiently offset by any amendments or clarifications that an audit may bring.

13.4 Many shareholders are not accountants and have no understanding of many of the items in full financial statements. Rather than sending them information they will not understand, shareholders may be sent simplified information containing those parts of the financial statements that they are both more likely to understand and more likely to be interested in having. This saves the companies (and their shareholders) money which, in itself, is a good thing. It also increases the possibility that shareholders will actually look at the financial statements.

## Review questions

**13.1** The following balances remained in the books of AK Ltd on 31 March 2017, *after* the statement of profit or loss had been drawn up. You are to draft the statement of financial position as at 31 March 2017 in accordance with the relevant accounting standards.

| | *Dr* | *Cr* |
|---|---|---|
| | *£000s* | *£000s* |
| Ordinary share capital: £1 shares | | 1,000 |
| Preference share capital: 50p shares | | 400 |
| Calls account (ordinary shares) | | 2 |
| Development costs | 128 | |
| Goodwill | 416 | |
| Land and buildings – at cost | 1,000 | |
| Plant and machinery – at cost | 300 | |
| Provision for depreciation: Buildings | | 80 |
| Provision for depreciation: Plant and machinery | | 120 |
| Shares in undertakings in which the company has a participating interest | 280 | |
| Inventory: Raw materials | 24 | |
| Inventory: Finished goods | 144 | |
| Accounts receivable: Trade | 96 | |
| Amounts owed by associate entities | 20 | |
| Prepayments | | 4 |
| Loan notes (*see* Note 1) | | 200 |
| Bank overdraft (repayable on demand) | | 62 |
| Accounts payable: Trade (payable within one year) | | 68 |
| Bills payable (*see* Note 2) | | 16 |
| Share premium | | 200 |
| Capital redemption reserve | | 40 |
| General reserve | | 80 |
| Retained profits | | 172 |
| | 2,438 | 2,438 |

*Notes:*

1 Of the loan notes, £80,000 is repayable in five months' time, while the other £12,000 is repayable in four years' time.

2 Of the bills payable, £12,000 is in respect of a bill to be paid in eight months' time and £4,000 for a bill payable in 14 months' time.

3 The depreciation charged for the year was: Buildings £10,000, Plant and machinery £15,000.

**13.2** After the statement of profit or loss and statement of changes in equity have been prepared for the year ending 30 April 2017, the following balances remain in the books of Tree plc. Prepare a statement of financial position in accordance with the relevant accounting standards.

| | *£000s* | *£000s* |
|---|---:|---:|
| Ordinary share capital | | 100 |
| Share premium | | 60 |
| Revaluation reserve | | 24 |
| General reserve | | 30 |
| Foreign exchange reserve | | 8 |
| Retained profits | | 36 |
| Patents, trade marks and licences | 6 | |
| Goodwill | 42 | |
| Land and buildings | 280 | |
| Provision for depreciation: Land and buildings | | 80 |
| Plant and machinery | 90 | |
| Provision for depreciation: Plant and machinery | | 48 |
| Inventory of raw materials: 30 April 2017 | 24 | |
| Work in progress: 30 April 2017 | 10 | |
| Finished goods: 30 April 2017 | 26 | |
| Accounts receivable: Trade | 84 | |
| Accounts receivable: Other | 4 | |
| Prepayments and accrued income | 2 | |
| Loan notes (redeemable in 6 months' time) | | 50 |
| Loan notes (redeemable in 4½ years' time) | | 40 |
| Bank overdraft (repayable in 3 months) | | 4 |
| Trade accounts payable (payable in next 12 months) | | 26 |
| Trade accounts payable (payable after 12 months) | | 2 |
| Bills of exchange (payable within 12 months) | | 6 |
| Corporation tax (payable in 9 months' time) | | 38 |
| National insurance (payable in next month) | | 2 |
| Pensions contribution owing | | 8 |
| Deferred taxation | | 6 |
| | 568 | 568 |

**13.3** The following trial balance has been extracted from the books of Baganza plc as at 30 September 2017:

| | £000 | £000 |
|---|---|---|
| Administrative expenses | 400 | |
| Called-up share capital (1,200,000 ordinary shares of £1 each) | | 1,200 |
| Cash at bank and in hand | 60 | |
| Corporation tax (overpayment for the year to 30 September 2016) | | 20 |
| Deferred taxation (at 1 October 2016) | | 460 |
| Distribution costs | 600 | |
| Dividends received (on 31 March 2017) | | 249 |
| Freehold property: | | |
| at cost | 2,700 | |
| accumulated depreciation (at 1 October 2016) | | 260 |
| Interim dividend (paid in June 2017) | 36 | |
| Investments in United Kingdom companies | 2,000 | |
| Plant and machinery: | | |
| at cost | 5,200 | |
| accumulated depreciation (at 1 October 2016) | | 3,600 |
| Purchases | 16,000 | |
| Research expenditure | 75 | |
| Retained profits (at 1 October 2016) | | 2,022 |
| Inventory (at 1 October 2016) | 2,300 | |
| Trade accounts payable | | 2,900 |
| Trade accounts receivable | 2,700 | |
| Revenue | | 21,360 |
| | £32,071 | £32,071 |

*Additional information*:

**1** The inventory at 30 September 2017 was valued at £3,600,000.

**2** Depreciation for the year to 30 September 2017 is to be charged on the historic cost of the non-current assets as follows:

Freehold property: 5%
Plant and machinery: 15%

**3** The basic rate of income tax is assumed to be 27%.

**4** The directors propose a final dividend of 60p per share.

**5** The company was incorporated in 2010.

**6** Corporation tax based on the profits for the year at a rate of 35% is estimated to be £850,000.

**7** A transfer of £40,000 is to be made to the deferred taxation account.

**Required:**

In so far as the information permits, prepare Baganza plc's statement of profit or loss for the year ending 30 September 2017, and a statement of financial position as at that date in accordance with the appropriate accounting standards.

However, formal notes to the accounts are not required, although detailed workings should be submitted with your answer, which should include your calculation of earnings per share.

*(Association of Accounting Technicians)*

**13.4A** The trial balance of Jeremina plc as at 31 March 2016 is as follows:

| | *Dr* £ | *Cr* £ |
|---|---|---|
| Preference share capital: 50p shares | | 200,000 |
| Ordinary share capital: £1 shares | | 300,000 |
| General reserve | | 25,000 |
| Exchange reserve | | 15,000 |
| Retained profits as on 31 March 2015 | | 21,000 |
| Inventory 31 March 2015 | 184,000 | |
| Revenue | | 1,320,000 |
| Returns inwards | 34,000 | |
| Purchases | 620,000 | |
| Carriage inwards | 6,000 | |
| Wages (putting goods into a saleable condition) | 104,000 | |
| Wages: Warehouse staff | 40,000 | |
| Wages and salaries: Sales staff | 67,000 | |
| Wages and salaries: Administrative staff | 59,000 | |
| Motor expenses (*see* Note (*ii*)) | 29,000 | |
| General distribution expenses | 17,000 | |
| General administrative expenses | 12,000 | |
| Loan-note interest | 2,000 | |
| Royalties receivable | | 5,000 |
| Directors' remuneration | 84,000 | |
| Bad debts | 10,000 | |
| Discounts allowed | 14,000 | |
| Discounts received | | 11,000 |
| Plant and machinery at cost (*see* Note (*iii*)) | 240,000 | |
| Provision for depreciation: Plant and machinery (*see* Note (*iv*)) | | 72,000 |
| Motor vehicles at cost (*see* Note (*ii*)) | 120,000 | |
| Provision for depreciation: Motors (*see* Note (*iv*)) | | 48,000 |
| Goodwill | 200,000 | |
| Development costs | 24,000 | |
| Trade accounts receivable | 188,000 | |
| Trade accounts payable | | 45,000 |
| Bank overdraft (repayable on demand) | | 7,000 |
| Bills of exchange payable (all due within one year) | | 7,000 |
| Loan notes (redeemable in three years' time) | | 30,000 |
| Preference dividend | 12,000 | |
| Ordinary dividend | 40,000 | |
| | 2,106,000 | 2,106,000 |

*Notes:*

(*i*) Inventory of finished goods on 31 March 2016 £163,000.

(*ii*) Motor expenses and depreciation on motors to be apportioned: distribution $^4/_5$, administrative $^1/_5$.

(*iii*) Plant and machinery depreciation to be apportioned: cost of sales $^7/_{10}$, distribution $^1/_5$, administrative $^1/_{10}$.

(*iv*) Depreciate the following non-current assets on cost: motor vehicles 20%, plant and machinery 15%.

(*v*) Accrue corporation tax on profits of the year £38,000. This is payable on 31 December 2016.

**You are to draw up:**

(*a*) a detailed statement of profit or loss for the year ending 31 March 2016 for internal use, and

(*b*) a statement of profit or loss for publication, also a statement of financial position as at 31 March 2016.

**13.5A** You are presented with the following information relating to Plott plc for the year to 31 March 2018:

| | £000 |
|---|---|
| Bank overdraft | 500 |
| Called-up share capital (issued and fully paid) | 2,100 |
| Corporation tax (based on the profit for the year to 31 March 2018) | 900 |
| Accounts payable | 300 |
| Accounts receivable | 200 |
| Deferred taxation (credit) | 80 |
| Non-current assets: at cost | 3,800 |
| accumulated depreciation (at 31 March 2018) | 1,400 |
| Non-current asset investments: at cost | 100 |
| Retained profits (at 1 April 2017: credit) | 1,200 |
| Proposed dividend | 420 |
| Retained profit (for the year to 31 March 2018) | 585 |
| Share premium account | 315 |
| Inventory: at cost (at 31 March 2018) | 400 |
| Trade accounts payable | 2,000 |
| Trade accounts receivable | 5,300 |

*Additional information*:

1 The above information has been obtained after the compilation of the company's statement of profit or loss for the year ending 31 March 2018.

2 Details of non-current assets for the year to 31 March 2018 are as follows:

| | £000 |
|---|---|
| (*a*) At cost | |
| At 1 April 2017 | 3,400 |
| Additions | 600 |
| Disposals | 200 |
| (*b*) Accumulated depreciation | |
| At 1 April 2017 | 1,200 |
| Additions | 500 |
| Disposals | 300 |

3 The market value of the non-current asset investments at 31 March 2018 was £110,000. There were no purchases or sales of non-current asset investments during the year.

4 Inventories comprise finished goods. The replacement cost of these goods is similar to the value indicated in the statement of financial position.

5 Assume that the basic rate of income tax is 25%.

6 The authorised share capital of the company consists of 2,500,000 ordinary shares of £1 each.

**Required:**

In so far as the information permits, prepare Plott plc's statement of financial position as at 31 March 2018 in accordance with the *minimum* requirements of the relevant accounting standards.

*Notes:*

1 Where appropriate, formal notes must be attached to your statement of financial position; and

2 Detailed working should be submitted with your answer.

(*Association of Accounting Technicians*)

**13.6A** The following information has been extracted from the books of Quire plc as at 30 September 2018.

| | *£000* | *£000* |
|---|---|---|
| Bank overdraft | | 2,400 |
| Called-up share capital (ordinary shares of £1 each) | | 4,000 |
| Deferred taxation | | 200 |
| Delivery expenses | 2,800 | |
| Non-current assets: at cost | 3,500 | |
| accumulated depreciation (at 1 October 2017) | | 1,100 |
| Loan notes held | 100 | |
| Loan-note interest (net) | | 40 |
| Interest payable | 400 | |
| Interim dividend paid | 60 | |
| Office expenses | 3,000 | |
| Other creditors | | 180 |
| Other debtors | 160 | |
| Retained profits (at 1 October 2017) | | 820 |
| Purchases | 12,000 | |
| Revenue | | 19,000 |
| Inventory (at 1 October 2017) | 500 | |
| Trade accounts payable | | 100 |
| Trade accounts receivable | 5,320 | |
| | £27,840 | £27,840 |

*The following additional information is to be taken into account*:

1 Inventory at 30 September 2018 was valued at £400,000.
2 All items in the above trial balance are shown net of value added tax.
3 At 30 September 2018, £130,000 was outstanding for office expenses, and £50,000 had been paid in advance for delivery van licences.
4 Depreciation at a rate of 50% is to be charged on the historic cost of the tangible non-current assets using the reducing balance method: it is to be apportioned as follows:

| | % |
|---|---|
| Cost of sales | 60 |
| Distribution | 30 |
| Administration | 10 |
| | 100 |

There were no purchases or sales of non-current assets during the year to 30 September 2018.

5 The following rates of taxation are to be assumed:

| | % |
|---|---|
| Corporation tax | 35 |
| Income tax | 25 |
| Value added tax | 17.5 |

The corporation tax payable based on the profits for the year to 30 September 2018 has been estimated at £80,000.

6 A transfer of £60,000 is to be made from the deferred taxation account.
7 The directors propose to pay a final ordinary dividend of 3p per share.

**Required:**
In so far as the information permits, prepare Quire plc's statement of profit or loss for the year ending 30 September 2018, and a statement of financial position as at that date in accordance with the requirements of the relevant accounting standards.

*Note*: Formal notes to the accounts are NOT required, but detailed workings should be submitted with your answer.

(*Association of Accounting Technicians*)

→

**13.7A** The following trial balance has been extracted from the books of Patt plc as at 31 March 2017:

| | *Dr* | *Cr* |
|---|---|---|
| | *£000* | *£000* |
| Bank overdraft | | 25 |
| Called-up share capital (ordinary shares of £1 each) | | 1,440 |
| Accounts payable | | 55 |
| Accounts receivable | 50 | |
| Non-current assets: at cost | 300 | |
| accumulated depreciation (at 1 April 2016) | | 120 |
| Marketing expenses | 100 | |
| Office expenses | 200 | |
| Retained profits (at 1 April 2016) | | 200 |
| Production expenses | 2,230 | |
| Purchases (net of VAT) | 3,700 | |
| Revenue (amounts invoiced, net of VAT) | | 7,000 |
| Inventory (at 1 April 2016) | 130 | |
| Trade accounts payable | | 160 |
| Trade accounts receivable | 2,290 | |
| | £9,000 | £9,000 |

*Additional information*:

1 Following the preparation of the above trial balance, the following additional matters need to be taken into account:
   (*a*) inventory at 31 March 2017 was valued at £170,000;
   (*b*) at 31 March 2017, £20,000 was owing for office expenses, and £15,000 had been paid in advance for marketing expenses;
   (*c*) a customer had gone into liquidation owing the company £290,000; the company does not expect to recover any of this debt;
   (*d*) the company decides to set up an allowance for doubtful debts amounting to 5% of the outstanding trade accounts receivable as at the end of each financial year; and
   (*e*) depreciation is to be charged on the non-current assets at a rate of 20% on cost; it is to be apportioned as follows:

| | % |
|---|---|
| Marketing | 20 |
| Office | 10 |
| Production | 70 |
| | 100 |

*Note*: There were no acquisitions or disposals of non-current assets during the year to 31 March 2017.

2 Corporation tax (based on the accounting profit for the year at a rate of 35%) is estimated to be £160,000. The basic rate of income tax is assumed to be 25%.

3 The directors are to recommend the payment of a dividend of 10p per ordinary share.

**Required:**

In so far as the information permits, prepare Patt plc's statement of profit or loss for the year ending 31 March 2017, and a statement of financial position as at that date in accordance with the relevant accounting standards.

*Notes*:

(*i*) Where appropriate, formal notes should be attached to your statement of profit or loss and statement of financial position. However, a statement of accounting policies is NOT required.

(*ii*) Detailed workings should also be submitted with your solution. They should be clearly designated as such, and they must not form part of your formal notes.

(*Association of Accounting Technicians*)

chapter 14

# Published financial statements of limited companies: accompanying notes

## Learning objectives

**After you have studied this chapter, you should be able to:**

- describe the additional notes to published financial statements that are required in the UK
- describe the requirement to include a directors' report with the published financial statements

## Introduction

In this chapter, you'll learn about the notes that must be included when company financial statements are published in the UK and about the report that must be prepared by the directors to accompany the financial statements.

## 14.1 Notes to accompany the financial statements

Companies may include as many notes as they wish when they publish their financial statements. In addition to those required under International GAAP, there are some notes that the Companies Acts require. These are currently under revision following publication of the Companies Act 2006. However, changes to previous requirements are unlikely to be significant. The principal requirements are:

### 1 Information about related undertakings unless doing so would be prejudicial to the business

### 2 Particulars of staff

(*a*) Average number employed by the company (or by the group), divided between categories of workers, e.g. between manufacturing and administration.

(*b*) (*i*) wages and salaries paid to staff;
(*ii*) social security costs of staff;
(*iii*) other pension costs for employees.

## 3 The directors' report and the strategic report

The directors' report for a financial year must state:

(*a*) the names of the persons who, at any time during the financial year, were directors of the company; and
(*b*) the principal activities of the company in the course of the year.

Except in the case of small companies, the report must state the amount (if any) that the directors recommend should be paid by way of dividend.

Unless the company is subject to the small companies' regime, the directors' report must contain a strategic report. The purpose of the business review is to inform members of the company and help them assess how the directors have performed their duty to promote the success of the company.

The strategic report must contain a fair review of the company's business, and a description of the principal risks and uncertainties facing the company. Overall, the strategic report must be balanced and comprehensive analysis of the development and performance of the company's business during the financial year, and the position of the company's business at the end of that year, consistent with the size and complexity of the business.

In the case of a quoted company, the strategic report must – to the extent necessary for an understanding of the development, performance or position of the company's business – include the main trends and factors likely to affect the future development, performance and position of the company's business; and information about:

- a description of the company's strategy;
- a description of the company's business model
- the number of people of each gender who were directors, managers, and employees of the company at the end of the reporting period.
- environmental matters (including the impact of the company's business on the environment);
- the company's employees; and
- social and community issues, including information about any policies of the company in relation to those matters and the effectiveness of those policies; and information about persons with whom the company has contractual or other arrangements which are essential to the business of the company (unless such disclosure would, in the opinion of the directors, be seriously prejudicial to that person and contrary to the public interest).

If the strategic report does not contain information of each kind mentioned above it must state which of those kinds of information it does not contain.

The strategic report must, to the extent necessary for an understanding of the development, performance or position of the company's business, include:

- analysis using financial key performance indicators (i.e. factors by reference to which the development, performance or position of the company's business can be measured effectively); and
- where appropriate, analysis using other key performance indicators, including information relating to environmental matters and employee matters.

(Medium-sized companies need not comply with these two bullet points so far as they relate to non-financial information.)

The strategic report must, where appropriate, include references to, and additional explanations of, amounts included in the company's annual accounts.

The disclosure of information about impending developments or matters in the course of negotiation is not required if the disclosure would, in the opinion of the directors, be seriously prejudicial to the interests of the company.

The directors' report of quoted companies must also include disclosures of greenhouse gas emissions. (This is described in detail in Section 33.8.)

In addition, all directors' reports must also contain a statement to the effect that, in the case of each of the persons who are directors at the time the report is approved:

- so far as the director is aware, there is no relevant audit information of which the company's auditor is unaware; and
- he has taken all the steps that he ought to have taken as a director in order to make himself aware of any relevant audit information and to establish that the company's auditor is aware of that information.

The directors' report must be approved by the board of directors and signed on behalf of the board by a director or the secretary of the company. If the report is prepared in accordance with the small companies regime, it must contain a statement to that effect in a prominent position above the signature.

**Activity 14.1** Why do you think the directors' report is audited?

The directors of a quoted company must also prepare a directors' remuneration report for each financial year of the company, disclosing within the report details of individual directors' remuneration packages, the company's remuneration policy, and the role of the board and remuneration committee in this area.

The directors' remuneration report must be approved by the board of directors and signed on behalf of the board by a director or the secretary of the company. It should include:

1 Aggregate amounts of:
   (*a*) emoluments, including pension contributions and benefits in kind. Distinction to be made between those emoluments as fees and those for executive duties;
   (*b*) pensions for past directors;
   (*c*) compensation for loss of office.
2 The chairman's emoluments and those of the highest-paid director, if paid more than the chairman. In both cases, pension contributions are to be excluded.
3 Number of directors whose emoluments, excluding pension contributions, fall within each bracket of £5,000.
4 Total amounts waived by directors and the number concerned.

The disclosures under 2 and 3 above are not needed for a company being neither a parent nor subsidiary undertaking where its directors' emoluments under 1 do not exceed £60,000. The disclosures under 2 and 3 are also not necessary for directors working wholly or mainly overseas.

An illustration is now given in Exhibit 14.1:

### Exhibit 14.1

| *Name* | *Fee (as directors)* | *Remuneration (as executives)* | *Pension contributions* |
|---|---|---|---|
| A (Chairman) | £5,000 | £85,000 | £20,000 |
| B | £2,500 | £95,000 | £30,000 |
| C | £2,500 | £55,000 | £15,000 |
| D | £1,500 | £54,000 | £12,500 |
| E | £1,500 | £30,000 | £10,000 |

*Note to accounts:*
Directors' remuneration: the amounts paid to directors were as follows:

| | |
|---|---|
| Fees as directors | £13,000 |
| Other emoluments, including pension contributions | £406,500 |

Emoluments of the Chairman – excluding pension contributions – amounted to £90,000, and those of the highest-paid director to £97,500. Other directors' emoluments were in the following ranges:

| | |
|---|---|
| £30,001 – £35,000 | 1 |
| £35,001 – £60,000 | 2 |

## 4 Various charges to be shown as notes

1 Auditors' remuneration, including expenses.
2 Hire of plant and machinery.
3 Interest payable on:
   (*a*) bank loans, overdrafts and other loans repayable by instalments or otherwise within five years;
   (*b*) loans of any other kind.
4 Depreciation:
   (*a*) amounts of provisions for both tangible and intangible assets;
   (*b*) effect on depreciation of change of depreciation method;
   (*c*) effect on depreciation of revaluation of assets.

## 5 Income from listed investments

## 6 Rents receivable from land, after deducting outgoings

## 7 Taxation (see also IAS 12 *Income taxes*)

1 Tax charges split between:
   (*a*) UK corporation tax, and basis of computation;
   (*b*) UK income tax, and basis of computation;
   (*c*) irrecoverable VAT;
   (*d*) tax attributable to franked investment income.
2 Show, as component part, charge for deferred tax.
3 Any other special circumstances affecting tax liability.

## 8 Prior period adjustments

See IAS 8 *Accounting policies, changes in accounting estimates and errors*, which is dealt with in Chapter 11.

## 9 Redemption of shares and loans

Show amounts set aside for these purposes.

## 10 Earnings per share (listed companies only)

See IAS 33 *Earnings per share*, which is dealt with in Section 11.26.

Why do you think these notes are required rather than leaving it up to companies to provide the information they believe to be worthwhile including?

Let's look at how all these requirements are enacted by working through two examples.

## 14.2 Illustrative company financial statements: worked example 1

F Clarke Ltd are specialist wholesalers. This is their trial balance at 31 December 2017.

| | *Dr* | *Cr* |
|---|---|---|
| | £ | £ |
| Ordinary share capital: £1 shares | | 1,000,000 |
| Share premium | | 120,000 |
| General reserve | | 48,000 |
| Retained profits as at 31.12.2016 | | 139,750 |
| Inventory: 31.12.2016 | 336,720 | |
| Revenue | | 5,090,370 |
| Purchases | 2,475,910 | |
| Returns outwards | | 121,220 |
| Returns inwards | 136,200 | |
| Carriage inwards | 6,340 | |
| Carriage outwards | 43,790 | |
| Warehouse wages (average number of workers 59) | 410,240 | |
| Salespeople's salaries (average number of workers 21) | 305,110 | |
| Administrative wages and salaries | 277,190 | |
| Plant and machinery | 610,000 | |
| Motor vehicle hire | 84,770 | |
| Provisions for depreciation: plant and machinery | | 216,290 |
| General distribution expenses | 27,130 | |
| General administrative expenses | 47,990 | |
| Directors' remuneration | 195,140 | |
| Ordinary dividend | 375,000 | |
| Rents receivable | | 37,150 |
| Trade accounts receivable | 1,623,570 | |
| Cash at bank and in hand | 179,250 | |
| Trade accounts payable (payable before 31.3.2018) | | 304,570 |
| Bills of exchange payable (payable 28.2.2018) | | 57,000 |
| | 7,134,350 | 7,134,350 |

*Notes*:

(*a*) Inventory at 31.12.2017: £412,780, consists of goods for resale.
(*b*) Plant and machinery is apportioned: distributive 60%; administrative 40%.
(*c*) Accrue auditors' remuneration: £71,000.
(*d*) Depreciate plant and machinery: 20% on cost.
(*e*) Of the motor hire, £55,000 is for distributive purposes.
(*f*) Corporation tax on profits, at a rate of 35%, is estimated at £238,500 and is payable on 1.10.2018.
(*g*) Pension contributions for staff amounted to £42,550 and social security contributions to £80,120. These figures are included in wages and salaries in the trial balance. No employee earned over £30,000.
(*h*) Plant of £75,000 had been bought during the year.
(*i*) Directors' remuneration has been as follows:

| | £ |
|---|---|
| Chairman | 46,640 |
| Managing Director | 51,500 |
| Finance Director | 46,000 |
| Marketing Director | 43,000 |
| | 187,140 |

In addition, each of them drew £2,000 as directors' fees. Pensions are the personal responsibility of directors.

**Required:**
Subject to the limits of the information given you, draw up a statement of profit or loss for the year ending 31 December 2017, and a statement of financial position as at that date. They should be in published form and accompanied by the necessary notes prescribed by statute.

## Answer to worked example 1

***Workings***

| | £ | | £ | £ |
|---|---|---|---|---|
| Revenue | 5,090,370 | Cost of sales: | | |
| *Less* Returns in | (136,200) | Opening inventory | | 336,720 |
| | 4,954,170 | *Add* Purchases | 2,475,910 | |
| | | *Less* Returns out | (121,220) | |
| | | | 2,354,690 | |
| | | *Add* Carriage in | 6,340 | 2,361,030 |
| | | | | 2,697,750 |
| | | *Less* Closing inventory | | (412,780) |
| | | | | 2,284,970 |
| Distribution costs: | | Administrative expenses: | | |
| Warehouse wages | 410,240 | Wages and salaries | | 277,190 |
| Salespeople's salaries | 305,110 | Motor hire | | 29,770 |
| Carriage out | 43,790 | General expenses | | 47,990 |
| General expenses | 27,130 | Directors' remuneration | | 150,140 |
| Motor hire | 55,000 | Auditors' remuneration | | 71,000 |
| Depreciation: plant | 73,200 | Depreciation: plant | | 48,800 |
| | | | | 624,890 |
| Marketing Director's remuneration | 45,000 | | | |
| | 959,470 | | | |

**F Clarke Ltd**
**Statement of Profit or Loss for the year ending 31 December 2017**

| | £ | £ |
|---|---|---|
| Revenue | | 4,954,170 |
| Cost of sales | | (2,284,970) |
| Gross profit | | 2,669,200 |
| Distribution costs | 959,470 | |
| Administrative expenses | 624,890 | |
| | | (1,584,360) |
| | | 1,084,840 |
| Other operating income | | 37,150 |
| Profit before taxation | | 1,121,990 |
| Taxation | | (238,500) |
| Profit for the year | | 883,490 |

**F Clarke Ltd**
**Statement of Financial Position as at 31 December 2017**

| | £ | £ |
|---|---|---|
| *Non-current assets* | | |
| Tangible assets: Plant and machinery | | 271,710 |
| *Current assets* | | |
| Inventory: Finished goods and goods for resale | 412,780 | |
| Trade accounts receivable | 1,623,570 | |
| Cash at bank and in hand | 179,250 | |
| | | 2,215,600 |
| Total assets | | 2,487,310 |
| *Current liabilities* | | |
| Trade and other accounts payable | 375,570 | |
| Bills of exchange payable | 57,000 | |
| Taxation | 238,500 | |
| | | (671,070) |
| *Net assets* | | 1,816,240 |
| *Equity* | | £ |
| Called-up share capital | | 1,000,000 |
| Share premium | | 120,000 |
| Other reserves: | | |
| General reserve | | 48,000 |
| Retained profits | | 648,240 |
| | | 1,816,240 |

## NOTES TO THE ACCOUNTS

### 1 Employees

Average number of workers was:

| | |
|---|---|
| Warehousing | 59 |
| Revenue | 21 |
| | 80 |

Remuneration of employees was:

| | £ |
|---|---|
| Wages and salaries | 869,870 |
| Social security costs | 80,120 |
| Pension contributions | 42,550 |
| | 992,540 |

### 2 Directors' remuneration

The amounts paid to directors were as follows:

| | £ |
|---|---|
| Fees as directors | 8,000 |
| Other emoluments | 187,140 |

Emoluments of the Chairman amounted to £46,640, and those of the highest-paid director £51,500. Other directors' emoluments were in the following ranges:

| | |
|---|---|
| £40,001–45,000 | 1 |
| £45,001–50,000 | 1 |

### 3 Operating profit is shown after charging

| | £ |
|---|---|
| Auditors' remuneration | 71,000 |
| Hire of motors | 84,770 |

### 4 Non-current assets

| Plant and machinery | £ | £ |
|---|---|---|
| Cost at 1.1.2017 | 535,000 | |
| Additions | 75,000 | |
| | | 610,000 |
| Depreciation to 31.12.2016 | 216,290 | |
| Charge for the year | 122,000 | |
| | | (338,290) |
| | | 271,710 |

**5 Trade and other accounts payable**

| | | |
|---|---|---|
| Trade accounts payable | 304,570 | |
| Auditors' remuneration | 71,000 | |
| | | 375,570 |

**6 Retained profits**

| | | |
|---|---|---|
| Balance at 31.12.2016 | 139,750 | |
| Profit for the year | 883,490 | |
| | 1,023,240 | |
| Dividends paid | (375,000) | |
| Balance at 31.12.2017 | | 648,240 |

***Note*: The retained profit information would be shown in the statement of changes in equity.**

## 14.3 Illustrative company financial statements: worked example 2

The trial balance of Quartz plc on 31 December 2016 was as follows:

| | *Dr* *£000* | *Cr* *£000* |
|---|---|---|
| Preference share capital: £1 shares | | 200 |
| Ordinary share capital: £1 shares | | 1,000 |
| Exchange reserve | | 75 |
| General reserve | | 150 |
| Retained profits 31.12.2015 | | 215 |
| Revenue | | 5,095 |
| Purchases | 2,196 | |
| Carriage inwards | 38 | |
| Inventory 31.12.2015 | 902 | |
| Wages (adding value to goods) | 35 | |
| Wages: warehousing | 380 | |
| Wages and salaries: administrative | 120 | |
| Wages and salaries: sales | 197 | |
| Motor expenses | 164 | |
| Bad debts | 31 | |
| Loan-note interest | 40 | |
| Preference dividend | 20 | |
| Ordinary dividend | 500 | |
| Bank overdraft interest | 19 | |
| General distribution expenses | 81 | |
| General administrative expenses | 73 | |
| Directors' remuneration | 210 | |
| Investments in associates | 340 | |
| Income from shares in associates | | 36 |
| Discounts allowed and received | 55 | 39 |
| Buildings: at cost | 1,200 | |
| Plant and machinery: at cost | 330 | |
| Motor vehicles: at cost | 480 | |
| Provisions for depreciation: | | |
| Land and buildings | | 375 |
| Plant and machinery | | 195 |
| Motors | | 160 |
| Goodwill | 40 | |
| Patents, licences and trade marks | 38 | |
| Trade accounts receivable and payable | 864 | 392 |
| Bank overdraft (repayable any time) | | 21 |
| Loan notes 10% | | 400 |
| | 8,353 | 8,353 |

*Notes*:

(*a*) Inventory at 31.12.2016: £1,103,000 at cost.

(*b*) Motor expenses and depreciation on motors to be apportioned: distribution 75%; administrative 25%.

(*c*) Depreciation on buildings and plant and machinery to be apportioned: distribution 50%; administrative 50%.

(*d*) Depreciate on cost: motor vehicles 25%; plant and machinery 20%.

(*e*) Accrued corporation tax on profits of the year £266,000. This is payable 1 October 2017.

(*f*) During the year new vehicles were purchased at a cost of £60,000.

(*g*) During June 2016 one of the buildings, which had originally cost £130,000, and which had a written-down value at the date of the sale of £80,000, was sold for £180,000. Depreciation on buildings to be charged against the year's profits £60,000. The buildings are revalued by B & Co., Chartered Surveyors, at £1,500,000 at 31.12.2016 (and this figure is to be included in the financial statements).

(*h*) Directors' remuneration was as follows:

| | £ |
|---|---|
| Marketing | 42,000 |
| Chairman | 37,000 |
| Managing | 61,000 |
| Finance | 50,000 |
| | 190,000 |

In addition each director drew £5,000 fees.

(*i*) The loan notes are to be redeemed in five equal annual instalments, starting in the following year, 2017.

(*j*) The investments are in listed companies with a market value at 31 December 2016 of £438,000.

(*k*) Accrue auditors' remuneration, including expenses, £7,000.

**You are required to** prepare a statement of profit or loss and a statement of financial position as at 31 December 2016 which should:

(*a*) conform to the requirements of the Companies Act 2006;

(*b*) conform to the relevant accounting standards;

(*c*) give the notes necessary to the accounts.

***Note*: Neither a statement of comprehensive income nor a statement of changes in equity is required.**

## Answer to worked example 2

***Workings***

| | *£000* | | *Dist.* *£000* | *Admin.* *£000* |
|---|---|---|---|---|
| Cost of sales: | | Wages | 577 | 120 |
| Opening inventory | 902 | Motor expenses | 123 | 41 |
| *Add* Purchases | 2,196 | General | 81 | 73 |
| *Add* Carriage in | 38 | Depreciation: plant | 33 | 33 |
| | 3,136 | motors | 90 | 30 |
| *Less* Closing inventory | (1,103) | buildings | 30 | 30 |
| | 2,033 | Directors | 47 | 163 |
| Wages (added value) | 35 | Auditors' remuneration | | 7 |
| | 2,068 | Discounts (net) 55–39 | | 16 |
| | | Bad debts | | 31 |
| | | | 981 | 544 |

**Quartz plc**
**Statement of profit or loss for the year ending 31 December 2016**

| | £000 | £000 |
|---|---|---|
| Revenue | | 5,095 |
| Cost of sales | | (2,068) |
| Gross profit | | 3,027 |
| Distribution costs | 981 | |
| Administrative expenses | 544 | |
| | | (1,525) |
| Operating profit | | 1,502 |
| Finance income | | |
| Income from associates | | 36 |
| | | 1,538 |
| Finance costs | | |
| Interest payable and similar charges | | (59) |
| Profit before taxation | | 1,479 |
| Taxation | | (266) |
| Profit for the year | | 1,213 |

**Quartz plc**
**Statement of Financial Position as at 31 December 2016**

| Non-current assets | £000 | £000 | £000 |
|---|---|---|---|
| *Intangible assets* | | | |
| Patents, licences and trade marks | | 38 | |
| Goodwill | | 40 | |
| | | 78 | |
| *Tangible assets* | | | |
| Buildings | 1,500 | | |
| Plant and machinery | 69 | | |
| Vehicles | 200 | | |
| | | 1,769 | |
| *Investments* | | | |
| Shares in associates | | 340 | |
| | | | 2,187 |
| *Current assets* | | | |
| Inventory | | 1,103 | |
| Trade accounts receivable | | 864 | |
| | | | 1,967 |
| Total assets | | | 4,154 |
| *Current liabilities* | | | |
| Loan notes | | 80 | |
| Bank overdraft | | 21 | |
| Trade and other accounts payable | | 399 | |
| Taxation | | 266 | |
| | | 766 | |
| Net current assets | | | |
| *Non-current liabilities* | | | |
| Loan notes | | 320 | |
| | | | (1,086) |
| Net assets | | | 3,068 |
| *Equity* | | | |
| Called-up share capital | | | 1,200 |
| Revaluation reserve | | | 735 |
| Retained profits | | | 908 |
| Other reserves | | | 225 |
| | | | 3,068 |

## NOTES TO THE ACCOUNTS

### 1 Share capital called up

| | £ |
|---|---|
| 200,000 10% preference shares of £1 each | 200,000 |
| 1,000,000 ordinary shares of £1 each | 1,000,000 |
| | 1,200,000 |

### 2 Tangible assets

| | *Buildings* | *Plant* | *Vehicles* |
|---|---|---|---|
| | *£000* | *£000* | *£000* |
| Cost at 1.1.2016 | 1,330 | 330 | 480 |
| Disposals (at cost) | (130) | – | – |
| Adjustment for revaluation | 735 | | |
| | 1,935 | 330 | 480 |
| Depreciation at 1.1.2016 | 425 | 195 | 160 |
| Provided in year | 60 | 66 | 120 |
| Disposals | (50) | | |
| | 435 | 261 | 280 |
| Net book values | 1,500 | 69 | 200 |

### 3 Investments

The market value of investments at 31 December 2016 was £438,000.

### 4 Ten per cent loan notes

These are redeemable in five equal annual instalments, starting next year. Interest of £40,000 is charged in this year's accounts.

### 5 Trade and other accounts payable

| | |
|---|---|
| Trade accounts payable | 392,000 |
| Auditors' remuneration | 7,000 |
| | 399,000 |

### 6 Other reserves

| | £ |
|---|---|
| Exchange reserve | 75,000 |
| General reserve | 150,000 |
| | 225,000 |

### 7 Directors' remuneration

The amounts paid to directors were as follows:

| | £ | £ |
|---|---|---|
| Fees as directors | 20,000 | |
| Other emoluments | 190,000 | 210,000 |

Emoluments of the chairman amounted to £42,000 and those of the highest-paid director £66,000. Other directors' emoluments were in the following ranges:

| | |
|---|---|
| £45,001–£50,000 | 1 |
| £50,001–£55,000 | 1 |

### 8 Operating profit is shown after charging

| | £ |
|---|---|
| Auditors' remuneration | 7,000 |
| Bank overdraft interest | 19,000 |

## Learning outcomes

**You should now have learnt:**

**1** The Companies Acts require that additional notes be prepared and included with the published financial statements.

**2** In many cases, the contents of these notes have been extended through the issuing of an accounting standard. For example, IFRS 8 *Operating segments* extended the disclosure required of all entities concerning segmental performance.

**3** Along with the notes to the financial statements, a directors' report must be presented which summarises the activities and performance of the entity, along with specific details on a number of matters, including directors' shareholdings and information concerning significant changes in non-current assets.

**4** The notes to the financial statements and the directors' report are both audited and the views of the auditors on their content are included in the auditors' report which is attached to companies' published annual reports.

## Answers to activities

14.1 The directors' report contains a review of the company's performance, activities and future intentions. It also contains many other qualitative and quantitative items of information considered likely to influence the economic decisions of the users of financial statements. The audit report indicates whether, in the opinion of the auditors, the directors' report presents a true and fair view of the items contained within it. If the directors' report was not audited, unscrupulous directors could paint pictures concerning the company that gave an overly favourable impression of its performance, so biasing the judgement of those taking economic decisions based on its content.

14.2 These items are all of a type considered to be important and likely to influence the economic decisions of the users of financial statements. They are subject to review by the auditors of the company in the same way as the financial statements.

## Review questions

**14.1** The following trial balance of X Limited, a non-listed company, has been extracted from the books after the preparation of the statement of profit or loss and statement of changes in equity for the year ending 31 March 2017.

| | *£000* | *£000* |
|---|---|---|
| Ordinary share capital – authorised, allotted and called-up fully paid shares of £1 each | | 1,000 |
| 12% loan notes (repayable in nine years) | | 500 |
| Deferred taxation | | 128 |
| Provisions for depreciation: | | |
| Plant and machinery at 31 March 2017 | | 650 |
| Freehold properties at 31 March 2017 | | 52 |
| Vehicles at 31 March 2017 | | 135 |
| Investments (listed), at cost | 200 | |
| Trade accounts receivable and prepayments | 825 | |
| Corporation tax | | 270 |
| Proposed final dividend | | 280 |
| Tangible non-current assets: | | |
| Freehold properties at 31 March 2017 | 1,092 | |
| Plant and machinery at 31 March 2017 | 1,500 | |
| Vehicles at 31 March 2017 | 420 | |
| Retained profits – balance at 31 March 2017 | | 356 |
| Share premium account | | 150 |
| Trade accounts payable and accruals | | 878 |
| Research and development costs | 35 | |
| Inventory: | | |
| Raw materials | 200 | |
| Work in progress | 50 | |
| Finished goods | 250 | |
| Bank balance | 439 | |
| Revaluation reserve on freehold properties | | 612 |
| | 5,011 | 5,011 |

You are also provided with the following information:

**1 Investments**
The listed investments consist of shares in W plc quoted on the Stock Exchange at £180,000 on 31 March 2017. This is not considered to be a permanent fall in the value of this asset.

**2 Trade accounts receivable and prepayments**
The company received notice, during April 2017, that one of its major customers, Z Limited, had gone into liquidation. The amount included in trade accounts receivable and prepayments is £225,000 and it is estimated that a dividend of 24p in the £ will be paid to unsecured creditors.

**3 Taxation**

(*a*) *Corporation tax*
The figure in the trial balance is made up as follows:

| | *£000* |
|---|---|
| Based on profits for the year | 174 |
| Tax on gain on sale of non-current asset (*see* Note 4) | 96 |
| | 270 |

(*b*) *Deferred taxation*
A charge of £50,000 was made to profit or loss during the year ended 31 March 2017.

**4 Tangible non-current assets**

(*a*) In arriving at the profit for the year, depreciation of £242,000 was charged, made up of freehold properties £12,000, plant and machinery £150,000 and vehicles £80,000.

(*b*) During the year to 31 March 2017, new vehicles were purchased at a cost of £200,000.

(*c*) During March 2017, the directors sold one of the freehold properties which had originally cost £320,000 and which had a written-down value at the date of the sale of £280,000. A profit of £320,000 on the sale has already been dealt with in arriving at the profit for the year. The estimated corporation tax liability in respect of the gain is £96,000, as shown in Note 3. After this sale, the directors decided to have the remaining freehold properties revalued, for the first time, by Messrs V & Co, Chartered Surveyors and to include the revalued figure of £1,040,000 in the 2017 accounts.

**5 Research and development costs**

The company carries out research and development and accounts for it in accordance with the relevant accounting standard. The amount shown in the trial balance relates to development expenditure on a new product scheduled to be launched in April 2017. Management is confident that this new product will earn substantial profits for the company in the coming years.

**6 Inventory**

The replacement cost of the finished goods, if valued at 31 March 2017, would amount to £342,000.

**You are required to** prepare a statement of financial position at 31 March 2017 to conform to the requirements of the Companies Acts and relevant accounting standards in so far as the information given allows. The vertical format must be used.

The notes necessary to accompany this statement should also be prepared.

Workings should be shown, but comparative figures are not required.

(*Chartered Institute of Management Accountants*)

**14.2** The following information has been extracted from the books of account of Billinge plc as at 30 June 2016:

| | *Dr* | *Cr* |
|---|---|---|
| | *£000* | *£000* |
| Administration expenses | 242 | |
| Cash at bank and in hand | 157 | |
| Cash received on sale of fittings | | 3 |
| Corporation tax (over-provision for the previous year) | | 10 |
| Deferred taxation | | 60 |
| Depreciation on fixtures, fittings, tools and equipment (1 July 2015) | | 132 |
| Distribution costs | 55 | |
| Factory closure costs | 30 | |
| Fixtures, fittings, tools and equipment at cost | 340 | |
| Retained profits (at 1 July 2015) | | 40 |
| Purchase of equipment | 60 | |
| Purchases of goods for resale | 855 | |
| Sales (net of VAT) | | 1,500 |
| Share capital (500,000 authorised, issued and fully paid ordinary shares of £1 each) | | 500 |
| Inventory (at 1 July 2015) | 70 | |
| Trade accounts payable | | 64 |
| Trade accounts receivable | 500 | |
| | £2,309 | £2,309 |

*Additional information*:

1 The company was incorporated in 2010.
2 The inventory at 30 June 2016 (valued at the lower of cost or net realisable value) was estimated to be worth £100,000.
3 Fixtures, fittings, tools and equipment all related to administrative expenses. Depreciation is charged on them at a rate of 20% per annum on cost. A full year's depreciation is charged in the year of acquisition, but no depreciation is charged in the year of disposal.
4 During the year to 30 June 2016, the company purchased £60,000 of equipment. It also sold some fittings (which had originally cost £20,000) for £3,000 and for which depreciation of £15,000 had been set aside.
5 The corporation tax based on the profits for the year at a rate of 35% is estimated to be £100,000. A transfer of £40,000 is to be made to the deferred taxation account.
6 The company proposes to pay a dividend of 20p per ordinary share.
7 The standard rate of income tax is 30%.

**Required:**

In so far as the information permits, prepare Billinge plc's statement of profit or loss for the year ending 30 June 2016, and a statement of financial position as at that date in accordance with the Companies Acts and appropriate accounting standards.

(*Association of Accounting Technicians*)

**14.3A** Cosnett Ltd is a company principally involved in the manufacture of aluminium accessories for camping enthusiasts. Its trial balance at 30 September 2018 was:

| | £ | £ |
|---|---:|---:|
| Issued ordinary share capital (£1 shares) | | 600,000 |
| Retained profits at 1 October 2017 | | 625,700 |
| Loan notes redeemable 2022 | | 150,000 |
| Bank loan | | 25,000 |
| Plant and machinery at cost | 1,475,800 | |
| Accumulated depreciation to 30 September 2018 | | 291,500 |
| Investments in UK companies at cost | 20,000 | |
| Revenue | | 3,058,000 |
| Dividends from investments | | 2,800 |
| Loss arising on factory closure | 86,100 | |
| Cost of sales | 2,083,500 | |
| Political and charitable contributions | 750 | |
| Distribution costs | 82,190 | |
| Salaries of office staff | 42,100 | |
| Directors' emoluments | 63,000 | |
| Rent and rates of offices | 82,180 | |
| Hire of plant and machinery | 6,700 | |
| Travel and entertainment expenses | 4,350 | |
| General expenses | 221,400 | |
| Trade accounts receivable | 396,100 | |
| Trade accounts payable and accruals | | 245,820 |
| Inventory | 421,440 | |
| Bank | 17,950 | |
| Interim dividend paid | 21,000 | |
| Interest charged | 19,360 | |
| Provision for deferred taxation | | 45,100 |
| | 5,043,920 | 5,043,920 |

→

*You are provided with the following additional information*:

(*a*) The company's shares are owned, equally, by three brothers: John, Peter and Henry Phillips; they are also the directors.

(*b*) The bank loan is repayable by five annual instalments of £5,000 commencing 31 December 2018.

(*c*) The investments were acquired with cash, surplus to existing operating requirements, which will be needed to pay for additional plant the directors plan to acquire early in 2019.

(*d*) On 1 January 2018 the company closed a factory which had previously contributed approximately 20% of the company's total production requirements.

(*e*) Trade accounts receivable include £80,000 due from a customer who went into liquidation on 1 September 2018; the directors estimate that a dividend of 20p in the £ will eventually be received.

(*f*) Trade accounts payable and accruals include:

(*i*) £50,000 due to a supplier of plant, of which £20,000 is payable on 1 January 2019 and the remainder at the end of the year;

(*ii*) accruals totalling £3,260.

(*g*) The mainstream corporation tax liability for the year is estimated at £120,000.

(*h*) The directors propose to pay a final dividend of 10.5p per share and to transfer £26,500 to the deferred tax account.

**Required:**

The statement of profit or loss of Cosnett Ltd for the year to 30 September 2018 and statement of financial position at that date together with relevant notes attached thereto. The accounts should comply with the minimum requirements of the Companies Acts and accounting standards so far as the information permits.

(*Institute of Chartered Secretaries and Administrators*)

**14.4A** The following trial balance has been extracted from the books of Arran plc as at 31 March 2017:

| | *£000* | *£000* |
|---|---|---|
| Administrative expenses | 95 | |
| Called-up share capital (all ordinary shares of £1 each) | | 200 |
| Cash at bank and in hand | 25 | |
| Accounts receivable | 230 | |
| Deferred taxation (at 1 April 2016) | | 60 |
| Distribution costs | 500 | |
| Non-current asset investments | 280 | |
| Income from non-current asset investments | | 12 |
| Interim dividend paid | 21 | |
| Overprovision of last year's corporation tax | | 5 |
| Land and buildings at cost | 200 | |
| Land and buildings: accumulated depreciation at 1 April 2016 | | 30 |
| Plant and machinery at cost | 400 | |
| Plant and machinery: accumulated depreciation at 1 April 2016 | | 170 |
| Retained profits (at 1 April 2016) | | 229 |
| Purchases | 1,210 | |
| Sales | | 2,265 |
| Inventory at 1 April 2016 | 140 | |
| Trade accounts payable | | 130 |
| | £3,101 | £3,101 |

*Additional information*:

1 Inventory at 31 March 2017 was valued at £150,000.
2 Depreciation for the year to 31 March 2017 is to be charged against administrative expenses as follows:

| | £000 |
|---|---|
| Land and buildings | 5 |
| Plant and machinery | 40 |

3 Assume that the basic rate of income tax is 30%.
4 Corporation tax of £180,000 is to be charged against profits on ordinary activities for the year to 31 March 2017.
5 £4,000 is to be transferred to the deferred taxation account.
6 The company proposes to pay a final ordinary dividend of 30p per share.

**Required:**

In so far as the information permits, prepare the company's statement of profit or loss for the year ending 31 March 2017 and a statement of financial position as at that date in accordance with the Companies Acts and related accounting standards. Note: statement of profit or loss and statement of financial position notes are not required, but you should show the basis and computation of earnings per share at the foot of the statement of profit or loss, and your workings should be submitted.

(*Association of Accounting Technicians*)

**14.5A** The following trial balance has been extracted from the books of account of Greet plc as at 31 March 2018:

| | *Dr* £000 | *Cr* £000 |
|---|---|---|
| Administrative expenses | 210 | |
| Called-up share capital (ordinary shares of £1 fully paid) | | 600 |
| Accounts receivable | 470 | |
| Cash at bank and in hand | 40 | |
| Corporation tax (overprovision in 2017) | | 25 |
| Deferred taxation (at 1 April 2017) | | 180 |
| Distribution costs | 420 | |
| Gain on sale of non-current asset | | 60 |
| Non-current asset investments | 560 | |
| Investment income | | 72 |
| Plant and machinery: at cost | 750 | |
| accumulated depreciation (at 31 March 2018) | | 220 |
| Retained profits (at 1 April 2017) | | 182 |
| Purchases | 960 | |
| Inventory (at 1 April 2017) | 140 | |
| Trade accounts payable | | 261 |
| Revenue | | 1,950 |
| | £3,550 | £3,550 |

*Additional information*:

1 Inventory at 31 March 2018 was valued at £150,000.
2 The following items *are already included* in the balances listed in the above trial balance:

| | *Distribution costs* £000 | *Administrative expenses* £000 |
|---|---|---|
| Depreciation (for the year to 31 March 2018) | 27 | 5 |
| Hire of plant and machinery | 20 | 15 |
| Auditors' remuneration | – | 30 |
| Directors' emoluments | – | 45 |

3 The following rates of taxation are to be assumed:

| | % |
|---|---|
| Corporation tax | 35 |
| Income tax | 27 |

4 The corporation tax charge based on the profits for the year is estimated to be £52,000.
5 A transfer of £16,000 is to be made to the credit of the deferred taxation account.
6 The gain made on the disposal of a non-current asset related to a factory in Belgium following the closure of the company's entire operations in that country.
7 The company's authorised share capital consists of 1,000,000 ordinary shares of £1 each.
8 A final ordinary payment of 50p per share is proposed.
9 There were no purchases or disposals of non-current assets during the year.
10 The market value of the non-current assets investments as at 31 March 2018 was £580,000. There were no purchases or sales of such investments during the year.

**Required:**
In so far as the information permits, prepare the company's published statement of profit or loss for the year ending 31 March 2018 and a statement of financial position as at that date in accordance with the Companies Acts and with related accounting standards.

Relevant notes to the statement of profit or loss and statement of financial position and detailed workings should be submitted with your answer, but a statement of the company's accounting policies is not required.

(*Association of Accounting Technicians*)

**14.6** The accountant of Scampion plc, a retailing company listed on the London Stock Exchange, has produced the following draft financial statements for the company for the year to 31 May 2016.

**Statement of Profit or Loss for year ending 31 May 2016**

| | *£000* | *£000* |
|---|---|---|
| Revenue | | 3,489 |
| Income from investments | | 15 |
| | | 3,504 |
| Purchases of goods and services | 1,929 | |
| Value added tax paid on sales | 257 | |
| Wages and salaries including pension scheme | 330 | |
| Depreciation | 51 | |
| Interest on loans | 18 | |
| General administration expenses | | |
| – Shops | 595 | |
| – Head office | 25 | |
| | | 3,205 |
| Net profit for year | | 299 |
| Corporation tax at 40% | | 120 |
| Profit after tax for year | | 179 |

**Statement of Financial Position at 31 May 2016**

| | £000 | £000 |
|---|---|---|
| *Non-current assets* | | |
| Land and buildings | | 1,178 |
| Fixtures, fittings, equipment and motor vehicles | | 194 |
| *Investments* | | 167 |
| | | 1,539 |
| *Current assets* | | |
| Inventory | 230 | |
| Accounts receivable | 67 | |
| Cash at bank and in hand | 84 | |
| | 381 | |
| *Current liabilities* | | |
| Accounts payable | 487 | |
| | | (106) |
| | | 1,433 |
| Ordinary share capital (£1 shares) | | 660 |
| Reserves | | 703 |
| Loans | | 70 |
| | | 1,433 |

You discover the following further information:

(*i*) Non-current assets details are as follows:

| | *Cost* | *Depreciation* | *Net* |
|---|---|---|---|
| | *£000* | *£000* | *£000* |
| Freehold land and buildings | 1,212 | 34 | 1,178 |
| Fixtures, fittings and equipment | 181 | 56 | 125 |
| Motor vehicles | 137 | 68 | 69 |

Purchases of non-current assets during the year were freehold land and buildings £50,000; fixtures, fittings and equipment £40,000; motor vehicles £20,000. The only non-current asset disposal during the year is referred to in note (*x*). Depreciation charged during the year was £5,000 for freehold buildings; £18,000 for fixtures, fittings and equipment; and £28,000 for motor vehicles. Straight line depreciation method is used assuming the following lives: Freehold buildings 40 years, fixtures, fittings and equipment 10 years and motor vehicles five years.

(*ii*) A dividend of 10p per share is proposed.

(*iii*) A valuation by Bloggs & Co Surveyors shows the freehold land and buildings to have a market value of £1,350,000.

(*iv*) Loans are:
£20,000 bank loan with a variable rate of interest repayable by 30 September 2016;
£50,000 12% loan notes repayable 2020;
£100,000 11% loan notes repaid during the year.
There were no other loans during the year.

(*v*) The income from investments is derived from non-current asset investments (shares in related companies) £5,000 and current asset investment (government securities) £10,000.

(*vi*) At the date of the statement of financial position the shares in related companies (cost £64,000) are valued by the directors at £60,000. The market value of the government securities is £115,000 (cost £103,000).

(*vii*) After the date of the statement of financial position but before the financial statements are finalised there is a very substantial fall in share and security prices. The market value of the government securities had fallen to £50,000 by the time the directors signed the accounts. No adjustment has been made for this item in the accounts.

(*viii*) Within two weeks of the date of the statement of financial position a notice of liquidation was received by Scampion plc concerning one of the company's debtors. £45,000 is included in the →

statement of financial position for this debtor and enquiries reveal that nothing is likely to be paid to any unsecured creditor. No adjustment has been made for this item in the accounts.

(*ix*) The corporation tax charge is based on the accounts for the year and there are no other amounts of tax owing by the company.

(*x*) Reserves at 31 May 2015 were:

| | £ |
|---|---|
| Revaluation reserve | 150,000 |
| Share premium account | 225,000 |
| Retained profits | 149,000 |

The revaluation reserve represents the after-tax surplus on a property which was valued in last year's statement of financial position at £400,000 and sold during the current year at book value.

**Required:**
A statement of profit or loss for the year ending 31 May 2016 and a statement of financial position at that date for Scampion plc complying with the Companies Acts in so far as the information given will allow.

Ignore advance corporation tax.

(*Association of Chartered Certified Accountants*)

**14.7A** The Companies Acts and accounting standards require a great deal of information to be disclosed in a company's annual report and accounts.

**Required:**
List the disclosure requirements for the following items:

(*a*) employees;
(*b*) directors' emoluments; and
(*c*) non-current assets.

(*Association of Accounting Technicians*)

chapter

# 15 Statements of cash flows

## Learning objectives

**After you have studied this chapter, you should be able to:**

- explain the purpose of cash flow information
- explain the difference between cash flow and profit
- explain the requirements of IAS 7
- prepare a statement of cash flows for a company following the format given in IAS 7 using the indirect method
- prepare a statement of cash flows for a company following the format given in IAS 7 using the direct method

## Introduction

In this chapter, you'll build on what you learnt in Chapter 39 of *Business Accounting 1* relating to statements of cash flows. You will be reminded of the layout of a statement of cash flows prepared on the basis of IAS 7 using the direct method and will learn how to prepare a statement of cash flows using both the direct method and the indirect method.

## 15.1 Background

*Business Accounting 1* introduced statements of cash flows and this chapter moves on to consider in more detail the accounting standard relating to these statements – IAS 7 *Statement of cash flows*.

IAS 7 requires that a statement of cash flows be prepared according to prescribed formats for all companies. The standard requires that the statement be included as a primary statement within the financial statements, i.e. it has the same status as the statement of comprehensive income and the statement of financial position.

## 15.2 IAS 7: Standard headings

The objective of IAS 7 requires the provision of information about the historic changes in cash and cash equivalents of an entity by means of a statement of cash flows which classifies cash flows during the period from operating, investing and financing activities. For this reason, the statement must show the flows of cash and cash equivalents for the period under the headings:

1 operating activities
2 investing activities
3 financing activities.

The headings should appear in that order and the statement should include a total for each heading. Operating cash flows can be presented by either the *direct* method (showing the relevant constituent cash flows) or the *indirect* method (calculating operating cash flows by adjustment to the operating profit reported in the statement of profit or loss).

The standard indicates in which section various items are to be located and these are described in Sections 15.4 to 15.6. Further guidance concerning where items appear in the statement can be seen in the examples presented later in this chapter.

At the foot of the statement, the net change in cash and cash equivalents is identified. This is then added to the opening cash and cash equivalent balance to produce the cash and cash equivalents balance at the end of the period.

## 15.3 Cash flow

'Cash flow' is defined in paragraph 6 of IAS 7 as 'inflows and outflows of cash and cash equivalents'. Anything that falls outside this definition is not a cash flow and should not appear in the statement (though it could appear in the notes).

'Cash' is defined as 'cash on hand and demand deposits repayable on demand with any qualifying financial institution, less overdrafts from any qualifying financial institution repayable on demand'.

'Demand deposits' are deposits that can be withdrawn at any time without notice and without penalty or if a maturity or period of notice of not more than 24 hours or one working day has been agreed.

'Cash equivalents' are defined as short-term, highly liquid investments that are readily convertible to known amounts of cash and which are subject to an insignificant risk of changes in value.

**Activity 15.1**

Imagine you are running a business and you have £500,000 that you won't need for three months. How will you invest it?

## 15.4 Operating activities and cash flows

*Operating activities* are the principal revenue-producing activities of the entity and other activities that are not investing or financing activities. The net cash flow from operating activities represents the net increase or decrease in cash resulting from the operations shown in the statement of profit or loss in arriving at operating profit.

The reconciliation between operating profit and net cash flow from operating activities for the period should disclose separately the changes during the period in inventory, accounts receivable, and accounts payable related to operating activities; other non-cash items, e.g. depreciation; and other items for which the cash effects are investing or financing cash flows.

In addition, cash flows from taxes on income should be disclosed separately under operating activities unless they can be attributed to specific financing or investing activities.

Also, interest and dividends must be disclosed separately under any of the three categories, so long as the same treatment is adopted from period to period.

In the statement of cash flows, *operating cash flows* may be shown using either the indirect method or the direct method. Using the *indirect method*, it would be laid out in a manner similar to that shown in Exhibit 15.1.

IAS 7 requires that in a statement of cash flows prepared using the indirect method a reconciliation be shown between the net cash flow from operating activities and the operating profit as shown in the statement of profit or loss.

**Exhibit 15.1**

| | £ |
|---|---|
| Operating profit | 12,000 |
| Depreciation charges | 500 |
| Loss on sale of tangible non-current assets | 10 |
| Increase in inventories | (200) |
| Increase in accounts receivable | (100) |
| Increase in accounts payable | 300 |
| Net cash inflow from operating activities | 12,510 |

The direct method would produce an analysis in the cash flow statement similar to that shown in Exhibit 15.2.

**Exhibit 15.2**

| *Operating activities* | £ |
|---|---|
| Cash received from customers | 120,000 |
| Cash payments to suppliers | (40,000) |
| Cash paid to and on behalf of employees | (60,000) |
| Other cash payments | (7,490) |
| Net cash inflow from operating activities | 12,510 |

As you can see, both methods produce the same figure for net cash flow from operating activities. However, it is generally easier for an entity to adopt the indirect method – the figures are readily available from the statement of profit or loss and statement of financial position. The direct method, on the other hand, requires that the cash book is analysed. Despite there being much more work involved in preparing it, the IASB recommends use of the direct method when the potential benefits to users outweigh the costs of doing so – it does help provide a far clearer view of cash flow than the bookkeeping adjustments to profit that are undertaken under the indirect method.

***Note*: In an examination, if sufficient information on cash flows is provided for you to adopt the *direct* method, you should assume that is the approach to take.**

## 15.5 Investing activities

These are activities involving the acquisition and disposal of non-current assets and other investments not included in cash equivalents. Examples include:

- cash payments to acquire property, plant and equipment;
- cash payments to acquire intangible non-current assets;
- cash receipts from sale of non-current assets;
- cash payments to acquire equity or debt instruments (such as loan notes) of other entities;
- cash payments to acquire an interest in a joint venture;
- cash receipts from sales of equity or debt instruments of other entities;
- cash receipts from sale of an interest in a joint venture;
- cash advances and loans made to other parties;
- cash receipts from repayments of advances and loans made to other parties.

## 15.6 Financing activities

These are activities that result in changes in the size and composition of the contributed equity and borrowings of the entity. Their disclosure is useful in predicting claims on future cash flows by providers of capital to the entity. Examples include:

- cash proceeds from issuing shares or other equity instruments;
- cash payments to owners to acquire or redeem the entity's shares;
- cash proceeds from issuing loan notes, bonds, mortgages and other short- or long-term borrowings;
- cash repayments of amounts borrowed;
- cash payments by a lessee for the reduction of the outstanding liability relating to a finance lease.

## 15.7 Foreign subsidiary cash flows

Under IAS 7, foreign subsidiary cash flows must be translated at the exchange rates prevailing at the dates of the cash flows (or an appropriate weighted average if this is infeasible).

## 15.8 Examples of statements of cash flows

Exhibit 15.3 presents a statement of cash flows using the indirect method.

### Exhibit 15.3 Format for an IAS 7 indirect method statement of cash flows

**X Limited**
**Statement of Cash Flows for the year ending 31 December 2017**

| | £000 | £000 |
|---|---|---|
| **Cash flows from operating activities** | | |
| Operating profit before taxation | XXX | |
| Adjustments for: | | |
| Depreciation | XXX | |
| (Profit)/Loss on sale of tangible non-current assets | XXX | |
| Operating cash flows before movements in working capital | | XXX |
| (Increase)/Decrease in inventories | XXX | |
| (Increase)/Decrease in accounts receivable | XXX | |
| Increase/(Decrease) in accounts payable | XXX | |
| | | XXX |
| Cash generated by operations | | XXX |
| Tax paid | (XXX) | |
| Interest paid | (XXX) | |
| | | (XXX) |
| *Net cash from/(used in) operating activities* | | XXX |
| **Cash flows from investing activities** | | |
| Dividends from joint ventures | XXX | |
| Dividends from associates | XXX | |
| Interest received | XXX | |
| Payments to acquire intangible non-current assets | (XXX) | |
| Payments to acquire tangible non-current assets | (XXX) | |
| Receipts from sales of tangible non-current assets | XXX | |
| Purchase of subsidiary undertaking | (XXX) | |
| Sale of business | XXX | |
| *Net cash from/(used in) investing activities* | | (XXX) |
| **Cash flows from financing activities** | | |
| Ordinary dividends paid | (XXX) | |
| Preference dividends paid | (XXX) | |
| Issue of ordinary share capital | XXX | |
| Repurchase of loan note | (XXX) | |
| Expenses paid in connection with share issues | (XXX) | |
| *Net cash from/(used in) financing activities* | | XXX |
| **Net increase/(decrease) in cash and cash equivalents** | | XXX |
| **Cash and cash equivalents at beginning of year** | | XXX |
| **Cash and cash equivalents at end of year** | | XXX |

**Note: The inclusion of the reconciliation of operating profit to net cash from/(used in) operating activities at the start of the statement of cash flows in Exhibit 15.3 follows the approach given in the Appendix to IAS 7. It is part of the IAS 7-based indirect method statement of cash flows.**

The layout using the direct method is shown in Exhibit 15.4. Note that the only difference between it and the indirect method presentation is the content of the operating activities section.

## Exhibit 15.4 Format for an IAS 7 direct method statement of cash flows

**X Limited**
**Statement of Cash Flows for the year ending 31 December 2017**

| | £000 | £000 |
|---|---|---|
| **Cash flows from operating activities** | | |
| Cash receipts from customers | XXX | |
| Cash paid to suppliers and employees | (XXX) | |
| Cash generated from operations | XXX | |
| Interest paid | (XXX) | |
| Tax paid | (XXX) | |
| *Net cash from/(used in) operating activities* | | XXX |
| **Cash flows from investing activities** | | |
| Dividends from joint ventures | XXX | |
| Dividends from associates | XXX | |
| Interest received | XXX | |
| Payments to acquire intangible non-current assets | (XXX) | |
| Payments to acquire tangible non-current assets | (XXX) | |
| Receipts from sales of tangible non-current assets | XXX | |
| Purchase of subsidiary undertaking | (XXX) | |
| Sale of business | XXX | |
| *Net cash from/(used in) investing activities* | | (XXX) |
| **Cash flows from financing activities** | | |
| Ordinary dividends paid | (XXX) | |
| Preference dividends paid | (XXX) | |
| Issue of ordinary share capital | XXX | |
| Repurchase of loan note | (XXX) | |
| Expenses paid in connection with share issues | (XXX) | |
| *Net cash from/(used in) financing activities* | | XXX |
| **Net increase/(decrease) in cash and cash equivalents** | | XXX |
| **Cash and cash equivalents at beginning of year** | | XXX |
| **Cash and cash equivalents at end of year** | | XXX |

**Activity 15.2**

When the items needed for the additional information required by the direct method are so easy to identify from the cash book, why do you think most companies prefer to use the indirect method?

## Learning outcomes

**You should now have learnt:**

1. The objective of IAS 7 is to require entities to provide information about the historical changes in their cash and cash equivalents in the form of a statement of cash flows which classifies cash flows during the period from operating, investing and financing activities.
2. This aids comparison between entities.
3. The IAS 7-based statement of cash flows must show the flows of cash for the period under the three headings:
   1. operating activities
   2. investing activities
   3. financing activities.
4. The headings in the statement of cash flows should be in that order and the statement should include a total for each heading.
5. Cash flow is inflows and outflows of cash and cash equivalents.
6. Operating activities are the principal revenue-producing activities of the entity and other activities that are not investing or financing activities.
7. Under IAS 7, operating cash flows can be shown using either the *indirect* method or the *direct* method.
8. The IASB recommends that companies applying IAS 7 use the *direct* method.
9. How to prepare a statement of cash flows under IAS 7 under both the indirect and direct methods.

## Answers to activities

15.1 Possible short-term investments include term deposits (e.g. 30-, 60- or 90-day deposit accounts all of which are considered to be cash equivalents under IAS 7), government stock (e.g. Treasury stock) and corporate bonds (i.e. loan stock issued by companies).

15.2 In principle, the direct method is very easy to calculate. You just add up all the cash inflows and outflows relating to trading activities shown in the cash book. However, in practice, the volume of cash flows generated by any but the smallest business means that this can be a difficult and time-consuming task. It is not surprising that very few companies adopt this approach.

## Review questions

**15.1** List the three headings in the statement of cash flows, as required by IAS 7.

**15.2A** Give an example of the information to be included under each of the headings in an IAS 7-based statement of cash flows and indicate why this information might be useful.

**15.3** Prepare a statement of cash flows for Chipsea Ltd for the year ended 31 December 2017 as required under IAS 7 using the direct method. The statement of profit or loss, statement of financial position and cash account of Chipsea Ltd for the year 2017 are given below:

**Statement of Profit or Loss for the year ending 31 December 2017**

| | £ | £ |
|---|---|---|
| Revenue | | 20,800 |
| *Less* Cost of goods sold | | (9,600) |
| | | 11,200 |
| *Less Expenses* | | |
| Wages | 6,400 | |
| Other costs | 1,920 | |
| Depreciation | 640 | |
| Interest | 320 | |
| | | (9,280) |
| Profit for the year | | 1,920 |

***Note*: During the year, dividends of £300 were paid.**

**Statement of Financial Position as at 31 December**

| | *2017* | | *2016* | |
|---|---|---|---|---|
| | £ | £ | £ | £ |
| *Non-current assets* at cost | | 14,400 | | 12,160 |
| *Less* Accumulated depreciation | | 3,520 | | 2,880 |
| Net book value | | 10,880 | | 9,280 |
| *Current assets* | | | | |
| Inventory | 1,280 | | 1,600 | |
| Trade accounts receivable | 480 | | 640 | |
| Cash | 500 | | 320 | |
| | | 2,260 | | 2,560 |
| Total assets | | 13,140 | | 11,840 |
| *Current liabilities* | | | | |
| Trade accounts payable | 1,040 | | 960 | |
| Accrued wages | 80 | | 160 | |
| | 1,120 | | 1,120 | |
| *Non-current liabilities* | | | | |
| Loan notes | 2,880 | | 3,200 | |
| Total liabilities | | 4,000 | | 4,320 |
| Net assets | | 9,140 | | 7,520 |
| *Equity* | | | | |
| Ordinary share capital | | 3,200 | | 3,200 |
| Retained profits | | 5,940 | | 4,320 |
| | | 9,140 | | 7,520 |

**Cash Account for 2017**

| | £ | | £ |
|---|---|---|---|
| Opening balance | 320 | Wages | 6,480 |
| Cash from customers | 20,960 | Other expenses | 1,920 |
| | | Cash paid to suppliers | 9,200 |
| | | Interest paid | 320 |
| | | Cash purchase of non-current assets | 2,240 |
| | | Cash paid to loan-note holders | 320 |
| | | Dividend paid | 300 |
| | | Closing balance | 500 |
| | 21,280 | | 21,280 |

**15.4A** The statements of financial position and additional information relating to Pennylane Ltd are given below. Prepare a statement of cash flows for Pennylane Ltd for the year ending 31 December 2016 as required under IAS 7 using the indirect method.

**Pennylane Ltd**
**Statements of Financial Position as at 31 December**

| | 2016 | 2015 |
|---|---|---|
| | £000 | £000 |
| *Non-current assets* | | |
| Tangible assets | 400 | 325 |
| Intangible assets | 230 | 180 |
| Investments | – | 25 |
| | 630 | 530 |
| *Current assets* | | |
| Inventory | 120 | 104 |
| Accounts receivable | 400 | 295 |
| 90-day deposit | 50 | – |
| Cash in hand | 10 | 4 |
| | 580 | 403 |
| Total assets | 1,210 | 933 |
| *Current liabilities* | | |
| Trade accounts payable | 122 | 108 |
| Bank overdraft | 188 | 185 |
| Taxation | 120 | 110 |
| | 430 | 403 |
| *Non-current liabilities* | | |
| Long-term loan | 100 | – |
| Deferred tax | 80 | 60 |
| | 180 | 60 |
| Total liabilities | 610 | 463 |
| Net assets | 600 | 470 |
| *Equity* | | |
| Share capital (£1 ordinary shares) | 200 | 150 |
| Share premium | 160 | 150 |
| Revaluation reserve | 100 | 90 |
| Retained profits | 140 | 80 |
| | 600 | 470 |

*Additional information*:

(*a*) During the year interest of £75,000 was paid, and interest of £25,000 was received.

(*b*) The following information relates to tangible non-current assets:

| *At 31 December* | 2016 | 2015 |
|---|---|---|
| | £000 | £000 |
| Cost | 740 | 615 |
| Accumulated depreciation | (340) | (290) |
| Net book value | 400 | 325 |

(*c*) The proceeds of the sale of non-current asset investments were £30,000.

(*d*) Plant, with an original cost of £90,000 and a net book value of £50,000, was sold for £37,000.

(*e*) Tax paid to Revenue and Customs during 2016 amounted to £110,000.

(*f*) Dividends of £80,000 were paid during 2016.

**15.5** State the purposes of a statement of cash flows.

*(Association of Chartered Certified Accountants)*

**15.6** The following information has been extracted from the books of Hayes Limited for the year to 31 December 2016:

**Statement of Profit or Loss extracts for the year ending 31 December**

| | 2016 | 2015 |
|---|---|---|
| | £000 | £000 |
| Profit before taxation | 59,920 | 26,600 |
| Taxation | (14,560) | (8,960) |
| Profit for the year | 45,360 | 17,640 |

| | 2016 | 2015 |
|---|---|---|
| *Note*: Dividends paid | £000 | £000 |
| Preference | 280 | 280 |
| Ordinary | 22,400 | 11,200 |
| | 22,680 | 11,480 |

**Statements of Financial Position at 31 December**

| | 2016 | 2015 |
|---|---|---|
| | £000 | £000 |
| *Non-current assets* | | |
| Plant, machinery and equipment, at cost | 66,920 | 49,280 |
| *Less* Accumulated depreciation | 27,300 | 26,600 |
| | 39,620 | 22,680 |
| *Current assets* | | |
| Inventory | 25,200 | 5,600 |
| Trade accounts receivable | 74,760 | 24,080 |
| Prepayments | 1,120 | 840 |
| Cash at bank and in hand | – | 1,680 |
| | 101,080 | 32,200 |
| Total assets | 140,700 | 54,880 |
| *Current liabilities* | | |
| Bank overdraft | 45,360 | |
| Trade accounts payable | 28,000 | 16,800 |
| Accruals | 2,800 | 2,240 |
| Taxation | 14,560 | 8,960 |
| | 90,720 | 28,000 |
| *Non-current liabilities* | | |
| 15% loan notes | 2,100 | 1,680 |
| Total liabilities | 92,820 | 29,680 |
| Net assets | 47,880 | 25,200 |
| *Equity* | | |
| Ordinary shares of £1 each | 14,000 | 14,000 |
| 10% preference shares of £1 each | 2,800 | 2,800 |
| Retained profits | 31,080 | 8,400 |
| | 47,880 | 25,200 |

*Additional information*:

1 The directors are extremely concerned about the large bank overdraft as at 31 December 2016 and they attribute this mainly to the increase in trade accounts receivable as a result of alleged poor credit control.

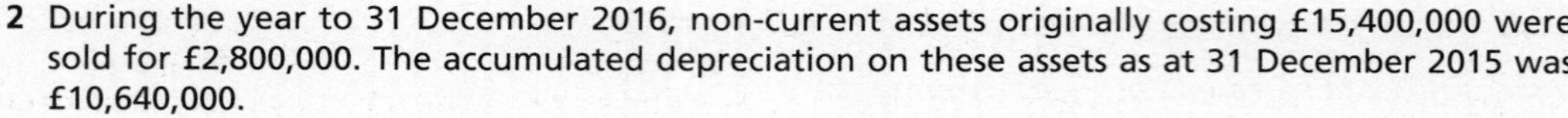

2 During the year to 31 December 2016, non-current assets originally costing £15,400,000 were sold for £2,800,000. The accumulated depreciation on these assets as at 31 December 2015 was £10,640,000.

**Required:**
Prepare a statement of cash flows using the IAS 7 indirect method for the year to 31 December 2016.

**15.7** The following summarised statements of financial position relate to Track Limited:

**Statements of Financial Position at 30 June**

| | *2018* | *2017* |
|---|---|---|
| | *£000* | *£000* |
| *Non-current assets* at cost | 650 | 500 |
| *Less* Accumulated depreciation | 300 | 200 |
| | 350 | 300 |
| Investments at cost | 50 | 200 |
| | 400 | 500 |
| *Current assets* | | |
| Inventory | 700 | 400 |
| Accounts receivable | 1,550 | 1,350 |
| Cash and bank | – | 100 |
| | 2,250 | 1,850 |
| Total assets | 2,650 | 2,350 |
| *Current liabilities* | | |
| Bank overdraft | 60 | – |
| Accounts payable | 920 | 800 |
| Taxation | 190 | 230 |
| Total liabilities | 1,170 | 1,030 |
| Net assets | 1,480 | 1,320 |
| *Equity* | | |
| Called-up share capital (£1 ordinary shares) | 750 | 500 |
| Share premium account | 200 | 150 |
| Retained profits | 530 | 670 |
| | 1,480 | 1,320 |

*Additional information*:

1 During the year to 30 June 2018, some non-current assets originally costing £25,000 had been sold for £20,000 in cash. The accumulated depreciation on these non-current assets at 30 June 2017 amounted to £10,000. Similarly, some of the investments originally costing £150,000 had been sold for cash at their book value.

2 The taxation balances disclosed in the above statements of financial position represent the actual amounts agreed with the Revenue and Customs. All taxes were paid on their due dates. Advance corporation tax may be ignored.

3 A dividend of £130,000 was paid during the year to 30 June 2018.

4 During the year to 30 June 2018, the company made a 1-for-2 rights issue of 250 ordinary £1 shares at 120p per share.

**Required:**
Prepare Track Ltd's statement of cash flows for the year to 30 June 2018 in accordance with the requirements of IAS 7 using the indirect method.

(*Association of Accounting Technicians*)

**15.8A** The accountant of a private company has been able to get the use of a computer to produce the spreadsheets shown below but as yet the computer lacks a program to print out final accounts. The accountant nevertheless expects to use the spreadsheet data to reconstruct a summary statement of profit or loss and a statement of cash flows for the year ending 30 April 2016.

**Movements of Assets during the year 2015/16 (£000)**

| | *Statement of financial position value last year* | *Depreciation or amortisation for year* | *Additions during year* | *Sales during year* | *Other changes* | *Statement of financial position value this year* |
|---|---|---|---|---|---|---|
| Goodwill | – | – | 40 | – | – | 40 |
| Property | 760 | (36) | – | – | – | 724 |
| Plant and vehicles | 540 | (84) | 420 | (60) | – | 816 |
| Inventories | 230 | – | – | – | 24 | 254 |
| Accounts receivable | 254 | – | – | – | 76 | 330 |
| Bank and cash | 50 | – | – | – | 14 | 64 |
| | 1,834 | (120) | 460 | (60) | 114 | |
| | | | | | | 2,228 |

**Movement of Liabilities and Reserves during the year 2015/16 (£000)**

| | *Statement of financial position value last year* | *New capital issued* | *Payments during year* | *Transfers to reserves and for provisions* | *Other changes* | *Statement of financial position value this year* |
|---|---|---|---|---|---|---|
| Ordinary shares (£1 each) | 1,060 | 440 | – | – | – | 1,500 |
| Deferred taxation | 36 | – | – | 176 | – | 212 |
| General reserve | 152 | – | – | 32 | – | 184 |
| Accounts payable | 136 | – | – | – | 24 | 160 |
| Provision for corporation tax | 450 | – | (450) | 172 | – | 172 |
| | 1,834 | 440 | (450) | 380 | 24 | 2,228 |

*Notes*:

(*i*) Proceeds of £40,000 were received from the sale of plant and vehicles.

(*ii*) During the year the company redeemed 10,000 of its £1 ordinary shares for £125,000 wholly out of distributable profits and this transaction has not been included in the spreadsheets.

**Required:**

(*a*) Reconstruct the statement of profit or loss for the year ending 30 April 2016.

(*b*) Prepare a statement of cash flows for the year ending 30 April 2016.

***Author's note*: Prepare the statement of cash flows under the rules of IAS 7.**

(*Institute of Chartered Secretaries and Administrators*)

→

**15.9** You are presented with the following forecast information relating to Baker Limited for the nine months to 30 September 2017.

Forecast statements of profit or loss (abridged) for the three quarters ending 30 September 2017:

| | *March 2017* | *June 2017* | *Sept 2017* |
|---|---|---|---|
| | *£000* | *£000* | *£000* |
| Revenue | 250 | 300 | 350 |
| Cost of goods sold | (200) | (240) | (280) |
| Gross profit | 50 | 60 | 70 |
| Depreciation | (3) | (20) | (4) |
| Administration, selling and distribution expenses | (37) | (40) | (42) |
| Forecast net profit | £10 | – | £24 |

| *Forecast balances at* | *31 Dec 2016* | *31 March 2017* | *30 June 2017* | *30 Sept 2017* |
|---|---|---|---|---|
| | *£000* | *£000* | *£000* | *£000* |
| *Debit balances* | | | | |
| Tangible non-current assets at cost | 360 | 240 | 480 | 480 |
| 90-day deposit at cost | 15 | 5 | 5 | 10 |
| Inventory at cost | 40 | 30 | 40 | 55 |
| Trade accounts receivable | 50 | 65 | 75 | 80 |
| Cash at bank and in hand | 80 | – | – | – |
| *Credit balances* | | | | |
| Loan notes (10%) | – | – | – | 50 |
| Trade accounts payable | 80 | 120 | 140 | 150 |
| Taxation | 8 | – | – | – |

*Additional information*:

1 Sales of tangible non-current assets in March 2017 were expected to realise £12,000 in cash.
2 Administration, selling and distribution expenses were expected to be settled in cash during the month in which they were incurred.
3 Baker Limited includes as liquid resources term deposits of less than one year.
4 The directors have proposed that a dividend of £15,000 be paid on 28 February 2017.

**Required:**

(*a*) Calculate Baker Limited's forecast net cash position at 31 March, 30 June and 30 September 2017 respectively.

(*b*) Prepare a forecast statement of cash flows for the nine months ending 30 September 2017.

***Author's note*: Prepare the forecast statement of cash flows under the rules of IAS 7.**

(*Association of Accounting Technicians*)

**15.10A** The following information has been extracted from the draft financial information of V Ltd:

**Statement of Profit or Loss for the year ending 31 December 2016**

| | £000 | £000 |
|---|---|---|
| Revenue | | 495 |
| Raw materials consumed | (49) | |
| Staff costs | (37) | |
| Depreciation | (74) | |
| Loss on disposal | (4) | |
| | | (164) |
| Operating profit | | 331 |
| Interest payable | | (23) |
| Profit before tax | | 308 |
| Taxation | | (87) |
| Profit for the year | | 221 |

*Note*: Dividend paid = £52,000

**Statements of Financial Position**

| | *31 December 2016* | | *31 December 2015* | |
|---|---|---|---|---|
| | *£000* | *£000* | *£000* | *£000* |
| *Non-current assets* (*see* below) | | 1,145 | | 957 |
| *Current assets* | | | | |
| Inventory | 19 | | 16 | |
| Trade accounts receivable | 38 | | 29 | |
| Bank | 31 | | 37 | |
| | | 88 | | 82 |
| Total assets | | 1,233 | | 1,039 |
| *Current liabilities* | | | | |
| Trade accounts payable | 12 | | 17 | |
| Taxation | 100 | | 81 | |
| | 112 | | 98 | |
| *Non-current liabilities* | | | | |
| Long-term loans | 70 | | 320 | |
| Total liabilities | | 182 | | 418 |
| Net assets | | 1,051 | | 621 |
| *Equity* | | | | |
| Share capital | | 182 | | 152 |
| Share premium | | 141 | | 80 |
| Revaluation reserve | | 170 | | – |
| Retained profits | | 558 | | 389 |
| | | 1,051 | | 621 |

→

| | Land & buildings £000 | Machinery £000 | Fixtures & fittings £000 | Total £000 |
|---|---|---|---|---|
| *Non-current assets* | | | | |
| Cost or valuation: | | | | |
| At 31 December 2015 | 830 | 470 | 197 | 1,497 |
| Additions | – | 43 | 55 | 98 |
| Disposals | – | (18) | – | (18) |
| Adjustment on revaluation | 70 | – | – | 70 |
| At 31 December 2016 | 900 | 495 | 252 | 1,647 |
| *Depreciation* | | | | |
| At 31 December 2015 | (90) | (270) | (180) | (540) |
| Charge for year | (10) | (56) | (8) | (74) |
| Disposals | – | 12 | – | 12 |
| Adjustment on revaluation | 100 | – | – | 100 |
| At 31 December 2016 | 0 | (314) | (188) | (502) |
| *Net book value* | | | | |
| At 31 December 2016 | 900 | 181 | 64 | 1,145 |
| At 31 December 2015 | 740 | 200 | 17 | 957 |

(*a*) **You are required to** prepare a statement of cash flows for V Ltd for the year ended 31 December 2016 in accordance with the requirements of IAS 7.

(*b*) It has been suggested that the management of long-term profitability is more important than short-term cash flow. Explain why this might be so.

(*Chartered Institute of Management Accountants*)

**15.11A** Indicate whether each of the following items would be associated with cash inflow (I), cash outflow (O) or non-cash item (N) and under which category each would be reported on a statement of cash flows: Operating Activities (OA); Investing Activities (IA); Financing Activities (FA) or not on the statement (NOS).

1. Fees collected for services
2. Interest paid
3. Proceeds from sale of equipment
4. Cash (principal) received from bank on loan note
5. Purchase of Treasury stock for cash
6. Collection of loan made to company officer
7. Cash dividend paid
8. Taxes paid
9. Wages paid to employees
10. Cash paid for inventory purchases
11. Proceeds from sale of common stock
12. Interest received on loan to company officer
13. Utility bill paid

**15.12A** Limedrop plc had the following selected transactions during the past year:

1. Sold (issued) 3,600 ordinary shares at £10 par for £35 per share.
2. Received £270,000 from various trade debtors.
3. Paid dividends of £220,000.
4. Received £3,200 interest on a note receivable from a company officer.
5. Paid an annual insurance premium of £9,200.

**Required:**

(*a*) Journal entries for each of the above transactions (omit explanations).

(*b*) For each transaction, indicate the amount of cash inflow or outflow and also how each cash flow would be classified in a statement of cash flows.

part 3

# GROUPS

## Introduction

**This part is concerned with group financial statements: how they are prepared, how various transactions should be dealt with, and how their presentation is regulated by the Companies Acts and accounting standards.**

chapter 16

# Group financial statements: an introduction

## Learning objectives

**After you have studied this chapter, you should be able to:**

- explain the difference between a parent and a subsidiary
- explain why it is important to produce consolidated financial statements
- describe some of the alternative methods whereby control can be acquired by one company over another
- explain the relevance of 'control' to the identification of a parent–subsidiary relationship

## Introduction

In this chapter, you'll learn about the three principal rights of shareholders; and about groups (of companies), how they come about, and the resulting need for consolidated financial statements.

## 16.1 Shareholders and their rights

As you know, the owners of a company are its shareholders, usually just the holders of ordinary shares but, when they exist, also holders of preference shares.

The rights of these two categories of shareholders are not identical. Anyone who buys ordinary shares in a company is usually given three rights:

1 The right to vote at shareholders' meetings.
2 A right to an interest in the net assets of the company.
3 A right to an interest in (i.e. share of) the profits earned by the company.

Preference shareholders do not normally have voting rights, except under special circumstances, such as when their dividends are in arrears, or their special rights are being changed by the company. Loan-note holders have no rights at all to vote at general meetings and are not 'owners' of the company.

By using their voting rights at shareholders' meetings, the shareholders are able to show their approval, or disapproval, of the election of directors and any proposals the directors make at such meetings. It is the directors who manage the affairs of the company. As a result, any group of shareholders who between them own more than 50% of the voting shares of a company can control the election of directors and, consequently, control the policies of the company through the directors. This would also be true if any one shareholder owned more than 50% of the voting shares.

One company may hold shares in another company. Therefore if one company wishes to obtain control of another company it can do so by obtaining more than 50% of the voting shares in that company.

**Activity 16.1** **Why do you think preference shareholders do not have the same voting rights as ordinary shareholders?**

Let's look at what happens when one company acquires sufficient share capital of another company to achieve control over it.

## 16.2 Parents and subsidiaries

We will consider this topic by working through an example.

- S Ltd has an issued share capital of 100,000 ordinary shares of £1 each.
- On 1 January 2018, P Ltd buys 50,001 of these shares from Jones, a shareholder, for £60,000.
- P Ltd will now have control of S Ltd because it has more than 50% of the voting shares.
- P Ltd is now called the 'parent'.
- S Ltd is now called the 'subsidiary' of P Ltd.

Just because the identity of S Ltd's shareholders has changed does not mean that the statement of financial position of S Ltd will be drafted in a different fashion. Looking only at the statement of financial position of S Ltd no one would be able to deduce that P Ltd owned more than 50% of the shares, or even that P Ltd owned any shares at all in S Ltd. After obtaining control of S Ltd, both P Ltd and S Ltd will continue to maintain their own sets of accounting records and to draft their own statements of financial position.

If the statements of financial position of P Ltd and S Ltd are looked at, both before and after the purchase of the shares, any differences can be noted.

### Exhibit 16.1

(*a*) Before P Ltd acquired control of S Ltd:

**P Ltd Statement of Financial Position as at 31 December 2017**

| | £ | £ |
|---|---|---|
| Non-current assets | | 200,000 |
| *Current assets* | | |
| Inventory | 29,000 | |
| Accounts receivable | 8,000 | |
| Bank | 63,000 | |
| | | 100,000 |
| | | 300,000 |
| Share capital | | 250,000 |
| Retained profits | | 50,000 |
| | | 300,000 |

**S Ltd Statement of Financial Position as at 31 December 2017**

| | £ | £ |
|---|---|---|
| Non-current assets | | 40,000 |
| *Current assets* | | |
| Inventory | 40,000 | |
| Accounts receivable | 20,000 | |
| Bank | 10,000 | |
| | | 70,000 |
| | | 110,000 |
| Share capital | | 100,000 |
| Retained profits | | 10,000 |
| | | 110,000 |

(*b*) After P Ltd acquired control of S Ltd the statements of financial position would appear as follows before any further trading took place:

**P Ltd Statement of Financial Position as at 1 January 2018**

| | £ | £ |
|---|---|---|
| Non-current assets | | 200,000 |
| Investment in subsidiary | | 60,000 |
| *Current assets* | | |
| Inventory | 29,000 | |
| Accounts receivable | 8,000 | |
| Bank | 3,000 | |
| | | 40,000 |
| | | 300,000 |
| Share capital | | 250,000 |
| Retained profits | | 50,000 |
| | | 300,000 |

**S Ltd Statement of Financial Position as at 1 January 2018**

| | £ | £ |
|---|---|---|
| Non-current assets | | 40,000 |
| *Current assets* | | |
| Inventory | 40,000 | |
| Accounts receivable | 20,000 | |
| Bank | 10,000 | |
| | | 70,000 |
| | | 110,000 |
| Share capital | | 100,000 |
| Retained profits | | 10,000 |
| | | 110,000 |

The only differences can be seen to be those in the statements of financial position of P Ltd. The bank balance has been reduced by £60,000 which is the cost of the shares in S Ltd, and the cost of the shares now appears as 'Investment in subsidiary undertaking £60,000'. The statements of financial position of S Ltd are completely unchanged.

We shall see later that IAS 27 (*Consolidated and separate financial statements*) gives a much wider meaning to 'subsidiary' than we have seen so far. This has been deliberately excluded up to this point to let you see the basic structure without complicating it.

## 16.3 Statements of profit or loss within a group

From the statement of profit or loss point of view of S Ltd, the entry for dividends paid in the statement of changes in equity would not change after P Ltd takes control. However, P Ltd would see a change in its statement of profit or loss when a dividend is received from S Ltd – in this case, the dividends received would be shown as investment income in the statement of profit or loss. **Remember that dividends paid are shown in the statement of changes in equity and may be shown as a note to the statement of profit or loss of the paying company, while dividends received are in the main part of the receiving company's statement of profit or loss.**

The terms '**parent**' and '**subsidiary**' have been in use for only a few years. Previously, a parent was called a '**holding company**', and a subsidiary was called a '**subsidiary company**'. In Chapter 26, we will see why the terms were changed. One of the reasons was that consolidated financial statements used to be concerned only with companies. Now, subsidiaries can also include unincorporated businesses.

In order to demonstrate the principles involved in company consolidations, the next nine chapters (17 to 25) focus solely upon that form of consolidation.

Chapter 26 examines accounting standards which cover the accounting treatment for parents and subsidiaries. The chapters which follow fully comply with all the requirements of the relevant accounting standards.

## 16.4 The need for consolidated financial statements

Imagine you are a shareholder of P Ltd from Section 16.2. Each year you receive a set of P Ltd's financial statements. After P's acquisition of the shares in S Ltd, £60,000 would appear as an asset in the statement of financial position of P Ltd. It would be normal for it to be shown at cost (i.e. £60,000) thus observing the historical cost concept.

When you look at the statement of profit or loss of P Ltd you would see the dividends received from S Ltd. This, and the cost of the investment in the statement of financial position would be the only things you would know about the subsidiary.

However, you have invested in P Ltd, and because of its majority shareholding in S Ltd you have, in effect, also invested in S Ltd. Being consistent, if you want to know how the assets and liabilities in P Ltd change over the years, you will now also like to know exactly the same for S Ltd.

You are not, however, a shareholder of S Ltd, and would not be sent a copy of its financial statements. As a result, you would not have any right to any further information about S Ltd.

This would be even worse if P Ltd, for example, had 20 subsidiaries and held a different percentage stake in each of them. It would also be almost certain that the companies would trade with each other, and owe money to one another or be owed money by them. This would also raise complications and make it hard for you to see what was truly happening across the group.

This would, clearly, be less than ideal. There is a remedy for this sort of problem. To overcome this situation, parent entities must distribute to their shareholders a set of consolidated financial statements. This is known as **consolidated accounting**. These bring together all of the financial statements for the parent and its subsidiaries in such a way that the shareholders can get an overall view of their investments.

**You will learn more about consolidated financial statements in Section 16.7.**

## 16.5 Different methods of acquiring control of one company by another

The acquisition of control in S Ltd by P Ltd involved P Ltd buying more than 50% of the shares in S Ltd from Jones. This is by no means the only way of acquiring control. Other methods of doing so include:

1. S Ltd may issue new shares to P Ltd amounting to over 50% of the voting shares. P Ltd pays for the shares in cash.
2. P Ltd could purchase over 50% of the voting shares of S Ltd on the open market by exchanging for them newly issued shares of P Ltd.

Or, acting through another company:

3. P Ltd acquires more than 50% of the voting shares in S1 Ltd for cash, and then S1 Ltd proceeds to acquire all of the voting shares of S2 Ltd. S2 Ltd would then be a sub-subsidiary of P Ltd.

These are only some of the more common ways by which one company becomes a subsidiary of another company.

## 16.6 Control other than by holding the majority of the voting power of a subsidiary

IAS 27 provides another way of looking at whether or not one company has control of another. If one company has 'the power to govern the financial and operating policies of an entity so as to obtain benefits from its activities', then it has control over it irrespective of its holding in the entity. **It is not, therefore, necessary to have over 50% of the voting share capital of a company in order to have control over it.** Control means that the holder of it has a right to give directions with regard to the operating and financial policies of another undertaking, and that the directors of that latter undertaking are obliged to follow those directions, whether or not the directors consider that those directions are for the benefit of the undertaking.

In other words, if one undertaking can tell another undertaking what to do, both from an operating and a financial point of view, and the directors of that latter undertaking have to carry out such instructions, then such an undertaking will be a subsidiary undertaking. This is a much wider definition than merely looking at the amounts of the shareholdings.

**Activity 16.2** How can an entity have control of another entity when it does not own over 50% of the voting share capital?

This topic is covered in more detail in Chapter 26.

## 16.7 The nature of a group

Wherever two or more companies are in the relationship of parent and subsidiary, a 'group' is said to exist. As you have already learnt in Section 16.4, when such a group exists, besides the financial statements of the parent undertaking itself there must be a set of financial statements prepared in respect of the group as a whole. These group financial statements are usually known as *consolidated financial statements*, because the financial statements of all the companies have had to be consolidated together to form one set of financial statements.

Sometimes parent undertakings carry on trading as well as investing in their subsidiaries. There are, however, many parent undertakings that do not trade, all of their activities being concerned with investing in other companies.

## 16.8 Subsidiaries which are not limited companies

At one time, group financial statements consolidated only financial statements of limited companies. In effect, subsidiaries had to be limited companies to 'merit' inclusion in the consolidated financial statements. This is no longer the case. Share of ownership or the existence of control will determine whether or not an entity is a subsidiary. If so, its financial statements are included in the preparation of the consolidated financial statements, in a similar fashion to those of limited companies.

Other forms of entity – associates and joint ventures – are, by definition, *not* subsidiaries and are not consolidated. They are included in the financial statements according to the rules contained in IAS 28 (*Investments in associates*) and IFRS 11 (*Joint arrangements*).

**See Chapter 26 for further details of these rules.**

## 16.9 Teaching method

This topic is normally taught and learnt using one of two methods. One focuses on the journal entries required; this is quite abstract and, many feel, more difficult to understand than the other method. Accordingly, the method used in this book for teaching consolidated financial statements is the alternative approach of showing the adjustments needed on the face of the consolidated statement of financial position, together with any workings required to explain the amounts included. This approach is adopted because:

1 We believe our job is to try to help you to understand the subject, and not just to be able to perform the necessary calculations. Given a clear explanation of what is happening, the necessary accounting entries are much easier to understand. Showing the adjustments on the face of the statement of financial position gives a 'bird's-eye view' so that it is easier to see what is happening, rather than having to trace your way laboriously through a complex set of double entry adjustments made in ledger accounts.
2 This would be a much lengthier and more costly book if all of the double entry accounts were shown. It is better for a first look at consolidated financial statements to be an introduction to the subject only, rather than both an introduction plus a very detailed analysis of the subject. If you can understand the consolidated financial statements shown in this book, you will have a firm foundation which will enable you, in your future studies, to tackle the more difficult and complicated aspects of the subject.

## Learning outcomes

**You should now have learnt:**

1 Ordinary shareholders generally have voting rights, a right in the net assets of the company, and a right to an interest in profits earned.
2 Preference shareholders do not usually have any voting rights.
3 Ordinary shareholders receive copies of the financial statements for the company whose shares they hold, but not for any company whose shares are owned by the company they hold their shares in.
4 Consolidated financial statements provide shareholders in parent entities with financial statements incorporating the relevant data for all companies in the group – not just the parent company's own accounts data.
5 The status of 'subsidiary' is dependent upon the existence of control over that undertaking by another entity.
6 'Control' does not depend upon the level of investment in the company.

## Answers to activities

16.1 Preference shareholders have far less risk in their investment than ordinary shareholders. In exchange for the greater risk they experience, the ordinary shareholders get voting rights that permit them to influence the decision-making of the company.

16.2 It could have control by virtue of some agreement made with the company. For example, a bank may have control over the major decisions of a company in exchange for a loan it has granted to the company. Control is generally able to exist because of agreements between shareholders that result in one of the shareholders being granted control.

## Review questions

**16.1** What determines whether or not one company is a subsidiary of another company?

**16.2** How should unincorporated subsidiaries be treated when preparing consolidated financial statements?

**16.3** What benefits accrue to the investor in a parent entity by the use of consolidated financial statements?

chapter 17

# Consolidation of statements of financial position: basic mechanics (I)

## Learning objectives

After you have studied this chapter, you should be able to:

- explain the principle of cancellation that is adopted when preparing consolidated financial statements
- explain why goodwill may arise on consolidation
- calculate goodwill and include it in the consolidated statement of financial position
- explain what is meant by the term 'non-controlling interest'
- explain how the existence of reserves at the time of acquisition affects the preparation of consolidated financial statements

## Introduction

In this chapter, you'll learn how to consolidate financial statements where a subsidiary is wholly owned or partially owned, how to calculate and include goodwill in the consolidated statement of financial position, and how to consolidate subsidiaries with reserves. Finally, you'll be reminded about how to deal with a gain on a bargain purchase in the consolidated financial statements.

## 17.1 Background

This chapter is concerned with the basic mechanics of consolidating statements of financial position. The figures used will be quite small, as there is no virtue in obscuring the principles involved by using more realistic amounts. For the sake of brevity, some abbreviations will be used. As the consolidation of the financial statements of either two or three companies, but no more, will be attempted, then the abbreviations will be: P for the parent, S1 for the first subsidiary, and S2 for the second subsidiary. Where there is only one subsidiary, it will be shown as S. Unless stated to the contrary, all the shares will be ordinary shares of £1 each.

It is far easier to understand this topic if relatively simple statements of financial position can be used to demonstrate the principles of consolidated financial statements. To this end, the statements of financial position which follow in the next few chapters will usually contain only two assets, those of inventory and cash at bank. This will save a great deal of time and effort. At this stage on this topic, if every time a consolidated statement of financial position had to be prepared it included land, buildings, patents, motor vehicles, plant and machinery, inventory, accounts receivable and bank balances, you'd find it far harder to understand the principles involved.

## 17.2 The principle of cancellation

The various financial statements of the parent and its subsidiaries have to be brought together and consolidated into one set of financial statements for the whole group. Some items in one entity's financial statements may refer to exactly the same transactions in the financial statements of one of the other entities in the group. If so, adjustments must be made to the figures 'to be used in the consolidation'.

Let us look at some of the more common examples:

1 An item which is an account receivable in one statement of financial position may be shown as an account payable in another statement of financial position. For example, if P Ltd had sold goods to S Ltd, its subsidiary, but S Ltd had not yet paid for them, then the item would be shown as an account receivable in the statement of financial position of P Ltd and as an account payable in the statement of financial position of S Ltd.
2 Sales by one of the group to another company in the group will appear as sales in one company's accounts and purchases in another company's financial statements.
3 Shares bought in one of the subsidiary undertakings by the parent undertaking will be shown as an investment on the assets side of the parent undertaking's statement of financial position. In the statement of financial position of the subsidiary, those same shares will be shown as issued share capital.
4 Dividends paid by a subsidiary undertaking to its parent undertaking will be shown as paid dividends in the financial statements of the subsidiary, and as dividends received in the financial statements of the parent undertaking.

Consolidated financial statements are supposed to show how groups as a whole have dealt with the world outside. Transactions which are between group entities do not represent dealings with the outside world. When all of the separate accounts of the companies within the group are put together such items need to be deleted, and will not appear in the consolidated financial statements of the group.

This therefore is the principle of cancellation. Similar things in different financial statements within the group should be cancelled out to arrive at the group's financial statements.

This can be shown in the form of the diagram in Exhibit 17.1:

**Exhibit 17.1 Consolidation of financial statements of a group**

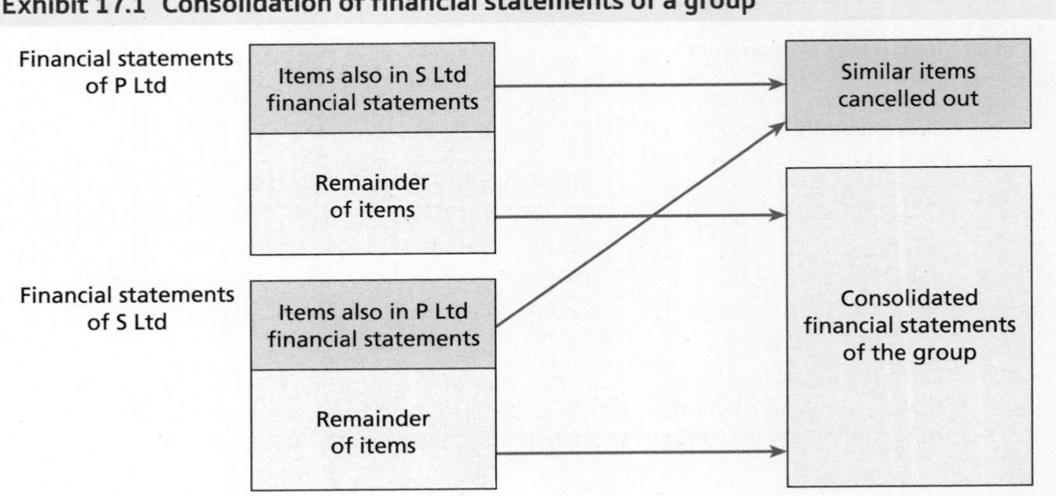


→

➔ This means that a consolidated statement of financial position, where the subsidiaries are 100% owned by the parent undertaking, will appear as follows:

**Consolidated Statement of Financial Position as at . . .**

| | £ |
|---|---|
| *Non-current assets* (*less* Cancelled items) | xxxx |
| *Current assets* (*less* Cancelled items) | xxxx |
| Total assets | xxxx |
| *Less Current liabilities* (*less* Cancelled items) | (xxxx) |
| | xxxx |
| *Equity* | |
| Share capital (of the parent undertaking only, as the purchase of shares in the subsidiaries have cancelled out) | xxxx |
| Reserves (*less* Cancelled items) | xxxx |
| | xxxx |

## 17.3 Rule 1

In consolidation, the first rule, therefore, is that like things cancel each other out. In fact, *cancellation accounts* are what consolidated financial statements are all about. It may help you to see the issue more clearly if we show an example of a consolidated statement of financial position constructed immediately after P has bought the shares in S.

### Exhibit 17.2 100% of the shares of S bought at statement of financial position value

P has just bought all the shares of S. Before consolidation the statements of financial position of P and S appear as follows:

**P Statement of Financial Position**

| | | £ |
|---|---|---|
| Investment in subsidiary S | (A) | 6 |
| Bank | | 4 |
| | | 10 |
| Share capital | | 10 |

**S Statement of Financial Position**

| | | £ |
|---|---|---|
| Inventory | | 5 |
| Bank | | 1 |
| | | 6 |
| Share capital | (B) | 6 |

The consolidated statement of financial position can now be drawn up. The rule about like things cancelling each other out can be applied. As can be seen, item (A) in P's statement of financial position and item (B) in S's statement of financial position are concerned with exactly the same thing, namely the six ordinary shares of S, and for the same amount, for the shares are shown in both statements of financial position at £6. These are cancelled out when the consolidated statement of financial position is drafted.

**P & S Consolidated Statement of Financial Position**

| | £ |
|---|---|
| Inventory | 5 |
| Bank (£4 + £1) | 5 |
| | 10 |
| Share capital | 10 |

However, sometimes the amount paid by the parent undertaking is not the same as the subsidiary's figure for share capital.

## Exhibit 17.3 100% of the shares of S bought for more than statement of financial position value

**P Statement of Financial Position**

| | | £ |
|---|---|---|
| Investment in subsidiary S: six shares | (C) | 9 |
| Bank | | 1 |
| | | 10 |
| Share capital | | 10 |

**S Statement of Financial Position**

| | | £ |
|---|---|---|
| Inventory | | 5 |
| Bank | | 1 |
| | | 6 |
| Share capital | (D) | 6 |

Now (C) and (D) refer to like things, but the amounts are unequal. What has happened is that P has paid £3 more than the book value for the shares of S. In accounting, where the amount paid (or 'consideration') for something exceeds the stated value, the difference is known as *goodwill*; and, when the consideration is less than the stated value, the difference is known as a '*gain from a bargain purchase*' or *negative goodwill*, the term it replaced in IFRS 3. (In practice, the accounting standards require that 'fair values', rather than book values, are used – see Section 22.3; however, for the sake of clarity, unless otherwise indicated, book values will be used throughout this book.) The consolidated statement of financial position is therefore:

**P and S Consolidated Statement of Financial Position**

| | £ |
|---|---|
| Goodwill (C) £9 − (D) £6 | 3 |
| Inventory | 5 |
| Bank (£1 + £1) | 2 |
| | 10 |
| Share capital | 10 |

Let's look at an example where a gain from a bargain purchase has been created.

## Exhibit 17.4 100% of the shares of S bought for less than statement of financial position value

**P Statement of Financial Position**

| | | £ |
|---|---|---|
| Investment in subsidiary S: six shares | (E) | 4 |
| Inventory | | 5 |
| Bank | | 1 |
| | | 10 |
| Share capital | | 10 |

**S Statement of Financial Position**

| | | £ |
|---|---|---|
| Inventory | | 5 |
| Bank | | 1 |
| | | 6 |
| Share capital | (F) | 6 |

P has bought all the shares of S, but has paid only £4 for £6 worth of shares at statement of financial position values. The £2 difference is a gain from a bargain purchase. Under IFRS 3 (*Business combinations*) a gain from a bargain purchase must be eliminated by writing it off immediately as a gain to profit or loss. P would immediately recognise the gain made on the acquisition in profit or loss (i.e. in its statement of profit or loss), which would result in its retained profits being increased. In this case, P's statement of financial position would be restated to reflect the increase in retained profits. The investment would increase by the amount of the gain from a bargain purchase and the reserves would increase by the same amount:

**P Statement of Financial Position (restated)**

| | £ |
|---|---|
| Investment in subsidiary S: six shares (revalued to reflect its fair value) | 6 |
| Inventory | 5 |
| Bank | 1 |
| | 12 |
| Share capital | 10 |
| Retained profits | 2 |
| | 12 |

The consolidated statement of financial position is then:

**P and S Consolidated Statement of Financial Position**

| | £ |
|---|---|
| Inventory (£5 + £5) | 10 |
| Bank | 2 |
| | 12 |
| Share capital | 10 |
| Retained profits | 2 |
| | 12 |

## 17.4 Cost of control

The expression **cost of control** could be used instead of 'goodwill'. This expression probably captures the essence of the purchase of the shares better than calling it goodwill. It is precisely for the sake of gaining control of the assets of the company that the shares are bought. However, the expression 'goodwill' is more widely used and is correspondingly the one that will be used through the remainder of this book.

**See Section 23.4 for details of how to record entries in a 'cost of control' account.**

**You can now attempt Review Questions 17.1, 17.2 and 17.3.**

## 17.5 Rule 2

Rule 2 states that, although the whole of the shares of the subsidiary have not been bought, nonetheless the whole of the assets of the subsidiary (subject to certain intercompany transactions described later) will be shown in the consolidated statement of financial position.

This rule comes about because of the choice made originally between two possible methods that could have been chosen. Suppose that P bought 75% of the shares of S, then the statements of financial position could be displayed in one of two ways:

**P and S Consolidated Statement of Financial Position – Method 1**

| | £ |
|---|---|
| Goodwill | xxxx |
| Assets of P: 100% | xxxx |
| Assets of S: 75% | xxxx |
| | xxxx |
| Share capital of P | xxxx |
| | xxxx |

**P and S Consolidated Statement of Financial Position – Method 2**

| | £ |
|---|---|
| Goodwill | xxxx |
| Assets of P: 100% | xxxx |
| Assets of S: 100% | xxxx |
| | xxxx |
| Share capital of P | xxxx |
| Non-controlling interest (i.e. claims of outsiders which equal 25% of the assets of S) | xxxx |
| | xxxx |

It can be seen that both statements of financial position show the amount of assets which P owns by virtue of its proportionate shareholding. On the other hand, the second statement of financial position gives a fuller picture, as it shows that P has control of all of the assets of S, although in fact it does not own all of them. The claims of outsiders come to 25% of S and obviously they cannot control the assets of S, whereas P, with 75%, can control the whole of the assets even though they are not fully owned by it. The second statement of financial position method gives rather more meaningful information and is the method that is used for consolidated financial statements in accordance with International GAAP.

Assume that S has six shares of £1 each and that it has one asset, namely inventory £6. P buys four shares for £1 each, £4. If the whole of the assets of S £6 are to be shown on the assets side of the consolidated statement of financial position, and the cancellation of only £4 is to take place on the other side, then the consolidated statement of financial position would not balance. Exhibit 17.5 shows this in detail before any attempt is made to get the consolidated statement of financial position to balance.

## Exhibit 17.5

**P Statement of Financial Position**

| | £ |
|---|---|
| Investment in subsidiary: four shares (bought today) | 4 |
| Inventory | 5 |
| Bank | 1 |
| | 10 |
| Share capital | 10 |

**S Statement of Financial Position**

| | £ |
|---|---|
| Inventory | 6 |
| Share capital | 6 |

As the two extra shares have not been bought by P, they cannot be brought into any calculation of goodwill. P has bought four shares with a statement of financial position value of £1 each, i.e. £4, for precisely £4. There is therefore no element of goodwill and no gain from a bargain purchase. On the other hand, the consolidated statement of financial position per Rule 2 must show the whole of the assets of S. This gives a consolidated statement of financial position as follows:

**P and S Consolidated Statement of Financial Position**

| | £ |
|---|---|
| Inventory (£5 + £6) | 11 |
| Bank | 1 |
| | |
| Share capital | 10 |

Quite obviously, if you now inserted the totals, they would differ by £2. What is this £2? On reflection it can be seen to be the £2 shares not bought by P. These shares belong to outsiders, they are not owned by the group. These outsiders also hold less than 50% of the voting shares of S. In fact, if they owned more, then S would probably not be a subsidiary of P. The original title given to the outside shareholders was **minority interest**. However, in an amendment made to IFRS 3 in January 2008, minority interest was renamed 'non-controlling interest'.

As the whole of the assets of S are shown in the consolidated statement of financial position then part of these assets are owned by the **non-controlling interest**. This claim against the assets is therefore shown in the equity section of the consolidated statement of financial position. The consolidated statement of financial position becomes:

**P and S Consolidated Statement of Financial Position**

| | £ |
|---|---|
| Inventory (£5 + £6) | 11 |
| Bank | 1 |
| | 12 |
| Share capital | 10 |
| Non-controlling interest | 2 |
| | 12 |

All the assets of the subsidiary (less certain intercompany transactions) are shown in the consolidated statement of financial position, with the claim of the non-controlling interest shown in the equity section of the statement of financial position.

## Exhibit 17.6 Where less than 100% of the subsidiary's shares are bought at more than book value

**P Statement of Financial Position**

| | | £ |
|---|---|---|
| Investment in subsidiary: six shares | (G) | 8 |
| Inventory | | 11 |
| Bank | | 1 |
| | | 20 |
| Share capital | | 20 |

**S Statement of Financial Position**

| | | £ |
|---|---|---|
| Inventory | | 7 |
| Bank | | 3 |
| | | 10 |
| Share capital | (I) | 10 |

P has bought six shares only, but has paid £8 for them. As the book value of the shares is £6, the £2 excess must therefore be goodwill. The cancellation is therefore £6 from (G) and £6 from (I), leaving £2 of (G) to be shown as goodwill in the consolidated statement of financial position. The remaining £4 of (I) is in respect of shares held by the non-controlling interest.

**P and S Consolidated Statement of Financial Position**

| | £ |
|---|---|
| Goodwill | 2 |
| Inventory (£11 + £7) | 18 |
| Bank (£1 + £3) | 4 |
| | 24 |
| Share capital | 20 |
| Non-controlling interest | 4 |
| | 24 |

## Exhibit 17.7 Where less than 100% of the shares in the subsidiary are bought at less than book value

**P Statement of Financial Position**

| | | £ |
|---|---|---|
| Investment in subsidiary: seven shares | (J) | 5 |
| Inventory | | 13 |
| Bank | | 2 |
| | | 20 |
| Share capital | | 20 |

→

**S Statement of Financial Position**

| | | £ |
|---|---|---|
| Inventory | | 9 |
| Bank | | 1 |
| | | 10 |
| Share capital | (K) | 10 |

Seven shares of S have now been bought for £5. This means that £5 of (J) and £5 of (K) cancel out with £2 of the share capital being represented by £2 of a gain from a bargain purchase. The remaining £3 of (K) is in respect of the shares held by the non-controlling interest and will be shown as such in the consolidated statement of financial position. However, the gain from a bargain purchase must first be eliminated. In this case, it was decided that the fair values in S's statement of financial position were correct, a gain of £2 would be recognised by P and the consolidated statement of financial position would be:

**P and S Consolidated Statement of Financial Position**

| | £ |
|---|---|
| Inventory (£13 + £9) | 22 |
| Bank (£2 + £1) | 3 |
| | 25 |
| Share capital | 20 |
| Retained profits | 2 |
| Non-controlling interest | 3 |
| | 25 |

**You can now attempt Review Questions 17.6 and 17.7.**

## 17.6 Goodwill and non-controlling interests

The calculations of goodwill in Section 17.5 all assumed that the non-controlling interest was measured at its proportionate share of the subsidiary's net assets. There is an alternative permitted under IFRS 3: the non-controlling interest may be measured at its fair value. If this is higher than its net asset value (which is likely), the goodwill calculated will also be higher. Section 17.9 contains an example illustrating this choice.

## 17.7 Taking over subsidiaries with reserves

So far, for reasons of simplification, the examples given have been of subsidiaries with share capital but no reserves. When reserves exist, as they do in the vast majority of cases, it must be remembered that they belong to the ordinary shareholders. This means that if P buys all the 10 shares of S for £15, and S at that point of time has a retained profits balance of £3 and a general reserve of £2, then what P acquires for its £15 is the full entitlement/rights of the 10 shares measured by/shown as:

| | £ |
|---|---|
| 10 shares | 10 |
| Retained profits | 3 |
| General reserve | 2 |
| | 15 |

This means that the £15 paid and the £15 entitlements as shown will cancel each other out and will not be shown in the consolidated statement of financial position. This is shown by the statements of financial position shown in Exhibit 17.8:

### Exhibit 17.8 Where 100% of the shares are bought at book value when the subsidiary has reserves

**P Statement of Financial Position**

| | | £ |
|---|---|---|
| Investment in subsidiary: 10 shares | (L) | 15 |
| Inventory | | 11 |
| Bank | | 2 |
| | | 28 |
| Share capital | | 20 |
| Retained profits | | 5 |
| General reserve | | 3 |
| | | 28 |

**S Statement of Financial Position**

| | | £ |
|---|---|---|
| Inventory | | 9 |
| Bank | | 6 |
| | | 15 |
| Share capital | (M1) | 10 |
| Retained profits | (M2) | 3 |
| General reserve | (M3) | 2 |
| | | 15 |

**P and S Consolidated Statement of Financial Position**

| | £ |
|---|---|
| Inventory (£11 + £9) | 20 |
| Bank (£2 + £6) | 8 |
| | 28 |
| Share capital | 20 |
| Retained profits | 5 |
| General reserve | 3 |
| | 28 |

The cost of the shares (L) £15 is cancelled out exactly against (M1) £10 + (M2) £3 + (M3) £2 = £15. These are therefore the only items cancelled out and the remainder of the two statements of financial position of P and S are then combined to be the consolidated statement of financial position.

## Exhibit 17.9 Where 100% of the shares are bought at more than book value when the subsidiary has reserves

**P Statement of Financial Position**

| | | £ |
|---|---|---|
| Investment in subsidiary: 10 shares | (N) | 23 |
| Inventory | | 7 |
| Bank | | 5 |
| | | 35 |
| Share capital | | 20 |
| Retained profits | | 9 |
| General reserve | | 6 |
| | | 35 |

**S Statement of Financial Position**

| | | £ |
|---|---|---|
| Inventory | | 15 |
| Bank | | 2 |
| | | 17 |
| Share capital | (O1) | 10 |
| Retained profits | (O2) | 4 |
| General reserve | (O3) | 3 |
| | | 17 |

P paid £23 (N) for the entitlements (O1) £10 + (O2) £4 + (O3) £3 = £17, so that a figure of £6 will be shown in the consolidated statement of financial position for goodwill.

**P and S Consolidated Statement of Financial Position**

| | £ |
|---|---|
| Goodwill | 6 |
| Inventory (£7 + £15) | 22 |
| Bank (£5 + £2) | 7 |
| | 35 |
| Share capital | 20 |
| Retained profits | 9 |
| General reserve | 6 |
| | 35 |

## Exhibit 17.10 Where 100% of the shares in the subsidiary are bought at below book value when the subsidiary has reserves

**P Statement of Financial Position**

| | | £ |
|---|---|---|
| Investment in subsidiary: 10 shares | (Z) | 17 |
| Inventory | | 10 |
| Bank | | 8 |
| | | 35 |
| Share capital | | 20 |
| Retained profits | | 6 |
| General reserve | | 9 |
| | | 35 |

**S Statement of Financial Position**

| | | £ |
|---|---|---|
| Inventory | | 16 |
| Bank | | 5 |
| | | 21 |
| Share capital | (Q1) | 10 |
| Retained profits | (Q2) | 8 |
| General reserve | (Q3) | 3 |
| | | 21 |

P has paid £17 (Z) for the benefits of (Q1) £10 + (Q2) £8 + (Q3) £3 = £21. This means that there will be a gain from a bargain purchase of £21 − £17 = £4 which must be eliminated, while (Z), (Q1), (Q2) and (Q3), having been cancelled out, will not appear.

A previous example (Exhibit 17.4) that included a gain from a bargain purchase involved restating the investment in the subsidiary to the fair value of the net assets acquired and introducing a reserve in the parent's statement of financial position. The same approach is adopted when the subsidiary has reserves:

**P and S Consolidated Statement of Financial Position**

| | £ |
|---|---|
| Inventory (£10 + £16) | 26 |
| Bank (£8 + £5) | 13 |
| | 39 |
| Share capital | 20 |
| Retained profits (£6 + £4) | 10 |
| General reserve | 9 |
| | 39 |

**Activity 17.1**

What would the consolidated statement of financial position look like if the amounts shown in S's statement of financial position were used rather than those in the restated statement of P's financial position?

## Exhibit 17.11 Where less than 100% of the shares are bought in a subsidiary which has reserves, and the shares are bought at the statement of financial position value

**P Statement of Financial Position**

| | | £ |
|---|---|---|
| Investment in subsidiary: eight shares | (R) | 24 |
| Inventory | | 15 |
| Bank | | 6 |
| | | 45 |
| Share capital | | 20 |
| Retained profits | | 17 |
| General reserve | | 8 |
| | | 45 |

**S Statement of Financial Position**

| | | £ |
|---|---|---|
| Inventory | | 21 |
| Bank | | 9 |
| | | 30 |
| Share capital | (T1) | 10 |
| Retained profits | (T2) | 5 |
| General reserve | (T3) | 15 |
| | | 30 |

The items (R) and the parts of (T1), (T2) and (T3) which are like things need to be cancelled out. The cancellation takes place from the share capital and reserves of S as follows:

| | *Total at acquisition date* | *Bought by P 80%* | *Held by non-controlling interest* |
|---|---|---|---|
| | £ | £ | £ |
| Share capital | 10 | 8 | 2 |
| Retained profits | 5 | 4 | 1 |
| General reserve | 15 | 12 | 3 |
| | 30 | 24 | 6 |

The amount paid by P was £24, and as P acquired a total of £24 value of shares and reserves, the cancellation takes place without there being any goodwill or gain from a bargain purchase. The consolidated statement of financial position is, therefore,

**P and S Consolidated Statement of Financial Position**

| | £ |
|---|---|
| Inventory (£15 + £21) | 36 |
| Bank (£6 + £9) | 15 |
| | 51 |
| Share capital | 20 |
| Retained profits | 17 |
| General reserve | 8 |
| Non-controlling interest | 6 |
| | 51 |

Activity 17.2 What are the two rules of consolidation?

## 17.8 Partial control at a price not equal to statement of financial position value

In Exhibit 17.11, the amount paid for the 80% of the shares of S was equal to the statement of financial position value of the shares in that it amounted to £24. This is unusual, as the price is normally different from the statement of financial position value. As you know, if an amount paid is greater than the statement of financial position value then the excess will be shown as goodwill in the consolidated statement of financial position; while, if a smaller amount than the statement of financial position value is paid, then the difference is a gain from a bargain purchase and must be eliminated. Using the consolidated statement of financial position figure of S in Exhibit 17.11, if P had paid £30 for 80% of the shares of S then the consolidated statement of financial position would show a goodwill figure of £6. If, instead, only £21 had been paid, a £3 gain from the bargain purchase would have been entered immediately to P's profit or loss (statement of profit or loss), resulting in an immediate increase in P's reserves of £3. At the same time, the investment in S would be increased by £3 to £24 in P's statement of financial position.

The next exhibit is a composite one, bringing in most of the points already shown, and includes an example of gain on a bargain purchase where there are non-controlling interests and the decision is taken to adjust the fair values.

## Exhibit 17.12 Where two subsidiaries have been acquired, both with reserves, full ownership being acquired of one subsidiary and a partial ownership of the other subsidiary

**P Statement of Financial Position**

| | | £ |
|---|---|---|
| Investment in subsidiaries: | | |
| S1 10 shares | (U) | 37 |
| S2 seven shares | (V) | 39 |
| Inventory | | 22 |
| Bank | | 2 |
| | | 100 |
| Share capital | | 40 |
| Retained profits | | 50 |
| General reserve | | 10 |
| | | 100 |

**S1 Statement of Financial Position**

| | | £ |
|---|---|---|
| Inventory | | 19 |
| Bank | | 11 |
| | | 30 |
| Share capital | (W1) | 10 |
| Retained profits | (W2) | 12 |
| General reserve | (W3) | 8 |
| | | 30 |

**S2 Statement of Financial Position**

| | | £ |
|---|---|---|
| Inventory | | 42 |
| Bank | | 18 |
| | | 60 |
| Share capital | (X1) | 10 |
| Retained profits | (X2) | 30 |
| General reserve | (X3) | 20 |
| | | 60 |

With the acquisition of S1 P has paid £37 for (W1) £10 + (W2) £12 + (W3) £8 = £30, giving a figure of £7 for goodwill. With the acquisition of S2 P has given £39 for $^{7}/_{10}$ of net assets of S2 (£60), i.e. £42, giving a gain from a bargain purchase of £3. The goodwill is shown in the consolidated statement of financial position. The gain from a bargain purchase must be eliminated by recording a gain to profit or loss.

The consolidated statement of financial position is:

**P and S1 and S2 Consolidated Statement of Financial Position**

| | | £ |
|---|---|---|
| Goodwill | | 7 |
| Inventory (£22 + £19 + £42) | | 83 |
| Bank (£2 + £11 + £18) | | 31 |
| | | 121 |
| Share capital | | 40 |
| Retained profits | | 53 |
| General reserve | | 10 |
| Non-controlling interest: | | |
| 3/10 of (X1) | 3 | |
| 3/10 of (X2) | 9 | |
| 3/10 of (X3) | 6 | |
| | | 18 |
| | | 121 |

***Note*: The non-controlling interest amount is not always shown in this way. Instead, it is simply shown as one amount representing the non-controlling interest in the restated net assets or restated total equity of S. The total amount is the same in both cases. We have shown this in detail here so as to emphasise that the non-controlling interest holds these amounts of the components of equity in S2. In future examples, we'll simply show the non-controlling interest in the total equity.**

**Now work through Review Questions 17.10 and 17.11.**

## 17.9 Calculating goodwill when there is a non-controlling interest

Not all acquisitions result in the acquiring entity obtaining control over the other. Smaller holdings, such as investments in 10% of a company, are accounted for according to the rules of IAS 39 (*Financial instruments*). Larger holdings, such as the acquisition of 40% of the equity of a company, which do not give control of the company to the investor, are accounted for as an associate under IAS 28 (*Investments in associates*). It is only when control is achieved, such as when an entity achieves control over 50% of the equity of a company, that a business combination is formed.

Under changes to IFRS 3 in 2008, this is the only time at which the measurement of goodwill occurs. Where the holding had previously been accounted for as an investment or as an associate, it is assumed that the original holding was disposed of at fair value and instantly reacquired for the same amount. The effect of this is that the fair value of the original holding is both included in the net assets acquired and added to the total consideration amount used in the calculation of goodwill.

When a business combination is formed but 100% ownership is not achieved, the acquiring entity must choose between two alternative methods to calculate goodwill. The difference between the two methods is the treatment of non-controlling interests. The impact of these alternatives can be seen in Exhibit 17.13.

### Exhibit 17.13

P acquired S in two stages.

- In 2011, P acquired a 30% equity interest in S for £60,000. At that time, the fair value of the net assets of S was £200,000.
- In 2016, P acquired a further 50% of the equity of S for £150,000. On the date of acquisition, the fair value of the net assets of S was £240,000. On that date, the fair value of P's original 30% holding was £80,000. The fair value of the 20% non-controlling interest in S on that date was £56,000.

The two alternatives are:

| | Non-controlling interest at a percentage of the fair value of the net assets (£) | Non-controlling interest at fair value (£) |
|---|---|---|
| Amount paid | 150,000 | 150,000 |
| Non-controlling interests | 48,000 (20% of £240,000) | 56,000 |
| Previous holding | 80,000 | 80,000 |
| | 278,000 | 286,000 |
| Fair value of net assets | 240,000 | 240,000 |
| Goodwill | 38,000 | 46,000 |

It is beyond the scope of this book to consider in detail why there is a difference between the two alternative amounts at which to state the value of the non-controlling interest. However, it is worthwhile drawing attention to the fact that fair value is dependent upon the context in which it is determined; and these two contexts are different: what S was valued at when P acquired control and what P would have to pay to acquire the non-controlling interests in S.

For simplicity, in Chapters 18 to 25 it will be assumed that the non-controlling interest is valued at its percentage of the fair value of the net assets. However, you will need to be aware of the alternative available in calculating goodwill in case your examiners choose to include it in your examination.

## Learning outcomes

**You should now have learnt:**

1. Some items in the financial statements of one of the group companies will refer to exactly the same transactions as in the financial statements of one of the other group companies and they will need to be cancelled out when the consolidated financial statements are prepared (*Rule 1*).
2. Where the consideration exceeds the statement of financial position value acquired, goodwill arises.
3. Where the consideration is less than the statement of financial position value acquired, the negative goodwill must be eliminated prior to consolidation (IFRS 3).
4. The treatment of goodwill is governed by IFRS 3. (*See* Chapter 25 for more detail on this topic.)
5. Non-controlling interests exist when less than 100% of the share capital of a subsidiary is owned at the date of the statement of financial position.
6. All the assets of a subsidiary are included in the consolidated financial statements, even where less than 100% of the share capital has been acquired (*Rule 2*).
7. When a subsidiary has reserves at the date of acquisition, those reserves are treated as part of the capital acquired and the calculation of goodwill includes the relevant proportion of the reserves.
8. When goodwill arises in respect of consolidation of one subsidiary and a gain from a bargain purchase arises on another, the positive goodwill is shown in the consolidated financial statements and the gain from a bargain purchase is eliminated by the parent

→

recognising the gain in profit or loss and increasing the amount of the investment as shown in its statement of financial position by the same amount, to reflect the fair value of the net assets acquired *before* consolidation.

**9** The alternative ways goodwill can be calculated when there are non-controlling interests in the acquired entity.

## Answers to activities

17.1 **P and S Consolidated Statement of Financial Position**

| | £ |
|---|---|
| Inventory (£10 + £16) | 26 |
| Bank (£8 + £5) | 13 |
| | 39 |
| Share capital | 20 |
| Retained profits | 10 |
| General reserve | 9 |
| | 39 |

17.2 Rule 1: items in the financial statements of one of the group companies that refer to exactly the same transactions as in the financial statements of one of the other group companies (e.g. a debtor balance in one company's ledger that corresponds to an equal creditor balance in another group company's ledger) need to be cancelled out when the consolidated financial statements are prepared.

Rule 2: all the assets of a subsidiary are included in the consolidated financial statements, even where less than 100% of the share capital has been acquired.

## Review questions

***Note*: In each of these review questions, the amounts have been kept low, so as to enable you to demonstrate an understanding of, and ability to apply, the principles involved.**

17.1 The following statements of financial position were drawn up immediately after Dad Ltd had acquired control of Son Ltd. You are to draw up a consolidated statement of financial position.

**Dad Statement of Financial Position**

| | £ |
|---|---|
| Investment in Son Ltd: 1,600 Ordinary £1 shares | 3,600 |
| Inventory | 1,500 |
| Bank | 900 |
| | 6,000 |
| Share capital – £1 Ordinary shares | 6,000 |

**Son Statement of Financial Position**

| | £ |
|---|---|
| Inventory | 1,200 |
| Bank | 400 |
| | 1,600 |
| Share capital – £1 Ordinary shares | 1,600 |

17.2 Prepare a consolidated statement of financial position from the following statements of financial position of Pop Ltd and Junior Ltd which were drawn up immediately after Pop Ltd had acquired the share capital of Junior Ltd.

**Pop Statement of Financial Position**

| | £ |
|---|---|
| Investment in Junior Ltd: 25,000 £1 Ordinary shares | 16,000 |
| Non-current assets | 48,000 |
| Inventory | 10,800 |
| Accounts receivable | 6,400 |
| Bank | 4,800 |
| | 86,000 |
| Share capital – £1 Ordinary shares | 86,000 |

**Junior Statement of Financial Position**

| | £ |
|---|---|
| Non-current assets | 18,000 |
| Inventory | 4,000 |
| Accounts receivable | 2,000 |
| Bank | 1,000 |
| | 25,000 |
| Share capital – £1 Ordinary shares | 25,000 |

17.3 Draw up a consolidated statement of financial position from the following statements of financial position which were drawn up as soon as Pa Ltd had acquired control of Sonny Ltd.

**Pa Statement of Financial Position**

| | £ |
|---|---|
| Investment in Sonny Ltd: 160,000 Ordinary £1 shares | 160,000 |
| Non-current assets | 148,000 |
| Inventory | 90,000 |
| Accounts receivable | 52,000 |
| Bank | 50,000 |
| | 500,000 |
| Share capital – Ordinary £1 shares | 500,000 |

**Sonny Statement of Financial Position**

| | £ |
|---|---|
| Non-current assets | 98,000 |
| Inventory | 48,000 |
| Accounts receivable | 8,000 |
| Bank | 6,000 |
| | 160,000 |
| Share capital – Ordinary £1 shares | 160,000 |

→

17.4A Papai Ltd acquired all the shares in Sister and Son Ltd and then the following statements of financial position were drawn up. You are to prepare a consolidated statement of financial position.

**Papai Statement of Financial Position**

| | £ |
|---|---|
| Investment in Sister and Son Ltd – Ordinary £1 shares | 90,000 |
| Non-current assets | 165,000 |
| Inventory | 41,000 |
| Accounts receivable | 37,000 |
| Bank | 7,000 |
| | 340,000 |
| Share capital – Ordinary £1 shares | 340,000 |

**Sister and Son Statement of Financial Position**

| | £ |
|---|---|
| Non-current assets | 52,000 |
| Inventory | 17,000 |
| Accounts receivable | 7,000 |
| Bank | 4,000 |
| | 80,000 |
| Share capital – Ordinary £1 shares | 80,000 |

17.5A Draw up a consolidated statement of financial position from the statements of financial position of Papi Ltd and Child Ltd that were drafted immediately after the shares in Child Ltd were acquired by Papi Ltd. The amounts shown in the statements of financial position are a correct reflection of the fair values.

**Papi Statement of Financial Position**

| | £ |
|---|---|
| Investment in Child Ltd: 140,000 Ordinary £1 shares | 140,000 |
| Non-current assets | 90,000 |
| Inventory | 31,000 |
| Accounts receivable | 63,000 |
| Bank | 16,000 |
| | 340,000 |
| Share capital – Ordinary shares of 50p each | 340,000 |

**Child Statement of Financial Position**

| | £ |
|---|---|
| Non-current assets | 108,000 |
| Inventory | 42,000 |
| Accounts receivable | 37,000 |
| Bank | 3,000 |
| | 190,000 |
| Share capital – Ordinary £1 shares | 190,000 |

17.6 Parental Ltd acquires 75% of the shares in Children United Ltd. Statements of financial position are then drafted immediately. You are to draw up the consolidated statement of financial position.

**Parental Statement of Financial Position**

| | £ |
|---|---|
| Investment in Children United Ltd: 30,000 Ordinary £1 shares | 60,000 |
| Non-current assets | 90,000 |
| Inventory | 25,000 |
| Accounts receivable | 18,000 |
| Bank | 7,000 |
| | 200,000 |
| Share capital – Ordinary shares of 25p each | 200,000 |

**Children United Statement of Financial Position**

| | £ |
|---|---|
| Non-current assets | 31,000 |
| Inventory | 4,000 |
| Accounts receivable | 2,000 |
| Bank | 3,000 |
| | 40,000 |
| Share capital – Ordinary £1 shares | 40,000 |

17.7 Parents Ltd acquires 90% of the shares of Sonny Jim Ltd. The following statements of financial position are then drafted. You are to draw up the consolidated statement of financial position. Any gain from a bargain purchase is to be eliminated by adjusting the non-current assets acquired.

**Parents Statement of Financial Position**

| | £ |
|---|---|
| Investment in Sonny Jim Ltd: 18,000 Ordinary £1 shares | 14,000 |
| Non-current assets | 82,000 |
| Inventory | 29,000 |
| Accounts receivable | 21,000 |
| Bank | 4,000 |
| | 150,000 |
| Share capital – Ordinary £1 shares | 150,000 |

**Sonny Jim Statement of Financial Position**

| | £ |
|---|---|
| Non-current assets | 12,000 |
| Inventory | 4,000 |
| Accounts receivable | 3,000 |
| Bank | 1,000 |
| | 20,000 |
| Share capital – Ordinary £1 shares | 20,000 |

→

**17.8A** Pops and Mom Ltd buys 60% of the shares in Kids Ltd. You are to draw up the consolidated statement of financial position from the following statements of financial position constructed immediately control had been achieved.

**Pops and Mom Statement of Financial Position**

| | £ |
|---|---:|
| Investment in Kids: 18,000 Ordinary £1 shares | 15,000 |
| Non-current assets | 90,000 |
| Inventory | 16,000 |
| Accounts receivable | 22,000 |
| Bank | 7,000 |
| | 150,000 |
| Share capital – Ordinary £1 shares | 150,000 |

**Kids Statement of Financial Position**

| | £ |
|---|---:|
| Non-current assets | 17,000 |
| Inventory | 8,000 |
| Accounts receivable | 3,000 |
| Bank | 2,000 |
| | 30,000 |
| Share capital – Ordinary £1 shares | 30,000 |

**17.9A** After Papai and Mamae Ltd acquired 70% of the shares of Siblings Ltd the following statements of financial position are drawn up. You are to draw up the consolidated statement of financial position.

**Papai and Mamae Statement of Financial Position**

| | £ |
|---|---:|
| Investments in Siblings Ltd: 25,200 Ordinary £1 shares | 30,000 |
| Non-current assets | 68,000 |
| Inventory | 14,000 |
| Accounts receivable | 19,000 |
| Bank | 9,000 |
| | 140,000 |
| Share capital – Ordinary shares of 10p each | 140,000 |

**Siblings Statement of Financial Position**

| | £ |
|---|---:|
| Non-current assets | 22,000 |
| Inventory | 6,000 |
| Accounts receivable | 5,000 |
| Bank | 3,000 |
| | 36,000 |
| Share capital – Ordinary £1 shares | 36,000 |

17.10 Immediately after Pop and Family Ltd had acquired control of Twin One Ltd and Twin Two Ltd the following statements of financial position were drawn up. You are to draw up a consolidated statement of financial position.

**Pop and Family Statement of Financial Position**

| | £ |
|---|---|
| Investments in subsidiaries: | |
| Twin One Ltd (16,000 Ordinary £1 shares) | 25,600 |
| Twin Two Ltd (19,200 Ordinary £1 shares) | 28,000 |
| Non-current assets | 116,800 |
| Current assets | 52,800 |
| | 224,000 |
| Share capital – Ordinary £1 shares | 164,000 |
| Retained profits | 60,000 |
| | 224,000 |

**Twin One Statement of Financial Position**

| | £ |
|---|---|
| Non-current assets | 17,600 |
| Current assets | 6,400 |
| | 24,000 |
| Share capital – Ordinary £1 shares | 16,000 |
| Retained profits | 3,200 |
| General reserve | 4,800 |
| | 24,000 |

**Twin Two Statement of Financial Position**

| | £ |
|---|---|
| Non-current assets | 30,400 |
| Current assets | 9,600 |
| | 40,000 |
| Share capital – Ordinary £1 shares | 24,000 |
| Retained profits | 9,600 |
| General reserve | 6,400 |
| | 40,000 |

17.11 Immediately after Parental Acquisition Ltd had acquired control of Daughter One Ltd and Daughter Two Ltd the following statements of financial position were drawn up. You are to draw up a consolidated statement of financial position. The amounts shown in the statements of financial position are a correct reflection of the fair values.

**Parental Acquisition's Statement of Financial Position**

| | £ |
|---|---|
| Investment in subsidiaries: | |
| Daughter One Ltd (60,000 Ordinary £1 shares) | 150,000 |
| Daughter Two Ltd (35,000 Ordinary £1 shares) | 48,000 |
| Non-current assets | 296,000 |
| Current assets | 84,000 |
| | 578,000 |
| Share capital – Ordinary £1 shares | 360,000 |
| Retained profits | 190,000 |
| General reserve | 28,000 |
| | 578,000 |

**Daughter One Statement of Financial Position**

| | £ |
|---|---|
| Non-current assets | 140,000 |
| Current assets | 40,000 |
| | 180,000 |
| Share capital – Ordinary £1 shares | 90,000 |
| Retained profits | 80,000 |
| General reserve | 10,000 |
| | 180,000 |

**Daughter Two Statement of Financial Position**

| | £ |
|---|---|
| Non-current assets | 41,000 |
| Current assets | 14,000 |
| | 55,000 |
| Share capital – Ordinary £1 shares | 35,000 |
| Retained profits | 8,000 |
| General reserve | 12,000 |
| | 55,000 |

17.12A Immediately after Pai, Mae and Co Ltd had achieved control of Sibling 1 Ltd and Sibling 2 Ltd the following statements of financial position are drawn up. You are to draw up the consolidated statement of financial position.

**Pai, Mae and Co Statement of Financial Position**

| | £ |
|---|---|
| Investments in subsidiaries: | |
| Sibling 1 Ltd 30,000 £1 Ordinary shares | 75,000 |
| Sibling 2 Ltd 30,000 £1 Ordinary shares | 53,000 |
| Non-current assets | 162,000 |
| Current assets | 41,000 |
| | 331,000 |
| Share capital – Ordinary £1 shares | 195,000 |
| Retained profits | 84,000 |
| General reserve | 52,000 |
| | 331,000 |

**Sibling 1 Statement of Financial Position**

| | £ |
|---|---|
| Non-current assets | 69,000 |
| Current assets | 20,000 |
| | 89,000 |
| Share capital – Ordinary £1 shares | 30,000 |
| Retained profits | 32,000 |
| General reserve | 27,000 |
| | 89,000 |

**Sibling 2 Statement of Financial Position**

| | £ |
|---|---|
| Non-current assets | 41,000 |
| Current assets | 19,000 |
| | 60,000 |
| Share capital – Ordinary £1 shares | 40,000 |
| Retained profits | 12,000 |
| General reserve | 8,000 |
| | 60,000 |

17.13A The following statements of financial position of Parental Times Ltd, Sons Ltd and Daughters Ltd were drawn up as soon as Parents Forever Ltd had acquired the shares in both subsidiaries. You are to draw up a consolidated statement of financial position.

**Parental Times Statement of Financial Position**

| | £ |
|---|---|
| Investments in subsidiaries: | |
| Sons Ltd 60,000 Ordinary £1 shares | 120,000 |
| Daughters Ltd 50,000 Ordinary £1 shares | 80,000 |
| Non-current assets | 140,000 |
| Current assets | 54,000 |
| | 394,000 |
| Share capital – Ordinary £1 shares | 260,000 |
| Retained profits | 124,000 |
| General reserve | 10,000 |
| | 394,000 |

**Sons Statement of Financial Position**

| | £ |
|---|---|
| Non-current assets | 123,000 |
| Current assets | 61,000 |
| | 184,000 |
| Share capital – Ordinary £1 shares | 100,000 |
| Retained profits | 58,000 |
| General reserve | 26,000 |
| | 184,000 |

→

**Daughters Statement of Financial Position**

| | £ |
|---|---|
| Non-current assets | 58,000 |
| Current assets | 14,000 |
| | 72,000 |
| Share capital – Ordinary £1 shares | 50,000 |
| Retained profits | 16,000 |
| General reserve | 6,000 |
| | 72,000 |

chapter 18

# Consolidation of statements of financial position: basic mechanics (II)

## Learning objectives

After you have studied this chapter, you should be able to:

- explain the implications when the dates of acquisition and of the group statement of financial position do not coincide
- explain that the calculation of goodwill is performed as at the date of acquisition
- describe the difference in treatment between pre- and post-acquisition reserves of subsidiary undertakings

## Introduction

In this chapter, you'll learn that goodwill is calculated on the basis of the financial position at the date of acquisition and that it does not change thereafter. You'll also learn that reserves acquired when an entity is acquired are not available for distribution and you'll learn how to show post-acquisition profits and losses in the consolidated statement of financial position and how to calculate any non-controlling interest when there are post-acquisition profits or losses.

## 18.1 Background

In the previous chapter, the consolidated statements of financial position were drawn up immediately the shares in the subsidiary had been acquired. **Even though the consolidation is normally performed at the end of the parent company's accounting period and, thus, frequently some time after the acquisition, it must also be prepared *as at the time the acquisition occurred*.** A similar thing must be done with the statement of profit or loss of the subsidiary and any of the balances on the other reserve accounts which have changed since the date of acquisition.

## 18.2 Goodwill financial statements of later years

Goodwill is calculated at the date of acquisition and remains unchanged as the years go by. It is important to remember this. Say, for instance, that the calculation of goodwill was done on an acquisition made on 31 December 2016 and that the goodwill figure was £5,000. Even if the calculation were made one year later, on 31 December 2017, the calculation must use the reserves etc. as on 31 December 2016 as this is when they were acquired, and so the figure of goodwill will always be £5,000. This would be true no matter how much time passed before anyone performed the calculation.

However, in examinations, the goodwill figure may still have to be calculated, even though the consolidated statement of financial position being drawn up is 5, 10 or 20 years after the company became a subsidiary. This has to be done because the previous financial statements and notes which show the figure to use are not available to an examinee.

## 18.3 Capital reserves

As you would expect, when companies purchase their own shares, previous holders of the shares have, effectively, had their investment returned to them and so cease to be shareholders in the company. The company has, in effect, returned some of its capital to those ex-shareholders. Unless special permission has been granted by the court, it is illegal for any company to return its capital to its shareholders in any other way. If a parent undertaking were to pay money to acquire a company as a subsidiary, and then distributed as dividends the assets it had bought, this would be the same as returning its capital to its shareholders and is, therefore, not allowed.

Let's look at an example. P pays £15 to acquire 100% of the shares of S, and the share capital of S consists of £10 of shares and £5 retained profits. Thus, to acquire a capital asset (i.e. ownership of S), the holding company has parted with £15. If the retained profits of S were merely added to those of P in the consolidated statement of financial position, the £5 balance of S could be regarded as being distributable as cash dividends to the shareholders of P. As this £5 of reserves has been bought as a capital asset, a dividend payment that was in part funded by this £5 of reserves would amount to a return of capital to the shareholders of P.

To prevent this, the balance of the retained profits of S on acquisition is capitalised, i.e. it is brought into the statement of financial position through the calculation of goodwill and is not shown in the consolidated statement of financial position as a retained profit balance. On the other hand, the whole of any profit made by S since acquisition will clearly belong to P's shareholders as P owns 100% of the shares of S.

Why do you think it would be a 'bad' thing to distribute as dividends the reserves acquired at the time of acquisition?

### Exhibit 18.1 Where the parent undertaking holds 100% of the subsidiary undertaking's shares

P acquires the shares on 31 December 2017. The statements of financial position one year later are as follows:

**P Statement of Financial Position as at 31 December 2018**

| | | £ |
|---|---|---|
| Investment in subsidiary: 10 shares bought 31.12.2017 | (A) | 18 |
| Inventory | | 11 |
| Bank | | 3 |
| | | 32 |
| Share capital | | 20 |
| Retained profits | | 12 |
| | | 32 |

**S Statement of Financial Position as at 31 December 2018**

| | | £ | £ |
|---|---|---|---|
| Inventory | | | 14 |
| Bank | | | 2 |
| | | | 16 |
| Share capital | (B) | | 10 |
| Retained profits: | | | |
| As at 31.12.2017 | (C) | 5 | |
| Profit for 2018 | (D) | 1 | |
| | | | 6 |
| | | | 16 |

The shares were acquired on 31 December 2017, therefore the calculation of the goodwill is based on the financial position of S at that date. Thus P obtained the following for (A) £18 at 31 December 2017: shares (B) £10 and retained profits (C) £5 = £15. Goodwill therefore amounted to £3. The profit made by S during 2018 was obviously made after acquisition and, therefore, does not come into the goodwill calculation. The figure of (D) £1 is a reserve which belongs wholly to P, as P in fact owns all of the shares of S. This (D) £1 is added to the reserves shown in the consolidated statement of financial position.

**P Consolidated Statement of Financial Position as at 31 December 2018**

| | £ |
|---|---|
| Goodwill | 3 |
| Inventory (£11 + £14) | 25 |
| Bank (£3 + £2) | 5 |
| | 33 |
| Share capital | 20 |
| Retained profits (P £12 + S £1) | 13 |
| | 33 |

## Exhibit 18.2 Where the parent holds 100% of the shares of the subsidiary and there is a post-acquisition loss

**P Statement of Financial Position as at 31 December 2018**

| | | £ | £ |
|---|---|---|---|
| Investment in subsidiary: | | | |
| 10 shares bought 31.12.2017 | (E) | | 19 |
| Inventory | | | 10 |
| Bank | | | 4 |
| | | | 33 |
| Share capital | | | 20 |
| Retained profits: | | | |
| As at 31.12.2017 | | 7 | |
| *Add* Profit 2018 | | 6 | |
| | | | 13 |
| | | | 33 |

**S Statement of Financial Position as at 31 December 2018**

| | | £ | £ |
|---|---|---|---|
| Inventory | | | 9 |
| Bank | | | 2 |
| | | | 11 |
| Share capital | (F) | | 10 |
| Retained profits: | | | |
| As at 31.12.2017 | (G) | 4 | |
| *Less* Loss 2018 | (I) | (3) | |
| | | | 1 |
| | | | 11 |

In calculating goodwill, the items (F) £10 and (G) £4 are cancelled against the amount paid (E) £19, thus the goodwill is £5. The loss (I) has been incurred since acquisition. A profit since acquisition, as in Exhibit 18.1, adds to the reserves in the consolidated statement of financial position, therefore a loss must be deducted.

**P Consolidated Statement of Financial Position as at 31 December 2018**

| | £ |
|---|---|
| Goodwill | 5 |
| Inventory (£10 + £9) | 19 |
| Bank (£4 + £2) | 6 |
| | 30 |
| Share capital | 20 |
| Retained profits (£13 − (I) £3) | 10 |
| | 30 |

## Exhibit 18.3 Where the parent acquires less than 100% of the shares of the subsidiary and there is a post-acquisition profit

**P Statement of Financial Position as at 31 December 2018**

| | | £ | £ |
|---|---|---|---|
| Investment in subsidiary: eight shares bought 31.12.2017 | (J) | | 28 |
| Inventory | | | 7 |
| Bank | | | 3 |
| | | | 38 |
| Share capital | | | 20 |
| Retained profits: | | | |
| As at 31.12.2017 | | 10 | |
| *Add* Profit 2018 | | 8 | |
| | | | 18 |
| | | | 38 |

**S Statement of Financial Position as at 31 December 2018**

| | | £ | £ |
|---|---|---|---|
| Inventory | | | 28 |
| Bank | | | 2 |
| | | | 30 |
| Share capital | (K) | | 10 |
| Retained profits: | | | |
| As at 31.12.2017 | (L) | 15 | |
| *Add* Profit 2018 | (M) | 5 | |
| | (N) | | 20 |
| | | | 30 |

P has given (J) £28 to take over 80% of (K) + (L), i.e. 80% of (£10 + £15) = £20. Therefore goodwill is £8. The profit for 2009 (M) £5 is also owned 80% by P = £4, and as this has been earned since the shares in S were bought, the whole of this belongs to the shareholders of P and is also distributable to them, therefore it can be combined with other retained profit balances in the consolidated statement of financial position.

The non-controlling interest is 20% of (K) £10 + (N) £20 = £6. It must be pointed out that, although the holding company splits up the retained profit balances into pre-acquisition and post-acquisition, there is no point in the non-controlling interest doing likewise. It would, however, amount to exactly the same answer if they did, because 20% of (K) £10 + (L) £15 + (M) £5 still comes to £6, i.e. exactly the same as 20% of (N) £20 + (K) £10 = £6.

**P Consolidated Statement of Financial Position as at 31 December 2018**

| | £ |
|---|---|
| Goodwill | 8 |
| Inventory (£7 + £28) | 35 |
| Bank (£3 + £2) | 5 |
| | 48 |
| Share capital | 20 |
| Retained profits (P £18 + £4) | 22 |
| Non-controlling interest (shares £2 + retained profits £4): | 6 |
| | 48 |

If there had been a post-acquisition loss, then this would have been deducted from P's retained profits of £18 when the consolidated statement of financial position was drawn up.

## Learning outcomes

**You should now have learnt:**

1 Goodwill must be calculated on the basis of the fair values at the date of acquisition of the consideration given and the net assets acquired.

2 Once calculated, there is no point in recalculating the goodwill on an acquisition at a future date of the statement of financial position as the value determined will not alter.

3 Pre-acquisition reserves of a subsidiary are part of the capital acquired and are cancelled out on consolidation; they are not treated as reserves of the group.

4 Pre-acquisition reserves acquired are not available for distribution to the shareholders of the parent company.

5 The group's share of a subsidiary undertaking's post-acquisition profits and losses are included on consolidation with the reserves of the rest of the group.

6 The non-controlling interest amount does not distinguish between pre- and post-acquisition reserves.

## Answer to activity

18.1 The £5 reserves acquired by P on acquisition of S were not earned by P and do not represent profits made by P. As such, it would be inappropriate to distribute them in this way.

## Review questions

***Note*: In all these review questions, the share capital of all the companies comprises ordinary shares of £1 each.**

**18.1** Dad Ltd buys 100% of the shares of Daughter Ltd on 31 December 2015. The statements of financial position of the two companies on 31 December 2016 are as shown. You are to draw up a consolidated statement of financial position as at 31 December 2016.

**Dad Statement of Financial Position as at 31 December 2016**

| | £ | £ |
|---|---|---|
| Investment in subsidiary: | | |
| 80,000 shares bought 31.12.2015 | | 120,000 |
| Non-current assets | | 102,000 |
| Current assets | | 64,000 |
| | | 286,000 |
| Share capital | | 150,000 |
| Retained profits: | | |
| As at 31.12.2015 | 59,000 | |
| *Add* Profit for 2016 | 77,000 | |
| | | 136,000 |
| | | 286,000 |

**Daughter Statement of Financial Position as at 31 December**

| | £ | £ |
|---|---|---|
| Non-current assets | | 98,000 |
| Current assets | | 23,000 |
| | | 121,000 |
| Share capital | | 80,000 |
| Retained profits: | | |
| As at 31.12.2015 | 10,000 | |
| *Add* Profit for 2016 | 31,000 | |
| | | 41,000 |
| | | 121,000 |

**18.2** Parents Pleasure Ltd bought 60% of the shares of Triplet Enterprise Ltd on 31 March 2017. The statements of financial position of the two companies on 31 March 2018 are as follows. You are to draw up a consolidated statement of financial position as at 31 March 2018. The amounts shown in the statements of financial position are a correct reflection of the fair values.

**Parents Pleasure Statement of Financial Position as at 31 March 2018**

| | £ | £ |
|---|---|---|
| Investment in Triplet Enterprise Ltd: | | |
| 72,000 shares bought 31.3.2017 | | 101,000 |
| Non-current assets | | 230,000 |
| Current assets | | 61,000 |
| | | 392,000 |
| Share capital | | 260,000 |
| Retained profits: | | |
| As at 31.3.2017 | 52,000 | |
| *Add* Profit for 2018 | 57,000 | |
| | | 109,000 |
| General reserve | | 23,000 |
| | | 392,000 |

→

**Triplet Enterprise Statement of Financial Position as at 31 March 2018**

| | £ | £ |
|---|---|---|
| Non-current assets | | 99,000 |
| Current assets | | 14,000 |
| | | 113,000 |
| Share capital | | 80,000 |
| Retained profits: | | |
| As at 31.3.2017 | 24,000 | |
| *Less* Loss for 2018 | (17,000) | |
| | | 7,000 |
| General reserve (unchanged since 2014) | | 26,000 |
| | | 113,000 |

**18.3A** Parents Ltd bought 52% of the shares in Offspring Ltd on 31 October 2017. From the following statements of financial position you are to draw up the consolidated statement of financial position as at 31 October 2018.

**Papai Statement of Financial Position as at 31 October 2018**

| | £ | £ |
|---|---|---|
| Investment in Offspring Ltd: 46,800 shares | | 80,000 |
| Non-current assets | | 121,000 |
| Current assets | | 41,000 |
| | | 242,000 |
| Share capital | | 160,000 |
| Retained profits: | | |
| As at 31.10.2017 | 31,000 | |
| *Add* Profit for 2018 | 51,000 | |
| | | 82,000 |
| | | 242,000 |

**Offspring Statement of Financial Position as at 31 October 2018**

| | £ | £ |
|---|---|---|
| Non-current assets | | 103,000 |
| Current assets | | 23,000 |
| | | 126,000 |
| Share capital | | 90,000 |
| Retained profits: | | |
| As at 31.10.2017 | 9,000 | |
| *Add* Profit for 2018 | 7,000 | |
| | | 16,000 |
| General reserve (unchanged since 2017) | | 20,000 |
| | | 126,000 |

→

**18.4** Parental Dream Company Ltd buys shares in Sibling 1 and Sibling 2 on 31 December 2017. You are to draft the consolidated statement of financial position as at 31 December 2018 from the following:

**Parent Company Statement of Financial Position as at 31 December 2018**

| | £ | £ |
|---|---|---|
| Sibling 1: 120,000 shares | | 185,000 |
| Sibling 2: 50,000 shares | | 95,000 |
| Non-current assets | | 317,000 |
| Current assets | | 92,000 |
| | | 689,000 |
| Share capital | | 500,000 |
| Retained profits: | | |
| As at 31.12.2017 | 68,000 | |
| *Add* Profit for 2018 | 81,000 | |
| | | 149,000 |
| | | 40,000 |
| | | 689,000 |

**Sibling 1 Statement of Financial Position as at 31 December 2018**

| | £ | £ |
|---|---|---|
| Non-current assets | | 225,000 |
| Current assets | | 64,000 |
| | | 289,000 |
| Share capital | | 160,000 |
| Retained profits: | | |
| As at 31.12.2017 | 44,000 | |
| *Add* Profit for 2018 | 45,000 | |
| | | 89,000 |
| General reserve (same as 31.12.2017) | | 40,000 |
| | | 289,000 |

**Sibling 2 Statement of Financial Position as at 31 December 2018**

| | £ | £ |
|---|---|---|
| Non-current assets | | 61,000 |
| Current assets | | 14,000 |
| | | 75,000 |
| Share capital | | 50,000 |
| Retained profits: | | |
| As at 31.12.2017 | 12,000 | |
| *Less* Loss for 2018 | (9,000) | |
| | | 3,000 |
| General reserve (same as 31.12.2017) | | 22,000 |
| | | 75,000 |

**18.5A** Parent plc bought 40,000 shares in Subsidiary 1 Ltd and 27,000 shares in Subsidiary 2 Ltd on 31 December 2015. The following statements of financial position were drafted as at 31 December 2016. You are to draw up a consolidated statement of financial position as at 31 December 2016.

**Parent Statement of Financial Position as at 31 December 2016**

| | £ | £ |
|---|---|---|
| Investments in subsidiaries | | |
| Subsidiary 1 Ltd 60,000 shares | | 73,000 |
| Subsidiary 2 Ltd 40,000 shares | | 38,000 |
| Non-current assets | | 130,000 |
| Current assets | | 140,000 |
| | | 381,000 |
| Share capital | | 300,000 |
| Retained profits: | | |
| As at 31.12.2015 | 17,000 | |
| *Add* Profit for 2016 | 24,000 | |
| | | 41,000 |
| General reserve | | 40,000 |
| | | 381,000 |

**Subsidiary 1 Statement of Financial Position as at 31 December 2016**

| | £ | £ |
|---|---|---|
| Non-current assets | | 79,000 |
| Current assets | | 34,000 |
| | | 113,000 |
| Share capital | | 100,000 |
| Retained profits: | | |
| As at 31.12.2015 | 5,000 | |
| *Less* Loss for 2016 | (3,000) | |
| | | 2,000 |
| General reserve (as at 31.12.2015) | | 11,000 |
| | | 113,000 |

**Subsidiary 2 Statement of Financial Position as at 31 December 2016**

| | £ | £ |
|---|---|---|
| Non-current assets | | 49,600 |
| Current assets | | 24,800 |
| | | 74,400 |
| Share capital | | 50,000 |
| Retained profits: | | |
| As at 31.12.2015 | 6,000 | |
| *Add* Profit for 2016 | 8,400 | |
| | | 14,400 |
| General reserve (as at 31.12.2015) | | 10,000 |
| | | 74,000 |

→

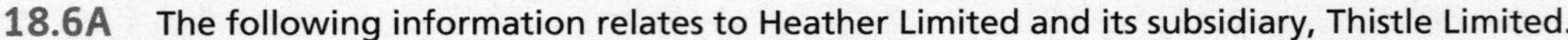

**18.6A** The following information relates to Heather Limited and its subsidiary, Thistle Limited.

1 *Heather Limited*
Retained profits as at 31 March 2018 £700,000.
80,000 ordinary shares were purchased in Thistle Limited on 1 April 2011 for £150,000.
2 *Thistle Limited*
Retained profits as at 1 April 2011 £50,000.
Retained profits as at 31 March 2018 £120,000.
There were no other capital or revenue account balances at either of these dates.
Issued share capital: 100,000 ordinary shares of £1 each.

**Required:**
Make the following calculations:

(*a*) the goodwill arising on the acquisition of Thistle Limited;
(*b*) the retained profits to be shown in the Heather Group statement of financial position as at 31 March 2018;
(*c*) the non-controlling interest in the Heather Group as at 31 March 2018.

(*Association of Accounting Technicians*)

chapter 19

# Intercompany dealings: indebtedness and unrealised profit in inventory

## Learning objectives

**After you have studied this chapter, you should be able to:**

- explain how to treat intra-group indebtedness upon consolidation
- explain how to treat unrealised intra-group profits upon consolidation

## Introduction

In this chapter, you'll learn how to deal with intra-group debts and unrealised profits in inventory sold between companies in a group, and so learn how to reduce the values shown in individual group financial statements so as to eliminate intra-group items prior to preparation of consolidated financial statements.

## 19.1 Intra-group debts

When a subsidiary owes money to its parent, the amount owing will be shown as a debtor in the parent's statement of financial position and as a creditor in the subsidiary's statement of financial position. IAS 24 (*Related party disclosures*) requires that such debtor and creditor balances are shown separately in the company statements of financial position from other accounts receivable and payable balances. When this type of situation exists it is really just 'two sides of the same coin'. That is, the debtor balance and the creditor balance of the two companies can be paired up and so cancel each other out when consolidated financial statements are prepared. As a result, neither amount is included in the consolidated financial statements.

The same treatment applies to debts owed by the parent to the subsidiary, or to debts owed by one subsidiary to another subsidiary. The treatment is exactly the same whether or not the subsidiary is 100% owned.

Let's look at an example (Exhibit 19.1).

**Exhibit 19.1 Where the subsidiary owes money to the parent**

**P Statement of Financial Position**

| | | £ | £ | £ |
|---|---|---|---|---|
| Investment in subsidiary: 10 shares | | | | 10 |
| Inventory | | | 13 | |
| Accounts receivable: | | | | |
| Owing from subsidiary | (A) | 4 | | |
| Other accounts receivable | | 7 | | |
| | | | 11 | |
| Bank | | | 1 | |
| | | | | 25 |
| | | | | 35 |
| Current liabilities: Accounts payable | | | | (9) |
| Net assets | | | | 26 |
| Share capital | | | | 20 |
| Retained profits | | | | 6 |
| | | | | 26 |

**S Statement of Financial Position**

| | | £ | £ |
|---|---|---|---|
| Inventory | | | 6 |
| Accounts receivable | | | 13 |
| Bank | | | 3 |
| | | | 22 |
| Current liabilities: Accounts payable | | | |
| Owing to parent | (B) | 4 | |
| Other accounts payable | | 8 | |
| | | | (12) |
| Net assets | | | 10 |
| Share capital | | | 10 |

**P & S Consolidated Statement of Financial Position**

| | £ |
|---|---|
| Inventory (£13 + £6) | 19 |
| Accounts receivable (£7 + £13) | 20 |
| Bank (£1 + £3) | 4 |
| | 43 |
| Accounts payable (£9 + £8) | (17) |
| Net assets | 26 |
| Share capital | 20 |
| Retained profits | 6 |
| | 26 |

## 19.2 Unrealised profit in inventory

Some companies in a group may not trade with each other. If so, the inventory held at the date of the statement of financial position will not include goods bought from another member of the group.

It is also possible that companies within a group may have traded with each other but, at the date of the statement of financial position, all such goods have been sold to individuals and organisations unconnected with the group. The result is that none of the companies in the group will have any such goods included in their year-end inventory.

However, when companies in a group have traded with each other, and one or more of the companies has inventory at the date of the statement of financial position which has been bought from another group member, adjustments to the inventory figure must be made before consolidation is carried out.

If the goods have been traded between members of the group at cost price, the goods would be included in the purchasing company's inventory in its statement of financial position. In this case, the consolidated statement of financial position will not be altered. Because the goods were transferred at cost price it would not be incorrect to add together all of the inventory figures in the group company statements of financial position and show the total in the consolidated statement of financial position, as the total will represent the total cost to the group of the unsold goods within the group.

However, goods are usually sold between companies within a group at prices above the original cost price paid by the selling company. If one or more of the companies in a group has goods in its inventory at the date of the statement of financial position which have been bought from another group member at above cost price, the goods would be included at the higher price in the purchasing company's inventory in its statement of financial position.

**If the amount at which the inventory is included in the statement of financial position of each company is the amount the inventory cost that company, why would the total derived not represent the total cost of the unsold goods within the group?**

When you have a situation like that described in Activity 19.1, you can't simply add together all of the inventory amounts in the group company statements of financial position and show the total in the consolidated statement of financial position. The total derived would not represent the total cost of the unsold goods held within the group because it would include the unrealised profit which the selling company added to the cost of the goods when it sold them to the other group company which has those goods in inventory at its statement of financial position date.

Suppose that the parent, P, owns all the shares in S, the subsidiary, and that P sold goods for £20 to S which had cost P £12. Also assume that S had sold none of these goods by the date of the statement of financial position. In the statement of financial position of S, the goods will be included in inventory at £20, while the profits made by P will include the £8 profit recorded in buying the goods for £12 and selling them for £20. Although this is a true reflection of what occurred from each company's point of view, it most certainly is not true from the perspective of the group. The goods have not passed to anyone outside the group. Therefore, the profit of £8 has not been realised by the group and so must be eliminated from both sets of financial statements before consolidation takes place.

**Why do you think this intra-group profit must be eliminated upon consolidation?**

If you are finding this difficult to understand, think back to when you were studying departmental accounts in *Frank Wood's Business Accounting 1* and what you needed to do when departments sold goods to each other at above or below cost.

**What could be the benefit to a group if companies within the group were to sell goods to other companies in the group at below cost?**

## 19.3 Realisation of profits

Going back to basic accounting concepts, the realisation concept states that profit should not be recognised until goods have been passed to the customer. You have just learnt that, as consolidated financial statements are concerned with an overall picture of a group, any profits on intra-group sales of goods that have not yet been sold to customers unconnected with the group are unearned and so must be eliminated before consolidation is performed. You saw an example of this in the previous section. Let's now consider some more complex examples.

If P had sold goods which had cost £12 to S, a 100% owned subsidiary, for £20, and S had sold $^3/_4$ of the goods for £22 by the date of the statement of financial position, the situation would obviously be different. P will have included a profit in its statement of profit or loss for these sales of £8. In addition, S will have shown a profit in its statement of profit or loss for the sales made of £7, i.e. £22 − $^3/_4$ of £20. The two statements of profit or loss show total profits of £8 + £7 = £15 on these goods.

However, looking at the group as a whole, these goods cost the group £12. Three-quarters of them have been sold to entities unconnected with the group, so that the cost of goods sold outside the group is $^3/_4$ of £12 = £9. As these were sold by S, the profit realised by the group is £22 − £9 = £13. This is £2 less than that shown by adding up the separate figures for each company in the group which, of course, is $^1/_4$ of the profit P charged S. (This is as you would expect because $^1/_4$ of the goods sold by P to S are still held in inventory by S.)

Thus, the group figures would be overstated by £2 if the separate figures were merely added together without any adjustment. In addition, the inventory would be overvalued by £2 if the inventory figures of the two companies were simply added together. The original cost to the group of the goods held in inventory by S was $^1/_4$ of £12 = £3. The adjustment needed in the consolidation process involves deducting £2 from the retained profits balance of P and £2 from the inventory of S. Doing so will remove the unrealised intra-group profits. This adjustment can be shown in tabular form as:

| | £ |
|---|---|
| (*a*) Cost of goods to P | 12 |
| (*b*) Sold to S for | 20 |
| (*c*) Sold by S, $^3/_4$ for | 22 |
| (*d*) Inventory of S at the statement of financial position date at cost to S $^1/_4$ of (*b*) | 5 |
| (*e*) Inventory of S at the statement of financial position date at cost to P $^1/_4$ of (*a*) | 3 |
| (*f*) Excess of S statement of financial position value of inventory over cost to group (*d*) − (*e*) | 2 |

(*g*) Profit shown in P statement of profit or loss (*b*) − (*a*) = £8
(*h*) Profit shown in S statement of profit or loss (*c*) £22 − $^3/_4$ of (*b*) = £7
(*i*) Profit shown in the statements of profit or loss of P and S = (*g*) + (*h*) = £15
(*j*) Actual profit made by the group dealing with outsiders (c) £22 less [$^3/_4$ of (*a*) £12] £9 = £13
(*k*) Profit recorded by individual companies exceeds profit made by the group's dealing with outsiders (*i*) − (*j*) = £2

This analysis confirms that the action needed before preparing the consolidated statement of financial position is to deduct (*f*) £2 from the combined inventory figure, and to deduct (*k*) £2 from the combined figure for retained profits.

Let's apply what you've just learnt by looking at another example.

## Exhibit 19.2 Where the inventory of one company includes goods bought from another company in the same group

**P Statement of Financial Position as at 31 December 2016**

| | | £ | £ |
|---|---|---|---|
| Investment in subsidiary: | | | |
| 10 shares bought 31.12.2015 | | | 16 |
| Inventory | | | 24 |
| Bank | | | 6 |
| | | | 46 |
| Share capital | | | 20 |
| Retained profits: | | | |
| As at 31.12.2015 | | 8 | |
| Profit for 2016 | (C) | 18 | |
| | | | 26 |
| | | | 46 |

**S Statement of Financial Position as at 31 December 2016**

| | | £ | £ |
|---|---|---|---|
| Inventory | (D) | | 22 |
| Bank | | | 3 |
| | | | 25 |
| Share capital | | | 10 |
| Retained profits: | | | |
| As at 31.12.2015 | | 6 | |
| Profit for 2016 | | 9 | |
| | | | 15 |
| | | | 25 |

During the year, P sold goods to S for £28. P paid £16 when it purchased the goods. The sale to S therefore resulted in a profit to P of £12. Of these goods, $^2/_3$ had been sold by S at the date of the statement of financial position. The inventory of S (D) therefore includes £4 unrealised profit ($^1/_3 \times$ £12). P's profit for the year of (C) £18 also includes £4 unrealised profit. When consolidating the two statements of financial position, £4 therefore needs to be deducted from each of those figures.

**P Consolidated Statement of Financial Position as at 31 December 2016**

| | £ |
|---|---|
| Inventory (S £22 − £4 + P £24) | 42 |
| Bank (P £6 + S £3) | 9 |
| | 51 |
| Share capital | 20 |
| Retained profits (S £9 + P £8 + £18 − £4) | 31 |
| | 51 |

*Note*: In Exhibit 19.2, the subsidiary was wholly owned by the parent. The final figures would have been exactly the same if the subsidiary had sold the goods to the parent instead of vice versa.

## 19.4 Partially owned subsidiaries and unrealised profits

In Exhibit 19.2 the subsidiary was 100% controlled and the unrealised profit in inventory was £4. A few years ago there were three possible methods of dealing with the adjustments needed – two of the methods took into account the actual percentage of shares owned. However, IAS 27 (*Separate financial statements*) requires that intra-group profits or losses are eliminated in full. As a result, those two proportional elimination methods can no longer be used.

This means that if in Exhibit 19.2 S had been 75% owned by P, the full intra-group profit of £4 would still be deducted from the inventory amount in the consolidated statement of financial position, and the full £4 would also be deducted from the retained profits of P when it is consolidated.

Why do you think the rules were changed?

### Learning outcomes

**You should now have learnt:**

1. Intra-group indebtedness must be eliminated upon consolidation, irrespective of the proportion of the holding in the subsidiary undertaking(s) involved.
2. Unrealised intra-group profits must be eliminated upon consolidation, irrespective of the proportion of the holding in the subsidiary undertaking(s) involved.

### Answers to activities

**19.1** Because the original cost when they were first purchased by a group company was lower. For example, imagine S1 bought £10 of goods from a company that was not part of the group and then sold them to S2 for £12. At the end of the accounting period, S2 still had all those goods in inventory so its inventory figure in the statement of financial position is £12, which is £2 more than the goods cost the group.

**19.2** If it wasn't eliminated, groups could show far greater profits than they are actually making. For example, imagine S1 bought £10 of goods from a company that was not part of the group and then sold them to S2 for £12. At the end of the accounting period, S2 still had all those goods in inventory so its inventory figure in the statement of financial position is £12. S1 would include a profit of £2 on these goods in its profit for the period. S2 would include the £12 in its purchases and in its closing inventory, resulting in no effect upon its profit. On consolidation, the group would include the £2 profit made by S1 in the group profit for the period.

**19.3** They could show far less profits by selling within the group at below cost, so delaying paying tax on some of their profits for a further 12 months.

**19.4** By definition, subsidiaries are members of a group because the parent company can control them. Unscrupulous parent companies could, therefore, require less than 100% subsidiaries to purchase goods at above or below cost from other companies in the group and could require them not to sell those goods. Before the rules were tightened up, this power could be abused to manipulate profits of the group, as the non-controlling interest share of the profits or losses could have been included in the profits or losses of the subsidiary and thus the group, making the group appear more or less profitable than it actually was. The change made eliminated the possibility of including such unrealised profits and losses in the consolidated financial statements.

## Review questions

***Note*: Unless otherwise indicated, the share capital of the companies in these review questions comprises ordinary shares of £1 each.**

**19.1** Prepare a consolidated statement of financial position from the following details as at 31 March 2016.

**Parent Statement of Financial Position as at 31 March 2016**

| | £ | £ |
|---|---|---|
| Non-current assets | | |
| Investment in subsidiary: 84,000 shares bought 31.3.2015 | | 140,000 |
| Other non-current assets | | 220,000 |
| | | 360,000 |
| Inventory | 47,000 | |
| Accounts receivable | 34,000 | |
| Bank | 11,000 | |
| | | 92,000 |
| | | 452,000 |
| Accounts payable | | (7,000) |
| | | 445,000 |
| Share capital | | 320,000 |
| Retained profits: | | |
| As at 31.3.2015 | 65,000 | |
| Profit for 2016 | 48,000 | |
| | | 113,000 |
| General reserve | | 12,000 |
| | | 445,000 |

**Subsidiary Statement of Financial Position as at 31 March 2016**

| | £ | £ |
|---|---|---|
| Non-current assets | | 208,000 |
| Inventory | | 30,000 |
| Accounts receivable | | 22,000 |
| Bank | | 8,000 |
| | | 268,000 |
| Current liabilities: Accounts payable | | (12,000) |
| | | 256,000 |
| Share capital | | 84,000 |
| Retained profits: | | |
| As at 31.3.2015 | 40,000 | |
| Profit for 2016 | 132,000 | |
| | | 172,000 |
| | | 256,000 |

During the year, Parent sold goods which had cost £2,300 to Subsidiary for £2,900. None of these goods had been sold by the date of the statement of financial position.

At the date of the statement of financial position Parent owes Subsidiary £3,600.

→

**19.2** Draw up a consolidated statement of financial position as at 31 December 2017 from the following:

**Mum and Dad's Statement of Financial Position as at 31 December 2017**

| | £ | £ |
|---|---|---|
| Non-current assets | | |
| Investment in subsidiary: 90,000 shares bought 31.12.2016 | | 135,000 |
| Other non-current assets | | 170,000 |
| | | 305,000 |
| Inventory | 37,000 | |
| Accounts receivable | 46,000 | |
| Bank | 13,000 | |
| | | 96,000 |
| | | 401,000 |
| Current liabilities: Accounts payable | | (11,000) |
| | | 390,000 |
| Share capital | | 260,000 |
| Retained profits: | | |
| As at 31.12.2016 | 172,000 | |
| *Less* Loss for 2017 | (42,000) | 130,000 |
| | | 390,000 |

**Daughter's Statement of Financial Position as at 31 December 2017**

| | £ | £ |
|---|---|---|
| Non-current assets | | 60,000 |
| Inventory | 55,000 | |
| Accounts receivable | 64,000 | |
| Bank | 4,000 | |
| | | 123,000 |
| | | 183,000 |
| Current liabilities: Accounts payable | | (7,000) |
| | | 176,000 |
| | | 100,000 |
| Share capital | | |
| Retained profits: | | |
| As at 31.12.2016 | 50,000 | |
| Profit for 2017 | 26,000 | |
| | | 76,000 |
| | | 176,000 |

At the date of the statement of financial position, Daughter Ltd owes Mum and Dad £2,200.

During the year Mum and Dad sold goods which had cost £5,000 to Daughter Ltd for £7,000. Four-fifths of these goods had been sold by Daughter Ltd by the date of the statement of financial position.

The amount paid for the investment in Daughter Ltd was £135,000. The fair value of the net assets of Daughter Ltd at that time was £150,000 and the £15,000 gain from a bargain purchase was recognised immediately in Mum and Dad's profit or loss.

**19.3** Prepare a consolidated statement of financial position from the following details as at 31 March 2016.

**Parents for Siblings Statement of Financial Position as at 31 March 2016**

| | £ | £ |
|---|---|---|
| Non-current assets | | |
| Investment in subsidiaries: | | |
| Sibling A 50,000 shares bought 31.3.2015 | | 76,000 |
| Sibling B 45,000 shares bought 31.3.2016 | | 58,000 |
| | | 134,000 |
| Other non-current assets | | 82,000 |
| Current assets | | 216,000 |
| Inventory | 31,000 | |
| Accounts receivable | 14,000 | |
| Bank | 7,000 | |
| | | 52,000 |
| | | 268,000 |
| Current liabilities: Accounts payable | | (11,000) |
| | | 257,000 |
| Share capital | | 175,000 |
| Retained profits: | | |
| As at 31.3.2015 | 47,000 | |
| *Add* Profit for 2016 | 15,000 | |
| | | 62,000 |
| General reserve | | 20,000 |
| | | 257,000 |

**Sibling A Statement of Financial Position as at 31 March 2016**

| | £ | £ |
|---|---|---|
| Non-current assets | | 39,000 |
| Inventory | 18,000 | |
| Accounts receivable | 9,000 | |
| Bank | 2,000 | |
| | | 29,000 |
| | | 68,000 |
| Current liabilities: Accounts payable | | (4,000) |
| | | 64,000 |
| Share capital | | 50,000 |
| Retained profits: | | |
| As at 31.3.2015 | 17,000 | |
| *Less* Loss for 2016 | (12,000) | |
| | | 5,000 |
| General reserve (as at 31.3.2015) | | 9,000 |
| | | 64,000 |

→

**Sibling B Statement of Financial Position as at 31 March 2016**

| | £ | £ |
|---|---|---|
| Non-current assets | | 54,000 |
| Inventory | 13,000 | |
| Accounts receivable | 16,000 | |
| Bank | 5,000 | |
| | | 34,000 |
| | | 88,000 |
| Current liabilities: Accounts payable | | (8,000) |
| | | 80,000 |
| Share capital | | 50,000 |
| Retained profits: | | |
| As at 31.3.2015 | 11,000 | |
| *Add* Profit for 2016 | 19,000 | |
| | | 30,000 |
| | | 80,000 |

At the date of the statement of financial position, Sibling B owed Sibling A £1,000 and Parents for Siblings owed Sibling B £1,500.

During the year, Parents for Siblings had sold to Sibling A for £3,220 goods costing £2,500. Of these goods, 1/3 had been sold by the year end. Parents for Siblings had also sold goods costing £700 to Sibling B for £1,050, of which none had been sold by the year end.

The amount paid for the investment in Sibling A was £65,000. The fair value of the net assets of Sibling A at that date was £76,000 and the £11,000 gain from a bargain purchase was recognised immediately in Parents for Siblings profit or loss.

**19.4A** You are presented with the following information from the Seneley group of companies for the year to 30 September 2016:

| | *Seneley plc* | *Lowe Ltd* | *Wright Ltd* |
|---|---|---|---|
| | *£000* | *£000* | *£000* |
| *Non-current assets* | | | |
| Tangible non-current assets | 225 | 300 | 220 |
| Investments | | | |
| Shares in group companies: | | | |
| Lowe Ltd | 450 | – | – |
| Wright Ltd | 182 | – | – |
| | 632 | – | – |
| Total non-current assets | 857 | 300 | 220 |
| *Current assets* | | | |
| Inventory | 225 | 150 | 45 |
| Accounts receivable | 240 | 180 | 50 |
| Cash at bank and in hand | 50 | 10 | 5 |
| | 515 | 340 | 100 |
| Total assets | 1,372 | 640 | 320 |
| *Current liabilities* | | | |
| Trade accounts payable | (320) | (90) | (70) |
| Net assets | 1,052 | 550 | 250 |
| *Equity* | | | |
| Called-up share capital | 800 | 400 | 200 |
| Retained profits | 252 | 150 | 50 |
| | 1,052 | 550 | 250 |

*Additional information*:

(*a*) The authorised, issued and fully paid share capital of all three companies consists of £1 ordinary shares.

(*b*) Seneley purchased 320,000 shares in Lowe Ltd on 1 October 2013, when Lowe's retained profits balance stood at £90,000.

(c) Seneley purchased 140,000 shares in Wright Ltd on 1 October 2015 for £130,000, when Wright's retained profits balance stood at £60,000. The £52,000 gain from a bargain purchase was recognised immediately in Seneley's profit or loss.

(d) During the year to 30 September 2016, Lowe had sold goods to Wright for £15,000. These goods had cost Lowe £7,000, and Wright still had half of these goods in inventory as at 30 September 2016.

(e) Included in the respective trade accounts payable and trade accounts receivable balances as at 30 September 2016 were the following intercompany debts:
- Seneley owed Wright £5,000
- Lowe owed Seneley £20,000
- Wright owed Lowe £25,000.

**Required:**
Prepare the Seneley group's consolidated statement of financial position as at 30 September 2016. Your workings should be submitted.

(*Association of Accounting Technicians*)

**19.5A** You are to draw up a consolidated statement of financial position as at 31 December 2018 from the following:

**Pa and Mum Statement of Financial Position as at 31 December 2018**

| | £ | £ |
|---|---|---|
| Investment in subsidiaries: | | |
| Son 1 90,000 shares bought 31.12.2017 | | 125,000 |
| Son 2 56,000 shares bought 31.12.2017 | | 85,000 |
| | | 210,000 |
| Other non-current assets | | 170,000 |
| | | 380,000 |
| Current assets | | |
| Inventory | 43,000 | |
| Accounts receivable | 38,000 | |
| Bank | 17,000 | |
| | | 98,000 |
| Total assets | | 478,000 |
| Current liabilities: Accounts payable | | (16,000) |
| | | 462,000 |
| Share capital | | 325,000 |
| Retained profits: | | |
| As at 31.12.2017 | 53,000 | |
| *Less* Loss for 2018 | (16,000) | |
| | | 37,000 |
| General reserve (as at 31.12.2017) | | 100,000 |
| | | 462,000 |

**Son 1 Statement of Financial Position as at 31 December 2018**

| | £ | £ |
|---|---|---|
| Non-current assets | | 72,000 |
| Inventory | 34,000 | |
| Accounts receivable | 21,000 | |
| Bank | 18,000 | |
| | | 73,000 |
| | | 145,000 |
| Current liabilities: Accounts payable | | (6,000) |
| | | 139,000 |
| Share capital | | 90,000 |
| Retained profits: | | |
| As at 31.12.2017 | 23,000 | |
| *Add* Profit for 2018 | 26,000 | |
| | | 49,000 |
| | | 139,000 |

→

**Son 2 Statement of Financial Position as at 31 December 2017**

| | £ | £ |
|---|---|---|
| Non-current assets | | 80,000 |
| Inventory | 24,000 | |
| Accounts receivable | 26,000 | |
| Bank | 13,000 | |
| | | 63,000 |
| | | 143,000 |
| Current liabilities: Accounts payable | | (8,000) |
| | | 135,000 |
| Share capital | | 100,000 |
| Retained profits: | | |
| As at 31.12.2017 | 27,000 | |
| *Less* Loss for 2018 | (4,000) | |
| | | 23,000 |
| General reserve (as at 31.12.2017) | | 12,000 |
| | | 135,000 |

At the date of the statement of financial position, Son 1 owed Pa and Mum £2,500 and Son 2 £1,100, and Pa and Mum owed Son 2 £2,100.

Pa and Mum had sold goods which had cost £1,400 to Son 2 for £2,100, and of these goods ½ had been sold by Son 2 by the year end.

**19.6** The following summarised information relates to the Pagg group of companies.

**Statement of Financial Position at 31 March 2017**

| | *Pagg plc* £000 | *Ragg Ltd* £000 | *Tagg Ltd* £000 |
|---|---|---|---|
| Non-current assets | | | |
| Tangible assets at net book value | 2,000 | 900 | 600 |
| *Investments* | | | |
| 800,000 ordinary shares in Ragg Ltd | 2,570 | – | – |
| 300,000 ordinary shares in Tagg Ltd | 968 | – | – |
| | 3,538 | – | – |
| Total non-current assets | 5,538 | 900 | 600 |
| *Current assets* | | | |
| Inventory | 1,300 | 350 | 100 |
| Debtors | 3,000 | 200 | 300 |
| Cash | 200 | 20 | 50 |
| | 4,500 | 570 | 450 |
| Total assets | 10,038 | 1,470 | 1,050 |
| Current liabilities: Accounts payable | (4,000) | (270) | (400) |
| | 6,038 | 1,200 | 650 |
| *Capital and reserves* | | | |
| Called-up share capital (all ordinary shares of £1 each) | 5,500 | 1,000 | 500 |
| Retained profits | 538 | 200 | 150 |
| | 6,038 | 1,200 | 650 |

*Additional information*:

1 Pagg acquired its shareholding in Ragg Ltd for £3,000 on 1 April 2012. Ragg's retained profits balance at that time was £600,000. Goodwill arising was £1,720.
2 The shares in Tagg Ltd were acquired on 1 April 2016 for £1,000 when Tagg's retained profits balance was £100,000. Goodwill arising was £640.
3 Impairment reviews of the goodwill amounts as required by IAS 38 have reduced the investments to the amounts shown above.
4 At 31 March 2017, Ragg had in inventory goods purchased from Tagg at a cost to Ragg of £60,000. These goods had been invoiced by Tagg at cost plus 20%.
5 Intercompany debts at 31 March 2017 were as follows: Pagg owed Ragg £200,000 and Ragg owed Tagg £35,000.

**Required:**
In so far as the information permits, prepare the Pagg group of companies' consolidated statement of financial position as at 31 March 2017 in accordance with the relevant accounting standards.

*Note*: Formal notes to the accounts are NOT required, although detailed working must be submitted with your answer.

(*Association of Chartered Certified Accountants*)

**19.7A** You are presented with the following summarised information relating to Block plc for the year to 30 September 2018:

| | *Block plc* | *Chip Ltd* | *Knot Ltd* |
|---|---|---|---|
| | *£000* | *£000* | *£000* |
| Non-current assets and equipment | 8,900 | 3,240 | 2,280 |
| *Investments* | | | |
| Shares in group companies: | | | |
| Chip Ltd | 2,560 | – | – |
| Knot Ltd | 1,600 | – | – |
| | 4,160 | – | – |
| Total non-current assets | 13,060 | 3,240 | 2,280 |
| *Current assets* | | | |
| Inventory | 300 | 160 | 80 |
| Trade accounts receivable | 1,600 | 130 | 50 |
| Cash at bank and in hand | 400 | 110 | 120 |
| | 2,300 | 400 | 250 |
| Current liabilities: Accounts payable | (300) | (140) | (130) |
| Net assets | 15,060 | 3,500 | 2,400 |
| *Capital and reserves* | | | |
| Called-up share capital (ordinary shares of £1 each) | 10,000 | 3,000 | 2,000 |
| Retained profits | 5,060 | 500 | 400 |
| | 15,060 | 3,500 | 2,400 |

*Additional information*:

1 Block purchased 80% of the share capital of Chip on 1 October 2013 for £2,500,000 when Chip's retained profits balance was £200,000 credit. The gain from a bargain purchase of £60,000 was recognised immediately in Block's profit or loss.

2 On 1 October 2017 Block purchased 60% of the share capital of Knot. Knot's retained profits balance at that date was £500,000 credit.

3 During the year to 30 September 2018, Block sold goods costing £200,000 to Chip for £300,000. Half of these goods remained in inventory at the year end.

4 Intercompany debts at the year end were as follows:

| | *£000* |
|---|---|
| Chip owed Block | 20 |
| Knot owed Chip | 30 |

**Required:**

Prepare the Block plc group of companies' consolidated statement of financial position as at 30 September 2018. Formal notes to the accounts are NOT required, although detailed working should be submitted with your answer.

(*Association of Chartered Certified Accountants*)

chapter 20

# Consolidated financial statements: acquisition of shares in subsidiaries at different dates

## Learning objectives

**After you have studied this chapter, you should be able to:**

- calculate goodwill when an interest in a subsidiary undertaking was acquired in blocks over a period of time
- calculate goodwill when a subsidiary undertaking was acquired part-way through its reporting period

## Introduction

In this chapter, you'll learn how to deal with piecemeal acquisitions, i.e. those situations where a subsidiary is acquired through a series of transactions. You will also learn how to calculate goodwill and pre-acquisition profits when a subsidiary is acquired part-way through its reporting period. In order to focus on the principles involved, we will use the threshold of ownership of over 50% of the share capital acquired to determine when the acquired company becomes a subsidiary.

## 20.1 Shares bought at different dates

Up to this point, in all our examples, the shares in subsidiaries have all been bought at one point in time for each company. However, it is a simple fact that shares are often bought in blocks at different times, and that the earlier purchases may not give the buyer a controlling interest. This is known as 'acquisition in stages' or 'piecemeal acquisition'.

There used to be two possible methods of calculating pre-acquisition profits, and therefore goodwill. However, IFRS 3 (*Business combinations*) states that only one method should be used, and this is the method used in this book. IFRS 3 requires that the consolidation be based on the fair values at the date the undertaking actually becomes a subsidiary, even though the acquisition has been made in stages. Any previously held interest is valued at its fair value when control is achieved and any resulting gains or losses are recognised in profit or loss.

However, goodwill arising on each transaction which together achieved control may also be calculated (there is more on this topic in Section 26.9).

**Activity 20.1** Why do you think this may be done – is there any benefit in calculating goodwill on these pre-control investments?

Let's look at an example of a piecemeal acquisition.

A company, S, has an issued share capital of 100 ordinary shares of £1 each. The only reserve of S is the balance of retained profits which was £50 on 31 December 2014, and two years later on 31 December 2016, it was £80. P buys 20 shares on 31 December 2014 for £36, and a further 40 shares on 31 December 2016 for £79. The date that S became a subsidiary was therefore 31 December 2016. The calculation of goodwill on acquisition is:

| | £ |
|---|---|
| Fair value of consideration given for controlling interest | 79 |
| Fair value of previously held interest | 36 |
| | 115 |
| Non-controlling interest (40% × £180) | 72 |
| | 187 |
| *Less* Fair value of net assets | (180) |
| Goodwill | 7 |

When the fair value of the initial investment of 20% is calculated on 31.12.2016 it is £36, which is what it cost, resulting in no entry being required to profit or loss.

Had the original investment cost £34, not £36, and P showed it at a value of £34 in its statement of financial position when it purchased the other 40% on 31.12.2016, there would be a £2 gain on the initial purchase. That gain would be taken to profit or loss and the initial investment would be restated at its fair value of £36 (i.e. 20% × £180) on 31.12.2016 in order to calculate the goodwill on the date control was achieved.

## 20.2 Shares bought during a reporting period

In addition, it has been conveniently assumed so far that all shares have been bought on exactly the last day of a reporting period. In reality, this is seldom the case. Most shares are bought part-way through a reporting period. Unless specially audited financial statements are drawn up as at the date of acquisition, there is no up-to-date figure for reserves as at the date of acquisition. As this amount is needed for the calculation of goodwill, some other method must be used to obtain it.

The approach adopted is that the reserves balance according to the last statement of financial position before the acquisition of the shares is taken, and an addition made (or deduction, if a loss) corresponding to the proportion of the year's profits that had been earned before acquisition took place. This is then taken as the figure of pre-acquisition profits for goodwill and capital reserve calculations.

Let's look at an example.

## Exhibit 20.1 Calculation of pre-acquisition profits, and goodwill, where the shares are bought part-way through a reporting period

P bought 20 of the 30 issued ordinary shares of S for £49 on 30 September 2018. The financial statements for S are drawn up annually to 31 December. The statement of financial position of S as at 31 December 2017 showed a balance of retained profits of £24. The statement of profit or loss of S for the year ending 31 December 2018 disclosed a profit of £12.

| | £ | £ |
|---|---|---|
| Shares bought | | 20 |
| Retained profits: | | |
| Balance at 31.12.2017 | 24 | |
| *Add* Proportion of 2018 profits before acquisition $^{9}/_{12} \times$ £12 | 9 | |
| | 33 | |
| Proportion of pre-acquisition profits | | |
| 20 shares owned out of 30, $^{2}/_{3} \times$ £33 | | 22 |
| | | 42 |

Paid for shares £49
Therefore goodwill is £49 − £42 = £7

*Note*: It may seem odd but, despite its name, goodwill is something parent entities seek to avoid. When, on the date of acquisition, goodwill is nil or a gain from a bargain purchase is identified, this is 'good'. The parent has done well. If goodwill on that date is positive, the parent has paid more than the net assets are worth. Put bluntly, this is 'bad'. Of course, parent entities do not acquire subsidiaries without reason. Goodwill will be considered 'acceptable' by the parent entity that allows it to arise. Future foreseen benefits make it seem worthwhile. Nevertheless, such future benefits carry risk of non-arrival. Hence, goodwill is not something a parent entity seeks. Goodwill can be a major element of the consideration paid. One recent study of UK plc acquisitions found that goodwill was, on average, 80& of the total consideration paid.

## Learning outcomes

**You should now have learnt:**

1 When an interest in a subsidiary is acquired in blocks over a period of time, goodwill is calculated as if all the blocks had been purchased at the date when control was achieved. However, goodwill may also be calculated at each purchase so that the pattern of its creation can be identified. It also has to be calculated when an entity invests in an associate accounted for using equity accounting.

2 When a subsidiary is acquired part-way through its reporting period, in the absence of specially audited financial statements, the proportion of profit (or loss) applicable to that part of the financial period that preceded the acquisition date should be treated as being part of the pre-acquisition reserves for the calculation of goodwill upon consolidation.

## Answer to activity

20.1 The subsidiary was actually acquired only when control passed to the parent company. As goodwill is to be calculated when that happens, it could be considered to be inappropriate to calculate parts of it at an earlier date. However, failure to calculate fair values of the net assets acquired and the goodwill arising each time the shareholding was increased would result in the true make-up of the final goodwill (i.e. the overall goodwill at the date of acquisition) not being known. By calculating goodwill after each transaction, it can be seen when each element of the overall goodwill arose. This might be useful, for example, if goodwill had dropped on the final transaction (good) or had suddenly risen (bad). Remember, goodwill is something a parent wishes to avoid. In addition, goodwill must be calculated when associates (not subsidiaries) are accounted for using equity accounting – see Section 26.8.

## Review questions

**20.1** On 31 March 2016, Sonny Ltd had issued share capital of 80,000 ordinary £1 shares and reserves of £48,000. Two years later, the reserves had risen to £72,000 but the share capital was unchanged. Pops Ltd purchased shares in Sonny Ltd: (i) 20,000 shares on 31 March 2016 for £51,200 and (ii) 28,800 shares on 31 March 2018 for £46,400. Calculate the figure for goodwill that will appear in the consolidated statement of financial position as at 31 March 2018 and identify the pattern of its creation.

**20.2A** On 31 October 2014, its date of the statement of financial position, Daughters Ahead Ltd had issued share capital of 840,000 ordinary £1 shares and reserves of £476,000. Four years later, the share capital is unchanged but the reserves have risen to £588,000. Parent Ltd purchased 210,000 shares in Daughters Ahead Ltd on 31 October 2014 for £364,000. On 31 October 2018, it paid £910,000 for another 420,000 shares. Calculate the goodwill to be shown in the consolidated statement of financial position as at 31 October 2018 and the pattern of its creation.

**20.3** Dad and Mum Ltd bought 84,000 of the 168,000 issued ordinary £1 shares of Child Ltd for £280,000 on 31 July 2017. The Child Ltd financial statements are drawn up annually to 31 December. The statement of financial position of Child Ltd on 31 December 2016 showed a balance of retained profits of £56,000. The statement of profit or loss of Child Ltd for the year ending 31 December 2017 showed a profit of £100,800. No other reserves appear in either statement of financial position. Calculate the figure for the goodwill to be shown in the consolidated statement of financial position as at 31 December 2017.

**20.4A** On 1 January 2018, Offspring and Co Ltd had an issued share capital of 360,000 ordinary £1 shares. The balance of retained profit was £36,000 and there was also a general reserve of £28,800. During the year ended 31 December 2018, Offspring and Co Ltd made a profit of £43,200, none of which was distributed. Father Ltd bought 315,000 shares on 1 April 2018 for £432,000. Calculate the figure of goodwill to be shown in the consolidated statement of financial position as at 31 December 2018.

chapter

# 21 Intra-group dividends

## Learning objectives

**After you have studied this chapter, you should be able to:**

- explain how to treat intra-group dividends
- explain how to treat dividends from a newly acquired subsidiary undertaking that were proposed prior to the acquisition date
- explain how to treat dividends proposed by subsidiary undertakings at the date of the statement of financial position

## Introduction

In this chapter, you'll learn how to treat dividends that have been received from a subsidiary and dividends that have been proposed by a subsidiary but not received at the end of the accounting period. You'll learn how to deal with dividends paid by a subsidiary out of pre-acquisition profits as compared with dividends paid by a subsidiary out of post-acquisition profits. You will also learn how to treat dividends proposed by a subsidiary at the acquisition date. Finally, you will learn how to treat dividends paid by non-wholly-owned subsidiaries.

## 21.1 Dividends paid from post-acquisition profits

Intra-group dividends are dividends paid by one member of a group to another, i.e. from one company in the group to another in the same group. They will, therefore, be shown in the receiving company's statement of profit or loss as finance activity income, with a subsequent increase in the bank balance. From the point of view of the paying company's financial statements, the dividend will appear as a transfer from distributable reserves in its statement of changes in equity. Also, when paid, there will be a reduction in the bank balance of that company.

If the dividend has been proposed, but not paid by the end of the accounting period, the proposed dividend appears only as a note to the statement of profit or loss of the company intending to make the payment. It does not appear anywhere in the notes or financial statements of the recipient company. No set-off is required, therefore, on dividends proposed.

**Activity 21.1**

What would be the impact upon the consolidated financial statements if the dividend had been paid before the end of the subsidiary's accounting period rather than simply being proposed?

## 21.2 Dividends paid from pre-acquisition profits

In Chapter 18, you learnt of the company law principle that dividends should not be paid out of capital. To prevent this from happening, any pre-acquisition profits are capitalised and brought into the goodwill calculation. A company cannot circumvent the principle by buying the shares of a company, part of the purchase price being for the reserves of the subsidiary, and then utilising those reserves by paying itself dividends, and consequently adding those dividends to its own profits and then declaring an increased dividend itself. The next two exhibits illustrate this. Exhibit 21.1 shows an example of dividends paid from post-acquisition profits. Exhibit 21.2 shows what occurs when dividends are paid from pre-acquisition profits.

As in previous chapters, to simplify things, we'll show retained profit adjustments including dividends paid as deductions from retained profits on the face of the statement of financial position. In 'real life', they would only be shown in the statement of changes in equity in the published financial statements. However, statements of financial position drawn up for internal use could be presented in the way shown in these examples.

### Exhibit 21.1 Dividends paid from post-acquisition profits

P buys 100% of the shares of S on 31 December 2017. In 2018, S pays a dividend of 50% to P. To simplify matters, the dividend is declared for 2018 and paid in 2018.

**P Statement of Financial Position as at 31 December 2017**

| | £ |
|---|---|
| Investment in subsidiary: | |
| 10 shares bought 31.12.2017 | 23 |
| Inventory | 3 |
| Bank | 1 |
| | 27 |
| Share capital | 20 |
| Retained profits | 7 |
| | 27 |

**S Statement of Financial Position as at 31 December 2017**

| | £ |
|---|---|
| Inventory | 16 |
| Bank | 6 |
| | 22 |
| Share capital | 10 |
| Retained profits | 12 |
| | 22 |

**Consolidated Statement of Financial Position as at 31 December 2017**
(immediately after acquisition)

| | £ |
|---|---|
| Goodwill (P £23 − S £10 − S £12) | 1 |
| Inventory | 19 |
| Bank (P £1 + S £6) | 7 |
| | 27 |
| Share capital | 20 |
| Retained profits | 7 |
| | 27 |

This consolidated statement of financial position was drafted immediately after acquisition of S by P. The following statements of financial position show the position one year later. Remember, the calculation of goodwill does not alter.

One year later, the statements of financial position are as follows:

**P Statement of Financial Position as at 31 December 2018**

| | £ | £ |
|---|---|---|
| Investment in subsidiary: | | |
| 10 shares bought 31.12.2017 | | 23 |
| Inventory | | 11 |
| Bank | | 1 |
| | | 35 |
| Share capital | | 20 |
| Retained profits: | | |
| As at 31.12.2017 | 7 | |
| *Add* Profit for 2018 (including dividend of £5 from S) | 8 | |
| | | 15 |
| | | 35 |

**S Statement of Financial Position as at 31 December 2018**

| | £ | £ |
|---|---|---|
| Inventory | | 19 |
| Bank | | 7 |
| | | 26 |
| Share capital | | 10 |
| Retained profits: | | |
| As at 31.12.2017 | 12 | |
| Profit for 2018 | 9 | |
| | 21 | |
| *Less* Dividend paid (to P) | (5) | |
| | | 16 |
| | | 26 |

To assess whether a dividend is paid out of pre- or post-acquisition reserves, we use the LEFO principle: **L**ast profits **E**arned are **F**irst profits **O**ut. The dividend of £5, therefore, has been paid out of profits made since the acquisition by P. The dividend, therefore, can be treated as being from post-acquisition profits and, therefore, can be shown in the statement of profit or loss of P as finance activity income, so increasing the profits of P available for dividend purposes.

**Consolidated Statement of Financial Position as at 31 December 2018**

| | £ |
|---|---|
| Goodwill (£23 − £10 − £12) | 1 |
| Inventory (P £11 + S £19) | 30 |
| Bank (P £1 + S £7) | 8 |
| | 39 |
| Share capital | 20 |
| Retained profits: | |
| [P £7 + £8 + S(£16 − £12 =) £4] | 19 |
| | 39 |

## Exhibit 21.2 Dividends paid from pre-acquisition profits

Once again, P buys 100% of the shares of S on 31 December 2017 and S pays a dividend for 2018 of 50% to P during 2018. However, in this case, S makes neither a profit nor a loss in 2018.

The statements of financial position at 31 December 2017 are obviously the same as in Exhibit 21.1. However, the statements of financial position a year later are now:

**P Statement of Financial Position as at 31 December 2018**

| | £ | £ |
|---|---|---|
| Investment in subsidiary: | | |
| (£23 originally calculated less dividend from pre-acquisition profits £5) | | 18 |
| Inventory | | 11 |
| Bank | | 1 |
| | | 30 |
| Share capital | | 20 |
| Retained profits: | | |
| As at 31.12.2017 | 7 | |
| *Add* Profit for 2018 (does not include the dividend from S) | 3 | |
| | | 10 |
| | | 30 |

**S Statement of Financial Position as at 31 December 2018**

| | £ | £ |
|---|---|---|
| Inventory | | 15 |
| Bank | | 2 |
| | | 17 |
| Share capital | | 10 |
| Retained profits: | | |
| As at 31.12.2017 | 12 | |
| *Add* Profit for 2018* | 0 | |
| | 12 | |
| *Less* Dividend paid (to P) | (5) | |
| | | 7 |
| | | 17 |

***For simplicity, the profit of S for 2018 is taken as being exactly nil.**

**Consolidated Statement of Financial Position as at 31 December 2018**

| | £ |
|---|---|
| Goodwill | 1 |
| Inventory | 26 |
| Bank | 3 |
| | 30 |
| Share capital | 20 |
| Retained profits | 10 |
| | 30 |

**When a dividend is paid by a subsidiary out of pre-acquisition profits it is, in fact, a return of capital to the parent company.** Accordingly, the dividend is deducted from the original cost of the investment – it is a return of the purchase money – rather than being treated as finance activity income of the holding company.

**Note: Examiners are always trying to identify the better candidates and award them marks to match their abilities. A common 'trick' used by some examiners is to treat the receipt of dividends paid from pre-acquisition reserves as finance activity income instead of treating the income as a refund of capital. Thus, the examiner's statement of financial position of P as at 31 December 2018 in Exhibit 21.2 would have read 'Retained profits £15' instead of 'Retained profits £10', and the investment would be shown as £23 instead of £18. The examiner wants the candidate to demonstrate an awareness of the error in the statement of financial position by adjusting it to show the correct amounts before proceeding with the consolidation of the statements of financial position of P and S.**

## 21.3 Dividends proposed at date of acquisition of shares

Sometimes when a company is acquired, it has already proposed but not yet paid a dividend. As a result, the new parent will receive the dividend even though it was paid from profits earned before acquisition took place. Clearly, the dividend is from pre-acquisition reserves. The action taken is similar to that in Exhibit 21.2: the dividend received is deducted from the price paid for the shares so that the net effective price paid may be calculated.

### Exhibit 21.3 Shares acquired in a subsidiary at a date when the acquired company has declared a proposed dividend which has not yet been paid

**Parent Statement of Financial Position as at 31 December 2016**

| | £ | £ |
|---|---|---|
| Investment in subsidiary: | | |
| 10 shares bought 31.12.2015 | 24 | |
| *Less* Dividend from pre-acquisition profits | (6) | |
| | | 18 |
| Inventory | | 9 |
| Bank | | 2 |
| | | 29 |
| Share capital | | 20 |
| Retained profits: | | |
| As at 31.12.2015 | 4 | |
| Profit for 2016 | 5 | |
| | | 9 |
| | | 29 |

**Subsidiary Statement of Financial Position as at 31 December 2016**

| | £ | £ |
|---|---|---|
| Inventory | | 19 |
| Bank | | 4 |
| | | 23 |
| Share capital | | 10 |
| Retained profits: | | |
| As at 31.12.2015 | 11 | |
| *Less* Dividend paid during 2016 | (6) | |
| | 5 | |
| *Add* Profit for 2016 | 8 | |
| | | 13 |
| | | 23 |

→

**Consolidated Statement of Financial Position as at 31 December 2016**

| | £ | £ |
|---|---|---|
| Goodwill* | | 3 |
| Inventory | | 28 |
| Bank | | 6 |
| | | 37 |
| Share capital | | 20 |
| Retained profits: (P £9 + S £8) | | 17 |
| | | 37 |

| **Calculation of goodwill* | £ | £ | £ |
|---|---|---|---|
| Paid | | | 24 |
| *Less* Shares | | 10 | |
| Retained profits at 31.12.2015 | | 11 | |
| | | | (21) |
| Goodwill | | | 3 |
| *or,* | | | |
| Paid | | | 24 |
| | | | (6) |
| *Less* Dividend from pre-acquisition reserves | | | 18 |
| Shares acquired | | 10 | |
| Retained profits at 31.12.2015 (11–6) | | 5 | |
| *Less* Dividend paid during 2016 | | | (15) |
| Goodwill | | | 3 |

***Note*: Goodwill is the same irrespective of how much of pre-acquisition dividends are paid.**

## Learning outcomes

**You should now have learnt:**

1. Intra-group dividends paid out of post-acquisition reserves will not appear in the consolidated financial statements, the entries in the individual company financial statements cancelling out upon consolidation.
2. Dividends from a newly acquired subsidiary that were declared prior to the date of acquisition are treated as repayment of capital and the investment in the subsidiary in the parent company statement of financial position is reduced by the amount received.
3. Dividends proposed by a subsidiary that are unpaid at the date of the statement of financial position will not appear in the financial statements of the parent and will appear only as a note to the statement of profit or loss of the subsidiary.

## Answer to activity

21.1 If the dividend has been paid, so far as the statements of financial position are concerned, the bank balance of the subsidiary has decreased while the bank balance of the parent has increased. The reserves of the subsidiary have been reduced while the reserves of the parent have risen. These all offset each other and have no impact upon the consolidated financial statements.

## Review questions

**Note: Unless otherwise indicated, the share capital of all the companies in these review questions comprises ordinary £1 shares. As in the text, movements on retained profits are shown in the statements of financial position in these questions, rather than (as they should be) shown in the statement of changes in equity. Consider these, therefore, as statements of financial position drawn up for internal use.**

**21.1** The following statements of financial position were drawn up as at 31 March 2018. The person drafting the statement of financial position of Parent Ltd was not too sure of an item and has shown it as a suspense amount.

**Parent Ltd Statement of Financial Position as at 31 March 2018**

| | £ | £ |
|---|---|---|
| Non-current assets | | |
| Investment in subsidiary: | | |
| 80,000 shares bought 31.3.2017 | | 108,000 |
| Other non-current assets | | 90,000 |
| Current assets | | 17,000 |
| | | 215,000 |
| Share capital | | 150,000 |
| Retained profits: | | |
| As at 31.3.2017 | 23,000 | |
| *Add* Profit for year to 31.3.2018 | 31,000 | |
| | | 54,000 |
| Suspense* | | 11,000 |
| | | 215,000 |

***The suspense item consists of the 2017 dividend received in June 2017 from Subsidiary Ltd.**

**Subsidiary Ltd Statement of Financial Position as at 31 March 2018**

| | £ | £ |
|---|---|---|
| Non-current assets | | 61,000 |
| Current assets | | 41,000 |
| | | 102,000 |
| Share capital | | 80,000 |
| Retained profits: | | |
| As at 31.3.2017* | 10,000 | |
| *Add* Profit for year to 31.3.2018 | 12,000 | |
| | | 22,000 |
| | | 102,000 |

***The balance of £10,000 is after deducting the dividend for 2017 of £11,000.**

**Required:**
Draw up the consolidated statement of financial position as at 31 March 2018.

→

**21.2A** The following statements of financial position of Father Ltd and Son Ltd were drawn up as at 31 December 2017. Draw up the consolidated statement of financial position as at that date.

**Father Ltd Statement of Financial Position as at 31 December 2017**

| | £ | £ |
|---|---|---|
| Non-current assets | | |
| Investment in subsidiary: | | |
| 100,000 shares bought 31.12.2016 | | 220,000 |
| Other non-current assets | | 380,000 |
| Current assets | | 120,000 |
| | | 720,000 |
| Share capital | | 500,000 |
| Retained profits: | | |
| As at 31.12.2016 | 149,000 | |
| *Add* Profit for 2017* | 71,000 | |
| | | 220,000 |
| | | 720,000 |

***The profit figure for 2017 includes the dividend of £40,000 received from Son Ltd for the year 2016.**

**Son Ltd Statement of Financial Position as at 31 December 2017**

| | £ | £ |
|---|---|---|
| Non-current assets | | 154,000 |
| Current assets | | 48,000 |
| | | 202,000 |
| Share capital | | 100,000 |
| Retained profits: | | |
| As at 31.12.2016* | 28,000 | |
| *Add* Profit for 2017 | 74,000 | |
| | | 102,000 |
| | | 202,000 |

***The balance of £28,000 is after deducting the dividend for 2016 of £40,000.**

**21.3** Draw up a consolidated statement of financial position as at 31 October 2016 from the following information.

**Parents United Ltd Statement of Financial Position as at 31 October 2016**

| | £ | £ |
|---|---|---|
| Non-current assets | | |
| Investment in subsidiary: 63,000 shares bought 31.10.2015 | | 120,000 |
| Other non-current assets | | 82,000 |
| Current assets | | 39,000 |
| | | 241,000 |
| Share capital | | 160,000 |
| Retained profits: | | |
| As at 31.10.2015 | 51,000 | |
| *Add* Profit for year to 31.10.2016 | 30,000 | |
| | | 81,000 |
| | | 241,000 |

**Twins Ltd Statement of Financial Position as at 31 October 2016**

| | £ | £ |
|---|---|---|
| Non-current assets | | 75,000 |
| Current assets | | 62,000 |
| | | 137,000 |
| Share capital | | 105,000 |
| Retained profits: | | |
| As at 31.10.2015 | 10,000 | |
| *Add* Profit for year to 31.10.2016 | 36,000 | |
| | 46.000 | |
| *Less* Dividend paid 2016 | (14,000) | |
| | | 32,000 |
| | | 137,000 |

***Note*: The dividend of Twins Ltd is for 2016 but has not yet been brought into the ledgers of Parents United Ltd as the accountant was unsure what entries should be made.**

**21.4A** The statements of financial position of Dad Ltd and Sibling Ltd are as follows:

**Dad Ltd Statement of Financial Position as at 31 December 2018**

| | £ | £ |
|---|---|---|
| Non-current assets | | |
| Investment in subsidiary: 350,000 shares bought 31.12.2017 | | 700,000 |
| Other non-current assets | | 210,000 |
| Current assets | | 70,000 |
| | | 980,000 |
| Share capital | | 800,000 |
| Retained profits: | | |
| As at 31.12.2017 | 110,000 | |
| *Add* Profit for 2018 | 70,000 | |
| | | 180,000 |
| | | 980,000 |

**Sibling Ltd Statement of Financial Position as at 31 December 2018**

| | £ | £ |
|---|---|---|
| Non-current assets | | 442,000 |
| Current assets | | 220,000 |
| Total assets | | 662,000 |
| Current liabilities | | (90,000) |
| Net assets | | 572,000 |
| Share capital | | 500,000 |
| Retained profits: | | |
| As at 31.12.2017 | 112,000 | |
| *Less* Loss for 2018 | (40,000) | |
| | | 72,000 |
| | | 572,000 |

**Required:**
Prepare the consolidated statement of financial position as at 31 December 2018.

**21.5** The following are the summarised statements of financial position of P Ltd and S Ltd at 31 December 2016.

| | *P Limited* | | *S Limited* | |
|---|---|---|---|---|
| Non-current assets | £ | £ | £ | £ |
| Tangible non-current assets (*see* Note (*a*)) | | 320,000 | | 360,000 |
| Loan to S Ltd | | 50,000 | | |
| Investment in S Ltd | | 250,000 | | |
| *Current assets* | | | | |
| Inventory | 110,000 | | 50,000 | |
| Accounts receivable | 98,000 | | 40,000 | |
| Loan interest | 2,000 | | | |
| Bank | 30,000 | | 10,000 | |
| | | 240,000 | | 100,000 |
| Total assets | | 860,000 | | 460,000 |
| Current liabilities | | | | |
| Trade accounts payable | 190,000 | | 28,000 | |
| Loan interest | – | | 2,000 | |
| | 190,000 | | 30,000 | |
| Non-current liabilities | | | | |
| Loan from P Ltd | – | | 50,000 | |
| | | (190,000) | | (80,000) |
| Net assets | | 670,000 | | 380,000 |
| Equity | | | | |
| Ordinary shares of £1 each, fully paid | | 500,000 | | 200,000 |
| 8% preference shares of £1 each, fully paid | | – | | 100,000 |
| Reserves | | 170,000 | | 80,000 |
| | | 670,000 | | 380,000 |

*Notes:*

(*a*) *Tangible non-current assets*

P Limited

| | *Cost* | *Cumulative depreciation* | *WDV* |
|---|---|---|---|
| | £ | £ | £ |
| Buildings | 120,000 | 10,000 | 110,000 |
| Plant and machinery | 200,000 | 40,000 | 160,000 |
| Motor vehicles | 80,000 | 30,000 | 50,000 |
| | 400,000 | 80,000 | 320,000 |

*Tangible non-current assets*
S Limited

| | *Cost* | *Cumulative depreciation* | *WDV* |
|---|---|---|---|
| | £ | £ | £ |
| Buildings | 300,000 | 100,000 | 200,000 |
| Plant and machinery | 120,000 | 30,000 | 90,000 |
| Motor vehicles | 130,000 | 60,000 | 70,000 |
| | 550,000 | 190,000 | 360,000 |

There were no additions or disposals of non-current assets by the group during the year.

(*b*) P Limited acquired its holding on 1 January 2016, when the balance on S Limited's reserves stood at £50,000. The investment consists of 150,000 ordinary shares of £1 each, fully paid, purchased for £250,000.

(*c*) P Limited included in its statement of profit or loss a dividend of £7,500 from S Limited in March 2016, in respect of the shares acquired on 1 January 2016. S Limited does not intend to pay an ordinary dividend for the year ended 31 December 2016.

**Required:**

Prepare a consolidated statement of financial position for P Limited and its subsidiary S Limited at 31 December 2016.

*Note:* Ignore taxation.

(*Chartered Institute of Management Accountants*)

**21.6** X plc acquired 80% of the ordinary share capital of Y plc on 1 January 2016 for £300,000. The lists of balances of the two companies at 31 December 2016 were as follows:

| | *X plc* | *Y plc* |
|---|---|---|
| | *£000* | *£000* |
| Called-up share capital: | | |
| 400,000 ordinary shares of £1 each, fully paid | 400 | |
| 300,000 ordinary shares of £0.50 each, fully paid | | 150 |
| Reserves as at 1 January 2016 | 220 | 90 |
| Profits for 2016 | 40 | 28 |
| Trade accounts payable | 130 | 80 |
| Taxation | 30 | 14 |
| Depreciation provisions: | | |
| Freehold property | 12 | 6 |
| Plant and machinery | 40 | 12 |
| Current account | – | 14 |
| | 872 | 394 |
| Tangible non-current assets: | | |
| Freehold property, at cost | 120 | 160 |
| Plant and machinery, at cost | 183 | 62 |
| Investment in Y plc | 300 | |
| Inventory | 80 | 70 |
| Accounts receivable | 160 | 90 |
| Bank | 10 | 12 |
| Current account | 19 | – |
| | 872 | 394 |

*Notes*:

(*a*) A remittance of £2,000 from Y plc to X plc in December 2016 was not received by X plc until January 2016.

(*b*) Goods, with an invoice value of £3,000, were despatched by X plc in December 2016 but not received by Y plc until January 2017. The profit element included in this amount was £400.

(*c*) Included in the inventory of Y plc at 31 December 2016 were goods purchased from X plc for £10,000. The profit element included in this amount was £2,000.

(*d*) No interim dividend was paid in 2016 by either company.

(*e*) Current accounts are the intra-group balances outstanding.

(*f*) Y plc has proposed a dividend of £10,000 be paid. It is unpaid at 31 December 2016 and is not provided for in the above trial balances.

**Required:**
Prepare a consolidated statement of financial position for X plc and its subsidiary Y plc as at 31 December 2016.

**(*Chartered Institute of Management Accountants*)**

**21.7A** P plc acquired 80% of the ordinary share capital of S plc for £150,000 and 50% of the issued 10% cumulative preference shares for £10,000, both purchases being effected on 1 May 2017. There have been no changes in the issued share capital of S plc since that date. The following balances are taken from the books of the two companies at 30 April 2018:

| | *P plc* | *S plc* |
|---|---|---|
| | *£000* | *£000* |
| Ordinary share capital (£1 shares) | 300 | 100 |
| 10% cumulative preference shares (50p shares) | – | 20 |
| Share premium account | 20 | 10 |
| General reserve | 68 | 15 |
| Retained profits | 65 | 45 |
| Trade accounts payable | 35 | 22 |
| Taxation | 50 | 30 |
| Depreciation | | |
| Freehold property | 40 | 15 |
| Plant and machinery | 100 | 48 |
| | 678 | 305 |
| Freehold property at cost | 86 | 55 |
| Plant and machinery at cost | 272 | 168 |
| Investment in S plc | 160 | – |
| Inventory | 111 | 65 |
| Accounts receivable | 30 | 15 |
| Cash | 19 | 2 |
| | 678 | 305 |

The following additional information is available:

(*a*) Inventory of P plc includes goods purchased from S plc for £20,000. S plc charged out this inventory at cost plus 25%.

(*b*) A proposed dividend of £10,000 by S plc includes a full year's preference dividend. No interim dividends were paid during the year by either company.

(*c*) Creditors of P plc include £6,000 payable to S plc in respect of inventory purchases. Debtors of S plc include £10,000 due from P plc. The parent sent a cheque for £4,000 to its subsidiary on 29 April 2018 which was not received by S plc until May 2018.

(*d*) At 1 May 2017 the balances on the reserves of S plc were as follows:

| | *£000* |
|---|---|
| Share premium | 10 |
| General reserve | 20 |
| Retained profits | 30 |

**Required:**

(*a*) Prepare a consolidated statement of financial position for P plc and its subsidiary S plc at 30 April 2018.
Notes to the accounts are not required. Workings must be shown.

(*b*) Explain what is meant by the term 'cost of control' and justify your treatment of this item in the above accounts.

(*Chartered Institute of Management Accountants*)

chapter

# 22 Consolidated statements of financial position: sundry matters

## Learning objectives

**After you have studied this chapter, you should be able to:**

- calculate goodwill on the purchase of preference shares
- treat unrealised profits and losses on intra-group asset sales
- describe the effect of 'fair value' on the calculation of goodwill and on the preparation of the consolidated financial statements

## Introduction

In this chapter, you'll learn how to calculate goodwill on preference shares and how to treat it in the consolidated financial statements. You'll also learn what to do with profits and losses on the sale of non-current assets between companies in the same group. Finally, you will learn more about what is meant by 'fair value' and how to calculate and incorporate it into consolidated financial statements.

## 22.1 Preference shares

You've already learnt that preference shares do not carry voting powers under normal conditions, nor do they possess a right to the reserves of the company. Contrast this with ordinary shares which, when bought by a parent entity, will give it voting rights and also a proportionate share of the reserves of the company.

The absence of any right to a share of the reserves for preference shareholders and the absence of voting rights for holders of preference shares means that preference shareholders cannot control a company, either by their holding a majority of the voting share capital through their preference shares which have no votes (impossible, even if share capital comprised 99% preference shares and 1% ordinary shares) or (as a result of their preference shareholding) being in a position to control the decision-making of the company, which, of course, is also impossible. As a result, the calculation of goodwill on the purchase of preference shares is very simple indeed: there is none, or is there?

If more is paid for preference shares than their nominal (or par) value, the difference is simply the result of market forces. The total paid is the total cost, nothing more, nothing less. You do not need to worry about this unless they are held (ultimately) by the company's parent.

If a parent buys preference shares of a subsidiary, the difference between the amount paid and the total nominal value of the preference shares purchased must be put somewhere in the consolidated statement of financial position. In the absence of any guidance in the standards, the only sensible place for it – if it is positive – is as goodwill. It could be shown as a combined figure with other goodwill, and the breakdown shown in a note. **If a gain from a bargain purchase is found, the gain could be taken to profit or loss.** Again, it must be stressed that there are no rules for the treatment of 'goodwill' arising on the purchase of preference shares in a subsidiary upon its acquisition.

It is almost unthinkable that anything other than the market value would be paid for preference shares on the open market so it is unlikely that this type of goodwill may arise.

Preference share dividends proposed but not paid and dividends not proposed or paid but due on cumulative preference shares of a subsidiary must be deducted from reserves when computing a parent's share of profits or losses of the subsidiary.

Preference shares owned by minority shareholders are simply shown as part of the non-controlling interest figure in the consolidated statement of financial position, each share being shown at nominal value.

***Note*: According to IAS 32 (*Financial instruments: disclosure and presentation*), when a preference share is redeemable at the option of the holder or redemption is mandatory at a given date, it is treated as a financial liability, not as equity. The 'dividend' payments made are treated as interest paid. As a result, such interest payments proposed but not paid at the year end should be accrued and included in the consolidated financial statements to the extent they are not set off within the group.**

## 22.2 Sale of non-current assets between members of the group

There is obviously nothing illegal in one company in a group selling some of its non-current assets to another company in the group. If the sale is at the original price paid for the non-current assets by the first company, then no adjustment will be needed in the consolidated statement of financial position. However, such sales are usually at a price which differs from their original cost. Any intra-group unrealised profit or loss arising in this way must be eliminated in a similar fashion to that taken for the unrealised profit in inventory as described in Chapter 19.

Not surprisingly, if a non-current asset is to be shown at its cost to the group in the consolidated statement of financial position rather than at the cost paid by one group company to another, the depreciation figure on that asset must be adjusted to that based on the original cost of the asset to the group, rather than on the amount paid by the group company that now owns it.

Let's look at an example.

### Exhibit 22.1

**Parent and Co Ltd Statement of Financial Position as at 31 December 2016**

| | £ | £ |
|---|---|---|
| Non-current assets | | |
| Investment in S: | | |
| 50 shares bought 31.12.2015 | | 95 |
| Other non-current assets | 78 | |
| *Less* Depreciation | (23) | |
| | | 55 |
| Current assets | | 20 |
| | | 170 |
| Share capital | | 100 |
| Retained profits: | | |
| As at 31.12.2015 | 30 | |
| For the year 2016 | 40 | |
| | | 70 |
| | | 170 |

**Subsidiary and Co Ltd Statement of Financial Position as at 31 December 2016**

| | £ | £ |
|---|---|---|
| Non-current assets | 80 | |
| *Less* Depreciation | (20) | |
| | | 60 |
| Current assets | | 35 |
| | | 95 |
| Share capital | | 50 |
| Retained profits: | | |
| As at 31.12.2015 | 20 | |
| For the year 2016 | 25 | |
| | | 45 |
| | | 95 |

During the year, Parent and Co Ltd had sold to Subsidiary and Co Ltd for £28 a non-current asset which had cost it £20. Of the figure of £20 depreciation in the statement of financial position of Subsidiary and Co Ltd, £7 refers to this asset and £13 to the other assets. The rate of depreciation is 25% straight line. The £8 profit is included in the figure of £40 profit for 2016 in the statement of financial position of Parent and Co Ltd.

Summarising all this:

(*a*) Parent and Co Ltd sold a non-current asset to Subsidiary and Co Ltd for £28 which had cost £20.

(*b*) Entries made in Parent and Co Ltd's accounts:

| | | |
|---|---|---|
| *Dr* Bank | £28 | |
| *Cr* Non-current assets | | £20 |
| *Cr* Gain on disposal of non-current asset | | £8 |

(*c*) Entries made in Subsidiary and Co Ltd's accounts:

| | | |
|---|---|---|
| *Dr* Non-current assets | £28 | |
| *Cr* Bank | | £28 |
| *Dr* Depreciation **(expense included in profit or loss)** | 7 | |
| *Cr* Accumulated depreciation (£28 × 25%) **(provision)** | | 7 |

This means that £8 needs to be removed from the asset costs in the consolidated statement of financial position and from the retained profits balance. In addition, the figure of depreciation needs adjusting downwards, from the £7 as shown on the statement of financial position of Subsidiary and Co Ltd, to the figure of £5, i.e. 25% depreciation based on the cost of the asset to the group. In turn, this means that the figure of profit for Subsidiary and Co Ltd of £25 needs to be increased by £2, as, instead of the expense of £7 depreciation, there will now be a reduced expense of £5. The consolidated statement of financial position becomes:

**Consolidated Statement of Financial Position as at 31 December 2016**

| | £ | £ |
|---|---|---|
| Non-current assets | | |
| Goodwill | | 25 |
| Other non-current assets | 150 | |
| *Less* Depreciation | (41) | |
| | | 109 |
| Current assets | | 55 |
| | | 189 |
| Share capital | | 100 |
| Retained profits: (Parent and Co: £70 − £8 + Subsidiary and Co £25 + £2) | | 89 |
| | | 189 |

## 22.3 Fair values in purchase method accounting

Under purchase method accounting, the consolidation process is looked at from the point of view that the parent undertaking acquires shares in a company, and thereby achieves control of that company. In addition, it is recognised that the reserves are also taken over. **(See Chapter 25 for fuller coverage of this topic.)**

The consolidated statement of financial position should give a picture of the group that is not clouded by the consolidation method adopted.

An entity is acquired to obtain control of its assets. The consolidated statement of financial position should give the same picture as that which would have been recorded if, instead of buying shares, the assets themselves had been bought.

One of the areas of greatest diversity before accounting standards on this topic were issued concerned the revaluation of assets and liabilities to 'fair values'. 'Fair value' is defined as the *amount for which an asset could be exchanged, or a liability settled, between knowledgeable, willing parties in an arm's-length transaction* (i.e. in an exchange between strangers).

Generally, acquiring companies follow the IFRS 3 rules to set their own 'fair values' on the assets and liabilities acquired, and then follow the IFRS 3 rule that the amount to be attributed to purchased goodwill should be the difference between the 'fair value' of the consideration given and the aggregate of the 'fair values' of the separable net assets acquired. This should apply to all the assets, liabilities and contingent liabilities including those attributable to non-controlling interests.

Under purchase method accounting, the investment is shown at cost (which equals the 'fair value' given) in the parent company's own financial statements. On consolidation, IFRS 3 requires that if the fair value of the net assets (excluding goodwill) acquired is *less than* the fair value of the purchase consideration, the difference is treated as goodwill and capitalised and subjected to annual impairment review. If the fair value of the net assets (excluding goodwill) acquired *exceeds* the fair value of the purchase consideration, the difference is treated as a gain from a bargain purchase and must be eliminated immediately. This is the treatment that has been adopted throughout the previous few chapters, the only difference being that fair values should always be used, rather than the values as shown in the statement of financial position of the acquired company.

IFRS 3 requires that upon acquisition, all assets and liabilities that existed in the acquired entity at that date are recorded at fair values reflecting their condition at that date. In doing so, it ensures that all changes to the acquired assets and liabilities and the resulting gains and losses *that arise after control of the acquired entity has passed to the acquirer*, are reported as part of the post-acquisition or post-combination financial performance of the reporting group.

IFRS 3 contains a number of rules governing the determination of appropriate fair values (for items where the use of present values is not mentioned, its use is permitted):

1 The fair value of land and buildings should be based upon *market value*.
2 Plant and equipment should be valued at *market value*.
3 The fair value of *intangible assets* should be based on their *replacement cost* in an active market or, if no active market exists, on what would have been paid in an arm's-length transaction between knowledgeable willing parties per IAS 38.
4 Inventory of finished goods and merchandise should be valued at selling price less (*a*) costs of disposal and (*b*) a reasonable profit allowance for the selling effort of the acquirer based on profit for similar finished goods and merchandise:
   (*i*) work in progress should be valued at selling price less costs to complete (*a*) and (*b*) above;
   (*ii*) raw materials should be valued at current replacement costs.
5 Financial instruments traded in an active market should be valued at *market* values.
6 Financial instruments not traded on an active market should be valued using estimated values that take into consideration features such as the price–earnings ratio, dividend yields and expected growth rates of comparable instruments of entities with similar characteristics.

7 Receivables and beneficial contracts and other identifiable assets should be valued using the present values of the amounts to be received, determined at appropriate current interest rates less allowances for uncollectability and collection costs, if necessary. Discounting is not required for short-term receivables, beneficial contracts and other identifiable assets when the difference between the nominal (i.e. existing) and discounted amounts is not material.
8 *Contingent* liabilities should be valued at the amounts a third party would charge to assume responsibility for them.
9 Net employee benefit assets or liabilities for defined benefit plans should be valued using the present value of the defined benefit obligation less the fair value of any plan assets. An asset is only recognised to the extent that it is probable that it is available to the acquirer in the form of refunds from a plan or a reduction in future contributions.
10 Tax assets and liabilities should be valued at the amount of tax benefit arising from tax losses or the taxes payable in respect of profit or loss in accordance with IAS 12 (*Income taxes*). The tax asset or liability is determined after allowing for the tax effect of restating identifiable assets, liabilities and contingent liabilities to their fair values. It is not discounted.
11 Accounts and notes payable, long-term debt, liabilities, accruals and other claims payable should be valued at the present values of the amounts to be paid to settle the liabilities determined at appropriate current interest rates. Discounting is not required for short-term liabilities where the difference between the nominal (i.e. existing) and discounted amounts is not material.
12 Onerous contracts and other identifiable liabilities should be valued using the present values of the amounts to be paid in settling the obligations determined at appropriate current interest rates.

What do you think is an 'onerous contract'?

The 'cost of acquisition' is the *aggregate of the fair values of the assets given, liabilities incurred or assumed and equity issued by the acquirer for control over the acquiree plus any costs directly attributable to the business combination*, all at the date of exchange.

The effect of the use of fair values can be seen from what would occur if fair values were used by the acquiring company in arriving at the price it wished to pay, but then were never incorporated into the financial statements. For instance, if P buys all the 10 £1 shares of S for £18 when the reserves are £5, then the goodwill calculation if fair values are not used is:

| | £ | £ |
|---|---|---|
| Cost | | 18 |
| *Less* Shares | 10 | |
| *Less* Reserves | 5 | |
| | | (15) |
| Goodwill | | 3 |

However, P might have bought the shares of S because it thought that the fair value of the net assets of S was £17.

What would be wrong with P recording goodwill as £3 in this case?

The revaluation upwards of the fixed assets by £2, and the consequent reduction of the goodwill figure by £2, brings the figures into line with how P views them. Where there are depreciation charges on the revalued assets, they also need to be adjusted.

Let's look at an example (Exhibit 22.2) of the amendments made when statement of financial position values are adjusted to fair values.

## Exhibit 22.2

**P Statement of Financial Position as at 31 December 2016**

| | £ | £ |
|---|---|---|
| Non-current assets | | |
| Investment in subsidiary: | | |
| 30 shares bought 31.12.2015 | | 56 |
| Other non-current assets | 80 | |
| *Less* Depreciation for the year | (16) | |
| | | 64 |
| Current assets | | 26 |
| | | 146 |
| Share capital | | 100 |
| Retained profits: | | |
| As at 31.12.2015 | 20 | |
| *Add* Profit 2016 | 26 | |
| | | 46 |
| | | 146 |

**S Statement of Financial Position as at 31 December 2016**

| | £ | £ |
|---|---|---|
| Non-current assets | 50 | |
| *Less* Depreciation for the year | (10) | |
| | | 40 |
| Current assets | | 14 |
| | | 54 |
| Share capital | | 30 |
| Retained profits: | | |
| As at 31.12.2015 | 3 | |
| *Add* Profit 2016 | 21 | |
| | | 24 |
| | | 54 |

At the time when P bought the shares in S, the assets in S were shown at a value of £33 in the statement of financial position of S. However, P valued the fair values of the non-current assets of S as being worth £20 more than that shown in S's statement of financial position. The consolidated statement of financial position, therefore, will show them at this higher figure. In turn, the depreciation on these non-current assets, which is at the rate of 20%, will be increased accordingly, by £4. The consolidated statement of financial position is therefore:

**P and S Consolidated Statement of Financial Position as at 31 December 2016**

| | £ | £ |
|---|---|---|
| Non-current assets | | |
| Goodwill | | 3 |
| Other non-current assets (£80 + £70) | 150 | |
| *Less* Depreciation (£16 + £14) | (30) | |
| | | 120 |
| Current assets | | 40 |
| | | 163 |
| Share capital | | 100 |
| Retained profits: | | |
| (P £46 + S £21 − increased depreciation £4) | | 63 |
| | | 163 |

## Learning outcomes

**You should now have learnt:**

1. Goodwill on the purchase of preference shares is the difference between their nominal value and the amount paid but that there is no guidance in accounting standards concerning how to treat this investment upon consolidation. It was suggested that if positive it should be treated as 'goodwill' and, if negative, treated as a gain on a bargain purchase.
2. Unrealised profit on the sale of non-current assets between companies in a group must be eliminated upon consolidation.
3. 'Fair values' at the time of acquisition should be used in the calculation of goodwill, rather than the value shown in the statement of financial position of the subsidiary, and the consolidation of the subsidiary should also be based on those fair values.
4. Fair value is dependent upon the nature of the item being valued. However, the general rule is that it represents the amount for which an asset or liability could be exchanged in an arm's-length transaction, i.e. in an exchange between strangers.
5. There are different rules for arriving at the fair values for different categories or assets, liabilities and contingent liabilities, and what those rules are.

## Answers to activities

22.1 An onerous contract is one where the only interest the acquirer had in it was in its termination, and valued it as such. This may arise, for example, when the acquirer advises the acquiree on or before the acquisition date that a contract would be terminated. That is, the acquirer did not seek any benefit from the contract, only that the contract be terminated, and valued it accordingly when deciding what to pay for the acquisition.

22.2 In P's eyes, it is giving £18 for physical assets worth £17 and the goodwill figure is correspondingly £18 − £17 = £1. Assuming that the difference is in the recorded value of non-current assets, then the consolidated statement of financial position will not be showing a true and fair view if it shows goodwill £3 and assets £15. The assets should be valued at £17 and goodwill recorded as £1.

## Review questions

***Note*: Unless indicated otherwise, assume that the issued share capital of all the companies in these review questions comprises ordinary £1 shares.**

**22.1** From the following statements of financial position and further information you are to draw up a consolidated statement of financial position as at 31 December 2016. →

**Parent Ltd Statement of Financial Position as at 31 December 2016**

| | £ | £ |
|---|---|---|
| Non-current assets | | |
| Investment in Subsidiary: | | |
| 700,000 shares bought 31.12.2015 | | 1,050,000 |
| Other non-current assets | 800,000 | |
| *Less* Depreciation | (380,000) | |
| | | 420,000 |
| Current assets | | 160,000 |
| | | 1,630,000 |
| Share capital | | 1,300,000 |
| Retained profits: | | |
| As at 31.12.2015 | 270,000 | |
| *Add* Profit for 2016 | 60,000 | |
| | | 330,000 |
| | | 1,630,000 |

**Subsidiary Ltd Statement of Financial Position as at 31 December 2016**

| | £ | £ |
|---|---|---|
| Non-current assets | | 750,000 |
| *Less* Depreciation | | (190,000) |
| | | 560,000 |
| Current assets | | 310,000 |
| | | 870,000 |
| Share capital | | 700,000 |
| Retained profits: | | |
| As at 31.12.2015 | 118,000 | |
| *Add* Profit for 2016 | 52,000 | |
| | | 170,000 |
| | | 870,000 |

During the year Parent Ltd had sold to Subsidiary Ltd for £80,000 a non-current asset which had cost it £64,000. Subsidiary Ltd has written off 25% of the amount it paid, i.e. £20,000 as depreciation for 2016.

**22.2A** From the following statements of financial position and supplementary information you are to draw up a consolidated statement of financial position as at 31 March 2017.

**Parent Holdings Ltd Consolidated Statement of Financial Position as at 31 March 2017**

| | £ | £ |
|---|---|---|
| Non-current assets | | |
| Investment in Subsidiary Ltd: 40,000 shares bought 31.3.2016 | | 90,000 |
| Other non-current assets | 190,000 | |
| *Less* Depreciation | (32,000) | |
| | | 158,000 |
| Current assets | | 52,000 |
| | | 300,000 |
| Share capital | | 180,000 |
| Retained profits: | | |
| As at 31.3.2016 | 84,000 | |
| *Add* Profit for 2017 | 36,000 | |
| | | 120,000 |
| | | 300,000 |

**Subsidiary Ltd Statement of Financial Position as at 31 March 2017**

| | £ | £ |
|---|---|---|
| Non-current assets | 114,000 | |
| *Less* Depreciation | (40,000) | |
| | | 74,000 |
| Current assets | | 24,000 |
| | | 98,000 |
| Share capital | | 40,000 |
| Retained profits: | | |
| As at 31.3.2016 | 26,000 | |
| *Add* Profit for 2017 | 12,000 | |
| | | 38,000 |
| General reserve (as at 31.3.2016) | | 20,000 |
| | | 98,000 |

During the year Parent Holdings Ltd sold a non-current asset to Subsidiary Ltd. It had cost Parent Holdings Ltd £3,000 and it was sold to Subsidiary Ltd for £4,000. Subsidiary Ltd had written off £800 as depreciation during 2017.

22.3

**Parent plc Statement of Financial Position as at 31 March 2018**

| | £ | £ |
|---|---|---|
| Non-current assets | | |
| Investment in Subsidiary: 100,000 shares bought on 31.3.2017 | | 190,000 |
| Other non-current assets | 124,000 | |
| *Less* Depreciation for year | (25,000) | |
| | | 99,000 |
| Current assets | | 31,000 |
| | | 320,000 |
| Share capital | | 240,000 |
| Retained profits: | | |
| As at 31.3.2017 | 50,000 | |
| *Add* Profit for 2018 | 30,000 | |
| | | 80,000 |
| | | 320,000 |

**Subsidiary Ltd Statement of Financial Position as at 31 March 2018**

| | £ | £ |
|---|---|---|
| Non-current assets | 121,000 | |
| *Less* Depreciation for year | (22,000) | |
| | | 99,000 |
| Current assets | | 49,000 |
| | | 148,000 |
| Share capital | | 100,000 |
| Retained profits: | | |
| As at 31.3.2017 | 26,000 | |
| *Add* Profit for 2018 | 22,000 | |
| | | 48,000 |
| | | 148,000 |

When Parent plc bought the shares of Subsidiary Ltd it valued the non-current assets at £132,000 instead of the figure of £121,000 as shown in the statement of financial position of Subsidiary Ltd.

Draw up a consolidated statement of financial position as at 31 March 2018.

→ **22.4A**

**Parental Venture plc Statement of Financial Position as at 31 December 2018**

| | £ | £ |
|---|---|---|
| Non-current assets | | |
| Investment in Subsidiary: 60,000 shares bought 31.12.2017 | | 98,000 |
| Other non-current assets | 120,000 | |
| *Less* Depreciation for year | (12,000) | |
| | | 108,000 |
| Current assets | | 18,000 |
| | | 224,000 |
| Share capital | | 150,000 |
| Retained profits: | | |
| As at 31.12.2017 | 51,000 | |
| *Add* Profit for 2018 | 23,000 | |
| | | 74,000 |
| | | 224,000 |

**Subsidiary Statement of Financial Position as at 31 December 2018**

| | £ | £ |
|---|---|---|
| Non-current assets | 80,000 | |
| *Less* Depreciation for year | (8,000) | |
| | | 72,000 |
| Current assets | | 12,000 |
| | | 84,000 |
| Share capital | | 60,000 |
| Retained profits: | | |
| As at 31.12.2017 | 16,000 | |
| *Add* Profit for 2018 | 8,000 | |
| | | 24,000 |
| | | 84,000 |

When Parental Venture plc took control of Subsidiary Ltd it valued the non-current assets at 31.12.2017 at £100,000 instead of £80,000 as shown.

Draw up the consolidated statement of financial position as at 31 December 2018.

chapter 23

# Consolidation of the financial statements of a group of companies

## Learning objectives

**After you have studied this chapter, you should be able to:**

- explain how a company that is the subsidiary of another is also a subsidiary of its parent's own parent entity
- consolidate groups that include subsidiaries of subsidiaries

## Introduction

In this chapter, you'll learn how to deal with situations where there are layers of subsidiaries beneath one overall parent company; and you will learn about the exemption that wholly owned subsidiaries have from preparing consolidated.

## 23.1 Subsidiaries that control other companies

So far, we have considered the case of parent entities having a direct interest in their subsidiaries. That is, in each example and review question, the parent itself bought over 50% of the voting shares in the subsidiary. In a straightforward case, where the parent company, P1, has bought shares in subsidiaries S1 and S2, it could be represented by a diagram (Exhibit 23.1).

**Exhibit 23.1**

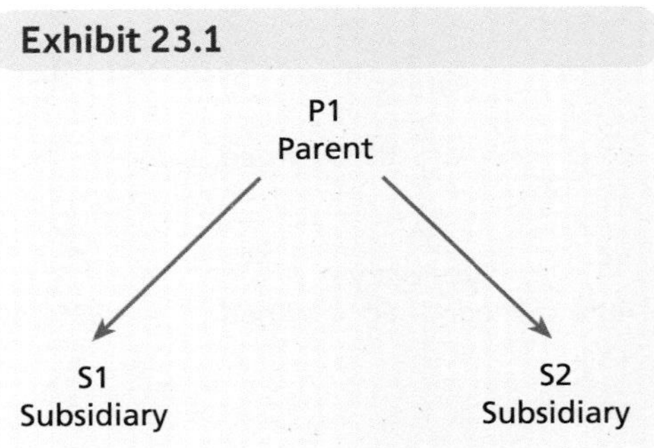

Suppose instead that another parent, P2, bought 100% of the shares in S3, and that S3 then bought 100% of the shares in S4. Because P2 controls S3 completely, and S3 controls S4 completely, P2 controls both S3 and S4. This is shown in Exhibit 23.2.

If another parent entity, P3, owned S5 100%, but S5 only owned 80% of S6, then we can say that P3 owns 100% of 80% of S6 = 80% (Exhibit 23.3). Similarly, if another parent entity, P4, owned 75% of S7, and S7 owns 80% of S8, then P4 owns 75% × 80% = 60% of S8 (Exhibit 23.4).

As can be seen in Exhibits 23.2, 23.3 and 23.4, the eventual ownership by the overall parent of each subsidiary's subsidiary exceeds 50%:

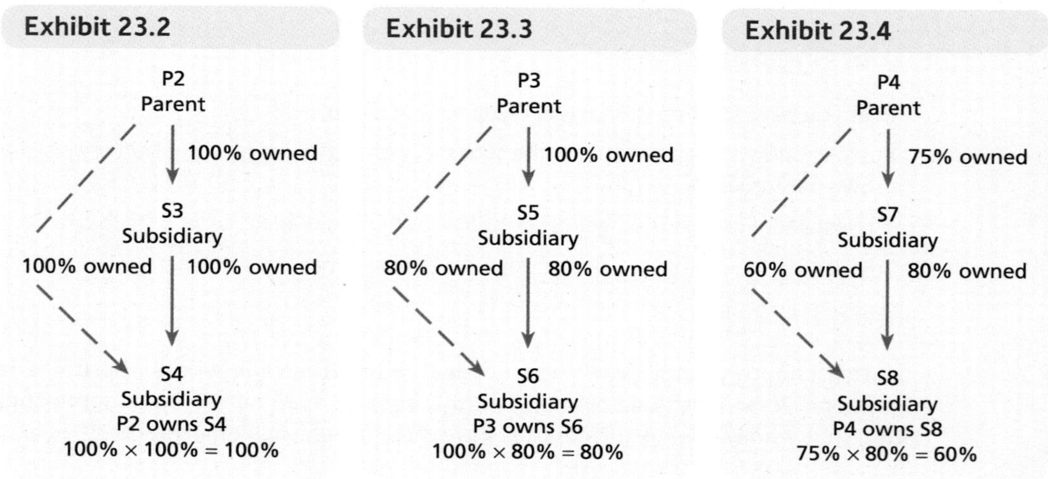


There will be cases where the ownership of the subsidiary of a subsidiary by the parent is less than 50%. Exhibit 23.5 shows an example of this where parent P5 owns 80% of S9, and S9 owns 60% of S10. This means that P5 owns 80% × 60% = 48% of S10. Exhibit 23.6 similarly shows that parent entity P6 owns 60% of S11 and S11 owns 55% of S12. Therefore, P6 owns 60% × 55% = 33% of S12:

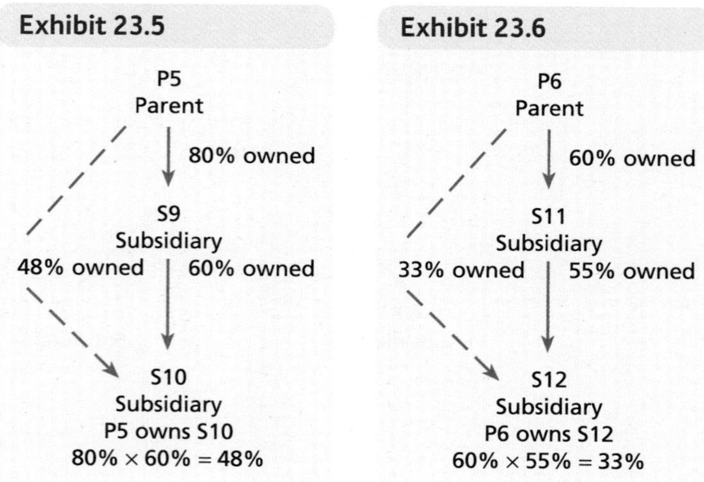

It might look as though S10 is not a subsidiary of P5, because P5 owns less than 50% of S10. However, P5 controls S9 as its ownership is over 50% and, in turn, S9 controls S10 as it owns more than 50%. In effect, therefore, P5 controls S10 and so S10 is its subsidiary even though P5 only controls 48% of the share capital of S10, *because it is able to control S10.*

**Activity 23.1** Would P6 be considered the ultimate parent company of S12?

## 23.2 Legal exemptions from preparing consolidated financial statements

IAS 27 (*Consolidated and separate financial statements*) exempts a wholly owned subsidiary from preparing consolidated financial statements. For instance, in Exhibit 23.2 the subsidiary S3 would not have to prepare consolidated financial statements; neither would S5 in Exhibit 23.3.

In each of cases S7, S9 and S11 in Exhibits 23.4, 23.5 and 23.6, there are minority shareholders. In practice, therefore, those subsidiary companies may have to prepare consolidated financial statements (for example, consolidating S7 and S8 in Exhibit 23.4) if sufficient of the non-controlling interests demand it.

However, in either case, three other conditions must be met for subsidiaries to have exemption from preparing consolidated financial statements:

1 the exempted entity's debt or equity is not traded in a public market;
2 the exempted entity did not file, nor is it in the process of filing, its financial statements with a securities commission or other regulatory organisation for the purpose of issuing any class of instruments in a public market;
3 the ultimate or any intermediate parent produces consolidated financial statements available for public use that comply with International GAAP.

**Activity 23.2** Why do you think wholly owned subsidiaries are normally exempted from preparing consolidated financial statements?

## 23.3 Methods of consolidating financial statements

There are two methods of consolidating the financial statements.

1 The 'indirect' or 'single-stage' method follows the reasoning already given in this chapter, i.e. computing the parent's interest in the subsidiaries and their subsidiaries and taking that percentage of the capital and reserves of these companies into the consolidation process. For instance, in Exhibit 23.5 the capital and reserves would give 100% of P5+80% of S9+48% of S10.
2 The 'multi-stage' method first consolidates the statements of financial position of the subsidiary and its subsidiary, and when that is done it is then consolidated with the statement of financial position of the holding company. This recognises the fact that subsidiaries with non-controlling interests have to produce consolidated financial statements and this method is more generally used in practice than the indirect method.

***Note*: For an examination, method 1 (the 'indirect' method) is to be preferred. It is a quicker method, and you will usually be short of time in an examination. Also, examination questions almost always ask for consolidation for the entire group only. As a result, there will be no need to do the intermediate consolidation. This book will therefore use method 1 only, the indirect method.**

## 23.4 The indirect method consolidation technique

The consolidation technique you learnt in previous chapters is very similar to the **indirect method** described in the previous section, but two points need stressing:

1 The entry for the cost of investment in the cost of control account:

(*a*) *For subsidiaries*: debit the total cost of investment to the cost of control account.
(*b*) *For subsidiaries of subsidiaries*: debit only **the proportion of the cost concerned with the parent's share in the subsidiary which controls the subsidiary** to the cost of control account. Debit the non-controlling interest account with the balance.

If P invests £20,000 to buy 80% of the shares of S1 and S1 then invests £10,000 to buy 60% of the shares of S2, the entries in the cost of control account of the P group would be:

**Cost of Control**

| | £ | | |
|---|---|---|---|
| Cost of shares in S1 | 20,000 | | |
| Cost of shares in S2 (80%) | 8,000 | | |

The remaining proportion of investment by S1 is then debited to a non-controlling interest account.

**Non-controlling Interest**

| | £ | | |
|---|---|---|---|
| Cost of shares in S2 (20%) | 2,000 | | |

2 The apportionment of share capital and reserves to the cost of control account and to the non-controlling interest account:

(*a*) *Cost of control*: take only the group's ultimate share of the subsidiary of subsidiary's share capital and reserves.
(*b*) *Non-controlling interest*: include the balance of the subsidiary of subsidiary's share capital and reserves.

In the illustration given in 1(*b*) where P bought 80% of S1, and S1 bought 60% of S2, the ultimate share of the group is 80% × 60% = 48%. Therefore, in the consolidated financial statements 48% should come into group calculations and 52% shown in non-controlling interest workings.

The double entry from the cost of control account when preparing the consolidated financial statements is:

*Dr* (appropriate) Reserve account
*Cr* Cost of control account

## 23.5 A worked example

P Ltd owns 80% of the ordinary share capital of S1 Ltd. In turn S1 Ltd owns 75% of the ordinary share capital of S2 Ltd. Both investments had been acquired on 31 December 2017, one year previous to the following statements of financial position:

**Statements of Financial Position as at 31 December 2018**

| | P Ltd | | S1 Ltd | | S2 Ltd | |
|---|---|---|---|---|---|---|
| | £000 | £000 | £000 | £000 | £000 | £000 |
| Non-current assets | | | | | | |
| Investments | | | | | | |
| Shares in S1 | | 41 | | | | |
| Shares in S2 | | | | 25 | | |
| Other non-current assets | | 40 | | 4 | | 27 |
| Current assets | | 19 | | 6 | | 28 |
| | | 100 | | 35 | | 55 |
| Share capital | | 40 | | 10 | | 20 |
| Retained profits: | | | | | | |
| As at 31.12.2017 | 24 | | 5 | | 15 | |
| *Add* Profit 2018 | 36 | | 10 | | 20 | |
| | | 60 | | 15 | | 35 |
| General reserve at 31.12.2017 | | – | | 10 | | – |
| | | 100 | | 35 | | 55 |

The statements of financial position show the fair values of the assets and liabilities. Ownership of P can be seen to be 80% of S1 and 80% × 75% = 60% of S2. Any goodwill on acquisition to be written off to profit or loss.

We now will prepare a consolidated statement of financial position on 31 December 2018, one year after both acquisitions. In previous chapters the illustrations have been given on the face of the statements of financial position. In this more complicated example we will use double entry accounts for the main items.

The first item to note is that International GAAP *does not permit* the initial (or any other) writing-off of positive goodwill. Goodwill can only be reduced following impairment review. The instruction given above to write off the goodwill, therefore, must be ignored. **You should be wary of examiners trying to trick you on this point.**

**P Ltd and its subsidiaries**
**Consolidated Statement of Financial Position as at 31 December 2018**

| | £000 |
|---|---|
| Non-current assets | |
| Goodwill | 20 |
| Other non-current assets | 71 |
| Current assets | 53 |
| | 144 |
| Share capital | 40 |
| Retained profits (*see* below) | 80 |
| | 120 |
| Non-controlling interest (*see* below) | 24 |
| | 144 |

**In the accounts that follow, 1(*a*), 1(*b*), 2(*a*) and 2(*b*) refer to the steps in the indirect consolidation method described in Section 23.4.**

**Cost of Control**

| | £000 | | £000 |
|---|---|---|---|
| Cost of shares in S1 (1(*a*)) | 41 | Share capital S1 80% × 10 | 8 |
| Cost of shares in S2 80% × 25 (1(*b*)) | 20 | Share capital S2 60% × 20 (2(*a*)) | 12 |
| | | Pre-acquisition reserves: | |
| | | Retained profits S1 80% × 5 | 4 |
| | | Retained profits S2 60% × 15 | 9 |
| | | General reserve S1 80% × 10 | 8 |
| | | **Goodwill** | 20 |
| | 61 | | 61 |

**Non-controlling Interest**

| | £000 | | £000 |
|---|---|---|---|
| Cost of shares in S2 20% × 20 (1(*b*)) | 5 | Share capital S1 20% × 10 | 2 |
| **Balance to consolidated statement of financial position** | **24** | Share capital S2 40% × 20 (2(*b*)) | 8 |
| | | Retained profits S1 20% × 15 | 3 |
| | | Retained profits S2 40% × 35 (2(*b*)) | 14 |
| | | General reserve S1 20% × 10 | 2 |
| | 29 | | 29 |

**Retained profits**

| | £000 | | £000 |
|---|---|---|---|
| Non-controlling interest S1 | 3 | P | 60 |
| Non-controlling interest S2 | 14 | S1 | 15 |
| Cost of control S1: pre-acquisition | 4 | S2 | 35 |
| Cost of control S2: pre-acquisition | 9 | | |
| **Balance to consolidated statement of financial position** | **80** | | |
| | 110 | | 110 |

**General Reserve**

| | £000 | | £000 |
|---|---|---|---|
| Cost of control 80% × 10 | 8 | S1 balance b/d | 10 |
| Non-controlling interest 20% × 10 | 2 | | |
| | 10 | | 10 |

## Learning outcomes

**You should now have learnt:**

1. A company that is the subsidiary of another is also a subsidiary of its parent's own parent entity, even where the ultimate parent's shareholding is below 50%.
2. There are two recognised methods of consolidating the financial statements of groups that contain subsidiaries of subsidiaries:
   (*a*) the multi-stage method is generally more common in practice, but
   (*b*) the indirect single-stage method is recommended for examinations.
3. The indirect method involves computing the parent entity's interest in the subsidiaries and their subsidiaries and taking that percentage of the capital and reserves of these companies into the consolidation process.
4. Goodwill cannot be written off other than following impairment review.

## Answers to activities

23.1 Yes. Although P6 has effective ownership of only 33% of S12, it can exercise control over S11, as it owns 60% of the company. S11, in turn, can exercise control over S12 through its 55% ownership. Consequently, P has control over both S11 and, through S11, of S12, and so P is the ultimate parent of S12.

23.2 There is no shareholder who would want to read them, other than the parent company, and it has access to far more detailed financial information about the subsidiary and its own subsidiaries than would ever be contained in the subsidiary's consolidated financial statements.

## Review questions

***Note***: **In all these review questions, unless otherwise indicated, assume that (*a*) the share capital of all the companies comprises ordinary £1 shares; and (*b*) all values shown are fair values.**

**23.1** From the following statements of financial position, you are to draft a consolidated statement of financial position for the group of Parent Ltd and its two subsidiaries, Sub 1 and Sub 2.

**Parent Ltd Statement of Financial Position as at 31 December 2017**

| | £ | £ |
|---|---|---|
| Non-current assets | | |
| Investment in Sub 1: 54,000 shares bought 31.12.2016 | | 128,000 |
| Other non-current assets | | 572,000 |
| Current assets | | 160,000 |
| | | 860,000 |
| Share capital | | 600,000 |
| Retained profits: | | |
| As at 31.12.2016 | 84,000 | |
| *Add* Profit for 2017 | 116,000 | |
| | | 200,000 |
| General reserve | | 60,000 |
| | | 860,000 |

**Sub 1 Ltd Statement of Financial Position as at 31 December 2017**

| | £ | £ |
|---|---|---|
| Non-current assets | | |
| Investment in Sub 2: 14,000 shares bought 31.12.2016 | | 60,000 |
| Other non-current assets | | 101,000 |
| Current assets | | 31,000 |
| | | 192,000 |
| Share capital | | 60,000 |
| Retained profits: | | |
| As at 31.12.2016 | 40,000 | |
| *Add* Profit for 2017 | 92,000 | |
| | | 132,000 |
| | | 192,000 |

**Sub 2 Ltd Statement of Financial Position as at 31 December 2017**

| | £ | £ |
|---|---|---|
| Non-current assets | | 24,000 |
| Current assets | | 14,000 |
| | | 38,000 |
| Share capital | | 20,000 |
| Retained profits: | | |
| As at 31.12.2016 | 8,000 | |
| *Add* Profit for 2017 | 10,000 | |
| | | 18,000 |
| | | 38,000 |

→

**23.2A** From the following statements of financial position prepare a consolidated statement of financial position for the group of Parenting Ltd, Sub A and Sub B.

**Parent plc Statement of Financial Position as at 31 March 2016**

| | £ | £ |
|---|---|---|
| Non-current assets | | |
| Investment in Sub A: 60,000 shares bought 31.3.2015 | | 130,000 |
| Other non-current assets | | 700,000 |
| Current assets | | 280,000 |
| | | 1,110,500 |
| Share capital | | 800,000 |
| Retained profits: | | |
| As at 31.3.2015 | 180,000 | |
| *Add* Profit for year ended 31.3.2016 | 130,000 | |
| | | 310,000 |
| | | 1,110,000 |

**Sub A Statement of Financial Position as at 31 March 2016**

| | £ | £ |
|---|---|---|
| Non-current assets | | |
| Investment in Sub B: 21,000 shares bought 31.3.2015 | | 42,000 |
| Other non-current assets | | 60,000 |
| Current assets | | 19,000 |
| | | 121,000 |
| Share capital | | 75,000 |
| Retained profits: | | |
| As at 31.3.2015 | 20,000 | |
| *Add* Profit for year ended 31.3.2016 | 16,000 | |
| | | 36,000 |
| General reserve (as at 31.3.2016) | | 10,000 |
| | | 121,000 |

**Sub B Statement of Financial Position as at 31 March 2016**

| | £ | £ |
|---|---|---|
| Non-current assets | | 30,000 |
| Current assets | | 22,000 |
| | | 52,000 |
| Share capital | | 30,000 |
| Retained profits: | | |
| As at 31.3.2015 | 7,000 | |
| *Add* Profit for year ended 31.3.2016 | 15,000 | |
| | | 22,000 |
| | | 52,000 |

**23.3** On 1 April 2014, Machinery Limited bought 80% of the ordinary share capital of Components Limited. On 1 April 2016, Machinery Limited was itself taken over by Sales Limited who purchased 75% of the ordinary shares in Machinery Limited.

The statements of financial position of the three companies at 31 October 2018 prepared for internal use showed the following position:

| | *Sales Ltd* | | *Machinery Ltd* | | *Components Ltd* | |
|---|---|---|---|---|---|---|
| | £ | £ | £ | £ | £ | £ |
| Non-current assets | | | | | | |
| Freehold land at cost | | 89,000 | | 30,000 | | 65,000 |
| Buildings at cost | 100,000 | | 120,000 | | 40,000 | |
| *Less* | | | | | | |
| Accumulated depreciation | (36,000) | | (40,000) | | (16,400) | |
| | | 64,000 | | 80,000 | | 23,600 |
| Plant and equipment at cost | 102,900 | | 170,000 | | 92,000 | |
| *Less* | | | | | | |
| Accumulated depreciation | (69,900) | | (86,000) | | (48,200) | |
| | | 33,000 | | 84,000 | | 43,800 |
| | | 186,000 | | 194,000 | | 132,400 |
| *Investments* | | | | | | |
| Shares in Machinery at cost | | 120,000 | | | | |
| Shares in Components at cost | | | | 128,000 | | |
| | | 306,000 | | 322,000 | | 132,400 |
| *Current assets* | | | | | | |
| Inventory | 108,500 | | 75,500 | | 68,400 | |
| Account receivable | 196,700 | | 124,800 | | 83,500 | |
| Cash at bank | 40,200 | | – | | 25,400 | |
| | | 345,400 | | 200,300 | | 177,300 |
| Total assets | | 651,400 | | 522,300 | | 309,700 |
| *Current liabilities* | | | | | | |
| Accounts payable | 240,000 | | 200,700 | | 71,200 | |
| Bank overdraft | – | | 69,400 | | – | |
| Corporation tax | 57,400 | | 47,200 | | 24,500 | |
| | | (297,400) | | (317,300) | | (95,700) |
| Net assets | | 354,000 | | 205,000 | | 214,000 |
| Ordinary shares | | 200,000 | | 120,000 | | 100,000 |
| 10% preference shares | | – | | – | | 40,000 |
| Revenue reserves | | 154,000 | | 85,000 | | 74,000 |
| | | 354,000 | | 205,000 | | 214,000 |

*Additional information*:

(*a*) All ordinary shares are £1 each, fully paid.

(*b*) Preference shares in Components Ltd are 50p each fully paid.

(*c*) All creditors are payable within one year.

(*d*) Items purchased by Machinery Ltd from Components Ltd and remaining in inventory at 31 October 2018 amounted to £25,000. The profit element is 20% of selling price for Components Ltd.

(*e*) Depreciation policy of the group is to provide for:

(*i*) buildings – at the rate of 2% on cost each year;

(*ii*) plant and equipment – at the rate of 10% on cost each year including full provision in the year of acquisition.

These policies are applied by all members of the group.

Included in the plant and equipment of Components Ltd is a machine purchased from the manufacturers, Machinery Ltd, on 1 January 2017 for £10,000. Machinery Ltd recorded a profit of £2,000 on the sale of the machine.

→

(*f*) Intra-group balances are included in accounts receivable and accounts payable respectively and are as follows:

| | | | £ |
|---|---|---|---|
| Sales Ltd | Accounts payable | – Machinery Ltd | 45,600 |
| | | – Components Ltd | 28,900 |
| Machinery Ltd | Accounts receivable | – Sales Ltd | 56,900 |
| Components Ltd | Accounts receivable | – Sales Ltd | 28,900 |

(*g*) A cheque drawn by Sales Ltd for £11,300 on 28 October 2018 was received by Machinery Ltd on 3 November 2018.

(*h*) At 1 April 2014, reserves in Machinery Ltd were £28,000 and in Components Ltd £20,000. At 1 April 2016 the figures were £40,000 and £60,000 respectively.

**Required:**
Prepare a group statement of financial position at 31 October 2018 for Sales Ltd and its subsidiaries complying, so far as the information will allow, with the accounting requirements of international accounting standards.

(*Association of Chartered Certified Accountants*)

chapter

# 24 Consolidated statements of profit or loss and statements of comprehensive income

## Learning objectives

**After you have studied this chapter, you should be able to:**

- prepare consolidated statements of profit or loss and comprehensive statements of profit or loss for groups with wholly owned subsidiaries
- prepare consolidated statements of profit or loss and comprehensive statements of profit or loss for groups with partly owned subsidiaries

## Introduction

In this chapter, you'll learn how to prepare consolidated statements of profit or loss and comprehensive statements of profit or loss for groups with either wholly owned subsidiaries, partly owned subsidiaries, or both.

## 24.1 The consolidated statement of profit or loss

So far, we've been looking at how to prepare the consolidated statement of financial position. However, consolidated financial statements comprise all the financial statements that must be prepared by individual companies, not just the statement of financial position.

The consolidated statement of profit or loss is drawn up to show the overall profit (or loss) of the companies in the group, treating the group as a single entity. If all of the subsidiaries are owned 100%, and there are no unrealised profits in inventory, then it is simply a case of adding together all the amounts contained in each of the individual company statements of profit or loss to form the consolidated statement of profit or loss. However, such a simple situation is very rarely found in practice.

Why can't we simply add together all of the separate statements of profit or loss to form the consolidated statement of profit or loss when the subsidiaries are partly owned and there are no unrealised profits on inventory?

Exhibit 24.1 shows the framework for preparing a consolidated statement of profit or loss giving details of the adjustments needed. As similar principles are applied to those used when preparing a consolidated statement of financial position, you will see that it is done in much the same way as was shown in Chapters 19–23.

***Note*: Exhibit 24.1 looks very complicated. It isn't. All I have done is summarised most of the equivalent statement of financial position adjustments into one exhibit, rather than distancing them out over four or five chapters. If you find it difficult to understand, refer back to the equivalent statement of financial position adjustments. This should help you follow what is being done.**

## Exhibit 24.1

**Specimen Statement of Profit or Loss for the year ending . . .**

| | | £000 | £000 | |
|---|---|---|---|---|
| Revenue | (a) | | 200 | Parent plus subsidiaries less cancellation of intra-group items |
| Cost of sales | (b) | | (120) | |
| Gross profit | | | 80 | |
| Distribution costs | | 10 | | |
| Administrative expenses | | 20 | | |
| | | | (30) | |
| Profit before taxation | | | 50 | |
| Taxation | (c) | | (14) | |
| Profit after taxation | | | 36 | |
| Non-controlling interest | (d) | | (4) | |
| Profit for the year | | | 32 | |

*Notes*:

(*a*) Turnover. Intra-group sales to be deducted.

(*b*) Cost of sales: (*i*) Intra-group purchases. This is the same figure as for (*a*), as the price at which sales are made by one group company is the same figure at which the other group company has bought them. (*ii*) Adjust for unrealised profit in inventory, by reducing closing inventory. As cost of sales = opening inventory + purchases − closing inventory, any reduction in closing inventory will increase 'cost of sales'. The statement of financial position inventory figure will be reduced by unrealised profits.

(*c*) This is the sum of taxation for all companies within the group.

(*d*) Non-controlling interest:

(*i*) If ordinary shares only are issued by subsidiary: deduct the non-controlling interest's percentage of the subsidiary's profits *after* taxation.

(*ii*) If preference shares are also issued by the subsidiary this figure is found by:
Non-controlling interest percentage of preference share capital × total preference dividend paid

*plus*

Non-controlling interest percentage of ordinary share capital × balance of profits (i.e. after tax and preference dividend) for the year, e.g.

Total preference shares £1,000: Non-controlling interest £400.
Total ordinary shares £2,000: Non-controlling interest £500.
Total preference dividend paid £150.
Profit of subsidiary after taxation: £950.

| Therefore, the non-controlling interest is: | £ |
|---|---|
| Share of preference dividend: 40% × £150 | 60 |
| Share of balance of after-tax profits: 25% × (£950 − £150) | 200 |
| | 260 |

Let's look at two more examples. One shows the consolidation of the statement of profit or loss when the subsidiary is wholly owned (Exhibit 24.2) and the other shows it where there is a non-controlling interest in the subsidiary company (Exhibit 24.3).

## Exhibit 24.2 Where the subsidiary is wholly owned

P Ltd owns 100% of the share capital of S Ltd. The statements of profit or loss of these companies for the year ending 31 December 2017 are:

| *Statements of profit or loss* | *P Ltd* | | *S Ltd* | |
|---|---|---|---|---|
| | *£000* | *£000* | *£000* | *£000* |
| Revenue | | 400 | | 280 |
| Cost of sales | | (270) | | (190) |
| Gross profit | | 130 | | 90 |
| Distribution costs | 20 | | 10 | |
| Administrative expenses | 30 | | 15 | |
| | | (50) | | (25) |
| Profit before taxation | | 80 | | 65 |
| Taxation | | (17) | | (11) |
| Profit for the year | | 63 | | 54 |

*Notes*:

(*a*) P Ltd had sold goods which cost £10,000 to S Ltd for £15,000.

(*b*) At the date of the statement of financial position, 40% of the goods in (*a*) had not been sold by S Ltd.

(*c*) Of the £7,000 retained profits from last year for S Ltd, £3,000 is in respect of post-acquisition profits.

The consolidated statement of profit or loss is:

**P Group Ltd**
**Consolidated Statement of Profit or Loss for the year ending 31 December 2017**

| | *£000* | *£000* |
|---|---|---|
| Revenue (W1) | | 665 |
| Cost of sales (W2) | | (447) |
| Gross profit | | 218 |
| Distribution costs | 30 | |
| Administrative expenses | 45 | |
| | | (75) |
| Profit before taxation | | 143 |
| Taxation | | (28) |
| Profit for the year | | 115 |

*Workings*:
Letters (*a*) to (*d*) refer to the descriptions given above and in Exhibit 24.1.

(W1) P 400 + S 280 − 15 intercompany sales = 665 (*a*).

(W2) P 270 + S 190 − 15 intercompany purchases + the unrealised profit in inventory (40% × 5 = 2) = 447 (*b*)(*i*) and (*ii*).

***Note*: The difference between the total profit found of £115 and the total of the two retained profits shown in the individual company statements of profit or loss (£63 + £54 = £117) is £2. This represents £2 unrealised profit (*b* (*ii*)).**

Why was the £2 unrealised profit in the inventory held by S Ltd added to the consolidated figure for cost of sales in Working 2?

## Exhibit 24.3 Where there is a non-controlling interest in the subsidiary

P2 Ltd owns 80% of shares in S2 Ltd. Statements of profit or loss of the companies for the year ending 31 December 2018 are as follows:

| *Statements of profit or loss* | *P2 Ltd* | | *S2 Ltd* | |
|---|---|---|---|---|
| | *£000* | *£000* | *£000* | *£000* |
| Revenue | | 640 | | 330 |
| Cost of sales | | (410) | | (200) |
| Gross profit | | 230 | | 130 |
| Distribution costs | 35 | | 20 | |
| Administrative expenses | 70 | | 55 | |
| | | (105) | | (75) |
| Profit before taxation | | 125 | | 55 |
| Taxation | | (26) | | (10) |
| Profit for the year | | 99 | | 45 |

*Notes:*

(*a*) S2 Ltd had sold goods which cost £20,000 to P2 Ltd for £30,000.

(*b*) At the date of the statement of financial position, 30% of the goods in (*a*) had not been sold by P2 Ltd.

(*c*) Of the £35,000 retained profits of S2 Ltd brought forward, £15,000 is post-acquisition profits.

**P2 Group Ltd**
**Consolidated Statement of Profit or Loss for the year ending 31 December 2018**

| | *£000* | *£000* |
|---|---|---|
| Revenue (W1) | | 940 |
| Cost of sales (W2) | | (583) |
| Gross profit | | 357 |
| Distribution costs | 55 | |
| Administrative expenses | 125 | |
| | | (180) |
| Profit before taxation | | 177 |
| Taxation | | (36) |
| Profit after taxation | | 141 |
| Non-controlling interest (W3) | | (9) |
| Profit for the financial year | | 132 |

*Workings:*

Letters (*a*) to (*d*) refer to the descriptions given above and in Exhibit 24.1.

(W1) P2 640 + S2 330 − intercompany sales 30 = 940 (*a*).

(W2) P2 410 + S2 200 − intercompany purchases 30 + unrealised profit in inventory (30% × 10 = 3) = 583 (*b*)(*i*) and (*ii*).

(W3) 20% × 45: profit after taxation of S2 Ltd = 9 (*d*)(*i*).

Explain the difference between the consolidated retained profits figure of £132 and the total of £144 found if you add together the profits for the year of P2 Ltd and S2 Ltd.

***Note*: If you remember the adjustments made to reconcile the consolidated profit figure in Activity 24.3, you should have no difficulty preparing consolidated statements of profit or loss.**

## 24.2 The consolidated statement of comprehensive income

In the examples shown above, there were no entries that belonged below 'profit for the year' in the statement of comprehensive income. **(See Section 12.10 for an example of this statement.)** When there are, the same principles apply as with the statement of financial position and the statements of profit or loss.

## 24.3 The consolidated statement of changes in equity

Dividends paid and transfers between reserves are among the items that appear in this statement. For consolidation:

(*a*) Transfers among reserves: show the parent's plus the group share of subsidiary transfers.
(*b*) Reserves of subsidiaries: only post-acquisition reserves are included.

### Learning outcomes

**You should now have learnt:**

1. When consolidating statements of profit or loss for groups with wholly owned subsidiaries with no intra-group transactions or indebtedness, it is simply a case of adding together all the separate statements of profit or loss to form the consolidated statement of profit or loss.
2. When consolidating statements of profit or loss, adjustments for unrealised profits on intra-group transactions and for intra-group indebtedness must be made where they exist (as per Chapters 19, 21 and 22).
3. When consolidating statements of profit or loss for groups with partly owned subsidiaries, the approaches detailed in Chapters 17 and 23 should be followed.

### Answers to activities

24.1 You need to deduct the non-controlling interest in the profits or losses of the subsidiary when combining the figures for profits and/or losses of the companies for the period.

24.2 It was added because it was deducted from the purchases of S Ltd when the cost of sales figure for S Ltd was calculated. As it represents unrealised profit, it needs to be added back, so increasing the cost of sales of the group to the correct figure – i.e. one that does not include any unrealised profit.

24.3 The difference of £12 comprises: £3 (unrealised profit in inventory) + £9 (non-controlling interest share of this year's profit of S2).

## Review questions

***Note*: Unless otherwise indicated, assume that the share capital of all the companies in these review questions comprises ordinary £1 shares.**

**24.1** The following information relates to the Brodick group of companies for the year to 30 April 2017:

| | *Brodick plc* | *Lamlash Ltd* | *Corrie Ltd* |
|---|---|---|---|
| | *£000* | *£000* | *£000* |
| Revenue | 1,100 | 500 | 130 |
| Cost of sales | (630) | (300) | (70) |
| Gross profit | 470 | 200 | 60 |
| Administrative expenses | (105) | (150) | (20) |
| Dividend received from Lamlash Ltd | 24 | – | – |
| Dividend received from Corrie Ltd | 6 | – | – |
| Profit before tax | 395 | 50 | 40 |
| Taxation | (65) | (10) | (20) |
| Profit for the year | 330 | 40 | 20 |

*Additional information*:

(*a*) The issued share capital of the group was as follows:
Brodick plc: 5,000,000 ordinary shares of £1 each;
Lamlash Ltd: 1,000,000 ordinary shares of £1 each; and
Corrie Ltd: 400,000 ordinary shares of £1 each.

(*b*) Brodick plc purchased 80% of the issued share capital of Lamlash Ltd in 2010. At that time, the retained profits of Lamlash amounted to £56,000.

(*c*) Brodick plc purchased 60% of the issued share capital of Corrie Ltd in 2014. At that time, the retained profits of Corrie amounted to £20,000.

**Required:**
In so far as the information permits, prepare the Brodick group of companies' consolidated statement of profit or loss for the year ending 30 April 2017 in accordance with IFRSs.

*Note*: Notes to the statement of profit or loss are not required, but you should append a statement showing the make-up of the 'profits for the year', and your workings should be submitted.

(*Association of Accounting Technicians*)

**24.2** You are presented with the following summarised information for Norbreck plc and its subsidiary, Bispham Ltd:

**Statements of Profit or Loss for the year ending 30 September 2017**

| | *Norbreck plc* | *Bispham Ltd* |
|---|---|---|
| | *£000* | *£000* |
| Revenue | 1,700 | 450 |
| Cost of sales | (920) | (75) |
| *Gross profit* | 780 | 375 |
| Administration expenses | (300) | (175) |
| Income from shares in group company | 120 | – |
| *Profit before taxation* | 600 | 200 |
| Taxation | (30) | (20) |
| *Profit for the year* | 570 | 180 |

**Statements of Financial Position at 30 September 2017**

| | Norbreck plc | Bispham Ltd |
|---|---|---|
| | £000 | £000 |
| Non-current tangible assets | 1,280 | 440 |
| Investments: Shares in group company | 400 | – |
| | 1,680 | 440 |
| *Current assets* | | |
| Inventory | 300 | 250 |
| Accounts receivable | 280 | 150 |
| Cash at bank and in hand | 40 | 10 |
| | 620 | 410 |
| Total assets | 2,300 | 850 |
| *Current liabilities* | | |
| Trade accounts payable | (80) | (160) |
| Other payables, taxation and social security | (160) | (70) |
| | (240) | (230) |
| *Non-current liabilities* | | |
| Deferred taxation | (460) | (20) |
| Total liabilities | (700) | (250) |
| Net assets | 1,600 | 600 |
| *Equity* | | |
| Called-up share capital (ordinary shares of £1 each) | 900 | 400 |
| Reserves (including retained profits) | 700 | 200 |
| | 1,600 | 600 |

*Additional information:*

*(a)* Norbreck plc acquired 80% of the shares in Bispham Ltd on 1 October 2014. Bispham's retained profits balance as at that date was £10,000.

*(b)* During the year, Norbreck paid dividends of £360,000 and Bispham paid dividends of £150,000.

**Required:**
Prepare Bispham plc's consolidated statement of profit or loss for the year ending 30 September 2017 and a consolidated statement of financial position as at that date.

*Note:* Formal notes to the account are not required, although detailed workings should be submitted with your answer. You should also append to the consolidated statement of profit or loss your calculation of earnings per share and a statement showing the make-up of 'retained profits carried forward'.

*(Association of Accounting Technicians)*

**24.3A** The following figures for the year to 30 April 2016 have been extracted from the books and records of three companies which form a group:

| | Old plc | Field Ltd | Lodge Ltd |
|---|---|---|---|
| | £ | £ | £ |
| Revenue reserves at 1 May 2015 | 30,000 | 40,000 | 50,000 |
| Inventory at 1 May 2015 | 90,000 | 150,000 | 80,000 |
| Sales | 1,250,000 | 875,000 | 650,000 |
| Purchases | 780,000 | 555,000 | 475,000 |
| Distribution expenses | 125,000 | 85,000 | 60,000 |
| Administration expenses | 28,000 | 40,000 | 72,000 |
| Share capital – fully paid ordinary shares of £1 each | 450,000 | 350,000 | 200,000 |
| 8% preference shares of £1 each | | 100,000 | |
| Inventory at 30 April 2016 | 110,000 | 135,000 | 85,000 |

Profits are deemed to accrue evenly throughout the year.

→

*Other information:*

(*a*) Corporation tax of the following amounts is to be provided on the profits of the year:

| | |
|---|---|
| Old plc | £125,000 |
| Field Ltd | £75,000 |
| Lodge Ltd | £20,000 |

(*b*) Field Ltd sells goods for resale to both Old plc and Lodge Ltd. At 30 April 2016, inventory of goods purchased from Field Ltd are:

| | |
|---|---|
| in Old plc | £40,000 |
| in Lodge Ltd | £28,000 |

The net profit percentage for Field Ltd on sales of these goods is 25%.
Old plc had £36,000 of these goods in inventory at 1 May 2015.
Total sales in the year by Field Ltd to Old plc were £150,000 and to Lodge Ltd £120,000.

(*c*) Old plc acquired the whole of the ordinary shares in Field Ltd many years ago. Old plc acquired 120,000 shares in Lodge Ltd on 1 August 2015.

**Required:**
A consolidated statement of profit or loss for Old plc and its subsidiaries for the year ending 30 April 2016, together with any relevant notes.

(*Association of Chartered Certified Accountants*)

**24.4A** The following are the trial balances of ATH Ltd, GLE Ltd, and FRN Ltd as at 31 December 2018.

| | *ATH Ltd* | *GLE Ltd* | *FRN Ltd* |
|---|---|---|---|
| | £ | £ | £ |
| Ordinary share capital (shares of £1 each, fully paid) | 100,000 | 30,000 | 20,000 |
| Retained profits – balance at 31.12.2017 | 15,600 | 6,000 | 1,900 |
| Current liabilities | 20,750 | 15,900 | 18,350 |
| Sales | 194,000 | 116,000 | 84,000 |
| Dividend received from GLE Ltd | 1,200 | – | – |
| | 331,550 | 167,900 | 124,250 |
| Non-current assets | 45,000 | 29,000 | 25,000 |
| Current assets | 46,000 | 27,500 | 17,500 |
| 24,000 ordinary shares in GLE Ltd at cost | 33,700 | – | – |
| 20,000 ordinary shares in FRN Ltd at cost | 21,250 | – | – |
| Cost of goods sold | 153,000 | 87,000 | 63,000 |
| General expenses | 32,600 | 22,900 | 18,750 |
| Dividend for 2018, paid on 31.12.2018 | – | 1,500 | – |
| | 331,550 | 167,900 | 124,250 |

ATH Ltd acquired the shares in FRN Ltd on 31 December 2016, when the balance of retained profits of FRN Ltd was £700, and acquired the shares in GLE Ltd on 31 December 2017. No dividend was paid by either ATH Ltd or GLE Ltd for the year 2017.

The sales of GLE Ltd for 2018 (£116,000) include £1,000 for goods sold to FRN Ltd and this amount has been debited to the purchases account in the books of FRN Ltd.

All these goods were sold by FRN Ltd during 2018.

**Required:**
A consolidated statement of profit or loss for the year 2018 and a consolidated statement of financial position as on 31 December 2018 (not necessarily in a form for publication).

Ignore depreciation of non-current assets and taxation.

(*Institute of Chartered Secretaries and Administrators*)

**24.5A** In recent years, Khang Plc has earned a reputation for buying modestly performing businesses and selling them at a substantial profit within a period of two to three years of their acquisition. On 1 July 2015, Khang Plc acquired 80% of the ordinary share capital of Yuan Ltd at a cost of £10,280,000. On the same date, it also acquired 50% of Yuan Ltd's 10% loan notes at par. The summarised draft financial statements of the two companies are:

**Statements of Profit or Loss for the year ending 31 March 2016**

| | *Khang Plc* | *Yuan Ltd* |
|---|---|---|
| | *£000* | *£000* |
| Turnover | 60,000 | 24,000 |
| Cost of sales | (42,000) | (20,000) |
| Gross profit | 18,000 | 4,000 |
| Operating expenses | (6,000) | (200) |
| Loan interest received (paid) | 75 | (200) |
| Operating profit | 12,075 | 3,600 |
| Taxation | (3,000) | (600) |
| Profit after tax for the year | 9,075 | 3,000 |
| Profit brought forward | 16,525 | 5,400 |
| Retained profit per statement of financial position | 25,600 | 8,400 |

**Statements of Financial Position as at 31 March 2016**

| | *Khang Plc* | | *Yuan Ltd* | |
|---|---|---|---|---|
| | *£000* | *£000* | *£000* | *£000* |
| Tangible non-current assets | | 19,320 | | 8,000 |
| Investments | | 11,280 | | Nil |
| | | 30,600 | | 8,000 |
| Current assets | 15,000 | | 8,000 | |
| Creditors: Amounts falling due after less than one year | (10,000) | | (3,600) | |
| Net current assets | | 5,000 | | 4,400 |
| Creditors: Amounts falling due after more than one year – 10% loan notes | | Nil | | (2,000) |
| Net assets | | 35,600 | | 10,400 |
| *Capital and reserves* | | | | |
| Ordinary shares of £1 each | | 10,000 | | 2,000 |
| Retained profits | | 25,600 | | 8,400 |
| | | 35,600 | | 10,400 |

The following information is relevant:

1 The fair values of Yuan Ltd assets were equal to their book values with the exception of its plant, which had a fair value of £3.2 million in excess of its book value at the date of acquisition. The remaining life of all of Yuan Ltd's plant at the date of its acquisition was four years and this period has not changed as a result of the acquisition. Depreciation of plant is on a straight-line basis and charged to cost of sales. Yuan Ltd has not adjusted the value of its plant as a result of the fair value exercise.
2 Khang Plc bears almost all of the administration costs incurred on behalf of the group (invoicing, credit control, etc). It does not charge Yuan Ltd for this service as to do so would not have a material effect on the group profit.
3 Revenues and profits should be deemed to accrue evenly throughout the year.
4 The goodwill impairment review at the year-end found goodwill to be overstated by £300,000.

**Required:**
Prepare a consolidated statement of profit or loss and statement of financial position for Khang Plc for the year to 31 March 2016.

chapter 25

# Business combinations: purchase method accounting

## Learning objectives

**After you have studied this chapter, you should be able to:**

- explain how to apply purchase method accounting
- explain how to recognise goodwill
- explain how the amount shown for any non-controlling interest is calculated

## Introduction

In this chapter, you'll learn in greater detail about the accounting method used to combine the accounting information when two companies join together to form one new overall organisation: purchase method accounting. Much of the contents of this chapter have been covered earlier, but here it is presented all in one place and should serve as good revision and a reminder of what you should know.

## 25.1 Introduction

When two companies join together to form one new overall organisation, it is obvious that the shares of both companies must come under common ownership. The accounting standards applied when business combinations exist or are formed are IAS 27 (*Separate financial statements*) and IFRS 3 (*Business combinations*). In this chapter we will look at IFRS 3. IAS 27 is covered in Chapter 26.

## 25.2 IFRS 3 Business combinations

A business combination is the bringing together of separate entities or businesses into one reporting entity. The result of nearly all business combinations is that one entity, the acquirer, obtains control of one or more other businesses, the acquirees. If an entity obtains control of one or more other entities that are not businesses, the bringing together of those entities is *not* a business combination. When an entity acquires a group of assets or net assets that does not constitute a business, it must allocate the cost of the group between the individual identifiable assets and liabilities in the group based on their relative fair values at the acquisition date.

Business combinations include those in which one entity obtains control of another entity but for which the date of obtaining control (the acquisition date) does not coincide with the date or dates of acquiring an ownership interest (the date or dates of exchange). For example, an investee may enter into share buy-back arrangements with some of its investors and, as a result, control of the investee changes.

All business combinations must be accounted for by applying the 'purchase method'. The purchase method views a business combination from the perspective of the combining entity that is identified as the acquirer. The acquirer purchases net assets and recognises the assets acquired and liabilities and contingent liabilities assumed, including those not previously recognised by the acquiree. The measurement of the acquirer's assets and liabilities is not affected by the transaction, nor are any additional assets or liabilities of the acquirer recognised as a result of the transaction, because they are not the subjects of the transaction.

At the acquisition date, the acquirer must allocate the cost of a business combination by recognising the acquiree's identifiable assets, liabilities and contingent liabilities at their fair values at that date [except for non-current assets (or disposal groups) that are classified as held for sale in accordance with IFRS 5 (*Non-current assets held for sale and discontinued operations*), which are recognised at fair value less costs to sell]. Any difference between the cost of the business combination and the acquirer's interest in the net fair value of the identifiable assets, liabilities and contingent liabilities is goodwill. Goodwill acquired in a business combination represents a payment made by the acquirer in anticipation of future economic benefits from assets that are not capable of being individually identified and separately recognised. It is accounted for at the acquisition date by the acquirer:

(*a*) recognising goodwill acquired in a business combination as an asset;
(*b*) initially measuring that goodwill at its cost, being the excess of the cost of the business combination over the acquirer's interest in the net fair value of the identifiable assets, liabilities and contingent liabilities;
(*c*) measuring, after initial recognition, such goodwill at cost less any accumulated impairment losses.

When the calculation of goodwill produces a negative amount, the acquirer must recognise the gain from a bargain purchase immediately *in profit or loss*.

Positive goodwill acquired in a business combination is *not* amortised. Instead, it must be tested annually for impairment, or more frequently if events or changes in circumstances indicate that it might be impaired, in accordance with IAS 36 (*Impairment of assets*).

Entities must disclose information that enables users of an entity's financial statements to evaluate the nature and financial effect of:

(*i*) business combinations that were effected during the period;
(*ii*) business combinations that were effected after the date of the statement of financial position but before the financial statements are authorised for issue;
(*iii*) some business combinations that were effected in previous periods;
(*iv*) changes in the carrying amount of goodwill during the period.

The acquirer's statement of profit or loss should incorporate the acquiree's profits and losses after the acquisition date by including the acquiree's income and expenses based on the cost of the business combination to the acquirer. For example, depreciation that relates to the acquiree's depreciable assets are based on the fair values of those depreciable assets at the acquisition date, i.e. their cost to the acquirer.

Any non-controlling interest in the acquiree is stated at the non-controlling interest's proportion of the fair value of the net assets acquired.

## 25.3 Purchase method accounting

As mentioned above, this is the method that has been adopted in Chapters 16–24. In the books of the parent undertaking:

(*a*) shares purchased in a subsidiary are shown at cost less dividends received out of pre-acquisition profits;

(*b*) dividends out of pre-acquisition profits cannot be regarded as available for distribution as dividends by the parent.

In the consolidated financial statements:

(*a*) assets *and* liabilities of the subsidiary at the date of acquisition are shown in the statement of financial position at their fair value at that date;
(*b*) the difference at the date of acquisition between the fair value of the purchase consideration and the fair value of the net assets acquired is treated as goodwill;
(*c*) only post-acquisition profits of the subsidiary attributable to members of the group should be included in the consolidated reserves of the group.

The idea underlying these rules is to stop capital receipts, i.e. dividends from pre-acquisition profits, being paid out as dividends. Clearly, they also prevent reserves attributable to minority shareholders from being treated as if they belong to the group.

The consolidation of statements of financial position using the *acquisition* method is now shown in Exhibit 25.1. You should know this well by now but, if you do find any items in the exhibit hard to follow, refer back to the chapter in which that item was first explained.

### Exhibit 25.1

A Ltd made an offer of £270,000 for the whole of the share capital of B Ltd and it was accepted. Payment was made in cash. The fair value placed on the tangible fixed assets of B Ltd for the purposes of the merger was £148,000. The statements of financial position of the two companies immediately before the merger on 31 December 2016 were:

| | *A Ltd* | | *B Ltd* | |
|---|---|---|---|---|
| | *£000* | *£000* | *£000* | *£000* |
| Tangible non-current assets | | 400 | | 120 |
| Current assets | | 450 | | 200 |
| | | 850 | | 320 |
| Current liabilities | | (130) | | (90) |
| | | 720 | | 230 |
| Ordinary shares £1 | | 500 | | 150 |
| Revenue reserves | | 220 | | 80 |
| | | 720 | | 230 |

The statements of financial position of A Ltd and of the group immediately following the merger were:

**Statement of Financial Position at 31 December 2016**

| | | *A Ltd* | | | *Group* | |
|---|---|---|---|---|---|---|
| | | *£000* | *£000* | | *£000* | *£000* |
| Non-current assets | | | | | | |
| Intangible (goodwill) | | – | | (W2) | 12 | |
| Tangible | | 400 | | (W3) | 548 | |
| Investments | | 270 | | | – | |
| | | | 670 | | | 560 |
| Current assets | (W1) | | 180 | (W4) | | 380 |
| Total assets | | | 850 | | | 940 |
| Current liabilities | | | (130) | | | (220) |
| Net assets | | | 720 | | | 720 |
| Share capital | | | 500 | | | 500 |
| Reserves | | | 220 | | | 220 |
| | | | 720 | | | 720 |

*Workings (£000):*

| | | | |
|---|---|---|---|
| (W1) | Original current assets 450 − cash paid 270 = 180 | | |
| (W2) | Paid for shares | | 270 |
| | *Less* Net assets of B at takeover date | 230 | |
| | *Add* Increase in value of non-current assets of B to a 'fair value' 148 − 120 = | 28 | |
| | | | (258) |
| | Goodwill (intangible non-current asset) | | 12 |
| (W3) | Non-current assets A Ltd 400 + B Ltd 148 = 548 | | |
| (W4) | A Ltd (after payment) 180 + B Ltd 200 = 380 | | |

## Learning outcomes

**You should now have learnt:**

1. IFRS 3 requires that all business combinations must be accounted for using purchase method accounting.
2. Under purchase method accounting, assets and liabilities must be restated to their fair values.
3. Positive goodwill must be recognised as an asset and must be tested annually for impairment.
4. Positive goodwill is not amortised.
5. When the goodwill calculation produces a regative number, the gain from the bargain purchase must be recognised in profit or loss and eliminated.
6. Any non-controlling interest is stated at the non-controlling interest's proportion of the fair value of the net assets acquired.

## Review question

**25.1** Large plc, a manufacturer and wholesaler, purchased 600,000 of the 800,000 issued ordinary shares of a smaller company, Small Ltd, on 1 January 2015 when the retained earnings account of Small Ltd had a credit balance of £72,000.

The latest accounts of the two companies are:

**Summary Statements of Profit or Loss for the year to 30 September 2016 (£000s)**

| | *Large plc* | *Small Ltd* |
|---|---|---|
| Revenue | 10,830 | 2,000 |
| Cost of sales and production services | (3,570) | (1,100) |
| Gross profit | 7,260 | 900 |
| Administrative and marketing expenses (including depreciation, audit fee and directors' remuneration) | (2,592) | (180) |
| Operating profit | 4,668 | 720 |
| Dividend received from Small Ltd | 180 | – |
| Net profit before tax | 4,848 | 720 |
| Taxation | (2,304) | (200) |
| Profit for the year | 2,544 | 520 |

**Summary Statements of Financial Position at 30 September 2016 (£000)**

| | *Large plc* | *Small Ltd* |
|---|---|---|
| Intangible non-current assets: | | |
| Research and development: | | |
| – research | 50 | – |
| – development | 228 | – |
| Goodwill – unpurchased | 50 | – |
| Other non-current assets at cost less depreciation | 3,920 | 728 |
| Investment in Small Ltd | 680 | – |
| Current account with Large plc | – | 75 |
| Inventory | 594 | 231 |
| Accounts receivable | 3,250 | 370 |
| Bank | 1,344 | 264 |
| | 10,116 | 1,668 |
| *Less* Current account with Small Ltd | (75) | (–) |
| Accounts payable for goods and services | (297) | (156) |
| | 9,744 | 1,512 |
| Share capital | 6,000 | 800 |
| Retained earnings | 3,744 | 712 |
| | 9,744 | 1,512 |

*Notes*:
The intangible non-current asset section of the statement of financial position of Large plc has not yet been amended prior to consolidation to take account of the provisions of accounting standards regarding intangible assets.

The inventory of Large plc contained goods valued at £108,000 purchased from Small Ltd at production cost plus 50%.

**Required:**

(*a*) Prepare the consolidated statement of profit or loss of Large plc and its subsidiary Small Ltd for the year to 30 September 2016.

(*b*) Prepare the consolidated statement of financial position of Large plc and its subsidiary Small Ltd at 30 September 2016.

(*Institute of Chartered Secretaries and Administrators*)

chapter

# 26 Standards covering subsidiaries, associates and joint arrangements

## Learning objectives

**After you have studied this chapter, you should be able to:**

- explain the importance of the control concept
- describe the circumstances under which a parent–subsidiary relationship is recognised
- describe the conditions whereby companies are exempt from preparing consolidated financial statements
- describe the conditions under which a subsidiary should not be included in the consolidated financial statements
- describe what to do when a company has investments in associate entities but does not prepare consolidated financial statements because it has no investments in subsidiaries
- describe the equity method of accounting

## Introduction

In this chapter, you'll learn more about various accounting standards that regulate the preparation of accounting information relating to subsidiaries and associates. These regulations have changed considerably in recent years and are now more standardised than in the past, enabling far greater comparability than was previously the case.

## 26.1 Background

In previous chapters you have learnt some of the rules in IAS 27 *Separate financial statements,* including:

- In preparing consolidated financial statements, the financial statements of the parent and its subsidiaries are combined line by line by adding together like items of assets, liabilities, equity, income, and expenses.
- Non-controlling interests in the profit or loss of consolidated subsidiaries are disclosed.
- Non-controlling interests in the net assets of consolidated subsidiaries are disclosed separately within equity and comprise the amount of non-controlling interests at the date of acquisition and the non-controlling interest's share of changes in equity since the date of the formation of the combination.
- Intra-group balances, transactions, income, expenses and dividends must be eliminated in full.
- Profits and losses resulting from intra-group transactions that are recognised in assets such as inventory and non-current assets (i.e. the profit or loss is unrealised) must be eliminated in full.

- Let's now look at some of the other requirements and definitions contained in IAS 27.

## 26.2 IAS 27 Separate financial statements

This standard applies to the preparation and presentation of consolidated financial statements for a group of entities under the control of a parent. That is, it applies to accounting for investments in subsidiaries, jointly controlled entities (joint arrangements) and associates in the financial statements of a parent, a venturer or investor. It also prescribes the accounting treatment for investments in subsidiaries, jointly controlled entities and associates when an entity elects, or is required by local regulations, to present separate financial statements and these investments must be accounted for at cost or in accordance with IAS 39 (*Financial instruments: recognition and measurement*) or IFRS 9 (*Financial instruments*). Consolidation is not required of a subsidiary acquired when there is evidence that control is intended to be temporary.

Control is defined as '*the power to govern the financial and operating policies of an entity so as to obtain benefits from its activities*'. Control is said to exist when the parent owns, directly or indirectly through subsidiaries, more than half of the voting power of an entity unless, in exceptional circumstances, it can be clearly demonstrated that such ownership does not constitute control. Control also exists when the parent owns half or less of the voting power of an entity when there is:

(*a*) power over more than half of the voting rights by virtue of an agreement with other investors;
(*b*) power to govern the financial and operating policies of the entity under a statute or an agreement;
(*c*) power to appoint or remove the majority of the members of the board of directors or equivalent governing body and control of the entity is by that board or body; or
(*d*) power to cast the majority of votes at meetings of the board of directors or equivalent governing body and control of the entity is by that board or body.

**Activity 26.1** **Why do you think control is now the key factor in determining the relationship between related companies, rather than ownership?**

When a parent or its subsidiary is an investor in an associate or a venturer in a jointly controlled entity, the consolidated financial statements must also comply with IAS 28 (*Investments in associates*) and IFRS 11 (*Joint arrangements*), respectively.

The reporting date of the parent and its subsidiaries must not be more than three months apart; and consolidated financial statements should be prepared using uniform accounting policies for like transactions and other events in similar circumstances.

When separate financial statements are prepared, investments in subsidiaries, jointly controlled entities and associates that are not classified as held for sale (or included in a disposal group that is classified as held for sale) in accordance with IFRS 5 shall be accounted for either at cost or in accordance with IAS 39 which would be at fair value if it can be ascertained.

## 26.3 Disclosure requirements

IAS 27 specifies the disclosures to be made in consolidated and separate financial statements:

(*a*) the nature of the relationship between the parent and a subsidiary when the parent does not own, directly or indirectly through subsidiaries, more than half of the voting power;
(*b*) the reasons why the ownership, directly or indirectly through subsidiaries, of more than half of the voting or potential voting power of an investee does not constitute control;

(*c*) the reporting date of the financial statements of a subsidiary when such financial statements are used to prepare consolidated financial statements and are as of a reporting date or for a period that is different from that of the parent, and the reason for using a different reporting date or period; and
(*d*) the nature and extent of any significant restrictions (e.g. resulting from borrowing arrangements or regulatory requirements) on the ability of subsidiaries to transfer funds to the parent in the form of cash dividends or to repay loans or advances.

When a parent, a venturer with an interest in a jointly controlled entity, or an investor in an associate prepares separate financial statements, those separate financial statements should disclose:

(*a*) the fact that the statements are separate financial statements and the reasons why those statements are prepared if not required by law;
(*b*) a list of significant investments in subsidiaries, jointly controlled entities and associates, including the name, country of incorporation or residence, proportion of ownership interest and, if different, proportion of voting power held; and
(*c*) a description of the method used to account for the investments listed under (*b*);

and shall identify the financial statements prepared in accordance with this standard, IAS 28, and IFRS 11 to which they relate.

When separate financial statements are prepared for a parent that elects not to prepare consolidated financial statements, those separate financial statements shall disclose:

(*a*) the fact that the financial statements are separate financial statements; that the exemption from consolidation has been used; the name and country of incorporation or residence of the entity whose consolidated financial statements that comply with IFRSs have been produced for public use; and the address where those consolidated financial statements are obtainable;
(*b*) a list of significant investments in subsidiaries, jointly controlled entities and associates, including the name, country of incorporation or residence, proportion of ownership interest and, if different, proportion of voting power held; and
(*c*) a description of the method used to account for the investments listed under (*b*).

In the remainder of this chapter, the more important provisions of the standards applicable to groups are discussed. As Chapters 16–25 have already incorporated the mechanics of implementing these standards, those points will not be looked at again. While this chapter is concerned with the other important aspects of these standards, it does not cover every detail. Such detail would only be needed at a later stage of your studies.

## 26.4 Exemption from preparing consolidated financial statements

In the UK, before the adoption of International GAAP, small and medium-sized companies could claim exemption from the requirements to prepare consolidated financial statements on the grounds of size. However, this option is not available under International GAAP. IAS 27 states that a parent is exempted from presenting consolidated financial statements if and only if:

(*a*) the parent is itself a wholly owned subsidiary, or is a partially owned subsidiary of another entity and its other owners, including those not otherwise entitled to vote, have been informed about, and do not object to, the parent not presenting consolidated financial statements;
(*b*) the parent's debt or equity instruments are not traded in a public market (a domestic or foreign stock exchange or an over-the-counter market, including local and regional markets);
(*c*) the parent did not file, and is not in the process of filing, its financial statements with a securities commission or other regulatory organisation for the purpose of issuing any class of instruments in a public market; and

(*d*) the ultimate or any intermediate parent of the parent produces consolidated financial statements available for public use that comply with International Financial Reporting Standards.

A parent that is exempted from presenting consolidated financial statements may present separate financial statements as its only financial statements.

## 26.5 Exemption from the inclusion of a subsidiary in consolidated financial statements

According to IAS 27, consolidated financial statements should include all subsidiaries of the parent *except* for a subsidiary that on acquisition meets the criteria to be classified as held for sale (see IFRS 5 *Non-current assets held for sale and discontinued operations*).

## 26.6 IAS 28 Investments in associates

An **associate** is an entity over which the investor has 'significant influence' and that is neither a subsidiary nor an interest in a joint venture. Significant influence is the power to participate in the financial and operating policy decisions of the investee but is not control or joint control over those policies. The main yardstick to apply is a threshold of 20% of the voting rights in the investee. If an investor holds, directly or indirectly (e.g. through subsidiaries), 20% or more of the voting power of the investee, it is presumed that the investor has significant influence, unless it can be clearly demonstrated that this is not the case. If it holds less than 20%, the existence of significant influence must be clearly demonstrable in at least one of the following ways:

(*i*) representation on the board of directors or equivalent governing body of the investee;
(*ii*) participation in policy-making processes, including participation in decisions about dividends or other distributions;
(*iii*) material transactions between the investor and the investee;
(*iv*) interchange of managerial personnel; or
(*v*) provision of essential technical information.

Associates are accounted for as non-current assets using the **equity accounting** method: the investment is recognised at cost and adjusted thereafter for the post-acquisition investor's share of net assets of the investee; and the investor's share of the profit or loss of the investee must be separately disclosed in the statement of profit or loss. The only investor entities that do not have to adopt the equity method are those where:

(*a*) the investment is classified as held for sale in accordance with IFRS 5; or
(*b*) the investor entity is exempt from producing consolidated financial statements under IAS 27 or, if it has no subsidiaries, would be exempt under IAS 27 if it had; or
(*c*) all of the following apply:
  (*i*) the investor is a wholly owned subsidiary, or is a partially owned subsidiary of another entity and its other owners, including those not otherwise entitled to vote, have been informed about, and do not object to, the investor not applying the equity method;
  (*ii*) the investor's debt or equity instruments are not traded in a public market (a domestic or foreign stock exchange or an over-the-counter market, including local and regional markets);
  (*iii*) the investor did not file, and is not in the process of filing, its financial statements with a securities commission or other regulatory organisation, for the purpose of issuing any class of instruments in a public market; and

(*iv*) the ultimate or any intermediate parent of the investor produces consolidated financial statements available for public use that comply with IFRSs.

When associates are not accounted for using the equity method, investor entities should disclose summarised financial information of the associates, either individually or in groups, including the amounts of total assets, total liabilities, revenues and profit or loss.

**Joint ventures** are defined in IFRS 11 (*Joint arrangements*) – *see* Section 26.7 – and their treatment is described in IAS 28: the entity recognises an investment and accounts for it using the equity method in accordance with IAS 28.

## 26.7 IFRS 11 Joint arrangements

A **joint arrangement** is either a joint operation or a joint venture in which two or more parties have joint control. It has the following attributes:

- the parties are bound by a contract, and
- the contract gives at least two of the parties joint control of the arrangement.

For joint control to exist, decisions about the activities require that the parties who share control agree unanimously in all cases.

A **joint operation** is defined in IFRS 11 as '*a joint arrangement whereby the parties that have joint control of the arrangement have rights to the assets, and obligations for the liabilities, relating to the arrangement*'. When the activity constitutes a business as defined in IFRS 3 (*Business combinations*), a joint operator must account for the assets, liabilities, revenues and expenses in accordance and must apply all the principles on accounting for business combinations in IFRS 3 and other IFRSs, except when they conflict with IFRS 11.

A **joint venture** is defined in IFRS 11 as '*a joint arrangement whereby the parties that have joint control of the arrangement have rights to the net assets of the arrangement*'. A joint venturer recognises its interest in a joint venture as an investment and must account for it using the equity method as prescribed in IAS 28 (*Investments in associates and joint ventures*) *unless* the entity is exempted in that standard from applying the equity method.

## 26.8 IFRS 12 Disclosure of interests in other entities

IFRS 12 presents the disclosure requirements relating to an entity's interest in subsidiaries, joint arrangements, associates, and unconsolidated 'structured entities'. Previously, these were dealt with in IAS 27 (*Consolidated and separate financial statements*), IAS 28 (*Investments in associates*) and IAS 31 (*Interests in joint ventures*). Combining these in one standard made it easier to identify the appropriate disclosures to make and provided an appropriate standard in which to present the disclosure requirements for unconsolidated structured entities.

A **structured entity** is defined in IFRS 12 as: '*A structured entity is an entity that has been designed so that voting or similar rights are not the dominant factor in deciding who controls the entity, such as when any voting rights relate to administrative tasks only and the relevant activities are directed by means of contractual arrangements.*'

The standard suggests that structured entities have some of the following attributes:

- restricted activities;
- a narrow and well-defined objective, such as to effect a tax-efficient lease, carry out research and development activities, provide a source of capital or funding to an entity or provide investment opportunities for investors by passing on risks and rewards associated with the assets of the structured entity to investors;

- insufficient equity to permit the structured entity to finance its activities without subordinated financial support;
- financing in the form of multiple contractually linked instruments to investors that create concentrations of credit or other risks (tranches).

Examples of structured entities include securitisation vehicles; asset-backed financings; and some investment funds.

## 26.9 An example of the equity method for a group

When the equity method is used to account for an associate or a joint venture in the consolidated statement of profit or loss, the investing company includes its full share of its earnings, whether or not the associate or joint venture has distributed the earnings as dividends. In the consolidated statement of financial position, the investment is shown at cost, adjusted each year by the share of retained profits belonging to the investor. Goodwill arising on acquisition of the investment is treated as per IFRS 3. Any subsequent impairment of goodwill is recognised by adjusting the carrying amount of the investment.

We will shortly see how this is carried out. You will learn that there are major differences between the equity method and consolidation accounting of a subsidiary's results. For example, under purchase method accounting, the group would take credit for the whole of the turnover, cost of sales, etc. and then make a one-line adjustment to remove any non-controlling interest. Under the equity method, the associate's turnover, cost of sales, etc. are not amalgamated with those of the group. Instead, only the items concerned with the group's share of the associate's or joint venture's profit or loss are included.

As it would be quite rare for a company with investments in associates not to have subsidiaries, we will use an example that demonstrates how to include the relevant equity accounting-based information into a set of consolidated financial statements.

### Effect upon the consolidated statement of profit or loss

*Take out:*

(*a*) dividends received.

*Include instead the group's share of the associate's:*

(*b*) pre-tax profit after eliminating the investor's share of profits or losses on transaction between the associate and other entities in the group;

(*c*) taxation charge;

(*d*) post-acquisition retained profits brought forward.

### Effect upon the consolidated statement of financial position

*Rather than* the cost of the investment

*Show instead* the cost of the investment

*plus*

the group's share of associate's post-acquisition retained profit.

Exhibit 26.1 shows how an associated undertaking's results are incorporated into a set of consolidated financial statements.

## Exhibit 26.1

A Ltd is a holding company with subsidiaries. It also has 25% of the equity share capital of B Ltd. This was bought for £100,000 three years ago when B Ltd had reserves (retained profits) of £20,000.

**Statements of Profit or Loss for the year ending 31 December 2016**

| | | *A Ltd & Subsidiaries (consolidated)* | | | *B Ltd (associate)* |
|---|---|---|---|---|---|
| | | *£000* | *£000* | *£000* | *£000* |
| Turnover | | | 540 | | 200 |
| Cost of sales | | | (370) | | (130) |
| Gross profit | | | 170 | | 70 |
| Distribution costs | | 20 | | 3 | |
| Administrative expenses | | 30 | | 5 | |
| Finance costs | | 10 | | 2 | |
| | | | (60) | | (10) |
| | | | 110 | | 60 |
| Dividends received from B Ltd | (A) | | 10 | | – |
| Profit before taxation | | | 120 | (B) | 60 |
| Taxation | | | (28) | (C) | (16) |
| Profit for the year | | | 92 | | 44 |

*Note:* During 2016, A Ltd paid a dividend of £60,000; B Ltd paid a dividend of £40,000 on 31 December 2016.

**Statement of Financial Position as at 31 December 2016 (abbreviated)**

| | *£000* | *£000* |
|---|---|---|
| Non-current assets | 145 | 130 |
| Investment in B Ltd at cost | 100 | – |
| Current assets | 280 | 164 |
| Total assets | 525 | 294 |
| Total liabilities | (100) | (50) |
| Net assets | 425 | 244 |
| | | |
| Share capital | 350 | 200 |
| Retained profits (A = 43 + 92 – 60 = 75; B = 40 + 44 – 40 = 44) | 75 | 44 |
| | 425 | 244 |

*Note:* Retained profits at 31 December 2015 were £43,000 (A Ltd group) and £40,000 (B Ltd).

We can now prepare the entries to incorporate B Ltd into the consolidation. As you have just learnt, the adjustments to be made are:

*Take out:* (A) Dividends received

*Include:* (B) Group share of pre-tax profit
(C) Group share of taxation
(D) Group's share of post-acquisition retained profit brought forward.

→

The answer is:

**A Ltd Group**

**Consolidated Statement of Profit or Loss for the year ending 31 December 2016**

| | | £000 | £000 |
|---|---|---|---|
| Turnover | | | 540 |
| Cost of sales | | | (370) |
| | | | 170 |
| Distribution costs | | 20 | |
| Administrative expenses | | 30 | |
| Finance costs | | 10 | |
| | | | (60) |
| | | | 110 |
| Share of profit of associate (W1) | (B) | | 15 |
| Profit before taxation | | | 125 |
| Taxation (W2) | (C) | | (32) |
| Profit for the year | | | 93 |

**Consolidated Statement of Financial Position as at 31 December 2016**

| | £000 |
|---|---|
| Non-current assets | 145 |
| Investment in B Ltd (W4) | 106 |
| Current assets | 280 |
| Total assets | 531 |
| Total liabilities | (100) |
| Net assets | 431 |
| Share capital | 350 |
| Retained profits (W5) | 81 |
| | 431 |

*Workings:*

(W1) 25% of profit before taxation of B Ltd × £60 = £15

(W2) A £28 + 25% of B £16 = £32

(W3) Retained profits at 31 December 2015 = A £43 + 25% of B's post-acquisition profits (£40 − £20) £20 = £43 + 5 = £48

| | | £000 |
|---|---|---|
| (W4) Cost of 25% share in B = | | 100 |
| *Add* Retained profits B c/d | 44 | |
| *Less* Pre-acquisition profits | (20) | |
| Post-acquisition profits | 24 | |
| 25% share | | 6 |
| | | 106 |
| (W5) Reserves A | | 75[Note] |
| *Add* 25% of post-acquisition profit of B (*see* W4) | | 6 |
| | | 81 |

* *Note:* This is after dividends paid during 2016.

## 26.10 Investing companies without subsidiaries

If no consolidated financial statements are produced by an investing company and that company is not exempt from preparing consolidated statements, or would not be if it had subsidiaries, a separate statement of profit or loss should be prepared showing the information that would have been included in respect of its associated entities had consolidated financial statements been prepared. Similar requirements apply to the statement of financial position. An example is shown in Exhibit 26.2:

**Exhibit 26.2**

**Statement of Profit or Loss of an Investing Company without Subsidiaries**

| | £000 | £000 |
|---|---|---|
| Turnover | | 2,000 |
| Cost of sales | | (1,400) |
| Gross profit | | 600 |
| Distribution costs | 175 | |
| Administrative expenses | 95 | |
| Finance costs | 20 | |
| | | (290) |
| | | 310 |
| Share of profits less loss of associates | | 35 |
| Profit before taxation | | 345 |
| Taxation | | (85) |
| Profit for the year | | 260 |

As you can see, this statement of profit or loss layout is like the one shown in Exhibit 26.1 – the only difference in layout would be the description of the reporting entity which, in this case, is a company rather than a group.

## 26.11 The control concept revisited

You have already learnt that the control concept underlies the presentation of consolidated financial statements for a group as a single economic entity. While the list given in Section 26.2 can be used to identify a parent–subsidiary relationship, it may result in more than one undertaking being classified as the parent. However, **control can only be held by one parent,** and the control that identifies entities as a parent and subsidiary should be distinguished from shared control, for example as in a joint venture. If more than one undertaking is identified as the parent, their interests in the subsidiary are, in effect, interests in a joint venture, and no parent– subsidiary relationship exists.

On the other hand, one or more of these parents may exercise a non-controlling but significant influence over the company in which it has invested. In that case it would be appropriate to account for it as an associate undertaking.

### Learning outcomes

**You should now have learnt:**

1. The existence of a parent–subsidiary relationship depends upon whether the 'parent' can exercise control over the 'subsidiary'.
2. The existence of a parent–associate relationship depends upon whether the 'parent' can exercise *significant* influence over the 'associate'.
3. Joint operations that constitute a business must be accounted for according to the requirements of IFRS 3 (*Business combinations*).
4. There are some circumstances where groups are exempted from the preparation of consolidated financial statements.
5. Equity accounting is used when including associates and joint ventures in financial statements.
6. Subsidiaries can have only one parent, however, more than one parent may have a significant influence over an associate.

## Answer to activity

26.1 Control is far more all-encompassing. Control in some cases can be exercised with very little ownership. It depends entirely upon the circumstances and may, in fact, depend on contractual agreements, as between lender and borrower, rather than equity ownership. By shifting the emphasis from ownership to control, the substance of the relationship is identified as the main deciding factor. As a result, parent–subsidiary relationships (and parent–associate relationships) are much more realistically defined, thus providing a more meaningful basis for the preparation of group financial statements.

## Review questions

**26.1** Q plc has three subsidiaries: L Ltd, M Ltd, and N Ltd. All three were acquired on 1 January at the start of the financial year which has just ended. Q has a 55%, 70% and 95% holding respectively and holds a majority of the voting equity in L and M. It has changed the composition of both these companies' boards since they were acquired. However, despite its 95% holding in N Ltd, it has only a 45% holding of the voting equity and has so far failed in all its attempts to have a director appointed to the board. How should these three investee companies be treated in the Q group consolidated financial statements?

**26.2** At the end of 2018, a parent company, P plc, with one subsidiary, had a holding representing 10% of the equity of R Ltd, a clothing company. It had cost £96,000 when purchased at the start of 2017. At the time of that investment, R Ltd had net assets of £72,000 which increased to £1,008,000 by the end of that year. At the start of the current year, the investment was increased by a further 11% of the equity at a cost of £132,000.

**Required:**

(*a*) How would the investment be shown in the financial statements if it were treated as an *investment,* i.e. as neither an associate nor as a subsidiary?

(*b*) How would the investment be shown in the financial statements if it were treated as an *associate?*

**26.3A** Relevant statements of financial position as at 31 March 2017 are set out below:

| | *Jasmin (Holdings) plc* | *Kasbah plc* | *Fortran plc* |
|---|---|---|---|
| | *£000* | *£000* | *£000* |
| Tangible non-current assets | 289,400 | 91,800 | 7,600 |
| Investments | | | |
| Shares in Kasbah (at cost) | 97,600 | | |
| Shares in Fortran (at cost) | 8,000 | | |
| | 395,000 | 91,800 | 7,600 |
| Current assets | | | |
| Inventory | 285,600 | 151,400 | 2,600 |
| Cash | 319,000 | 500 | 6,800 |
| | 604,600 | 151,900 | 9,400 |
| Total assets | 999,600 | 243,700 | 17,000 |
| Current liabilities | | | |
| Creditors | (289,600) | (238,500) | (2,200) |
| Net assets | 710,000 | 5,200 | 14,800 |
| Equity | | | |
| Called-up share capital | | | |
| Ordinary £1 shares | 60,000 | 20,000 | 10,000 |
| 10% £1 Preference shares | | 4,000 | |
| Revaluation reserve | 40,000 | | 1,200 |
| Retained profits | 610,000 | (18,800) | 3,600 |
| | 710,000 | 5,200 | 14,800 |

You have recently been appointed chief accountant of Jasmin (Holdings) plc and are about to prepare the group statement of financial position at 31 March 2017. The following points are relevant to the preparation of those accounts.

(*i*) Jasmin (Holdings) plc owns 90% of the ordinary £1 shares and 20% of the 10% £1 preference shares of Kasbah plc. On 1 April 2016 Jasmin (Holdings) plc paid £96 million for the ordinary £1 shares and £1.6 million for the 10% £1 preference shares when Kasbah's reserves were a credit balance of £45 million.

(*ii*) Jasmin (Holdings) plc sells part of its output to Kasbah plc. The inventory of Kasbah plc on 31 March 2017 includes £1.2 million of inventory purchased from Jasmin (Holdings) plc at cost plus one-third.

(*iii*) The policy of the group is to revalue its tangible non-current assets on a yearly basis. However, the directors of Kasbah plc have always resisted this policy, preferring to show tangible non-current assets at historical cost. The market value of the tangible non-current assets of Kasbah plc at 31 March 2017 is £90 million. The directors of Jasmin (Holdings) plc wish to follow the requirements of IFRS 3 (*Business combinations*) and IAS 16 (*Property, plant and equipment*) in respect of the value of tangible non-current assets to be included in the group accounts.

(*iv*) The ordinary £1 shares of Fortran plc are split into 6 million 'A' ordinary £1 shares and 4 million 'B' ordinary £1 shares. Holders of 'A' shares are assigned one vote and holders of 'B' ordinary shares are assigned two votes per share. On 1 April 2016 Jasmin (Holdings) plc acquired 80% of the 'A' ordinary shares and 10% of the 'B' ordinary shares when the retained profits of Fortran plc were £1.6 million and the revaluation reserve was £2 million. The 'A' ordinary shares and 'B' ordinary shares carry equal rights to share in the company's profits and losses.

(*v*) The fair values of Kasbah plc and Fortran plc were not materially different from their book values at the time of acquisition of their shares by Jasmin (Holdings) plc.

(*vi*) Kasbah plc has paid its preference dividend for the current year but no other dividends are proposed by the group companies. The preference dividend was paid shortly after the interim results of Kasbah plc were announced and was deemed to be a legal dividend by the auditors.

***Authors' note*: Impairment reviews indicate that no further adjustments to goodwill are required.**

**Required:**

(*a*) Prepare a consolidated statement of financial position for Jasmin (Holdings) Group plc for the year ending 31 March 2017. (All calculations should be made to the nearest thousand pounds.)

(*b*) Comment briefly on the possible implications of the size of Kasbah plc's losses for the year for the group accounts and the individual accounts of Jasmin (Holdings) plc.

(*Association of Chartered Certified Accountants*)

**26.4A** Huge plc acquired a holding of 600,000 of the 800,000 ordinary £1 shares of Large plc on 1 October 2015 when the revenue reserves of Large stood at £320,000.

On 1 October 2016, the directors of Medium plc agreed to appoint the commercial manager of Huge as one of its directors to enable Huge to participate in its commercial, financial and dividend policy decisions. In exchange, Huge agreed to provide finance to Medium for working capital. On the same day, Huge acquired its holding of 100,000 of the 400,000 ordinary £1 shares of Medium when the revenue reserves of Medium were £150,000. Three months later, the directors of Small plc, who supplied materials to Large, heard of the arrangement between Huge and Medium and suggested that they would be pleased to enter into a similar relationship. The board of Huge were interested in the proposal and showed their good faith by acquiring a 10% holding in Small which at that time had a debit balance of £2,000 on its retained profits reserve. →

**Statements of Financial Position of the four companies on 30 September 2017**

| | *Huge* | *Large* | *Medium* | *Small* |
|---|---|---|---|---|
| | *£000* | *£000* | *£000* | *£000* |
| Property, plant and machinery | 2,004 | 780 | 553 | 85 |
| Investment in Large | 900 | | | |
| Investment in Medium | 180 | | | |
| Investment in Small | 12 | | | |
| Current a/c Medium | 40 | | | |
| Current a/c Small | | 10 | | |
| Inventory | 489 | 303 | 72 | 28 |
| Accounts receivable | 488 | 235 | 96 | 22 |
| Bank/cash | 45 | 62 | 19 | 5 |
| | 4,158 | 1,390 | 740 | 140 |
| Current liabilities: Creditors | (318) | (170) | (90) | (10) |
| | 3,840 | 1,220 | 650 | 130 |
| Ordinary share capital | 2,400 | 800 | 400 | 80 |
| Revenue reserves | 1,440 | 420 | 210 | 40 |
| Current a/c Huge | | | 40 | |
| Current a/c Large | | | | 10 |
| | 3,840 | 1,220 | 650 | 130 |

**Required:**

(*a*) Identify which of the four companies should be included in a group consolidation, explaining how and why the treatment of one company in the consolidation may be different from another. Mention any appropriate accounting standards or legislation applicable.

(*b*) Prepare the consolidated statement of financial position of the group at 30 September 2017 using the purchase method of accounting.

(*Institute of Chartered Secretaries and Administrators*)

part 4

# FINANCIAL CALCULATIONS AND ANALYSIS

## Introduction

**This part considers how accounting information is traditionally analysed and used.**

chapter 27

# Interest, annuities and leasing

## Learning objectives

**After you have studied this chapter, you should be able to:**

- explain the difference between simple and compound interest
- explain what is meant by and be able to calculate the annual percentage rate (APR)
- calculate the present value of a series of cash flows
- describe what an annuity is and be able to calculate the value of ordinary annuities
- describe the difference between operating and finance leases and be able to calculate the relevant figures to use in financial statements

## Introduction

In this chapter, you'll learn about the nature of interest rates, of the difference between *simple* interest and *compound* interest and how to calculate them. You'll also learn how to calculate the annual percentage rate (APR) and how to calculate the cost and value of annuities and leases. Finally, you'll learn how to apply the accounting rules relating to leases.

## 27.1 Different values

Would you rather be given £10 today or in 12 months' time? As time passes, money loses value due to the effects of inflation – prices generally rise over time. When a transaction involves a delay in payment for the item purchased (e.g. a new car), the (inflation-caused) loss in value of the amount paid will be recovered by the seller charging the buyer interest. The delay also represents a period during which the seller could have invested the money and earned interest. **This 'opportunity cost' of interest lost will also be charged to the buyer.**

The seller may have had to borrow money to provide the item purchased, and the interest cost incurred will be charged to the buyer. **In addition, the seller will also add interest to the amount due in order to compensate for risk** – the risk that the buyer will not pay the debt when due. Thus, the amount the buyer will be required to pay depends upon inflation, the market rate of interest, and the degree of risk in the debt as perceived by the seller.

## 27.2 Interest rates

If a seller adds 10% interest to a debt of £100, the required payment if made one year later is £100 + (10% × £100 = £10) = £110. The interest in this case is known as '*simple interest*' – 'simple' because the rate (10%) is for one year, which matches the length of the debt. Interest rates generally indicate the percentage of the amount due that will be charged as interest if the debt is unpaid for a year.

If a 10% interest rate is used, but the buyer is allowed to wait two years before paying the debt, the second year's interest will be based on the amount due at the end of the first year – £110 (i.e. the original debt of £100 plus the £10 interest charged for the first year). The interest for the second year is therefore 10% × £110 = £11, and the amount due at the end of the second year is the original debt (£100) + the first year's interest (£10) + the second year's interest (£11) = £121. This is known as '*compound interest*' – 'compound' because the amount of interest due for years beyond the first year is calculated on the basis of how much is owed at the start of each year, i.e. the original amount plus all the interest to that date.

If a buyer offers to pay £121 in two years' time, instead of paying £100 today, and the seller charges debtors 10% interest per annum, the value today to the seller of the £121 which will be received in two years' time is £100. However, if the seller uses a 20% interest rate, the £121 will only be worth £84.03. On the other hand, if the seller uses a 5% interest rate, the £121 will be worth £109.75. These different values can be checked by applying the same approach as with the 10% interest rate.

At 20%, the interest for the first year on a debt of £84.03 will be £16.80, and the amount due at the end of one year will be £100.84. The second year's interest will be 20% of £100.84, i.e. £20.17, and the total due at the end of the second year will be £121.

At 5%, the interest for the first year on a debt of £109.75 will be £5.49, and the amount due at the end of one year will be £115.24. The second year's interest will be 5% of £115.24, i.e. £5.76, and the total due at the end of the second year will be £121.

This is not as complicated as it may appear. Easy to follow statistical tables can be used to find the values involved quickly. Alternatively, it is straightforward to prepare a spreadsheet that will provide the values required for any combination of the variables involved.

## 27.3 Simple interest

Simple interest on a debt of one year is, therefore, calculated using the formula:

**Amount of interest ($Y$) = Amount due ($A$) × Interest rate ($r$)**

However, simple interest also applies to periods of less than a year. In order to calculate the interest on a shorter period, the period in question is expressed as a proportion of a year, and the formula is adjusted to:

**Amount of interest ($Y$) = Amount due ($A$) × Interest rate ($r$) × Fraction of a year ($t$)**

Let's look at an example.

### Example

Interest on a debt of £100 is to be charged at 10% per annum. The debt will be repaid after 60 days. The interest due can be calculated using the formula:

$$\begin{aligned} Y &= £100 \times 10\% \times (60/365) \\ &= £10 \times (60/365) \\ &= £1.64 \end{aligned}$$

## 27.4 Annual percentage rate (APR)

Sometimes, an interest rate that appears to be a 'simple interest' rate does not actually represent the 'real' rate charged. This can arise where, for example, a 10% rate is charged on a debt for a year, but part of the debt must be repaid part-way through the year, and the interest charge ignores the fact that there is early payment of part of the debt. This 'real' rate is known as the '*annual percentage rate*' (APR). Hire purchase agreements are examples of debts where APR must be calculated to determine the 'real' cost incurred by the debtor.

Let's look at two examples.

### Example 1

Interest on a debt of £100 is to be charged at 10% per annum. However, £40 must be paid after six months, and the balance plus the interest at the end of the year.

| | | | £ |
|---|---|---|---|
| The interest to be paid is | 10% of £100 | $= Y$ | $=$ 10 |
| The amount due is | £100 for ½ year | $=$ | 50 |
| | £60 for ½ year | $=$ | 30 |
| The equivalent amount due for a year is | | $= q$ | $=$ 80 |
| The 'real' rate of interest | | $= r$ | $= Y/q$ |
| | | | $=$ 10/80 |
| | | | $=$ 12.5% $=$ the APR |

Another typical example of APR arises when a business is owed money by its customers and it decides to sell the debt to a factor in order to obtain cash now. In these cases, the factor will pay the business an amount equal to the amount of the debt less a discount.

### Example 2

A business is due £10,000 from a customer and the customer has agreed to make the payment in 90 days' time. The business approaches a debt factor who agrees to pay the amount due now, less a discount rate of 10%. Applying the formula for debts of less than one year

**Amount of interest (*Y*) = Amount due (*A*) × Interest rate (*r*) × Fraction of a year (*t*)**

the discount charged is:

$$\begin{aligned} Y &= £10{,}000 \times 10\% \times (90/365) \\ &= £1{,}000 \times (90/365) \\ &= £246.58 \end{aligned}$$

The debt factor will pay the business £10,000 less £246.58, i.e. £9,753.42. **However, £246.58 does not represent a charge based on the amount of the advance (£9,753.42). Rather, it is based on the higher original amount of the customer's debt of £10,000.** As a proportion of the £9,753.42 advanced by the debt factor, £246.58 represents an interest rate of 10.25%. This can be seen by rewriting the formula for debts of less than year to:

$$r = \frac{Y}{A \times t}$$

which, substituting the example values, gives:

$$r = \frac{246.58}{9{,}753.42 \times (90/365)} = 10.25\%$$

**A similar approach is used with *bills of exchange* and *trade bill* interest rate calculations.**

## 27.5 Compound interest and investments

As mentioned in Section 27.2, when more than a year is involved, the interest due is compounded, i.e. each year's interest charge is based on the amount outstanding, including all interest relating to previous years, at the beginning of the year.

Rather than looking at how compound interest charges to be paid are calculated, let's look at another application of compound interest – the interest earned on investments.

The graph shown in Exhibit 27.1 illustrates the difference between two investments of £1,000 at 10% per annum for 20 years. In the first case, the interest is reinvested at the same 10% rate and the final value of the investment is £6,727.50. In the other case, the interest is withdrawn as soon as it is paid, leaving only the original £1,000 invested, which is also the final value of the investment. However, 20 times £100, i.e. £2,000, has been received in interest over the 20 years, resulting in the overall value (ignoring inflation) being £3,000.

**Exhibit 27.1**

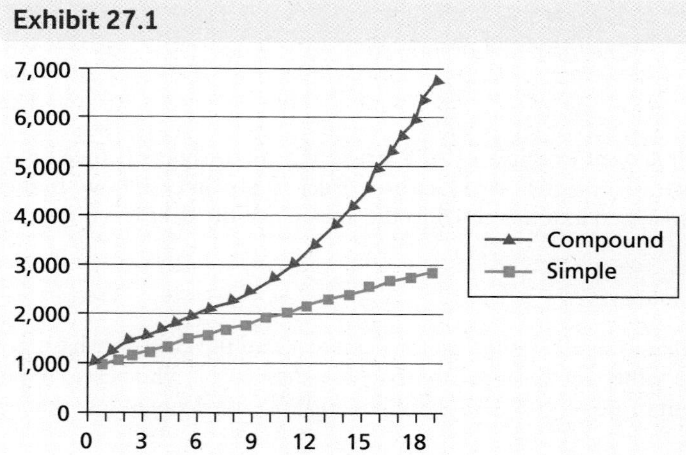


The final value of an investment that is subject to compound interest can be calculated laboriously by calculating the value at the end of the first year, calculating the interest on that amount for the next year, adding that interest to the amount at the start of the year to get the amount at the end of the year, and repeating the process for each year. However, there is a formula which enables the amount to be calculated swiftly:

**Final value ($V$) = Amount invested ($I$) × $(1 + r)^n$, where $n$ = the number of years**

**Example**

£1,000 invested today for five years at 10% would have a final value ($V$) of:

$$\begin{aligned} V &= £1{,}000 \times (1 + 0.10)^5 \\ &= £1{,}000 \times (1.1)^5 \\ &= £1{,}000 \times 1.61051 \\ &= £1{,}610.51 \end{aligned}$$

Calculations of this type are easily performed on most calculators, or by the use of tables. Where such calculations are performed regularly, it is quite common for a spreadsheet to be used to perform the calculation, often using the structure of a compound interest table within the spreadsheet to make it clear how the numbers used were derived. A compound interest table is included in Appendix 1 (Table 1), but a shorter example is reproduced in Exhibit 27.2:

## Exhibit 27.2 An example of a compound interest table

**Compound Interest Table**
**Period**
**Length £1 compounded at the end of each period at the interest rate shown**

| *n* | *1%* | *2%* | *3%* | *4%* | *5%* | *6%* | *7%* | *8%* | *9%* | *10%* | *n* |
|---|---|---|---|---|---|---|---|---|---|---|---|
| 1 | 1.010 | 1.020 | 1.030 | 1.040 | 1.050 | 1.060 | 1.070 | 1.080 | 1.090 | 1.100 | 1 |
| 2 | 1.202 | 1.040 | 1.061 | 1.082 | 1.103 | 1.124 | 1.145 | 1.166 | 1.188 | 1.210 | 2 |
| 3 | 1.030 | 1.061 | 1.093 | 1.125 | 1.158 | 1.191 | 1.225 | 1.260 | 1.295 | 1.331 | 3 |
| 4 | 1.041 | 1.082 | 1.126 | 1.170 | 1.216 | 1.262 | 1.311 | 1.360 | 1.412 | 1.464 | 4 |
| 5 | 1.051 | 1.104 | 1.159 | 1.217 | 1.276 | 1.338 | 1.403 | 1.469 | 1.539 | 1.611 | 5 |
| 6 | 1.062 | 1.126 | 1.194 | 1.265 | 1.340 | 1.419 | 1.501 | 1.587 | 1.677 | 1.772 | 6 |
| 7 | 1.072 | 1.149 | 1.230 | 1.316 | 1.407 | 1.504 | 1.606 | 1.714 | 1.828 | 1.949 | 7 |
| 8 | 1.083 | 1.172 | 1.267 | 1.369 | 1.477 | 1.594 | 1.718 | 1.851 | 1.993 | 2.144 | 8 |
| 9 | 1.094 | 1.195 | 1.305 | 1.423 | 1.551 | 1.689 | 1.838 | 1.999 | 2.172 | 2.358 | 9 |
| 10 | 1.105 | 1.219 | 1.344 | 1.480 | 1.629 | 1.791 | 1.967 | 2.159 | 2.367 | 2.594 | 10 |
| *n* | *11%* | *12%* | *13%* | *14%* | *15%* | *16%* | *17%* | *18%* | *19%* | *20%* | *n* |
| 1 | 1.110 | 1.120 | 1.130 | 1.140 | 1.150 | 1.160 | 1.170 | 1.180 | 1.190 | 1.200 | 1 |
| 2 | 1.232 | 1.254 | 1.277 | 1.300 | 1.323 | 1.346 | 1.369 | 1.392 | 1.416 | 1.440 | 2 |
| 3 | 1.368 | 1.405 | 1.443 | 1.482 | 1.521 | 1.561 | 1.602 | 1.643 | 1.685 | 1.728 | 3 |
| 4 | 1.518 | 1.574 | 1.630 | 1.689 | 1.749 | 1.811 | 1.874 | 1.939 | 2.005 | 2.074 | 4 |
| 5 | 1.685 | 1.762 | 1.842 | 1.925 | 2.011 | 2.100 | 2.192 | 2.288 | 2.386 | 2.488 | 5 |
| 6 | 1.870 | 1.974 | 2.082 | 2.195 | 2.313 | 2.436 | 2.565 | 2.700 | 2.840 | 2.986 | 6 |
| 7 | 2.076 | 2.211 | 2.353 | 2.502 | 2.660 | 2.826 | 3.001 | 3.185 | 3.379 | 3.583 | 7 |
| 8 | 2.305 | 2.476 | 2.658 | 2.853 | 3.059 | 3.278 | 3.511 | 3.759 | 4.021 | 4.300 | 8 |
| 9 | 2.558 | 2.773 | 3.004 | 3.252 | 3.518 | 3.803 | 4.108 | 4.435 | 4.785 | 5.160 | 9 |
| 10 | 2.839 | 3.106 | 3.395 | 3.707 | 4.046 | 4.411 | 4.807 | 5.234 | 5.695 | 6.192 | 10 |

**Example**

As you can see highlighted in Exhibit 27.2, if you want to know how much will be held at the end of seven years if you invest £100 at 6% compound interest per annum, the table shows that it would be £100 times **1.504** = £150.40.

Interest often accumulates more frequently than once a year, for example, daily, monthly, or quarterly. If so, the rate of interest used in the formula must be changed to reflect this. To do this, the number of periods is multiplied by the number of payments being made each year, and the interest rate used is divided by the same amount. The formula can then be used with these adjusted values, as shown in the following example.

**Example**

If £100 is invested for two years at 12% compound interest paid quarterly, the interest rate used in the calculation is 3% (i.e. 12% divided by four). The number of periods to use is eight (i.e. two multiplied by four). Looking up the table, the amount accumulated at the end of the two years will be £126.70.

Compare that to the compounded amount if interest was paid annually, £125.40. The difference is very small. However, the investment was for a short period of time. Had it been for a longer period, the difference would have become progressively greater. When large amounts of money are being invested over a long period, an increased frequency of interest payments will have a significant effect upon the amount of interest received.

Over time, most investments change their value. Investments, whether in the stock market, houses, or anything else, are made without knowing what the rate of return (the amount earned from the investment) will be. When the investment is ended and the final amount received is known, it is often useful to know what the rate of return was over the period of the investment.

This can be done using the table. If an investment was made for five years, it is the five-year row in the table that would be consulted. In that row, you would search for the number that represents the proportion that the final amount received represented of the initial investment. The interest rate column in which that proportion lay would represent the average rate of return on the investment.

Let's look at two examples.

**Example 1**

If a house was bought for £100,000 on 1 January 2014 and sold for £140,300 on 31 December 2018, a five-year investment was made. The proportion that £140,300 represents of the £100,000 invested is 1.403 : 1. Looking up the table in the row where $n = 5$, a value of 1.403 can be seen in the 7% interest rate column. The rate of return is equivalent to 7% compound per annum. Where the proportion calculated is not shown in the table, the table can be used to identify an approximate rate which can then be adjusted in order to arrive at the accurate rate.

**Example 2**

If a house was bought for £100,000 on 1 January 2014 and sold for £160,000 on 31 December 2017, a four-year investment was made. The proportion that £160,000 represents of the £100,000 invested is 1.6 : 1. Looking up the table in the row where $n = 4$, a value of 1.574 can be seen in the 12% column and 1.630 can be seen in the 13% column. The difference between these two values is 0.056 (i.e. 1.630 − 1.574). The difference between 1.574 and the amount being searched for of 1.6 is 0.026, which represents 46% of the total difference of 0.056 between the 12% and 13% amounts. Adding 0.46 to 12 produces a percentage return of 12.46%.

Rather than using the tables to identify the rate of return, a formula can be used which rewrites the final value formula [Final value ($V$) = Amount invested ($I$) × $(1 + r)^n$, where $n$ = the number of years] to identify $r$:

$$r = \sqrt[n]{\left(\frac{V}{I}\right)} - 1$$

Substituting the values from the last example, we can confirm the answer found:

$$\begin{aligned} r &= \sqrt[4]{160{,}000/100{,}000)} - 1 \\ &= 12.46\% \end{aligned}$$

## 27.6 Annuities

An **annuity** is an income-generating investment whereby, in return for the payment of a single lump sum, the 'annuitant' receives regular amounts of income over a predefined term (i.e. number of years). The frequency of the payments to the annuitant will depend upon the agreement reached, but would generally be monthly, quarterly, six-monthly or annually.

The timing of the payments to the annuitant varies from annuity to annuity. For example, some involve regular payments being made to the annuitant at the start of each period, while others make the payments at the end of each period.

In some cases, the original investment is repaid at the end of the agreed term, in others it is not. It is also possible for the agreement to include the annuitant making the investment in a series of payments, rather than in a single lump sum.

As this suggests, there is a large range of possible arrangements that can be incorporated into an annuity, and it is not possible to describe how to deal with the computations relating to each of them. However, in the next section, we will focus upon one specific form of annuity – one in which equal payments are made to the annuitant at the end of each period. From that example, the basic principles involved can be identified which can then be applied to more complex situations. As a result, there should be very few circumstances when the form of an annuity means that you find it impossible to perform the necessary calculations.

Contrary to what many people think, knowledge of how to perform an annuity calculation can be a very useful business skill because many forms of business transactions, including rental agreements, hire purchase agreements and leases, involve similar calculations to an annuity.

## 27.7 Calculation of the value of ordinary annuities

When calculating the value of an annuity, **it can be helpful to think of it as being similar to the calculation of compound interest, *but one period in arrears.*** For example, when considering compound interest on a straightforward investment, it would be assumed that an investment of £1,000 in year two was made at the start of the year. In contrast, for an annuity, all the payments are assumed to arise at the end of a year, so interest on a payment made in year two would only start to accumulate during year three – there would be no interest in year two on that part of the annuity.

The following formula can be used to calculate the value of an annuity which provides a series of regular payments and, upon which, a set rate of interest is being earned.

$$\text{Value} = \text{Annuity per period} \times \frac{(1 + r)^n - 1}{r}$$

For example, if £1,000 is being saved at the end of each year for five years and the interest rate is 10%, the amount accumulated by the end of the fifth year will be:

$$\begin{aligned}\text{Value} &= £1{,}000 \times \frac{(1 + 0.10)^5 - 1}{0.10} \\ &= £1{,}000 \times 6.1051 \\ &= £6{,}105.10\end{aligned}$$

This can be confirmed by treating each of the five payments as individual compound interest calculations:

| *Year* | *Invested* £ | *Formula* | *Value* £ |
|---|---|---|---|
| 1 | 1,000 | $£1{,}000 \times (1 + 0.10)^4$ | 1,464.10 |
| 2 | 1,000 | $£1{,}000 \times (1 + 0.10)^3$ | 1,331.00 |
| 3 | 1,000 | $£1{,}000 \times (1 + 0.10)^2$ | 1,210.00 |
| 4 | 1,000 | $£1{,}000 \times (1 + 0.10)^1$ | 1,100.00 |
| 5 | 1,000 | $£1{,}000 \times (1 + 0.10)^0$ | 1,000.00 |
| | | | 6,105.10 |

Tables can also be used. Table 3 in Appendix 1 also confirms that the value of an annuity of £1 for five years at 10% would be £6.105, i.e. £1 times the multiplier of 6.105 given in the table.

**Example**

As an alternative to calculating the value of an annuity when the amounts paid are known, it can often be useful to know how much should be set aside regularly in order to accumulate a certain amount at the end of a given period. For example, if it was intended to purchase equipment estimated to cost £10,000 in five years' time, and a 10% interest rate was being offered for regular investments over a five-year period, the annuity formula can be rewritten so as to provide the amount to set aside each year:

$$\text{Annuity per period} = \frac{\text{Value} \times (r)}{(1 + r)^{n-1}}$$

For our example, this gives:

$$\frac{£10{,}000 \times 0.10}{(1.10)^5 - 1} = £1{,}637.97$$

As mentioned previously, the multiplier given in the annuity table for a five-year annuity at 10% is 6.105. If £1,637.97 is multiplied by 6.105, it confirms the annuity has a final value (to the nearest £1) of £10,000. It is also possible to confirm the annuity per period does result in the correct final value of £10,000 by creating a payment plus interest table:

| *Annuity paid* | *Payment* £ | *Interest* £ | *Increase in fund* £ | *Balance of fund* £ |
|---|---|---|---|---|
| End of year 1 | 1,637.97 | – | 1,637.97 | 1,637.97 |
| End of year 2 | 1,637.97 | 163.80 | 1,801.77 | 3,439.74 |
| End of year 3 | 1,637.97 | 343.97 | 1,981.94 | 5,421.68 |
| End of year 4 | 1,637.97 | 542.17 | 2,180.14 | 7,601.82 |
| End of year 5 | 1,637.97 | 760.18 | 2,398.15 | 9,999.97 |

## 27.8 Calculation of the present value of ordinary annuities

If faced with a choice of paying for something now, or paying for it in a series of instalments, it would obviously be useful to know which is the cheaper of the two alternatives. For example, a business may purchase a new computer costing £1,000 and have a choice of paying £1,000 now, or £200 per month for six months. At first glance, the second option appears to be more expensive because £1,200 (i.e. six times £200) would be paid instead of £1,000.

However, first impressions can be misleading. In order to be able to compare the two alternatives properly, the payments must all be discounted to arrive at their cost expressed in terms of today's money. This is known as their **present value**. Whether it really is more expensive to pay by instalments will depend on the discount rate used in the calculation.

As with the calculation of the value of an ordinary annuity, tables are available for the calculation of the present value of an ordinary annuity. A full table is provided in Appendix 1 (Table 4) and it shows the value now of £1 per period for $n$ periods when an organisation uses a discount rate of $r$. When payments are made more frequently than once per annum, the discount rate used should be reduced accordingly – that is, if payments are half-yearly, the rate is halved; if they are made every month, the rate is divided by 12.

The formula for calculating the present value of an ordinary annuity is:

$$\textbf{Present value} = \textbf{Regular payment} \times \left[\frac{1 - \dfrac{1}{(1 \times r)^n}}{r}\right]$$

If a 12% rate were used in the example at the start of this section, the rate of 12% would be divided by 12 (because payments are made monthly) and the present value would be:

$$\text{Present value} = £200 \times \left[\frac{1 - \dfrac{1}{(1 + 0.01)^6}}{0.01}\right]$$

$$= £1{,}159.10$$

The multiplier in Table 4 in Appendix 1 for 1% over six periods is 5.795 which, when multiplied by the payment of £200, gives a present value of £1,159.10.

It can be shown that this is the amount required if a table of interest and withdrawals is constructed (interest is at the same rate as above – 1% per month):

| *Period* | *Balance b/d* £ | *Interest* £ | *Payment* £ | *Balance c/d* £ |
|---|---|---|---|---|
| 1 | 1,159.10 | 11.60 | (200) | 970.70 |
| 2 | 970.70 | 9.70 | (200) | 780.40 |
| 3 | 780.40 | 7.80 | (200) | 588.20 |
| 4 | 588.20 | 5.88 | (200) | 394.08 |
| 5 | 394.08 | 3.94 | (200) | 198.02 |
| 6 | 198.02 | 1.98 | (200) | – |

## 27.9 Leasing

Under a lease, the lessee agrees to pay a rental to the lessor for use of something for a period of time. Lease rental payments are treated as allowable expenses for tax, whereas assets that are purchased are only eligible for a partial deduction against tax in the form of a capital allowance. The lessor claims the capital allowances on the assets leased. The lessee charges all the lease rental payments against income.

Why do you think leasing is usually financially advantageous for both the lessor and the lessee?

An organisation acquiring an asset will often consider whether leasing may be preferable to outright purchase. As the cost, expected useful economic life, anticipated scrap value, and leasing charges can all be identified, it is possible to identify the APR of the lease. That can then be used to assess whether it would be preferable to lease rather than buy the asset.

Let's look at an example.

### Example

A printing machine costing £200,000 has an expected useful economic life of ten years. Scrap value of the machine is expected to be zero, as the rate of obsolescence on machinery of this type is very high. The machine could be leased for £32,547 per annum. **The APR is the interest rate that is found when the cost of the machine is equal to the present value of the annual rental payments.** That is, it is the interest rate for which the ten-year multiplier will convert £32,547 into £200,000.

£200,000 divided by £32,547 is 6.145 and, in the 10-year row of the annuity table (Table 4) in Appendix 1, 6.145 is the multiplier for an interest rate of 10%. This is, therefore, the APR of the lease. If the multiplier being sought lies between two values in the annuity table, the APR would be identified by interpolation, as you will see when you learn about accounting for leases in Section 27.11.

Normally, tax is taken into account in identifying the APR of a lease. Ignoring the time lags inherent in the tax system, as the expense is charged directly against income, if the tax rate is 40%, in the above example the net of tax cost of the lease would be 60% of £32,547 (i.e. £19,528) and the APR would be 60% of 10%, i.e. 6%. This can be compared to the organisation's *cost of capital after tax* in order to assess whether to lease or purchase the machine.

So far as the option to purchase is concerned, an annualised cost approach can be used. The cost of £200,000 is assumed to occur immediately, so its real cost is £200,000. Technically, the cost is said to have occurred in 'year zero', i.e. before inflation could make any impact on monetary values.

If 100% capital allowances were available on the machine, at a tax rate of 40%, there would be a tax saving equivalent to 40% of £200,000 in year one. **Net present value (NPV)** is the sum of the present values of all the cash flows. That is, it represents the net overall gain or loss on the investment in the machine after expressing all cash flows in terms of their equivalent value at year zero.

If the organisation's net of tax cost of capital is 8%, the £80,000 tax saving would be discounted to £74,080 (i.e. £80,000 × 0.926), leaving a net present value of £125,920. The annualised cost is, therefore, £125,920 ÷ 6.710 (which is the annuity multiplier for 10 years at 8%), i.e. £18,766. When compared to the net of tax cost of the lease of £19,528, this suggests that it might be preferable to purchase the machine.

As an alternative to the above approach, the £125,920 net present value of buying the machine (as derived in the annualised cost calculation) can be compared to the NPV of the lease payments. The net of tax NPV of leasing is the net of tax rental (£19,528) multiplied by the present value multiplier of a 10-year annuity at 8% (6.710), i.e. £131,033.

## 27.10 Financial implications of leasing

Despite the existence of a legal obligation to continue paying rental on a lease, neither the extent of the obligation to the lessor, nor the benefits obtainable under the lease appear in the lessee's statement of financial position. However, a lease often represents the equivalent of a loan. The equivalent loan is the NPV of the outstanding lease payments discounted at the pre-tax rate of interest. For example, the NPV of a 10-year lease with rental of £32,547 and a pre-tax rate of interest of 10% would be £32,547 × 6.145 = £200,000.

## 27.11 Accounting for leases

Leases are either finance leases or operating leases. IAS 17 *Leases* defines the difference between them. (You learnt about the rules of IAS 17 in Chapter 2.) The principal characteristic of a finance lease is that substantially all the risks and rewards of ownership are transferred to the lessee.

Various steps are described in IAS 17 that should be followed in order to determine whether a finance lease exists. These involve determining whether the present value of the minimum lease payments amounts to substantially all (normally 90%) of the fair value of the asset.

However, if the substance of the lease is to have the opposite effect, then it should be categorised accordingly. At the end of the day, it is the substance (i.e. what is actually happening to the risks and rewards of ownership) rather than the form of the transaction that decides whether there exists a finance or an operating lease.

Hire purchase contracts will usually be of a financing nature and treated in the same way as finance leases.

When a lease is classified as 'operating', it is deemed to still be an asset of the lessor. Both lessor and lessee take the rentals to the statement of profit or loss. The lessor should also record the non-current asset and depreciate it over its useful life.

An asset held under a finance lease is deemed to 'belong' to the lessee, who should capitalise it and make a corresponding entry in accounts payable. The initial value used should be the present value of the minimum lease payments. Depreciation should then be provided over the shorter of the lease term and the asset's useful life, except in the case of a hire purchase contract, under which circumstances the asset should be depreciated over its useful life. As each payment is made, the proportion which relates to the creditor balance should be applied to reduce that balance. The rest of the payment should be treated as a lease charge in the statement of profit or loss for the period.

Lessors should initially record the amount due under a finance lease as an account receivable using the amount of the net investment in the lease. As each payment is received, the proportion which relates to payment of the account receivable balance should be applied to reduce that balance. The rest of the receipt should be treated as lease income in the statement of profit or loss for the period.

Operating leases are accounted for in the same way as most revenue expenditure and income. Finance leases, however, are much more complex. The rental payments comprise a mixture of capital and revenue, and they must be separated and recorded differently. An approach called the actuarial method is generally used. Under this approach, it is first necessary to calculate the real rate of interest implied in the lease. This requires that information is available concerning the rental payments, the lease period and the cash value of the asset at the start of the lease.

**Example**

Quarterly rental on a leased computer is £400, the lease period is 12 quarters from 1 January 2016, and the cash value of the computer at 1 January 2016 is £4,000. The interest rate implied in the lease is that which produces a present value for the 12 payments of £400 equal to £4,000. Note, the first payment is at the start of the lease, yet ordinary annuity calculations relate to payments at the end of periods. In order to bring the example into line with this assumption, the first payment is offset against the cash value, reducing it to £3,600 and the annuity is calculated over 11 periods rather than 12.

$$\text{The factor for 11 periods is } \frac{£3{,}600}{400} = 9$$

$$\text{From the tables } 3\% = 9.253$$

$$4\% = 8.760$$

By interpolation, the gap between 3% and the rate is 253/493 = 0.513, therefore, the interest rate implied in the lease is 3.513%. This can be verified by substituting the rate and other information into the formula given in Section 27.8:

$$\text{Present value} = \text{Payment} \times \left[\frac{1 - \dfrac{1}{(1 + r)^n}}{r}\right]$$

$$3{,}600 = 400 \times \left[\frac{1 - \dfrac{1}{(1 + 0.03513)^{11}}}{0.03513}\right]$$

$$3{,}600 = £400 \times 9$$

Applying the rate of interest of 3.513 to the lease data produces the data in Exhibit 27.3:

**Exhibit 27.3 Calculation of the periodic finance charge in the lease**

| *Quarter* | *Capital sum at start of period* £ | *Rental paid at start of period* £ | *Capital sum during period* £ | *Finance charge (3.513% per quarter)* £ | *Capital sum at end of period* £ |
|---|---|---|---|---|---|
| 2016 –1 | 4,000 | 400 | 3,600 | 126 | 3,726 |
| 2 | 3,726 | 400 | 3,326 | 117 | 3,443 |
| 3 | 3,443 | 400 | 3,043 | 107 | 3,150 |
| 4 | 3,150 | 400 | 2,750 | 96 | 2,846 |
| 2017 –1 | 2,846 | 400 | 2,446 | 86 | 2,532 |
| 2 | 2,532 | 400 | 2,132 | 75 | 2,207 |
| 3 | 2,207 | 400 | 1,807 | 63 | 1,870 |
| 4 | 1,870 | 400 | 1,470 | 51 | 1,521 |
| 2018 –1 | 1,521 | 400 | 1,121 | 39 | 1,160 |
| 2 | 1,160 | 400 | 760 | 27 | 787 |
| 3 | 787 | 400 | 387 | 13 | 400 |
| 4 | 400 | 400 | – | – | – |
| | | 4,800 | | 800 | |

The finance charges for each year of the lease are:

| | | £ |
|---|---|---|
| 2016 (126 + 117 + 107 + 96) | = | 446 |
| 2017 (86 + 75 + 63 + 51) | = | 275 |
| 2018 (39 + 27 + 13) | = | 79 |
| | | 800 |

The overall picture in each of the three years is:

| *Year* | *Total rental* £ | *less* | *Finance charge* £ | = | *Capital repayment* £ |
|---|---|---|---|---|---|
| 2016 | 1,600 | | 446 | | 1,154 |
| 2017 | 1,600 | | 275 | | 1,325 |
| 2018 | 1,600 | | 79 | | 1,521 |

In the statement of financial position of the lessee, the liability under the finance lease would be:

| *Year* | *Obligations under finance lease at start of year* £ | *less* | *Capital repayment* £ | = | *Obligations under finance lease at end of year* £ |
|---|---|---|---|---|---|
| 2016 | 4,000 | | 1,154 | | 2,846 |
| 2017 | 2,846 | | 1,325 | | 1,521 |
| 2018 | 1,521 | | 1,521 | | – |

## 27.12 The rule of 78

Before spreadsheets became commonplace, these actuarial method-based lease calculations were often considered too complex and, in their place, a simple rule-of-thumb approach was adopted: the rule of 78.

The '78' in its name represents the sum of the numbers 1 to 12, and is used because these calculations originally focused on 12-month periods. Each month receives a proportion in reverse to its position. Thus, month 1 of 12 would be accorded $^{12}/_{78}$ of the total, and month 12 of 12, $^{1}/_{78}$.

Similarly to the actuarial method, under the rule of 78, earlier periods will carry the majority of the allocation. For the purpose of lease calculations, the proportion is applied to the difference between the total payments under the leasing agreement and the cash value of the asset at the start.

Using the example from Exhibit 27.3, the rule of 78 produces the following:

| *Quarter* | *Rental payment number* | *Rule of 78* | *Allocation × £800* | *Annual allocation* £ |
|---|---|---|---|---|
| 2016 –1 | 1 | 11 | 11/66 × £800 = 133 | |
| 2 | 2 | 10 | 121 | |
| 3 | 3 | 9 | 109 | |
| 4 | 4 | 8 | 97 | 460 |
| 2017 –1 | 5 | 7 | 85 | |
| 2 | 6 | 6 | 73 | |
| 3 | 7 | 5 | 61 | |
| 4 | 8 | 4 | 49 | 268 |
| 2018 –1 | 9 | 3 | 36 | |
| 2 | 10 | 2 | 24 | |
| 3 | 11 | 1 | 12 | |
| 4 | – | – | – | 72 |
| | | 66 | 800 | 800 |

(There is no allocation to the final quarter as the payments are made at the start of each quarter.) Comparison of the two methods shows that while the rule of 78 provides a general indication of the pattern flows, it is not particularly accurate.

| *Year* | *Actuarial method* £ | *Rule of 78* £ |
|---|---|---|
| 2016 | 446 | 460 |
| 2017 | 275 | 268 |
| 2018 | 79 | 72 |
| | 800 | 800 |

## Learning outcomes

**You should now have learnt:**

1. As time passes, money loses value and this loss of value must be allowed for when considering long-term investments.
2. Interest rates may be simple or compound, and interest may be paid at any appropriate frequency. Compound interest will generate significantly greater values than the same rate of simple interest the longer the time period involved and the greater the frequency of interest payments.
3. How to calculate simple interest, compound interest, APR, annuities and leases.
4. The real rate of interest often differs from the apparent rate and an annual percentage rate (APR) must be calculated in order to compare alternatives.
5. Annuity calculations are useful when considering rental agreements, hire purchase and leases.
6. Operating leases are accounted for differently from finance leases.

## Answer to activity

27.1 Leasing exists because both lessee and lessor can benefit from the arrangement as a result of their differing tax positions and capital-raising abilities. A small company may find it very expensive, possibly impossible, to borrow £200,000 for some new equipment, whereas a large leasing company would be able to raise the funds at a very competitive rate.

## Review questions

**27.1**

(*a*) If you were lent £20,000 for 86 days at 5%, how much interest would you pay?

(*b*) If a debt factor offered to discount a £5,000 bill of exchange at 10%, and if the bill had an outstanding period of 180 days, how much would the debt factor pay for the bill?

**27.2** What is the real rate of interest of discounting the bill of exchange in Question 27.1?

**27.3**

(*a*) If you were lent £9,000 for 99 days at 6%, how much interest would you pay?

(*b*) If a debt factor offered to discount an £14,000 bill of exchange at 8%, and if the bill had an outstanding period of 30 days, how much would the debt factor pay for the bill?

**27.4** What is the real rate of interest of discounting the bill of exchange in Question 27.3?

**27.5** Interest of £800 is charged and included in a loan of £5,400, i.e. the £4,600 is received. The loan has to be repaid at £1,350 per quarter over the next 12 months. What is the real rate of interest of the loan?

**27.6** If £8,000 is invested for 5 years at 6% compound per annum, how much interest is earned over the five years?

**27.7A** If the interest on the investment in Question 27.6 had been compounded every six months, how much interest would have been earned over the four years?

**27.8A** Shares bought on 1 January 2014 for £4,000 were sold on 31 December 2019 for £7,900. What was the rate of annual compound interest on the investment?

**27.9** Should you accept an offer of £60,000 for your rights over the next 15 years to the £4,800 annual rent from shop premises you own and have leased to a local company? You could invest the £60,000 at 5% per annum.

**27.10A** In relation to the rental income, what rate of interest does the offer made in Question 27.9 represent? Having made this calculation should you change your decision taken in Question 27.9?

**27.11** A condition of a seven-year loan of £70,000 is that the borrower will pay equal annual amounts into a sinking fund so that it accumulates at the end of the seven years to the amount of the loan. The sinking fund will earn interest at 6% per annum. How much should be paid into the sinking fund each year?

**27.12A** If the interest on the sinking fund in Question 27.11 were at 8%, how much would the annual payments into it be?

**27.13** What is the implied interest rate if equipment can be leased for four years at £10,000 per annum and the cash price is £36,000?

**27.14** The annual rental payments on a finance lease are £16,000. If the rate of interest on borrowing for this purpose is 8%, what is the capital value of the lease?

chapter

# 28 Accounting ratios

## Learning objectives

**After you have studied this chapter, you should be able to:**

- describe various groups of accounting ratios, where they would be used, why they would be of interest, and to whom they would be of interest
- calculate a number of commonly used accounting ratios
- describe some of the difficulties that may arise in the calculation and interpretation of accounting ratios
- describe the dangers of overtrading and how ratio analysis can be used to detect it

## Introduction

This chapter revises what you learnt in *Business Accounting 1* concerning ratios and introduces some that are more commonly used. You will also learn about one of the main causes of small business failure, overtrading, and of how ratios can be used to minimise the risk of its occurring undetected.

## 28.1 Background

Without ratios, financial statements would be largely uninformative to all but the very skilled. By using ratios, financial statements can be interpreted and usefully applied to satisfy the needs of the reader, whether skilled or not.

The subject of accounting ratios and their use when analysing financial statements was introduced in *Frank Wood's Business Accounting Volume 1*. This chapter takes that material forward, re-examining it for reinforcement, and then developing it so as to increase the depth of your knowledge and understanding.

Information can be defined as 'data organised for a purpose'. Information in financial statements is organised to enable users of the financial statements to draw conclusions concerning the financial well-being and performance of the reporting entity. In the case of the financial statements of companies, independent auditors review the manner in which the data has been presented and provide a filter mechanism attesting to the reliability of the information presented.

For partnerships and sole proprietors, there is generally no such independent review. However, as the financial statements are generally subject to review by the tax authorities, there is some justification in assuming that they are a reasonable reflection of reality and, in fact, many are prepared by qualified accountants who are governed by the ethical standards of their professional body and so, while not required to do so by the business involved will, nevertheless, strive to produce financial statements that represent a 'true and fair view' of the performance and financial position of the business.

Yet, being 'reasonably assured' of the reliability of such financial statements is not generally sufficient for tax authorities. As a result, they often review the financial statements of partnerships and sole proprietors to determine whether there may be cause to doubt their reliability. One of the key instruments at their disposal is ratios, and they use ratio analysis to compare those found in the entity under review with those typically existing in that sector of the economy. Hence, through ratio analysis, unusual characteristics and deviations from the norm can be identified that would not otherwise be apparent.

**Activity 28.1** What sort of 'deviations from the norm' do you think they may be looking for?

As you learnt in *Business Accounting 1,* ratio analysis can also be used to review trends and compare entities with each other. A number of financial analysis organisations specialise in this service, providing detailed ratio analysis of the financial statements of plcs to anyone who subscribes to their service, thereby enabling analysts to see, at a glance, how one company is performing, or how its financial structure compares with that of others of a similar nature.

This is fine for analysts, academic researchers and business competitors who can afford the services of such an organisation. However, there are a vast number of other stakeholders interested in analysing financial statements, including shareholders, lenders, customers, suppliers, employees and government agencies, not all of whom would either want this information or wish to pay for it. In many cases, each stakeholder group will be interested in different things, and so there is no definitive, all-encompassing list of points for analysis that would be useful to all the groups even if some organisation endeavoured to do so.

Nevertheless, it is possible to construct a series of ratios that together will provide all these groups with something that they will find relevant, and from which they can choose to investigate further, if necessary.

**Ratio analysis is, therefore, a first step in assessing the performance and financial position of an entity. It removes some of the mystique surrounding the financial statements and makes it easier to pinpoint items which would be interesting to investigate further.**

Exhibit 28.1 shows some categories of ratios and indicates some of the groups that would be interested in them. You will recall a similar list in *Frank Wood's Business Accounting 1.* However, note that the term 'solvency' has been substituted for 'liquidity' in the list here. 'Solvency' is a broader term and more clearly indicative of precisely what we are trying to identify when we consider the ratios that fall within its group. **Despite 'solvency' being the more appropriate term, many examiners use the term 'liquidity' when referring to this group of ratios.**

## Exhibit 28.1

| *Ratio category* | *Examples of interested groups* |
|---|---|
| **Profitability** | Shareholders, management, employees, creditors, competitors, potential investors |
| **Solvency** | Shareholders, suppliers, creditors, competitors |
| **Efficiency** | Shareholders, potential purchasers, competitors |
| **Shareholder** | Shareholders, potential investors |
| **Capital structure** | Shareholders, lenders, creditors, potential investors |

Let's now revise the main features of each category of ratios.

## 28.2 Profitability

These measures indicate whether the company is performing satisfactorily. They are used, among other things, to measure the performance of management, to identify whether a company may be a worthwhile investment opportunity, and to determine a company's performance relative to its competitors.

There are a large number of these ratios. You will recall that we covered three in *Frank Wood's Business Accounting 1* – *gross profit : sales; net profit after tax : sales;* and *return on capital employed.* We shall review them once more and add some others that are commonly used.

### Gross profit : Sales

If gross profit is £120,000 and sales are £480,000, the ratio would be 25%. (This should not be confused with the gross margin : cost of sales ratio which compares the gross profit to the cost of goods sold which, in this case, would have a value of 33.33%.) This ratio is also called '*gross profit : revenue*'.

### Net profit after tax : Sales

If net profit is £38,400 and sales are £480,000, the ratio would be 8%. It indicates how much safety there is in the price, i.e. current prices could be reduced by up to 8% without causing the company to make a loss. Of course, it is much more complex than this. As any student of economics knows only too well, if a commodity's price falls, generally demand for it rises. This could result in costs increasing (if unexpected demand has to be met in a hurry) or falling (as bulk discounts become available that were not previously obtainable owing to the lower level of demand). Nevertheless, as a general guide, it is a sensible indicator of safety, as well as an indicator of success.

While a high value for this ratio may suggest successful performance, it is not always the case. It is possible for selling prices to be so high that demand is reduced, causing overall profitability to be significantly lower than it could be were a lower price being used. In this circumstance, the ratio would produce a high percentage, but performance would certainly not be as good as it ought to have been.

This ratio is also called '*net profit after tax : revenue*'.

### Return on capital employed

An adequate return on capital employed is what many investors seek and is, therefore, one of the main reasons why people invest their money in a business in the first place. As a result, this is an extremely important ratio. First, let's remind ourselves of what we learnt in *Business Accounting 1*.

#### (i) Sole proprietors

In this chapter, we will use the average of the capital account as the figure for capital employed, i.e. (opening balance + closing balance) / 2.

In businesses *C* and *D* in Exhibit 28.2 the same amount of net profit has been made, but the capitals employed are different.

## Exhibit 28.2

**Statements of Financial Position**

| | *C* | *D* |
|---|---|---|
| | £ | £ |
| Non-current + Current assets − Current liabilities | 10,000 | 16,000 |
| Capital accounts | | |
| Opening balance | 8,000 | 14,000 |
| *Add* Net profit | 3,600 | 3,600 |
| | 11,600 | 17,600 |
| *Less* Drawings | (1,600) | (1,600) |
| | 10,000 | 16,000 |

Return on capital employed (ROCE) is:

$$\text{ROCE} = \frac{\text{Net profit}}{\text{Capital employed}} \times 100$$

therefore

$$C: \quad \frac{3{,}600}{(8{,}000 + 10{,}000) \div 2} \times \frac{100}{1} = 40\% \qquad D: \quad \frac{3{,}600}{(14{,}000 + 16{,}000) \div 2} \times \frac{100}{1} = 24\%$$

The ratio illustrates that **what is important is not simply how much profit has been made but how well the capital has been employed.** Business *C* has made far better use of its capital, achieving a return of £40 net profit for every £100 invested, whereas *D* has received only a net profit of £24 per £100.

### (ii) Limited companies

There is no universally agreed definition of **capital employed** for companies. The main ones used are:

(*a*) return on capital employed by ordinary shareholders;
(*b*) return on capital employed by all long-term suppliers of capital.

Let's now look at each of these:

(*a*) In a limited company this is known as 'return on owners' equity' (ROOE) or, more commonly, 'return on shareholders' funds' (ROSF).

**From now on, we shall use the second of these terms, 'return on shareholders' funds', but you will need to remember that when you see 'return on owners' equity', it is the same as ROSF.**

The word 'return' is the net profit for the period. The term 'shareholders' funds' means the book value of all things in the statement of financial position that describe the owners' capital and reserves. As the 'owners' are the holders of the *ordinary* share capital, shareholders' funds = ordinary share capital + all reserves.

(*b*) This is often known as 'return on capital employed' (ROCE). The word 'return' in this case means net profit + any preference share dividends + loan note and long-term loan interest. The word 'capital' means ordinary share capital + reserves + preference shares + loan notes and other long-term loans.

Now, let's calculate ROSF and ROCE for P Ltd and Q Ltd. Q Ltd has issued loan notes, so its ROSF and ROCE will not be the same. P Ltd's capital employed is sourced solely from shareholders' funds, so its ROSF and ROCE will be identical.

**Statements of Financial Position as at 31 December**

| | P Ltd | | Q Ltd | |
|---|---|---|---|---|
| | £ | £ | £ | £ |
| | *2015* | *2016* | *2015* | *2016* |
| Non-current assets | 5,200 | 5,600 | 8,400 | 9,300 |
| Net current assets | 2,800 | 3,400 | 1,600 | 2,700 |
| | 8,000 | 9,000 | 10,000 | 12,000 |
| 10% loan notes | – | – | (1,200) | (1,200) |
| | 8,000 | 9,000 | 8,800 | 10,800 |
| Share capital (ordinary) | 3,000 | 3,000 | 5,000 | 5,000 |
| Reserves | 5,000 | 6,000 | 3,800 | 5,800 |
| | 8,000 | 9,000 | 8,800 | 10,800 |

**Changes in Equity for year to 31 December 2016**

| | P Ltd | Q Ltd |
|---|---|---|
| | £ | £ |
| Net profit | 2,200 | 3,800 |
| Dividends | (1,200) | (1,800) |
| | 1,000 | 2,000 |

**Return on Shareholders' Funds (ROSF)**

*P Ltd*

$$\frac{2{,}200}{(8{,}000 + 9{,}000) \div 2} \times \frac{100}{1} = 25.9\%$$

*Q Ltd*

$$\frac{3{,}800}{(8{,}800 + 10{,}800) \div 2} \times \frac{100}{1} = 38.8\%$$

**Return on Capital Employed (ROCE)**

*P Ltd*

Same as ROSF$^{\text{(Note 1)}}$ = 25.9%

*Q Ltd*

$$\frac{3{,}800 + 120^{\text{(Note 2)}}}{(10{,}000 + 12{,}000) \div 2} \times \frac{100}{1} = 35.6\%$$

***Note 1*: The return on capital employed by all long-term sources of capital (in Q Ltd's case, the shareholders' funds and the loan notes) is the same as the ROSF in the case of P Ltd, as it has no loan notes.**

***Note 2*: The loan-note interest (i.e. 10% of £1,200 = £120) must be added back, as it was an expense in calculating the £3,800 net profit.**

To summarise: return on capital employed is one of the more awkward ratios to deal with. Unlike, for example, the current ratio, there is no widely agreed definition for ROCE – even the ones given here are but examples of how it may be defined. Hence, care must be taken when comparing this ratio as calculated for one company and as reported by another 'so as to confirm that like is being compared with like'. Using the services of financial analysis organisations which use the same formulae to calculate the ratios of all the companies they consider is one way around this difficulty. Another is to ensure that the formula used by the companies with which comparison is being made is known and, where necessary, the ratio result is recalculated in order to bring it into line with the internally calculated ratio.

***Note*: A problem you face as a student is that you will never be quite sure what an examiner wants if the exam paper refers to this ratio. You should always write down the formula you are using on your exam script.**

To avoid confusion, unless otherwise indicated by, for example, the examiner, for companies use the definition of ROCE given above. The ratio compares the profit earned (usually *before* interest and tax) to the funds used to generate that return (often the total of shareholders' funds at the beginning of the accounting period plus long-term payables). If the profit before interest and tax was £40,000 and the opening capital employed shown in the statement of financial position was £800,000 the return on capital employed would be 5%.

**In theory, the higher the ratio, the more profitably the resources of the company have been used.**

## Return on share capital

In theory, the higher this ratio is, the more profitably the shareholders' investment in the company has been used. It is often used to compare a company's performance across accounting periods, rather than to make comparisons with the ROSC of other companies. As with ROCE, there are a number of different ways in which return on share capital may be calculated. One is to compare profit on ordinary activities before tax with share capital and reserves. For example, if profit on ordinary activities before tax was £40,000 and the share capital and reserves at the start of the accounting period were £720,000 the return on share capital (ROSC) would be 5.56%.

## Net profit after tax : total assets

Net profit after tax is compared with the total of all non-current assets, plus working capital (i.e. current assets less current liabilities). If working capital is £20,000 and all non-current assets total £820,000, total assets are £840,000. If net profit after tax is £30,000, the ratio is £30,000/£840,000, i.e. 3.57%.

There are problems with the validity of this ratio: it is really concerned with the operating profit generated by the net assets. However, some items of expenditure, e.g. interest on loan notes, will have been charged against the profit in arriving at the figure for profit after tax. Strictly speaking, these other payments to investors and creditors ought to be excluded from this ratio and so should be added back to arrive at the profit figure used in the ratio, otherwise the profit may be significantly understated, giving a less healthy view than would be appropriate to present.

In addition, intangible assets, such as goodwill, are included in the value of total assets used in the ratio. Many would argue that this is inappropriate, as there is not an agreed view on how such assets should be valued.

These issues result in variations of this ratio being used – some add back expenditure, some exclude all intangible assets, some don't – which may not be apparent if only the ratio result is available. As a result, intercompany comparisons may be misleading.

## Net operating profit : operating assets

This is an alternative to the *net profit after tax : total assets* ratio. It takes the net profit before interest, taxes and dividends, and before inclusion of any investment income. This is then compared with the assets other than intangibles and investments outside the company. Working capital would be included, but bank overdrafts would be excluded from the current liabilities on the basis that they are not generally short term in nature. Assume that net operating profit before interest, tax and dividends is £36,000 and tangible non-current assets excluding investments made outside the company are £600,000, working capital is £20,000 and there is a bank overdraft of £5,000. The ratio is:

$$\frac{£36,000}{£625,000} = 5.76\%$$

## 28.3 Solvency

Being solvent means having sufficient resources to meet your debts when due. Your resources must be sufficiently liquid to do so, hence the frequent use of the term 'liquidity' when referring to this group of ratios. As you learnt in *Business Accounting 1*, the solvency of individuals is often performed through credit checks undertaken by credit rating agencies. Many lenders, such as banks, use a checklist of questions concerning financial status before they will lend or grant credit to a private individual. For companies, information can be purchased that indicates their solvency, i.e. whether they are liable to be bad credit risks. Such information is usually based, at least in part, upon ratio analysis of their financial statements.

When it comes to the solvency of a business, both its own ability to pay its debts when due *and* the ability of its debtors to pay the amount they owe to the business are of great importance. Ratio analysis that focuses upon solvency (or liquidity) of the business generally starts with a look at two ratios that are affected most by these two aspects of liquidity: the *current ratio* and the *acid test ratio*.

### Current ratio

The *current ratio* compares total current assets to total current liabilities and indicates whether there are sufficient short-term assets to pay the short-term liabilities. This ratio is so sector-dependent that it would be and is inappropriate to suggest a ratio result that may be seen generally as being the 'norm'. Consequently, no such guidance will be given here. Rather, a set of issues to consider are offered below:

1 What is the norm in this industrial sector?
2 Is this company significantly above or below that norm?
3 If so, can this be justified after an analysis of the nature of these assets and liabilities, and of the reasons for the amounts of each held?

The ratio may be expressed as either a ratio to 1, with current liabilities being set to 1, or as a 'number of times', representing the relative size of the amount of total current assets compared with total current liabilities.

**Example**

If total current assets are £40,000 and total current liabilities are £20,000, the current ratio could be expressed as either:

$$\pounds 40{,}000 : \pounds 20{,}000 = 2 : 1$$

or as:

$$\frac{\pounds 40{,}000}{\pounds 20{,}000} = 2 \text{ times}$$

### Acid test ratio

As with the current ratio, there is no point in suggesting a norm for the ratio result to expect. The only difference in the items involved between the two ratios is that the acid test ratio (or 'quick' ratio) does not include inventory. Otherwise, it is identical to the current ratio, comparing current assets, excluding inventory, with current liabilities. Inventory is omitted as it is considered to be relatively illiquid, because it depends upon prevailing and future market forces and may be impossible to convert to cash in a relatively short time.

Many companies operate with acid test ratios below 1 : 1; that is, they have insufficient liquid assets to meet their short-term liabilities. The great majority of companies in this situation have no problem paying their creditors when due. Consideration of a simple example should explain how this is possible.

**Activity 28.2**

**The only difference between the current and acid test ratios is that inventory is omitted from the acid test ratio. Why is it appropriate to remove inventory from the analysis?**

**Example**

**If total current assets, including inventory of £22,000, are worth £40,000 and total current liabilities stand at £20,000, the acid test ratio will be £18,000 : £20,000 = 0.9 : 1 (or 0.9 times). This means that at the statement of financial position date, had all current liabilities been due for payment, it would not have been possible to do so without converting some other assets (e.g. inventory, or some non-current assets) into cash even though it would be unlikely that they could be converted quickly into cash without offering a discount on their true value. In other words, the company would have had to pay a premium in order to meet its obligations, clearly something it would not be able to do indefinitely.**

However, the reality is generally that the current liabilities shown in the statement of financial position are due for payment at varying times over the coming financial period and some, for example a bank overdraft, may not in reality ever be likely to be subject to a demand for swift repayment.

The current assets, on the other hand, are within the control of the company and can be adjusted in their timing to match the due dates for payment to creditors. They can be renewed many times before one or other of the current liabilities is due for payment. For example, account receivables may be on a 10-day cycle while trade account payables are only paid after 90 days' credit has expired. Clearly, in this case, cash receipts from nine times the statement of financial position account receivables figure could be received and available to meet the trade account payables figure shown in the statement of financial position when it falls due.

As with the current ratio, the acid test ratio should be compared with the norms for the industrial sector, and then the underlying assets and liabilities should be considered to determine whether there is any cause for concern in the result obtained.

**Activity 28.3**

**If inventory is removed from the analysis when calculating the acid test ratio, why isn't the figure for accounts receivable also removed? Accounts receivable can be just as difficult to turn into cash.**

## 28.4 Efficiency ratios

Profitability is affected by the way that the assets of a business are used. If plant and machinery are used for only a few hours a day, the business is probably failing to utilise these assets efficiently. This may be because there is limited demand for the product produced. It could be due to the business restricting supply to maximise profitability per item produced. On the other hand, it could be that there is a shortage of skilled labour and that there is no one to operate the plant and machinery the rest of the time. Alternatively, it could be that the plant and machinery are unreliable, breaking down a lot, and that the limited level of use is a precautionary measure designed to ensure that production targets are met.

In common with all accounting ratios, it is important that the results of efficiency ratio computations are not treated as definitively good or bad. They must be investigated further through consideration both of the underlying variables in the ratios, and of the broader context of the business and its relation to the industrial sector in which it operates.

Efficiency ratios include:

## Asset turnover

Asset turnover is a measure of how effectively the assets are being used to generate sales. It is one of the ratios that would be considered when interpreting the results of profitability ratio analyses like ROCE, but is of sufficient importance to be calculated and analysed irrespective of its relevance to other ratios. The calculation involves dividing revenue by total assets less current liabilities.

As a general guide, where a company's asset turnover is significantly lower than that of its competitors, it suggests there may be overinvestment in assets which could, in turn, make the company vulnerable to takeover by a company interested in selling off any surplus assets while otherwise retaining the business in its current form. However, considerable care must be taken when interpreting this ratio: the assets may be much newer than those of other companies; the company may use a lower rate of depreciation than its competitors; or the company may purchase its plant and machinery, whereas the industry norm is to lease them. On the other side of the ratio, the result may be high because, for example, selling prices are being suppressed in order to maximise volume.

## Inventory turnover

Included in virtually every case where accounting ratios are being calculated, inventory turnover measures the number of times (approximately) that inventory is replenished in an accounting period. If average inventory is £100,000 and cost of goods sold is £800,000, the inventory turnover ratio would be 8 times. The ratio can also be expressed as a number of days – the number of days inventory held. In this example, 365 would be divided by 8 producing a result of 45.6 days.

There are two major difficulties in computing the inventory turnover ratio: if cost of goods sold is not available, it is tempting to use revenue instead. This should not be done. Revenue is expressed at selling prices; inventory is expressed at cost price. Use of revenue instead of cost of goods sold in the equation will not be comparing like with like.

In addition, there are at least three possible inventory values that could be used: opening, closing and the average of these figures. The average figure is the more commonly used, but use of any of the three can be justified.

Whichever approach is taken, the result will, at best, be a crude estimate. Due to seasonality of the business, inventory as shown in the statement of financial position may not be representative of the 'normal' level of inventory. However, it is still useful for comparing trends over time and should be used mainly for that purpose. The result it produces needs to be handled with care. A rising inventory turnover may indicate greater efficiency; or it may be an indicator that inventory is being run down and that there may be problems in meeting demand in future. A falling inventory turnover may indicate lower efficiency, perhaps with a build-up of obsolete inventory; or it could indicate that higher inventory volumes are being held because inventory purchasing has become more efficient and the higher inventory levels are financially beneficial for the company. In addition, it is important not to overlook the fact that any change in the ratio may have nothing to do with inventory but, instead, may be due to changes in factors relating to the sales for the period. (This ratio is also known as '*stock turnover*' and as '*stockturn*'.)

## Accounts receivable days

Accounts receivable days indicates how efficient the company is at controlling its accounts receivable. If accounts receivable are £50,000 and sales £800,000, debtors are taking, on average, 22.8 days credit, i.e.

$$\frac{\pounds 50{,}000}{\pounds 800{,}000} \times 365 = 22.8$$

Strictly speaking, the two figures are not comparable. Accounts receivable include the VAT on sales; the figure for revenue excludes VAT. However, the adjustment is not difficult to make if required for clarity.

As with inventory, the amount shown in the statement of financial position for accounts receivable may not be representative of the 'normal' level of accounts receivable. Nevertheless, this is generally a useful ratio to calculate and comparison with that of other companies in the same industrial sector may be very interesting. However, as with inventory turnover, its strength lies in trend analysis between periods. (The ratio is also known as '*debtor days*'.)

### Accounts payable days

The accounts payable days ratio indicates one aspect of how the company uses short-term financing to fund its activities, and further investigation will reveal whether or not the result found is due to efficiency. It is calculated by dividing accounts payable by purchases, and multiplying the result by 365. The purchases figure is not usually available in published financial statements, the cost of sales amount being used in its place. As with inventory turnover and accounts receivable days, its strength lies in trend analysis between periods. (The ratio is also known as '*creditor days*'.)

## 28.5 Shareholder ratios

Shareholder ratios are those most commonly used by anyone interested in an investment in a company. They indicate how well a company is performing in relation to the price of its shares and other related items including dividends and the number of shares in issue. The ratios usually calculated are described below.

### Dividend yield

Dividend yield measures the real rate of return by comparing the dividend paid to the market price of a share. It is calculated as:

$$\frac{\text{Gross dividend per share}}{\text{Market price per share}}$$

### Earnings per share (EPS)

EPS is the most frequently used of all the accounting ratios and is generally felt to give the best view of performance. It indicates how much of a company's profit can be attributed to each ordinary share in the company. IAS 33 *Earnings per share* provides the formula to be used when calculating this ratio:

$$\frac{\text{Net profit or loss attributable to ordinary shareholders}}{\text{The weighted average number of ordinary shares outstanding during the period}}$$

### Dividend cover

Dividend cover compares the amount of profit earned per ordinary share with the amount of dividend paid, thereby showing the proportion of profits that could have been distributed and where. It differs from EPS only in having a different denominator. The formula is:

$$\frac{\text{Net profit or loss attributable to ordinary shareholders}}{\text{Net dividend on ordinary shares}}$$

### Price earnings (P/E) ratio

The P/E ratio relates the earnings per share to the market price of the shares. It is calculated as:

$$\frac{\text{Market price}}{\text{Earnings per share}}$$

and is a useful indicator of how the stock market assesses the company. It is also very useful when a company proposes an issue of new shares, in that it enables potential investors to better assess whether the expected future earnings make the share a worthwhile investment.

## 28.6 Capital structure

There are a number of ratios that can be used to assess the way in which a company finances its activities. One, accounts payable days, was referred to in the last section. The ratios discussed in this section differ in that they are longer term in nature, being concerned more with the strategic rather than with the operational level of corporate decision-making. Some of the more commonly analysed ratios of this type are described below.

### Net worth : total assets

This ratio indicates the proportion of non-current and current assets that are financed by net worth (the total of shareholders' funds, i.e. share capital plus reserves). If non-current assets are shown at a value of £500,000, current assets £100,000 and net worth is £300,000, then 50% of total assets are financed by shareholders' funds. As with many accounting ratios, it is the trend in this ratio between periods that is important.

### Non-current assets : net worth

This ratio focuses on the longer-term aspects of the net worth : total assets ratio. By matching long-term investment with long-term finance it is possible to determine whether borrowing has been used to finance some long-term investment in assets. Where this has occurred, there may be a problem when the borrowing is to be repaid (as the non-current assets it used to acquire cannot be readily converted into cash). Again, this ratio is of most use when the trend over time is analysed.

### Non-current assets : net worth + long-term liabilities

This ratio focuses on whether sufficient long-term finance has been obtained to meet the investment in non-current assets.

### Debt ratio

This ratio compares the total debts to total assets and is concerned with whether the company has sufficient assets to meet all its liabilities when due. For example, if total liabilities are £150,000 and total assets are £600,000, the debts represent 25% of total assets. Whether this is good or bad will, as with all accounting ratios, depend upon the norm for the industrial sector in which the company operates and on the underlying items within the figures included in the ratio.

### Capital gearing ratio

This ratio provides the proportion of a company's total capital that has a prior claim to profits over those of ordinary shareholders. Prior claim (or prior charge) capital includes loan notes, other long-term loans, and preference share capital and is any capital carrying a right to a fixed return. Total capital includes ordinary share capital and reserves, preference shares and non-current liabilities.

### Debt : equity ratio

This is the ratio of prior charge capital to ordinary share capital and reserves.

### Borrowing : net worth

This ratio indicates the proportion that borrowing represents of a company's net worth. If long-term liabilities are £100,000 and current liabilities are £50,000, then total borrowing is £150,000. If net worth is £300,000, the ratio is 1 : 2, or 50%.

This and the debt : equity ratio indicate the degree of risk to investors in ordinary shares in a company. The higher these ratios are, the greater the possibility of risk to ordinary shareholders – both in respect of expectations of future dividends (especially in times of depressed performance where much of the profits may be paid to the holders of prior charge capital), and from the threat of liquidation should there be a slump in performance that leads to a failure to meet payments to holders of prior charge capital. Whether these risks may be relevant can be investigated by reference to the next ratio.

### Interest cover

This ratio shows whether enough profits are being earned to meet interest payments when due. It is calculated by dividing profit before interest and tax by the interest charges. Thus, the interest cover is 20 times if profit before interest and tax is £400,000 and the total interest charges are £20,000. In this case, there would be little cause for immediate concern that there was any risk of the company's failing to meet its interest charges when due. However, just because a company is making profits does not guarantee that there will be sufficient cash available to make the interest charge payments when due.

## 28.7 Overtrading

A very high proportion of new businesses fail within the first two years of trading. This can occur because there was insufficient demand for the goods or services provided, because of poor management, or for any of a number of other reasons; the most common of these is possibly *overtrading*. However, unlike the other common causes of business failure, overtrading often arises when a business is performing profitably. Furthermore, overtrading can just as easily affect established businesses as new businesses.

Overtrading occurs when poor control over working capital results in there being insufficient liquid funds to meet the demands of creditors. As the cash dries up, so do the sources of supply of raw materials and other essential inputs – suppliers will not continue to supply a business that fails to settle its bills when due. Overtrading is generally the result of sales growth being at too fast a rate in relation to the level of trade accounts receivable, trade accounts payable and inventory.

Take an example where, over a 12-month period, profits increased by 20%; revenue doubled from £1 million to £2 million; trade accounts receivable doubled from £80,000 to £160,000; trade accounts payable quadrupled from £60,000 to £240,000; inventory quadrupled from £50,000 to £200,000; and the bank balance moved from positive £20,000 to an overdraft of £80,000.

No changes occurred during the period in long-term financing of the business, though £100,000 was spent on some new equipment needed as a result of the expansion.

Working capital was 2.5 : 1; now it is 1.125 : 1 and the acid test ratio is now 0.5 : 1 from 1.67 : 1. Liquidity appears to have deteriorated significantly (but may have been high previously compared with other businesses in the same sector). Accounts receivable days are unchanged (as the ratio of revenue to accounts receivable is unaltered). However, accounts payable days have probably doubled (subject to a slight reduction due to some cheaper purchasing costs as a result of the higher volumes involved). If the bank overdraft is currently at its limit, the business would be unable to meet any requests from creditors for immediate payment, never mind pay wages and other regular expenses.

This situation can be addressed by raising long-term finance, or by cutting back on the expansion – clearly, the first option is likely to be the more acceptable one to the owners of the business.

Signals suggesting overtrading include:

(*a*) significant increases in the volume of good sold;
(*b*) lower profit margins;
(*c*) deteriorating accounts receivable, accounts payable, and inventory turnover;
(*d*) increasing reliance on short-term finance.

## 28.8 Summary of ratios

### Profitability

Gross profit : revenue $$\frac{\text{Gross profit}}{\text{Sales}}$$

Net profit after tax : revenue $$\frac{\text{Net profit after tax}}{\text{Sales}}$$

Return on capital employed $$\frac{\text{Profit before interest and tax}}{\text{Total assets} - \text{Current liabilities}}$$

Return on share capital $$\frac{\text{Profit before tax}}{\text{Share capital} + \text{Reserves}}$$

Net profit after tax : total assets $$\frac{\text{Net profit after tax}}{\text{Non-current assets} + \text{Working capital}}$$

Net operating profit : operating assets $$\frac{\text{Net profit before interest, tax, dividends, and investment income}}{\text{Tangible non-current assets} - \text{Outside investments} + \text{Working capital} + \text{Bank overdraft}}$$

### Solvency

Current ratio $$\frac{\text{Current assets}}{\text{Current liabilities}}$$

Acid test ratio $$\frac{\text{Current assets} - \text{Inventory}}{\text{Current liabilities}}$$

### Efficiency

Asset turnover $$\frac{\text{Revenue}}{\text{Total assets} - \text{Current liabilities}}$$

Inventory turnover $\dfrac{\text{Cost of goods sold}}{\text{Average inventory}}$

Accounts receivable days $\dfrac{\text{Accounts receivable}}{\text{Revenue}} \times 365$

Accounts payable days $\dfrac{\text{Accounts payable}}{\text{Purchases}} \times 365$

## Shareholder ratios

Dividend yield $\dfrac{\text{Gross dividend per share}}{\text{Market price per share}}$

Earnings per share $\dfrac{\text{Net profit or loss attributable to ordinary shareholders}}{\text{Weighted average number of ordinary shares outstanding during the period}}$

Dividend cover $\dfrac{\text{Net profit or loss attributable to ordinary shareholders}}{\text{Net dividend on ordinary shares}}$

Price/earnings ratio $\dfrac{\text{Market price}}{\text{Earnings per share}}$

## Capital structure

Net worth : Total assets $\dfrac{\text{Shareholders' funds}}{\text{Total assets}}$

Non-current assets : net worth $\dfrac{\text{Fixed assets}}{\text{Shareholders' funds}}$

Non-current assets : net worth + long-term liabilities $\dfrac{\text{Fixed assets}}{\text{Shareholders' funds + Long-term liabilities}}$

Debt ratio $\dfrac{\text{Total liabilities}}{\text{Total assets}}$

Capital gearing ratio $\dfrac{\text{Prior charge capital}}{\text{Total capital}}$

Debt : equity ratio $\dfrac{\text{Prior charge capital}}{\text{Ordinary share capital and reserves}}$

Borrowing : net worth $\dfrac{\text{Total borrowing}}{\text{Shareholders' funds}}$

Interest cover $\dfrac{\text{Profit before interest and tax}}{\text{Interest charges}}$

***Note*: If you wish to read more about the topic of ratios, there are many worthwhile books available, such as Ciaran Walsh's *Key Management Ratios*, published by FT Prentice Hall. However, don't forget that there is no 'correct' formula for many of the financial ratios you have learnt about in this chapter. If you do read further on this topic *do not* make changes to these formulae. These are generally accepted formulae and ones your examiners will recognise.**

## Learning outcomes

**You should now have learnt:**

1. There are many different categories of accounting ratios and many different ratios within each category.
2. Ratios that are of interest to one group of readers of financial statements may not be of interest to another.
3. Ratios may be used to review reliability of financial statements.
4. Ratios may be used to review trends between periods for the same company.
5. Ratios may be used to compare a company to others in the same industrial sector.
6. Some ratios in wide use have no agreed 'correct' formula to calculate them. This makes comparison between analysis reported elsewhere of limited value unless the formula used can be identified.
7. The ratios derived can be misleading if taken at face value. It is essential that they are placed in context and that interpretation goes beyond a superficial comparison to general norms.
8. Used casually, accounting ratios can mislead and result in poor-quality decision-making.
9. Used carefully, accounting ratios can provide pointers towards areas of interest in an entity, and provide a far more complete picture of an entity than that given by the financial statements.
10. Overtrading can be financially disastrous for a business and ratios can be used to help detect it.

## Answers to activities

28.1 Lower levels of gross profit than the industry norm, which might indicate goods were being taken out of the business for the owner's own use but not being recorded as drawings. Alternatively, lower levels of gross profit than the industry norm may indicate sales for cash were not all being recorded. Revenue and Customs use ratios to detect anything that might indicate the possibility that a proprietor is understating the profit earned.

28.2 Inventory is sometimes very difficult to convert into cash, particularly at the value placed upon it in the statement of financial position. Because it can be difficult to generate liquid funds through the sale of inventory, it is inappropriate to consider it when looking at the issue of whether an organisation is able to pay its debts quickly.

28.3 Accounts receivable can be very difficult to turn into cash. However, there are three aspects of accounts receivable that make them less problematic than inventory in this context. Firstly, specialist financial agencies called 'factors' will take over debts in many instances in exchange for a percentage of the amount owing. Through this medium, organisations can convert some of their accounts receivable into cash quickly and at relatively little cost. Secondly, accounts receivable can be pursued through the courts. Thus, when an organisation urgently needs money owing from accounts receivable that is already overdue, it can threaten legal action, thereby accelerating the receipt of the money due. Finally, most debtors do eventually pay their debts; inventory may never be sold.

In the context of the cash it will generate, inventory is usually sold at above the value placed upon it in the statement of financial position while, apart from overestimation of doubtful debts, accounts receivable never realise more than the value shown for them in the statement of financial position. However, so far as the acid test ratio is concerned, the key difference is that money owing by debtors will generally be received more quickly than money tied up in inventory.

## Review questions

**28.1** Five categories of accounting ratios were described in this chapter. What are they?

**28.2A** Why should different groups of people be interested in different categories of accounting ratios?

**28.3** Describe two ratios from each of the five groups of ratios, including how to calculate them.

**28.4A** What is the purpose in using each of the following ratios:

(*a*) current ratio
(*b*) net profit after tax : revenue
(*c*) asset turnover
(*d*) interest cover
(*e*) dividend cover?

**28.5** If you wished to assess the efficiency of a company, which of these ratios would you use:

(*a*) inventory turnover
(*b*) interest cover
(*c*) return on capital employed
(*d*) acid test ratio
(*e*) dividend yield?

**28.6A** A company has capital of 5 million ordinary shares of £1 each. It pays a dividend of 5% of its profits after tax of £800,000 on sales of £8 million. The market price of the shares is £2.50. What is the:

(*a*) net profit after tax : revenue
(*b*) dividend yield
(*c*) earnings per share
(*d*) price earnings ratio?

**28.7** In respect of each of the following events, select all the effects resulting from that event that are shown in the list of effects:

(*i*) a bad debt written off;
(*ii*) an increase in the bank overdraft;
(*iii*) a purchase of six months' inventory;
(*iv*) payment of all amounts due to trade accounts payable that had been outstanding for longer than 90 days;
(*v*) an offer of 5% discount to all customers who settle their accounts within two weeks.

*Effects*
(*a*) increased current ratio
(*b*) reduced current ratio
(*c*) increased acid test ratio
(*d*) reduced acid test ratio.

**28.8A** Using the following statement of financial position and statement of profit or loss, calculate ten accounting ratios (each to 2 decimal places). Comment on each ratio calculated (ignore taxation).

**Statement of Financial Position as at 31 March 2016 (£000)**

| | | |
|---|---|---|
| *Non-current assets* | | |
| Equipment at cost | | 720 |
| *Less* Depreciation to date | | (240) |
| | | 480 |
| *Current assets* | | |
| Inventory | 360 | |
| Accounts receivable | 72 | |
| Bank | – | |
| | | 432 |
| *Total assets* | | 912 |
| *Current liabilities* | | |
| Accounts payable | 192 | |
| Dividends payable | 14 | |
| Bank overdraft | 202 | |
| | 408 | |
| *Non-current liabilities* | | |
| 5% Loan notes | (120) | |
| | | (528) |
| Net assets | | 384 |
| *Equity* | | |
| Share capital – ordinary shares of 50p each | | 300 |
| *Reserves* | | |
| General reserve | | 481 |
| Retained profits | | 36 |
| | | 384 |

**Statement of Profit or Loss for period ending 31 March 2016 (£000)**

| | | |
|---|---|---|
| Revenue | | 2,400 |
| *Less* Cost of goods sold | | |
| Opening inventory | 300 | |
| *Add* Purchases | 1,740 | |
| | 2,040 | |
| *Less* Closing inventory | (360) | |
| | | (1,680) |
| Gross profit | | 720 |
| *Less* Depreciation | 96 | |
| Other expenses | 572 | |
| | | (668) |
| Operating profit | | 52 |
| Loan-note interest | | (6) |
| Profit for the year | | 46 |

***Note*: The statement of changes in equity shows that retained profits at 1 April 2015 were £28,800; that £24,000 has been transferred from retained profit to the general reserve; and that a dividend of £14,400 was paid during the year. (The statement of financial position reflects these items.)**

**28.9** Study the following financial statements for two very similar privately owned department stores that each have one store in the city centre of the same large city and then answer the questions which follow.

**Summary of Financial Statements**

| *Statements of financial position* | *A* | | *B* | |
|---|---|---|---|---|
| | £000s | £000s | £000s | £000s |
| *Non-current assets* | | | | |
| Building at cost | 480 | | 704 | |
| *Less* Depreciation to date | (408) | | (352) | |
| | | 72 | | 352 |
| Equipment at cost | 224 | | 288 | |
| *Less* Depreciation to date | (190) | | (144) | |
| | | 34 | | 144 |
| | | 106 | | 496 |
| *Current assets* | | | | |
| Inventory | 224 | | 416 | |
| Accounts receivable | 424 | | 192 | |
| Bank | 6 | | 3 | |
| | | 654 | | 611 |
| Total assets | | 760 | | 1,107 |
| *Current liabilities* | | | | |
| Accounts payable | | (392) | | (403) |
| Net assets | | 368 | | 704 |
| *Financed by:* | | | | |
| *Capital accounts* | | | | |
| Balance at start of year | | 384 | | 688 |
| *Add* Net profit | | 96 | | 144 |
| | | 480 | | 832 |
| *Less* Drawings | | (112) | | (128) |
| | | 368 | | 704 |
| *Statements of profit or loss* | | | | |
| Revenue | | 2,880 | | 4,320 |
| *Less:* Cost of goods sold | | | | |
| Opening inventory | 384 | | 480 | |
| *Add* Purchases | 2,080 | | 3,600 | |
| | 2,464 | | 4,080 | |
| *Less* Closing inventory | (224) | | (416) | |
| | | (2,240) | | (3,664) |
| Gross profit | | 640 | | 656 |
| *Less* Depreciation | 35 | | 64 | |
| Other expenses | 509 | | 448 | |
| | | (544) | | (512) |
| Net profit | | 96 | | 144 |

**Required:**

(a) Calculate the following ratios to one decimal place:
   (*i*) gross profit as % of revenue;
   (*ii*) net profit as % of revenue;
   (*iii*) expenses as % of revenue;
   (*iv*) inventory turnover;
   (*v*) rate of return of net profit on capital employed (use the average of the capital account for this purpose);
   (*vi*) current ratio;
   (*vii*) acid test ratio;
   (*viii*) accounts receivable : revenue ratio;
   (*ix*) accounts payable : purchases ratio.

(b) Drawing upon all your knowledge of accounting, comment upon the differences and similarities of the accounting ratios for *A* and *B*. Which business seems to be the most efficient? Justify your opinion.

**28.10A** Study the following financial statements of two companies and then answer the questions which follow. Both companies are stores selling carpets and other floor coverings; each company has a single store in the same 10-year-old custom-built shopping complex located on the outskirts of a major UK city.

**Statements of Profit or Loss**

| | *R Ltd* | | *T Ltd* | |
|---|---|---|---|---|
| | £000s | £000s | £000s | £000s |
| Revenue | | 2,000 | | 1,400 |
| *Less Cost of goods sold* | | | | |
| Opening inventory | 440 | | 144 | |
| *Add* Purchases | 1,550 | | 996 | |
| | 1,990 | | 1,140 | |
| *Less* Closing inventory | (490) | | (240) | |
| | | (1,500) | | (900) |
| Gross profit | | 500 | | 500 |
| *Less Expenses* | | | | |
| Depreciation | 27 | | 14 | |
| Wages and salaries | 180 | | 160 | |
| Directors' remuneration | 210 | | 210 | |
| Other expenses | 23 | | 16 | |
| | | (440) | | (400) |
| Net profit | | 60 | | 100 |

***Note*: The statement of changes in equity shows that retained profits at the start of the year were £60,000 (R Ltd) and £20,000 (T Ltd); that dividends paid during the year were £50,000 (R Ltd) and £40,000 (T Ltd); and that both companies made transfers from retained profit to general reserve at the end of the year: £20,000 (R Ltd) and £20,000 (T Ltd).**

**Statements of Financial Position**

| | R Ltd | | T Ltd | |
|---|---|---|---|---|
| | £000s | £000s | £000s | £000s |
| *Non-current assets* | | | | |
| Building at cost | 300 | | 100 | |
| *Less* Depreciation to date | (150) | | (50) | |
| | | 150 | | 50 |
| Equipment at cost | 60 | | 30 | |
| *Less* Depreciation to date | (40) | | (20) | |
| | | 20 | | 10 |
| Motor vans | 40 | | 35 | |
| *Less* Depreciation to date | (16) | | (14) | |
| | | 24 | | 21 |
| | | 194 | | 81 |
| *Current assets* | | | | |
| Inventory | 490 | | 240 | |
| Accounts receivable | 680 | | 320 | |
| Bank | 80 | | 127 | |
| | | 1,250 | | 687 |
| Total assets | | 1,444 | | 768 |
| *Current liabilities* | | | | |
| Accounts payable | | (324) | | (90) |
| Net assets | | 1,120 | | 678 |
| *Equity* | | | | |
| Issued share capital | | 1,000 | | 500 |
| Reserves | | | | |
| General reserve | 70 | | 120 | |
| Retained profits | 50 | | 58 | |
| | | 120 | | 178 |
| | | 1,120 | | 678 |

**Required:**

(*a*) Calculate the following ratios for each of R Ltd and T Ltd:

- (*i*) gross profit as % of revenue;
- (*ii*) net profit as % of revenue;
- (*iii*) expenses as % of revenue;
- (*iv*) inventory turnover;
- (*v*) rate of return of net profit on capital employed (for the purpose of this question only, take capital as being total of share capital + reserves at the date of the statement of financial position);
- (*vi*) current ratio;
- (*vii*) acid test ratio;
- (*viii*) accounts receivable : revenue ratio;
- (*ix*) accounts payable : purchases ratio.

(*b*) Comment briefly on the comparison of each ratio as between the two companies. State which company appears to be the more efficient, giving what you consider to be possible reasons.

**28.11** The directors of L Ltd appointed a new sales manager towards the end of 2015. This manager devised a plan to increase revenue and profit by means of a reduction in selling price and extended credit terms to customers. This involved considerable investment in new machinery early in 2016 in order to meet the demand which the change in sales policy had created.

The financial statements for the years ended 31 December 2015 and 2016 are shown below. The sales manager has argued that the new policy has been a resounding success because revenue and, more importantly, profits have increased dramatically.

| **Statements of profit or loss** | *2016* | *2015* |
|---|---|---|
| | *£000* | *£000* |
| Revenue | 2,800 | 900 |
| Cost of sales | (1,680) | (360) |
| Gross profit | 1,120 | 540 |
| Selling expenses | (270) | (150) |
| Bad debts | (140) | (18) |
| Depreciation | (208) | (58) |
| Interest | (192) | (12) |
| Net profit | 310 | 302 |

| **Statements of financial position** | *2016* | | *2015* | |
|---|---|---|---|---|
| | *£000* | *£000* | *£000* | *£000* |
| Non-current assets | | | | |
| Factory | | 441 | | 450 |
| Machinery | | 1,791 | | 490 |
| | | 2,232 | | 940 |
| Current assets | | | | |
| Inventory | 238 | | 30 | |
| Accounts receivable | 583 | | 83 | |
| Bank | – | | 12 | |
| | | 821 | | 125 |
| Total assets | | 3,053 | | 1,065 |
| Current liabilities | | | | |
| Accounts payable | 175 | | 36 | |
| Bank | 11 | | – | |
| | 186 | | 36 | |
| Non-current liabilities | | | | |
| Borrowings | 1,600 | | 100 | |
| | | (1,786) | | (136) |
| | | 1,267 | | 929 |
| Equity | | | | |
| Share capital | | 328 | | 300 |
| Retained profits | | 939 | | 629 |
| | | 1,267 | | 929 |

*Note:* The balance on the retained profits reserve at the end of 2015 was £327,000.

(*a*) You are required to explain whether you believe that the performance for the year ended 31 December 2016 and the financial position at that date have improved as a result of the new policies adopted by the company. You should support your answer with appropriate ratios.

(*b*) All of L Ltd's sales are on credit. The finance director has asked you to calculate the immediate financial impact of reducing the credit period offered to customers. Calculate the amount of cash which would be released if the company could impose a collection period of 45 days.

(*Chartered Institute of Management Accountants*)

chapter 29

# Interpretation of financial information

## Learning objectives

**After you have studied this chapter, you should be able to:**

- explain the importance of trend analysis when analysing financial statements
- explain that there is no such thing as a generally 'good' or 'bad' value for any ratio
- describe the need to compare like with like if attempting to assess the quality of the result found from ratio analysis
- explain the pyramid of ratios that can be used in order to enhance the view obtained from ratio analysis
- explain that different groups of users of financial statements have access to different sources of information that may help in developing an understanding of and explanation for the results of ratio analysis
- explain earnings management and its relevance to accounting ratios and to any attempt to interpret financial information

## Introduction

In this chapter, you'll learn more about ratio analysis and how to use it effectively. You'll revisit how to perform comparisons between organisations and the need for effective and appropriate comparators if valid and worthwhile conclusions are to be made. You'll also learn about the interlinked relationships between ratios and look in greater detail at return on capital employed. Finally, you'll learn about the role that earnings management plays in arriving at accounting values and of examples of how and why it is done.

## 29.1 Background

When shareholders receive the financial statements of the company they have invested in, many simply look to see whether the business has made a profit, and then put the document away. (This is one reason why the introduction of an option to send shareholders abbreviated financial statements, rather than the far more costly to produce full set of financial statements, was introduced a few years ago.) They are aware of only one thing – that the company made a profit of £*x*. They do not know if it was a 'good' profit. Nor do they know whether it was any different from the profit earned in previous years. (Even if they had noticed the previous period's profit figure in the comparative column, they would be unaware of the equivalent figures for the periods that preceded it.) In addition, they would have no perception of how the performance compared with that of other companies operating in the same sector.

As explained in the previous chapter, ratio analysis can be used to assess company performance and financial position. However, as you learnt in *Business Accounting 1*, such analysis is relatively useless unless a similar task is undertaken on the financial figures for previous periods, so providing a view of the changes that have occurred over time. Trend analysis of this type is very important in the interpretation of financial statements, for it is only then that the position found can be truly placed in context and statements made concerning whether things are improving, etc.

Of similar importance if financial statements are to be usefully interpreted is comparison of the position shown with that of other companies operating in the same sector, both now and over a period of time.

## 29.2 Sector relevance

Analysis and interpretation of any phenomenon are all very well if conducted in isolation from the rest of the world. However, it can be of only limited use without comparators with which to develop an understanding of what is being examined. Even when this is done, it is important that the comparators are valid – there is not much point in comparing the performance of a Rolls-Royce with that of a bicycle. Like must be compared with like. Racing bike to racing bike, mountain bike to mountain bike, Premier League football team to Premier League football team, and so on. **For companies, the easiest way to ensure that like is being compared with like is to compare companies that operate in the same business sector.**

The importance of ensuring that any comparison undertaken between companies involves companies in the same sector can best be illustrated through an extreme example: that of the contrast between service companies and manufacturing companies.

Stating the obvious, a firm of consultants which advises its clients on marketing strategies will have far fewer tangible assets than a company with the same revenue and the same capital employed which manufactures forklift trucks. The firm of consultants will need premises, but these could easily be rented ready for use, whereas a manufacturing company would need to make major adjustments to the premises before using them. In addition, the firm of consultants would need very little in the way of machinery, possibly just some computer equipment and office equipment.

In comparison, the manufacturing company would need a great deal of machinery as well as lorries and various types of buildings, and so on. The manufacturing firm would also have inventory of materials and unsold forklift trucks. The consultancy would not have any inventory.

**What effect would these types of differences have on the ratios of the two businesses?**

With wider use and increasing levels of personal ownership of PCs with broadband Internet access, an increasing number of employees are working from home, especially in the service sector. This trend is set to continue with a resultant reduction in the need for many service industry organisations to maintain offices of the size required in the past.

All of this has an effect on the ratios of performance calculated from the financial statements of manufacturers and service industry firms. The figure of return on capital employed for a service firm, simply because of the far lower amount of tangible assets needed, may appear to be quite high. For a manufacturing firm the opposite may well be the case.

If this distinction between these completely different types of organisation is understood, then the interpreter of the financial statements is able to judge them appropriately. Failure to understand the distinction will bring forth some very strange conclusions.

## 29.3 Trend analysis

Looking internally at one organisation, sensible comparisons can clearly be made between the situation it was in at various points in time.

**Activity 29.2**

What two key things does an inward-looking analysis of this type NOT tell you? (*Hint*: think about the overall context.)

In *Business Accounting 1*, an example was shown of two companies, G and H. The example is now reintroduced and further developed. Exhibit 29.1 presents four ratios derived from the financial statements of G over this and the previous four years.

### Exhibit 29.1

| *Year:* | *1* | *2* | *3* | *4* | *5 (now)* |
|---|---|---|---|---|---|
| Gross profit as % of revenue | 40 | 38 | 36 | 35 | 34 |
| Net profit as % of revenue | 15 | 13 | 12 | 12 | 11 |
| Net profit as % of capital employed | 13 | 12 | 11 | 11 | 10 |
| Current ratio | 3.0 | 2.8 | 2.6 | 2.3 | 2.0 |

All other thing being equal, you would expect it to be more likely that all four of these ratios would rise over time. However, it is clear that they are all decreasing, but there is no other information available which might clarify whether or not this should be cause for concern. For example, the industry may be becoming more competitive, causing margins to shrink, and the falling current ratio may be due to an increase in efficiency over the control of working capital.

A company with this trend of figures could provide an explanation for the decline in margins and for the reduction in liquidity in its annual report. A reader of the financial statements could then decide to accept the explanation and put the calculations away. However, there is no guarantee that an explanation of this kind actually indicates a beneficial situation, irrespective of whether or not it is accurate.

In order to gain a better understanding of the analysis, comparison with other comparable companies in the same sector is needed. Exhibit 29.2 presents the information from Exhibit 29.1 for company G plus information on another company of a similar size operating in the same sector, company H.

### Exhibit 29.2

| | | | | *Years* | | |
|---|---|---|---|---|---|---|
| | | 1 | 2 | 3 | 4 | 5 (current) |
| Gross profit as % of revenue | *G* | 40 | 38 | 36 | 35 | 34 |
| | *H* | 30 | 32 | 33 | 33 | 34 |
| Net profit as % of revenue | *G* | 15 | 13 | 12 | 12 | 11 |
| | *H* | 10 | 10 | 10 | 11 | 11 |
| Net profit as % of capital employed | *G* | 13 | 12 | 11 | 11 | 10 |
| | *H* | 8 | 8 | 9 | 9 | 10 |
| Current ratio | *G* | 3.0 | 2.8 | 2.6 | 2.3 | 2.0 |
| | *H* | 1.5 | 1.7 | 1.9 | 1.0 | 2.0 |

This form of presentation can be difficult to digest and interpret. As an alternative, these results may be compared through graphs, as shown by the example in Exhibit 29.3 which compares the trend in gross profit as a percentage of revenue of the two companies. (Note that the vertical axis does not show the percentage below 30 as there is no percentage below that amount in Exhibit 29.2. Omitting the lower figures on the graph in these circumstances allows for a more informative display of the information.)

**Exhibit 29.3 The trend of gross profit as a percentage of revenue**

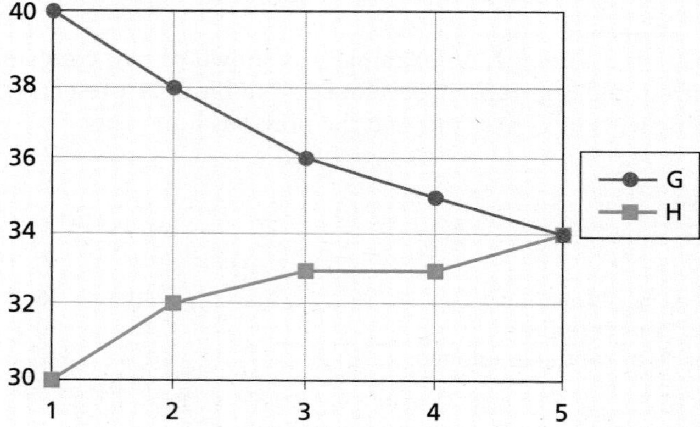


Now, you should see the importance of placing trends in context. The companies have identical ratios for the current period – does that make them equally desirable as investments? Given one year's financial statements it appears so, but the five-year trend analysis reveals a different picture.

From these figures, G appears to be the worse investment for the future, as the trend for it appears to be downwards, while that of H is upwards. It suggests that the explanation made earlier for the falling margins may not be valid. If the trend for G is continued it could be in a very dangerous financial situation in a year or two's time. H, on the other hand, is strengthening its position all the time.

While it would be ridiculous to state without reservation that H will continue on an upward trend, or that G will continue downwards, a consistent trend of this type does suggest that the situation may well continue into the foreseeable future. It is certainly cause for further investigation.

## 29.4 Comparisons over time

As shown in the previous section, one of the best ways of using ratios is to compare them with the ratios for the same organisation in respect of previous years. Take another example, the net profit percentage of a company for the past six years, including the current year 2018:

| | *2013* | *2014* | *2015* | *2016* | *2017* | *2018 (now)* |
|---|---|---|---|---|---|---|
| Net profit % | 5.4 | 5.2 | 4.7 | 4.8 | 4.8 | 4.5 |

This could be presented in a graph as shown in Exhibit 29.4:

**Exhibit 29.4**

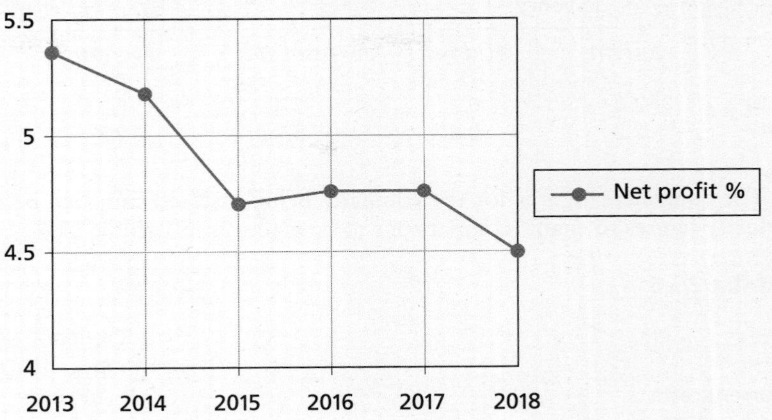


It is obvious that there is a long-term decline in the net profit percentage. This prompts us to examine why this should be so. Without measuring against past years our understanding of the direction in which the business seems to be heading would be much diminished.

We would not only look at the long-term changes in net profit percentages, but also compare similar long-term figures in relation to other aspects of the business.

Of course, other factors outside an organisation, particularly changes in the economy, may make the interpretation of trends an extremely complex process. For example, the use of the historical cost accounting concept during periods of high inflation can make effective comparison of monetary amounts over time very problematic.

## 29.5 Comparisons with other businesses

We've already looked at some of the benefits of undertaking comparisons with other businesses in Section 29.3. Now, we'll consider it in more detail. No one can say in isolation that a business is very profitable. A business may have made an average net profit over the last few years of £6 million which, to most people, may seem profitable. On the other hand, if businesses of a similar size in the same industry are making £20 million a year, then the business making £6 million a year cannot be said to be very profitable.

Ideally, we would like to be able to compare the results of one business with those of similar businesses in the same industry. Then, and only then, would we be able to judge how well, or how badly, that business was doing.

The size of a business can have an important effect upon ratios. Just as we would not try to compare a chemist's shop with a building firm, it would also be wrong to judge a small independent supermarket against Sainsbury's, which owns hundreds of supermarkets.

Interfirm comparisons are also sometimes misleading because of the different accounting treatment of various items, and the location and ages of assets. Some industries have, however, set up interfirm comparisons with guidelines to the companies to ensure that the figures have been constructed using the same bases so that the information is comparable. The information does not disclose data which can be traced to any one firm, ensuring that full confidentiality is observed.

The information available may take the form shown in Exhibit 29.5:

**Exhibit 29.5 Published ratios for the widget industry (extract)**

| | *Solvency* | | *Efficiency* | | | |
|---|---|---|---|---|---|---|
| | *Current* | *Acid test* | *Asset T/O* | *Inventory T/O* | *Debtor days* | *Creditor days* |
| 2016 | 2.4 | 0.7 | 5.4 | 8.2 | 56.4 | 80.4 |
| 2017 | 2.2 | 0.8 | 5.7 | 9.3 | 52.6 | 66.8 |

The equivalent figures for the company being assessed can then be tabulated alongside the industry figures to enable comparisons to be made, as in Exhibit 29.6.

**Exhibit 29.6**

| | *Company ratios* | | *Industry ratios* | |
|---|---|---|---|---|
| | *2016* | *2017* | *2016* | *2017* |
| Current ratio | 2.9 | 2.8 | 2.4 | 2.2 |
| Acid test ratio | 0.5 | 0.6 | 0.7 | 0.8 |
| Asset turnover | 5.2 | 5.3 | 5.4 | 5.7 |
| Inventory turnover | 4.4 | 4.7 | 8.2 | 9.3 |
| Accounts receivable days | 65.9 | 65.2 | 56.4 | 52.6 |
| Accounts payable days | 58.3 | 56.8 | 80.4 | 66.8 |

The financial status of the company is now much clearer. What appeared to be a situation of improving liquidity and efficiency is now shown to be an increasingly poorer liquidity and efficiency position compared with the industry as a whole.

However, it should be borne in mind that the industry figures probably include many companies that are either much larger or much smaller than the company being assessed. To obtain a more complete picture, information is needed concerning companies of a similar size, such as in the comparison between G and H earlier in this chapter (see Section 29.3). This information may be available from the source of the interfirm comparison. If not, other sources would need to be used, for example the published financial statements of appropriate companies.

The other information missing from the above comparison is data from previous periods. While not so relevant to the current position, it can be useful in explaining why a situation has developed, and in determining whether the current position is likely to persist.

**Activity 29.3** When an organisation operates in more than one sector, how do you identify other appropriate organisations with which to make comparisons?

## 29.6 Pyramid of ratios

Once ratios have been analysed and compared, explanations must be sought for the results obtained. Sometimes it will be obvious why a certain result was obtained – for example, if a company has moved from traditional stock-keeping to a just-in-time system during the period, its stock turnover will bear no resemblance to that which it had in the previous period.

For those inside the company – its directors and management – the management accounting records are available to assist in finding explanations, as are the company's staff. Outsiders – shareholders, analysts, lenders, suppliers, customers, etc. – do not have access to all this internal information (though some of these user groups will have access to more internal information than others – banks, for example, can usually obtain copies of a company's confidential internal accounting information upon request). They must, instead, fall back upon other sources of information, such as newspaper reports and industry publications.

One source of additional information available to everyone is a result of the fact that most ratios can be further subdivided into secondary ratios which, themselves, can also be subdivided, so building into a *pyramid of ratios*. By following through the pyramid of a given ratio, the source of the original ratio can often be isolated, enabling a far more focused investigation than would otherwise be possible.

For example, one of the most important ratios is the return on the capital employed (ROCE). This ratio has not happened by itself. If the ratio of net profit to revenue had not been a particular figure and the ratio of revenue to capital employed had not been a particular figure, then the ROCE would not have turned out to be the figure that it is.

Thus, the ROCE comes about as a result of all the other ratios which have underpinned it. It is the final summation of all that has happened in the various aspects of the business. The ROCE pyramid of ratios is shown in Exhibit 29.7:

**Exhibit 29.7**

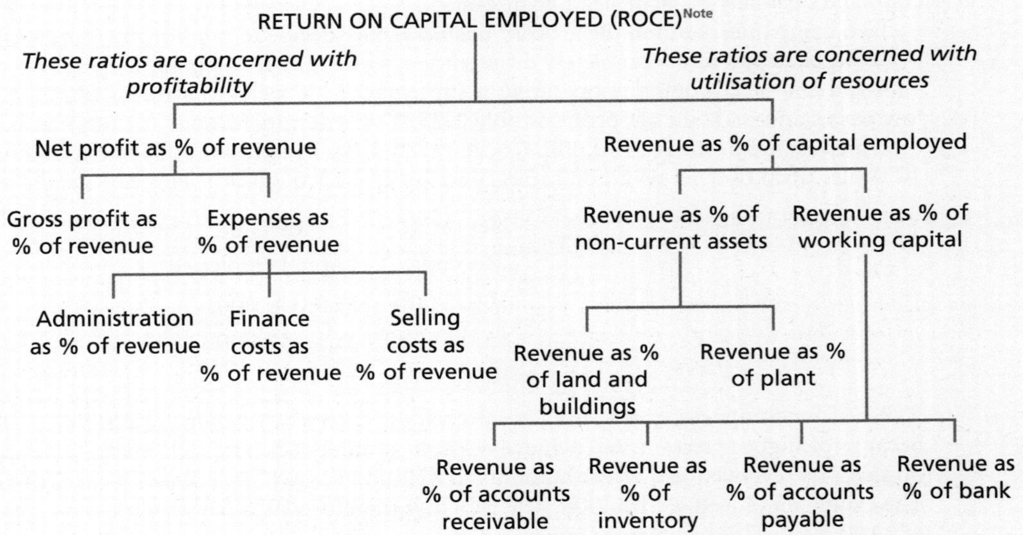


***Note*: The formula for ROCE used here is a (very) simplified version of the formula listed in Section 28.8. Nevertheless, to all intents and purposes, it is the same formula.**

By itself, the pyramid of ratios does not tell you everything. It comes into full effect when compared with similar ratios from previous years, or with similar pyramids of ratios in respect of other businesses. If the ROCE has been falling over the past year, a study of the pyramid of ratios for each of the previous two years may enable you to pinpoint exactly where the changes have been made to bring about the worsening position. Investigation of these matters may then give you some indication of the action to take.

## 29.7 Return on capital employed: company policy

The pyramid of ratios in Exhibit 29.7 illustrates the interdependence of each ratio. This can be examined in greater detail by investigating the policies of two companies to achieve their desired return on capital employed.

The first part of the pyramid tells us that the ROCE is dependent on both net profit as a percentage of revenue and also revenue as a percentage of capital employed. This means that:

$$\text{ROCE} = \frac{\text{Net profit}}{\text{Capital employed}}$$

which by splitting the equation between profitability ratios and resource utilisation ratios means also that:

$$\text{ROCE} = \frac{\text{Net profit}}{\text{Revenue}} \times \frac{\text{Revenue}}{\text{Capital employed}}$$

This interrelationship of the subsidiary ratios can be illustrated through an example. At the same time, it can be seen that the result of computing a primary ratio is dependent upon the items which it comprises; and that there is no guarantee that a value of $x$ will be 'good', and $y$ 'bad'. Whether the result obtained is 'good' or 'bad' depends on the underlying factors that give rise to the result obtained (what, for example, is the company's policy on depreciation and replacement of assets, as this can significantly affect the ROCE?), the sector in which the business operates and its relative size. Without knowledge of these items, comparison of the ratio analysis of two companies is likely to be misleading at best.

Two companies, both in the grocery business, may decide to aim for the same ROCE of 10%. This can be achieved in completely different ways by the two companies.

A Ltd is a large company operating a supermarket. It seeks to attract customers by offering low prices and makes a net profit of only 1.25% on sales. Its revenue for the year is £8,000,000 on which its net profit is £100,000. Its capital employed is £1,000,000. The ROCE is, therefore, 10% (i.e. £100,000 net profit on capital employed of £1,000,000). This can also be expressed as:

$$\begin{aligned}\text{ROCE} &= \frac{\text{Net profit}}{\text{Revenue}} \times \frac{\text{Revenue}}{\text{Capital employed}}\\ &= \frac{£100{,}000}{£8{,}000{,}000} \times \frac{£8{,}000{,}000}{£1{,}000{,}000}\\ &= 10\%\end{aligned}$$

B Ltd by comparison is a small local retailer. It seeks a higher margin per £100 sales, but because of higher prices it will achieve a lower volume of business. It makes a net profit of 5% on sales. Its revenue for the year amounts to £200,000 on which it makes a net profit of £10,000. The capital employed is £100,000. The ROCE is therefore 10% (i.e. £10,000 on capital employed of £100,000). This can also be expressed as:

$$\begin{aligned}\text{ROCE} &= \frac{\text{Net profit}}{\text{Revenue}} \times \frac{\text{Revenue}}{\text{Capital employed}}\\ &= \frac{£10{,}000}{£200{,}000} \times \frac{£200{,}000}{£100{,}000}\\ &= 10\%\end{aligned}$$

It can be seen that two companies, despite different sizes of business and operating different pricing policies, can have the same ROCE.

## 29.8 Earnings management

Sometimes the benefits of undertaking financial analysis can be compromised by companies making alterations to the amounts that appear in their financial statements. They do this because they wish to present a specific view of their performance and financial position that cannot be achieved if they did not make these alterations. This process is called '**earnings management**'.

Earnings management is *'the use of accounting techniques to deliberately manipulate the company's earnings so that the figures match a pre-determined target'*. Its use can be traced back hundreds of years to periods when companies used earnings management techniques to 'smooth earnings'. The term used for this motivation for companies to adopt earnings management is '**income smoothing**': *'the use of accounting techniques to level out net income fluctuations from one period to the next'*. Companies do this because investors prefer to hold shares in companies with steady and predictable earnings rather than those whose earnings are subject to wild fluctuations. However, this is not the only reason why adjustments of these types are made.

You will learn in Chapter 30 that when companies enter into a loan agreement with a bank, in exchange for a lower interest rate and the granting of the loan they often agree to conditions relating to the loan that are linked to their financial performance, or their financial position, or their share price. These agreements are called **debt covenants**. Typically, a debt covenant will include a clause relating to a specific accounting ratio. The agreement would state that if the ratio deteriorates below a certain level, penalties may be exacted by the bank and the loan may be recalled.

When this happens, it can be disastrous for the company involved. As a result, when companies are close to breaching clauses of this type, they often behave 'opportunistically' and engage in earnings management in an attempt to avoid technical default (by failing to meet the condition set).

Why might having to repay a loan in these circumstances be disastrous for a company?

Earnings management using similar techniques is also undertaken by managers seeking to preserve their bonus when it is linked to earnings or market price of the company's shares.

There are two main forms of earnings management:

(*a*) *'Accruals-based earnings management'*: the deliberate manipulation of earnings without direct cash flow impact; and
(*b*) *'Real earnings management'*, which does not focus on the immediate manipulation of financial accounts but, instead, involves actions that change the timing and structuring of real transactions and thus alter financial results.

Both of these tactics affect reported earnings, financial position, gearing, and the ratios used to analyse company performance and financial position. All of these, in turn, and especially earnings, affect share price.

## Accruals-based earnings management

**Accruals-based earnings management** focuses upon changing accounting numbers to achieve the desired financial position. Many of these accruals are used to increase income. They include reducing depreciation rates; reducing allowances for doubtful debts; reducing amounts written off for bad debts; accruing less expenses than would normally be the case; and increasing prepayments to levels higher than would normally be the case. A similar effect can result from changing depreciation method or increasing the anticipated economic life of an asset.

Activity 29.5

What effect would increasing income in this way have upon gearing?

Some other accruals-based adjustments have the initial effect of increasing assets. They include a switch from historic cost to fair value, revaluation of an existing non-current asset, reclassifying development expenditure as a capital expense and recognising development expenditure as a non-current asset rather than as a revenue expense that would be charged to profit and loss.

**Activity 29.6** What effect would increasing non-current asset values in these ways have upon gearing?

Eventually, accruals-based earnings management must be reversed – it cannot go on forever.

When this occurs, the company will likely report that it had a particularly bad year. However, the following year, all the potential accrual adjustments are once again available and the whole process may start all over again. The point when a company decides that it needs to stop this process is known as taking a '**big bath**' because all the 'dirty' things that have accumulated are washed away.

This often occurs when a new CEO is appointed. In taking a 'big bath', the new CEO reveals how poor a job his predecessor did and, at the same time, is placed in a position to show how good a job he or she does over subsequent years – if reported earnings are usually £20 million and the 'big bath' causes them to fall to only £12 million in the year when the CEO was appointed, future earnings of £20 million will look very good, even though they would have been expected prior to the arrival of the new CEO.

## Real earnings management

**Real earnings management** is concerned with manipulating transactions before they are entered into the accounting system so as to achieve the desired financial position; for example, by delaying the entry of transactions into the system, accelerating their entry into the accounting system, or by inventing transactions that are subsequently reversed. Among possible examples are: including physical inventory in a stock-count the purchase of which is not entered in the accounting system until the following period; or having customers place orders for goods at the end of the period that are then reversed a few weeks into the next period. The result is that earnings and/or asset values are changed, resulting in changes in the ratios of interest, the ones that would have signalled a problem for the company had they not been changed as a result of the earnings management actions it took.

## Ratios and earnings management

Ratios can be used to identify earnings management, though it is very difficult to do so because it requires that the cause of a ratio not being as expected may be very difficult to trace. Even when it is traced, if the cause is an accrual adjustment it can be very difficult to prove that it was done for any other purpose than a genuine belief that the changes made were appropriate in pursuit of arriving at a true and fair view.

Many banks safeguard themselves against accruals-based earnings management by requiring companies to apply the same basis for their accruals and the same accounting methods and policies year-on-year. However, it can be very difficult to monitor all adjustments made, particularly as financial reports are an extreme summary of all that they portray; and it is not particularly difficult for an accountant to hide many such adjustments in a way that is virtually impossible to detect. This is one reason why, although it is well known that companies and managers engage widely in earnings management, these practices only tend to be discovered when disaster strikes. Examples over the past few years include Enron, WorldCom, Xerox, Parmalat, ABC Learning and Tesco.

## Learning outcomes

**You should now have learnt:**

1. Ratios on their own are frequently misleading – they should not be considered in isolation from similar computations:
   (*a*) in previous periods; and/or
   (*b*) on similar-sized firms in the same sector.
2. The items in the financial statements are affected by company policy – for example, the rate of depreciation to use, and the policy of asset replacement; the policies adopted, therefore, directly affect the ratio analysis.
3. Companies of very different size and in very different sectors can have the same ratio results despite their being different in every respect.
4. The importance and impact of size, sector and company policies upon ratios mean that there is no such thing as a 'good' or 'bad' value that can be treated as a yardstick for any ratio.
5. All ratios are part of one or more pyramids of ratios.
6. When the results of ratio analysis are being investigated further, the relevant pyramid of ratios can be analysed in order to pinpoint the element giving rise to the situation being investigated.
7. What earnings management is and how it often involves the manipulation of accounting numbers or manipulation of the timing of the recording of transactions so as to improve accounting ratios and improve perceptions of performance and financial position.

## Answers to activities

29.1 The service business will probably have a lower current ratio – it has no inventory. Its accounts payable days are probably near zero. Its return on capital employed is probably much higher. Its asset turnover may be extremely high – it may not have very many non-current assets. Overall, trying to draw any sensible conclusions by comparing the ratios of these two businesses will be a waste of time.

29.2 It won't tell you whether the organisation is or was in a good position relative to its competitors or other organisations in the same sector. Nor will it tell you if changes in the ratios are actually moving in the appropriate direction for the sector in which the organisation operates.

29.3 In this case, you can try to identify other organisations with a similar range of activities. However, it would probably be of more benefit to separate out the data relating to each type of activity and then compare the reduced data against appropriate comparators.

29.4 The company might struggle to find the cash to repay the loan. It may have to sell off non-current assets at below market value. It may find it impossible to obtain further funding, or find that it was significantly more expensive to do so. Its share price would fall, perhaps significantly. The impact upon its reputation – its 'legitimacy' (*see* Chapter 30) – would be threatened and its place in the market may come under threat as competitors take advantage of its financial weakness to move into its markets.

29.5 If earnings increase, equity increases, which results in a reduction in gearing.

29.6 If assets increase, equity increases, which results in a reduction in gearing.

## Advice

Ratio analysis is a topic that causes more marks to be thrown away in exams than probably every other topic combined. No other accounting topic is as concerned with understanding rather than knowledge, and examiners increasingly expect you to be able to demonstrate understanding rather than simply your ability to prepare the financial statements or calculate the ratios.

There is no one set pattern to the questions, which depend upon the examiner's ingenuity and background experience. The usual shortcomings in the answers handed in by examinees, particularly on questions relating to this topic but also on questions in other areas, can be listed as follows:

1 Not following the instructions as laid down. If the question says 'list the' then the examiner expects a list as an answer, 'discuss the' means exactly that, 'write a report' needs a report as the answer, and so on. You will lose a lot of marks for not giving the examiner exactly what has been asked for.
2 Very often all the ratios etc. are calculated, but then the candidate does not offer any comments even though they have been asked for. *Make certain you cover this part of the question in an appropriate amount of detail.*
3 Even where students have written something about the ratios, they often repeat what the calculations are and offer nothing else, e.g. 'you can see that the gross profit ratio has increased from 18 to 20%' and the answer has finished there. The examiner can already see from your calculations that the gross profit percentage has increased, and wants you to write about *why* it might have increased, what conclusions, if any, can be arrived at, or what further information may be needed to discover why it has changed.
4 Remember that when the examiner asks you 'what other information you would like to have' about a firm when trying to interpret the financial statements so as to give advice to someone then, ideally, you would like to know more about the plans for the future of the business, how it compares with others in the same industry, whether or not there are going to be changes in the management and so on. We should not limit ourselves to information about the past, we really need to know as much about the future as we possibly can.
5 Do not restrict your examination answers to what you have read in a textbook. Keep your eyes and ears open as you go shopping, visit factories, work, buy petrol at a filling station, go to the theatre, and so on. Reading a 'quality' newspaper helps, as there are quite a lot of items about business. Bring all of this sort of knowledge and experience into your answers. You will impress the examiners. They are extremely bored reading regurgitations of textbook learning with nothing added.
6 Quite a few questions will concern the type of business of which you will have first-hand experience, so you can introduce personal knowledge into your answer. A typical instance would be comparing two grocery businesses. One would be a large supermarket and the other would be a small corner shop. The policies of the two firms would be quite different. The supermarket would have decided on a policy of attracting new customers by lowering sales margins and yet boosting ROCE. The corner shop might have a policy of high margins, but remain open on Sundays and late at nights, and thus be a 'convenience shop', i.e. customers might well go there when other shops are closed or are too far away to be worth the extra cost in petrol, etc. when compared with the extra cost of shopping at the corner shop.
7 Last, but not least, *show your workings*. If you make a mistake in your calculations and do not show your workings you cannot be awarded any credit for a partially incorrect calculation. Consider how much longer it takes to show the detail contained in Section 29.7 above, rather than simply the result of the calculation – maybe 30 seconds. *Now consider whether you would rather spend five minutes in an exam showing the workings of ten ratio calculations, or six months studying to retake the exam you failed because you made a mistake in two of your calculations and lost five marks because the examiner could not tell why you got the answer wrong.*

## Review questions

**29.1** Adrian Frampton was considering the purchase of one of two businesses. However, Frampton had only been provided with limited information about the businesses, as follows:

**Summarised Financial Information for the year ended 31 December 2016**

| *Information* | *Business X* | *Business Y* |
|---|---|---|
| Cost of goods sold | £400,000 | £600,000 |
| Administrative expenses | £50,000 | £60,000 |
| Average inventory at cost | £40,000 | £50,000 |
| Working capital as at 31 December 2016 | £90,000 | £250,000 |
| Selling and distribution expenses | £15,000 | £35,000 |
| Proprietor's capital at 1 January 2016 | £200,000 | £350,000 |
| Gross profit percentage mark-up on cost | 20 | 25 |

*Additional information:*

1 Average inventory had been calculated by using the year's opening and closing inventories. Subsequently it was discovered that Business Y had overvalued its inventory on 31 December 2016 by £10,000.
2 Business X's administrative expenses included a payment for rent of £15,000 which covered a three-year period to 31 December 2018.
3 A sum of £2,500 was included in the administrative expenses of Business Y in respect of a holiday taken by the owner and his family.
4 Cash drawings for the year ended 31 December 2016 were:

| | £ |
|---|---|
| Business X | 20,000 |
| Business Y | 25,000 |

5 The owners of the businesses had stipulated the following prices for their businesses:

| | £ |
|---|---|
| Business X | 190,000 |
| Business Y | 400,000 |

**Required:**

(*a*) Based on the information available prepare comparative statements of profit or loss for the year ending 31 December 2016.

(*b*) Using the information provided and the accounting statements prepared in (*a*), calculate relevant accounting ratios in order to give Frampton a basis for assessing the performances of the two businesses. Comment on the results.

(*c*) What additional information is needed in order to assess more accurately
  (*a*) the liquidity of the businesses;
  (*b*) the future prospects of the businesses?

*(AQA (Associated Examining Board): GCE A-level)*

**29.2** Three companies have the capital structures shown below.

| *Company* | *A* | *B* | *C* |
|---|---|---|---|
| | *£000* | *£000* | *£000* |
| Ordinary shares | 600 | 400 | 50 |
| 12% loan notes | – | 200 | 550 |
| | 600 | 600 | 600 |

→

The return on capital employed was 20% for each firm in 2016, and in 2017 was 10%. Corporation tax in both years was assumed to be 55%, and loan note interest is an allowable expense against corporation tax.

(*a*) Calculate the percentage return on the shareholders' capital for each company for 2016 and 2017. Assume that all profits are distributed.

(*b*) Use your answer to explain the merits and the dangers of high gearing.

(*Edexcel: University of London GCE A-level*)

**29.3A** Martha is the accountant of a trading business. During the past year she produced interim accounts for the six months ended 30 November 2015, and draft final accounts for the year ended 31 May 2016, as follows:

| | *Interim accounts* | *Draft final accounts* |
|---|---|---|
| | £ | £ |
| Revenue (all on credit terms) | 140,000 | 336,000 |
| Cost of sales (Note 1) | 42,000 | 112,000 |
| Gross profit | 98,000 | 224,000 |
| *Less* Expenses | 56,000 | 168,000 |
| Net profit | 42,000 | 56,000 |
| Non-current assets | 70,000 | 63,000 |
| Current assets (Note 2) | 42,000 | 71,000 |
| Current liabilities (Note 3) | (22,000) | (30,000) |
| | 90,000 | 104,000 |
| Share capital | 30,000 | 30,000 |
| Retained earnings | 60,000 | 74,000 |
| | 90,000 | 104,000 |

*Notes:*

1 Average inventory was £14,000 during the first six months.

2 Current assets were:

| | *30 Nov 2015* | *31 May 2016* |
|---|---|---|
| | £ | £ |
| Inventory | 16,000 | 25,000 |
| Accounts receivable | 24,000 | 28,000 |
| Bank | 2,000 | 18,000 |
| | 42,000 | 71,000 |

3 Current liabilities consisted entirely of trade accounts payable.

Martha informs you that the business leased additional premises from 1 December 2015, and that sales arising therefrom totalled £70,000 for the six months to 31 May 2016, with an average mark-up on cost prices of 150% being made on those goods.

Expenses relating to these additional premises totalled £21,000 for the period. Two-fifths of the closing inventory of the business was located at these premises.

**Prepare a report,** using appropriate accounting ratios, to explain the changes in the financial situation of the business during the year ended 31 May 2016.

(*Edexcel: University of London GCE A-level*)

**29.4** John Jones is considering purchasing shares in one of two companies and has extracted the following information from the statement of financial position of each company.

| | *Company A Plc* | *Company B Plc* |
|---|---|---|
| | *£000* | *£000* |
| *Authorised share capital* | | |
| £1 ordinary shares | 600 | 1,000 |
| 8% £1 preference shares | 400 | |
| *Issued share capital* | | |
| £1 ordinary shares | 300 | 800 |
| 8% £1 preference shares | 200 | |
| *Reserves* | | |
| Share premium | 300 | 400 |
| Retained earnings | 400 | 200 |
| *Non-current liabilities: loan notes* | | |
| 10% loan notes (2017) | | 200 |
| 12% loan notes (2023) | 400 | |

**Required:**

(*a*) Define the term 'gearing' stating clearly what is meant by a low gearing ratio.

(*b*) Calculate the gearing factor for each company.

(*c*) Explain to John Jones the significance of gearing to an ordinary shareholder in each of the companies above.

(*d*) Assuming for each company a trading profit of £200,000 before interest and an ordinary dividend of 15% show the movement on retained earnings for a year for each company. You should ignore taxation.

*(AQA (Associated Examining Board): GCE A-level)*

**29.5A** The following are extracted from the statements of financial position as at 31 March 2017 and 31 March 2018 of Glebe Ltd:

| | *31 March 2017* | | *31 March 2018* | |
|---|---|---|---|---|
| | £ | £ | £ | £ |
| Current assets | | | | |
| Inventory | 20,000 | | 25,000 | |
| Trade accounts receivable | 10,000 | | 17,000 | |
| Cash | 5,000 | | 3,000 | |
| | | 35,000 | | 45,000 |
| Current liabilities | | | | |
| Trade accounts payable | 12,000 | | 16,000 | |
| Bank overdraft | 7,000 | | 34,000 | |
| | | (19,000) | | (50,000) |
| | | 16,000 | | (5,000) |

**Required:**

(*a*) Calculate for each of the two years two ratios that indicate the liquidity position of the company.

(*b*) (*i*) From the information given, give reasons for the changes which have occurred in the working capital.

(*ii*) What other information regarding the current assets and current liabilities would you consider necessary to assess the ability of the business to continue in operation?

(*c*) Discuss any other information available from a statement of financial position that may affect an assessment of the liquidity of a business.

*(AQA (Associated Examining Board): GCE A-level)*

**29.6** Colin Black is considering investing a substantial sum in the ordinary shares of Jacks Ltd. Having some accounting knowledge he has extracted the following information from the accounts for the last two financial years.

| | *As at 31 March 2015* | *As at 31 March 2016* |
|---|---|---|
| | £ | £ |
| Issued share capital | | |
| £1 ordinary shares, fully paid | 100,000 | 150,000 |
| Reserves | | |
| Share premium | 10,000 | 60,000 |
| Retained earnings | 140,000 | 160,000 |
| Loan capital | | |
| 10% loan notes 2022–2023 | 40,000 | 40,000 |
| | For year ended 31 March 2015 | For year ended 31 March 2016 |
| | £ | £ |
| Net profit after tax | 60,000 | 70,000 |

Because he was disappointed with the result he obtained when he calculated the return on the equity capital employed, Colin Black has asked for your advice.

**Required:**

(*a*) Calculate the figures which prompted Colin Black's reaction.

(*b*) Prepare a memorandum to Colin Black pointing out other information to be considered when comparing the return on equity capital employed over two years as a basis for his investment decision.

(*c*) Explain why a company builds up and maintains reserves.

*(AQA (Associated Examining Board): GCE A-level)*

**29.7A** The following information has been extracted from the accounts of Witton Way Ltd:

**Statement of Profit or Loss for the year ending 30 April**

| | *2015* | *2016* |
|---|---|---|
| | *£000* | *£000* |
| Revenue (all credit sales) | 7,650 | 11,500 |
| *Less* Cost of sales | (5,800) | (9,430) |
| *Gross profit* | 1,850 | 2,070 |
| Other expenses | (150) | (170) |
| Loan interest | (50) | (350) |
| *Profit before taxation* | 1,650 | 1,550 |
| Taxation | (600) | (550) |
| *Profit after taxation* | 1,050 | 1,000 |

***Note*: Dividends paid in 2016 were £300,000 (2015: £300,000).**

**Statement of Financial Position at 30 April**

| | 2015 £000 | 2016 £000 |
|---|---|---|
| *Non-current assets* | | |
| Tangible assets | 10,050 | 11,350 |
| *Current assets* | | |
| Inventory | 1,500 | 2,450 |
| Trade accounts receivable | 1,200 | 3,800 |
| Cash | 900 | 50 |
| | 3,600 | 6,300 |
| Total assets | 13,650 | 17,650 |
| Current liabilities: accounts payable | (2,400) | (2,700) |
| Non-current liabilities | | |
| Loans and other borrowings | (350) | (3,350) |
| Total liabilities | (2,750) | (6,050) |
| Net assets | 10,900 | 11,600 |
| Equity | | |
| Called-up share capital | 5,900 | 5,900 |
| Retained profits | 5,000 | 5,700 |
| | 10,900 | 11,600 |

*Additional information:*

During the year to 30 April 2016, the company tried to stimulate sales by reducing the selling price of its products and by offering more generous credit terms to its customers.

**Required:**

(*a*) Calculate six accounting ratios specifying the basis of your calculations for each of the two years to 30 April 2015 and 2016 respectively which will enable you to examine the company's progress during 2016.

(*b*) From the information available to you, including the ratios calculated in part (*a*) of the question, comment upon the company's results for the year to 30 April 2016 under the heads of 'profitability', 'liquidity', 'efficiency' and 'shareholders' interests'.

(*c*) State what additional information you would require in order to assess the company's attempts to stimulate sales during the year to 30 April 2016.

(*Association of Accounting Technicians*)

**29.8** You are presented with the following information for three quite separate and independent companies:

**Summarised Statements of Financial Position at 31 March 2017**

| | Chan plc £000 | Ling plc £000 | Wong plc £000 |
|---|---|---|---|
| Total assets *less* current liabilities | 600 | 600 | 700 |
| Non-current liabilities 10% loan | – | – | (100) |
| | £600 | £600 | £600 |
| Capital and reserves: | | | |
| Called-up share capital | | | |
| Ordinary shares of £1 each | 500 | 300 | 200 |
| 10% cumulative preference shares of £1 each | – | 200 | 300 |
| Retained profits | 100 | 100 | 100 |
| | £600 | £600 | £600 |

→

*Additional information:*

1 The operating profit before interest and tax for the year to 31 March 2018 earned by each of the three companies was £300,000.
2 The effective rate of corporation tax for all three companies for the year to 31 March 2018 is 30%. This rate is to be used in calculating each company's tax payable on ordinary profit.
3 An ordinary dividend of 20p for the year to 31 March 2018 was paid by all three companies, as were the preference dividends.
4 The market prices per ordinary share at 31 March 2018 were as follows:

| | £ |
|---|---|
| Chan plc | 8.40 |
| Ling plc | 9.50 |
| Wong plc | 10.38 |

5 There were no changes in the share capital structure or in long-term loans of any of the companies during the year to 31 March 2018.

**Required:**

(*a*) In so far as the information permits, prepare the statement of profit or loss for each of the three companies (in columnar format) for the year ending 31 March 2018 (formal notes to the accounts are not required).

(*b*) Show the change in retained profits for each company over the year.

(*c*) Calculate the following accounting ratios for each company:
(*i*) earnings per share;
(*ii*) price earnings; and
(*iii*) gearing [taken as total borrowings (preference share capital and long-term loans) to ordinary shareholders' funds].

(*d*) Using the gearing ratios calculated in answering part (*c*) of the question, briefly examine the importance of gearing if you were thinking of investing in some ordinary shares in one of the three companies assuming that the profits of the three companies were fluctuating.

(*Association of Accounting Technicians*)

**28.9A** The chairman of a family business has been examining the following summary of the accounts of the company since it began three years ago.

**Statement of Financial Position (at 30 June) £000**

| | *2014* | *Actual* | *2015* | *Actual* | *2016* | *Actual* |
|---|---|---|---|---|---|---|
| Freehold land and buildings | | 150 | | 150 | | 150 |
| Plant | 150 | | 150 | | 450 | |
| *Less* Depreciation | (15) | | (30) | | (75) | |
| | | 135 | | 120 | | 375 |
| | | 285 | | 270 | | 525 |
| Inventory: goods and work in progress | 20 | | 45 | | 85 | |
| Accounts receivable | 33 | | 101 | | 124 | |
| Bank and cash | 10 | 63 | 15 | 161 | – | 209 |
| | | 348 | | 431 | | 734 |
| Accounts payable | 20 | | 80 | | 35 | |
| Taxation | 4 | | 17 | | 6 | |
| Overdraft | – | | – | | 25 | |
| | | 24 | | 97 | | 66 |
| Loan | – | | – | | 200 | |
| Deferred tax | 7 | | 9 | | 23 | |
| | | 7 | | 9 | | 223 |
| | | (31) | | (106) | | (289) |
| Net assets | | 317 | | 325 | | 445 |
| Ordinary share capital (£1 shares) | | 300 | | 300 | | 400 |
| General reserve | | 17 | | 25 | | 45 |
| | | 317 | | 325 | | 445 |

**Statement of Profit or Loss (for year ending 30 June) £000**

| | | *2014 Actual* | | *2015 Actual* | | *2016 Actual* |
|---|---|---|---|---|---|---|
| Revenue | | 260 | | 265 | | 510 |
| Trading profit | | 53 | | 50 | | 137 |
| Depreciation | 15 | | 15 | | 45 | |
| Loan interest | – | | – | | 30 | |
| | | (15) | | (15) | | (75) |
| Net profit | | 38 | | 35 | | 62 |
| Taxation | | (11) | | (15) | | (15) |
| Net profit after tax | | 27 | | 20 | | 47 |
| Dividends proposed | | 10 | | 12 | | 14 |

The company's products are popular in the locality and in the first two years sales could have been higher if there had been extra machine capacity available.

On 1 January 2016, additional share and loan capital was obtained which enabled extra machinery to be purchased. This gave an immediate increase in sales and profits.

Although 2015/16 showed the best yet results, the chairman is not very happy; the accountant has suggested that a dividend should not be proposed this year (2016) because of the overdraft. The accountant has proposed, however, that the directors consider a dividend of £14,000 (£2,000 up on last year).

Naturally, the chairman is displeased and wants some explanations from the accountant regarding the figures in the accounts. He specifically asks:

(*i*) Why, if profits are the best ever and considering the company has obtained extra capital during the year, has the company gone into overdraft? Can there really be a profit if there is no cash left in the bank to pay a dividend next year?

(*ii*) Why is the freehold still valued at the same price as in 2014? The real value seems to be about £225,000. Why is this real value not in the statement of financial position?

**Required:**

Write a report to the chairman:

(*a*) commenting on the state and progress of the business as disclosed by the accounts and the above information, supporting your analysis by appropriate key accounting ratios; and

(*b*) giving reasoned answers, in the context of recognised accounting law, rules and practices, to each of the questions raised by the chairman.

(*Institute of Chartered Secretaries and Administrators*)

**29.10** The following information is provided for Bessemer Ltd which operates in an industry subject to marked variations in consumer demand.

| | | *£000* |
|---|---|---|
| (*i*) | Shareholders' equity at 30 September 2018: | |
| | Issued ordinary shares of £1 each fully paid | 5,000 |
| | Retained profits | 1,650 |
| | | 6,650 |

There were no loans outstanding at the date of the statement of financial position.

| | | *£000* |
|---|---|---|
| (*ii*) | Statement of profit or loss extracts: year to 30 September 2018: | |
| | Net profit before tax | 900 |
| | *Less* Corporation tax | 270 |
| | | 630 |

→

(*iii*) Changes in retained profits: year ending 30 September 2018:

| | |
|---|---:|
| Retained profit at 1 October 2017 | 1,620 |
| Dividends paid during year ending 30 September 2018 | (600) |
| | 1,020 |
| Profit after tax for year ending 30 September 2018 | 630 |
| Retained profit at 30 September 2018 | 1,650 |

(*iv*) The directors are planning to expand output. This will require an additional investment of £2,000,000 which may be financed either by issuing 1,000,000 ordinary shares each with a nominal value of £1, or by raising a 12% loan note.

(*v*) Forecast profits before interest charges, if any, for the year to 30 September:

| | *£000* |
|---|---:|
| 2019 | 1,800 |
| 2020 | 500 |
| 2021 | 2,200 |

A corporation tax rate of 30% on reported profit before tax may be assumed; the directors plan to pay out the entire post-tax profit as dividends.

**Required:**

(*a*) The forecast dividends for each of the next three years and year-end statement of financial position extracts, so far as the information permits, assuming that the expansion is financed by:
   (*i*) issuing additional shares; or
   (*ii*) issuing loan notes.

(*b*) Calculate the forecast return on shareholders' equity, for each of the next three years, under the alternative methods for financing the planned expansion.

(*c*) An assessment of the merits and demerits of the alternative methods of finance based on the calculations made under (*a*) and (*b*) and any other relevant methods of comparison.

(*Institute of Chartered Secretaries and Administrators*)

**29.11A** An investor is considering the purchase of shares in either AA plc or BB plc whose latest accounts are summarised below. Both companies carry on similar manufacturing activities with similar selling prices and costs of materials, labour and services.

**Statements of Financial Position at 30 September 2017 (£000)**

| | | *AA plc* | | *BB plc* |
|---|---:|---:|---:|---:|
| Freehold property at revaluation 2017 | | 2,400 | | – |
| Plant, machinery and equipment: | | | | |
| at cost | 1,800 | | 1,800 | |
| depreciation | 1,200 | 600 | 400 | 1,400 |
| Goodwill | | – | | 800 |
| | | 3,000 | | 2,200 |
| Inventory: finished goods | | 400 | | 200 |
| work in progress | | 300 | | 100 |
| Accounts receivable | | 800 | | 500 |
| Bank deposit | | – | | 400 |
| Total assets | | 4,500 | | 3,400 |
| Current liabilities | | | | |
| Accounts payable | 600 | | 900 | |
| Overdraft | 200 | | – | |
| | 800 | | 900 | |
| Non-current liabilities | 1,400 | | 1,000 | |
| Total liabilities | | (2,200) | | (1,900) |
| Net assets | | 2,300 | | 1,500 |
| Equity | | | | |
| Ordinary £1 shares | | 1,000 | | 500 |
| Reserves | | 1,300 | | 1,000 |
| | | 2,300 | | 1,500 |

**Statements of Profit or Loss – year ending 30 September 2017 (£000)**

| | AA plc | | BB plc | |
|---|---|---|---|---|
| Revenue | | 2,500 | | 2,500 |
| Operating profit | | 400 | | 600 |
| Depreciation – plant, machinery and equipment | | (180) | | (180) |
| | | 220 | | 420 |
| Finance income: Bank interest | | – | | 100 |
| | | 220 | | 520 |
| Finance costs: Interest | | (150) | | (160) |
| | | 70 | | 360 |
| Taxation | | (20) | | (90) |
| Profit for the year | | 50 | | 270 |
| *Note*: | | | | |
| Dividend proposed | | 40 | | 130 |
| Price/earnings ratio | 30 | | 5 | |
| Market value of share | £1.50 | | £2.70 | |

**Required:**

(*a*) write a report to the investor, giving an appraisal of the results and state of each business; and

(*b*) advise the investor whether, in your opinion, the price/earnings ratios and market price of the shares can be justified in the light of the figures in the accounts, giving your reasons.

(*Institute of Chartered Secretaries and Administrators*)

**29.12** The following are the summarised accounts for B Limited, a company with an accounting year ending on 30 September.

| **Summarised Statements of Financial Position for** | *2015/16* | | *2016/17* | |
|---|---|---|---|---|
| | *£000* | *£000* | *£000* | *£000* |
| Tangible non-current assets – at cost | | | | |
| *Less* Depreciation | | 4,995 | | 12,700 |
| Current assets: | | | | |
| Inventory | 40,145 | | 50,455 | |
| Accounts receivable | 40,210 | | 43,370 | |
| Cash at bank | 12,092 | | 5,790 | |
| | | 92,447 | | 99,615 |
| Total assets | | 97,442 | | 112,315 |
| Current liabilities | | | | |
| Trade accounts payable | 34,389 | | 39,215 | |
| Taxation | 2,473 | | 3,260 | |
| | 36,862 | | 42,475 | |
| Long-term liabilities | | | | |
| 10% loan notes 2016/2019 | 19,840 | | 19,840 | |
| Total liabilities | | (56,702) | | (62,315) |
| Net assets | | 40,740 | | 50,000 |
| Equity | | | | |
| Called-up share capital of £0.25 per share | | 9,920 | | 9,920 |
| Retained profits | | 30,820 | | 40,080 |
| Shareholders' funds | | 40,740 | | 50,000 |

→

| Summarised Statements of Profit or Loss for | 2015/16 | 2016/17 |
|---|---|---|
| | £000 | £000 |
| Revenue | 486,300 | 583,900 |
| Operating profit | 17,238 | 20,670 |
| Interest payable | (1,984) | (1,984) |
| Profit before taxation | 15,254 | 18,686 |
| Taxation | (5,734) | (7,026) |
| Profit for the year | 9,520 | 11,660 |
| *Notes:* | | |
| **1** Retained profit brought forward: | 23,540 | 30,820 |
| **2** Dividends paid during the year were: | 2,240 | 2,400 |

**Required:**

(*a*) calculate, for each year, two ratios for each of the following user groups, which are of particular significance to them: (*i*) shareholders; (*ii*) trade accounts payable; (*iii*) internal management;

(*b*) make brief comments upon the changes, between the two years, in the ratios calculated in (*a*) above.

(*Chartered Institute of Management Accountants*)

**29.13A** The following are the financial statements of D Limited, a wholesaling company, for the year ended 31 December:

| Statements of Profit or Loss | 2017 | 2017 | 2018 | 2018 |
|---|---|---|---|---|
| | £000 | £000 | £000 | £000 |
| Revenue – credit sales | 2,200 | | 2,640 | |
| cash sales | 200 | | 160 | |
| | | 2,400 | | 2,800 |
| Cost of sales | | (1,872) | | (2,212) |
| Gross profit | | 528 | | 588 |
| Distribution costs | | (278) | | (300) |
| Administration expenses | | (112) | | (114) |
| Operating profit | | 138 | | 174 |
| Interest payable | | – | | (32) |
| Profit before tax | | 138 | | 142 |

| Statements of Financial Position as at 31 December | 2017 | 2017 | 2018 | 2018 |
|---|---|---|---|---|
| | £000 | £000 | £000 | £000 |
| Tangible non-current assets | | 220 | | 286 |
| Current assets: Inventory | 544 | | 660 | |
| Accounts receivable | 384 | | 644 | |
| Cash at bank | 8 | | 110 | |
| | | 936 | | 1,414 |
| Total assets | | 1,156 | | 1,700 |
| Current liabilities: | | | | |
| Trade accounts payable | 256 | | 338 | |
| Non-current liabilities | | | | |
| Loan notes | – | | 320 | |
| | | (256) | | (658) |
| Shareholders' funds | | 900 | | 1,042 |

The following information should be taken into consideration.

1 You may assume that:

(*i*) the range of products sold by D Limited remained unchanged over the two years;

(*ii*) the company managed to acquire its products in 2018 at the same prices as it acquired them for in 2017;

(*iii*) the effects of any inflationary aspects have been taken into account in the figures.

2 Ignore taxation.
3 All calculations must be shown to one decimal place.

**You are required,** using the information above, to assess and comment briefly on the company, from the point of view of:
(*a*) profitability;
(*b*) liquidity.

(*Chartered Institute of Management Accountants*)

**29.14** G plc is a holding company with subsidiaries that have diversified interests. G plc's board of directors is interested in the group acquiring a subsidiary in the machine tool manufacturing sector. Two companies have been identified as potential acquisitions, A Ltd and B Ltd. Summaries of both these companies' accounts are shown below:

**Statements of Profit or Loss for the year ending 30 April 2018**

| | *A Ltd* | *B Ltd* |
|---|---|---|
| | *£000* | *£000* |
| Revenue | 985 | 560 |
| Cost of goods sold | | |
| Opening inventory | 150 | 145 |
| Materials | 255 | 136 |
| Labour | 160 | 125 |
| Factory overheads | 205 | 111 |
| Depreciation | 35 | 20 |
| Closing inventory | (155) | (140) |
| | 650 | 397 |
| Gross profit | 335 | 163 |
| Selling and administration expenses | (124) | (75) |
| Interest | (35) | (10) |
| Profit before taxation | 176 | 78 |
| Taxation | (65) | (25) |
| Profit for the year | 111 | 53 |

**Statements of Financial Position at 30 April 2018**

| | *A Ltd* | | *B Ltd* | |
|---|---|---|---|---|
| | *£000* | *£000* | *£000* | *£000* |
| Non-current assets | | 765 | | 410 |
| Current assets | | | | |
| Inventory | 155 | | 140 | |
| Accounts receivable | 170 | | 395 | |
| Bank | 50 | 375 | 45 | 580 |
| Total assets | | 1,140 | | 990 |
| Current liabilities | | | | |
| Trade accounts payable | 235 | | 300 | |
| Other | 130 | | 125 | |
| | 365 | | 425 | |
| Non-current liabilities | | | | |
| Loan notes | 220 | | 70 | |
| Total liabilities | | 585 | | 495 |
| Net assets | | 555 | | 495 |
| Share capital | | 450 | | 440 |
| Retained profits | | 105 | | 55 |
| | | 555 | | 495 |

**You are required to** prepare a report for the board of G plc assessing the financial performance and position of A Ltd and B Ltd. Your report should be prepared in the context of G plc's interests in these two companies and should be illustrated with financial ratios where appropriate. You should state any assumptions you make as well as any limitations of your analysis.

(*Chartered Institute of Management Accountants*)

**29.15A** J plc supplies and fits car tyres, exhaust pipes and other components. The company has branches throughout the country. Roughly 60% of sales are for cash (retail sales). The remainder are credit sales made to car hire companies and large organisations with fleets of company cars (business sales). Business sales tend to be more profitable than retail and the company is keen to expand in this area. There is, however, considerable competition. Branch managers are responsible for obtaining business customers and have some discretion over terms of trade and discounts.

The company's computerised accounting system has recently produced the following report for the manager of the Eastown branch for the six months ended 30 September 2017:

| | *Eastown branch* | *Average for all branches* |
|---|---|---|
| Return on capital employed | 22% | 16% |
| Gross profit | 38% | 45% |
| Selling and promotion costs/revenue | 9% | 6% |
| Wages/revenue | 19% | 14% |
| Accounts receivable turnover (based on credit sales only) | 63 days | 52 days |
| Inventory turnover | 37 days | 49 days |

The Eastown branch manager has only recently been appointed and is unsure whether his branch appears well managed. He has asked for your advice.

**You are required to** compare the performance of the Eastown branch with the average for all branches. Suggest reasons for the differences you identify.

(*Chartered Institute of Management Accountants*)

**29.16A** Company managers are aware that the readers of financial statements often use accounting ratios to evaluate their performance. **Explain** how this could lead to decisions which are against the company's best interests.

(*Chartered Institute of Management Accountants*)

**29.17** What are the two forms of earnings management? Provide examples of both.

**29.18** What would cause a manager to engage in earnings management when doing so did not benefit the company the manager works for?

**29.19** Why would a company with no debt covenants engage in earnings management?

part 5

# ISSUES IN FINANCIAL REPORTING

## Introduction

**This part looks at the theories that help to explain why particular accounting choices might be made. It then presents theories upon which accounting practice is based, considers issues affecting accounting and financial reporting, and reviews the place of accounting information in the context of the environment in which business entities operate.**

chapter

# 30 Theories of accounting-related choice

## Learning objectives

**After you have studied this chapter, you should be able to:**

- explain and describe three groups of theories that relate to accounting
- describe the differences between normative theories, positive theories and social judgement theories
- describe and apply several positive theories of accounting to explain and predict accounting-related decisions
- describe and apply several social judgement theories to explain how some accounting-related decisions are taken

## Introduction

This chapter presents an overview of various theories that can be used to explain accounting choice – why particular decisions are made relating to accounting data and accounting information.

## 30.1 Background

Accounting is not a physical science where everything complies to a rigid framework of complex and constant relationships. It is a social science and is the result of choices made by those who record and adjust accounting data, prepare accounting reports, and present accounting information. This is why, for example, no two accountants will ever prepare identical financial statements of large companies from identical data, why one bank will lend funds to a company while another will not, and why one auditor will declare a company a going concern while another will not. Choice of action is part of accounting as much as debits and credits, accounts, statements of profit or loss, statements of financial position, or statements of cash flow.

When anyone or any organisation takes a decision, their motivation in selecting the choice they make is sometimes not as straightforward as it appears. This is particularly the case for accountants for they have choices to make in virtually everything they do, and have so much flexibility in what they decide that it can sometimes be hard to identify their reasoning.

These decisions include deciding which accounts should be used to enter a transaction; deciding what depreciation method to use; what depreciation rate to use; what amount to accrue for an expense or an item of income; what amount to treat as a prepayment; what to write off as a bad debt; what provision to make for doubtful debts; what to treat as a non-current asset; whether to treat development costs as expenses or capitalise them; and many, many others.

Many of these decisions are guided by accounting standards, but even those that are directed in this way always leave some room for alternatives to be selected. Sometimes the choice made can be explained using economic factors, such as that it was the cost-effective alternative whereas what could have been done instead would have been far too complicated and costly to do. This could be the case, for example, if choosing between using straight-line depreciation and using a depreciation charge based on the actual reduction in the future economic benefits arising from the asset. The latter would comply directly with the intention of depreciation whereas the former is an approximation, a compromise that is widely used.

In other cases, while a decision taken can be explained away by talk of cost, benefit, and a true and fair view, the reality of what caused a choice to be made may only be identified by considering the wider context. That is, by considering external factors that may have motivated the accountant, factors that have very little to do with portraying a true and fair view. To this end, a number of theories have been developed that can help explain the choices made by accountants and by businesses in their presentation of accounting information; by investors; and by governments and regulators in their pronouncements on accounting practices. Knowing about these theories helps stakeholders to understand what is being reported or what has occurred.

## 30.2 Theories of accounting-related choice

Most theories relevant to accounting are either **normative** theories or **positive** theories. Normative theories *prescribe* what *should* happen. Examples of the results of normative theories are accounting standards and any other form of regulation. Chapter 31 discusses these **theories of accounting practice**. Positive theories are theories and hypotheses that (*exante*) provide valid and meaningful predictions about things that have not yet been observed and (*expost*) can be used to describe and explain what has happened. That is, **they *describe* what *has* happened, *explain* what *has* happened, and *predict* what *will* happen in response to specific stimuli.**

**Theories of accounting-related choice are almost entirely positive theories.** They are often labelled or linked under the umbrella term *'Positive Accounting Theory'*.

There is another group of theories that relate to individuals which also apply to accounting-related choice: **social judgement theories**. These *describe* **how** individuals take decisions.

Positive theories assume that everyone is rational and motivated constantly by self-interest, maximising personal benefit in all decisions taken. They assume everyone will do the same thing. As a result they predict what the most likely response will be to a given situation. While this is clearly unrealistic, research has found that these theories can generally be used to explain decisions of particular types. These types of decision are characterised by the context in which they arise:

### Positive accounting theories

Theories relating to choice of accounting method:

- Rational choice theory

Theories relating to companies and stock markets:

- Efficient market hypothesis

Theories relating to the relationships between two parties, such as a manager and an owner or a company and a bank:

- Agency theory
- Efficient contracting
- Opportunistic perspective
- Management bonus hypothesis
- Debt covenant hypothesis

Theories relating to the relationship between an organisation and its stakeholders:

- Social contract
- Legitimacy theory
- Stakeholder theory

Theories relating to regulation:

- Public interest theory
- Political cost hypothesis
- Capture theory
- Private interest theory

Theories relating to individuals:

- Enlightened self-interest

### Social judgement theories

Social judgement theories focus on the individual. They recognise that everyone is different, that people do not always do what is rational or logical, and that people are not motivated at all times by self-interest.

Theories relating to individual decision-making:

- Brunswick lens
- Anchoring and adjustment
- Representativeness
- Availability

## 30.3 Theories relating to choice of accounting method

### Rational choice theory

This theory assumes that accountants will select the accounting method that most efficiently presents a true and fair view of what is being portrayed. That is, they seek the most cost-effective means to fairly present information.

For example, this theory predicts that the method adopted for valuing inventory at the end of a period is the one that is most efficient at arriving at an appropriate value for the item of inventory. Doing so requires that the nature of what is being assessed is considered.

Imagine a coal distributor that receives supplies of coal in lorry-loads of loose coal that are kept in a large single store; and that each new delivery is placed on top of what is already in store. Issues from the store are taken from the top of the pile of coal. The most appropriate method of inventory valuation to use to value the cost of each batch of coal that is sold would be 'last in, first out' (LIFO) – the cost of the last batch received is used until the quantity sold exceeds the amount received in that batch, at which point the cost of remaining coal sold is valued at the cost of the second last batch received, etc. After deducting the cost of all the coal sold, the value of the final inventory is set at those costs not yet included in the cost of coal sold. No other valuation basis is capable of identifying as appropriate a value for the inventory, so the coal distributor will not wish to change to a different method.

This theory explains why businesses and groups of businesses sometimes resist changes in accounting regulations or legislation that remove the possibility of using the method that they had been using.

LIFO is not permitted under IFRS. How does this affect the coal distributor's ability to identify an appropriate value for its inventory?

## 30.4 Theories relating to companies and stock markets

### Efficient market hypothesis

This theory explains why share prices on stock markets change in response to the availability of information relating to a company, the market in which it operates, or the wider environment.

Share prices are the result of investors considering how much they will receive in dividends over the lifetime of their investment. Dividends are based on the earnings of a company. If its profits increase, dividends are likely to increase, and so the share price will increase, and vice versa.

The theory proposes that there are three possibilities:

1 Market prices change in response only to historic information, such as the latest statement of profit or loss and the latest statement of financial position. This is known as the '*weak*' form of the hypothesis.
2 Market prices change in response to historic information and all other publicly available information; and that any newly released information will immediately be compounded into the market price. This is known as the '*semi-strong*' form.
3 Market prices are based on all information, historic, public and private (i.e. information known only to company insiders). This is known as the '*strong*' form.

The semi-strong form is considered to be the most realistic. New information that indicates that earnings will increase leads to the share price increasing. Share prices will fall if new information indicates that company earnings will reduce. Companies will seek to ensure that their earnings do not decline, but that they are rising in a relatively steady manner that is in line with or exceeds expectations of analysts and investors.

Because companies are aware of this theory, they may be tempted to alter their accounting figures in their financial statements so as to avoid a fall in the price of their shares. **This is one cause of companies engaging in earnings management**, which you learnt about in Chapter 29.

## 30.5 Theories relating to the relationships between two parties

### Agency theory

Agency theory concerns the relationship between 'agents' (e.g. employees) and 'principals' (e.g. employers). It states that agents are always self-interested and that principals need to align the objectives of their agents to match their own. Doing so completely is impossible. There will always be a **residual cost** to the principal but by **negotiating efficiently** with the agent, this can be minimised. Doing so incurs two types of cost for the principal: **bonding costs** (the extra benefits paid to the agent in order to encourage the agent to commit to the objectives of the principal) and **monitoring costs** (the costs of checking that the agent acts in the best interests of the principal).

**Agency is why managers are paid performance bonuses.**

### Opportunistic perspective

Because people are self-interested, they will take any opportunity available to maximise the benefit to them. The opportunistic perspective predicts that if managers (agents) can do something that is beneficial to them, they will do it whatever the costs to their employer (principal) – *see* the *management bonus hypothesis* below. Alternatively, if a company is close to breaching an agreement with a bank concerning a loan, and can do something that cost-effectively results in it not breaching the agreement, it will do so – *see* the *debt covenant hypothesis* below.

### Efficient contracting

This theory predicts that both agents and principals will engage in a form of negotiation that maximises the benefit to themselves. An employment contract that has been efficiently negotiated will result in agents maximising their benefits *and* principals minimising their **agency costs** – the total of the bonding costs, maintenance costs and residual costs.

### Management bonus hypothesis

When an agent has a performance-related bonus plan, if the bonus is under threat, the agent will do whatever is necessary in order to achieve it, including manipulating accounting numbers by adjusting accruals and changing the choices of accounting methods, deferring expenditure, and bringing forward revenue receipts that ought to belong in the next period.

Alternatively, if there is no prospect of an agent reaching the target level of performance to trigger a bonus payment, a 'big bath' will be taken whereby recorded performance is reduced to a level that provides an increased probability the target will be reached in the following period. The opposite forms of adjustments will be done: accounting numbers will be manipulated by adjusting accruals and changing accounting methods, bringing forward expenditure originally intended to be incurred in the next period, and delaying revenue transactions until the next period.

**This is a cause of managers of companies engaging in earnings management.**

### Debt covenant hypothesis

When a company borrows funds from a bank, it will enter into negotiations with the bank concerning the rate of interest charged. A bank will typically reduce interest rates if loans are secured on the non-current assets of the company. It will reduce them further if the company enters into a debt covenant whereby the company agrees to certain conditions that, if broken, will result in its paying a penalty or, more typically, forfeiting the loan. Such a breach of covenant can be very expensive for a company, involving a combination of the costs of attempting to renegotiate the existing loan, attempting to arrange a new loan, and having to raise cash quickly by selling off assets at below their market value.

Debt covenants usually involve conditions relating to a company's gearing with one or more ratios acting as triggers for breach. For example, a debt covenant may state that a company must not have a debt to equity ratio of above 40 per cent. Alternatively debt covenants may be linked to the market price of the company's shares.

The debt covenant hypothesis states that when a company is close to breaching its debt covenants it will engage in earnings management that will result in increasing its earnings or in increasing its assets. This may involve manipulating accruals to alter the accounting numbers or making physical adjustments to transaction entries, such as shifting the period in which they appear.

**This is another cause of companies engaging in earnings management.**

## 30.6 Theories relating to the relationship between an organisation and its stakeholders

### Social contract

This theory states that unwritten and unvoiced agreements exist between entities and their stakeholders. Stakeholders have expectations of entities and if they do anything that breaches such an understanding, the stakeholders who have been let down will be alienated.

So, for example, stakeholders would generally expect a company not to use child labour, not to pollute the environment, not to cause damage to society, not to mislead, and so on. It is important, sometimes vital, for organisations **to maintain their *legitimacy*** in the eyes of their stakeholders or, just as shareholders will start selling shares in companies that are not achieving the returns they expected, their stakeholders will react in ways that may generate a negative impact on the organisation and its future viability.

## Legitimacy theory

When an entity breaches its social contract, legitimacy theory states that it will do what it can to restore it. This may entail trying to show that it has not broken the *social contract* or it may involve the entity trying to create a new social contract that aligns to what it is doing rather than what its stakeholders perceived it should be doing or, more probably, a mixture of these two tactics.

One common response is to make voluntary disclosures, often of accounting-related information. When an entity volunteers some financial information for this purpose, it may not be audited information and it may be in a summary form that makes it easier for a non-accountant to understand. This lack of the quality control of the audit upon what is being disclosed is not something non-accountants have much awareness of. The information disclosed will tend to be accepted at face value.

Consequently, unscrupulous organisations may elect to manipulate accounting numbers in order to produce a summary statement to support the image they are trying to portray. Doing so may remove or reduce the level of discontent among its stakeholders and, by the time it is revealed that the information disclosed was misleading, it may be much easier to deal with the issues that its discovery brings.

Take, for example, a company accused of causing its employees to become ill from asbestos poisoning. It may react by creating a trust fund for the victims which it publicises as something that guarantees they will all be very well looked after. None of the stakeholders checks whether the amount put into the fund will be sufficient. The perceived legitimacy of the company is improved and the *social contract* begins to be reinstated. Even if it is subsequently discovered that the company exaggerated the degree to which the fund was adequate, the present problem for the company is much reduced.

## Stakeholder theory

There are two branches of stakeholder theory: the ethical branch and the managerial branch. The *ethical branch* is a *normative theory* that states that **entities that break their *social contracts* should take actions that do not discriminate between groups of stakeholders.** That is, no stakeholder group is favoured above any other.

For example, if a company pollutes the environment in a remote jungle location, it should do everything it can to neutralise the pollution and return everything to how it was before the incident that caused the pollution, compensating victims fairly and replacing destroyed and damaged man-made and natural resources, irrespective of the extent to which any of its various groups of stakeholders perceive that the company has broken its *social contract*. In responding in this way, no one stakeholder group is favoured over another.

Under the *managerial branch of stakeholder theory*, **entities will respond to perceived breaches of their *social contract* only when primary stakeholders may respond negatively if they do not.** Primary stakeholders are those that are in a position to damage the future well-being of an entity.

So, for example, if a company causes the beach shoreline next to a large city to be heavily polluted, but no one complains except a few surfers, it won't do anything. On the other hand, if the Government starts to threaten fines and sanctions, such as cancelling the company's licence to operate, it will do whatever is necessary to convince this primary stakeholder (the Government) that it is doing everything possible to repair the damage caused and to ensure it will not happen again. That is, **the company will strive to repair its legitimacy in the eyes of its primary stakeholder and attain a *social contract* which the Government accepts.**

## 30.7 Theories relating to regulation

### Public interest theory

This theory states that governments will step in and issue regulations to prevent entities acting in a manner that is against the public interest, i.e. not good for society as a whole. An example would be where a pharmaceutical company is taking advantage of its monopoly hold over the market for one of its products and this is resulting in a drug that would cure thousands of people only being available to the very wealthy. This is certainly not 'good' for society as a whole. In this case, the Government would be motivated to pass legislation that requires that the drug be provided at a price everyone can afford because doing so would be 'in the public interest'.

This is the justification for all legislation, including all company regulations. Because this is so well known, companies will avoid placing themselves in a visible position where their activities could be affected in this way.

Why do you think the phrase 'visible position' is used here, rather than simply the word 'position'?

### Political cost hypothesis

When an entity is being very successful, it is difficult not to draw attention to itself. It can hardly hide the level of its success: it must publish its financial statements every year. Not everyone likes to see an entity being highly successful and some public criticism is likely to result. If the entity is perceived by legislators to be too successful, i.e. that it is acting in ways that are against the public interest by taking advantage of its position, it may be subject to some legislation that restricts its activities, forces it to share its secrets with competitors, or even forces the organisation to be broken up into a number of separate entities.

When an entity feels that there is a possibility that it is being successful in a way that may be considered to *not* be in the public interest, it will seek to avoid being subject to any legislation that restricts its ability to continue as at present. In order to do so, the *political cost hypothesis* states that **it will seek to look legitimate** (*legitimacy theory*) by any means available to it. Typically, these include making voluntary disclosures that are intended to diminish the perceived threat of legislation. Another obvious tactic would be to reduce earnings (profits) to a level that would be considered acceptable.

**This is another cause of companies engaging in earnings management.**

### Capture theory

Whenever new legislation is proposed, there are usually individuals and groups who do not agree with the proposals. They do what they can to have the proposals modified or dropped, typically by lobbying the legislators. This theory states that **regulatory capture** occurs when the people or organisations whom legislation is intended to control become the regulators. That is, they have achieved a dominant influence over the content of the regulations that are issued.

In accounting this is most clearly seen in the manner in which accounting standards are issued by the very stakeholder group whose actions they are intended to control: accountants.

### Private interest theory

This is also referred to as 'economic interest group theory' and 'special interest theory'. It states that when faced with a perceived threat from potential or proposed legislation, interest groups form of like-minded individuals and organisations are formed. These groups influence the legislators by promoting their interests to the exclusion of others.

Typically, there may be competing interest groups seeking to gain the attention of the regulator, but none of these groups achieves monopoly control or a dominant influence over the regulators, though the group that gains the greatest consideration will benefit more than the rest and, in doing so, will cause other interest groups to get less than they were seeking.

For example, if a government proposes to build a new dam so that farmland around it might benefit from year-round irrigation, it would please the farmers. But, it would not please the inhabitants of the town that had to be demolished in order to build the dam. Nor would it please the fishermen or the fish processing plant that had previously experienced great success due to the vast freshwater fish stock that inhabits the 20-mile-long river that is being redirected 10 miles east to provide water for the new dam. The town's inhabitants, the fishermen and the fish processing plant might form a private interest group and would compete for the attention of the legislators with the private interest group of the farmers.

Both groups cannot be successful but, so long as one does not capture the legislators, a compromise of sorts will result. This could, for example, take the form of creating a fork in the river rather than diverting all of it to the dam and providing high-quality new accommodation for the inhabitants of the old town rather than simply giving them compensation based upon an artificially low market price for their property.

Sometimes, there is no compromise and only one group achieves (at least some of) its objectives. For example, if it is proposed by the IASB that goodwill is to be amortised at a rate of 5 per cent straight-line, one group may lobby for there to be no amortisation, another for a set percentage, another for the rate to be 2 per cent, and another may petition in support of a 10 per cent rate. When the amended accounting standard is issued, the rate set is 2 per cent but the group that wished that outcome did not become influential to the extent that it took over the IASB. It simply made a convincing case for the rate it was proposing.

## 30.8 Theories relating to individuals

### Enlightened self-interest

This theory states that because everyone is self-interested and motivated to maximise their personal wealth, when a choice is given that involves doing something that would not be against a person's best interests, they will decline to do it, and vice versa Similarly, this can be applied to companies and other entities for which profit maximisation or some other target such as market growth is their primary goal.

It is argued that even legislators exhibit this trait, passing legislation that is in their own personal best interests rather than legislation that is primarily in the public interest. A politician facing re-election will be unlikely to pass legislation that will lose votes but, if this were occurring two years into a four-year term of office, when the risks to the politician's future are virtually non-existent, a different form of legislation would be likely, one that is far more in the public interest.

**Enlightened self-interest explains why companies and their employees engage in earnings management relating to debt covenants and management bonuses.**

## 30.9 Theories relating to individual decision-making

### Brunswick lens

This theory concerns how individuals take decisions. It involves identifying the 'cues' that a decision-maker uses. 'Cues' are the questions a decision-maker seeks to answer before arriving at a decision. Once a cue is identified, the weighting placed upon it by the decision-maker is also sought. Then, once all the cues the decision-maker used are identified and weighted, the decision taken can be analysed and explained.

For example, a bank may be willing to offer a loan to a major company but its loan officer will need to discover the answer to the questions that she always asks when approached for a loan by companies of this size. The list of questions (cues) may be very long indeed, and the weightings used may not even all be consciously known to the loan officer – some may be being applied by instinct. If a bank wants to ensure that all its loan officers are taking these decisions in the best interests of the bank, it will need to discover what cues the loan officer is using, which cues the loan officer perceives to be important, and how the loan officer combines these cues in reaching a decision. This is not a simple task but banks have done it successfully in the past, working with their most successful loan officers in building a computer simulation of the cues and the weightings placed upon them. Once completed, they then made this captured expertise available to all their loan officers. Thereafter, all the loan officers were guided to a higher level of consistency and a higher level of financially beneficial loan decisions.

One of the factors that makes identification of the cues used and their weighting difficult to identify is that most decision-makers adopt **heuristics** ('rules of thumb') that involve them in short-cutting the decision-making process by focusing upon some, but not all, of the cues that they could use. When a very experienced specialist does this, it can be virtually as effective as taking the same decision using a far lengthier list of cues with far more complex weighting structures. The benefit to the decision-maker is that it saves time and it saves costs.

The disadvantages are that the quality of the decisions taken is compromised – perhaps losing a few percentage points of accuracy, maybe much more.

A simplifying heuristic is not a wise approach to use in the long term. It can only be the 'best long-term option' if it truly is all that needs to be considered to obtain the 'best' decision. But, as a short-term device to speed up decisions temporarily, using such a heuristic is an attractive option when time is short or the costs of applying a full range of cues is high.

An expert using a heuristic that she has devised will probably do so more successfully than a novice who is told to use the same heuristic – the expert will, for example, have a far greater sense of something being 'not quite right' and will adjust the way she is using the heuristic accordingly. Imagine an expert in mental arithmetic using a calculator compared to someone who is not very good at arithmetic doing so. The expert will work out an approximate answer for each calculation mentally and then check that the result shown by the calculator looks OK before trusting that she pressed the correct keys. Most of us do make mistakes from time to time when using a calculator, just as we make mistakes using a word processor, or in entering formulae in a spreadsheet. An expert will detect far more of the errors she makes than a novice.

Accountants who use ratios to assess the financial performance and financial position of an entity are almost certainly using a heuristic. You learnt how ratios can be used in Chapter 29, but it takes far more than a few ratio calculations to construct a complete picture. Even where a large number of ratios are used, qualitative and contextual factors are also needed before any realistically sound conclusion can be drawn. If the need for a complete set of cues and weightings is consistently ignored, wrong conclusions will eventually be made and incorrect decisions taken as a result. The next three theories provide examples of the type of errors that can result if heuristics are over-used.

## Anchoring and adjustment

This form of heuristic involves decision-makers relying on past results or past data to establish the foundations of what they are attempting to do (**anchoring**). They then make **adjustments** to that base position as they move towards reaching a decision.

For example, if an accountant wishes to forecast the profit for the next 12 months, she can use the statement of profit or loss from the previous 12 months as a starting point. Those items considered unlikely to change very much can be adjusted slightly and only those that are sure to be different are investigated in detail to find more appropriate figures to insert in the calculation. As a result, the forecast is only of limited use. It is certainly inferior to one prepared by looking in detail at what is expected to occur during the next 12 months, and placing values on each item based on actual anticipated outcomes rather than a rough figure based mainly on last year's amount.

Another example relates to auditing. Where an auditor relies too much on the findings of the previous year's audit, problems may be overlooked because they did not exist last year and nobody felt it was worthwhile making sure nothing had changed. The result may be a 'clean' audit report, one that declares that the company is a going concern and that the financial statements present a true and fair view of the financial performance and position of the company. The reality may be very different, resulting in the company failing rapidly, so causing significant losses to be suffered by investors and creditors who relied upon the audit report. The reputation of the audit firm would also be affected, perhaps leading to loss of business and potential reductions in staff.

## Representativeness

When decision-makers apply this heuristic, they classify the item they are considering according to the features of something that is ***apparently*** similar. Doing so saves a lot of time and effort, not to mention cost, but it is a very dangerous heuristic to adopt. For example, if someone holds shares in two companies, one in the hotel industry and the other in electronics, and needs to sell one of the holdings, he may look at how other companies in the same industries are faring. If a leading electronics company is experiencing problems and its share price is falling, he may assume that his investment in the same industry will soon start to drop in value, so he sells the shares in that company. Then, within a month, the shares he sold increase in value by 20 per cent, while shares in the company he retained fall by 5 per cent. He did not make the correct decision because he relied on a flawed heuristic.

What people who apply the **representativeness** heuristic fail to do is ensure that the 'similarities' between the two companies are close enough for this conclusion to be drawn. They often are not. Just being in the same industrial sector does not guarantee similar performances, or similar movements in share prices. One company may be significantly larger than the other, the markets they trade in may be very different, the products they supply may be as similar as chalk and cheese – calculators and tablets are both electronic goods, but would a company specialising in calculators really be a good guide to the financial future of one specialising in tablets?

## Availability

Decision-makers who adopt the **availability** heuristic use information that is easy to obtain. They think they can make good decisions without having to refer to the difficult-to-obtain information, even though they know that the information they are ignoring is a very important guide to the correct decision to make. It is like picking low-hanging fruit just because it is there, rather than climbing a tree and selecting the best fruit on the tree. You get fruit, but it is not of the quality you would have got had you put more effort into obtaining it.

Decisions that do not incorporate all the information (cues) considered to be important can rarely if ever be as good as those that do. Strategic decisions that are based on partial information are a recipe for financial stress. Investment decisions made on this basis are destined to be much more risky and much less rewarding.

In short, there is no long-term financial advantage in adopting a strategy of using heuristics like these when you know that there is a better approach to take. The only benefits are increased speed of the decision and the avoidance of the costs of obtaining better or more appropriate information.

These savings are likely to be minimal compared with the eventual losses that arise from such decisions, whether they be real, identifiable costs or opportunity cost, as represented by potential profits missed. Yet decision-makers do often adopt these heuristics, mostly in situations where it does not really matter but, when it does matter if the decision is incorrect, it can be a very costly tactic indeed.

## 30.10 Conclusion

This chapter presented an overview of various theories that can be used to explain accounting choice – why particular decisions are made relating to accounting data and accounting information.

These theories are a mix of indicators of cause and effect that:

- explain why some decisions might be taken, including
  - decisions relating to buying and selling shares;
  - a sudden increase in voluntary disclosure by a company;
  - manipulation of accounting numbers;
  - alterations to the timing of transactions;
- explain events that occur when new accounting standards are being proposed and drafted; or
- describe what decision-makers do in the process of taking a decision.

**They can all be used to explain accounting-related choices, and much more besides.**

### Learning outcomes

**You should now have learnt:**

1. About three groups of theories that relate to accounting.
2. The differences between normative theories, positive theories and social judgement theories.
3. How to apply several positive theories of accounting to explain and predict accounting-related decisions.
4. How to apply several social judgement theories to explain accounting-related decisions.

### Answers to activities

30.1 The company must use a different method, one that is less 'efficient' and so less capable of presenting a true and fair view of the value of the inventory.

30.2 Companies will be reluctant to call attention to themselves and will not publicise the fact that they are taking advantage of a monopoly position in their market. If they can continue to operate in the same way, they will do so. When what they are doing becomes 'visible', i.e. becomes public knowledge, it will be considered a breach of their social contract, and the stakeholders, such as the Government, will respond if they believe the breach to be sufficiently important that they should do so.

## Review questions

**30.1** What is the difference between capture theory and private interest group theory?

**30.2** What is the relationship between legitimacy theory, social contracts, and the stakeholders of an entity?

**30.3** A bank uses a set of 20 questions to assess the financial position of applicants for loans. Since introducing this approach 5 years ago, it has found that only 1 per cent of loans granted have proved to be irrecoverable. Previously, a far less complex and more informal approach was used in the lending decision and 5 per cent of loans were irrecoverable. A loan officer has recommended that the number of questions used be reduced to 4 because the other 16 do not seem to have been relevant in the case of any of the defaulting loans that arose in the past year. He argues that this will save time and money and that it will avoid any need to undertake some of the more complex and harder-to-resolve investigations that are required in the current approach. Which form of heuristic does this suggestion represent?

**30.4** If you were the senior loan officer in the bank in Question 30.3, would you support this suggestion?

**30.5** A manager is responsible for monitoring his employer's debt covenants. These are linked to the debt to equity ratio, which must not rise above 40 per cent. The manager has noticed that the draft financial statements are showing that this is now at 42 per cent. The manager recommends that the accountants adjust the accruals at the period-end so that this figure drops to 35 per cent. What types of changes could the accountants legally make?

**30.6** If the covenant in Question 30.5 was related to the price of the company's shares, what steps could be taken to raise the price of its shares?

**30.7** What would be the long-term impact upon the company of the measures adopted in Questions 30.5 and 30.6?

**30.8** Why is knowledge of double entry important in identifying whether some of these theories have correctly predicted behaviour?

chapter 31

# Theories of accounting practice

## Learning objectives

**After you have studied this chapter, you should be able to:**

- explain that there is no one overall general theory of accounting practice
- describe some of the possible valuation alternatives to the historical cost basis for valuation
- explain the difference between current purchasing power and current cost accounting

## Introduction

This chapter is in two parts: general theories of accounting practice, in which you will learn about asset valuation, the concept of wealth measurement, and capital maintenance; and accounting for changing price levels, such as occur in periods of inflation.

# Part 1 GENERAL THEORIES OF ACCOUNTING PRACTICE

## 31.1 Background

You may find it strange that a discussion of the theory of accounting practice has been left until now. The reason for not dealing with this earlier is simple: it could have distracted you, and made it more difficult for you to learn the basic practices of accounting. The terms used in explaining accounting are those you have learnt up to this point – terms such as 'capital', 'liabilities', 'assets' and 'net profit'. If you had not learnt how these terms are used in accounting before considering the theories of accounting practice, you would have found it very difficult to understand what these theories seek to explain. Leaving it until now, if theory points out what is wrong with accounting methods, at least you know what those methods are.

As this is your first look at theories of accounting practice, the rest of this chapter presents an introduction to this topic.

## 31.2 An overall accepted theory of accounting practice?

It would not be surprising if you were expecting to read here about the overall accepted theory of accounting practice. Unfortunately, there is no such 'accepted' theory. This is much regretted by those accountants who have chosen an academic life. To practising accountants, however, accounting is what accountants do, and they feel theory has little place in their world. The reality, however, is that theories of accounting practice provide a general framework against which accounting practices can be judged and also provide a means by which new practices and procedures may be developed.

The lack of an accepted overall theory of accounting practice does not mean that it has not been attempted; there have been numerous attempts. At first an *inductive approach* was tried – i.e. one that tried to create a theory from a few examples. For example, if you saw a white swan, you might induce the theory that all swans are white (which they are not). Applying an inductive approach, the practices of accountants were observed and analysed to see if any consistent behaviour could be detected. This was done in the hope that if a general principle was identified, everyone could be led towards applying it. The attempt failed.

It was impossible to find consistent patterns of behaviour amongst the mass of practices that had developed over the years. Also, such an approach would not have brought about any important improvements in accounting practices, as it looked at 'what accountants do' rather than 'what accountants should be doing'.

A different approach emerged in the 1950s. It was a *normative approach,* which looked at what accountants should be doing rather than at what they did. To do so, it also included elements of the inductive approach in attempting to derive accounting rules designed to meet a set of objectives. The combination of these approaches has been promising, but the main problem has been a lack of a general agreement upon the objectives of accounting.

As you might expect, over time, attention then switched towards a less ambitious approach. This is based, first, on identifying the users of financial statements, and then upon identifying what kind of information they require. Such an approach was used in *The Corporate Report,* sponsored by the UK government and published in 1975. We will look later at the user groups which were identified. The other important report using this approach was that of the Sandilands Committee (also sponsored by the UK government and published in 1975). This will also be considered more fully later.

**Activity 31.1**

Should accountants give the user groups the information they are asking for, or the information for which they should be asking?

Another point is whether only one report should be issued for all user groups, or whether each group should have its own report.

At present, this appears to have been resolved. After 80 years of discussion, analysis, and various attempts to satisfy everyone, accounting information produced for external use is now considered to be primarily for investors and creditors. Having narrowed down the 'target audience', it should now be easier to produce accounting information that is more useful and better suited to the needs of those principal user groups; and to produce accounting standards better able to assist in achieving that objective.

Having had an overview of the principal attempts to develop overall theories of accounting practice, let's now look at theories of accounting practice that have been developed.

## 31.3 Measurement of income

One term we use in accounting is '*income*', a term that, in accounting, means the same as the term '*net profit*'. We use the term '*revenue*' when describing receipts net of VAT arising from sales transactions. In accounting, the term '*income*' does *not* have the same meaning as '*revenue*'. In this book the calculation of net profit is done within fairly strict guidelines. Chapter 10 in *Frank Wood's Business Accounting 1* provided guidance on the overall concepts ruling such calculations. However, just because the business world and the accounting profession use this basic approach does not mean it is the only one available. We will now describe some alternative approaches.

Let's start by looking at the simplest possible example of the calculation of profit, where everyone would agree with the way it is calculated. John is starting in business, his only asset being £1,000 in cash. He rents a stall in a market for the day, which costs him £40. He then buys fruit for cash £90, and sells it all during the day for cash £160. At the end of the day, John's only asset is still cash: £1,000 − £40 − £90 + £160 = £1,030. Everyone would agree that his profit for that day was £30, i.e. £160 sales − £90 purchases − £40 expenses = £30. In this case his profit equals the increase in his cash.

Suppose that John now changes his style of trading. He buys the market stall, and he also starts selling nuts and dried fruit, of which he can keep an inventory from one day to another. If we now want to calculate his daily profit, we cannot do so purely in terms of cash: we also have to place a value both on his inventory of fruit and nuts and on his stall; and we would need to do this at both the beginning and the end of each day.

The argument just put forward assumes that we can all agree that profit represents an increase in wealth. It assumes that John will make a profit for a period if either:

(*a*) he is better off at the end of the period than he was at the beginning; or
(*b*) he would have been better off at the end than at the beginning had he not consumed some of the profits by taking drawings.

The Nobel Prize-winning economist Sir John Hicks expressed the view that profit was the maximum value which a person could consume during a period and still be as well off at the end of the period as at the beginning. You will learn later about the rules governing the calculation of profit. In a sense, as we said above, profit is very much the same as income – what you have left after you subtract all your expenses from your receipts is your 'income'. (Accountants call it 'net income' or 'net profit' but, for simplicity, let's just call it 'income' for the time being.)

In terms of a limited company, the 1970s Sandilands Committee said that a company's profit for the year is the maximum value which the company can distribute as dividends during the year and still be as well off at the end of the year as it was at the beginning. There are some important questions here which need answering:

1 How can we measure wealth at the beginning and end of a period?
2 How do we measure the change in wealth over a period?
3 Having measured wealth over a period, how much can be available for consumption and how much should not be consumed?

There are two main approaches to the measurement of wealth of a business:

(*a*) by finding the values of the individual assets of a business and then subtracting from them the value of the individual liabilities of the business;
(*b*) by measuring the expectation of future benefits. (This involves calculating something known as 'the present value of expected future net cash flows'. You will be covering this topic in Chapters 50 and 51.)

From these, you can see that in order to measure wealth, you must first identify the value of your assets and liabilities or the value of your future net cash flows.

**If you paid £1,000 for a computer, what value would you say it had?**

Arriving at an acceptable value for an asset is not nearly as simple as it appears. Firstly, you need to know what the term 'value' means. It is rather more than just the amount paid or the amount something is sold for. You need to consider the context – a glass of water has a lot more value in a desert than in London. If you have studied any economics, you will know that the availability of something dictates its value to the purchaser. Also, from an accounting perspective, once you own something, the value you place on it may not be what you paid for it and the basis of valuation that you use needs to be acceptable in the context of accounting.

Let's now look at the different methods that can be used to value assets.

## 31.4 Asset valuation alternatives

### 1 Historical cost

This is the most commonly applied valuation basis, or 'method', in accounting. You have been using it and will continue to use it throughout your accounting studies. The principles underpinning it are quite simple. An asset is valued at what it cost, less an amount representing the impact of its use so far upon that value.

Take the computer costing £1,000 as an example. Let's assume it was expected to be used for four years before being scrapped. As it would last four years, each year you could reduce its value by a quarter of what it cost. That is, it would be reduced by £250 every year. At the end of two years, it would have a value of £500 (£1,000 − £250 − £250).

This seems quite simple, except that someone needs to decide how much to reduce its value by each year. Why was four years chosen for the useful economic life of the computer? Why not three or five? Why was it assumed that it would lose value equally each year? This depreciation adjustment is just one example of how imprecise accounting can be in relation to arriving at a value for something. There is no one 'true' answer; the choice of method and expected length of use of the asset, etc. are quite arbitrary.

Let's look at a couple of other examples.

1 Inventory to be used during a period can be charged out at FIFO (first in, first out), LIFO (last in, first out), AVCO (average cost method) for inventory valuation, and so on. There is no one 'true' figure.
2 Suppose we buy a block of assets, e.g. we take over the net assets of another organisation. How do we allocate the cost exactly? There is no precise way – we simply use a 'fair value' for each asset. As you know, the amount by which the total cost exceeds the total of the fair values is treated as goodwill.

### 2 Adjusted historical cost

Because the value or purchasing power of money changes over time, the historical cost approach can be very unsatisfactory. Take the case of a buildings account. In it we find that two items have been debited. One was a warehouse bought in 1970 for £100,000 and the other an almost identical warehouse bought in 2002 for £400,000. These two figures are added together to show cost of warehouses £500,000 – quite clearly a misleading value for these assets today.

To remedy this defect, the original historical cost of an asset could be adjusted for the changes in the value or purchasing power of money over the period from acquisition to the present date of the statement of financial position. These calculations are made using a price index, such as is issued by the government as a measure of inflation.

This method does not mean that the asset itself is revalued. What is revalued is the amount for which the asset was originally bought. This method forms the basis of what is known as *current purchasing power* accounting, abbreviated as CPP. During the early 1980s when inflation in the UK was high, many companies produced financial accounting information based on CPP.

The method does not remove the problem of the 'true' cost. All it does is to assume the original historical cost was accurate and then adjust the value of the business (and, hence, the owner's wealth) to allow for the impact of changing price levels over time.

To illustrate how it works, let's look at an example of a CPP-based valuation.

A machine which will last for five years, depreciated using the straight line method, was bought on 1 January 2014 for £5,000. On 1 January 2016 exactly the same kind of machine (there have been no technological improvements) is bought for £6,000. The price index was 100 at 1 January 2014, 120 at 1 January 2016 and 130 at 31 December 2016. The machines would appear in the statement of financial position at 31 December 2016 as follows, the workings being shown in the box alongside.

| | *Historical cost* | *Conversion factor* | | **Statement of financial position CPP at 31 Dec 2016** |
|---|---|---|---|---|
| | £ | £ | | £ |
| Machine 1 | 5,000 | 130/100 | 6,500 | |
| Machine 2 | 6,000 | 130/120 | 6,500 | 13,000 |
| *Less* Depreciation | | | | |
| Machine 1 | 3,000 | 130/100 | 3,900 | |
| Machine 2 | 1,200 | 130/120 | 1,300 | (5,200) |
| | | | | 7,800 |

You can see that the CPP statement of financial position shows two exactly similar machines at the same cost, and each has been depreciated £1,300 for each year of use. In this particular case CPP has achieved exactly what it sets out to do, namely put similar things on a similar basis.

Underlying this method are the problems inherent in the price index used to adjust the historical cost figures. Any drawbacks in the index will result in a distortion of the adjusted historical cost figures.

**Activity 31.3** Summarise the potential flaws in this method.

## 3 Replacement cost

Replacement cost is the estimated amount that would have to be paid to replace the asset at the date of valuation. You will often see it referred to as an 'entry value' as it is the cost of an asset entering the business.

How do we 'estimate' the replacement cost? As we are not, in fact, replacing the asset we will have to look at the state of the market at the date of valuation. If the asset is exactly the same as those currently being traded, perhaps we can look at suppliers' price lists.

Even with exactly the same item, there are still problems. Until you have actually negotiated a purchase it is impossible to say how much discount you could get – you might guess but you could not be certain. Also, if the asset consists of, say, ten computers, how much discount could you get for buying ten computers instead of one?

And that's the 'easy' one! What do you do when you are trying to find out these figures for assets that are no longer available? Technological change has greatly speeded up in recent years. If there is a second-hand market, it may be possible to get a valuation. However, in second-hand markets the price is often even more subject to negotiation. It becomes even more complicated when the original asset was specially made and there is no exactly comparable item, new or second-hand.

The difficulties outlined above mean that solutions to replacement cost-based valuation can be sought under three headings:

1 **Market prices.** There will often be a market, new or second-hand, for the assets. For instance, this is particularly true for motor vehicles. However, if your asset differs in some way from the one you found the price of, an adjustment may be necessary to the value, thus decreasing the reliability of the value you place on the asset.

2 **Units of service.** Where a market price cannot be found, a value can be placed based upon the units of service (or output) which the asset can provide; for example, if a machine is estimated to be able to produce another 1,000 items before it is scrapped and a new but different machine would be expected to produce 5,000 of the same items before being scrapped. The old machine can be given a value equal to one-fifth of the cost of the new machine. However, if the costs of operating the two machines differ, this would need to be taken into account when arriving at the valuation figure for the old machine.

3 **Cost of inputs.** If the asset was made or constructed by the owner, it may be possible to calculate the cost of replacing it at the date of the statement of financial position. Present rates of labour and materials costs could be worked out to give the replacement cost.

**Activity 31.4** What flaw can you see in this method?

## 4 Net realisable value

Net realisable value means the estimated amount that would be received from the sale of the asset less the estimated costs of its disposal. The term '*exit value*' is often used as it is the amount receivable when an asset leaves the business.

A very important factor affecting such a valuation concerns the conditions under which the assets are to be sold. To dispose of an asset in a hurry often means accepting a very low price. Look at the prices received from sales of bankruptcy inventories – usually very low figures. The standard way of approaching this problem is to value the asset as though the realisation were 'in the normal course of business'. This is not capable of a precise valuation, as economic conditions change and the firm might never sell such an asset 'in the normal course of business'.

The difficulties of establishing an asset's net realisable value are similar to those of the replacement value method when similar assets are not being bought and sold in the marketplace. However, the problems are more severe as the units of service approach cannot be used, as you do not know how many units of service a buyer of your asset may expect it to produce.

## 5 Economic value (present value)

Economists would tell you that they would value an asset as the sum of the future expected net cash flows associated with the asset, discounted (adjusted) to its present value (what the cash flows would be worth today). For example, £20 in a year's time might only be able to buy goods that today could be purchased for £19. The technicalities of discounting are discussed in Chapters 27 and 50.

Certainly, if you really did know (not guess) the future net cash flows associated with the asset and you had the correct discount rate, your valuation would be absolutely correct. The trouble is that it is impossible to forecast future net cash flows with certainty, and we will not necessarily have chosen the correct discount rate. It is also very difficult to relate cash flows to a particular asset, since a business's assets combine together to generate revenue.

Before considering the next method, you may find it helpful to see four of these methods compared in the contexts of time and valuation basis (Exhibit 31.1).

### Exhibit 31.1 Four methods of valuation in the contexts of time and valuation basis

| | *Past* | *Present* | *Future* |
|---|---|---|---|
| *Entry value* | Historical cost | Replacement cost | |
| *Exit value* | | Net realisable value | Present value |

## 6 Deprival value

The final concept of value we shall consider is based on ideas propounded in the USA by Professor Bonbright in the 1930s, and later developed in the UK for profit measurement by Professor WT Baxter.

**Deprival value** is based on the concept of the value of an asset being the amount of money the owner would have to receive to compensate him for being deprived of it. We had better point out immediately that the owner does not have to be deprived of the asset to ascertain this value; it is a hypothetical exercise. This leads to a number of consequences.

(*a*) Deprival value cannot exceed replacement cost, since if the owner were deprived of the asset he could replace it for a lesser amount. Here we will ignore any costs concerned with a delay in replacement.

(*b*) If the owner feels that the asset is not worth replacing, its replacement cost would be more than its deprival value. The owner simply would not pay the replacement cost, so the value to the owner is less than that figure.

(*c*) If the asset's deprival value is to be taken as its net realisable value, that value must be less than its replacement cost. It would otherwise make sense for someone to sell the asset at net realisable value and buy a replacement at a lower cost. Again, delays in replacement are ignored.

(*d*) Take the case where an owner would not replace the asset, but neither would he sell it. It is possible to envisage an asset, such as a machine, which has become obsolete but might possibly be used, for example, when other machines break down. It is not worth buying a new machine, as the replacement cost is more than the value of the machine to the business. Such a machine may well have a very low net realisable value. The benefit to the business of keeping such a machine can be said to be its 'value in use'. This value must be less than its replacement cost, as pointed out above, but more than its net realisable value, for otherwise the owner would sell it.

It is probably easier to summarise how to find deprival value by means of the diagram in Exhibit 31.2:

### Exhibit 31.2 Deprival value

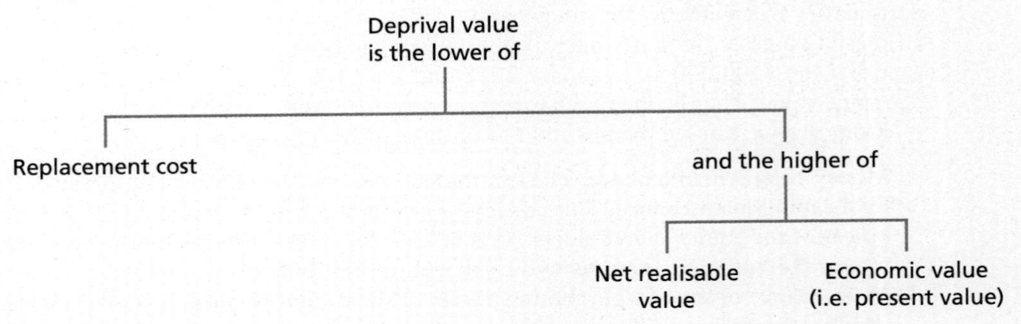


Deprival values can be illustrated by a few examples, using assets A, B and C.

| | *Asset A* | *Asset B* | *Asset C* |
|---|---|---|---|
| | £ | £ | £ |
| Replacement cost (RC) | 1,000 | 800 | 600 |
| Net realisable value (NRV) | 900 | 500 | 400 |
| Economic value (EV) | 2,000 | 700 | 300 |

The deprival values can be explained as follows. (Check them against Exhibit 31.2.)

(*a*) ***Asset A.*** If the firm were deprived of asset A, what would it do? As economic value is greater than replacement cost it would buy another asset A. The deprival value to the business is therefore £1,000, i.e. replacement cost.
(*b*) ***Asset B.*** If deprived of asset B, what would the firm do? It would not replace it, as the replacement cost of £800 is greater than its value to the business – its economic value £700. If deprived, the firm would therefore lose the present value of future cash flows, i.e. economic value £700. This then is the deprival value for asset B.
(*c*) ***Asset C.*** With this asset there would be no point in keeping it, as its economic value to the firm is less than the firm could sell it for. Selling it is the logical way, so the deprival value is net realisable value £400.

## 31.5 Capital maintenance

Let's go back to Sir John Hicks's definition of income (profit): 'A man's income is the maximum value which he can consume during a week, and still expect to be as well off at the end of the week as he was at the beginning.'

We've looked at the different ways assets may be valued so that they can be added together to find the wealth or 'well-offness' of a business at a particular date. Now, let's examine the problems of measuring the maintenance of wealth over a period. This is called *capital maintenance*.

Capital maintenance is the basic method of measuring maintenance of wealth used in accounting. If a business has a value (called its 'net worth') according to its financial statements of £100,000 on 1 January 2017 it must also have a value in its financial statements of £100,000 at 31 December 2017 to be as well off at the end of the period. Take the example of a company that has neither issued (sold) nor redeemed (bought back) any of its share capital (shares) and has paid no dividends. If it started with a value according to its financial statements of £100,000 on 1 January 2018 and finished with a value in its financial statements of £170,000 on 31 December 2018, it must have made a profit of £70,000.

This approach is known as 'money capital maintenance'. It would be acceptable to everyone in a period when there is no change in price levels. However, most people would agree that it is not satisfactory when either prices in general, or specific prices affecting the business, are changing. In these two cases, to state that £70,000 profit has been made in 2018 completely ignores the fact that the £100,000 at 1 January 2018 and the £100,000 at 31 December 2018 do not have the same value. That is, the purchasing power of £100,000 has changed between the two dates.

From this we can see the possibilities of three different concepts.

1 **Money capital maintenance.** The traditional system of accounting as already described.
2 **Real capital maintenance.** This concept is concerned with maintaining the general purchasing power of the equity shareholders. This takes into account changes in the purchasing power of money (i.e. inflation) as measured by the retail price index.
3 **Maintenance of specific purchasing power of the capital of the equity.** This uses a price index which is related to the specific price changes of the goods in which the firm deals.

From these we can look at the following example, which illustrates three different figures of profit being thrown up for a company.

## 31.6 A worked example

A company has only one class of share capital. Its net assets on 1 January 2018 were £1,000 and on 31 December 2018 they are £1,400. There have been no issues or withdrawal of share capital during the year. The general rate of inflation, as measured by the retail price index, is 10%, whereas the specific rate of price increase for the type of goods in which the company deals is 15%. The profits for the three measures are as follows:

| | *(a)* *Money maintenance of capital* | *(b)* *Real capital maintenance* | *(c)* *Maintenance of specific purchasing power* |
|---|---|---|---|
| | £ | £ | £ |
| Net assets 31 Dec 2018 | 1,400 | 1,400 | 1,400 |
| *Less* What net assets would have to be at 31 Dec 2018 to be as well off on 1 Jan 2018 | | | |
| (*a*) Money maintenance | (1,000) | | |
| (*b*) Real capital £1,000 + 10% | | (1,100) | |
| (*c*) Specific purchasing power maintenance £1,000 + 15% | | | (1,150) |
| Profit | 400 | 300 | 250 |

Note that under the three methods:

(*a*) here the normal accounting method gives £400 profit;
(*b*) this case recognises that there has been a fall in the purchasing power of money;
(*c*) this takes into account that it would cost £1,150 for goods whose value at the start of the year was £1,000.

## 31.7 Combinations of different values and capital maintenance concepts

We have just looked at three ways of calculating profits based on historical cost allied with three capital maintenance concepts. This can be extended by using replacement cost or net realisable value instead. Each of these, when adjusted by each capital maintenance concept, will give three separate figures for profit. Together the three different means of valuation, multiplied by three different concepts of capital maintenance, will give us nine different profit figures.

At this stage in your studies it will be difficult to understand how such different profit measures could be useful for different purposes. We can leave this until your studies progress to more advanced examinations. However, we can use one simple example to illustrate how using only the traditional way of calculating profits can have dire consequences.

## 31.8 Another worked example

A company has net assets on 1 January 2017 of £100,000 financed purely by equity share capital. During 2017 there has been no injection or withdrawal of capital. At 31 December 2017 net assets have risen to £115,000. Both the retail price index and the specific price index for the goods dealt in have risen by 25%. Taxation, based on traditional historical cost calculations (maintenance of money capital), is at the rate of 40%. The profit may be calculated as follows.

| | *Maintenance of money capital* | *Maintenance of real capital and of specific purchasing power* |
|---|---|---|
| | £ | £ |
| Net assets on 31 Dec 2017 | 115,000 | 115,000 |
| *Less* Net assets needed to be as well off at 31 Dec 2017 as with £100,000 on 1 Jan 2017 | | |
| (*a*) Money capital | (100,000) | |
| (*b*) Both real capital and specific purchasing power £100,000 + 25% | | (125,000) |
| Profit/loss | 15,000 | (10,000) |

Tax payable is £15,000 × 40% = £6,000. Yet the real capital or that of specific purchasing power has fallen by £10,000. When tax is paid, that would leave us with net assets of £115,000 − £6,000 = £109,000. Because of price changes, £109,000 could not finance the amount of activity financed by £100,000 one year before. The operating capacity of the company, therefore, would be reduced.

Obviously, it is not equitable for a company to have to pay tax on what is in fact a loss. It is only the traditional way of measuring profits that has thrown up a profit figure.

## 31.9 Operating capital maintenance concept

This approach looks at the output that could be generated by the initial holding of assets. A profit will only be made if the assets held at the end of the period are able to maintain the same level of output.

A simple example of this is that of a newspaper seller who sells newspapers on a street corner. The only costs the newspaper seller incurs are those of buying the newspapers. No other products are sold and the newspaper seller has no assets apart from the newspapers. In this case the operating capital consists solely of newspapers.

Under historical cost, a newspaper seller will recognise a profit if the revenue from the sale of newspapers is greater than the historical cost of the newspapers. Using the operating capital maintenance concept, the newspaper seller will recognise a profit only if the revenue from the sale is greater than the cost of buying the newspapers to replace the newspapers sold.

## 31.10 Summary

You should now be aware that there are a large number of alternative ways in which wealth can be measured. Accounting has tended always to use the simplest: historical cost. However, there have been occasions – during periods of high inflation, for example – when another method has been used. Another exception to historical cost is that net realisable value and replacement cost are both used when businesses need to value their unsold goods for resale at the end of periods.

In any consideration of asset valuation and wealth measurement, it is important to remember why the calculations are being made. At the end of the day, the reason is that the users of the accounting information wish them to be done in order to provide the financial information they need.

# Part II ACCOUNTING FOR CHANGING PRICE LEVELS

## 31.11 Background

As you have seen already in this chapter, changes in price levels can lead to both profit and asset valuation figures being far from reality if the original historical cost figures are used for their statement of financial position amounts. This is not a recently observed phenomenon. As far back as 1938, Sir Ronald Edwards wrote several classic articles which were published in *The Accountant*. You can find these in the book *Studies in Accounting Theory*, edited by WT Baxter and S Davidson and published by the Institute of Chartered Accountants in England and Wales (ICAEW: London, 1977).

The greater the rate of change in price levels, the greater the distortion. The clamour for changes to simple historical cost accounting is noticeably greater when the inflation rate is high – at such times the deficiencies of historical cost financial statements are most obvious. If there were a period of deflation, however, the historical cost financial statements would still be misleading.

In certain countries the annual rate of inflation in recent years has been several hundred per cent. Historical cost financial statements in those countries would certainly be at odds with financial statements adjusted for inflation. In the UK the highest rate in recent years, based on the retail price index (RPI), was 17.8% for 1979, falling to less than 3% in recent years.

We can now look, in outline only, at suggestions made in the UK since 1968 as to methods which could be used to adjust financial statements for changing price levels.

## 31.12 Current purchasing power (CPP)

This is something you have already read about. It is the adjustment of historical cost accounting figures by a price index figure to give figures showing what was called 'real capital maintenance'. It will convey more of the problems and uncertainties facing the accounting profession in this regard, if we look at the history of the various proposals.

First came *Accounting for Stewardship in a Period of Inflation*, published in 1968 by the Research Foundation of the Institute of Chartered Accountants in England and Wales (ICAEW). Stemming from this came Exposure Draft No 8 (ED 8), published in 1973. ED 8 contained the proposal that companies should be required to publish, in addition to their conventional financial statements, supplementary statements which would be, in effect, their final financial statements amended to conform to CPP principles. In May 1974 a Provisional Statement of Standard Accounting Practice No 7 ([P]SSAP 7) was published. Notice the sign of uncertainty; it was a *provisional* standard – the only one ever published by either the Accounting Standards Committee (ASC) or the Accounting Standards Board (ASB). Compared with ED 8, which said that a company should be *required* to publish CPP financial statements, [P]SSAP 7 simply *requested* them to publish such financial statements. Many companies did not.

[P]SSAP 7 stipulated that the price index to be used in the conversion of financial statements from historical cost should be the retail price index (RPI). However, the actual price index relating to the goods dealt in by the firm could be very different from RPI. As a result, the CPP financial statements could show values that were misleadingly unrealistic.

The exact nature of the calculations needed for CPP financial statements is not part of your syllabus, and we will not repeat the calculations here.

Many people, including the government, were completely dissatisfied with the CPP approach. After ED 8 was issued, the government set up its own committee of inquiry into inflation accounting. The chairman of the committee was Sir Francis Sandilands. The report, known as the Sandilands Report, was published in September 1975.

## 31.13 Current cost accounting (CCA)

The Sandilands Committee's approach was quite different from ED 8 and [P]SSAP 7. The committee recommended a system called *current cost accounting* (CCA). This basically approved the concept of capital maintenance as the maintenance of operating capacity.

After the Sandilands Report appeared, the accounting bodies, as represented by their own Accounting Standards Committee (ASC), abandoned their proposals in [P]SSAP 7. A working party, the Inflation Accounting Steering Group (IASG), was set up to prepare a Statement of Standard Accounting Practice based on the Sandilands Report.

This group published ED 18 *Current cost accounting* in November 1976. It was attacked by many members of the ICAEW, whose members passed, in July 1977, a resolution rejecting compulsory use of CCA. However, the government continued its support, and in November 1977 the accounting profession issued a set of interim recommendations called the Hyde Guidelines (named after the chairman of the committee). A second exposure draft, ED 24, was issued in April 1979, followed by SSAP 16 in March 1980. SSAP 16 was to last three years to permit the evaluation of the introduction of CCA. After this, ED 35 was published in July 1984.

In November 1986 the CCAB Accounting Standards Committee published its handbook, *Accounting for the Effects of Changing Prices*. At the same time presidents of five of the leading accountancy bodies issued the following statement:

> The presidents of five of the leading accountancy bodies welcome the publication by the CCAB Accounting Standards Committee of its Handbook on *Accounting for the effects of changing prices*.
>
> The presidents endorse the CCAB Accounting Standards Committee's view that, where a company's results and financial position are materially affected by changing prices, historical cost accounts alone are insufficient and that information on the effects of changing prices is important for an appreciation of the company's results and financial position. The presidents join the Accounting Standards Committee in encouraging companies to appraise and, where material, report the effects of changing prices.
>
> The five bodies have proposed that SSAP 16, 'Current cost accounting', which was made non-mandatory by all the CCAB bodies in June 1985, should now be formally withdrawn. They take the view, however, that the subject of accounting for the effects of changing prices is one of great importance. Accordingly, they support the Accounting Standards Committee in its continuing work on the subject and agree that an acceptable accounting standard should be developed.
>
> *The Institute of Chartered Accountants in England and Wales; The Institute of Chartered Accountants of Scotland; The Institute of Chartered Accountants in Ireland; The Chartered Institute of Management Accountants; The Chartered Institute of Public Finance and Accountancy.*

So, once again, the idea of forcing companies to produce financial statements adjusted for changing prices was rejected. The emphasis became one of encouragement, rather than trying to force companies to do it.

The reason why, at this early stage in your studies, we have given you some of the history behind the efforts to compel companies to produce CCA financial statements is to illustrate the conflicts that have taken place inside and outside the accountancy profession. Opinions on the merits of CCA financial statements are widely divided, but it should be made clear at the outset that it is a controversial topic. This subject is covered in greater detail in Chapter 32.

## 31.14 Handbook on *Accounting for the Effects of Changing Prices*

We can now look at the main outline of this handbook. The ASC encouraged companies to co-operate in an attempt to produce financial statements suitable for the effects of changing price levels. In doing this it did not try to recommend any one method, or even recommend one way only of publishing the results. The handbook says that the information may be presented:

(*a*) as the main financial statements; or
(*b*) in the notes to the financial statements; or
(*c*) as information supplemental to the financial statements.

The handbook first examines the problems.

## 31.15 Problems during a period of changing price levels

Obviously, the greater the rate of change, the greater will be the problems. We can now list some of them.

1 **Fixing selling prices.** If you can change your prices very quickly, an extreme case being a market trader, this problem hardly exists. For a company setting prices which it is expected to maintain for a reasonably long period, the problems are severe. It dare not price too highly, as early demand may be reduced by an excessive price; on the other hand, the company has to guess how prices are going to change over a period so that sufficient profit is made.
2 **Financial planning.** As it is so difficult to guess how prices are going to change over a period, planning the firm's finances becomes particularly trying. Obviously, it would be better if the plans were revised frequently as conditions changed.
3 **Paying taxation and replacing assets.** We have seen earlier how, during a period of inflation, traditional historical accounting will tend to overstate profits. Such artificial profits are then taxed. Unless various supplementary tax allowances are given, the taxation paid is both excessive and more than true profits, adjusted for inflation, can bear easily. This tends to lead to companies being short of cash, too much having been taken in tax. Therefore, when assets which have risen in price have to be replaced, adequate finance may not be available.
4 **Monetary assets.** If inventories of goods are held, they will tend to rise in money terms during a period of inflation. On the other hand, holding monetary assets, e.g. cash, bank and debtors, will be counterproductive. A bank balance of £1,000 held for six months, during which the purchasing power of money has fallen 10%, will in real terms be worth only 90% of its value six months before. Similarly, in real terms, a debt of £5,000 owed continually over that same period will have seen its real value fall by 10%.
5 **Dividend distribution.** Just as it is difficult to calculate profits, so is it equally difficult to decide how much to pay as dividends without impairing the efficiency and operating capability of the company. At the same time the shareholders will be looking to payment of adequate dividends.

## 31.16 Solutions to the problems

The handbook recommends the use of one of two concepts. These will now be examined fairly briefly, in as much detail as is needed at this stage of your examinations.

### 1 Profit under the operating capital maintenance concept

This has been mentioned previously, with a simple example given of a trader buying and selling newspapers. Under this concept several adjustments are needed to the profit calculated on the historical cost basis. Each adjustment is now considered.

#### Adjustment 1: holding gains and operating gains

Nearly all companies hold fixed assets and inventories. For each of these assets the opportunity cost will bear little relationship to its historical cost. Instead it is the asset's value to the business at date of consumption, and this is usually the replacement cost of the asset.

Accordingly the historical cost profit, which was based on money capital maintenance, can be divided into two parts.

1 Current cost profit, or operating gains. This is the difference between sales revenue and the replacement cost of the assets.
2 Holding gains. This is the replacement cost of the assets less the historical cost of those assets.

For example, a company buys an asset for £1,000 on 1 January 2017. It holds it for one year and sells it for £1,600 when the replacement cost is £1,200. There has been a historical cost profit of £600. This can be analysed as in Exhibit 31.3.

### Exhibit 31.3

**Profit for 2017**

| | £ |
|---|---|
| Historical cost profit (£1,600 – £1,000) | 600 |
| *Less* Holding gain (£1,200 – £1,000) | (200) |
| Current cost profit (or operating gain) | 400 |

To put it another way, the company makes £200 historical profit by simply holding the asset from when its replacement cost (i.e. original cost) was £1,000, until the date of sale when its replacement cost was £1,200. The actual current cost profit at point of sale must reflect conditions at the date of sale, i.e. the company has sold for £1,600 something which would currently cost £1,200 to replace. The current cost profit is therefore £400.

The holding gains are often described as a 'cost of sales adjustment' (COSA).

### Adjustment 2: depreciation

Depreciation is to be adjusted to current replacement cost values. Without going into complicated examples, this means that if the historical cost of depreciation is £4,000 and the current cost of depreciation, based on current replacement cost values, is £7,000, then the adjustment should be £3,000 as follows:

| | £ |
|---|---|
| Depreciation based on historical cost | 4,000 |
| Adjustment needed to bring depreciation charge to CCA basis | 3,000 |
| CCA depreciation | 7,000 |

### Adjustment 3: monetary working capital adjustment

The monetary working capital needed to support the operating capability of the business will be affected by inflation. An adjustment will be needed to the historical profits in respect of this.

### Adjustment 4: gearing adjustment

If we borrow £1,000 now, and have to pay back exactly £1,000 in five years' time, we will gain during a period of inflation. We will be able to put the £1,000 to use at current purchasing power. In five years' time, if £1 now is worth only 60p then, we will have gained because we will only be giving up £600 of current purchasing power now. The gearing adjustment is an attempt to adjust current cost operating profits for this factor.

## 2 Statement of profit or loss based on the operating capital maintenance concept

A general idea of how such an statement of profit or loss could appear can now be shown.

**RST Ltd**
**Statement of Profit or Loss incorporating Operating Capital Maintenance Concept adjustments**

| | £ | £ |
|---|---|---|
| Profit on the historical cost basis, before interest and taxation | | 100,000 |
| *Less* Current cost operating adjustments: | | |
| (1) Holding gains (COSA) | 15,000 | |
| (2) Depreciation | 10,000 | |
| (3) Monetary working capital | 5,000 | |
| | | (30,000) |
| Current cost operating profit | | 70,000 |
| (4) Gearing adjustment | (2,000) | |
| Interest payable less receivable | 6,000 | |
| | | (4,000) |
| Current cost profit before taxation | | 66,000 |
| Taxation | | (25,000) |
| Current cost profit attributable to shareholders | | 41,000 |

*Note*: Dividends proposed are £30,000.

## 3 Profit under the financial capital maintenance concept

According to the handbook, this method is sometimes known as the 'real terms' system of accounting. The steps by which the profit is calculated can be summarised as:

(*a*) calculate shareholders' funds at the beginning of the period, based on current cost asset values; then
(*b*) restate that opening amount in terms of pounds at the end of the period, by adjusting (*a*) by the relevant change in a general price index (e.g. RPI); then
(*c*) calculate shareholders' funds at the end of the period, based on current cost values.

Assuming that there have been no introductions or withdrawals of capital, including dividends, if (*c*) is greater than (*b*) a 'real terms' profit will have been made. Otherwise a loss will have been incurred.

Allowance will have to be made in steps (*a*) to (*c*) above where there have been introductions or withdrawals of capital, or where there have been dividends.

The calculation of 'real terms' profit, as described, has been by way of comparing opening and closing statements of financial position. If, for example, the 'real terms' profit figure had been £10,000, it could in fact have been calculated as follows:

| | £ | £ |
|---|---|---|
| Historical cost profit | | 7,800 |
| *Add* Holding gains: the amount by which the current costs of the assets have increased over the period | 3,400 | |
| *Less* Inflation adjustment: the amount by which general inflation has eroded shareholders' funds | (1,200) | |
| Real holding gains | | 2,200 |
| Total real gains | | 10,000 |

The statement of financial position approach was described first, as it is probably the easier to understand in the first instance. Obviously the link between opening and closing statements of financial position can be traced to total real gains, which can also be explained using the concept of profit or loss calculation shown above.

### 4 Current cost statement of financial position

The two main differences between a current cost statement of financial position and a historical cost statement of financial position are as follows. Under current cost:

1 Assets are shown at value to the business on the date of the statement of financial position, rather than at any figure based on historical cost or at any previous revaluation.
2 Obviously the statement of financial position would not balance if asset values were altered without an amendment somewhere else. A current cost reserve account is opened, additions to historical cost account values are debited to each asset account, while a credit will be made in the current cost reserve account. Entries are also made here to complete the double entry in respect of the four adjustments in the current cost statement of profit or loss. As a result, all double entry adjustments are made in this account and so the statement of financial position will now balance.

## 31.17 IAS 29 Financial reporting in hyperinflationary economies

This standard was covered briefly in Section 11.24. So far as the basis used, when current cost is used, statement of financial position amounts are not restated before bringing them into the parent entity's currency. Current cost statement of profit or loss amounts must be restated to the period end equivalents using a general price index before bringing them into the parent entity's currency. IAS 29 indicates that current cost accounting may be used by entities operating in hyperinflationary economies. Chapter 32 describes current cost accounting in detail.

## Learning outcomes

**You should now have learnt:**

**1** That there is no one overall general theory of accounting practice.

**2** Changing price levels distort historical cost values and that various approaches have been suggested to deal with this issue.

**3** Some of the possible valuation alternatives to historical cost.

**4** The difference between current purchasing power and current cost accounting.

## Answers to activities

31.1 This isn't a problem for management accounting (which is concerned with providing information for internal use) – management and the management accountants agree on what should be produced and the management accountants do what they can to provide it. With financial accounting information, there is no such close relationship between the accountant and the user groups. There are also the legal and other regulations governing financial reports that the accountant must observe. It would not be appropriate to give all users what they want – some user groups, such as competitors, would prefer information that is sensitive to the business. At the same time, no one can foretell what information a particular user should be asking for at a given time.

31.2 This may appear to be an easy question. If you said it was £1,000 because that is what it cost, you would be correct so far as its *cost* to you was concerned, but no accountant would say that that was its *value*. It may have cost you that amount but do you really believe you could get someone else to pay you £1,000 for it? And how much would it cost to replace it? More, or less than £1,000?

31.3 CPP does not remove the problem of the 'true' cost. All it does is to assume the original historical cost was accurate and then adjust the value of the business to allow for the different timings. Also, any inaccuracies, inconsistencies, inappropriateness or other drawbacks inherent in the price index used to adjust the historical cost figures will result in a distortion of the adjusted historical cost figures.

31.4 Replacement cost rarely arrives at asset values that everyone would agree upon. It can be very subjective and can often be easy to dispute.

## Review questions

**31.1** Complete the following table by entering the appropriate valuation base in each unshaded box.

| | Entry value | Exit value |
|---|---|---|
| Past | | (shaded) |
| Present | | |
| Future | (shaded) | |

**31.2** Explain the relationship between deprival value; replacement cost; net realisable value; and economic value.

**31.3** What is the difference between current purchasing power (CCP) and current cost accounting (CCA)?

**31.4** Which groups of users of published financial statements take precedence in the development of accounting standards? Why?

chapter 32

# Current cost accounting

## Learning objectives

**After you have studied this chapter, you should be able to:**

- explain why historical cost financial statements are deficient in times of rising prices
- describe different valuation methods
- describe the purposes of specific price indices for assets and liabilities
- explain the adjustments necessary in order to convert historical costs to current costs
- prepare a current cost statement of financial position and a current cost statement of profit or loss

## Introduction

In this chapter, you'll learn more about the issues behind the development of current cost accounting which were outlined in Chapter 31; and of how to prepare current cost financial statements. There is no international accounting standard that describes a method which could be applied, though IAS 29 (*Financial reporting in hyperinflationary economies*) makes it clear that current cost accounting is an acceptable basis for financial statements of individual entities operating in a hyperinflationary environment. An indicator of the existence of such an environment is where cumulative inflation over a three-year period is approaching or exceeds 100%.

## 32.1 Background

Financial statements have traditionally been prepared for two main purposes, stewardship and decision-making. The IASB's *Framework for the Preparation and Presentation of Financial Statements* lists several user groups with varying needs, all of whom are interested in financial information. Shareholders are interested in different information than trade creditors. This information has traditionally been provided by financial statements prepared under the historical cost convention. However, there are circumstances when financial statements prepared under this traditional approach can present financial information in a misleading way.

Consider the following example. On 1 January 2017, a company buys 500 widgets for £1,000, i.e. £2 per widget. Shortly before the year end, when the replacement cost of a widget is £2.20, the widgets are sold for £1,200. On a historical cost basis, the profit is recorded as follows:

| | £ |
|---|---|
| Sales | 1,200 |
| Cost of sales | (1,000) |
| Profit | 200 |

However, in order to maintain the same operating capacity, the company will need to invest in more widgets at a cost of £1,100 (500 • £2.20). If the company distributes the £200 as a dividend, it will only be left with £1,000 and cannot make this investment.

**Activity 32.1**

**If you replaced the £1,000 cost of the widgets in the above calculation of profit with the £1,100 it will cost to replace it, does it remind you of any of the alternatives to historical cost accounting you learnt about in Chapter 31?**

From this simple example, one of the major criticisms of historical cost accounting is evident – its inability to reflect the effects of changing prices. Obviously, this criticism is dependent upon the level of inflation at the time.

An acceptable alternative to historical cost accounting has been sought by the accountancy profession in the UK for several years. The attempts of the Accounting Standards Committee (ASC) to introduce a system of inflation accounting, which are outlined in Chapter 31, failed.

The culmination of great effort and numerous exposure drafts and standards was the ASC handbook, *Accounting for the Effects of Changing Prices,* published in 1986. In Chapter 31, you started looking at some of the aspects covered in the handbook. In this chapter, we'll consider several of the issues dealt with in the handbook in the context of the preparation of a set of current cost accounts.

## 32.2 Valuation

Under historical cost accounting, assets and liabilities are recorded at their actual cost at the date of transaction. For example, when a new machine is purchased, the price per the invoice can be recorded in the books of the business. While this is a familiar and reasonably cheap method of recording the assets and liabilities of an entity, its main advantage is its objectivity. The historical cost of an item is an objective, verifiable fact that can easily be ascertained from the records of the business.

It is worth remembering that there is an element of subjectivity in the preparation of historical cost financial statements. Consider, for example, the choice of suitable depreciation method for an asset which is left to the discretion of the directors of the company. The size of the allowance for doubtful debts is also dependent upon the exercise of judgement. Notwithstanding this, it is fair to say that historical values have a high degree of reliability.

**Activity 32.2**

**Apart from the subjectivity in some of the adjustments made to the original figures, such as for depreciation, if you were asked for the main disadvantage of historical cost accounting, especially in times of rising prices, what would you say it was?**

Current value accounting considers the following valuation methods which were covered in Chapter 31: economic value, value to the business (i.e. deprival value), replacement cost, net realisable value and recoverable amount.

To recap what you learnt in Chapter 31, the *economic value* of an asset is the sum of the future expected net cash flows associated with the asset, discounted to its present value. The value to the business, or *deprival value*, can be considered an appropriate valuation basis for accounting purposes. If a business is deprived of an asset, it can either replace it, or choose not to. If the asset is replaced, then its current value to the business is its net current *replacement cost*. This is normally the current cost of a non-current asset, except where it has suffered a permanent diminution in value, in which case it will be written down to its *recoverable amount*. This may happen, for example, because there is no longer a market for the product the asset (e.g. equipment) is used to create. Alternatively, if the business chooses not to replace the asset which has diminished in value, it could sell it and its current cost becomes its *net realisable value*, i.e. the price at which it can be sold.

How are these values determined by a business? The replacement cost of an asset can be approximated using a relevant index. Indices published, for example, by the UK Government Statistical Service, are usually specific to a class of asset. A company may prepare its own index based on experience. The index will indicate the change in value of the asset or class of asset. Where it is not appropriate to use an index, a valuer may be relied upon. This is normal practice, for example, when revaluing property.

Consider the following example. A machine was purchased on 1 January 2015 for £75,000 when the relevant specific price index was 90. Its current value at 31 December 2017, when the relevant specific price index is 120, is:

$$\frac{\text{Index at accounting date}}{\text{Index at date of purchase}} \times £75{,}000 = \frac{120}{90} \times £75{,}000 = £100{,}000$$

Replacement does not necessarily mean replacement of the asset with a similar asset. Rather, it focuses on replacement of the service potential of the asset and its contribution to the business.

Net realisable value is the price at which the asset could be sold in an arm's-length transaction. A problem may arise where no market exists for the asset. The main problem with current values is the level of subjectivity involved in ascertaining valuations. A business may need to spend considerable time and effort ascertaining current values for its assets and liabilities.

Let's now look in detail at the principles of current cost accounting.

## 32.3 Current cost financial statements

In order to prepare current cost financial statements, a number of adjustments to the historical cost figures must be made. Specifically, **adjustments are needed relating to:**

- **non-current assets**
- **depreciation**
- **inventory**
- **cost of sales**
- **monetary working capital**
- **gearing.**

**Other than the gearing adjustment, no adjustment is made to monetary assets, such as accounts receivable, bank and cash, or to monetary liabilities such as accounts payable or long-term loans.**

We shall use Hillcrest Ltd to show how these adjustments are made.

The directors of Hillcrest Ltd are interested in preparing current cost accounts to reflect changing prices. They have prepared a historical cost statement of financial position and statement of profit or loss (Exhibit 32.1). The relevant price indices for plant and machinery, inventory, accounts receivable and accounts payable, are given in Exhibit 32.2.

## Exhibit 32.1

**Hillcrest Ltd**
**Statement of Financial Position as at 30 June (£000)**

| | | 2018 | | 2017 |
|---|---|---|---|---|
| *Non-current assets* | | | | |
| Plant and machinery | | | | |
| Cost | | 800 | | 800 |
| Depreciation | | (320) | | (240) |
| Net book value | | 480 | | 560 |
| *Current assets* | | | | |
| Inventory | 250 | | 200 | |
| Trade accounts receivable | 180 | | 110 | |
| Cash | 105 | 535 | 75 | 385 |
| | | 1,015 | | 945 |
| *Current liabilities* | | | | |
| Trade accounts payable | 90 | | 100 | |
| *Non-current liabilities* | | | | |
| 10% loan notes | 310 | | 310 | |
| | | (400) | | (410) |
| | | 615 | | 535 |
| *Equity* | | | | |
| Ordinary shares | | 200 | | 200 |
| Reserves | | 415 | | 335 |
| | | 615 | | 535 |

**Hillcrest Ltd**
**Statement of Profit or Loss for year ending 30 June 2018 (£000)**

| | | |
|---|---|---|
| Revenues | | 1,700 |
| Cost of sales | | |
| Opening inventory | 200 | |
| Purchases | 1,375 | |
| | 1,575 | |
| *Less* Closing inventory | (250) | |
| | | (1,325) |
| Gross profit | | 375 |
| Depreciation | 80 | |
| Other expenses | 184 | |
| | | (264) |
| Operating profit | | 111 |
| Interest | | (31) |
| Profit for the year | | 80 |

## Exhibit 32.2

*Price index for inventory at the end of each month:*

| | | |
|---|---|---|
| March | 2017 | 109 |
| April | 2017 | 112 |
| June | 2017 | 114 |
| December | 2017 | 116 |
| March | 2018 | 122 |
| April | 2018 | 126 |
| June | 2018 | 130 |
| Average for the year ending 30 June 2018 | | 126 |

| *Plant and machinery index* | | | *Accounts receivable and accounts payable index* | | |
|---|---|---|---|---|---|
| June | 2014 | 80 | June | 2017 | 110 |
| June | 2015 | 90 | June | 2018 | 200 |
| June | 2016 | 100 | | | |
| June | 2017 | 105 | | | |
| June | 2018 | 110 | Average for | 2018 | 155 |

In order to prepare current cost accounts, **the first step is to calculate current values for the assets.** Hillcrest Ltd's plant and machinery was purchased for £800,000 on 1 July 2014. The current value of the plant and machinery at 30 June 2018 is:

$$\text{Plant and machinery at cost} \times \frac{\text{Index at date of the statement of financial position}}{\text{Index at date of purchase}}$$

$$= £800{,}000 \times \frac{110}{80}$$

$$= £1{,}100{,}000$$

**The accumulated depreciation of £320,000 charged in the historical cost financial statements, representing 40% of the asset which has been consumed, is also restated.** The current value of the depreciation is:

$$£320{,}000 \times \frac{110}{80} = £440{,}000$$

On average, Hillcrest Ltd's inventory was acquired three months before the year end. Hence, its current value, rounded to the nearest £000, at 30 June 2018 is:

$$£250{,}000 \times \frac{130}{122} = £266{,}393$$

**Monetary assets, for example trade accounts receivable and cash, and monetary liabilities, including trade accounts payable, are not restated.** These items have a fixed monetary value which does not change. For example, if you borrow £1,000 today under an agreement to repay in 12 months' time, the monetary value of the amount borrowed will not change, that is you will repay £1,000. However, in times of rising prices, the market value of the amount will decrease. This gain will be dealt with later in this chapter.

## 32.4 Current cost reserve

Having revalued both plant and machinery and inventory to their current values, the following revaluation gains are recorded:

| | *Plant & machinery (£)* | *Inventory (£)* | *Total (£)* |
|---|---|---|---|
| Current book value | 660,000* | 266,393 | |
| Historical book value | (480,000) | (250,000) | |
| Surplus on revaluation | 180,000 | 16,393 | 196,393 |

***Note: At current cost less accumulated depreciation, i.e. £1,100,000 – £440,000.**

**The total gain of £196,393 is not a gain which has been realised through a transaction,** for example, sale of goods at a profit. In addition, Hillcrest Ltd cannot distribute this revaluation gain as a dividend if it wishes to maintain its operating capacity. In this example **the gain of £196,393 will be credited to a non-distributable reserve called the current cost reserve.** The statement of financial position incorporating these revaluations is shown in Exhibit 32.3:

### Exhibit 32.3

**Hillcrest Ltd**
**Statement of Financial Position (with some items restated to current cost)**
**as at 30 June 2018 (£000)**

| | | |
|---|---|---|
| *Non-current assets* | | |
| Plant and machinery | | |
| Current value | | 1,100 |
| Depreciation | | (440) |
| Net book value | | 660 |
| *Current assets* | | |
| Inventory | 266 | |
| Accounts receivable | 180 | |
| Cash | 105 | 551 |
| | | 1,211 |
| *Current liabilities* | | |
| Trade creditors | 90 | |
| *Non-current liabilities* | | |
| 10% loan notes | 310 | |
| | | (400) |
| | | 811 |
| *Equity* | | |
| Ordinary shares | | 200 |
| Reserves | | 415 |
| Current cost reserve | | 196 |
| | | 811 |

**Exhibit 32.3, however, does not incorporate the effect of changing prices on the profit for the year.** The reserves figure of £415,000 includes historical cost profit of £80,000 for the year ended 30 June 2018. We will now consider adjustments necessary in order to calculate the current cost profit for Hillcrest Ltd for the year.

## 32.5 Cost of sales adjustment

In calculating the profit for an accounting period, the cost of the goods sold (or cost of sales) is charged against sales. In Exhibit 32.1, sales of £1,700,000 are recorded at their invoiced prices during the year to 30 June 2018. Likewise, purchases of £1,375,000 are recorded at their actual cost prices during the year. If we assume that activity occurs evenly throughout the year, a reasonable assumption unless trade is seasonal, then these figures will reflect the average prices for the period. The opening and closing inventory valuations, in times of rising prices, will not reflect average prices under the historical cost convention. It is therefore necessary to adjust these figures in order to calculate the current cost of sales. This is carried out using an averaging method.

Using the price index for inventory, the current cost of sales for Hillcrest Ltd is:

| | | £ |
|---|---|---|
| Opening inventory at average prices: £200,000 × $\frac{130}{109}$ | = | 238,532 |
| Purchases (assume occur evenly through year) | = | 1,375,000 |
| | | 1,613,532 |
| Closing inventory at average prices: £250,000 × $\frac{130}{122}$ | = | (266,393) |
| Current cost of sales | = | 1,347,139 |

The cost of sales adjustment is the difference between the current cost of sales of £1,347,139 and the historical cost of sales of £1,325,000, i.e. £22,139. This is charged to the historical cost statement of profit or loss as an adjustment in order to arrive at the current cost profit. A corresponding amount will be credited to the current cost reserve.

## 32.6 Depreciation adjustment

**Depreciation charged to profit and loss should be based on the value of the asset as stated in the statement of financial position. Hence, an adjustment is necessary where depreciation has been based on the historical cost of a non-current asset.**

Consider the following example in which the depreciation charge is based on the value of the asset at the year end. A non-current asset is purchased on 1 January 2016 for £10,000 when the relevant price index is 100. It is planned to depreciate this asset on a straight line basis at 20% per annum. At the end of 2016, when the index has moved to 110, the current value of the asset is:

$$£10{,}000 \times \frac{110}{100} = £11{,}000$$

and depreciation based on current cost of the asset is:

$$£10{,}000 \times \frac{110}{100} \times 20\% = £2{,}200$$

The net book value of the asset as stated in the current cost statement of financial position is:

| | £ |
|---|---|
| Asset at current value | 11,000 |
| Accumulated depreciation | (2,200) |
| | 8,800 |

At the end of 2017 the relevant index is 120, and the current value of the asset is:

$$£10{,}000 \times \frac{120}{100} = £12{,}000$$

and the depreciation charge based on current cost is:

$$£10{,}000 \times \frac{120}{100} \times 20\% = £2{,}400$$

Hence, at the end of 2017, the net book value of the asset in the current cost statement of financial position is:

| | £ |
|---|---|
| Asset at current value | 12,000 |
| Accumulated depreciation | (4,600) |
| | 7,400 |

While 40% of the value of the asset has been consumed at 31 December 2017, it is noted that £4,600 is not 40% of £12,000. This is due to an undercharge of £200 depreciation in 2016 in current value terms. **As the original cost of the asset is altered to reflect current values, the aggregate depreciation must also be adjusted.**

The term given to depreciation relating to earlier years is '*backlog depreciation*'. Backlog depreciation is not charged against this period's profit. As we saw in the Hillcrest example, only an adjustment for this year's depreciation is charged against profit. **Backlog depreciation is charged to the current cost reserve.**

For Hillcrest Ltd, depreciation charged at 10% on the current value of the plant and machinery of £1,100,000 is £110,000. Comparing this with the historical cost depreciation charge in the historical cost statement of profit or loss of £80,000 gives an additional, i.e. backlog depreciation adjustment of £30,000. This is a charge in arriving at current cost profit for the year, the corresponding credit going to the current cost reserve.

## 32.7 Monetary working capital adjustment

The effect of changing prices on inventory values has already been considered. In addition, during inflationary periods, the market value of monetary assets, e.g. trade accounts receivable, trade accounts payable and cash, will change. In order for a business to maintain its operating capacity, this change needs to be reflected in the financial statements. **The monetary working capital adjustment represents the increase (or decrease) in finance necessary to provide an appropriate level of monetary working capital due to price changes, rather than a change in the volume of working capital.**

Cash is usually excluded from the calculation as the amount of cash held by a business may not relate to its operating activities. For example, cash may be held in order to make a capital investment. However, in the case of a bank, cash balances which are required to support daily operations are included in the **monetary working capital adjustment.**

**Calculation of the monetary working capital adjustment is similar to the calculation of the cost of sales adjustment.**

The index for accounts receivable should reflect changes in the cost of goods or services sold which are included in accounts receivable. Likewise, the index for accounts payable should reflect changes in the cost of goods or services purchased which are included in accounts payable. A single index may be appropriate, and in some businesses, a fair approximation may be the index used for inventory. Consider the following example:

| | *31 December 2017* | *31 December 2018* |
|---|---|---|
| | £ | £ |
| Trade accounts receivable | 9,000 | 12,000 |
| Trade accounts payable | (7,500) | (11,000) |
| Monetary working capital | 1,500 | 1,000 |

Relevant indices applicable to the business are:

| | |
|---|---|
| 31 December 2017 | 100 |
| 31 December 2018 | 200 |
| Average for the year | 150 |

The monetary working capital at 31 December 2017 in the historical cost financial statements is £1,500 (£9,000 − £7,500). Stating this at average values for the year gives:

$$£1,500 \times \frac{150}{100} = £1,125$$

The monetary working capital at 31 December 2018 in the historical cost financial statements is £1,000 (£12,000 − £11,000). Stating this at average values for the year gives:

$$£1,000 \times \frac{150}{200} = £750$$

The historical cost financial statements show a decrease in monetary working capital over the year of £500. However, at average values for the year, the monetary working capital is reduced by £375 (£1,125 − £750).

**What does the difference between the change under the historical cost convention and under the current cost convention of £1,000 (£1,500 − £500) – the monetary working capital adjustment – represent?**

Now, let's do the same thing for Hillcrest Ltd. The monetary working capital adjustment is calculated as follows:

| | *2018* | *2017* |
|---|---|---|
| | £ | £ |
| Trade accounts receivable | 180,000 | 110,000 |
| Trade accounts payable | (90,000) | (100,000) |
| Net monetary working capital | 90,000 | 10,000 |

Hence, the increase in monetary working capital in historical cost terms is £80,000 (£90,000 − £10,000).

Restating opening monetary working capital at average prices gives (to the nearest £000):

$$£10,000 \times \frac{155}{110} = £14,000$$

The value of closing monetary working capital at average prices is (to the nearest £000):

$$£90,000 \times \frac{155}{200} = £70,000$$

The increase in monetary working capital which is due to change in volume is £56,000 (£70,000 − £14,000). The increase due to price changes – the monetary working capital adjustment – is £24,000 (£80,000 − £56,000).

## 32.8 Current cost operating profit

Hillcrest Ltd's current cost operating profit for the year ending 30 June 2018, having applied the above adjustments, is given in Exhibit 32.4.

**Exhibit 32.4**

**Hillcrest Ltd**
**Current Cost Operating Profit for year ending 30 June 2018 (£000)**

| | | |
|---|---|---|
| Sales | | 1,700 |
| Net profit | | 80 |
| *Add* Interest | | 31 |
| | | 111 |
| *Adjustments* | | |
| Cost of sales adjustment | 22 | |
| Monetary working capital adjustment | 24 | |
| Additional depreciation adjustment | 30 | |
| | | (76) |
| Current cost operating profit | | 35 |

From the point of view of a business and maintenance of its operating capacity, the current cost operating profit is relevant. However, maintenance of financial capital is also relevant where a business is not financed solely by equity. In this case, account should be taken of the capital structure of the business.

## 32.9 Gearing adjustment

If a company is financed by debt, and prices increase, whilst the monetary value of the loan has not changed, the market value has reduced. This gain for shareholders is recorded by making a gearing adjustment. The gearing adjustment is calculated in the following way.

**Firstly, a gearing proportion is calculated:**

$$\text{Average net borrowings for the year (L)} : \text{Shareholders' interest (S)} + \text{L}$$

For Hillcrest Ltd, its net borrowings for the two years to 30 June 2018 are:

| | *2018* | *2017* |
|---|---|---|
| | £ | £ |
| Loan notes | 310,000 | 310,000 |
| Cash | (105,000) | (75,000) |
| Net borrowing | 205,000 | 235,000 |

Hence, average net borrowings for the year to 30 June 2018 are:

$$\frac{£205{,}000 + £235{,}000}{2} = £220{,}000$$

Shareholders' interest for both years are:

| | *2018* | *2017* |
|---|---|---|
| | £ | £ |
| Ordinary shares | 200,000 | 200,000 |
| Reserves | 415,000 | 335,000 |
| | 615,000 | 535,000 |

Average shareholders' interest (S) for the year to 30 June 2018 is:

$$\frac{£615,000 + £535,000}{2} = £575,000$$

The gearing proportion is:

$$\frac{L}{L + S} = \frac{£220,000}{£220,000 + £575,000} = 27.67\%$$

**To calculate the gearing adjustment, this proportion is applied to the sum of the current cost adjustments for the year, that is:**

| | £ |
|---|---|
| Cost of sales adjustment | 23,000 |
| Depreciation adjustment | 30,000 |
| Monetary working capital adjustment | 24,000 |
| | 77,000 |

The gearing adjustment for Hillcrest Ltd (to the nearest £000) is:

$$27.67\% \times £77,000 = £21,000$$

Exhibit 32.5 shows the current cost reserve having made the above adjustments:

## Exhibit 32.5

| Current cost reserve | *£000* |
|---|---|
| Surplus on revaluation of plant and machinery | 180 |
| Additional depreciation adjustment | 30 |
| Surplus on revaluation of inventory | 16 |
| Cost of sales adjustment | 22 |
| Monetary working capital adjustment | 24 |
| Gearing adjustment | (21) |
| Balance at 30 June 2018 | 251 |

The current cost profit for the year ending 30 June 2018 is given in Exhibit 32.6:

## Exhibit 32.6

**Hillcrest Ltd**
**Current cost Statement of Profit or Loss for year ending 30 June 2018**

| | | *£000* |
|---|---|---|
| Sales | | 1,700 |
| Trading profit (after adding back interest) | | 111 |
| *Adjustments* | | |
| Cost of sales adjustment | 22 | |
| Monetary working capital adjustment | 24 | |
| Additional depreciation adjustment | 30 | |
| | | (76) |
| Current cost operating profit | | 35 |
| Gearing adjustment | 21 | |
| *Less* Interest payable | (31) | |
| | | (10) |
| Current cost profit | | 25 |

The statement of financial position for Hillcrest Ltd for 30 June 2018, based on current costs, is given in Exhibit 32.7.

## Exhibit 32.7

**Hillcrest Ltd**
**Current Cost Statement of Financial Position as at 30 June 2018**

| | | £000 |
|---|---|---|
| *Non-current assets* | | |
| Plant and machinery | | |
| Cost | | 1,100 |
| Depreciation | | (440) |
| Net book value | | 660 |
| *Current assets* | | |
| Inventory | 266 | |
| Accounts receivable | 180 | |
| Cash | 105 | 551 |
| | | 1,211 |
| *Current liabilities* | | |
| Trade accounts payable | 90 | |
| *Non-current liabilities* | | |
| 10% loan notes | 310 | |
| | | (400) |
| | | 811 |
| *Equity* | | |
| Ordinary shares | | 200 |
| Reserves (335 + 25) | | 360 |
| Current cost reserve | | 251 |
| | | 811 |

## Learning outcomes

**You should now have learnt:**

1. During inflationary periods, one of the main criticisms of historical cost accounting is its inability to reflect changing prices.
2. Deprival value is a suitable valuation basis for accounting purposes.
3. One of the major difficulties with current cost accounting is the level of subjectivity which can be involved in converting historical costs to current costs.
4. Relevant price indices, specific to an asset or class of assets, can approximate replacement cost.
5. The purpose of the cost of sales adjustment is to restate historical cost of sales in current cost terms by including opening and closing inventory at average prices.
6. The depreciation adjustment ensures that the depreciation charge in the current cost statement of profit or loss is based on the current value of the asset as stated in the current cost statement of financial position.
7. The monetary working capital adjustment reflects the change in the market value of monetary assets and liabilities, usually trade accounts receivable and trade accounts payable, in the current cost financial statements.

8 Gains or losses for shareholders, which arise due to debt financing in times of changing prices, are accounted for in the gearing adjustment.

9 Surpluses and deficits on revaluations are credited or charged to the current cost reserve, which is a non-distributable reserve.

## Answers to activities

32.1 Substituting the £1,100 it would cost to replace the inventory in place of the £1,000 the inventory cost would produce a profit of £100. This is an example of the concept of 'maintenance of specific purchasing power' you learnt about in Section 31.5.

32.2 The main disadvantage of historical cost accounting, particularly in times of changing prices, is its relevance to decision-making. This was demonstrated in the widget example in the previous section, when any business that relied purely on the historical cost-based profit calculation to determine how much profit was available for distribution could find it impossible to replace all the inventory it had sold.

32.3 The change in working capital due to price changes during the year.

## Review questions

**32.1** State whether you consider the following statements to be true or false:

(*a*) During inflationary periods, historical cost financial statements do not reflect a true and fair view.
(*b*) The preparation of historical cost financial statements does not involve subjectivity.
(*c*) Current cost accounting involves estimating future events.
(*d*) An index number must relate to a specific asset in order to be useful in converting historical cost accounts to current cost accounts.
(*e*) Where no market exists for an asset, conversion from historical cost to current cost can be difficult.

**32.2A** State whether you consider the following statements to be true or false:

(*a*) The current cost of plant and machinery is likely to be its net realisable value.
(*b*) A company should distribute dividends from the current cost reserve.
(*c*) The market value of a monetary asset, for example trade accounts receivable, will decrease during inflationary periods.
(*d*) A gearing adjustment is necessary where a company is financed solely by equity capital.
(*e*) Backlog depreciation is charged to the current cost reserve.

**32.3A** What are the practical difficulties a company may encounter in ascertaining the current values of its assets?

**32.4** Plant and equipment was purchased on 1 January 2016 for £64,000, when the relevant specific price index was 80. What is the current cost value of the asset at 31 December 2017 if the index at that date is 120?

**32.5A** The plant and equipment, details of which are given in Question 32.4, is depreciated on a straight line basis at 12% per annum. The depreciation charge is based on year-end values. What is the current cost depreciation charge for the year ended 31 December 2018, if the index at that date is 180?

**32.6** Calculate backlog depreciation at 31 December 2018 for the plant and equipment, the details of which are given in Question 32.5A.

**32.7A** A company purchased equipment on 1 January 2017 for £120,000, at which date the relevant price index for equipment was 100. Depreciation is charged on a straight line basis at 20% per annum. The index at 31 December 2017 had moved to 160, and at 31 December 2018 it was 200. Show the current cost statement of financial position entries for equipment at 31 December 2017 and 31 December 2018. Calculate the adjustments to the current cost reserve in respect of equipment.

**32.8** The historical cost of sales figure for Lemon Ltd for the year ended 31 December 2016 is calculated as follows:

| | £ |
|---|---|
| Opening inventory | 100,000 |
| Purchases | 800,000 |
| | 900,000 |
| Closing inventory | (150,000) |
| Cost of sales | 750,000 |

Price indices for inventory are as follows:

| | |
|---|---|
| Index at date of purchase of opening inventory | 70 |
| Index at date of purchase of closing inventory | 110 |
| Average index for 2016 | 90 |
| Index at 31 December 2016 | 120 |

**Required:**
Assuming that purchases occur evenly throughout the year, calculate the cost of sales adjustment for Lemon Ltd for 2016.

**32.9A** The statement of financial position of Aberdeen Ltd at 31 December shows the following balances:

| | *31 December 2017* | *31 December 2016* |
|---|---|---|
| | £ | £ |
| Trade accounts receivable | 60,000 | 50,000 |
| Trade accounts payable | 40,000 | 38,000 |

The relevant price indices for trade accounts receivable and trade accounts payable are:

| | |
|---|---|
| 31 December 2016 | 110 |
| 31 December 2017 | 170 |
| Average for the year ending 31 December 2017 | 140 |

**Required:**
Using the above information, calculate the monetary working capital adjustment at 31 December 2017 for Aberdeen Ltd.

**32.10** If the relevant price indices for trade accounts receivable and trade accounts payable are as follows, calculate the monetary working capital adjustment for Aberdeen Ltd, using the details given in Question 32.9A.

| | |
|---|---|
| 31 December 2016 | 220 |
| 31 December 2017 | 260 |
| Average for the year ending 31 December 2017 | 250 |

**32.11A** The information given below has been extracted from the accounting records of Beechgrove Ltd for the year ending 30 June 2017. Prepare a statement showing the current cost operating profit to 30 June 2017.

| | £ |
|---|---|
| Revenue | 4,000,000 |
| Historical cost operating profit | 2,600,000 |
| *Current cost adjustments* | |
| Additional depreciation adjustment | 800,000 |
| Cost of sales adjustment | 1,050,000 |
| Monetary working capital adjustment | 44,000 |

→

**32.12** The statement of financial position for Glencoe Ltd at 31 December is given below (£000):

| | *2016* | | *2015* | |
|---|---|---|---|---|
| *Non-current assets* | | | | |
| Plant and equipment | | | | |
| Cost | | 960 | | 960 |
| Depreciation | | (384) | | (192) |
| | | 576 | | 768 |
| *Current assets* | | | | |
| Inventory | 252 | | 156 | |
| Accounts receivable | 120 | | 72 | |
| Cash | 174 | 546 | 60 | 288 |
| | | 1,122 | | 1,056 |
| *Current liabilities* | | | | |
| Trade accounts payable | 96 | | 72 | |
| *Non-current liabilities* | | | | |
| 10% loan notes | 240 | | 240 | |
| | | (336) | | (312) |
| | | 786 | | 744 |
| *Financed by*: | | | | |
| Ordinary shares | | 300 | | 300 |
| Reserves | | 444 | | 408 |
| Current cost reserve | | 42 | | 36 |
| | | 786 | | 744 |

**Required:**
Using the above information, calculate the gearing adjustment percentage:

$$\frac{L}{L + S}$$

**32.13A** The following information has been extracted from the accounting records of Barry Bucknell Ltd for the year ended 30 June 2016.

| | £ |
|---|---|
| Revenue | 9,500,000 |
| Historical cost trading profit | 6,400,000 |
| Interest payable | 800,000 |
| Corporation tax charge for the year | 2,100,000 |
| Ordinary dividend proposed | 700,000 |
| Additional depreciation adjustment | 300,000 |
| Cost of sales adjustment | 600,000 |
| Monetary working capital adjustment | 220,000 |
| Gearing adjustment: $\frac{L}{L + S}$ | 15% |

**Required:**
Prepare a current cost statement of profit or loss for Barry Bucknell Ltd for the year ending 30 June 2016.

**32.14** During a period of inflation, many accountants believe that financial reports prepared under the historical cost convention are subject to the following major limitations:

1 inventories are undervalued;
2 depreciation is understated;
3 gains and losses on net monetary assets are undisclosed;
4 statement of financial position values are unrealistic; and
5 meaningful periodic comparisons are difficult to make.

**Required:**
Explain briefly the limitations of historical cost accounting in periods of inflation with reference to each of the items listed above.

*(Association of Accounting Technicians)*

**32.15A** You are presented with the following information relating to Messiter plc:

| **Year to 31 December** | *2017* | *2018* |
|---|---|---|
| | *£m* | *£m* |
| **Statements of profit or loss** | | |
| Revenue, all on credit terms | 1,300 | 1,400 |
| Cost of sales | 650 | 770 |
| Gross profit | 650 | 630 |
| Profit before taxation | 115 | 130 |
| **Statements of financial position at 31 December:** | | |
| Non-current assets at cost | 850 | 850 |
| *Less* Accumulated depreciation | 510 | 595 |
| Net book value | 340 | 255 |
| Inventory at cost | 105 | 135 |
| Trade accounts receivable | 142 | 190 |

**Required:**
(*a*) Using the historical cost financial statements and stating the formulae you use, calculate the following accounting ratios for both 2017 and 2018:
  (*i*) Gross profit percentage;
  (*ii*) Net profit percentage;
  (*iii*) Inventory turnover, stated in days;
  (*iv*) Trade accounts receivable collection period, stated in days; and
  (*v*) Non-current asset turnover.

(*b*) Using the following additional information:
  (*i*) Restate the turnover for 2017 and 2018 incorporating the following average retail price indices:

| | |
|---|---|
| Year to 31.12.2017 | 85 |
| Year to 31.12.2018 | 111 |

  (*ii*) Calculate the additional depreciation charge required to finance the replacement of non-current assets at their replacement cost. The company's depreciation policy is to provide 10% per annum on original cost, assuming no residual value.
  The replacement cost of non-current assets at 31 December was as follows:

| | *£ millions* |
|---|---|
| 2017 | 1,140 |
| 2018 | 1,200 |

  (*iii*) Based upon these two inflation adjustments, why may it be misleading to compare a company's results for one year with that of another without adjusting for changes in general (RPI) or specific inflation?

*(Association of Accounting Technicians)*

chapter 33

# Social and environmental reporting and integrated reporting

## Learning objectives

**After you have studied this chapter, you should be able to:**

- explain the term 'social and environmental accounting'
- describe the implications of social and environmental accounting for the accounting function
- describe some of the difficulties in the measurement of qualitative factors
- describe the conflict between social and environmental considerations and the interests of shareholders
- describe triple bottom line reporting, its benefits, and the difficulties in adopting it
- describe integrated reporting, its benefits, and the difficulties in adopting it

## Introduction

In this chapter you'll learn about some of the issues underlying the development of social accounting, of five general areas to which social and environmental accounting has traditionally been applied, and of the extent to which social and environmental reporting and integrated reporting are becoming increasingly important elements of corporate reporting.

## 33.1 Background

Over time, the objective of financial statements has changed. Initially financial statements were prepared to meet the financial information needs of investors so that they could assess the quality of the stewardship – i.e. the management of the resources – of the company in which they had invested. For a period, this extended to endeavouring to provide financial information that would be useful to all other interested groups, such as customers, suppliers, employees, trade unions, communities where the company operated, and government. However, this was never a practical option and now, under IFRS, the primary objective is to assist two specific groups in their economic decision-making: investors and creditors,

However, in addition to reporting to these two interest groups, entities are aware of a wide range of other user groups who are interested in obtaining information about them. These user groups include employees of the company, customers, government, and the public at large.

In many cases, these other groups are not interested in financial information relating to an entity's performance and financial position. Instead, they are interested in learning about the entity's policies and practices relating to the environment and to society, both locally and as a whole. They want to know if the entity is being socially and environmentally aware – if it pursues, advocates and successfully achieves sustainability of the resources it uses and affects, so that future generations may have sufficient for their needs.

The background to this lies in the many warnings that have been given over at least the past 50 years: that we are using the world's resources too quickly, that we are depleting them to a point where many will cease to exist, and that doing so is also having an impact upon our environment. Global warming, for example, was predicted many years ago as we kept burning vast quantities of fossil fuel (such as wood, coal and oil) that slowly made holes in the atmosphere, so weakening our protection against the rays of the sun.

As these predictions have slowly come to pass, so business and government have begun to shift towards embracing the need for greater social and environmental responsibility. Initially, this was typified by multinational companies that expressed their sincerity about their aim of achieving sustainability. But this was often more to do with sustainability of the business, rather than of society or the environment.

Some companies issued sustainability reports along with their annual report and many embraced the Internet to ensure that these were freely available. But reports on the social and environmental activities of an entity are typically qualitative (full of text) not quantitative (full of numbers). Accountants do not have the expertise to prepare such reports and auditors do not have the expertise to audit them. And, so, an impasse arose, one in which companies could issue these reports and did so, but without the same level of validity checking that goes into the preparation of financial reports.

Meanwhile, in 1981, it was first suggested that companies should report on three distinct aspects of performance: social, environmental and financial. In 1994, this form of reporting was first described as *triple bottom line* (TBL). And by 1997, companies such as Shell were publishing a TBL report. Unfortunately, while this was an admirable concept, for the reasons indicated above, *triple bottom line* reports did not have the impact on business practice or on stakeholder awareness that was envisaged. Consequently, these interest groups continue to seek the information they desire that will make clear what an entity's impact is upon society and the environment, and what it is doing to ensure the sustainability of the resources it uses and affects.

The latest attempt to address this by inviting business entities to report openly on these issues is integrated reporting, a topic that will be covered in Section 33.12. The rest of this chapter revisits these issues and describes the role of accounting and accountants in social and environmental reporting.

## 33.2 Difficulties in determining social and environmental costs and benefits

Many attempts have been made to attribute financial amounts to social and environmental activities and impacts. But identifying costs and measuring the effects of (often intangible) factors is difficult. At its simplest, consider how to place a value on the loyalty of an employee, or how to place a value on a commitment to quality performance. Such intangible factors cannot be measured using objective and verifiable techniques. How then do you measure the impact in long-term financial terms of cutting down a forest to build a city – the impact on the environment, on wildlife, on the atmosphere, on the quality of the life of those who lived in and around the forest? If a river is diverted to enable this to happen, these intangible impacts increase and it is still no easier to attribute financial values to the costs and benefits that arise.

**Activity 33.1** How would you value employee loyalty?

Some of the input costs of 'social' activities can be evaluated reasonably accurately. Providing some of the 'social' information required under the Companies Act 2006 is not particularly difficult. Ever since it was first issued, companies have been required to provide information about their employees in the financial statements, including numbers of employees, wages and salaries data, and details regarding the company's policy on disabled persons. Even where social and environmental disclosure was required by subsequent legislation, such as greenhouse gas emissions, these can often be costed reasonably accurately.

These costs have become a basic and essential part of financial statements. But, when they are included in the financial statements rather than solely in the *directors' report* or in the *strategic report,* net profit has clearly reduced without any clear financial benefits flowing to the business. Companies would like to be able to place appropriate values on the benefits of their social and environmental actions. But how can the benefits of controlling pollution from a factory be evaluated? It is no easier than attempting to place an appropriate value on employee loyalty. Why then should an attempt be made to evaluate these benefits? Would they not be better reported in qualitative or non-financial quantitative terms? That is what *triple bottom line* reporting sought to achieve.

Unfortunately, as soon as a company seeks to incorporate social and environmental criteria alongside other, more traditional performance measures, problems arise with objectivity, comparability and usefulness. For example, the social criteria for a paper manufacturer may include environmental issues concerning reforestation; and an oil extraction company would include the environmentally safe disposal of oil rigs at the end of their useful economic lives among its social criteria. Conventional accounting techniques are not the answer.

For example, when environmental projects are viewed using conventional capital appraisal techniques, issues of this type become problematic. Not only may the measurable financial payback period be so long as to be immaterial – as in the case of an environmental project such as reforestation – it may be virtually non-existent, as in the case of the disposal of obsolete oil rigs. Assessment of issues of this type requires different techniques from those traditionally used, and corporate information systems must take this into account, not just in terms of embracing more qualitative criteria, but also in selecting the information required to assist in the decision-making process of those for whom the information is being prepared.

Clearly, it is no simple process arriving at appropriate and valid amounts for such costs and benefits, and no solution has yet been found to make this possible. Instead, social reports and environmental reports use mixed forms of data, some quantitative and some qualitative, to produce a valid, reliable and understandable view of what has occurred and of its impact upon society and the environment. And, even before attempting to do so, organisations must consider the wishes of their stakeholders for whom any additional costs that do not bring financial benefits are intuitively undesirable: their shareholders.

## 33.3 Conflict between shareholders' interests and social considerations

Organisations that adopt socially and environmentally friendly practices do so within the context of the impact such practices will have on their shareholders. For instance, a company could treat its employees so well in terms of pay, pensions and welfare that the extra costs would mean very low profits or even losses. In such cases, a compromise is sought that satisfies those who expect the company to be socially and environmentally aware while avoiding alienating its shareholders and other investors.

However, there are instances where, no matter what the effect on profits, the expenses just have to be incurred. If, for example, a company owns a chemical plant that, if not effectively safeguarded, could explode and cause widespread destruction, then there cannot be any justification for not spending the money either to keep the plant safe or to demolish it. If the company did not do so, the legally imposed costs resulting from such an incident could cripple it and may even force it out of business.

All the facts of the particular case must be taken into account. Let's consider the case of workers in underdeveloped countries. They are usually paid far lower wages than those in developed countries. What happens if a large multinational company pays its workers in one of those countries three or four times as much as the local wage? Everyone wants to work for the multinational company. It can then take its pick of the labour force, leaving the less suitable workers to be employed by the local businesses.

Is that sensible? What chance is there for the development of the country's own home-based businesses if foreign companies constantly take all the best brains and the most able people? In such cases, it would make sense for the multinational company to pay wages similar to those in the local economy, and to help that country in other ways, such as by improving the level of health care, financing improved levels of education, and so on. But, how do you identify the social and environmental cost and benefits of either of these options?

Nevertheless, despite the inherent likelihood of shareholder resistance to spending resources on something that does not generate any immediate return, 74% of CEOs now believe that companies should engage in social and environmental reporting.

## 33.4 What has led to this change in corporate reporting?

Despite the existence of many environmental laws, much of the pressure for social actions comes from pressure groups like Greenpeace, which was founded in Canada in 1969. These groups can have an enormous impact upon an organisation's profitability, in ways that governments have singularly failed to do. For example, an air pollution law may concentrate on monitoring the quality of air around a factory, rather than on measuring emissions from the factory, making it far more difficult to enforce action against the factory – it can always argue that another factory is the cause of any pollution found.

This type of outcome is often the result of pressure from powerful cartels or less sinister 'economic interest groups' that influence the legislators, resulting in enormous delays in introducing socially and environmentally responsible legislative controls, and in their being ineffective when they are finally issued. Government fails to control the problem, but a pressure group can force the company to take action by shaming it into doing so.

**This example of ineffective legislation can be explained by one of the theories you learnt about in Chapter 30. Which one?**

Why this is so can be explained by two of the theories you learnt about in Chapter 30. Companies wish to maintain their legitimacy, to make it appear as if they are upholding their side of their social contract with their stakeholders. It sometimes does not take a lot of action by a prominent pressure group for a company's legitimacy to be called into question by some of its stakeholders. Consequently, pressure groups can ultimately cause considerable harm to an organisation that resists their demands. They can influence customers to stop buying its products, make it difficult for it to send its products to its customers, and may give it so much negative publicity that it can find its public image materially and irreversibly altered in a very short time. Clearly, this is something that companies seek to avoid. The *managerial branch of stakeholder theory* tells you that as soon as a company perceives that key stakeholders may be influenced against the company, *legitimacy theory* tells you that it will act to preserve its legitimacy: the pressure group can succeed where the Government fails.

While pressure groups are not a new phenomenon, heightened public awareness of the importance of social and environmental responsibility has made their power far greater than it has ever been. Nowadays, organisations involved in activities with social or environmental consequences need to be aware of them and in a position to assess how best to deal with them. To do so, they need to identify all the variables, both quantitative and qualitative, and both the inputs (costs) and the outputs (effects) of these variables, and determine what actions to take; and to do so before they become contentious. But, very little guidance in how to do so is available, particularly from accountants, who are ill-equipped to advise management on these qualitative issues.

Social and environmental reporting is concerned with how to report upon the application of the social and environmental policies adopted by an organisation, and upon how they have impacted upon the organisation, its environment, and society. An organisation that does so effectively will not only be providing user groups with rich information from which to form a view concerning its social ethos, it will also be enhancing its ability to take decisions appropriate for its own longer-term survival and prosperity.

## 33.5 Corporate social and environmental reporting

The reporting of the social and environmental effects of a company's activities became an issue in the UK in the 1970s. The reporting of non-financial information usually takes the form of narrative disclosure, sometimes supported by a statistical summary. As much social and environmental reporting is non-mandatory, comparison with other companies is difficult, if not pointless and misleading. This is partially due to a positive bias in what is reported – most companies have tended to report only 'good news' in their social reports. It is also due to the lack of standards governing what to include and how to present social reports.

Environmental issues have been firmly on the political agenda since the early 1980s and large corporations have responded to public demands for more information about 'green issues'. Oil companies, in particular, produce a notable amount of additional information in their annual reports. This environmental information usually includes details about the company's waste disposal practices and attitudes towards pollution and natural resource depletion, as well as the overall corporate environmental policy. However, many continue to avoid any non-mandatory social reporting, and many instances have been reported of organisations claiming to be socially responsible when they were, in fact, anything but. However, this is beginning to change.

### Government intervention

In 2001, all companies listed on the Paris stock exchange were required to prepare triple bottom line reports. The UK was much slower. In 2002, the Government made the inclusion of a *Directors' Remuneration Report* compulsory for all quoted companies. Then, in 2003, it announced that all listed companies would need to include an Operating and Financial Review in their annual reports from January 2005. In November 2005, this statutory requirement was removed, with effect from January 2006.

While this false start set back the move towards a greater amount of corporate social and environmental reporting in the UK, from October 2008 UK listed companies were required to prepare an *Enhanced Business Review* and include it within their *Directors' Report*. The review was intended to allow *shareholders* to make an informed assessment of the performance and prospects of the company and it included information on environmental, employment, social and community issues and the main factors likely to affect the company's future business. **It was not, however, intended to be used to report in detail on corporate social and environmental issues that might be of interest to other stakeholder groups.** It was a step forward, but not one that met the needs of those most likely to wish to know what a company was doing with respect to its social and environmental responsibilities.

In 2012, the UK became the first country to make it compulsory for companies to report on their greenhouse gas emissions as part of their annual Directors' Report. However, a far greater change occurred in 2013 when the 2006 Companies Act was amended to require all but the smallest companies to include a *Strategic Report* in their annual reports.

The *Strategic Report* contains all the items previously included in the *Business Review* section of the *Directors' Report*. It must present a fair review of the company's business and a description of the principal risks it faces. Furthermore, to enable an understanding of the development, performance or position of the business, it must include an analysis based upon key performance indicators (KPIs), both financial and non-financial where appropriate. As you will see when you read Section 33.12, this represents a huge step towards embracing the concepts of integrated reporting.

### Social accounting

How then have social and environmental issues typically been presented up until now? They have often been presented under the banner of 'social accounting' rather than 'social and environmental accounting', though environmental issues are just as relevant to what is being reported. Social accounting can be divided into five general areas:

(*a*) national social income accounting;
(*b*) social auditing;
(*c*) financial social accounting in profit-oriented organisations;
(*d*) managerial social accounting in profit-oriented organisations;
(*e*) financial and/or managerial social accounting for non-profit organisations.

## 33.6 National social income accounting

National social income accounts have now been in existence for many years. The measure of the nation's productivity recorded in the accounts – basically in sales terms – gives an income called the gross national product, usually referred to as GNP.

To an outsider, an increase in GNP would seem to indicate a betterment or progress in the state of affairs existing in the country. This is not necessarily so. The following example illustrates this point.

A new chemical factory is built in a town. Fumes are emitted during production which cause houses in the surrounding areas to suffer destruction of paintwork and rotting woodwork, and it also causes extensive corrosion of bodywork on motor vehicles in the neighbourhood. In addition it also affects the health of the people living nearby. An increase in GNP results because the profit elements in the above add to GNP. These profit elements include:

- to construction companies and suppliers of building materials: profit made on construction of plant;
- to house paint dealers and paint manufacturers, painters and decorators, joiners and carpenters: profit made on all work effected in extra painting, woodwork, etc.;
- to garages and car paint manufacturers: profit made on all extra work needed on motor vehicles;
- to chemists and medical requirement manufacturers: profit made on dealing with effects on residents' health, because of extra medical purchases, etc.

However, in real terms one can hardly say that there has been progress. Obviously, the quality of life has been seriously undermined for many people.

As national income accounts do not record the 'social' well-being of a country, other national measures have been proposed. The one most often mentioned is a system of 'social indicators'. These measure social progress in such ways as:

- national life expectancies
- living conditions
- levels of disease
- nutritional levels
- amount of crime
- road deaths.

Thus, if national life expectancies rose, or road deaths per 100,000 people decreased, there could be said to be social progress, while the converse would apply were the opposite signals found to be occurring.

The main difficulty with this approach is that (given present knowledge and techniques) it cannot be measured in monetary terms. Because of this, the national social income accounts cannot be adjusted to take account of social indicators. On the level of an individual organisation, however, social indicators similar to the above are used in Planning, Programming, Budgeting Systems (PPBS). This will be discussed in more detail in Section 33.10.

## 33.7 Social auditing

While national social accounting would measure national social progress, many individuals and organisations are interested in their own social progress. This form of social progress is usually called 'social responsibility'.

To identify activities to be measured, a 'social audit' is required, investigating:

(*a*) which of their activities contribute to, or detract from, being socially responsible;
(*b*) measurement of those activities;
(*c*) a report on the results disclosed by the investigation.

An example of this might be to discover how the organisation had performed in respect of such matters as:

- employment of women
- employment of disabled people
- occupational safety
- occupational health
- benefits at pensionable age
- air pollution
- water pollution
- charitable activities
- help to developing countries.

Social audits may be carried out by an organisation's own staff or by external auditors. The reports may be for internal use only or for general publication.

## 33.8 Financial social accounting in profit-oriented organisations

Financial social accounting is an extension to normal financial accounting. The objective may either be to show how the social actions have affected financial performance, or otherwise to put a social value on the financial statements of the organisations. The three main types of financial social accounting envisaged to date are those of human resource accounting, greenhouse gas emissions, and how the organisation has responded to governmental or professional bodies' regulations concerning environmental matters.

## Human resource accounting

One of the main limitations of 'normal' financial accounting is the lack of any inclusion of the 'value' of the workforce to an organisation. The value may be determined by:

(*a*) capitalising recruitment and training costs of employees and apportioning value over employees' period of employment; or
(*b*) calculating the 'replacement cost' of the workforce and taking this as the value of human resources; or
(*c*) extending either of the above to include the organisation's suppliers and customers.

It is contended that such measurements have the benefits that (1) financial statements are more complete, and (2) managerial decisions can be made with a fuller understanding of their implications. For instance, suppose that a short-term drop in demand for a firm's goods led to a manufacturer laying off part of the workforce. This might mean higher profits in the short term, because of wages and salaries saved. In the long term, it could do irreparable damage, as recruitment could then be made difficult, or because of the effect on the morale of the rest of the workforce, or changes in attitudes of suppliers and customers.

## Greenhouse gas emissions

UK quoted companies must report on greenhouse gas emissions for which they are responsible. The emissions must be expressed as an intensity ratio or ratios, such as emissions per unit of sales revenue or floor space. If companies fail to report on all the gas emissions for which they are responsible, they must point out the omissions.

The report must:

- enable readers to have a clear understanding of the operations for which emissions data have been reported;
- indicate if and how this differs from operations within the consolidated financial statements;
- provide comparative data for the previous period alongside information on emissions for the current period.

Most benefits of greenhouse gas emissions reporting come from the reduction in risks relating to non-disclosure, including reduced profit exposure; enhanced market value; increased brand value; improved stakeholder/customer reputation; reduced insurance premiums; and improved credit ratings. Market value has been found to increase as well, but only by 0.005%. Other benefits include greater understanding within reporting organisations of the issues involved which, in turn, enable more realistic targets for emission reductions to be set.

For further details on greenhouse gas emissions reporting, the perceived costs, benefits, and risks, *see* http://ec.europa.eu/environment/pubs/pdf/ERM_GHG_Reporting_final.pdf

## Compliance costs of statutory/professional requirements

As the effects of organisations upon societies are more widely recognised there will be more and more regulations with which to comply. The costs of compliance will obviously then become a basic and essential part of financial statements.

## 33.9 Managerial social accounting in profit-oriented organisations

The identification and preparation of social and environmental information for reporting have an impact upon the information system of an organisation, requiring it to be extended to embrace this new data and information. As to how this is done will depend on the nature of each organisation and its existing information system. Some will simply add additional data capture, processing and reporting routines without making major changes to the existing system. Others, particularly organisations that embrace integrated reporting, may have to redesign their entire information system, switching to software capable of producing the reports such an innovation requires.

Whatever is done to change the information system, changes will continue to be made as new ways of reporting are found, so any change made to the information system needs to be flexible and adaptable.

The social and environmental information that it produces will not just be reported and used by a variety of stakeholders, it will be used internally on an ongoing basis to influence the day-to-day and strategic decision-making of the organisation.

**Activity 33.3** Why is this information used on an ongoing basis?

## 33.10 Financial and/or managerial social accounting for non-profit organisations

As profit is not relevant to these organisations it can be difficult to measure how well they are performing. Two approaches to measurement have been used: *planning, programming, budgeting systems (PPBS)* and *social programme measurement.*

Both of these approaches can be said to be part of what is sometimes referred to as 'value for money' accounting. The view of most governments has long been that while there is a need for a wide range of social programmes, including health, it is imperative that resources are not wasted. In essence, care should be taken to ensure that we get 'value for money' by making sure that the benefits arising from such schemes are worth at least the cost of providing them. But, returning to a theme expressed earlier in this chapter, how do you ensure this is the case when the benefits are hard to quantify and evaluate in monetary terms?

### Planning, programming, budgeting systems (PPBS)

In the past, there was a great deal of confusion between planning and budgeting. Annual budgeting takes a short-term financial view. Planning, on the other hand, should be long-term and also be concerned with strategic thinking.

PPBS enables management of non-profit organisations to make decisions on a better-informed basis about the allocation of resources to achieve their overall objectives. PPBS works in four stages:

1 Review organisational objectives.
2 Identify programmes to achieve objectives.
3 Identify and evaluate alternative ways of achieving each specific programme.
4 On the basis of cost–benefit principles, select appropriate programme.

PPBS necessitates the drawing up of a long-term corporate plan. This shows the objectives which the organisation is aiming to achieve. Such objectives may not be in accord with the existing organisational structure.

For instance, suppose that the objective of a local government authority, such as a city, is the care of the elderly. This could include providing:

- services to help them keep fit
- medical services when they are ill
- old people's housing
- sheltered accommodation
- recreational facilities
- educational facilities.

These services will usually be provided by separate departments, e.g. housing, welfare, education. PPBS relates the total costs to the care of the elderly, rather than to individual departmental budgets.

Management is therefore forced by PPBS to identify exactly which services or activities should be provided, otherwise the worthiness of the programme could not be evaluated. PPBS also provides information which enables management to assess the effectiveness of their plans, such as giving them a base to decide whether, for every thousand pounds, they are giving as good a service as possible.

As the structure of the programme will not match up with the structure of the organisation, e.g. the services provided will cut across departmental borders, a specific individual must be made responsible for controlling and supervising the programme.

### Social programme measurement

The idea that governmental social programmes should be measured effectively is, as yet, in its infancy.

A government auditor would determine whether the agency had complied with the relevant laws, and had exercised adequate cost controls. The auditor would determine whether or not the results expected were being achieved and whether there were alternatives to the programmes at a lower cost.

There should be cost–benefit analyses to show that the benefits are worth the costs they incur. However, the benefit side of the analysis is often very difficult to measure. How, for instance, do you measure the benefits of not dumping a particular substance or an obsolete oil rig into the sea?

As a consequence, most social programmes do not measure results (benefits). Instead they measure 'outputs', e.g. how many prosecutions for dumping waste: a high number of prosecutions is 'good', a low number 'bad'. This is hardly a rational way of assessing results, and quite a lot of research is going into better methods of audit.

## 33.11 Reports from companies

Many companies now report upon their practices relating to social and environmental issues. Where legislation does not require that this is reported, they will usually include it in their annual reports, and may also provide it on their company website.

Such reports vary greatly between organisations but one could, for example, include the following 10 principles of environmental policy:

1. To comply with both governmental and community standards of environmental excellence.
2. To use only materials and packaging selected to be good for the health of consumers, and for the safety and quality of the environment.
3. To keep energy use per unit of output down to a low level.
4. To minimise waste.

5 To get to as low a level as possible the discharge of pollutants.
6 To use other firms which have shown commitment to environmental excellence.
7 To research fully the ecological effect of the company's products and packaging.
8 To carry on business operations in an open, honest and co-operative manner.
9 To make certain that on the board of directors there would be scientifically knowledgeable directors, and ensure that they were regularly provided with environmental reports.
10 To ensure that all the above principles are fully observed and that challenges posed by the environment are vigorously and effectively pursued.

A company that reports voluntarily on social and environmental issues will include a mixture of information, some quantitative and some qualitative. As a result, its stakeholders will have a greater awareness of its principles and strategies with respect to social and environmental sustainability, but no overall financial view of the net cost or benefit of the company doing so because it is not possible to put a price on everything. The resulting mixed view needs considerable care in its interpretation – the 'normal' conventions of what an accountant or an analyst would look for in a financial report no longer apply.

In some instances, companies have taken this form of reporting beyond a simple list of features such as that presented above to one where all the elements are interlinked, showing their impact upon each other. This is known as 'integrated reporting', a form of report that goes much further to place social and environmental issues in context than was possible under conventional financial reporting or even when triple bottom line reporting was used.

## 33.12 Integrated reporting

Integrated reporting involves analysing all material factors affecting the long-term sustainability of an organisation. It has been described by the International Integrated Reporting Committee (IIRC) as bringing *'together material information about an organization's strategy, governance, performance and prospects in a way that reflects the commercial, social and environmental context within which it operates'*.

The IIRC believes that integrated reporting results in a broader explanation of performance than traditional reporting. It makes visible an organisation's use of and dependence on different resources and relationships or 'capitals' (financial, manufactured, human, intellectual, natural and social), and the organisation's access to and impact on them. Reporting this information is critical to:

- a meaningful assessment of the long-term viability of the organisation's business model;
- a meaningful assessment of the long-term viability of its strategy;
- meeting the information needs of investors and other stakeholders; and
- the effective allocation of scarce resources.

In South Africa, integrated reporting has been compulsory for companies listed on the Johannesburg stock market since 2010. Other countries have not yet adopted it and there is no agreed standard format, but it is significantly more comprehensive than a triple bottom line report and many companies are currently experimenting with the concept and producing integrated reports on a regular, but unregulated basis.

Exhibit 33.1 presents an integrated reporting model developed by the accounting firm, Pricewaterhouse Coopers (PWC) that shows four categories of information and the links between them, both internally and externally. Traditional financial reporting and triple bottom line reporting are in the lower left quadrant. Under integrated reporting, these would be linked to each other and to the elements within the other three quadrants.

An alternative perspective is presented in Exhibit 33.2. It shows the main information areas in an integrated report and their interdependencies in the context of the organisation's environment.

## Exhibit 33.1 The PwC integrated reporting model

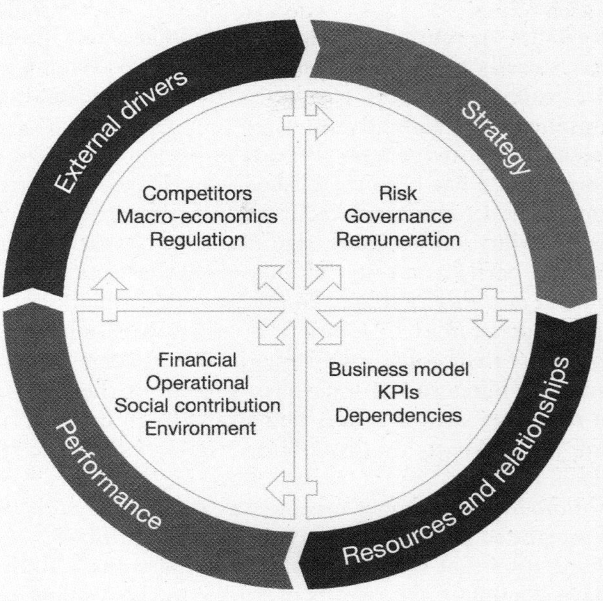


Source: PwC www.pwc.com/en_GX/gx/audit-services/corporate-reporting/assets/cr_ftse350.pdf

## Exhibit 33.2 Information areas and their interdependencies in an *integrated report*

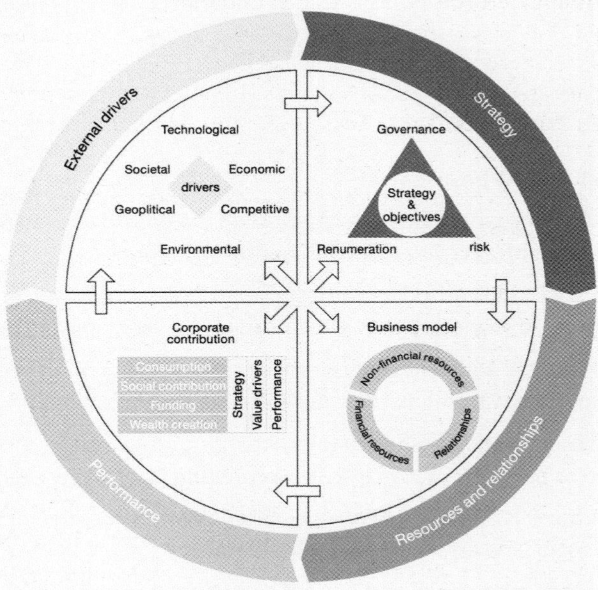


Source: PwC (2012) *Integrated Reporting – The Future of Corporate Reporting,* p.7

## 33.13 Finally

Organisations that operate consistently in a way that is socially and environmentally responsible are also being socially and environmentally sustainable. Yet, few organisations are successfully so and pressure groups continue to play a key role in their efforts to raise awareness of and within those organisations that blatantly fail to do so.

It now seems that after at least 50 years of pressure to be more socially and environmentally aware, a compromise has been established whereby the short-term benefits to the shareholders of many companies are being reduced in exchange for long-term benefits to the environment and society. Sustainability has become a significant factor, partly as a result of the influence of pressure groups, and partly as a result of increased awareness of what the consequences will be for the environment and society if they do not pay more attention to it.

A study conducted in 2014 found that 74% of CEOs believe that measuring and reporting the total impact of their company's activities across social, environmental, fiscal and economic dimensions contributes to the long-term success of their company. However, the problems inherent in reporting such practices and strategies in financial reports have not been resolved and, instead, those aspects that cannot be reliably valued are typically expressed or described in other terms.

*Triple bottom line* reporting is making way for *integrated reporting* and, while a standard format for an integrated report does not exist, there is sufficient guidance and sufficient exemplars for any organisation that wishes to do so to prepare one – all the major accountancy firms, for example, have exemplars and reports of studies freely available on their corporate websites.

Governments are now far more aware and far more involved in promoting social and environmental disclosures so, perhaps, we are now at a stage when integrated reports will become the norm. But, if they do, and if they require to be audited – social and environmental information that was previously included in the *Director's Report* and is now included in the *Strategic Report,* as is required by UK law, is subject to audit – accountants and auditors will need to develop the skills to prepare them and audit them. This presents a challenge to accountants, auditors, and to the accountancy profession as a whole, and only time will tell how they respond.

### Learning outcomes

**You should now have learnt:**

1. To whom organisations are responsible is a controversial area, and there is no exact definition of 'social and environmental accounting'.
2. That social indicators measure social progress, but as yet, given their inability to measure progress in monetary terms, they cannot be incorporated into social income accounts.
3. That a social audit will test the social responsibility of an organisation, including compliance with regulations, for example legislation relating to employees.
4. If an organisation wishes to take account of social and environmental factors, these items need to be incorporated into its accounting information system.
5. That there is a conflict between shareholders' interests, for example profit maximisation, and social and environmental considerations.
6. That corporate social and environmental reporting is the reporting of a company's activities and how they are related to social, including environmental, issues.

**7** That there are five areas into which social and environmental accounting has traditionally been divided:
(*a*) national social income accounting;
(*b*) social auditing;
(*c*) financial social accounting in profit-oriented organisations;
(*d*) managerial social accounting in profit-oriented organisations;
(*e*) financial and/or managerial social accounting in non-profit organisations.

**8** That social and environmental reporting, of which social and environmental is but part of a much larger picture, is as yet in its infancy. There is obviously a great difficulty in trying to put money values on the various aspects of being better off or worse off. There are also problems connected with exactly what 'better off' and 'worse off' mean. One person's worsening in some way may be someone else's betterment.

**9** That triple bottom line reporting is an approach that presents three reports, one financial, one social and one environmental, but does not relate each to the other.

**10** That integrated reporting embraces social and environmental reporting along with many other aspects of the business, its stakeholders and its environment in an attempt to present as complete a picture as possible of the impacts of its operations.

## Answers to activities

33.1 There isn't a correct answer to this question but there are examples of values being placed on employee loyalty, for example, clocks for 25 years of service, gold watches for 50 years of service, etc. But do acts like this actually place a value on employee loyalty? Hardly – what is the cost per year of a clock costing £25 that is presented to an employee for 25 years' loyal service to the organisation: £1 per year. Professional footballers who stay longer than the norm with one club are entitled to a testimonial game where all the proceeds are given to the loyal player. Similar schemes also exist in cricket, though, in cricket, it is usually a 'benefit year' where many events are held for the benefit of an individual player. Yet there have been cases where footballers have ended up out-of-pocket because the gifts they gave all the players who took part in the testimonial match – they don't get paid – and other expenses were greater than the income from the game – hardly a case of loyalty being rewarded.

Clearly, organisations don't tend to put a value on loyalty in such a way as to reward the loyal individual directly. They also cannot include a figure for employee loyalty in the statement of financial position as an asset. However, when a business is sold, employee loyalty is one of the factors that will be taken into account when deciding what the business is worth.

Just about the only way a business can recognise loyalty and endeavour to give it a value is to publicise it. This can be done through the media (Internet, social media, TV, radio, newspapers, etc.). It can also be done in the Annual Report, the document containing all the financial statements and accompanying reports that is sent to shareholders each year. The share price may rise slightly as a result but, even if it does, it is hardly the same as the company placing a value on the loyalty of its employees.

33.2 Private interest theory, which is also known as 'economic interest group theory' and 'special interest theory'.

33.3 Being socially and environmentally aware means that you monitor constantly the extent to which you are achieving your social and environmental goals. You can't simply check once a year whether you are putting too much pollution in the local river or whether your employees are being loyal and are happy, or whether your supplies are coming from companies that do not employ child labour. If an organisation becomes socially aware and adopts socially and environmentally aware practices and social and environmental reporting, its information system needs to be amended to reflect the change.

## Review questions

**33.1** Explain why social and environmental reporting is now generally considered to be important.

**33.2** Describe triple bottom line reporting.

**33.3** What are the benefits of companies adopting triple bottom line reporting?

**33.4** What problems do companies face in preparing triple bottom line reports?

**33.5** What problems do stakeholders face in interpreting triple bottom line reports?

**33.6** What problems do accountants face in preparing triple bottom line reports?

**33.7** What problems do auditors face in auditing triple bottom line reports?

**33.8** Describe how an increase in gross national product may not have a positive effect on the well-being of the country.

**33.9A** What types of measure could be used to measure social well-being? What difficulties would be discovered in trying to use accounting in measuring these?

**33.10** What aspects of an organisation's activities could be measured in a social audit?

**33.11** Describe how there could be conflicts between short-term and long-term benefits.

**33.12** Describe how PPBS may conflict with departmental budgets.

**33.13A** Review a set of company financial statements for social disclosures. Consider the usefulness of such disclosures to different user groups.

**33.14** Why has the traditional model of income measurement failed to account for the impact of business activities on the environment (Association of Chartered Certified Accountants)

**33.15A** Providing social and environmental information is costly for shareholders. Other than legislation, stock market requirements, or accounting regulations, what motivates companies to provide this information?

**33.16** Describe integrated reporting.

**33.17** What are the benefits of companies adopting integrated reporting?

**33.18** What problem do companies face in preparing integrated reports?

**33.19** What problems do stakeholders face in interpreting integrated reports?

**33.20** What problems do accountants face in preparing integrated reports?

**33.21** What problems do auditors face in auditing integrated reports?

chapter

# 34 Corporate governance

## Learning objectives

**After you have studied this chapter, you should be able to:**

- explain why it is important for companies to adopt sound practices of corporate governance
- describe the background to the development of the *UK Corporate Governance Code*
- outline the nature of the contents of the *UK Corporate Governance Code*

## Introduction

In this chapter, you'll learn about the increasingly important issue of corporate governance, of the background to the development of a code on corporate governance that UK listed companies must follow and on which they must report their compliance annually, and of the nature of its contents.

## 34.1 The importance of corporate governance

Corporate governance is concerned with the manner in which directors carry out their stewardship responsibilities. It has been defined as 'the exercise of power over and responsibility for corporate entities'. According to the ICAEW, the purpose of corporate governance is to facilitate effective, entrepreneurial and prudent management that can deliver the long-term success of the company. It is the system by which companies are directed and controlled. Boards of directors are responsible for the governance of their companies. If the directors of a company are failing to act in the interests of the shareholders, they are not performing the role to which they were appointed. Where this occurs, the shareholders need to be aware of it and take the steps necessary to ensure the directors do perform their role properly.

However, it is all very well saying this should happen. In the absence of any regulation that must be adhered to, it can take a long time for it to become clear to a company's shareholders that the directors are acting inappropriately. To this end, over the last decade two sets of guidelines have been developed. *The UK Corporate Governance Code* was developed for directors and the *UK Stewardship Code* was developed for institutional investors.

The *Stewardship Code* sets standards for investors in monitoring and engaging with the companies they own. Its objective is to improve the quality of communications between institutional investors and companies, so leading to improved long-term returns to shareholders and making institutional investors more accountable to their clients and beneficiaries. It was first issued in 2010 and then revised in 2012.

## 34.2 The *UK Corporate Governance Code*

In 2003, in response to continuing public concerns about the actions and motivation of some company directors who appeared to have their own interests at heart, rather than those of the shareholders they were appointed to represent, a revised version of a document called the *Combined Code on Corporate Governance* was published by the Financial Reporting Council. The latest version, now renamed the *UK Corporate Governance Code*, was issued in 2014. It is available at https://www.frc.org.uk/corporate/ukcgcode.cfm

The *UK Corporate Governance Code* contains a set of guidelines which can be used to determine whether directors have adequately performed their primary task of corporate stewardship. That is, whether the directors have carried out their duties adequately and in an appropriate manner, and in the best interests of the shareholders that they represent.

## 34.3 The policing of effective corporate governance

Both the *UK Stewardship Code* and the *UK Corporate Governance Code* are voluntary codes of conduct. They are neither legally enforceable codes nor have the status of an accounting standard. However, the UK *Financial Conduct Authority* (www.fca.org.uk/) requires UK authorised asset managers to report on whether or not they apply the Stewardship Code; and compliance with the *UK Corporate Governance Code* is required by the listing rules of the Stock Exchange.

As a result, when a company is listed on a UK Stock Exchange, the Directors' Report (which is included in the annual report of all UK companies) must include a statement indicating how they have applied the *UK Corporate Governance Code* in their annual report and accounts. Along with the financial statements and notes, the Directors' Report is subject to review by a company's external auditors, thus minimising the possibility of spurious claims being made by the directors.

**Activity 34.1**

If corporate governance is so important, why do you think unlisted companies are not required to apply the *UK Corporate Governance Code?*

## 34.4 The development of the *UK Corporate Governance Code*

The development of the *UK Corporate Governance Code* began with the *Cadbury Report*. This was the report of a committee set up in May 1991 by the Financial Reporting Council, the London Stock Exchange and the accountancy profession, under the chairmanship of Sir Adrian Cadbury, to consider the financial aspects of corporate governance. The *Cadbury Report* was published in December 1992.

Its main recommendation was that the boards of all the listed companies registered in the UK should comply with a code of practice and state in their financial accounts whether or not they have complied with it, identifying any areas of non-compliance. It also stated that non-executive directors should be appointed for specified terms and re-appointment should not be automatic, that such directors should be selected through a formal process and that both their selection and their appointment should be a matter for the board as a whole.

This was followed by the establishment of a committee chaired by Sir Richard Greenbury. The committee's main remit was to look into various aspects of directors' remuneration. The *Greenbury Report* was published in July 1995 and it recommended a Code of Best Practice based on the fundamental principles of accountability, transparency, and linkage of rewards to performance.

The *Cadbury Report* and the *Greenbury Report* were then reviewed together and the report on this review, *The Committee on Corporate Governance – Final Report* (often referred to as the *Hampel Report*), was published in January 1998. This report led to the first version of the *Combined Code* being published in June 1998.

Using that version as a starting point, the next version of the *Combined Code* was developed with reference to the *Turnbull Report on Internal Control* (2002–03), the *Smith Guidance on Audit Committees* (2003) and the *Higgs Report on Reviewing the Role and Effectiveness of Non-Executive Directors* (2003) and contained elements of all three reports within it.

## 34.5 Justification for a *UK Corporate Governance Code*

Following the issue of the *Combined Code on Corporate Governance* in 2003, the need for such a code was confirmed in a report called *Enterprise Governance: Getting the Balance Right,* prepared by the Professional Accountants in Business Committee of the International Federation of Accountants (IFAC) and published by IFAC in 2004. It looked at 27 corporate case studies – 11 outstandingly successful companies and 16 companies that had failed. It found evidence of clear failures in corporate governance in the recent well-known cases, including Enron, WorldCom and Vivendi. The report can be found using a browser search utility, such as Google. It is available at both the IFAC and the CIMA websites.

The study analysed information for each company including:

- whether the role of the chairman and chief executive was split
- how long the chairman, chief executive and financial director had been in place and where they had been recruited from
- the executive remuneration package
- the composition and background of the board
- information about mergers and acquisitions
- strategy development and implementation
- the use of complex financial engineering techniques.

### Corporate governance – key failure factors

High on the list of the key failure factors identified by the study were the culture and tone at the top level of the company. By their own poor example and failure to uphold high ethical standards, senior managers allowed a culture to flourish in which secrecy, rule-breaking and fraudulent behaviour became acceptable. Many examples were found of dominant charismatic chief executives who went unchallenged by senior executives and board directors.

The study found that strategic factors were more important than good corporate governance. This confirmed what many commentators and business analysts had always felt to be the case – while poor corporate governance can ruin a company, good corporate governance cannot, on its own, ensure success.

## 34.6 The content of The *UK Corporate Governance Code* 2010

There have been six versions of the *Combined Code/UK Corporate Governance Code:* 1998, 2003, 2006, 2008, 2010 and 2014. The latest version of the *UK Corporate Governance Code* comprises five sections and two schedules:

Sections:

A: Leadership
B: Effectiveness
C: Accountability
D: Remuneration
E: Relations with Shareholders

Schedule A: The design of performance-related remuneration for executive directors
Schedule B: Disclosure of corporate governance arrangements.

It contains a set of main and supporting principles and all listed companies have to report on how it applies to them. The form and content of this report are not prescribed, it being felt that companies should be free to explain their governance policies in the light of the principles, including any special circumstances which have led to a particular approach being adopted.

Listed companies must either confirm they have complied with these provisions, or provide an explanation where they have not done so. However, companies outside the FTSE 350 (i.e. those companies that are not among the 350 largest companies) are exempt from some of the provisions.

Schedule B of the Code contains guidance which suggests ways of applying the relevant principles and of complying with the relevant provisions on risk management and internal control (B.2 and part of B.3 in the Code); and on the provisions concerning audit committees and auditors (B.3 of the Code).

At times, the text of the *UK Corporate Governance Code* lacks the precision of, for instance, an accounting standard. For example, the main principle in Section A concerning leadership states that 'Every company should be headed by an effective board which is collectively responsible for the long-term success of the company.' What precisely is meant by 'effective' is a matter of interpretation based on the detailed contents of the *UK Corporate Governance Code.*

The supporting principles concerning leadership in Section A are similarly broadly presented: 'The board's role is to provide entrepreneurial leadership of the company within a framework of prudent and effective controls which enables risk to be assessed and managed. The board should set the company's strategic aims, ensure that the necessary financial and human resources are in place for the company to meet its objectives and review management performance. The board should set the company's values and standards and ensure that its obligations to its shareholders and others are understood and met.'

'All directors must act in what they consider to be the best interests of the company, consistent with their statutory duties.'

Concerning non-executive directors: 'As part of their role as members of a unitary board, non-executive directors should constructively challenge and help develop proposals on strategy. Non-executive directors should scrutinise the performance of management in meeting agreed goals and objectives and monitor the reporting of performance. They should satisfy themselves on the integrity of financial information and that financial controls and systems of risk management are robust and defensible. They are responsible for determining appropriate levels of remuneration of executive directors and have a prime role in appointing, and where necessary removing, executive directors, and in succession planning.'

While this may appear less likely to be effective than the heavily defined terminology of accounting standards, the nature of what is being dealt with in the *UK Corporate Governance Code* lends itself to this approach and there is no doubt that it is proving an effective instrument in improving corporate governance in the UK.

The full text of the *UK Corporate Governance Code* includes a number of related URLs which anyone wishing to look further into this topic would be well advised consulting. Similar resources can be found on the IFAC website and those of many professional accountancy bodies.

## Learning outcomes

**You should now have learnt:**

1. Why it is important for companies to adopt sound practices of corporate governance.
2. About the background to the development of the *UK Corporate Governance Code.*
3. About the nature of the content of the *UK Corporate Governance Code.*

## Answer to activity

34.1 The *UK Corporate Governance Code* has been imposed upon listed companies following high-profile incidences of financial irregularities that resulted in heightened public concerns about financial reporting, accounting procedures and the remuneration of directors. Unlisted companies are, by definition, much smaller enterprises where, typically, the directors own the majority, if not all, of the shares of the company. Many of these companies are exempt from an annual audit and, in the case of those that are externally audited, the only people likely to be affected by poor corporate governance are those same people who are failing in the performance of their stewardship role. Consequently, it makes little sense to require unlisted companies to apply the *UK Corporate Governance Code.*

## Review questions

**34.1** Define corporate governance.

**34.2** Why is it considered necessary to have an official set of corporate governance guidelines?

**34.3** If the *UK Corporate Governance Code* is a *voluntary* code of conduct for the directors of all UK limited companies, why is it that all listed UK companies must report annually on their compliance with it?

**34.4** Briefly describe the development of the *UK Corporate Governance Code* from 1991 to the present day.

**34.5** Briefly describe the main and supporting principles relating to directors contained in the *UK Corporate Governance Code.*

chapter

# 35 Public sector accounting

## Learning objectives

After you have studied this chapter, you should be able to:

- explain the differences between the public sector and the private sector
- describe the accounting arrangements in place in central government, local government, and the National Health Service
- describe the structure of public sector auditing in the UK for central government, local government, and the National Health Service
- outline some key differences between the structure of public sector auditing in Scotland and that which exists in the rest of the UK

## Introduction

In this chapter, you'll learn about the special aspects of accounting in the public sector, particularly the accounting arrangements in place in central government, local government, and the National Health Service. You will also learn about auditing of the public sector and of the main differences between the structure of the audit system in Scotland compared to the rest of the UK.

## 35.1 The nature of the 'public sector'

The public sector has been defined as 'all organisations which are not privately owned or operated'. It consists of organisations the control of which is in the hands of 'public', as opposed to 'private' owners, and whose objectives involve the provision of services where profit is not a primary objective. The word 'public' as used in the phrase 'in the hands of the public' is often taken to mean 'government', either local or national.

Unlike the private sector of the economy, where there is a clear objective and motivation in making profits or a return on capital, the public sector has a multitude of demands and objectives.

> ***'In the private sector, you are able to focus very clearly on the bottom line. You've got a clear objective. That's not always true in the public sector. In the public sector, you often have many conflicting objectives and grappling with those is part of the skill of public sector management and part of what makes it so interesting.'*** **(Steve Bundred, former Chief Executive, Audit Commission)**

The public sector is concerned primarily with providing services to the general public which would not otherwise be available or provided adequately within the financial resources of all individual members of the public. Consequently, it exists primarily in order to:

- provide services which are beyond the private means of people using those services
- provide a benefit to everyone within socially acceptable norms
- achieve certain minimum standards of service, e.g. roads, education and training schemes
- substitute central or local planning in place of consumer choice
- ensure a consistent approach to certain practices or procedures
- aid control and economic regulation in key areas.

These objectives within the public sector are significantly influenced by the central government. The relationship between central control and local democracy is an important political consideration and, while the concept of what the public sector provides is fairly universal, the means of control over the different organisations providing these services can differ.

## 35.2 Types of public sector organisations in the UK

Public sector organisations can be classified into five major groups in the UK:

- nationalised industries, public corporations
- departments of central government
- local authorities
- health authorities
- bodies set up for a specific purpose: universities; the Royal Mint; and HM Stationery Office.

## 35.3 The relevance of legislation

The nationalised industries and public corporations are required to meet certain criteria set by the government in the form of a return on capital. The other four categories of public sector organisations are given other forms of performance targets. The obligation to provide public services by the different types of organisation is generally derived from statutes or legislation passed by Parliament. This legislation may be either 'general', i.e. applicable to the whole country, or 'local', relating to just one area.

For anyone looking at these organisations from an accounting perspective, a knowledge of certain aspects of this legislation is important. Not only will the relevant statutes set out the powers of the organisation for raising money to pay for the provision of services, associated regulations may provide details of the accounting and audit requirements relating to the organisation.

## 35.4 The objectives of public sector organisations

> ***'Many public bodies are effective monopolies, providing services to very vulnerable people or services that people can't choose to opt out of. So there's a necessity in the public sector to have other means to ensure effectiveness, stimulate innovation and drive improvement.'***
> **(Steve Bundred, former Chief Executive, Audit Commission)**

Each type of public sector organisation has its own accounting objectives which influence the form and content of its financial statements and accounting arrangements. Some of the underlying factors necessary to achieve those objectives are common to all public sector organisations.

### Stewardship

The use of public money, particularly if it is acquired through taxation, demands that the accounts show that monies have been properly and lawfully used. This requires the publication of sufficient information which can be easily understood by the public.

### Maintaining systematic records

All public sector organisations must maintain systematic records so that (*i*) financial requirements can be estimated and (*ii*) the measurement of the use of these financial resources can be established and the relative efficiency and effectiveness of the organisation in using them can be assessed. Value for money is of the utmost importance, especially when taxation or charging levels are high or are increasing rapidly. Accounting procedures must be directed towards ensuring that the maximum benefit is obtained from the limited resources.

### Financial control

Total planned public expenditure for 2010 was £704 billion, financed by receipts of £541 billion and borrowing of £163 billion. When amounts of this magnitude are involved, there is a significant need for effective financial control, particularly given the lack of any profit objective and the motivation and discipline that go with it. Even more than in the case of the private sector, financial control in the public sector must be exercised through a sound budgeting and accounting system. Such a control system will normally be supported by written internal regulations or instructions concerning expenditure and income procedures and their associated accounting arrangements, and the control system used by one organisation is often virtually identical to those in other similar public sector organisations.

**Activity 35.1** Why do you think similar public sector organisations are likely to use virtually identical control systems?

In the rest of this chapter, we'll look at the accounting arrangements in place in central government, local government, and the National Health Service, focusing mainly on the system that operates in England and Wales.

## 35.5 Central government accounting

Central government services are administered through the various government departments which operate their accounting systems on a fund basis. The basic system is that all government income, from taxes and other revenues, is paid into a central Consolidated Fund and the various departments draw off this Fund to finance the services that they provide. Any deficit in the Consolidated Fund is financed from the National Loans Fund, and vice versa.

The funds available to finance public expenditure are allocated between the various government departments. The size of the allocation to an individual department depends on the political and social priorities of the government. Of particular importance in recent years has been the government's increase in the level of public expenditure coupled with achieving better value for money from every pound spent providing the various government services.

The amount of money available for public expenditure is subject to cash limits. Spending by a department in any year is stated in cash terms. That is, the prices prevailing in the November of the previous year plus an amount to cover forecast inflation in the next year. The total level of expenditure is controlled within this cash limited amount, and the Treasury is responsible for monitoring spending and reporting to the government on the level of spending by the various departments throughout the financial year.

Following an announcement in the 1993 budget speech a major change in government accounting took place from the 2001/2002 financial year when a system called '**Resource Accounting**' was adopted. This resulted in a switch from a receipts-and-payments-based accounting system (i.e. **cash-based accounting**) to a system based on normal commercial practice complete with accruals and movements in cash flows. This system was introduced by the Government Resources and Accounts Act 2000 and is part of a longer-term aim to publish fully audited 'Whole of Government Accounts' (WGA) covering the whole of the UK public sector based on generally accepted accounting principles (GAAP).

Under this Act, each department is required to prepare resource accounts for each financial year, in conformity with a Treasury direction, detailing the resources acquired or disposed of during the year and the use of resources by the department during the year.

The resource accounts are prepared on an accruals basis and must give a true and fair view of the state of affairs of the department, the net resource outturn, resources applied to objectives, recognised gains and losses, and cash flows for the financial year.

HM Treasury appointed the Permanent Head of Department as Accounting Officer of each government department, with responsibility for preparing the department's accounts and for transmitting them to the *Comptroller and Auditor General* (who is head of the National Audit Office).

In preparing the accounts, the Accounting Officer is required to comply with the *Resource Accounting Manual* prepared by HM Treasury, and in particular to:

- observe the relevant accounting and disclosure requirements, and apply suitable accounting policies on a consistent basis;
- make judgements and estimates on a reasonable basis;
- state whether applicable accounting standards, as set out in the *Resource Accounting Manual*, have been followed, and disclose and explain any material departures in the accounts;
- prepare the accounts on a going-concern basis.

The responsibilities of an Accounting Officer, including responsibility (*i*) for the propriety and regularity of the public finances for which an Accounting Officer is answerable and (*ii*) for keeping proper records and for safeguarding the department's assets, are set out in the *Accounting Officers' Memorandum* issued by HM Treasury and published in *Government Accounting*.

## 35.6 Local government accounting

The Local Government Acts 1972 and 1985 contain the statutory provisions which broadly established the present structure of London and Metropolitan Boroughs, Unitary Authorities, and County District and Parish Councils. Total planned expenditure on local government services for 2014/15 was £115 billion with approximately 31% on local education services and 19% on welfare.

The changing role of local government has accelerated during the past 30 years. In early 1994, the Financial Secretary to the Treasury told an audience of prominent local government and public sector figures that he would like to see their role diminish to that of a purchaser of services, which would almost wholly be provided by the private sector. The 'enabling' authority is seen as one mainly concerned with policy direction, the allocation of resources, determining standards and priorities and then monitoring the results. The widening of compulsory competitive tendering (CCT) was an important move in this direction, as is 'outsourcing', where local services are provided by a private company under contract, without the need for CCT and, more recently, Best Value measures (performance against a range of measurable criteria) in the provision of public services.

### The role of the Chief Financial Officer

The Local Government Act 1972 abolished specific statutory reference to the need to appoint a 'treasurer' and to the 'making of safe and efficient arrangements for receipts and payments'.

What it did do, however, was to impose wider but more general responsibilities for the financial administration of local authority affairs. The 1972 Act stated:

> ***'A local authority shall appoint such officers as they think necessary for the proper discharge . . . of their functions . . . Every local authority shall make arrangements for the proper administration of their financial affairs and shall ensure that one of their officers has responsibility for the administration of those affairs.'***

The Local Government Act 1988 strengthened the position of the 1972 Act by:

- requiring all Section 151 officers to have appropriate qualifications for the job
- specifying those issues on which Section 151 officers must report to the council.

The title 'Chief Financial Officer' is widely used, but other titles also exist (e.g. 'Treasurer' and 'Director of Finance'). In practice it is for the members of an authority to determine the role of the Chief Financial Officer and to specify the terms and conditions of this appointment.

Government regulations place upon the 'responsible financial officer' (subject to instructions from the employer) the responsibility for determining the accounting system, form of accounts and supporting records. Further, that officer has a duty to ensure that the accounting systems are observed and that the accounts and supporting records are kept up to date.

The regulations contain several sections that are particularly relevant to the financial officer. In particular, the responsible officer is required to maintain an adequate and effective internal audit of the accounts of the body and have right of access at all times to such documents of the body which relate to the accounts of the body as they appear to him or her to be necessary for the purpose of the audit and shall be entitled to require from any officer of the body such information and explanation as is required for that purpose.

## Local authority financial reporting

Local authorities prepare four main types of financial reports.

(*a*) an annual revenue budget and capital programme (budget);
(*b*) an information leaflet or mini-report to be sent to all council taxpayers with the council tax demand note;
(*c*) a statement of accounts (traditionally referred to as an 'abstract of accounts'; they are legally required to publish this);
(*d*) an annual report.

The form and content of these reports are largely standardised, and must comply with four types of external requirements:

- statutory requirements, including Acts of Parliament and Accounts and Audit regulations;
- government directions in the form of codes of practice and notes of guidance;
- professional standards: the IFRS-based *Code of Practice on Local Authority Accounting* (which specifies the form and content of the individual financial statements which make up the statement of accounts);
- International GAAP.

## The Accounting Code of Practice

The CIPFA/LASAAC (Local Authority, Scotland, Accounts Advisory Committee, Accounting Code of Practice (ACOP)) was recognised by the UK Accounting Standards Board as a SORP (Statement of Recommended Accounting Practice) and, since its introduction in 1991, was regularly updated, until being replaced in April 2010 by the IFRS-based Code of Practice on Local Authority Accounting in the United Kingdom. It is updated annually.

A typical Statement of Accounts published by a district or borough council is now prepared under International GAAP and may contain the following sections:

(*a*) an Explanatory Foreword setting out the main financial features of the year;
(*b*) a Statement of Accounting Policies, Changes in Estimates and Errors;
(*c*) a Statement of the responsibilities of the Local Authority and its Chief Financial Officer in respect of the statement of accounts;
(*d*) Comprehensive Income and Expenditure Statement;
(*e*) Movements in Reserves Statement;
(*f*) the Statement of Financial Position;
(*g*) the Statement of Cash Flows;
(*h*) Notes to the financial statements, including segment reporting;
(*i*) a Statement summarising the collection of Council Tax and Business Rates and the appropriation of that money to the relevant providers of local services.

County Councils publish sections (*a*) to (*h*) only, but would also include the accounts of the Superannuation Fund (revenue account and net assets statement covering employees of all local authorities in its area). Police and Fire Authorities prepare separate income and expenditure accounts and statements of financial position.

## Audit arrangements in local government

Until March 2015, local authority audits in England and Wales were overseen by the National Audit Office (**www.audit-commission.gov.uk**). A slightly different system operates in Scotland where Audit Scotland (**www.audit-scotland.gov.uk**) oversees the audits on behalf of and reports to the Audit General and the Accounts Commission. In Northern Ireland, the Northern Ireland Audit Office (**www.niauditoffice.gov.uk**) oversees the audits and reports to the Department of the Environment. As when we looked at central government auditing, we will focus on the system in England and Wales.

Auditing is performed to a national legislative standard (Audit Commission Act 1998) and a detailed Code of Audit Practice, the latest version of which was issued by the National Audit Office in April 2015.

For over 160 years, the audit was usually performed by District Auditors appointed by the Audit Commission with approximately 30% of these audits performed by private sector auditing firms. However, all audits have been outsourced to the private sector since 2012/13.

This audit is as thorough as a private sector company audit and the impact on those responsible for the stewardship of a local authority who are found to have been acting inappropriately can be very severe indeed. The highest-profile case involved the Audit Commission's role as auditor of Westminster Council which resulted in a 15-year battle conducted by the District Auditor to recover amounts lost to the council from Dame Shirley Porter, former leader of the council, for her role in what was referred to as the 'homes for votes scandal'.

### The 'homes for votes scandal'

Between 1987 and 1989, Dame Shirley Porter, who was then the leader (i.e. in charge of the stewardship) of Westminster Council, kept council homes empty and sold them cheaply in the hope of boosting support for her political party in eight marginal wards (districts). By doing so, she hoped to prevent the Labour Party from winning control of the council. This policy was found to have cost the council £27,023,376! The case was finally settled after three appeals by a payment of £12.3 million in 2004.

When the auditors are satisfied that nothing materially incorrect has been done, an unqualified audit opinion is issued, similar to the example shown in Exhibit 35.1:

**Exhibit 35.1 An unqualified audit opinion**

*Opinion*:

'In our opinion, the financial statements present fairly the financial position of the XYZ Borough Council as at 31 March 2015 and its income and expenditure for the year then ended.'

The Audit Commission closed on 1 April 2015 with its role transferred permanently to the private sector. By 2019, all outsourced contracts to provide this service will have expired and the service will be entirely operated by the private sector.

## 35.7 National Health Service accounting

The National Health Service is almost wholly dependent upon central government funding. It has no independent source of revenue equivalent to business rates or the community charge. The planned NHS expenditure for 2014/15 was £113 billion. Some of that funding is derived from employers' and employees' National Insurance contributions, but the bulk of it comes from general taxation. Some diagnostic services and treatments are free, as are consultations with NHS doctors and specialists, as well as NHS hospital treatment. Most patients bear at least part of other costs, such as spectacles, dentistry and drugs prescribed by doctors.

The provision of national health services is devolved to each of the four parts of the United Kingdom, with a separate national health service for England, Northern Ireland, Scotland, and Wales. In England, it is overseen by the Secretary of State for Health, and by ministers of the devolved governments in Northern Ireland, Scotland, and Wales. Details of the differences across these four parts of the UK can be found in *The organisation of the NHS in the UK: comparing structures in the four countries – Research Paper* (available at http://www.assembly.wales/researchdocuments/15-020 – the organisation of the NHS in the UK comparing structures in the four countries/15-020.pdf).

For example, in England, highly specialist services and primary care are commissioned by NHS England: primary healthcare including GP services and dentists, specialised healthcare services, offender healthcare, and military healthcare. Secondary care, community services, hospitals, mental health services, and rehabilitation services are administered by 211 clinical commissioning groups (CCGs). Public Health England (PHE), an executive agency of the Department of Health, is responsible for commissioning immunisation, screening, and child health services. Local authorities provide local health services.

The majority of NHS services, such as hospitals, belong to either an NHS trust or an NHS foundation trust, an independent legal entity accountable to local people; with a board of governors including staff, patients, members of the public and other external organisations. Each foundation trust has financial freedom, can raise capital within cash flow (i.e. affordable) limits. Financial surpluses can be invested to provide new NHS services.

Healthcare is regulated by and licensed by Monitor. It is responsible for regulating prices for NHS services and addressing restrictions on competition that act against patients' interests. The Trust Development Authority is responsible for ensuring that NHS trusts fix problems and improve standards.

NHS trusts are monitored against two financial categories:

*(a)* In-year financial delivery;
*(b)* Monitor's Risk Assessment Framework – Continuity of Service.

The chief executive officer of each trust is accountable for internal financial controls on a daily basis; and is responsible for (i) maintaining a sound system of internal control that supports the achievement of its objectives and (ii) reviewing its effectiveness. The system of internal control is based on an ongoing risk management process designed to identify the principal risks to the achievement of the organisation's objectives; to evaluate the nature and extent of those risks; and to manage them efficiently, effectively, and economically.

### NHS broad financial arrangements

Financial directives are issued by the Health Secretary and set down the responsibilities and requirements for financial control. These form the basis upon which authorities develop their own financial control policies.

The purpose of the accounts of NHS organisations is to satisfy the 'primary requirements of public accountability for the use of NHS financial resources'. The annual report and financial statements of each foundation trust is laid before parliament and presented at a public meeting. (This part of the process is different in Scotland, as you will see in Section 35.9.)

Financial reporting of foundation trusts is overseen by Monitor through its *NHS Foundations Trust Annual Reporting Manual*. Four IASB-based financial statements must be published annually by each foundation trust:

1. a statement of comprehensive income;
2. a statement of financial position;
3. a statement of cash flows;
4. a statement of changes in taxpayers' equity.

However, the government considers certain principles under IASB pronouncements to be inappropriate to trusts and alternative treatments are prescribed in those cases. The annual accounts must be accompanied by a statement of accounting practice, certified by the director of finance and acknowledged by the chairman prior to audit. Annual accounts must be completed by 30 June after the financial year to which they relate.

### NHS Audit arrangements

Auditors of NHS trusts and NHS foundation trusts follow an audit code issued by the National Audit Office on behalf of the Comptroller and Auditor General. From 1 April 2015, NHS auditors are appointed by Public Sector Audit Appointments Limited. It took over this role after the closure of the Audit Commission on 31 March 2015.

## 35.8 The National Audit Office (NAO)

The NAO (www.nao.org.uk) audits the financial statements of all government departments and agencies, and those of many other public bodies, and reports to Parliament on the spending of central government funds, specifically in the context of value for money. There are separate national audit offices for Scotland, Northern Ireland and Wales.

## 35.9 Public sector auditing in Scotland

You have already learnt that the audit arrangement for local government in Scotland is slightly different from that which exists in England and Wales. For the rest of the public sector, the differences are considerably greater. In the rest of the UK, the audits of government departments are the responsibility of the *Comptroller and Auditor General*. In Scotland, Audit Scotland conducts the audits on behalf of the *Auditor General* (**www.audit-scotland.gov.uk/about/ags**) who reports to the Scottish Parliament.

The role of the *Auditor General* is to:

- examine how public bodies spend public money;
- make sure they manage their finances to the highest standards;
- make sure they achieve value for money.

Public bodies that the *Auditor General* reviews include:

- Departments of the Scottish government;
- NHS boards;
- further education colleges;
- Scottish Water;
- government agencies and non-departmental public bodies such as Scottish Enterprise, the Scottish Prison Service, and Historic Scotland.

## Learning outcomes

**You should now have learnt:**

1. What distinguishes the public sector from the private sector.
2. About the accounting arrangements in place in central government, local government, and the National Health Service.
3. About the structure of public sector auditing in the UK for central government, local government, and the National Health Service.
4. That there are some differences between the structure of public sector auditing in Scotland and that which exists in the rest of the UK.

## Answer to activity

35.1 The public sector organisations will all have similar regulations governing what they do, and performance targets set using the same criteria. As in any situation where organisations are ultimately owned by one entity, efforts will be made to achieve economies of scale (i.e. savings) and benefit from the increased efficiency and effectiveness that a control system developed using the resources of all organisations within the group can bring.

## Review questions

**35.1** What is the public sector?

**35.2** Briefly describe the role of the accounting officer of a central government department.

**35.3** Briefly describe the differences between the structure of local authority auditing in Northern Ireland compared to England and Wales.

**35.4** Briefly describe the differences between the structure of public sector auditing in Scotland compared to the rest of the UK.

chapter 36

# Accounting for management control

## Learning objectives

**After you have studied this chapter, you should be able to:**

- describe some of the deficiencies of financial accounting if it were used for management control purposes
- describe the need to avoid potential conflicts between alternative or competing objectives that may be adopted within an organisation
- explain that decision-making should involve more than just the financial figures involved
- explain that the information needs of organisations are, in part at least, a function of their size
- describe the difference between the three areas in which management operates, and their different information needs
- explain that accounting information is only one part of the overall system in which organisations operate
- describe how the accounting system is affected by the surrounding environment both inside and outside the organisation in which it operates

## Introduction

In this chapter, you'll learn about the deficiencies of financial accounting information for decision-making. You'll also learn about the impact of organisational objectives, people and organisation size on decision-making and about the three-part role of management. Finally, you will learn about the manner in which the accounting system interacts with its environment and of the relationship between quantitative and qualitative data and formal and informal information systems.

## 36.1 The part played by financial accounting

So far your studies have been concerned primarily with the recording function of accounting, often called bookkeeping, and the drafting of the financial statements of different types of organisations, such as partnerships and limited companies. The term generally used for your studies up to this point is '*financial accounting*'. Much of financial accounting is concerned with legal requirements, such as complying with the provisions of accounting standards and the Companies Acts when drafting financial statements, or keeping an accounting record of a customer's legal indebtedness, i.e. a debtor's account.

With companies, the annual report represents the information given to the shareholders by the directors of their running of the company during a particular year. In other words, it is a description of the directors' 'stewardship' of the company. The financial statements are also given to other interested parties, such as the company's bankers, creditors, inspectors of taxes, etc.

While financial accounting is necessary from a legal point of view, it cannot be said to be ideal from the point of view of controlling the activities of a firm. Your studies, therefore, would be incomplete if you had seen only the 'stewardship' function of accounting as represented by financial accounting. The use of accounting for controlling the activities of an organisation is probably more important. In this chapter, we shall briefly consider accounting for 'management control'.

The word 'management' has nothing at all to do with whether or not an entity is a limited company, a plc, a small family-run business, a partnership, or a club or society or other not-for-profit organisation. It means the people who are managing the affairs of the organisation, whether they are directors; partners; sole proprietors; 'managers', i.e. employees who are in charge of other employees; or volunteers.

## 36.2 Deficiencies of financial accounting for management control

Before starting to examine accounting for management control, let's look first at the deficiencies of financial accounting when used to control the activities of an organisation.

**The first major deficiency of financial accounting is that it deals with events that have already occurred.** It deals with the past, not the future. It is possible to control something while it is happening, and control can be arranged for something that is going to happen but, when it has already happened without being controlled, the activity has ended and we are too late to do anything about it; for example, if a company incurs a loss and we do not realise it until long after it has happened, by which time the loss obviously cannot be prevented.

What we really want to do is to control affairs so that a loss is not incurred if at all possible, and to be able to call on accounting techniques to help us do so. However, it certainly does not mean that we are not interested in the past. We can learn lessons from the past which can be very useful in understanding what is going on now, and what is likely to be happening in the future.

**The second major deficiency of financial accounting is that it is concerned with the whole of the organisation.** Thus the trading account of a business may show a gross profit of £60,000 but, while it is better to know that than to have no idea at all of what the gross profit is, it does not tell management much about past transactions. Suppose, for example, that it manufactures three products – watches, pens and zips. Some possibilities of how much of the gross profit was attributable to each of the products are shown in Exhibit 36.1:

### Exhibit 36.1

| | *Various possibilities of profits and loss for each product (£s)* | | | |
|---|---|---|---|---|
| | 1 | 2 | 3 | 4 |
| Watches | 20,000 | 5,000 | 30,000 | (30,000)* |
| Pens | 20,000 | 70,000 | 28,000 | 65,000 |
| Zips | 20,000 | (15,000)* | 2,000 | 25,000 |
| Total gross profit | 60,000 | 60,000 | 60,000 | 60,000 |

***Losses are shown in brackets.**

These are only some of the possible figures of gross profit and loss for each product which could result in an overall gross profit of £60,000. The figure of total gross profit alone provides very few clues as to what lessons can be learnt. If, say, possibility number 2 was, in fact, the real situation, it would stimulate further discussion and investigation as to why these results had occurred.

It could, perhaps, result in the closing down of the section of the business which makes zips if, after investigation, it was found to be in the interests of the business to cease manufacturing them. (As you will learn later, simply because it is making a gross loss may not necessarily mean it would be wrong to continue manufacturing zips.) Many more lessons can therefore be learnt if the business's activities can be examined piece by piece instead of looking at the overall, summarised results.

The third major deficiency of financial accounting is that it reports aggregated data, and each figure in the financial statements may be a total of any number of individual data items, including some that could have legitimately been incorporated instead into a different item shown in the financial statements. Users of financial statements have no means of disaggregating the items they show and so can never be sure of what is contained in each item they see in the financial statements, even when, as for example in the case of non-current assets, additional information may be given in a note to the financial statements.

For these and a number of other reasons, **financial accounting is of little use by itself for management control purposes.** It does not mean that it is of no use at all for control purposes – for example, the financial accounting system may reveal that the accounts receivable at a point in time are £50,000, something that management need to know if they are to control their finances properly – but much of the financial accounting information produced is of little use in controlling the business.

Imagine we bought a building in 2000 for £400,000 that is now worth £1,200,000. If we rented a similar building now it might cost us £100,000 a year. What use would you make of the knowledge that the building originally cost £400,000 when deciding whether or not to rent a similar building now, or buy another one for £1,200,000?

Let's consider in more detail, what management control seeks to do, and why.

## 36.3 Objectives of the organisation

If we want to discuss management control we must first of all ask ourselves: what is its purpose? We can only have control if it is for a particular purpose, otherwise how can we possibly determine what we may need to control, never mind start doing anything at all.

It might seem obvious that the objectives of an organisation should be spelled out clearly and unambiguously. In fact, the writing down of a formal set of objectives for an organisation is very often overlooked. It is often, instead, assumed in such cases that the objectives are obvious. As a result, in many cases, the employees of the organisation could be pulling in many different directions, as they all have different ideas of the objectives of the organisation.

Some of the possible objectives an organisation may include:

- To ensure that the maximum profit is made. This still is not clear; do we mean profits in the long term or the short term?
- To obtain a minimum specific share of the market for its goods or services.
- To have the greatest share of the market for its goods or services.
- To achieve the highest possible level of quality in the goods being manufactured or services offered.
- To ensure that its customers are fully satisfied with its goods and services.
- To ensure full employment for its employees.
- To ensure that its employees' welfare is maintained at a high level, in terms of such things as back-up facilities and adequate pension schemes.

- To ensure that its employees receive the best training and are kept fully up to date with the latest technology for our sort of business.
- To cause as little environmental damage as possible.
- To take over all its major competitors progressively.

Activity 36.2

What other objectives can you think of? Try to think of another two. If you can, try to make them objectives which cannot be identified or demonstrated using information provided by financial accounting.

You should now be beginning to see for yourself that there are many things which it would be useful to know about an organisation that cannot be provided by financial accounting.

If you look at the above list of possible objectives, you will see that some simply cannot be achieved at the same time – they contradict, or are incompatible with, one another. Let's look at how this problem of conflict between objectives can be addressed.

## 36.4 Conflicts between objectives

Most organisations have more than one objective, some compatible with some others and some not. By that we mean that pursuit of one objective may impact upon the organisation's ability to achieve some of its other objectives, and that, as a result, no objective can be considered completely on its own.

Take, for example, the objective of maximising profit being pursued at the same time as the objective of causing as little environmental damage as possible. If any funds have to be spent in order to achieve the second objective, the first objective is automatically undermined. There would be an additional level of conflict if the environmental expenditure was being made voluntarily rather than being forced on the organisation by the authorities. Even where it was being forced on the organisation, it would raise a conflict as the firm would want to do so in the cheapest possible way so as to maintain its objective of profit maximisation. Cheapness may be achieved by relaxing controls so that a small but noticeable level of environmental damage occurred which just happened to be within the limit set by the government, thus enabling maximisation of the profit objective within the constraints of the environmental objectives.

Similarly, maintaining a very high quality of goods could mean lower profits if a large number of items manufactured are scrapped because they are not up to standard. Lowering the quality could possibly increase profits but would result in non-attainment of the quality objective.

Activity 36.3

Both these examples have something in common relating to the time-frame in which the actions taken can be justified. What is it?

**It is thus essential to ensure that the objectives are very clearly spelled out *and prioritised*.** In effect, the objectives should be stated in terms of Objective A being sought, subject to the constraint that Objective B must be achieved, etc. Otherwise, people will easily misunderstand them and because of this the firm may not proceed in the direction that is desired. **It is also essential that an appropriate time-frame is considered when resolving conflicting objectives.**

## 36.5 People and management control

**The *most* important resource of any organisation is the people who work for it.** A danger exists that a great deal of care and attention may be given to designing a management control system and operating it, but it is a complete failure because the people in the organisation did not use it effectively. Systems and figures do not themselves do anything. It is the people in the organisation who take (or do not take) the necessary action that determines if a successful outcome is to result.

Figures thrown up by control systems are only part of the evidence available when a decision has to be made as to the necessary action to take. A department may be incurring losses now, but the sales manager may state that he believes sales will increase soon and that the department will then rapidly become profitable. **If decision-makers use accounting figures as the only criteria on which action should be based, there would be some very poor decisions taken by management.** Many very successful products have incurred losses at first, but have eventually proved successful because the organisation had faith in the product and persevered with it.

One important feature of any effective management control system is that it is integrated into the operations of the existing systems and used in an appropriate way. For example, if exactly the same system of management control was used in three different organisations, A may find that its control system was useless because no one acted on the data produced. In B, the control system might have damaged the organisation because management used the data as though it were the only criterion in gauging the actions it should take. In C, it might be very effective because the management saw the data as a useful guide in planning and control and had also made certain that the rest of the organisation took the same view.

How human beings use and react to a management control system is, therefore, at the heart of the problem of ensuring that management control systems are effective.

## 36.6 Different sizes of organisations and the decision-making process

Part of this book is about information which is intended to be used by the management of an organisation. For a small and simple organisation the information needs of management may be limited and can be obtained by direct observation – using the eyes to look and the voice to ask questions.

For example, a person managing a greengrocer's stall in a street market can often operate the business effectively without the assistance of any formal records or analysis. What he buys is determined by the goods available in the local wholesale market and his personal knowledge of what his customers are prepared to buy at a given price. His records will probably centre around the recording of cash – the details of his sales and his expenditure. However, apart from the essential requirement of maintaining an appropriate level of cash, these records do not help him in the day-to-day management of his business operations.

In contrast, if we look at the buyer responsible for buying fresh fruit and vegetables for a large supermarket chain, certain differences emerge. The basic decision about what to buy at a given price remains the same. However, a large organisation has a much wider choice of where and how to buy than a small one. The buyer from the large organisation may, for example, be able to enter into contracts directly with growers and to enter forward contracts for the supply of produce (for example, a farmer agrees at the start of the summer to sell all his summer output of potatoes and peas to a frozen foods manufacturer at a fixed price).

In a large supermarket chain, the buyer will not be in regular direct contact with each of the many different sales outlets and therefore relies upon written information to keep him in touch with demand. He does not have to listen to complaining customers! Similarly because there will be many more potential sources of supply than exist for a smaller business, he needs more formal information to keep him in touch with market prices than would be the case were he employed by a smaller organisation.

One of the other features about large organisations which distinguishes them from smaller ones is that responsibility for running the business is shared between many different people. In order to ensure that the operations of the organisation are carried out efficiently and effectively, there needs to be some criterion to measure the performance of the managers. In a small organisation, the poorly informed proprietor will either, at best, make a poor living or at the other extreme, go out of business. Thus success or failure is clearly the sole proprietor's own responsibility. In a large organisation, the same things can happen overall, but the situation may be obscured by a swings and roundabouts effect of some good sections making up for some bad. A management control system should help identify the problems and problem areas within an organisation.

## 36.7 The management process

The way that management operates in an organisation can be divided into three distinct activities:

(*a*) forecasting and planning;
(*b*) controlling operations;
(*c*) evaluating performance.

### (a) Forecasting and planning

Forecasting and planning is the process by which senior management decides on major overall issues concerning what the business is going to do and how it is going to do it. It involves an assessment of information about the future which is produced through a process known as 'forecasting'. When a forecast has been prepared, senior management can plan how to achieve the organisation's objectives. 'Planning' is the process of co-ordinating the resources available to attain an objective.

### (b) Controlling operations

Controlling operations involves management in a number of processes and requires several different kinds of information. The plans produced by senior management must be converted into an operating pattern which matches the parts into which the organisation is divided. This process breaks down the overall plan into detailed operating plans, each of which relates to the management structure of the company. This process is called 'budgeting'.

When actual events occur, the information recording those events needs to be measured in such a way that it can be compared with the plan. This provides feedback on the success of the plan.

Controlling operations effectively also requires that information is provided in a form designed to help managers take the decisions which their jobs require. For example, information about the profit from one product as compared to another will enable a decision to be made about how many of each product to make.

### (c) Evaluating performance

Evaluating performance involves the analysis and assessment of actual results. This is partly, but not exclusively, a process of comparison with plans. The information on which plans were based may have been inaccurate. Thus, the analysis of performance, while involving comparison of actual results with planned results, needs considerable judgement as to what the plans should have been had all the information now available been known when the plans were drawn up.

The three activities we have described are by no means independent of each other. In reality, they follow a distinct sequence. One way of looking at this is in the form of a cycle in which information is circulating continually from one activity to another, as shown in Exhibit 36.2.

In this diagram, information is shown flowing around from one activity to another. Thus, for example, forecasts for a period may be improved before the period they apply to ends by taking

**Exhibit 36.2**

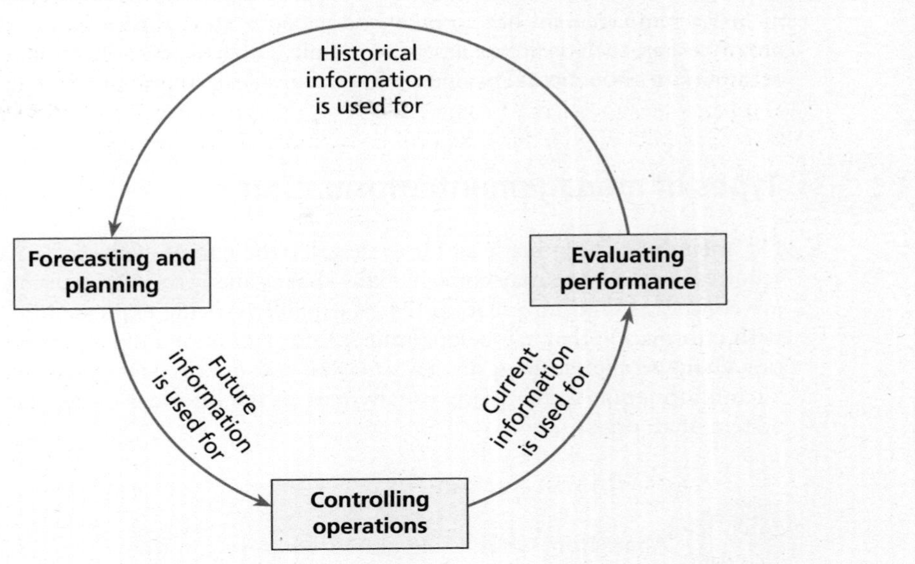


account of the analysis of what happened during the previous period *and* during the period to which the forecast relates.

As shown in Exhibit 36.2, forecasting and planning relate to the future. Controlling operations relates to concurrent events – the here and now. Evaluating performance can only be concerned with the past.

The diagram we have just considered only looks at internal information. Exhibit 36.3 recognises that information is being fed into the process from outside the organisation, both from the

**Exhibit 36.3**

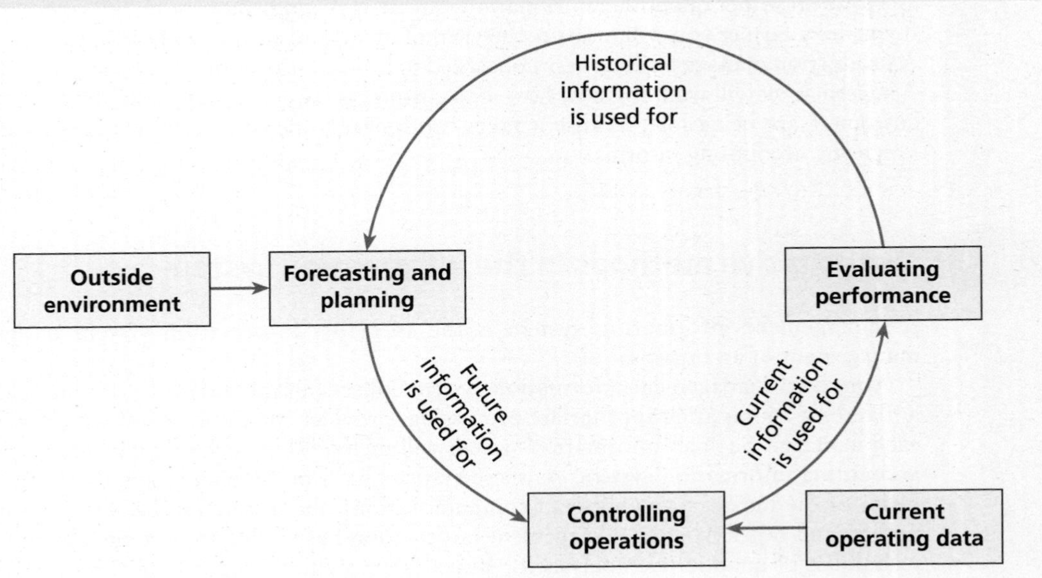

general environment in which the organisation operates and as a result of interactions between the organisation and its operating environment.

Senior management has to take into account all the information it can about the external environment, such as competition, economic cutbacks, etc. Controlling operations also receives information about actual business events, e.g. sales activity, purchasing activity, etc.

## 36.8 Types of management information

No attempt has been made so far to describe the nature of the information which management requires. Information may come in many shapes and forms. Accounting and, therefore, this book are concerned with information that is capable of being expressed in numerical terms. That is, with information that can be quantified. Information of a more general nature, such as information about people's feelings or views, may be very useful to management but cannot be quantified. Such information is, therefore, usually part of the informal rather than the formal information system of an organisation.

Apart from what is said above, what do you think is the main difference between formal and informal information systems?

Within the body of quantified information, it is normal to identify that part which can be measured in monetary terms. This part of the information system is called the 'accounting information system'. The accounting information system is a very important element of the organisation's information system since the organisation is basically an economic unit which must survive in conditions of economic scarcity and competition. In other words, an organisation which does not meet its economic objectives will eventually fail or be taken over, hence the central importance of accounting information.

However, other quantified information may be very important for management. For example, if you are a farmer you will measure the yield of milk from your cows in the first instance in litres. A production manager will be very concerned to monitor the tonnages produced on his machines. A supermarket will want to know how long customers have to queue at the checkout (and whether customers are being lost because it takes too long). None of these items is of interest to those preparing accounting information.

## 36.9 Quantitative methods in the information system

A management information system is the specialist information system designed for the management of an organisation.

A modern management information system collects all the data together (into what is called a 'database') and, after appropriate processing, provides the information which is important to each manager. Such an information system will include some information that originated in the accounting information system. As these systems have become more sophisticated (largely as a result of the impact of widespread computerisation), the distinction between accounting information and other types of management information has tended to become less meaningful. The techniques of quantitative analysis (or statistics) apply to all the data in this system, whether or not it is accounting data.

## Learning outcomes

**You should now have learnt:**

1 Financial accounting fulfils a stewardship function by reporting past performance and financial position.

2 Financial accounting information is of only limited use for management control purposes, for which other forms of data and information are required.

3 It is important that organisational objectives are clearly defined and that the financial accounting information system is designed to meet and support those objectives in the most efficient and effective way.

4 Management is concerned with three areas of activity:
   (*a*) forecasting and planning;
   (*b*) control;
   (*c*) evaluating performance.

5 The financial accounting information system does not exist in a vacuum, it interacts with, and is affected by, the environment in which it is operating and must be designed accordingly.

## Answers to activities

36.1 The original cost is now completely irrelevant for decision-making purposes, whether at this time or at some point in the future. Yet, in many cases, it is the £400,000 that will appear in the current year's statement of financial position and, in that case, the £400,000 is included in the amounts used to calculate ROCE and other key profitability and efficiency ratios. This is one of the reasons why IAS 16 allows non-current assets such as buildings to be revalued on a regular basis.

36.2 (i) To be identified as the most innovative company in the field and (ii) to have the lowest rate of staff turnover in the industry are two, neither of which can be identified or demonstrated through the use of information provided by financial accounting.

36.3 Lowering the standard of pollution control or the quality of product could possibly increase profits in the short term, but it could mean lower profits in the long term if customers deserted the organisation because it had a reputation for causing pollution or its goods were considered to be second-rate. Short-termism can be very counterproductive and often leads to the wrong decisions being taken, from a long-term perspective. However, conflicting objectives can often become compatible objectives when a long-term view is taken. For example, in the environmental example, by eliminating pollution an organisation may be able to enhance its reputation sufficiently to recoup the additional cost through increased revenues and, thus, maximise its profits in the long term.

36.4 At its simplest, an informal information system is one that operates without rules and procedures. Information gets passed through it virtually accidentally, in the same way as you may learn what someone did last weekend during a casual conversation. An informal information system has no firm structure. It does not have a hierarchy and information does not undergo any uniform or routine transformation as it passes around the information system. Information is not constrained by the nature of the information system and can be both qualitative and quantitative.

A formal information system is everything an informal information system is not. It has rules, procedures, a hierarchy, a routing system for data and information flow and set procedures for data and information processing. The data and information within it tend to be quantitative, though this is changing as computer systems become capable of greater storage. One key aspect of the formal information system is that nothing gets into it that isn't identified beforehand as an appropriate form of input. Formal information systems also tend to be fairly inflexible and slow to change compared with informal ones. Thus, for example, if the VAT rate changes and the information system cannot be easily or quickly amended to accept the new VAT rate, it may be some time before the necessary changes can be made and the information adjusted to reflect the change.

## Review questions

**36.1** 'Financial accounting looks behind, whilst management accounting looks ahead.' To what extent does this quotation accurately reflect the role of the two branches of accountancy?

*(Edexcel: University of London GCE A-level)*

**36.2** 'Financial accounting is non-dynamic, backward looking, conservative, as objective as possible, and subject to statutory and other regulation. Management accounting is future oriented, is dynamic, produces forward looking figures, should not be too concerned with objectivity, and is not generally subject to external regulation.' (Prof. Michael Bromwich) Justify this statement, giving examples to illustrate your answer.

*(Edexcel: University of London GCE A-level)*

**36.3** What are some of the deficiencies of financial accounting?

**36.4** Why is it important that the employees of an organisation should clearly understand what the objectives of the organisation are?

**36.5** How can there be a conflict between the various objectives of an organisation?

**36.6** Describe the management process and how it operates.

part 6

# THE EMERGING BUSINESS ENVIRONMENT OF ACCOUNTING

## Introduction

This part reviews increasingly popular recently developed approaches to managing the flow of information and data and enhancing the management of resources. It also looks at the emerging Internet-based business environment and the impact of e-commerce upon accounting.

chapter

# 37 The supply chain and enterprise resource planning systems

## Learning objectives

**After you have studied this chapter, you should be able to:**

- describe what is meant by the term 'supply chain'
- describe what is meant by the term 'supply chain management'
- describe some of the advantages of supply chain management
- describe what is meant by the term 'enterprise resource planning'
- describe what the differences are between an enterprise planning system and a traditional information system
- explain why organisations that integrate their ERP systems with supply chain management stand to benefit compared with those that do not
- explain why supply chain management and ERP systems are both important concepts for accounting and accountants

## Introduction

In this chapter you'll learn how organisations can improve their overall efficiency, reduce costs and increase revenues by adopting supply chain management. You'll also learn about the advantages of adopting enterprise resource planning and of the advantages of integrating an enterprise resource planning system with supply chain management. Finally, you'll learn why enterprise resource planning and supply chain management are important concepts for accounting and accountants.

## 37.1 Supply chain management

Manufacturing organisations purchase raw materials, convert them into finished goods, and then sell the finished goods. The term used to describe this sequence or chain of events is the **supply chain**. Everything within the two end-points of the chain is encompassed by the term. Thus, it includes demand forecasting, scheduling of production, supplier identification, ordering, inventory management, carriage, warehousing at all stages, production, and customer service. **The more the supply chain can be made a seamless and seemingly continuous process (where each stage acts as the trigger for the stage that follows it and where all the links operate automatically when appropriate), the more successful a business will be.**

An example of a supply chain is shown in Exhibit 37.1. For simplicity, warehousing has been omitted and purchasing is shown as being triggered by customer orders. Obviously, ordering often anticipates demand rather than being led by it.

**Exhibit 37.1**

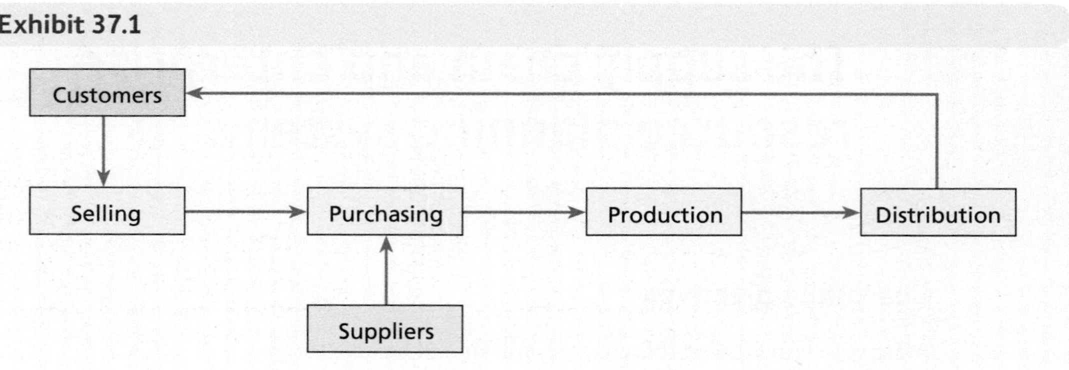


To achieve effective **supply chain management**, the organisation needs to have control over information and/or item flows both within and outwith the organisation. That is, all the external parties involved in the chain – suppliers, carriers, information systems providers, and customers – need to be linked through the supply chain management system into the supply chain at the appropriate points.

Supply chain management decisions fall into two broad categories: strategic and operational. Strategic decisions guide the design of the supply chain (by virtue of the supply chain needing to comply with and adhere to the strategic decisions of the organisation). The operational decisions relate to the flow through the supply chain and need to be compatible with the strategic decisions if the supply chain is to operate effectively and appropriately.

There are four stages at which these decisions need to be taken in supply chain management:

1 **Location.** The location of suppliers, warehouse facilities, and production facilities. Decisions need to be taken regarding physical location, size and number of such facilities. The location of each of these classes of facility determines the possible range of routes through the supply chain from supplier to customer and has a major impact on cost, time in the supply chain and level of service.
2 **Production.** At the strategic level, decisions must be made concerning what to produce and where, and which suppliers to use. The decisions made have a major impact upon costs. The strategic decisions include: what products to produce, which plants should produce them, and the allocation of suppliers to plants, plants to distribution channels, and DCs to customer markets. They define the flow through the supply chain in yet greater detail than that defined by the location choices. Operational decisions at this stage are concerned with production scheduling, equipment maintenance scheduling, workload planning, and quality control. As with location, both categories of decision at this stage have a big impact on the costs, revenues, and the level of customer service.
3 **Inventory.** The key impact of the decisions at this stage is upon customer service. However, there is an obvious and clear impact upon production scheduling and upon costs that arise from whatever decisions are taken. The principal decisions to be taken concern the levels of inventory to hold. Whether any should be held at all at the start of the chain is a key strategic decision – should a just-in-time approach be taken whereby the supplier holds the inventory of raw materials until ordered and orders are dispatched immediately by the supplier? The cost implications of such a decision are both obvious (there would be no need for raw material warehouse facilities) and less than obvious (there needs to be an excellent relationship with the supplier; access may well be needed to the supplier's inventory system, resulting in increased IT facility requirements and costs). Where a conventional inventory system is adopted, warehouse facilities will be required and an effective inventory control and ordering system must be established and maintained.

What operational decisions would need to be taken in order to establish and maintain an effective inventory control and ordering system?

4 **Distribution.** Decisions here are mainly strategic and relate to what form of distribution is to be used: lorry, van, train, plane, courier, etc. The decisions made need to consider distribution at all stages of the supply chain, i.e. receipts from suppliers, movements to storage facilities of finished and part-finished goods, and delivery to customers. While decisions at this stage often have less of an impact on cost to the business than some of the others that must be made, they are nonetheless crucial to the effective and efficient operation of the business and have both a direct and indirect impact upon customer service.

In what way can distribution decisions have both a direct and indirect impact upon customer service?

## 37.2 Advantages of effective supply chain management

A number of advantages have been identified as resulting from effective supply chain management:

- reduced costs
- reduced supply chain cycle times
- reduced lead times
- improved customer service
- improved inventory management
- improved distribution systems
- greater synergy between the objectives and actions of various elements of the organisation.

***Note*: Product quality is *not* seen as being improved through supply chain management, but the level of customer service and the utilisation of resources are.**

## 37.3 Difficulties in establishing supply chain management

The supply chain is a complex and dynamic network of facilities, departments and organisations with different, conflicting objectives. There are three principal difficulties encountered when a supply chain management system is being established:

(*a*) **Bringing together all the conflicting objectives of the parties involved** in the supply chain so as to produce an effective, efficient and manageable process.

(*b*) **Establishing effective relationships at all stages and between all elements of the supply chain.** Often this represents a significant change from the previous position. Suppliers, for example, may need to provide access to their inventory database or, at the very least, agree to prioritise orders and expedite deliveries. Inventory control must be strengthened and the relationships between production and ordering and production and selling must become seamless where, previously, they may have been very informal and distant. Both the systems and the interpersonal relationships of those involved must be changed to accommodate the shift to supply chain management.

(*c*) **IT systems need to be changed, frequently involving considerable initial and increased ongoing expense and changes in working practices.** There is certainly a requirement for many individuals to retrain in the new systems and software. Also, auditors have an enhanced and altered role in respect of the controls that are needed in such a system compared with a traditional purchasing/production/selling/distribution environment.

## 37.4 Accounting and supply chain management

Traditional approaches to accounting can identify some of the costs relating to supply chain management. However, because accounting focuses on transactions rather than business processes, it is only the directly visible costs and savings that arise from a supply chain management system that traditional accounting can record, monitor, and report.

Where an activity-based costing system has been adopted, there is an increased level of accounting-related information available (as it focuses upon the drivers of costs within business processes). As a result, many organisations that have adopted supply chain management have also adopted activity-based costing.

Nevertheless, there are considerable hidden costs and savings of introducing and operating a supply chain management system that even ABC cannot isolate and report. For example, it is difficult to put an accurate financial value on reductions in supply chain cycle times or on an increased synergy between the objectives of the various functions of an organisation involved in or affected by a supply chain. It is also hard to quantify the benefits of having stronger links with suppliers.

**As accountants are generally involved in costing new projects, they are usually heavily involved in assessing the merits of proposals for new or amended supply chain management systems. Failure to capture the appropriate data and information means that the models and techniques of the accountant can be very inadequate in assessing the viability and worth of such proposals.**

To play a meaningful role in supply chain management, accountants need to adopt a business process perspective and gather data relating to business events rather than individual transactions. Qualitative data needs to be gathered, processed, monitored and made available as well as quantitative data. At the same time, the range of quantitative data needs to be extended to include non-financial aspects of business events and processes, such as the names and other demographic information relating to customers, suppliers and employees.

This is seen as a sufficiently important area for accountants to become involved that a few years ago the American Institute of Management Accountants published two reports, *Implementing Integrated Supply Chain Management for Competitive Advantage* (which includes a cost and performance measurement system effectively to control the activities of the supply chain) and *Tools and Techniques for Implementing Integrated Supply Chain Management.*

Software suppliers are developing and offer a range of supply chain management software. Some products include fully integrated accounting systems, others enable existing accounting systems to be linked into the supply chain management system. Either approach results in new challenges for accountants as they become more involved in looking beyond the numbers and in communicating effectively to managers on aspects of the organisation with which they were not previously involved.

## 37.5 Enterprise resource planning

The supply chain crosses outside the organisation at two points – to the customers and to the suppliers. As such, much of the philosophy of supply chain management entails involving these outside agents in working with the organisation in the pursuit of its objectives. This is not a simple task – only the largest organisations can put pressure on their suppliers to the extent that they will agree to prioritise the organisation over all others. Similarly, most customers have a choice and may choose to avoid dealing with organisations that look for clearer indications of demand such as allowing them to access their inventory database and automatically provide new goods when the inventory reaches its reorder level.

Not surprisingly, supply chain management is a relatively recent development and the main beneficiaries have been the larger organisations that have embraced it. While small and medium-sized organisations can and do also adopt supply chain management, they have far greater difficulty in achieving the commitment of the outside entities to their objectives.

Another integrating approach, but one that is internal to the organisation, is the **enterprise resource planning (ERP) system**. ERP integrates the internal functions of the organisation and achieves savings through the efficiencies that result.

An ERP system is a suite of software modules. Each relates to a function of the organisation, such as order processing, production, creditor control, debtor control, payroll, marketing and human resources. The software modules are positioned on top of a centralised database, resulting in data being entered only once into the system but being accessible to all modules within it. Because the software modules all come from the same supplier, they are fully and seamlessly integrated from the start. There is no need to bolt together a range of software from different suppliers in order to achieve data integration.

There are two groups of applications within an ERP system:

(*a*) **Core applications.** The applications that need to work or the organisation will be unable to function. They include production, sales, distribution and planning. These are always fully integrated within the ERP system.

(*b*) **Business analysis applications.** Examples include modelling, decision support, information retrieval, reporting, accounting, simulation and 'what if' analysis. Some ERP software includes these. Some provide links into the ERP system to third-party software that performs these tasks.

## 37.6 Difficulties of justifying ERP

Integrating all the functions of an organisation in this way is a non-trivial exercise. It has been estimated that the implementation cost of a large ERP system is more than £25 million and the average annual cost of an ERP system is £11 million. As with supply chain management, the benefits of such systems are hard to quantify in traditional accounting terms or through the use of traditional accounting data and techniques.

Instead, as with supply chain management, less quantifiable advantages must be considered and weighed up against the identifiable costs.

## 37.7 Advantages of ERP systems

The advantages of ERP systems compared to traditional information system architectures include:

- increased data consistency;
- reduced data redundancy;
- greatly enriched data, including access to qualitative data by functions that do not typically have access to it;
- greatly increased depth and breadth of data analysis;
- reduced response times to information requests;
- reduced need for manual intervention in data access and analysis;
- reduced risk of errors in data or in its analysis;
- greatly enhanced exception reporting facility (due to the increase in the range of variables that can be flagged for monitoring);
- reduced time spent analysing exception reports (as the level of detail provided by the system is greatly enhanced);

- greatly reduced lead times in report generation;
- greatly increased efficiency in materials ordering, requisition and deployment;
- much closer ties between ordering, inventory control and production.

## 37.8 Organisational size

Since they first appeared, ERP systems have been developed in the largest organisations. Software vendors have produced their products with this in mind. However, computing power has increased and its price has dropped to such an extent that medium-sized and even small organisations can now take advantage of the software and develop ERP systems. While ERP systems are costly, the benefits are generally seen as outweighing the costs, provided the installation of ERP systems is effective and appropriate.

It is likely that within a few years, ERP software will be far cheaper and as commonplace in organisations of all sizes as general accounting packages are at present and that, in some cases, it will provide all the functionality of those accounting packages along with everything else they currently provide as standard.

## 37.9 ERP systems and supply chain management

Those organisations that add supply chain management to their ERP systems achieve the greatest benefit. An efficient and effective ERP system enhances the ability to integrate all the internal functions of the supply chain while also integrating other support functions, such as human resources and accounting. **Supply chain management enhances the capability of the ERP system to record and monitor all aspects of the organisation's business and bring suppliers and customers within the co-ordinated control of the organisation.**

Many organisations are moving in this direction and their accountants are being seen as playing a vital role in the success of the emerging information systems. For their part, ERP software providers have recognised the pivotal role of the accountant and have for some years funded American universities to integrate their software into accounting courses. Whether this occurs elsewhere remains to be seen. However, there is no doubt that ERP and supply chain management are two subjects that accountants need to be aware of and prepared to be involved with.

### Learning outcomes

**You should now have learnt:**

1. What is meant by the term 'supply chain'.
2. What is meant by the term 'supply chain management'.
3. About the advantages of supply chain management.
4. What is meant by the term 'enterprise resource planning'.
5. What the differences are between an enterprise planning system and a traditional information system.
6. Why organisations that integrate their ERP systems with supply chain management stand to benefit compared with those that do not.
7. Why supply chain management and ERP systems are both important concepts for accounting and accountants.

## Answers to activities

37.1 Inventory holding levels would need to be established for each item of raw materials: minimum level, safety inventory level, reorder level (see Section 43.8).

37.2 Customer service is directly affected by the speed at which delivery is made and by the amount charged for the service. It is indirectly affected by the decisions made concerning shipping raw materials in from suppliers and, once again, it is the time factor that matters. A just-in-time system that allows suppliers a week to deliver raw material orders is going to result in a level of customer service that is somewhat less than one that requires delivery within 24 hours.

## Review questions

**37.1** What is the supply chain?

**37.2** What is meant by the term 'supply chain management'?

**37.3** What are the advantages of effective supply chain management?

**37.4** Why does supply chain management bring new challenges for accounting and accountants?

**37.5** What is enterprise resource planning?

**37.6** What are the advantages of an ERP system?

**37.7** Why will those organisations that integrate their ERP systems with supply chain management benefit more than those that introduce only one or the other of these two concepts?

chapter

# 38 E-commerce and accounting

## Learning objectives

**After you have studied this chapter, you should be able to:**

- explain what is meant by 'e-commerce'
- explain what is meant by 'business-to-business' transactions
- explain what is meant by 'business-to-consumer' transactions
- describe a typical business-to-consumer transaction
- describe some of the benefits of e-commerce to sellers
- describe some of the benefits of e-commerce to buyers
- describe the impact of e-commerce upon the role of the financial accountant
- describe the impact of e-commerce upon the role of the management accountant
- describe the impact of e-commerce upon the role of the auditor, both internal and external
- explain why many retail businesses cannot afford to stay out of e-commerce

## Introduction

In this chapter, you'll learn about e-commerce and its impact upon sellers, buyers and accountants.

## 38.1 Background

For many years, all business was undertaken face-to-face. Gradually, orders started to be placed by other means – letter, telegram, telex, fax, telephone, etc. However, when transactions were undertaken between businesses, paper was normally exchanged indicating an order was being placed and, subsequently, indicating how much the seller required to be paid for the goods ordered.

This is the business environment in which accounting developed. Accountants learnt to use the documents relating to the transaction in order to make entries in the accounting books. They ensured there was an audit trail running from the original paperwork right through to each entry in the ledger. Checking these entries was time-consuming but always possible and, where original records did not exist, auditors would get very concerned as to the validity of transactions. Sometimes they accepted the word of the proprietor that transactions were valid. On other occasions, they did not and an investigation was launched in pursuit of evidence that things were recorded inaccurately.

What sorts of things were done in this investigation phase?

Other forms of business started to emerge. Ones where communication was electronic but, initially, all payment was by traditional means. Then payments too became increasingly electronic. Now, not only can communication and payment all be done electronically, but the seller may never physically possess the goods or services being sold and, in fact, the seller may not even be aware that a transaction has occurred (as the sale process is entirely automated). Also, products that were traditionally physical – books and CDs, for example – can now be sold as electronic files downloaded off the Internet directly into the customer's PC.

This is **electronic commerce (e-commerce)** and is the environment in which an increasing proportion of business is now conducted. It was expected that the total value of e-commerce transactions would rise by 400% between 2001 and 2004 to around US$5,000 billion. By 2013, it had risen to US$1.2 trillion.

In a report issued in 2001, *The Global Online Retailing Study,* the accounting firm Ernst & Young stated that online retailing is no longer an option, but a *business requirement.* Retail businesses must move into e-commerce or watch their markets disappear into the hands of their competitors. That was 14 years ago. If it was important then, it is even more so now. One obvious change that has occurred in this period is the massive switch to purchasing music by downloading it from the Internet. In 2001, this was rare: music was bought on CDs from shops. Now, many music shops have disappeared as buyers have switched to other sellers who are operating virtual shops and conducting their business as e-commerce organisations. Bookshops are also disappearing rapidly for the same reason and because of the rise of e-books.

Not surprisingly, data on the growth, trends and size of the e-commerce market are difficult to derive, inconsistent, and sometimes conflicting, depending on the source used. However, sufficient data is publicly available from which a view can be formed. In 2013, 1.42 billion individuals (41.3% of the world's Internet users) made online purchases. In Europe, 565 million individuals (69%) use the Internet and 264 million (32%) shop online. In 2013, online retailing in Europe totalled £111 billion. Online retail sales in the UK that year were £45 billion and were expected to grow by 12–15% each year, reaching £80 billion in 2018. In the UK, 38.8 million people used the Internet in May 2014 and 74% made online purchases during the year. Total retail sales in the UK in November 2014 were £7.9 billion.

Focusing on sales made in the UK, Internet sales represented between 11 and 13.5% of all retail spending in 2014. This makes the UK the market with the greatest penetration of Internet sales, followed by the USA, Germany, and Sweden. The average across Europe was 7.2% compared with 5.5% in 2010. In the five years since 2009, average weekly online spending in the UK rose from £342 million to £718 million.

Why do you think there may be problems for anyone trying to gather data of this type.

If you would like more information on this topic, *see*, for example, www.statista.com; www.retailresearch.org/onlineretailing.php; and The Office for National Statistics (www.ons.gov.uk/).

## 38.2 Electronic commerce

Electronic commerce can be defined as the use of electronic telecommunication technology to conduct business transactions over the Internet. It allows goods to be exchanged any time, 24 hours a day, seven days a week, anywhere the buyer has access to the Internet. It expands the market of every seller – in many cases, the market becomes global.

There are two principal e-commerce models:

1 **Business-to-business (B2B).** Businesses purchase from other businesses and/or sell their goods and services to other businesses; and
2 **Business-to-consumer (B2C).** Businesses sell to consumers. For B2C to work:
   (*a*) the customer must have access to the Internet;
   (*b*) the customer must have a means of making payment electronically (normally, a credit or debit card);
   (*c*) there must be a viable means of delivering the item(s) purchased to the consumer.

E-commerce involves the transmission of confidential, sensitive and valued information. To operate in this environment effectively, not only customers, but also business partners, must be convinced that a B2B or B2C business's systems are secure, reliable, available and properly controlled. While this is very much a necessity for effective supply chain management (Chapter 37), it is much more critical in an e-commerce environment and is the aspect of e-commerce that, more than any other, is impacting upon the role of the accountant and, in particular, the role of the auditor.

## 38.3 Business-to-business

B2B transactions are very similar to how transactions occur in a traditional business environment. Request for payment is often by traditional invoicing and payment follows at some date in the future.

### The seller

B2B e-commerce offers the seller many advantages over a traditional business environment, including:

- cost savings by removing the need for a human salesperson to be involved in the transaction;
- faster transaction times;
- lower clerical costs as there is now a reduced level of paper records to be prepared and maintained;
- richer analysis of sales due to greatly enhanced knowledge about the pattern of sale.

However, the major differences that e-commerce can bring to this form of e-commerce lie in the ability to integrate the B2B e-commerce system into the seller's accounting system. There is a growing range of integrated software available, including many of the ERP software packages referred to in Chapter 37.

Doing so has many advantages for the seller, including:

- better credit control at the time of sale;
- better control over debtor balances;
- potential to cut costs by automating the sale process, leaving it to be triggered by the level of inventory shown in the purchaser's inventory database.

### The buyer

The buyer benefits from:

- faster transaction times;
- greater confidence that orders will be filled in a timely manner;
- (in many cases) a greatly increased market (geographically) in which to make a purchase;

- cost savings arising from increased competition among sellers;
- (often) visual confirmation that what is being ordered is what is required (as there is no longer a possibility that an ill-informed salesperson is dealing with the order/enquiry).

## The accountant

There is less of a paper trail than under a traditional system. However, this has little effect on the day-to-day work of accountants working within the seller or buyer organisation. **Thus, accountants who work for the seller or buyer are relatively unaffected by the shift from a traditional business environment.** Transaction data is entered automatically into the accounting records rather than manually by a clerk. Thereafter, the internal accountant handles the data in the normal way and can create and provide all the 'normal' accounting information that would be provided were this a traditional business environment.

### Management accountants

There is the possibility of the management accountant providing more detailed and richer information to the decision-maker, as B2B transactions are information-rich compared with traditional ones. For example, far more qualitative and non-financial quantitative data is available or is available from a more reliable source.

### Financial accountants

Financial accountants will not experience very much change in the nature of data from that experienced under a traditional computerised accounting environment. However, when the audit is being conducted, there will be a need to be able to explain to the auditor where the data within the accounting system comes from and the controls that are in place to ensure that it is both accurate and reliable.

### Auditors

In contrast to the two main groups of accountants, auditors (both internal and external) are greatly affected by the introduction of B2B e-commerce. As mentioned earlier, there is less of a paper trail than under a traditional system. In fact, there may be nothing on paper until a goods delivery note is prepared in order to ship the goods. Thus, they have an increased need to focus on the technology involved in each transaction. As a result, they need to focus on assurance. In particular, online assurance, i.e. whether the B2B system is working correctly and whether all the transaction details being recorded are accurate, reliable and complete.

This represents a major change in the nature of the audit, even where previously an organisation's accounting system was computerised. Often in that case, auditors audited around the computer – that is, they checked that what came out was what they would have expected. In a B2B organisation, they need to audit through the computer – that is, they need to be assured that the computer is doing the correct things and that there are appropriate controls in place to ensure that errors are not made. This is particularly needed in the seller organisation because there is typically no human intervention in the transaction. In this case, the assurance should, preferably, be in real time. That is, the check on the controls on transactions should be done as transactions are being processed.

## 38.4 Business-to-consumer

This is the side of e-commerce that is most different from the traditional business environment. The seller is represented by a computer program which responds as appropriate to enquiries made by a consumer who can not only place an order but who will also provide a shipping address and make payment, all at the same time.

The consumer accesses the Internet and navigates to the seller's website. At the website, the consumer checks the seller's catalogue for the item(s) required, often through a series of searches of the seller's inventory database. This in itself may be very different from a traditional high-street purchase, for the seller may actually have little or no physical inventory. Instead, the seller has built an inventory database of the items that can be shipped to a customer in a reasonable period of time. (You can see examples of this at sites such as **www.amazon.co.uk**)

When the decision is made to purchase something, the customer is directed to the seller's *online transaction server,* where all the customer's information, including personal details, the item(s) required, and credit or debit card details are entered. This information, particularly the credit card information, is usually encrypted as it is received. The information is then passed to the bank that issued the credit or debit card and to the seller's bank (i.e. the bank that operates the receipt of funds in this form for the seller). If both banks accept the transaction, the seller is informed it has been accepted and provided with an order number for reference and an indication of when the item(s) will be shipped.

This B2C e-commerce system is presented in Exhibit 38.1:

**Exhibit 38.1**

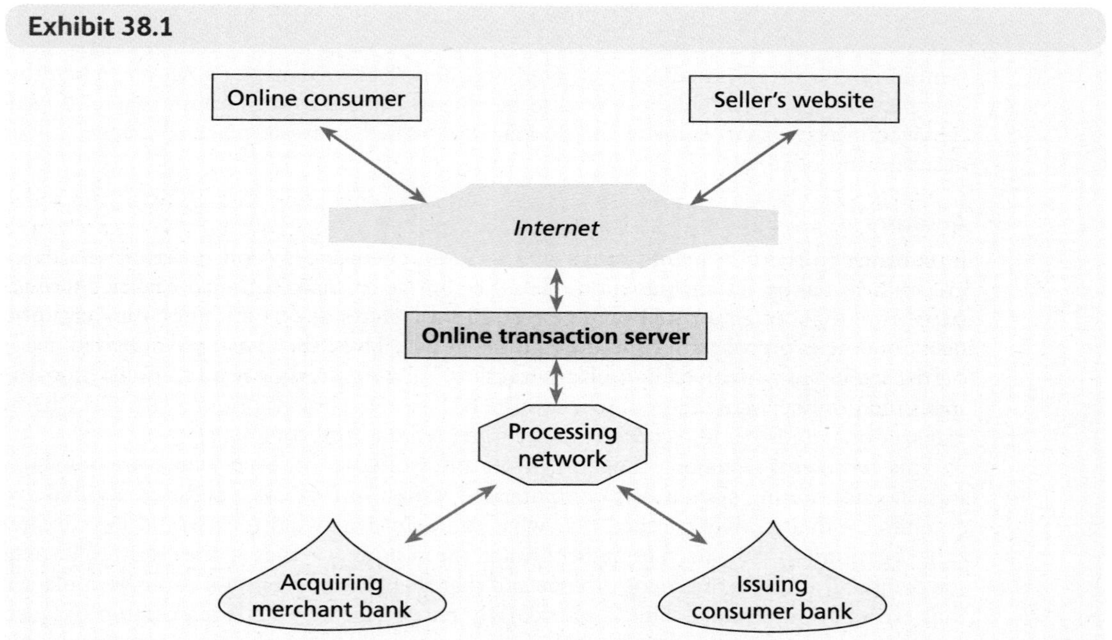


**Activity 38.3**

Compared with businesses operating in a traditional trading environment, what advantages concerning receipt of payment can you see for a business operating in a B2C environment?

## 38.5 Accountants and B2C e-commerce

B2C e-commerce has an impact upon the routine work of financial and management accountants similar to B2B. However, there are major issues with which accountants must be involved when the business first moves into a B2C environment:

1 The size of the transaction database. Is it going to be capable of handling a significant increase in transactions? In fact, what is that level of transactions likely to be?
2 The interface between the B2C systems and the accounting system.
3 The internal controls – the accountants need to emphasise the need for effective internal controls – checks built into the system to ensure entries are correct and correctly authorised – at the design stage, when it is easiest to incorporate them into the B2C system.

These are particularly difficult issues to deal with when the business is new and has no existing customer base, especially the question of size.

Auditors have similar issues to deal with as under B2B but, often, far more transactions to deal with. As individuals rather than other businesses are normally involved on the consumer side, there is a need to ensure that effective controls are in place in the system concerning credit card fraud and data security, for the liability if the system is breached may be far greater than if a B2B system is breached.

There is a further dimension for accountants to be concerned with concerning B2C transactions – globalisation.

## 38.6 Globalisation

In the UK, 23% of consumers use B2C to purchase goods they wish to buy from sellers in the EU and 21% from the rest of the world, either because the goods they want are not available in their own country or because they have found it cheaper to buy overseas. In 2013, in the UK 15.9 million shoppers spent £8.5 billion on online cross-border goods. The five most common categories of goods purchased in this were clothes, shoes and accessories; personal electronics; health and beauty products; computer hardware; and jewellery, gems and watches.

For accountants, this adds problems concerning international tax and, for auditors especially, opens the possibility of international fraud.

## 38.7 E-commerce and accounting

E-commerce is changing and will continue to change the manner in which accountants carry out their role and, more importantly, it will change the nature of that role.

We already have a wide range of accounting software that eliminates the need to use traditional double entry to record transactions. Accountants have remained outside the system changes by continuing to do what they've always done and, instead, they have developed computer packages to check that the accounting software was working properly.

The accountants did not need to be retrained and, for many years, no attention was paid in the training of accountants to this shift in the environment of accounting. This was possible because business was still conducted in traditional ways. It was only the manner by which transactions were recorded that changed.

E-commerce changed this. An increasing proportion of transactions are now conducted electronically, both between businesses and between businesses and consumers. In many cases, there are no paper records and no written entries relating to these transactions. As a result, **accountants can no longer check a transaction against the original invoice or order document. Neither can they check that someone with appropriate authority has approved an order by signing an authorisation.**

Take away the paper, take away the written signature, and take away the double entry and what have you left for an accountant to do? Even more to the point, what can an auditor do to check the validity and accuracy of the accounting records?

A knowledge of double entry is still important. No financial accountant will be able to function effectively all the time without it. Accountants need to understand the entries in the accounting records and need to be able to tell if they are appropriate and correct. They also need to know how to produce financial statements and how to make appropriate adjustments to the accounting figures when doing so. Thus, there is still a need for the traditional techniques, skills and understanding that have been covered in both volumes of *Business Accounting*.

However, they now need to add further techniques, skills and understanding to their role. They need to shift towards real-time assurance – verifying that things are as they should be *in real time*. To do so, accountants need to become technologically competent. They need to know and understand the technological infrastructure of e-commerce in the same way as they have always needed to know the infrastructure of traditional business and the manner in which it is conducted and performed. They need to know how to recognise weaknesses and loopholes, and how to trap errors in an electronic business environment. They need to know how to distinguish between valid entries and those that are erroneous or falsified when the only evidence they have is electronic.

There are great changes coming in the role of the accountant. Some of the professional accounting bodies already have examinations which consider these issues, but those examinations are being sat by people who have already been working as accountants for a few years. Pre-work education always lags behind real life and it will be many years before it is normal to include these skills in accounting courses at schools, colleges and universities. Instead, they will be learnt later, on the job, by attending training courses, or while studying for the examinations of the professional accountancy bodies.

As a student of accounting, you will be wise to become aware of this changing environment and to understand how it differs from the world as presented in the classroom and in your textbooks. Don't let it take you by surprise. Look at the Internet, learn how business is conducted upon it and consider how different it is from doing business face-to-face.

## Learning outcomes

**You should now have learnt:**

1. What is meant by 'e-commerce'.
2. What is meant by 'business-to-business' transactions.
3. What is meant by 'business-to-consumer' transactions.
4. What occurs in a typical business-to-consumer transaction.
5. About some of the benefits of e-commerce to sellers and buyers.
6. About the impact of e-commerce upon the role of the financial accountant, management accountant, internal auditor, and external auditor.
7. Why retail businesses cannot afford to stay out of e-commerce.

## Answers to activities

38.1 Contacting the customer or supplier and asking for confirmation; checking inventory to confirm that it had existed; checking the existence of non-current assets; etc.

38.2 There are many reasons, including: data being difficult to collect; definitions of 'Internet sales' vary; some personal consumption items, such as petrol for a car, cannot be purchased online, so some analysts exclude this type of expenditure when calculating the proportion of all spending that is made online, but others do not.

38.3 No sales take place without prior payment which is guaranteed by the issuing consumer bank. There will, therefore, be no bad debts for the seller. Also, there is far greater control over cash flow as payment will always be received on time.

## Review questions

**38.1** What is e-commerce?

**38.2** What happens in a typical business-to-consumer transaction?

**38.3** What impact is e-commerce having upon the role of the accountant?

**38.4** Why can retail businesses not afford to ignore e-commerce?

chapter

# 39 Forensic accounting

## Learning objectives

**After you have studied this chapter, you should be able to:**

- Define the term 'forensic accounting'
- Describe a range of tasks undertaken by forensic accountants
- Explain the difference in the approach to their jobs taken by forensic accountants compared to that taken by accountants
- Describe how the accounting profession is responding to a growth in demand for forensic accounting services

## Introduction

In this chapter, you'll learn about forensic accounting and the nature of the activities performed by forensic accountants

## 39.1 What is forensic accounting?

Forensic accounting has been defined by the Association of Certified Fraud Examiners as '*the use of professional accounting skills in matters involving potential or actual civil or criminal litigation, including, but not limited to, generally acceptable accounting and audit principles; the determination of lost profits, income, assets, or damages; evaluation of internal controls; fraud; and any other matter involving accounting expertise in the legal system*'.

More recently, a more comprehensive definition was offered by two leading American scholars, Dennis Huber and Jim DiGabriele. They drew to our attention that forensic accounting is considerably more than an area in which accountants may practise; it is a field of activity in which people from many different professions participate. Their definition states that forensic accounting is:

> **A multidisciplinary field that encompasses both a profession and an industry, where civil or criminal economic and financial claims, whether business or personal, are contested within established political structures, recognized and accepted social parameters, and well-defined legal jurisdictions, and informed by the theories, methods, and procedures from the fields of law, auditing, accounting, finance, economics, psychology, sociology, and criminology.**

Forensic accounting can be broken down into two main aspects: litigation support and investigative services. Traditionally, it has been in the role of an expert witness that most people assume forensic accountants are engaged; and being an expert witness may involve the forensic accountant in work involving either of these two main categories.

Litigation support involves providing the data or information or opinion to support expert testimony. This would include finding the evidence relating to testimony on tax matters; insurance litigation claims; misuse of computer systems; divorce; equitable property settlements; contractual disputes; bankruptcy; and accounting and auditing litigation issues.

Investigative forensic accounting is concerned with looking for and discovering inaccuracies. While auditors are interested in the numbers and the systems of internal control, forensic accountants go beyond both. In particular they look for indicators of fraud and criminal transactions in banks, businesses and any other entity's financial records. In doing so, they analyse seemingly ordinary documents and transaction records, looking primarily for inconsistencies. They have a far more sceptical approach than accountants and auditors, one which is embedded in the lack of any assumption concerning the integrity of management or employees.

However, as will be shown in Section 39.5, there is more to the role of a forensic accountant than being an expert witness, i.e. making testimony on issues on which the witness is an expert.

## 39.2 Who can act as a forensic accountant

A forensic accountant will typically specialise in one or more of the areas of forensic accounting work. For obvious reasons, a qualified accountant is most likely to have the necessary expertise to act as an expert witness on accounting, auditing and taxation matters. However, due to the different focus of their work, forensic accountants will be more qualified in the other forensic accounting tasks and activities than accountants would normally be expected to be. For this reason, many of those who work as forensic accountants are not qualified accountants but lawyers, systems specialists, surveyors, real estate experts, or members of other professional groups who may not actually know very much about accounting.

## 39.3 The skill set of a forensic accountant

Anyone wishing to perform across the entire range of forensic accounting activities would need to be skilled in financial accounting; cost accounting; taxation; economics; finance; statistics and quantitative analysis; information technology; business law; and knowledge of professional standards (i.e. how professionals should behave and perform in given situations). Forensic accounting also involves considerable communication, both when investigating and when reporting. Consequently, forensic accountants also need good communication skills as well as good investigative skills. It is fairly obvious that, just as being a proficient accountant does not automatically make someone a good tax accountant, being a proficient accountant does not automatically make someone a capable forensic accountant.

**Activity 39.1**

Why do you think a forensic accountant needs to be knowledgeable about professional standards?

## 39.4 The development of forensic accounting

Forensic accounting can be traced back to 13th-century England when auditors would carry out investigative activities along with their other duties. However, the roots of modern forensic accounting can be found in 18th-century Scotland, when solicitors (lawyers) appointed accountants to rank the claims of creditors.

However, it is only since the late 20th century that forensic accounting has begun to establish itself as a profession in the UK. Now, all the larger accounting firms have specialist forensic accounting departments and there are over 300 independent forensic accounting firms in the UK.

## 39.5 The response of the accountancy profession to the growth of forensic accounting practice in the UK

The professional accountancy bodies have begun to respond to the growth in demand for and existence of forensic accounting practitioners. In 1999, the Institute of Chartered Accountants in England and Wales (ICAEW) formed a forensic special interest group for its members to maintain a list of authorised forensic practitioners, develop a formal apprenticeship, and introduce professional examinations. Only the first of these has occurred.

More recently, in 2009 the ICAEW launched a voluntary accreditation scheme for forensic accountants and expert witnesses. Obtaining ICAEW forensic accountant or expert witness accreditation depends upon experience. For forensic accounting accreditation, evidence must be provided of experience in eight areas:

1 Accounting expertise;
2 Forensic technique A – evidence;
3 Forensic technique B – interviewing and negotiation;
4 Forensic technique C – general application;
5 Understanding of law/regulation;
6 Commercial knowledge;
7 Management skills; and,
8 Written communications skills.

Expert witness accreditation requires experience in these eight areas plus experience in:

- Court or other adjudication forum; and
- Expert meetings.

In 2012, Chartered Accountants Ireland (CAI) launched a diploma in forensic accounting for their members. The diploma comprised of six modules:

(*i*) An Introduction to Forensic Accounting
(*ii*) Expert Witness Assignments (Part 1)
(*iii*) Expert Witness Assignments (Part 2)
(*iv*) Fraud, Theft and Other Financial Investigations (Part 1)
(*v*) Fraud, Theft and Other Financial Investigations (Part 2)
(*vi*) Case Study – Putting it into Practice

However, no other major initiatives have been launched in the UK and Ireland and it now seems that the accountancy profession in this part of the world has accepted that it cannot drive the establishment of forensic accounting as something belonging to the profession of accounting.

The reasons for this are not difficult to identify. Forensic accounting is a line of activity in which accountants participate but, as shown in Exhibit 39.1, a recent study of UK and Irish forensic accountants found that it is a field of activity that has great variability in the expertise required, none of which is necessarily something for which accountants are the best prepared.

Too much of forensic accounting activity requires skills other than accounting. The skills shown in Exhibit 39.1 do not just apply to accounting assignments, they apply to issues relating to people, to organisations, to computer systems, computer programs, data analytics in general, and many other situations that have little direct involvement of or need for accounting expertise.

In addition, there is too much involvement in forensic accounting from other professional groups, to permit one single profession to take ownership and leadership in establishing

**Exhibit 39.1 Skills considered essential and desirable in forensic accounting**

| | | Essential or desirable % | Essential % |
|---|---|---|---|
| 1 | Effective written communication skills | 100.0 | 89.3 |
| 2 | Ability to analyse & interpret financial information | 100.0 | 87.5 |
| 3 | Analytical skills | 98.2 | 82.1 |
| 4 | Effective oral communication skills | 100.0 | 73.2 |
| 5 | Problem solving skills | 100.0 | 60.7 |
| 6 | Fraud investigation skills | 100.0 | 55.4 |
| 7 | Knowledge of rules of evidence & court procedure | 98.2 | 53.6 |
| 8 | Loss quantification skills | 96.4 | 48.2 |
| 9 | Ability to synthesise results of discovery & analysis | 96.4 | 48.2 |
| 10 | Presentation skills | 100.0 | 46.4 |

forensic accounting as a stand-alone profession in its own right. Any such development will depend upon those engaged in forensic accounting determining that there is enough similarity in the nature of their work to form a professional association that may ultimately lead this group of specialists.

## 39.6 The future of forensic accounting in the UK

There is no doubt that forensic accounting will continue to grow in importance, especially at a time, such as now, when a series of high-profile corporate scandals at the beginning of this century was followed by a loss of credibility of the banking sector, a collapse of the property market, and a shortage of credit, all since 2007/8. These have all combined to generate a major increase in demand for forensic accounting services as businesses and individuals struggle to maintain liquidity while faced with significantly less valuable assets to underpin their business activities. Financial crime is at a peak and a shortage of accountants capable of performing forensic accounting tasks that, as described in Section 39.5, are often beyond the expertise of an accountant has led to an influx of non-accountants into an emerging professional area that accountants would traditionally see as theirs by right. So much so, that the accounting profession is no longer indicating any significant interest in doing so.

The situation is different in this respect elsewhere. In the United States, Canada, Australia and New Zealand, for example the accounting profession has been far more proactive in endeavouring to retain control of forensic accounting, establishing codes of practice and promoting education initiatives both for their members and in universities. Yet, no widely accepted professional body has emerged and there is no more evidence to suggest that accountants have control of this field of activity elsewhere than they have in the UK and Ireland.

For those accountants who choose to switch into forensic accounting, there is a great deal of opportunity – salaries, for example, are likely to be higher, especially for the more experienced. However, forensic accounting is clearly a very different activity from those traditionally performed by professional accountants. A desire by accountants to continue doing what they have always done and consequently distance themselves from forensic accounting, which is what seems to be happening just now, may lead to an entirely new profession emerging. While it might continue to be linked to but separate from the accountancy profession, it is very likely that the majority of its members would be qualified in other professional areas more suited to the role of a forensic accountant.

## Learning outcomes

**You should now be able to:**

**1** Define the term 'forensic accounting'.

**2** Describe the range of tasks undertaken by forensic accountants.

**3** Describe the difference in the approach to their jobs taken by forensic accountants compared to that taken by accountants.

**4** Describe how the accounting profession is responding to the growth in demand for forensic accounting services.

## Answer to activity

39.1 So that what occurred may be compared with what should have occurred and a judgement made concerning whether or not what happened was acceptable.

## Review question

**39.1** Define forensic accounting and explain how it differs from traditional accounting and auditing.

part 7

# COSTING

## Introduction

**This part looks at what constitutes cost and at four techniques used to derive cost.**

chapter 40

# Elements of costing

## Learning objectives

After you have studied this chapter, you should be able to:

- explain why information must fit the purpose for which it is prepared
- discuss why the costs of obtaining information should be less than the benefits of having the information
- describe the flow of costs through financial accounts
- describe the flow of costs through a manufacturing business
- classify expenses appropriately
- explain the importance of an effective costing system
- explain the importance of cost allocation in the context of control

## Introduction

In this chapter, you'll learn how costs flow through financial accounts and through a manufacturing business's accounting system into its manufacturing account. You will also be introduced to, and reminded of, terminology relating to costs and expenses and learn the difference between them through an exercise in cost classification.

## 40.1 Management accounting

So far you have learnt about bookkeeping and the preparation of financial statements. These are the two principal components of financial accounting. As you learnt in Chapter 40, the information as produced by financial accounting is usually historic, backward-looking and produced (mainly) for the use of decision-makers external to the organisation.

There is a second side to accounting. This one is generally forward-looking and capable of being used to aid managerial control, forecasting and planning. Similarly to financial accounting, it also consists of two components. One where costs are recorded, the other where the data is processed and converted into reports for managers and other decision-makers. The cost recording component is called '*cost accounting*' and the processing and reporting component is called '*management accounting*', which is also the name used to refer to this side of accounting. It is also sometimes referred to as 'managerial accounting'.

**Cost accounting data also feeds into financial accounting,** where it is used to derive the cost and expenditure figures that appear in the statement of profit or loss. However, the two branches of accounting use the data and information differently. Referring once more to the third exhibit in

Chapter 36, reproduced here as Exhibit 40.1, you can follow the flow of data and information within it and see how and where management accounting information is used.

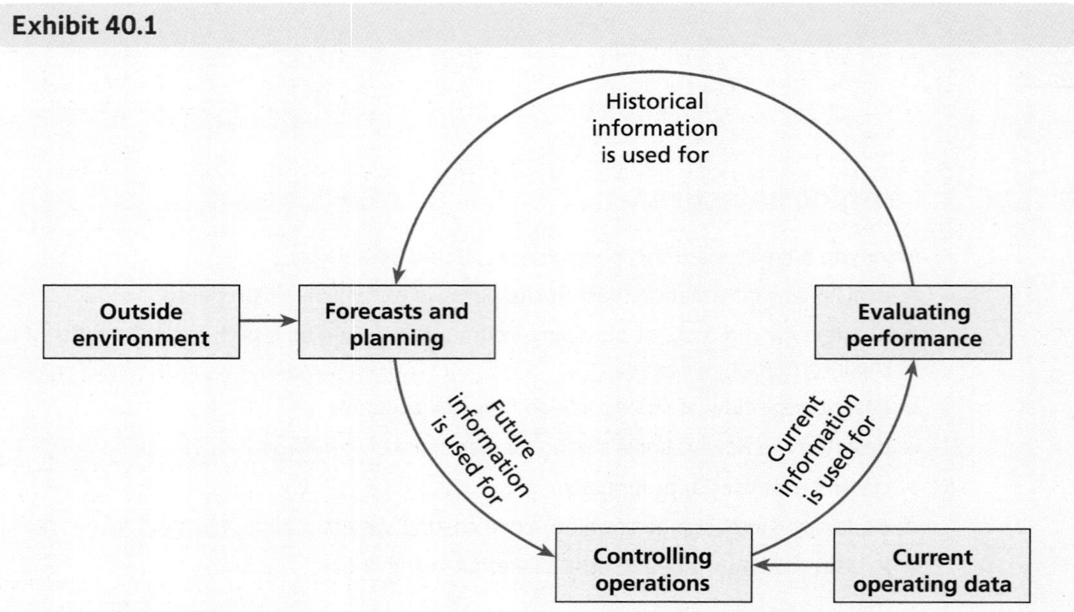


Management accounting produces the financial forecasts that guide planning. It embeds controls into the flow of operating data and uses them to control activities within the context of the plans. It evaluates performance and uses the information that is produced to underpin the forecasts that guide planning.

As you can see, while it frequently looks backwards to gather information, the main focus of management accounting is on producing information (*i*) for control over current operations, and (*ii*) to forecast and plan for the future.

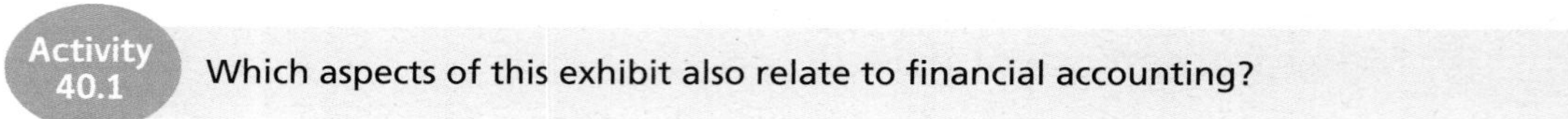


Which aspects of this exhibit also relate to financial accounting?

For financial accounting and management accounting to operate effectively, they both need the raw data that is then built up and processed into the information they produce. As mentioned earlier, the process whereby this data is gathered is known as cost accounting.

## 40.2 Costs for different purposes

Cost accounting underpins both the management accounting system and the financial accounting system of an organisation. Without cost accounting, such systems could not exist as they would be unable to determine with any accuracy the costs and expenditures relating to each aspect of their activities. Before entering into any detailed review of costs, it is better if we **ask ourselves first of all what use we are going to make of information about costs**. By doing so, the context and motivations for cost accounting will be revealed, thus making it easier to understand the nature of the costs themselves.

Let's do so, first, by referring to something that is not accounting, and then relating it to accounting. Suppose you had a job in a local business and that your employer has just left you a message asking you to measure the distance between Manchester and London. As you thought about this request, the following thoughts might go through your head:

1 ***How*** does he want the distance measured? Some possibilities are:
   (*a*) from the southern outskirts of Manchester to the northern outskirts of London;
   (*b*) from the accepted geographical centre of London to the accepted geographical centre of Manchester;
   (*c*) to the centres of the two cities calculated as mathematically precise points;
   (*d*) from a Manchester postcode to a London postcode;
   (*e*) by road – this could be just major roads, just minor roads, or could be a mixture of both – the main requirement being the quickest route by road;
   (*f*) by canal;
   (*g*) by train;
   (*h*) by air; allowance may or may not be made for the distance covered by the aircraft which would include climbing to an altitude of 5,000 feet or perhaps 40,000 feet, or might ignore the distance travelling in achieving an altitude.
2 The ***cost*** of obtaining the information. Measuring distances (or measuring costs) is not costless itself. Using very sophisticated instruments to get accurate measurement can be very expensive indeed, especially if you have to purchase the equipment first in order to do so. On the other hand it might just be a matter of measuring the distance on a map with a rule and converting it into miles – this would cost hardly anything at all.
3 At first glance, it may seem obvious that this should be done either online using websites like Google Maps and Mappy, or by using a GPS route application you may have on your phone. However, you could be wrong to do so. You must first consider the ***purpose*** for which the measurement will be used. This has been deliberately left as the last point, but in fact it should have been the first question that came into your mind. Illustrations of the use could have been as follows:
   (*a*) he is going to drive from Manchester to London by car and wants a rough idea of the mileage so that he can gauge what time to set off if he is to arrive before it gets dark in London;
   (*b*) he might conceivably want to walk it;
   (*c*) he might be submitting a tender for the building of a motorway by the shortest possible route, cutting tunnels through ranges of hills;
   (*d*) perhaps he wants to send goods by canal;
   (*e*) maybe he wants to arrive as close as possible to an underground station;
   (*f*) he might be an amateur pilot who wants to fly from Manchester Airport to one of the London airports.

You may also wonder about how accurate an answer is required.

The lesson to be learnt from all this is that the measurement required depends entirely on the use that is to be made of it, i.e. of the data. Too often, businesses make measurements of financial and other data without looking first at the use that is going to be made of it. In fact, it is sometimes said that 'information' is useful data that is provided for someone to use for a specific purpose and that, unless it is suitable for that purpose, it is worthless.

**Thus, data given to someone which is not relevant to the purpose for which it is required is simply *not* information.** Data which is provided for a particular purpose, and which is completely wrong for the purpose, is worse than having no data at all. At least when there is no data, the decision-maker knows that the best that can be done is to guess.

Apart from the obvious fact that it is irrelevant, why is useless data such a bad thing?

Now, let's assume that instead of being asked for the distance from Manchester to London, you were asked to discover what something cost. You need to consider the following:

1 ***What is the data on costs wanted for?***
It might be needed for the preparation of the financial statements, for management control or for decision-making. Different data on costs is wanted for different purposes.
For example, the cost of each item of inventory held at the end of the financial year is needed for the preparation of the financial statements; the cost of each item in inventory is needed for management control to verify whether items are being manufactured or purchased at an appropriate price; and the cost of each unit of inventory held is required to decide what price to sell it at. Three very different uses of three very similar items.

2 ***How are the costs to be measured?***
Only when the purpose for which costs are to be used has been identified can the measurement process be selected. Sometimes, financial accounting needs a precision in calculating certain costs which is not needed in management accounting; sometimes the opposite is the case. It depends on the costs involved and why they are required.

3 ***The cost of obtaining data should not exceed the benefits to be gained from having it.***
This does not apply when data on cost is needed to comply with various provisions of the law but such exceptions are rare.
Let's look at some examples to illustrate the cost/benefit factor:
(*a*) Spending £100 to obtain cost data which will be used as a basis for pricing many of a company's products. If the costs used were 'guessed' rather than actual figures, errors in the sales prices derived from those costs could lead to large losses, as some items were sold at prices lower than their actual cost while others were priced so high they could not be sold.
(*b*) Spending £10,000 to find data on sales which the sales manager will not use because it is not the data she wants is obviously money wasted.
(*c*) Spending a lot of time and money to find that the inventory value on a particular day was exactly £2,532,198 when the chairman was having an informal chat with the bank manager, and all he needed to know was an approximate inventory valuation. The approximate figure could have been found easily and at little cost, so here the costs of obtaining the information have exceeded the benefits of having it.

**When it is known what the costs are for, and how much may be spent on obtaining them, an appropriate method to be used to obtain them can be selected. The same applies to information about anything – the benefits of obtaining the information should always exceed the cost of doing so.**

## 40.3 Past costs in trading companies

There are many classifications of cost. As we go through the rest of this chapter, we'll summarise briefly those that you already know about. The first of these is historical cost.

### Historical cost

Historical costs underpin financial accounting as we know it today. Historical cost is the amount something actually cost. Exhibit 40.2 shows a simplified view of costs flowing through the financial accounting system from original transaction to the ledgers to the financial statements and the calculation of profit. Revenue from sales has been included simply so as to enable profits to be shown. All items in this case have been entered on the basis of their historical cost.

When calculating net profit some of the items may be included at a 'cost' that is different from their historical cost. Buildings, for example, may have been revalued to reflect their market value.

**Exhibit 40.2**

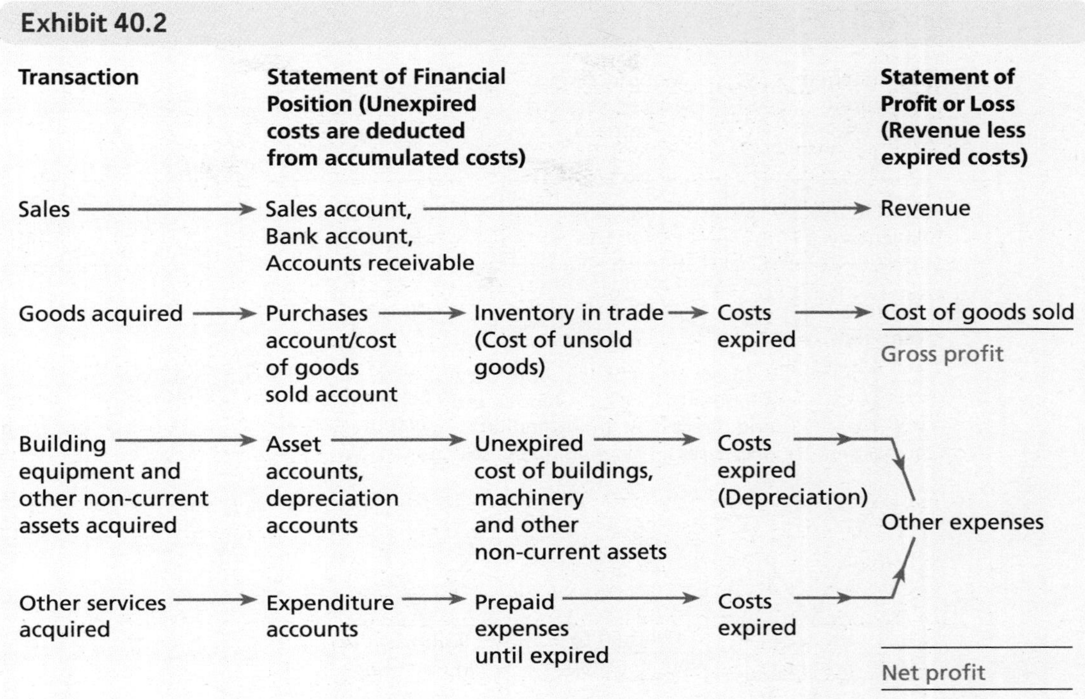


If so, depreciation would be based on the revalued amount, not the historical cost of the buildings; and the amount the buildings are shown at in the statement of financial position would be based on their revalued amounts, not their historical cost. However, the flow of 'cost' information shown in Exhibit 40.2 would not change. It is the nature or bases of the amounts shown that change.

When a company manufactures goods for sale, other costs need to be included.

## 40.4 Past costs in manufacturing companies

You probably covered the topic of manufacturing accounts when you studied *Business Accounting 1*. In this chapter, we will look at it in more detail, as it is essential for a study of cost accounting. First, a couple of definitions:

### Product costs

These are the costs attributed to the units of goods manufactured. They are included in the calculation of the cost of goods manufactured in the trading account, and would normally be part of the valuation of unsold goods if the goods to which they refer had not been sold by the end of the period. Product costs are, therefore, charged against revenue only when the goods they relate to are sold.

### Period costs

Period costs are non-manufacturing in nature, i.e. selling and distribution, administration and financial expenses. They are treated as expenses of the period in which they are incurred irrespective of the volume of goods sold.

**Exhibit 40.3**

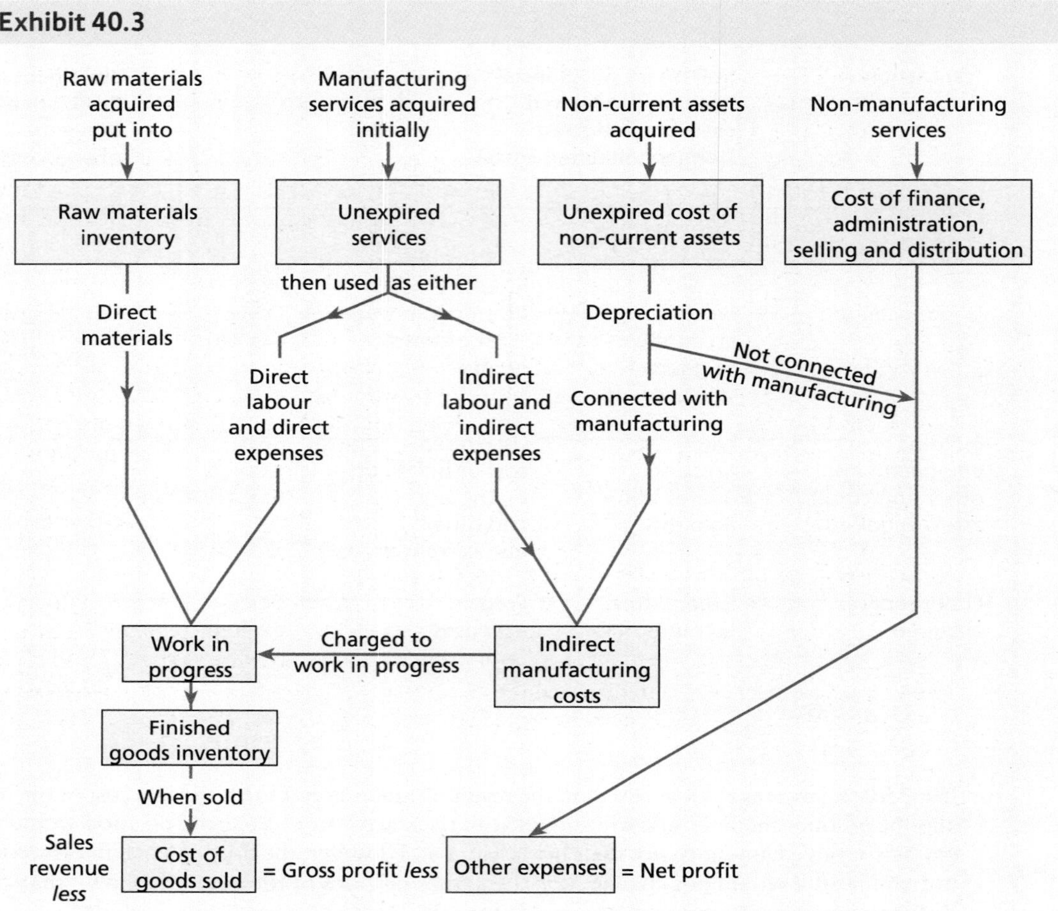


Knowledge of the differences between these two types of costs is acquired so that manufacturing accounts may be produced. Exhibit 40.3 shows the flow of costs through a manufacturing company from initial transaction to their inclusion in the cost of work in progress and finished products.

***Note*: Exhibits 40.2 and 40.3 show what you use cost information for in financial accounting: to produce the information you need in order to prepare the financial statements. In management accounting, there is a different emphasis, some of which overlaps with the needs of financial accounting, but much of which is for completely different purposes.**

## 40.5 Further costs defined

The following is a more detailed description of costs than you will have encountered previously.

- *Direct materials* are those materials which become part of the finished goods, subject to the proviso that the expense involved in tracing the cost is worthwhile. Some items which, strictly speaking, are direct costs may be treated as indirect materials even though they are part of the finished product because the cost cannot be ascertained easily. (This is an example of application of the cost/benefit test.)

- *Direct labour* comprises those labour costs which are incurred in converting direct materials into finished goods, also subject to the proviso that the expense involved in tracing this cost is worthwhile.
- *Direct expenses* are those expenses which can be traced directly to the product being manufactured. These are fairly rare, but an example would be a royalty payment where the production of each unit produced resulted in, say, £1 being due to the owner of a patent on that product.
- *Prime cost*: the total of direct materials + direct labour + direct expenses is called prime cost.

  Accountants each have their own opinion as to whether certain costs are worth tracing as being of a direct type, as it will often be a matter of judgement which defies any easy proof whether or not the expense of tracing the cost exceeds the benefit from so doing. Thus, if two different accountants independently determine the prime cost of a range of products, it is unlikely that all of the amounts calculated will be the same. You should get used to the idea in accounting that disagreements of this kind will often occur. When such differences are brought to light (as may occur if an auditor decides to check the amounts calculated by the company's accountants), they may only be settled by a compromise or appeal to someone in higher authority to settle the argument. This relates to many things in accounting besides the decision as to whether a cost is direct or not.
- *Indirect manufacturing costs* or *factory indirect expenses* or *manufacturing overheads* are three names for the same thing – all the expenses concerned with the manufacturing process which have not been treated as being of the direct type. Because there is no easily traceable direct connection between them and the goods being manufactured, these costs must be apportioned between the goods being manufactured in a logical fashion. (We will look at how this is done later.)

***Note*: These expenses are often simply referred to as 'overheads'. As we progress through the chapters that follow, we will gradually increase use of that term. However, in order to emphasise the true nature of these expenses, we will start by using the more complete and more informative term, 'factory indirect expenses'. Do not forget that the two terms are simply different names for the same thing. Examiners usually use the term 'overheads'.**

- *Production cost*: the total of prime cost + indirect manufacturing costs is called production cost.
- *Administration, selling and distribution and finance expenses* are common to both trading and manufacturing firms.
- *Total cost*: if we add together production cost and administration, selling and distribution, and finance expenses, the resultant figure is known as total cost. To summarise:

| | | £ |
|---|---|---|
| | Direct materials | xxx |
| *Add* | Direct labour | xxx |
| *Add* | Direct expenses | xxx |
| Gives: | Prime cost | xxx |
| *Add* | Indirect manufacturing costs | xxx |
| Gives: | Production cost | xxx |
| *Add* | Administration expenses | xxx |
| *Add* | Selling and distribution expenses | xxx |
| *Add* | Finance expenses | xxx |
| Gives: | Total cost | xxx |

Here is a list of typical types of expenses found in a manufacturing firm. These can be classified as direct materials, direct labour, direct expenses, indirect manufacturing costs, administration expenses, selling and distribution expenses, or finance expenses. In the right-hand column, write down what type of expense each item is.

| *Cost* | *Cost analysis* |
|---|---|
| 1 Raw materials for goods – identifiable with product made | 1 ______________ |
| 2 Rent of factory buildings | 2 ______________ |
| 3 Sales staff salaries | 3 ______________ |
| 4 Wages of machine operators in factory | 4 ______________ |
| 5 Wages of accounting machine operators in office | 5 ______________ |
| 6 Depreciation of lathes in factory | 6 ______________ |
| 7 Depreciation of computers in office | 7 ______________ |
| 8 Depreciation of fixtures in sales showrooms | 8 ______________ |
| 9 Supervisors' wages in factory | 9 ______________ |
| 10 Royalty paid for each item manufactured | 10 ______________ |
| 11 Works manager's salary: he reckons that he spends $^{3}/_{4}$ of his time in the factory and $^{1}/_{4}$ in general administration of the business | 11 ______________ |
| 12 Raw materials incorporated in goods sold, but too difficult to trace to the goods being made | 12 ______________ |
| 13 Depreciation of motor vehicles used for delivery of finished goods to customers | 13 ______________ |
| 14 Interest on bank overdraft | 14 ______________ |
| 15 Wages of crane drivers in factory | 15 ______________ |
| 16 Discounts allowed | 16 ______________ |
| 17 Company secretary's salary | 17 ______________ |
| 18 Advertising | 18 ______________ |
| 19 Wages of staff of canteen used by factory staff only | 19 ______________ |
| 20 Cost of hiring special machinery for use in manufacturing one special item | 20 ______________ |

## 40.6 Advantages of a costing system

So far, we have looked at the various elements of cost from the perspective of the whole organisation. A classification of costs from that perspective is necessary so that the overall production cost can be ascertained, so enabling cost of sales, valuation of the closing inventory of finished goods and the valuation of work-in-progress to be calculated.

What most businesses want to know is how much each item it produced has cost to make. As a result, simply knowing the total cost is not sufficient. These costs must be analysed further. They also want to know what costs are likely to be in the future. Again, more analysis is needed. Cost accounting is the process of measuring and recording all these costs.

To be worth the effort, any costing system must bring about better control of the business in guiding it towards its objectives, and **the benefits to be derived from the costing system must be**

**greater than the expense of operating the costing system.** We must, therefore, look at the possible advantages to be gained in carrying on further analyses of cost:

1 Once expenditure is traced down to each item produced, or each batch of items produced, it becomes possible to ascertain the contribution of each item to the profitability of the business. The desirability of stopping apparently unprofitable activities can then be assessed.
2 Once the profitability of each item produced is known, the reasons for increases or decreases in profits can be seen more clearly.
3 It becomes easier to forecast future results if we know more about the operations of all the various parts of the business. When forecast results are not achieved, the availability of detailed cost information makes it possible to highlight any cost-based reasons for the failure to achieve the forecast results.
4 Estimates and tenders can be prepared in future with far greater confidence – previously such calculations as were done must have been largely guesswork. Fewer errors, therefore, should arise because of the greater knowledge gained via the costing system.
5 Improvements in various activities of the business may come about because of the more relevant information that can be supplied. Thus a machine which had always been thought to be quite cheap to use may turn out to be very expensive. This may result in an investigation which would not otherwise have happened and it may, consequently, be found that a simple attachment to the machine costing, say, £10 would achieve a saving of £100 a year.
6 As you will see, a very important advantage is a major increase in the level of control that can be exercised over expenditure, and it can be achieved because an individual can be made responsible for the expenditure under his/her control.

Many advantages are gained by having a cost accounting system that provides this level of detail of cost information. **It is, however, now a convenient point to remind you that accounting techniques themselves do not solve problems; people are needed to do that.** When armed with the cost information that management accounting techniques can provide, managers and other internal decision-makers are able to make much more sensible decisions about what should be done to aid the progress of the business towards its objectives.

For example, imagine trying to decide which item to stop producing out of 12 items made by a business if you have little information as to the amount each item contributes towards the profitability of the business. The best solution could be to change the layout of the factory; or provide special training to certain employees; or to make changes in the system of remunerating employees and so on. Without appropriate information, you can only guess at what to do.

The information provided by accounting is only one part of the whole story for any problem requiring a decision to be made. Sometimes *it will be the least important information* available, as far as the decision-maker is concerned. However, rarely indeed is a decision made concerning a business that does not rely to some extent on accounting information.

## 40.7 The control of costs

**One of the most important features of cost accounting is its use for control purposes,** meaning, in this context, the *control of expenditure*. But control of expenditure is possible only if you can trace the costs down to the employees who are responsible for such costs. A convenient and frequently adopted approach to collecting costs is through a **cost centre** – a production or service location, function, activity, or item of equipment that can be identified as an item which incurs costs.

Costs are collected from a cost centre for an individual **cost unit** – unit of product or service. For example, in a manufacturing firm all direct materials, direct labour and direct expenses are traced to cost centres. (In this case, they may be known as 'product centres'.)

A cost centre may be a single machine used for jobbing work, i.e. separate jobs performed specially to conform with the customer's specifications. It could be a group of similar machines or a production department. Thus, if a business makes metal boxes on one machine, all the costs *incurred directly* relating to that machine (cost centre) would be gathered and then shared (allocated) among all the metal boxes (cost units) made by that machine.

Direct costs are easy to allocate in this way. However, so far as indirect costs are concerned, things can be far from simple. Indirect costs are, instead, traced to cost centres which give service (called '*service centres*') rather than being concerned with work directly on the products. Examples of service centres include factory canteens and maintenance departments. The costs from these service centres are then apportioned to the product centres on an appropriate basis – for example, canteen costs may be allocated to product cost centres according to the number of employees working at each product cost centre.

In practice, there are a number of possible ways of attributing costs to cost centres. **What must not be lost sight of is the endeavour to trace costs to a person responsible for the expenditure so that the costs can be controlled. If that is to be done effectively, so that cost control is improved, any apportionment of indirect costs must be done carefully and must be done using a base that is acceptable to all those affected by its use.**

## 40.8 Costing: manufacturing organisations compared with retailing, wholesaling, and service organisations

It is quite wrong to think that costing is concerned only with manufacturing firms. Both textbooks and examination papers often give the impression that costing is only needed or found in manufacturing organisations. This is incorrect. **Costing is just as relevant to retailing and wholesaling firms and service industries as it is to those in manufacturing.** It is simply that manufacturing, which usually has more complex sorts of activities because of the manufacturing element, has attracted greater attention than other types of organisations. In addition, there are many other forms of organisations such as farming, shipping, banking and even charitable organisations where costing can aid management control. It would indeed be difficult to find any organisation which could not profitably use some form of costing system.

### Learning outcomes

**You should now have learnt:**

1. Cost accounting is needed for there to be an effective management accounting system.
2. The benefits of operating a costing system should always outweigh the costs of operating it.
3. To be useful, information must be 'fit for purpose'.
4. When it is known what costs are for, and how much is to be spent on studying them, the appropriate method for measuring them can be decided.
5. In the case of a manufacturing company, classifying costs appropriately is necessary so that the overall production cost can be ascertained and so enable appropriate valuation of the closing inventory of finished goods and of work-in-progress.

6 Accounting techniques themselves do not solve problems; people within the organisation are far more able to make sensible decisions about what should be done to aid the progress of the organisation towards its objectives when armed with the information that accounting techniques can provide.

7 Appropriate cost allocation is very important for control.

8 When costs are assigned to an individual cost centre, they are 'allocated'; when they are assigned to two or more cost centres, they are 'apportioned'.

## Answers to activities

40.1 Very little. Financial accounting gathers data relating to current performance in ledger accounts and then summarises it in order to evaluate performance through the preparation of financial statements which convey historic performance information to stakeholders in the organisation and other interested parties. It has no involvement in forecasting and planning and no interest in future information. In addition, the evaluation of performance conducted by financial accounting is very different from that undertaken by management accounting.

40.2 Useless data has cost time and money to collect, in itself a waste of resources. Secondly, it is often assumed to be useful and so misleads a decision-maker into taking decisions that are completely inappropriate. Thirdly, it clogs up the communication system within a business, so that other data is not acted on properly because of the general confusion that has been caused by the misleading data.

40.3

| *Cost* | *Cost analysis* |
|---|---|
| 1 Raw materials for goods – identifiable with product made | 1 Direct materials |
| 2 Rent of factory buildings | 2 Indirect manufacturing costs |
| 3 Sales staff salaries | 3 Selling and distribution |
| 4 Wages of machine operators in factory | 4 Direct labour |
| 5 Wages of accounting machine operators in office | 5 Administration expenses |
| 6 Depreciation of lathes in factory | 6 Indirect manufacturing costs |
| 7 Depreciation of computers in office | 7 Administration expenses |
| 8 Depreciation of fixtures in sales showrooms | 8 Selling and distribution expenses |
| 9 Supervisors' wages in factory | 9 Indirect manufacturing costs |
| 10 Royalty paid for each item manufactured | 10 Direct expenses |
| 11 Works manager's salary: he reckons that he spends $^3/_4$ of his time in the factory and $^1/_4$ in general administration of the business | 11 Factory indirect expenses $^3/_4$ Administration expenses $^1/_4$ |
| 12 Raw materials incorporated in goods sold, but too difficult to trace to the goods being made | 12 Indirect manufacturing costs |
| 13 Depreciation of motor vehicles used for delivery of finished goods to customers | 13 Selling and distribution expenses |
| 14 Interest on bank overdraft | 14 Finance expenses |
| 15 Wages of crane drivers in factory | 15 Indirect manufacturing costs |
| 16 Discounts allowed | 16 Finance expenses |
| 17 Company secretary's salary | 17 Administration expenses |
| 18 Advertising | 18 Selling and distribution expenses |
| 19 Wages of staff of canteen used by factory staff only | 19 Indirect manufacturing costs |
| 20 Cost of hiring special machinery for use in manufacturing one special item | 20 Direct expenses |

## Review questions

**40.1** Categorise each of the following costs into one of these six categories:

(*i*) Direct materials
(*ii*) Direct labour
(*iii*) Indirect manufacturing costs
(*iv*) Administration expenses
(*v*) Selling and distribution expenses
(*vi*) Finance expenses

- (*a*) Wages for staff maintaining machines in factory
- (*b*) Wages for staff maintaining computing equipment
- (*c*) Expenses of canteen run exclusively for factory workers
- (*d*) Expenses of canteen run exclusively for administrative workers
- (*e*) Grease used for factory machinery
- (*f*) Cost of raw materials
- (*g*) Carriage inwards on fuel used in factory boiler-house
- (*h*) Carriage inwards on raw material
- (*i*) Wages of managing director's chauffeur
- (*j*) Wages of cleaners in factory
- (*k*) Discounts allowed
- (*l*) Rent of salesrooms
- (*m*) Wages of lathe operators in factory
- (*n*) Wages of security guards; the area of the factory buildings is four times as great as the other buildings
- (*o*) Loan-note interest
- (*p*) Rent of annexe used by accounting staff
- (*q*) Managing director's remuneration
- (*r*) Sales staff salaries
- (*s*) Running costs of sales staff cars
- (*t*) Repairs to factory buildings
- (*u*) Audit fees
- (*v*) Power for machines in factory
- (*w*) Business rates: $^3/_4$ for factory buildings and $^1/_4$ for other buildings
- (*x*) Rent of internal telephone system in factory
- (*y*) Bank charges
- (*z*) Costs of advertising products on television.

**40.2A** Categorise each of the following costs into one of these six categories:

(*i*) Direct materials
(*ii*) Direct labour
(*iii*) Indirect manufacturing costs
(*iv*) Administration expenses
(*v*) Selling and distribution expenses
(*vi*) Finance expenses

- (*a*) Interest on bank overdraft
- (*b*) Factory storekeepers' wages
- (*c*) Hire of a Rolls-Royce for managing director's use
- (*d*) Repairs to factory roof
- (*e*) Hotel bills incurred by sales staff
- (*f*) Motor tax for vans used for delivering goods to customers
- (*g*) Chief accountant's salary
- (*h*) Lubricants for factory machinery
- (*i*) Cost of USB sticks for the company's computers
- (*j*) Helicopter hire charges re special demonstration of company's products

(*k*) Debt collection costs
(*l*) Costs of displaying advertising signs on London buses
(*m*) Cost of flight tickets for sales staff
(*n*) Wages of painters engaged in production
(*o*) Wages of timekeepers in factory
(*p*) Postal charges for letters
(*q*) Wages of office boy in general office
(*r*) Postal charges – parcels sent to customers
(*s*) Repairs to vans used for taking goods to customers
(*t*) Cost of raw materials included in product
(*u*) Wages for cleaners engaged in administration block
(*v*) Carriage inwards on raw materials
(*w*) Repairs to neon sign in Piccadilly Circus
(*x*) Advertising agency fees
(*y*) Wages of crane drivers in factory
(*z*) Power costs of computer equipment.

**40.3** From the following information, calculate:

(*a*) Prime cost
(*b*) Production cost
(*c*) Total cost.

| | £ | £ |
|---|---|---|
| Wages and salaries of employees: | | |
| In factory (70% is directly concerned with units being manufactured) | | 220,000 |
| Salaries: Sales staff | | 8,000 |
| Commission on sales paid to sales staff | | 1,400 |
| Salaries of administrative staff | | 72,000 |
| Travelling expenses: | | |
| Sales staff | 2,900 | |
| Factory workers not directly concerned with production | 100 | |
| Administrative staff | 200 | |
| | | 3,200 |
| Haulage costs on raw material bought | | 4,000 |
| Carriage costs on goods sold | | 7,800 |
| Depreciation: | | |
| Factory equipment | 38,000 | |
| Accounting and office equipment | 2,000 | |
| Motor vehicles: | | |
| Sales staff cars | 3,800 | |
| Administrative staff | 1,600 | |
| Sales display equipment | 300 | |
| | | 45,700 |
| Royalties payable per unit of production | | 1,600 |
| Canteen costs used by all the workers, 2/3 work in the factory, 1/3 in other parts of the firm | | 6,000 |
| Raw materials: | | |
| Inventory at start of period | | 120,000 |
| Inventory at close of period | | 160,000 |
| Bought in the period | | 400,000 |
| Interest on loans and overdrafts | | 3,800 |
| Other indirect manufacturing costs | | 58,000 |
| Other administrative expenses | | 42,000 |
| Other selling expenses | | 65,000 |

**40.4A** From the following information work out:

(*a*) Prime cost
(*b*) Production cost
(*c*) Total cost.

| | £ | £ |
|---|---|---|
| Wages and salaries of employees: | | |
| In factory (60% is directly concerned with units being manufactured) | | 150,000 |
| In sales team | | 15,000 |
| In administration | | 26,000 |
| Carriage costs: | | |
| On raw materials brought into the firm | | 1,800 |
| On finished goods delivered to customers | | 1,100 |
| Rent and rates: | | |
| Of factory block | 4,900 | |
| Of sales department and showrooms | 1,000 | |
| Of administrative block | 1,100 | |
| | | 7,000 |
| Travelling expenses: | | |
| Sales team | 3,400 | |
| Administrative staff | 300 | |
| Factory workers not connected directly with production | 200 | |
| | | 3,900 |
| Raw materials: | | |
| Inventory at start of period | | 11,400 |
| Bought in the period | | 209,000 |
| Inventory at close of the period | | 15,600 |
| Royalties: payable per unit of production | | 400 |
| Depreciation: | | |
| Sales team cars | 500 | |
| Vehicles used for deliveries to customers | 300 | |
| Cars of administrative staff | 400 | |
| Machinery in factory | 1,800 | |
| Office equipment | 200 | |
| | | 3,200 |
| Interest costs on borrowed money | | 800 |
| Other indirect manufacturing costs | | 6,000 |
| Other administrative expenses | | 4,000 |
| Other selling expenses | | 1,000 |

**40.5A**

(*a*) The terms *cost behaviour* and *analysis of total cost* are regularly used in cost accounting to classify costs. Distinguish between the two terms.
(*b*) Explain how the following costs will:
  (*i*) behave;
  (*ii*) be analysed:
  - factory power and lighting
  - production line workers' wages
  - sales manager's salary
  - office rent.

(*Edexcel: University of London GCE A-level*)

**40.6** Explain the difference between financial accounting and management accounting and the relationship between cost accounting, financial accounting, and management accounting.

chapter

# 41 Absorption and marginal costing

## Learning objectives

**After you have studied this chapter, you should be able to:**

- explain why the costs relevant for decision-making are often different from those used for the calculation of net profit
- explain the difference between fixed, variable, semi-variable, and step-variable costs
- explain the difference between absorption and marginal costing
- discuss various factors underlying the pricing policy adopted by an organisation
- explain why marginal costing, not absorption costing, should be used when deciding how to utilise spare capacity through additional production
- explain what is meant by 'full cost pricing'
- explain the importance of contribution to pricing, production, and selling decisions
- explain what is meant by activity-based costing (ABC)
- discuss the advantages and limitations of ABC

## Introduction

In this chapter, you'll learn more about the nature of different types of costs, including fixed, variable and semi-variable costs. You will also learn how to arrive at a cost per unit that can then be used to set an appropriate selling price for a good or service. Two contrasting approaches – absorption (or 'full') costing and marginal costing – are reviewed; and the concept of contribution is introduced and its importance in pricing and production decisions is explored. Finally, you will learn about another approach to cost attribution: activity-based costing.

## 41.1 Allocation of indirect manufacturing costs

As you learnt in the previous chapter, all indirect manufacturing costs are allocated to the products manufactured. Indirect manufacturing costs, therefore, add to the value of work in progress and, so, to the value of finished goods inventory. After apportioning all indirect manufacturing costs to the products produced, the production cost of any item comprises direct materials, direct labour, any direct expenses, plus a share of indirect manufacturing costs.

After a financial period has ended, it is possible to look back and accurately calculate the indirect costs. It is this figure that is used when calculating the valuation of closing inventory. Consider a company which had produced 1,000 units, of which 200 units have not yet been sold, at a total production cost of £100,000. The closing inventory valuation becomes:

$$\frac{\text{Unsold units}}{\text{Total units produced}} \times \text{Production cost of goods completed} = \frac{200}{1{,}000} \times £100{,}000$$

$$= £20{,}000 \text{ closing inventory valuation}$$

The method we have just used above, which includes allocating all indirect manufacturing costs to products, is known as **absorption costing**, sometimes called 'full costing'. While you proceed through the rest of this chapter, try to decide for yourself whether or not it would always be appropriate to use absorption costing in order to determine the cost of something produced (a good) or provided (a service).

## 41.2 Absorption costing: effect upon future action

Let's consider a decision you may have to make concerning a future action. Exhibit 41.1 concerns a decision about whether or not to take on an extra order, something that arises from time to time in all forms of business.

### Exhibit 41.1

Donald Ltd's factory has been making 100,000 units annually of a particular product for the past few years. Last year, costs were:

| | £ |
|---|---|
| Direct labour | 200,000 |
| Direct materials | 300,000 |
| Indirect manufacturing costs | 400,000 |
| Production cost | 900,000 |
| Administration and other expenses | 150,000 |
| | 1,050,000 |

The 100,000 units were sold for £12 each = £1,200,000

The production cost per unit can be seen to be $\frac{£900{,}000}{100{,}000} = £9$

The current year is following exactly the same pattern of production and costs. Suddenly, part-way through the year, a foreign buyer sends a request for 20,000 units if the price per unit can be cut from £12 to £8. A meeting is held and the managing director says, 'What a pity. This could have been our first export order, something we have been waiting to happen for several years. The selling price overseas has no bearing on our selling price at home. But it costs us £9 to produce a unit, so we would lose £1 per unit if we accepted this order. We just cannot afford to lose money in order to achieve some export sales. Our shareholders would not tolerate the annual profit of the company falling below £150,000.'

'I think you're wrong,' says John, the accountant. 'Let's look at this year's results (*a*) if we do not accept the order and (*b*) if the order is accepted':

| | *(a) Order not taken* | | *(b) Order taken* | |
|---|---|---|---|---|
| | £ | £ | £ | £ |
| Revenue 100,000 × £12 | | 1,200,000 | | |
| 100,000 × £12 + 20,000 × £8 | | | | 1,360,000 |
| *Less Expenses:* | | | | |
| Direct labour | 200,000 | | 240,000 | |
| Direct materials | 300,000 | | 360,000 | |
| Indirect manufacturing costs | 400,000 | | 420,000 | |
| Other expenses | 150,000 | | 150,000 | |
| | | (1,050,000) | | (1,170,000) |
| Net profit | | 150,000 | | 190,000 |

'More profit. This means that we take the order,' says the sales director enthusiastically.

'Surely you've got your figures wrong, John', says the managing director. 'Check your arithmetic.'

'There's nothing wrong with my arithmetic,' says John; 'all I've done is to illustrate the benefits of using a different approach to product costing in these circumstances compared to the one we use when valuing our inventory. It is known as "marginal costing". Perhaps it will be a little clearer if I add some more details.'

| | *(a) Order not taken* | | *(b) Order taken* | |
|---|---|---|---|---|
| | £ | £ | £ | £ |
| Revenue | | 1,200,000 | | 1,360,000 |
| *Less* Costs which vary with production: | | | | |
| *Direct labour.* The workers are on piece-work (i.e. they are paid according to how much they produce. In this case, this means 20% more production brings 20% more wages (i.e. £200,000 for 100,000 units; £240,000 for 120,000 units) | 200,000 | | 240,000 | |
| *Direct materials.* 20% greater production gives 20% more materials (£300,000 + £60,000) | 300,000 | | 360,000 | |
| *Indirect manufacturing costs.* Some would not change at all, e.g. factory rent, factory rates. Some would alter, e.g. cost of electric power because machines are used more. Of the indirect manufacturing costs, 1/4 is variable. For this variable part, £100,000 costs for 100,000 units becomes £120,000 costs for 120,000 units. | 100,000 | | 120,000 | |
| Marginal cost | | (600,000) | | (720,000) |
| Revenue *Less* Variable costs | | 600,000 | | 640,000 |
| Fixed costs (i.e. costs which will not alter at all if 20,000 more units are produced): | | | | |
| Indirect manufacturing costs; fixed part | 300,000 | | 300,000 | |
| Administration and other expenses | 150,000 | | 150,000 | |
| | | (450,000) | | (450,000) |
| Net profit | | 150,000 | | 190,000 |

'We can do all this without borrowing any money,' says the managing director, 'so I'll phone now to tell them we will start production immediately. By the way, John, come to my office this afternoon and tell me more about variable and fixed costs.'

## 41.3 The lesson to be learnt

You must not get lost in the technicalities of accounting. It is easy to think that calculations which look complicated must give the right answer. Logic must be brought to bear on such problems. The example presented in Exhibit 41.1 shows that **the costs needed when making decisions about the future will often be different from those which were used for calculating profit earned in the past.** In the example, £9 per unit had been used for inventory valuation, but this example demonstrates how an organisation can manufacture units and sell them for less than their cost, as calculated using absorption costing, and still increase its profit. The reason for this is the very essence of the differences between fixed and variable costs which we will now consider.

## 41.4 Fixed and variable costs

The division of costs into those that are fixed and those that are variable is not always straightforward. Even something often assumed to be a fixed cost, such as factory rent, is not always 'fixed'. For example, if production had to be increased above a certain figure, the business might have to rent additional premises. Such a change would not usually happen in the short term: it would take a while to rent and set up a new factory or extra premises before production could start. **When fixed costs are mentioned it is normally assumed that these costs are fixed in the short term.**

In the Donald Ltd example in Exhibit 41.1, it was assumed that variable costs were 100% variable. That is, if production rose 20% then the cost would rise 20%; if the production rose 47% then the cost would also rise 47%. This is not necessarily true. The cost of power may rise 20% if production rose 20%, but the cost of repairing and maintaining the machines may rise by only 10% if production rose 20%. In this case, the machine maintenance would be a 'semi-variable cost', this being the term for a cost which varies with changes in the level of production, but not at the same rate as the changes in the level of production.

## 41.5 Cost behaviour

Appropriate cost planning and control is dependent on possessing sound knowledge of how individual costs behave under certain conditions. In particular, how costs behave in the organisation

**Exhibit 41.2**

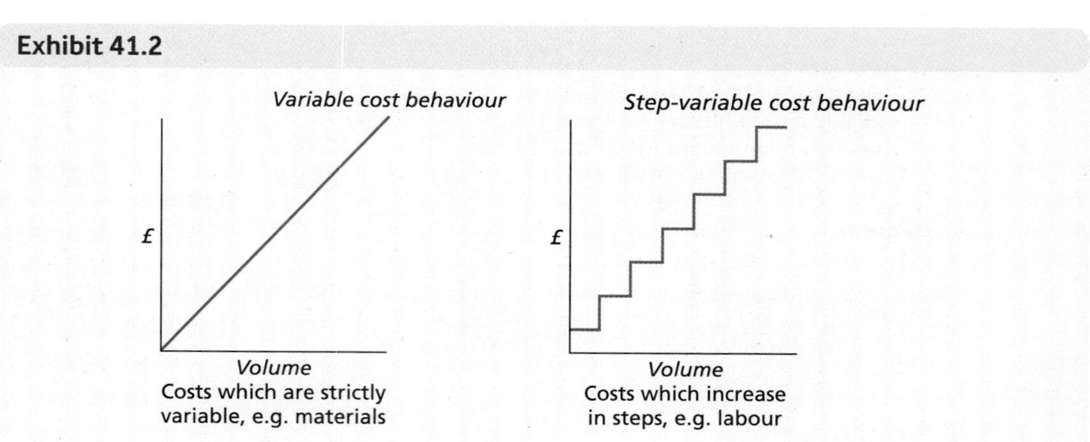

in question. There is no substitute for experience when it comes to understanding cost behaviour. As a result, accountants often require the assistance of specialists in other aspects of the business when endeavouring to understand the nature of cost behaviour.

Raw materials are an example of a variable cost which normally varies *in total* in strict proportion to the units manufactured. Labour costs, on the other hand, usually move in steps, thus the term 'step-variable' cost. For instance, a job may be done by two people, and then a slight increase in production activity means that the two people cannot manage it so that a third person is added. In fact, the increase in production activity may only represent 2⅓ people's work, but **the acquisition of workers comes in indivisible chunks.** There can still be a further increase in activity without any more workers, but then the time will come when a fourth person is needed. This is illustrated in the two graphs in Exhibit 41.2.

## 41.6 Marginal costing and absorption costing contrasted

Where costing is used which takes account of the variable cost of products rather than the full production cost, this is known as **marginal costing.** We have seen that a marginal costing approach to the decision whether or not to accept the foreign order by Donald Ltd gave an answer which increased the firm's profitability, whereas blindly using absorption costing of £9 a unit would have meant the order being rejected and the opportunity presented to increase profits and break into the foreign market being lost.

Let's look now at what would happen to gross profit if we used either marginal costing or absorption costing for a whole organisation.

### Exhibit 41.3

The calculations of the annual gross profit of Burke Ltd are shown drafted as if (A) marginal costing had been used, and (B) absorption costing had been used. The following information is available:

1 Fixed manufacturing costs amounted to £400,000 per annum.
2 Variable overheads amounted to £2 per unit.
3 Direct labour and direct materials total £3 per unit.
4 Sales remain constant at 100,000 units per annum at £13 per unit.
5 Production in year 1 is 120,000 units, year 2 is 150,000 units and year 3 is 90,000 units.

| **Year 1** | (A) *Marginal costing* | | (B) *Absorption costing* | |
|---|---|---|---|---|
| | £ | £ | £ | £ |
| Revenue | | 1,300,000 | | 1,300,000 |
| *Less Variable costs:* | | | | |
| Direct labour and material: 120,000 × £3 | 360,000 | | 360,000 | |
| Variable overheads: 120,000 × £2 | 240,000 | | 240,000 | |
| Total variable cost | 600,000 | | | |
| *Less* in (A) Valuation of closing inventory | | | | |
| $\frac{20,000}{120,000}$ × £600,000 | (100,000)* | | | |
| Marginal cost of goods sold | 500,000 | | | |
| Fixed manufacturing costs | 400,000 | | 400,000 | |
| | | (900,000) | | |
| Total production costs | | | 1,000,000 | |
| *Less* in (B) Valuation of closing inventory | | | | |
| $\frac{20,000}{120,000}$ × £1,000,000 | | | (166,667)* | |
| | | | | (833,333) |
| Gross profit | | 400,000 | | 466,667 |

→

| **Year 2** | (A) *Marginal costing* | | (B) *Absorption costing* | |
|---|---|---|---|---|
| | £ | £ | £ | £ |
| Revenue | | 1,300,000 | | 1,300,000 |
| *Less Variable costs:* | | | | |
| Direct labour and material 150,000 × £3 | 450,000 | | 450,000 | |
| Variable overheads, 150,000 × £2 | 300,000 | | 300,000 | |
| Total variable cost | 750,000 | | | |
| *Add* in (A) Opening inventory b/d | 100,000 | | | |
| | 850,000 | | | |
| *Less* in (A) Closing inventory $\frac{70,000}{150,000}$ × £750,000 | (350,000)* | | | |
| Marginal cost of goods sold | 500,000 | | | |
| Fixed manufacturing costs | 400,000 | | 400,000 | |
| | | (900,000) | | |
| Total production costs | | | 1,150,000 | |
| *Add* Opening inventory in (B) b/d | | | 166,667 | |
| | | | 1,316,667 | |
| *Less* Closing inventory in (B) $\frac{70,000}{150,000}$ × £1,150,000 | | | (536,667)* | |
| | | | | (780,000) |
| Gross profit | | 400,000 | | 520,000 |

| **Year 3** | (A) *Marginal costing* | | (B) *Absorption costing* | |
|---|---|---|---|---|
| | £ | £ | £ | £ |
| Revenue | | 1,300,000 | | 1,300,000 |
| *Less Variable costs:* | | | | |
| Direct labour and material, 90,000 × £3 | 270,000 | | 270,000 | |
| Variable overheads, 90,000 × £2 | 180,000 | | 180,000 | |
| Total variable cost | 450,000 | | | |
| *Add* in (A) Opening inventory b/d | 350,000 | | | |
| | 800,000 | | | |
| *Less* in (A) Closing inventory $\frac{60,000}{90,000}$ × £450,000 | (300,000)* | | | |
| Marginal cost of goods sold | 500,000 | | | |
| Fixed manufacturing costs | 400,000 | | 400,000 | |
| | | (900,000) | | |
| | | | 850,000 | |
| *Add* in (B) Opening inventory b/d | | | 536,667 | |
| | | | 1,386,667 | |
| *Less* in (B) Closing inventory $\frac{60,000}{90,000}$ × 850,000 | | | 566,667* | |
| | | | | (820,000) |
| Gross profit | | 400,000 | | 480,000 |

***Note:***
**The closing inventory each year for (A) is made up of:**

$$\frac{\text{Unsold units}}{\text{Number of units produced in year}} \times \text{Total variable cost of that year}$$

**Units produced Year 1 120,000 − 100,000 = Closing inventory 20,000 units**
**Units produced Year 2 150,000 + 20,000 opening inventory − sales 100,000 = Closing inventory of 70,000 units**
**Units produced Year 3 90,000 + 70,000 opening inventory − sales 100,000 = Closing inventory of 60,000 units**

**So in Year 1 unsold units are 20,000 units; units produced 120,000; total variable cost is £600,000; therefore inventory valuation is:**

$$\frac{20,000}{120,000} \times £600,000 = £100,000$$

**and the cost per unit is £5.**

**The closing inventory each year for (B) is made up of:**

$$\frac{\text{Unsold units}}{\text{Number of units produced in year}} \times \text{Total production cost of that year}$$

**So in Year 1 inventory valuation becomes** $\frac{20,000}{120,000} \times £1,000,000 = £166,667$ **and the cost per unit is £8.33.**

Exhibit 41.4 shows in diagrammatic form the reported gross profits shown in Exhibit 41.3.

**Exhibit 41.4**

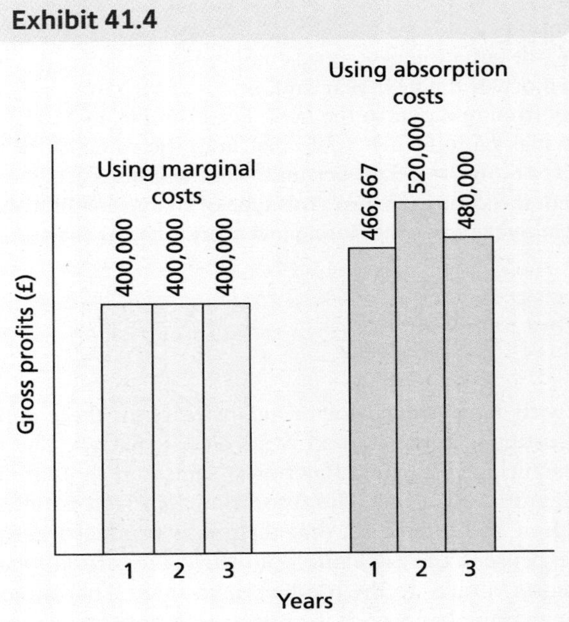


You can see from the note that if 'cost' is used to set selling prices, under absorption costing, selling prices would be much higher than under marginal costing.

## 41.7 Comparison of reported profits – constant sales and uneven production

Exhibits 41.3 and 41.4 have illustrated that Burke Ltd, a business which had the same volume of sales each year at the same prices, and the same variable cost per unit, shows quite different gross profit figures using marginal costing compared with the gross profits under absorption costing. As these were the gross profits that were calculated let us assume that the selling, distribution, administration and finance expenses were £100,000 for each of these years. The net profits would therefore be as follows:

| | (A) *Marginal costing* | (B) *Absorption costing* |
|---|---|---|
| | £ | £ |
| Year 1 | 300,000 | 366,667 |
| Year 2 | 300,000 | 420,000 |
| Year 3 | 300,000 | 380,000 |

Under absorption costing, Year 2 shows the biggest profit. As sales, etc. are the same, only production being different, this means that the year which has the greatest closing inventory has shown the greatest profit. Because of greater production, the amount of fixed factory manufacturing cost per unit is less. For instance, in Year 1 with 120,000 units produced and £400,000 fixed manufacturing costs this means fixed manufacturing costs in Year 1 are £3.33 per unit:

$$\frac{£400{,}000}{120{,}000} = £3.33 \text{ per unit; Year 2 } \frac{£400{,}000}{150{,}000} = £2.67 \text{ per unit; Year 3 } \frac{£400{,}000}{90{,}000} = £4.44 \text{ per unit}$$

Under absorption costing, the value of closing inventory includes the fixed indirect manufacturing costs and less gets charged per unit for fixed indirect manufacturing costs when production increases, and vice versa. Also, as shown in Exhibits 41.3 and 41.4, a greater gross profit is shown under absorption costing than under marginal costing.

Of course, the situation gets more complicated because the closing inventory of one year is the opening inventory of the next year and, under absorption costing, the value of each unit of inventory will vary from one year to the next. For example, in Year 3, the opening inventory of 70,000 units is shown as £536,667 = £7.67 per unit; the value of the closing inventory of 60,000 units is shown as £566,667 = £9.44 per unit. Yet these units are of exactly the same product and costs have been kept the same each year. **This type of change in unit value can be confusing and showing a higher profit in a year when the closing inventory is higher than usual can give a false sense of security.**

**Activity 41.1** Why?

Many experts have argued for or against each of these approaches – marginal costing and absorption costing – in the context of profit calculation. The marginal approach assumes that fixed manufacturing costs are a function of time and should not be carried forward to the next period in inventory valuations. The absorption approach assumes that such overhead is concerned with production and, therefore, that the goods produced in that year but not yet sold should include the expense in the calculation of their value carried forward to the next period.

Do such costs 'attach' to the product or to time? They attach to time. Consequently, it does seem that the marginal approach is more appropriate for closing inventory valuation.

## 41.8 Understanding the difference between marginal cost-based gross profit and absorption cost-based gross profit

Under absorption costing, both the closing inventory *and* the opening inventory values will be *greater* than under marginal costing. This is because fixed costs are included in the inventory value under absorption costing but not under marginal costing.

*When there is no opening inventory*

The gross profit under absorption costing will be *higher* than under marginal costing by the difference between the two closing inventory values: the absorption costing inventory value *minus* the marginal costing inventory value.

You can prove this to yourself if you *add* the difference between the two closing inventory values to the marginal cost-based gross profit: the result is the absorption cost-based gross profit.

*When there is opening inventory, and no closing inventory*
The gross profit under absorption costing will be *lower* than under marginal costing because the opening inventory value is *always* higher under absorption costing.

*Where there is both opening and closing inventory **and** inventory levels are **rising***
The negative impact upon the absorption cost-based gross profit of its higher opening inventory values is more than offset by the positive impact upon the gross profit made by the higher absorption cost-based closing inventory values. The gap between the absorption cost-based gross profit and the marginal cost-based gross profit will be greater than it was in the previous period.

*Where there is both opening and closing inventory **and** inventory levels are **falling***
The negative impact upon the absorption cost-based gross profit of its higher opening inventory values is greater than the positive impact upon the gross profit made by the higher absorption cost-based closing inventory values. The gap between the absorption cost-based gross profit and the marginal cost-based gross profit will be less than it was in the previous period.

You can demonstrate each of the above situations by entering appropriate values into the following table:

**Table 41.1**

| | £ |
|---|---|
| Gross profit per marginal costing | A |
| *Add:* Closing absorption cost inventory – Closing marginal cost inventory | B |
| | C |
| *Less:* Opening absorption cost inventory – Opening marginal cost inventory | D |
| Gross profit per absorption costing | E |

**Activity 41.2**

Enter the relevant amounts for each of the three years from Exhibit 41.3 in the columns labelled 1 to 3 in the following table:

| | 1 | 2 | 3 | 4 | Total |
|---|---|---|---|---|---|
| Gross profit per marginal costing | | | | | |
| *Add*: Closing absorption cost inventory – Closing marginal cost inventory | | | | | |
| | | | | | |
| *Less*: Opening absorption cost inventory – Opening marginal cost inventory | | | | | |
| Gross profit per absorption costing | | | | | |

Assume that in Year 4, Burke Ltd's costs per unit and fixed costs were unchanged from Year 3. Production in Year 4 was 40,000 units and all inventory was sold. Enter the appropriate amounts for that year into the table. Finally, add up the four values for gross profit per marginal costing and the four values for gross profit per absorption costing and place the two totals in the totals column. What does this tell you about the difference in long-term gross profit of using one of these valuation bases rather than the other?

Of course, **during the life of a business, its recorded profits will be the same in total irrespective of which method is in use.** If Burke Ltd exists for 20 years before it closes down, the profits as calculated for each year using the different methods will result in different recorded profits year by year (except by coincidence). The total profit during the complete life of the business of (say) £20 million will be the same. However, the intermediate reporting of profits may induce decisions which change the pattern of activities and, therefore, affect the future profitability of the business. Use of an inappropriate basis for calculating profits can lead to inappropriate decisions being made.

## 41.9 Pricing policy

One thing is clear: **in the long term, revenues must exceed costs or else the entity will fail and go out of business.** If it was a company, it would have to be liquidated. If it was a business run by a sole proprietor, she could be declared bankrupt. On the other hand, businesses may find that, in the short term, costs sometimes exceed revenues. In other words, the business makes a net loss. Many do make losses from time to time without being forced out of business because, in other periods, they make sufficient profits to offset those losses.

This being so, the way in which prices are determined for the goods or services sold by a business is of great importance. You may well expect that there are some definite rules which will be observed by a business when it fixes its prices, and that these rules are followed by all businesses. Your expectations would, however, be quite wrong.

With pricing, each business is unique. That is, each business has certain features that do not apply to other businesses. These differences affect pricing policy. For instance, let's look at the price of sugar sold by three different businesses. The first (A) is a grocer's shop in a village; it is the only grocer's shop, and the next shop at which the villagers can buy sugar is 30 miles away. The second (B) is a grocer's shop in a town where there are plenty of other shops selling sugar. The third (C) is a very large supermarket in a city, in a street where there are other large supermarkets.

For a bag of sugar, you have to pay at (A) 90p; (B) 80p; (C) 60p. The sugar is of exactly the same quality and is manufactured by the same company. (A) buys in small quantities; consequently it pays a higher price than (B) or (C) for its sugar, but it knows that none of its customers want to go 30 miles for sugar. The owner does not want to lose self-respect by overcharging anyway, so he settles for 90p. He always reflects that if he charged more, his customers might decide to buy sugar in larger quantities when they went to the nearest town to shop. (B) makes hardly any profit at all out of its sugar sales. It fears that if its regular customers were to go elsewhere for their sugar they might well decide to buy other things as well, resulting in (B) losing not only its sugar sales but also a great deal of its other sales as well. (C) sells sugar at a loss – it does this quite deliberately to tempt customers who come to buy cheap sugar, and then buy other items on which the supermarket makes reasonable profits.

If there can be such differences in the selling price of a bag of sugar when sold by three different businesses, none of which had, in fact, produced the sugar, then how much more complex is the position where businesses manufacture goods and then each has to decide the prices to sell them at? This is where a study of economics helps to get this in better perspective. Along with other economic factors, the elasticity of demand (i.e. the impact upon demand of a change in price) must be considered as well as whether or not the business has a dominant position in the market. Knowledge of economics provides a framework for your thinking but it is not the purpose of this book to be an economics text. Nevertheless, pricing relies on economic analysis as much as on information about costs. We will content ourselves with accepting that this is so, and will focus upon how accounting information impacts upon pricing.

## 41.10 Full cost pricing

Although there may be no clearly defined rules on pricing, it can at least be said that views of pricing can be traced to one of two attitudes. These are:

1 Ascertain the cost of the product and then add something to that for profit, the sum being the selling price. This is usually known as *full cost pricing*.
2 Ascertain the price at which similar products are selling, and then attempt to keep costs below that level so as to make an acceptable profit.

Many of the problems connected with full cost pricing are the same as those that arise with absorption costing and marginal costing.

Activity 41.3

What are these problems of absorption costing and marginal costing?

Despite the inflexibility of the approach, many businesses use the full cost basis to price their goods and services, very probably because it is easy to apply and guarantees an acceptable profit on each unit of product or service that it manages to sell; and is easy to explain, justify, and understand. This is not meant as a criticism – after all, the accounting process it requires is the simplest one available. There is no advantage to be gained by using complicated methods when simple ones will meet the needs of the end users of the accounting information.

The more complicated the costing (and thus pricing) approach adopted, the greater will be the costs of creating it and of maintaining it. If the benefits to be obtained from a complex approach do not exceed the costs of the additional complexity in the approach, a simpler, more cost-effective approach should be adopted. On the other hand, using a simple approach because it is simple and, therefore, cheap to operate, can be extremely costly in the long run if the information it produces and provides is less accurate than is required for effective decision-making. Both these aspects need to be considered when selecting the accounting approach to adopt.

The information shown in Exhibit 41.5 has been drawn up on a full cost basis. Full cost pricing finds the cost of direct materials and direct labour and then adds relevant amounts to represent indirect manufacturing costs, selling, admin and finance expenses, and profit. The selling price is calculated as follows:

**Exhibit 41.5**

| | £ |
|---|---|
| Cost of direct materials and direct labour | 10 |
| *Add* Variable manufacturing costs | 5 |
| *Add* Share of fixed manufacturing costs | 1 |
| Absorption cost | 16 |
| *Add* Percentage (50% in this case) for selling, administration and finance expenses | 8 |
| Full cost | 24 |
| *Add* Percentage for profit (in this case, 25%) | 6 |
| Selling price | 30 |

The 50% for selling, administration and finance costs is probably based on the figures for the previous year, when, as a total for the year, they would have approximated to 50% of the total of direct materials + direct labour + variable manufacturing costs + fixed manufacturing costs (i.e. in this case it would have amounted to £16 for one unit). Therefore, taking 50% of that figure (£8) as an addition is really saying that it is assumed that the pattern of costs incurred is similar to that of the previous year.

Remember that this was just an example of how full cost pricing may be applied. In other situations and even in the same situation but in another business, differences in the way the figures used are found will be commonplace. As you have already seen earlier in this book, the allocation of fixed costs is very arbitrary, yet when full cost pricing is adopted, the selling price is based upon figures produced as a direct consequence of such arbitrary allocation. Unsurprisingly, sometimes the price arrived at turns out to have been incorrect.

## 41.11 Example of full cost pricing

In Exhibit 41.6, three businesses are making identical products. For the purpose of illustration, we will assume that the variable and fixed costs for each of them are the same. Different accountants use different methods of allocating fixed costs between products even though, in each case, the allocation may seem to be quite rational. **There is usually no one 'right' way of allocating fixed costs.** Instead, there are 'possible' ways. In this exhibit, each of them manufactures two products and, because of the different ways in which they have allocated fixed costs, they have each come up with different selling prices for their products.

### Exhibit 41.6

| | *Blue Ltd Products* | | *Green Ltd Products* | | *Red Ltd Products* | |
|---|---|---|---|---|---|---|
| | *A* | *B* | *A* | *B* | *A* | *B* |
| | £ | £ | £ | £ | £ | £ |
| Direct labour and materials | 10 | 12 | 10 | 12 | 10 | 12 |
| Variable manufacturing costs | 16 | 10 | 16 | 10 | 16 | 10 |
| Marginal cost | 26 | 22 | 26 | 22 | 26 | 22 |
| Fixed manufacturing costs | 6 | 26 | 22 | 10 | 14 | 18 |
| Full cost | 32 | 48 | 48 | 32 | 40 | 40 |
| *Add* Profit: 12.5% of full cost | 4 | 6 | 6 | 4 | 5 | 5 |
| | 36 | 54 | 54 | 36 | 45 | 45 |

In real life, once selling prices have been calculated, the market prices of similar goods are looked at, and the price is arrived at after taking account of what competitors are charging. In this case, the prices set by Red Ltd might well have been the result of its having calculated the average market price as given by finding the average of the prices set by Blue Ltd and Green Ltd.

Suppose Blue Ltd and Green Ltd placed their faith in their full cost pricing-based selling prices but now realise they also need to set their selling prices at £45. Blue might think that as the full cost of product B is £48, it would lose £3 for every unit sold of product B. Green Ltd might, on the other hand, think that as the full cost of product A is £48, it would lose £3 on every unit sold of product A. If they rigidly apply full cost pricing, Blue Ltd might decide to cease production of B, and Green Ltd might decide to cease production of A. This is unlikely to be a wise decision for either company.

If the plans had been for each company to sell 100 of each of products A and B, then the plans have now altered to Blue Ltd producing and selling 100 of A only, Green Ltd producing and selling 100 of B only, and Red Ltd producing and selling 100 of A and 100 of B. The summarised profit and loss accounts of the three companies will now be as shown in Exhibit 41.7.

Exhibit 41.7 shows that Blue Ltd and Green Ltd would incur losses if they ceased production of product B and product A respectively. Yet, if they had not ceased production they would both have made profits of £1,000 (as Red Ltd has done). After all, they are *similar* organisations with *exactly* the same costs – the only difference was the way they allocated fixed costs. The fixed costs in each company totalled £3,200. Blue allocated this between products as A £6, B £26.

**Exhibit 41.7**

| | *Blue Ltd* | *Green Ltd* | *Red Ltd* |
|---|---|---|---|
| | £ | £ | £ |
| *Sales:* 100 of A @ £45 | 4,500 | | 4,500 |
| 100 of B @ £45 | | 4,500 | 4,500 |
| Total revenue | 4,500 | 4,500 | 9,000 |
| *Less* Costs: Direct labour and materials | | | |
| Product A 100 × £10 | 1,000 | | 1,000 |
| Product B 100 × £12 | | 1,200 | 1,200 |
| Variable manufacturing costs | | | |
| Product A 100 × £16 | 1,600 | | 1,600 |
| Product B 100 × £10 | | 1,000 | 1,000 |
| Fixed manufacturing costs: does not change as a consequence of cessation of production in Blue Ltd and Green Ltd as it is a fixed cost. | 3,200 | 3,200 | 3,200 |
| Total costs | (5,800) | (5,400) | (8,000) |
| Net profit | | | 1,000 |
| Net loss | (1,300) | (900) | |

Green allocated it A £22, B £2. Red allocated it A £14, B £18. With 100 units of each product being produced, this amounted to an allocation overall apportionment of fixed costs of £3,200 by each company. **Fixed overhead does not change just because of ceasing production of one type of product.** The factory rent and rates will remain the same, as will the secretaries' salaries and other fixed costs.

## 41.12 Contribution

The question arises therefore as to **which costing approach, absorption costing or marginal costing, is more appropriate when deciding whether or not to continue manufacturing a product or providing a service. The answer to this is that it is the *marginal cost* – i.e. the variable cost – which is relevant and so should be used.** If marginal cost is *less* than selling price, the difference will make a **contribution** towards fixed costs, thus reducing the burden of the fixed costs on the other products.

This can be seen in the following example (Exhibit 41.8) concerning which of the two products we introduced in Section 41.11, A and B, to make when there is some spare production capacity. **Remember, as absorption costing includes an element of fixed cost, it is not appropriate to use it when considering decisions of this type:**

**Exhibit 41.8**

| | *Product A* | *Product B* |
|---|---|---|
| | £ | £ |
| Selling price | 45 | 45 |
| *Less* Marginal cost | (26) | (22) |
| Contribution towards fixed costs and profit | 19 | 23 |

Either product could be usefully considered; both make a positive contribution towards fixed costs. However, all other things being equal, product B appears to be the better option. Thus, if there is spare capacity, and an opportunity arises to use some of it, marginal costing can be used in order to determine whether the projected income arising from 'extra' sales exceeds the marginal cost of the 'extra' items produced. If it does, it is worthwhile considering taking on the work. This is based on an important rule:

**Contribution = Selling price − Variable cost**

Contribution is also the basis of another important rule for decision-making:

$$\textbf{Breakeven point} = \frac{\textbf{Fixed costs}}{\textbf{Selling price per unit} - \textbf{Variable cost per unit}}$$

Breakeven point is the volume of sales required in order to make neither a profit nor a loss.

**In Chapter 49, you will learn more about these rules when you look at breakeven analysis (also called cost–volume–profit analysis).**

***Note***: **Marginal costing uses variable costs. The variable cost is often referred to as the marginal cost. They are essentially the same thing.**

## 41.13 Using marginal costs

Let's test what you've just learnt in another example. A company produces five products and has the following cost and sales data. It can sell exactly 100 of each product it manufactures. Total fixed costs are £4,800, apportioned: A £5 (100), B £7 (100), C £11 (100), D £15 (100), E £10 (100), i.e. £4,800 total. Exhibit 41.9 presents this in a table.

**Exhibit 41.9**

| *Violet Ltd* | *Products* | | | | |
|---|---|---|---|---|---|
| | *A* | *B* | *C* | *D* | *E* |
| Cost per unit: | £ | £ | £ | £ | £ |
| Direct labour and materials | 8 | 9 | 16 | 25 | 11 |
| Variable manufacturing costs | 7 | 8 | 10 | 13 | 14 |
| Marginal cost | 15 | 17 | 26 | 38 | 25 |
| Fixed costs | 5 | 7 | 11 | 15 | 10 |
| Full cost | 20 | 24 | 37 | 53 | 35 |
| Selling price per unit | 30 | 21 | 31 | 80 | 20 |

On the full cost basis, only A and D appear to be profitable. Should production of B, C and E be discontinued? You know that production should cease only when the selling price is less than marginal cost. In Exhibit 41.10, you can see if following this brings more profit than following the result of the full cost calculation. You can also see what would have happened if production levels of all products continued as before.

## Exhibit 41.10

| | (1) Following full cost pricing, cease producing *B, C* and *E* | (2) Using marginal costing, cease producing *E* only | (3) Ignore costing altogether and produce all items |
|---|---|---|---|
| | £ | £ | £ |
| Sales: A 100 × £30 | 3,000 | 3,000 | 3,000 |
| B 100 × £21 | | 2,100 | 2,100 |
| C 100 × £31 | | 3,100 | 3,100 |
| D 100 × £80 | 8,000 | 8,000 | 8,000 |
| E 100 × £20 | | | 2,000 |
| Total revenue | 11,000 | 16,200 | 18,200 |
| *Less* Costs: | | | |
| Direct labour and materials: | | | |
| 100 × cost per product | (£33) 3,300 | (£58) 5,800 | (£69) 6,900 |
| Variable manufacturing costs: | (£20) 2,000 | (£38) 3,800 | (£52) 5,200 |
| 100 × cost per product | | | |
| Fixed costs (do not change) | 4,800 | 4,800 | 4,800 |
| Total costs | (10,100) | (14,400) | (16,900) |
| Net profit | 900 | 1,800 | 1,300 |

The £ amounts in brackets show the cost of each product, e.g. in (1) the direct labour and materials are A £8 + D £25 = £33.

As you can see from Exhibit 41.10, it would be just as well if we followed our own advice. This would give a profit of £1,800 compared with £900 using the full cost approach or £1,300 if we disregarded costing altogether. Sometimes the full cost approach will give far better results than ignoring costing altogether, but this case shows that **using an inappropriate costing base can be even worse than having no costing system at all.** Marginal costing always gives the most appropriate answer in this sort of situation.

**There is, however, a danger in thinking that if the marginal cost of each product is less than the selling price then all products produced will be profitable. This is not the case,** and full consideration must be given to the fact that the *total* contribution from all the products *must* exceed the fixed costs, otherwise there will be an overall loss. Different volumes of activity on each product will also affect this. Exhibit 41.11 looks at a two-product firm making products A and B at different volumes of activity. Product A has a marginal cost of £10 and a selling price of £14. Product B has a marginal cost of £6 and a selling price of £8. Fixed costs are £1,400.

**Exhibit 41.11**

| | *Profit, or loss, at different volumes of activity* | | | | | | | |
|---|---|---|---|---|---|---|---|---|
| | A | B | A | B | A | B | A | B |
| Units sold | 100 | 100 | 200 | 200 | 300 | 300 | 400 | 400 |
| | £ | £ | £ | £ | £ | £ | £ | £ |
| Contribution (Selling price *Less* Marginal cost) A £4 per unit, B £2 per unit | 400 | 200 | 800 | 400 | 1,200 | 600 | 1,600 | 800 |
| Total contributions | 600 | | 1,200 | | 1,800 | | 2,400 | |
| Fixed costs | (1,400) | | (1,400) | | (1,400) | | (1,400) | |
| Net loss | (800) | | (200) | | | | | |
| Net profit | | | | | 400 | | 1,000 | |

Here the selling price always exceeds marginal cost, but if activity is low the firm will incur a loss. This is shown where activity is only 100 or 200 units of each product.

To summarise, the main lessons to be learned about selling prices are:

(*a*) a product should make a positive contribution (unless there is some overriding matter which makes the product a viable loss-leader, as in the case of the supermarket's sugar price in Section 41.9). That is, selling prices should exceed marginal costs; and

(*b*) the volume of sales should be sufficient so that, in the long term (it may be different in the short term) the fixed costs are less than the total of the contributions from all the products.

## 41.14 Maximisation of total contribution

**It is the maximisation of the total contribution from a product that is important.** Because of this, the volumes of activity cannot be ignored. Suppose, for instance, that a company could only manufacture two products in future whereas, to date, it had manufactured three. It may be that per unit the contribution may well have been (A) £10, (B) £8 and (C) £6. If a decision was made on this basis only then (C) would be discontinued. However, if the volumes were (A) 20, (B) 15 and (C) 30, the total contributions would be (A) 20 × £10 = £200; (B) 15 × £8 = £120; (C) 30 × £6 = £180. As (B) has the lowest *total* contribution it should be (B) that is discontinued, not (C).

**Where there is a limit of one of the items used in production of the product, the contribution per product per unit of that limiting factor (or 'key factor') should be used as the basis for the decision taken. (*Note: this topic appears frequently in examinations.*)**

Take, for example, a situation where there are 200 spare hours of machine capacity available and a decision has to be made concerning which, if any, of its products should have their production levels increased. The contribution per machine hour of each product is: A £2; B £3; C £5; D £1. Based on this information, more of product C should be produced. It will generate the greatest amount of contribution. If there is any spare capacity remaining after all of product C has been produced (for example, if there is only enough material available to make a few more of product C) then product B should be produced, etc.

## 41.15 Activity-based costing (ABC)

A single measure of volume is used for each production/service cost centre when apportioning indirect costs under traditional absorption costing. For example:

- machine hours
- direct labour hours
- direct materials cost
- direct labour cost.

These bases are often difficult to justify when the nature of the activity at the cost centre and, more particularly, the nature of the item that is absorbing the cost is considered. In reality, the amount of overhead incurred may depend on any of a range of factors. **An appropriate basis for cost absorption ought to adopt a basis that as truly as possible reflects the changes in overhead arising from the activities undertaken.**

Unfortunately, traditional cross-activity bases such as these can only be truly appropriate to all production when either the nature of the products produced and their production processes are virtually identical *or* when only a small range of products are produced.

Let's look now at an approach to cost apportionment that is considered far more 'accurate' than the traditional marginal and absorption costing bases.

## Cost drivers

Cost drivers are activities that generate cost. They are the factors that cause variable manufacturing costs to be incurred. A cost driver may be related to a short-term variable expense (e.g. machine running costs) – where the cost is driven by production volume and the cost driver will be volume-based (e.g. machine hours). Alternatively, it could be related to a long-term variable overhead (e.g. quality inspection costs) – where the cost is driven by the number of occasions the relevant activity occurs and where the cost driver will be transaction-based (e.g. the number of quality inspections).

**Activity-based costing** **is the process of using cost drivers as the basis for the apportionment of indirect manufacturing costs to individual products.** Costs are attributed to cost units on the basis of the benefit received from indirect activities, e.g. ordering, setting up equipment so that the item to be produced can be manufactured, and assuring quality.

While this sounds more appropriate than absorption costing, the information required to apply ABC is not generally available from traditional accounting records, and organisations that embrace ABC often require to develop a new accounting information system in order to provide that information.

## Cost pools

A cost pool is a collection of individual costs within a single heading. In traditional marginal and absorption costing, cost pools is simply another term for production cost centres. This is not the case under ABC, where a cost pool is created for each activity area. Then, in order to attribute costs held in a cost pool to an item, the amount in the cost pool is divided by the quantity of the related cost driver. This process of cost attribution is very similar to that used in traditional costing – it is the terminology, the manner in which costs are built up, and the type of basis used for cost apportionment that differ.

## ABC vs. traditional costing

It is claimed that traditional marginal and absorption costing underapportions indirect costs to lower-volume products and overapportions them to higher-volume products – that is, they produce potentially misleading information at the two extremes. ABC does not suffer from these defects. As a result, it directs attention to matters of interest that traditional overhead allocation and apportionment are insufficiently sensitive to identify. It should, therefore, be capable of producing more useful information for decision-making.

Because administration, selling and distribution overheads are excluded from both financial accounting inventory values and cost of sales calculations, traditional indirect cost apportionment stops at the edge of the factory floor. A full analysis of product profitability requires consideration of these non-production overheads, which is one reason why some organisations have chosen to adopt ABC, which *does* include these indirect costs. When companies that use ABC to evaluate inventory and cost of sales have to produce their financial statements, it is not difficult removing these non-production costs from the calculated amounts.

## Limitations of ABC

While it is possible to implement an ABC system in most organisations, in many cases it is not worthwhile:

1 The costs of implementing and operating such a system often outweigh the benefits, especially for smaller organisations.
2 It can often be the case that the additional precision and accuracy that ABC brings are immaterial in the context of managerial decision-making.
3 For single-product or single-service organisations, ABC is of little benefit.
4 Because of the need to exclude administration, selling and distribution costs from the calculation of inventory and cost of sales in financial statements, many organisations that implement ABC operate a more traditional costing accounting system in parallel with it. This simply adds to the complexity of the accounting system and can confuse non-accounting-aware managers when they have two different 'cost' figures for the same product or item of inventory.

However, where organisations have multiple products or services, ABC can prove to be a worthwhile and cost-effective way of increasing the reliability of managerial decision-making concerning product pricing.

## Learning outcomes

**You should now have learnt:**

1 Why different costs are often relevant for decision-making rather than those used for the calculation of net profit.
2 The costs needed when making decisions about the future will often be different from those used when calculating profit in the past.
3 The difference between fixed, variable, semi-variable and step-variable costs.
4 The difference between absorption and marginal costing.
5 How various factors underlie the pricing policy adopted by an organisation.
6 Why marginal cost, not full (or absorption) cost, is the relevant cost when considering a change in what and/or how much is produced.
7 What is meant by full cost pricing.
8 The importance of contribution to pricing, production and selling decisions.
9 That selling prices should exceed marginal costs. (Almost the only exception to this would be where a product was being promoted as a loss-leader.)
10 That, in the long term, the total contributions at given volumes must exceed the fixed costs of the business.
11 What is activity-based costing (ABC).
12 The advantages and limitations of ABC.

## Answers to activities

41.1 The inventory may be rising because we cannot sell the goods, i.e. the business is getting into trouble, yet the financial statements sublimely show a higher profit.

41.2

| | 1 | 2 | 3 | 4 | Total |
|---|---|---|---|---|---|
| Gross profit per marginal costing | 400,000 | 400,000 | 400,000 | 800,000 | 2,000,000 |
| *Add:* Closing absorption cost inventory – Closing marginal cost inventory | 66,667 | 186,667 | 266,667 | | |
| | 466,667 | 586,667 | 666,667 | 800,000 | |
| *Less:* Opening absorption cost inventory – Opening marginal cost inventory | | 66,667 | 186,667 | 266,667 | |
| Gross profit per absorption costing | 466,667 | 520,000 | 480,000 | 533,333 | 2,000,000 |

*Workings:* Year 4
Revenue = 100,000 × £13 = £1,300,000
Variable costs = direct labour and material cost: 40,000 × £3 = £120,000;
variable overheads: 40,000 × £2 = £80,000; total = £200,000
Fixed manufacturing costs = £400,000
Marginal costing gross profit = £1,300,000 − (£200,000 + 300,000) = £800,000
Absorption costing gross profit = £1,300,000 − (£200,000 + 566,667) = £533,333

Over the life of a business, the overall gross profit (and net profit) will be the same, irrespective of whether the business uses absorption costing or marginal costing.

41.3 In absorption costing, the whole of the fixed costs were allocated to products, whereas in marginal costing the 'contribution' was found (i.e. revenue *less* variable cost) out of which fixed costs would have to come, leaving the profit as the difference. The problem is how to decide the amount of fixed cost per unit to arrive at 'full cost'.

## Review questions

**41.1** Raleigh Ltd's costs for the current year are expected to be:

| | £ | £ |
|---|---|---|
| Direct labour | | 600,000 |
| Direct materials | | 700,000 |
| Indirect manufacturing costs: | | |
| Variable | 450,000 | |
| Fixed | 50,000 | |
| | | 500,000 |
| Administration expenses | | 120,000 |
| Selling and distribution expenses | | 60,000 |
| Finance expenses | | 20,000 |
| | | 2,000,000 |

It was expected that 200,000 units would be manufactured and sold, the selling price being £12 each.
Suddenly during the year two enquiries were made at the same time which would result in extra production being necessary. They were:

→

(A) An existing customer said that he would take an extra 10,000 units, but the price would have to be reduced to £10 per unit on this extra 10,000 units. The only extra costs that would be involved would be in respect of variable costs.

(B) A new customer would take 15,000 units annually. This would mean extra variable costs and an extra machine would have to be bought costing £15,000 which would last for five years before being scrapped. It would have no scrap value. Extra running costs of this machine would be £6,000 per annum. The units are needed for an underdeveloped country and owing to currency difficulties the highest price that could be paid for the units was £9.25 per unit.

On this information, and assuming that there are no alternatives open to Raleigh Ltd, should the company accept or reject these orders? **Draft the memo** that you would give to the managing director of Raleigh Ltd.

**41.2A** Jack Ltd expects its cost per unit, assuming a production level of 200,000 units per annum, to be:

| | £ |
|---|---|
| Direct materials | 3.2 |
| Direct labour | 4.8 |
| Indirect manufacturing costs: Variable | 1.6 |
| Fixed | 0.8 |
| Selling and distribution expenses | 0.4 |
| Administration expenses | 0.6 |
| Finance | 0.2 |
| | 11.6 |

Selling price is £15 per unit.

The following propositions are put to the managing director. Each proposition is to be considered on its own without reference to the other propositions.

(*a*) If the selling price is reduced to £14.80 per unit, sales could be raised to 240,000 units per annum instead of the current 200,000 units. Apart from direct materials, direct labour and indirect fixed manufacturing costs, there would be no change in costs.

(*b*) If the selling price is put up to £15.40 per unit, sales would be 160,000 per annum instead of 200,000. Apart from variable costs, there would also be a saving of £4,000 per annum in finance costs.

(*c*) To satisfy a special order, which would not be repeated, 10,000 extra units could be sold at £9.80 each. This would have no effect on fixed expenses.

(*d*) To satisfy a special order, which would not be repeated, 6,000 extra units could be sold for £9.20 each. This would have no effect on fixed expenses.

**Draft a memo** stating what you would advise the managing director to do, giving your reasons and workings.

**41.3** Assume that two companies have exactly the same pattern of costs and revenue and both use FIFO when valuing inventory, but that Lima Ltd uses a marginal costing approach to the valuation of inventory in its financial statements, while Delfina Ltd values its inventory using absorption costing. **Calculate** the gross profit for each company in each of their first three years in business from the following information:

(*a*) Total fixed indirect manufacturing cost is £60,000 per year.
(*b*) Direct labour costs over each of the three years were £8 per unit.
(*c*) Direct material costs over each of the three years were £12 per unit.
(*d*) Variable expenses which vary in direct ratio to production were £10 per unit.
(*e*) Sales were: Year 1: 2,400 units; Year 2: 3,600 units; Year 3: 3,000 units.
The selling price remained constant at £120 per unit.
(*f*) Production is at the rate of: Year 1: 3,200 units; Year 2: 4,000 units; Year 3: 3,400 units.

**41.4** Using the data from the solution to Review Question 41.3: (*a*) explain why there is a difference between the total gross profits of Lima over the three years and that of Delfina; and (*b*) how is the difference between the two total gross profits reflected in the assets shown in the statement of financial position of Lima Ltd?

**41.5A** Your company has been trading for three years. It has used a marginal costing approach to value its inventory in its financial statements. The directors are interested to know what the recorded profits would have been if absorption costing had been used instead. **Using the following information, prepare a statement for each of the three years comparing both methods.**

(*a*) Fixed indirect manufacturing costs are £64,000 per year.
(*b*) Direct labour costs per unit over each of the three years were £16 per unit.
(*c*) Direct material costs over each of the three years were £12 per unit.
(*d*) Variable expenses which vary in direct ratio to production were £20 per unit.
(*e*) Sales are: Year 1: 36,000 units; Year 2: 40,000 units; Year 3: 60,000 units. All at £64 per unit.
(*f*) Production volumes were: Year 1: 40,000 units; Year 2: 48,000 units; Year 3: 51,000 units.

**41.6** Greatsound Ltd manufactures and sells compact disc players, the cost of which is made up as follows:

| | £ |
|---|---|
| Direct material | 74.80 |
| Direct labour | 18.70 |
| Variable overhead | 7.50 |
| Fixed overhead | 30.00 |
| Total cost | 131.00 |

The current selling price is £187.

Greatsound Ltd works a day shift only, at present producing 120,000 compact disc players per annum, and has no spare capacity.

Market research has shown that there is a demand for an additional 60,000 compact disc players in the forthcoming year. However, these additional sales would have a selling price of £150 each. One way of achieving the extra production required is to work a night shift. However, this would increase fixed costs by £2,500,000 and the labour force would have to be paid an extra 20% over the day shift rate.

The company supplying the materials to Greatsound Ltd has indicated that it will offer a special discount of 10% on total purchases if the annual purchases of materials increase by 50%.

The selling price and all other costs will remain the same.

Assuming that the additional purchases will only be made if the night shift runs, **you are required to:**

(*a*) Advise Greatsound Ltd whether it should proceed with the proposal to commence the night shift, based on financial considerations.
(*b*) Calculate the minimum increase in sales and production required to justify the night shift.
(*c*) Give **four** other matters which should be taken into consideration when making a decision of this nature.

*(AQA (Northern Examinations and Assessment Board): GCE A-level)*

**41.7A**

(*a*) What is meant by the terms *contribution* and *marginal cost?*
(*b*) Barton & Co Ltd make and sell 2,000 units per month of a product 'Barco'. The selling price is £65 per unit, and unit costs are: direct labour £8; direct materials £17; variable overheads £11. Fixed costs per month are £29,400.

The company receives two export orders for completion in September 2016. Order A requests 600 items at a special total price of £20,000; order B requires 750 items at a total price of £34,000. Order A will require no special treatment, but order B will demand extra processing at a cost of £6 per item. The company has sufficient capacity to undertake *either* A *or* B in addition to its current production, but only by paying its direct labour force an overtime premium of 25%.

Calculate the company's contribution and the profits for the month if:
(*i*) normal production only takes place
(*ii*) order A is accepted in addition to normal production
(*iii*) order B is accepted in addition to normal production.

(*c*) Use your answer to (*b*) to demonstrate that a company will normally accept an order which produces a *contribution* towards overheads.

*(Edexcel: GCE A-level)*

**41.8** Arncliffe Limited manufactures two types of product marketed under the brand names of 'Crowns' and 'Kings'. All the company's production is sold to a large firm of wholesalers.

Arncliffe is in something of a crisis because the chief accountant has been taken ill just as the company was about to begin negotiating the terms of future contracts with its customer. You have been called in to help and are given the following information relating to each product for the last year. This information has been prepared by a junior assistant.

Report on revenues/costs for the year just ended:

| | *Crowns* | *Kings* |
|---|---|---|
| | £ | £ |
| Sales | 60,000 | 25,000 |
| Floor space costs (rent and rates) | 10,000 | 5,000 |
| Raw materials | 8,000 | 2,000 |
| Direct labour | 20,000 | 10,000 |
| Insurances | 400 | 200 |
| Machine running costs | 12,000 | 3,000 |
| Net profit | 9,600 | 4,800 |

The junior assistant says in his report, 'As you can see, Crowns make twice as much profit as Kings and we should therefore stop manufacturing Kings if we wish to maximise our profits. I have allocated floor space costs and insurances on the basis of the labour costs for each product. All other costs/revenues can be directly related to the individual product.'

Further investigation reveals the following information:

(*i*) The wholesaler bought all the 20,000 Crowns and 10,000 Kings produced last year, selling them to his customers at £4 and £3 each respectively. The wholesaler is experiencing an increasing demand for Crowns and intends to raise his price next year to £4.50 each.

(*ii*) Crowns took 8,000 hours to process on the one machine the company owns, whereas Kings took 2,000 hours. The machine has a maximum capacity of 10,000 hours per year.

(*iii*) Because all production is immediately sold to the wholesaler no inventory is kept.

**Required:**

(*a*) Prepare the revenue/cost statement for the year just ended on a marginal cost basis, and calculate the rate of contribution to sales for each product.

(*b*) You are told that in the coming year the maximum market demand for the two products will be 40,000 Crowns and 36,000 Kings and that the wholesaler wishes to sell a minimum of 6,000 units of each product. Calculate the best product mix and resulting profit for Arncliffe Limited.

(*c*) Calculate the best product mix and resulting profit for Arncliffe Limited if another machine with identical running costs and capacity can be hired for £20,000 per annum. Floor space and insurance costs would not change and the maximum and minimum conditions set out in (*b*) above continue to apply.

(*d*) What points does Arncliffe Limited need to bear in mind when negotiating next year's contract with the wholesaler?

*(Reproduced with the kind permission of OCR: from the University of Cambridge Local Examinations Syndicate)*

**41.9A** Reed Ltd manufactures three products A, B and C. Budgeted costs and selling prices for the three months ending 30 September 2016 are as follows:

| | *A* | *B* | *C* |
|---|---|---|---|
| Sales (units per month) | 6,000 | 8,000 | 5,000 |
| | £ | £ | £ |
| Selling price per unit | 45 | 44 | 37 |
| *Unit costs* | | | |
| Direct labour | 6 | 9 | 6 |
| Direct materials[Authors' note] | 20 | 24 | 16 |
| Variable overhead | 4 | 3 | 2 |
| Fixed overhead | 5 | 5 | 6 |

* ***Note*: Assume that the materials used in each product are of the same kind.**

Labour costs are £3 per hour, and material costs are £4 per kilo for all products. The total fixed costs are of a general factory nature, and are unavoidable.

The company has been advised by its supplier that due to a material shortage, its material requirement for the month of September will be reduced by 15%. No other changes are anticipated.

**Required:**

A A statement to show the maximum net profit for the three months ending 30 September 2016, taking into account the material shortage for the month of September.

B Explain how the fixed cost element is dealt with in marginal costing and in absorption costing. Briefly explain how this affects any closing inventory valuation.

*(Reproduced with the kind permission of OCR – University of Oxford Delegacy of Local Examinations: GCE A-level)*

**41.10** Paul Wagtail started a small manufacturing business on 1 May 2015. He has kept his records on the double entry system, and has drawn up a trial balance at 30 April 2016 before attempting to prepare his first final accounts.

**Extract from the Trial Balance of Paul Wagtail at 30 April 2016**

| | £ | £ |
|---|---|---|
| Purchases of raw materials | 125,000 | |
| Sales | | 464,360 |
| Selling expenses | 23,800 | |
| Insurance | 4,800 | |
| Factory repairs and maintenance | 19,360 | |
| Carriage on raw materials | 1,500 | |
| Heating and lighting | 3,600 | |
| Direct factory power | 12,430 | |
| Distribution expenses | 25,400 | |
| Production wages | 105,270 | |
| Factory supervisor's wages | 29,600 | |
| Administration expenses | 46,700 | |
| Plant and machinery at cost | 88,000 | |
| Delivery vehicles at cost | 88,000 | |
| Raw materials returned to supplier | | 2,100 |

At 30 April 2016, he has closing inventory of raw materials costing £8,900. He has manufactured 9,500 completed units of his product, and sold 8,900. He has a further 625 units that are 80% complete for raw materials and production labour, and also 80% complete for factory indirect costs.

He has decided to divide his insurance costs and his heating and lighting costs 40% for the factory and 60% for the office/showroom.

He wishes to depreciate his plant and machinery at 20% p.a. on cost, and his delivery vehicles using the reducing balance method at 40% p.a.

He has not yet made up his mind how to value his inventories of work in progress and finished goods. He has heard that he could use either marginal or absorption costing to do this, and has received different advice from a friend running a similar business and from an accountant.

**Required:**

(*a*) Prepare Paul Wagtail's manufacturing account and statement of profit or loss for the year ending 30 April 2016 using *both* marginal and absorption costing methods, preferably in columnar format.

(*b*) Advise Paul Wagtail of the advantages and disadvantages of using each method.

*(Reproduced with the kind permission of OCR – University of Oxford Local Delegacy Examinations: GCE A-level)*

→

**41.11A** The figures given below are all that could be salvaged from the records after a recent fire in the offices of Firelighters Limited. The company manufactures a single product, has no raw materials or work in progress and values its inventory at marginal cost (i.e. at variable manufacturing cost) using the FIFO basis. It is known that the unit closing inventory valuation in 2017 was the same as in 2016.

| | *2017* | *2018* |
|---|---|---|
| Selling price per unit | £10.00 | £10.00 |
| Variable manufacturing cost (per unit produced) | £4.00 | £4.00 |
| Variable selling cost (per unit sold) | £1.25 | ? |
| Quantity sold (units) | 100,000 | ? |
| Quantity manufactured (units) | 105,000 | 130,000 |
| Contribution | ? | £585,000 |
| Fixed manufacturing costs | £105,000 | £117,000 |
| Other fixed costs | £155,000 | ? |
| Operating profit before interest charges | ? | £292,000 |
| Interest charges | £70,000 | ? |
| Opening finished inventory (units) | ? | ? |
| Closing finished inventory (units) | 20,000 | 20,000 |
| Net profit for the year | ? | £210,000 |

**Required:**
Prepare a revenue statement for management showing contribution, operating profit and net profit for each year in as much detail as the information given above permits.

*(Reproduced with the kind permission of OCR: from the University of Cambridge Local Examinations Syndicate)*

**41.12A** Gainford Ltd is a manufacturing company which produces three specialist products – A, B and C. For costing purposes the company's financial year is divided into 13 periods of four weeks. There is always sufficient raw material in inventory to meet any planned level of production but there is a maximum number of labour hours available to the company. The production of each product requires a different physical layout of the factory equipment although the labour tasks are broadly similar. For this reason the company only produces one type of product at any time, and the decision as to which product to manufacture is taken before each four week period commences.

A 40-hour working week is in operation and the following factory staff are employed:

Grade 1 28 staff paid at a rate of £8 per hour
Grade 2 12 staff paid at a rate of £6 per hour

In addition, a limited number of qualified part-time staff can be employed when required. Both full-time and part-time staff are paid at the same rate. The next four week period is number 7 and the following maximum part-time hours are available for that period:

Grade 1 2,240 hours
Grade 2 1,104 hours

The production costs and selling costs per unit for each product are:

| | | A | B | C |
|---|---|---|---|---|
| | | £ | £ | £ |
| Direct raw material | | 147 | 87 | 185 |
| Direct labour: | Grade 1 | 64 | 56 | 60 |
| | Grade 2 | 24 | 27 | 21 |
| Variable overheads | | 15 | 10 | 15 |
| Fixed overheads | | 12 | 12 | 12 |
| Selling price of each product | | 400 | 350 | 450 |

There is a strong demand for all three products and every unit produced is sold.

**Required:**

(*a*) Explain the terms:
 (*i*) 'contribution'
 (*ii*) 'key factor'.

(*b*) Calculate the contribution and profit obtained when **each** product is sold.

(*c*) Prepare a statement from the available information, for period number 7 which will assist management to decide which product to produce in order to maximise contribution. This statement should include details of the:
 (*i*) total production labour hours available
 (*ii*) number of hours required to produce one unit of **each** type of product
 (*iii*) maximum production (in units) possible of **each** type of product
 (*iv*) product which will give the greatest contribution in period number 7.

(*d*) Outline the main steps in the manufacturing decision-making process which ought to be adopted by a business.

*(AQA (Associated Examining Board): GCE A-level)*

**41.13A** Vale Manufacturing started in business on 1 April 2015, and incurred the following costs during its first three years.

| Year ending 31 March | *2016* | *2017* | *2018* |
|---|---|---|---|
| | £ | £ | £ |
| Direct materials | 60,000 | 49,900 | 52,200 |
| Direct labour | 48,000 | 44,000 | 45,000 |
| Variable overheads | 24,000 | 30,000 | 40,000 |
| Fixed costs | 40,000 | 40,600 | 41,300 |

Sales during the first three years were all at £20 per unit.

| | | | |
|---|---|---|---|
| Production each year (units) | 16,000 | 14,000 | 14,000 |
| Sales each year (units) | 14,000 | 14,000 | 15,000 |

**Required:**

(*a*) Prepare a statement showing the gross profit for each of the three years if the company used:
 (*i*) the marginal costing approach to valuing inventory;
 (*ii*) the absorption costing approach to valuing inventory.

(*b*) Advise the company of the advantages and disadvantages of using each method.

*(Reproduced with the kind permission of OCR – University of Oxford Delegacy of Local Examinations: GCE A-level)*

**41.14** Frames Ltd make four different products: K, L, M and N. They have ascertained the cost of direct materials and direct labour and the variable overhead for each unit of product. An attempt is made to apportion the other costs in a logical manner. When this is done, 20% is added for profit. The cost of direct labour and materials per unit is K: £28; L: £56; M: £120; N: £64. Variable overheads per unit are K: £8; L: £16; M: £26; N: £24. Fixed overhead costs of £3,800 are allocated per unit as K: £4; L: £8; M: £14; N: £12.

**You are required to:**

(*a*) Calculate the prices at which the units would be sold by Frames Ltd if the full cost system of pricing was adhered to.

(*b*) What would you advise the company to do if, because of market competition, prices had to be fixed at K: £66; L: £78; M: £140; N: £98?

(*c*) Assuming production of 100 units of each item per accounting period, what would be the net profit (*i*) if your advice given in your answer to (*b*) was followed; (*ii*) if the company continued to produce all of the items?

(*d*) What would you advise the company to do if, because of market competition, prices had to be fixed at K: £34; L: £96; M: £280; N: £78?

(e) Assuming production of 100 units of each item per accounting period, what would be the net profit (*i*) if your advice given in your answer to (*d*) was followed; (*ii*) if the company continued to produce all of the items?

**41.15A** Lenses Ltd makes six different products: P, Q, R, S, T and U. An analysis of costs ascertains the following:

| *Per unit* | *P* | *Q* | *R* | *S* | *T* | *U* |
|---|---|---|---|---|---|---|
| | £ | £ | £ | £ | £ | £ |
| Direct labour and direct materials | 45 | 51 | 114 | 147 | 186 | 342 |
| Variable manufacturing expenses | 18 | 33 | 30 | 63 | 66 | 69 |

Fixed costs of £34,200 are allocated per unit as P: £12; Q: £21; R: £21; S: £30; T: £48; U: £39. Using full cost pricing, 10% is to be added per unit for profit.

**You are required to:**

(*a*) Calculate the prices that would be charged by Lenses Ltd if full cost pricing was adhered to.

(*b*) What advice would you give the company if a survey of the market showed that the prices charged could be P: £78; Q: £78; R: £198; S: £225; T: £240; U: £660?

(*c*) Assuming production of 600 units per period of each unit manufactured, what would be the profit of the firm (*i*) if your advice in (*b*) was followed, (*ii*) if the company continued to produce all of the items?

(*d*) Suppose that in fact the market survey had revealed instead that the prices charged could be P: £90; Q: £99; R: £225; S: £198; T: £435; U: £390, what would your advice have been to the company?

(*e*) Assuming that production of each item manufactured was 600 units per month, then what would have been the profit (*i*) if your advice in (*d*) had been followed, (*ii*) if the company chose to continue manufacturing all items?

**41.16A**

(*a*) What are the differences between marginal cost pricing and full cost pricing?

(*b*) How far is it true to state that marginal cost pricing is a short-term strategy?

(*c*) A.S. Teriod Ltd makes five different products – Ceres, Eros, Hermes, Icarus and Vesta. The various costs per unit of the products are respectively: direct labour, £14, £8, £22, £18 and £26; direct materials, £8, £10, £13, £12 and £17; variable overheads, £11, £9, £16, £15 and £19.

The fixed expenses for the month of February 2018 are estimated at £8,200, and this has been allocated to the units produced as Ceres £17, Eros £13, Hermes £19, Icarus £15 and Vesta £18. The company adds 20% on to the total cost of each product by way of profit.

(*i*) Calculate the prices based upon full cost pricing.

(*ii*) Advise the company on which products to produce, if competition forces the prices to: Ceres £59, Eros £25, Hermes £80, Icarus £44 and Vesta £92.

(*iii*) Assuming that output for the month amounts to 100 units of each model, that fixed costs remain the same irrespective of output and that unused capacity cannot be used for other products: calculate the profit or loss if the company continued to produce the whole range at the new prices; AND if the company followed your advice in (*ii*) above.

(*Edexcel: GCE A-level*)

**41.17A** A Khang Ltd manufactures digital photo albums. The following information is available for the year ending 31 December 2018.

| | |
|---|---|
| Opening inventory | zero |
| Production | 60,000 units |
| Sales | 45,000 units |
| Selling price per unit | £18 |
| Direct labour cost per unit | £3 |
| Direct material cost per unit | £5 |
| Variable selling and administration per unit | £2 |
| Fixed selling and administration costs | £25,000 |
| Variable manufacturing overhead per unit | £1 |
| Fixed manufacturing costs | £240,000 |

**Required:**

(*a*) Prepare the statement of profit or loss for Khang Ltd for the year ending 31 December 2018 using:
   (*i*) absorption costing
   (*ii*) marginal costing

(*b*) Provide a reconciliation of the two profit (or loss) amounts in (a) above.

(*c*) Calculate the contribution earned at this level of output and sales.

chapter

# 42 Job, batch and process costing

## Learning objectives

**After you have studied this chapter, you should be able to:**

- explain how indirect costs are apportioned among cost centres
- explain the difference between the accounting treatment of normal and abnormal losses
- explain the difference between scrap, by-products, and joint products
- discuss some of the issues relating to cost allocation between joint products
- describe the system of job costing
- describe the system of process costing
- explain the appropriate treatment for under- and overabsorbed overheads

## Introduction

In this chapter, you'll learn about the differences between costing for continuous production processes and costing for short-term production runs or one-off production activity. You'll learn more about attributing costs to cost centres, in this case, indirect costs such as service centre costs. Finally, you'll learn about how to deal with costs and revenues relating to by-products and joint products.

## 42.1 Background

The earlier chapters on costing have been concerned mainly with the business as a whole. You have seen the effects of and differences between applying marginal and absorption costing, and you have seen the flow of costs through manufacturing and retail businesses. Now we have to consider the actual use of these concepts in the application of costing in businesses. So far, things have been simplified so that the concepts could be seen and understood. For instance, it has been assumed in most of the *exhibits* that the businesses have been making only one kind of product, and that there has really been only one cost centre. Without stretching your imagination greatly, you will realise that businesses often manufacture many different items, and that most have a large number of cost centres.

Costing systems can usually be divided into two main types, (*a*) **job costing**, and (*b*) **process costing**. These two main types of costing system may adopt either an absorption or marginal costing approach, and may use FIFO or LIFO or AVCO methods of pricing issues from inventory, etc.

***Note*: It is important to realise that absorption costing and marginal costing *are not* costing *systems*. Rather, they are approaches to costing which are adopted when job or process costing systems are used.**

## 42.2 Process costing or job costing?

Job costing is used when a finite number of units of a single product are made in one continuous batch. A job may be one single unit, as in the case of a bicycle manufacturer which produces bikes to the precise and very individual requirements of its customers. Alternatively, a job may comprise many units. However, irrespective of the number of units involved, jobs are not often repeated and tend to all be uniquely different.

Process costing is used when production of identical products is continuous and lasts for a significant time. Unlike jobs, process products tend to be repeated as, for example, in a jam factory where the same five different jams are produced each week, each one being produced for an entire day.

**Thus, process costing is relevant where production is a continuous flow**, and is most applicable in industries where production is repetitive and continuous; for example, an oil refinery where crude oil is processed continually, emerging as different grades of petrol, paraffin, motor oil, etc. Another instance would be a salt works where brine (salt water) is pumped into the works, and the product is slabs or packets of salt. Salt works and oil refineries will have a repetitive and continuous flow of production and would, therefore, use process costing.

### Exhibit 42.1

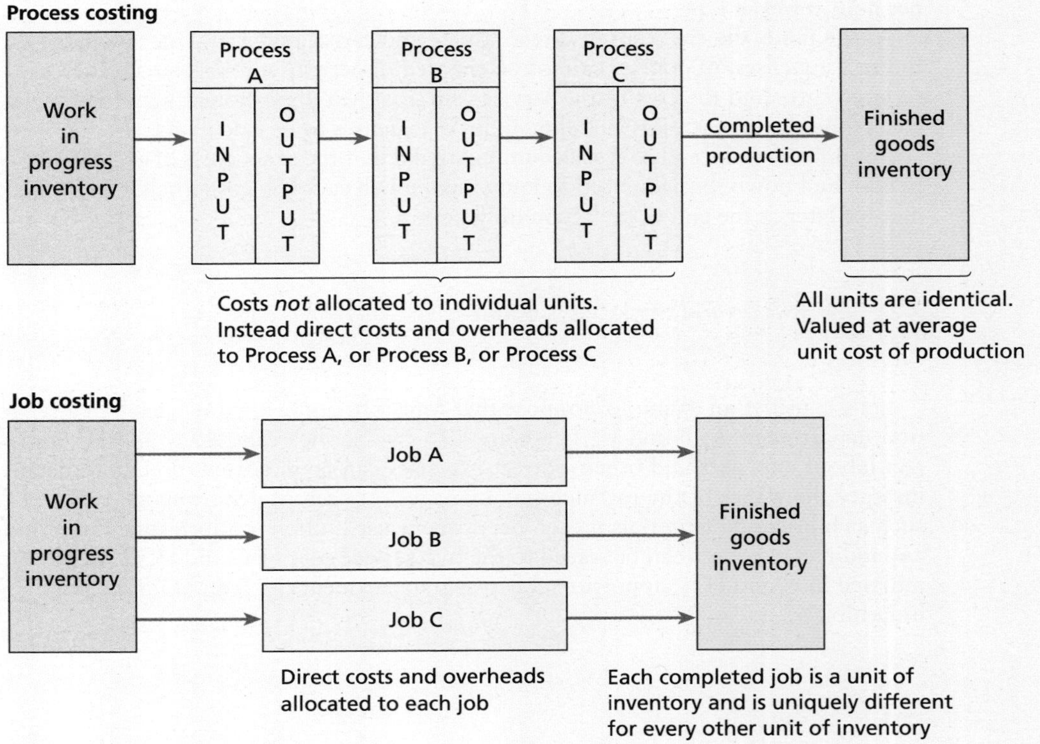

**Process costing**



**Job costing**

Contrasted with this would be production comprising separate jobs for special orders which could be just one item or of a batch of items. For instance, where bodies of Rolls-Royce cars are made to each customer's specifications, each car can be regarded as a separate job. Compared with this would be a printer's business where books are printed, so that the printing of, say, 5,000 copies of a book can also be regarded as a job. **The 'job' can thus be one item or a batch of similar items.**

Two terms are used to describe this *specific order* form of costing. 'Job costing', when costs are to be attributed to an individual job (a customer order or task of relatively short duration); and '*batch costing*', when costs are to be attributed to a specific batch of a product [a group of similar items which is treated as a separate cost unit (a unit of product or service in relation to which costs are ascertained)].

The accounting treatment is the same. For our purposes, **in this chapter, we will only refer to job costing. If you are asked to perform batch costing, remember that the accounting approach is the same.** (Review Question 42.9 is on batch costing.)

We can compare process costing to job costing by using diagrams of the different types of costing. These are shown above in Exhibit 42.1.

Let's now look in detail at job costing.

## 42.3 Job costing

**When job costing is used, each job is given a separate job number, and direct materials and direct labour used on the job are charged to the job.** As a result, the job *is* the cost centre. The accumulation of the costs is done on a 'job cost sheet', which is simply a formal record of the costs incurred. (You will see examples of job cost sheets later in this chapter.) The materials will be charged to a job on a FIFO, LIFO, or AVCO basis. The direct labour costs will be found by recording the number of direct labour hours of each type of direct worker, and multiplying by the labour cost per hour for each type.

**As the job is the cost centre,** direct labour and direct materials can be charged directly to it. Indirect expenses, of course, cannot be charged directly to a job. Instead, they are charged to a service centre and the cost of the service centre is then apportioned between the various jobs to enable the cost of each job including indirect expenses to be calculated.

It is only after the end of the accounting period that the exact costs of each service centre for the period are known, but you need to know how much each job cost when it is finished, not several months later at the end of the accounting period.

**Activity 42.1** How do you think this is done?

Let's consider an example. Suppose that four jobs are being done, each in a separate production department: A, B and C. There are also two service centres, G and H. Some of the indirect labour expenses and other indirect expenses can be allocated directly to departments – for instance the wages of the foremen (i.e. manager) of each of departments A, B and C; and items such as lubricating materials if each department used different lubricants. Other indirect labour and indirect expenses can be traced to the two service centres G and H. How will the costs accumulated in G and H be apportioned between departments A, B and C? One possibility is shown in Exhibit 42.2:

### Exhibit 42.2

Indirect labour costs and other indirect expenses have been allocated to production departments A, B and C and service departments G and H as follows:

| | *Production departments (£s)* | | | *Service departments (£s)* | |
|---|---|---|---|---|---|
| | A | B | C | G | H |
| Indirect labour | 2,000 | 3,000 | 4,000 | 500 | 1,000 |
| Other indirect expenses | 1,000 | 2,000 | 3,000 | 1,500 | 2,000 |
| | 3,000 | 5,000 | 7,000 | 2,000 | 3,000 |

The problem is to apportion the costs of G and H to the production departments. Department G maintains the factory buildings while Department H maintains the factory machinery.

A study of the costs of Department G made it obvious how its costs should be apportioned. There was no doubt that the costs were in direct relationship to the floor space occupied by each department. But it must not be overlooked that Department H also needed the attention of Department G's workforce so that part of the costs of G must be apportioned to Department H.

These costs increase the total of the costs of Department H, which must then be apportioned between the three production departments. Floor space in square feet was A 2,000, B 4,000, C 3,000 and H 1,000. The £2,000 costs of Department G were therefore apportioned using the formula:

$$\frac{\text{Floor space in the department}}{\text{Total floor space}} \times £2{,}000$$

Therefore:

| | | £ |
|---|---|---|
| A | $\frac{2{,}000}{10{,}000} \times £2{,}000 =$ | 400 |
| B | $\frac{4{,}000}{10{,}000} \times £2{,}000 =$ | 800 |
| C | $\frac{3{,}000}{10{,}000} \times £2{,}000 =$ | 600 |
| H | $\frac{1{,}000}{10{,}000} \times £2{,}000 =$ | 200 |
| | | 2,000 |

Department H's costs have now increased by £200 to £3,200.

The apportionment of Department H's costs is far less straightforward. Apportionment based on the number of pieces of equipment (machines), volume of production, and type of equipment were all considered. However, let's suppose it was felt that there was a high relationship in this case between the value of the equipment in use and the costs of maintaining it. The more costly equipment was very complicated and needed a lot of attention. Consequently, it was decided to apportion Department H's costs between A, B and C on the basis of the value of equipment in each department: A £3,000; B £6,000; and C £7,000. The costs were therefore apportioned using the formula:

$$\frac{\text{Value of equipment in department}}{\text{Total value of equipment in all three departments}} \times £3{,}200$$

Therefore:

| | | £ |
|---|---|---|
| A | $\frac{3{,}000}{16{,}000} \times £3{,}200 =$ | 600 |
| B | $\frac{6{,}000}{16{,}000} \times £3{,}200 =$ | 1,200 |
| C | $\frac{7{,}000}{16{,}000} \times £3{,}200 =$ | 1,400 |
| | | 3,200 |

→

➔ The costs and their apportionment can, therefore, be shown:

| | Production departments (£s) | | | Service departments (£s) | |
|---|---|---|---|---|---|
| | A | B | C | G | H |
| Indirect labour | 2,000 | 3,000 | 4,000 | 500 | 1,000 |
| Other expenses | 1,000 | 2,000 | 3,000 | 1,500 | 2,000 |
| | 3,000 | 5,000 | 7,000 | 2,000 | 3,000 |
| Department G's costs apportioned | 400 | 800 | 600 | (2,000) | 200 |
| | | | | | 3,200 |
| Department H's costs apportioned | 600 | 1,200 | 1,400 | | (3,200) |
| | 4,000 | 7,000 | 9,000 | – | – |

This continuous method of apportioning service department overheads is sometimes called the **repeated distribution method.**

**See Review Question 42.7 for a discussion of this and another method, the elimination method.**

We have now identified the indirect expenses for each department. We now have another problem – how are these costs to be taken into the calculation of the cost of each job in these departments?

After investigation, Departments A and B are found to have a direct relationship between direct labour hours and indirect expenses but, in Department C, the guiding factor is machine hours.

If the total overheads of Departments A and B are divided by the total direct labour hours in those departments, this will give the indirect expenses rate per direct labour hour while, in Department C, the total indirect expenses will be divided by the total machine hours. The calculations of the indirect expenses rates are therefore:

| | Production departments | | |
|---|---|---|---|
| | A | B | C |
| Direct labour hours | 5,000 | 4,000 | |
| Machine hours | | | 6,000 |
| Indirect expenses rate per direct labour hour | £4,000 / 5,000 = £0.8 | £7,000 / 4,000 = £1.75 | |
| Indirect expenses rate per machine hour | | | £9,000 / 6,000 = £1.5 |

***Note*: The indirect expenses rate is often referred to as the 'overhead rate'. As this is the term preferred by most examiners, we will use it from now on.**

We can now calculate the costs of the four jobs being done in this factory:

*Department A*

Job A/70/144 Started 1.7.2018. Completed 13.7.2018
Cost of direct materials £130
Number of direct labour hours 100
Cost rate of direct labour per hour £0.9

*Department B*

Job B/96/121 Started 4.7.2018. Completed 9.7.2018
Cost of direct materials £89
Number of direct labour hours 40
Cost rate of direct labour per hour £1.1

*Department C*

Job C/67/198 Started 8.7.2018. Completed 16.7.2018
Cost of direct materials £58
Number of direct labour hours 50
Cost rate of direct labour per hour £1.0
Number of machine hours 40

| | *Departments A and C* |
|---|---|
| Job AC/45/34 | Started in A 3.7.2018. Passed on to C 11.7.2018. Completed in C 16.7.2018 |
| | Cost of materials £115 |
| | Number of direct labour hours (in Dept A) 80 |
| | Number of direct labour hours (in Dept C) 90 |
| | Cost rate per direct labour hour Dept A £0.9 |
| | Dept C £1.0 |
| | Number of machine hours, Dept C 70 |

The job cost sheets for these four jobs are shown below. If an absorption costing approach had been used, indirect expenses (i.e. overheads) would include both fixed and variable indirect expenses. If a marginal costing approach had been used, the indirect expenses brought into the calculations of job costs would exclude fixed indirect expenses and, consequently, the overhead rate would be a variable one.

*Job Cost Sheet. Job No. A/70/144*

| Started 1.7.2018 | Completed 13.7.2018 | | |
|---|---|---|---|
| | *Hours* | *Overhead Rates (£s)* | £ |
| Direct materials | | | 130 |
| Direct labour | 100 | 0.9 | 90 |
| Indirect manufacturing costs | 100 | 0.8 | 80 |
| Total job cost | | | 300 |

*Job Cost Sheet. Job No. B/96/121*

| Started 4.7.2018 | Completed 9.7.2018 | | |
|---|---|---|---|
| | *Hours* | *Overhead Rates (£s)* | £ |
| Direct materials | | | 89 |
| Direct labour | 40 | 1.1 | 44 |
| Indirect manufacturing costs | 40 | 1.75 | 70 |
| Total job cost | | | 203 |

*Job Cost Sheet. Job No. C/67/198*

| Started 8.7.2018 | Completed 16.7.2014 | | |
|---|---|---|---|
| | *Hours* | *Overhead Rates (£s)* | £ |
| Direct materials | | | 58 |
| Direct labour | 50 | 1.0 | 50 |
| Indirect manufacturing costs | 40 | 1.5 | 60 |
| Total job cost | | | 168 |

*Job Cost Sheet. Job No. AC/45/34*

| Started 3.7.2018 | Completed 16.7.2018 | | |
|---|---|---|---|
| | *Hours* | *Overhead Rates (£s)* | £ |
| Direct materials | | | 115 |
| Direct labour (Dept A) | 80 | 0.9 | 72 |
| Direct labour (Dept C) | 90 | 1.0 | 90 |
| Indirect manufacturing costs (Dept A) | 80 | 0.8 | 64 |
| Indirect manufacturing costs (Dept C) | 70 | 1.5 | 105 |
| Total job cost | | | 446 |

## 42.4 Cost centres – job costing and responsibility

It must be pointed out that the use of a cost centre for job costing is not necessarily the same as tracing the costs down to the individual who is responsible for controlling them. There are two requirements here: (*a*) finding the cost of a job to check on its profitability and (*b*) controlling the costs by making someone responsible for them so that he/she will have to answer for any variations from planned results. As a result, many organisations keep separate records of costs to fulfil each of these functions when the appropriate cost centre to use for job costing is inappropriate for matching costs to the individuals responsible for those costs.

Now, let's look at process costing.

## 42.5 Process costing

Job costing treats production as comprising a number of separate jobs, whereas process costing sees production as a continuous flow. **In process costing, no attempt is made to allocate costs to specific units being produced.**

There is, however, usually more than one process in the manufacture of goods. Take, for example, a bakery producing cakes. There are three processes: (*A*) the mixing of the cake ingredients, (*B*) the baking of the cakes, and (*C*) the packaging of the cakes. Each process is treated as a cost centre.

The costs for (*A*), (*B*) and (*C*) are, therefore, collected separately. Overhead rates are then calculated for each cost centre in a similar fashion to that in job costing.

In the case of the bakery, each accounting period would probably start and finish without any half-mixed or half-baked cakes, but many businesses which use process costing have processes which take rather longer to complete than baking cakes. A typical case would be the brewing of beer. At the beginning and end of each period there is an inventory of partly processed units. It is a simple arithmetic exercise to convert unfinished units in production into 'equivalent units produced' (which is also known as *equivalent production*). For example, production during a particular period may be as in Exhibit 42.3:

### Exhibit 42.3

| | |
|---|---|
| Started and $^3/_4$ completed in previous period and $^1/_4$ completed in current period, 400 units: $400 \times {}^1/_4$ | 100 |
| Started and completed in current period | 680 |
| Started in current period and $^1/_8$ completed by end of period, 160 units: $160 \times {}^1/_8$ | 20 |
| Equivalent production | 800 units |

If the total costs of the cost centre amounted to £4,000 then the unit cost would be:

$$\frac{£4{,}000}{800} = £5$$

Process costing becomes more complicated if some of the part-produced items are, for example, complete in terms of materials, but incomplete in terms of labour; or $^2/_3$ complete for material and $^1/_4$ complete for labour. Although the situation is more complicated, the principles are no different from those described for calculating equivalent production when the proportion used of all items is the same.

We can now look at an example of process costing in Exhibit 42.4. So that we do not get involved in too many arithmetical complications, we will assume that there are no partly completed goods in any process either at the start or end of the period.

## Exhibit 42.4

A bakery making cakes has three processes, process (A) the mixing of the cake ingredients, (B) the baking of the cakes, and (C) the packaging of the cakes.

Activity in January was:

| | £ |
|---|---|
| *Direct materials used:* | |
| Process (A) | 4,000 |
| Process (B) | – |
| Process (C) | 1,000 |
| *Direct labour:* | |
| Process (A) | 1,500 |
| Process (B) | 500 |
| Process (C) | 800 |
| *Indirect manufacturing costs:* | |
| Variable: | |
| Process (A) | 400 |
| Process (B) | 1,300 |
| Process (C) | 700 |
| Fixed: (allocated to processes) | |
| Process (A) | 600 |
| Process (B) | 500 |
| Process (C) | 400 |

100,000 cakes were made during January. The process cost accounts are:

*Process (A)*

| | £ | | £ |
|---|---|---|---|
| Direct materials | 4,000 | Transferred to process (B) | |
| Direct labour | 1,500 | 100,000 units at £0.065 | 6,500 |
| Variable factory indirect costs | 400 | | |
| Fixed factory indirect costs | 600 | | |
| | 6,500 | | 6,500 |

*Process (B)*

| | £ | | £ |
|---|---|---|---|
| Transferred from process (A) | | Transferred to process (C) | |
| 100,000 units at £0.065 | 6,500 | 100,000 units at £0.088 | 8,800 |
| Direct labour | 500 | | |
| Variable indirect manufacturing costs | 1,300 | | |
| Fixed indirect manufacturing costs | 500 | | |
| | 8,800 | | 8,800 |

*Process (C)*

| | £ | | £ |
|---|---|---|---|
| Transferred from process (B) | | Transferred to finished goods inventory | |
| 100,000 units at £0.088 | 8,800 | 100,000 units at £0.117 | 11,700 |
| Direct materials | 1,000 | | |
| Direct labour | 800 | | |
| Variable indirect manufacturing costs | 700 | | |
| Fixed indirect manufacturing costs | 400 | | |
| | 11,700 | | 11,700 |

Now, let's look at what is done when fewer units are produced during a process than was expected.

## 42.6 Normal and abnormal losses

There are some production losses that are a result of the production process which cannot be avoided and, as a result, the costs they represent cannot be eliminated from the total cost of the products produced. For instance, when printing books, losses of paper occur when paper is cut to the required size; when brewing beer there will be losses due to evaporation, when cutting steel the amount of cut steel will be less than the amount of steel before it was cut. These losses are inevitable, even in the most efficient businesses. They are called **normal losses** (sometimes called 'uncontrollable losses').

On the other hand, there are losses which should be avoided if the production process is efficient. Such things as the incorrect cutting of cloth so that it is wasted unnecessarily, not mixing ingredients properly so that some of the product is unusable, and the use of inferior materials so that much of the product cannot pass quality inspection tests and is scrapped. These are all examples of **abnormal losses** (sometimes called 'controllable losses').

The accounting treatments of these two very different types of losses are:

- **Normal losses.** These are not transferred from the process account but are treated as part of the process costs.
- **Abnormal losses.** These are transferred out of the process account and into an abnormal loss account. The double entry is:

*Dr* Abnormal loss account
*Cr* Process account

As a result, an abnormal loss is not included in the cost of items produced. Instead, it is treated as a period cost.

How do you think this is done?

## 42.7 Under/overabsorption of overheads

When an overhead rate is based on estimated annual indirect expenditure and estimated activity, it is not usually the same as it would have been had it been calculated at the end of the accounting period, when all costs are known. Either the costs themselves will differ from expectations, or the activity will not have proceeded as expected, or both.

For example, if £300,000 has been allocated for indirect costs to the year's production, but actual indirect costs were £298,000 then too much has been allocated. In other words, an overabsorption of indirect expenses has occurred amounting to £2,000. (Overabsorption is sometimes referred to as 'over-recovery'.)

If, on the other hand, £305,000 had been allocated but the actual costs were £311,000 then too little has been allocated. This would represent an underabsorption of indirect costs (i.e. overheads) amounting to £6,000. (Underabsorption is sometimes referred to as 'under-recovery'.)

At the closing date of the statement of financial position, inventory has been valued and this value includes something for indirect costs. In the case of an underabsorption, the question arises as to whether the closing inventory valuation should be amended to include something for the underabsorbed overheads. The accounting answer is that no adjustment should be made to the inventory valuation. Similarly, the inventory valuation should not be reduced to take account of overabsorption of overheads.

Exhibit 42.5 shows how the indirect costs should be treated when there is an underabsorption of those costs which was caused by abnormal losses.

**Exhibit 42.5**

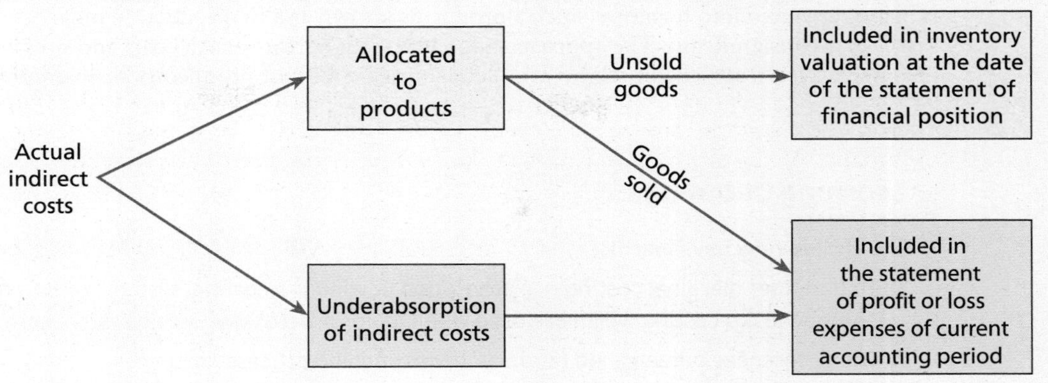


Any overabsorption is also included in the statement of profit or loss, but as a credit.

## 42.8 Other kinds of businesses

Process costing is found most often in industries such as oil, canning, paint manufacture, steel, textiles and food processing.

## 42.9 The problem of joint costs

A manufacturing operation often results in only one product being produced. Any excess output other than the product itself is regarded as scrap, and the small cost that could be traced to it is ignored. For example, in the manufacture of a suit, when the cost is traced to the suit, the small unusable bits of cloth that are left over are ignored.

This is not always the case. **Where a group of separate products is produced simultaneously, each of the products having relatively substantial sales values, then the products are referred to as joint products**; for example, crude oil taken to an oil refinery where it is processed into different grades of petrol, paraffin, motor oil, etc., all of which are joint products. The costs of the materials and processes, etc. must then be split between the joint products.

Many problems exist in doing so. Perhaps you will see why when you consider the problem of allocating the costs of cutting up a cow for beef. From a cow there is rump steak, fillet steaks, T-bone steaks, sirloin, silverside, brisket, etc. If cutting up the cow cost £20, then how would you allocate the cost between all of these various joint products? This gives you some idea of the type of problems which can exist – in many industries this becomes increasingly problematic as the production technology in use increases in complexity.

**Activity 42.3** How would you split the cost of cutting up the cow between joint products?

***Note*: In fact, you could allocate the costs on any basis and none would be indisputably 'correct'. With joint products, there is no rational reason or basis for splitting their costs that cannot be argued against.**

Sometimes, a minor (i.e. much lower value) but, nevertheless, distinguishable product is produced at the same time as the main product. One example is the sawdust that is created when wood is being converted into furniture. Such a product is known as a **by-product.** In most cases, the costs involved are insignificant. The approach adopted is to ignore any such costs and simply credit any income derived from sale of the by-product against the cost of producing the main product(s).

## Learning outcomes

**You should now have learnt:**

1. That neither marginal costing nor absorption costing is a costing 'system'; rather, they are approaches to costing which are used when job or processing costing systems are used.
2. The differences between job (and batch) costing and process costing.
3. That direct costs can be allocated directly to the relevant cost centre. However, indirect costs have to be apportioned among cost centres on an appropriate basis, as there is no way of knowing precisely how much indirect cost was incurred on each item produced.
4. How indirect costs can be apportioned across cost centres.
5. How to deal with normal and abnormal losses.
6. About the problems relating to cost allocation between joint products.

## Answers to activities

42.1 The indirect expenses attributed to each service centre are estimated and then apportioned using an appropriate base to each job.

42.2 It is included in the costs charged to the statement of profit or loss at the end of the period.

42.3 Among the obvious choices, you could allocate the joint costs on the basis of the sale price of each of the joint products, or on the basis of the relative weight or volume of the joint products.

## Review questions

***Advice*: Questions on job costing and process costing are usually fairly easy to answer and it is also relatively simple to gain quite high marks by tackling them. Don't forget, if a question refers to 'batch costing', this is accounted for using the same accounting procedures as job costing.**

**42.1** In a factory, four types of jobs are performed in separate production departments A, B, C and D. In addition there are three service departments, K, L and M. Costs have been allocated to the departments as follows:

| | *Production departments* | | | | *Service departments* | | |
|---|---|---|---|---|---|---|---|
| | *A* | *B* | *C* | *D* | *K* | *L* | *M* |
| | *£* | *£* | *£* | *£* | *£* | *£* | *£* |
| Indirect labour | 8,000 | 12,000 | 16,000 | 4,000 | 3,000 | 6,000 | 8,200 |
| Other expenses | 5,400 | 6,200 | 7,200 | 3,000 | 9,000 | 4,000 | 4,000 |

The expenses of the service departments are to be allocated between other departments as follows:

Dept K to Depts A 20%; B 25%; C 30%; D 15%; M 10%.
Dept L to Depts A 35%; C 45%; D 20%.
Dept M to Depts B 40%; C 25%; D 35%.

In departments A and C the job costing is to use an overhead rate per direct labour hour, while in B and D a machine hour rate will be used. The number of direct hours and machine hours per department is expected to be:

| | *A* | *B* | *C* | *D* |
|---|---|---|---|---|
| Direct labour hours | 4,000 | 8,000 | 8,900 | 5,400 |
| Machine hours | 3,800 | 5,200 | 5,800 | 4,800 |

**You are required to calculate:**
(*a*) The overhead rates for departments A and C.
(*b*) The overhead rates for departments B and D.

**Keep your answer – it will be used as a basis for the next question.**

**42.2** For the factory in Question 42.1, what would be the costs of the following jobs given that the direct labour costs per hour are: Dept A £5; B £4; C £6; D £7?

| | | |
|---|---|---|
| Job 351: Dept A | Direct materials cost | £760 |
| | Number of direct labour hours | 112 |
| | Number of machine hours | 80 |
| Job 352: Dept B | Direct materials cost | £3,597 |
| | Number of direct labour hours | 256 |
| | Number of machine hours | 252 |
| Job 353: Dept C | Direct materials cost | £2,000 |
| | Number of direct labour hours | 390 |
| | Number of machine hours | 300 |
| Job 354: Dept D | Direct materials cost | £1,998 |
| | Number of direct labour hours | 180 |
| | Number of machine hours | 128 |
| Job 355: Dept C | Direct materials cost | £1,680 |
| | Number of direct labour hours | 320 |
| | Number of machine hours | 300 |
| Dept B | Job passed on to Dept B where additional direct materials cost | £204 |
| | Number of direct labour hours | 60 |
| | Number of machine hours | 40 |

**42.3A** A manufacturer is producing five types of job, each in a separate production department P, Q, R, S and T. In addition, there are two service departments F and G. Costs have been allocated to the departments as follows:

| | *Production departments* | | | | | *Service departments* | |
|---|---|---|---|---|---|---|---|
| | *P* | *Q* | *R* | *S* | *T* | *F* | *G* |
| | *£* | *£* | *£* | *£* | *£* | *£* | *£* |
| Indirect labour | 15,000 | 21,000 | 9,000 | 18,000 | 12,000 | 20,000 | 18,000 |
| Other expenses | 2,000 | 3,000 | 4,000 | 4,500 | 1,500 | 8,000 | 10,000 |

The expenses of the service departments are to be allocated between other departments as follows:

Dept F to Depts P 15%; Q 10%; S 40%; T 20%; G 15%.
Dept G to Depts P 20%; Q 15%; R 30%; S 25%; T 10%.

In departments R and T the job costing is to use an overhead rate per direct labour hour, while in the other production departments a machine hour rate will be used. The number of direct labour hours and machine hours per department is expected to be:

| | *P* | *Q* | *R* | *S* | *T* |
|---|---|---|---|---|---|
| Direct labour hours | 10,000 | 12,000 | 8,000 | 15,000 | 5,000 |
| Machine hours | 7,000 | 9,000 | 5,000 | 14,000 | 3,000 |

**You are required to calculate:**

(*a*) The overhead rates for departments R and T.

(*b*) The overhead rates for departments P, Q and S.

**Keep your answer – it will be used for Question 42.4A.**

**42.4A** For the company in Question 42.3A, what would be the costs of the following jobs, given that the direct labour rate per hour is Dept P £6; Q £9; R £8; S £11; T £10?

| | | |
|---|---|---|
| Job 701: Dept R | Direct materials cost | £345 |
| | Number of direct labour hours | 105 |
| | Number of machine hours | 87 |
| Job 702: Dept T | Direct materials cost | £3,240 |
| | Number of direct labour hours | 540 |
| | Number of machine hours | 480 |
| Job 703: Dept P | Direct materials cost | £1,560 |
| | Number of direct labour hours | 400 |
| | Number of machine hours | 280 |
| Job 704: Dept S | Direct materials cost | £196 |
| | Number of direct labour hours | 620 |
| | Number of machine hours | 90 |
| Job 705: Dept Q | Direct materials cost | £11,330 |
| | Number of direct labour hours | 860 |
| | Number of machine hours | 610 |
| Job 706: Dept P | Direct materials cost | £1,480 |
| | Number of direct labour hours | 600 |
| | Number of machine hours | 540 |
| Dept T | Then passed to Dept T for completion where direct materials cost | £32 |
| | Number of direct labour hours | 36 |
| | Number of machine hours | 6 |

**42.5**

(*a*) Define the term *equivalent production* and state when the principle is used.

(*b*) During May 2017, M Wurzel & Co. Limited's output was 4,000 finished items plus 600 partly finished items. There was no work in progress on 1 May 2017.

| | *Materials* | *Labour* | *Overheads* | *Total* |
|---|---|---|---|---|
| Total cost (£) | 8,172 | 7,120 | 5,196 | 20,488 |
| WIP degree of completion % | 90 | 75 | 55 | – |

**Calculate for the month of May 2017:**

(*i*) the total equivalent production for each cost element;

(*ii*) the cost per complete unit;

(*iii*) the value of the work in progress.

(*Edexcel: GCE A-level*)

## 42.6A

(a) What is meant by the term *equivalent production?*

(b) At Earith Industries at the beginning of April there were no partially finished goods on hand. During the month, 6,000 completed units were produced, together with 800 units partially completed. Details of the partially finished items were:

| | *Total cost (£)* | *Percentage completed* |
|---|---|---|
| Materials | 12,540 | 75 |
| Labour | 8,476 | 65 |
| Overheads | 7,084 | 55 |

**Calculate:**

(*i*) the total equivalent production,
(*ii*) the cost per complete unit,
(*iii*) the total value of work in progress.

*(Edexcel: GCE A-level)*

## 42.7

(a) Explain the difference between the terms *overhead allotment, overhead apportionment* and *overhead absorption.*

(b) Why are *estimated* figures used in calculating overhead absorption rates?

(c) The following information relates to Flyby Knight plc for the six months ended 31 December 2017:

| | *Production Departments* | | | *Service Departments* | |
|---|---|---|---|---|---|
| | *A* | *B* | *C* | *X* | *Y* |
| Overheads (£) | 14,000 | 12,000 | 8,000 | 4,000 | 3,000 |
| Overheads to be apportioned: | | | | | |
| Dept X (%) | 35 | 30 | 20 | – | 15 |
| Dept Y (%) | 30 | 40 | 25 | 5 | – |

(*i*) Use the continuous apportionment (repeated distribution) method to apportion the service departments' overheads between each other.
(*ii*) Apportion the service departments' overheads calculated in (*i*) to the production departments.
(*iii*) Show how the overheads apportioned to the production departments would have differed if the elimination method had been used for the service departments.
(*iv*) State how far it is true to say that the elimination method produces an inaccurate answer, and is therefore not to be recommended.

*(Edexcel: GCE A-level)*

**42.8A** Kalmo Ltd offers a subcontracting service in assembly, painting and packing. Components are supplied by customers to the company, the required operations are then carried out, and the completed work returned to the customer. The company is labour intensive, with only a relatively small amount of materials purchased.

Currently, one factory overhead recovery rate is used which is a percentage of total direct labour costs. This is calculated from the following budgeted costs.

| *Department* | *Direct labour costs* | *Direct labour hours* | *Machine hours* | *Factory overheads* |
|---|---|---|---|---|
| | £ | | | £ |
| Assembly | 450,000 | 150,000 | 6,000 | 180,000 |
| Painting | 500,000 | 140,625 | – | 225,000 |
| Packing | 250,000 | 100,000 | 8,000 | 75,000 |

→

The cost sheet for Job 131190 shows the following information:

| *Department* | *Direct labour costs* | *Direct labour hours* | *Machine hours* | *Direct material costs* |
|---|---|---|---|---|
| | £ | | | £ |
| Assembly | 2,500 | 1,000 | 120 | 100 |
| Painting | 2,200 | 900 | – | 400 |
| Packing | 4,800 | 960 | 80 | 500 |

General administration expenses of 20% are added to the total factory costs, and then a further 25% of the total cost is added as profit, to arrive at the selling price.

Although the company has been using the blanket factory overhead recovery rate for a number of years, one of the directors has questioned this method, and asks if it would be possible to apply overhead recovery rates for each department.

**Required:**

(*a*) Calculate the current factory overhead recovery rate, and apply this to arrive at the selling price for Job 131190.

(*b*) In line with the director's comments, calculate overhead recovery rates for each department, using two alternative methods, and apply both to arrive at new selling prices for Job 131190.

(*c*) Briefly evaluate the methods you have used for the recovery of factory overheads, justifying which one you consider to be most appropriate.

(*d*) Outline how an unsatisfactory method of overhead absorption can affect the profits of a business.

*(Reproduced with the kind permission of OCR – University of Oxford Delegacy of Local Examinations: GCE A-level* )

**42.9**

(*a*) What is meant by the term 'specific order costing'?

(*b*) In what ways does specific order costing differ from process costing?

(*c*) The Acme Shelving Co. Ltd manufactures shelving brackets in batches of 300. During May, Batch No. 23 was machined at a rate of 15 per hour. Sixty of the brackets failed to pass inspection, but of these, 40 were thought to be rectifiable. The remaining 20 were scrapped, and the scrap value was credited to the batch cost account. Rectification work took nine hours.

*Batch No. 23*

| | £ |
|---|---|
| Raw materials per bracket | 1.60 |
| Scrap value per bracket | 0.86 |
| Machinists' hourly rate | 4.20 |
| Machine hour overhead rate (running time only) | 3.60 |
| Setting up of machine: normal machining | 21.00 |
| rectification | 18.00 |

**Calculate:**

(*i*) the cost of Batch No. 23 in total and per unit, if all units pass inspection;

(*ii*) the *actual* cost of Batch No. 23, in total and per unit, after crediting the recovery value of the scrapped components, and including the rectification costs;

(*iii*) the loss incurred because of defective work.

(*Edexcel: GCE A-level*)

**42.10A** Horden Products Ltd manufactures goods which could involve any or all of three production departments. These departments are simply entitled **A**, **B** and **C**. A direct wages cost percentage absorption rate for the recovery of production overheads is applied to individual job costs.

Details from the company's budgets for the year ended 31 March 2018 are as follows:

| | *Dept A* | *Dept B* | *Dept C* |
|---|---|---|---|
| Indirect materials | £23,000 | £35,000 | £57,000 |
| Indirect wages | £21,000 | £34,000 | £55,000 |
| Direct wages | £140,000 | £200,000 | £125,000 |
| Direct labour hours | 25,000 | 50,000 | 60,000 |
| Machine hours | 100,000 | 40,000 | 10,000 |

The following information is also available for the production departments:

| | *Dept A* | *Dept B* | *Dept C* |
|---|---|---|---|
| Area (square metres) | 30,000 | 20,000 | 10,000 |
| Cost of machinery | £220,000 | £160,000 | £20,000 |
| Horsepower of machinery | 55 | 30 | 15 |

| Other budgeted figures are: | £ |
|---|---|
| Power | 120,000 |
| Rent, rates, light, heat | 90,000 |
| Insurance (machinery) | 20,000 |
| Depreciation | 80,000 |

Machinery is depreciated on the basis of 20% on cost.

Job No. 347 passed through all three departments and incurred the following actual direct costs and times:

| | *Direct material* | *Direct wages* | *Direct labour hours* | *Machine hours* |
|---|---|---|---|---|
| | £ | £ | £ | £ |
| **Dept A** | 152 | 88 | 35 | 60 |
| **Dept B** | 85 | 192 | 90 | 30 |
| **Dept C** | 52 | 105 | 45 | 10 |

A sum amounting to 30% of the production cost is added to every job to enable a selling price to be quoted.

**Required:**

(*a*) A statement to show the total production overheads per department and calculate the absorption rate which the company has adopted.

(*b*) Calculate the selling price to be quoted for Job No. 347.

(*c*) Using the available data, calculate absorption rates when based on:

(*i*) direct labour hour rate;

(*ii*) machine hour rate.

(*d*) Explain clearly the meaning of the following terms relating to overheads:

(*i*) allotment;

(*ii*) allocation;

(*iii*) apportionment.

*(AQA (Associated Examining Board): GCE A-level )*

## 42.11A

(*a*) Explain the following terms as used in process costing:

(*i*) normal losses

(*ii*) abnormal losses

(*iii*) equivalent production

(*iv*) joint cost

(*v*) split-off point.

(*b*) In process costing, it is neither the technology nor the costs incurred, but the market price of the item, which determines whether an item is classed as:

(*i*) scrap or waste; and

(*ii*) a joint product or a by-product.

How far do you agree?

*(Edexcel: GCE A-level)*

**42.12A** From the information given below, you are required to:

(*a*) Prepare a standard cost sheet for one unit and enter on the standard cost sheet the costs to show sub-totals for:

(*i*) Prime cost
(*ii*) Variable production costs
(*iii*) Total production cost
(*iv*) Total cost

(*b*) Calculate the selling price per unit allowing for a profit of 15% of the selling price.

***The following data are given:***

| | |
|---|---|
| Budgeted output for the year | 9,800 units |

*Standard details for one unit:*

Direct materials 40 square metres at £5.30 per square metre.

Direct wages:
Bonding Department – 48 hours @ £2.50 per hour
Finishing Department – 30 hours @ £1.90 per hour

Budgeted costs and hours per annum:

| | £ | Hours |
|---|---|---|
| Variable overhead: | | |
| Bonding Department | 375,000 | 500,000 |
| Finishing Department | 150,000 | 300,000 |

| | £ |
|---|---|
| Fixed overhead: | |
| Production | 392,000 |
| Selling and distribution | 196,000 |
| Administration | 98,000 |

part 8

# BUDGETS

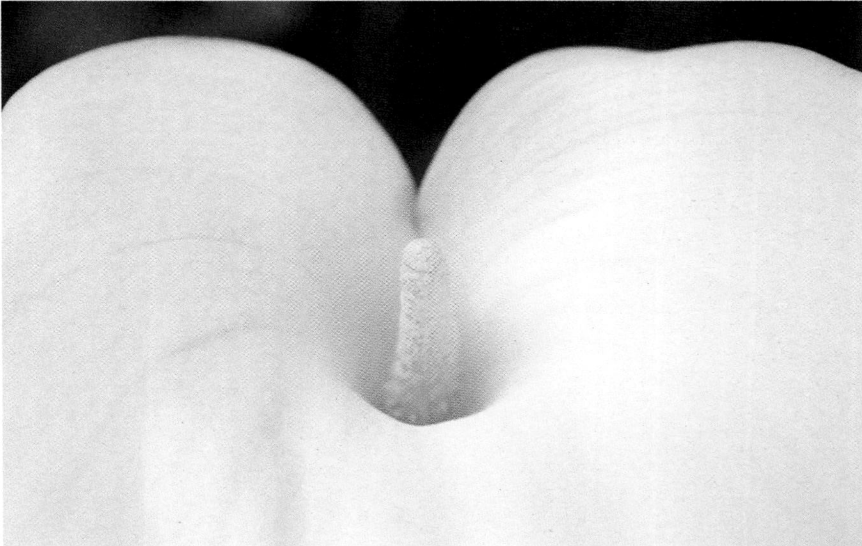

## Introduction

**This part looks at how management can institute a system to support planning, evaluation and control through the use of budgets.**

chapter

# 43 Budgeting and budgetary control

## Learning objectives

**After you have studied this chapter, you should be able to:**

- describe the budgetary process
- explain the importance of budgets for planning and control
- explain how to apply the economic order quantity approach to stock control

## Introduction

In this chapter, you'll learn about the need for budgeting, how production budgets can be set, both when production is to be at a constant level and when it is to vary according to demand. You will also learn about how to determine the most appropriate point in time to order new supplies and about alternatives to traditional methods of ensuring that sufficient but not too many raw materials and bought-in goods for resale are available for production and sale when required.

## 43.1 Background

In Chapters 36 and 40, you learnt that management control is needed if organisations are to achieve their objectives. Once the objectives of an organisation have been agreed, plans need to be drawn up so that the objectives can be met.

Don't assume that plans can only be expressed in monetary terms and values. For example, quality of the product might be best shown in engineering terms, or social objectives shown in a plan concerned with employee welfare. But some of the objectives, such as the attainment of a desired profit, or of the attainment of a desired growth in assets, can be expressed and measured in monetary terms and values.

When a plan is expressed quantitatively (i.e. in numbers – monetary amounts or quantities) it is known as a **budget** and the process of converting plans into budgets is known as '*budgeting*'. In this book, we are concerned primarily with budgets shown in monetary terms, i.e. 'financial budgets'.

A budget is like a lane on a motorway. You may enjoy being able to switch lanes and, at times, you may need to do so but, if you want to reach your destination at a specific time, you need to spend as much of the journey as possible in the lane that is most appropriate for the time you have available.

The budgeting process may be very formal, as it typically is in most large organisations. Sometimes it may be so formal a process that committees are set up to co-ordinate and review the task. On the other hand, in a very small organisation the owner may note down his budget on a piece of scrap paper or the back of a used envelope. Some even manage without writing anything down at all, they have done the budgets in their heads and can remember them easily. In this book, we will focus upon budgeting in a formal manner.

## 43.2 Budgets and people

**In no other part of accounting is there a greater need for understanding people than in the processes of budgeting.** Budgets are prepared in order to try to guide the organisation towards its objectives. Yet, there is no doubt that some budgets are even more harmful to the organisation than if none were drawn up at all. The main cause of such a mismatch between a budget and the organisation is a failure to consider the human side of budgeting.

Activity 43.1

What does this statement concerning the harm budgets may bring to an organisation remind you of from earlier chapters?

Budgets are drawn up for control purposes, that is, they represent an attempt to control the direction in which the organisation is moving. Many people, however, look upon budgets, not as a guide, but as a straitjacket. Let's look at a few undesirable actions that can result from people regarding budgets as a straitjacket rather than as a guide.

1 A sales manager refuses to let a salesman go to Sweden in response to an urgent and unexpected request from a Swedish firm. The reason: the overseas sales expenses budget has already been spent. The result: the most profitable order that the company would have received for many years is lost to a competitor.
2 The factory manager turns down requests for overtime work on a job because the budgeted overtime has already been exceeded. The result: the job is not completed on time and the company has to pay a large sum under a penalty clause in the contract.
3 Towards the end of the accounting period, a manager realises that she has not spent all of her budget for a particular item. She is worried that failing to do so will result in a cut in her budget for the next accounting period. As a result, she launches on a spending spree, buying many completely unnecessary items. The result: a lot of unusable and unnecessary equipment.
4 The staff training budget has been spent early in the year. As a result, the human resources manager will not let anyone go on courses for the rest of the year. The result: the company starts to fall behind in a fast-changing industry which is highly dependent on advanced technology, the staff concerned become disillusioned (as they know they need to 'keep up') and the better ones start to look for jobs in other companies which are more responsive to the need to allow personnel to keep in touch with changing technology.

Research studies have shown that the more that managers are brought into the budgeting process, then the more successful budgetary control is likely to be. A manager on whom a budget is imposed is likely to pay less attention to the budget and use it less wisely in the control process compared to a manager who had an active part in the drafting of his budget.

Having sounded the warning that needs to be borne in mind constantly when budgeting, we can now look at the positive end of budgeting – the advantages of a good budgetary control system.

## 43.3 Budgets, planning and control

The methodology of budgetary control is probably accounting's major contribution to the process of management. Before we get down to the actual mechanics of preparing a budget, we will first look briefly at the main steps involved in drafting a budget.

When budgets are being prepared, two principal objectives must be uppermost in the mind of top management. Budgets exist in order to implement:

1 **Planning.** This means a properly co-ordinated and comprehensive plan *for the whole business*. Each part *must* interlock with the other parts.
2 **Control.** Just because a plan is set down on paper does not guarantee that the plan will be followed automatically and that there will be no deviations from it. Control is needed to ensure a plan is followed and control is exercised via the budgets, thus the term 'budgetary control'. To achieve real control, the responsibility of managers and budgets must be so linked that the manager responsible for a certain part of the plan is given a guide to help her produce the desired results and, also, that the actual results achieved are then compared against the expected results, i.e. actual compared with budget.

## 43.4 Preparation of estimates and the sales budget

The first budget that should be prepared is the sales budget. However, before doing so, the first thing to establish when preparing a budget is what limiting factors exist that affect it. For example, it may well be that sales cannot be pushed above a certain amount, or it might be that the company could sell as much as it can produce, but productive capacity is limited. There is no doubt that identification of the limiting factors is crucial if an achievable budget is to be set. There would not, for instance, be much point in budgeting for the sale of 1,000 units a year if production could not manufacture more than 700; or in budgeting to manufacture 2,000 units a year if only 1,300 of them could be sold.

The most difficult estimate to make when preparing a company's budget is that of sales volume and, then, sales revenue. This can be done using one of two methods:

1 Make a statistical forecast on the basis of the economic conditions relating to the goods sold (e.g. how demand reacts to price changes) and what is known about the actions of competitors.

   This approach has an *external* rather than an *internal* focus. When adopted, it tends to be performed at a high level in the organisation, with relatively little consultation involving employees actually engaged in the selling process.
2 The alternative approach uses information gathered lower down in the organisation. This is usually done by asking each salesperson, or group of salespeople, to estimate the sales in their own areas, and then adding together all the estimates.

If you have studied, or are studying, economics, you will find it very useful in helping you understand some of the issues mentioned above. In particular, a knowledge of elasticity of demand; whether the product is a complementary product (e.g. the price of egg cups is linked to the demand for eggs); or whether it is a substitute (e.g. a rise in the price of butter may induce consumers to use butter substitutes instead), is very relevant. Factors of crucial importance include whether the company has a monopoly dominance of its market; whether the company has many small customers, a few large customers, or just one large customer. When estimating sales revenue all relevant economic factors must be considered.

The sales budget is, however, more than just a forecast of sales volume and sales revenue. **Budgets should show the actions that management is taking to influence future events.** If an increase in sales is desired, the sales budget may show extra sales, which may well also indicate that management is going to attempt to increase sales by means such as extra television advertising, making a better product, or giving retailers better profit margins.

Now, let's look at another key budget, the production budget.

## 43.5 The production budget

**The production budget must be compatible with the sales budget.** However, some other factors are also highly relevant, such as the level of inventory of finished goods which will be held by the business.

If sales are at the same level over the year, production can be too and the inventory figure can remain constant. For example, if a company sells 50 units every month, it can produce 50 units per month. In almost every business, a minimum inventory level will have to be maintained, the quantity of inventory being dependent on factors such as the amount of storage space, the estimated amount needed to cater for breakdowns in production or for delays in receiving raw materials, etc. The minimum level of inventory to be held is a separate issue from the level of production. Consequently, whether the inventory level was to be a minimum of 70 units, 100 units or any other level, production in the above example would be 50 units per month.

On the other hand, sales may not be constant. For example, sales may *average* 50 units per month, but the monthly figures may be as follows:

| | | | | | |
|---|---|---|---|---|---|
| January | 20 units | February | 30 units | March | 60 units |
| April | 80 units | May | 70 units | June | 40 units |

If production levels were kept at 50 units per month, there would be a shortage of 10 units in May – when 70 were demanded but only 60 were available for sale (10 left over from April plus 50 produced in May). An extra 10 units would need to be held to cover this shortfall. If production each month is to be the same, 10 units would need to be held in inventory at the start of the year.

Any calculation of minimum inventory levels must include these 10 units. For example, if minimum inventory of 100 is required, inventory at the beginning of the year would need to be 110 units, otherwise inventory at the end of May would only be 90, not 100.

However, instead of producing the same number of units each month, the monthly production could be set to equal the sales figures. If a minimum inventory level of 100 units is required, the number of units held at the beginning of the year would then be 100.

We can now compare the two levels of production in Sections 43.6 and 43.7.

## 43.6 Even production levels

The problem here is to find the inventory level that the business would need on 1 January if (*a*) sales are as shown, (*b*) the inventory must not fall below 100 units, and (*c*) production is to be 50 units per month.

The inventory level can be found by trial and error. For example, if you decided to see what would happen if the business had 100 units in inventory on 1 January, you would find that after adding production and deducting sales each month, the inventory level would fall to 90 units in May. As 100 units of inventory is the minimum, you would need to start off on 1 January with 110 units.

The method simply requires that you start off your calculation with an estimated figure of inventory at the start of the period, which must not be less than the minimum inventory level, and then find the lowest figure of inventory during the period. If this is, for example, 10 units less than the minimum inventory required, go back and add 10 units to the inventory to be held at the start. If the lowest figure is 30 units less than required, add 30 units to the opening inventory, and so on. Let's look at this in Exhibit 43.1.

**Exhibit 43.1**

| *Units* | *January* | *February* | *March* | *April* | *May* | *June* |
|---|---|---|---|---|---|---|
| Opening inventory | 110 | 140 | 160 | 150 | 120 | 100 |
| *Add* Units produced | 50 | 50 | 50 | 50 | 50 | 50 |
| | 160 | 190 | 210 | 200 | 170 | 150 |
| *Less* Sales | (20) | (30) | (60) | (80) | (70) | (40) |
| Closing inventory | 140 | 160 | 150 | 120 | 100 | 110 |

**Activity 43.2**

**Sales are expected to be: January 70, February 40, March 50, April 120, May 140 and June 70. The inventory level must not fall below 120 units, which is the level at the end of May, and an even production flow of 80 units is required. What inventory level would have to have been held on 1 January?**

In many organisations, it is felt to be more important to ensure a smooth production flow than to bother unduly about inventory levels. They simply assume that the minimum inventory level is always attained. If the work is skilled, the labour force may take several years to become trained, and skilled labour in many industries does not take kindly to being sacked and re-employed as the demand for the goods they produce fluctuates. Of course, there are exceptions. For example, in the building industry, bricklayers may go to a builder until they have completed a contract such as building a college, a hospital or a housing estate, and then leave and look for another employer.

On the other hand, a skilled engineer concerned with the manufacture of, say, diesel engines would not expect to be fired and re-employed continuously. The bricklayer has a skill that is easily transferable to many other building employers in an area, whereas the diesel engineer may have only one firm within 50 miles of her home where she can perform her skills properly. A person employed as a labourer might work on a building site in one part of the year and in a brewery during the rest of the year.

Whether a business could carry on production with widely uneven production levels depends so much on the type of firm and the type of labour involved. A business would only sack skilled labour which it needed to rehire soon afterwards if it could persuade them to come back when required. If the people who had been sacked were likely to find other employment, and not return to their previous employer when required, they would probably be kept on the payroll instead of being temporarily sacked. Production could continue but inventory of finished goods would begin to pile up.

Many businesses do accept their social obligations by only laying off workers when no other reasonable alternative exists. In some organisations, there are probably more workers from time to time than are actually needed – this is known as 'organisational slack' so that there is a leeway between the increasing of production and having to take on extra workers.

## 43.7 Uneven production levels

Some organisations, by their very nature, have uneven production levels, and this is accepted by their labour force. An ice-cream firm would find its sales at their highest levels in summer, tailing off in winter. It is not really possible to build up inventory of ice-cream very much in the winter for summer sales. Even if it could be done, the costs of refrigerating large quantities of ice-cream for several months could hardly be economical. The large labour force used in the summer months probably includes quite a few students occupying their vacation periods profitably, who are not able to work at the job all the year round, even if they wanted to. Such a business will normally have a far stronger relationship between its current inventory levels and current sales than one which has even production levels.

The calculation of the quantity to be produced in any one period is:

**Units sold − Opening inventory + Closing inventory = Units produced**

This can also be stated as:

**Opening inventory + Units produced − Units sold = Closing inventory**

Thus, if the opening inventory is 80 units, units sold are expected to be 100, and the desired closing inventory is 50 units, the quantity to be produced becomes:

| | *Units* |
|---|---|
| Opening inventory | 80 |
| *Add* Production | ? |
| | ? |
| *Less* Sales | (100) |
| Closing inventory | 50 |

Production will, therefore, be the missing figure, i.e. 70 units (80 + production 70 = 150 for sale less actually sold 100 = closing inventory 50).

Exhibit 43.2 shows the units to be produced if the following information is known: inventory required 1 January 40, at end of each month, January 60, February 110, March 170, April 100, May 60, June 20. Sales are expected to be January 100, February 150, March 110, April 190, May 70, June 50.

**Exhibit 43.2**

| *Units* | *January* | *February* | *March* | *April* | *May* | *June* |
|---|---|---|---|---|---|---|
| Opening inventory | 40 | 60 | 110 | 170 | 100 | 60 |
| Production required (?) | 120 | 200 | 170 | 120 | 30 | 10 |
| | 160 | 260 | 280 | 290 | 130 | 70 |
| *Less* Sales | (100) | (150) | (110) | (190) | (70) | (50) |
| Closing inventory | 60 | 110 | 170 | 100 | 60 | 20 |

**Linked with the production budget will be a materials purchase budget. It may well be that an order will have to be placed in January, received in March and issued to production in April. The purchase of materials will have to be planned as scientifically as possible.**

**What is the relationship between the sales budget, the production budget and the materials purchase budget?**

## 43.8 Inventory control

In your earlier studies of accounting, you probably examined the different methods by which inventory is valued – see, for example, *Frank Wood's Business Accounting Volume 1*, Chapter 29. Apart from valuation of inventory, accountants are also interested in knowing if the quantity of inventory being carried is greater than it need be.

Let's look at what makes this information interesting – holding excessive inventory can have a detrimental effect upon the financial results of a business:

1 Money tied up in unnecessarily large inventory is not earning anything. If, therefore, an extra £1 million is tied up unnecessarily in inventory, the money which could have been earned from utilising that extra £1 million somewhere else has been lost. If a 10% return could have been earned on that money, the unnecessary inventory has cost £100,000 a year, even before the cost of storing this excess inventory is considered.
2 Too much inventory needs extra storage space. Therefore the rent for the extra space, heating, lighting, insurance, wages of extra storekeepers, etc. is all money being spent for no benefit.

One thing that anyone should look for when examining the affairs of a business is to see if inventory is larger than it need be. For someone controlling a business, there are three commonly used methods of cutting down on unnecessarily high inventory:

1 **Economic order quantity (EOQ).** This is a mathematical method which finds the lowest amount of inventory that should be ordered at a time so that the costs of purchasing and holding inventory are minimised.

 The formula for this is:

$$\text{EOQ} = \sqrt{\frac{2CO}{S}}$$

 where:
 $C$ = consumption (usage) per annum in units
 $O$ = cost of placing one order
 $S$ = cost of storage and holding of one unit per year

$S$ includes the costs of operating the stores where the inventory is kept, transport and insurance, and also the costs concerned with interest on capital which has been invested in inventory.

Exhibit 43.3 shows an example of the calculation.

## Exhibit 43.3

Annual consumption = 800 units
Cost of reordering = £4
Storage and holding costs per unit = £1

$$\text{EOQ} = \sqrt{\frac{2 \times 800 \times 4}{1}} = \sqrt{\frac{6{,}400}{1}} = 80 \text{ units per order (i.e. 10 orders per year)}$$

2 *Just-in-time (JIT).* This has been seen as one of the major factors which have resulted in the success of Japanese manufacturers over the last 30 or so years. It is not just an approach which is concerned with inventory levels, but that is part of it.

 The JIT approach requires that delivery of materials should occur immediately before their use. If arrangements are made with suppliers for more frequent deliveries, then inventory can be cut to a minimum. Getting suppliers to inspect the materials before they deliver them, and getting them to guarantee their quality, also cuts down on costs, including the need to keep larger inventory in case there are deficiencies.

 This sort of service is obtained by giving more business to fewer suppliers, and also placing longer-term orders. This enables the supplier to plan ahead more effectively to give you a better service.

3 *Optimised production technology (OPT).* The object of this approach to the management of production is to distinguish between 'bottleneck' and 'non-bottleneck' resources. For example, the 'bottleneck' resource might be a machine which has a limited capacity. As a result, everything else can only be operated at that same level. Rather than other parts of the business produce more than the 'bottleneck' machine can absorb, a lower overall level of activity takes place. This needs less inventory.

Of course, if a 'bottleneck' can be eliminated, it will be. The above applies when a bottleneck, for whatever reason, cannot be eliminated.

It is better to have a smooth-running business, operating within its 'bottleneck' capacities, than to have one which operates very irregularly. One run irregularly would have to have parts of the business shut down at times. One running smoothly, besides all the other economies, needs less inventory.

**Of these three methods, the existence of a formula which gives a precise and easily justified answer makes EOQ particularly easy to use and, for the same reason, examine. It is a useful aid to management in ensuring that they are making the best use of their inventory-related resources. Also, because of the precise nature of the calculation, it lends itself to incorporation within a computerised managerial decision-support system.**

## 43.9 Safety inventory

Safety inventory (also shown as 'safety stock') is quantity of inventory carried in excess of expected usage. It is held in order to reduce the possibility of running out of inventory. For example, if 100 units of inventory are expected to be sold in a period, but there is a possibility that as many as 110 units might be sold, an extra 10 units (i.e. 110 − 100) would be held. That is, 110 units would be held in inventory. The extra 10 units are the 'safety inventory'.

### Learning outcomes

**You should now have learnt:**

1. That budgets are prepared in order to guide the firm towards its objectives.
2. That they should be drawn up within the context of *planning* and *control*.
3. Budgets should be drawn up in consultation with those who will be affected by them.
4. That while budgets are drawn up for control purposes, a budget should not be seen as a straitjacket.
5. That there are a number of methods or techniques available to management wishing to ensure that excessive inventory is not carried by their organisations. These include economic order quantity (EOQ), just-in-time (JIT), and optimised production technology (OPT).

### Answers to activities

**43.1** 'Data which is provided for a particular purpose, and which is completely wrong for the purpose, is worse than having no data at all.' (Section 40.2)
'Using an inappropriate costing base can be even worse than having no costing at all.' (Section 41.13)

**43.2**

| *Units* | *January* | *February* | *March* | *April* | *May* | *June* |
|---|---|---|---|---|---|---|
| Opening inventory | 140 | 150 | 190 | 220 | 180 | 120 |
| *Add* Units produced | 80 | 80 | 80 | 80 | 80 | 80 |
| | 220 | 230 | 270 | 300 | 260 | 200 |
| *Less* Sales | (70) | (40) | (50) | (120) | (140) | (70) |
| Closing inventory | 150 | 190 | 220 | 180 | 120 | 130 |

**43.3** The sales budget is used to set the levels of activity required in the production budget which, in turn, is used to set the quantities required to be obtained in the materials purchase budget.

## Review questions

**43.1** Explain the concept of economic order quantity (EOQ); its advantages to businesses that use it; and the assumptions made in using it.

**43.2** Using the data provided below, what production levels should be set for each month?

| *Units 2018* | *Jul* | *Aug* | *Sept* | *Oct* | *Nov* | *Dec* |
|---|---|---|---|---|---|---|
| (*a*) Inventory levels wanted at the end of each month | 138 | 156 | 220 | 280 | 232 | 188 |
| (*b*) Expected sales each month | 160 | 184 | 218 | 264 | 296 | 204 |

(*c*) The inventory level at 1 July 2018 will be 148 units.

**43.3** For the year ended 31 December 2017, the quantities of units sold are expected to be:

| | | | |
|---|---|---|---|
| January | 330 | July | 210 |
| February | 540 | August | 290 |
| March | 310 | September | 510 |
| April | 450 | October | 330 |
| May | 360 | November | 450 |
| June | 300 | December | 570 |

The opening inventory at 1 January 2017 will be 144 units. The closing inventory desired at 31 December 2017 is 150 units.

**Required:**

(*a*) What will production be per month if an even production flow is required and inventory levels during the year can fall to zero because that minimises the cost of holding inventory?

(*b*) Given the same information plus the constraint that inventory levels must never fall below 80 units, and that extra production will be undertaken in January 2017 to ensure this happens, what will be the January production figure?

**43.4A**

(*a*) For each of the following, state three reasons why a firm may wish to keep:

(*i*) a minimum inventory level of finished goods, and

(*ii*) an even level of production in the face of fluctuating demand.

(*b*) The sales forecast for Douglas & Co for July–December 2017 is:

| | *J* | *A* | *S* | *O* | *N* | *D* |
|---|---|---|---|---|---|---|
| Units | 280 | 200 | 260 | 360 | 400 | 420 |

Produce a production budget showing monthly opening and closing inventory figures if the firm wishes to maintain an even level of producing 300 units each month, and a minimum inventory level of 150 units.

What must the opening inventory be at 1 July to achieve this?

(*c*) Under what circumstances, in budgetary control, may a firm's productive capacity prove to be its limiting or key factor?

*(AQA (Associated Examining Board): GCE A-level)*

→

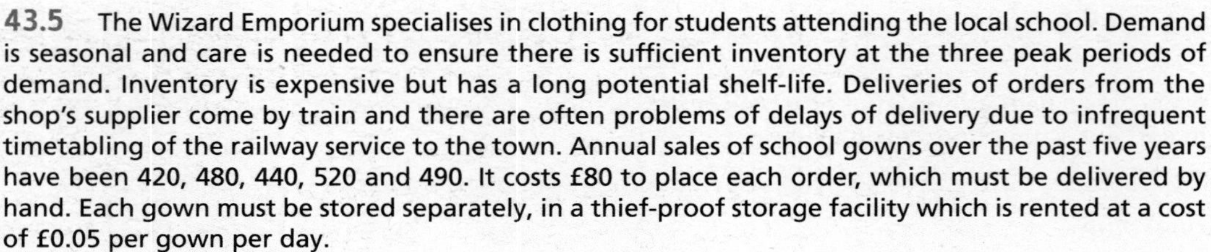

**43.5** The Wizard Emporium specialises in clothing for students attending the local school. Demand is seasonal and care is needed to ensure there is sufficient inventory at the three peak periods of demand. Inventory is expensive but has a long potential shelf-life. Deliveries of orders from the shop's supplier come by train and there are often problems of delays of delivery due to infrequent timetabling of the railway service to the town. Annual sales of school gowns over the past five years have been 420, 480, 440, 520 and 490. It costs £80 to place each order, which must be delivered by hand. Each gown must be stored separately, in a thief-proof storage facility which is rented at a cost of £0.05 per gown per day.

**Required:**

(*a*) Using EOQ, what is the lowest number of gowns that should be ordered so that the costs of purchasing and holding inventory are minimised?

(*b*) Does this answer appear sensible?

chapter

# 44 Cash budgets

## Learning objectives

**After you have studied this chapter, you should be able to:**

- explain the importance of cash funds to an organisation
- explain what is meant by the term 'cash budget'
- prepare a cash budget
- explain the importance of cash budgeting in the control of cash funds
- explain why a cash budget may be prepared
- explain the difference between profits and cash in the context of organisational survival

## Introduction

In this chapter, you'll learn how to prepare a cash budget, of the advantages of cash budgets and, in the context of business survival, of the relationship between profit, cash and a shortage of cash funds.

## 44.1 The need for cash budgets

**It is no use budgeting for production and for sales if, during the budget period, the business runs out of cash funds.** When talking about cash in budgets we are also usually including bank funds. For that reason, in this book we will not differentiate between cash and cheque payments or between cash and cheques received.

As cash is so important, a budget is created for it. As a result, any shortage of cash can be foreseen and action taken in good time to obtain a loan or a bank overdraft to cover the shortfall when it occurs. Bank managers do not like it when one of their customers needs a loan or a bank overdraft without prior warning. If a cash budget had been prepared, the customer would have known well in advance that there would be a need for additional cash funds on a particular date.

The finance needed may not be found by borrowing from a bank or finance house. It may well be a long-term need that can only be satisfied by an issue of shares or loan notes. Such issues need planning well in advance, and a cash budget can reveal (*a*) that they will be needed, (*b*) how much is needed and (*c*) when it will be needed.

We can now look at a very simple case. Without being concerned in this first example with exactly what the receipts and payments are for (just to keep things simple at this stage) you can see the dangers that are inherent in not budgeting for cash.

**Exhibit 44.1**

Mr Muddlem had a meeting with his accountant on 1 July 2015. He was feeling very pleased with himself. He had managed to get some very good orders from customers, mainly because he was now allowing them extra time in which to pay their accounts. Sprite, the accountant, said, 'Can you afford to do all that you are hoping to do?'

Muddlem laughed, 'Why, I'll be making so much money I won't know how to spend it.'

'But have you got the cash to finance everything?' asked Sprite.

'If I'm making a good profit, of course I'll have the cash,' said Muddlem. 'I know the bank manager says that the bank overdraft cannot be more than £1,000, but I doubt if I'll ever need it.'

'Let's not rely on guesses,' says Sprite. 'Let's work it out.'

After an hour's work the following facts emerge.

(*a*) Present cash balance (including bank balance) £800.
(*b*) Receipts from debtors are expected to be: July £2,000; August £2,600; September £5,000; October £7,000; November £8,000; December £15,000.
(*c*) Payments are expected to be: July £2,500; August £2,700; September £6,900; October £7,800; November £9,900; December £10,300.

This is then summarised:

| | *July* | *Aug* | *Sep* | *Oct* | *Nov* | *Dec* |
|---|---|---|---|---|---|---|
| | £ | £ | £ | £ | £ | £ |
| Balance at the start of the month: | 800 | 300 | 200 | | | |
| Deficit at the start of the month: | | | | (1,700) | (2,500) | (4,400) |
| Receipts | 2,000 | 2,600 | 5,000 | 7,000 | 8,000 | 15,000 |
| | 2,800 | 2,900 | 5,200 | 5,300 | 5,500 | 10,600 |
| Payments | (2,500) | (2,700) | (6,900) | (7,800) | (9,900) | (10,300) |
| Balance at end of the month | 300 | 200 | | | | 300 |
| Deficit at the end of the month | | | (1,700) | (2,500) | (4,400) | |

'I'm in an awkward position then,' says Muddlem. 'I just cannot borrow £4,400 and it would be stupid for me to try to reduce my sales; and, anyway, I don't really want to as these new sales are very profitable indeed. If only I'd known this, I could have borrowed the money from my brother only last week but he's invested it elsewhere now.'

'Come and see me tomorrow,' says Sprite. 'There may well be something we can do.'

Fortunately for Muddlem his luck was in. He arrived to see his accountant the following morning waving a cheque. 'My wife won £5,000 on a jackpot bingo last night,' he said.

'Thank goodness for that. At least in future you'll learn to budget ahead for cash requirements. You can't be lucky all the time,' says Sprite.

## 44.2 Timing of cash receipts and payments

In drawing up a cash budget, you need to be aware that all the payments made relating to units produced are very rarely made at the same time as production itself. For instance, raw materials might be bought in March, incorporated in goods being produced in April, and paid for in May. On the other hand, the raw materials may have been in inventory for some time, bought in January, paid for in February, and used in production the following August.

In contrast, the direct labour part of a product is usually paid for at almost the same time as the unit is produced. Even here, a unit may be produced in one week and the wages paid one week later, so that a unit might be produced on, say, 27 June and the wages for the direct labour involved paid on 3 July.

Similarly, except for supermarkets and retail stores where most of the goods sold are paid for at the time of sale, the date of sale and the date of receipt of cash will not usually be the same. Goods might be sold in May and the money received in August, or even paid for in advance so that the goods might be paid for in February but the goods not shipped to the buyer until May. This is especially true, at least for part of the goods, when a cash deposit is left for custom-made goods which will take some time to manufacture. A simple example of this would be a made-to-measure suit on which a deposit would be paid at the time of order, the final payment being made when the completed suit is collected by the buyer.

### Exhibit 44.2

A cash budget for the six months ended 30 June 2015 is to be drafted from the following information.

(*a*) Opening cash balance at 1 January 2015 £3,200.

(*b*) Sales, at £12 per unit, cash received three months after sale: in units.

| 2014 | | | 2015 | | | | | | | | |
|---|---|---|---|---|---|---|---|---|---|---|---|
| *Oct* | *Nov* | *Dec* | *Jan* | *Feb* | *Mar* | *Apr* | *May* | *June* | *July* | *Aug* | *Sept* |
| 80 | 90 | 70 | 100 | 60 | 120 | 150 | 140 | 130 | 110 | 100 | 160 |

(*c*) Production: in units.

| 2014 | | | 2015 | | | | | | | | |
|---|---|---|---|---|---|---|---|---|---|---|---|
| *Oct* | *Nov* | *Dec* | *Jan* | *Feb* | *Mar* | *Apr* | *May* | *June* | *July* | *Aug* | *Sept* |
| 70 | 80 | 90 | 100 | 110 | 130 | 140 | 150 | 120 | 160 | 170 | 180 |

(*d*) Raw materials used in production cost £4 per unit of production. They are paid for two months before being used in production.

(*e*) Direct labour, £3 per unit paid for in the same month as the unit is produced.

(*f*) Other variable expenses, £2 per unit, $^{3}/_{4}$ of the cost being paid for in the same month as production, the other $^{1}/_{4}$ paid in the month after production.

(*g*) Fixed expenses of £100 per month are paid monthly.

(*h*) A van is to be bought and paid for in April for £800.

Schedules of payments and receipts are as follows:

*Payments* (the month shown in brackets is the month in which the units are produced):

| *January* | £ | *February* | £ |
|---|---|---|---|
| Raw materials: 130 (March) × £4 | 520 | 140 (April) × £4 | 560 |
| Direct labour: 100 (January) × £3 | 300 | 110 (February) × £3 | 330 |
| Variable: 100 (January) × $^{3}/_{4}$ × £2 | 150 | 110 (February) × $^{3}/_{4}$ × £2 | 165 |
| 90 (December) × $^{1}/_{4}$ × £2 | 45 | 100 (January) × $^{1}/_{4}$ × £2 | 50 |
| Fixed | 100 | | 100 |
| | 1,115 | | 1,205 |
| *March* | £ | *April* | £ |
| Raw materials: 150 (May) × £4 | 600 | 120 (June) × £4 | 480 |
| Direct labour: 130 (March) × £3 | 390 | 140 (April) × £3 | 420 |
| Variable: 130 (March) × $^{3}/_{4}$ × £2 | 195 | 140 (April) × $^{3}/_{4}$ × £2 | 210 |
| 110 (February) × $^{1}/_{4}$ × £2 | 55 | 130 (March) × $^{1}/_{4}$ × £2 | 65 |
| Fixed | 100 | | 100 |
| Motor van | | | 800 |
| | 1,340 | | 2,075 |
| *May* | £ | *June* | £ |
| Raw materials: 160 (July) × £4 | 640 | 170 (August) × £4 | 680 |
| Direct labour: 150 (May) × £3 | 450 | 120 (June) × £3 | 360 |
| Variable: 150 (May) × $^{3}/_{4}$ × £2 | 225 | 120 (June) × $^{3}/_{4}$ × £2 | 180 |
| 140 (April) × $^{1}/_{4}$ × £2 | 70 | 150 (May) × $^{1}/_{4}$ × £2 | 75 |
| Fixed | 100 | | 100 |
| | 1,485 | | 1,395 |

→

*Receipts:* (the month shown in brackets is the month in which the sale was made):

| | | | | £ |
|---|---|---|---|---|
| January | 80 | (October) | × £12 | 960 |
| February | 90 | (November) | × £12 | 1,080 |
| March | 70 | (December) | × £12 | 840 |
| April | 100 | (January) | × £12 | 1,200 |
| May | 60 | (February) | × £12 | 720 |
| June | 120 | (March) | × £12 | 1,440 |

*Cash Budget*

| | *Jan* | *Feb* | *Mar* | *Apr* | *May* | *June* |
|---|---|---|---|---|---|---|
| | £ | £ | £ | £ | £ | £ |
| Balance from previous month | 3,200 | 3,045 | 2,920 | 2,420 | 1,545 | 780 |
| *Add* Receipts (per schedule) | 960 | 1,080 | 840 | 1,200 | 720 | 1,440 |
| | 4,160 | 4,125 | 3,760 | 3,620 | 2,265 | 2,220 |
| *Less* Payments (per schedule) | (1,115) | (1,205) | (1,340) | (2,075) | (1,485) | (1,395) |
| Balance carried next month | 3,045 | 2,920 | 2,420 | 1,545 | 780 | 825 |

## 44.3 Advantages of cash budgets

These can be said to be:

1 Having to think ahead and plan for the future and express plans in figures **focuses the mind** in a way that thinking in a general fashion about the future will not do – a general optimistic feeling that 'all will be well' often fails to stand up to scrutiny when the views of the future are expressed in a cash budget.

2 Seeing that money will have to be borrowed at a particular date will mean that **you can negotiate for a loan in advance**, rather than at the time when you have actually run out of cash. Bankers and other lenders do not like someone attempting to borrow money in a panic.

When borrowing money, you have to give the lender the confidence that the loan will be repaid at the agreed time, plus any interest and charges that may accrue. Last-minute borrowing, unsupported by any calmly thought-out plan, will not inspire such confidence, and will often lead to the loan being refused as the lender may think that the risk is too great.

Activity 44.1

What other disadvantages do you think there might be in waiting until the last minute to arrange a loan of this type?

3 Knowing about the need to borrow in advance also **widens the possible pool of lenders**. Such people as friends, relations and businesspeople or investors other than bankers rarely have large sums of cash quickly available. They need time to turn their own investments into cash before they can lend to you.

4 Alternatively, you may find that you will have cash funds surplus to requirements. Knowing this in advance **enables you to investigate carefully how you can invest this surplus cash until required**, thus earning interest or other investment income. Surplus cash lying in bank current accounts very often earns absolutely no interest at all, no matter how large the amount. Banks often offer deposit accounts linked to current accounts that automatically transfer funds from one to the other so that any surplus funds in the current account are moved immediately to the deposit account and reversed back to the current account when required.

There are also other sorts of short-term investments which banks and accountants can advise businesses to put their surplus cash into at appropriate times.

## 44.4 Profits and shortages of cash funds

As you've just learnt, making good profits does not mean there cannot be a shortage of cash funds. But how can this happen? Let's look at how some businesses may have good profits and yet still be short of cash funds, possibly having bank overdrafts or loans which are getting steadily bigger.

1 A has increased its sales by 50%. It is making the same percentage gross profit and its expenses have hardly increased, yet its overdraft has got bigger. The reason is that it increased its sales by giving all of its customers four months to pay instead of the usual one month. This has attracted a lot of new customers.

   This means that the debtors are increasing by very large amounts, as they can wait another three months in which to pay their bills. Thus, the equivalent of three months' cash receipts have not come into the bank. Meanwhile, the business is making extra purchases for goods for the new customers, with a consequent outflow of more cash than usual, especially if it has not got longer credit terms from its suppliers. So, hardly any cash is coming in in the short term, while more cash than usual is going out.

   The answer to this is: large increase in profits and fewer cash funds probably resulting in higher bank overdrafts or loans.

2 B has the same sales, purchases and expenses as usual. However, the proprietor is now taking much higher drawings than before. In fact, his drawings are exceeding the profits he is making.

   Such a situation cannot go on for ever. He will start to find his cash funds in the business are decreasing, possibly meaning higher loans or overdrafts being needed.

3 C has just spent a lot of money on non-current assets. It will be several years before the business recoups the money it has paid out. In the meantime, only the depreciation provisions are charged against profits. However, the cash funds have been reduced by the whole amount paid for non-current assets.

   The net result is that profits may be recorded but the business is hard-up for cash funds.

4 D is going through a bad patch in that sales are very difficult to make, but it does not want to get rid of any of its workforce. Production is kept going at normal rates, and the products not sold are simply kept in inventory. Thus the inventory is increasing at an alarming rate.

   If inventory is not being sold, then cash is obviously not being received in respect of such production. Meanwhile, all the expenses and wages are still being paid for. This can result in a severe shortage of funds if carried on for long unless further finance is received.

5 A long-term loan has been paid off but no extra finance from anywhere else has been received. Or, a partner retires and the balance due to him is paid out of the firm's funds, without a new partner being introduced. Or a company buys back its shares without making a new issue of shares.

   **In the long term, there is a connection between profits and cash funds available, even though it may not be that marked. In the short term, you can see that there may be no relationship at all. This simple fact is one that surprises most people. It is because the calculation of profits follows one set of concepts, whereas the calculation of cash funds follows a completely different set of rules.**

**Go back to Section 28.7 for a discussion on overtrading.**

## Learning outcomes

**You should now have learnt:**

1. The difference between profit and cash funds.
2. When undertaking a cash budget, 'cash' includes both money held in the form of cash and amounts held in the bank.
3. The importance of cash funds to an organisation.
4. What is meant by the term 'cash budget'.
5. The importance of preparing and monitoring a cash budget.
6. How to prepare a cash budget.
7. The difference between profits and cash in the context of organisational survival.

## Answer to activity

44.1 It is not only that you risk the loan being refused. Lenders will often realise that they have you at their mercy, and will charge much higher rates of interest and impose other conditions than they would otherwise have done.

## Review questions

***Advice*: Cash budgeting is an extremely important part of accounting. Questions on this topic are relatively easy to do, and high marks can be gained quite easily.**

**40.1** Took comes to see you in March 2016. He is full of enthusiasm for a new product that he is about to launch on to the market. Unfortunately his financial recklessness in the past has led him into being bankrupt twice, and he has only just been discharged by the court from his second bankruptcy.

'Look here, laddie,' he says, 'with my new idea I'll be a wealthy man before Christmas.'

'Calm down,' you say, 'and tell me all about it.'

Took's plans as far as cash is concerned for the next six months are:

(*a*) Present cash balance (including bank) £200.
(*b*) Legacy under a will – being received on 1 April, 2016, £10,000. This will be paid into the business bank account by Took.
(*c*) Receipts from debtors will be: April £800; May £8,000; June £16,000; July £24,000; August £18,000; September £10,000.
(*d*) Payments will be: April £200; May £10,000; June £22,000; July £40,000; August £24,000; September £14,000.

**You are required:**
(*a*) To draw up a cash budget, showing the balances each month, for the six months to 30 September 2016.
(*b*) The only person Took could borrow money from would charge interest at the rate of 70% per annum. This is not excessive considering Took's past record. Advise Took.

**40.2** Draw up a cash budget for F. Jack showing the balance at the end of each month, from the following information for the six months ended 31 December 2017:

(*a*) Opening cash (including bank) balance on 1 July 2017 £3,600
(*b*) Production in units:

| 2017 March | April | May | June | July | Aug | Sep | Oct | Nov | Dec | 2018 Jan |
|---|---|---|---|---|---|---|---|---|---|---|
| 720 | 810 | 900 | 960 | 1,050 | 1,110 | 1,140 | 1,020 | 930 | 780 | 750 |

(*c*) Raw materials used in production cost £15 per unit. Of this, 90% is paid in the month of production and 10% in the month after production.
(*d*) Direct labour costs of £24 per unit are payable in the month of production.
(*e*) Variable expenses are £6 per unit, payable 40% in the same month as production and 60% in the month following production.
(*f*) Sales at £60 per unit:

| 2017 Feb | Mar | Apr | May | Jun | July | Aug | Sep | Oct | Nov |
|---|---|---|---|---|---|---|---|---|---|
| 780 | 600 | 960 | 870 | 1,200 | 900 | 1,050 | 1,200 | 1,170 | 1,200 |

Debtors to pay their accounts three months after that in which sales are made.
(*g*) Fixed expenses of £1,200 per month payable each month.
(*h*) Machinery costing £6,000 to be paid for in September 2017.
(*i*) Will receive a legacy of £7,500 in November 2017.
(*j*) Drawings will be £900 per month.

**44.3** Herbert Limited make a single product, whose unit budget details are as follows:

| | £ | £ |
|---|---|---|
| Selling price | | 30 |
| *Less Costs* | | |
| Direct material | 9 | |
| Direct labour | 4 | |
| Direct production expenses | 6 | |
| Variable selling expenses | 4 | |
| | | (23) |
| Contribution | | 7 |

*Additional information:*

1 Unit sales are expected to be:

| *June* | *July* | *August* | *September* | *October* |
|---|---|---|---|---|
| 1,000 | 800 | 400 | 600 | 900 |

2 Credit sales will account for 60% of total sales. Debtors are expected to pay in the month following sale for which there will be a cash discount of 2%.
3 Inventory levels will be arranged so that the production in one month will meet the next month's sales demand.
4 The purchases of direct materials in one month will just meet the next month's production requirements.
5 Suppliers of direct materials will be paid in the month following purchase.
6 Labour costs will be paid in the month in which they are incurred. All other expenses will be paid in the month following that in which they are incurred.
7 Fixed expenses are £2,000 per month and include £180 for depreciation.
8 The bank balance at 1 July 2016 is £3,900 favourable to the business.

**Required:**
(*a*) A cash budget for Herbert Limited for the three month period ending on 30 September 2016 showing the balance of cash at the end of each month.
(*b*) List and explain **three** ways in which the preparation of a cash flow budget could be of advantage to the management of Herbert Limited.

*(AQA (Associated Examining Board): GCE A-level)*

**44.4A** Mtoto Ltd operate as wholesale 'cash and carry' stores and in addition to its main store have two other depots. The company's summarised statement of financial position as at 31 August 2018 was as follows.

| | £ | £ |
|---|---|---|
| *Non-current assets* | | |
| (at net book value) | | 549,600 |
| *Current assets* | | |
| Inventory | 399,900 | |
| Trade accounts receivable | 21,000 | 420,900 |
| | | 970,500 |
| *Less* Current liabilities | | |
| Trade (and other) accounts payable | 110,500 | |
| Bank overdraft | 240,000 | |
| | | (350,500) |
| | | 620,000 |
| Authorised and issued capital | | |
| 450,000 £1 Ordinary shares fully paid | | 450,000 |
| Retained earnings at 1 Sept 2017 | 300,000 | |
| *Less* Loss for year ending 31 Aug 2018 | (130,000) | |
| | | 170,000 |
| | | 620,000 |

- Over the past year the company has experienced increased competition and as a consequence reported a net trading loss for the year ended 31 August 2018.
- The company has decided that in the new financial year tighter control must be exercised over cash resources.

The following information is available:

1 All goods are purchased by the main store.

**Purchases 2018**

| *Actual* | | *Forecast* | | | |
|---|---|---|---|---|---|
| *July* | *Aug* | *Sept* | *Oct* | *Nov* | *Dec* |
| £ | £ | £ | £ | £ | £ |
| 55,800 | 61,200 | 64,300 | 41,000 | 46,000 | 41,800 |

- Mtoto Ltd pays suppliers two months after the month of purchase.
- Forecast purchases are being reduced since the managing director regarded current inventory levels as too high.
- In addition, shop-soiled inventory which cost £20,000 is to be sold for cash in October. It is anticipated that this inventory will be sold for £17,000. This sale is not included in the sales of Note 2 below.

2 All sales are on a cash basis only except for several important customers who trade only with Mtoto's main store.

**Sales 2018**

| | *Actual* | | *Forecast* | | | |
|---|---|---|---|---|---|---|
| | *July* | *Aug* | *Sept* | *Oct* | *Nov* | *Dec* |
| | £ | £ | £ | £ | £ | £ |
| Main store | | | | | | |
| Cash sales | 21,500 | 21,600 | 18,000 | 26,300 | 19,200 | 24,700 |
| Credit sales | 24,000 | 21,000 | 32,500 | 26,000 | 25,400 | 27,800 |
| Depot 1 | 15,500 | 17,400 | 19,700 | 18,000 | 17,600 | 17,900 |
| Depot 2 | 21,000 | 24,000 | 26,300 | 19,700 | 21,000 | 19,100 |

3 Mtoto Ltd pays £9,500 fixed overhead costs per month.

4 Wages and salaries are paid each month through a centralised payroll system.

**Wages and salaries 2018**

| Actual | Forecast | | | |
|---|---|---|---|---|
| Aug | Sept | Oct | Nov | Dec |
| £ | £ | £ | £ | £ |
| 16,000 | 17,000 | 19,000 | 13,000 | 12,000 |

In October, 10 staff were made redundant and are to receive their redundancy compensation of £12,000 in December. This amount is not included in the above figures.

5 Other variable overhead charges are paid by Mtoto Ltd in the month following the month they are incurred.

**Variable overhead charges 2018**

| Actual | Forecast | | | |
|---|---|---|---|---|
| Aug | Sept | Oct | Nov | Dec |
| £ | £ | £ | £ | £ |
| 5,600 | 6,800 | 6,100 | 7,400 | 6,900 |

6 Plant surplus to requirement is to be sold in September for £26,500 cash. The plant cost £55,000 and depreciation to date is £20,000.

**Required:**

(*a*) A detailed cash budget, on a month by month basis, for the first four months of the financial year ending 31 December 2018 for Mtoto Ltd.

(*b*) A report commenting on:
 (*i*) the current and forecast liquidity position.
 (*ii*) the action that Mtoto Ltd could take to attempt a return to a profit situation.

*(AQA (Associated Examining Board): GCE A-level)*

**44.5** David Llewelyn has been advised by his bank manager that he ought to provide a forecast of his cash position at the end of each month. This is to ensure that his cash inputs will be sufficient to allow a bank loan to be repaid when due and to check that his outgoings are properly controlled. It is estimated that at 30 June 2017 his current account will be £5,000 in credit, whereas the amount owing in respect of the bank loan taken out on 1 July 2012 will be £15,000. Monthly deductions from the current account balance amount to £242 including interest charges on account of this loan. In addition to these outgoings, David has to allow for the following:

(*i*) The payment of wages of £2,000 per month.

(*ii*) Personal drawings of £500 per month.

(*iii*) On average David earns a margin of 15% (of sales) and expects to sell inventory purchased in the previous month. Of the sales in any one month, 20% are paid for within that month, 70% the following month and the remainder two months after sale. Other receipts from debtors are expected to be £40,000 in July 2017, £32,000 in August 2017 and £4,000 in September 2017.

(*iv*) Purchases of supplies will amount to £38,250 per month from July 2017 payable one month in arrears. In addition, purchases of £7,500 to increase inventory will be delivered in September 2017 and must be paid for in October 2017. Creditors of £34,000 for purchases made in June 2017 are to be paid in July 2017.

(*v*) Monthly payments to the Revenue and Customs for the taxation of his employees' earnings will amount to £500 per month.

(*vi*) Rent which has to be paid quarterly in advance amounts to £5,000 per annum. These payments commenced in January 2017.

(*vii*) Business rates are to be paid in two instalments as due in October 2017 and in March 2018. This estimated expenditure will amount to £4,500 per annum.

(*viii*) Payment of Value Added Tax to H.M. Revenue and Customs of £5,000 in July 2017 and every third month thereafter (but see also (*ix*)).

(*ix*) David intends to purchase a van for £8,150 in August 2017. He will then be entitled to deduct £1,050 from the VAT payment due to H.M. Revenue and Customs in October 2017.

**Required:**

A forecast cash flow statement in columnar form showing the estimated current account balance at the close of each of the four months ending 31 October 2017.

*(Welsh Joint Examining Board: GCE A-level)*

**44.6** The managing director of Pumpkin Ltd was reviewing the results of the company for the financial year ended 31 March 2017. The following summarised information was available:

| | £ |
|---|---|
| *Balances as at 1 April 2016* | |
| Issued ordinary share capital: | |
| £1 fully paid shares | 150,000 |
| Share premium account | 100,000 |
| Balance of retained earnings | 40,000 |
| *Balances as at 31 March 2017* | |
| Net profit for year 2016/17 | 70,000 |
| Non-current assets | 300,000 |
| Bank overdraft | 150,000 |
| Other net current assets | 210,000 |

**Note: There were no other accounts with balances. The balances as at 1 April 2016 had remained unchanged throughout the year.**

The managing director was pleased that the company had made a good profit, but he was rather concerned that a healthy bank balance at the beginning of the year had now become a large bank overdraft.

Consequently he asked the company accountant to prepare forecast information for 2017/18 in order that the cash situation could be improved.

The following information was prepared by the accountant:

1 Company sales – March 2017

| | £ |
|---|---|
| Cash sales | 30,000 |
| Credit sales | 65,000 |

In each month April to September (inclusive) the sales per month would be:

| | £ |
|---|---|
| Cash sales | 40,000 |
| Credit sales | 70,000 |

All credit sales are settled the month after the sale.

2 All goods purchased are from a single supplier. The goods are purchased on credit and each month's purchases are paid for three months after the month of purchase.

The following purchase schedule had been prepared for the first 9 months of 2017:

| | *January* | *February* | *March* |
|---|---|---|---|
| Purchases | £60,000 | £58,000 | £61,000 |

Purchases in April, May and June
£55,000 in each month
Purchases in July, August and September
£45,000 in each month

**Note: The company had successfully negotiated lower prices from its supplier commencing 1 July 2017.**

3 Dividends would be paid as follows:
(*i*) Final ordinary dividend of 5p per share payable on 31 May 2017 in respect of financial year 2016/17.
(*ii*) Interim ordinary dividend of 2p per share payable on 31 July 2017 in respect of financial year 2017/18.

4 Selling and distribution expenses are expected to be 6% of a given month's total sales. They are paid one month in arrears.

5 Administration charges would be incurred as follows:

| | |
|---|---|
| 2017 February, March, April | £10,000 per month |
| 2017 May to September (inclusive) | £13,500 per month |

Administration charges are settled two months after the month in which they were incurred.

6 The company had decided to make a bonus issue of shares of one share for every three held. The issue would be made on 30 April 2017. The bonus shares would not qualify for the final dividend of 2016/17, but would qualify for the interim dividend to be paid on 31 July 2017.

**Required:**

(*a*) Comment on the liquidity of the company as at 31 March 2017 and explain to the managing director why a company can apparently make a good profit but have no cash in the bank.

(*b*) Prepare a cash budget for each of the four months ending 31 July 2017.

(*c*) Comment on the forecast bank balance as shown by your cash budget. Identify ways in which the bank overdraft could be reduced over the last five months of 2017.

*(AQA (Associated Examining Board): GCE A-level)*

**44.7A** Belinda Raglan owns a clothing factory. Trading over the last two years has been very successful and she feels that having achieved good results it is now time to request an increase in the overdraft facility.

- In the past the bank has been willing to offer business overdraft facilities and at present there is an agreed limit of £15,000.
- On 1 May 2017 the overdraft stands at £5,000.
- In order to support her request for the increased facility, she has produced a forecast profit statement for the four months ended 31 August 2017 as follows:

| | *May* | | *June* | | *July* | | *August* | |
|---|---|---|---|---|---|---|---|---|
| | *£000* | *£000* | *£000* | *£000* | *£000* | *£000* | *£000* | *£000* |
| Sales | | 74 | | 28 | | 116 | | 168 |
| Cost of sales | | 51 | | 12 | | 78 | | 101 |
| Gross profit | | 23 | | 16 | | 38 | | 67 |
| *Less* Rent | 4 | | 4 | | 4 | | 4 | |
| Other expenses | 8 | | 3 | | 10 | | 14 | |
| Depreciation | 5 | | 5 | | 5 | | 5 | |
| | | (17) | | (12) | | (19) | | (23) |
| Net profit | | 6 | | 4 | | 19 | | 44 |

Although Belinda thought these figures would be sufficient to satisfy the requirements of the bank, the manager has asked for a cash budget for the period concerned to be submitted.

The following additional information concerning the business is available.

1 Rent is paid quarterly in advance on the first day of May, August, November and February.
2 All other expenses are payable in the month in which they are incurred.
3 Purchases for the period are expected to be – May £60,000; June £120,000; July £40,000 and August £43,000. These will be paid for in the month of purchase. Purchases will be unusually high in May and June because they will be subject to a special reduction of 3% of the amounts quoted.
4 80% of the sales are on a credit basis payable two months later. Sales in March and April were £88,000 and £84,000 respectively.
5 A compensation payment of £10,000 to a former employee for an industrial injury, not covered by insurance, is due to be paid in May.

**Required:**

(*a*) Prepare a forecast cash budget on a month by month basis for the period May to August 2017.

(*b*) Discuss the advantages and disadvantages of cash budgeting.

(*c*) Draft notes, to be used by the bank manager for a letter to Ms Raglan, indicating why the request for an increased overdraft facility may be refused.

*(AQA (Associated Examining Board): GCE A-level)*

→ **44.8A** Ian Spiro, formerly a taxi-driver, decided to establish a car-hire business after inheriting £50,000.

His business year would be divided into budget periods each being four weeks.

He commenced business on a Monday the first day of Period 1, by paying into a business bank account £34,000 as his initial capital.

All receipts and payments would be passed through his bank account.

The following additional forecast information is available on the first four budget periods of his proposed business venture.

1 At the beginning of Period 1 he would purchase six saloon cars of a standard type; list price £6,000 each, on which he had negotiated a trade discount of 11%.

2 He estimates that four of the cars will be on the road each Monday to Friday inclusive, and at weekends all six cars will be on the road. Hire charges as follows:

Weekday rate £10 per day per car
Weekend rate £18 per day per car

He estimates that this business trading pattern will commence on the Monday of the second week of Period 1, and then continue thereafter.

All hire transactions are to be settled for cash.

***Note*: a weekend consists of Saturday and Sunday. All remaining days are weekdays.**

3 An account was established with a local garage for fuel, and it was agreed to settle the account two periods in arrear. The forecast litre usage is as follows:

| *Period 1* | *Period 2* | *Period 3* | *Period 4* |
|---|---|---|---|
| 200 | 200 | 400 | 500 |

The fuel costs £1.80 per litre.

4 Servicing costs for the vehicles would amount to £300 per period, paid during the period following the service. Servicing would commence in Period 1.

5 Each of his vehicles would be depreciated at 25% per annum on a reducing balance basis.

6 Fixed costs of £200 per period would be paid each period.

7 He had agreed with a local firm to provide two cars on a regular basis, Monday to Friday inclusive, as chauffeur driven cars. The agreed rate was £60 a day (per car), payment being made in the following period.

This contract would not commence until the first day of Period 2, a Monday.

8 Drawings: Periods 1 and 2: £400 a period.
Periods 3 and 4: £800 a period.

9 Wages and salaries:
(*a*) Initially he would employ three staff, each on £320 a budget period. Employment would commence at the beginning of Period 1.
(*b*) On commencement of the contract the two additional staff employed as chauffeurs would each receive £360 a budget period. Payments are to be made at the end of the relevant period.

10 In anticipation of more business being developed he planned to buy a further three cars for cash in Period 4. The cars would cost £6,500 each and it was agreed he would be allowed a trade discount of 10%.

**Required:**
(*a*) A detailed cash budget for the first four budget periods.
(*b*) An explanation as to why it is important that a business should prepare a cash budget.
(*c*) Identify how a sole proprietor may finance a forecast cash deficit distinguishing between internal and external financial sources.

*(AQA (Associated Examining Board): GCE A-level)*

**44.9** Using detailed examples, write a report explaining the differences between a cash budget, a cash flow forecast, and a statement of cash flows.

chapter

# 45 Co-ordination of budgets

## Learning objectives

**After you have studied this chapter, you should be able to:**

- explain the benefits of budgeting to an organisation
- explain the importance of effective co-ordination of budgets for the organisation
- prepare a master budget
- describe the benefits of operating a system of flexible budgeting

## Introduction

In this chapter, you'll learn about the process of preparing a budget and of how budgets are co-ordinated and used to monitor and identify deviations between them and actual performance. You'll also learn about the importance of investigating these differences and of the benefits of adopting a system of flexible budgeting as compared to budgets being set that remain fixed during the entire period they cover.

## 45.1 Master budgets

Once prepared, all the various budgets have to be linked together to draw up a **master budget**, which is really a budgeted set of financial statements. We have looked at the sales, production and cash budgets. However, many more budgets are typically prepared, including:

- a selling budget
- an administration expense budget
- a manufacturing overhead budget
- a direct labour budget
- a purchases budget
- a capital expenditure budget

and so on. In this book, we do not wish to get entangled in too many details, but in a real business with a proper set of budgeting techniques there will be a great deal of detailed computations behind the figures that are incorporated in the budgets.

It may be that when all the budgets have been co-ordinated, or slotted together, the master budget shows a smaller profit than the directors are prepared to accept. This will mean recasting budgets to see whether a greater profit can be earned and, if at all possible, the budgets will then be altered. Eventually, there will be a master budget that the directors can agree to. This then gives the target for the results that the business hopes to achieve in financial terms.

***Remember*: there are other targets, such as employee welfare, product quality, etc., that cannot be expressed in financial terms but which will impact upon and influence the setting of budgets.**

The rest of this chapter is concerned with the drawing up of budgets for an imaginary company, Walsh Ltd, culminating in the drawing up of the master budget.

Let's start with a look at the statement of financial position of Walsh Ltd, as at 31 December 2017. This gives us our opening figures for inventory of raw materials, inventory of finished goods, cash (including bank) balance, accounts payable, accounts receivable, etc. Next, we'll produce budgets for the six months ending 30 June 2018.

**Walsh Ltd**
**Statement of Financial Position as at 31 December 2017**

| *Non-current assets* | *Cost* | *Depreciation to date* | *Net* |
|---|---|---|---|
| | £ | £ | £ |
| Machinery | 4,000 | 1,600 | 2,400 |
| Motor vehicles | 2,000 | 800 | 1,200 |
| | 6,000 | 2,400 | 3,600 |
| *Current assets* | | | |
| Inventory: Finished goods (75 units) | | 900 | |
| Raw materials | | 500 | |
| Accounts receivable (2017 October £540 + November £360 + December £450) | | 1,350 | |
| Cash and bank balances | | 650 | 3,400 |
| | | | 7,000 |
| *Less Current liabilities* | | | |
| Accounts payable for raw materials (November £120 + December £180) | | 300 | |
| Accounts payable for indirect manufacturing expenses (December) | | 100 | |
| | | | (400) |
| Net assets | | | 6,600 |
| *Equity* | | | |
| Share capital: 4,000 shares £1 each | | | 4,000 |
| Retained profit | | | 2,600 |
| | | | 6,600 |

The plans for the six months ended 30 June 2018 are as follows:

(*a*) Production will be 60 units per month for the first four months, followed by 70 units per month for May and June.

(*b*) Production costs will be (per unit):

| | £ |
|---|---|
| Direct materials | 5 |
| Direct labour | 4 |
| Variable overhead | 3 |
| | 12 |

(*c*) Fixed indirect manufacturing expenses are £100 per month, payable always one month in arrears.

(*d*) Sales, at a price of £18 per unit, are expected to be:

| | *January* | *February* | *March* | *April* | *May* | *June* |
|---|---|---|---|---|---|---|
| No. of units | 40 | 50 | 60 | 90 | 90 | 70 |

(*e*) Purchases of direct materials (raw materials) will be:

| *January* | *February* | *March* | *April* | *May* | *June* |
|---|---|---|---|---|---|
| £ | £ | £ | £ | £ | £ |
| 150 | 200 | 250 | 300 | 400 | 320 |

(*f*) The creditors for raw materials bought are paid two months after purchase.
(*g*) Debtors are expected to pay their accounts three months after they bought the goods.
(*h*) Direct labour and variable indirect manufacturing expenses are paid in the same month as the units are produced.
(*i*) A machine costing £2,000 will be bought and paid for in March.
(*j*) 3,000 shares of £1 each are to be issued at par in May.
(*k*) Depreciation for the six months: machinery £450; motor vehicles £200.

We must first of all draw up the various budgets and then incorporate them into the master budget. Some of the more detailed budgets which can be dispensed within this illustration will be omitted.

**Materials Budget (£s)**

| | *January* | *February* | *March* | *April* | *May* | *June* |
|---|---|---|---|---|---|---|
| Opening inventory | 500 | 350 | 250 | 200 | 200 | 250 |
| *Add* Purchases | 150 | 200 | 250 | 300 | 400 | 320 |
| | 650 | 550 | 500 | 500 | 600 | 570 |
| *Less* Used in production: | | | | | | |
| Jan–April 60 × £5 | (300) | (300) | (300) | (300) | | |
| May and June 70 × £5 | | | | | (350) | (350) |
| Closing inventory | 350 | 250 | 200 | 200 | 250 | 220 |

**Production Budget (in units)**

| | *January* | *February* | *March* | *April* | *May* | *June* |
|---|---|---|---|---|---|---|
| Opening inventory | 75 | 95 | 105 | 105 | 75 | 55 |
| *Add* Produced | 60 | 60 | 60 | 60 | 70 | 70 |
| | 135 | 155 | 165 | 165 | 145 | 125 |
| *Less* Sales | (40) | (50) | (60) | (90) | (90) | (70) |
| Closing inventory | 95 | 105 | 105 | 75 | 55 | 55 |

**Production Cost Budget (£s)**

| | *January* | *February* | *March* | *April* | *May* | *June* | *Total* |
|---|---|---|---|---|---|---|---|
| Materials cost | 300 | 300 | 300 | 300 | 350 | 350 | 1,900 |
| Labour cost | 240 | 240 | 240 | 240 | 280 | 280 | 1,520 |
| Variable indirect manufacturing expenses | 180 | 180 | 180 | 180 | 210 | 210 | 1,140 |
| | 720 | 720 | 720 | 720 | 840 | 840 | 4,560 |

**Accounts Payable Budget (£s)**

| | *January* | *February* | *March* | *April* | *May* | *June* |
|---|---|---|---|---|---|---|
| Opening balance | 300 | 330 | 350 | 450 | 550 | 700 |
| *Add* Purchases | 150 | 200 | 250 | 300 | 400 | 320 |
| | 450 | 530 | 600 | 750 | 950 | 1,020 |
| *Less* Payments | (120) | (180) | (150) | (200) | (250) | (300) |
| Closing balance | 330 | 350 | 450 | 550 | 700 | 720 |

**Accounts Receivable Budget (£s)**

| | *January* | *February* | *March* | *April* | *May* | *June* |
|---|---|---|---|---|---|---|
| Opening balances | 1,350 | 1,530 | 2,070 | 2,700 | 3,600 | 4,320 |
| *Add* Sales | 720 | 900 | 1,080 | 1,620 | 1,620 | 1,260 |
| | 2,070 | 2,430 | 3,150 | 4,320 | 5,220 | 5,580 |
| *Less* Received | (540) | (360) | (450) | (720) | (900) | (1,080) |
| Closing balances | 1,530 | 2,070 | 2,700 | 3,600 | 4,320 | 4,500 |

**Cash Budget (£s)**

| | January | February | March | April | May | June |
|---|---|---|---|---|---|---|
| Opening balance | 650 | 550 | 210 | | | 1,050 |
| Opening overdraft | | | | (2,010) | (2,010) | |
| Received (see schedule) | 540 | 360 | 450 | 720 | 3,900 | 1,080 |
| | 1,190 | 910 | 660 | (1,290) | 1,890 | 2,130 |
| Payments (see schedule) | (640) | (700) | (2,670) | (720) | (840) | (890) |
| Closing balance | 550 | 210 | | | 1,050 | 1,240 |
| Closing overdraft | | | (2,010) | (2,010) | | |

**Cash Payments Schedule (£s)**

| | January | February | March | April | May | June |
|---|---|---|---|---|---|---|
| Creditors for goods bought two months previously | 120 | 180 | 150 | 200 | 250 | 300 |
| Fixed indirect manufacturing expenses | 100 | 100 | 100 | 100 | 100 | 100 |
| Direct labour | 240 | 240 | 240 | 240 | 280 | 280 |
| Variable indirect manufacturing expenses | 180 | 180 | 180 | 180 | 210 | 210 |
| Machinery | | | 2,000 | | | |
| | 640 | 700 | 2,670 | 720 | 840 | 890 |

**Cash Receipts Schedule (£s)**

| | January | February | March | April | May | June |
|---|---|---|---|---|---|---|
| Debtors for goods sold three months previously | 540 | 360 | 450 | 720 | 900 | 1,080 |
| Shares issued | | | | | 3,000 | |
| | | | | | 3,900 | |

**Master Budget**
**Forecast Operating Statement for the six months ending 30 June 2018**

| | £ | £ | £ |
|---|---|---|---|
| Sales | | | 7,200 |
| *Less* Cost of goods sold: | | | |
| Opening inventory of finished goods | | 900 | |
| *Add* Cost of goods completed | | 4,560 | |
| | | 5,460 | |
| *Less* Closing inventory of finished goods | | (660) | |
| | | | (4,800) |
| Gross profit | | | 2,400 |
| *Less* | | | |
| Fixed indirect manufacturing expenses | | 600 | |
| Depreciation: Machinery | 450 | | |
| Motors | 200 | | |
| | | 650 | |
| | | | (1,250) |
| Net profit | | | 1,150 |

**Forecast Statement of Financial Position as at 30 June 2018**

| *Non-current assets* | *Cost* | *Depreciation to date* | *Net* |
|---|---|---|---|
| | £ | £ | £ |
| Machinery | 6,000 | 2,050 | 3,950 |
| Motor vehicles | 2,000 | 1,000 | 1,000 |
| | 8,000 | 3,050 | 4,950 |
| *Current assets* | | | |
| Inventory: Finished goods | | 660 | |
| Raw materials | | 220 | |
| Accounts receivable | | 4,500 | |
| Cash and bank balances | | 1,240 | 6,620 |
| | | | 11,570 |
| *Current liabilities* | | | |
| Accounts payable for goods | | 720 | |
| Accounts payable for indirect manufacturing expenses | | 100 | |
| | | | (820) |
| Net assets | | | 10,750 |
| *Equity* | | | |
| Called-up share capital | | | 7,000 |
| Retained profits (2,600 + 1,150) | | | 3,750 |
| | | | 10,750 |

## 45.2 Capital budgeting

You'll have noticed that the cash budget included £2,000 for the machine paid for in March. The other side of the double entry will also have been entered in a budget – the *capital expenditure budget*. This is where all the plans for the acquisition of non-current assets such as machinery, buildings, etc. are entered. Management will evaluate the various possibilities open to it, and will compare the alternatives. This is a very important part of budgeting. However, for the purposes of demonstrating how budgets are co-ordinated, we shall stick to the budgets we have demonstrated in this example. Suffice to say that the process for the capital expenditure budget and other budgets omitted from the detail of this example is broadly similar to those you have seen so far.

## 45.3 The advantages of budgeting

The process of preparing budgets, including the involvement of employees in all areas of the organisation, and finally producing a profit plan, is a regular feature in all but the smallest businesses. Very often, this is the one period each year when the various parts of management can really get together and work as a team rather than as separate parts of an organisation.

What is it that you learnt about earlier in this book which involved all the functional areas and departments across the organisation that needs to be 'right' if appropriate budgets are to be agreed?

When budgeting is conducted under favourable conditions, there is no doubt that **an organisation which uses budgeting will tend to perform rather better than a similar business that does not.** Using budgeting means that managers can no longer give general answers affecting the running of the business. They have to express their plans in financial terms and they know that, in the end, their estimated figures are going to be compared with what the actual figures turn out to be.

It has often been said that **the act of budgeting is possibly of more benefit than the budgets that are produced.** However, the following benefits can be claimed for good budgeting:

1 **The strategic planning carried out by the board of directors or owners can be more easily linked to the decisions made by managers concerning how the resources of the business will be used to try to achieve the objectives of the business.** The strategic plan has to be converted into action, and budgeting provides the ideal device for converting such plans into financial terms.
2 **Standards of performance can be agreed for the various parts of the business.** If sales and production targets are set as part of a co-ordinated plan, then the sales department cannot really complain that production is insufficient if they had agreed previously to a production level and this is being achieved. Nor can production complain if its output exceeds the amount it budgeted for and the excess output remains unsold.
3 **The expression of plans in comparable financial terms.** Some managers think mainly in terms of, say, units of production, or of tonnes of inputs or outputs, or of lorry mileage, etc. The effect that the actions of each manager has upon financial results must be brought home to them. For instance, a transport manager might be unconcerned about the number of miles that his fleet of lorries covers until the cost of a large mileage is brought home to him, often during budgeting, and it may be then and only then that he starts to search for possible economies. It is possible in many cases to use mathematical formulae to find the best ways of loading vehicles, or to plan routes taken by vehicles so that fewer miles are covered and yet the same delivery service is maintained. This is just one example of many where the expression of the plans of a section of a business in financial terms sparks off a search for economies, when otherwise it may never have started at all.
4 **Managers can see how their work slots into the activities of the organisation.** It can help to get rid of the feeling of 'I'm only a number not a person', because they can identify their positions within the organisation and can see that their jobs really are essential to the proper functioning of the business.
5 **The budgets for an organisation cannot be set in isolation.** This means that the situation of the business, the nature of its products and its workforce, etc., must be seen against the economic background of the country. For instance, it is no use budgeting for extra labour when labour is in extremely short supply, without realising the implications, such as having to pay higher than normal wage rates. Increasing the sales target during a credit squeeze needs a full investigation of the effect of the shortage of money upon the demand for the firm's goods and so on.

What disadvantages you learnt about earlier in this book may arise if an organisation's managers are not allowed to vary their activities from budget?

**However, budgets can be misused. Too often they are set at one level of sales or production and remain unchanged throughout the budget period when, in fact, flexible budgets ought to be used – see Section 45.5.** Sometimes, budgets are forced upon managers against their will. Instead, a 'selling job' should be conducted to try to convince managers that their budgets are not unreasonable. A trial run for part of a business is often much better than starting off with a fully detailed budget for the whole of the business.

Learning to use budgets is rather like learning to swim. Let a child get used to the water first and remove its fear of the water, then it will learn to swim fairly easily. For most children (but not all), if the first visit to a swimming pool meant being pushed into the deep end immediately, then reaction against swimming would probably set in. In organisations that introduce budgeting for the first time, it is best to let managers become used to the idea of budgeting during a trial period, without the fear of being dealt with severely if they don't adhere to their budgets. Most managers will then accept the idea and participate appropriately and effectively in the budgeting process.

## 45.4 The use of computers in budgeting

Years ago, budgeting was a task which most accountants hated. It was not the concept of budgeting that accountants disliked. Far from it: it suited their needs perfectly. Rather, it was the multitude of numerical manipulations that had to be performed time and time again that made the task both boring and formidable, never mind very prone to errors.

Everyone who has prepared financial statements from a trial balance and a list of adjustments knows the feeling when, after a lot of work, the statement of financial position fails to balance. Searching through all the entries and workings to find the error(s) can be a daunting prospect. With budgets, the problem is even greater – you do not have anything to tell you if you have made an error. Imagine how much more complicated it is in a real business dealing with real figures, rather than with the simple sets of data which form your exercises. Also, imagine the thoughts going through the head of the accountant in the days before spreadsheets when the managing director said 'What would happen to net profit if we increased our prices by 5% and took an extra month to pay creditors?' The accountant would then have to plough his way through a large number of extra calculations.

Most of that is now a thing of the past. Computers are used instead. They either have software specially written for the task, or spreadsheets are used. By keying in the necessary data, the computer will automatically produce the budgets and any 'what if'-based amended budgets within a very short space of time.

This enables management to see the results that would be expected from many separate propositions, thus enhancing the chance of choosing the best solution in setting the most acceptable budget. Also, as the accounting period unfolds, the changes that have occurred since the period started can be incorporated very easily so as to adjust (or 'flex') the budgets as the accounting period progresses.

Let's now look at how budgets may be adjusted using a process called 'flexible budgeting'.

## 45.5 Flexible budgets

So far in this book, budgets have been drawn up on the basis of one set of expectations, based on just one level of sales and production. Inevitably – no one can foretell the future with 100% accuracy – when the actual results are compared with the budgeted results, they will not be identical. This occurs for two reasons:

1 While the actual and budgeted volumes of production and sales may be the same, there may be a difference between the actual and the budgeted costs.
2 The volumes of actual and budgeted units of sales and production may vary. If they do, the costs and revenues will be different because of the different volumes of units involved.

The difference between budget and actual is called **variance**. Variances coming under (**1**) above will probably be under the control of the relevant department. On the other hand, variances under (**2**) arise because of variations in plans brought about by changing sales, and/or production levels.

Budgets are used for guiding activity and for control. A manager does not take kindly to being held responsible for a variance in her spending if she is working to a fixed budget and the variance is caused by a type (**2**) occurrence. To avoid this, budgets are created for several levels of volume, to show what costs, etc. should arise at each level of activity.

For example, if a budget had been fixed at a volume of 500 units and the actual volume is 550, the production manager would undoubtedly feel aggrieved if his costs for producing 550 units were compared with the costs he should have incurred for 500 units. A budget which does allow for changing levels of activity is called a **flexible budget**.

To draft a full set of flexible budgets is outside the scope of this book, but an instance of one department's flexible budget for manufacturing overhead is shown in Exhibit 45.1.

**Exhibit 45.1**

**Data Ltd**
**Budget for Manufacturing Overhead, Department S***

| | | | | | |
|---|---|---|---|---|---|
| Units | 400 | 450 | 500 | 550 | 600 |
| Variable indirect manufacturing expenses (£) | 510 | 550 | 600 | 680 | 770 |
| Fixed indirect manufacturing expenses (£) | 400 | 400 | 400 | 400 | 400 |
| Total indirect manufacturing expenses (A) (£) | 910 | 950 | 1,000 | 1,080 | 1,170 |
| Direct labour hours (B) | 200 | 225 | 250 | 275 | 300 |
| Overhead rates (A) divided by (B) (£) | 4.55 | 4.22 | 4.00 | 3.92 | 3.90 |

***In real life, this would be in greater detail and, using a spreadsheet, would be capable of showing the flexed budget for *any* level of activity.**

Notice that the variable costs in Exhibit 45.1 do not vary in direct proportion to production. Once 500 units production have been exceeded, they start to climb rapidly. The flexible budget makes far greater sense than a fixed budget. For instance, if a fixed budget had been agreed at 400 units, with variable overhead £510; if production levels rose to 600 units, the manager would think the whole system unfair if he were expected to incur only £510 variable overhead (the figure for 400 units). On the contrary, if the comparison was on a flexible budget then costs at 600 units production would, instead, be compared with £770 (the budgeted variable overhead at 600 units).

## Learning outcomes

**You should now have learnt:**

**1** There are a number of budgets that together make up the master budget and they must all reconcile to each other and to the master budget.

**2** That budget preparation is often an iterative process as the master budget is focused more and more tightly to the objectives of the organisation.

**3** How to prepare a master budget.

**4** That flexible budgeting permits managers to adjust their budgets in the light of variations in plan, often involving items over which they have no control.

## Answers to activities

45.1 The various objectives of each of the functional areas and departments need to be compatible with each other and with the overall goals of the organisation. (Section 35.3)

45.2 Budgets that are too rigorously applied generate a situation of inflexibility that can be extremely counterproductive. There must be scope for managers to depart from budget when it is in the best interests of the organisation to do so. (Section 39.2)

## Review questions

***Note*: In many ways, preparing a set of budgeted financial statements is very much like preparing financial statements from single-entry records. However, financial statements prepared from single-entry records are based on facts and concern the past; whereas budgeted financial statements are based on estimates and concern the future.**

**45.1** Richard Toms has agreed to purchase the business of Norman Soul with effect from 1 August 2017. Soul's budgeted working capital at 1 August 2017 is as follows:

| | £ | £ | £ |
|---|---|---|---|
| Current assets | | | |
| Inventory at cost | 13,000 | | |
| Accounts receivable | 25,000 | | |
| | | 38,000 | |
| Current liabilities | | | |
| Accounts payable | 10,000 | | |
| Bank overdraft | 20,000 | | |
| | | (30,000) | |
| | | | 8,000 |

In addition to paying Soul for the acquisition of the business, Toms intends to improve the liquidity position of the business by introducing £10,000 capital on 1 August 2017. He has also negotiated a bank overdraft limit of £15,000. It is probable that 10% of Soul's debtors will in fact be bad debts and that the remaining debtors will settle their accounts during August subject to a cash discount of 10%. The opening accounts payable are to be paid during August. The sales for the first four months of Toms's ownership of the business are expected to be as follows: August £24,000, September £30,000, October £30,000 and November £36,000. All sales will be on credit and debtors will receive a two-month credit period. Gross profit will be at a standard rate of 25% of selling price. In addition, in order to further improve the bank position and to reduce his opening inventory, Toms intends to sell on 1 August 2017 at cost price £8,000 of inventory for cash. In order to operate within the overdraft limit Toms intends to control inventory levels and to organise his purchases to achieve a monthly rate of inventory turnover of 3. He will receive one month's credit from his suppliers.

General cash expenses are expected to be £700 per month.

**Required:**

(*a*) An inventory budget for the four months ending 30 November 2017 showing clearly the inventory held at the end of each month.

(*b*) A cash budget for the four months ending 30 November 2017 showing clearly the bank balance at the end of each month.

*(AQA (Associated Examining Board): GCE A-level)*

**45.2A** A company's estimated pattern of costs and revenues for the first four months of 2017 is as follows:

**Costs and Revenues: January–April 2017 (£000)**

| *Month* | *Sales* | *Materials* | *Wages* | *Overheads* |
|---|---|---|---|---|
| January | 410.4 | 81.6 | 16.2 | 273.6 |
| February | 423.6 | 84.8 | 16.8 | 282.4 |
| March | 460.8 | 93.6 | 18.3 | 306.7 |
| April | 456.3 | 91.2 | 18.6 | 304.5 |

→

1 One-quarter of the materials are paid for in the month of production and the remainder two months later: deliveries received in November 2017 were £78,400, and in December 2016 £74,800.
2 Customers are expected to pay 1/3 of their debts a month after the sale and the remainder after two months: sales expected for November 2016 are £398,400, and for December 2016, £402,600.
3 Old factory equipment is to be sold in February 2017 for £9,600. Receipt of the money is expected in April 2017. New equipment will be installed at a cost of £38,000. One-half of the amount is payable in March 2017 and the remainder in August 2017.
4 Two-thirds of the wages are payable in the month they fall due, and 1/3 a month later: wages for December 2016 are estimated at £15,900.
5 £50,000 of total monthly overheads are payable in the month they occur, and the remainder one month later: total overheads for December 2016 are expected to be £265,200.
6 The opening bank balance at 1 January 2017 is expected to be an overdraft of £10,600.

**Required:**
(*a*) Using the information above, prepare the firm's cash budget for the period January–April 2017.
(*b*) Provide a statement to show those items in part (*a*) which would appear in a budgeted statement of financial position as at 30 April 2017.

(*Edexcel: GCE A-level*)

**45.3** F. Tain is opening his first boutique on 1 July 2018. He is investing £30,000 as capital. His plans are as follows:

(*i*) On 1 July 2018 to buy and pay for premises £60,000; shop fixtures £4,000; motor van £8,000.
(*ii*) To employ two assistants, each to get a salary of £130 per month, to be paid at the end of each month. (PAYE tax, National Insurance contributions, etc., are to be ignored.)
(*iii*) To buy the following quantities of goods for resale (shown in units):

| | *July* | *Aug* | *Sep* | *Oct* | *Nov* | *Dec* |
|---|---|---|---|---|---|---|
| Units | 600 | 660 | 840 | 1,050 | 1,200 | 990 |

(*iv*) To sell the following number of units of these goods:

| | *Jul* | *Aug* | *Sep* | *Oct* | *Nov* | *Dec* |
|---|---|---|---|---|---|---|
| Units | 360 | 540 | 720 | 900 | 1,170 | 1,260 |

(*v*) Based on similar ventures in shops selling other products, he has decided to sell all goods at the same price – £30. Two-thirds of the sales are for cash, the other 1/3 being on credit. These latter customers are expected to pay their accounts in the third month following that in which they received their goods.
(*vi*) The goods will cost £7 each for July to October inclusive, and £8 each thereafter. Creditors will be paid in the second month following purchase. (Value inventory on FIFO basis.)
(*vii*) The other expenses of the shop will be £450 per month payable in the month following that in which they were incurred.
(*viii*) Part of the premises will be sub-let as an office at a rent of £8,000 per annum. This is paid in equal instalments in March, June, September and December.
(*ix*) His cash drawings will be £1,400 per month.
(*x*) Depreciation is to be provided on premises at 5% per annum straight line; shop fixtures at 15% per annum and on the motor van at 25% per annum, both using the reducing balance method.

**You are required to:**
(*a*) Draw up a cash budget for the six months ended 31 December 2018, showing the balance of cash at the end of each month.
(*b*) Draw up a forecast statement of profit or loss for the six months ending 31 December 2018, and a forecast statement of financial position as at that date.

**45.4A** M. Lamb is going to set up a new business on 1 April 2018. She estimates that her first six months in business will be as follows:

(*i*) She will put £60,000 into a bank account for the business on 1 April 2018.
(*ii*) On 1 April 2018, she will buy machinery for £8,000, a motor van for £6,400 and premises for £35,000, paying for them immediately out of the business bank account.
(*iii*) All purchases will be on credit. She will buy £10,000 of goods on 1 April and will pay for these in May. She will purchase another £12,000 of goods in April and £16,000 of goods each month during May, June, July, August, and September. Other than the first £10,000 purchase in April, all other purchases will be paid for two months after purchase.
(iv) Sales (all on credit) will be £26,000 for April and £28,000 for each month after that. Debtors will pay for the goods in the second month after purchase.
(*v*) Inventory on 30 September 2018 will be £8,000.
(*vi*) Wages and salaries will be £2,100 per month and will be paid on the last day of each month.
(*vii*) General expenses will be £200 per month, payable in the month following that in which they were incurred.
(*viii*) She has an endowment assurance policy maturing on 15 July 2018. She will receive £17,500 on that date and it will be paid into the business bank account immediately.
(ix) Insurance covering the 12 months to 31 March 2019 will be paid by cheque on 30 September 2018, £560.
(*x*) Business rates will be paid as follows: for the three months to 30 June 2018 by cheque on 31 May 2018: for the 12 months ended 30 June 2019 by cheque on 31 October 2018. Business rates are £1,440 per annum.
(*xi*) She will make drawings of £1,800 per month by cheque.
(*xii*) She has substantial investments in public companies. Her bank manager will give her any overdraft that she may require.
(*xiii*) Depreciate premises 5% per annum, van 25% per annum, and machinery 20% per annum, all using the straight line method.

**You are required to:**
(*a*) Draft a cash budget (includes bank) month by month showing clearly the amount of bank balance or overdraft at the end of each month.
(*b*) Draft the projected statement of profit or loss for the first six months' trading, and a statement of financial position as at 30 September 2018.

**45.5A**
(*a*) What is meant by the terms:
(*i*) Budget
(*ii*) Operating budget
(*iii*) Master budget?

→

(b) The information below relates to the business of Madingley Ltd:

**Statement of Financial Position as at 30 May 2017 (£000)**

| | Cost | Aggregate depreciation | Book value |
|---|---|---|---|
| *Non-current assets* | | | |
| Land and buildings | 134.00 | – | 134.00 |
| Plant and machinery | 9.40 | 3.76 | 5.64 |
| Fixtures and fittings | 2.30 | 1.05 | 1.25 |
| | 145.70 | 4.81 | 145.89 |
| *Current assets* | | | |
| Inventory: Raw materials | | 91.70 | |
| Finished goods | | 142.40 | |
| Accounts receivable | | 594.40 | |
| Bank | | 12.40 | 845.90 |
| | | | 981.79 |
| *Less Current liabilities* | | | |
| Accounts payable: Raw materials | | 82.20 | |
| Overheads | | 127.40 | |
| | | | (209.60) |
| Net assets | | | 772.19 |
| *Equity* | | | |
| Share capital | | 500.00 | |
| Retained profits | | 272.19 | |
| | | | 772.19 |

The following is a schedule of the budgeted income and expenditure for the six months ended 30 November 2017 (£000):

| | *Sales* | *Materials* | *Wages* | *Overheads* |
|---|---|---|---|---|
| June | 193.20 | 45.20 | 7.60 | 123.00 |
| July | 201.40 | 42.40 | 7.90 | 119.20 |
| August | 216.10 | 49.60 | 8.80 | 131.40 |
| September | 200.50 | 31.40 | 6.10 | 91.50 |
| October | 190.30 | 21.20 | 3.70 | 59.30 |
| November | 183.70 | 19.80 | 2.60 | 42.60 |

*Notes:*

(*i*) Generally, materials are paid for two months after receipt, and customers pay on average after three months.

(*ii*) Payments outstanding for materials at 1 June 2017 were: April £38,500; May £43,700.

(*iii*) Accounts receivable were: March £194,300; April £203,600; May £196,500.

(*iv*) Wages are to be paid in the month in which they fall due.

(*v*) Overheads are to be paid one month after they are incurred: the figure for May was £127,400.

(*vi*) Inventory of raw materials are to be kept at £91,700.

(*vii*) The inventory of finished goods at 30 November 2017 are to be £136,200.

(*viii*) There is no inventory of semi-finished items on 31 May 2017, and none are expected in inventory on 30 November.

(*ix*) 40% of the overheads are to be considered as fixed.

(*x*) Depreciation on plant and machinery is to be allowed at 10% per annum on cost; the fixtures and fittings are thought to have a value at 30 November of £980.

(*xi*) There are no sales of finished goods or purchases of raw materials for cash planned during the period.

**Prepare:**

(*a*) A forecast operating statement for the period June to November 2017; and

(*b*) A forecast statement of financial position as at 30 November 2017.

(*Edexcel: GCEA-level*)

**45.6** The following information has been extracted from the books of Issa Ltd for the financial year ended 31 December 2017.

**Statement of Profit or Loss for the year ending 31 December 2017**

| | £000 | | £000 |
|---|---|---|---|
| Opening inventory | 90 | Sales | 750 |
| Purchases | 490 | | |
| | 580 | | |
| *Less* Closing inventory | 80 | | |
| Cost of goods sold | 500 | | |
| Gross profit | 250 | | |
| | 750 | | 750 |
| Administration expenses | 60 | Gross profit | 250 |
| Selling and distribution expenses | 50 | | |
| Financial charges | 20 | | |
| Depreciation of non-current assets | 20 | | |
| Net profit | 100 | | |
| | 250 | | 250 |

**Statement of Financial Position as at 31 December 2017**[Authors' note]

| | | £000 | £000 | | £000 | £000 |
|---|---|---|---|---|---|---|
| Non-current assets at cost | | | 750 | £1 Ordinary shares fully paid | | 200 |
| *Less* Aggregate depreciation | | | | 9% £1 Preference shares, | | |
| | | | 144 | fully paid | | 100 |
| | | | 606 | | | |
| *Current assets* | | | | Share premium | | 150 |
| Inventory | | 80 | | Retained earnings | | 350 |
| Trade accounts receivable | 75 | | | | | |
| *Less* Allowance for | | | | *Current liabilities* | | |
| doubtful debts | 5 | 70 | | Trade accounts payable | 50 | |
| Balance at bank | | 100 | 250 | Accrued expenses | 6 | 56 |
| | | | 856 | | | 856 |

The company had commenced the preparation of its budget for the year ending 31 December 2018 and the following information is the basis of its forecast.

1 An intensive advertising campaign will be carried out in the first six months of 2018 at a cost of £15,000. It is anticipated that as a result of this, sales will increase to £900,000 in 2018.
2 The gross profit/sales ratio will be increased to 35%.
3 A new inventory control system is to be installed in 2018 and it is expected that the inventory level will be reduced by £15,000 as compared to the 2017 closing inventory.
4 Land and buildings which cost £50,000 (nil depreciation to date) will be sold in 2018 for £200,000 cash. Half of the proceeds will be used to buy ordinary shares in another company, Yates Ltd, at an agreed price of £4 per share. (Ignore share commission, etc.)
5 The company planned to capitalise some of its reserves on 1 April 2018. New ordinary shares are to be issued on a one for two basis. Half the funds required will be drawn from the share premium account and the remainder will be taken from retained earnings.
6 Preference share dividends will be paid on 1 May 2018 and 1 November 2018. The company planned to pay an interim ordinary share dividend on the increased share capital of 2.5p per share on 1 July 2018. No final dividend is proposed.
7 Owing to inflation revenue expenses are expected to rise as follows:
Administration expenses will increase by 6%.
Selling and distribution expenses will increase by 8%.

The advertising campaign expenses are in addition to the increase above.
Financial charges will increase by 4%.
These percentage increases are based on the figures for the year ended 31 December 2017.

8 With the projected sales increases trade accounts receivable are expected to rise to £100,000 by 31 December 2018. The allowance for doubtful debts is to be adjusted to 7 1/2% of forecast accounts receivable.

9 Other forecast figures as at 31 December 2018.

| | £000 |
|---|---|
| Balance at bank | 350.1 |
| Trade accounts payable | 56.0 |
| Expense accounts payable | 15.0 |

10 Depreciation of 10% per annum on cost is to be provided on £600,000 of the company's fixed assets.

**Required:**

(*a*) A budgeted statement of profit or loss for the year ending 31 December 2018. Show the full details of the trading account.

(*b*) A budgeted statement of financial position as at 31 December 2018.

(*c*) What advantages accrue to a business by preparing a budget with respect to
  (*i*) forecast profitability;
  (*ii*) forecast liquidity?

(*AQA (Associated Examining Board): GCE A-level*)

***Author's note*: This statement of profit or loss and statement of financial position are presented in the rarely used 'horizontal format'. They are presented in this way because examiners do, occasionally use them. You should find it a simple process to identify or calculate the figures you are used to finding in vertical statements of profit or loss and statements of financial position.**

**45.7** The statement of financial position of Pies and Cakes Ltd at 30 June 2018 was expected to be as follows:

**Statement of Financial Position 30 June 2018 (£)**

| | | | |
|---|---|---|---|
| *Non-current assets* | *Cost* | *Depreciation to date* | *Net* |
| Buildings | 300,000 | 120,000 | 180,000 |
| Plant and machinery | 50,000 | 30,000 | 20,000 |
| Motor vehicles | 30,000 | 14,000 | 16,000 |
| Office fixtures | 2,500 | 1,100 | 1,400 |
| | 382,500 | 165,100 | 217,400 |
| *Current assets* | | | |
| Inventory: Finished goods (570 units at £12 each) | | 6,840 | |
| Raw materials | | 1,500 | |
| Accounts receivable (June 2018 sales) | | 9,500 | |
| Cash and bank balances | | 35,500 | 53,340 |
| | | | 270,740 |
| *Less: Current liabilities* | | | |
| Accounts payable for raw materials (May £300 + June £240) | | 540 | |
| Accounts payable for indirect manufacturing expenses | | 1,050 | |
| | | | (1,590) |
| | | | 269,150 |
| *Equity* | | | |
| Share capital | | | 225,000 |
| Retained profits | | | 44,150 |
| | | | 269,150 |

The plans for the six months to 31 December 2018 can be summarised as:

(*i*) Production costs per unit will be:

| | £ |
|---|---|
| Direct materials | 2 |
| Direct labour | 6 |
| Variable indirect manufacturing expenses | 4 |
| | 12 |

(*ii*) Sales will be at a price of £20 per unit for the three months to 30 September and at £21 subsequently. The number of units sold will be:

| | *Jul* | *Aug* | *Sept* | *Oct* | *Nov* | *Dec* |
|---|---|---|---|---|---|---|
| Units | 300 | 400 | 500 | 500 | 450 | 350 |

All sales will be on credit, and debtors will pay their accounts one month after they bought the goods.

(*iii*) Production will be consistent at 450 units per month.

(*iv*) Purchases of direct materials – all on credit – will be:

| *Jul* | *Aug* | *Sept* | *Oct* | *Nov* | *Dec* |
|---|---|---|---|---|---|
| £ | £ | £ | £ | £ | £ |
| 1,100 | 1,000 | 800 | 700 | 700 | 900 |

Creditors for direct materials will be paid two months after purchase.

(*v*) Direct labour is paid in the same month as production occurs.

(*vi*) Variable indirect manufacturing expenses are paid in the month following that in which the units are produced.

(*vii*) Fixed indirect manufacturing expenses of £450 per month are paid each month and never in arrears.

(*viii*) A machine costing £2,500 will be bought and paid for in July. A motor vehicle costing £10,000 will be bought and paid for in September.

(*ix*) Loan notes of £25,000 will be issued and the cash received in November. Interest will not be charged until 2019.

(*x*) Provide for depreciation for the six months: Buildings £15,000; Motor vehicles £4,000; Office fixtures £220; Plant and machinery £5,000.

**You are required to draw up as a minimum:**

(*a*) Cash budget, showing figures each month.
(*b*) Accounts receivable budget, showing figures each month.
(*c*) Accounts payable budget, showing figures each month.
(*d*) Raw materials budget, showing figures each month.
(*e*) Forecast operating statement for the six months.
(*f*) Forecast statement of financial position as at 31 December 2018.

In addition, draw up any other budgets which show the workings behind the above budgets.

**45.8** The following information relates to the actual sales of Griffton Ltd during the last four months of its financial year.

| | *March* | *April* | *May* | *June* |
|---|---|---|---|---|
| Quantity (units) | 900 | 900 | 900 | 1,000 |
| Price each | £55 | £55 | £55 | £55 |

The budgeted information below relates to the next financial year commencing 1 July 2018:

(*i*) The company forecasts that sales quantity will decrease in July by 10% of the level in June. The reduced quantity will remain for August and September, but will then increase by 10% in October, and remain fixed for the next three months.

→

The sales price will remain at £55 each until 1 September when it will be increased to £60 per unit, this price will be effective for a minimum of six months.

50% of sales are on a cash basis and attract a 2% cash discount, the remaining 50% of sales are paid two months in arrears.

The company arranges its purchases of raw materials such that the closing inventory at the end of each month exactly meets the requirement for the following month's sales. Each unit sold requires 2 kg of material at £15 per kg; this price is fixed until December 2019.

(*ii*) As a separate exercise, the managing director asks for inventory levels to be reviewed, and asks you about the use of economic order quantities at some time in 2019. The following budgeted data would apply to this exercise:

| | |
|---|---|
| Material | 2,000 kg per month |
| Price | £15 per kg |
| Inventory holding costs | 20% p.a. on average inventory value |
| Ordering costs | £10 per order |

**Required:**

A. Draw up monthly budgets for the four-month period commencing 1 July 2018 for:
   (*a*) Accounts receivable in £s;
   (*b*) Raw material purchases in kg.

B. From the budgeted information given in note (*ii*) calculate the economic order quantity for the company. Briefly outline the limitations of this ordering method.

*(Reproduced with the kind permission of OCR – University of Oxford Delegacy of Local Examinations: GCE A-level)*

***Author's note*: EOQ was covered in Section 40.8.**

**45.9** Bedford Ltd is a manufacturing business with several production departments. Benjamin Kent, the manager of the machining department, submitted the following figures for the firm's annual budget for his department:

| | |
|---|---|
| Units produced (normal production level) | 64,000 |
| | £ |
| Raw materials | 294,400 |
| Direct labour | 236,800 |
| Power | 38,400 |
| Repairs and maintenance (25% variable at this level of budgeted cost) | 51,200 |
| Insurance | 1,300 |
| Heating and lighting | 1,250 |
| Indirect wages (15% variable at this level of budgeted cost) | 64,000 |
| Total cost | 687,350 |

Total capacity for machining department — 80,000 units

Actual production for the period is 68,000 units, and costs are:

| | |
|---|---|
| Materials | 310,750 |
| Labour | 249,100 |
| Power | 39,800 |
| Repairs and maintenance | 53,050 |
| Insurance | 1,350 |
| Heating and lighting | 1,200 |
| Indirect wages | 65,250 |
| Total cost | 720,500 |

Benjamin is being criticised for overspending £33,150 compared with his normal budget. It is appreciated that he has made a saving on heating and lighting, but concern is being expressed over the spending on materials and labour. Benjamin feels that he has been able to control the department's costs efficiently.

**Required:**

A. Construct a flexible budget for 60%, 70%, 75%, 85% and 90% of production capacity, calculate any savings or overspending by Benjamin's department and comment on its efficiency.

B. Describe the operation of an efficient system of budgetary control.

*(Reproduced with the kind permission of OCR – University of Oxford Delegacy of Local Examinations: GCE A-level)*

**45.10A** The summarised statement of financial position of Newland Traders at 30 May 2017 was as follows:

| | £000 | £000 |
|---|---|---|
| Non-current assets at cost | | 610 |
| *Less* Depreciation | | 264 |
| | | 346 |
| Current assets | | |
| Inventory | 210 | |
| Accounts receivable | 315 | |
| Cash at bank and in hand | 48 | 573 |
| | | 919 |
| *Less* Current liabilities | | |
| Accounts payable | | (128) |
| | | 791 |
| Equity | | |
| Issued capital | | 600 |
| General reserve | | 150 |
| Retained profits | | 41 |
| | | 791 |

Selling and materials prices at 30 May 2017 provide for a gross profit at the rate of 25% of sales.

The accounts payable at 30 May 2017 represent the purchases for May 2017, and the accounts receivable the sales for April of £150,000 and May of £165,000.

Estimates of sales and expenditure for the six months to 30 November 2017 are as follows:

(*i*) Sales for the period at current prices will be £800,000. Sales for the months of September and October will each be twice those of the sales in each of the other months.

(*ii*) Inventory at the end of each month will be the same as at 30 May 2017 except that at 30 November 2017 it will be increased to 20% above that level.

(*iii*) Creditors will be paid one month after the goods are supplied and debtors will pay two months after the goods are supplied.

(*iv*) Wages and expenses will be £20,000 a month and will be paid in the month in which they are incurred.

(*v*) Depreciation will be at the rate of £5,000 a month.

(*vi*) There will be capital expenditure of £80,000 on 1 September 2017. Depreciation, in addition to that given in (*v*) above, will be at the rate of 10% per annum on cost.

(*vii*) There will be no changes in issued capital, general reserve or prices of sales or purchases.

**Required:**

(*a*) Sales and purchases budgets and a budgeted statement of profit or loss for the six months ending 30 November 2017.

(*b*) A budgeted statement of financial position as at 30 November 2017.

(*c*) A cash flow budget for the six months ended 30 November 2017 indicating whether or not it will be necessary to make arrangements for extra finance and, if so, your recommendation as to what form it should take.

*Show all your calculations.*

*(Welsh Joint Education Committee: GCE A-level)*

→ **45.11A** Len Auck and Brian Land trade as partners in Auckland Manufacturing Company making components for minicomputers. To cope with increasing demand the partners intend to extend their manufacturing capacity but are concerned about the effect of the expansion on their cash resources during the build-up period from January to April 2016.

The following information is available.

(*a*) The statement of financial position of Auckland Manufacturing Company at 31 December 2015 is expected to be:

| | £ | £ |
|---|---|---|
| *Non-current assets* | | |
| Plant and machinery at cost | | 65,000 |
| *Less* Depreciation | | 28,000 |
| | | 37,000 |
| *Current assets* | | |
| Inventory – raw materials | 10,500 | |
| – finished goods | 18,500 | |
| Accounts receivable | 36,000 | |
| Cash at bank | 4,550 | 69,550 |
| | | 106,550 |
| *Current liabilities* | | |
| Accounts payable | | (27,550) |
| | | 79,000 |
| *Partners' capital accounts* | | |
| Len Auck | | 40,000 |
| Brian Land | | 39,000 |
| | | 79,000 |

(*b*) Accounts payable at 31 December 2015 are made up of:

| | |
|---|---|
| Accounts payable for materials supplied in November and December at £13,000 per month | 26,000 |
| Accounts payable for overheads | 1,550 |
| | 27,550 |

(*c*) New plant costing £25,000 will be delivered and paid for in January 2016.

(*d*) Raw material inventory are to be increased to £12,000 by the end of January 2016, thereafter raw material inventory will be maintained at that level. Payment for raw materials is made two months after the month of delivery. Finished goods inventory will be maintained at £18,500 throughout the period. There is no work in progress.

(*e*) Sales for the four months are expected to be:

| | £ |
|---|---|
| January | 18,000 |
| February | 22,000 |
| March | 22,000 |
| April | 24,000 |

Sales for several months prior to 31 December had been running at the rate of £18,000 per month. It is anticipated that all sales will continue to be paid for two months following the month of delivery.

(*f*) The cost structure of the product is expected to be:

| | % |
|---|---|
| Raw materials | 50 |
| Direct wages | 20 |
| Overheads, including depreciation | 17½ |
| Profit | 12½ |
| Selling price | 100 |

(*g*) Indirect wages and salaries included in overheads amount to £900 for the month of January and £1,000 per month thereafter.
(*h*) Depreciation of plant and machinery (including the new plant) is to be provided at £700 per month and is included in the total overheads.
(*i*) Wages and salaries are to be paid in the month to which they relate; all other expenses are to be paid for in the month following the month to which they relate.
(*j*) The partners share profits equally and drawings are £400 per month each.
(*k*) During the period to April an overdraft facility is being requested.

**Required:**
(*a*) A forecast statement of profit or loss for the four months January to April 2016 and a statement of financial position as at 30 April 2016.
(*b*) A month by month cash forecast for the four months showing the maximum amount of finance required during the period.
(*c*) A calculation of the month in which the overdraft facility would be repaid on the assumption that the level of activity in April is maintained.

For the purposes of this question, taxation and bank interest may be ignored.

(*Association of Chartered Certified Accountants*)

part 9

# STANDARD COSTING AND VARIANCE ANALYSIS

## Introduction

This part looks at how budgetary control can be exercised in a timely manner through the establishment of estimates for cost and income and the subsequent monitoring of those estimates against the actual costs and income as they arise.

chapter

# 46 Standard costing

## Learning objectives

**After you have studied this chapter, you should be able to:**

- explain the difference between a standard costing system and an actual cost system
- explain the advantages of adopting a standard costing system
- distinguish between ideal standards and attainable standards
- explain the importance of selecting appropriate standards

## Introduction

In this chapter, you'll learn about standard costing, its benefits, and the difference between 'ideal' and 'attainable' standards and of the importance of recognising the difference between them.

## 46.1 Comparison with actual costs

A cost accounting system can be of two types: one that uses *actual* costs or one that uses something called **standard costs**. The difference is not in the systems themselves but in the *kind* of costs that are used. In the costing systems already shown, we have seen that they have consisted of the actual costs for direct materials and direct labour, and that overhead has been charged by reference to a predetermined overhead rate. Standard costing uses instead the costs that *should have been incurred*. **So standard costing has costs that *should* have been incurred, while other systems use costs that *have* been incurred.**

In a cost accounting system that uses 'actual costs', costs are traced through the records as product costs. On the other hand, **standard costing** uses standards of performance and of costs and prices derived from studying operations and on estimates of future costs and prices. Each unit being produced is given a standard material cost, a standard direct labour cost and a standard overhead cost. As with any form of management accounting, this does not have to be carried out in full. For example, some companies will use *standard* labour and *standard* overhead costs but *actual* material costs. In the rest of this chapter, we will consider organisations that use standard costs for everything.

As with all management accounting tools, the benefits flowing from using standard costing should exceed the costs of doing so. Advantages that may arise as a result of having a standard costing system include:

1 **Usually a standard costing system is simpler and needs less work than a costing system based on actual costs.** This is because once the standards have been set they are adhered to, and the standard costs remain unchanged for fairly long periods. Costing systems based on actual costs need constant recalculations of cost. For example, the average cost method of pricing issues of materials needs a recalculation of the price each time there are further receipts, whereas standard cost of materials will remain at a constant figure. This can bring about a reduction in the costs of clerical work.

2 **The unit costs for each identical product will be the same, whereas this may not be the same with actual costing systems.** For instance, in an actual cost system two people making identical units may be paid at different wage rates, the materials issued to one person may have come from a slightly later lot of raw materials received which cost more than the previous lot and therefore the issue price may be higher, and so on. In a standard costing system the same amount would be charged for each of these people until such time as the standards were altered.

3 **A standard cost system provides a better means of checking on the efficiency with which production is carried on,** in that the differences between the standard costs and the actual costs, i.e. the **variances**, throw up the changes in efficiency.

4 **Standard costing increases the speed of reporting.** This is certainly important, as generally the later that information is received the less useful it is. Standard costing has a great deal of predetermined data when compared with an actual costing system; therefore entering up job order sheets, job sheets and many other tasks can be speeded up if the actual costs do not have to be awaited.

By definition, the costs that flow through a standard costing system are standard costs. As actual costs will normally be different from the equivalent standard costs, the difference (i.e. 'variance') if adverse (i.e. actual costs have exceeded standard costs) is debited to the profit and loss account. If the variance is a favourable one (i.e. actual costs have been less than the standard costs) it is credited to the profit and loss account. This must be done, as all the costs used for the calculation of gross profit, etc. have been standard costs, and if the variances were not included in the profit and loss account then the net profit it shows would not be the net profit actually made.

## 46.2 Setting standards

Standard costing is a classic case of the use of the principle of 'management by exception'. Put roughly, this means that **when things are going according to plan leave them alone, and concentrate instead on the things that are deviating from planned results.** With standard costing, the actual results that conform to the standards require little attention. Instead, management's interest is centred on the exceptions to standards. The approach whereby this information is given to management is known as 'exception reporting'.

**Getting the standard costs, quantities and prices 'right' is, therefore, of prime importance.** If the 'wrong' standards are used, not only will a lot of time and money have been wasted, but they may bring worse results than if no standard had been set at all.

**Activity 46.1** What does this last statement remind you of from earlier chapters?

Standards may be unsuitable because they were not set properly, or because conditions have changed greatly since they were set.

Standards can be of two types:

1 **Ideal standards.** These are based on maximum levels of efficiency. They thus represent standards of performance that can rarely, if ever, be attained. Adoption of this type of standard is never appropriate. Quite apart from the unrealistic view it gives of everything, it is misleading and can be demotivating if the standards set are perceived to be unachievable by those employees who are meant to be striving to achieve them.
2 **Attainable standards.** It is simple for someone to say that individuals will be motivated to attain standards that they are capable of, that they will not exert very much effort to exceed standards, and that standards outside their capabilities will not motivate them. From this follows the easy conclusion that standards should be neither 'too easy' nor 'too difficult' but should be 'just right'. The difficult part of this is in saying what the 'just right' figures are. There is no doubt that the work of behavioural scientists in this area has brought about a far greater insight into such problems. In a very large firm, such specialists may be members of the team setting the standards.

The standards for materials and for labour can be divided between those which are concerned with (*a*) prices and (*b*) quantities. Standard overhead costs are divided between standard variable overhead costs and standard fixed overhead costs. The standard fixed overhead costs will be used in absorption costing only, as marginal costing does not bring the fixed costs into its figures.

**Activity 46.2**

Think back to Activity 46.1. What message have you taken from these four statements:

1 'Data which is provided for a particular purpose, and which is completely wrong for the purpose, is worse than having no data at all.' (Section 40.2)
2 'Using an inappropriate costing base can be even worse than having no costing at all.' (Section 41.12)
3 'Some budgets [that are drawn up] are even more harmful to a firm than if none were drawn up at all.' (Section 43.2)
4 'If the "wrong" standards are used, not only will a lot of time and money have been wasted, but they may bring worse results than if no standard had been set at all.' (Section 46.2)

## Learning outcomes

**You should now have learnt:**

1 That standard costing is based upon costs that should have been incurred, while other costing systems are based upon actual costs, i.e. costs that have been incurred.
2 About the benefits of standard costing.
3 That under a standard costing system, management focuses upon the exceptions to the standards.
4 That it is essential that the standards adopted are appropriate and attainable.

## Answers to activities

46.1 'Data which is provided for a particular purpose, and which is completely wrong for the purpose, is worse than having no data at all.' (Section 40.2)
'Using an inappropriate costing base can be even worse than having no costing at all.' (Section 37.12)
'Some budgets [that are drawn up] are even more harmful to a firm than if none were drawn up at all.' (Section 43.2)

46.2 In order to obtain maximum benefit from costing systems and management accounting systems, it is vital that appropriate data and management accounting techniques are used and that they are used in an appropriate and effective manner. Failure to do this is both directly wasteful of resources and can be not just counterproductive, but harmful to the organisation.

## Review questions

***Note*: This chapter gives background information only. You will not find many computational questions limited to its contents.**

**46.1** Rimham plc prepares its budgets annually and as the accountant you are responsible for this task. The following standard data is available:

| *Material content* | *Product X* | *Product Y* | *Product Z* |
|---|---|---|---|
| | *kg* | *kg* | *kg* |
| Material 1 | – | 18 | 24 |
| Material 2 | 4 | 14 | – |
| Material 3 | 12 | 10 | 6 |
| Material 4 | 8 | – | 18 |

| *Material prices* | *Price per kg* |
|---|---|
| | £ |
| Material 1 | 0.1 |
| Material 2 | 0.15 |
| Material 3 | 0.25 |
| Material 4 | 0.05 |

| *Labour content* | *Product X* | *Product Y* | *Product Z* |
|---|---|---|---|
| | *hours* | *hours* | *hours* |
| Department A | 2.5 | 1.5 | 3 |
| Department B | 2.5 | 1.5 | 3 |

| *Labour rates* | *Rate per hour* |
|---|---|
| | £ |
| Department A | 1.6 |
| Department B | 1.2 |

| *Additional budgeted information* | |
|---|---|
| Direct labour hours | 635,000 |
| Production overheads | £1,143,000 |

- Production overheads are absorbed in the direct labour hour rate method.
- Administration and selling overheads are absorbed as a percentage of production cost at the rates of 50% and 25%, respectively.
- Profit is estimated at $12\frac{1}{2}$% on budgeted selling price.
- Sales, at standard selling price, for the following year are budgeted as follows:

| *Product* | £ |
|---|---|
| X | 800,000 |
| Y | 1,280,000 |
| Z | 2,400,000 |

- In order to meet the needs of an expansion programme the company considers it necessary to increase inventory as follows:

| | |
|---|---|
| Material 1 | 90,000 kg |
| Material 2 | 36,000 kg |
| Material 3 | 42,000 kg |
| Material 4 | 54,000 kg |
| Finished goods | |
| Product X | 5,000 units |
| Product Y | 10,000 units |
| Product Z | 10,000 units |

**You are required to prepare the following:**

(*a*) A schedule giving a detailed standard cost and standard selling price per unit for **each** product.
(*b*) The sales budget in units.
(*c*) The production budget in units.
(*d*) The direct material purchases budget in both units and value.

(*Northern Examinations and Assessment Board: GCE A-level*)

**46.2A** Define the terms:

(*i*) standard costing
(*ii*) standard cost
(*iii*) standard hours
(*iv*) variance.

chapter

# 47 Materials and labour variances

## Learning objectives

**After you have studied this chapter, you should be able to:**

- explain the difference between a favourable and an adverse variance
- calculate materials usage and price variances
- calculate labour efficiency and wage rate variances
- explain the similarity between the calculation of the materials usage variance and the labour efficiency variance
- explain the similarity between the calculation of the materials price variance and the wage rate variance
- suggest possible explanations for variances

## Introduction

In this chapter, you'll learn about two of the main groups of variances, those relating to materials and labour, and how to calculate them.

## 47.1 Background

**Variance analysis** is a means of assessing the difference between budgeted and actual amounts. These can be monetary amounts or physical quantities.

Properly used, variance analysis can improve the operating efficiency of a business by, first of all, setting up the predetermined standard cost structures and, then, measuring actual costs against them to assess efficiency.

Variance analysis makes use of the principle of management by exception. When things are going according to plan they can be left alone. Management can then concentrate on the things that deviate from the planned results and, as mentioned in Chapter 46, can adopt exception reporting in order to do so.

## 47.2 Adverse and favourable variances

The difference between standard cost and actual cost has already been stated to be a variance. Remember these are classified:

- **Adverse variance:** actual cost amount *greater* than standard cost amount
- **Favourable variance:** actual cost amount *less* than standard cost amount.

The use of the words 'adverse' and 'favourable' should not be confused with their meaning in ordinary language. They are technical terms. Whether a variance is 'good' or 'bad' can only be determined after the causes of the variance have been fully investigated and ascertained. For example, the actual cost of a unit of a product may be less than the standard cost because more units than expected were produced, resulting in lower unit costs – a good thing. Alternatively, actual cost may be lower because the standard cost was based on an error by the person who calculated it – a bad thing.

## 47.3 Computation of variances

There is a big difference between the *computation* of the variances and their *analysis*. The computation simply requires the use of straightforward formulae. In contrast, the analysis of a variance is a matter requiring a good deal of judgement which, by its very nature, cannot be done in a mechanical fashion.

We can now look at the computation of some variances. There are many variances which can be computed, but we will concentrate on a few of the more important ones. In order that sense can be made of the computations and a reasonable job of analysis done, it will be assumed that the standards set were calculated on a rational basis – i.e. they were appropriate.

***Note*: In the computations of variances which follow, exhibits are used to illustrate the variances which have been calculated. The lines drawn on the exhibits represent:**

Standard costs - - - - - - - - - - - -
Actual costs ————————
Where actual costs and standard costs are the same —·—·—·—·—·—·—·—·—·—.

**The shaded part(s) in each exhibit represent the variance. The value of each variance can be confirmed by multiplying price by quantity, i.e. it is the area of the shaded rectangle.**

### 1 Materials price variances

#### Favourable variance

| *Material J* | |
|---|---|
| Standard price per metre | £4 |
| Standard usage per unit | 5 metres |
| Actual price per metre | £3 |
| Actual usage per unit | 5 metres |

Usage is the same as standard, therefore the only variance is that of price calculated:

| | £ |
|---|---|
| Actual cost per unit £3 × 5 | 15 |
| Standard cost per unit £4 × 5 | 20 |
| Variance (favourable) | 5 |

**Exhibit 47.1 shows the £5 variance (represented by the shaded area).** This is the £1 difference in price multiplied by a quantity of 5, therefore the variance is £5. **The variance extends to the price line and not the quantity line, so it is a price variance.**

Exhibit 47.1

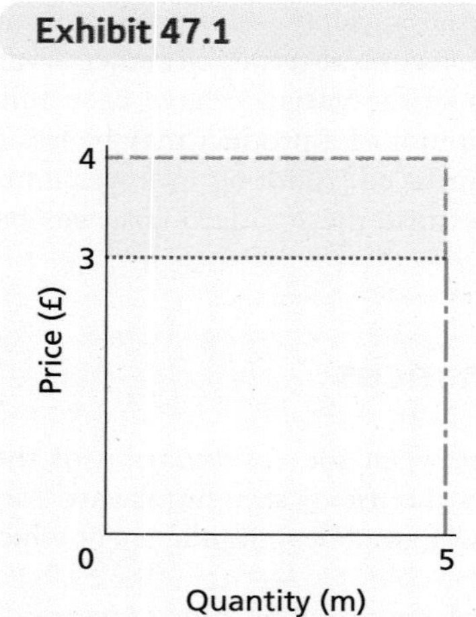


**Adverse variance**

| | |
|---|---|
| *Material K* | |
| Standard price per metre | £9 |
| Standard usage per unit | 8 metres |
| Actual price per metre | £11 |
| Actual usage per unit | 8 metres |

Exhibit 47.2

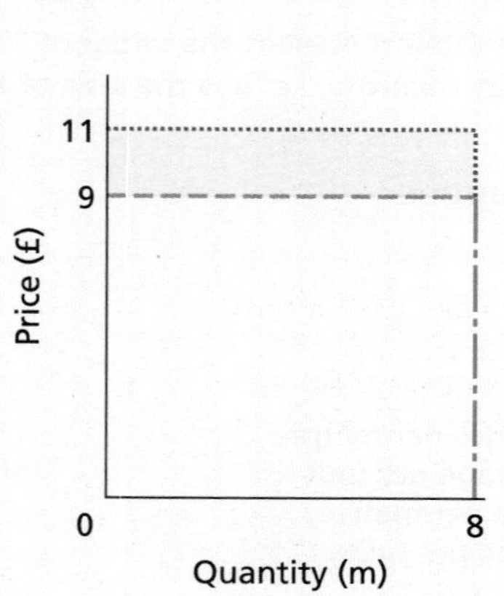


| | |
|---|---|
| Variance computed: | £ |
| Actual cost per unit £11 × 8 units | 88 |
| Standard cost per unit £9 × 8 units | 72 |
| Variance (adverse) | 16 |

The variance is shown in Exhibit 47.2 – £2 times a quantity of 8, i.e. £16. Notice that the shaded area is outside the lines marked – – – – – – representing standard costs.

***Note*: In the exhibits, when the variance is outside the standard cost area as marked by the standard cost lines, it will be an adverse variance. When it is inside the standard cost area as marked by the standard cost lines, it will be a favourable variance.**

## 2 Materials usage variances

### Favourable variance

| *Material L* | |
|---|---|
| Standard price per tonne | £5 |
| Standard usage per unit | 100 tonnes |
| Actual price per tonne | £5 |
| Actual usage per unit | 95 tonnes |

Cost is the same as standard, therefore the only variance is that of usage calculated:

| | £ |
|---|---|
| Actual cost per unit £5 × 95 | 475 |
| Standard cost per unit £5 × 100 | 500 |
| Variance (favourable) | 25 |

Exhibit 47.3

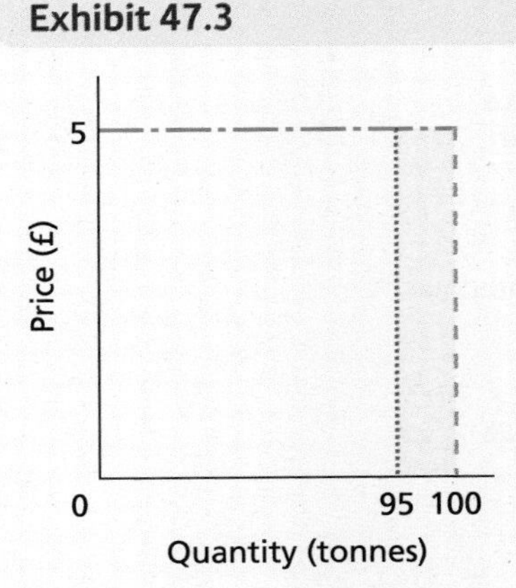


### Adverse variance

| *Material M* | |
|---|---|
| Standard price per centimetre | £8 |
| Standard usage per unit | 11 cm |
| Actual price per centimetre | £8 |
| Actual usage per unit | 13 cm |

Exhibit 47.4

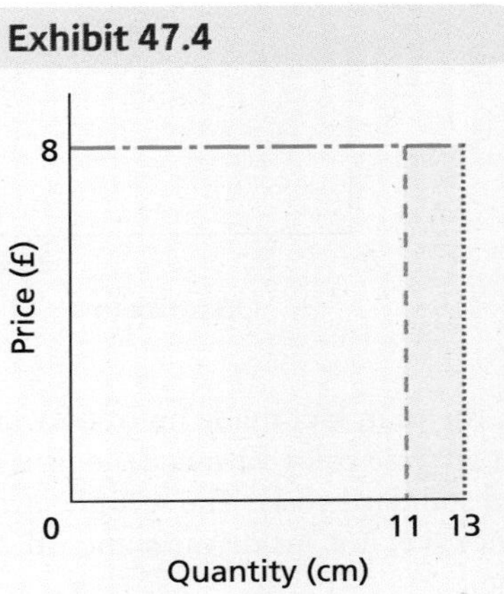

| Variance computed: | £ |
|---|---|
| Actual cost per unit £8 × 13 | 104 |
| Standard cost per unit £8 × 11 | 88 |
| Variance (adverse) | 16 |

Here again the variances for materials L and M are shown in exhibits by means of shaded areas. **The variances extend to the quantity lines and are, therefore, usage variances.** With material L, the variance is shown inside the standard cost area, and is, therefore, a favourable variance, whereas material M shows an adverse variance as it is outside the standard cost area.

## 3 Combinations of materials price and usage variances

Most variances are combinations of both materials price and usage variances. Sometimes one variance will be favourable while the other is adverse; sometimes both will be adverse variances; and at other times both will be favourable variances.

### Favourable and adverse variances combined

| *Material N* | |
|---|---|
| Standard price per metre | £6 |
| Standard usage per unit | 25 m |
| Actual price per metre | £7 |
| Actual usage per metre | 24 m |

The net variance is calculated as:

| | £ |
|---|---|
| Actual cost per unit £7 × 24 | 168 |
| Standard cost per unit £6 × 25 | 150 |
| Variance (adverse) | 18 |

Exhibit 47.5

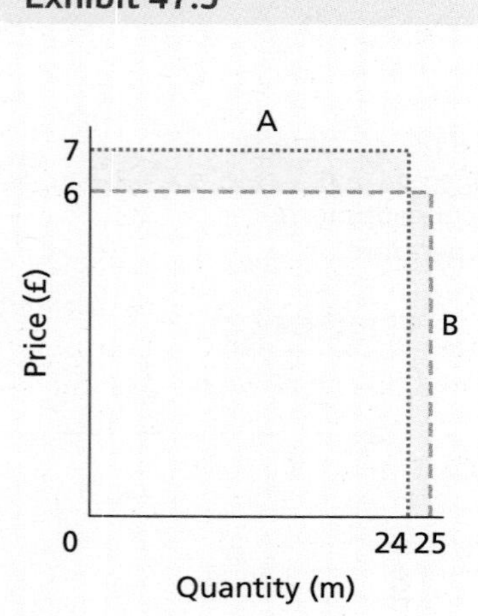


As Exhibit 47.5 shows, this is in fact made up of two variances. The first variance, shown as the shaded portion A, is an adverse price variance (i.e. it is outside the standard cost lines, therefore actual cost has exceeded standard cost). The second variance, shown as the shaded portion B, is a favourable usage variance (i.e. it is inside the standard cost lines, therefore actual usage has been less than standard usage).

The adverse price variance can therefore be seen to be £1 by a quantity of 24 = £24. The favourable usage variance can be seen to be a length of 1 metre by a price of £6 = £6. The net (adverse) variance is therefore made up:

| | £ |
|---|---|
| Adverse materials price variance | 24 |
| Favourable materials usage variance | 6 |
| Net (adverse) variance | 18 |

## Both adverse variances combined

| *Material O* | |
|---|---|
| Standard price per kg | £9 |
| Standard usage per unit | 13 kg |
| Actual price per kg | £11 |
| Actual usage per unit | 15 kg |

The net variance is computed:

| | £ |
|---|---|
| Actual cost per unit £11 × 15 | 165 |
| Standard cost per unit £9 × 13 | 117 |
| Variance (adverse) | 48 |

Exhibit 47.6

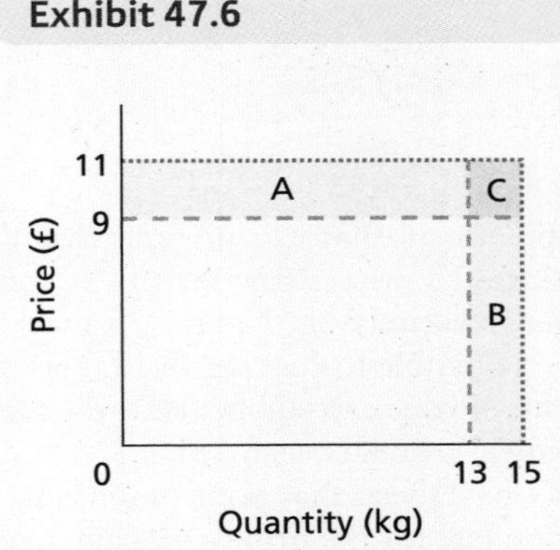


Exhibit 47.6 shows the shaded area A which is definitely a price variance of £2 × 13 = £26 adverse. Shaded area B is definitely a usage variance of 2 × £9 = £18 adverse. This makes up £44 of the variance, but there is the double-shaded area, C, of 2 × £2 = £4. This is really an area which is common to both usage and price. Sometimes, although not very often, this would be treated as a separate variance, but as detail is necessarily limited, in this book we will just add it to the price variance, making it £26 + £4 = £30, the usage variance being left at £18.

## Both favourable variances combined

| *Material P* | |
|---|---|
| Standard price per tonne | £20 |
| Standard usage per unit | 15 tonnes |
| Actual price per tonne | £19 |
| Actual usage per unit | 13 tonnes |

The net variance is computed:

| | £ |
|---|---|
| Actual cost per unit £19 × 13 | 247 |
| Standard cost per unit £20 × 15 | 300 |
| Variance (favourable) | 53 |

Exhibit 47.7

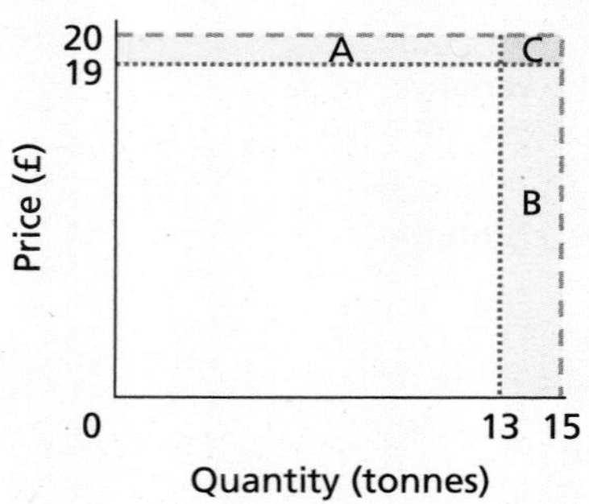


Exhibit 47.7 shows the shaded area A which is definitely a price variance of £1 × 13 = £13 favourable. Shaded area B is a usage variance of 2 × £19 = £38 favourable. The double-shaded area C of £1 × 2 = £2, making up the total variance of 53, would normally be added to the usage variance to make it £38 + £2 = £40.

## 47.4 Materials variances – analysis

### 1 Price variances

The price variance is a simple one in that it is obvious that the purchasing department has not been able to buy at the anticipated price. How far this is completely outside the powers of the purchasing department depends entirely on the facts. It may simply be that the rate of inflation is far greater than it had been possible to foresee, or that special forms of extra taxes have been introduced by the government. No one can surely blame the purchasing department for not knowing the secrets of the government's budget each year.

On the other hand, it may have been that poor purchasing control has meant that orders for materials have been placed too late for the firm to manage to get the right price in the market, or that materials which ought to have been bought in bulk have, in fact, been bought in small lots at uneconomic prices. If there are regular suppliers, a short-term gain by buying a cheaper lot from somewhere else could act against the business's benefit in the long run if its regular suppliers took umbrage.

Buying the cheapest materials does not always result in the greatest possible profit being attained.

**Activity 47.1** Why do you think this is the case?

In the end, after all the variance analysis has been undertaken, there must be someone to whom the responsibility for the price variance can be traced and who is then accountable for it. However, as Activity 47.1 illustrated, care must be taken not to give praise blindly or to criticise unfairly.

### 2 Usage variances

There are many reasons for excessive use of materials. Inferior materials can bring about a lot of waste, so can workers who are not as skilled as they ought to be. Perhaps the machinery is not suitable for the job, or there might even be deliberate wastage of material, e.g. wood wasted so that it can be taken home by workers as fuel, etc. The theft of material obviously aggravates a usage variance. Here again responsibility must be traced.

When you prepare one of these variance diagrams, there are two simple rules you can use to identify the type (price or usage) and nature (favourable or adverse) of the variance. What are they?

## 47.5 Key questions of variances

Before we look at the computation or analysis of any further variances, this is a convenient point to raise some fundamental questions about variances. They are:

1 Why do we wish to calculate this particular variance?
2 When it has been calculated, what action are we going to take based on it?
3 If we are not going to make an effective use of the variance, then why bother to calculate it?

## 47.6 Formulae for materials variances

We have deliberately waited until now to give you the formula for calculating each variance. We wanted you to understand what the variances were, rather than simply give you the formula to calculate them. They are as follows:

**Materials price variance** = **(Standard price − Actual price per unit) × Quantity purchased**
= **(SP − AP) × QP**

**Materials usage variance** = **(Standard quantity required − Actual quantity) × Standard price**
= **(SQ − AQ) × SP**

## 47.7 Inventory records under standard costing

It is worth noting at this point that when a business adopts a standard costing system it avoids the difficulties involving FIFO, LIFO or average inventory methods. In a standard costing system all materials received and issued are valued at the standard cost in the inventory account. There is no recording problem associated with changing prices during the period since they are separately recorded as variances.

Provided that standards are reviewed sufficiently often this system should ensure that the values of inventories are maintained close to their current value.

## 47.8 Disposition of variances

The question arises as to how the variances are to be brought into the financial statements of the business. There are, in fact, several methods of dealing with them.

They can be treated entirely as costs (if adverse variances) which are period costs and, therefore, are not included in the valuation of closing inventory of finished goods or work in progress. Alternatively, they may be brought in as product costs and therefore used in the valuation of closing inventory. Another variation is to treat those variances which are controllable as period costs, but to treat the uncontrollable variances as product costs.

All of these methods are acceptable for the financial statements which are prepared for external reporting.

**Before you read further, attempt Review Questions 47.1 and 47.2A.**

## 47.9 Costing for labour

Before looking at labour variances, we first need to consider the range of basis upon which labour may be paid. There is no exact definition of 'wages' and 'salaries'. In general, it is accepted that wages are earnings paid on a weekly basis, while salaries are paid monthly.

The methods can vary widely between employers and also as regards different employees in the same organisation. The main methods are:

1 Fixed amount salaries or wages – these are an agreed annual amount.
2 Piece rate – based on the number of units produced by the employee.
3 Commission – a percentage based on the amount of sales made by the employee.
4 Basic rate per hour – a fixed rate multiplied by number of hours worked.

Arrangements for rewarding people for working overtime (time exceeding normal hours worked) will vary widely. The rate will usually be in excess of that paid during normal working hours. People being paid salaries will often not be paid for overtime.

In addition, bonuses may be paid on top of the above earnings. Bonus schemes will also vary widely and may depend on the amount of net profit made by the company, or on the amount of work performed or production achieved, either by the whole company or else the department in which the employee works.

**It is important that the nature of payment to the employees is known before attempting to interpret the results of labour variance calculations. There will be significant differences in the possible explanations when employees are on salaries as opposed to basic rate as opposed to overtime, etc.**

## 47.10 Labour variances

The computation of labour variances is similar to that of material variances. With labour variances the analysis can be broken down into:

(*a*) wage rate variances
(*b*) labour efficiency variances.

***Note*: As you read and work through this section, you will notice great similarity between the labour variance formulae and the materials variance formulae. In actual fact, the only difference is a terminological one. The wage rate formula is identical in method to the materials price formula; and the labour efficiency formula is similarly identical to the materials usage formula. This is something that students frequently fail to grasp. In effect, it means that you need only learn one of the pairs of formulae, along with the terminology for the other pair. You can then complete any variance computation using both pairs of formulae.**

Because the computation of labour variances is so similar to those of materials variances only a few examples will be given.

### 1 Wage rate variance

| *Product A* | |
|---|---|
| Standard hours to produce | 100 |
| Actual hours to produce | 100 |
| Standard wage rate per hour | £0.9 |
| Actual wage rate per hour | £1.0 |

**Exhibit 47.8**

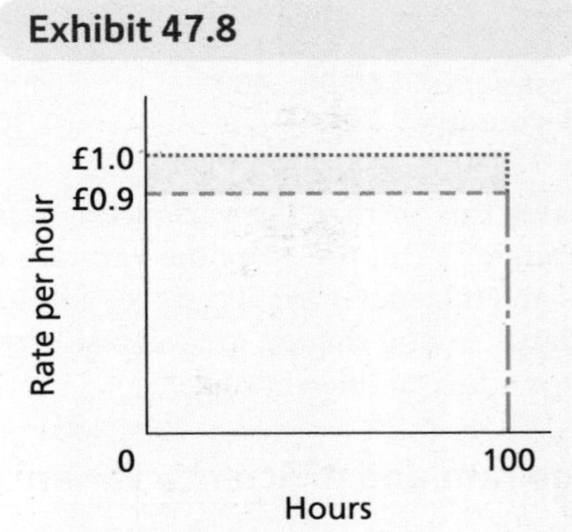


As the actual and standard hours are the same, then the only variance will be a wage rate variance, computed as follows:

| | £ |
|---|---|
| Actual cost per unit £1.0 × 100 | 100 |
| Standard cost per unit £0.9 × 100 | 90 |
| Variance (adverse) | 10 |

Exhibit 47.8 illustrates this in that the variance is represented by the shaded area. This is £0.1 by a quantity of 100, therefore the variance is £10. The variance extends to the wage rate line and it is thus a wage rate variance, and as the shaded area is outside the standard cost lines, indicated by lines marked ––––––, then it is an adverse variance.

## 2 Labour efficiency variance

| *Product B* | |
|---|---|
| Standard hours to produce | 400 |
| Actual hours to produce | 370 |
| Standard wage rate per hour | £1.0 |
| Actual wage rate per hour | £1.0 |

**Exhibit 47.9**

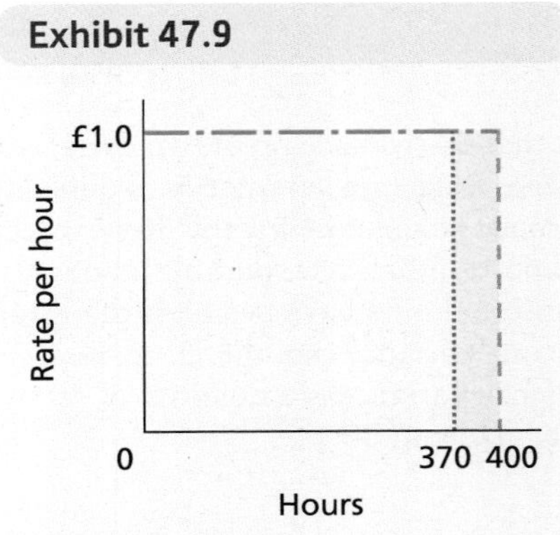


As the actual and standard wage rates are the same, then the only variance will be a labour efficiency variance, computed as follows:

| | £ |
|---|---|
| Actual cost per unit £1.0 × 370 | 370 |
| Standard cost per unit £1.0 × 400 | 400 |
| Variance (favourable) | 30 |

Exhibit 47.9 illustrates this in that the variance is represented by the shaded area. This is a quantity of 30 by a rate of £1.0, therefore the variance is £30. The variance extends to the time line, therefore this is an efficiency variance, as the job has been completed in a different number of hours from standard. As the shaded area is inside the standard cost lines indicated by lines marked -------, it is a favourable variance.

## 3 Combined wage rate and efficiency variance

| *Product C* | |
|---|---|
| Standard hours to produce | 500 |
| Actual hours to produce | 460 |
| Standard wage rate per hour | £0.9 |
| Actual wage rate per hour | £1.1 |

**Exhibit 47.10**

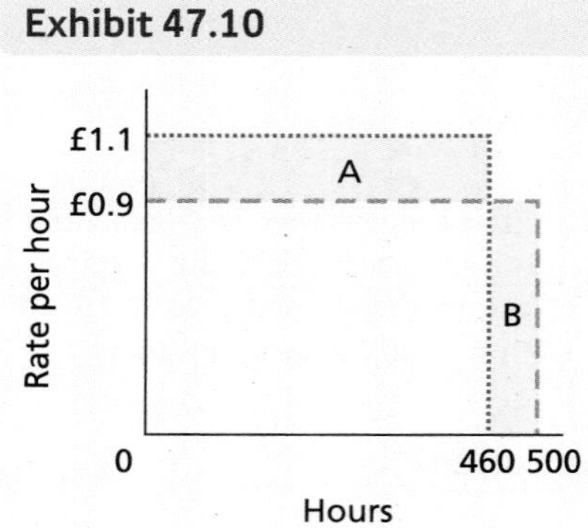


The net variance can be computed as:

| | £ |
|---|---|
| Actual cost per unit £1.1 × 460 | 506 |
| Standard cost per unit £0.9 × 500 | 450 |
| Variance (adverse) | 56 |

Exhibit 47.10 shows that this is made up of two variances. The first variance, shown as the shaded portion A, is an adverse wage rate variance (it is outside the standard cost lines, therefore it is an adverse variance because actual cost for this has exceeded standard cost). The second variance, shown as the shaded portion B, is a favourable labour efficiency variance (it is inside the standard cost lines, therefore actual hours have been less than standard hours).

The adverse wage rate variance can, therefore, be seen to be £0.2 by a quantity of 460 = £92. The favourable efficiency variance is a quantity of 40 by a price of £0.9 = £36. The net adverse variance is, therefore, made up of:

| | £ |
|---|---|
| Adverse wage rate variance | 92 |
| Favourable labour efficiency variance | 36 |
| Variance (adverse) | 56 |

## 47.11 Labour variances – analysis

Labour wage rates will probably be set in conjunction with the trade unions involved, so that this variance may not really be subject to control at any other level other than at the bargaining table with the unions involved. Nevertheless such a variance could arise because a higher grade of labour was being used than was necessary, even taking into account trade union needs. It might reflect a job running behind schedule that had to be finished off quickly even though higher grade labour was used. It might have been a rush job that also meant bringing in a higher grade of labour as well. The staffing policy of the firm may have come adrift because the firm had not recruited sufficient numbers of the various grades of labour.

Labour efficiency variances can be caused by a great number of things. Using unsuitable labour, unsuitable machinery, workers trying to slow work up so that more overtime rates of pay are earned, the day after a bank holiday, or the day before it, can affect performance; the morale of workers, the physical state of workers, using poor materials which slows up production, hold-ups because of bottlenecks in production, and so on. The possibilities are almost endless. At the same time, if the variance was worth calculating, some form of action should follow. Otherwise, there is no point at all in calculating such variances.

## 47.12 Formulae for labour variances

**Wage rate variance** = **(Standard wage rate per hour − Actual wage rate) × Actual hours worked**
= **(SR − AR) × AH**

**Labour efficiency variance** = **(Standard labour hours for actual production − Actual labour hours worked) × Standard wage rate per hour**
= **(SH − AH) × SR**

**Don't forget, if you compare these formulae to the materials variance formulae, you will see that they are actually the same, only the terminology is different, i.e. 'wage rate' instead of 'price'; 'efficiency' instead of 'usage'.**

### Learning outcomes

**You should now have learnt:**

1. Variance analysis can improve the operating efficiency of a business by pinpointing items in need of investigation.
2. Adverse variances are not necessarily 'bad'. They result from more having been used or spent than was anticipated. Similarly, favourable variances are not necessarily 'good'. It is the reason for the variance, not the effect, that determines whether it is 'good' or 'bad'.
3. The materials usage variance formula is identical to the labour efficiency variance formula. Only the terminology differs.
4. The materials price variance formula is identical to the wage rate variance formula. Only the terminology differs.

## Answers to activities

**47.1** Buying cheaply may produce a favourable variance for the purchasing manager. This makes that individual appear efficient. However, doing so may result in poor quality materials being used, resulting in more wastage, a greater amount of labour time because the workers take longer to do the job with inferior materials, and a product made up of poor materials may well damage the image of the firm because its products do not last as long as they used to. This will make the production manager look inefficient. Clearly, it is not fair that the production manager takes the blame while the purchasing manager is congratulated for a job well done. This is one very good reason why it is important that overall variances are broken down into their constituent parts. Only then can blame be attributed to the correct individual and praise given to those that deserve it.

**47.2** **Rule 1:** if the shaded box is horizontal, it is a price variance; if vertical, it is a usage variance. **Rule 2:** if the shaded box lies inside the standard cost line, the variance is favourable; if it lies outside, it is adverse.

## Review questions

***Advice*: Work carefully through Review Questions 47.1 and 47.3. If you have any difficulty, repeat them after 24 hours. Questions on this topic rarely contain any surprises. Once you get used to doing them, you will find they are actually quite easy to answer.**

**47.1** Calculate the materials variances from the following data

| | | | | |
|---|---|---|---|---|
| (*i*) | Material A: | Standard price per tonne | £10 | |
| | | Standard usage per unit | 30 | tonnes |
| | | Actual price per tonne | £9 | |
| | | Actual usage per unit | 35 | tonnes |
| (*ii*) | Material B: | Standard price per metre | £15 | |
| | | Standard usage per unit | 60 | metres |
| | | Actual price per metre | £16 | |
| | | Actual usage per unit | 54 | metres |
| (*iii*) | Material C: | Standard price per metre | £24 | |
| | | Standard usage per unit | 30 | metres |
| | | Actual price per metre | £28 | |
| | | Actual usage per unit | 38 | metres |
| (*iv*) | Material D: | Standard price per roll | £20 | |
| | | Standard usage per unit | 31 | rolls |
| | | Actual price per roll | £18 | |
| | | Actual usage per unit | 28 | rolls |
| (*v*) | Material E: | Standard price per kilo | £4 | |
| | | Standard usage per unit | 280 | kg |
| | | Actual price per kilo | £5 | |
| | | Actual usage per unit | 310 | kg |
| (*vi*) | Material F: | Standard price per litre | £75 | |
| | | Standard usage per unit | 5,000 | litres |
| | | Actual price per litre | £66 | |
| | | Actual usage per unit | 4,950 | litres |

**47.2A** Calculate the materials variances from the following data:

| | | | | |
|---|---|---|---|---|
| (*i*) | Material T: | Standard price per metre | £11 | |
| | | Standard usage per unit | 176 | metres |
| | | Actual price per metre | £11 | |
| | | Actual usage per unit | 171 | metres |
| (*ii*) | Material U: | Standard price per tonne | £42 | |
| | | Standard usage per unit | 50 | tonnes |
| | | Actual price per tonne | £45 | |
| | | Actual usage per unit | 50 | tonnes |
| (*iii*) | Material V: | Standard price per litre | £22 | |
| | | Standard usage per unit | 79 | litres |
| | | Actual price per litre | £22 | |
| | | Actual usage per unit | 83 | litres |
| (*iv*) | Material W: | Standard price per metre | £8 | |
| | | Standard usage per unit | 41 | metres |
| | | Actual price per metre | £10 | |
| | | Actual usage per unit | 41 | metres |
| (*v*) | Material X: | Standard price per tonne | £29 | |
| | | Standard usage per unit | 60 | tonnes |
| | | Actual price per tonne | £30 | |
| | | Actual usage per unit | 60 | tonnes |
| (*vi*) | Material Y: | Standard price per kilo | £55 | |
| | | Standard usage per unit | 84 | kg |
| | | Actual price per kilo | £55 | |
| | | Actual usage per unit | 78 | kg |

**47.3** Calculate the labour variances from the following data:

| | | *Standard hours* | *Actual hours* | *Standard wage rate (£)* | *Actual wage rate (£)* |
|---|---|---|---|---|---|
| (*i*) | Job J | 440 | 432 | 6.00 | 6.00 |
| (*ii*) | Job K | 230 | 230 | 5.60 | 5.80 |
| (*iii*) | Job L | 400 | 480 | 5.70 | 5.70 |
| (*iv*) | Job M | 280 | 206 | 7.00 | 7.00 |
| (*v*) | Job N | 136 | 136 | 5.70 | 5.10 |
| (*vi*) | Job O | 60 | 68 | 5.60 | 5.60 |
| (*vii*) | Job P | 140 | 154 | 5.50 | 5.50 |
| (*viii*) | Job Q | 200 | 200 | 5.80 | 6.10 |

**47.4A** Calculate the labour variances from the following data:

| | | *Standard hours* | *Actual hours* | *Standard wage rate (£)* | *Actual wage rate (£)* |
|---|---|---|---|---|---|
| (*i*) | Job a | 450 | 426 | 5.20 | 5.60 |
| (*ii*) | Job b | 660 | 680 | 4.90 | 4.70 |
| (*iii*) | Job c | 150 | 140 | 5.30 | 4.90 |
| (*iv*) | Job d | 510 | 520 | 5.10 | 5.40 |
| (*v*) | Job e | 420 | 450 | 5.20 | 4.80 |
| (*vi*) | Job f | 810 | 780 | 4.60 | 5.00 |

**47.5** The company for which you are the accountant manufactures three related, but different, products. These are dishwashers, washing machines and refrigerators. Each product has a standard time per unit of production. These are:

→

| | |
|---|---|
| dishwashers | 10 hours |
| washing machines | 12 hours |
| refrigerators | 14 hours |

In the month of March the actual production was:

| | |
|---|---|
| dishwashers | 150 |
| washing machines | 100 |
| refrigerators | 90 |

and the labour details were:

| | |
|---|---|
| actual hours worked | 4,100 |
| standard hourly rate of pay | £4 |
| actual wages incurred | £18,450 |

**You are required to:**

(*a*) Explain the term 'standard hour'.

(*b*) Calculate the standard hours produced in the month of March.

(*c*) Calculate the following variances, using the above data:

(*i*) total direct labour variance

(*ii*) direct labour rate variance

(*iii*) direct labour efficiency variance.

(*d*) Give **two** possible causes for **each** of the labour rate and efficiency variances in (*c*).

*(AQA (Northern Examinations and Assessment Board): GCE A-level)*

**47.6A** Central Grid plc manufactures tungsten parts which pass through two processes, machining and polishing, before being transferred to finished goods. The management of the company have in operation a system of standard costing and budgetary control. The standard cost and budget information for April 2018 has been established by the management accountant as follows:

**Standard Cost and Budget Details for April 2018**

| | *Machining* | *Polishing* |
|---|---|---|
| Standard cost per unit | | |
| Direct material | £5 | – |
| Direct labour | £12 | £4.50 |
| Budgeted output – units (See Note below) | 16,000 | 16,000 |
| Budgeted direct labour hours | 48,000 | 24,000 |

*Note:* Output passes through both processes and there is no opening or closing work in progress.

*Additional information:*

1 The actual production costs and details for April 2018 are as follows:

(*i*) The output that passed through the two processes was 12,000 units and there was no opening or closing work in progress.

(*ii*) Direct material used at standard prices was £64,150.

(*iii*) Direct material used at actual prices was £60,390.

(*iv*) The direct wages bill and the direct labour hours clocked for the machining department were:

| | £ | *Hours* |
|---|---|---|
| Machining department | 153,000 | 34,000 |

2 Variances for the polishing department have been calculated and reveal the following:

| | |
|---|---|
| Labour efficiency variance | £3,000 Adverse |
| Labour rate variance | Nil |

**Required:**

(*a*) Calculate the total direct materials variance and its analysis into:
  (*i*) direct materials usage variance
  (*ii*) direct materials price variance.

(*b*) Calculate the overall direct labour variance for the machining department and analyse this variance into:
  (*i*) direct labour efficiency variance
  (*ii*) direct labour rate variance.

(*c*) Identify the possible reasons for each of the variances calculated for the machining department in (*a*) and (*b*) above and also for the variances given for the polishing department.

(*d*) Discuss possible interrelationships between these variances.

*(AQA (Associated Examining Board): GCE A-level)*

**47.7** Borrico Ltd manufacture a single product and they had recently introduced a system of budgeting and variance analysis. The following information is available for the month of July 2018:

| 1 | *Budget* | *Actual* |
|---|---|---|
| | £ | £ |
| Direct materials | 200,000 | 201,285 |
| Direct labour | 313,625 | 337,500 |
| Variable manufacturing overhead | 141,400 | 143,000 |
| Variable sales overhead | 64,400 | 69,500 |
| Fixed manufacturing overhead | 75,000 | 71,000 |
| Administration costs | 150,000 | 148,650 |

**2** Standard costs were:
Direct labour 48,250 hours at £6.50 per hour.
Direct materials 20,000 kilograms at £10 a kilogram.

**3** Actual manufacturing costs were:
Direct labour 50,000 hours at £6.75 per hour.
Direct materials 18,900 kilograms at £10.65 a kilogram.

**4** Budgeted sales were 20,000 units at £50 a unit.
Actual sales were
  15,000 units at £52 a unit
  5,200 units at £56 a unit

**5** There was no work in progress or inventory of finished goods.

**Required:**

(*a*) An accounting statement showing the budgeted and actual gross and net profits or losses for July 2018.

(*b*) The following variances for July 2018.
  (*i*) Direct materials cost variance, direct materials price variance and direct materials usage variance.
  (*ii*) Direct labour cost variance, direct labour rate variance and direct labour efficiency variance.

(*c*) What use can the management of Borrico Ltd make of the variances calculated in (*b*) above?

*(AQA (Associated Examining Board): GCE A-level)*

**47.8A**

(*a*) How does a system of standard costing enable a business to operate on the principle of management by exception?

(*b*) Some of the following materials and labour variances have been wrongly calculated, although the figures used are correct. Recalculate the variances, showing clearly the formulae you have used, and state whether the variances are adverse or favourable.

| | | |
|---|---|---|
| (*i*) | *Total Materials Variance* | |
| | (Standard price − Actual price) | (Standard quantity − Actual quantity) |
| | = (£8.42 − £8.24) | (1,940 litres − 2,270 litres) |
| | = (£0.18) | (−330 litres) |
| | = £59.40 *adverse* | |
| (*ii*) | *Materials Price Variance* | |
| | (Standard price − Actual price) | Standard quantity |
| | = (£8.42 − £8.24) | 1,940 |
| | = £349.20 *favourable* | |
| (*iii*) | *Materials Usage Variance* | |
| | (Standard quantity − Actual quantity) | Standard price |
| | = (1,940 − 2,270) | £8.42 |
| | = £2,778.6 *adverse* | |
| (*iv*) | *Total Labour Variance* | |
| | (Actual hours − Standard hours) | (Actual rate − Standard rate) |
| | = (860 − 800) | (£6.14 − £6.53) |
| | = (60 hours) | (−£0.39) |
| | = £23.4 *adverse* | |
| (*v*) | *Wage Rate Variance* | |
| | (Standard rate − Actual rate) | Actual hours |
| | = (£6.53 − £6.14) | 860 |
| | = £335.4 *favourable* | |
| (*vi*) | *Labour Efficiency Variance* | |
| | (Actual hours − Standard hours) | Standard rate |
| | = (860 − 800) | £6.53 |
| | = £391.80 *favourable* | |

(*Edexcel: GCE A-level*)

**47.9A** Makers Ltd assembles computer games machines. Standard costs have been prepared as follows:

| | *Gamesmaster* | *Gotchya* |
|---|---|---|
| | £ | £ |
| Standard cost: | | |
| *Direct material:* boards | 5 | 10 |
| components | 20 | 30 |
| *Direct labour:* assembly | 5 | 5 |
| testing | 5 | 10 |
| Overheads charged at 200% | 20 | 30 |
| | 55 | 85 |
| Profit margin | 11 | 15 |
| Standard selling price | 66 | 100 |

The standard direct labour rate is £5 per hour.
During May 2018, 5,000 Gamesmasters were sold at £60 each and 2,000 Gotchyas at £110 each.

Actual costs were incurred as follows:

| | £ |
|---|---|
| 5,050 Gamesmaster boards | 26,000 |
| 5,060 sets Gamesmaster components | 75,000 |
| 2,010 Gotchya boards | 28,390 |
| 2,025 sets Gotchya components | 56,409 |
| 10,000 assembly labour hours @ £4.90 | 49,000 |
| 7,000 testing labour hours at £5.10 | 35,700 |
| Overheads | 160,000 |
| | 430,499 |

There is no opening or closing inventory.

**Required:**
A schedule of direct materials and direct labour variances for the month.

(*Welsh Joint Education Committee: GCE A-level*)

**47.10A** The following diagram reflects costs under a standard costing system. Assume that all the variances are *unfavourable*. State, with reasons, which rectangle(s) represent:

(*i*) the standard cost
(*ii*) the actual cost
(*iii*) the total labour cost variance
(*iv*) the efficiency variance
(*v*) the wage rate variance.

(*Edexcel: GCE A-level*)

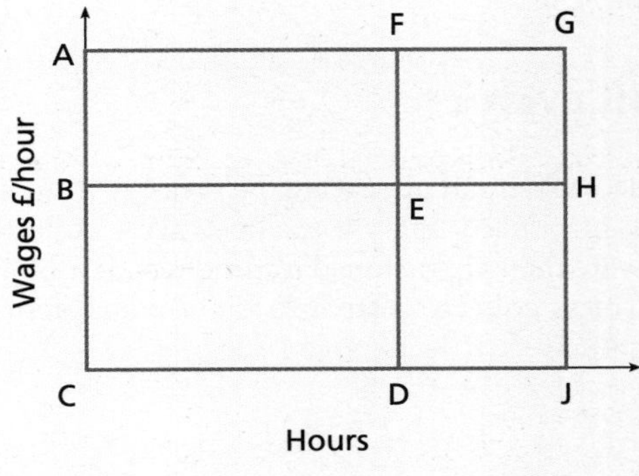

chapter 48

# Overhead and sales variances

## Learning objectives

**After you have studied this chapter, you should be able to:**

- calculate overhead expenditure variances, volume variances, efficiency variances, and capacity variances
- calculate sales price, volume and mix variances
- describe the similarities between the variable production overhead efficiency variance and both the labour efficiency variance and the materials usage variance
- identify appropriate reasons why variances found have occurred

## Introduction

In this chapter, you'll learn about another two groups of variances: those relating to overheads (both variable and fixed) and sales, and how to calculate them and interpret the results.

## 48.1 Management overheads

In Chapter 42, the problem of allocating overheads (i.e. indirect manufacturing expenses) to jobs or processes was introduced. First, these costs were collected in cost centres. The total costs of each cost centre were then apportioned to products or jobs as they passed through the cost centre.

Suppose a business collects costs into three manufacturing departments, with the result as shown in Exhibit 48.1:

**Exhibit 48.1**

| | *Department* | | |
|---|---|---|---|
| | *A* | *B* | *C* |
| | £ | £ | £ |
| Fixed overhead cost | 50,000 | 40,000 | 20,000 |
| Variable overhead cost | 30,000 | 35,000 | 40,000 |
| Total overhead | 80,000 | 75,000 | 60,000 |
| Direct labour hours | 10,000 | 30,000 | 15,000 |
| Machine hours | 20,000 | 2,000 | 15,000 |

A decision has to be taken as to which activity, either labour hours or machine time, is the *dominant factor* in the department and will, therefore, provide the most appropriate basis for apportioning the overheads to products or jobs manufactured in each department.

***Note*: The focus on the 'dominant factor'. This is the key to appropriate selection of the apportionment basis to use.**

In the case of Department A, machine hours is the dominant factor. Overheads, therefore, will be charged on the basis £80,000/20,000 hours = £4 per machine hour. The business will record for each job or process the number of machine hours taken and the overheads will be allocated on this total of hours at £4 per hour.

In Department B, labour is the dominant factor. Overheads will be charged on a labour hour rate calculated at £75,000/30,000 hours = £2.50 per hour.

Department C does not exhibit any dominant activity and could be expressed in either a machine hour rate or a labour hour rate. Some businesses, where rates of pay in a department are stable and the mix of labour at different rates of pay stays the same, prefer to express the overheads as a percentage of labour cost. In Department C, if the direct labour cost was £75,000 it could be £60,000/£75,000 = 80%. Thus the labour cost for all work going through Department C would be collected and overheads allocated at 80% of the labour cost figure. Alternatively, either the direct labour hours or the machine hours could be used. Both give an overhead rate of £60,000/15,000 = £4 per hour.

## 48.2 Predetermined rates

The usual procedure, whether or not standard costing is being used, is to predetermine the overhead absorption rates using budgeted figures for both the overhead costs and the activity measure, whether it be machine or labour hours or something else, such as the direct labour cost. This process has a number of advantages. It not only allows appropriate current estimates to be made for things such as price quotations, but also avoids the problem of overhead rates that fluctuate at different times of the year due to seasonal factors.

For example, an ice-cream manufacturer is likely to be much more active in the summer months than in the winter. Because activity is low in winter, the overhead absorption rate is likely to rise steeply in the winter, as overhead costs will not all reduce proportionately – i.e. they will not all be purely variable in nature. It therefore makes more sense to view the overheads in this type of business on an annual cycle and recover the same amount of overhead throughout the year.

## 48.3 Variances in overhead recovery

In all situations where budgeted figures are used, there are almost certainly going to be variances at the end of a budget period. Let's take figures from Exhibit 48.1 for Department A as the budget, and compare them with actual performance. This is shown in Exhibit 48.2 on the next page.

The actual machine hours worked of 25,000 will have been used to allocate overheads to production at the rate of £4 per hour. As a result, £100,000 will have been allocated. Compared to actual overheads of £89,000 this represents an overabsorption of £11,000. The recovery would only have been exactly equal to actual overhead costs if 22,250 machine hours had been worked, i.e. 22,250 × £4 = £89,000.

Section 47.8 described the treatment of variances identified when standard costing is used. In a cost accounting system *not* using standard costing, any overabsorption or underabsorption of overheads would be either:

(*a*) transferred wholly to profit or loss for the period;
(*b*) allocated between closing inventories and cost of goods sold; or
(*c*) carried forward to the next period.

**Exhibit 48.2**

| | Department A | |
|---|---|---|
| | *Budget figures* | *Actual figures* |
| | £ | £ |
| Fixed overhead | 50,000 | 52,000 |
| Variable overhead | 30,000 | 37,000 |
| Total overhead | 80,000 | 89,000 |
| Machine hours | 20,000 | 25,000 |
| Machine hour rate £4 | | |

The first would be used if the difference was felt to be due to below 'normal' levels of achievement that could and should have been avoided – i.e. if it represents an 'abnormal' loss or an 'abnormal' gain; for example, if the number of hours worked had dropped due to bad management planning. (This is what you learnt in Section 42.6, when normal and abnormal losses were discussed.)

The second would be used if the differences were felt to be due to poor estimates of the original budgets. That is, if the activity levels achieved were 'normal' but the budget was based on something either above or below 'normal' activity. As a result, the overheads overabsorbed or underabsorbed represent costs that should be removed/added to the production cost for the period.

**The third would apply only to interim financial statements, not those prepared at a period end.**

Activity 48.1

Why?

## Analysing the variances

The £11,000 variance found in Exhibit 48.2 between the amount recovered of £100,000 and the actual overhead cost of £89,000 can be analysed into a group of constituent variances in the normal manner of standard costing. In the example we have used, the variance can be due to either:

(*a*) the prices paid for goods and services were different from original estimates or standards – an 'expenditure' variance (sometimes called a 'budget' variance – both terms mean the same thing); or

(*b*) the volume of activity during the period was different from the original estimate – a 'volume' variance (for fixed overheads) or an 'efficiency' variance (for variable overheads).

Let's look at both these types of variances.

### (a) Expenditure variance

An expenditure variance represents the difference between the actual cost of an overhead and its budgeted overhead cost after the level of activity used to calculate the total budgeted overhead cost is adjusted to the actual level of operational activity and the budgeted overhead cost recalculated.

From Exhibit 48.2 the budget figures need to be increased to take account of the fact that activity measured in machine hours has increased from 20,000 to 25,000 hours. **This will not, of**

**course, increase the fixed overhead** – only the variable overheads, which we will assume increase by 25% in line with the increase in the machine hours. (You can see from Exhibit 48.2 that the £4 overhead recovery rate comprised 5/8 (£2.50) for the fixed element and 3/8 (£1.50) for the variable element.) The adjusted budget figures are shown in Exhibit 48.3.

## Exhibit 48.3

| | *Department A* | | | |
|---|---|---|---|---|
| | a<br>*Original budget* | b<br>*Adjusted budget* | c<br>*Actual* | b − c<br>*Variance* |
| Fixed overhead | 50,000 | 50,000 | 52,000 | (2,000) |
| Variable overhead | 30,000 | 37,500 | 37,000 | 500 |
| | 80,000 | 87,500 | 89,000 | (1,500) |

The actual expenditure of £89,000 exceeds the adjusted budget by £1,500. You can see from Exhibit 48.3 that this represents an adverse fixed overhead expenditure variance of £2,000 and a favourable variable expenditure variance of £500.

### (b) Volume variance

Apart from the cost of the overheads, another factor was included in the calculations when the budgets were originally calculated – the estimated number of machine hours that would be worked. In the above example, we estimated that 20,000 machine hours would be worked. In fact, 25,000 machine hours were worked. This additional 5,000 hours would not matter if *all* the overheads were variable, since the rate per hour would be constant at different activities. However, where fixed costs are concerned, increasing the activity will increase the amount recovered above the level required and, if activity is below budget, insufficient fixed overhead will be recovered.

As you know, in this example the overhead rate of £4 per machine hour was split:

$$\text{Fixed} \quad \frac{50{,}000}{80{,}000} \times £4 = £2.50$$

$$\text{Variable} \quad \frac{30{,}000}{80{,}000} \times £4 = £1.50$$

As a result, when the actual machine hours increased from 20,000 to 25,000 we recovered 5,000 × £2.50 = £12,500 more than was actually incurred on the fixed overheads, i.e. there is a favourable variance (a volume variance) of £12,500.

An alternative way of viewing this is to compare the amount of overheads recovered at 25,000 hours with the flexible budget for this level of activity:

| | | *Total* | *Fixed* | *Variable* |
|---|---|---|---|---|
| Recovered 25,000 × £4 = | | 100,000 | 62,500 | 37,500 |
| Budget variable cost 25,000 × £1.50 | 37,500 | | | (37,500) |
| Fixed cost | 50,000 | | (50,000) | |
| | | (87,500) | | |
| Volume variance | | 12,500 | 12,500 | – |

This volume variance shows that by increasing the utilisation of the fixed resources, considerable savings were made. (This is often the case.) The £12,500 is, therefore, a favourable variance in terms of the original machine-hours-rate-based budget.

## Summary of variances

The analysis so far shows:

| | £ | £ |
|---|---|---|
| Overhead recovered at actual level of activity (25,000 × £4) | | 100,000 |
| Fixed overhead variance at this level of activity – adverse | 2,000 | |
| Variable overhead variance at this level of activity – favourable | (500) | |
| | | 1,500 |
| | | 101,500 |
| Volume variance – favourable | | (12,500) |
| Actual level of expenditure overhead | | 89,000 |

This analysis has revealed that the variances to be investigated are the adverse fixed expenditure variance of £2,000 and the favourable variable expenditure variance of £500. The remaining £12,500 volume variance was due to the increase in activity and has been eliminated from further investigation after the budget was adjusted (i.e. flexed) for the change in activity.

However, while it does not apparently require further investigation, the volume variance does require to be dealt with. As it stands, £12,500 too much has been recovered. That is, production has been charged with £12,500 too much. If you are not operating a standard costing system and if it was due to an error in the estimation of 'normal' activity, you would need to deal with it using the second of the three approaches described earlier in this section – allocate it between closing inventories and the cost of goods sold. (We will return to this variance at the end of the next section.)

This is not the end of the analysis required of the variable variances. You need to do more than simply find the difference between what it should have cost at the actual level of activity (i.e. the flexed budget) and what it actually cost. You need to look at what was actually produced and use that information to identify precisely which variances are to be investigated.

## 48.4 Assessing variances

In an organisation manufacturing products that has adopted a standard costing system, the cost of the overheads are normally directly related to the products produced. For example, if a Superwidget is manufactured in Department A and it is estimated that it requires two machine hours to produce each Superwidget, the standard overhead cost per Superwidget will be 2 × £4 = £8.

If in the actual period, a Superwidget takes less than two hours to make there will be a favourable variance which will be costed at £4 per hour. Similarly, if more than two hours are taken, there will be an adverse (i.e. unfavourable) variance costed on the same basis.

Let's again use the example from Exhibit 48.1 and assume Department A manufactures only Superwidgets, that the original budget is to make 10,000 Superwidgets, and that the actual production of Superwidgets is 12,000. We can now flex the budget using the number of Superwidgets produced. This is shown in Exhibit 48.4.

Now that we are no longer using the machine hours to flex the budget, we can see another variance: 12,000 widgets should take 24,000 hours at the standard rate of two machine hours per Superwidget. Since the actual hours are 25,000, 1,000 times £4, i.e. £4,000 too much has been charged to production. In effect, this represents a favourable variance from the machine-hour-based flexed budget as actual costs do not include this £4,000. (This is quite complex as the number of machine hours worked is 1,000 higher than expected, so ought to be an adverse

**Exhibit 48.4**

| | Department A | | |
|---|---|---|---|
| | *Original budget* | *Flexed budget* | *Actual* |
| | £ | £ | £ |
| Total overhead expenditure | 80,000 | 96,000 | 89,000 |
| Machine hours | 20,000 | 24,000 | 25,000 |
| Machine hours per Superwidget | 2 | 2 | |
| Number of units produced | 10,000 | 12,000 | 12,000 |

variance. It would have been had the machine-hour-based overhead rate been used to flex the budget. It was not.) *Note:* This is made up of both fixed *and* variable overhead.

Using the flexed budget, we get a standard overhead recovery at the actual level of output (now based on units produced) of £96,000 (i.e. 12,000 Superwidgets at two machine hours each equals 24,000 machine hours at £4 per hour). Actual costs were £89,000. The total variance between the flexed budget figure of £96,000 and the actual expenditure of £89,000 is therefore £7,000. This can be broken down as shown below. *Note*: The first two lines would not normally be included as the basis for the budgeted activity has been changed from machine hours to quantity produced. It is included here to illustrate the link between the effect of using the different overhead rate.

| | £ |
|---|---|
| Overhead recovered at actual level of activity (25,000 × £4) | 100,000 |
| Variable overhead efficiency variance favourable | (4,000) |
| Standard cost of overheads for 12,000 actual Superwidgets produced × £8 = | 96,000 |
| Variable overhead expenditure variance – favourable (*see* below) | (500) |
| Variable overhead efficiency variance – adverse (*see* below) | 1,500 |
| Fixed overhead expenditure variance – adverse (*see* below) | 2,000 |
| Fixed overhead volume variance – favourable (*see* below) | (10,000) |
| Actual overhead expenditure | 89,000 |

The £4,000 favourable variance represents the amount the overhead over-recovery would have increased had the original machine-hour-based overhead rate been used throughout rather than the output-based rate.

Compare this analysis with the one shown at the end of the *summary of variances* part of Section 48.3. The comparison should tell you three things. Firstly, the choice of the basis on which to flex a budget can significantly affect the information provided concerning the existence of variances and their cause. Secondly, if budgets are not flexed in a timely manner, variances can arise that need to be dealt with in the financial statements and in the valuation of stock that may be significantly greater than they should have been.

Finally, you can now see that the original £12,500 favourable volume variance comprised favourable variances of £4,000 for the machine hours and a fixed volume variance of £10,000 and an adverse efficiency variance of £1,500. You will see an alternative interpretation of the £12,500 variance in the next section.

## 48.5 Formulae for variances

In this section, we will use the Superwidget example data. The formula for each overhead variance is as follows:

Variable overhead expenditure variance
= Actual cost − (Actual hours worked × Standard rate)
= AC − (AH × SR)
= £37,000 − (25,000 × £1.50) = £500 *Favourable*

Variable overhead efficiency variance
= (Actual hours worked − Actual production in standard hours) × Standard rate
= (AH − APSH) × SR
= (25,000 − 24,000) × £1.50 = £1,500 *Adverse* (Note 2)

Fixed overhead expenditure variance
= Budgeted fixed production overheads − Actual fixed production overheads
= BFPO − AFPO
= £50,000 − £52,000 = £2,000 *Adverse*

Fixed overhead volume variance (Note 1)
= (Actual production in standard hours × Standard rate) − Budgeted fixed production overheads
= (APSH × SR) − BFPO
= (24,000 × £2.50) − £50,000 = £10,000 *Favourable*

The fixed overhead volume variance can be further divided into:

Fixed overhead efficiency variance (Note 1)
= (Actual hours worked − Actual production in standard hours) × Standard rate
= (AH − APSH) × SR
= (25,000 − 24,000) × £2.50 = £2,500 *Adverse*

Fixed overhead capacity variance (Note 1)
= (Actual hours worked − Budgeted hours to be worked) × Standard rate
= (AH − BH) × SR
= (25,000 − 20,000) × £2.50 = £12,500 *Favourable*

*Note 1*: The last three variances – the fixed overhead volume variance and its component variances, the fixed overhead efficiency and capacity variances – *are only calculated when absorption costing is being used*. When the basis of the costing system is marginal costing, only the first three are used (because you do not link fixed costs to the level of output). In a marginal-costing-based environment, the total standard overhead cost for the 12,000 Superwidgets would be 12,000 at £3.00 variable overhead cost per Superwidget (= £36,000) plus the budgeted fixed cost of £50,000.

Rather than simply calculating the fixed overhead volume variance, you should normally calculate the efficiency and capacity variances. However, you need to be aware that together they represent the fixed overhead volume variance and so you should be able to calculate it if required. Replacing the favourable fixed overhead volume variance of £10,000 in the Superwidgets example with the fixed overhead efficiency and capacity variances produces the following breakdown of costs and variances:

| | £ |
|---|---|
| Standard cost of overheads for 12,000 actual Superwidgets produced × £8 = | 96,000 |
| Variable overhead expenditure variance – *favourable* | (500) |
| Variable overhead efficiency variance – *adverse* | 1,500 |
| Fixed overhead expenditure variance – *adverse* | 2,000 |
| Fixed overhead efficiency variance – *adverse* | 2,500 |
| Fixed overhead capacity variance – *favourable* | (12,500) |
| Actual overhead expenditure | 89,000 |

**The formula for the variable overhead efficiency variance is the same formula as is used for the fixed overhead efficiency variance. As you will soon learn, it is also the same as the formula for the labour efficiency variance and the material usage variance.**

***Note 2*: Efficiency variances are *always* adverse when less is recovered than should have been.**

## 48.6 A comprehensive example

The organisation in this example operates standard costing based on absorption costing. The data set out below refers to a cost centre for a particular period:

### Budget

Variable overheads (extract) flexible budget

| *Output* | | *Cost* |
|---|---|---|
| *In units* | *In standard hours* | £ |
| 9,800 | 49,000 | 98,000 |
| 9,900 | 49,500 | 99,000 |
| 10,000 | 50,000 | 100,000 |
| 10,100 | 50,500 | 101,000 |
| 10,200 | 51,000 | 102,000 |
| Fixed overheads | | 150,000 |

Budgeted volume of production 10,000 units

Standard labour hours per unit = 5

### Actual

| | |
|---|---|
| Variable overhead | £104,000 |
| Fixed overhead | £160,000 |
| Direct labour hours worked | 49,000 hours |
| Units of production | 9,900 units |

The 9,900 units of production are the equivalent of 9,900 × 5 = 49,500 standard direct labour hours.

Before calculating the variances, let's consider the data we've been given. The flexible budget shows that each unit of production has a standard variable overhead cost of £10. Alternatively, this can be expressed as £10 ÷ 5 = £2 per standard hour of labour. **It should not be assumed that this rate of £2 also applies to levels of production outside the range shown** – there may well be step costs, such as additional supervision, which **would alter** the standard variable overhead rate at levels of output outside the range shown.

The fixed costs are thought likely to remain fixed provided the range of output does not extend too far above or below the budgeted volume of production. The fixed standard rate is based on the budgeted volume of production and is therefore £150,000 ÷ 50,000 = £3 per standard hour of labour, or £150,000 ÷ 10,000 = £15 per unit.

The standard unit overhead cost is: £10 + £15 = £25 per unit or £2 + £3 = £5 per labour hour.

**This budgeted volume of production is likely to be the level of output thought of as being 'normal' and acceptable in the long run. It is referred to as the normal volume of production or, more commonly, as the 'normal level of activity'.**

### Calculation of variances

Firstly, it is helpful to calculate the overall net variance which is to be analysed. This is found using the standard cost of the actual units produced:

| | | | £ |
|---|---|---|---|
| Actual total overhead costs | | | 264,000 |
| Standard cost of actual production 9,900 × £25 = | | | 247,500 |
| Total variance | | *Adverse* | (16,500) |

This is broken down into the five component variances as follows.

**Variable overhead expenditure variance**

| | | | £ |
|---|---|---|---|
| Actual cost | | | 104,000 |
| Actual hours worked at standard rate = 49,000 × £2 | | | 98,000 |
| Variable expenditure variance | | *Adverse* | (6,000) |

**Variable overhead efficiency variance**

| | | | | |
|---|---|---|---|---|
| Actual hours worked | 49,000 | | | |
| Actual production in standard hours | 49,500 | | | |
| Variable efficiency variance | 500 | × £2 | *Favourable* | 1,000 |

**Fixed overhead expenditure variance**

| | | |
|---|---|---|
| Budgeted fixed production overheads | | 150,000 |
| Actual fixed production overheads | | 160,000 |
| Fixed expenditure variance | *Adverse* | (10,000) |

**Fixed overhead efficiency variance**

| | | | | |
|---|---|---|---|---|
| Actual hours worked | 49,000 | | | |
| Actual production in standard hours | 49,500 | | | |
| Variable efficiency variance | 500 | × £3 | *Favourable* | 1,500 |

**Fixed overhead capacity variance**

| | | | | |
|---|---|---|---|---|
| Actual hours worked | 49,000 | | | |
| Budgeted hours to be worked | 50,000 | | | |
| Fixed volume variance | 1000 | × £3 | *Adverse* | (3,000) |

**Summary of variances**

| | | |
|---|---|---|
| Variable expenditure | *Adverse* | (6,000) |
| Variable efficiency | *Favourable* | 1,000 |
| Fixed expenditure | *Adverse* | (10,000) |
| Fixed efficiency | *Favourable* | 1,500 |
| Fixed capacity | *Adverse* | (3,000) |
| | *Net Adverse* | (16,500) |

## Reconciliation of standard and actual cost

| | |
|---|---|
| Standard cost of actual production 9,900 units × £25 | (247,500) |
| Variable expenditure – *adverse* | (6,000) |
| Efficiency variance – *favourable* | 1,000 |
| Fixed expenditure – *adverse* | (10,000) |
| Fixed efficiency variance – *favourable* | 1,500 |
| Fixed capacity variance – *adverse* | (3,000) |
| Actual cost of overheads | (264,000) |

## 48.7 Variances and management action

**The calculation of variances and their explanation to managers is of no value unless the information so revealed is used when making decisions which change subsequent activities. The question then arises as to whether every variance needs some form of action. It is not possible to be dogmatic here. It really does depend on the circumstances. In some cases, a fairly large variance may be insignificant whereas, in others, even a small amount may call for urgent action.**

There is no doubt that variance calculations of the *right* type, given to the *right* people at the *right* time, which have an effect upon subsequent operations, can make a significant positive impact.

On the other hand, much of the effort put into variance calculation in many organisations just goes to waste, as managers do not act appropriately on the information they have received. There are many reasons why this may occur, some obvious, some less so. However, it is often because a poor 'selling' job has been done by the management accountant on the managers concerned: either the information provided is not really what the managers require to enable them to tackle their jobs properly or they have not been able to convince the managers that variance analysis is worthwhile. This is the major problem of variance analysis. Many managers and other decision-makers view it as an accounting tool which is far too difficult to understand, so they ignore it.

## 48.8 Sales variances

The analysis of the difference between budgeted sales levels and actual sales levels can obviously have an important bearing on the depth of understanding of results. The main issues which are important in analysing sales are the sales price, volume, and mix. These are analysed using three variances:

(*a*) selling price variances
(*b*) volume variances
(*c*) mix variances.

**The selling price variance measures the overall profit difference caused by the budgeted unit selling price and actual unit selling price being different.** If the budget was to sell 100 widgets at £5 each and the actual sales were 100 widgets of £4.50 each, there would be a profit reduction of £50 due to the adverse selling price variance of 50p per unit on the 100 units sold.

The volume variances in sales is measured in terms of the difference between the budgeted and the actual quantity sold. The impact of changes in volume of sales on profit can only be measured if we know the profitability of the units sold. This is considered at gross profit level. Thus, if the budget is to sell 100 widgets with a unit gross margin of £2 but only 90 are sold, this represents an adverse variance of 10 units at the margin of £2, i.e. a loss of profit of £20. If several products are being sold, the variance is calculated on the basis of the total units actually sold in the proportions originally budgeted.

Let's look at an example.

### Exhibit 48.5

| *Product* | *Budget sales units* | *Budget %* | *Budget unit gross profit margin* | *Total budget gross profit margin* | *Actual sales units* | *Actual sales in budget %* |
|---|---|---|---|---|---|---|
| | | | £ | £ | | |
| X | 200 | 33.3 | 1.00 | 200 | 250 | 240 |
| Y | 200 | 33.3 | 1.50 | 300 | 190 | 240 |
| Z | 200 | 33.3 | 3.50 | 700 | 280 | 240 |
| | 600 | 100.0 | | 1,200 | 720 | 720 |

The *volume variance* is calculated by comparing actual sales (in the same proportion of total sales as was used in the budget percentage mix) with the original budget using the budgeted gross profit margins:

| Product | Actual sales in same proportions as budget sales units* | Budget sales units | Difference in units | Budget unit gross profit margin £ | Volume variances £ |
|---|---|---|---|---|---|
| X | 240 | 200 | 40 | 1.00 | 40.00 |
| Y | 240 | 200 | 40 | 1.50 | 60.00 |
| Z | 240 | 200 | 40 | 3.50 | 140.00 |
| | 720 | 600 | 120 | | 240.00 |

***Note: Actual sales = 720 therefore, in budget proportions, 720 units would have been sold, $^1/_3$ X + $^1/_3$ Y + $^1/_3$ Z = 240 + 240 + 240.**

The *mix variance* arises where more than one product is being sold and the different products have different profit margins. If the proportions of the actual sales of the products vary from budget, the overall profit will vary as a consequence, even if the total sales revenue is the same as in the budget.

In the volume variance calculation, the original budget was compared with actual total overall sales volume split between the products in the budget mix. For the mix variance, the actual sales in the budget mix are compared with the actual sales and the differences evaluated at the budgeted gross profit margin.

## Exhibit 48.6

| Product | Actual units sold | Actual sales in same proportions as budget sales units | Difference in units | Budget unit gross profit margin £ | Mix variance £ |
|---|---|---|---|---|---|
| X | 250 | 240 | 10 | 1.00 | 10 |
| Y | 190 | 240 | (50) | 1.50 | (75) |
| Z | 280 | 240 | 40 | 3.50 | 140 |
| | 720 | 720 | – | | 75 |

The difference in mix between budget and actual has increased profit by £75 due to the influence of a higher proportion of sales of product Z which has a higher gross margin than the other products. That is, there is a favourable sales mix variance of £75.

In this example, we assumed the budget and actual selling prices per unit were identical. This is often not the case. Let's look at another example. This time, we will calculate the price variance, then the volume variance and, finally, the mix variance.

## Exhibit 48.7

| | | Budget | | | | Actual | | | |
|---|---|---|---|---|---|---|---|---|---|
| Product | Budget % | Units | Unit selling price £ | Unit gross profit margin £ | Total profit £ | Units | Unit selling price £ | Unit gross profit margin £ | Total profit £ |
| A | 16.7 | 100 | 20 | 5 | 500 | 90 | 21 | 6 | 540 |
| B | 33.3 | 200 | 25 | 10 | 2,000 | 220 | 24 | 9 | 1,980 |
| C | 50 | 300 | 10 | 2 | 600 | 350 | 10 | 2 | 700 |
| | 100 | 600 | | | 3,100 | 660 | | | 3,220 |

| Total variance = | Actual profit | 3,220 |
|---|---|---|
| | Budget profit | (3,100) |
| | Favourable variance | 120 |

**(i) Eliminate the price variance using the actual units sold as the basis.**

| | *Actual units sold* 1 | *Budget price* 2 £ | *Actual price* 3 £ | *Unit variance* 3 − 2 = 4 £ | *Price variance* 1 × 4 = 5 £ |
|---|---|---|---|---|---|
| A | 90 | 20 | 21 | 1 | 90 |
| B | 220 | 25 | 24 | (1) | (220) |
| C | 350 | 10 | 10 | – | – |
| | | | | *Adverse price variance* | (130) |

**(ii) Eliminate the volume variance using the unit budgeted gross profit to evaluate the variance.**

| | *Actual units sold* 1 | *Budget %* 2 | *Actual sales in same proportions as budget sales units* 3 £ | *Budget sales units* 4 £ | *Difference in units* 3 − 4 = 5 £ | *Budget unit gross margin* 6 £ | *Volume variance* 5 × 6 = 7 £ |
|---|---|---|---|---|---|---|---|
| A | 90 | 16.7 | 110 | 100 | 10 | 5 | 50 |
| B | 220 | 33.3 | 220 | 200 | 20 | 10 | 200 |
| C | 350 | 50 | 330 | 300 | 30 | 2 | 60 |
| | 660 | 100 | 660 | 600 | 60 | | |
| | | | | | *Favourable volume variance* | | 310 |

**(iii) Calculate the mix variance.**

| | *Actual units sold* 1 | *Budget %* 2 | *Actual sales in same proportions as budget sales units* 3 £ | *Difference in units* 1 − 3 = 4 £ | *Budget unit gross margin* 5 £ | *Mix variance* 4 × 5 = 6 £ |
|---|---|---|---|---|---|---|
| A | 90 | 16.7 | 110 | (20) | 5 | (100) |
| B | 220 | 33.3 | 220 | – | 10 | – |
| C | 350 | 50.0 | 330 | 20 | 2 | 40 |
| | 660 | | 660 | | | |
| | | | | *Adverse mix variance* | | (60) |

Summary of variance:

| | £ |
|---|---|
| Adverse price variance | (130) |
| Favourable volume variance | 310 |
| Adverse mix variance | (60) |
| Favourable total sales variance | 120 |

The gross profit margin may change for many reasons other than changes in sales volume. For example, if the cost of materials varies from budgets or wage rates change, the sales price may be raised in order to preserve the gross profit margin. This type of variance has, however, already been dealt with under materials and labour variances.

## Learning outcomes

**You should now have learnt:**

1. How to calculate overhead and sales variances.
2. The similarities between the variable production overhead efficiency variance and both the labour efficiency variance and the materials usage variance.
3. How to identify appropriate reasons why variances found have occurred.
4. That the calculation of variances and their explanation to managers is of no value unless the information so revealed is put to use in making decisions which change subsequent activities.

## Answer to activity

48.1 Because they are period costs that must be charged to profit or loss during the reporting period.

## Review questions

***Advice*: Remember that the overhead variances consist of the difference between the standard costs at the actual level of activity and the actual costs. Remember also that the total sales variance comprises three variances – price, volume and mix.**

**It is important that you answer the parts of the questions that ask you to comment on exactly what might be behind the variances and what action is needed.**

**48.1** Calculate the appropriate overhead variances from the following data.

(*a*) Budgeted for £9,000 variable overhead expenditure and 1,500 labour hours of production activity.

| | |
|---|---|
| Actual variable overhead expenditure | £8,400 |
| Actual labour hours | 1,500 |

(*b*) Budgeted for £60,000 variable overhead expenditure and 12,000 machine hours of production activity.

| | |
|---|---|
| Actual variable overhead expenditure | £61,000 |
| Actual machine hours | 14,000 |

(*c*) Budgeted for £9,750 fixed overhead and the actual fixed overhead is found to be £9,400.

(*d*) Budgeted for £16,320 fixed overhead and the actual fixed overhead is found to be £16,400.

(*e*) Budgeted production of 17,000 units in 19,000 hours. Standard variable overhead rate is £4 per hour. In fact, 17,000 units are produced in 18,100 hours.

(*f*) Budgeted production of 11,500 units in 23,000 hours. Standard variable overhead rate is £6 per hour. In fact, 11,320 units are produced in 26,000 hours.

→

**48.2A** Calculate the overhead variances in the following cases:

(*a*) Budgeted for £19,000 fixed overhead. The actual fixed overhead turns out to be £18,109.
(*b*) Budgeted for production of 6,000 units in 300 machine hours. The variable overhead rate is £12 per machine hour. In fact, 6,000 units are produced in 280 machine hours.
(*c*) Budgeted for £28,000 variable overhead and 14,000 labour hours. Actual variable overhead is £28,000 and actual labour hours 13,800.
(*d*) Budgeted for £12,000 variable overhead and 6,000 machine hours. Actual variable overhead is £11,400 and actual machine hours 6,000.
(*e*) Budgeted for £84,100 fixed overhead. The actual fixed overhead turns out to be £88,700.
(*f*) Budgeted for production of 15,000 units in 20,000 machine hours. Standard variable overhead rate is £10 an hour. In fact, 14,600 units are produced in 20,000 machine hours.

**48.3** Calculate the overhead variances of Mark & Son Ltd. The budget is prepared as:

(*a*) Total budgeted variable overhead: £120,000.
(*b*) Total budgeted fixed overhead: £48,000.
(*c*) Budgeted level of production activity: 60,000 direct labour hours to produce 50,000 units.

The actual results turn out to be:

(*i*) Actual variable overhead: £128,000.
(*ii*) Actual fixed overhead: £46,000.
(*iii*) Actual level of production activity was 59,000 direct labour hours which resulted in 52,000 units of production.

**48.4A** Calculate the overhead variances of Changes Ltd. The budget is prepared as:

(*a*) Total budgeted variable overhead: £80,000.
(*b*) Total budgeted fixed overhead: £120,000.
(*c*) Budgeted level of production activity: 60,000 direct labour hours to produce 240,000 units.

The actual results turn out to be:

(*i*) Actual variable overhead: £78,000.
(*ii*) Actual fixed overhead: £104,000.
(*iii*) Actual level of production activity was 64,000 direct labour hours which resulted in 236,000 units being produced.

**48.5** The Morningside Company Ltd had the following results for the year to 31 December 2017. A single product – a woggley – was made by the company.

| | *Budget* | *Actual* |
|---|---|---|
| Sales in units | 140,000 | 168,000 |
| Sales in £ | 350,000 | 403,200 |

The standard cost of manufacturing each unit was £2.20.

What are the price and volume variances on sales in 2017?

**48.6A** Felicidade plc manufactures a detergent in one of its factories. The information for the year to 30 June 2018 was as follows:

| | *Budget* | *Actual* |
|---|---|---|
| Sales in litres | 80,000 | 75,000 |
| Sales in £ | 480,000 | 480,000 |

The standard cost of manufacturing a litre was £3.10.

Calculate the price and volume variances for the year.

**48.7** The following data was collected for Metal Chain Ltd for the year ended 31 October 2018.

| Product | Budget selling price £ | Budget sales units | % | Budget gross profit per unit £ | Budget gross profit total £ | Actual selling price £ | Actual sales unit | % | Actual gross profit per unit £ | Actual gross profit total £ |
|---|---|---|---|---|---|---|---|---|---|---|
| A | 6 | 1,000 | 25 | 2.00 | 2,000 | 8.20 | 1,224 | 34 | 1.90 | 2,325.60 |
| B | 9 | 2,000 | 50 | 2.50 | 3,000 | 11.60 | 2,160 | 60 | 2.30 | 4,830.00 |
| C | 8 | 1,000 | 25 | 2.20 | 2,200 | 10.90 | 216 | 6 | 2.20 | 475.20 |
| | | 4,000 | 100 | | 7,200 | | 3,600 | 100 | | 7,630.80 |

Calculate the price, volume and mix variances for the year.

**48.8A** The following information relates to The Melted Cheese Company Ltd for the year to 31 December 2018:

| Product | Budget units | Sales % | Budget selling price per unit £ | Budget gross profit per unit £ | Actual units | Sales % | Actual unit selling price £ | Actual unit gross profit £ |
|---|---|---|---|---|---|---|---|---|
| X | 800 | 14.3 | 60 | 10 | 1,000 | 20.8 | 58 | 8 |
| Y | 1,200 | 21.4 | 50 | 8 | 800 | 16.7 | 54 | 10 |
| Z | 3,600 | 64.3 | 80 | 20 | 3,000 | 62.5 | 78 | 18 |
| | 5,600 | 100.0 | | | 4,800 | 100.0 | | |

Calculate the price, volume and mix variances for 2018.

**48.9** Singleton has been operating for some years as a manufacturer of a single product, and after several years' growth has decided to form a company Singleton Ltd.

His accountant advised him that in an increasingly competitive world he really should achieve greater financial control of his business, and to assist Singleton in this objective the accountant prepared a simple manufacturing budget for the financial year ending 31 August 2016.

The following schedule provides the detail of the budget and the actual results for the year ended 31 August 2016. The actual results have been extracted from the ledger as at that date without any adjustments made.

| | Budget £ | Actual £ |
|---|---|---|
| Raw materials consumed | 80,000 | 90,000 |
| Factory rent | 10,000 | 12,500 |
| Factory maintenance expenses | 6,700 | 6,100 |
| Heating and lighting | 2,900 | 3,000 |
| Direct labour wages | 120,000 | 110,500 |
| Direct expenses | 5,800 | 6,000 |
| Depreciation of plant and machinery | 8,900 | 10,500 |
| Wages, maintenance labour | 18,000 | 24,000 |
| Other factory overheads | 12,700 | 9,600 |

*Additional information:*

1 At 31 August 2016 the following amounts were still owing:

| | £ |
|---|---|
| Direct labour wages | 5,100 |
| Heating and lighting | 900 |
| Other factory overheads | 400 |

**2** The factory rent paid covered the period from 1 September 2015 to 30 November 2016.
**3** During the year the firm sold 90,000 units of its product at £4.50 a unit.
**4** There was no work in progress. The inventories of finished goods were:

| | £ |
|---|---|
| 1 September 2015 | 28,900 |
| 31 August 2016 | 35,000 |

**Required:**

(*a*) What is variance analysis and how can it contribute to the operating efficiency of Singleton's business?

(*b*) For the year ended 31 August 2016 prepare:
 (*i*) A manufacturing account and a schedule of the relevant variances;
 (*ii*) A trading account.

(*c*) Write a report to advise Singleton whether the principles of budgeting can be applied to:
 (*i*) Non-manufacturing costs;
 (*ii*) The control of cash resources.

Your report should indicate in each case the potential benefits that the firm could achieve through extending its use of budgeting.

*(AQA (Associated Examining Board): GCE A-level)*

**48.10A** Flint Palatignium Ltd calculates the prices of its output by adding a mark-up of 15% to standard costs. These standard costs are arrived at by reference to budgeted outputs and estimated direct costs as follows:

| | *£ each* | *Standard price/rate* |
|---|---|---|
| Materials | 5.00 | £1 per unit |
| Direct labour | 2.50 | £1.25 per hour |
| Overheads | 7.50 | £3.75 per direct labour hour |
| | 15.00 | |
| Mark-up | 2.25 | |
| Selling price | 17.25 | |

Management accounts for April, 2018 provide an analysis of operations as follows:

| | £ |
|---|---|
| Sales – at standard price | 534,750 |
| Standard margin on sales | 69,750 |
| Favourable sales price variance | 8,691 |
| | 78,441 |
| Other favourable variances | |
| Material price | 4,662 |
| Labour rate | 600 |
| Overhead expenditure | 147 |
| | 83,850 |
| Adverse variances | |
| Material usage | (1,743) |
| Labour efficiency | (292) |
| Overhead capacity | (9) |
| Actual operating profit | 81,806 |

Materials in inventory are valued at standard cost. At 1 April, 1,000 units of material were held, whereas at 30 April the inventory of this material increased to 1,750 units.

**Required:**

(*i*) A trading account for the month of April 2018 comparing the budgeted income and expenditure appropriate to actual output, to actual income and expenditure.

(*ii*) An explanation of the value of standard costing and variance analysis to a service business whose custom is to negotiate fixed price contracts.

(*Welsh Joint Education Committee: GCE A-level*)

*Note*: The following question covers material from both Chapters 47 and 48.

**48.11A** HGW Limited produces a product called a Lexton. The standard selling price and the manufacturing costs of this product are as follows:

| | | £ |
|---|---|---|
| Standard selling price per unit | | 86 |
| Standard production costs: | | |
| Direct material | 1.5 kilos at £12 per kilo | 18 |
| Direct labour | 4.4 hours at £7.50 per hour | 33 |
| Variable overheads | 4.4 hours at £5 per hour | 22 |
| | | 73 |

The projected production and sales for March 2017 were 520 units.

On 1 April 2017 the following actual figures were determined.

| | |
|---|---|
| Sales | 550 units at £85 each |
| Production | 550 units |
| Direct material | 785 kilos at £12.40 per kilo |
| Direct labour | 2,400 hours at £7.80 per hour |
| Overheads | £12,500 (overall variance £400 adverse) |

There was no opening inventory of the product Lexton.

**Required:**

(*a*) Prepare an actual statement of profit or loss for HGW Ltd for March 2017.

(*b*) Calculate the following variances and their respective sub-variances:
  (*i*) sales – price and volume
  (*ii*) direct materials – price and usage
  (*iii*) direct labour – rate and efficiency.

(*c*) Prepare a statement reconciling the actual profit calculated in part (*a*) with the budgeted profit on actual sales. (Use the variances calculated in part (*b*) and the given overhead variance.)

(*d*) Write a report to the management outlining the factors that need to be considered when standards are being established.

(*AQA (Associated Examining Board): GCE A-level*)

part 10

# PLANNING, CONTROL AND DECISION-MAKING

## Introduction

This part looks at how accounting information may be used to guide decision-making within an entity, at how the cost of investment is calculated, and at how organisations are beginning to use the information available to them to provide a richer view of the performance of the organisation than is possible from straightforward ratio analysis.

chapter

# 49 Breakeven analysis

## Learning objectives

**After you have studied this chapter, you should be able to:**

- explain what is meant by 'breakeven'
- prepare breakeven graphs and contribution graphs
- explain the importance of contribution and fixed costs in identifying the breakeven level of sales
- use graphs to identify breakeven point, the margin of safety, and the contribution for any level of activity
- use breakeven graphs to show the impact of changes in costs, volume and selling price upon profitability
- describe some of the limitations of breakeven charts
- use a formula in order to calculate the breakeven point
- explain the relevance of contribution to decision-making

## Introduction

In this chapter, you'll learn about breakeven analysis and, at the same time, about the relationship between costs, volume, selling price and profit.

## 49.1 Introduction

The level of activity achieved by a business is of great importance in determining both whether or not it makes a profit or loss, and the size of such profits or losses. Let's take an example to which the answer is obvious. If a business has fixed costs of £100,000 and its total revenue is £80,000 then, no matter how much the variable costs are, the business is bound to make a loss. A business has to cover both its fixed costs and its variable costs before it can make a profit. With revenue below the level of fixed costs, as in this case, a loss is bound to arise.

There is, therefore, a great deal of interest in exactly how much revenue (i.e. sales) has to be earned before a profit can be made. If revenue is below fixed costs, a loss will be incurred; if revenue is below total costs (i.e. fixed costs + variable costs) a loss will still be incurred. However, when revenue is greater than the combined total of the fixed and variable costs, a profit will have been made. The question is, at what level of sales does the business stop incurring a loss and, with the next unit of revenue, make a profit? That is, at what point does it break even and make neither a profit nor a loss?

**Fixed costs stay unchanged over stated ranges in the volume of production, but variable costs change *in total* when the volume of production changes within a stated range.** As revenue increases so do variable costs, so that the only item that remains unchanged is that of fixed costs. Let's look at an example showing the changing costs and revenues over differing volumes of production.

Apollo Ltd has fixed costs of £5,000. The variable costs are £2 per unit. The revenue (selling price) is £3 per unit. Looking at production in stages of 1,000 units we can see (Exhibit 49.1):

## Exhibit 49.1

| *No. of units* | *Fixed cost* | *Variable cost* | *Total cost: Variable + Fixed* | *Revenue (Sales)* | *Profit* | *Loss* |
|---|---|---|---|---|---|---|
| | £ | £ | £ | £ | £ | £ |
| 0 | 5,000 | nil | 5,000 | nil | | 5,000 |
| 1,000 | 5,000 | 2,000 | 7,000 | 3,000 | | 4,000 |
| 2,000 | 5,000 | 4,000 | 9,000 | 6,000 | | 3,000 |
| 3,000 | 5,000 | 6,000 | 11,000 | 9,000 | | 2,000 |
| 4,000 | 5,000 | 8,000 | 13,000 | 12,000 | | 1,000 |
| 5,000 | 5,000 | 10,000 | 15,000 | 15,000 | nil | nil |
| 6,000 | 5,000 | 12,000 | 17,000 | 18,000 | 1,000 | |
| 7,000 | 5,000 | 14,000 | 19,000 | 21,000 | 2,000 | |
| 8,000 | 5,000 | 16,000 | 21,000 | 24,000 | 3,000 | |
| 9,000 | 5,000 | 18,000 | 23,000 | 27,000 | 4,000 | |

With an activity level of 5,000 units, the business will break even. It will make neither a profit nor a loss. Above that it moves into profit; below that, it never makes a profit.

We could have calculated the breakeven point without drawing up a schedule of costs, etc. as in Exhibit 49.1. Instead we could have said that for one unit the revenue is £3 and the variable cost is £2, so that the remaining £1 is the amount out of which the fixed costs have to be paid, and that anything left over is profit.

The £1 is the 'contribution' towards fixed costs and profit. If the contribution was only just enough to cover fixed costs, there would be no profit, but neither would there be any loss. There are £5,000 fixed costs, so that with a contribution of £1 per unit there would have to be 5,000 units to provide a contribution of £5,000 to cover fixed costs. It could be stated as:

$$\textbf{Breakeven point} = \frac{\textbf{Fixed costs}}{\textbf{Selling price per unit} - \textbf{Variable costs per unit}}$$

i.e. in the case of Apollo Ltd

$$\frac{£5{,}000}{£3 - £2} = \frac{5{,}000}{1} = 5{,}000 \text{ units}$$

If fixed costs were £7,000 and the contribution per unit were £2, what would be the breakeven level of sales?

## 49.2 The breakeven chart

The information given in Exhibit 49.1 can also be shown in the form of a chart. Many people seem to grasp the idea of breakeven analysis rather more easily when they see it in chart form. This is particularly true for anyone who is not used to dealing with accounting information. We will, therefore, plot the figures from Exhibit 49.1 on a chart which is shown as Exhibit 49.2.

The use of the chart can now be looked at. It would be extremely useful if you could draw the chart as shown in Exhibit 49.2 on a piece of graph paper. The larger the scale that you use, the easier it will be to take accurate readings. Plot the lines from the figures shown in Exhibit 49.1.

**Exhibit 49.2**

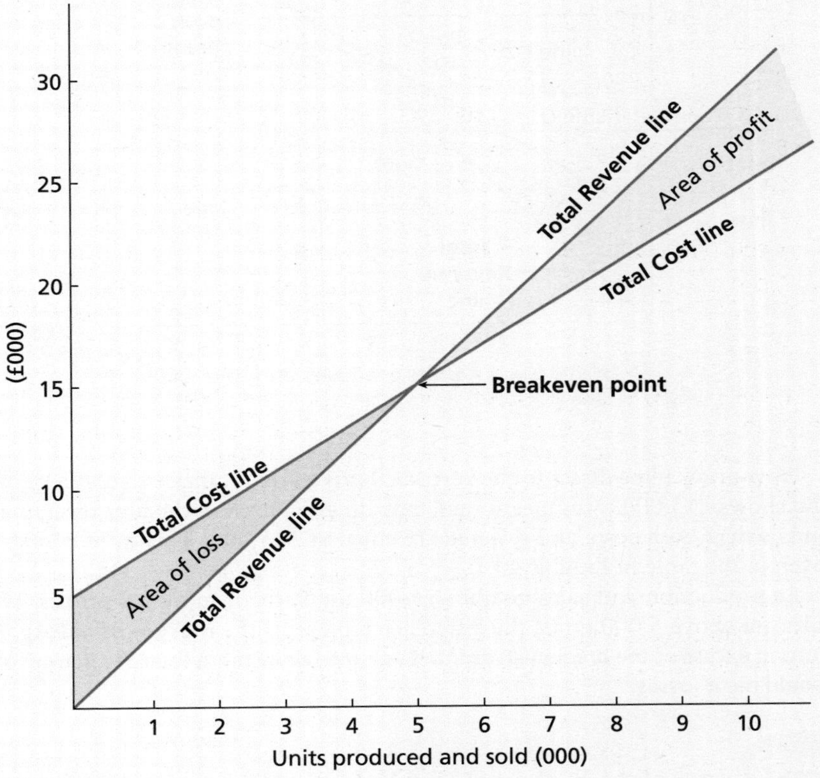


**To find the breakeven point in terms of units of product, draw a line straight down from the breakeven point so that it meets the horizontal axis at right angles.** This is shown in Exhibit 49.3 as line A which, when read off, gives units of production and sales as 5,000 units.

Exhibit 49.3

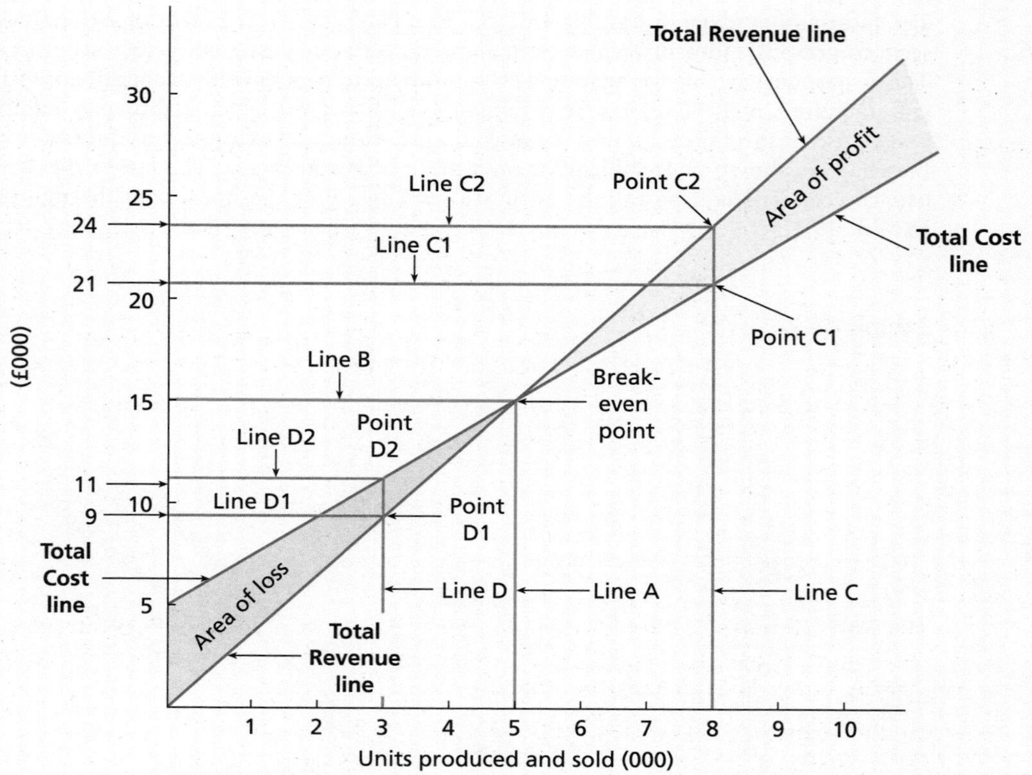


Now draw a line direct to the vertical £ axis so that it meets that at a right angle. This is line B and shows £15,000. This means that according to the chart the breakeven point is shown at 5,000 units where both costs and revenue are equal at £15,000. This is, of course, the same answer as given in the table in Exhibit 49.1.

As production and sales go above 5,000 units, the firm makes profits. When production and sales are above 5,000 units, the difference represents the **margin of safety**. **This is the number of units in excess of the breakeven point. If volume fell by more than the margin of safety, the business would incur losses.**

Look at the chart again and, without looking back at what you have just read, attempt to answer the following two questions by taking readings off your chart:

*(i)* What would the total costs of the firm be at (*a*) 2,000 units, (*b*) 7,000 units, (*c*) 8,500 units?

***Remember*: Take a line up from the product line for the figure needed then, from where the cost line is bisected, draw a line to the £s line to meet it at right angles.**

*(ii)* What is the revenue for (*a*) 3,000 units, (*b*) 6,000 units, (*c*) 7,500 units?

Before proceeding further, look at the answers to this activity.

Now we will try to find the amount of profit or loss at various levels by looking at the chart in Exhibit 49.3. First, let's calculate the profit made if 8,000 units are going to be made and sold. Draw a line up from the product line (horizontal axis) at right angles (shown as line C) until it bisects both the Total Cost line and the Total Revenue line, the points of intersection being shown as C1 for the Total Cost line and C2 for the Total Revenue line. Read off the amounts in £s by taking lines across to the £s vertical axis until they meet it at right angles. These are shown as lines C1 and C2. The line from C1 will give a reading of £21,000 and from C2 of £24,000. As the Total Revenue exceeds the Total Costs there is a profit. In this case, the profit is £3,000.

If we now try for 3,000 units, the line drawn up from the product line will meet the Total Revenue line at point D1 and the Total Cost line at D2. Reading off to the £s line D1 shows as £9,000 while D2 shows as £11,000. In this case, the Total Cost exceeds the Total Revenue by £2,000 and there is, therefore, a loss of £2,000.

**Activity 49.3**

Look at your chart again and use it to find the profit or loss recorded at (*a*) 1,000 units, (*b*) 4,000 units, (*c*) 6,500 units and (*d*) 8,500 units.

Before proceeding, look at the answers to this activity at the end of the chapter.

## 49.3 Changes and breakeven charts

The effect of changes on profits can easily be shown by drawing fresh lines on the chart to show the changes, or intended changes, in the circumstances of the firm. Let's first consider some factors that can bring about a change in profits:

(*a*) the selling price per unit could be increased (or decreased);
(*b*) a possible decrease (or increase) in fixed costs;
(*c*) a possible decrease (or increase) in variable costs per unit;
(*d*) increase the volume of production and sales.

We will investigate these by starting with some basic information for a business and then seeing what would happen if each of the changes (*a*) to (*d*) were to happen.

The basic information is shown in Exhibit 49.4:

**Exhibit 49.4**

| *No. of units* | *Fixed cost* | *Variable cost* | *Total cost: Variable + Fixed* | *Revenue (Sales)* | *Profit* | *Loss* |
|---|---|---|---|---|---|---|
| | £ | £ | £ | £ | £ | £ |
| 100 | 2,000 | 400 | 2,400 | 900 | | 1,500 |
| 200 | 2,000 | 800 | 2,800 | 1,800 | | 1,000 |
| 300 | 2,000 | 1,200 | 3,200 | 2,700 | | 500 |
| 400 | 2,000 | 1,600 | 3,600 | 3,600 | nil | nil |
| 500 | 2,000 | 2,000 | 4,000 | 4,500 | 500 | |
| 600 | 2,000 | 2,400 | 4,400 | 5,400 | 1,000 | |
| 700 | 2,000 | 2,800 | 4,800 | 6,300 | 1,500 | |
| 800 | 2,000 | 3,200 | 5,200 | 7,200 | 2,000 | |
| 900 | 2,000 | 3,600 | 5,600 | 8,100 | 2,500 | |

The table in Exhibit 49.4 shows that variable costs are £4 per unit and selling price £9 per unit. (These figures are found by dividing the variable cost and revenue values at any number of units by that number of units. For example, dividing £400 variable cost by 100 gives £4 variable cost per unit.)

We can draw a chart to incorporate this information before considering the changes being contemplated. This is shown in Exhibit 49.5.

**Exhibit 49.5**

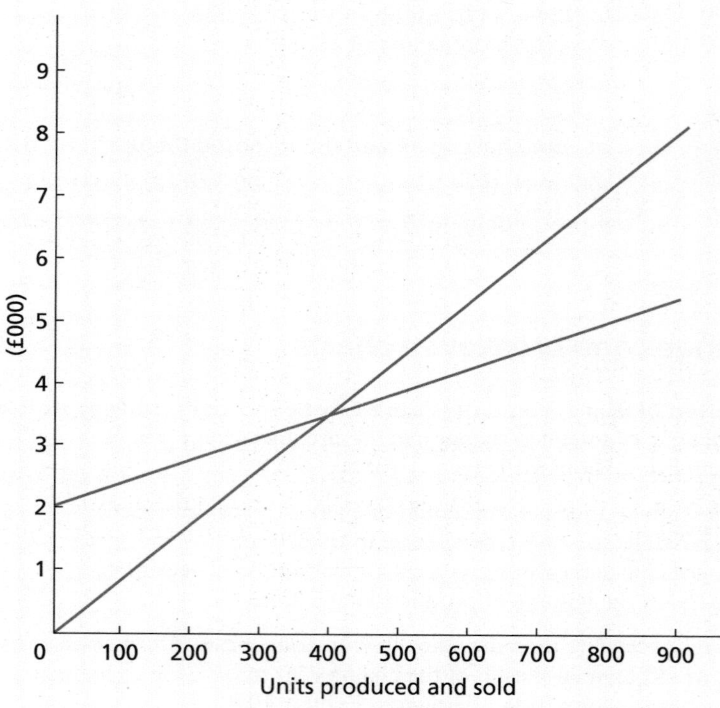


## (a) Increase selling price

Taking the chart shown in Exhibit 49.5 as a base, we can now draw an extra line on it to represent an increase in selling price. Let us suppose that the selling price could be increased by £2 per unit. This can now be shown on a breakeven chart in Exhibit 49.6. The line shown as New Total Revenue can then be added. This would mean that the breakeven point would change as the increased revenue means that costs can be covered sooner. The lilac shaded area shows the reduction in the loss area that would be incurred at the same volume of sales, while the blue shaded area shows the increase in profit at the various volumes of sales.

**Exhibit 49.6**

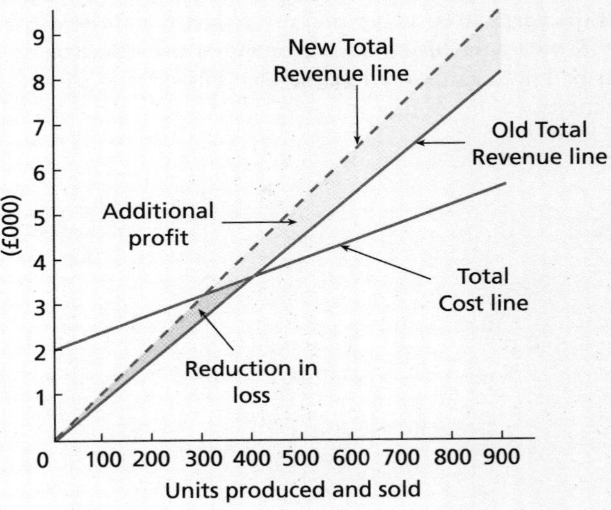


## (b) Reduce fixed costs

We can now draw some more lines on the chart shown in Exhibit 49.6, this time to reflect a reduction of £800 in fixed costs. This can be seen in Exhibit 49.7, where a line entitled New Total Cost has been added. The reduction in loss if sales were at a low volume is represented by the lilac shaded area, while the blue shaded area shows the additional profit at various volumes of activity. The change in profit or loss will be constant at £800 over these volumes.

**Exhibit 49.7**

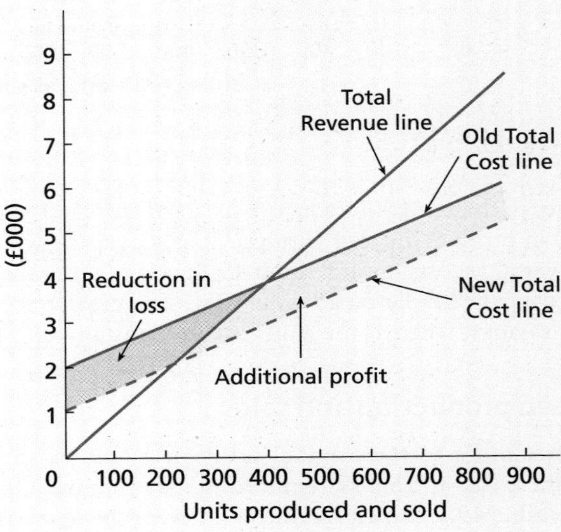

### (c) Reduce variable costs

Reverting to the chart shown in Exhibit 49.6 (where the fixed costs are £2,000), we can see what happens if the variable costs per unit are reduced, in this case by £2 per unit. This is shown in Exhibit 49.8, where the lilac shaded area shows the reduction in loss compared with the position if the costs had not changed, while the blue shaded area shows the additional profit at different levels of activity.

**Exhibit 49.8**

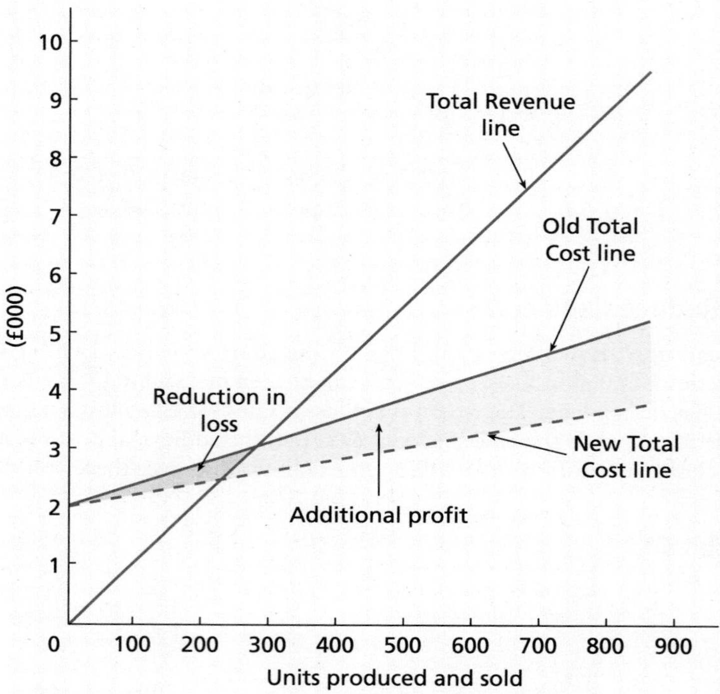


You will recall that an £800 reduction in fixed costs in Exhibit 49.7 showed a constant difference of £800 in profit compared with previously over the whole range of activity. In contrast, a reduction in variable costs (as in Exhibit 49.8) brings about different increases of profit, or reduction of loss, over the whole range of activity. The greater the activity the greater the gain with variable cost savings, whereas the gain remains constant with fixed cost savings.

### (d) Increased production and sales

Reverting once more to the original position as shown in Exhibit 49.5, when sales and/or production increase, all that is required is that the lines Total Revenue and Total Cost are extended. Exhibit 49.9 shows Exhibit 49.5 with the level of activity increased by 300 units. The new profit indicated will be greater than the old profit because all extra units are being sold at a profit.

Exhibit 49.9

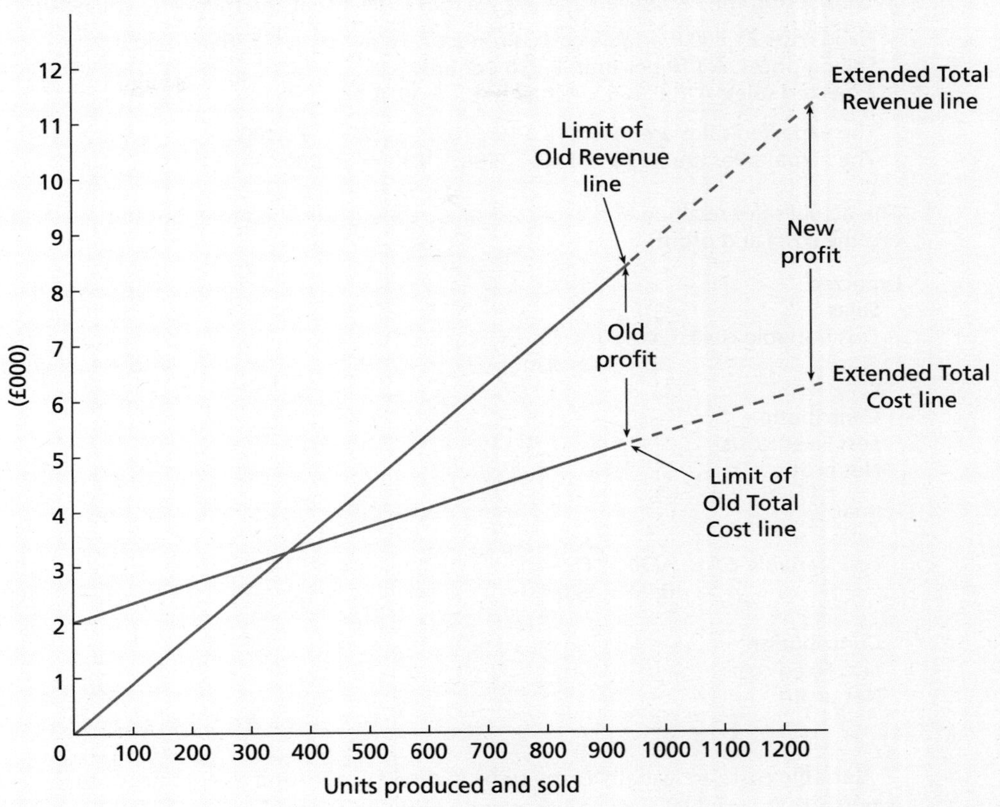


## 49.4 The limitations of breakeven charts

In each of the cases looked at it has been assumed that only one of the factors of variable cost, fixed cost, selling price or volume of sales has altered. This is not usually the case. An increase in price may well reduce the number sold. There may well be an increase in fixed cost which has an effect which brings down variable costs. The changes in the various factors should, therefore, be studied simultaneously rather than separately.

In addition, **where there is more than one product, the proportions in which the products are sold, i.e. the product mix, can have a very important bearing on costs.** Suppose that there are two products, one has a large amount of fixed costs but hardly any variable costs, and the other has a large amount of variable costs but little fixed costs. If the proportions in which each is sold change very much then this could mean that the costs and profit could vary tremendously, even though the total figures of sales stayed constant. An illustration of this can be seen in Exhibit 49.10:

**Exhibit 49.10**

In considering the breakeven analysis we may expect that the following will occur.

Fixed costs £1,000, Variable costs: Product A £5 per unit, B £20 per unit.
Selling prices: A £10 per unit, B £30 per unit.
Expected sales: A 150, B 50. Actual sales: A 30, B 90.

The expected sales are: A 150 × £10 + B 50 × £30 = £3,000.
The actual sales are: A 30 × £10 + B 90 × £30 = £3,000.

The actual sales revenue and expected sales revenue are the same, but the sales mix is different, as are the costs and profit:

| | | | £ |
|---|---|---|---|
| Expected: | | | |
| Sales | | | 3,000 |
| *Less* Variable costs: | A 150 × £5 = | 750 | |
| | B 50 × £20 = | 1,000 | |
| | | | (1,750) |
| Contribution | | | 1,250 |
| *Less* Fixed costs | | | 1,000 |
| Net profit | | | 250 |
| Actual: | | | |
| Sales | | | 3,000 |
| *Less* Variable costs: | A 30 × £5 = | 150 | |
| | B 90 × £20 = | 1,800 | |
| | | | (1,950) |
| Contribution | | | 1,050 |
| *Less* Fixed costs | | | (1,000) |
| Net profit | | | 50 |

Variable costs are usually taken to be in direct proportion to volume, so that 1,000 units means (say) £5,000 variable costs and therefore 2,000 units would mean £10,000 variable costs, 3,000 units equal £15,000 variable costs and so on. This is often a reasonable estimation of the situation, but may well hold true only within fairly tight limits. For instance 3,100 units could mean £16,000 costs instead of the £15,500 that it would be if a linear relationship existed. This is also true of sales, because to increase sales beyond certain points some units may be sold cheaply. Thus 1,000 units might be sold for £9,000; 2,000 units sold for £18,000; but to sell 2,200 units the revenue might be only £19,100 instead of the £19,800 (2,200 × £9) that might be expected if a linear relationship existed over all ranges.

It is assumed that everything produced is sold, and that inventory-in-trade remain constant. It would be difficult to do otherwise as both sales revenue and costs relate to one and the same measure of volume.

Another limitation is more of a complication than a hindrance. Organisations considering a change in the level of activity outside the current range may well be faced with changed fixed costs as a result. For example, a new warehouse may need to be leased in order to cope with the extra production. In that case, the breakeven graphs produced need to incorporate stepped fixed costs that increase to a new fixed level once the threshold in activity for the higher cost has been reached. This can result in multiple breakeven points.

## 49.5 Contribution graph

Exhibit 49.11 is a redrafting of Exhibit 49.5 that includes the addition of a line representing variable cost. It runs parallel to and below the Total Cost line. This is an alternative method of presentation. It highlights the total contribution. The vertical gap between the Total Cost line and the Variable Cost line at any particular number of units represents the contribution at that number of units.

**Exhibit 49.11**

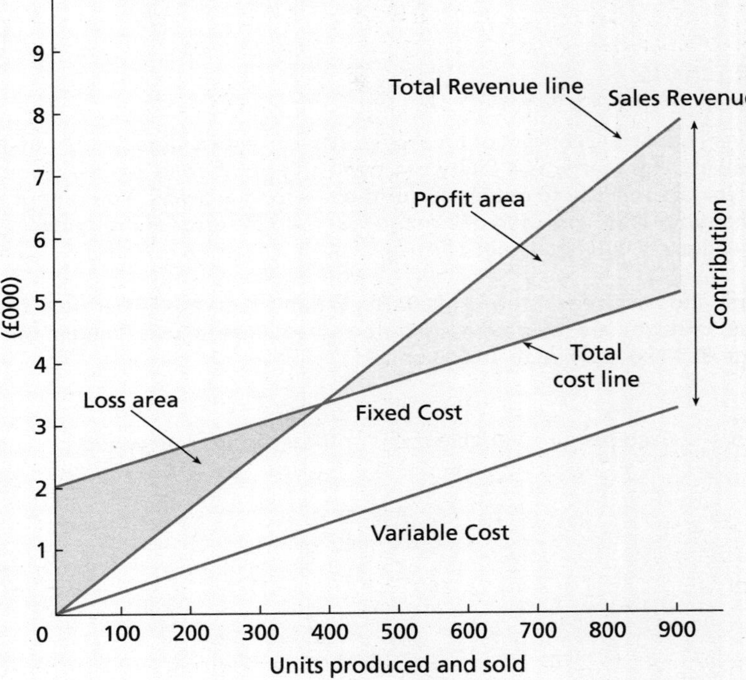


## Learning outcomes

**You should now have learnt:**

1. How to prepare breakeven graphs and contribution graphs.
2. That breakeven analysis can be performed using either a formula or a graph.
3. How to use graphs to identify breakeven point, the margin of safety and the contribution for any level of activity.
4. How to use a formula in order to calculate the breakeven point.
5. That fixed costs are assumed to be fixed for the range of activity being considered, and variable costs per unit and sales revenue per unit are assumed to be constant within that range of activity. It is important to check whether these assumptions are correct when carrying out a breakeven analysis. If they are not, the format of the analysis should be adjusted appropriately.
6. How to use breakeven graphs to show the impact of changes in costs, volume and selling price upon profitability.
7. How to explain the relevance of contribution to decision-making.

## Answers to activities

49.1 3,500 units.

49.2 (*i*) (*a*) £9,000 (*b*) £19,000 (*c*) £22,000

(*ii*) (*a*) £9,000 (*b*) £18,000 (*c*) £22,500

49.3 (*a*) Loss £4,000 (*b*) Loss £1,000 (*c*) Profit £1,500 (*d*) Profit £3,500

## Review questions

*Advice*: **The very important concept of breakeven attracts quite a large number of questions. Be careful when drawing any charts, as a faulty chart will give you wrong answers for every part of your answer and you are unlikely to get marks for those wrong answers. You cannot expect examiners to assume that your faulty drawing of a graph was a simple error of draughtsmanship instead of a lack of knowledge or understanding.**

**49.1** Hedges Ltd has fixed costs of £8,000. The variable costs are £4 per unit. The revenue (selling price) is £6 per unit. You are required (*i*) to draft a schedule as follows filling in the columns (*a*) to (*f*) for each stage of 1,000 units up to 10,000 units.

| *No. of units* | (*a*) *Fixed cost* £ | (*b*) *Variable cost* £ | (*c*) *Total cost* £ | (*d*) *Revenue* £ | (*e*) *Profit* £ | (*f*) *Loss* £ |
|---|---|---|---|---|---|---|
| 0 | | | | | | |
| 1,000 | | | | | | |
| 2,000 | | | | | | |
| 3,000 | | | | | | |
| 4,000 | | | | | | |
| 5,000 | | | | | | |
| 6,000 | | | | | | |
| 7,000 | | | | | | |
| 8,000 | | | | | | |
| 9,000 | | | | | | |
| 10,000 | | | | | | |

(*i*) **You are also required to** draw a breakeven chart from the data in this schedule. Draw it carefully to scale on a piece of graph paper. Retain your answer, you will need it for some questions which follow later.

**49.2** Cover up the schedule you constructed as your answer to 49.1(*i*) and look instead at the breakeven chart constructed as the answer to 49.1(*ii*). **Answer the following**:

(*a*) What are the total costs at production levels of (*i*) 4,000 units; (*ii*) 7,000 units; (*iii*) 9,000 units; (*iv*) 5,500 units?

(*b*) What is the total revenue at (*i*) 3,000 units; (*ii*) 8,000 units; (*iii*) 5,500 units?

**49.3A** Look at your schedule in answer to 49.1(*i*) and **answer the following**:

(*a*) What are the total costs at production levels of (*i*) 4,000 units; (*ii*) 7,000 units; (*iii*) 9,000 units; (*iv*) 5,500 units? You will have to deduce this amount as it is not shown as a figure on the schedule.

(*b*) What is the total revenue at (*i*) 3,000 units; (*ii*) 8,000 units; (*iii*) 5,500 units?

**49.4** From your breakeven chart for 49.1(*ii*), **calculate** the profit or loss that will be made at levels of (*i*) 3,000 units; (*ii*) 10,000 units; (*iii*) 4,000 units; (*iv*) 7,000 units; (*v*) 8,500 units.

**49.5A** From the schedule in 49.1(*i*), **calculate** the profit or loss that would be made at levels of (*i*) 3,000 units; (*ii*) 10,000 units; (*iii*) 4,000 units; (*iv*) 7,000 units; (*v*) 8,500 units (this last figure will have to be deduced as it is not a figure on the schedule).

**49.6** If fixed costs are £70,000; selling price per unit is £14; and the variable cost of each unit in £6:

(*a*) What is the number of units sold at which a profit will be made for the first time?
(*b*) What is the revenue required to be achieved in order to break even?

**49.7** Polemic Ltd manufacture and sell a single product. The following information is available for three financial years ending 30 September.

| | *Price per unit* | *Unit volume* |
|---|---|---|
| | £ | *000s* |
| *Sales* | | |
| Actual 2001 | 130 | 50 |
| Forecast 2002 | 129 | 52 |
| Forecast 2003 | 128.5 | 53 |

| *Costs per unit Produced* | *Actual* 2016 | *Forecast* 2017 | 2018 |
|---|---|---|---|
| | £ | £ | £ |
| Direct materials | 50 | 55 | 55 |
| Direct labour | 30 | 31.5 | 33 |
| Variable production overhead | 10 | 11 | 12 |
| Direct expenses | 5 | 5 | 6 |
| Variable sales overhead | 15 | 16 | 16 |
| *Other costs for the year* | £ | £ | £ |
| | *000* | *000* | *000* |
| Fixed production overhead | 50 | 55 | 55 |
| Other fixed overhead | 200 | 220 | 220 |

*Additional information*:

**(1)** When the management of Polemic prepared its direct labour forecast unit cost for 2017 and 2018, direct wages were increased only by the forecast rate of inflation.

**(2)** The trade union representatives of the production workers wished to press for a greater wage increase. They suggested that:

(*i*) Direct wages be increased at twice the rate of inflation. The effect of this would be to increase direct labour costs per unit as follows:

| | *2017* | *2018* |
|---|---|---|
| | £ | £ |
| Direct labour | 33.0 | 35.0 |

(*ii*) Unit selling prices be increased in order to cover the increased labour costs.

**(3)** It is to be assumed that all expense and revenue relationships will be unchanged except where indicated.

**Required:**

(*a*) A schedule for 2016, 2017 and 2018 for Polemic Ltd showing:
(*i*) the breakeven points;
(*ii*) the net profit for each year.
Base your calculations on the original labour costs.

(*b*) A graph showing a breakeven point for 2017.

(*c*) Advise Polemic Ltd's management as to their response to the trade union's claim for higher wages. Include relevant financial analysis.

(*d*) Explain the limitation of breakeven analysis.

**(*AQA (Associated Examining Board)*: *GCE A-level*)**

→

**49.8A** The relationship between income/cost/volume suggests that there are four ways by which profit can be increased. These are:

**1** Increase unit selling price.
**2** Decrease unit variable cost.
**3** Decrease fixed costs.
**4** Increase volume.

Assume that the current situation for a product is as follows:

| | |
|---|---|
| Sales volume | 1,000 units |
| Selling price | £2 each |
| Variable cost | £1 per unit |
| Fixed costs | £500 |

**You are required to:**

(*a*) draw **four** separate breakeven charts showing the effect of the following changes on the current situation:
   (*i*) a 10% increase in volume,
   (*ii*) a 10% increase in unit selling price,
   (*iii*) a 10% decrease in unit variable cost,
   (*iv*) a 10% reduction in fixed costs.

(*b*) Use your charts to state the additional profit resulting from **each** change.

*(AQA (Northern Examinations and Assessment Board): GCE A-level)*

**49.9** At the monthly senior management meeting of Hampshire plc on 1 May 2017, various suggestions were made to improve the profit to be made by selling the firm's single product in the last quarter of the year ending 30 September 2017. The product is not subject to seasonal demand fluctuations, but there are several competitors producing similar items. In the first quarter of the year a suggestion was made that profit could be improved if the selling price were reduced by 5%, and this was put into effect at the beginning of the second quarter. As the new price undercut that of the rival firms, demand increased, and the firm's breakeven point was reduced.

The following suggestions have now been raised:

(*i*) Differentiate the product from its rivals by giving it a more distinctive shape, colour and packaging. This would increase material costs per unit by £0.30, but selling price would not be raised. Demand is then predicted to rise by 10%;

(*ii*) Improve the quality of the product by strengthening it and giving it a one-year guarantee – material costs would then increase by £0.15 per unit and labour costs by £0.30 per unit. Selling price would rise by £0.40 per unit, and demand increase by 7%;

(*iii*) Further reduce the selling price by 10% – demand to rise by 20%;

(*iv*) Pay commission plus salaries instead of fixed salaries only to all sales staff. Variable selling costs would then rise by £0.20 per unit, but fixed costs would fall by £4,100 per quarter;

(*v*) Subcontract the making of some components, and close the department responsible, making six staff redundant at an estimated cost to the firm of £12,000. 30,000 components are currently made per quarter. Each component's variable cost is £0.55. They can be bought from a recently established firm for £0.60 per unit. The department's share of the firm's fixed costs is 20% and £2,500 fixed costs per quarter would cease to arise if the department were to be closed.

| *Data for:* | *First quarter* | *Second quarter* |
|---|---|---|
| Number of units produced and sold | 9,000 | 10,800 |
| | £ | £ |
| Selling price per unit | 14 | 13.30 |
| Materials per unit | 3.65 | 3.65 |
| Labour per unit | 2.10 | 2.10 |
| Variable factory overhead per unit | 1.40 | 1.40 |
| Variable selling costs per unit | 0.85 | 0.85 |
| Fixed factory overhead | 21,375 | 21,375 |
| Fixed selling and administration costs | 16,125 | 16,125 |

**Required:**

A. Calculate the profit made in each of the first and second quarters, showing clearly the contribution per unit in each case.

B. Draw one breakeven chart showing the total costs and total revenues for the first and second quarters. You should label clearly the two breakeven points and margins of safety.

C. Taking each suggestion independently, calculate the profit that might be made in the last quarter if each of them were to be implemented.

D. Discuss the implications for the firm of undertaking suggestions (*i*)–(*iv*), and for the firm and the local community of undertaking suggestion (*v*).

E. Explain to the senior managers how, while breakeven analysis is useful, it has limitations.

*(Reproduced with the kind permission of OCR – University of Oxford Delegacy of Local Examinations: GCE A-level)*

**49.10A** You are employed by Monarch Ltd which manufactures specialist hydraulic seals for the aircraft industry. The company has developed a new seal with the following budgeted data.

| | |
|---|---|
| Variable cost per unit | £ |
| Direct materials | 8 |
| Direct labour | 4 |
| Variable overheads | 4 |
| | 16 |

The draft budget for the following year is as follows.

| | | |
|---|---|---|
| Production and sales | | 60,000 units |
| | | £ |
| Fixed cost: | Production | 260,000 |
| | Administration | 90,000 |
| | Selling, marketing and distribution | 100,000 |
| Contribution | | 840,000 |

Certain departmental managers within the company believe there is room for improvement on the budgeted figures, and the following options have been suggested.

(*i*) The sales manager has suggested that if the selling price was reduced by 10%, then an extra 30% units could be sold. The purchasing manager has indicated that if materials requirements were increased in line, then a materials price reduction of 6.25% could be negotiated. With this additional output, fixed production costs would increase by £30,000, administration by £5,000 and selling, marketing and distribution by £10,000. Other costs would remain unchanged.

(*ii*) The export manager has suggested that if the company increased overseas marketing by £15,000 then exports would increase from 15,000 units to 17,000 units. With this suggestion, distribution costs would increase by £12,000, and all other costs would remain unchanged.

(*iii*) The marketing manager has suggested that if an extra £40,000 were spent on advertising, then sales quantity would increase by 25%. The purchasing manager has indicated that in such circumstances, materials costs would reduce by £0.30 per unit. With this suggestion fixed production costs would increase by £25,000, administration by £4,000 and other selling, marketing and distribution costs by £7,000. All other costs would remain unchanged.

(*iv*) The managing director believes the company should be aiming for a profit of £486,000. He asks what the selling price would be per unit if marketing were increased by £50,000, this leading to an estimated increase in sales quantity of 30%. Other fixed costs would increase by £67,000, whilst material prices would decrease by 6.25% per unit. All other costs would remain unchanged.

**Required:**

(*a*) Taking each suggestion independently, compile a profit statement for options (*i*) to (*iii*), showing clearly the contribution per unit in each case. For suggestion (*iv*), calculate the selling price per unit as requested by the managing director.

→

(*b*) Calculate the breakeven quantity in units if the managing director's suggestion were implemented. Draw a contribution/sales graph to illustrate your calculations.
Read from the graph the profit if 60,000 units were sold.

(*c*) Whilst marginal costing has a number of applications, it also has disadvantages. In a report to the managing director, outline the main applications of marginal costing and explain its disadvantages.

*(Reproduced with the kind permission of OCR – University of Oxford Delegacy of Local Examinations: GCE A-level)*

**49.11** Magwitch Limited's finance director produced the following forecast breakeven chart for the year ending 31 May 2018:

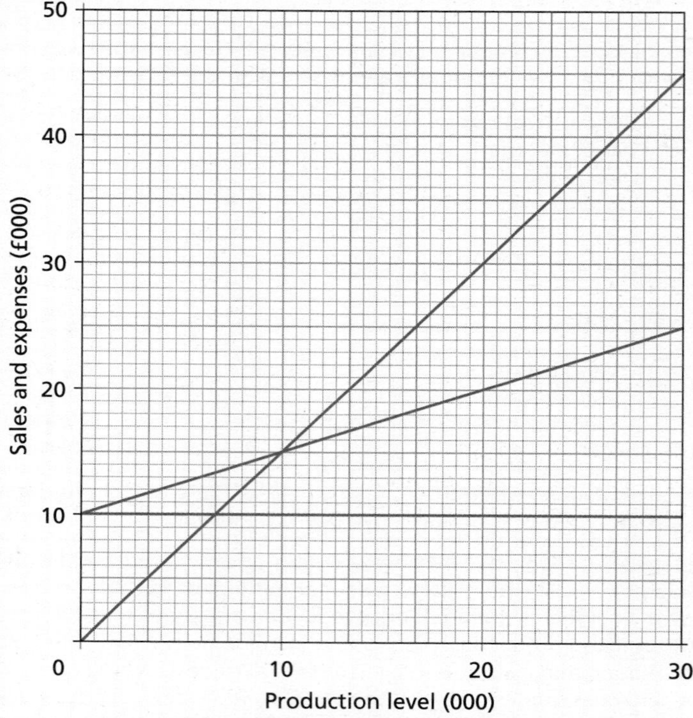


During the year the company produced and sold 20,000 units, and both revenue and expenses were 10% higher than forecast.

Compeyson plc has made an agreed takeover bid for the company at a value of 12 times the net profit for the year ending 31 May 2018.

Magwitch's assets and liabilities are to be taken over at their statement of financial position values, with the exception of non-current assets, which are to be revalued at £40,000.

The summarised statements of financial position of Magwitch Limited and Compeyson plc at the takeover date of 31 May 2018 are as follows:

| | *Magwitch* | *Compeyson* |
|---|---|---|
| | *£000* | *£000* |
| Non-current assets | 32 | 160 |
| Current assets | 65 | 340 |
| Current liabilities | (26) | (110) |
| | 71 | 390 |
| Share capital (£1 shares) | 40 | 200 |
| Reserves | 31 | 190 |
| | 71 | 390 |

The terms of the takeover are that Compeyson plc will give three of its shares (value £1.80 each) for every two shares in Magwitch Limited, plus a cash payment to make up the total agreed takeover price.

Magwitch Limited will cease to trade on 31 May 2018, and its assets and liabilities will be assumed by Compeyson plc. Any goodwill arising is to be written-off immediately against reserves.

(*a*) Draw up a summarised statement of profit or loss for Magwitch Limited for the year ending 31 May 2018.
(*b*) Draw up a statement of financial position for Compeyson plc after the takeover of Magwitch Limited has taken place.
(*c*) Calculate how many shares and how much cash would be received by a holder of 6,000 shares in Magwitch Limited as a result of the takeover.

(*Edexcel: GCE A-level*)

## 49.12A

(*a*) How far is it true to state that a company's breakeven point occurs where the contribution just equals the fixed costs?
(*b*) A company's detailed information of costs and sales has been destroyed because of a computer malfunction. The following data has, however, been gleaned from various sources:

| | | |
|---|---|---|
| Sales volume (units) | 10,000 | 12,000 |
| Costs (£): | | |
| direct materials | 30,000 | 36,000 |
| direct labour | 28,000 | 33,000 |
| overheads | 20,500 | 24,100 |

Selling price per unit at all volumes of output is £12.30

**Calculate:**
(*i*) the cost of an additional 2,000 units of output;
(*ii*) the variable costs of 10,000 units of output;
(*iii*) the fixed element – if any – of each component cost;
(*iv*) the breakeven point.

(*Edexcel: GCE A-level*)

chapter 50

# Capital expenditure appraisal

## Learning objectives

**After you have studied this chapter, you should be able to:**

- explain why interest rates are important in financial decision-making
- calculate and compare the net present value (NPV), internal rate of return (IRR), and payback of a series of cash flows
- choose between alternative projects on the basis of NPV, IRR and payback
- describe and compute the effects of taxation upon capital expenditure appraisal
- calculate the annualised amount of a series of cash flows and select between alternative projects on that basis

## Introduction

In this chapter, you'll learn how to assess and choose between alternative capital expenditure proposals using a variety of appraisal techniques. You'll also learn about 'relevant' and 'irrelevant' costs, sunk costs, and of the impact of uncertainty and uneven project lengths upon capital expenditure decisions.

## 50.1 Present value

You were introduced to the concept of present value in Chapter 27. You will recall that it is the amount that a future cash flow is worth in terms of today's money. £1,000 invested for five years at 10% compound results in a final amount of £1,610.51, but what would be the value of that £1,610.51 at the date of the initial investment (i.e. today)? If it were known, it would be possible to tell whether the investment might be worthwhile.

To calculate present value, the formula to use has the same variables as that used to calculate compound interest that you learnt about in Section 27.5, but it is rewritten to reflect that it is really the reciprocal of the compound interest formula:

$$\text{Amount invested } (I) = \frac{\text{Final value } (V)}{(1 + r)^n}$$

However, it would be more appropriate to describe the amount calculated as 'present value' rather than 'amount invested' and the formula becomes:

$$\text{Present value } (PV) = \frac{\text{Final value } (V)}{(1 + r)^n}$$

Let's look at an example.

**Example**

A bank is offering a guaranteed return at the end of five years of £1,500 for every £1,000 invested. If you could usually expect to obtain a rate of interest of 8% on your investments, what would be the present value of investing £1,000 in the bank?

$$PV = \frac{£1{,}500}{(1.08)^5} = £1{,}020.87$$

The 8% interest rate used in this example is generally referred to as the *discount rate* , i.e. the rate at which the future flow of cash is discounted to arrive at its present value. As with compound interest, present value tables are generally used, and will often be created and used on spreadsheets. A present value table is included in Appendix 1 (Table 2). An extract is presented in Exhibit 50.1:

### Exhibit 50.1 An example of a present value table

**Present Value Table**
**Period**
**Length PV of £1 discounted over the period at the rate shown**

| *n* | *1%* | *2%* | *3%* | *4%* | *5%* | *6%* | *7%* | *8%* | *9%* | *10%* | *n* |
|---|---|---|---|---|---|---|---|---|---|---|---|
| 1 | 0.990 | 0.980 | 0.971 | 0.961 | 0.952 | 0.943 | 0.935 | 0.926 | 0.917 | 0.909 | 1 |
| 2 | 0.980 | 0.961 | 0.943 | 0.925 | 0.907 | 0.890 | 0.873 | 0.857 | 0.842 | 0.826 | 2 |
| 3 | 0.971 | 0.942 | 0.915 | 0.889 | 0.864 | 0.840 | 0.816 | 0.794 | 0.772 | 0.751 | 3 |
| 4 | 0.961 | 0.924 | 0.889 | 0.855 | 0.823 | 0.792 | 0.763 | 0.735 | 0.708 | 0.683 | 4 |
| 5 | 0.951 | 0.906 | 0.863 | 0.822 | 0.784 | 0.747 | 0.713 | 0.681 | 0.650 | 0.621 | 5 |
| 6 | 0.942 | 0.888 | 0.838 | 0.790 | 0.746 | 0.705 | 0.666 | 0.630 | 0.596 | 0.564 | 6 |
| 7 | 0.933 | 0.871 | 0.813 | 0.760 | 0.711 | 0.665 | 0.623 | 0.583 | 0.547 | 0.513 | 7 |
| 8 | 0.923 | 0.853 | 0.789 | 0.731 | 0.677 | 0.627 | 0.582 | 0.540 | 0.502 | 0.467 | 8 |
| 9 | 0.914 | 0.837 | 0.766 | 0.703 | 0.645 | 0.592 | 0.544 | 0.500 | 0.460 | 0.424 | 9 |
| 10 | 0.905 | 0.820 | 0.744 | 0.676 | 0.614 | 0.558 | 0.508 | 0.463 | 0.422 | 0.386 | 10 |

| *n* | *11%* | *12%* | *13%* | *14%* | *15%* | *16%* | *17%* | *18%* | *19%* | *20%* | *n* |
|---|---|---|---|---|---|---|---|---|---|---|---|
| 1 | 0.901 | 0.893 | 0.885 | 0.877 | 0.870 | 0.862 | 0.855 | 0.847 | 0.840 | 0.833 | 1 |
| 2 | 0.812 | 0.797 | 0.783 | 0.769 | 0.756 | 0.743 | 0.731 | 0.718 | 0.706 | 0.694 | 2 |
| 3 | 0.731 | 0.712 | 0.693 | 0.675 | 0.658 | 0.641 | 0.624 | 0.609 | 0.593 | 0.579 | 3 |
| 4 | 0.659 | 0.636 | 0.613 | 0.592 | 0.572 | 0.552 | 0.534 | 0.516 | 0.499 | 0.482 | 4 |
| 5 | 0.593 | 0.567 | 0.543 | 0.519 | 0.497 | 0.476 | 0.456 | 0.437 | 0.419 | 0.402 | 5 |
| 6 | 0.535 | 0.507 | 0.480 | 0.456 | 0.432 | 0.410 | 0.390 | 0.370 | 0.352 | 0.335 | 6 |
| 7 | 0.482 | 0.452 | 0.425 | 0.400 | 0.376 | 0.354 | 0.333 | 0.314 | 0.296 | 0.279 | 7 |
| 8 | 0.434 | 0.404 | 0.376 | 0.351 | 0.327 | 0.305 | 0.285 | 0.266 | 0.249 | 0.233 | 8 |
| 9 | 0.391 | 0.361 | 0.333 | 0.308 | 0.284 | 0.263 | 0.243 | 0.226 | 0.209 | 0.194 | 9 |
| 10 | 0.352 | 0.322 | 0.295 | 0.270 | 0.247 | 0.227 | 0.208 | 0.191 | 0.176 | 0.162 | 10 |

Frequently, the cash flows arising from an investment arise throughout the period of the investment, not simply at the end. To calculate the overall present value of all the cash flows, each is calculated separately, and all the resulting present values are added together.

**Example**

An investment of £10,000 is made for five years. The net cash flows at the end of each of the five years are:

| *Period* | *Amount* £ |
|---|---|
| 1 | 2,000 |
| 2 | 3,000 |
| 3 | 4,000 |
| 4 | 3,000 |
| 5 | 1,000 |

If the discount rate used is 10%, the overall present value of the net cash flows is calculated as:

| *Period* | *Amount* £ | *Discount factor* *10%* | *Present value* £ |
|---|---|---|---|
| 1 | 2,000 | 0.909 | 1,818 |
| 2 | 3,000 | 0.826 | 2,478 |
| 3 | 4,000 | 0.751 | 3,004 |
| 4 | 3,000 | 0.683 | 2,049 |
| 5 | 1,000 | 0.621 | 621 |
| | | Overall present value of cash flows | 9,970 |

When compared to the initial investment of £10,000, it can be seen that this investment would lose £30 (i.e. £10,000 – £9,970). To make it easier to see this figure, these calculations usually incorporate the initial investment (which is not discounted as it is already at today's value) and produce a figure known as the net present value, or NPV. Incorporating the initial investment into this example produces the following table:

| *Period* | *Amount* £ | *Discount factor* *10%* | *Present value* £ |
|---|---|---|---|
| 0 | (10,000) | 1.000 | (10,000) |
| 1 | 2,000 | 0.909 | 1,818 |
| 2 | 3,000 | 0.826 | 2,478 |
| 3 | 4,000 | 0.751 | 3,004 |
| 4 | 3,000 | 0.683 | 2,049 |
| 5 | 1,000 | 0.621 | 621 |
| | | Net present value | (30) |

Many businesses have a rate of return that they require to achieve on investments. If a potential investment is not expected to achieve that rate of return, the investment will not be made. It is always possible to adopt the NPV approach in order to determine whether the return exceeds the required rate (which is shown by a positive NPV). **However, it is often useful to know what the actual rate of return is – the proposed investment may, for example, require that some additional financing be obtained that would be at a higher rate than the business's normal rate of return.**

The actual rate of return is known as the '*internal rate of return*', or *IRR*. It is the discount rate that results in an NPV of zero. It can be calculated very easily using a spreadsheet – a table similar to the one above would be written in the spreadsheet, but the discount factor would be left blank. Then, by instigating an appropriate command, the spreadsheet would identify and insert the IRR into the table so as to arrive at an NPV of zero.

**However, spreadsheets are not always available and IRR may need to be calculated manually. The method to adopt is similar to that adopted in the final example in Section 45.5 – a guess is made as to an appropriate IRR and the NPV calculation is made using that rate.** If the NPV is positive, a higher rate is selected (a lower rate is selected if the NPV is negative) and the NPV is again calculated. This continues until one positive NPV and one negative NPV are identified. The absolute difference between the two NPVs is calculated and the proportion of that difference that represents the difference between the NPV of the lower of the rates involved and zero is added to the lower rate to produce the IRR.

**Example**

You have been asked if you would be willing to lend £100,000 to a taxi company in order that it may expand its fleet of taxis. The money would be repaid at the rate of £30,000 per annum for four years. What is the IRR?

Step 1 is to select a rate that may be approximately correct. There is no simple way to select such a rate, and what would often be done is that the same rate would be used as the first step with most IRR calculations, and then the choice of the second rate to use would depend on how close to zero the first attempt came, and on whether the NPV it gave was positive or negative. If an 8% rate is used, the following results:

| *Period* | *Amount* | *Discount factor* | | *Present value* |
|---|---|---|---|---|
| | £ | *8%* | | £ |
| 0 | (100,000) | 1.000 | | (100,000) |
| 1 | 30,000 | 0.926 | | 27,780 |
| 2 | 30,000 | 0.857 | | 25,710 |
| 3 | 30,000 | 0.794 | | 23,820 |
| 4 | 30,000 | 0.735 | | 22,050 |
| | | | Net present value | (640) |

Using the 8% rate resulted in an NPV that was less than zero. The next rate chosen must, therefore, be less than 8%. A 7% rate produces the following:

| *Period* | *Amount* | *Discount factor* | | *Present value* |
|---|---|---|---|---|
| | £ | *7%* | | £ |
| 0 | (100,000) | 1.000 | | (100,000) |
| 1 | 30,000 | 0.935 | | 28,050 |
| 2 | 30,000 | 0.873 | | 26,190 |
| 3 | 30,000 | 0.816 | | 24,480 |
| 4 | 30,000 | 0.763 | | 22,890 |
| | | | Net present value | 1,610 |

Therefore, the IRR lies between 7% and 8%. The difference between the two NPVs is 2,250 (i.e. 640 + 1,610). A zero NPV will result if the rate is set to 7% plus 1,610/2,250 (as 7% is 1,610 away from zero). Expressed as a decimal, 1,610/2,250 = 0.72 and the IRR is, therefore, 7.72%.

## 50.2 Capital expenditure appraisal

If you had £5,000 to spend today and had the choice of investing it in a five-year bond with a bank, or lending it to a friend who had just opened a restaurant and who offered you 10% of the profits for five years, plus the return of your £5,000 at the end of the five years, which alternative would you choose and why?

Organisations make vast numbers of short-term decisions. They make comparatively few long-term decisions. These long-term decisions involve investing resources in something and then receiving the benefits. Examples include:

- building a new production facility
- buying a new delivery truck
- sponsoring a local football team for three years
- building a bridge
- buying an airline
- making a new product
- starting a new business.

**Generally, only the incremental cash payments and receipts arising from the decision to invest are relevant.** The relevant costs include interest, but not items that normally appear in the calculation of profit but which do not involve cash – depreciation, for example. There are two aspects of the incremental cash flows that should be distinguished: the cash outflows resulting from the decision to invest, and the cash inflows arising as a result of investing. The difference between these two groups of incremental cash flows determines whether or not an investment is made.

The techniques used to aid the selection of the appropriate long-term decision are referred to collectively as '*capital expenditure appraisal*'. There are three generally acceptable capital expenditure appraisal techniques in common use. Two have already been introduced in Section 50.1 – *net present value* and *internal rate of return*. Collectively, these two are known as '*discounted cash flow*' (*DCF*) techniques, as they involve the discounting of future net cash flows of a capital project to find their present value. Both techniques assume that all cash flows occur at the end of a period.

The third technique, '*payback*', involves selecting the alternative that repays the initial investment in the shortest time, provided that it does not exceed the business's maximum acceptable payback period – its payback hurdle period. It is useful when cash resources are limited and swift repayment of the investment is vital for the maintenance of working capital. Also, because risks of problems arising increase with the length of an investment, payback reduces the risk by minimising the relevant length of investment. **In contrast to the DCF techniques, payback assumes all cash flows occur evenly over a period, other than identifying when the total investment will be repaid.**

A fourth technique, '*accounting rate of return*' (*ARR*), having once been very popular, is now rarely used. The technique uses profits rather than cash flows and it involves dividing the average return by the average investment over the period. For example, if £10,000 is invested and the return is £30,000 over a 10-year period, there would be a return of £3,000 per year (£30,000 ÷ 10). If the £10,000 is repaid at the end of the 10 years, the average investment is £10,000 (i.e. [£10,000 + £10,000] ÷ 2). Therefore, the (annual) accounting rate of return is £3,000 divided by £10,000 i.e. 30%.

**Although it is generally easy to calculate, ARR produces a percentage figure that is of little practical use.** It cannot, for example, be compared with an organisation's cost of capital in order to assess whether a project would achieve a greater return than the cost of the capital that financed it. It also ignores the timing of cash flows – a project whose profits all arose at the start would be rejected in favour of one with a higher ARR whose profits all came at the end, even if inflation meant that those later period profits were worth significantly less in present value terms than the earlier profits of the rejected project. **There is no rational reason for using ARR.**

## Example

When considering a capital expenditure (or 'capital project') proposal, the first step is to identify all the incremental cash flows that would arise were the decision taken to proceed with the investment. As most decisions of this type involve cash flows over a number of years, once identified, the cash flows are mapped against the year in which they arise.

A new machine would cost £10,000 and installation would cost a further £1,000. It would replace an existing machine that would be sold for £2,000. The machine would generate cash income of £2,500 per annum for four years, at the end of which it would be sold for £3,000.

The cash flows are:

| *Period* | | *Amount* £ |
|---|---|---|
| 0 | Purchase + installation – sale proceeds | (9,000) |
| 1 | Income | 2,500 |
| 2 | Income | 2,500 |
| 3 | Income | 2,500 |
| 4 | Income (including sale proceeds) | 5,500 |
| | | 4,000 |

If the business's cost of capital is 10%, that would be the discount rate used and the net present value (as previously illustrated in Section 50.1) would be:

| *Period* | *Amount* £ | *Discount factor* 10% | *Present value* £ |
|---|---|---|---|
| 0 | (9,000) | 1.000 | (9,000.00) |
| 1 | 2,500 | 0.909 | 2,272.50 |
| 2 | 2,500 | 0.826 | 2,065.00 |
| 3 | 2,500 | 0.751 | 1,877.50 |
| 4 | 5,500 | 0.683 | 3,756.50 |
| | | Overall net present value of cash flows | 971.50 |

As the NPV is positive, the internal rate of return is higher than 10%. A 15% discount factor produces a negative NPV of £144:

| *Period* | *Amount* £ | *Discount factor* 15% | *Present value* £ |
|---|---|---|---|
| 0 | (9,000) | 1.000 | (9,000) |
| 1 | 2,500 | 0.870 | 2,175 |
| 2 | 2,500 | 0.756 | 1,890 |
| 3 | 2,500 | 0.658 | 1,645 |
| 4 | 5,500 | 0.572 | 3,146 |
| | | Overall net present value of cash flows | (144) |

Interpolating between these two values, as in Section 50.1, the IRR is found to be 14.35%. [The absolute difference is £1,115.50 (i.e. £971.50 + £144), of which approximately 87% (£971.50) is represented by the proportion relating to the 10% NPV. Multiplying the difference between the two discount rates (15% – 10% = 5%) by 87% gives an answer to two decimal places of 4.35%. This is then added to 10% to produce the IRR of 14.35%.] On the basis that the business's cost of capital is 10%, this project will be financially beneficial. Substituting the discount rate of 14.35% into the table produces a net present value of –10, the failure to reach a value of zero being due to rounding.

| *Period* | *Amount* £ | *Discount factor* 14.35% | *Present value* £ |
|---|---|---|---|
| 0 | (9,000) | 1.000 | (9,000.00) |
| 1 | 2,500 | 0.875 | 2,187.50 |
| 2 | 2,500 | 0.765 | 1,912.50 |
| 3 | 2,500 | 0.669 | 1,672.50 |
| 4 | 5,500 | 0.585 | 3,217.50 |
| | | Overall net present value of cash flows | (10.00) |

These two DCF techniques generally arrive at the selection of the same alternative when faced with a choice between two or more projects. However, they can produce different choices, and when they do, it is the NPV choice that should be selected.

As the following schedule shows, payback on the machine occurs after 3.27 years:

| *Period* £ | *Amount* £ | *Balance* £ | |
|---|---|---|---|
| 0 | (9,000) | (9,000) | |
| 1 | 2,500 | (6,500) | |
| 2 | 2,500 | (4,000) | |
| 3 | 2,500 | (1,500) | |
| 4 | 5,500 | – | Payback at 3 plus 1,500/5,500 years = 3.27 years |

This will then be compared to the business's hurdle period (i.e. its maximum permitted period) for payback. If it is later than the hurdle period, the project will be rejected. When cash flow is important, for example when the cost of capital is high, or when the risks in a project increase significantly the longer it runs, payback provides a measure of how quickly the investment in the project will be repaid, any subsequent cash flows being viewed as a bonus. However, it can result in a project being selected that is considerably less profitable than another that happens to take longer to repay the investment in it. It also ignores the time value of money. ('Real' payback will always be later than revealed by calculation as later receipts are not worth so much in today's money as early ones because of inflation.)

**How could you address these deficiencies to ensure payback was effectively applied?**

Closer inspection of the approach reveals that payback ignores everything after the (first) break-even point. Applied blindly, it is not concerned about whether a project breaks even overall, only that the amount invested in a project is reduced to zero at some stage. The fact that a project may break even in three years, but then requires more investment in year five, only finally breaking even in year six, can easily be overlooked when calculating payback.

## 50.3 Taxation

One factor often overlooked in consideration of capital projects is taxation. Items of equipment acquired will give rise to tax allowances that can be used to reduce tax payable, and any incremental profits arising from a capital project will give rise to payments of tax.

Taxation allowances are granted in place of depreciation and, when the equipment is sold or scrapped, its tax-written-down value (i.e. cost less taxation allowances claimed) less any amount received upon its disposal is allowed as a deduction against income for tax purposes.

Once calculated, the impact of taxation on the incremental cash flows is taken into account in the same way as any other item of incremental income or expenditure.

**Example**

A new machine costing £10,000 has an estimated useful life of four years, after which it will be scrapped. During those four years, it is expected to generate sales of £5,000 per annum. Production costs are anticipated to be 40% of sales revenue. Working capital of £3,000 will be required for this activity, all of which will be recovered when the machine is scrapped. Depreciation is by the straight line method, i.e. £2,500 per annum starting in Year 1. Corporation tax of 40% is paid nine months after the end of each accounting period. A taxation allowance of 25% (reducing balance) will be available if the machine is acquired.

The expected annual profit is:

| | £ | £ |
|---|---|---|
| Sales | | 5,000 |
| Production costs | 2,000 | |
| Depreciation | 2,500 | |
| | | (4,500) |
| | | 500 |
| Corporation tax | | (200) |
| Net profit after tax | | 300 |

The expected cash flows that would be used for the capital expenditure appraisal are:

| *Investment (£)* | *Year 1* | *2* | *3* | *4* | *5* |
|---|---|---|---|---|---|
| Machine | (10,000) | | | | |
| Working capital | (3,000) | | | 3,000 | |
| Tax allowance | | 1,000 | 750 | 562.50 | 1,687.50 |
| | (13,000) | 1,000 | 750 | 3,562.50 | 1,687.50 |
| *Cash flows (£)* | | | | | |
| Sales | 5,000 | 5,000 | 5,000 | 5,000 | |
| Production costs | (2,000) | (2,000) | (2,000) | (2,000) | |
| Tax (40% × £3,000) | | (1,200) | (1,200) | (1,200) | (1,200) |
| | 3,000 | 1,800 | 1,800 | 1,800 | (1,200) |
| *Net cash flows (£)* | (10,000) | 2,800 | 2,550 | 5,362.50 | 487.50 |

**Note: The overall tax allowances are £4,000, which is 40% of the cost of the equipment, for which it has been assumed that there will be no scrap proceeds. Also, the cost of the machine and additional working capital would be treated as having arisen in Year 0 for the purposes of the capital expenditure appraisal techniques. They are shown in Year 1 in the above table so as to clarify the timing of the tax and tax allowance cash flows.**

## 50.4 Annualised figures

It can be difficult comparing projects that have different lengths. To overcome this complication, it is possible to use annualised amounts. Notionally, this approach assumes that the comparison would then be made over a period that represented the lowest common multiple of the projects – a 12-year cycle would be used for two projects, one of three years' duration, the other four. However, as will be seen, once the annualised amounts are calculated, the decision can be taken without reference to any particular length of time.

The first step is to calculate the present value of the projects and then identify the amount of the annuity for the period of each project that has the same present value as that project's NPV. For example, if a discount rate of 10% is used and the NPV of the three-year project is £500, the annuity multiplier (from Table 4 in Appendix 1) is 2.487 and the three-year annuity with a present value of £500 is therefore £201 (i.e. £500 ÷ 2.487). If the four-year project has an NPV of £800, the four-year annuity is £252 (i.e. £800 ÷ 3.170). On the basis of these annualised amounts, the four-year project would be selected.

## 50.5 Relevant and irrelevant costs

When decision-making, some costs and revenues are relevant to a decision that is to be taken, whilst other costs and revenues are **irrelevant costs.** The **relevant costs** and *relevant revenues* are those costs and revenues of the future that will be affected by the decision, whereas irrelevant costs and revenues will not be so affected.

Take as an example a decision as to whether or not we should telephone a lot of our customers in a sales campaign. The cost of the telephone rental is irrelevant in the decision whether or not to conduct the campaign, as we will have to pay exactly the same rental whether or not we engage in the campaign. On the other hand, the cost of making the extra calls will be a relevant cost as they would not have been incurred if the campaign had not gone ahead.

With revenues, take the case of buying a new car for a salesperson. If the revenues he would help create by sales would remain unchanged no matter which car he were to have, then the revenues would be completely irrelevant in taking the decision as to the type of car to be bought.

However, take the case of a salesperson who sells some of his products to farmers. With a four-wheel-drive car he could get to farms which would otherwise be inaccessible to a two-wheel-drive car. In this case the revenues would be relevant to the decision as to the type of car to be bought, as they would be affected by the decision.

## 50.6 Sunk costs

**Sunk cost** is a term which can be confusing, since it really means an irrelevant cost which has already occurred. It is a past cost, not a future cost.

Let's take the case of a machine which was bought several years ago, and now has a written-down value of £10,000. The scrap value is nil. We can either use the machine on a project we are considering or else we can scrap it. Let us suppose that the revenue from the project will be £25,000 and the future relevant costs will be £18,000. If we added the written-down value of the machine to the £18,000 costs then we would make a loss of £3,000 (£25,000 − £28,000). Looking at it that way, we would not tackle the project.

However, the cost of the machine was a past cost. If we do not use the machine on this project the only other alternative is to scrap it. Such a past cost is said to be a *sunk cost* and is irrelevant to the decision to be taken. We therefore take on the project (assuming there is no better alternative project) and are better off by £7,000 (£25,000 − £18,000).

## 50.7 A comparison of the methods

We will now look at a case where each of the methods already described will be used to try to select the best investment. You will see that the different methods can give different answers as to which project should be chosen.

## Exhibit 50.2

ABC Ltd is wondering whether or not to invest in one of three possible projects. The initial investment will be £10,000 and the cost of capital is 10%. There is no scrap value for the non-current assets used in these projects. Details of the net cash inflows are as follows:

| | *M* | *N* | *P* |
|---|---|---|---|
| | £ | £ | £ |
| Year 1 | 3,000 | 5,000 | 4,000 |
| Year 2 | 6,000 | 5,000 | 5,000 |
| Year 3 | 4,000 | 2,000 | 3,000 |
| Year 4 | – | 1,600 | 1,000 |
| Year 5 | – | – | 1,400 |
| | 13,000 | 13,600 | 14,400 |

**1 Accounting rate of return method**

$$\frac{\text{Average yearly profit}}{\text{Average investment}} \times \frac{100}{1} \qquad \frac{1,000}{5,000} = 20\% \qquad \frac{900}{5,000} = 18\% \qquad \frac{880}{5,000} = 17.6\%$$

**2 Payback method**

| *M* | *N* | *P* |
|---|---|---|
| 2.25 years | 2 years | 2 years |

**3 Net present value method (cost of capital 10%)**

| *Discount factors per tables* | *M* | | *N* | | *P* | |
|---|---|---|---|---|---|---|
| | | | *Present values (£)* | | | |
| 1.000 | × (10,000) = | (10,000) | × (10,000) = | (10,000) | × (10,000) = | (10,000) |
| 0.909 | × 3,000 = | 2,727 | × 5,000 = | 4,545 | × 4,000 = | 3,636 |
| 0.826 | × 6,000 = | 4,956 | × 5,000 = | 4,130 | × 5,000 = | 4,130 |
| 0.751 | × 4,000 = | 3,004 | × 2,000 = | 1,502 | × 3,000 = | 2,253 |
| 0.683 | | | × 1,600 = | 1,093 | × 1,000 = | 683 |
| 0.621 | | | | | × 1,400 = | 869 |
| Net present values | | 687 | | 1,270 | | 1,571 |

**4 Internal rate of return**

*Stage 1:* Use a rate of return which will give negative net present values. In this instance it is taken to be 18%.

| *Discount factors per tables at 18%* | *M* | | *N* | | *P* | |
|---|---|---|---|---|---|---|
| | | | *Present values (£)* | | | |
| 1.000 | × (10,000) = | (10,000) | × (10,000) = | (10,000) | × (10,000) = | (10,000) |
| 0.847 | × 3,000 = | 2,541 | × 5,000 = | 4,235 | × 4,000 = | 3,388 |
| 0.718 | × 6,000 = | 4,308 | × 5,000 = | 3,590 | × 5,000 = | 3,590 |
| 0.609 | × 4,000 = | 2,436 | × 2,000 = | 1,218 | × 3,000 = | 1,827 |
| 0.516 | | | × 1,600 = | 826 | × 1,000 = | 516 |
| 0.437 | | | | | × 1,400 = | 612 |
| Net present values | | (715) | | (131) | | (67) |

*Stage 2:* Calculate the internal rate of return (IRR), using figures for positive present values already calculated in 3 above.

$$M \quad 10\% + \left(8\% \times \frac{687}{687 + 715}\right) = 13.92\%$$

$$N \quad 10\% + \left(8\% \times \frac{1,270}{1,270 + 131}\right) = 17.25\%$$

$$P \quad 10\% + \left(8\% \times \frac{1,571}{1,571 + 67}\right) = 17.67\%$$

If used on its own, without reference to the other methods:

1 Accounting rate of return would choose project M, as it gives highest rate of 20%.
2 Payback would choose project N, as it pays back in the shortest time of two years.
3 Net present value would choose project P as it gives the highest net present value of £1,571.
4 Internal rate of return would choose project P, as it shows highest return of 17.67%, which is itself higher than the cost of capital.

## 50.8 Uncertainty

Many of the values used in the calculations and formulae described in this chapter are, at best, objectively based estimates of future cash flows and interest rates. It is, for example, virtually inconceivable that the figures forecast in a capital expenditure appraisal will be confirmed to have been 100% accurate when the project is completed.

Proposers of a course of action tend to be over-optimistic and, in order to avoid the risk of non-achievement of forecasted results, a number of measures have been adopted. The two most common are the adoption of a higher cost of capital rate than is actually required in practice, and reducing estimates of income by a fixed percentage and using the same percentage to increase all costs. However, such arbitrary adjustments can no more guarantee accuracy than the original estimates, and they will often cause the decision taken to be different from that which the original, possibly more meaningful, data would have produced.

A more rational adjustment that can be adopted is to change the amounts forecast according to their subjective probabilities. The probabilities would be provided by the proposers of a project.

**Example**

| *Estimated sales* × | *Probability of occurrence* = | *Expected sales* |
|---|---|---|
| £ | £ | |
| 2,000 | 0.2 | 400 |
| 4,000 | 0.5 | 2,000 |
| 6,000 | 0.2 | 1,200 |
| 8,000 | 0.1 | 800 |
| | 1.0 | 4,400 |

In this case, the expected value of £4,400 will be used, rather than the most likely value of £4,000. While this approach appears more rational than the other possible methods of dealing with uncertainty, it is dependent upon the probabilities used being soundly based.

If two projects both require the same investment and one has an NPV of £100 and the other an NPV of £240, which should be selected? Would this always be the case?

## 50.9 Sensitivity analysis

One of the greatest benefits of spreadsheets is the facility to perform unlimited numbers of sensitivity analysis computations on a given set of data. Cash flows can be adjusted marginally to see if the change turns a positive NPV negative; interest rates can be altered to see if the same decision would be made; the timing of cash flows can be altered to see what the impact of doing so is upon NPV. Sensitivity analysis enables information generated using the formulae and methods described in this chapter to be manipulated to maximise the understanding of the flexibility and limits of that information.

The importance of discounting has been recognised by the Institute of Chartered Accountants in England and Wales, which issued Technical Release 773: *The Use of Discounting in Financial Statements*. It is an excellent source of discussion on this topic, and on its application in practice.

## Learning outcomes

**You should now have learnt:**

1. That as time passes, money loses value and this loss of value must be allowed for when considering long-term investments.
2. That net present value (NPV) and internal rate of return (IRR) usually lead to the same selection being made between mutually exclusive projects. When they differ, it is the NPV selection that should be followed.
3. That accounting rate of return (ARR) is still used, but the rate it produces cannot be compared to the cost of capital and the technique is not recommended.
4. How to calculate NPV, IRR, payback and ARR.
5. The relative merits of the four methods.
6. What is meant by relevant and irrelevant costs.
7. What is meant by sunk cost.
8. How to select the 'best' project for an organisation to pursue at a given time from a range of possible alternative projects.
9. How to explain why, from a financial perspective, the selected project is the 'best' one for the organisation to pursue.
10. That where alternative projects are of unequal length, annualised amounts can be calculated to enable comparison.

## Answers to activities

50.1 It would depend on many factors, not least the rate of interest you would receive from the bank and the anticipated profits from the restaurant. You would need to consider the probability of the estimates concerning the profitability of the restaurant. You would also need to take into account your relationship with your friend and your own willingness to run the risk that you may not be able to recover your investment without damaging your relationship with your friend should you need the money back before the five years had passed. There are many non-financial factors that often need to be taken into account when considering long-term investments.

50.2 These deficiencies in the payback approach can be addressed by discounting all cash flows to their present values, and by ensuring that the calculation includes a check for there being multiple payback points. While the first is generally sensible, the second is essential if payback is to be effectively applied.

50.3 The project with the higher NPV should normally be chosen. Where the NPV is very small relative to the investment, it may not be so important that the one with the higher NPV is chosen. For example, if the investment required for these NPVs is £7,500 the NPVs are relatively very small indeed. Other factors would be more important, such as the likelihood that the figures would prove to be accurate; the potential impact of each alternative on the general image and reputation of the organisation; whether the projects would involve any opportunity costs that are not accounted for in the NPV calculation (such as employees being unavailable for other work), etc.

## Review questions

**50.1** The following project costs have been estimated relating to the upgrading of some equipment; all the costs are being incurred solely because of the project:

| *2017* | | | £ |
|---|---|---|---|
| January | 1 | One year's rent on premises paid | 20,400 |
| | 31 | Equipment purchased | 34,000 |
| March | 31 | Installation of equipment completed and paid | 6,800 |
| December | 31 | Costs incurred in commissioning equipment | 13,600 |
| *2018* | | | |
| January | 1 | One year's rent on premises paid | 20,400 |
| March | 31 | Additional commissioning costs paid | 4,000 |
| May | 31 | Training costs paid | 5,100 |
| June | 30 | Additional working capital provided | 27,200 |
| December | 31 | Cash proceeds from sale of old equipment | 8,500 |

Ignoring tax, prepare a statement showing the outlays of cash on the project in 2017 and 2018. The new facility will be in full use from 1 July 2018.

**50.2** Assume the company in Question 50.1 pays tax at 30%, on 30 September each year, nine months after the end of its financial period. The company receives 25% writing-down allowances on the cost of equipment and will receive the allowances for 2017 expenditure to be offset against the tax payable on the profits for 2017. 100% capital allowances were received on the old equipment sold in 2018 and the receipts from the sale of the old equipment must, therefore, be treated as taxable income of 2018. Show the impact on the cash flows of these tax items.

**50.3** Assuming an interest rate of 5%, what is the net present value of the net of tax cash flows in Question 50.2 for 2017, 2018, 2019 and 2020?

**50.4A** The annual forecasted profit from a project is:

| | £ | £ |
|---|---|---|
| Sales | | 300,000 |
| Labour, materials, and overheads | 88,000 | |
| Depreciation | 20,000 | |
| | | (108,000) |
| Net profit before tax | | 192,000 |
| Tax at 30% | | (57,600) |
| Net profit after tax | | 134,400 |

Equipment with a four-year useful economic life and no residual value will be purchased on 1 September for £80,000. £45,000 additional working capital, which will be recovered in full at the end of the four years, will be required from 1 September. A 25% writing-down allowance (i.e. reducing balance) will be available throughout the period of the project. Tax at 30% will be payable on 1 June each year, nine months after the end of the company's financial period on 31 August. Prepare a cash flow budget for the project.

**50.5A** If the interest rate is 6%, what is the net present value of the net cash flows arising from the project in Question 50.4A?

**50.6A** If retained, a machine would be depreciated £3,000 for each of the next five years, at which point it would be fully written-down and scrapped. The machine could be sold at any point in the next year for £18,000, the gain being subject to tax at 30%, payable the following year. If it were sold, a new machine costing £90,000 would be bought. The new machine would receive 20% writing-down allowances to be offset annually against profits. It is estimated that the new machine would save material costs of £30,000 per year compared to the current machine. Profits are subject to tax at 30%, payable nine months after the end of the company's financial period. The new machinery would have a five-year life, with a residual value of zero, and would be depreciated by the straight line method over that period. Prepare a cash flow forecast for the replacement option, and indicate how the profits reported in the financial statements would be altered were the existing machine to be replaced.

**50.7** What is the payback period on the following project cash flows? (Brackets indicate expenditure.)

| *Year* | *Net cash flows* |
|---|---|
| | *£* |
| 0 | (20,000) |
| 1 | 15,000 |
| 2 | 8,000 |
| 3 | 4,000 |
| 4 | 3,000 |

**50.8** Using a discount rate of 5%, what is the net present value of the project in Question 50.7?

**50.9** What is the internal rate of return on the project in Question 50.7?

**50.10** What is the annualised amount of the net benefits from the project in Question 50.7?

**50.11A** What is the payback on a project requiring £60,000 initial investment that has a net cash inflow of £41,000 in Year 1, £23,000 in Year 2, and £8,000 in Year 3?

**50.12A** Using a discount rate of 4%, what is the net present value of the project in Question 50.11A?

**50.13A** What is the internal rate of return on the project in Question 50.11A?

**50.14A** What is the annualised amount of the net benefits from the project in Question 50.11A?

**50.15A** The annual profit forecast for a project is:

| | *£* | *£* |
|---|---|---|
| Revenue | | 210,000 |
| Labour, materials, and overheads | 70,000 | |
| Depreciation | 42,000 | |
| | | 112,000 |
| Net profit before tax | | 98,000 |

The project requires that a new machine be purchased for £180,000. It will be depreciated using the straight line method over five years to a residual value of £15,000. The project will cease when the machine is sold for £15,000 at the end of the fifth year. Ignoring taxation, what is the accounting rate of return? (No additional working capital is required for this project.)

**50.16A** Assuming that all sales are for cash, what is the internal rate of return on the project in Question 50.15A?

→

**50.17** Which of the following two mutually exclusive alternatives should be selected if a 6% interest rate is used for the calculation of net present value?

| | *Net cash flow Year 0* | *Net cash flow Year 3* |
|---|---|---|
| | *£* | *£* |
| Machine X project | (36,000) | 61,000 |
| Machine Y project | (104,000) | 210,000 |

**50.18** Using internal rate of return, which of the two projects in Question 50.17 would be preferred?

**50.19A** Which of the following two mutually exclusive alternatives should be selected if a 7% interest rate is used for the calculation of net present value?

| | *Net cash flow Year 0* | *Net cash flow Year 1* | *Net cash flow Year 3* |
|---|---|---|---|
| | *£* | *£* | *£* |
| Project X | (68,000) | 30,000 | 48,000 |
| Project Y | (58,000) | 42,000 | 21,000 |

**50.20A** Using internal rate of return, which of the two projects in Question 50.19A would be preferred?

**50.21** Equipment with an estimated useful economic life of four years has an NPV of £4,200 using an 8% discount rate. What is the annualised equivalent of the £4,200 NPV?

**50.22A** Two mutually exclusive alternatives are available. Project X will require initial investment of £50,000 and run for three years at a cost of £8,000 per annum. Project Y will require initial investment of £110,000 and last for five years at a cost of £12,000 for the first two years and £2,000 in Years 3, 4 and 5. Calculate the annualised cost of both projects over a five-year period, assuming that reinvestment in Project X would cost £4,000 at the end of Year 2 and an interest rate of 6%. Which alternative should be selected?

**50.23** A machine with a four-year useful life could be purchased for £50,000. It would have zero residual value at the end of the four years. Alternatively, the machine could be rented at £15,180 per annum for four years. Assuming a tax rate of 30% and that tax relief is obtained in the same period as the payments, what is the implicit interest rate in the lease?

**50.24** Roadwheelers Ltd were considering buying an additional lorry but the company had not yet decided which particular lorry to purchase. The lorries had broadly similar technical specifications and each was expected to have a working life of five years.

The following information was available on the lorries being considered:

1

| | | *Lorries* | |
|---|---|---|---|
| | *BN* | *FX* | *VR* |
| | *Roadhog* | *Sprinter* | *Rocket* |
| Purchase price | £40,000 | £45,000 | £50,000 |
| Estimated scrap value after five years | £8,000 | £9,000 | £14,000 |
| Fixed costs other than depreciation | £ | £ | £ |
| Year 1 | 2,000 | 1,800 | 1,500 |
| Year 2 | 2,000 | 1,800 | 1,500 |
| Year 3 | 2,200 | 1,800 | 1,400 |
| Year 4 | 2,400 | 2,000 | 1,400 |
| Year 5 | 2,400 | 2,200 | 1,400 |
| Variable costs per road mile | 6p | 8p | 7p |

**2** The company charges 25p per mile for all journeys irrespective of the length of journey and the expected annual mileages over the five-year period are:

| | *Miles* |
|---|---|
| Year 1 | 50,000 |
| Year 2 | 60,000 |
| Year 3 | 80,000 |
| Year 4 | 80,000 |
| Year 5 | 80,000 |

**3** The company's cost of capital is 10% per annum.
**4** It should be assumed that all operating costs are paid and revenues received at the end of year.
**5** Present value of £1 at interest rate of 10% per annum:

| | |
|---|---|
| Year 1 | £0.909 |
| Year 2 | £0.826 |
| Year 3 | £0.751 |
| Year 4 | £0.683 |
| Year 5 | £0.621 |

**Required:**
(*a*) (*i*) Appropriate computations using the net present value method for each of the lorries under consideration.

(*ii*) A report to the directors of Roadwheelers Ltd advising them as to which specific lorry should be purchased.

(*b*) A brief outline of the problems encountered in evaluating capital projects.

*(AQA (Associated Examining Board): GCE A-level)*

**50.25A** Hirwaun Pig Iron Co. operate a single blast furnace producing pig iron. The present blast furnace is obsolete and the company is considering its replacement. The alternatives the company is considering are:

(*i*) Blast furnace type Exco. Cost £2 million.
This furnace is of a standard size capable of a monthly output of 10,000 tonnes. The company expects to sell 80% of its output annually at £150 per tonne on a fixed price contract. The remaining output will be sold on the open market at the following expected prices:

| | *2015* | *2016* | *2017* | *2018* |
|---|---|---|---|---|
| Price per tonne | £150 | £140 | £140 | £160 |

(*ii*) Blast furnace type Ohio. Cost £3.5 million.
This large furnace is capable of a monthly output of 20,000 tonnes. A single buyer has agreed to buy all the monthly output at a fixed price which is applicable from 1 January each year. The prices fixed for the next four years are as follows:

| | *Payments per tonne of output* | | | |
|---|---|---|---|---|
| | *2015* | *2016* | *2017* | *2018* |
| Price per tonne | £130 | £130 | £140 | £170 |

*Additional information:*
**1** Blast furnaces operate continuously and the operating labour is regarded as a fixed cost. During the next four years the operating labour costs will be as follows:

Exco £1.2 million per annum
Ohio £2.5 million per annum

2 Other forecast operating payments (excluding labour) per tonne:

| | *2015* | *2016* | *2017* | *2018* |
|---|---|---|---|---|
| Exco | £130 | £130 | £135 | £135 |
| Ohio | £120 | £120 | £125 | £125 |

3 It can be assumed that both blast furnaces will have a life of 10 years.
4 The company's cost of capital is 12% per annum.
5 It should be assumed that all costs are paid and revenues received at the end of each year.
6 The following is an extract from the present value table for £1:

| | *11%* | *12%* | *13%* | *14%* |
|---|---|---|---|---|
| Year 1 | £0.901 | £0.893 | £0.885 | £0.877 |
| Year 2 | £0.812 | £0.797 | £0.783 | £0.769 |
| Year 3 | £0.731 | £0.712 | £0.693 | £0.675 |
| Year 4 | £0.659 | £0.636 | £0.613 | £0.592 |

**Required:**

(*a*) The forecast budgets for each of the years 2015–2018 and for each of the blast furnaces being considered. Show the expected yearly net cash flows.

(*b*) Appropriate computations using the net present value method for each of the blast furnaces, Exco and Ohio, for the first four years.

(*c*) A report providing a recommendation to the management of Hirwaun Pig Iron Co. as to which blast furnace should be purchased. Your report should include a critical evaluation of the method used to assess the capital project.

*(AQA (Associated Examining Board): GCE A-level)*

**50.26** Moray Ferries Ltd own a single ship which provides a short sea ferry service for passengers, private vehicles and commercial traffic. The present ship is nearing the end of its useful life and the company is considering the purchase of a new ship.

The forecast operating budgets using the present ship are as follows:

| | *2017* | *2018* | *2019* | *2020* | *2021* |
|---|---|---|---|---|---|
| Estimated revenue receipts | *£m* | *£m* | *£m* | *£m* | *£m* |
| Private traffic | 2 | 3 | 4.5 | 6 | 7 |
| Commercial traffic | 3 | 4 | 4.5 | 5 | 6 |
| | 5 | 7 | 9.0 | 11 | 13 |
| Estimated operating payments | 4 | 5 | 6.5 | 7.5 | 9 |
| | 1 | 2 | 2.5 | 3.5 | 4 |

The ships being considered as a replacement are as described below.

1 Ship A. Cost £10m
This ship is of similar capacity to the one being replaced, but being a more modern ship it is expected that extra business would be attracted from competitors. It is anticipated therefore that estimated revenue receipts would be 10% higher in each year of the present forecast. There would be no change in operating payments.

2 Ship B. Cost £14m
This modern ship has a carrying capacity 30% greater than the present ship. It is expected that private traffic receipts would increase by £½m a year in each year of the forecast. Commercial traffic receipts are expected to increase by 15% in each of the first two years and by 30% in each of the remaining years.
Operating payments would increase by 20% in each year of the forecast.

*Additional information:*

3 The company's cost of capital is 15% per annum.
4 It is company policy to assume that ships have a life of 20 years.
5 It should be assumed that all costs are paid and revenues received at the end of each year.

**6** The following is an extract from the present value table for £1:

| | *12%* | *14%* | *15%* | *16%* |
|---|---|---|---|---|
| Year 1 | £0.893 | £0.877 | £0.870 | £0.862 |
| Year 2 | £0.797 | £0.769 | £0.756 | £0.743 |
| Year 3 | £0.712 | £0.675 | £0.658 | £0.641 |
| Year 4 | £0.636 | £0.592 | £0.572 | £0.552 |
| Year 5 | £0.567 | £0.519 | £0.497 | £0.476 |

**7** All calculations should be made correct to three places of decimals.

**Required:**

(*a*) Revised operating budgets for 2017–2021 for each of the alternatives being considered.
(*b*) Appropriate computations using the net present value method for each of the ships, A and B.
(*c*) A report providing a recommendation to the management of Moray Ferries Ltd as to which course of action should be followed. Your report should include any reservations that you may have.

*(AQA (Associated Examining Board): GCE A-level)*

**50.27A** The Rovers Football Club are languishing in the middle of the Premier Division of the Football League. The Club have suffered a loss of £200,000 in their last financial year and whilst receipts from spectators have declined over the last five years, recently receipts have stabilised at approximately £1,000,000 per season. The Club is considering the purchase of the services of one of two new football players, Jimmy Jam or Johnny Star.

Jimmy Jam is 21 years old and considered to be a future international footballer. He is prepared to sign a five-year contract with Rovers for a salary of £50,000 per annum. His present club would require a transfer fee of £200,000 for the transfer of his existing contract. With J. Jam in the team the Rovers Club would expect receipts to increase by 20%.

Johnny Star is 32 years old and a leading international footballer who is prepared to sign for Rovers on a two-year contract before retiring completely from football. He would expect a salary of £200,000 per annum and his present club would require a transfer fee of £100,000 for the transfer of his existing contract. Rovers believe that as a result of signing Star receipts would increase by 40%.

The rate of interest applicable to the transaction is 12% and the following is an extract from the present value table for £1:

| | *12%* |
|---|---|
| Year 1 | 0.893 |
| Year 2 | 0.797 |
| Year 3 | 0.712 |
| Year 4 | 0.636 |
| Year 5 | 0.567 |

It should be assumed that all costs are paid and revenues received at the end of each year.

**Required:**

A report, incorporating an evaluation of the financial result of engaging each player by the net present value method, providing the Rovers Football Club with information to assist it in deciding which alternative to adopt. Indicate any other factors that may be taken into consideration.

*(AQA (Associated Examining Board): GCE A-level)*

chapter

# 51 The balanced scorecard

## Learning objectives

**After you have studied this chapter, you should be able to:**

- describe the aims of the balanced scorecard
- explain the four perspectives of the balanced scorecard
- explain the two types of measure inherent in the balanced scorecard
- explain the difference between the balanced scorecard and a traditional financial-accounting-based performance appraisal system
- describe some advantages of adopting the balanced scorecard
- describe some of the problems that can arise when the balanced scorecard is adopted

## Introduction

In this chapter, you'll learn about the balanced scorecard, its four perspectives, its two measures and its advantages compared with more traditional financial-accounting-based performance appraisal systems. You'll also learn about some of the problems that can arise when the balanced scorecard is adopted.

## 51.1 Background

Much has changed in the way that organisations operate today compared with even five years ago. The change over the past 40 years has been immense. In 1980, only the largest organisations had computers, the spreadsheet had only just been invented, the Internet was something only academics and some government employees had heard of, email was used by only a few, the *World Wide Web* was 10 years away from being invented, electronic commerce was something from science fiction, and most business records were still recorded and maintained by hand.

The business environment of today is far more competitive, far more open, and far more volatile than it has ever been. In order to survive, businesses need to be far more efficient in the use of their resources, have a far better understanding of the needs of their customers, have far better organised internal systems and procedures, and have employees who have a far greater level of interpersonal skills than in the past. Above all, they need to have a well-defined organisational strategy and to have both defined the objectives that ensure the strategy is pursued and identified the measures required in order to ensure that the objectives not only are being achieved but will continue to be achieved in future.

This means that **organisations need to look beyond the historical perspective of their traditional financial reporting systems** which were mainly backwards-looking, focusing upon reporting achievements rather than upon the attainment and pursuit of objectives. They need to incorporate data capture and analysis of non-financial measures, such as customer profiles, customer satisfaction, employee performance, employee satisfaction, product quality, service quality, organisational transformation and development. They need to pay attention to the long term and think less about the short term.

One performance evaluation technique that supports this shift in emphasis and focus has emerged over the last 20 years, Kaplan and Norton's **balanced scorecard**. It bridges the strengths of the traditional financial measures of past performance with the benefits of measuring factors that impact upon or 'drive' future performance. It does so at all levels of the business, not just at the overall level typified by the traditional measures of financial performance.

## 51.2 The framework of the balanced scorecard

The balanced scorecard assesses performance across a balanced set of four perspectives: customers, internal processes, organisational learning and growth, and financial. It does not replace the traditional focus upon financial measurement as a critical summary of managerial and business performance. Rather, it complements it by the addition of the other three perspectives.

Thus, the traditional financial measures are still there for those that require them and for the purposes to which they are most suited but new measures are provided that enrich the information available at all levels of the organisation and so facilitate the co-ordinated achievement of organisational objectives, particularly in the long term.

### The four perspectives of the balanced scorecard

Exhibit 51.1 shows the relationship between the four perspectives, and organisational vision and strategy:

**Exhibit 51.1**

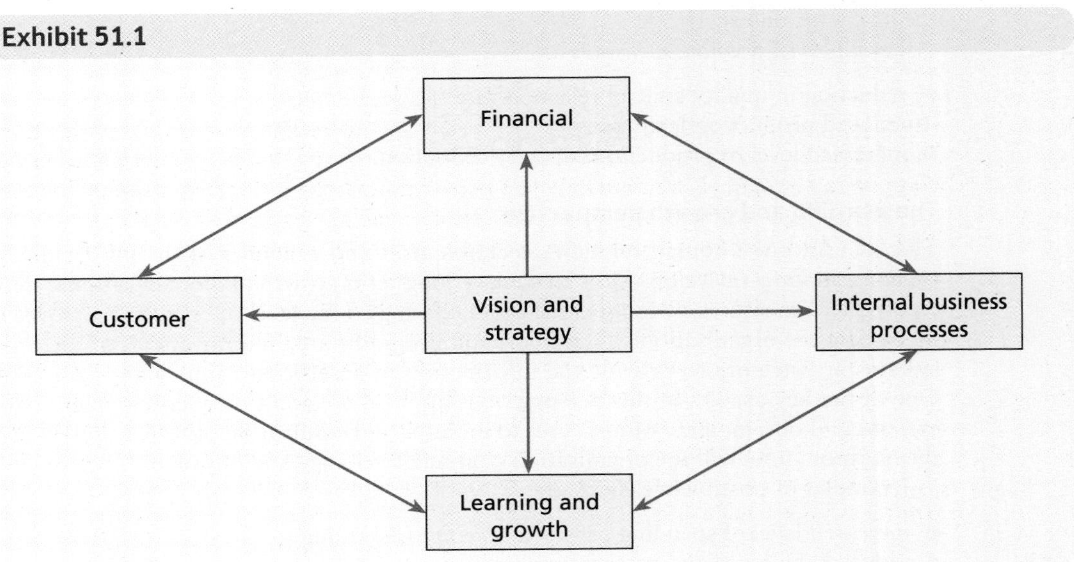

### The financial perspective

Here you identify the financial objectives that the organisation wishes to pursue and develop measures that indicate how successful the organisation has been in achieving those objectives. In essence, this is the aspect of the balanced scorecard that accounting has long been associated with and includes the use of such measures as return on capital employed, earnings per share, and the other financial ratios you learnt about in Chapter 28. It answers the question, how does the organisation appear to its owners?

Examples of possible measures are:

- return on capital employed
- return on net assets
- reduction of administrative expenses
- reduction in bad debts
- reduction in accounts receivable days
- reduction in gearing.

### The customer perspective

You must identify the customer and market segments in which the organisation operates. Measurements should then be made of factors such as customer satisfaction, retention, acquisition, profitability and market share. It answers the question, how does the organisation appear to its customers?

Examples of possible measures are:

- customer satisfaction
- customer retention
- increasing customer base
- reduction in delivery times
- reduction in rate of goods returned by customers.

### The internal business processes perspective

You need to identify and measure the internal processes that are critical to the organisation being able to improve the drivers that will attract and retain customers in targeted markets and satisfy owner expectations concerning financial returns. It answers the question, at what must the organisation excel?

Examples of possible measures are:

- reduction in quality control rejection rate
- reduced production lead times
- increased level of production capacity utilisation.

### The learning and growth perspective

This identifies the human relations, technological and general systems infrastructure that the organisation must develop if it is to achieve long-term growth and organisational improvement. Appropriate measures would include those relating to the level of relevant employee skills, how up to date the organisation's IT systems and programs are, and the ability of the organisation's systems architecture to provide the information in an efficient, timely and cost-effective way. One of the key aspects in this perspective is appropriate and timely development of people and systems and development of measures to monitor and confirm that this is being done. It answers the question, how will the organisation continue to change and improve?

Examples of possible measures are:

- increased level of spending per head on employee training
- reduced employee absenteeism rate

- reduced staff turnover rate
- increased range of products
- increased proportion of new product sales as a proportion of total sales
- greater reporting flexibility in the information system
- increase in the range of information available on demand from the information system.

## 51.3 Measures

Two forms of measures are used in the balanced scorecard approach:

(*a*) *outcome measures,* which assess past performance;
(*b*) *performance measures (or drivers),* which are indicators that drive future performance.

Performance measures need to be aligned to organisation strategy and, therefore, to outcomes. There is no point in having a measure that has no bearing on strategy or its pursuit. Typically, three to five measures for each of the four perspectives should be adequate. Once the organisation strategy has been identified and converted into objectives, those factors that will achieve the desired objectives (i.e. the performance measures) are identified, along with those that can confirm the objectives are being achieved (i.e. the outcome measures).

As a result of articulating the outcomes the organisation desires and pinpointing the drivers of those outcomes, the energies, abilities and specific knowledge of people throughout the organisation can be aligned to achieve the goals of the organisation.

Once they have been established, there is no reason why the measures inherent in the balanced scorecard should remain fixed. Organisational strategy may change at any time. When it does, the objectives will obviously be changed to keep them in line with the revised strategy. Clearly, the measures of both output and performance will also change as appropriate.

## 51.4 The relationship between the four perspectives

There needs to be a series of cause-and-effect relationships between the four perspectives and the factors within them. Specifically, there must be a clear and logical relationship between each performance driver and one or more of the outcome measures. If there is not, the overall strategy of the organisation cannot be achieved.

**Activity 51.1** Why is this the case?

## 51.5 Benefits of adopting the balanced scorecard

There are a number of benefits to those organisations that adopt the balanced scorecard:

1 **It provides the organisation with a strategic management system that:**

(*a*) clarifies and encourages consensus about organisational vision and strategy;
(*b*) communicates strategy, objectives, drives and measures of performance;
(*c*) facilitates the linking of strategic objectives to budgets;
(*d*) facilitates strategic reviews, especially periodic but also *ad hoc;*
(*e*) facilitates the identification and promotion of new strategic initiatives;
(*f*) facilitates fine-tuning and amendment of strategy in the light of performance.

In effect, the balanced scorecard provides management with a tool to focus strategy and move the organisation in a co-ordinated and transparent manner towards the achievement of its objectives.

2 **It helps people understand how they can contribute to the strategic success of the organisation.** By making it clear what items are important indicators of success, people become aware of what actually leads to the organisation achieving its objectives. They then know which aspects of their work are vital and know that to focus upon them will be beneficial to the organisation. Previously, they would have had to choose to focus upon one or more of a range of alternative activities, many of which may have made no worthwhile contribution to the achievement of the organisational goals.

3 **It guides the transformation of the organisation's vision and strategy into a set of performance measures.** The chain of development of the balanced scorecard is quite straightforward. First, the organisation's mission must be established, then its strategy to pursue its mission, then the objectives that will underpin its strategy, then output measures must be defined so that performance can be assessed and the performance measures (or drivers) established so that it can be seen whether the organisation is moving in the right direction. By creating and providing such a framework to management, the balanced scorecard approach supports the organisation's move towards a greater and more consistent performance that is in line with the organisation's objectives and strategy.

## 51.6 Problems that may arise in introducing the balanced scorecard

There are a number of problems that may arise when introducing the balanced scorecard. Each of them can result in its being less than successful and care needs to be taken to ensure they do not arise, or, if they do arise, that they are eliminated as quickly as possible. The problems include:

(*a*) **A lack of a clearly defined organisational vision or strategy.** It is very difficult to establish objectives if there is no overall organisational vision or strategy. Many organisations have no statement of their mission and many that do have developed no clear organisational strategy. This slows down implementation of the balanced scorecard, as it first requires that a mission, vision and strategy be developed and agreed. Not surprisingly, unless this is done, the balanced scorecard can do little to improve the overall ability of the organisation to achieve its strategic objectives.

(*b*) **Developing and implementing a balanced scorecard before appropriate objectives have been identified.** It can only be wasteful and misleading to develop a balanced scorecard in this case, as there will be aspects of it that are wasteful of resources and other aspects that simply fail to address the appropriate measures. Once the mission, vision and strategy have been developed, it will become obvious that the objectives that existed previously and formed the basis for the development of a balanced scorecard were inappropriate. At that point the incorrect balanced scorecard must be amended and replaced with one that is consistent with the 'real' objectives. As most people are naturally resistant to change, this can create human relations problems that seriously undermine the effort to install an appropriate balanced scorecard. It is far better to wait for appropriate objectives to be identified before starting to develop the balanced scorecard.

(*c*) **Failing to achieve consensus and acceptance at all levels of the organisation.** In this aspect, there are similarities with the need to ensure all individuals accept, understand and appropriately apply a system of budgetary control. As the extent of the measures and drivers of the four perspectives of the balanced scorecard are far greater than for a budgetary control system, the need for consensus is considerably greater. Dysfunctional responses to the balanced scorecard seriously undermine its potential to motivate development of the organisation in the directions established by the clear definition of the organisational strategy which the balanced scorecard provides.

(*d*) **When first attempted, definition of the objectives inherent in the financial, customer and internal business process perspectives often reveals gaps between the existing capabilities of people, organisational systems and procedures and the objectives that are sought.** Management must close these gaps by retraining employees, improving the organisational systems (often through more effective use of IT), and realigning organisational procedures and routines so that they are more compatible with the systems to which they relate.

(*e*) **The organisational objectives across all four perspectives must be compatible and moving in the same direction in the long term.** If the balanced scorecard is to be successfully adopted, it needs to be done with a view to the long term. For example, an objective to enhance customer satisfaction may require that employees are retrained and that systems and quality control procedures are altered so as to improve product quality.

These changes will impact the financial performance measures negatively in the short term. If the organisation has a financial strategy objective to improve return on capital employed, this will only be achieved once the changes made have resulted in increased customer satisfaction which, in turn, results in increased customer loyalty, higher demand for the organisation's products, increased profitability, and an improved return on capital employed.

(*f*) **The organisation's ability to offer current and accurate information to support the balanced scorecard may be undermined because it is currently capable of providing only a few of the outcomes and measures identified by the balanced scorecard analysis.** If the underlying systems and technology are incapable of providing the outcomes and measures required by the balanced scorecard, they must be reorganised and replaced if the balanced scorecard is to be implemented successfully.

(*g*) **The performance measures selected are not aligned with the organisation's strategy.** One cause may be a desire to retain traditional measures because they have always been used rather than to abandon them. Developing a balanced scorecard requires that management reappraise the organisation and switch the emphasis from monitoring output and performance that fails to support the organisation's strategy in a meaningful way.

Change is crucial to the successful implementation of the balanced scorecard. The difference between a traditional financial-performance-related monitoring focus and the far broader and more focused balanced scorecard requires a major shift in perceptions and practices. Reluctance to change can seriously undermine the success of the balanced scorecard approach.

## 51.7 Strategic planning and budgeting

If you investigate when most organisations carry out these two activities, you will find that strategic planning and budgeting are typically done at different times of the year and led by different parts of the organisation.

Kaplan and Norton recommended that the budgeting process be integrated with the strategic planning process. To do so, the budgeting process should follow the strategic planning process. They also believe that the budget should represent Year 1 of a three- or a five-year plan and that companies should be budgeting not only for financial measures but also for the measures in the other three perspectives as well.

They argued that by comparing the gap between where the organisation wants to be in three to five years and where it is today, the managers can assign new resources and strategic initiatives to close the gaps. This motivates additional spending in Year 1. Discretionary spending, both operating and capital, is aimed at closing the forecast future gaps, rather than being devoted to the pursuit of short-term gains.

At the same time, if management specify how the initial spending and investment will start to improve measures in the customer, internal business processes and learning and growth perspectives, they will provide a ready-made yardstick by which to measure performance in pursuit of these changes.

The benefit of this approach is that costs rise in the short term but in a way that does not result in the perspectives being out of balance with each other. In the long term, all the perspectives benefit.

As a result, by integrating strategic planning and budgeting, managers can reach a consensus about the trade-offs between short-term financial performance and long-term benefit. There are potentially enormous benefits to be gained by organisations that adopt such an approach over those that stick with traditional financial-based performance measures.

## 51.8 Adoption of the balanced scorecard

It is not surprising that the balanced scorecard is becoming increasingly adopted as a means of offering a more focused approach to performance monitoring and measurement. It provides a far more focused approach than traditional financial-based performance measures and organisations that adopt it experience a greatly enhanced synergy between their mission, strategy and objectives and the means used to measure output and performance.

It is likely that adoption of the balanced scorecard will become ever more popular as organisations of all sizes and types become aware of its potential. However, it should not be overlooked that the traditional financial measures still have a significant role to play and that the balanced scorecard adds a new and complementary dimension to performance measurement rather than offering an outright alternative.

### Learning outcomes

**You should now have learnt:**

1 The aims of the balanced scorecard.

2 The four perspectives of the balanced scorecard.

3 The two types of measures inherent in the balanced scorecard.

4 Some advantages of adopting the balanced scorecard.

5 Some of the problems that can arise when the balanced scorecard is adopted.

6 The difference between the balanced scorecard and a traditional financial accounting-based performance appraisal system.

### Answer to activity

51.1 It is very difficult to establish objectives if there is no overall organisational vision or strategy. Without a mission, vision and strategy, the organisational objectives can be little more than guesses concerning whether or not they help the organisation pursue its strategy in a meaningful way. Establishing measures to achieve false objectives serves no meaningful purpose.

## Review questions

**51.1** What is the balanced scorecard?

**51.2** Compare the balanced scorecard to a traditional financial-accounting-based performance measurement.

**51.3** Compare and contrast the two forms of measure applied by the balanced scorecard.

**51.4** Compare and contrast the four perspectives of the balanced scorecard.

appendix 1

# Interest tables

## Table 1 Compound sum of £1

| Year | 1% | 2% | 3% | 4% | 5% | 6% | 7% | 8% | 9% | 10% |
|---|---|---|---|---|---|---|---|---|---|---|
| 1 | 1.010 | 1.020 | 1.030 | 1.040 | 1.050 | 1.060 | 1.070 | 1.080 | 1.090 | 1.100 |
| 2 | 1.020 | 1.040 | 1.061 | 1.082 | 1.103 | 1.124 | 1.145 | 1.166 | 1.188 | 1.210 |
| 3 | 1.030 | 1.061 | 1.093 | 1.125 | 1.158 | 1.191 | 1.225 | 1.260 | 1.295 | 1.331 |
| 4 | 1.041 | 1.082 | 1.126 | 1.170 | 1.216 | 1.262 | 1.311 | 1.360 | 1.412 | 1.464 |
| 5 | 1.051 | 1.104 | 1.159 | 1.217 | 1.276 | 1.338 | 1.403 | 1.469 | 1.539 | 1.611 |
| 6 | 1.062 | 1.126 | 1.194 | 1.265 | 1.340 | 1.419 | 1.501 | 1.587 | 1.677 | 1.772 |
| 7 | 1.072 | 1.149 | 1.230 | 1.316 | 1.407 | 1.504 | 1.606 | 1.714 | 1.828 | 1.949 |
| 8 | 1.083 | 1.172 | 1.267 | 1.369 | 1.477 | 1.594 | 1.718 | 1.851 | 1.993 | 2.144 |
| 9 | 1.094 | 1.195 | 1.305 | 1.423 | 1.551 | 1.689 | 1.838 | 1.999 | 2.172 | 2.358 |
| 10 | 1.105 | 1.219 | 1.344 | 1.480 | 1.629 | 1.791 | 1.967 | 2.159 | 2.367 | 2.594 |
| 11 | 1.116 | 1.243 | 1.384 | 1.539 | 1.710 | 1.898 | 2.105 | 2.332 | 2.580 | 2.853 |
| 12 | 1.127 | 1.268 | 1.426 | 1.601 | 1.796 | 2.012 | 2.252 | 2.518 | 2.813 | 3.138 |
| 13 | 1.138 | 1.294 | 1.469 | 1.665 | 1.886 | 2.133 | 2.410 | 2.720 | 3.066 | 3.452 |
| 14 | 1.149 | 1.319 | 1.513 | 1.732 | 1.980 | 2.261 | 2.579 | 2.937 | 3.342 | 3.797 |
| 15 | 1.161 | 1.346 | 1.558 | 1.801 | 2.079 | 2.397 | 2.759 | 3.172 | 3.642 | 4.177 |

| Year | 12% | 14% | 15% | 16% | 18% | 20% | 24% | 28% | 32% |
|---|---|---|---|---|---|---|---|---|---|
| 1 | 1.120 | 1.140 | 1.150 | 1.160 | 1.180 | 1.200 | 1.240 | 1.280 | 1.320 |
| 2 | 1.254 | 1.300 | 1.323 | 1.346 | 1.392 | 1.440 | 1.538 | 1.638 | 1.742 |
| 3 | 1.405 | 1.482 | 1.521 | 1.561 | 1.643 | 1.728 | 1.907 | 2.097 | 2.300 |
| 4 | 1.574 | 1.689 | 1.749 | 1.811 | 1.939 | 2.074 | 2.364 | 2.684 | 3.036 |
| 5 | 1.762 | 1.925 | 2.011 | 2.100 | 2.288 | 2.488 | 2.932 | 3.436 | 4.007 |
| 6 | 1.974 | 2.195 | 2.313 | 2.436 | 2.700 | 2.986 | 3.635 | 4.398 | 5.290 |
| 7 | 2.211 | 2.502 | 2.660 | 2.826 | 3.185 | 3.583 | 4.508 | 5.629 | 6.983 |
| 8 | 2.476 | 2.853 | 3.059 | 3.278 | 3.759 | 4.300 | 5.590 | 7.206 | 9.217 |
| 9 | 2.773 | 3.252 | 3.518 | 3.803 | 4.435 | 5.160 | 6.931 | 9.223 | 12.166 |
| 10 | 3.106 | 3.707 | 4.046 | 4.411 | 5.234 | 6.192 | 8.594 | 11.806 | 16.060 |
| 11 | 3.479 | 4.226 | 4.652 | 5.117 | 6.176 | 7.430 | 10.657 | 15.112 | 21.199 |
| 12 | 3.896 | 4.818 | 5.350 | 5.936 | 7.288 | 8.916 | 13.215 | 19.343 | 27.983 |
| 13 | 4.363 | 5.492 | 6.153 | 6.886 | 8.599 | 10.699 | 16.386 | 24.759 | 36.937 |
| 14 | 4.887 | 6.261 | 7.076 | 7.988 | 10.147 | 12.839 | 20.319 | 31.691 | 48.757 |
| 15 | 5.474 | 7.138 | 8.137 | 9.266 | 11.974 | 15.407 | 25.196 | 40.565 | 64.359 |

| Year | 36% | 40% | 50% | 60% | 70% | 80% | 90% |
|---|---|---|---|---|---|---|---|
| 1 | 1.360 | 1.400 | 1.500 | 1.600 | 1.700 | 1.800 | 1.900 |
| 2 | 1.850 | 1.960 | 2.250 | 2.560 | 2.890 | 3.240 | 3.610 |
| 3 | 2.515 | 2.744 | 3.375 | 4.096 | 4.913 | 5.832 | 6.859 |
| 4 | 3.421 | 3.842 | 5.062 | 6.544 | 8.352 | 10.498 | 13.032 |
| 5 | 4.653 | 5.378 | 7.594 | 10.486 | 14.199 | 18.896 | 24.761 |
| 6 | 6.328 | 7.530 | 11.391 | 16.777 | 24.138 | 34.012 | 47.046 |
| 7 | 8.605 | 10.541 | 17.086 | 26.844 | 41.034 | 61.222 | 89.387 |
| 8 | 11.703 | 14.758 | 25.629 | 42.950 | 69.758 | 110.200 | 169.836 |
| 9 | 15.917 | 20.661 | 38.443 | 68.720 | 118.588 | 198.359 | 322.688 |
| 10 | 21.647 | 28.925 | 57.665 | 109.951 | 201.599 | 357.047 | 613.107 |
| 11 | 29.439 | 40.496 | 86.498 | 175.922 | 342.719 | 642.684 | 1164.902 |
| 12 | 40.037 | 56.694 | 129.746 | 281.475 | 582.622 | 1156.831 | 2213.314 |
| 13 | 54.451 | 79.372 | 194.619 | 450.360 | 990.457 | 2082.295 | 4205.297 |
| 14 | 74.053 | 111.120 | 291.929 | 720.576 | 1683.777 | 3748.131 | 7990.065 |
| 15 | 100.712 | 155.568 | 437.894 | 1152.921 | 2862.421 | 6746.636 | 15181.122 |

## Table 2 Present value of £1

| Year | 1% | 2% | 3% | 4% | 5% | 6% | 7% | 8% | 9% | 10% | 12% | 14% | 15% |
|---|---|---|---|---|---|---|---|---|---|---|---|---|---|
| **1** | 0.990 | 0.980 | 0.971 | 0.961 | 0.952 | 0.943 | 0.935 | 0.926 | 0.917 | 0.909 | 0.893 | 0.877 | 0.870 |
| **2** | 0.980 | 0.961 | 0.943 | 0.925 | 0.907 | 0.890 | 0.873 | 0.857 | 0.842 | 0.826 | 0.797 | 0.769 | 0.756 |
| **3** | 0.971 | 0.942 | 0.915 | 0.889 | 0.864 | 0.840 | 0.816 | 0.794 | 0.772 | 0.751 | 0.712 | 0.675 | 0.658 |
| **4** | 0.961 | 0.924 | 0.889 | 0.855 | 0.823 | 0.792 | 0.763 | 0.735 | 0.708 | 0.683 | 0.636 | 0.592 | 0.572 |
| **5** | 0.951 | 0.906 | 0.863 | 0.822 | 0.784 | 0.747 | 0.713 | 0.681 | 0.650 | 0.621 | 0.567 | 0.519 | 0.497 |
| **6** | 0.942 | 0.888 | 0.838 | 0.790 | 0.746 | 0.705 | 0.666 | 0.630 | 0.596 | 0.564 | 0.507 | 0.456 | 0.432 |
| **7** | 0.933 | 0.871 | 0.813 | 0.760 | 0.711 | 0.665 | 0.623 | 0.583 | 0.547 | 0.513 | 0.452 | 0.400 | 0.376 |
| **8** | 0.923 | 0.853 | 0.789 | 0.731 | 0.677 | 0.627 | 0.582 | 0.540 | 0.502 | 0.467 | 0.404 | 0.351 | 0.327 |
| **9** | 0.914 | 0.837 | 0.766 | 0.703 | 0.645 | 0.592 | 0.544 | 0.500 | 0.460 | 0.424 | 0.361 | 0.308 | 0.284 |
| **10** | 0.905 | 0.820 | 0.744 | 0.676 | 0.614 | 0.558 | 0.508 | 0.463 | 0.422 | 0.386 | 0.322 | 0.270 | 0.247 |
| **11** | 0.896 | 0.804 | 0.722 | 0.650 | 0.585 | 0.527 | 0.475 | 0.429 | 0.388 | 0.350 | 0.287 | 0.237 | 0.215 |
| **12** | 0.887 | 0.788 | 0.701 | 0.625 | 0.557 | 0.497 | 0.444 | 0.397 | 0.356 | 0.319 | 0.257 | 0.208 | 0.187 |
| **13** | 0.879 | 0.773 | 0.681 | 0.601 | 0.530 | 0.469 | 0.415 | 0.368 | 0.326 | 0.290 | 0.229 | 0.182 | 0.163 |
| **14** | 0.870 | 0.758 | 0.661 | 0.577 | 0.505 | 0.442 | 0.388 | 0.340 | 0.299 | 0.263 | 0.205 | 0.160 | 0.141 |
| **15** | 0.861 | 0.743 | 0.642 | 0.555 | 0.481 | 0.417 | 0.362 | 0.315 | 0.275 | 0.239 | 0.183 | 0.140 | 0.123 |
| **16** | 0.853 | 0.728 | 0.623 | 0.534 | 0.458 | 0.394 | 0.339 | 0.292 | 0.252 | 0.218 | 0.163 | 0.123 | 0.107 |
| **17** | 0.844 | 0.714 | 0.605 | 0.513 | 0.436 | 0.371 | 0.317 | 0.270 | 0.231 | 0.198 | 0.146 | 0.108 | 0.093 |
| **18** | 0.836 | 0.700 | 0.587 | 0.494 | 0.416 | 0.350 | 0.296 | 0.250 | 0.212 | 0.180 | 0.130 | 0.095 | 0.081 |
| **19** | 0.828 | 0.686 | 0.570 | 0.475 | 0.396 | 0.331 | 0.276 | 0.232 | 0.194 | 0.164 | 0.116 | 0.083 | 0.070 |
| **20** | 0.820 | 0.673 | 0.554 | 0.456 | 0.377 | 0.319 | 0.258 | 0.215 | 0.178 | 0.149 | 0.104 | 0.073 | 0.061 |
| **25** | 0.780 | 0.610 | 0.478 | 0.375 | 0.295 | 0.233 | 0.184 | 0.146 | 0.116 | 0.092 | 0.059 | 0.038 | 0.030 |
| **30** | 0.742 | 0.552 | 0.412 | 0.308 | 0.231 | 0.174 | 0.131 | 0.099 | 0.075 | 0.057 | 0.033 | 0.020 | 0.015 |

| Year | 16% | 18% | 20% | 24% | 28% | 32% | 36% | 40% | 50% | 60% | 70% | 80% | 90% |
|---|---|---|---|---|---|---|---|---|---|---|---|---|---|
| **1** | 0.862 | 0.847 | 0.833 | 0.806 | 0.781 | 0.758 | 0.735 | 0.714 | 0.667 | 0.625 | 0.588 | 0.556 | 0.526 |
| **2** | 0.743 | 0.718 | 0.694 | 0.650 | 0.610 | 0.574 | 0.541 | 0.510 | 0.444 | 0.391 | 0.346 | 0.309 | 0.277 |
| **3** | 0.641 | 0.609 | 0.579 | 0.524 | 0.477 | 0.435 | 0.398 | 0.364 | 0.296 | 0.244 | 0.204 | 0.171 | 0.146 |
| **4** | 0.552 | 0.516 | 0.482 | 0.423 | 0.373 | 0.329 | 0.292 | 0.260 | 0.198 | 0.153 | 0.120 | 0.095 | 0.077 |
| **5** | 0.476 | 0.437 | 0.402 | 0.341 | 0.291 | 0.250 | 0.215 | 0.186 | 0.132 | 0.095 | 0.070 | 0.053 | 0.040 |
| **6** | 0.410 | 0.370 | 0.335 | 0.275 | 0.227 | 0.189 | 0.158 | 0.133 | 0.088 | 0.060 | 0.041 | 0.029 | 0.021 |
| **7** | 0.354 | 0.314 | 0.279 | 0.222 | 0.178 | 0.143 | 0.116 | 0.095 | 0.059 | 0.037 | 0.024 | 0.016 | 0.011 |
| **8** | 0.305 | 0.266 | 0.233 | 0.179 | 0.139 | 0.108 | 0.085 | 0.068 | 0.039 | 0.023 | 0.014 | 0.009 | 0.006 |
| **9** | 0.263 | 0.226 | 0.194 | 0.144 | 0.108 | 0.082 | 0.063 | 0.048 | 0.026 | 0.015 | 0.008 | 0.005 | 0.003 |
| **10** | 0.227 | 0.191 | 0.162 | 0.116 | 0.085 | 0.062 | 0.046 | 0.035 | 0.017 | 0.009 | 0.005 | 0.003 | 0.002 |
| **11** | 0.195 | 0.162 | 0.135 | 0.094 | 0.066 | 0.047 | 0.034 | 0.025 | 0.012 | 0.006 | 0.003 | 0.002 | 0.001 |
| **12** | 0.168 | 0.137 | 0.112 | 0.076 | 0.052 | 0.036 | 0.025 | 0.018 | 0.008 | 0.004 | 0.002 | 0.001 | 0.001 |
| **13** | 0.145 | 0.116 | 0.093 | 0.061 | 0.040 | 0.027 | 0.018 | 0.013 | 0.005 | 0.002 | 0.001 | 0.001 | 0.000 |
| **14** | 0.125 | 0.099 | 0.078 | 0.049 | 0.032 | 0.021 | 0.014 | 0.009 | 0.003 | 0.001 | 0.001 | 0.000 | 0.000 |
| **15** | 0.108 | 0.084 | 0.065 | 0.040 | 0.025 | 0.016 | 0.010 | 0.006 | 0.002 | 0.001 | 0.000 | 0.000 | 0.000 |
| **16** | 0.093 | 0.071 | 0.054 | 0.032 | 0.019 | 0.012 | 0.007 | 0.005 | 0.002 | 0.001 | 0.000 | 0.000 | |
| **17** | 0.080 | 0.060 | 0.045 | 0.026 | 0.015 | 0.009 | 0.005 | 0.003 | 0.001 | 0.000 | 0.000 | | |
| **18** | 0.069 | 0.051 | 0.038 | 0.021 | 0.012 | 0.007 | 0.004 | 0.002 | 0.001 | 0.000 | 0.000 | | |
| **19** | 0.060 | 0.043 | 0.031 | 0.017 | 0.009 | 0.005 | 0.003 | 0.002 | 0.000 | 0.000 | | | |
| **20** | 0.051 | 0.037 | 0.026 | 0.014 | 0.007 | 0.004 | 0.002 | 0.001 | 0.000 | 0.000 | | | |
| **25** | 0.024 | 0.016 | 0.010 | 0.005 | 0.002 | 0.001 | 0.000 | 0.000 | | | | | |
| **30** | 0.012 | 0.007 | 0.004 | 0.002 | 0.001 | 0.000 | 0.000 | | | | | | |

## Table 3 Sum of an annuity of £1 for *n* years

| Year | 1% | 2% | 3% | 4% | 5% | 6% | 7% | 8% |
|---|---|---|---|---|---|---|---|---|
| 1 | 1.000 | 1.000 | 1.000 | 1.000 | 1.000 | 1.000 | 1.000 | 1.000 |
| 2 | 2.010 | 2.020 | 2.030 | 2.040 | 2.050 | 2.060 | 2.070 | 2.080 |
| 3 | 3.030 | 3.060 | 3.091 | 3.122 | 3.152 | 3.184 | 3.215 | 3.246 |
| 4 | 4.060 | 4.122 | 4.184 | 4.246 | 4.310 | 4.375 | 4.440 | 4.506 |
| 5 | 5.101 | 5.204 | 5.309 | 5.416 | 5.526 | 5.637 | 5.751 | 5.867 |
| 6 | 6.152 | 6.308 | 6.468 | 6.633 | 6.802 | 6.975 | 7.153 | 7.336 |
| 7 | 7.214 | 7.434 | 7.662 | 7.898 | 8.142 | 8.394 | 8.654 | 8.923 |
| 8 | 8.286 | 8.583 | 8.892 | 9.214 | 9.549 | 9.897 | 10.260 | 10.637 |
| 9 | 9.369 | 9.755 | 10.159 | 10.583 | 11.027 | 11.491 | 11.978 | 12.488 |
| 10 | 10.462 | 10.950 | 11.464 | 12.006 | 12.578 | 13.181 | 13.816 | 14.487 |
| 11 | 11.567 | 12.169 | 12.808 | 13.486 | 14.207 | 14.972 | 15.784 | 16.645 |
| 12 | 12.683 | 13.412 | 14.192 | 15.026 | 15.917 | 16.870 | 17.888 | 18.977 |
| 13 | 13.809 | 14.680 | 15.618 | 16.627 | 17.713 | 18.882 | 20.141 | 21.495 |
| 14 | 14.947 | 15.974 | 17.086 | 18.292 | 19.599 | 21.051 | 22.550 | 24.215 |
| 15 | 16.097 | 17.293 | 18.599 | 20.024 | 21.579 | 23.276 | 25.129 | 27.152 |
| 16 | 17.258 | 18.639 | 20.157 | 21.825 | 23.657 | 25.673 | 27.888 | 30.324 |
| 17 | 18.430 | 20.012 | 21.762 | 23.698 | 25.840 | 28.213 | 30.840 | 33.750 |
| 18 | 19.615 | 21.412 | 23.414 | 25.645 | 28.132 | 30.906 | 33.999 | 37.450 |
| 19 | 20.811 | 22.841 | 25.117 | 27.671 | 30.539 | 33.760 | 37.379 | 41.446 |
| 20 | 22.019 | 24.297 | 26.870 | 29.778 | 33.066 | 36.786 | 40.995 | 45.762 |
| 25 | 28.243 | 32.030 | 36.459 | 41.646 | 47.727 | 54.865 | 63.249 | 73.106 |
| 30 | 34.785 | 40.568 | 47.575 | 56.085 | 66.439 | 79.058 | 94.461 | 113.283 |

| Year | 9% | 10% | 12% | 14% | 16% | 18% | 20% | 24% |
|---|---|---|---|---|---|---|---|---|
| 1 | 1.000 | 1.000 | 1.000 | 1.000 | 1.000 | 1.000 | 1.000 | 1.000 |
| 2 | 2.090 | 2.100 | 2.120 | 2.140 | 2.160 | 2.180 | 2.200 | 2.240 |
| 3 | 3.278 | 3.310 | 3.374 | 3.440 | 3.506 | 3.572 | 3.640 | 3.778 |
| 4 | 4.573 | 4.641 | 4.779 | 4.921 | 5.066 | 5.215 | 5.368 | 5.684 |
| 5 | 5.985 | 6.105 | 6.353 | 6.610 | 6.877 | 7.154 | 7.442 | 8.048 |
| 6 | 7.523 | 7.716 | 8.115 | 8.536 | 8.977 | 9.442 | 9.930 | 10.980 |
| 7 | 9.200 | 9.487 | 10.089 | 10.730 | 11.414 | 12.142 | 12.916 | 14.615 |
| 8 | 11.028 | 11.436 | 12.300 | 13.233 | 14.240 | 15.327 | 16.499 | 19.123 |
| 9 | 13.021 | 13.579 | 14.776 | 16.085 | 17.518 | 19.086 | 20.799 | 24.712 |
| 10 | 15.193 | 15.937 | 17.549 | 19.337 | 21.321 | 23.521 | 25.959 | 31.643 |
| 11 | 17.560 | 18.531 | 20.655 | 23.044 | 25.738 | 28.755 | 32.150 | 40.238 |
| 12 | 20.141 | 21.384 | 24.133 | 27.271 | 30.350 | 34.931 | 39.580 | 50.895 |
| 13 | 22.953 | 24.523 | 28.029 | 32.089 | 36.766 | 42.219 | 48.497 | 64.110 |
| 14 | 26.019 | 27.975 | 32.393 | 37.581 | 43.672 | 50.818 | 59.196 | 80.496 |
| 15 | 29.361 | 31.722 | 37.280 | 43.842 | 51.659 | 60.965 | 72.035 | 100.815 |

| Year | 28% | 32% | 36% | 40% | 50% | 60% | 70% | 80% |
|---|---|---|---|---|---|---|---|---|
| 1 | 1.000 | 1.000 | 1.000 | 1.000 | 1.000 | 1.000 | 1.000 | 1.000 |
| 2 | 2.280 | 2.320 | 2.360 | 2.400 | 2.500 | 2.600 | 2.700 | 2.800 |
| 3 | 3.918 | 4.062 | 4.210 | 4.360 | 4.750 | 5.160 | 5.590 | 6.040 |
| 4 | 6.016 | 6.326 | 6.725 | 7.104 | 8.125 | 9.256 | 10.503 | 11.872 |
| 5 | 8.700 | 9.398 | 10.146 | 10.846 | 13.188 | 15.810 | 18.855 | 22.370 |
| 6 | 12.136 | 13.406 | 14.799 | 16.324 | 20.781 | 26.295 | 33.054 | 41.265 |
| 7 | 16.534 | 18.696 | 21.126 | 23.853 | 32.172 | 43.073 | 57.191 | 75.278 |
| 8 | 22.163 | 25.678 | 29.732 | 34.395 | 49.258 | 69.916 | 98.225 | 136.500 |
| 9 | 29.369 | 34.895 | 41.435 | 49.153 | 74.887 | 112.866 | 167.983 | 246.699 |
| 10 | 38.592 | 47.062 | 57.352 | 69.814 | 113.330 | 181.585 | 286.570 | 445.058 |
| 11 | 50.399 | 63.122 | 78.998 | 98.739 | 170.995 | 291.536 | 488.170 | 802.105 |
| 12 | 65.510 | 84.320 | 108.437 | 139.235 | 257.493 | 467.458 | 830.888 | 1444.788 |
| 13 | 84.853 | 112.303 | 148.475 | 195.929 | 387.239 | 748.933 | 1413.510 | 2601.619 |
| 14 | 109.612 | 149.240 | 202.926 | 275.300 | 581.859 | 1199.293 | 2403.968 | 4683.914 |
| 15 | 141.303 | 197.997 | 276.979 | 386.420 | 873.788 | 1919.869 | 4087.745 | 8432.045 |

## Table 4 Present value of annuity of £1 per period

| *Year* | *1%* | *2%* | *3%* | *4%* | *5%* | *6%* | *7%* | *8%* | *9%* | *10%* |
|---|---|---|---|---|---|---|---|---|---|---|
| **1** | 0.990 | 0.980 | 0.971 | 0.962 | 0.952 | 0.943 | 0.935 | 0.926 | 0.917 | 0.909 |
| **2** | 1.970 | 1.942 | 1.913 | 1.886 | 1.859 | 1.833 | 1.808 | 1.783 | 1.759 | 1.736 |
| **3** | 2.941 | 2.884 | 2.829 | 2.775 | 2.723 | 2.673 | 2.624 | 2.577 | 2.531 | 2.487 |
| **4** | 3.902 | 3.808 | 3.717 | 3.630 | 3.546 | 3.465 | 3.387 | 3.312 | 3.240 | 3.170 |
| **5** | 4.853 | 4.713 | 4.580 | 4.452 | 4.329 | 4.212 | 4.100 | 3.993 | 3.890 | 3.791 |
| **6** | 5.795 | 5.601 | 5.417 | 5.424 | 5.076 | 4.917 | 4.766 | 4.623 | 4.486 | 4.355 |
| **7** | 6.728 | 6.472 | 6.230 | 6.002 | 5.786 | 5.582 | 5.389 | 5.206 | 5.033 | 4.868 |
| **8** | 7.652 | 7.325 | 7.020 | 6.733 | 6.463 | 6.210 | 5.971 | 5.747 | 5.535 | 5.335 |
| **9** | 8.566 | 8.162 | 7.786 | 7.435 | 7.108 | 6.802 | 6.515 | 6.247 | 5.985 | 5.759 |
| **10** | 9.471 | 8.983 | 8.530 | 8.111 | 7.722 | 7.360 | 7.024 | 6.710 | 6.418 | 6.145 |
| **11** | 10.368 | 9.787 | 9.253 | 8.760 | 8.306 | 7.887 | 7.499 | 7.139 | 6.805 | 6.495 |
| **12** | 11.255 | 10.575 | 9.954 | 9.385 | 8.863 | 8.384 | 7.943 | 7.536 | 7.161 | 6.814 |
| **13** | 12.134 | 11.348 | 10.635 | 9.986 | 9.394 | 8.853 | 8.358 | 7.904 | 7.487 | 7.103 |
| **14** | 13.004 | 12.106 | 11.296 | 10.563 | 8.899 | 9.295 | 8.745 | 8.244 | 7.786 | 7.367 |
| **15** | 13.865 | 12.849 | 11.938 | 11.118 | 10.380 | 9.712 | 9.108 | 8.559 | 8.060 | 7.606 |
| **16** | 14.718 | 13.578 | 12.561 | 11.652 | 10.838 | 10.106 | 9.447 | 8.851 | 8.312 | 7.824 |
| **17** | 15.562 | 14.292 | 13.166 | 12.166 | 11.274 | 10.477 | 9.763 | 9.122 | 8.544 | 8.022 |
| **18** | 16.398 | 14.992 | 13.754 | 12.659 | 11.690 | 10.828 | 10.059 | 9.372 | 8.756 | 8.201 |
| **19** | 17.226 | 15.678 | 14.324 | 13.134 | 12.085 | 11.158 | 10.336 | 9.604 | 8.950 | 8.365 |
| **20** | 18.046 | 16.351 | 14.877 | 13.590 | 12.462 | 11.470 | 10.594 | 9.818 | 9.128 | 8.514 |
| **25** | 22.023 | 19.523 | 17.413 | 15.622 | 14.094 | 12.783 | 11.654 | 10.675 | 9.823 | 9.077 |
| **30** | 25.808 | 22.397 | 19.600 | 17.292 | 15.373 | 13.765 | 12.409 | 11.258 | 10.274 | 9.427 |

| *Year* | *12%* | *14%* | *16%* | *18%* | *20%* | *24%* | *28%* | *32%* | *36%* |
|---|---|---|---|---|---|---|---|---|---|
| **1** | 0.893 | 0.877 | 0.862 | 0.847 | 0.833 | 0.806 | 0.781 | 0.758 | 0.735 |
| **2** | 1.690 | 1.647 | 1.605 | 1.566 | 1.528 | 1.457 | 1.392 | 1.332 | 1.276 |
| **3** | 2.402 | 2.322 | 2.246 | 2.174 | 2.106 | 1.981 | 1.868 | 1.766 | 1.674 |
| **4** | 3.037 | 2.914 | 2.798 | 2.690 | 2.589 | 2.404 | 2.241 | 2.096 | 1.966 |
| **5** | 3.605 | 3.433 | 3.274 | 3.127 | 2.991 | 2.745 | 2.532 | 2.345 | 2.181 |
| **6** | 4.111 | 3.889 | 3.685 | 3.498 | 3.326 | 3.020 | 2.759 | 2.534 | 2.339 |
| **7** | 4.564 | 4.288 | 4.089 | 3.812 | 3.605 | 3.242 | 2.937 | 2.678 | 2.455 |
| **8** | 4.968 | 4.639 | 4.344 | 4.078 | 3.837 | 3.421 | 3.076 | 2.786 | 2.540 |
| **9** | 5.328 | 4.946 | 4.607 | 4.303 | 4.031 | 3.566 | 3.184 | 2.868 | 2.603 |
| **10** | 5.650 | 5.216 | 4.833 | 4.494 | 4.193 | 3.682 | 3.269 | 2.930 | 2.650 |
| **11** | 5.988 | 5.453 | 5.029 | 4.656 | 4.327 | 3.776 | 3.335 | 2.978 | 2.683 |
| **12** | 6.194 | 5.660 | 5.197 | 4.793 | 4.439 | 3.851 | 3.387 | 3.013 | 2.708 |
| **13** | 6.424 | 5.842 | 5.342 | 4.910 | 4.533 | 3.912 | 3.427 | 3.040 | 2.727 |
| **14** | 6.628 | 6.002 | 5.468 | 5.008 | 4.611 | 3.962 | 3.459 | 3.061 | 2.740 |
| **15** | 6.811 | 6.142 | 5.575 | 5.092 | 4.675 | 4.001 | 3.483 | 3.076 | 2.750 |
| **16** | 6.974 | 6.265 | 5.669 | 5.162 | 4.730 | 4.033 | 3.503 | 3.088 | 2.758 |
| **17** | 7.120 | 5.373 | 5.749 | 4.222 | 4.775 | 4.059 | 3.518 | 3.097 | 2.763 |
| **18** | 7.250 | 6.467 | 5.818 | 5.273 | 4.812 | 4.080 | 3.529 | 3.104 | 2.767 |
| **19** | 7.366 | 6.550 | 5.877 | 5.316 | 4.844 | 4.097 | 3.539 | 3.109 | 2.770 |
| **20** | 7.469 | 6.623 | 5.929 | 5.353 | 4.870 | 4.110 | 3.546 | 3.113 | 2.772 |
| **25** | 7.843 | 6.873 | 6.907 | 5.467 | 4.948 | 4.147 | 3.564 | 3.122 | 2.776 |
| **30** | 8.055 | 7.003 | 6.177 | 5.517 | 4.979 | 4.160 | 3.569 | 3.124 | 2.778 |

# Answers to review questions

*Note*: All the answers are the work of the author. None has been supplied by an examining body. The examining bodies accept no responsibility whatsoever for the accuracy or method of working in the answers given.

In order to save space, £ signs have been omitted from columns of figures, except where the figures refer to £000, or where the denomination needs to be specified. For the same reason, names of the organisations and dates are sometimes omitted, but only where they add little to an understanding of the answer.

**1.1**

(*a*) (dates omitted)

*Branch Current Account*

| | | | |
|---|---|---|---|
| Balance b/d | 181,440 | Cash | 270,000 |
| Goods sent | 208,440 | Goods returned | 3,600 |
| Expenses paid | 33,000 | | |
| Net profit | 120,000 | Balance c/d | 269,280 |
| | 542,880 | | 542,880 |

(*b*) Proof:

| | |
|---|---|
| Branch assets | xxx |
| *Less* Branch liabilities | xxx |
| = Balance of branch current account | xxx |

Indicates: Amount of money invested in branch

**1.2**

*Branch Inventory (dates omitted)*

| | Memo | | | Memo | |
|---|---|---|---|---|---|
| Balance b/d | 80,320 | 50,200 | Branch accounts receivable | 387,000 | 387,000 |
| Goods from head office | 446,400 | 279,000 | Cash sales | 21,600 | 21,600 |
| Gross profit | | 197,520 | Returns to HO | 18,000 | 11,250 |
| | | | Goods stolen | 10,800 | 6,750 |
| | | | Profit and loss: Normal wastage | 1,800 | 1,125 |
| | | | Profit and loss: Abnormal wastage | 16,400 | 10,250 |
| | | | Balance c/d | 71,120 | 88,745 |
| | 526,720 | 526,720 | | 526,720 | 526,720 |

*Branch Accounts Receivable*

| | | | |
|---|---|---|---|
| Balances b/d | 33,514 | Bad debts | 1,332 |
| Branch inventory: Sales | 387,000 | Discounts allowed | 3,852 |
| | | Bank | 403,200 |
| | | Balance c/d | 12,130 |
| | 420,514 | | 420,514 |

**1.3**

(*a*) (*i*)

*Branch Inventory (Selling Prices)*

| | | | |
|---|---|---|---|
| Goods from head office (82,400 + 10% 8,240 = 90,640 + 25%) | 113,300 | Cash sales | 89,940 |
| | | Sales: Branch accounts receivable | 1,870 |
| | | Goods to other branches | 3,300 |
| | | Branch inventory adjustment: Reductions | 2,250 |
| | | Balance c/d | 15,940 |
| | 113,300 | | 113,300 |

(*ii*)

*Branch Inventory Adjustment* *(profit margin)

| | | | |
|---|---|---|---|
| Goods to other branches | 660 | Branch inventory (113,300 − 90,640) | 22,660 |
| Branch inventory: Reductions | 2,250 | | |
| Profit and loss | 16,562 | | |
| Balance c/d | 3,188 | | |
| | 22,660 | | 22,660 |

*As cost to branch (original cost + 10%) is subject to further mark-up of 25%, therefore margin is 20%, and this is profit margin used in this account.

(*b*)

| | |
|---|---|
| Book inventory per branch inventory account | 15,940 |
| Physical inventory | 14,850 |
| | 1,090 |

Four possible reasons for deficiency:
(*i*) thefts by customers;
(*ii*) thefts by staff;
(*iii*) wastages due to breakages, miscounting, etc.;
(*iv*) cash misappropriated.

(*c*) Figure to be taken for RST statement of financial position:

| | |
|---|---|
| Actual inventory at selling price | 14,850 |
| *Less* 20% margin | 2,970 |
| Cost to branch | 11,880 |
| *Less* Head office loading (+10%=1/11th of adjusted figure) 1/11th | 1,080 |
| Actual cost to company | 10,800 |

Therefore (*iii*) 10,800 is correct answer.

**1.5**

Packer & Stringer

*Statement of Profit or Loss for the year ending 31 December 2017*

| | *Head Office* | | *Branch* | |
|---|---|---|---|---|
| Revenue | | 39,000 | | 26,000 |
| *Less* Cost of goods sold | | | | |
| Opening inventory | 13,000 | | 4,400 | |
| *Add* Purchases | 37,000 | | | |
| | 50,000 | | | |
| Goods to branch | 17,200 | | 17,200 | |
| | 32,800 | | 21,600 | |
| *Less* Closing inventory | 15,240 | 17,560 | 6,570 | 15,030 |
| | | 21,440 | | 10,970 |
| Allowance for doubtful debt not required | | | | 20 |
| | | | | 10,990 |
| Salaries | 4,500 | | 3,200 | |
| Administrative expenses | 1,440 | | 960 | |
| Carriage | 2,200 | | 960 | |
| General expenses | 3,200 | | 1,800 | |
| Allowance for doubtful debts | 50 | | | |
| Depreciation | 150 | | 110 | |
| Manager's commission | – | 11,540 | 360 | 7,390 |
| Net profit | | 9,900 | | 3,600 |
| | | | 13,500 | |
| Packer: Commission | | 900 | | |
| Interest on capital: Packer | 840 | | | |
| Stringer | 240 | 1,080 | | |
| | | 1,980 | | |
| Balance of profits: Packer $^3/_4$ | 8,640 | | | |
| Stringer $^1/_4$ | 2,880 | 11,520 | 13,500 | |

*Statement of Financial Position as at 31 December 2017*

| | | | |
|---|---|---|---|
| *Non-current assets* | | | |
| Furniture | | 2,600 | |
| *Less* Depreciation | | 1,110 | 1,490 |
| *Current assets* | | | |
| Inventory | | 21,810 | |
| Accounts receivable | 10,000 | | |
| *Less* Allowance for doubtful debts | 830 | 9,170 | |
| Cash and bank | | 3,000 | 33,980 |
| *Less Current liabilities* | | | 35,470 |
| Accounts payable | | 6,200 | |
| Bank overdraft | | 1,350 | |
| Manager's commission | | 120 | |
| | | | (7,670) |
| | | | 27,800 |

**1.7**

Nion

*Statement of Profit or Loss for the year ending 31 October 2018*

| | *Head Office* | | *Branch* | |
|---|---|---|---|---|
| | | £000 | | £000 |
| Revenue | | 850 | | 437 |
| Transfers to branch | | 380 | | |
| | | 1,230 | | |
| *Less* Cost of goods sold: | | | | |
| Opening inventory | 8 | | 20 | |
| *Add* Purchases | 914 | | | |
| *Add* Goods from head office | | | 375 | |
| | 922 | | 395 | |
| *Less* Closing inventory | 12 | 910 | 15 | 380 |
| Gross profit | | 320 | | 57 |
| *Less* Expenses: | | | | |
| Administrative | 200 | | 16.5 | |
| Distribution | 80.5 | | 5 | |
| Depreciation | 35 | | 10 | |
| Changes in allowance for doubtful debts | (6) | 309.5 | 0.5 | 32 |
| Net profit | | 10.5 | | 25 |

*Statement of Financial Position as at 31 October 2018*

| | £000 | £000 | £000 |
|---|---|---|---|
| Non-current assets at cost | | | 450 |
| *Less* Depreciation to date | | | 215 |
| | | | 235 |
| *Current assets* | | | |
| Inventory (12 + 12 + 4*) | | 28 | |
| Accounts receivable | 120 | | |
| *Less* Provision | 6 | 114 | |
| Cash and bank (15.5 + 13 + 50) | | 78.5 | |
| | | 220.5 | 220.5 |
| | | | 455.5 |
| *Less Current liabilities* | | | |
| Accounts payable | | | 50.0 |
| | | | 405.5 |
| Capital | | | |
| Balance at 1.11.2014 | | | 410 |
| *Add* Net profit | | | 35.5 |
| | | | 445.5 |
| *Less* Drawings | | | 40 |
| | | | 405.5 |

$*5 \times ^4/_5$

**1.9**

*(a)* *Conversion of Branch Trial Balance to Pounds Sterling*

| | *Fl.* | *Fl.* | *Rate* | £ | £ |
|---|---|---|---|---|---|
| Freehold buildings | 63,000 | | 7 | 9,000 | |
| Accounts receivable and accounts payable | 36,000 | 1,560 | 8 | 4,460 | 195 |
| Revenue | | 432,000 | 9 | | 48,000 |
| Head office | | 504,260 | Actual | | 60,100 |
| Branch cost of sales | 360,000 | | Below* | 40,400 | |
| Depreciation: Machinery | | 56,700 | 7 | | 8,100 |
| Administration costs | 18,000 | | 9 | 2,000 | |
| Stock 30.6.2018 | 11,520 | | 8 | 1,440 | |
| Machinery at cost | 126,000 | | 7 | 18,000 | |
| Remittances | 272,000 | | Actual | 29,990 | |
| Balances at bank | 79,200 | | 8 | 9,900 | |
| Selling and distribution | 28,800 | | 9 | 3,200 | |
| Profit on exchange | | – | – | | 1,995 |
| | 994,520 | 994,520 | | 118,390 | 118,390 |

*Cost of sales: Branch Fl. 360,000
*Less* Depreciation Fl. 12,600 ÷ 7 = £1,800
Fl. 347,400 ÷ 9 = £38,600
£40,400

*EG Company Ltd*
*Statement of Profit or Loss for the year ending 30 June 2018*

| | | Head Office | | Branch |
|---|---|---|---|---|
| Revenue | | 104,000 | | 48,000 |
| *Less* Cost of sales | 58,400 | | 38,600 | |
| Depreciation | 600 | | 1,800 | 40,400 |
| | 59,000 | | | |
| Goods to branch | 35,000 | 24,000 | | |
| Gross profit | | 80,000 | | 7,600 |
| Administration costs | 15,200 | | 2,000 | |
| Selling and distribution | 23,300 | | 3,200 | |
| Provison for unrealised profit on branch inventory | 300 | | | |
| Manager's commission | – | | 114 | |
| | | 38,800 | | 5,314 |
| Net profit | | 41,200 | | 2,286 |
| | | | 43,486 | |
| *Add* Balance from last year | | | 2,000 | |
| Balance carried forward to next year | | | 45,486 | |

*(b)* *Statement of Financial Position as at 30 June 2018*

| | | |
|---|---|---|
| *Non-current assets* | | |
| Freehold buildings at cost | | 23,000 |
| Machinery at cost | 24,000 | |
| *Less* Depreciation | 9,600 | 14,400 |
| | | 37,400 |
| *Current assets* | | |
| Inventory | 30,040 | |
| Accounts receivable | 13,360 | |
| Bank | 14,500 | |
| Cash in transit | 1,990 | 59,890 |
| | | 97,290 |
| *Less Current liabilities* | | |
| Accounts payable* | | 9,809 |
| | | 87,481 |
| *Equity* | | |
| Share capital: Authorised and issued | | 40,000 |
| Reserves: | | |
| Difference on exchange | 1,995 | |
| Retained profits | 45,486 | 47,481 |
| | | 87,481 |

*Accounts payable HO 9,500 + *Branch* 195 + *Manager* 114 = 9,809.

*(c)* **(HO Books)** *Branch Account*

| | £ | *Fl.* | | £ | *Fl.* |
|---|---|---|---|---|---|
| Balance b/d | 25,136 | 189,260 | Cash from debtors | 36 | 320 |
| Components | 35,000 | 315,000 | Remittances | 28,000 | 256,000 |
| Net profit | 2,286 | **24,000 | Cash in transit | 1,990 | 16,000 |
| Difference on exchange | 1,995 | – | Balance c/d | 34,391 | 255,940 |
| | 64,417 | 528,260 | | 64,417 | 528,260 |

**This represents the profit per branch statement of profit or loss if it had been drawn up using florins.

**1.10**

*(a)* *Trial Balance as at 31 December 2017*

| | *Crowns* | *Crowns* | *Rate* | £ | £ |
|---|---|---|---|---|---|
| Bank | 66,000 | | 4 | 16,500 | |
| Accounts payable | | 92,400 | 4 | | 23,100 |
| Accounts receivable | 158,400 | | 4 | 39,600 | |
| Non-current assets | 145,200 | | 5 | 29,040 | |
| Head office | | 316,800 | Actual | | 65,280 |
| Retained profits | | 79,200 | 4.4 | | 18,000 |
| Inventory | 118,800 | | 4 | 29,700 | |
| Difference on exchange | | | | | 8,460 |
| | 488,400 | 488,400 | | 114,840 | 114,840 |

**1.10** *(cont'd)*

*(b)* (**Books of head office**) *Highland Branch*

| | | | |
|---|---|---|---|
| Balance b/d | 65,280 | Balance c/d | 91,740 |
| Difference on exchange | 8,460 | | |
| Net profit | 18,000 | | |
| | 91,740 | | 91,740 |

*(c)* *Statement of Financial Position as at 31 December 2017*

| | | |
|---|---|---|
| Non-current assets | | 68,640 |
| *Current assets* | | |
| Inventory | 56,100 | |
| Accounts receivable | 58,080 | |
| Bank | 27,060 | 141,240 |
| | | 209,880 |
| *Less Current liabilities* | | |
| Accounts payable | | 44,220 |
| | | 165,660 |
| *Equity* | | |
| Issued share capital | | 86,400 |
| Reserves: | | |
| Retained profits | 70,800 | |
| Difference on exchange | 8,460 | 79,260 |
| | | 165,660 |

**2.1**

*Equipment*

| | | | |
|---|---|---|---|
| 2016 | | | |
| Jan 1 | Vendor | | 120,000 |

*Vendor's Account*

| | | | | | | | | |
|---|---|---|---|---|---|---|---|---|
| 2016 | | | | 2016 | | | | |
| Jan 1 | Bank | | 9,980 | Jan 1 | | | | 120,000 |
| Dec 31 | Bank | | 40,400 | Dec 31 | HP interest | | | 5,501* |
| 31 | Balance | c/d | 75,121 | | | | | |
| | | | 125,501 | | | | | 125,501 |
| 2017 | | | | 2017 | | | | |
| Dec 31 | Bank | | 40,400 | Jan 1 | Balance | | c/d | 75,121 |
| 31 | Balance | c/d | 38,477 | Dec 31 | HP interest | | | 3,756 |
| | | | 78,877 | | | | | 78,877 |
| 2018 | | | | 2018 | | | | |
| Dec 31 | Bank | | 40,401 | Jan 1 | Balance | | b/d | 38,477 |
| | | | | Dec 31 | HP interest | | | 1,924 |
| | | | 40,401 | | | | | 40,401 |

*Provision for Depreciation: Equipment*

| | | | | | | | |
|---|---|---|---|---|---|---|---|
| 2016 | | | | 2016 | | | |
| Dec 31 | Balance | c/d | 16,000 | Dec 31 | Profit and loss | | 12,000 |
| 2017 | | | | 2017 | | | |
| Dec 31 | Balance | c/d | 24,000 | Jan 1 | Balance | b/d | 12,000 |
| | | | | Dec 31 | Profit and loss | | 12,000 |
| | | | 24,000 | | | | 24,000 |
| 2018 | | | | 2018 | | | |
| Dec 31 | Balance | c/d | 36,000 | Jan 1 | Balance | b/d | 24,000 |
| | | | | Dec 31 | Profit and loss | | 12,000 |
| | | | 36,000 | | | | 36,000 |

*Statement of Financial Position as at 31 December 2016*

| | | |
|---|---|---|
| Equipment at cost | 120,000 | |
| *Less* Depreciation | 12,000 | 108,000 |
| (included in Liabilities) Owing on HP | | 75,121 |

*120,000 − 9,980 = 110,020 × 0.05 = 5,501

**2.3**

*(a)*

**Bulwell's books**

*Motor Lorries*

| | | |
|---|---|---|
| 2015 | Granby Garages | 54,000 |

*Hire Purchase Interest*

| | | | | | |
|---|---|---|---|---|---|
| 2015 | Granby Garages | 11,250 | 2015 | Profit and loss | 11,250 |
| 2016 | Granby Garages | 8,063 | 2016 | Profit and loss | 8,063 |
| 2017 | Granby Garages | 4,078 | 2017 | Profit and loss | 4,078 |

*Bank*

| | | | | | |
|---|---|---|---|---|---|
| | | | 2015 | Granby (Jan 1) | 9,000 |
| | | | | Granby (Dec 31) | 24,000 |
| | | | 2016 | Granby | 24,000 |
| | | | 2017 | Granby | 20,391 |

*Granby Garages*

| | | | | | |
|---|---|---|---|---|---|
| 2015 | Bank | 9,000 | 2015 | Motor lorries | 54,000 |
| | Bank | 24,000 | | HP interest | 11,250 |
| | Balance c/d | 32,250 | | | |
| | | 65,250 | | | 65,250 |
| 2016 | Bank | 24,000 | 2016 | Balance b/d | 32,250 |
| | Balance c/d | 16,313 | | HP interest | 8,063 |
| | | 40,313 | | | 40,313 |
| 2017 | Bank | 20,391 | 2017 | Balance b/d | 16,313 |
| | | | | Interest | 4,078 |
| | | 20,391 | | | 20,391 |

*Depreciation*

| | | | | | | |
|---|---|---|---|---|---|---|
| 2015 | Balance c/d | 12,500 | 2015 | Profit and loss | 12,500 |
| 2016 | Balance c/d | 25,000 | 2016 | Balance b/d | 12,500 |
| | | | | Profit and loss | 12,500 |
| | | 25,000 | | | 25,000 |
| 2017 | Balance c/d | 37,500 | 2017 | Balance b/d | 25,000 |
| | | | | Profit and loss | 12,500 |
| | | 37,500 | | | 37,500 |
| 2018 | Balance c/d | 50,000 | 2018 | Balance b/d | 37,500 |
| | | | | Profit and loss | 12,500 |
| | | 50,000 | | | 50,000 |

*Statement of Financial Position as at 31 December*

| | *2015* | *2016* | *2017* | *2018* |
|---|---|---|---|---|
| Motor lorries cost | 54,000 | 54,000 | 54,000 | 54,000 |
| *Less* Depreciation to date | 12,500 | 25,000 | 37,500 | 50,000 |
| | 41,500 | 29,000 | 16,500 | 4,000 |
| *Liabilities:* | | | | |
| HP debt outstanding | 32,250 | 16,313 | | |
| Charge against profit: | | | | |
| HP interest | 11,250 | 8,063 | 4,078 | – |
| Depreciation | 12,500 | 12,500 | 12,500 | 12,500 |

NB: Calculation of interest

| | |
|---|---|
| 2001 25% × £45,000 = | £11,250 |
| 2002 25% × £32,250 = | £8,063 |
| 2003 25% × £16,313 = | £4,078 |

(*b*)

**Granby's books**

*Bulwell Aggregates*

| | | | | | |
|---|---|---|---|---|---|
| 2015 | HP sales | 54,000 | 2015 | Bank – deposit | 9,000 |
| | HP interest | 11,250 | | – instalment | 24,000 |
| | | | | Balance c/d | 32,250 |
| | | 65,250 | | | 65,250 |
| 2016 | Balance b/d | 32,250 | 2016 | Bank – instalment | 24,000 |
| | HP interest | 8,063 | | Balance c/d | 16,313 |
| | | 40,313 | | | 40,313 |
| 2017 | Balance b/d | 16,313 | 2017 | Bank – instalment | 20,391 |
| | HP interest | 4,078 | | | |
| | | 20,391 | | | 20,391 |

*Bank*

| | | |
|---|---|---|
| 2015 | Bulwell | 9,000 |
| | Bulwell | 24,000 |
| 2016 | Bulwell | 24,000 |
| 2017 | Bulwell | 20,391 |

*HP Interest*

| | | | | | |
|---|---|---|---|---|---|
| 2015 | HP trading | 11,250 | 2015 | Bulwell | 11,250 |
| 2016 | HP trading | 8,063 | 2016 | Bulwell | 8,063 |
| 2017 | HP trading | 4,078 | 2017 | Bulwell | 4,078 |

*Hire Purchase Trading*

| | | | | | |
|---|---|---|---|---|---|
| 2015 | Cost of lorries | 43,200 | 2015 | HP Sales | 54,000 |
| | HP Profit deferred c/d | 6,450 | | HP Interest | 11,250 |
| | Gross profit | 15,600 | | | |
| | | 65,250 | | | 65,250 |
| 2016 | HP Profit deferred c/d | 3,263 | 2016 | HP Profit deferred b/d | 6,450 |
| | Gross profit | 11,250 | | HP Interest | 8,063 |
| | | 14,513 | | | 14,513 |
| 2017 | Gross profit | 7,341 | 2017 | HP Profit deferred b/d | 3,263 |
| | | | | HP Interest | 4,078 |
| | | 7,341 | | | 7,341 |

Working: $\frac{\text{Unrealised profit}}{\text{Profit margin}} \quad \frac{10,800}{54,000} \times \frac{100}{1} = 20\%$

| | |
|---|---|
| 20% × £32,250 = | £6,450 |
| 20% × £16,313 = | £3,263 |

**2.5**

(*a*) (*i*)

*Truck Fleet Ltd*

| | | | | | |
|---|---|---|---|---|---|
| 2014 | | | 2014 | | |
| Mar 31 | Cash | 20,000 | Mar 31 | Lorry | 61,620 |
| Mar 31 | Balance c/d | 41,620 | | | |
| | | 61,620 | | | 61,620 |
| | | | Apr 1 | Balance b/d | 41,620 |
| 2015 | | | 2015 | | |
| Mar 31 | Cash | 23,981 | Mar 31 | HP interest 10% of 41,620 | 4,160 |
| Mar 31 | Balance c/d | 21,801 | | | |
| | | 45,782 | | | 45,782 |
| | | | Apr 1 | Balance b/d | 21,801 |
| 2016 | | | 2016 | | |
| Mar 31 | Cash | 23,981 | Mar 31 | HP interest 10% of 21,802 | 2,180 |
| | | 23,981 | | | 23,981 |

**2.5** *(cont'd)*

*(ii)* *Lorry*

| | | | | | | |
|---|---|---|---|---|---|---|
| 2014 | | | | | | |
| Mar 31 | Truck Fleet Ltd | 61,620 | | | | |

*(iii)* *Provision for Depreciation: Lorry*

| | | | | | | |
|---|---|---|---|---|---|---|
| | | | 2014 | | | |
| | | | Mar 31 | Profit and loss | 24,648 |
| | | | 2015 | | | |
| | | | Mar 31 | Profit and loss | 14,789 |
| | | | 2016 | | | |
| | | | Mar 31 | Profit and loss | 8,873 |

*(iv)* *Hire Purchase Interest*

| | | | | | |
|---|---|---|---|---|---|
| 2015 | | | 2015 | | |
| Mar 31 | Vehicles and finance | 4,162 | Mar 31 | Profit and loss | 4,162 |
| 2016 | | | 2016 | | |
| Mar 31 | Vehicles and finance | 2,180 | Mar 31 | Profit and loss | 2,180 |

*(b)* *Statement of Financial Position as at 31 March 2015*

| | | |
|---|---|---|
| Lorry at cost | 61,620 | |
| *Less* Depreciation to date | 39,437 | 22,183 |
| (Included in Liabilities) Owing on hire purchase | | 21,801 |

**2.6**

**J Tocher**

*Hire Purchase Statement of Profit or Loss for the year ending 31 March 2017*

| | | |
|---|---|---|
| Sales at hire purchase price (1,900 × 165) | | 313,500 |
| Purchases | 220,000 | |
| *Less* Inventory (100 × 110) | 11,000 | |
| | 209,000 | |
| Provision for unrealised profit and interest* | 43,700 | 252,700 |
| Gross profit | | 60,800 |
| *Less* Rent business rates and insurance | 5,000 | |
| Wages | 27,000 | |
| General expenses | 5,100 | 37,100 |
| Net profit | | 23,700 |

*Cash yet to be collected 313,500 − 131,100 = 182,400

Therefore *profit* + *interest* to recognise $\frac{182,400}{313,500} \times 55 = 32 \times 1,900 = 60,800$

∴ profit plus interest to *ignore* = 55 − 32 = 23 × 1,900 = 43,700

*Statement of Financial Position as at 31 March 2017*

| | | | |
|---|---|---|---|
| Non-current assets | | | 9,500 |
| *Current assets* | | | |
| Inventory | | 11,000 | |
| HP accounts receivable | 182,400 | | |
| *Less* Provision: unrealised profit and interest | 43,700 | 138,700 | |
| Bank | | 13,026 | 162,726 |
| | | | 172,226 |
| *Less Current liabilities* | | | |
| Accounts payable | | | 12,600 |
| | | | 159,626 |
| *Equity* | | | |
| Capital at 1.10.2017 | | | 175,926 |
| *Add* Net profit | | | 23,700 |
| | | | 199,626 |
| *Less* Drawings | | | 40,000 |
| | | | 159,626 |

**2.7**

**RJ**

*Hire Purchase Trading*

| | | | | | |
|---|---|---|---|---|---|
| 2018 | Cost of refrigerators | 170,000 | 2018 | HP sales (W1) | 170,000 |
| | HP profit deferred (W2) | 59,500 | | HP interest (W1) | 85,000 |
| | Gross profit | 25,500 | | | |
| | | 255,000 | | | 255,000 |

(W1) To separate cost from interest, it is assumed that the difference between cost price and selling price is interest. The HP sales amount is, therefore, the same as the cost of the units sold, i.e. £170,000. HP interest is, therefore, £85,000.

(W2) Receipts = £76,500 which is 30% of the amount invoiced of £255,000. Profit (i.e. interest) is recognised at that percentage (30%) of profit received = 30% × £85,000 = £25,500 so the HP profit deferred = £85,000 − £25,500 = £59,500.

*Authors' note*: It is assumed that the question is asking for a separate T-account showing the HP trading account, plus an income statement. If you wish, you could simply provide the HP details in the income statement and include a note saying you assumed that you did not need to also provide the T-account. This ambiguity in this question is quite common in questions on this topic. Be careful to ensure you make it clear that you could have prepared the T-account when you do not prepare one. Generally, the examiners are looking only for the statement of profit or loss with the trading account details shown unless they request a T-account. However, in this case, it is likely the T-account was required as well.

*Hire Purchase Trading Account and Statement of Profit or Loss for the year ending 31 December 2018*

| | | |
|---|---|---|
| Sales at hire purchase price (850 × 300) | | 255,000 |
| Purchases | 180,000 | |
| *Less* Inventory (50 × 200) | 10,000 | |
| Cost of goods sold | 170,000 | |
| Provision of unrealised profit | 59,500 | 229,500 |
| Gross profit | | 25,500 |
| *Less* Wages and salaries | 12,800 | |
| General expenses | 5,500 | |
| Bank interest | 400 | 18,700 |
| Net profit | | 6,800 |

*Statement of Financial Position as at 31 December 2018*

| | | | |
|---|---|---|---|
| Non-current assets | | | 10,000 |
| *Current assets* | | | |
| Inventory in warehouse | | 10,000 | |
| Hire purchase accounts receivable | 178,500 | | |
| *Less* Provision for unrealised profit | 59,500 | 119,000 | |
| | | 129,000 | |
| *Less Current liabilities* | | | |
| Accounts payable | 16,600 | | |
| Bank overdraft | 19,600 | 36,200 | 92,800 |
| | | | 102,800 |
| *Financed by:* | | | |
| Capital | | | |
| Cash introduced | | | 100,000 |
| *Add* Net profit | | | 6,800 |
| | | | 106,800 |
| *Less* Drawings | | | 4,000 |
| | | | 102,800 |

**2.11**

(*a*) (*i*)

*Machine Hire Purchase*

| | | | | | |
|---|---|---|---|---|---|
| 1.1.15 | Bank | 2,000 | 1.1.15 | Machine | 10,000 |
| 30.6.15 | Bank | 3,056 | 1.1.15 | HP interest | 7,280 |
| 31.12.15 | Bank | 3,056 | | | |
| 31.12.15 | Balance c/d | 9,168 | | | |
| | | 17,280 | | | 17,280 |
| 30.6.16 | Bank | 3,056 | 1.1.16 | Balance b/d | 9,168 |
| 31.12.16 | Bank | 3,056 | | | |
| 31.12.16 | Balance c/d | 3,056 | | | |
| | | 9,168 | | | 9,168 |
| 30.6.17 | Bank | 3,056 | 1.1.17 | Balance b/d | 3,056 |

(*ii*)

*Machine Hire Purchase (see workings)*

| | | | | | |
|---|---|---|---|---|---|
| 1.1.15 | Machine HP | 7,280 | 31.12.15 | Profit and loss | 4,368 |
| | | | 31.12.15 | Balance c/d | 2,912 |
| | | 7,280 | | | 7,280 |
| 1.1.16 | Balance b/d | 2,912 | 31.12.16 | Profit and loss | 2,427 |
| | | | 31.12.16 | Balance c/d | 485 |
| | | 2,912 | | | 2,912 |
| 1.1.17 | Balance b/d | 485 | 31.12.17 | Profit and loss | 485 |

(*b*) *(Extracts) Statements of Financial Position as at 31 December*

| | 2015 | 2016 | 2017 |
|---|---|---|---|
| *Non-current assets* | | | |
| Machinery at cost | 10,000 | 10,000 | 10,000 |
| *Less* Depreciation to date | 1,800 | 3,600 | 5,400 |
| | 8,200 | 6,400 | 4,600 |
| *Creditors* | | | |
| Falling due within one year | | | |
| Hire purchase | 3,685 | 2,571 | |
| Falling due after one year | | | |
| Hire purchase | 2,571 | | |

(2015 3,056 + 3,056 − 2,427)
(2016 3,056 − 485)

*Workings*: Interest (sum of digits is 15)
To 31.12.2015 (5/15 × 7,280) 2,427 + (4/15 × 7,280) = 4,368
To 31.12.2016 (3/15 × 7,280) 1,456 + (2/15 × 7,280) 971 = 2,427
To 31.12.2017 1/15 × 7,280 = 485
Depreciation (10,000 − 1,000) ÷ 5 = 1,800 *p.a.*

**3.1**

*Contract 32*

| | | | |
|---|---|---|---|
| Year to 31.03.17 | | Year to 31.03.17 | |
| Plant | 76,800 | Work certified | 400,000 |
| Materials | 163,200 | Plant c/d | 40,800 |
| Wages | 182,400 | Inventory and work in progress c/d | 130,080 |
| Direct expenses | 12,800 | | |
| Gross profit to profit or loss | 135,680 | | |
| | 570,880 | | 570,880 |
| Year to 31.03.18 | | Year to 31.03.18 | |
| Plant b/d | 40,800 | Work certified | 800,000 |
| Inventory and work in progress | 130,080 | Sale of plant | 19,200 |
| Materials | 214,400 | | |
| Wages | 291,200 | | |
| Direct expenses | 19,200 | | |
| Penalty | 120,000 | | |
| Gross profit to profit or loss | 3,520 | | |
| | 819,200 | | 819,200 |

**3.1** *(cont'd)*

*Workings:*

(i) Computation profit of year to 31.03.17

| | | |
|---|---|---|
| Contract price | | 1,200,000 |
| *Less* Actual expenditure | | |
| (163,200 + 182,400 + 12,800) | 358,400 | |
| Estimated cost of plant (76,800 − 4,800) | 72,000 | |
| Estimated expenses year to 31.03.18 | 515,200 | 945,600 |
| Estimated total contract profit: estimate made at end of year to 31.03.17 | | 254,400 |

Using formula given by question:

$$\frac{\text{Work certified}}{\text{Total contract price}} \times \text{Total estimated profit} = \text{Profit for year to 31.03.17}$$

$$= \frac{360{,}000 + 40{,}000}{1{,}200{,}000} \times 254{,}400 = \underline{135{,}680}$$

(*ii*) Depreciation of plant to 31.03.17 = (76,800 − 4,800) ÷ 18 = 4,000 per month = 36,000.

(*iii*) Work certified in year to 31.03.18 = 1,200,000 − 400,000 = 800,000.

**3.2**

**Stannard and Sykes Ltd**
**Pier Contract Account**

*Contract for Seafront Development Corporation valued at £300,000*

| | | | | |
|---|---|---|---|---|
| Materials: direct | 58,966 | | Materials on site c/d | 11,660 |
| from store | 10,180 | 69,146 | Work in progress c/d | 151,167 |
| Wages | | 41,260 | | |
| Hire of plant | | 21,030 | | |
| Direct expenditure | | 3,065 | | |
| Overheads | | 8,330 | | |
| Wages accrued c/d | | 2,826 | | |
| | | 145,657 | | |
| Profit and loss account (proportion of profit to date) | | 17,170 | | |
| | | 162,827 | | 162,827 |
| Materials on site b/d | | 11,660 | Wages accrued b/d | 2,826 |
| Work in progress b/d | | 151,167 | | |

A suggested method for prudently estimating the amount of profit to be taken to November 30 is:

$$\frac{2}{3} \times \frac{\text{Cash received}}{\text{Value of work certified}} \times \text{Estimated profit (Value of work certified less cost of work certified)}$$

| | | |
|---|---|---|
| Total expenditure to date | | 145,657 |
| *Less* Materials on site at November 30 2018 | 11,660 | |
| Cost of work not yet certified | 12,613 | 24,273 |
| Cost of work certified (*a*) | | 121,384 |
| Value of work certified (*b*) | | 150,000 |
| Total profit to date (*b*) − (*a*) | | 28,616 |

**5.1**

*Bank*

| | | | |
|---|---|---|---|
| Application | 100,000 | Balance c/d | 601,250 |
| Allotment (150,000 less excess applications 40,000) | 110,000 | | |
| First call (595,000 × 0.35) | 208,250 | | |
| Second call (595,000 × 0.30) | 178,500 | | |
| E Kershaw (5,000 × 0.9) | 4,500 | | |
| | 601,250 | | 601,250 |

*E Kershaw*

| | | | |
|---|---|---|---|
| Ordinary share capital | 5,000 | Bank | 4,500 |
| | | Forfeited shares | 500 |
| | 5,000 | | 5,000 |

*Application and Allotment*

| | | | |
|---|---|---|---|
| Ordinary share capital | 210,000 | Bank | 100,000 |
| | | Bank | 110,000 |
| | 210,000 | | 210,000 |

*Ordinary Share Capital*

| | | | |
|---|---|---|---|
| Forfeited shares | 5,000 | Application and allotment | 210,000 |
| | | First call | 210,000 |
| Balance c/d | 600,000 | Second call | 180,000 |
| | | E Kershaw | 5,000 |
| | 605,000 | | 605,000 |

*First Call*

| | | | |
|---|---|---|---|
| Ordinary share capital | 210,000 | Bank | 208,250 |
| | | Forfeited shares | 1,750 |
| | 210,000 | | 210,000 |

*Second Call*

| | | | |
|---|---|---|---|
| Ordinary share capital | 180,000 | Bank | 178,500 |
| | | Forfeited shares | 1,500 |
| | 180,000 | | 180,000 |

*Forfeited Shares*

| | | | |
|---|---|---|---|
| First call | 1,750 | Ordinary share capital | 5,000 |
| Second call | 1,500 | | |
| E Kershaw | 500 | | |
| Transfer to share premium | 1,250 | | |
| | 5,000 | | 5,000 |

*Statement of Financial Position (extract)*

| | |
|---|---|
| Bank | 601,250 |
| | 601,250 |
| Ordinary share capital | 600,000 |
| Share premium | 1,250 |
| | 601,250 |

**5.2**

*Bank*

| | | | |
|---|---|---|---|
| Application (1.08 million × 0.20) | 216,000 | Application and allotment: Refund of application monies | 16,000 |
| Allotment (800,000 × 0.28 less excess application monies 40,000) | 184,000 | Balance c/d | 802,500 |
| First call (795,000 × 0.27) | 214,650 | | |
| Second call (793,000 × 0.25) | 198,250 | | |
| H Vipond (7,000 × 0.80) | 5,600 | | |
| | 818,500 | | 818,500 |

*Application and Allotment*

| | | | |
|---|---|---|---|
| Bank: Refunds | 16,000 | Bank | 216,000 |
| Ordinary share capital | 384,000 | Bank | 184,000 |
| | 400,000 | | 400,000 |

*First Call Account*

| | | | |
|---|---|---|---|
| Ordinary share capital | 216,000 | Bank | 214,650 |
| | | Forfeited shares | 1,350 |
| | 216,000 | | 216,000 |

*Second Call Account*

| | | | |
|---|---|---|---|
| Ordinary share capital | 200,000 | Bank | 198,250 |
| | | Forfeited shares | 1,750 |
| | 200,000 | | 200,000 |

*Ordinary Share Capital*

| | | | |
|---|---|---|---|
| Forfeited shares | 7,000 | Application and allotment | 384,000 |
| Balance c/d | 800,000 | First call | 216,000 |
| | | Second call | 204,000 |
| | | H Vipond | 7,000 |
| | 807,000 | | 807,000 |

*Forfeited Shares*

| | | | |
|---|---|---|---|
| First call | 1,350 | Ordinary share capital | 7,000 |
| Second call | 1,750 | | |
| H Vipond | 1,400 | | |
| Transfer to share premium | 2,500 | | |
| | 7,000 | | 7,000 |

*H Vipond*

| | | | |
|---|---|---|---|
| Ordinary share capital | 7,000 | Bank | 5,600 |
| | | Forfeited shares | 1,400 |
| | 7,000 | | 7,000 |

**5.3**

*(a)*

**Cosy Fires Ltd**

*Application and Allotment*

| | | | | |
|---|---|---|---|---|
| Cash: Return of unsuccessful applications 5,000 × 0.60 | 3,000 | Cash application for 65,000 × 0.60 | | 39,000 |
| Share capital: Due on application and allotment: 40,000 × 0.70 | 28,000 | Cash: Balance due on allotment (*see* workings)* | | 1,975 |
| Share premium: 40,000 × 0.25 | 10,000 | Balance c/d: Due from allottee in respect of 500 shares: 500 × 0.35 = | 175 | |
| | | *Less* o/paid on application 250 × 0.60 = | 150 | 25 |
| | 41,000 | | | 41,000 |
| Balance b/d | 25 | Forfeited shares | | 25 |

*Share Capital*

| | | | |
|---|---|---|---|
| Forfeited shares: Amount called on shares forfeited: 500 × 0.70 | 350 | Balance b/d | 75,000 |
| Balance c/d | 115,000 | Application and allotment | 28,000 |
| | | Call | 11,850 |
| | | Forfeited shares | 500 |
| | 115,350 | | 115,350 |

*Share Premium*

| | | | |
|---|---|---|---|
| Balance c/d | 10,375 | Application and allotment | 10,000 |
| | | Forfeited shares | 375 |
| | 10,375 | | 10,375 |

*Forfeited Shares*

| | | | |
|---|---|---|---|
| Application and allotment | 25 | Share capital | 350 |
| Share capital | 500 | Cash: 500 × 1.10 per share | 550 |
| Share premium | 375 | | |
| | 900 | | 900 |

*Call*

| | | | |
|---|---|---|---|
| Share capital 39,500 × 0.30 | 11,850 | Cash | 11,850 |

**5.3** *(cont'd)*

*(b)* *Statement of Financial Position as at 31 May 2017*

| | | | |
|---|---|---|---|
| Share capital | | | |
| Authorised: 160,000 ordinary shares of 1 each | | | 160,000 |
| Issued and fully paid: 115,000 ordinary shares of 1 each | | | 115,000 |
| Capital reserve: | | | |
| Share premium | | | 10,375 |
| *Workings: | Due on application 0.60 × 40,000 | 24,000 | |
| | Due on allotment 0.35 × 40,000 | 14,000 | 38,000 |
| | Received on application: 0.60 × 65,000 | 39,000 | |
| | *Less* Refunded 5,000 × 0.60 | 3,000 | 36,000 |
| | Balance due on allotment | | 2,000 |
| | *Less* | | |
| | Amount due on application and allotment 500 × 0.95 | 475 | |
| | Received on application 750 × 0.60 | 450 | 25 |
| | | | 1,975 |

**5.5**

M Ltd

*Ledger Accounts (dates omitted)*

*Cash*

| | | | |
|---|---|---|---|
| Application and allotment (750,000 × 85p) | 637,500 | Application and allotment (Refund 125,000 × 85*p*) | 106,250 |
| Application and allotment (500,000 × 25p − overpaid 125,000 × 85p) | 18,750 | | |
| First and final call (495,000 × 50p) | 247,500 | | |
| Forfeited shares (5,000 × 90p) | 4,500 | | |

*Application and Allotment*

| | | | |
|---|---|---|---|
| Share capital | 250,000 | Cash | 637,500 |
| Share premium | 300,000 | Cash | 18,750 |
| Cash | 106,250 | | |
| | 656,250 | | 656,250 |

*Share Premium*

| | | | |
|---|---|---|---|
| | | Application and allotment | 300,000 |
| Balance c/d | 302,000 | Forfeited shares | 2,000 |
| | 302,000 | | 302,000 |

*Share Capital*

| | | | |
|---|---|---|---|
| Forfeited shares | 5,000 | Balance b/d | 500,000 |
| | | Application and allotment | 250,000 |
| Balance c/d | 1,000,000 | First and final call | 250,000 |
| | | Forfeited shares | 5,000 |
| | 1,005,000 | | 1,005,000 |

*First and Final Call*

| | | | |
|---|---|---|---|
| Share capital | 250,000 | Cash | 247,500 |
| | | Forfeited shares | 2,500 |
| | 250,000 | | 250,000 |

*Forfeited Shares*

| | | | |
|---|---|---|---|
| First and final call | 2,500 | Share capital | 5,000 |
| Share capital | 5,000 | Cash | 4,500 |
| Share premium | 2,000 | | |
| | 9,500 | | 9,500 |

*Current assets*

| | |
|---|---|
| Accounts receivable: called-up share capital not paid | 2,500 |
| Issued share capital: | |
| 1,000,000 ordinary shares of £1 each | 1,000,000 |
| Reserves: | |
| Share premium | 302,000 |

The authorised share capital should be shown also as a note only.

The increase in share premium would also be shown as a note in the statement showing changes in reserves.

**6.1**

*(a)*

| | | *Dr* | *Cr* |
|---|---|---|---|
| (A1) | Bank | 8,000 | |
| | (A2) Ordinary share applicants | | 8,000 |
| Cash received from applicants. | | | |
| (B1) | Ordinary share applicants | 8,000 | |
| | (B2) Ordinary share capital | | 8,000 |
| Ordinary shares allotted. | | | |
| (C1) | Preference share capital | 8,000 | |
| | (C2) Preference share redemption | | 8,000 |
| Shares to be redeemed. | | | |
| (D1) | Preference share redemption | 8,000 | |
| | (D2) Bank | | 8,000 |
| Payment made to redeem shares. | | | |

| | Balances before | Effect Dr | Effect Cr | Balances after |
|---|---|---|---|---|
| Net assets (except bank) | 32,000 | | | 32,000 |
| Bank | 20,800 | (A1) 8,000 | (D2) 8,000 | 20,800 |
| | 52,800 | | | 52,800 |
| Preference share capital | 8,000 | (C1) 8,000 | | |
| Preference share redemption | – | (D1) 8,000 | (C2) 8,000 | – |
| Ordinary share capital | 24,000 | | (B2) 8,000 | 32,000 |
| Ordinary share applicants | – | (B1) 8,000 | (A2) 8,000 | – |
| Share premium | 3,200 | | | 3,200 |
| | 35,200 | | | 35,200 |
| Retained profits | 17,600 | | | 17,600 |
| | 52,800 | | | 52,800 |

(*b*)

| | | Dr | Cr |
|---|---|---|---|
| (A1) | Preference share capital | 8,000 | |
| | (A2) Preference share redemption | | 8,000 |
| Shares to be redeemed. | | | |
| (B1) | Preference share redemption | 8,000 | |
| | (B2) Bank | | 8,000 |
| Cash paid on redemption. | | | |
| (C1) | Retained profits | 8,000 | |
| | (C2) Capital redemption reserve | | 8,000 |
| Transfer per Companies Act. | | | |

| | Balances before | Effect Dr | Effect Cr | Balances after |
|---|---|---|---|---|
| Net assets (except bank) | 32,000 | | | 32,000 |
| Bank | 20,800 | | (B2) 8,000 | 12,800 |
| | 52,800 | | | 44,800 |
| Preference share capital | 8,000 | (A1) 8,000 | | – |
| Preference share redemption | – | (B1) 8,000 | (A2) 8,000 | – |
| Ordinary share capital | 24,000 | | | 24,000 |
| Capital redemption reserve | – | | (C2) 8,000 | 8,000 |
| Share premium | 3,200 | | | 3,200 |
| | 35,200 | | | 35,200 |
| Retained profits | 17,600 | (C1) 8,000 | | 9,600 |
| | 52,800 | | | 44,800 |

(*c*)

| | | Dr | Cr |
|---|---|---|---|
| (A1) | Bank | 2,400 | |
| | (A2) Ordinary share applicants | | 2,400 |
| Cash received from applicants. | | | |
| (B1) | Ordinary share applicants | 2,400 | |
| | (B2) Ordinary share capital | | 2,400 |
| Ordinary shares allotted. | | | |
| (C1) | Retained profits | 5,600 | |
| | (C2) Capital redemption reserve | | 5,600 |
| Part of redemption not covered by new issue, to comply with Companies Act. | | | |
| (D1) | Preference share capital | 8,000 | |
| | (D2) Preference share redemption | | 8,000 |
| Shares to be redeemed. | | | |
| (E1) | Preference share redemption | 8,000 | |
| | (E2) Bank | | 8,000 |
| Payment made for redemption. | | | |

| | Balances before | Effect Dr | Effect Cr | Balances after |
|---|---|---|---|---|
| Net assets (except bank) | 32,000 | | | 32,000 |
| Bank | 20,800 | (A1) 2,400 | (E2) 8,000 | 15,200 |
| | 52,800 | | | 47,200 |
| Preference share capital | 8,000 | (D1) 8,000 | | – |
| Preference share redemption | – | (E1) 8,000 | (D2) 8,000 | – |
| Ordinary share capital | 24,000 | | (B2) 2,400 | 26,400 |
| Ordinary share applicants | – | (B1) 2,400 | (A2) 2,400 | – |
| Capital redemption reserve | – | | (C2) 5,600 | 5,600 |
| Share premium | 3,200 | | | 3,200 |
| | 35,200 | | | 35,200 |
| Retained profits | 17,600 | (C1) 5,600 | | 12,000 |
| | 52,800 | | | 47,200 |

(*d*)

| | | Dr | Cr |
|---|---|---|---|
| (A1) | Preference share capital | 8,000 | |
| | (A2) Preference share redemption | | 8,000 |
| Shares to be redeemed. | | | |
| (B1) | Retained profits | 2,000 | |
| | (B2) Preference share redemption | | 2,000 |
| Premium on redemption of shares *not* previously issued at premium. | | | |
| (C1) | Retained profits | 8,000 | |
| | (C2) Capital redemption reserve | | 8,000 |
| Transfer because shares redeemed out of distributable profits. | | | |
| (D1) | Preference share redemption | 10,000 | |
| | (D2) Bank | | 10,000 |
| Payment on redemption. | | | |

**6.1** *(cont'd)*

| | *Balances before* | *Effect Dr* | *Effect Cr* | *Balances after* |
|---|---|---|---|---|
| Net assets (except bank) | 32,000 | | | 32,000 |
| Bank | 20,800 | | (D2) 10,000 | 10,800 |
| | 52,800 | | | 42,800 |
| Preference share capital | 8,000 | (A1) 8,000 | | |
| Preference share redemption | – | (D1) 10,000 | (A2) 8,000 | – |
| | | | (B2) 2,000 | – |
| Ordinary share capital | 24,000 | | | 24,000 |
| Capital redemption reserve | – | | (C2) 8,000 | 8,000 |
| Share premium | 3,200 | | | 3,200 |
| | 35,200 | | | 35,200 |
| Retained profits | 17,600 | (C1) 8,000<br>(B1) 2,000 | | 7,600 |
| | 52,800 | | | 42,800 |

*(e)*

| | *Dr* | *Cr* |
|---|---|---|
| (A1) Bank | 10,400 | |
| (A2) Ordinary share applicants | | 10,400 |
| Cash received from applicants. | | |
| (B1) Ordinary share applicants | 10,400 | |
| (B2) Ordinary share capital | | 10,400 |
| Ordinary shares allotted. | | |
| (C1) Preference share capital | 8,000 | |
| (C2) Preference share redemption | | 8,000 |
| Shares being redeemed. | | |
| (D1) Share premium account | 2,000 | |
| (D2) Preference share redemption | | 2,000 |
| Amount of share premium account used for redemption. | | |
| (E1) Retained profits | 400 | |
| (E2) Preference share redemption | | 400 |
| Excess of premium payable over amount of share premium account usable for the purpose. | | |
| (F1) Preference share redemption | 10,400 | |
| (F2) Bank | | 10,400 |
| Amount payable on redemption. | | |

| | *Balances before* | *Effect Dr* | *Effect Cr* | *Balances after* |
|---|---|---|---|---|
| Net assets (except bank) | 32,000 | | | 32,000 |
| Bank | 20,800 | (A1) 10,400 | (F2) 10,400 | 20,800 |
| | 52,800 | | | 52,800 |
| Preference share capital | 8,000 | (C1) 8,000 | | – |
| Preference share redemption | – | (F1) 10,400 | (C2) 8,000<br>(D2) 2,000<br>(E2) 400 | – |
| Ordinary share capital | 24,000 | | (B2) 10,400 | 34,400 |
| Ordinary share applicants | – | (B1) 10,400 | (A2) 10,400 | – |
| Share premium account | 3,200 | (D1) 2,000 | | 1,200 |
| | 35,200 | | | 35,600 |
| Retained profits | 17,600 | (E1) 400 | | 17,200 |
| | 52,800 | | | 52,800 |

**6.3**

*(a)*

| | *Dr* | *Cr* |
|---|---|---|
| (A1) Ordinary share capital | 19,200 | |
| (A2) Ordinary share purchase | | 19,200 |
| Shares to be purchased. | | |
| (B1) Ordinary share purchase | 19,200 | |
| (B2) Bank | | 19,200 |
| Payment for shares purchased. | | |
| (C1) Retained profits | 14,400 | |
| (C2) Capital redemption reserve | | 14,400 |
| Transfer of deficiency of permissible capital payment to comply with Companies Act. | | |

| | *Balances before* | *Effect Dr* | *Effect Cr* | *Balances after* |
|---|---|---|---|---|
| Net assets (except bank) | 40,000 | | | 40,000 |
| Bank | 41,600 | | (B2) 19,200 | 22,400 |
| | 81,600 | | | 62,400 |
| Preference share capital | 16,000 | | | 16,000 |
| Ordinary share capital | 32,000 | (A1) 19,200 | | 12,800 |
| Ordinary share purchase | – | (B1) 19,200 | (A2) 19,200 | – |
| Non-distributable reserves | 19,200 | | | 19,200 |
| Capital redemption reserve | – | | (B2) 14,400 | 14,400 |
| | 67,200 | | | 62,400 |
| Retained profits | 14,400 | (C1) 14,400 | | – |
| | 81,600 | | | 62,400 |

(*b*)

| | | *Dr* | *Cr* |
|---|---|---|---|
| (A1) | Ordinary share capital | 19,200 | |
| | (A2) Ordinary share purchase | | 19,200 |
| Shares to be purchased. | | | |
| (B1a) | Retained profits | 14,400 | |
| (B2b) | Non-distributable reserves | 960 | |
| | (B2) Ordinary share capital | | 15,360 |
| Transfers of retained profits and non-distributable reserves per Companies Act. | | | |
| (C1) | Ordinary share purchase | 34,560 | |
| | (C2) Bank | | 34,560 |
| Payment to shareholders. | | | |

| | *Balances before* | *Effect* Dr | *Effect* Cr | *Balances after* |
|---|---|---|---|---|
| Net assets (except bank) | 40,000 | | | 40,000 |
| Bank | 41,600 | | (C2) 34,560 | 7,040 |
| | 81,600 | | | 47,040 |
| Preference share capital | 16,000 | | | 16,000 |
| Ordinary share capital | 32,000 | (A1) 19,200 | | 12,800 |
| Ordinary share purchase | – | (C1) 34,560 | (A2) 19,200<br>(B2) 15,360 | – |
| Non-distributable reserves | 19,200 | (B1b) 960 | | 18,240 |
| | 67,200 | | | 47,040 |
| Retained profits | 14,400 | (B1a) 14,400 | | – |
| | 81,600 | | | 47,040 |

**6.5**

*Workings:* Opening balance 10% loan notes (a/c below)

| | | |
|---|---|---|
| Originally issued | 375,000 | |
| *Less* Redeemed previously | 150,000 | 225,000 |

*10% Loan notes*

| | | | |
|---|---|---|---|
| 30/9 Loan-note redemption | 225,000 | 1/7 Balance b/d | 225,000 |

*Workings:* Sinking fund investments (a/c below)

| | |
|---|---|
| Appropriations to date | 334,485 |
| Interest invested (39,480 – 2,475) | 37,005 |
| | 371,490 |
| *Less* Sold – at cost | 144,915 |
| | 226,575 |

*Sinking Fund Investments*

| | | | | | |
|---|---|---|---|---|---|
| 1/7 | Balance b/d | 226,575 | 2/8 | Bank No. 2 Sale | 73,215 |
| 2/8 | Sinking fund: Profit (73,215 – 69,322) | 3,893 | 25/9 | Bank No. 2 Sale | 160,238 |
| 25/9 | Sinking fund: Profit (Cost 226,575 – 69,322 = 157,253. Sold for 160,238) | 2,985 | | | |
| | | 233,453 | | | 233,453 |

*Workings*: Sinking fund (a/c below)

| | |
|---|---|
| Previous contributions | 334,485 |
| Interest on investments | 39,480 |
| Profit: Previous sales of investments (147,243 – 144,915) | 2,328 |
| Profit: Previous purchase loan notes (150,000 – 147,243) | 2,757 |
| | 379,050 |
| *Less* Transfer to general reserve sum equal to loan notes redeemed | 150,000 |
| | 229,050 |

*Sinking Fund A/c*

| | | | | | |
|---|---|---|---|---|---|
| 30/9 | Loan-notes redemption (Premium 1%) | 2,250 | 1/7 | Balance b/d | 229,050 |
| | | | 7/7 | No 2 Bank: Interest | 1,756 |
| 30/9 | General reserve | 236,889 | 2/8 | SF Investments: Profit | 3,893 |
| | | | 13/9 | No 2 Bank: Interest | 1,455 |
| | | | 25/9 | SF Investments: Profit | 2,985 |
| | | 239,139 | | | 239,139 |

*No. 2 Bank A/c*

| | | | | | |
|---|---|---|---|---|---|
| 1/7 | Balance b/d | 2,475 | 30/9 | W Bank plc (deposit) | 15,150 |
| 7/7 | Sinking fund: Interest | 1,756 | 30/9 | Loan notes redemption | 212,100 |
| 2/8 | SF investments: Sale | 73,215 | 30/9 | No. 1 Bank transfer of balance | 11,889 |
| 13/9 | Sinking fund: Interest | 1,455 | | | |
| 25/9 | SF investments: Sale | 160,238 | | | |
| | | 239,139 | | | 239,139 |

*Loan-note Redemption A/c*

| | | | | | |
|---|---|---|---|---|---|
| 30/9 | No. 2 Bank (225,000 Loan notes −15,000 B Ltd = 210,000 at 1% premium) | 212,100 | 30/9 | 10% Loan notes | 225,000 |
| | | | 30/9 | Sinking fund (premium) | 2,250 |
| 30/9 | Balance c/d (15,000 outstanding at premium 1%) | 15,150 | | | |
| | | 227,250 | | | 227,250 |

*W Bank plc*

| | | |
|---|---|---|
| 30/9 | No. 2 Bank | 15,150 |

**6.7**

(Dates omitted – all figures shown in £000)

*Application and Allotment*

| | | | |
|---|---|---|---|
| Ordinary shares | 80 | Bank | 60 |
| Share premium | 20 | Bank | 40 |
| | 100 | | 100 |

*Call Account*

| | | | |
|---|---|---|---|
| Ordinary shares | 20 | Bank | 18 |
| | | Investments | 2 |
| | 20 | | 20 |

*Investments (own shares)*

| | | | |
|---|---|---|---|
| Call | 2 | Bank | 11 |
| Share premium | 9 | | |
| | 11 | | 11 |

**6.9**

(*Note:* Some abbreviations are used.)

(*a*) *10% Loan notes*

| | | | | | |
|---|---|---|---|---|---|
| 31.12.18 | Loan-note redemption | 12,000 | 1.4.18 | Balance b/d | 100,000 |
| 31.3.19 | Balance c/d | 88,000 | | | |
| | | 100,000 | | | 100,000 |

(*b*) *Loan-note Redemption Fund*

| | | | | | |
|---|---|---|---|---|---|
| 31.12.18 | Reserve (equal to loan notes redeemed) | 12,000 | 1.4.18 | Balance b/d | 20,000 |
| | | | 31.12.18 | LNRFI profit on redemption) | 1,400 |
| | | | 31.12.18 | LN (profit on purchase) | 900 |
| | | | 31.12.19 | Bank | 1,600 |
| | | | 31.3.19 | Profit and loss (annual appropriation) | 2,000 |
| 31.3.19 | Balance c/d | 13,900 | | | |
| | | 25,900 | | | 25,900 |

(*c*) *Loan-note Redemption Fund Investment*

| | | | | | |
|---|---|---|---|---|---|
| 1.4.18 | Balance b/d | 20,000 | 31.12.18 | Bank (sale) | 11,400 |
| 31.12.18 | LN Fund (profit on sale) | 1,400 | | | |
| 31.3.19 | Bank (2,000 + 300 + 1,600) | 3,900 | 31.3.19 | Balance c/d | 13,900 |
| | | 25,300 | | | 25,300 |

(*d*) *Loan-note Redemption*

| | | | | | |
|---|---|---|---|---|---|
| 31.12.18 | Bank (purchase) | 11,400 | 31.12.18 | 10% Loan notes | 12,000 |
| 31.12.18 | LNR Fund (profit on redemption) | 900 | 31.12.18 | Loan-note interest accrued | 300 |
| | | 12,300 | | | 12,300 |

(*e*) *Loan-note Interest*

| | | | | | |
|---|---|---|---|---|---|
| 30.9.18 | Bank (100,000 × 10% ÷ 2) | 5,000 | | | |
| 31.12.18 | Loan-note redemption (interest included in price 12,000 × 10% × ¼) | 300 | | | |
| 31.3.19 | Bank (88,000 × 10% ÷ 2) | 4,400 | 31.3.19 | Profit and loss | 9,700 |
| | | 9,700 | | | 9,700 |

**7.1**

(*a*)

**Club Ltd**

*Statement of Profit or Loss for the year ending 31 May 2018*

| | *Total* | *Basis of allocation* | *Pre-incorporation* | *Post incorporation* |
|---|---|---|---|---|
| Gross profit | 224,000 | Turnover | 64,000 | 160,000 |
| *Less* | | | | |
| Salary of vendor | 13,560 | Actual | 13,560 | |
| Wages | 69,120 | Time | 17,280 | 51,840 |
| Rent | 6,880 | Time | 1,720 | 5,160 |
| Distribution | 13,440 | Turnover | 3,840 | 9,600 |
| Commission | 5,600 | Turnover | 1,600 | 4,000 |
| Bad debts | 2,512 | Actual | 832 | 1,680 |
| Interest | 13,200 | Time | 7,920 | 5,280 |
| Directors' remuneration | 32,000 | Actual | | 32,000 |
| Directors' expenses | 4,120 | Actual | | 4,120 |
| Depreciation | | | | |
| Vans* | 15,200 | Actual | 3,200 | 12,000 |
| Machinery | 4,600 | Actual | 1,000 | 3,600 |
| Bank interest | 1,344 | Actual | | 1,344 |
| | 181,576 | | 50,952 | 130,624 |
| Net profit | 42,424 | | 13,048 | 29,376 |
| | 224,000 | | 64,000 | 160,000 |

*Depreciation on vans:

Vans to 31 March 2018 20% × 3 months × 56,000 + 20% × 1 month × 24,000 = 3,200

After 20% × 9 months × 56,000 + 20% × 9 months × 24,000 = 12,000

(*b*) Transfer to capital reserve.

(*c*) Charge to a pre-incorporation loss account.

**7.2**

*Adjusted Profits*

| | *2015* | | *2016* | | *2017* | |
|---|---|---|---|---|---|---|
| Profit per accounts | | 185,360 | | 226,960 | | 192,224 |
| *Add* Motor expenses saved | 3,760 | | 3,960 | | 4,120 | |
| Depreciation overcharged | 9,600 | | 5,760 | | 2,688 | |
| Wrapping expenses saved | 4,008 | | 4,584 | | 4,896 | |
| Bank interest | 704 | | 1,792 | | 2,176 | |
| Preliminary expenses | – | 18,072 | 7,040 | 23,136 | – | 13,880 |
| | | 203,432 | | 250,096 | | 206,104 |
| *Less* Extra management salaries | 56,000 | | 56,000 | | 56,000 | |
| Investment income | 3,360 | | 4,640 | | 6,720 | |
| Rents received | 12,480 | | 5,280 | | – | |
| Opening inventory | – | | 7,520 | | – | |
| Profit on property | – | 71,840 | 37,120 | 110,560 | – | 62,720 |
| Profits as adjusted | | 131,592 | | 139,536 | | 143,384 |

Average profit
131,592
139,536
143,384
414,512 ÷ 3 = 138,171

If 138,171 is a return of 20% on investment, then

$$\frac{138{,}171}{20} \times 100 = 690{,}855 \text{ purchase price.}$$

**7.3**

(*a*)

**CK**

*Realisation*

| | | | |
|---|---|---|---|
| Freehold premises | 8,000 | CK Ltd: Value at which assets taken over | 27,200 |
| Plant | 4,000 | Discount on accounts payable | 150 |
| Inventory | 2,000 | | |
| Accounts receivable | 5,000 | | |
| Profit on realisation | 8,350 | | |
| | 27,350 | | 27,350 |

*Capital*

| | | | |
|---|---|---|---|
| CK Ltd: Shares | 24,150 | Balance b/d | 16,000 |
| Cash | 200 | Profit on realisation | 8,350 |
| | 24,350 | | 24,350 |

*CK Ltd (not asked for in question)*

| | | | |
|---|---|---|---|
| Realisation | 27,200 | Accounts payable | 3,050 |
| | | Shares | 24,150 |
| | 27,200 | | 27,200 |

**RP Ltd**

*Realisation*

| | | | |
|---|---|---|---|
| Freehold premises | 4,500 | CK Ltd: Value at which assets taken over | 13,000 |
| Plant | 2,000 | | |
| Inventory | 1,600 | | |
| Accounts receivable | 3,400 | | |
| Profit on realisation | 1,500 | | |
| | 13,000 | | 13,000 |

*Sundry Shareholders*

| | | | |
|---|---|---|---|
| CK Ltd | | Share capital | 4,000 |
| Cash | 5,000 | Profit on realisation | 1,500 |
| Shares | 3,000 | Revenue surplus | 2,500 |
| | 8,000 | | 8,000 |

**CK Ltd** (not asked for in question)

| | | | |
|---|---|---|---|
| Realisation | 13,000 | Bank overdraft | 3,500 |
| | | Accounts payable | 1,500 |
| | | Sundry shareholders: Cash | 5,000 |
| | | Shares | 3,000 |
| | 13,000 | | 13,000 |

*Journal of CJK Ltd*

(*b*) (Narratives omitted)

| | Dr | Cr |
|---|---|---|
| Cash | 5,000 | |
| Share premium | | 3,000 |
| Ordinary shares | | 2,000 |
| Cash | 7,840 | |
| Discount on issue | 160 | |
| 7% loan notes | | 8,000 |
| Goodwill | 7,000 | |
| Freehold premises | 10,000 | |
| Plant | 3,500 | |
| Inventory | 2,000 | |
| Accounts receivable | 5,000 | |
| Provision for discounts receivable | 150 | |
| Accounts payable | | 3,200 |
| Allowance for doubtful debts | | 300 |
| Ordinary shares | | 24,150 |
| Goodwill | 500 | |
| Freehold premises | 5,500 | |
| Plant | 2,000 | |
| Inventory | 1,600 | |
| Accounts receivable | 3,400 | |
| Accounts payable | | 1,500 |
| Bank overdraft | | 3,500 |
| Cash | | 5,000 |
| Ordinary share capital | | 3,000 |
| Formation expenses | 1,200 | |
| Cash | | 1,200 |

**7.3** *(cont'd)*

*(c)*

CJK Ltd

*Statement of Financial Position as at 1 January 2017**

| | | | |
|---|---|---|---|
| *Non-current assets: at cost* | | | |
| Freehold premises | | | 15,500 |
| Plant | | | 5,500 |
| Goodwill | | | 7,500 |
| Formation expenses | | | 1,200 |
| | | | 29,700 |
| *Current assets* | | | |
| Inventory | | 3,600 | |
| Accounts receivable | 8,400 | | |
| *Less* Allowance for doubtful debts | 300 | 8,100 | |
| Cash at bank | | 3,140 | 14,840 |
| Total assets | | | 44,540 |
| *Current liabilities* | | | |
| Accounts payable | 4,700 | | |
| *Less* Provision | 150 | 4,550 | |
| Non-current liability | | | |
| Loan notes 7% | | 8,000 | 12,550 |
| Net assets | | | 31,990 |
| *Equity* | | | |
| Share capital | 29,150 | | |
| Share premium | 3,000 | | |
| Retained profits** | (160) | | |
| | 31,990 | | |

*This could be 31 December 2016.
**Discount on issue of loan notes to be written off against retained profits.

**8.1**

*(a)*

*Loan note Interest*

| 2016 | | | 2016 | | |
|---|---|---|---|---|---|
| Dec 31 | Bank | 14,000 | Dec 31 | Profit and loss | 17,500 |
| Dec 31 | Income tax | 3,500 | | | |
| | | 17,500 | | | 17,500 |

*Income Tax*

| 2016 | | | 2016 | | |
|---|---|---|---|---|---|
| Dec 31 | Balance c/d | 3,500 | Dec 31 | Loan-note interest | 3,500 |

*Ordinary Dividends*

| 2016 | | | 2016 | | |
|---|---|---|---|---|---|
| Jul 1 | Bank | 32,000 | Dec 31 | Profit and loss | 32,000 |

*Deferred Taxation*

| 2016 | | | 2016 | | |
|---|---|---|---|---|---|
| Dec 31 | Balance c/d | 16,000 | Dec 31 | Profit and loss* | 16,000 |

*40% of (110,000 − £70,000) = £16,000

*Corporation Tax*

| 2016 | | | 2016 | | |
|---|---|---|---|---|---|
| Dec 31 | Balance c/d | 145,000 | Dec 31 | Profit and loss | 145,000 |

*(b)* *Statement of Profit or Loss (extracts) for the year ending 31 December 2016*

| | | |
|---|---|---|
| Net trading profit | | 390,000 |
| *Less* Loan-note interest | | 17,500 |
| Profit before taxation | | 372,500 |
| *Less* Corporation tax | 145,000 | |
| Deferred tax | 16,000 | 161,000 |
| Profit for the year | | 211,500 |

*Statement of Financial Position (extracts) as at 31 December 2016*

| | |
|---|---|
| *Current liabilities* | |
| Corporation tax | 145,000 |
| Income tax | 3,500 |
| *Non-current liabilities* | |
| Deferred tax | 16,000 |

**8.3**

*Workings:*

(W1) Tax deducted from fixed interest income is $^1/_4 \times$ £30,000 = £7,500

(W2) Changes in deferred taxation account.

Timing difference:

| | |
|---|---|
| Capital allowances allowable for tax (D) | 130,000 |
| Depreciation actually charged (D) | 90,000 |
| | 40,000 |

Transferred to deferred tax account £40,000 × 40% = £16,000

*Deferred Tax*

| 2015 | | | 2015 | | | |
|---|---|---|---|---|---|---|
| Dec 31 | Balance c/d | 101,000 | Jan 1 | Balance b/d | (J) | 85,000 |
| | | | Dec 31 | Profit and loss | (W2) | 16,000 |
| | | 101,000 | | | | 101,000 |

*Income Tax*

| 2015 | | | | 2015 | | | |
|---|---|---|---|---|---|---|---|
| Nov 9 | Interest received | (C1) | 7,500 | Dec 5 | Loan-note interest | (B) | 20,000 |
| Dec 19 | Bank | | 12,500 | | | | |
| | | | 20,000 | | | | 20,000 |

*Interest Received*

| 2015 | | | | 2015 | | | |
|---|---|---|---|---|---|---|---|
| Dec 31 | Profit and loss | | 37,500 | Nov 9 | Bank | (C1) | 30,000 |
| | | | | Nov 9 | Income tax | (C1) | 7,500 |
| | | | 37,500 | | | | 37,500 |

*Loan-note Interest*

| 2015 | | | | 2015 | | | |
|---|---|---|---|---|---|---|---|
| Dec 5 | Bank | (B) | 80,000 | Dec 31 | Profit and loss | | 100,000 |
| Dec 5 | Income tax | (B) | 20,000 | | | | |
| | | | 100,000 | | | | 100,000 |

*Investment Income*

| 2015 | | | | 2015 | | | |
|---|---|---|---|---|---|---|---|
| Dec 31 | Profit and loss | | 1,000 | Oct 1 | Bank | (C2) | 1,000 |
| | | | 1,000 | | | | 1,000 |

*Corporation Tax*

| 2015 | | | | 2015 | | | |
|---|---|---|---|---|---|---|---|
| Sept 30 | Bank* | | 136,000 | Jan 1 | Balance b/d | (K) | 140,000 |
| Sept 30 | Profit and loss† | (K) | 4,000 | Dec 31 | Profit and loss | (L) | 170,000 |
| Dec 31 | Balance c/d | (L) | 170,000 | | | | |
| | | | 310,000 | | | | 310,000 |

* £140,000 *owing* – £4,000 *reduction* (K) = £136,000.
† Adjustment for amendment in tax bill.

*Preference Dividends*

| 2015 | | | | 2015 | | | |
|---|---|---|---|---|---|---|---|
| Jun 30 | Bank | (F) | 16,000 | Dec 31 | Profit and loss | | 16,000 |

*Ordinary Dividends*

| 2015 | | | | 2015 | | | |
|---|---|---|---|---|---|---|---|
| Mar 10 | Bank | (I) | 120,000 | Dec 31 | Profit and loss | | 210,000 |
| Aug 8 | Bank | (G) | 90,000 | | | | |
| | | | 210,000 | | | | 210,000 |

**Tilt Ltd**

*Statement of Profit or Loss (extracts) for the year ending 31 December 2015*

| | | | |
|---|---|---|---|
| Net trading profit | (A) | | 600,000 |
| *Add* Fixed rate interest (C1) (gross) | | 37,500 | |
| Investment income (C2) (gross) | | 1,000 | 38,500 |
| | | | 638,500 |
| *Less* Loan-note interest (B) (gross) | | | 100,000 |
| Profit before taxation | | | 538,500 |
| *Less* Taxation: Corporation tax | | 166,000* | |
| Deferred tax | | 16,000 | 182,000 |
| Profit for the year | | | 356,500 |

*Notes attached to the financial statements giving make-up of this figure.

*Statement of Financial Position (extracts) as at 31 December 2015*

| | |
|---|---|
| *Current liabilities* | |
| Corporation tax | 170,000 |
| *Non-current liabilities* | |
| Deferred tax | 101,000 |

A final point concerns the difference in treatment of tax on investment income as compared with tax on other income, such as interest. It is only the tax on investment income which is treated as part of the final tax costs, while the tax on interest is simply deducted from charges paid by the company. You would have to study taxation in detail to understand why this happens.

**8.5** **Sunset Ltd**

*Statement of Profit or Loss for the year ending 31 December 2016*

| | | |
|---|---|---|
| Trading profit | | 150,000 |
| Income from shares in related companies | 3,600* | |
| Other interest receivable and similar income | 1,000** | 4,600 |
| | | 154,600 |
| Interest payable and similar charges | | 3,000 |
| Profit before taxation | | 151,600 |
| Taxation | | 54,000 |
| Profit for the year | | 97,600 |

*£30,000 × 12% = £3,600
**£20,000 × 5% = £1,000

**8.6**

(All in £million)

(*i*) *Ordinary Dividends*

| | | | | | |
|---|---|---|---|---|---|
| 31.8.15 | Bank (07 final) | 28 | | | |
| 31.12.15 | Bank (08 interim) | 12 | 31.3.16 | Profit and loss | 40 |
| | | 40 | | | 40 |

(*ii*) *Deferred Taxation*

| | | | | | |
|---|---|---|---|---|---|
| 31.3.16 | Balance c/d | 8 | 1.4.15 | Balance b/d | 3 |
| | | | 31.3.16 | Profit and loss | 5 |
| | | 8 | | | 8 |

**9.1**

(*a*)

**Either Ltd**

| | + | – | £000 |
|---|---|---|---|
| Profit per draft financial statements | | | 157 |
| (*i*) Inventory: reduce to net realisable value | | 35 | |
| (*ii*) Directors' remuneration | | 43 | |
| (*iii*) Bad debt | | 30 | |
| (*iv*) Corporation tax saved on (*i*) + (*ii*) + (*iii*) × 50% | 54 | | |
| (*v*) Depreciation adjustment (W1) | | 30 | |
| (*vi*) Revaluation reserve (realised on sale) | 125 | | |
| (*vii*) General reserve | 80 | | |
| (*viii*) Loss brought forward (W2) | | 144 | |
| | 259 | 282 | |
| | | net (23) | (23) |
| Maximum possible dividend | | | 134 |
| Preference dividend 6% | £9,000 | | |
| Ordinary dividend | £125,000 | | |

*Research and development expenditure:* assumed to have been carried forward in accordance with IAS 38 and can be justified. Failing this it would have to be a realised loss.

(*b*) For a plc no changes required, except that the payment should not reduce net assets below called-up share capital and undistributable reserves = 400 + 150 + 100 = 650.
A further bad debt might change this position.

(W1) *Reducing balance*

| | |
|---|---|
| Cost 1.12.2014 | 100,000 |
| Depreciation 2015 | 25,000 |
| | 75,000 |
| Cost 1.6.2016 | 25,000 |
| | 100,000 |
| Depreciation 2016 | 25,000 |
| | 75,000 |
| Cost 29.2.2017 | 28,000 |
| 31.5.2017 | 45,000 |
| | 148,000 |
| Depreciation 2017 | 37,000 |
| | 111,000 |
| Cost 1.12.2017 | 50,000 |
| | 161,000 |
| Depreciation 2018 | 40,250 |
| | 120,750 |
| Total 25,000 + 25,000 + 37,000 + 40,250 = | 127,250 |

| *Straight line* | | *2015* | *2016* | *2017* | *2018* |
|---|---|---|---|---|---|
| Cost 1.12.2015 | 100,000 | 25,000 | 25,000 | 25,000 | 25,000 |
| 1.6.2016 | 25,000 | | 3,125 | 6,250 | 6,250 |
| 29.2.2017 | 28,000 | | | 5,250 | 7,000 |
| 31.5.2017 | 45,000 | | | 5,625 | 11,250 |
| 1.12.2017 | 50,000 | | | | 12,500 |
| | | 25,000 | 28,125 | 42,125 | 62,000 |
| | | Total 157,250 | | | |

Extra depreciation 157,250 − 127,250 = 30,000

(W2) As profits after tax were £157,000 but were shown in the statement of financial position as £13,000, this means that a deficit of £144,000 had been brought forward from last year.

**10.1**

(*a*)

**Merton Manufacturing Co Ltd**

*Statement of Financial Position as at . . .*

| | | | |
|---|---|---|---|
| *Non-current tangible assets* | | | |
| Freehold land and buildings at cost | | | 95,000 |
| Plant and equipment at written-down value | (W1) | | 104,350 |
| | | | 199,350 |
| *Current assets* | | | |
| Inventory | | 25,000 | |
| Accounts receivable | | 50,000 | |
| Bank | (W2) | 14,150 | |
| | | | 89,150 |
| | | | 288,500 |
| *Current liabilities* | | | |
| Accounts payable | | 63,500 | |
| *Non-current liabilities* | | | |
| 8% loan notes | (W3) | 150,000 | |
| | | | 213,500 |
| Net assets | | | 75,000 |
| *Equity* | | | |
| Called-up share capital | | | |
| 150,000 50p ordinary shares | (W4) | | 75,000 |

*Workings:*

(W1) *Capital Reduction*

| | | | |
|---|---|---|---|
| Ordinary shares 50p (new) | | Ordinary shares £1 (old) | 90,000 |
| (1 for 6 = 15,000 × 50*p*) | 7,500 | 6% preference shares (old) | 150,000 |
| Ordinary shares 50p (new) | | $11^1/_2$% loan notes (old) | 100,000 |
| (1 for 3 – *preference* – 50,000 × 50*p*) | 25,000 | Share premium written off | 25,000 |
| 8% loan notes | | | |
| (exchange for $11^1/_2$%) | 150,000 | | |
| Ordinary shares 50p | | | |
| (1 for every £4 old loan note) | 12,500 | | |
| Goodwill impaired written off | 50,000 | | |
| Retained profits written off | 38,850 | | |
| Plant and equipment* | 81,150 | | |
| | 365,000 | | 365,000 |

*Per (*vii*) of question – amount needed to balance.

(W2) Shares issued 60,000 shares × 50p = 30,000
Cash 30,000 – overdraft 15,850 = balance 14,150

(W3) See capital reduction – debit side (W1) new loan notes 150,000

(W4) See (W1) 7,500 + 25,000 + 12,500 + new shares issued for cash 30,000 = 75,000

(*b*) (Main points)

| | *Old shareholdings* | *New shareholdings* |
|---|---|---|
| Expected profit | 22,500 | 22,500 |
| *Less* Interest $11^1/_2$% | 11,500 | |
| 8% | | 12,000 |
| Taxable profits | 11,000 | 10,500 |
| *Less* Corporation tax $33^1/_3$% | 3,667 | 3,500 |
| Profits before dividends | 7,333 | 7,000 |
| Preference dividends – if profits sufficient | 9,000 | – |

*Before reconstruction*

(Old) Preference shareholders

Before reconstruction it would have taken over five years at this rate before preference dividends payable, as the deficit of 38,850 of retained profits would have to be cleared off first.

(Old) Ordinary shares

Even forgetting the retained profits deficit, the preference dividends were bigger than available profits. This would leave nothing for the ordinary shareholder.

*After reconstruction*

The EPS is £7,000 ÷ 150,000 = 4.67p

If all profits are distributed the following benefits will be gained:

| | |
|---|---|
| By old preference shareholders | |
| 50,000 shares × 4.67p | 2,335 |
| Plus any benefits from tax credits. | |
| By old ordinary shareholders | |
| 15,000 shares × 4.67p | 700 |
| Plus any benefits from tax credits. | |

(*c*) Preference shareholders – points to be considered:

(*i*) What were prospects for income?

Based on projected earnings would have been no income for over five years, then earnings of 7,333 per annum if all profits distributed.

(*ii*) What are new prospects for income?

Total earnings of 7,000 per annum immediately.

(*iii*) Is it worth exchanging (*i*) for (*ii*)?

Obviously depends on whether forecasts are accurate or not. If the above are accurate would seem worthwhile.

(*iv*) What have preference shareholders given up?

The exchange consists of ordinary shares which are more risky than preference shares, both in terms of dividends and of payments on liquidation. Dividends will be lower than the 6% they were due previously, but it was not being paid.

(*v*) What have they gained?

Likelihood of dividends much sooner than the minimum of five years anticipated above.

**10.2**

(*a*)

| (*Narratives omitted*) | *Dr* | *Cr* |
|---|---|---|
| Preference share capital | 37,500 | |
| Ordinary share capital | 175,000 | |
| Capital reduction | | 212,500 |
| Preference shares reduced 25p each (0.25 × 150,000) and Ordinary shares reduced by 0.875 (200,000 × 0.875). | | |
| Capital reduction | 3,375 | |
| Ordinary share capital | | 3,375 |
| Ordinary shares issued repreference dividend arrears, 27,000 × 0.125. | | |
| Share premium | 40,000 | |
| Capital reduction | | 40,000 |
| Share premium balance utilised. | | |
| Provision for depreciation | 62,500 | |
| Capital reduction | 72,500 | |
| Plant and machinery | | 135,000 |
| Plant and machinery written down to 75,000. | | |
| Capital reduction | 176,625 | |
| Retained profits | | 114,375 |
| Preliminary expenses | | 7,250 |
| Goodwill | | 55,000 |
| Retained profits and intangible assets written off. | | |
| Cash | 62,500 | |
| Ordinary share applicants | | 62,500 |
| Applications for shares 500,000 × 0.125. | | |
| Ordinary share applicants | 62,500 | |
| Ordinary share capital | | 62,500 |
| 500,000 ordinary shares issued. | | |

(*b*)

*Statement of Financial Position as at 31 December 2016*

| | | |
|---|---|---|
| *Non-current assets* | | |
| Leasehold property at cost | 80,000 | |
| *Less* Provision for depreciation | 30,000 | 50,000 |
| Plant and machinery at valuation | | 75,000 |
| | | 125,000 |
| *Current assets* | | |
| Inventory | 79,175 | |
| Accounts receivable | 31,200 | |
| Bank | 11,500 | 121,875 |
| Total assets | | 246,875 |
| *Current liabilities* | | |
| Accounts payable | | 43,500 |
| Net assets | | 203,375 |
| *Equity* | | |
| Share capital: | | |
| Preference shares | | |
| 150,000 shares £0.75 | | 112,500 |
| Ordinary shares | | |
| 727,000 ordinary shares £0.125 | | 90,875 |
| | | 203,375 |

**10.3**

*The Journal* (narratives omitted)

| | *Dr* | *Cr* |
|---|---|---|
| (*a*) Preference share capital | 64,000 | |
| Capital reduction | | 64,000 |
| (*b*) Ordinary share capital | 1,400,000 | |
| Capital reduction | | 1,400,000 |
| (*c*) Capital reserve | 192,000 | |
| Capital reduction | | 192,000 |
| (*d*) Preference share capital | 256,000 | |
| Ordinary share capital | 1,400,000 | |
| New ordinary share capital | | 1,656,000 |
| (*e*) (*i*) Loan-note holders | 960,000 | |
| Loan notes | | 960,000 |
| (*ii*) Bank | 960,000 | |
| Loan-note holders | | 960,000 |
| (*f*) Capital reduction | 1,656,000 | |
| Goodwill etc. | | 800,000 |
| Plant and machinery | | 76,800 |
| Furniture | | 14,080 |
| Retained profits | | 765,120 |

**Greenmantle Ltd**

*Statement of Financial Position as at 31 March 2016*

| | | |
|---|---|---|
| *Non-current assets* | | |
| Intangible: Goodwill and trademarks | | 96,000 |
| Tangible: Plant and machinery | | 947,200 |
| Furniture and fittings | | 12,800 |
| | | 1,056,000 |
| *Current assets* | | |
| Inventory | 608,640 | |
| Accounts receivable | 238,720 | |
| Bank | 817,920 | |
| Cash | 960 | 1,666,240 |
| Total assets | | 2,722,240 |
| *Current liabilities* | | |
| Accounts payable | 106,240 | |
| *Non-current liabilities* | | |
| Loan notes | 960,000 | |
| | | 1,066,240 |
| | | 1,656,000 |
| *Equity* | | |
| Called-up share capital | | 1,656,000 |

**11.1**

(*a*) Following is a brief answer:

(*i*) Such closure costs should be disclosed separately.

(*ii*) This should be adjusted in tax charge for 2017. Because it is not material (probably) it does not need to be disclosed separately.

(*iii*) The excess should be credited to a reserve account, and a note attached to the statement of financial position. Depreciation to be based on revalued amount and on new estimate of remaining life of the asset, to be disclosed in a note to the accounts.

(*iv*) Treat as bad debt and write off to profit and loss.

(*v*) This is a prior period adjustment. The retained profit brought forward should be amended to allow for the change in accounting policy in the current year. The reasons: (1) it is material, (2) relates to a previous year, (3) as a result of change in accounting policy. The adjustment should be disclosed in a note to the financial statements.

**11.2**

(*i*) The replacement cost is irrelevant. The inventory should be shown at the cost of £26,500. This assumes historic cost accounts.

(*ii*) *Paramite:* inventory to be valued at direct costs £72,600 plus fixed factory overhead £15,300 = £87,900. Under no circumstances should selling expenses be included.

*Paraton:* as net realisable value is lower than the costs involved, this figure of £9,520 should be used (IAS 2).

(*iii*) In this case there is a change of accounting policy. Accordingly a prior period adjustment will be made. On a straight line basis, net book value would have been:

| | |
|---|---|
| Cost 160,000 less $12\frac{1}{2}\% \times 2$ *years* = | 120,000 |
| Value shown | 90,000 |
| Therefore prior period adjustment of to be added to retained profit at 1 November 2017. | 30,000 |

For 2018 and each of the following five years depreciation will be charged at the rate of £20,000 per annum (IAS 16).

(*iv*) The cost subject to depreciation is £250,000 less land £50,000 = £200,000. With a life of 40 years this is £5,000 per annum.

This also will result in a prior period adjustment, in this case 10 × £5,000 = £50,000. This will be debited to retained profits at 1 November 2017. For 2018 and each of the following 29 years the yearly charge of depreciation will be £5,000 (IAS 16).

(*v*) Write off £17,500 to profit or loss (IAS 38).

(*vi*) As this development expenditure is almost definitely going to be recovered over the next four years it can be written off over that period (IAS 38).

(*vii*) Charge to profit and loss.

(*viii*) As this is over 20%, it is material and appears to be long term. This means that Lilleshall Ltd is an associate company and should be included in the financial statements on the equity basis. The post-acquisition profits to be brought in are 30% × £40,000 = £12,000.

**11.5**

The fact that this is a partnership does not mean that accounting standards are not applicable; they are just as applicable to a partnership as they are to a limited company.

(*a*) (*i*) These should be included as sales of £60,000 in the accounts for the year to 31 May 2017. This is because the matching concept requires that revenue, and the costs used up in achieving it, should be matched up. Profits: increase of £60,000.

(*ii*) Inventory values are normally based on the lower of cost or net realisable value. In this case it depends how certain it is that the inventory can be sold for £40,000. If a firm order can definitely be anticipated, then the figure of £40,000 can be used as this then represents the lower figure of net realisable value. Profit: an increase of £15,000. However, should the sale not be expected, then the concept of prudence dictates that the scrap value of £1,000 be used. Profit: a reduction of £24,000.

(*b*) It is important to establish the probability of the payment of the debt of £80,000. If it is as certain as it possibly can be that payment will be made, even though it may be delayed then no provision is needed. Profit change: nil.

However, the effect on future profits can be substantial. A note to the accounts detailing the possibilities of such changes should be given.

**11.5** *(cont'd)*

(*c*) The concepts which are applicable here are (*i*) going concern, (*ii*) consistency, (*iii*) accruals, (*iv*) prudence.

Following on the revelations in (*b*) and the effect on sales so far of the advertising campaign, is the partnership still able to see itself as a going concern? This would obviously affect the treatment of valuations of all assets.

Given that it can be treated as a going concern, the next point to be considered is that of consistency. The treatment of the expense item should be treated consistently.

The accruals concept is concerned with matching up revenues and costs, and will affect the decision as to how much of the costs should be carried forward. Some revenue in future periods needs to be expected with a high degree of certainty before any of this expenditure should be carried forward. It does not seem highly likely that large revenues can be expected in future in this case. In any case 75% is a very large proportion of such expenditure to be carried forward. There is no easy test of the validity of the partners' estimates. Granted that under IAS 38 for development expenditure some of it, under very stringent conditions, can be carried forward. If the partners' estimates can be accepted under this, then profits would be increased by 75% × (50,000 + 60,000) = £82,500.

(*d*) The expected profit/loss is as follows:

| | *Project A* | *Project B* | *Project C* |
|---|---|---|---|
| Direct costs to date | 30,000 | 25,000 | 6,000 |
| Overheads to date | 4,000 | 2,000 | 500 |
| Future expected direct costs | 10,000 | 25,000 | 40,000 |
| Future expected overheads | 2,000 | 2,000 | 3,000 |
| Total of expected costs | 46,000 | 54,000 | 49,500 |
| Sale price of project | 55,000 | 50,000 | 57,500 |
| Expected total profit/loss | 9,000 | (4,000) | 8,000 |
| % Complete | 75% | 50% | 15% |

When a project is sufficiently near completion then a proportion of the profits can be taken as being realised.

Project A is 75% complete and this indicates profit being taken. Whether or not 75% can be taken, i.e. £6,750, will depend on the facts of the case. If completion at the above figures can be taken for granted then it might be reasonable to do so. Prudence dictates that a lesser figure be taken.

With Project B there is an expected loss. Following the prudence concept losses should always be accounted for in full as soon as they become known.

It is too early in Project C, only 15% completed, to be certain about the outcome. No profit should therefore be brought into account.

Profit, dependent on comments about Project A, will therefore be increased by £6,750 − £4,000 = £2,750.

(*e*) This is a case where the examiner has dipped into topics from other subjects. What is needed here is a tree diagram to show the probabilities.

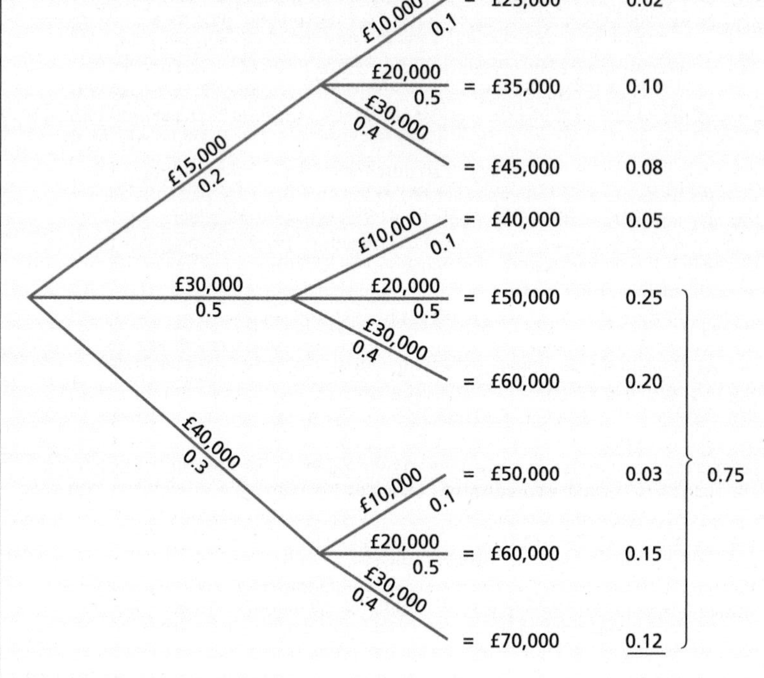


There is a probability of 0.75 of achieving £50,000 sales. As this is greater than the specified figure of 0.70 then the inventory should not be written down. Effect on profits: nil.

(*f*) The opening inventory should be shown as the revised figure. If error had not been found this year's profit would have been £7,000 greater.

The adjustment should be shown as a prior period adjustment in the comparative information in the current financial statements.

**11.6**

*(a)*

Address
Date

The Chief Accountant
Uncertain Ltd

Dear Sir/Mr . . . ,

*Report on Draft Statement of Profit or Loss for the year ending 30 September 2017*

Further to your letter/our meeting of . . . I would like to offer my suggestions for the appropriate accounting treatment of items (*i*) to (*v*).

(*i*) Redundancy payments: £100,000

The reorganisation had a material effect on the nature and focus of the reporting entity's operations. As a result, the costs should be shown separately on the face of the income statement along with the relevant taxation effect as one figure.

(*ii*) Closure costs of a factory

Profits or losses on the termination of an operation should be shown separately on the face of the statement of profit or loss. In calculating the profit or loss in respect of the termination, consideration should only be given to revenue and costs directly related to it. Clearly, the costs have been identified and are known and there is a loss on the termination. It should not have been deducted from reserves; it must go through the income statement.

(*iii*) Change of basis of depreciation: £258,000

There should only be a change in the basis of depreciation if it brings about a fairer presentation of the accounting results and financial position of the company – see IAS 16. This should be treated as a change in accounting estimate (IAS 8) and should be recognised in profit or loss for this period. It is not a change in accounting policy.

Because the item is material, a note as to the details should be appended to the accounts.

(*iv*) Additional expenses covered by fire: £350,000

These expenses are covered by IAS 10 as post-reporting period non-adjusting events. The fire happened after the end of the reporting period, and therefore did not affect conditions as at that date. The figures in this year's financial statements, therefore, should not be altered.

If the event was such as to call into question the continuation of the business, then there should be a note to the financial statements on the going-concern basis. In this particular instance this does not seem to be the case, but good practice, although not necessary, would be to give details of the event in notes to the financial statements.

(*v*) Bad debt: £125,000

The accounts have not yet been approved by the directors, and it does affect the valuation of assets at the year end. IAS 10 would treat it as a post-reporting period adjusting event. It should therefore be written off as a bad debt.

Where it is considered to be material there should also be a note attached to the financial statements.

Should you like to have further discussions concerning any of the points raised, will you please contact me. I hope that you will find my comments to be of use.

Yours faithfully,

CACA

*(b)*

**Uncertain Ltd**

*Statement of Profit or Loss for the year ending 30 September 2017*

| | | |
|---|---|---|
| Sales | | 5,450,490 |
| Manufacturing cost of sales (W1) | | 2,834,500 |
| | | 2,615,990 |
| Administration expenses | 785,420 | |
| Selling expenses (W2) | 1,013,600 | |
| | | 1,799,020 |
| Operating profit | | 816,970 |
| Redundancy payments | 100,000 | |
| Discontinued operations – factory closure costs | 575,000 | |
| | | 675,000 |
| Profit before tax | | 141,970 |
| Corporation tax (50%) (W3) | | 70,985 |
| Profit for the year | | 70,985 |

Reduction in profits for the period from draft statement of profit or loss = £304,400

(W1) £3,284,500 − £100,000 (*i*) − £350,000 (*iv*) = £2,834,500
(W2) £629,800 + £258,800 (*iii*) + £125,000 (*v*) = £1,013,600
(W3) 50% of profits before tax

**11.7**

*(a)* (*i*) Post-reporting period events consist of those events (also known as events after the date of the statement of financial position), whether favourable or unfavourable, which take place between the date of the statement of financial position and the date on which the financial accounts and notes are approved by the directors.

(*ii*) Adjusting events are post-reporting period events which give extra evidence of what was happening at the date of the statement of financial position. The events included may be included because they are either of a statutory nature or taken into account by convention.

(*iii*) Non-adjusting events are post-reporting period concerned with matters which did not exist at the date of the statement of financial position.

(*iv*) A contingent asset/liability is concerned with something which seems to be apparent at the end of the reporting period but can only be verified by future events which are uncertain.

*(b)* Adjusting events: (*i*) debtor's inability to pay; (*ii*) subsequent discovery of frauds rendering accounts incorrect; (*iii*) when net realisable value is used for inventory valuation and later shown to be wrong when inventory sold; (*iv*) subsequent discovery of errors rendering accounts incorrect.

Non-adjusting events: (*i*) change in foreign exchange rates; (*ii*) strikes; (*iii*) nationalisation; (*iv*) share issues.

*(c)* (*i*) A material contingent liability should be accrued where some future event will give evidence of the loss, subject to the fact that it should be able to be determined with reasonable accuracy when the accounts are agreed by the directors.

(*ii*) Material contingent assets should be disclosed in the financial statements if it is very probable that they will be realised.

**12.1**

(*i*) (Internal) **Royal Oak plc**

*Statement of Profit or Loss for the year ending 31 March 2018 (£000)*

| | | | |
|---|---|---|---|
| Sales | | 9,824 | |
| *Less* Returns inwards | | 432 | 9,392 |
| *Less* Cost of sales: | | | |
| Inventory 1 April 2017 | | 336 | |
| *Add* Purchases | 5,848 | | |
| *Less* Returns outwards | 148 | 5,700 | |
| Carriage inwards | | 56 | |
| | | 6,092 | |
| *Less* Inventory 31 March 2018 | | 408 | 5,684 |
| Gross profit | | | 3,708 |
| *Distribution costs:* | | | |
| Salaries and wages | 136 | | |
| Rent and business rates | 36 | | |
| General distribution expenses | 112 | | |
| Motor expenses | 36 | | |
| Depreciation: Motors | 46 | | |
| Equipment | 2 | 368 | |
| *Administrative expenses:* | | | |
| Salaries and wages | 408 | | |
| Rent and business rates | 24 | | |
| General administrative expenses | 96 | | |
| Motor expenses | 18 | | |
| Auditors' remuneration | 44 | | |
| Discounts allowed | 144 | | |
| Bad debts | 20 | | |
| Depreciation: Motors | 54 | | |
| Equipment | 4 | 812 | 1,180 |
| | | | 2,528 |
| Other operating income: Royalties receivable | | | 16 |
| | | | 2,544 |
| Operating profit | | | |
| Income from associates and joint ventures | | 12 | |
| Interest on bank deposit | | 24 | 36 |
| | | | 2,580 |
| Interest payable: Loan-note interest | | | 48 |
| Profit before taxation | | | 2,532 |
| Taxation | | | 1,456 |
| Profit for the year | | | 1,076 |
| Retained profits from last year | | | 408 |
| | | | 1484 |
| Transfer to general reserve | | 60 | |
| Dividend paid | | 420 | 480 |
| Retained profits carried forward to next year | | | 1,004 |

(*ii*) (Published) **Royal Oak plc**

*Statement of Profit or Loss for the year ending 31 March 2018 (£000)*

| | | |
|---|---|---|
| Revenue | | 9,392 |
| Cost of sales | | 5,684 |
| Gross profit | | 3,708 |
| Distribution costs | 368 | |
| Administrative expenses | 812 | 1,180 |
| | | 2528 |
| Other operating income | | 16 |
| | | 2544 |
| Operating profit | | |
| Income from associates and joint ventures | 12 | |
| Other interest receivable | 24 | 36 |
| | | 2,580 |
| Interest payable | | 48 |
| Profit before taxation | | 2,532 |
| Taxation | | 1,456 |
| Profit for the year | | 1,076 |

**12.2**

(*i*) (Internal) **District plc**

*Statement of Profit or Loss for the year ending 31 December 2018 (£000)*

| | | | |
|---|---|---|---|
| Sales | | 6,696 | |
| *Less* Returns inwards | | 32 | 6,664 |
| *Less* Cost of sales: | | | |
| Inventory 1 January 2018 | | 504 | |
| *Add* Purchases | 4,104 | | |
| *Less* Returns outwards | 18 | 4,086 | |
| Carriage inwards | | 29 | |
| | | 4,619 | |
| *Less* Inventory 31 December 2018 | | 576 | |
| Cost of goods sold | | 4,043 | |
| Wages | | 317 | |
| Depreciation of plant and machinery | | 30 | |
| | | | 4,390 |
| Gross profit | | | 2,274 |
| *Distribution costs* | | | |
| Salaries and wages | 223 | | |
| Rent and business rates | 44 | | |
| Motor expenses | 66 | | |
| General distribution expenses | 43 | | |
| Haulage costs | 14 | | |
| Depreciation: Motors | 60 | | |
| Plant and machinery | 27 | 477 | |

| | | | |
|---|---|---|---|
| *Administrative expenses* | | | |
| Salaries and wages | 266 | | |
| Rent and business rates | 66 | | |
| Motor expenses | 22 | | |
| General administrative expenses | 22 | | |
| Bad debts | 7 | | |
| Discounts allowed | 40 | | |
| Auditors' remuneration | 50 | | |
| Directors' remuneration | 130 | | |
| Depreciation: Motors | 23 | | |
| Plant and machinery | 18 | | |
| | 644 | | |
| *Less* Discounts received | 50 | 594 | 1,071 |
| | | | 1,203 |
| Operating profit | | | |
| Income from associates | | 18 | |
| Interest from government securities | | 11 | 29 |
| | | | 1,232 |
| Amount written off investment in related companies | | 94 | |
| Loan-note interest | | 7 | 101 |
| Profit before taxation | | | 1,131 |
| Taxation | | | 394 |
| Profit for the year | | | 757 |
| Retained profits from last year | | | 338 |
| | | | 1,095 |
| Transfer to loan-note redemption reserve | | 90 | |
| Dividend paid | | 216 | 306 |
| Retained profits for the year | | | 789 |

(*ii*) (Published) **District plc**

*Statement of Profit or Loss for the year ending 31 December 2018* (£000)

| | | |
|---|---|---|
| Revenue | | 6,664 |
| Cost of sales | | 4,390 |
| Gross profit | | 2,274 |
| Distribution costs | 477 | |
| Administrative expenses | 594 | 1,071 |
| | | 1,203 |
| Operating profit | | |
| Income from associates | 18 | |
| Other interest receivable | 11 | 29 |
| | | 1,232 |
| Amount written off investments | 94 | |
| Interest payable | 7 | 101 |
| Profit before taxation | | 1,131 |
| Taxation | | 374 |
| Profit for the year | | 757 |

**12.3**

(*a*) **Rufford plc**

*Statement of Profit or Loss for the year ended 31 March 2016*

| | *Notes* | *£000* | *£000* |
|---|---|---|---|
| Revenue | (1) | | 642 |
| Cost of sales (60 + 401 − 71) | | | 390 |
| *Gross profit* | | | 252 |
| Distribution costs (33 + 19) | | 52 | |
| Administrative expenses (97 + 8) | | 105 | 157 |
| *Operating profit* | (2) | | 95 |
| Loss on disposal of discontinued operations | (3) | | 12 |
| | | | 83 |
| Income from other non-current asset investments | (4) | 14 | |
| Other interest receivable | | 25 | 39 |
| | | | 122 |
| Interest payable | (5) | | 6 |
| *Profit before taxation* | | | 116 |
| Taxation: Current tax | (6) | 35 | |
| Deferred tax | | 9 | 44 |
| Profit for the year | | | 72 |

*Notes to the accounts:*

1 Turnover is net of VAT.

2 Operating profit is shown after charging the following:

| | *£000* | *£000* |
|---|---|---|
| Depreciation: distribution costs | 19 | |
| administrative expenses | 8 | 27 |
| Auditor's remuneration | | 20 |
| Directors' emoluments | | 45 |
| Hire of plant | | 12 |

3 Factory closure expenses.

4 Income from non-current asset investment is in respect of a listed company.

5 Interest payable is on a bank overdraft, repayable within five years.

6 Tax on profit:

| | *£000* |
|---|---|
| Corporation tax at 50% on profits | 38 |
| Overprovision in 2005 | (3) |
| | 35 |

7 Dividends:

| | *£000* |
|---|---|
| Interim 5p per share | 21 |
| Final: proposed 10p per share | 42 |
| | 63 |

8 Earnings per share:
EPS of 17.1p per share based on earnings of £72,000 and on average 420,000 shares on issue throughout the year.

**12.3** *(cont'd)*

*(b)* *Statement of Financial Position extracts as at 31 March 2016*

| | £000 | £000 |
|---|---|---|
| *Current liabilities* | | |
| Taxation (W1) | | 35 |
| *Non-current liabilities* | | |
| Deferred taxation (W2) | | 33 |

| *Workings:* | £000 |
|---|---|
| (W1) Corporation tax for year to 31 March 2016 | 35 |
| (W2) Deferred tax as given | 24 |
| Charged to profit or loss | 9 |
| | 33 |

**13.1**

**AK Ltd**

*Statement of Financial Position as at 31 March 2017 (£000)*

| | | | |
|---|---|---|---|
| Called-up share capital not paid | | | 2 |
| *Non-current assets* | | | |
| *Intangible assets* | | | |
| Development costs | 128 | | |
| Goodwill | 416 | 544 | |
| *Tangible assets* | | | |
| Land and buildings | 920 | | |
| Plant and machinery | 180 | 1,100 | |
| *Investments* | | | |
| Shares in associate entities | | 280 | 1,924 |
| *Current assets* | | | |
| Inventory: | | | |
| Raw materials and consumables | 24 | | |
| Finished goods and goods for resale | 144 | 168 | |
| Trade accounts receivable | 96 | | |
| Amounts owed by associate entities | 40 | | |
| Prepayments | 8 | 144 | 312 |
| Total assets | | | 2,238 |
| *Current liabilities* | | | |
| Loan notes | 80 | | |
| Bank overdrafts | 62 | | |
| Trade accounts payable | 68 | | |
| Bills of exchange payable | 12 | 222 | |
| *Non-current liabilities* | | | |
| Loan notes | 120 | | |
| Bills of exchange payable | 4 | 124 | 346 |
| Net assets | | | 1,892 |
| *Equity* | | | |
| Called-up share capital | | | 1,400 |
| Share premium account | | | 200 |
| Other reserves: | | | |
| Capital redemption reserve | | 40 | |
| General reserve | | 80 | 120 |
| Retained profits | | | 172 |
| | | | 1,892 |

*Notes:*

| | | |
|---|---|---|
| *(i)* Called-up share capital consists of: | | |
| 50,000 £1 ordinary shares | | 1000 |
| 50,000 preference shares of 50p each | | 400 |
| | | 1,400 |
| *(ii)* Land and buildings: | | |
| Cost | | 1,000 |
| Depreciation to 31 March 2016 | 70 | |
| Depreciation for year to 31 March 2017 | 10 | 80 |
| | | 920 |
| *(iii)* Plant and machinery: | | |
| Cost | | 300 |
| Depreciation to 31 March 2016 | 105 | |
| Depreciation for year to 31 March 2017 | 15 | 120 |
| | | 180 |

**13.2**

**Tree plc**

*Statement of Financial Position as at 30 April 2017 (£000)*

| | | | |
|---|---|---|---|
| *Non-current assets* | | | |
| *Intangible assets* | | | |
| Concessions, patents, licences, trade marks and similar rights and assets | 6 | | |
| Goodwill | 42 | 48 | |
| *Tangible assets* | | | |
| Land and buildings | 200 | | |
| Plant and machinery | 42 | 242 | |
| | | | 290 |
| *Current assets* | | | |
| Inventory: | | | |
| Raw materials and consumables | 24 | | |
| Work in progress | 10 | | |
| Finished goods and goods for resale | 26 | 60 | |
| Trade accounts receivable | 84 | | |
| Other accounts receivable | 4 | | |
| Prepayments and accrued income | 2 | 90 | 150 |
| Total assets | | | 440 |

| | | | |
|---|---|---|---|
| *Current assets* | | | |
| *Current liabilities* | | | |
| Loan notes | 50 | | |
| Bank loans and overdrafts | 4 | | |
| Trade accounts payable | 26 | | |
| Bills of exchange payable | 6 | | |
| Other accounts payable including taxation and social security | 40 | 126 | |
| *Non-current liabilities* | | | |
| Loan notes | 40 | | |
| Trade accounts payable | 2 | 42 | |
| *Provisions*: | | | |
| Pensions and similar obligations | 8 | | |
| Taxation, including deferred taxation | 6 | 14 | 182 |
| Net assets | | | 258 |
| *Equity* | | | |
| Called-up share capital | | | 100 |
| Share premium | 60 | | |
| Revaluation reserve | 24 | | |
| General reserve | 30 | | |
| Foreign exchange reserve | 8 | | |
| Retained profits | 36 | | 158 |
| | | | 258 |

Notes appended to the accounts on the details of tangible assets and depreciation, also exact details of items lumped under group descriptions.

**13.3** **Baganza plc**

*Statement of Profit or Loss for the year ending 30 September 2017 (£000)*

| | | |
|---|---|---|
| Revenue | | 21,360 |
| Cost of sales (W1) | | 14,700 |
| *Gross profit* | | 6,660 |
| Distribution costs | 600 | |
| Administrative expenses (W2) | 1,390 | 1,990 |
| | | 4,670 |
| Other operating income (W3) | | 249 |
| *Profit before taxation* | | 4,919 |
| Taxation: Current tax (W4) | 830 | |
| Deferred tax | 40 | 870 |
| Profit for the year | | 4,049 |
| Earnings per share (W6) | 337.4p | |

*Workings* (in £000):

(W1) Opening inventory 2,300 + Purchases 16,000 − Closing inventory 3,600 = 14,700

(W2) Per trial balance 400 + Research 75 + Depreciation: Property (5% × 2,700) 135 + Plant (15% × 5,200) 780 = 1,390

(W3) Dividends received 249

(W4) Corporation tax 850 − Overpayment last year 20 = 830

(W6) EPS = Profit 4,049,000 ÷ Shares 1,200,000 = 337.4p

**Baganza plc**

*Statement of Financial Position as at 30 September 2017*

| | £000 | £000 | £000 |
|---|---|---|---|
| *Non-current assets* | | | |
| Tangible assets | | | |
| Land and buildings | 2,305 | | |
| Plant and machinery | 820 | 3,125 | |
| Investments | | 2,000 | 5,125 |
| *Current assets* | | | |
| Inventory | | 3,600 | |
| Accounts receivable | | 2,700 | |
| Cash at bank | | 60 | 6,360 |
| Total assets | | | 11,485 |
| *Current liabilities* | | | |
| Trade accounts payable | 2,900 | | |
| Corporation tax | 850 | | |
| *Non-current liabilities* | 3,750 | | |
| Deferred tax | 500 | | 4,250 |
| | | | 7,235 |
| *Equity* | | | |
| Called-up share capital | | | 1,200 |
| Retained profits (2,022 − 36 + 4,049) | | | 6,035 |
| | | | 7,235 |

*Note*: The proposed dividend should appear as a note to the statement of profit or loss.

**14.1**

## X Limited

*Statement of Financial Position at 31 March 2017*

| | Notes | £000 | £000 | £000 |
|---|---|---|---|---|
| *Non-current assets* | | | | |
| Intangible assets | | | | |
| Development costs | (1) | 35 | | |
| Tangible assets | (2) | | | |
| Freehold properties | | 1,040 | | |
| Plant and machinery | | 850 | | |
| Vehicles | | 285 | | |
| | | 2,210 | | |
| Investments | (3) | | | |
| Investments in listed shares | | 200 | | 2,410 |
| *Current assets* | | | | |
| Inventory | (4) | 500 | | |
| Accounts receivable (see workings) | | 654 | | |
| Cash at bank | | 439 | | 1,593 |
| Total assets | | | | 4,003 |
| *Current liabilities* | | | | |
| Trade and other accounts payable | | 878 | | |
| Taxation | | 270 | 1,148 | |
| *Non-current liabilities* | | | | |
| 12% loan notes 2026 | | 500 | | |
| Deferred tax | (5) | 128 | 628 | |
| Total liabilities | | | | 1,776 |
| Net assets | | | | 2,227 |
| *Equity* | (6) | | | |
| Called-up share capital | | | | 1,000 |
| Share premium | | | | 150 |
| Revaluation reserve | | | | 612 |
| Retained profits (see workings) | | | | 465 |
| | | | | 2,227 |

*Workings:*

| | £000 | £000 |
|---|---|---|
| Retained profits (356 + 280) | 636 | |
| *Less* Bad debt (225,000 × 76%) | 171 | 465 |
| Accounts receivable | 825 | |
| *Less* Bad debt (225,000 × 76%) | 171 | 654 |

*Notes to the statement of financial position*

1 *Research and development*

Research costs are written off immediately. Development costs are carried forward when there is a reasonable certainty of profitable outcome of the project and amortised over the useful life of the project.

2 *Tangible non-current assets*

| | Freehold property £000 | Plant and machinery £000 | Vehicles £000 |
|---|---|---|---|
| Cost on 1 April 2016* | 800 | 1,500 | 220 |
| Disposal at cost | (320) | | |
| Addition | | | 200 |
| Revaluation adjustment | 612 | | |
| On 31 March 2017 | 1,092 | 1,500 | 420 |
| Depreciation at 1 April 2016* | 80 | 500 | 55 |
| Depreciation on disposals | (40) | | |
| Provision in year | 12 | 150 | 80 |
| | 52 | 650 | 135 |
| *Net book values* | 1,040 | 850 | 285 |

* *Exam note only:* Found by working backwards, leaving these figures as difference.

*Note:* Freehold property was valued by Messrs V & Co, Chartered Surveyors, at a market value of £1,040,000 as compared with net book value of £428,000. The valuation figure has been included in statement of financial position, and £612,000 has been credited to a revaluation reserve. Depreciation for 2017 has been based on the revalued figure.

3 *Investments*

These had a market value of £180,000 on 31 March 2017, but as this is not considered by the directors to be a permanent fall in value, the cost figure has been retained.

4 *Inventory*

| | £000 |
|---|---|
| Finished goods | 250 |
| Raw materials | 200 |
| Work in progress | 50 |
| | 500 |

The current replacement cost of goods is £342,000.

5 *Deferred taxation*

| | | |
|---|---|---|
| Provision as at 1 April 2016 | 78 | |
| *Add* Provision during year | 50 | 128 |

6 *Share capital*

1,000,000 ordinary shares of £1 each is the authorised capital, which has been fully issued and called up.

**14.2**

## Billinge plc

*Statement of Profit or Loss for the year ending 30 June 2016*

| | Notes | £000 | £000 |
|---|---|---|---|
| Revenue | | | 1,500 |
| Cost of sales (W1) | | | 825 |
| Gross profit | | | 675 |
| Distribution costs | | 55 | |
| Administrative expenses (W2) | (2) | 320 | 375 |
| | | | 300 |
| Loss on disposal of discontinued operations | (3) | | 30 |
| Profit before taxation | | | 270 |
| Taxation: Current tax | | 100 | |
| Deferred tax | (4) | 30 | 130 |
| Profit after taxation | | | 140 |
| Earnings per share | (5) | 28.0p | |

## Billinge plc

*Statement of Financial Position as at 30 June 2016*

| | Notes | £000 | £000 | £000 |
|---|---|---|---|---|
| *Non-current assets* | | | | |
| Tangible assets | | | | |
| Fixtures and fittings | (7) | | | 187 |
| *Current assets* | | | | |
| Inventory: Finished goods and goods for resale | | | 100 | |
| Accounts receivable | | | 500 | |
| Cash at bank | | | 157 | 757 |
| Total assets | | | | 944 |
| *Current liabilities* | | | | |
| Trade accounts payable | | | 64 | |
| Taxation | | | 100 | |
| | | | 164 | |
| *Non-current liabilities* | | | | |
| Deferred tax | (8) | | 100 | 264 |
| Net assets | | | | 680 |
| *Equity* | | | | |
| Called-up share capital | (9) | | | 500 |
| Retained profits (40 + 140) | | | | 180 |
| | | | | 680 |

*Workings*:

| (W1) Opening inventory | 70 | |
|---|---|---|
| Purchases | 855 | 925 |
| *Less* Closing inventory | | 100 |
| | | 825 |

| (W2) Depreciation | 340 | |
|---|---|---|
| *Less* disposals | 20 | 320 |
| Additions | | 60 |
| | | 380 |

| (W2) (*cont'd*) | | |
|---|---|---|
| 20% × 380 | | 76 |
| Loss on disposals | 20 | |
| *Less* Depreciation | (15) | |
| *Less* Cash | (3) | 2 |
| | | 78 |

| (W3) C/T for year | 100 |
|---|---|
| Deferred taxation | 40 |
| | 140 |
| *Less* Previous overprovision | 10 |
| | 130 |

| (W4) Other creditors, taxation and social security: | | | |
|---|---|---|---|
| Corporation tax | 100 | Administrative expenses | 242 |
| | | | 320 |

*Notes to the accounts*:

1 Accounting policies
   (*a*) The financial statements have been drawn up using the historical cost convention.
   (*b*) Revenue consists of sales to external customers less VAT.
   (*c*) Inventory is valued at the lower of cost or net realisable value.
   (*d*) Depreciation of non-current assets is based on cost, using the straight line method over five years, salvage values being ignored.
   (*e*) Deferred taxation is at the anticipated rate, taking into account the differing periods and the probability that a liability will occur.

2 Administrative expenses include depreciation £78,000.

3 Charges of £30,000 resulted from the closure of a factory.

4 Taxation

| | £000 |
|---|---|
| Corporation tax at 35% on profit for the period | 100 |
| Deferred taxation | 40 |
| | 140 |
| *Less* Adjustment re last year's corporation tax | 10 |
| | 130 |

5 EPS calculated by dividing profit after taxation by number of ordinary shares on issue during the period.

6 Proposed ordinary dividend of 20p per share = £100,000.

7 Tangible non-current assets:

| | £000 | £000 | £000 |
|---|---|---|---|
| Fixtures, etc. at 1.7.2015 | | 340 | |
| Additions | | 60 | 400 |
| *Less* Disposals | | | 20 |
| | | | 380 |
| Depreciation at 1.7.2015 | 132 | | |
| For the period | 76 | 208 | |
| *Less* Disposals | | 15 | 193 |
| | | | 187 |

8 Deferred taxation at 1.7.2015

| | | |
|---|---|---|
| Deferred taxation at 1.7.2015 | 60 | |
| Charge to profit or loss | 40 | 100 |

9 Authorised, issued and fully paid ordinary £1 shares 500

**14.6**

**Scampion plc**

*Statement of Profit or Loss for the year ending 31 May 2016*

| | £000 | £000 |
|---|---|---|
| Revenue (3,489 − VAT 257) | | 3,232 |
| Cost of sales (1,929 + 330 + 51) | | 2,310 |
| Gross profit | | 922 |
| Administrative expenses (595 + 25 + 45) | | 665 |
| Operating profit | | 257 |
| Income from shares in related companies | 5 | |
| Other interest receivable (Note 2) | 10 | 15 |
| | | 272 |
| Interest payable (Note 3) | 18 | |
| Written-off investments (Note 7) | 4 | 22 |
| Profit before taxation | | 250 |
| Taxation (Note 4) | | 100 |
| Profit for the year | | 150 |
| Earnings per share (Note 5) | 22.73p | |

**Scampion plc**

*Statement of Financial Position as at 31 May 2016*

| | £000 | £000 |
|---|---|---|
| *Non-current assets* | | |
| Tangible assets (Note 6) | | 1,372 |
| Investments (Note 7) | | 60 |
| | | 1,432 |
| *Current assets* | | |
| Inventory | 230 | |
| Accounts receivable (67 − 45) | 22 | |
| Investments (market value £115,000) | 103 | |
| Cash at bank and in hand | 84 | 439 |
| Total assets | | 1,871 |
| *Current liabilities* | | |
| Accounts payable | 367 | |
| Taxation | 100 | |
| Bank loan | 20 | |
| | 487 | |
| *Non-current liabilities* | | |
| 12% loan notes 2020 | 50 | |
| Total liabilities | | 537 |
| Net assets | | 1,334 |
| *Equity* | | |
| Called-up share capital | | 660 |
| Share premium account | | 225 |
| Retained profits (Note 10) | | 449 |
| | | 1,334 |

*Notes:*

1 Accounting policies

The historical cost convention has been used.

Provisions for depreciation are to write off the cost or valuation over the expected useful lives of the assets, by equal instalments, as follows:

| | |
|---|---|
| Freehold buildings | 40 years |
| Fixtures, fittings or equipment | 10 years |
| Motor vehicles | 5 years |

Depreciation provisions have not been made on freehold land. The basis of the valuation of inventory is at the lower of cost or net realisable value.

2 Other interest receivable

This is income from government securities £10,000.

3 Interest payable

| | |
|---|---|
| Interest on loans repayable within one year | 12,000 |
| Interest on loans repayable in more than five years' time | 6,000 |
| | £18,000 |

4 Taxation

(It has been assumed that 'tax charge based on the accounts for the year' means that the profit shown of £250 is same as the taxable profits.)

Corporation tax at the rate of 40% on profits has been provided for.

5 Earnings per share $= \frac{150}{660} = 22.73\text{p}$

6 Tangible assets (£000)

| | *Valuation or cost at 31.5.15* | *Additions at cost* | *Less disposals* | *Depreciation to: 31.5.15* | *31.5.16* | *Net* |
|---|---|---|---|---|---|---|
| Freehold land and buildings | 1,562 | 50 | 400 | 29 | 5 | 1,178 |
| Fittings, fixtures and equipment | 141 | 40 | | 38 | 18 | 125 |
| Motor vehicles | 117 | 20 | | 40 | 28 | 69 |
| | 1,820 | 110 | 400 | 107 | 51 | 1,372 |

7 Investments

| | |
|---|---|
| Valuation by directors of shares in related companies | 64,000 |
| *Less* Written off during the year | 4,000 |
| | 60,000 |

8 Current liabilities

| | |
|---|---|
| Accounts payable (487,000 − *Tax* 120,000) | 367,000 |
| Corporation tax | 100,000 |
| Bank loan | 20,000 |
| | 487,000 |

9 Non-current liabilities – amounts falling due after more than one year £50,000 12% loan notes repayable in four years' time.

| 10 *Reserves* | *Share premium* | *Revaluation* | *Retained profits* |
|---|---|---|---|
| Balance 31.5.2015 | 225 | 150 | 149 |
| Transfer to retained profits | – | (150) | 150 |
| Profit for year to 31.5.16 | – | – | 150 |
| | 225 | – | 449 |

**15.1**

Operating activities; investing activities; financing activities.

**15.3**

Chipsea Ltd

*Statement of Cash Flows (using the direct method) for the year ending 31 December 2017*

| | | |
|---|---|---|
| **Cash flows from operating activities** | | |
| Cash received from customers | 20,960 | |
| Cash paid to suppliers | (9,200) | |
| Cash paid to employees | (6,480) | |
| Other cash payments | (1,920) | |
| Cash generated from operations | 3,360 | |
| Interest paid | (320) | |
| *Net cash from operating activities* | | 3,040 |
| **Cash flows from investing activities** | | |
| Payments to acquire tangible assets | (2,240) | |
| *Net cash used in investing activities* | | (2,240) |
| **Cash flows from financing activities** | | 800 |
| Payment to repurchase loan notes | (320) | |
| Equity dividends paid | (300) | |
| *Net cash used in financing activities* | | (620) |
| **Net decrease in cash and cash equivalents** | | (120) |
| **Cash and cash equivalents at beginning of period** | | 320 |
| **Cash and cash equivalents at end of period** | | 200 |

**15.5**

*See* text of Chapter 15, Section 15.2.

**15.6**

Hayes Limited

*Statement of Cash Flows (using the indirect method) for the year ending 31 December 2016 (£000)*

| | | |
|---|---|---|
| **Cash flows from operating activities** | | |
| Profit before taxation | | 59,920 |
| Adjustments for: | | |
| Depreciation | 11,340 | |
| Loss on sale of non-current assets | 1,960 | |
| Increase in inventories | (19,600) | |
| Increase in trade accounts receivable | (50,680) | |
| Increase in prepayments | (280) | |
| Increase in trade accounts payable | 11,200 | |
| Increase in accruals | 560 | |
| | | (45,500) |
| Cash generated from operations | | 14,420 |
| Taxation paid | | (8,960) |
| Net cash from operating activities | | 5,460 |
| **Cash flows from investing activities** | | |
| Purchase of tangible non-current assets | (33,040) | |
| Proceeds from sale of tangible non-current assets | 2,800 | |
| Net cash used in investing activities | | (30,240) |
| **Cash flows from financing activities** | | |
| Proceeds from issue of loan notes | 420 | |
| Dividends paid | (22,680) | |
| Net cash used in financing activities | | (22,260) |
| **Net decrease in cash and cash equivalents** | | (47,040) |
| **Cash and cash equivalents at beginning of period** | | 1,680 |
| **Cash and cash equivalents at end of period** | | (45,360) |

*Workings*:

Depreciation = 26,600 − 10,640 = 15,960 − 27,300 = 11,340

Loss on sale of non-current asset = 2,800 − (15,400 − 10,640) = (1,960)

**15.7**

### Track Limited

*Statement of Cash Flows (using the indirect method) for the year ending 30 June 2018 (£000)*

| | | |
|---|---|---|
| **Cash flows from operating activities** | | |
| Profit before tax | | 180 |
| Adjustments for: | | |
| Depreciation | 110 | |
| Profit on sale of non-current assets | (5) | |
| Increase in inventories | (300) | |
| Increase in trade accounts receivable | (200) | |
| Increase in trade accounts payable | 120 | |
| | | (275) |
| Cash generated from operations | | |
| Taxation paid | | (95) |
| Net cash used in operating activities | | (230) |
| | | (325) |
| **Cash flows from investing activities** | | |
| Purchase of non-current assets | (175) | |
| Proceeds from sale of non-current assets | 150 | |
| Proceeds from sale of investments | 20 | |
| Net cash used in investing activities | | (5) |
| **Cash flows from financing activities** | | |
| Proceeds from issue of share capital | 300 | |
| Dividend paid | (130) | |
| Net cash from financing activities | | 170 |
| **Net decrease in cash and cash equivalents** | | (160) |
| **Cash and cash equivalents at beginning of period** | | 100 |
| **Cash and cash equivalents at end of period** | | (60) |

*Working*:
Profit on sale of non-current assets = 20 − (25 − 10) = (5)

**15.9**

(*a*)

### Baker Limited

*Forecast net cash position for the three quarters ending 30 September 2017*

| | *Quarter to* | | |
|---|---|---|---|
| | *31 March 2017* | *30 June 2017* | *30 Sept 2017* |
| | £000 | £000 | £000 |
| *Receipts* | | | |
| Trade accounts receivable (W1) | 235 | 290 | 345 |
| Tangible non-current assets | 12 | – | – |
| Investments | 10 | – | – |
| Loan notes | – | – | 50 |
| | 257 | 290 | 395 |
| *Payments* | | | |
| Trade accounts payable (W2) | 150 | 230 | 285 |
| Administration, selling and distribution expenses | 37 | 40 | 42 |
| Tangible non-current assets | – | 240 | – |
| Investments | – | – | 5 |
| Taxation | 8 | – | – |
| Dividend | 15 | | |
| | 210 | 510 | 332 |
| Forecast net cash flow | 47 | (220) | 63 |
| *Add* Opening cash | 80 | 127 | (93) |
| Forecast closing cash | 127 | (93) | (30) |

*Workings*:
(W1) Trade accounts receivable: forecast cash receivable:

| | *31 March 2017* | *30 June 2017* | *30 Sept 2017* |
|---|---|---|---|
| | £000 | £000 | £000 |
| Sales | 250 | 300 | 350 |
| *Less* Closing trade accounts receivable | 65 | 75 | 80 |
| | 185 | 225 | 270 |
| *Add* Opening trade accounts receivable | 50 | 65 | 75 |
| Forecast cash receipts from trade accounts receivable | 235 | 290 | 345 |

(W2) Trade accounts payable: forecast cash payable

| | 31 March 2017 £000 | 30 June 2017 £000 | 30 Sept 2017 £000 |
|---|---|---|---|
| Opening inventory | 40 | 30 | 40 |
| Purchases (by deduction) | 190 | 250 | 295 |
| | 230 | 280 | 335 |
| *Less* Closing inventory | 30 | 40 | 55 |
| Cost of sales | 200 | 240 | 280 |
| Purchases (as above) | 190 | 250 | 295 |
| *Less* Closing trade accounts payable | 120 | 140 | 150 |
| | 70 | 110 | 145 |
| *Add* Opening trade accounts payable | 80 | 120 | 140 |
| Forecast cash payments to trade accounts payable | 150 | 230 | 285 |

(*b*) **Baker Limited**

*Forecast Statement of Cash Flows (using the direct method) for the nine months ending 30 September 2017 (£000)*

| | | |
|---|---|---|
| **Cash flows from operating activities** | | |
| Profit before tax | | 34 |
| Adjustments for: | | |
| Depreciation | 27 | |
| Increase in inventory | (15) | |
| Increase in trade accounts receivable | (30) | |
| Increase in trade accounts payable | 70 | |
| | | 52 |
| Cash generated from operations | | 86 |
| Taxation | | (23) |
| Net cash from operating activities | | 63 |
| **Cash flows from investing activities** | | |
| Purchase of non-current assets | (240) | |
| Proceeds from sale of non-current assets | 12 | |
| Net cash used in investing activities | | (228) |
| **Cash flows from financing activities** | | |
| Proceeds from issue of loan notes | 50 | |
| Net cash from financing activities | | 50 |
| **Net decrease in cash and cash equivalents** | | (115) |
| **Cash and cash equivalents at beginning of period** | | 95 |
| **Cash and cash equivalents at end of period** | | (20) |

*Workings*:

Cash and cash equivalents at beginning of period = 80 + 15

Cash and cash equivalents at end of period = (30) + 10

**16.1**

*See* text Section 16.6.

**16.2**

*See* text Section 16.8.

**16.3**

*See* text Section 16.4.

**17.1** *Consolidated Statement of Financial Position*

| | |
|---|---|
| Goodwill | 2,000 |
| Inventory | 2,700 |
| Bank | 1,300 |
| | 6,000 |
| Share capital | 6,000 |

**17.2** *Consolidated Statement of Financial Position*

| | |
|---|---|
| Non-current assets | 66,000 |
| Inventory | 14,800 |
| Accounts receivable | 8,400 |
| Bank | 5,800 |
| | 95,000 |
| Share capital and reserves | 95,000 |

**17.3** *Consolidated Statement of Financial Position*

| | |
|---|---|
| Non-current assets | 246,000 |
| Inventory | 138,000 |
| Accounts receivable | 60,000 |
| Bank | 56,000 |
| | 500,000 |
| Share capital | 500,000 |

**17.6** *Consolidated Statement of Financial Position*

| | |
|---|---|
| Goodwill (60,000 − (¾ × 40,000)) | 30,000 |
| Non-current assets | 121,000 |
| Inventory | 29,000 |
| Accounts receivable | 20,000 |
| Bank | 10,000 |
| | 210,000 |
| Share capital | 200,000 |
| Non-controlling interest | 10,000 |
| | 210,000 |

**17.7** *Consolidated Statement of Financial Position*

| | |
|---|---|
| Non-current assets [82,000 + 12,000] | 94,000 |
| Inventory | 33,000 |
| Accounts receivable | 24,000 |
| Bank | 5,000 |
| | 156,000 |
| Share capital | 150,000 |
| Reserves | 4,000 |
| Non-controlling interest [10% of 20,000] | 2,000 |
| | 156,000 |

**17.10** *Consolidated Statement of Financial Position*

| | |
|---|---|
| Goodwill | 1,600 |
| Non-current assets | 164,800 |
| Current assets | 68,800 |
| | 235,200 |
| Share capital | 164,000 |
| Retained profits (60,000 + 3,200) | 63,200 |
| Non-controlling interest (20% × 40,000) | 8,000 |
| | 235,200 |

**17.11** *Consolidated Statement of Financial Position*

| | |
|---|---|
| Goodwill | 30,000 |
| Non-current assets | 477,000 |
| Current assets | 138,000 |
| | 645,000 |
| Share capital | 360,000 |
| Retained profits (190,000 + 7,000) | 197,000 |
| General reserve | 28,000 |
| Non-controlling interest | 60,000 |
| | 645,000 |

Elimination of gain from a bargain purchase of 17,000 by Parental Acquisition Ltd recognising the gain in profit or loss.

**18.1** *Consolidated Statement of Financial Position as at 31 December 2016*

| | |
|---|---|
| Goodwill | 30,000 |
| Non-current assets | 200,000 |
| Current assets | 87,000 |
| | 317,000 |
| Share capital | 150,000 |
| Retained profits (136,000 + 31,000) | 167,000 |
| | 317,000 |

**18.2** *Consolidated Statement of Financial Position as at 31 March 2018*

| | |
|---|---|
| Non-current assets | 329,000 |
| Current assets | 75,000 |
| | 404,000 |
| Share capital | 260,000 |
| Retained profits [109,000 + 16,000 − (90% of 17,000 = 15,300)] | 109,700 |
| General reserve | 23,000 |
| Non-controlling interest (8,000 + 700 + 2,600) | 11,300 |
| | 404,000 |

Elimination of gain from a bargain purchase of 16,000 by Parents Pleasure Ltd recognising the gain in profit or loss.

**18.4** *Consolidated Statement of Financial Position as at 31 December 2018*

| | |
|---|---|
| Goodwill | 13,000 |
| Non-current assets | 603,000 |
| Current assets | 170,000 |
| | 786,000 |
| Share capital | 500,000 |
| Retained profits | 173,750 |
| General reserve | 40,000 |
| Non-controlling interest | 72,250 |
| | 786,000 |

Non-controlling interest 25% of (160,000 + 89,000 + 40,000) = 72,250.
Goodwill 185,000 − [75% of (160,000 + 44,000 + 40,000) = 183,000] = 2,000; 95,000 − [(50,000 + 12,000 + 22,000) = 84,000] = 11,000; 2,000 + 11,000 = 13,000.
Retained profits 149,000 + 33,750 − 9,000 = 173,750.

**19.1** *Consolidated Statement of Financial Position as at 31 March 2016*

| | | |
|---|---|---|
| Goodwill | | 16,000 |
| Non-current assets | | 428,000 |
| *Current assets* | | |
| Inventory (47,000 + 30,000 − 600) | 76,400 | |
| Accounts receivable (34,000 + 22,000 − 3,600) | 52,400 | |
| Bank | 19,000 | 147,800 |
| Total assets | | 591,800 |
| *Current liabilities* | | |
| Accounts payable (7,000 + 12,000 − 3,600) | | 15,400 |
| *Net assets* | | 576,400 |
| *Equity* | | |
| Share capital | | 320,000 |
| Retained profits (113,000 − 600 + 132,000) | | 244,400 |
| General reserve | | 12,000 |
| | | 576,400 |

**19.2** *Consolidated Statement of Financial Position as at 31 December 2017*

| | | |
|---|---|---|
| Non-current assets | | 230,000 |
| *Current assets* | | |
| Inventory (37,000 + 55,000 − 400) | 91,600 | |
| Accounts receivable (46,000 − 2,200 + 64,000) | 107,800 | |
| Bank | 17,000 | |
| | 216,400 | |
| *Less Current liabilities* | | |
| Accounts payable (11,000 + 7,000 − 2,200) | (15,800) | |
| Net current assets | | 200,600 |
| | | 430,600 |
| *Equity* | | |
| Share capital | | 260,000 |
| Retained profits (130,000 − 400 + (90% × 26,000)) | | 153,000 |
| Non-controlling interest (10% × (100,000 + 76,000)) | | 17,600 |
| | | 430,600 |

**19.3** *Consolidated Statement of Financial Position as at 31 March 2016*

| | | |
|---|---|---|
| Non-current assets | | |
| Goodwill | | 3,100 |
| Other non-current assets | | 175,000 |
| Total non-current assets | | 178,100 |
| *Current assets* | | |
| Inventory (62,000 − 830) | 61,170 | |
| Accounts receivable (39,000 − 2,500) | 36,500 | |
| Bank | 14,000 | 111,670 |
| Total assets | | 289,770 |
| *Current liabilities* | | |
| Accounts payable (23,000 − 2,500) | | (20,500) |
| Net assets | | 269,270 |
| *Equity* | | |
| Share capital | | 175,000 |
| Retained profits | | |
| (62,000 − 480 − 350 − 12,000 + (90% × 19,000)) | | 66,270 |
| General reserve | | 20,000 |
| Non-controlling interest (10% × (50,000 + 30,000)) | | 8,000 |
| | | 269,270 |

Goodwill: 58,000 − 90% × (50,000 + 11,000) = 3,100.

**19.6** **Pagg Group of Companies**

*Consolidated Statement of Financial Position as at 31 March 2017*

| | | £000 |
|---|---|---|
| Non-current assets | | |
| Intangible assets: Goodwill (Note 1) | | 1,898 |
| Tangible assets | | 3,500 |
| | | 5,398 |
| Current assets | | |
| Inventory (1,300 + 350 + 100 − 10) | 1,740 | |
| Accounts receivable (3,000 + 300 + 200 − 200 − 35) | 3,265 | |
| Cash at bank and in hand | 270 | 5,275 |
| Total assets | | 10,673 |
| Current liabilities | | |
| Accounts payable (270 + 400 + 4,000 − 200 − 35) | | 4,435 |
| | | 6,238 |
| Equity | | |
| Called-up share capital | | 5,500 |
| Retained profits (Note 2) | | 238 |
| | | 5,738 |
| Non-controlling interest (Note 3) | | 500 |
| | | 6,238 |

Notes:

| | | | Ragg | | | Tagg |
|---|---|---|---|---|---|---|
| 1 *Cost of control* | | | | | | |
| Consideration | | | 3,000 | | | 1,000 |
| *Less* Shares | (80%) | 800 | | (60%) | 300 | |
| Profit and loss | (80% × 600) | 480 | 1,280 | (60% × 100) | 60 | 360 |
| Goodwill arising on acquisition | | | 1,720 | | | 640 |
| Impairment review deductions | | | 430 | | | 32 |
| Goodwill remaining | | | 1,290 | | | 608 |
| | | | 1,898 | | | |

| 2 Retained profits: | |
|---|---|
| Pagg | 538 |
| Ragg 80% of (200 − 600) | (320) |
| Tagg 60% of (150 − 100) | 30 |
| Intra-group profit on inventory ($^1/_6$ of 60) | (10) |
| | 238 |

| 3 Non-controlling interest | | Ragg | | Tagg |
|---|---|---|---|---|
| Share capital called up | | 1,000 | | 500 |
| Retained profits | | 200 | | 150 |
| | | 1,200 | | 650 |
| | (20%) | 240 | (40%) | 260 |
| | | 500 | | |

**20.1**

| | |
|---|---|
| Loss on initial investment | |
| Fair value at 31.3.2018 (25% × 152,000) | 38,000 |
| Carrying amount | 51,200 |
| Loss taken to profit or loss | 13,200 |
| Goodwill / Gain from a bargain purchase | |
| Fair value of consideration given for controlling interest | 46,400 |
| Fair value of previously held interest | 38,000 |
| Non-controlling interest (39% × £152,000) | 59,280 |
| | 143,680 |
| *Less* Fair value of net assets | 152,000 |
| Gain from a bargain purchase | (8,320) |

**20.3**

| | | |
|---|---|---|
| Shares bought | | 84,000 |
| Retained profits 31.12.2016 | 56,000 | |
| *Add* Proportion 2017 profits before acquisition 7/12 × 100,800 | 58,800 | |
| | 114,800 | |
| Proportion of pre-acquisition profit: $\frac{84,000}{168,000} \times 114,800 =$ | | 57,400 |
| | | 141,400 |

Paid-for shares 280,000
Therefore goodwill is 280,000 − 141,400 = 138,600.

**21.1** *Consolidated Statement of Financial Position as at 31 March 2018*

| | |
|---|---|
| Goodwill | 7,000 |
| Other non-current assets | 15,000 |
| Current assets | 58,000 |
| | 216,000 |
| Share capital | 150,000 |
| Retained profits (54,000 + 12,000) | 66,000 |
| | 216,000 |

*Workings*: Goodwill: Cost 108,000 − 80,000 − 10,000 − Dividend 11,000 = 7,000.

**21.3** *Consolidated Statement of Financial Position as at 31 October 2016*

| | |
|---|---|
| Goodwill (Note 1) | 51,000 |
| Other non-current assets | 157,000 |
| Current assets (Note 2) | 109,400 |
| | 317,400 |
| Share capital | 160,000 |
| Retained profits: (Note 3) (89,400 + 60% of (36,000 − 14,000)) | 102,600 |
| Non-controlling interest [40% of (105,000 + 32,000)] | 54,800 |
| | 317,400 |

*Notes*:
1 Goodwill: Cost 120,000 − 60% of (105,000 + 10,000) = 51,000.
2 The current assets in Parents United Ltd were increased by 60% of £74,000 = £8,400.
3 The retained profits of Parents United Ltd were increased by the dividend received of £8,400.
4 It is presumed that the dividend was paid out of post-acquisition reserves.

**21.5** *Consolidated Statement of Financial Position of P Ltd & S Ltd as at 31 December 2016*

| | | |
|---|---|---|
| *Non-current assets* | | |
| Intangible assets: | | |
| Goodwill (see *Workings (a)*) | | 55,000 |
| Tangible assets (Note 1) | | 680,000 |
| | | 735,000 |
| *Current assets* | | |
| Inventory | 160,000 | |
| Accounts receivable | 138,000 | |
| Bank | 40,000 | 338,000 |
| Total assets | | 1,073,000 |
| *Current liabilities* | | |
| Trade accounts payable | | 218,000 |
| | | 855,000 |
| *Capital and reserves* | | |
| Called-up share capital: ordinary shares £1 fully paid | | 500,000 |
| Reserves (see *Workings (c)*) | | 185,000 |
| Non-controlling interest (see *Workings (b)*) | | 170,000 |
| | | 855,000 |

| *Note 1 Tangible non-current assets* | *Cost* | *Depreciation to date* | *Net* |
|---|---|---|---|
| Buildings | 420,000 | 110,000 | 310,000 |
| Plant and machinery | 320,000 | 70,000 | 250,000 |
| Motor vehicles | 210,000 | 90,000 | 120,000 |
| | 950,000 | 270,000 | 680,000 |

*Workings*:

| | | |
|---|---|---|
| *(a) Goodwill* | | |
| Cost of investment | | 250,000 |
| *Less* Ordinary shares (75%) | 150,000 | |
| Reserves (75% of £50,000) | 37,500 | |
| | | 187,500 |
| | | 62,500 |
| *Less* Dividend from pre-acquisition profits | | 7,500 |
| | | 55,000 |
| *(b) Non-controlling interest* | | |
| Preference shares | | 100,000 |
| Reserves 25% × 80,000 | | 20,000 |
| Ordinary shares 25% | | 50,000 |
| | | 170,000 |
| *(c) Reserves* | | |
| P Ltd (170,000 − £7,500) | | 162,500 |
| S Ltd 75% of extra reserves since acquisition 80,000 − 50,000 = 30,000 | | 22,500 |
| | | 192,500 |
| *Less* Dividends received by P Ltd which were from pre-acquisition profits | | 7,500 |
| | | 185,000 |

*Note:* The loan interest of £2,000 on each statement of financial position is set off and does not appear in the consolidated statement of financial position. The same applies to the loan of £50,000.

**21.6**

(*a*) *Reconciliating Adjustments*

| | X | Y |
|---|---|---|
| Amended profits for 2016 | X | Y |
| Per balances | 40 | 28 |
| Profit in goods in transit | (0.4) | |
| Profit in inventory | 2.0 | (2.0) |
| | 41.6 | 26 |
| Current accounts in books of: | X | Y |
| Per balances | 19 | (14) |
| Remittance not received by X | (3) | (2) |
| Goods in transit | 16 | 16 |

(*b*) Amendments to balances

| | | X | Y |
|---|---|---|---|
| (*a*) *Dr* | Bank Y | 2 | |
| *Cr* | Current A/c with X | | 2 |
| (*b*) *Dr* | Profit 2016 X | 0.4 | |
| | Inventory X | 2.6 | |
| *Cr* | Current A/c with Y | | 3 |
| (*c*) *Dr* | Profit 2016 X | 2 | |
| *Cr* | Inventory Y | | 2 |

(*c*) Amended figures in balances

| | X | Y |
|---|---|---|
| Profits for 2016 (40 − 0.4 − 2) | 37.6 | |
| Current account (14 + 2) | | 16 |
| Inventory (80 + 2.6) | 82.6 | |
| Inventory (70 − 2) | | 68 |
| Bank (12 + 2) | | 14 |
| Current account (19 − 3) | 16 | |

*Consolidated Statement of Financial Position for X plc & subsidiary Y plc as at 31 December 2016*

| | Cost | Depreciation to date | Net |
|---|---|---|---|
| | £000 | £000 | £000 |
| Non-current assets | | | |
| Goodwill (see *Workings*) | | | 108 |
| Other non-current assets: | | | |
| Freehold property | 280 | 18 | 262 |
| Plant and machinery | 245 | 52 | 193 |
| | 525 | 70 | 455 |
| Total assets | | | 563 |
| *Current assets* | | | |
| Inventory (see *Workings*) | | 150.6 | |
| Accounts receivable | | 250 | |
| Bank | | 24 | 424.6 |
| Total assets | | | 987.6 |
| *Less Current liabilities* | | | |
| Trade accounts payable (130 + 80) | 210 | | |
| Taxation | 44 | | 254 |
| | | | 733.6 |
| Called-up share capital | | | |
| 400,000 ordinary shares £1 | | | 400 |
| Reserves [220 + 37.6 + (80% of 28 = ) 22.4] | | | 280 |
| | | | 680 |
| Non-controlling interest (see *Workings*) | | | 53.6 |
| | | | 733.6 |

*Workings:*

*Cost of control* (remember to calculate it as on 1.1.16) £000

| | | |
|---|---|---|
| Cost of investment | | 300 |
| *Less* Nominal value shares bought 80% | 120 | |
| Reserves 80% × 90 | 72 | 192 |
| | | 108 |

| | | |
|---|---|---|
| *Non-controlling interest* | | |
| 20% of reserves at 1.1.16 | 18 | |
| 20% of 2016 profit | 5.6 | |
| 20% of *shares* × 150 | 30 | 53.6 |
| *Inventory* | | |
| X | 82.6 | |
| Y | 68 | |
| | 150.6 | |
| *Bank* | | |
| X 10 + Y 14 | | 24 |

*Note:* The proposed dividend is irrelevant to the preparation of the consolidated statement of financial position.

**22.1** *Consolidated Statement of Financial Position as at 31 December 2016*

| | | |
|---|---|---|
| *Non-current assets* | | |
| Goodwill (1,050,000 – 700,000 – 118,000) | | 232,000 |
| Other non-current assets (800,000 + (750,000 – 16,000)) | 1,534,000 | |
| *Less* Depreciation (380,000 + 190,000 – 4,000*) | 566,000 | 968,000 |
| Current assets | | 470,000 |
| | | 1,670,000 |
| Share capital | | 1,300,000 |
| Retained profits: (330,000 – 16,000) + (52,000 + 4,000*) | | 370,000 |
| | | 1,670,000 |

*Depreciation of £20,000 on an asset which cost £80,000 but which cost the group £64,000 ∴ depreciation should be reduced by $^1/_5$, i.e. £4,000.

**22.3** *Consolidated Statement of Financial Position as at 31 March 2016*

| | | |
|---|---|---|
| Non-current assets | | |
| Goodwill (190,000 – 100,000 – 26,000 – 11,000) | | 53,000 |
| Other non-current assets (124,000 + 121,000 + 11,000) | 256,000 | |
| *Less* Depreciation (25,000 + 22,000 + 2,000) | 49,000 | 207,000 |
| Current assets | | 80,000 |
| | | 340,000 |
| Share capital | | 240,000 |
| Retained profits (80,000 + 22,000 – 2,000) | | 100,000 |
| | | 340,000 |

**23.1** *Consolidated Statement of Financial Position as at 31 December 2017*

| | | |
|---|---|---|
| Non-current assets | | |
| Goodwill | | 74,360 |
| Other non-current assets | | 697,000 |
| | | 771,360 |
| Current assets | | 205,000 |
| | | 976,360 |
| Share capital | | 600,000 |
| Retained profits (200,000 + 90% of 92,000 + 63% of 10,000) | | 289,100 |
| General reserve | | 60,000 |
| Non-controlling interest | | 27,260 |
| | | 976,360 |

| | | |
|---|---|---|
| *Non-controlling interest* | | |
| Shares in Sub1 | 6,000 | |
| Shares in Sub2 37% of 20,000 | 7,400 | 13,400 |
| Retained profits: Sub1 10% of 132,000 | 13,200 | |
| Sub2 37% of 18,000 | 6,660 | 19,860 |
| | | 33,260 |
| *Less* Cost of shares in Sub2 for non-controlling interest of Sub1 10% of 60,000 | | 6,000 |
| | | 27,260 |

| | | |
|---|---|---|
| *Goodwill:* Cost of shares to group in: Sub1 | 128,000 | |
| Sub2 90% of 60,000 | 54,000 | 182,000 |
| *Less* Shares: In Sub1 | 54,000 | |
| In Sub2 63% of 20,000 | 12,600 | |
| Retained profits: Sub1 90% of 40,000 | 36,000 | |
| Sub2 63% of 8,000 | 5,040 | 107,640 |
| | | 74,360 |

**23.3**

**Sales Ltd & subsidiaries**

*Statement of Financial Position as at 31 October 2018*

| | *Cost* | *Depreciation* | *Net* | |
|---|---|---|---|---|
| *Non-current assets* | | | | |
| Land | 184,000 | – | 184,000 | |
| Buildings | 260,000 | 92,400 | 167,600 | |
| Plant (W1) | 362,900 | 203,700 | 159,200 | |
| | 806,900 | 296,100 | | 510,800 |
| *Current assets* | | | | |
| Inventory (W2) | | | 247,400 | |
| Accounts receivable (W3) | | | 319,200 | |
| Bank | | | 65,600 | 632,200 |
| | | | | 1,143,000 |
| *Current liabilities* | | | | |
| Accounts payable (W4) | | 437,400 | | |
| Bank overdraft (W5) | | 58,100 | | |
| Corporation tax | | 129,100 | | (624,600) |
| Net assets | | | | 518,400 |
| Ordinary share capital | | | | 200,000 |
| Revenue reserves (W6) | | | | 189,390 |
| | | | | 389,390 |
| Non-controlling interest (W8) | | | | 129,010 |
| | | | | 518,400 |

*Workings:*

*Note:* S Ltd owns 75% of M Ltd & 75% × 80% = 60% of C Ltd

| | |
|---|---|
| Plant 102,900 + 170,000 + 92,000 = | 364,900 |
| (W1) *Less* (Note (*e*)) intercompany profit | 2,000 |
| | 362,900 |
| Depreciation 69,900 + 86,000 + 48,200 = | 204,100 |
| *Less* two years on intercompany profit element 10% × 2,000 × 2 | 400 |
| | 203,700 |
| (W2) Inventory 108,500 + 75,500 + 68,400 | 252,400 |
| – Unrealised profit (Note (*d*)) 20% × 25,000 | 5,000 |
| | 247,400 |

| | | | |
|---|---|---|---|
| (W3) | Accounts receivable 196,700 + 124,800 + 83,500 | | 405,000 |
| | –Inter-indebtedness (Note (*f*)) | 56,900 | |
| | | 28,900 | 85,800 |
| | | | 319,200 |
| (W4) | Accounts payable 240,000 + 200,700 + 71,200 | | 511,900 |
| | – Inter-indebtedness (Note (*f*)) | 28,900 | |
| | | 45,600 | 74,500 |
| | | | 437,400 |
| (W5) | Overdraft | | 69,400 |
| | – cheque in transit (Note (*g*)) | | 11,300 |
| | | | 58,100 |
| (W6) | Reserves S Ltd | 154,000 | |
| | M Ltd | 85,000 | |
| | C Ltd | 74,000 | 313,000 |
| | *Add* Reduction in depreciation of components 2,000 × 10% × 2 years = 400 × 60% ownership of components | | 240 |
| | | | 313,240 |
| | *Less* Profit on machinery | 2,000 | |
| | Unrealised profit on inventory | 5,000 | |
| | Pre-acquisition reserves of C Ltd on 1.4.16 60% × 60,000 | 36,000 | |
| | Non-controlling interest in C Ltd 40% × 74,000 | 29,600 | |
| | Pre-acquisition reserves of M Ltd on 1.4.16 75% × 40,000 | 30,000 | |
| | Non-controlling interest in M Ltd 25% × 85,000 | 21,250 | 123,850 |
| | | | 189,390 |
| (W7) | Cost of control | | |
| | C Ltd at date of purchase: Capital: | | |
| | Ordinary shares | 100,000 | |
| | Reserves | 60,000 | |
| | | 160,000 | |
| | M Ltd owns 80% = | 128,000 | |
| | M Ltd paid | 128,000 | |
| | Bringing about | – | |
| | Of this 25% is owned by non-controlling interest of M Ltd | – | – |
| | M Ltd at date of purchase: Capital | 120,000 | |
| | Reserve | 40,000 | |
| | | 160,000 | |
| | S Ltd owns 75% = | 120,000 | |
| | S Ltd paid | 120,000 | |
| | Cost of control: Goodwill | – | – |
| | Overall Goodwill | | Nil |
| (W8) | Non-controlling interest | | |
| | Ordinary shares: 25% M Ltd | 30,000 | |
| | 40% C Ltd | 40,000 | |
| | Preference shares | 40,000 | |
| | Increase in retained profits because of depreciation change 40% × 400 | 160 | |
| | 25% revenue reserves M Ltd × 85,000 | 21,250 | |
| | 40% revenue reserves C Ltd × 74,000 | 29,600 | |
| | | 161,010 | |
| | *Less* 25% payment made by M Ltd for investment in C Ltd × 128,000 | 32,000 | 129,010 |

**24.1** **Brodick plc & subsidiaries**

*Consolidated Statement of Profit or Loss for the year ending 30 April 2017*

| | £000 | £000 |
|---|---|---|
| Revenue (1,100 + 500 + 130) | | 1,730 |
| Cost of sales (630 + 300 + 70) | | 1,000 |
| Gross profit | | 730 |
| Administrative expenses (105 + 150 + 20) | | 275 |
| Profit before taxation | | 455 |
| Taxation (65 + 10 + 20) | | 95 |
| Profit after taxation | | 360 |
| Non-controlling interests (20% × 40 + 40% × 20) | | 16 |
| Profit for the year | | 344 |

*Note 1*

| | |
|---|---|
| Profits for the year comprise: | |
| Brodick plc (*see* W1) | 300 |
| Subsidiaries (*see* W1) | 44 |
| | 344 |

*Workings:*

| | | | |
|---|---|---|---|
| (W1) | Brodick profits for the year 330 − (24 + 6) | | 300 |
| | Lamlash profits for the year 40 − (20% × 40 = 8) | 32 | |
| | Corrie profits for the year 20 − (40% × 20 = 8) | 12 | 44 |
| | | | 344 |

*Note:* The dividends received from the subsidiary are ignored as they represent a transfer of reserves and will be shown in the consolidated statement of changes in equity.

**24.2** **Norbreck plc & its subsidiary Bispham Ltd**

*Consolidated Statement of Profit or Loss for the year ending 30 September 2017*

| | | £000 |
|---|---|---|
| Revenue | | 2,150 |
| Cost of sales | | 995 |
| Gross profit | | 1,155 |
| Administrative expenses | | 475 |
| Profit before taxation | | 680 |
| Taxation | | 50 |
| Profit after taxation | | 630 |
| Non-controlling interest (20% × 180) | | 36 |
| Profit for the year | | 594 |
| Earnings per share (594/900) | 66p | |

**Norbreck plc & its subsidiary Bispham Ltd**

*Consolidated Statement of Financial Position as at 30 September 2017*

| | £000 | £000 | £000 |
|---|---|---|---|
| *Non-current assets* | | | |
| Goodwill | | | 72 |
| *Other non-current assets* | | | |
| Tangible assets | | | 1,720 |
| | | | 1,792 |
| *Current assets* | | | |
| Inventory | 550 | | |
| Accounts receivable (280 + 150) | 430 | | |
| Cash and bank | 50 | | 1,030 |
| Total assets | | | 2,822 |
| *Current liabilities* | | | |
| Trade accounts payable | 240 | | |
| Other payables, taxation and social security | 230 | | |
| | | 470 | |
| Non-current liabilities | | | |
| Deferred taxation | | 480 | 950 |
| | | | 1,872 |
| *Equity* | | | |
| Called-up share capital | | | 900 |
| Reserves (including retained profits)* | | | 852 |
| | | | 1,752 |
| *Non-controlling interest* (20% × £600) | | | 120 |
| | | | 1,872 |

*700 + [80% of (200 − 10) = 152]

| *Workings:* | £000 | £000 |
|---|---|---|
| Goodwill | | |
| Investment | | 400 |
| Nominal value of shares (80% of 400) | 320 | |
| Retained profits (80% of 10) | 8 | 328 |
| Goodwill on acquisition | | 72 |
| Retained profits b/d | | |
| Norbreck (700 + 360 − 570) | | 490 |
| Bispham (200 + 150 − 180) | 170 | |
| – Pre-acquisition | (10) | |
| | 160 | |
| – Dividend paid | (150) | |
| | 10 | |
| – Non-controlling interest (20%) | (2) | 8 |
| Retained profits of Group b/d | | 498 |
| For the year (per consolidated P/L 594 − 360) | | 234 |
| | | 732 |
| Plus dividend received by Norbreck from Bispham | | 120 |
| | | 852 |

**25.1**

*(a)* **Large Ltd & its subsidiary Small Ltd**

*Consolidated Statement of Profit or Loss for the year ending 30 September 2016*

| | £000 | £000 |
|---|---|---|
| Revenue (10,830 + 2,000 − 108) | | 12,722 |
| Cost of sales and production [(3,570 + 1,100) − (⅔ of 108)] | | 4,598 |
| | | 8,124 |
| Administrative and marketing expenses | 2,772 | |
| Unpurchased goodwill written off (per IFRS 3) | 50 | |
| Research costs written off (per IAS 38) | 50 | 2,872 |
| Profit before taxation | | 5,252 |
| Taxation | | 2,504 |
| Profit after taxation | | 2,748 |
| Non-controlling interest (520 − 36) × ¼ | | 121 |
| Profit for the year | | 2,627 |

(*b*) **Large Ltd & its subsidiary Small Ltd**

*Consolidated Statement of Financial Position as at 30 September 2016*

| | £000 | £000 |
|---|---|---|
| *Non-current assets* | | |
| Intangible assets | | |
| Development costs | 228 | |
| Goodwill (W1) | 26 | |
| | 254 | |
| Tangible assets | | |
| At cost less depreciation | 4,648 | 4,902 |
| *Current assets* | | |
| Inventory (594 + 231 − 36) | 789 | |
| Accounts receivable | 3,620 | |
| Bank | 1,608 | 6,017 |
| Total assets | | 10,919 |
| *Current liabilities* | | |
| Trade accounts payable | | 453 |
| | | 10,466 |
| *Capital and reserves* | | |
| Called-up share capital | | 6,000 |
| Retained profits [(3,744 − 100) + [(712 − 36 − 72) × 0.75]] | | 4,097 |
| Non-controlling interest (W2) | | 369 |
| | | 10,466 |

*Workings:*

| | | |
|---|---|---|
| (W1) Investment in Small cost | | 680 |
| *Less* Share capital | 600 | |
| 75% Retained earnings of 72 | 54 | 654 |
| Goodwill on acquisition | | 26 |
| (W2) Share capital | | 200 |
| 25% Retained earnings of 676 | | 169 |
| | | 369 |

*Note:* The adjustments necessary were:

(*a*) Remove intragroup sale from group revenue.
(*b*) Remove unrealised profit in inventory from net profit on Small's Statement of Profit or Loss sheet, reducing it from 520 to 484 and calculating non-controlling interest for Statement of Profit or Loss based on this amount.
(*c*) Remove unrealised profit of 36 from Small's retained earnings, reducing them from 712 to 676 and using this amount to calculate non-controlling interest for statement of financial position.
(*d*) Remove research (50) and unpurchased goodwill (50) from Large's statement of financial position and reduce Large's retained earnings by 100 to complete the double entry, so reducing them from 3,744 to 3,644.
(*e*) Remove unrealised profit of 36 from inventory in Large for consolidation.

**26.1**

If Q plc is unable to control or to exercise significant influence over N Ltd, the group comprises the parent undertaking (Q) and two subsidiaries (L and M). N Ltd should be excluded from consolidation and treated as a non-current asset investment at fair value if it can be ascertained. However, if Q plc is able to exercise significant influence over N Ltd, it should treat it as an associated undertaking using the equity method.

**26.2**

(*a*) There are two acquisition points. Any dividends received from the pre-acquisition (of the first investment) profits should be applied to reduce the initial investment of £96,000. (Similar treatment should be applied to the £132,000 investment.) The initial investment should be shown in the P's company statement of financial position at fair value if it can be ascertained and at cost of £96,000 less any such dividends received if its fair value cannot be identified.

(*b*) At the time the investment became 21%, the net assets of the clothing company were £1,008,000. The company's share of this is £211,200. The premium paid on acquisition, subject to adjustment for pre-acquisition reserves distributed, is £16,320 (£96,000 + £132,000 − £211,680). (This figure appears nowhere in the financial statements.) Disclosure in the company's own financial statements is as for investments. The group statement of profit or loss should use the equity method to show the company's share of the publishing company's profit or loss for the year. The group statement of financial position carrying value in respect of this investment will comprise the cost of the investment plus the company's share of post-acquisition retained profits, less any amounts written off either of these amounts.

**27.1**

(*a*) $£20,000 \times 0.05 \times \frac{86}{365} = £235.62$

(*b*) $£5,000 \times 0.10 \times \frac{180}{365} = £246.58$

therefore amount paid = £4,753.42

**27.2**

The amount borrowed is £4,753.42 and the interest charged is £246.58; therefore, the real rate of interest is:

$$r = \frac{246.58}{4{,}753.42 \times \frac{180}{365}} = 10.52\%$$

**27.3**

(*a*) $£9{,}000 \times 0.06 \times \frac{99}{365} = £146.47$

(*b*) $£14{,}000 \times 0.08 \times \frac{30}{365} = £92.05$ discount

therefore amount paid = £14,000 − £92.05 = £13,907.95

**27.4**

The amount borrowed is £13,907.95 and the interest charged is £92.05; therefore, the real rate of interest is:

$$r = \frac{92.05}{13{,}907.95 \times \frac{30}{365}} = 8.05\%$$

**27.5**

The amount borrowed is:

$$\begin{aligned} 5{,}400 \times \tfrac{1}{4} &= 1{,}350.00 \\ 4{,}050 \times \tfrac{1}{4} &= 1{,}012.50 \\ 2{,}700 \times \tfrac{1}{4} &= 675.00 \\ 1{,}350 \times \tfrac{1}{4} &= \underline{337.50} \\ \text{Equivalent loan for one year} &\ \underline{3{,}375.00} \end{aligned}$$

$$r = \frac{800}{3{,}375} = 0.2370 \text{ or } 23.70\%$$

**27.6**

£8,000 will accumulate to $£8{,}000 \times (1 + 0.06)^5 = £10{,}705.80$
£10,705.80 − £8,000 = £2,705.80

**27.9**

From Table 4 in Appendix 1, the present value of an annuity of £4,800 p.a. for 15 years at 5% = £4,800 × 10.380 = £49,824 or:

$$\text{Present value} = £4{,}800 \times \left[\frac{1 - \frac{1}{(1 + 0.05)^{15}}}{0.05}\right] = £49{,}822$$

As the offer of £60,000 exceeds the present value of the rent, you should accept the offer.

**27.11**

$$\begin{aligned} \text{Paid in per year} &= \frac{\text{Value} \times (r)}{(1 + r)^n - 1} \\ &= \frac{£70{,}000 \times 0.06}{(1.06)^7 - 1} \\ &= £8{,}339.45 \text{ per year} \end{aligned}$$

**27.13**

£10,000 × present value factor of an annuity = £36,000. Therefore, the present value factor = 36,000/10,000 = 3.6, which is 4% according to four-year row of Table 4 in Appendix 1.

**27.14**

The present value factor of an annuity of £1 for six years at 8% = 4.623
£16,000 × 4.623 = £73,968 capital value of the lease.

**28.1**

Solvency, profitability, efficiency, capital structure and shareholder.

**28.3**

| | |
|---|---|
| Solvency | – *see* text, Section 28.3 |
| Profitability | – *see* text, Section 28.2 |
| Efficiency | – *see* text, Section 28.4 |
| Capital structure | – *see* text, Section 28.6 |
| Shareholder | – *see* text, Section 28.5 |

**28.5**

(*a*) inventory turnover

**28.7**

(*i*) (*b*) and (*d*).
(*ii*) (*b*) and (*d*).
(*iii*) (*d*).
(*iv*) If current liabilities greater than current assets, (*b*) and (*d*); if current assets greater than current liabilities, (*a*) and (*c*).
(*v*) (*b*) and (*d*) but only after a customer takes up the offer.

**28.9**

(*a*)

(*i*) Gross profit as % of revenue: $\frac{640}{2,880} \times \frac{100}{1} = 22.2\%$ $\frac{656}{4,320} \times \frac{100}{1} = 15.2\%$

(*ii*) Net profit as % of revenue: $\frac{96}{2,880} \times \frac{100}{1} = 3.3\%$ $\frac{144}{4,320} \times \frac{100}{1} = 3.3\%$

(*iii*) Expenses as % of revenue: $\frac{544}{2,880} \times \frac{100}{1} = 18.9\%$ $\frac{512}{4,320} \times \frac{100}{1} = 11.9\%$

(*iv*) Inventory turnover: $\frac{2,240}{(384 + 224) \div 2}$ $= 7.4$ times $\frac{3,664}{(480 + 416) \div 2}$ $= 8.2$ times

(*v*) Rate of return (ROCE): $\frac{96}{(384 + 368) \div 2} \times \frac{100}{1}$ $= 25.5\%$ $\frac{144}{(688 + 704) \div 2 \times \frac{100}{1}}$ $= 20.7\%$

(*vi*) Current ratio: $\frac{654}{392} = 1.67$ $\frac{611}{403} = 1.52$

(*vii*) Acid test ratio: $\frac{430}{392} = 1.10$ $\frac{195}{403} = 0.48$

(*viii*) Accounts receivable : revenue ratio: $\frac{424}{2,880} \times 12$ $= 1.77$ months $\frac{192}{4,320} \times 12$ $= 0.53$ month

(*ix*) Accounts payable : purchases ratio: $\frac{392}{2,080} \times 12$ $= 2.26$ months $\frac{403}{3,600} \times 12$ $= 1.34$ months

(*b*) Business B has made more net profit (£144,000 compared with £96,000) but, in terms of capital employed, B has only managed to achieve a return of 20.7% whereas A has managed a return of 25.5%. A is clearly more efficient in the use of its resources. Reasons as follows – possibly – as not until you know more about the business could you give a definite answer.

(*i*) B managed to sell far more merchandise but at lower prices, i.e. took only 15.2% margin as compared with A's 22.2% margin.
(*ii*) Maybe less efficient use of mechanised means in the business by B. Note that assuming A and B both use similar depreciation rates, B has more equipment and it is considerably newer than A's.
(*iii*) B did not have as much inventory lying idle. B turned over inventory 8.2 times in the year as compared with 7.4. This could indicate inefficient purchasing by A and/or a likelihood of zero inventory and, so, loss of sales.
(*iv*) While A waited (on average) 1.77 months to be paid by customers. B managed to collect in 0.53 months on average. Money represented by debts is money lying idle. However, A took longer (2.26 months) to pay its creditors than B (1.34 months). It appears that A was therefore less efficient in controlling its debtors whereas B was less efficient in controlling its creditors' payments. Overall, these two results probably cancel each other out so far as explaining A's higher rate of return.
It appears that the key factor may be the less efficient use of its assets by B. A has less than $^1/_5$ of the resources tied up in fixed assets than B, yet has 67% of B's sales and 67% of B's net profit.

**28.11**

(*a*) The ratios reveal that L Ltd's relative profitability has fallen between the two years. The gross and net profit margins have both fallen, but this may be due to the new sales manager's price-cutting policy, rather than because of any change in costs.

The fall in return on capital employed is not what was hoped for from the new sales price policy. A drop from 31% to 18% is significant and suggests that the change in sales price policy and the investment in new machinery, although with the related increased borrowings, have led to short-term depressed returns. If the increased market resulting from the new sales policy can be retained, it would be worthwhile considering an increase in sales price to a point where a higher rate of return would be achieved.

The company appears solvent – there is no shortage of liquid assets. However, it has taken on considerably more long-term debt in order to fund the market expansion. This will have to be serviced and the level of profit should be monitored to ensure that margins do not fall further, raising the current level of risk to unacceptable levels. As 38.2% (£192,000) of net profits before interest (£502,000) is already being used to meet debt interest payments, compared with only 3.8% in 2015, it would not take very large changes in costs or selling price to cause this to become a major problem. The current level of gearing will also inhibit the company's ability to raise additional loan funding in future.

| *Profitability* | *2015* | *2016* |
|---|---|---|
| Gross profit : revenue | $\frac{540}{900} \times 100 = 60\%$ | $\frac{1,120}{2,800} \times 100 = 40\%$ |
| Net profit : revenue | $\frac{302}{900} \times 100 = 34\%$ | $\frac{310}{2,800} \times 100 = 11\%$ |
| ROCE | $\frac{302 + 12}{929 + 100} = 31\%$ | $\frac{310 + 192}{1,267 + 1,600} = 18\%$ |
| *Solvency* | | |
| Current ratio | $\frac{125}{36} = 3.47 : 1$ | $\frac{821}{186} = 4.41 : 1$ |
| Acid test ratio | $\frac{125 - 30}{36} = 2.63 : 1$ | $\frac{821 - 238}{186} = 3.13 : 1$ |
| *Capital structure* | | |
| Capital gearing | $\frac{100}{100 + 929} = 10\%$ | $\frac{1,600}{1,600 + 1,267} = 56\%$ |

(*b*) Current accounts receivable collection period $= \frac{583}{2{,}800} \times 365 = 76$ days.

If the collection period were 45 days, the new accounts receivable amount would be:

$$\frac{45}{76} \times 583{,}000 = 345{,}200$$

The amount released if a 45-day accounts receivable collection period could be imposed would be £237,800.

**29.1**

(*a*) *Statements of Profit or Loss for the year ended 31 December 2016*

| | | X | | | Y |
|---|---|---|---|---|---|
| Revenue | | 480,000 | | | 762,500* |
| *Less* Cost of goods sold | | 400,000 | (+10,000) | | 610,000 |
| Gross profit | | 80,000 | | | 152,500 |
| *Less* Admin. expenses (−10,000) | 40,000 | | (−2,500) | 57,500 | |
| Selling expenses | 15,000 | 55,000 | | 35,000 | 92,500 |
| Net profit | | 25,000 | | | 60,000 |

*Assumed 25% mark-up despite wrong inventory valuation.

(*b*) *Profitability:*

| | X | | Y | |
|---|---|---|---|---|
| Gross profit % | 20% | | 25% | |
| Net profit % $\frac{25}{480} \times \frac{100}{1}$ | = 5.2% | $\frac{60}{762.5} \times \frac{100}{1}$ | = 7.87% | |
| Inventory turnover $\frac{400{,}000}{40{,}000}$ | = 10 times | $\frac{610{,}000}{45{,}000^*}$ | = 13.6 times | |

*Adjusted to take into account inaccurate valuation.

Return on capital employed (ROCE) (previous owners)

$$\frac{25{,}000}{200{,}000} \times \frac{100}{1} = 12.5\% \qquad \frac{60{,}000}{350{,}000} \times \frac{100}{1} = 17.14\%$$

Based on purchase price of business the ROCE for Adrian Frampton would be:

$$X: \frac{25{,}000}{190{,}000} \times \frac{100}{1} = 13.15\% \qquad Y: \frac{60{,}000}{400{,}000} \times \frac{100}{1} = 15\%$$

All ratios are favourable for Y. If gross profit ratios remained the same in future together with other expenses then Y business is best value.

However:

(*i*) Can gross profit ratios of X be improved as compared with those of Y?
(*ii*) Can inventory turnover be improved?

If so, then X could be cheapest business to buy as it gives a better ROCE.

(*c*) (*i*) Need to know current assets and current liabilities in detail.
(*ii*) Are these similar businesses?
Type of business
Areas in which situated
Competition
Prefer several years' financial statements to gauge trends
Quality of staff and whether they would continue.

**29.2**

(*a*)

| 2016 | A | | B | | C |
|---|---|---|---|---|---|
| | £000 | | £000 | | £000 |
| Return on capital of 20% = Profit* | 120.0 | | 120.0 | | 120.0 |
| Interest *less* tax | – | 24.0 | | 66.0 | |
| | | 13.2 | 10.8 | 36.3 | 29.7 |
| Profit for ordinary shares | 120.0 | | 109.2 | | 90.3 |
| Ordinary share capital | 600 | | 400 | | 50 |
| Profit return (%) | 20 | | 27.3 | | 180.6 |
| **2017** | | | | | |
| Return on capital of 10% = Profit | 60.0 | | 60.0 | | 60.0 |
| Interest *less* tax | | | | | |
| | – | 24.0 | | 66.0 | |
| | | 13.2 | 10.8 | 36.3 | 29.7 |
| Profit for ordinary shares | 60.0 | | 49.2 | | 30.3 |
| Ordinary share capital | 600 | | 400 | | 50 |
| Profit return (%) | 10 | | 12.3 | | 60.6 |

*Profit is assumed to be after tax but before interest.

(*b*) High gearing accentuates the rate of return to the ordinary shareholder. In the zero-geared position of Company A the return to the shareholder simply reflects the change in profits earned on trading. In the high-geared position of Company C the return to the shareholder decreases from 180.6% to 60.6%, i.e. to a reduction of 66.5% as profits reduce by only 50%. Company B reflects an intermediate position with a relatively moderate level of gearing.

High gearing increases risk to shareholders for two reasons. First, if the profits earned are not sufficiently high to meet interest charges then the company may find itself failing since the lenders may seek a winding-up order. Second, the risk is increased simply because of exaggerated fluctuations in the returns which are accentuated in the high-geared situation.

However, it can be seen that if profits earned are higher than the interest rate, this will produce a significantly higher return to the shareholder in a high-geared company. The fact that interest is allowed as a deduction for tax purposes indicates that gearing may give an overall advantage. The market's assessment of the risk position will counter this, and will be based on the nature of the business and management.

**29.4**

(*a*) Refer to the text.

(*b*)

| | Company A £000 | % | Company B £000 | % |
|---|---|---|---|---|
| Ordinary shares | 300 | | 800 | |
| *Revenue:* Share premium | 300 | | 400 | |
| Retained profit | 400 | | 200 | |
| | 1,000 | 62.5 | 1,400 | 87.5 |
| 8% preference shares | 200 | | – | |
| 10% loan notes | | | 200 | |
| 12% loan notes | 400 | | | |
| | 600 | 37.5 | 200 | 12.5 |
| Total share capital and loan notes | 1,600 | 100.0 | 1,600 | 100.0 |

Company A Debt : *Equity* $= \frac{37.5}{62.5} = 60\%$

B Debt : *Equity* $= \frac{12.5}{87.5} = 14.3\%$

(*c*) Company A is more highly geared than B since it is committed to paying a higher proportion of fixed dividend and interest payments for its profits. A higher level of gearing increases risk. (Note the answer in 28.2 (*b*) is appropriate.)

(*d*)

| | | A | B |
|---|---|---|---|
| Trading profit before interest | | 200,000 | 200,000 |
| *Less* Interest charges | | 48,000 | 20,000 |
| Net profit after interest charge | | 152,000 | 180,000 |
| Preference dividend | 16,000 | | – |
| Ordinary dividend | 45,000 | 61,000 | 120,000 |
| Retained profit | | 91,000 | 60,000 |

**29.6**

(*a*)

| | 2015 | 2016 |
|---|---|---|
| Equity shares | 100,000 | 150,000 |
| Reserves | 150,000 | 220,000 |
| Total equity capital | 250,000 | 370,000 |
| Loans | 40,000 | 40,000 |
| Total capital employed | 290,000 | 410,000 |
| Profits (net after tax) | 60,000 | 70,000 |
| Return on total equity | 24% | 18.9% |

(*b*) To Mr C. Black

The reduction in profits from 24% to 18.9% of total equity needs to be analysed into its causal factors. During the year the net profits have increased but not as fast as the equity capital which has gone up by £120,000 over the year. If the increase reflected an investment late in 2015/16 it would reduce returns because a full year's profit could not be earned.

It is therefore essential to examine the nature of the investment and the future. Before shares are bought it is essential to examine future prospects. If these are good, the historic analysis may not be important. However, if the new funds were used – clearly prospects may not be good and shares should not be bought.

(*c*) Reserves are profits retained within the business. The profits may be from revenue, i.e. from profits which could be distributed as dividends to shareholders or capital – for example where fixed amounts are revalued upwards to reflect current market value.

The creation of reserves reflects an increase in capital in the organisation which would normally be to reflect an increasing scale of operation. In this sense reserves reflect an alternative to issuing new shares. In the case of capital reserves from revaluation – these are simply 'paper adjustments' to value which do not in themselves indicate more resources in the organisation.

Revenue reserves may in fact be distributed as dividends whereas capital reserves would not normally be available for this purpose and are more akin to share capital.

**29.8**

(*a*) *Statements of Profit or Loss for the year to 31 March 2018*

| | Chan plc £000 | Ling plc £000 | Wong plc £000 |
|---|---|---|---|
| Operating profit | 300 | 300 | 300 |
| Interest payable | – | – | (10) |
| *Profit on ordinary activities before tax* | 300 | 300 | 290 |
| Taxation (30%) | (90) | (90) | (87) |
| Profit after tax | 210 | 210 | 203 |

(*b*)

| *Changes in retained profits* | Chan plc | Ling plc | Wong plc |
|---|---|---|---|
| Opening balance | ? | ? | ? |
| Profit for the year | 210 | 210 | 203 |
| Dividends paid: Preference | – | (20) | (30) |
| Ordinary | (100) | (60) | (40) |
| Increase over the year | 110 | 130 | 133 |

(*c*) (*i*) *Earnings per share*

| | | Chan plc | Ling plc | Wong plc |
|---|---|---|---|---|
| Net profit after tax and preference dividend | | 210 | 210–20 | 203–30 |
| Number of ordinary shares in issue | = | 500 | 300 | 200 |
| | = | 42p | 63.3p | 86.5p |

(*ii*) *Price/earnings ratio*

| | | Chan plc | Ling plc | Wong plc |
|---|---|---|---|---|
| Market price of ordinary shares | = | 840 / 42 | 950 / 63.3 | 1,038 / 86.5 |
| Earnings per share | = | 20 | 15 | 12 |

(*iii*) *Gearing ratio*

$$\frac{\text{Loan capital + preference shares} \times 100}{\text{Shareholders' funds}}$$

Chan plc = Nil

$$\text{Ling plc} = \frac{200}{300 + 100 + 130} \times 100 = 37.7\%$$

$$\text{Wong plc} = \frac{300 + 100}{200 + 100 + 133} \times 100 = 92.4\%$$

(*d*) A gearing ratio expresses the relationship that exists between total borrowings (that is, preference share capital and long-term loans), and the total amount of ordinary shareholders' funds. It should be noted that other definitions of gearing are possible and are sometimes used.

Any company with a gearing ratio of, say, 70% would be considered to be high-geared, while a company with a gearing ratio of, say, 20% would be low-geared.

Gearing is an important matter to consider when investing in ordinary shares in a particular company. A *high*-geared company means that a high proportion of the company's earnings are committed to paying either interest on any loan notes and/or dividends on any preference share capital *before* an ordinary dividend can be declared. If a company is low geared, then a high proportion of the company's earnings can be paid out as ordinary dividends.

Chan plc has not issued any loan notes or any preference share capital. Gearing does not, therefore, apply to this company, and all of the earnings may be paid out to the ordinary shareholders.

Ling plc is a relatively low-geared company. It has no loan notes, and only a small proportion of its earnings are committed to paying its preference shareholders. The balance may then all be declared as an ordinary dividend.

Wong plc is an extremely high-geared company. A high proportion of borrowings (in this case consisting of both loan notes and preference share capital) means that a high proportion of its earnings has to be set aside for both its loan-note holders and its preference shareholders before any ordinary dividend can be declared. As a result, if the profits of the company are low, no ordinary dividend may be payable.

If profits are rising, a high-geared company may not be a particularly risky company in which to purchase some ordinary shares, but the reverse may apply if profits are falling.

For the year to 31 March 2018, Chan, Ling and Wong's operating profit is identical. Wong is committed to paying interest on its loan notes (which is allowable against tax), and both Ling and Wong have to pay a preference dividend (which is *not* allowable against tax).

In deciding whether to invest in any of the three companies, there are a great many other factors to be considered, including future prospects of all three companies. However, when profits are fluctuating an ordinary shareholder is more likely to receive a higher return by investing in Chan than by investing in either Ling or Wong. Similarly, an ordinary shareholder can expect a higher return by investing in Wong.

Based on the limited amount of information given in the question, therefore, an investor considering purchasing ordinary shares in only one of these three companies would be recommended to buy shares in Chan plc.

It should be noted that if profits were *increasing*, an investor would be recommended to buy shares first in Wong, then in Ling and finally in Chan. The earnings per share in both Ling and Wong are far higher than in Chan, so there is a much greater chance of an increase in the ordinary dividend, but this is not necessarily the case if profits are falling or fluctuating.

**29.10**

(*a*) (*i*)

*Forecast Dividends*

| | *2019* | *2020* | *2021* |
|---|---|---|---|
| | *£000* | *£000* | *£000* |
| Forecast profits | 1,800 | 500 | 2,200 |
| *Less* Corporation tax (30%) | 540 | 150 | 660 |
| | 1,260 | 350 | 1,540 |
| Dividends to be paid in following year | 1,260 | 350 | 1,540 |

*Statement of Financial Position extracts*

| | | | |
|---|---|---|---|
| *Shareholders' equity* | | | |
| Issued ordinary shares of £1 each fully paid | 6,000 | 6,000 | 6,000 |
| Share premium account | 1,000 | 1,000 | 1,000 |
| Retained profits (1,650 + 1,260 − 630; | 2,280 | 2,000 | 3,190 |
| 2,910 − 1,260 + 350; 2,000 − 350 + 1,540) | 9,280 | 9,000 | 10,190 |
| *Note* | | | |
| Dividends paid | 630 | 1,260 | 350 |

(*ii*)

*Forecast Dividends*

| | *2019* | *2020* | *2021* |
|---|---|---|---|
| | *£000* | *£000* | *£000* |
| Forecast profits | 1,800 | 500 | 2,200 |
| *Less* interest (12% × £2*m*) | 240 | 240 | 240 |
| | 1,560 | 260 | 1,960 |
| *Less* Corporation tax (30%) | 468 | 78 | 588 |
| | 1,092 | 182 | 1,372 |
| Dividends to be paid in following year | 1,092 | 182 | 1,372 |

*Statement of Financial Position extracts*

| | | | |
|---|---|---|---|
| *Shareholders' equity* | | | |
| Issued ordinary shares of £1, each fully paid | 5,000 | 5,000 | 5,000 |
| Retained profits (1,650 + 1,092; | 2,742 | 1,832 | 3,022 |
| 2,742 − 1,092 + 182; 1,832 − 182 + 1,372) | 7,742 | 6,832 | 8,022 |
| *Non-current liabilities* | | | |
| 12% loan notes | 2,000 | 2,000 | 2,000 |
| *Note* | | | |
| Dividends paid | 630 | 1,092 | 182 |

(*b*) (*i*) If planned expansion is financed by share issue, the forecast return on shareholders' equity for the next three years will be:

2019 1,260/9,910 × 100 = 12.7%
2020 350/9,000 × 100 = 3.9%
2021 1,540/10,190 × 100 = 15.1%

(*ii*) If planned expansion is financed by issuing loan, the forecast return on shareholders' equity for the next three years will be:

2019 1,092/7,742 × 100 = 14.1%
2020 182/6,832 × 100 = 2.7%
2021 1,372/8,022 × 100 = 17.1%

*Note:* All the above figures are, of course, net of tax and should be grossed by a factor of 100/70 if comparison with gross interest rates is to be made (on the assumption of 30% tax rate).

(*c*) The return on shareholders' equity for the year ended 30 September 2018 was 630/6,650 = 9.5% (although the shareholders only received 600 of the 630 profit so their actual return received was slightly less). To have the return fluctuate between 2.7% and 17.1%, as it will do if the planned expansion is financed by the loan-notes issue, will surely unnerve all but the most sturdy shareholders. Such a violent swing from year to year will confuse, confound and alarm anyone looking at the shares as an investment.

To finance the planned expansion by a share issue does not improve matters greatly, as it will be seen that the return fluctuates between 3.9% and 15.1%. But since we are told that the industry is 'subject to marked variations in consumer demand' it does seem more appropriate to use share capital (by definition risk-bearing) rather than a loan note. The poor profits forecast for 2020 suggest that it would not take much of a variation from the expected results to show no profit at all, and were this to occur, is there not a possibility that the loan-note holders could not be paid their due interest? Failure to pay loan-note interest on time would bring in a receiver (assuming the loan notes were secured): his function would then be to collect not only the unpaid interest but the capital as well, as failure to pay interest would be a breach of the conditions under which the loan notes were issued.

Under both options shareholders are to miss a year's dividends as a result of the dividend for 2018 having been paid during the year and the 2019 dividend not being paid until 2020. The directors can expect a stormy annual general meeting, but that is far less dangerous than the entry of a receiver.

In practice, of course, it is unusual for a company to pay out all profits as dividends, and since shareholders will pay more attention usually to the level of dividends paid than to profits earned, it would make better financial sense if the 2019 dividend were maintained at or slightly above the 2018 level, enabling an addition to be made to retained profits. This in turn would enable a fund to be built up to supplement current profits for dividends and/or to redeem the loan notes.

The all-shares or all-loan-notes choice is also an unrealistic one. Although there is much to be said for a broad share base to support what is obviously a risky business, it could make better sense to raise part of the required £2,000,000 by shares and part by loan notes. A restrained dividend policy coupled with the use of the (probably enlarged) depreciation charge arising after the expansion had taken place could enable a loan-note redemption programme to be established over the course of the next few years.

**29.12**

| (*a*) (*i*) *Shareholders* | *2016* | *2017* |
|---|---|---|
| Earnings per share (EPS) | $\frac{9{,}520}{39{,}680} = 24p$ | $\frac{11{,}600}{39{,}680} = 29.4p$ |
| Dividend cover (= EPS ÷ dividend per share) | $\frac{24p}{(2{,}240 \div 39{,}680)} = \frac{24p}{5.6p} = 4.3$ times | $\frac{29.4p}{(2{,}400 \div 39{,}680)} = \frac{29.4p}{6p} = 4.9$ times |
| (*ii*) *Trade accounts payable* | | |
| Current ratio | $\frac{92{,}447}{36{,}882} = 2.5$ | $\frac{99{,}615}{42{,}475} = 2.3$ |
| Acid test | $\frac{40{,}210 + 12{,}092}{36{,}862} = 1.4:1$ | $\frac{43{,}370 + 5{,}790}{42{,}475} = 1.2:1$ |
| (*iii*) *Internal management* | | |
| Accounts receivable ratio/Sales* | | |
| *Assumed credit sales | $\frac{40{,}210}{486{,}300} \times 52 = 4.3$ weeks | $\frac{43{,}370}{583{,}900} \times 52 = 3.9$ |
| Return on capital employed (before tax) | $\frac{15{,}254}{40{,}740} = 37.4\%$ | $\frac{18{,}686}{50{,}000} = 37.4\%$ |

(*b*) *Shareholders*

EPS. An increase of 5.4p per share has occurred. This was due to an increase in profit without any increase in share capital.

Dividend cover. Increased by 0.6 times because increase in profit not fully reflected in dividends.

*Trade creditors*

Current ratio. This has fallen but only marginally and it still appears to be quite sound.

Acid test. This has also fallen, but still seems to be quite reasonable.

*Internal management*

Accounts receivable ratio. There appears to have been an increase in the efficiency of our credit control.

Return on capital employed. This has stayed the same for each of the two years. The increase in capital employed has seen a proportional increase in profits.

**29.14**

To the Board of G plc

**From** AN Other, Accountant

**Subject:** *Potential acquisition of either of companies A Ltd and B Ltd as subsidiaries in the machine tool manufacturing sector. Financial performances assessed.*

As instructed by you I have investigated the financial performances of these two companies to assist in the evaluation of them as potential acquisitions.

It should be borne in mind that financial ratio analysis is only partial information. There are many other factors which will need to be borne in mind before a decision can be taken.

The calculations of the various ratios are given as an appendix.

*Profitability*

While the main interest to the board is what G plc could obtain in profitability from A Ltd and B Ltd, all I can comment on at present is the current profitability enjoyed by these two companies.

Here the most important ratio is that of ROCE (return on capital employed). A's ROCE is 27.2% as compared with B's 15.6%.

The great difference in ROCE can be explained by reference to the secondary ratios of profit and asset utilisation. Both ratios are in A's favour. The profit ratios are A 34%: B 29%. The asset utilisation ratios are A 0.9%: B 0.6%, showing that A is utilising its assets 50% better than B. It is the effects of these two ratios that give the ROCE for each company.

The very low working capital employed by A Ltd very much affects the asset utilisation ratio. How far such a low working capital is representative of that throughout the whole year is impossible to say.

*Liquidity*

It would not be sensible to draw a final conclusion as to the liquidity positions of the two companies based on the statement of financial position figures. As a statement of financial position is based at one point in time it can sometimes be misleading, as a reading of figures over a period would be more appropriate.

A Ltd does appear to have a short-term liquidity problem, as the current assets only just cover current liabilities. The 'quick' or 'acid test ratio' on the face of it appears to be very inadequate at 0.6.

By contrast, B Ltd with a current ratio of 1.4 and a 'quick ratio' of 1.0 would appear to be reasonably liquid.

However, much more light is shed on the position of the companies when the debtor collection period is examined. A collects its debts with a credit period of nine weeks. In the case of B Ltd this rises to an astonishing 36.7 weeks. Why is this so? It could be due simply to very poor credit control by B Ltd. Such a long credit period casts considerable doubt on the real worth of the accounts receivable. There is a high probability that many of the debts may prove difficult to collect. It might be that B Ltd, in order to maintain sales, has lowered its requirements as to the creditworthiness of its customers. If the credit period were reduced to a normal one for the industry it might be found that many of the customers might go elsewhere.

The problem with accounts receivable in the case of B Ltd is also carried on to inventory. In the case of A Ltd the inventory turnover is 4.3 falling to 2.8 in B Ltd. There could be a danger that B Ltd has inventory increasing simply because it is finding it difficult to sell its products.

*Capital gearing*

A Ltd is far more highly geared than B Ltd: 39.6% as compared with 14.1%. A comparison with this particular industry by means of interfirm comparison should be undertaken.

*Limitations of ratio analysis*

You should bear in mind the following limitations of the analysis undertaken:

(*i*) One year's financial statements are insufficient for proper analysis to be undertaken. The analysis of trends, taken from, say, five years' accounts would give a better insight.
(*ii*) Differences in accounting policies between A Ltd and B Ltd will affect comparisons.
(*iii*) The use of historical costs brings about many distortions.
(*iv*) The use of industry interfirm comparisons would make the ratios more capable of being interpreted.
(*v*) The plans of the companies for the future expressed in their budgets would be of more interest than past figures.

*Conclusions*

Depending on the price which would have to be paid for acquisition, I would suggest that A Ltd is the company more suitable for takeover.

A N Other
Accountant

***Appendix***

(*i*) *Return on capital employed* — *A Ltd* / *B Ltd*

$$\frac{\text{Profits before interest and tax}}{\text{Capital employed}} \qquad \frac{211}{775} \times 100 = 27.2\% \qquad \frac{88}{565} \times 100 = 15.6\%$$

(*ii*) *Assets utilisation ratios*

$$\text{Total assets revenue: } \frac{\text{Revenue}}{\text{Total assets}} \qquad \frac{985}{1{,}140} = 0.9 \qquad \frac{560}{990} = 0.6$$

$$\text{Non-current assets revenue: } \frac{\text{Revenue}}{\text{Non-current assets}} \qquad \frac{985}{765} = 1.3 \qquad \frac{560}{410} = 1.4$$

$$\text{Working capital revenue: } \frac{\text{Revenue}}{\text{Working capital}} \qquad \frac{985}{10} = 98.5 \qquad \frac{560}{150} = 3.7$$

(*iii*) *Profitability ratios*

$$\text{Gross profit \% Revenue } \frac{\text{Gross profit}}{\text{Revenue}} \qquad \frac{335}{985} \times 100 = 34\% \qquad \frac{163}{560} \times 100 = 29\%$$

$$\text{Profit before taxation and interest as \% revenue} \qquad \frac{211}{985} \times 100 = 21\% \qquad \frac{88}{560} \times 100 = 16\%$$

(*iv*) *Liquidity ratios*

$$\text{Current ratio: } \frac{\text{Current assets}}{\text{Current liabilities}} \qquad \frac{375}{365} = 1.0 \qquad \frac{580}{425} = 1.4$$

Acid test or Quick ratio:

$$\frac{\text{Current assets} - \text{inventory}}{\text{Current liabilities}} \qquad \frac{220}{365} = 0.6 \qquad \frac{440}{425} = 1.0$$

Accounts receivable weeks:

$$\frac{\text{Trade accounts receivable}}{\text{Credit sales}} \times 52 \qquad \frac{170}{985} \times 52 = 9 \text{ weeks} \qquad \frac{395}{560} \times 52 = 36.7 \text{ weeks}$$

(*v*) *Capital structure*

Gearing ratio:

$$\frac{\text{Long-term borrowing}}{\text{Shareholders' funds}} \qquad \frac{220}{555} \times 100 = 39.6\% \qquad \frac{70}{495} \times 100 = 14.1\%$$

Proprietory ratio:

$$\frac{\text{Shareholders' funds}}{\text{Tangible assets}} \qquad \frac{555}{1{,}140} = 0.5 \qquad \frac{495}{990} = 0.5$$

**29.17**

*Accruals-based earnings management* and *real earnings management;* for examples, *see* Section 29.8

**29.18**

Managers typically engage in earnings management in order to qualify for a bonus. As you will learn in Chapter 30, when they do so, they are motivated by their own self-interest and often do things that are detrimental to the organisation. For example, a senior manager in a chemical company may delay major expenditure on research and development until the next accounting period so that earnings for the current period are not reduced by the expense and, as a result, he receives his bonus. The impact on the company may be significant. In this instance, the delay in injecting the expenditure into research and development may mean the company is beaten to the development of a new product by a competitor and loses millions of pounds compared to the manager's bonus of, say, £100,000.

**29.19**

There are many reasons why a company may wish to increase its income or the value of its assets in this way. Apart from doing so motivated by a desire to smooth earnings, it may do so if it wished to increase its earnings and so cause an increase in its share price prior to offering of shares in the company on the stock market, or before a rights issue - *see* Chapter 10.

**30.1**

Capture theory involves the regulated taking over the regulatory process. This is only possible if the regulated monopolise the process. Private interest group theory applies where competing stakeholder groups compete to have their viewpoint embraced in legislation. No one stakeholder group gains dominance over the process, so there is no instance of regulatory capture.

**30.2**

Legitimacy theory states that entities avoid conflicts and ensure that they operate within the boundaries and norms expected of them so their activities are perceived as legitimate by society (i.e. their stakeholders). When entities breach their social contract, this can threaten not only their image and reputation, but also their long-term existence. Entities that are perceived to have breached their social contract will endeavour to raise perceptions of their legitimacy by such tactics as increasing voluntary disclosure.

**30.3**

Availability.

**30.4**

No, not in the long-term unless either (*a*) further investigations found that this group of four questions was the best identifiable approach to take; or (*b*) the benefits of adopting this simplifying heuristic permanently outweigh the costs of its adoption.

**30.5**

The accountants will be constrained by the requirements of GAAP. They can increase income by, for example, reducing depreciation rates; reducing allowances for doubtful debts; reducing amounts written off for bad debts; and reclassifying some items, such as development costs, from expenses to non-current assets; switching the basis of inventory valuation from FIFO to Weighted Average, or vice versa, if this increases the amount shown for closing inventory. Alternatively, they can increase the value of non-current assets by revaluing them or by switching from historic cost to fair value.

**30.6**

The company could manage its earning as in Question 30.5 and it could also manage the timing of its transactions in a way that increases earnings in the present period. For example, it could delay processing invoices for purchases until the following period but include the items received in the inventory for this period. It could also start issuing press releases that indicate that it is doing better than anticipated – announcements of new products, new markets, and profit announcements indicating what its likely earnings for the period would be (after those earnings had been increased through the various earnings management tactics adopted). All of these approaches would be likely to have an impact upon the price of the company's shares, and most are permitted under GAAP if they can be justified by reference to achieving a true and fair view, which is usually something an accountant can successfully argue with an auditor.

**30.7**

Once a company starts to manage its earnings, particularly by adjusting accruals and by adjusting the timing of transactions, it needs to continue to do so. Eventually, this will prove impossible and it will usually end up taking a 'big bath' so that it can begin the process all over again in the following period, if it feels it needs to do so. (Investors can be convinced a big bath is a good thing if companies do it in a way that it is not clear that they were doing anything inappropriate up to that point.) A company also cannot keep changing its methods of making accounting adjustments, which means that, eventually, it will need to adopt one method and stick more closely to it. If it does not, this form of earnings management is relatively easy for analysts to detect, much easier than it is to detect manipulation of accruals. Once that happens, the company's legitimacy is threatened, stakeholders react, and it may be extremely difficult for the company to regain their trust.

**30.8**

Knowledge of double entry enables an understanding of what has occurred when accounting numbers are manipulated. It enables entries to be traced and understood. It also helps to understand why increasing income or increasing assets will improve gearing ratios, and to assess the impact of such decisions upon earnings.

**31.1**

| | Entry value | Exit value |
|---|---|---|
| Past | Historical cost | |
| Present | Replacement cost | Realisable value |
| Future | | Present value |

**31.2** *See* text, Section 31.4

**31.3** *See* text, Section 31.12

**31.4** Shareholders and lenders/creditors. (*See* text, Section 31.19.)

**32.1**
(*a*) T (*b*) F (*c*) T (*d*) F (*e*) T

**32.4**
£96,000

**32.6**
At 31 December 2018, accumulated depreciation is:

$36\% \times 64{,}000 \times \frac{180}{80} = 51{,}840$

At 31 December 2017, accumulated depreciation is:

$24\% \times 64{,}000 \times \frac{120}{80} = 23{,}040$

Depreciation charge for the year ended 31 December 2018 is:

$12\% \times 64{,}000 \times \frac{180}{80} = 17{,}280$

Hence, depreciation provision at 31 December 2018 is:

$23{,}040 + 17{,}280 = 40{,}320$

Backlog depreciation is $51{,}840 - 40{,}320 = 11{,}520$

**32.8**

| | | |
|---|---|---|
| Opening inventory at average prices $= 100{,}000 \times \frac{90}{70}$ | = | 128,521 |
| Purchases | = | 800,000 |
| Closing inventory at average prices $= 150{,}000 \times \frac{90}{110}$ | = | (122,727) |
| Current cost of sales | = | 805,794 |
| Historic cost of sales | = | 750,000 |
| Cost of sales adjustment | = | 55,794 |

**32.10**

| | | | | |
|---|---|---|---|---|
| Opening working capital | = | 12,000 | | |
| Closing working capital | = | 20,000 | | |
| Change in the year | = | 8,000 | | |
| At average values: | | | | |
| Opening working capital | = | $12{,}000 \times \frac{250}{220}$ | = | 13,636 |
| Closing working capital | = | $20{,}000 \times \frac{250}{260}$ | = | 19,231 |
| Change in the year | | | = | 5,595 |

The monetary working capital adjustment is $8{,}000 - 5{,}595 = 2{,}405$

**32.12**

| | *2016* | *2015* |
|---|---|---|
| | *£000* | *£000* |
| Loan notes | 240 | 240 |
| Cash | 174 | 60 |
| Net borrowings | 66 | 180 |

$$\text{Average net borrowings*} = \frac{66{,}000 + 180{,}000}{2} = 123{,}000$$

*Loan Cash

| | *2016* | *2015* |
|---|---|---|
| | *£000* | *£000* |
| Ordinary shares | 300 | 300 |
| Reserves | 444 | 408 |
| Current cost reserve | 42 | 36 |
| Shareholder interest | 786 | 744 |

$$\text{Average shareholder interest} = \frac{786{,}000 + 744{,}000}{2} = 765{,}000$$

$$\text{Gearing adjustment percentage is: } \frac{123{,}000}{123{,}000 + 765{,}000} = 15.81\%$$

**32.14**
Many accountants believe that during a period of inflation financial reports prepared under the historical cost convention are subject to a number of severe limitations. The question lists five such limitations, and a brief explanation of each one is as follows.

1 *Inventories are undervalued.*
Inventory values are normally based on historical costs. This means that the historical closing inventory will usually have cost less than its current economic value. Hence the cost of sales will tend to be higher than it would be if the closing inventory was revalued at its current cost. As a result, the gross profit will be higher, and the entity may then pay out a higher level of net profit.

If the entity pays out a high level of profit and at the same time it has to pay more for its inventory (because prices are rising), it may be left with insufficient funds for it to be able to replace its inventory with the same *quantity* of goods that it had sold during the previous period. Hence it will not be able to operate at the same level of activity as it had previously experienced.

2 *Depreciation is understated.*
Depreciation is usually based on the historical cost of non-current assets. Such assets will normally increase in price during a period of inflation. The annual depreciation charge, therefore, may not reflect the amount needed to be able to replace the assets at their increased cost. Consequently, the accounting profit tends to be overstated, and this may mean that too much profit is withdrawn from the business. The cash resources may then prove insufficient to replace the assets at the end of their useful life. Like the inventory valuation problem, therefore, the business may not be able to operate at the same level of activity that it has previously experienced.

3 *Gains and losses on net monetary assets are undisclosed.*
Net monetary assets include both long- and short-term loans made to and by the entity, for example, loan notes, and trade accounts receivable and trade accounts payable. During a period of inflation, an entity gains on both long- and short-term borrowings. The gain arises because although the amount originally borrowed will eventually be repaid at its face value, its purchasing power will have been reduced; for example, £5,000 borrowed in 2014 will not purchase the same quantity of goods in 2018 as it did in 2014. In 2018 the borrower may have to pay (say) £8,000 to purchase the same quantity of goods as he might have done in 2018. Hence the entity will have, in effect, gained £3,000 by borrowing during an inflationary period, because it is effectively having to pay back less in purchasing power (or in real terms, as it is known) than it borrowed.

By contrast, if the entity has *loaned* money during a similar period (perhaps by allowing its customers to buy goods on credit), it loses money because the purchasing power of the respective debts (which are fixed in monetary terms) will purchase fewer goods when they are eventually settled than they would have done when they were first incurred.

In financial reports prepared under the historical cost system, neither the gross nor the net effect of these types of transactions is disclosed.

4 *Statement of financial position values are unrealistic.*
Non-current assets are normally recorded in the statement of financial position at their original cost, that is, at their historical cost. During a period of inflation, the historical cost of the assets may be far less than their *current* cost, that is, at the value the entity places on them at the time that the financial reports are prepared. Hence, the financial reports give a misleading impression of the entity's net worth as at the time that they are prepared.

5 *Meaningful periodic comparisons are difficult to make.*
A meaningful comparison of financial reports prepared under the historical cost convention over several accounting periods may be misleading since such accounts will normally have been prepared using, say, pounds sterling in one period and pounds sterling in all subsequent periods.

Financial reports prepared in such a way are not, however, strictly comparable. For example, £100 in 2014 is not the same as £100 in 2018, because £100 would not purchase the same amount of goods in 2018 as it did in 2014. In fact, the comparison is just as meaningless as comparing financial reports prepared, say, in dollars with, say, reports prepared in euros. It is obvious to most users of such reports that 100 dollars are not the same as 100 euros, but it is less obvious that £100 in 2014 are not the same as £100 in 2018.

In order to be able to make a meaningful comparison between financial reports prepared in different time periods, therefore, it is desirable to translate them into the same currency, that is, to use the same price base. The argument behind this point is similar in principle to that used in translating dollars into euros or euros into dollars.

**33.1**
See Section 33.1.

**33.2**
See Section 33.1.

**33.3**
They present a more complete view of their activities and their impact on society and the environment. This reduces pressure from pressure groups and enhances their relationship with their stakeholders.

**33.4**
See Section 33.2.

**33.5**
Triple bottom line reports combine quantitative and qualitative information, some of which may be subjective in nature. This results in it being less reliable. Stakeholders reading an a triple bottom line report need to be aware of this and take it into account in making any judgement about the report. Also, many potentially relevant items of information may not be included because they cannot be reported reliably. Stakeholders need to take this into account also.

**33.6**
See Section 33.1.

**33.7**
See Section 33.1.

**33.8**
See text, Section 33.6.

**33.10**
See text, Section 33.7.

**33.11**
Basically, there are many things that could be done to improve the various parts of 'social well-being'. However, (*a*) benefits cost a lot of money in the short term, and (*b*) beneficial effects are felt only in the long term. Examples are better education and better housing.

**33.12**
*See* text, Section 33.10, social programme measurement.

**33.14**
The accountant's model of income measurement, with its reliance upon data that can be expressed in financial terms, can be said to be too narrow and fails to consider wider social and environmental issues. The air we breathe does not have a 'price' in financial terms. Yet, what businesses do may cause costs to be incurred by others as a result of their abuse of the air in their environment. Similarly, the true cost of a natural resource may never be accounted for – the rainforests being a very well-known example: they are being removed upon payment of a financially stated price, but the price only satisfies the seller, it does little to replace the environment being destroyed. Thus the price being added into the cost of manufacturing paper from the trees in the rainforests does not include the social and environmental cost of their destruction.

Thus, in the income model, it could be argued only in a narrow sense of the term that 'capital' is being maintained. In reality, the destruction of natural resources that are not or cannot be replaced means that the 'capital' is being consumed and future consumption impaired as a result.

It is for reasons of this type that it can be argued that accountants ought to be involved in disclosing the effects of a company's business activities upon its environment, for only by doing so will a true view of a company's activities be revealed.

**33.16**
See Section 33.12.

**33.17**
See Section 33.12.

**33.18**
See Section 33.12.

**33.19**
Integrated reports combine quantitative and qualitative information, some of which may be subjective in nature. This results in it being less reliable. Stakeholders reading an integrated report need to be aware of this and take it into account in making any judgment about the report. Also, many potentially relevant items of information may not be included because it cannot be reported reliably. Stakeholders need to take this into account also.

**33.20**
See Section 33.1.

**33.21**
See Section 33.1.

**34.1**
*See* text, Section 34.1.

**34.2**
*See* text, Sections 34.1 and 34.2.

**34.3**
*See* text, Section 34.3.

**34.4**
*See* text, Section 34.4.

**34.5**
*See* text, Section 34.6.

**35.1**
*See* text, Section 35.1.

**35.2**
*See* text, Section 35.5.

**35.3**
*See* text, Section 35.6.

**35.4**
*See* text, Section 35.9.

**35.5**
*See* text, Section 35.7.

**36.1**
*See* text, Sections 36.1 and 36.2.

**36.2**
*See* text, Sections 36.1 and 36.2.

**36.3**
*See* text, Section 36.2.

**36.4**
*See* text, Section 36.3.

**36.5**
*See* text, Section 36.4.

**36.6**
*See* text, Section 36.7.

**37.1**
*See* text.

**37.2**
*See* text.

**37.3**
*See* text.

**37.4**
*See* text.

**37.5**
*See* text.

**37.6**
*See* text.

**37.7**
*See* text.

**38.1**
*See* text.

**38.2**
*See* text.

**38.3**
*See* text.

**38.4**
*See* text.

**39.1**
*See* text.

**40.1**
*(i) f, h.* *(ii) m.* *(iii) a, c, e, g, j,* $^4/_5$ of *n, t, v,* $^3/_4$ of *w, x.* *(iv) b, d, i,* $^1/_5$ of *n, p, q,* part of $^1/_4$ of *w.* *(v) l, r, s, z,* part of $^1/_4$ of *w.* *(vi) o, k, u, y.*

**40.3**

| | | |
|---|---|---|
| Raw materials consumed (120,000 + 400,000 − 160,000) | | 360,000 |
| Haulage costs | | 4,000 |
| Direct labour 70% × 220,000 | | 154,000 |
| Royalties | | 1,600 |
| (*a*) **Prime cost** | | 519,600 |
| *Factory overhead* | | |
| Factory indirect labour | 66,000 | |
| Other factory indirect expenses | 58,000 | |
| Travelling expenses | 100 | |
| Depreciation: Factory equipment | 38,000 | |
| Firm's canteen expenses | 4,000 | |
| | | 166,100 |
| (*b*) **Production cost** | | 685,700 |
| *Administration expenses* | | |
| Salaries | 72,000 | |
| Travelling expenses | 200 | |
| Firm's canteen expenses | 2,000 | |
| Depreciation: Acctg. and office equipment | 2,000 | |
| Cars of admin. staff | 1,600 | |
| Other administrative expenses | 42,000 | |
| | | 119,800 |
| *Selling and distribution expenses* | | |
| Salaries | 8,000 | |
| Commission | 1,400 | |
| Travelling expenses | 2,900 | |
| Depreciation: Equipment | 300 | |
| Sales staff cars | 3,800 | |
| Other selling expenses | 65,000 | |
| Carriage costs on sales | 7,800 | |
| | | 89,200 |
| *Finance costs* | | |
| Interest on loans and overdrafts | | 3,800 |
| (*c*) **Total cost** | | 898,500 |

**40.6**
*See* text, Section 40.1.

**41.1**

(*a*) Answers to be drafted by students in proper memo form.

Introduction:

| Marginal cost is: | |
|---|---|
| Direct labour | 3.00 |
| Direct materials | 3.50 |
| Variable expenses | 2.25 |
| | 8.75 |

As selling price of £10 exceeds marginal cost of £8.75 we should accept (but see below).*

| *Proof* | *Without new order* | *With new order* |
|---|---|---|
| Direct labour | 600,000 | 630,000 |
| Direct materials | 700,000 | 735,000 |
| Indirect manufacturing costs | | |
| Variable | 450,000 | 472,500 |
| Fixed | 50,000 | 50,000 |
| Administration expenses | 120,000 | 120,000 |
| Selling and distribution expenses | 60,000 | 60,000 |
| Finance expenses | 20,000 | 20,000 |
| | 2,000,000 | 2,087,500 |
| Revenue | 2,400,000 | |
| Sales (2,400,000 + 100,000) | | 2,500,000 |
| Profit | 400,000 | 412,500 |

*Depends on how other things affected besides simple accounting calculation, such as whether there is sufficient spare manufacturing capacity to produce the extra units.

(*b*) For extra order:

| | |
|---|---|
| Marginal costs per unit (*see* (*a*)) | 8.75 |
| Depreciation (£3,000 *p.a.* ÷ 15,000) | 0.20 |
| Running costs (£6,000 *p.a.* ÷ 15,000) | 0.40 |
| Marginal costs per unit | 9.35 |

As £9.35 is greater than selling price of £9.25 do NOT accept.

**41.3**

| *Year 1* | | *(A) Lima Ltd (Marginal)* | | *(B) Delfina Ltd (Absorption)* |
|---|---|---|---|---|
| Revenue £120 × 2,400 | | 288,000 | | 288,000 |
| *Less* Variable costs | | | | |
| Direct labour £8 × 3,200 | 25,600 | | 25,600 | |
| Direct materials £12 × 3,200 | 38,400 | | 38,400 | |
| Variable expenses £10 × 3,200 | 32,000 | | 32,000 | |
| Total variable cost | 96,000 | | 96,000 | |
| *Less* in (A) Valuation closing inventory $\frac{800}{3,200} \times £96,000$ | 24,000 | | | |
| | 72,000 | | | |
| Fixed indirect manufacturing costs | 160,000 | | 160,000 | |
| | | | 256,000 | |
| *Less* in (B) Valuation closing inventory $\frac{800}{3,200} \times £256,000$ | | | 64,000 | |
| Total costs | | 232,000 | | 192,000 |
| Gross profit | | 56,000 | | 96,000 |
| *Year 2* | | *(A)* | | *(B)* |
| Revenue £120 × 3,600 | | 432,000 | | 432,000 |
| *Less* Variable costs | | | | |
| Direct labour £8 × 4,000 | 32,000 | | 32,000 | |
| Direct materials £12 × 4,000 | 48,000 | | 48,000 | |
| Variable expenses £10 × 4,000 | 40,000 | | 40,000 | |
| Total variable cost | 120,000 | | 120,000 | |
| *Add* in (A) Opening inventory b/d | 24,000 | | | |
| *Add* in (B) Opening inventory b/d | | | 64,000 | |
| | 144,000 | | 184,000 | |
| *Less* in (A) Valuation closing inventory $\frac{1,200}{4,000} \times 120,000$ | 36,000 | | | |
| | 108,000 | | | |
| Fixed indirect manufacturing costs | 160,000 | | 160,000 | |
| | | | 344,000 | |
| *Less* in (B) Valuation of closing inventory $\frac{1,200}{4,000} \times (£120,000 + £160,000)$ | | | 84,000 | |
| Total costs | | 26,000 | | 260,000 |
| Gross profit | | 164,000 | | 172,000 |

**41.3** *(cont'd)*

| *Year 3* | | *(A)* | | *(B)* |
|---|---|---|---|---|
| Revenue £120 × 3,000 | | 360,000 | | 360,000 |
| *Less* Variable costs | | | | |
| Direct labour £8 × 3,400 | 27,200 | | 27,200 | |
| Direct materials £12 × 3,400 | 40,800 | | 40,800 | |
| Var. expenses £10 × 3,400 | 34,000 | | 34,000 | |
| Total variable cost | 102,000 | | 102,000 | |
| *Add* in (A) Op. inventory b/d | 36,000 | | | |
| *Add* in (B) Op. inventory b/d | | | 84,000 | |
| | 138,000 | | 186,000 | |
| *Less* in (A) Valuation of closing inventory $\frac{1,600}{3,400} \times 102,000$ | 48,000 | | | |
| | 90,000 | | | |
| Fixed indirect manufacturing costs | 160,000 | | 160,000 | |
| | | | 346,000 | |
| *Less* in (B) Valuation of closing inventory $\frac{1,600}{3,400} \times (102,000 + 160,000)$ | | | 123,294 | |
| Total costs | | 250,000 | | 222,706 |
| Gross profit | | 110,000 | | 137,294 |

**41.4**

(*a*) *See* text

(*b*) Lima Ltd has an inventory value of £48,000 in its statement of financial position; Delfina Ltd has an inventory valuation of £123,294. The difference of £75,294 is the difference in the overall gross profits of the two companies.

**41.6**

(*a*) Subject to points raised in (*c*) the extra production should be taken on, as this results in greater profits amounting to £1,562,000. Proof is as follows:

| | | |
|---|---|---|
| Extra revenue 60,000 × £150 | | 9,000,000 |
| *Less* Extra costs | | |
| Direct materials (W1) | 3,141,600 | |
| Direct labour 60,000 × 18.70 × 120% = | 1,346,400 | |
| Variable overhead 60,000 × 7.50 | 450,000 | |
| Fixed costs | 2,500,000 | 7,438,000 |
| Extra profit | | 1,562,000 |
| (W1) 60,000 × 74.80 | | 4,488,000 |
| *Less* Saving 10% on extra materials | 448,800 | |
| Saving 10% on materials used on day shift 10% × 120,000 × 74.80 | 897,600 | 1,346,400 |
| | | 3,141,600 |

(*b*) Breakeven point to justify night shift

| | | |
|---|---|---|
| Sale price per unit | | 150.00 |
| *Less* Costs per unit | | |
| Material | 74.80 | |
| Direct labour 18.70 + 20% | 22.44 | |
| Variable overhead | 7.50 | 104.74 |
| Contribution per unit | | 45.26 |

Total fixed costs $\frac{2,500,000}{45.26}$ = Breakeven at 55,236 units

*Note*: No 10% reduction on materials because demand less than extra 60,000 units.

(*c*) (*i*) Would firm be able to maintain selling price of £187 on first 120,000 units per year?

(*ii*) Would it have been more profitable to subcontract extra units needed?

(*iii*) Could we diversify into a more profitable alternative product?

(*iv*) Could extra day facilities have been more profitable?

**41.8**

(*a*)

**Arncliffe Ltd**

*Revenue Statement for the year ending . . .*

| | | *Crowns* | | *Kings* | | *Total* |
|---|---|---|---|---|---|---|
| Revenue | | 60,000 | | 25,000 | | 85,000 |
| Direct costs: | | | | | | |
| Raw mats | 8,000 | | 2,000 | | 10,000 | |
| Labour | 20,000 | | 10,000 | | 30,000 | |
| M/c running costs | 12,000 | 40,000 | 3,000 | 15,000 | 15,000 | 55,000 |
| Contribution | | 20,000 | | 10,000 | | 30,000 |
| Rate of contribution to revenue | | 33.3% | | 40% | | 35.3% |

**41.8** *(cont'd)*

*(b)* Best product mix for next year:
Crowns manufactured per hour = 20,000/8,000 = 2.5 per hour
Kings manufactured per hour = 10,000/2,000 = 5 per hour
Kings gives best contribution rate, so produce Kings up to maximum requirements.

| | *Crowns* | | *Kings* | |
|---|---|---|---|---|
| | *Units* | *Hours* | *Units* | *Hours* |
| Minimum required | 6,000 ÷ 2.5 | 2,400 | 6,000 ÷ 5 | 1,200 |
| Produce up to maximum of 36,000 Kings | | | 30,000 ÷ 5 | 6,000 |
| | | 2,400 | | 7,200 |
| Still (10,000 − 7,200 − 2,400) = 400 hours left, left, so now produce Crowns | 1,000 ÷ 25 | 400 | | |
| | | 2,800 | | 7,200 |

Best mix is therefore: Crowns (6,000 + 1,000) = 7,000
Kings (6,000 + 30,000) = 36,000

Revenue therefore: 7,000 × £3 = 21,000 : 36,000 × £2.5 = 90,000

| | | | |
|---|---|---|---|
| Contributions: | Crowns (33.3%) | 7,000 | |
| | Kings (40%) | 36,000 | 43,000 |
| Floor space costs | | 15,000 | |
| Insurance | | 600 | 15,600 |
| Profit | | | 27,400 |

*(c)* Product mix with extra machine
As maximum requirements for Kings have already been met in *(b)*, all new output will be of Crowns.

| | *Crowns* | | *Kings* |
|---|---|---|---|
| Revenue (as before) in £ | 21,000 | | 90,000 |
| Extra (10,000 hours × 2.5) = 25,000 × £3 = | 75,000 | | |
| | 96,000 | | 90,000 |
| Contributions: Crowns (33.3%) | | 32,000 | |
| Kings (40%) | | 36,000 | 68,000 |
| Hire of extra machine | | 20,000 | |
| Floor space costs | | 15,000 | |
| Insurance | | 600 | 35,600 |
| | | | 32,400 |

*(d)* Briefly:
*(i)* Market demand maintained.
*(ii)* Flexibility of return of extra machine if demand falls.
*(iii)* To see if wholesaler will guarantee minimum orders.
*(iv)* Are there outlets possible other than wholesaler?
*(v)* Selling price to wholesaler.

**41.10**

*(a)*

**Paul Wagtail**
*Manufacturing Account and Statement of Profit or Loss for the year ending 30 April 2016*

| | | *Marginal method* | | *Absorption method* |
|---|---|---|---|---|
| Purchases of raw mats (125,000 − 2,100) | | 122,900 | | 122,900 |
| Carriage of raw materials | | 1,500 | | 1,500 |
| | | 124,400 | | 124,400 |
| *Less* Inventory raw materials | | 8,900 | | 8,900 |
| Cost of raw materials consumed | | 115,500 | | 115,500 |
| Production wages | | 105,270 | | 105,270 |
| Prime cost | | 220,770 | | 220,770 |
| Factory overhead expenses: | | | | |
| Factory power | 12,430 | | 12,430 | |
| Factory supervisors' wages | 29,600 | | 29,600 | |
| Factory repairs | 19,360 | | 19,360 | |
| Factory insurance (40%) | 1,920 | | 1,920 | |
| Factory heating & light (40%) | 1,440 | | 1,440 | |
| Depreciation of plant | 17,600 | 82,350 | 17,600 | 82,350 |
| | | 303,120 | | 303,120 |
| *Less* Work in progress (W1) | | 11,038 | | 15,156 |
| Production cost of goods completed c/d | | 292,082 | | 287,964 |
| Revenue | | 464,360 | | 464,360 |
| Production cost b/d | 292,082 | | 287,964 | |
| *Less* Inventory finished goods (W2) | 18,447 | 273,635 | 18,187 | 269,777 |
| Gross profit | | 190,725 | | 194,583 |
| *Less* Expenses: | | | | |
| Administration expenses | 46,700 | | 46,700 | |
| Distribution expenses | 25,400 | | 25,400 | |
| Selling expenses | 23,800 | | 23,800 | |
| Insurance (60%) | 2,880 | | 2,880 | |
| Heating and lighting (60%) | 2,160 | | 2,160 | |
| Depn: delivery vehicles | 35,200 | 136,140 | 35,200 | 136,140 |
| Net profit | | 54,585 | | 58,443 |

*Workings:*
(W1) 625 × 80% = 500 equivalent making total 9,500 + 500 = 10,000

Valuations: *Marginal* $\frac{500}{10,000} \times 220,770 = 11,038$

*Absorption* $\frac{500}{10,000} \times 303,120 = 15,156$

(W2) *Marginal* $\frac{600}{9,500} \times 292,082 = 18,447$

*Absorption* $\frac{600}{9,500} \times 287,964 = 18,187$

*(b) See* text.

**41.14**

(a)

| | K | L | M | N |
|---|---|---|---|---|
| Direct labour and materials | 28 | 56 | 120 | 64 |
| Variable overheads | 8 | 16 | 26 | 24 |
| Fixed overhead | 4 | 8 | 14 | 12 |
| Total cost per unit | 40 | 80 | 160 | 100 |
| *Add* Profit 20% | 8 | 16 | 32 | 20 |
| Selling price | 48 | 96 | 192 | 120 |

(b) Discontinue M. The others are above marginal cost whereas M is below it.

(c)

| | (i) Followed our advice | | (ii) Produced all items | |
|---|---|---|---|---|
| Revenue K 100 × £66 | 6,600 | | 6,600 | |
| L 100 × £78 | 7,800 | | 7,800 | |
| M 100 × £140 | – | | 14,000 | |
| N 100 × £98 | 9,800 | | 9,800 | |
| | 24,200 | | 38,200 | |
| *Less Costs* | | | | |
| Direct labour and materials | | | | |
| (i) (28 + 56 + 64) × 100 | 14,800 | | | |
| (ii) (28 + 56 + 120 + 64) × 100 | | | 26,800 | |
| Variable overhead | | | | |
| (i) (8 + 16 + 24) × 100 | 4,800 | | | |
| (ii) (8 + 16 + 26 + 24) × 100 | | | 7,400 | |
| Fixed overhead | 3,800 | | 3,800 | |
| | 23,400 | | 38,000 | |
| Net profit | 800 | | 200 | |

*Note*: The net profit or loss could have been worked out using contributions per items e.g. (i) Contributions per unit (i.e. Selling price *less* Marginal cost).

| | | |
|---|---|---|
| K 66 − (28 + 8) = 30 | | |
| L 78 − (56 + 16) = 6 | | |
| N 98 − (64 + 24) = 10 | 46 × 100 of each = | 4,600 |
| *Less* Fixed costs | | 3,800 |
| Net profit | | 800 |

In (ii) the contribution from M would be negative.

(d) Discontinue K and N. All other items are above marginal cost.

(e)

| | (i) Followed our advice | (ii) Produced all items |
|---|---|---|
| Revenue K 100 × £34 | – | 3,400 |
| L 100 × £96 | 9,600 | 9,600 |
| M 100 × £280 | 28,000 | 28,000 |
| N 100 × £78 | – | 7,800 |
| | 37,600 | 48,800 |
| *Less Costs* | | |
| Direct labour and materials | | |
| (i) (56 + 120) × 100 | 17,600 | |
| (ii) (28 + 56 + 120 + 64) × 100 | | 26,800 |
| Variable costs | | |
| (i) (16 + 26) × 100 | 4,200 | |
| (ii) (8 + 16 + 26 + 24) × 100 | | 7,400 |
| Fixed overhead | 3,800 | 3,800 |
| | 25,600 | 38,000 |
| Net profit | 12,000 | 10,800 |

**42.1**

| | *Production departments* | | | | *Service departments* | | |
|---|---|---|---|---|---|---|---|
| | A | B | C | D | K | L | M |
| Indirect lab. | 8,000 | 12,000 | 16,000 | 4,000 | 3,000 | 6,000 | 8,200 |
| Other exp. | 5,400 | 6,200 | 7,200 | 3,000 | 9,000 | 4,000 | 4,000 |
| | 13,400 | 18,200 | 23,200 | 7,000 | 12,000 | 10,000 | 12,200 |
| *Apportionment of costs:* | | | | | | | |
| Dept K | 2,400 | 3,000 | 3,600 | 1,800 | (12,000) | – | 1,200 |
| Dept L | 3,500 | – | 4,500 | 2,000 | – | (10,000) | – |
| | | | | | | | 13,400 |
| Dept M | – | 5,360 | 3,350 | 4,690 | | | (13,400) |
| | 19,300 | 26,560 | 34,650 | 15,490 | – | – | – |

(a) Overhead rates per direct labour hour

Department A $£\frac{19,300}{4,000} = £4.825$

Department C $£\frac{34,650}{8,900} = £3.89$

(b) Overhead rates per machine hour

Department B $£\frac{26,560}{5,200} = £5.11$

Department D $£\frac{15,490}{4,800} = £3.23$

**42.2**

*Job Cost Sheet Job 351 Dept. A*

| | | |
|---|---|---|
| Direct materials | | 760.00 |
| Direct labour | 112 × £5 | 560.00 |
| Factory overhead | 112 × £4.825 | 540.40 |
| | | 1,860.40 |

*Job Cost Sheet Job 352 Dept. B*

| | | |
|---|---|---|
| Direct materials | | 3,597.00 |
| Direct labour | 256 × £4 | 1,024.00 |
| Factory overhead | 252 × £5.11 | 1,287.72 |
| | | 5,908.72 |

*Job Cost Sheet Job 353 Dept. C*

| | | |
|---|---|---|
| Direct materials | | 2,000.00 |
| Direct labour | 390 × £6 | 2,340.00 |
| Factory overhead | 390 × £3.89 | 1,517.10 |
| | | 5,857.10 |

*Job Cost Sheet Job 354 Dept. D*

| | | |
|---|---|---|
| Direct materials | | 1,998.00 |
| Direct labour | 180 × £6 | 1,080.00 |
| Direct overhead | 128 × £3.23 | 413.44 |
| | | 3,491.44 |

*Job Cost Sheet Job 355 Depts. C and B*

| | | |
|---|---|---|
| Dept C Direct materials | | 1,680.00 |
| Direct labour | 320 × £6 | 1,920.00 |
| Factory overhead | 320 × £3.89 | 1,244.80 |
| Dept B Direct materials | | 204.00 |
| Direct labour | 60 × £4 | 240.00 |
| Factory overhead | 40 × £5.11 | 204.40 |
| | | 5,493.20 |

**42.5**

(*a*) *See* text, Section 42.5.

(*b*) (*i*)

| | Materials | | Labour | | Overhead | |
|---|---|---|---|---|---|---|
| Finished items | 4,000 | | 4,000 | | 4,000 | |
| WIP (600) | 540 | (90%) | 450 | (75%) | 330 | (55%) |
| Total units | 4,540 | | 4,450 | | 4,330 | |

(*ii*) Cost per complete unit

| | | | |
|---|---|---|---|
| Material | £8,172 ÷ 4,540 = | 1.80 | |
| Labour | £7,120 ÷ 4,450 = | 1.60 | |
| Overhead | £5,196 ÷ 4,330 = | 1.20 | £4.60 |

(*iii*) Value of work-in-progress

| | | | | |
|---|---|---|---|---|
| Material | 540 × 1.80 | = | 972 | |
| Labour | 450 × 1.60 | = | 720 | |
| Overhead | 330 × 1.20 | = | 396 | £2,088 |

**42.7**

(*a*) Allotment: where overheads traced directly to units.
Apportionment: where overheads not directly traceable and have to be apportioned between units.
Absorption rates: the total amount of overheads calculated as being charged to each unit.

(*b*) Because the figures belong to the future and therefore cannot be known precisely.

(*c*) (*i*) and (*ii*). Note that parts (*i*) and (*ii*) illustrate two different methods in use. The method in (*iii*) is not in the text.
Continuous apportionment (repeated distribution) method:

| *Line* | *Production departments* A | | B | | C | | *Service departments* X | | Y |
|---|---|---|---|---|---|---|---|---|---|
| 1 Allocation per analysis | 14,000 | | 12,000 | | 8,000 | | 4,000 | | 3,000 |
| 2 Allocation of X (4,000) (35%) | 1,400 | (30%) | 1,200 | (20%) | 800 | | (4,000) | (15%) | 600 |
| | | | | | | | | | 3,600 |
| 3 Allocation of Y (3,600) (30%) | 1,080 | (40%) | 1,440 | (25%) | 900 | (5%) | 180 | | (3,600) |
| 4 Allocation of X (180) (35%) | 63 | (30%) | 54 | (20%) | 36 | | (180) | (15%) | 27 |
| 5 Allocation of Y (27) (30%) | 8 | (40%) | 12* | (25%) | 7 | (5%) | 0 | | (27) |
| | 16,551 | | 14,706 | | 9,743 | | (= total 41,000) | | |

*Rounded

*Explanation*:
Steps:
(1) Allocate X overheads to others by % shown.
(2) Allocate Y overheads to others by % shown.
Keep repeating (1) and (2) until the figures left under X and Y are insignificant.

(*iii*) Elimination method:

| *Line* | *Production departments* A | | B | | C | *Service departments* X | | Y |
|---|---|---|---|---|---|---|---|---|
| 1 Allocation per analysis | 14,000 | | 12,000 | | 8,000 | 4,000 | | 3,000 |
| 2 Allocate service (35%) dept X | 1,400 | (30%) | 1,200 | (20%) | 800 | (4,000) | (15%) | 600 |
| | | | | | | – | | |
| 3 Allocate service dept Y (30/95) | 1,137 | (40/95) | 1,516 | (25/95) | 947 | | | (3,600) |
| | 16,537 | | 14,716 | | 9,747 | (= total 41,000) | | – |

*Explanation*:
Steps:

(1) Allocate service department overheads which does largest proportion of work for other departments, i.e. department X.
(2) Allocate next service department per (1), in this case is only Y.
(3) When doing (2) nothing is charged to service departments already allocated, i.e. in this case X.
(4) Note that since (3) happens the ratios in the next allocation change. As X 5% of Y is not returned then A gets 30/95 of Y, not 30% and so on.

(*iv*) The answer will depend on whichever approach is adopted. No one can categorically state which method is the most accurate; there is no 'ideal' method.

**42.9**

(*a*) and (*b*) *See* text.

(*c*) (*i*) *Batch No. 23*

| | |
|---|---|
| Raw materials 300 × 1.60 | 480 |
| Direct labour 4.20 × 20 hours | 84 |
| Setting up of machine | 21 |
| Overheads 3.60 × 20 hours | 72 |
| Total cost | 657 |

Cost per unit 657 ÷ 300 = £2.19

(*ii*) *Batch No. 23*

| | | |
|---|---|---|
| Raw materials 300 × 1.60 | 480.00 | |
| *Less* Received for scrap 20 × 0.86 | 17.20 | 462.80 |
| Direct labour: | | |
| Normal 20 × 4.20 | 84.00 | |
| Rectification 9 × 4.20 | 37.80 | 121.80 |
| Setting up: | | |
| Normal | 21.00 | |
| Rectification | 18.00 | 39.00 |
| Overheads: Running time 3.60 × 20 | 72.00 | |
| Rectification 3.60 × 9 | 32.40 | 104.40 |
| | | 728.00 |

Per usable unit £728 ÷ 280 = 2.60

| | |
|---|---|
| (*iii*) Loss because of extra costs 728 − 657 = | 71.00 |
| Loss because of faulty products 657 × 20/300 | 43.80 |
| | 114.80 |

**43.1** *See* text, Section 43.8, the main assumption is that consumption, ordering costs, and storage/holding cost remain constant.

**43.2**

| | *July* | *Aug* | *Sept* | *Oct* | *Nov* | *Dec* |
|---|---|---|---|---|---|---|
| Opening inventory | 148 | 138 | 156 | 220 | 280 | 232 |
| *Add* Production | 150 | 202 | 282 | 324 | 248 | 160 |
| | 298 | 340 | 438 | 544 | 528 | 392 |
| *Less* Sales | 160 | 184 | 218 | 264 | 296 | 204 |
| Closing inventory | 138 | 156 | 220 | 280 | 232 | 188 |

**43.3**

| | | | |
|---|---|---|---|
| (*a*) Opening inventory | | | 144 |
| *Add* Production | ? | (C) | |
| | | (B) | |
| *Less* Sales total – *see* question | | | 4,650 |
| Closing inventory | | | 150 |

Missing figure (B) must be 4,800
Missing figure (C) must then be 4,656
Equal production per month 4,656 ÷ 12 = 388 units.

(*b*) Given figures per (*a*)

| | J | F | M | A | M | J | J | A | S | O | N | D |
|---|---|---|---|---|---|---|---|---|---|---|---|---|
| Opening inventory | 144 | 202 | 50 | 128 | 66 | 94 | 182 | 360 | 458 | 336 | 394 | 332 |
| *Add* Production | 388 | 388 | 388 | 388 | 388 | 388 | 388 | 388 | 388 | 388 | 388 | 388 |
| | 532 | 590 | 438 | 516 | 454 | 482 | 570 | 748 | 846 | 724 | 782 | 720 |
| *Less* Sales | 330 | 540 | 310 | 450 | 360 | 300 | 210 | 290 | 510 | 330 | 450 | 570 |
| Closing inventory | 202 | 50 | 128 | 66 | 94 | 182 | 360 | 458 | 336 | 394 | 332 | 150 |

Lowest closing figure is 50 units in February. It is also below 80 in April. If inventory is not to fall below 80 units an extra 80 − 50 = 30 units will have to be produced in February, making production for that month of 418 units; and an extra 14 will need to be produced in April, making production for that month 402 units.

**43.4**

(*a*) Using EOQ, the average annual sales are (420 + 480 + 440 + 520 + 490) ÷ 5 = 470. Therefore,

C = 470
O = £80
S = £0.05 × 365 = £18.25

$$\text{and EOQ} = \sqrt{\frac{2 \times 470 \times 80}{18.25}}$$

$$= \sqrt{\frac{75{,}200}{18.25}}$$

= 64.2
= 64 gowns

(*b*) No. Demand is seasonal and ordering in batches of 64 gowns when demand peaks three times a year would result in high levels of increasing inveritory during three periods each year. Another approach should be adopted instead of EOQ.

**44.1**

(*a*)

*Took: Cash Budget*

| | May | Jun | Jul | Aug | Sept | Oct |
|---|---|---|---|---|---|---|
| Balance b/d | 200 | 10,800 | 8,800 | 2,800 | | |
| Overdraft b/d | | | | | 13,200 | 19,200 |
| Receipts from debtors | 800 | 8,000 | 16,000 | 24,000 | 18,000 | 10,000 |
| Capital | 10,000 | | | | | |
| | 11,000 | 18,800 | 24,800 | 26,800 | 4,800 | (9,200) |
| Payments | 200 | 10,000 | 22,000 | 40,000 | 24,000 | 14,000 |
| Balance c/d | 10,800 | 8,800 | 2,800 | | | |
| Overdraft c/d | | | | 13,200 | 19,200 | (23,200) |

(*b*) There are the possibilities of delaying payments to creditors, delaying purchases or somehow getting debtors to pay up more quickly. Apart from these it is possible that a credit factoring firm could help in 'buying' the amounts of accounts receivable from Ukridge.

If none of these is possible only a really fantastic product could warrant interest at 70% per annum. This would rarely be the case, although there are many people whose optimism about their products exceeds their true potential profitability.

**44.2**

*F. Jack: Cash Budget*

| | Jul | Aug | Sept | Oct | Nov | Dec |
|---|---|---|---|---|---|---|
| Balance b/d | 3,600 | 12,309 | 12,765 | 25,518 | 30,906 | 56,997 |
| Receipts | 57,600 | 52,200 | 72,000 | 54,000 | 70,500* | 72,000 |
| | 61,200 | 64,509 | 84,765 | 79,518 | 101,406 | 128,997 |
| Payments (see schedule) | 48,891 | 51,744 | 59,247 | 48,612 | 44,409 | 37,965 |
| Balance c/d | 12,309 | 12,765 | 25,518 | 30,906 | 56,997 | 91,032 |

*Includes £7,500 legacy

Payments schedule

| | *July* | | *Aug* | |
|---|---|---|---|---|
| Raw materials | 1,050 (Jul) × £13.5 | 14,175 | 1,110 (Aug) × £13.5 | 14,985 |
| | 960 (Jun) × £1.5 | 1,440 | 1,050 (July) × £1.5 | 15,750 |
| Direct labour | 1,050 × £24 | 25,200 | 1,110 × £24 | 26,640 |
| Variable | 960 × £3.6 + 1,050 × £2.40 | 5,976 | 1,050 × £3.6 + 1,110 × £2.40 | 6,444 |
| Fixed expenses | | 1,200 | | 1,200 |
| Drawings | | 900 | | 900 |
| | | 48,891 | | 65,919 |

| | *Sept* | | *Oct* | |
|---|---|---|---|---|
| Raw materials | 1,140 (Sept) × £13.5 | 15,390 | 1,020 (Oct) × £13.5 | 13,770 |
| | 1,110 (Aug) × £1.5 | 1,665 | 1,140 (Sep) × £1.5 | 1,710 |
| Direct labour | 1,140 × £24 | 27,360 | 1,020 × £24 | 24,480 |
| Variable | 1,110 × £3.6 + 1,140 × £2.4 | 6,732 | 1,140 × £3.6 + 1,020 × £2.4 | 6,552 |
| Fixed expenses | | 1,200 | | 1,200 |
| Drawings | | 900 | | 900 |
| Machinery | | 6,000 | | |
| | | 59,247 | | 48,612 |

| | *Nov* | | *Dec* | |
|---|---|---|---|---|
| Raw materials | 930 (Nov) × £13.5 | 12,555 | 780 (Dec) × £13.5 | 10,530 |
| | 1,020 (Oct) × £1.5 | 1,530 | 930 (Nov) × £1.5 | 1,395 |
| Direct labour | 930 × £24 | 22,320 | 780 × £24 | 18,720 |
| Variable | 1,020 × £3.6 + 930 × £2.4 | 5,904 | 930 × £3.6 + 780 × £2.4 | 5,220 |
| Fixed expenses | | 1,200 | | 1,200 |
| Drawings | | 900 | | 900 |
| | | 44,409 | | 37,965 |

**44.3**

(*a*)

*Cash Budget*

| | July | Aug | Sept |
|---|---|---|---|
| *Receipts* | | | |
| Cash sales (W1) | 9,600 | 4,800 | 7,200 |
| Credit sales (W2) | 17,640 | 14,112 | 7,056 |
| | 27,240 | 18,912 | 14,256 |
| *Payments* | | | |
| Purchases | 3,600 | 5,400 | 8,100 |
| Direct labour | 1,600 | 2,400 | 3,600 |
| Direct production expenses | 4,800 | 2,400 | 3,600 |
| Variable selling expenses | 4,000 | 3,200 | 1,600 |
| Fixed expenses | 1,820 | 1,820 | 1,820 |
| | 15,820 | 15,220 | 18,720 |
| Balance start of month | 3,900 | 15,320 | 19,012 |
| Balance at end of month | 15,320 | 19,012 | 14,548 |

| | | |
|---|---|---|
| (W1) | July | 800 × 40% × £30 = 9,600 |
| | August | 400 × 40% × £30 = 4,800 |
| | September | 600 × 40% × £30 = 7,200 |
| (W2) | July | 1,000 × 60% × £30 = 18,000 − 2% = 17,640 |
| | August | 800 × 60% × £30 = 14,400 − 2% = 14,112 |
| | September | 400 × 60% × £30 = 7,200 − 2% = 7,056 |

(*b*) (*i*) Can forecast when and if money needs to be borrowed.

(*ii*) Can forecast when surplus funds are available so that they can be invested elsewhere.

(*iii*) To use as basis when dealing with supplier as to creditworthiness or bank for borrowing powers.

**44.5**

| *Receipts* | *July* | *Aug* | *Sept* | *Oct* |
|---|---|---|---|---|
| Sales this month 20% | | 9,000 | 9,000 | 9,000 |
| Sales last month 70% | | | 31,500 | 31,500 |
| Sales two months ago 10% | | | | 4,500 |
| Other receipts from debtors | 40,000 | 32,000 | 4,000 | |
| | 40,000 | 41,000 | 44,500 | 45,000 |
| *Payments* | | | | |
| Wages | 2,000 | 2,000 | 2,000 | 2,000 |
| Bank loan and interest | 242 | 242 | 242 | 242 |
| Drawings | 500 | 500 | 500 | 500 |
| Purchases | 34,000 | 38,250 | 38,250 | 45,750 |
| PAYE tax | 500 | 500 | 500 | 500 |
| Rent | 1,250 | | | 1,250 |
| Rates | | | | 2,250 |
| Value added tax | 5,000 | | | 3,950 |
| Motor van | | 8,150 | | |
| | 43,492 | 49,642 | 41,492 | 56,442 |
| *Current account balances* | | | | |
| Start of month | 5,000 | 1,508 | (7,134) | (4,126) |
| End of month | 1,508 | (7,134) | (4,126) | (15,568) |

**44.6**

(*a*) In brief:

Current ratio of 210,000 : 150,000 = 1.4 : 1

Acid test ratio not known. Very dangerous situation because if bank manager asks for repayment of overdraft it is unlikely it can be repaid in the short term.

Profits get ploughed back into the company in all sorts of ways, e.g. extra non-current assets, more inventory. It has no direct connection with the balance at the bank. (Use cash flow statements as an illustration.)

(*b*)

*Cash Budget*

| *Receipts* | *Apr* | *May* | *June* | *July* |
|---|---|---|---|---|
| Cash sales | 40,000 | 40,000 | 40,000 | 40,000 |
| Credit sales | 65,000 | 70,000 | 70,000 | 70,000 |
| | 105,000 | 110,000 | 110,000 | 110,000 |
| *Payments* | | | | |
| Purchases | 60,000 | 58,000 | 61,000 | 55,000 |
| Selling and administration | 5,700 | 6,600 | 6,600 | 6,600 |
| Administration charges | 10,000 | 10,000 | 10,000 | 13,500 |
| Final dividend 2016/17 | | 7,500 | | |
| Interim dividend 2017/18 | | | | 4,000 |
| | 75,700 | 82,100 | 77,600 | 79,100 |
| Balance overdraft start of month | (150,000) | (120,700) | (92,800) | (60,400) |
| Balance overdraft end of month | (120,700) | (92,800) | (60,400) | (29,500) |

(*c*) Would seem to be proceeding satisfactorily to eliminate overdraft.
Could be further reduced by:
(*i*) Issuing new shares
(*ii*) Getting debtors to pay more quickly
(*iii*) Delaying payment of creditors
(*iv*) Selling off non-current assets
(*v*) Issuing loan notes

**44.9**

A cash budget is the same thing as a cash flow forecast: they are two terms for the same thing. They are prepared in order to identify cash surpluses and deficits during a period of time in the future. Doing so enables additional funds to be sourced when they are likely to be required and enables surplus cash to be used productively when it would otherwise be idle. Examples and a fuller description can be seen in the text of Chapter 44.

A statement of cash flows is prepared to show what caused the balance of cash and cash equivalents to change between two dates in the past. Examples and a fuller description can be found in Chapter 15.

**45.1**

| (*a*) *Inventory Budget 2017* | | *Aug* | *Sept* | *Oct* | *Nov* |
|---|---|---|---|---|---|
| Opening inventory | (A) | 5,000* | 7,000 | 8,000 | 7,000 |
| *Add* Purchases | (B) | 20,000 | 23,500 | 21,500 | 31,000 |
| | (C) | 25,000 | 30,500 | 29,500 | 38,000 |
| *Less* Cost of sales | (D) | 18,000 | 22,500 | 22,500 | 27,000 |
| Closing inventory | (E) | 7,000 | 8,000 | 7,000 | 11,000 |

*After special sale of £8,000 goods at cost.

To work out missing figures:
August (A) is known. (D) is 24,000 − 25%

Therefore, as inventory turnover is 3, $\frac{\text{(D) } 18{,}000}{[\text{(A) } 5{,}000 + \text{(E) question}] \div 2} = 3$

Therefore bottom line is 6,000 so (E) must be 7,000.
Repeat following months.

| (*b*) *Cash Budget 2017* | *Aug* | *Sept* | *Oct* | *Nov* |
|---|---|---|---|---|
| *Receipts:* | | | | |
| Capital | 10,000 | | | |
| Soul's accounts receivable | 20,250 | | | |
| Accounts receivable | – | – | 24,000 | 30,000 |
| Special sale | 8,000 | | | |
| | 38,250 | – | 24,000 | 30,000 |
| *Payments:* | | | | |
| Accounts payable | 10,000 | 20,000 | 23,500 | 21,500 |
| General expenses | 700 | 700 | 700 | 700 |
| | 10,700 | 20,700 | 24,200 | 22,200 |
| *Bank:* Opening | (20,000) | 7,550 | (13,150) | (13,350) |
| Closing | 7,550 | (13,150) | (13,350) | (5,550) |

**45.3**

(*a*)

| *Cash Budget* | *July* | *Aug* | *Sept* | *Oct* | *Nov* | *Dec* |
|---|---|---|---|---|---|---|
| Opening balance | 30,000 | | | | | 18,000 |
| Opening overdraft | | (36,460) | (27,770) | (17,680) | (2,810) | |
| Received (*see* schedule) | 7,200 | 10,800 | 16,400 | 21,600 | 28,800 | 34,400 |
| | 37,200 | (25,660) | (11,370) | 3,920 | 25,990 | 52,400 |
| Payments (*see* schedule) | 73,660 | 2,110 | 6,310 | 6,730 | 7,990 | 9,460 |
| Closing balance | (36,460) | (27,770) | (17,680) | (2,810) | 18,000 | 42,940 |
| Closing overdraft | | | | | | |

| *Cash Receipts Schedule* | *July* | *Aug* | *Sept* | *Oct* | *Nov* | *Dec* |
|---|---|---|---|---|---|---|
| Cash sales | 7,200 | 10,800 | 14,400 | 18,000 | 23,400 | 25,200 |
| Credit sales | – | – | – | 3,600 | 5,400 | 7,200 |
| Rent received | | | 2,000 | | | 2,000 |
| | 7,200 | 10,800 | 16,400 | 21,600 | 28,800 | 34,400 |

| *Cash Payments Schedule* | *July* | *Aug* | *Sept* | *Oct* | *Nov* | *Dec* |
|---|---|---|---|---|---|---|
| Drawings | 1,400 | 1,400 | 1,400 | 1,400 | 1,400 | 1,400 |
| Premises | 60,000 | | | | | |
| Shop fixtures | 4,000 | | | | | |
| Motor van | 8,000 | | | | | |
| Salaries of assistants | 260 | 260 | 260 | 260 | 260 | 260 |
| Payments to creditors | | | 4,200 | 4,620 | 5,880 | 7,350 |
| Other expenses | | 450 | 450 | 450 | 450 | 450 |
| | 73,660 | 2,110 | 6,310 | 6,730 | 7,990 | 9,460 |

(*b*)

**F Tain**

*Forecast Statement of Profit or Los for the six months ending 31 December 2018*

| | | |
|---|---|---|
| Revenue | | 148,500 |
| *Less* Cost of goods sold: | | |
| Purchases | 39,570 | |
| *Less* Closing inventory (390 × £8) | 3,120 | 36,450 |
| Gross profit | | 112,050 |
| *Add* Rent received | | 4,000 |
| | | 116,050 |
| *Less* Expenses: | | |
| Assistants' salaries | 1,560 | |
| Other expenses | 2,700 | |
| Depreciation: Premises | 1,500 | |
| Shop fixtures | 300 | |
| Motor van | 1,000 | 7,060 |
| Net profit | | 108,990 |

*Forecast Statement of Financial Position as at 31 December 2018*

| *Non-current assets* | *Cost* | *Depn* | *NBV* |
|---|---|---|---|
| Premises | 60,000 | 1,500 | 58,500 |
| Shop fixtures | 4,000 | 300 | 3,700 |
| Motor van | 8,000 | 1,000 | 7,000 |
| | 72,000 | 2,800 | 69,200 |
| *Current assets* | | | |
| Inventory | | 3,120 | |
| Accounts receivable | | 33,300 | |
| Bank | | 42,940 | 79,360 |
| Current liabilities | | | 148,560 |
| Accounts payable | | 17,520 | |
| Other expenses owing | | 450 | (17,970) |
| Working capital | | | 130,590 |
| *Financed by:* | | | |
| Capital | | | |
| Cash introduced | | | 30,000 |
| *Add* Net profit | | | 108,990 |
| | | | 138,990 |
| *Less* Drawings | | | (8,400) |
| | | | 130,590 |

**45.6**

(*a*)

**Issa Ltd**

*Budgeted Statement of Profit or Los for the year ending 31 December 2018*

| | | £000 |
|---|---|---|
| Revenue | | 900.0 |
| *Less* Cost of goods sold | | |
| Opening inventory | 80.0 | |
| Purchases (difference) | 570.0 | |
| | 650.0 | |
| *Less* Closing inventory | 65.0 | 585.0 |
| Gross profit | | 315.0 |
| *Less* Expenses | | |
| Administration expenses | 63.6 | |
| Selling and distribution expenses (54 + 15) | 69.0 | |
| Financial charges | 20.8 | |
| Allowance for doubtful debts | 2.5 | |
| Depreciation | 60.0 | 215.9 |
| | | 99.1 |
| Gain on sale of land and buildings | | 150.0 |
| Profit for the year | | 249.1 |
| *Note:* Bonus share issue | 50.0 | |
| Preference share dividends | 9.0 | |
| Ordinary dividend | 7.5 | |
| Total appropriation of retained profits | 66.5 | |

*(b) Budgeted Statement of Financial Position as at 31 December 2018*

| | £000 | £000 | £000 |
|---|---|---|---|
| Non-current assets at cost (750 − 50) | | 700.0 | |
| *Less* Depreciation to date | | 204.0 | 496.0 |
| Investment in Yates Ltd at cost | | | 100.0 |
| | | | 596.0 |
| *Current assets* | | | |
| Inventory | | 65.0 | |
| Trade accounts receivable | 100.0 | | |
| *Less* Allowance for doubtful debts | 7.5 | 92.5 | |
| Bank | | 350.1 | 507.6 |
| *Total assets* | | | 1,103.6 |
| *Current liabilities* | | | |
| Trade accounts payable | | 56.0 | |
| Expense accounts payable | | 15.0 | (71.0) |
| | | | 1,032.6 |
| *Equity* | | | |
| Ordinary share capital (200 + 100) | | | 300.0 |
| Share premium (150 − 50) | | | 100.0 |
| 9% Preference shares | | | 100.0 |
| Retained profits (350.0 + 249.1 − 66.5) | | | 532.6 |
| | | | 1,032.6 |

(c) Advantages:

(i) Business can establish desired profit in advance. It can then take necessary action to try to achieve it.
Desired ROCE can be set as target.
Also helps in forecasting dividends/planning for taxation purposes/organising necessary finance/for use with financial backers.

(ii) Manage working capital to ensure its sufficiency when needed.
Manage cash balances to seek overdrafts/loans from bank when needed.
Ensure accounts payable are paid on time to gain discounts. Invest surpluses as and when they may occur.

**45.7** *Cash Payments Schedule*

| | Jul | Aug | Sept | Oct | Nov | Dec |
|---|---|---|---|---|---|---|
| Direct materials | 300 | 240 | 1,100 | 1,000 | 800 | 700 |
| Direct labour | 2,700 | 2,700 | 2,700 | 2,700 | 2,700 | 2,700 |
| Variable indirect manufacturing expenses | 1,050 | 1,800 | 1,800 | 1,800 | 1,800 | 1,800 |
| Fixed indirect manufacturing expenses | 450 | 450 | 450 | 450 | 450 | 450 |
| Machine | 2,500 | | | | | |
| Motor vehicle | | | 10,000 | | | |
| | 7,000 | 5,190 | 16,050 | 5,950 | 5,750 | 5,650 |

*Cash Receipts Schedule*

| | Jul | Aug | Sept | Oct | Nov | Dec |
|---|---|---|---|---|---|---|
| Loan notes | | | | | 25,000 | |
| Receipts from accounts receivable | 9,500 | 6,000 | 8,000 | 10,000 | 10,500 | 9,450 |
| | 9,500 | 6,000 | 8,000 | 10,000 | 35,500 | 9,450 |

(a) *Cash Budget (£)*

| | Jul | Aug | Sept | Oct | Nov | Dec |
|---|---|---|---|---|---|---|
| Opening balance | 35,500 | 38,000 | 38,810 | 30,760 | 34,810 | 64,560 |
| *Add* Receipts | 9,500 | 6,000 | 8,000 | 10,000 | 35,500 | 9,450 |
| | 45,000 | 44,000 | 46,810 | 40,760 | 70,310 | 74,010 |
| *Less* Payments | 7,000 | 5,190 | 16,050 | 5,950 | 5,750 | 5,650 |
| Closing balance | 38,000 | 38,810 | 30,760 | 34,810 | 64,560 | 68,360 |

(b) *Accounts Receivable Budget (£)*

| | Jul | Aug | Sept | Oct | Nov | Dec |
|---|---|---|---|---|---|---|
| Opening balance | 9,500 | 6,000 | 8,000 | 10,000 | 10,500 | 9,450 |
| *Add* Sales | 6,000 | 8,000 | 10,000 | 10,500 | 9,450 | 7,350 |
| | 15,500 | 14,000 | 18,000 | 20,500 | 19,950 | 16,800 |
| *Less* Receipts | 9,500 | 6,000 | 8,000 | 10,000 | 10,500 | 9,450 |
| Closing balance | 6,000 | 8,000 | 10,000 | 10,500 | 9,450 | 7,350 |

(c) *Accounts Payable Budget (£)*

| | Jul | Aug | Sept | Oct | Nov | Dec |
|---|---|---|---|---|---|---|
| Opening balance | 540 | 1,340 | 2,100 | 1,800 | 1,500 | 1,400 |
| *Add* Purchases | 1,100 | 1,000 | 800 | 700 | 700 | 900 |
| | 1,640 | 2,340 | 2,900 | 2,500 | 2,200 | 2,300 |
| *Less* Payments | 300 | 240 | 1,100 | 1,000 | 800 | 700 |
| Closing balance | 1,340 | 2,100 | 1,800 | 1,500 | 1,400 | 1,600 |

(d) *Raw Materials Budget (£)*

| | Jul | Aug | Sept | Oct | Nov | Dec |
|---|---|---|---|---|---|---|
| Opening inventory | 1,500 | 1,700 | 1,800 | 1,700 | 1,500 | 1,300 |
| *Add* Purchases | 1,100 | 1,000 | 800 | 700 | 700 | 900 |
| | 2,600 | 2,700 | 2,600 | 2,400 | 2,200 | 2,200 |
| *Less* Used in production | 900 | 900 | 900 | 900 | 900 | 900 |
| Closing inventory | 1,700 | 1,800 | 1,700 | 1,500 | 1,300 | 1,300 |

**45.7** *(cont'd)*

**Pies and Cakes Ltd**

(e) *Forecast Operating Statement for the six months ending 31 December 2018*

| | | | | |
|---|---|---|---|---|
| Revenue | | | | 51,300 |
| *Less* Cost of goods sold | | | | |
| Opening inventory finished goods | | | 6,840 | |
| *Add* Cost of goods completed (£12 × 2,700) | | | 32,400 | |
| | | | 39,240 | |
| *Less* Closing inventory finished goods (£12 × 770) | | | 9,240 | 30,000 |
| Gross profit | | | | 21,300 |
| *Less* Expenses | | | | |
| Fixed indirect manufacturing expenses | | | 2,700 | |
| Depreciation: Buildings | 15,000 | | | |
| Plant and machinery | 5,000 | | | |
| Motor vehicles | 4,000 | | | |
| Office fixtures | 220 | 24,220 | | 26,920 |
| Net loss | | | | (5,620) |

(f) *Forecast Statement of Financial Position as at 31 December 2018*

| *Non-current assets* | | | |
|---|---|---|---|
| Tangible assets | *Cost* | *Acc Depn* | *NBV* |
| Buildings | 300,000 | 135,000 | 165,000 |
| Plant and machinery | 52,500 | 35,000 | 17,500 |
| Motor vehicles | 40,000 | 18,000 | 22,000 |
| Office fixtures | 2,500 | 1,320 | 1,180 |
| | 395,000 | 189,320 | 205,680 |
| *Current assets* | | | |
| Inventory: Finished goods | | 9,240 | |
| Raw materials | | 1,300 | |
| Accounts receivable | | 7,350 | |
| Cash and bank | | 68,360 | 86,250 |
| | | | 291,930 |
| *Current liabilities* | | | |
| Accounts payable for raw materials | | 1,600 | |
| Accounts payable for variable indirect manufacturing overheads | | 1,800 | |
| | | 3,400 | |
| *Non-current liabilities* | | | |
| Loan notes | | 25,000 | |
| Total liabilities | | | (28,400) |
| Net assets | | | 263,530 |
| *Equity* | | | |
| Called-up share capital | | | 225,000 |
| Retained profits (44,150 − 5,620) | | | 38,530 |
| | | | 263,530 |

**45.8**

| (A) (a) *Accounts receivable budget* | *July* | *Aug* | *Sept* | *Oct* |
|---|---|---|---|---|
| Balances from last month | 52,250 | 52,250 | 49,500 | 51,750 |
| *Add* Credit sales | 24,750 | 24,750 | 27,000 | 33,000 |
| | 77,000 | 77,000 | 76,500 | 84,750 |
| *Less* Paid by debtors | 24,750 | 27,500 | 24,750 | 24,750 |
| Balances at end of month | 52,250 | 49,500 | 51,750 | 60,000 |

*Note*: Sales are July 900, Aug 900, Sept 900, Oct 1,100. October is taken to be June figure + 10%.

| (b) *Raw material budget* (in kg) | July | Aug | Sept | Oct |
|---|---|---|---|---|
| Inventory from last month | 1,800 | 1,800 | 1,800 | 2,200 |
| *Add* purchases | 1,800 | 1,800 | 2,200 | 2,200 |
| | 3,600 | 3,600 | 4,000 | 4,400 |
| *Less* Used | 1,800 | 1,800 | 1,800 | 2,200 |
| Inventory at end of month | 1,800 | 1,800 | 2,200 | 2,200 |

B *See* text, Section 43.8

$$\text{EOQ} = \sqrt{\frac{2 \times 12{,}000 \times £10}{£6}} = 200 \text{ units}$$

(*i*) Based on estimates which obviously can vary a lot from actual.
(*ii*) Consumption may be uneven at times; EOQ assumes even usage.
(*iii*) Such things as strikes, catastrophes, etc. can render it useless.

**45.9**

A *Workings*:

1 Raw materials 294,400 ÷ 64,000 = 4.6 per unit
2 Direct labour 236,800 ÷ 64,000 = 3.7 per unit
3 Power 38,400 ÷ 64,000 = 0.60 per unit
4 Repairs are 51,200 − 25% × (12,800) = 48,000 fixed.
Variable 12,800 ÷ 64,000 = 0.20
5 Indirect wages 64,000 − 15% × (9,600) = 62,560 fixed.
Variable 9,600 ÷ 64,000 = 0.15.

**Bedford Ltd**

*Flexible Budget at Varying Levels of Production*

| | *Level of Production* | | | | | | |
|---|---|---|---|---|---|---|---|
| | 60% | 70% | 75% | 90% | 85% | *Actual* | *Variance* |
| *Units* | 48,000 | 56,000 | 60,000 | 72,000 | 68,000 | 68,000 | +(−) |
| *Variable costs* (£) | | | | | | | |
| Raw materials | 220,800 | 257,600 | 276,000 | 331,200 | 312,800 | 310,750 | 2,050 |
| Direct labour | 177,600 | 207,200 | 222,000 | 266,400 | 251,600 | 249,100 | 2,500 |
| Power | 28,800 | 33,600 | 36,000 | 43,200 | 40,800 | 39,800 | 1,000 |
| Repairs and maintenance | 9,600 | 11,200 | 12,000 | 14,400 | 13,600 | 14,650 | (1,050) |
| Indirect wages | 7,200 | 8,400 | 9,000 | 10,800 | 10,200 | 10,850 | (650) |
| | 444,000 | 518,000 | 555,000 | 666,000 | 629,000 | 625,150 | 3,850 |

**45.9** *(cont'd)*

| *Fixed costs* | | | | | | | |
|---|---|---|---|---|---|---|---|
| Repairs and maintenance | 48,000 | 48,000 | 48,000 | 48,000 | 48,000 | 48,000 | – |
| Insurance | 1,300 | 1,300 | 1,300 | 1,300 | 1,300 | 1,350 | (50) |
| Heating/lighting | 1,250 | 1,250 | 1,250 | 1,250 | 1,250 | 1,200 | 50 |
| Indirect wages | 62,560 | 62,560 | 62,560 | 62,560 | 62,560 | 62,560 | – |
| | 13,110 | 13,110 | 13,110 | 13,110 | 13,110 | 13,110 | – |
| *Total costs* | 557,110 | 631,110 | 668,110 | 779,110 | 742,110 | 734,260 | 3,850 |

Briefly: generally efficient as most variances are favourable. Comment in detail on each variance.

B *See text.*

**46.1**

| *(a) Standard cost per unit* | X | | Y | | Z | |
|---|---|---|---|---|---|---|
| Material 1 | | | 1.8 | | 2.4 | |
| Material 2 | 0.6 | | 2.1 | | | |
| Material 3 | 3.0 | | 2.5 | | 1.5 | |
| Material 4 | 0.4 | 4.0 | — | 6.4 | 0.9 | 4.8 |
| Labour: Dept A | 4.0 | | 2.4 | | 4.8 | |
| Dept B | 3.0 | 7.0 | 1.8 | 4.2 | 3.6 | 8.4 |
| Production cost | | 11.0 | | 10.6 | | 13.2 |
| *Overheads* | | | | | | |
| Production (1.8 per hour) | | 9.0 | | 5.4 | | 10.8 |
| | | 20.0 | | 16.0 | | 24.0 |
| Administration (50%) | | 10.0 | | 8.0 | | 12.0 |
| Selling | | 5.0 | | 4.0 | | 6.0 |
| Standard cost | | 35.0 | | 28.0 | | 42.0 |
| Profit (1/7 of standard cost) | | 5.0 | | 4.0 | | 6.0 |
| Standard selling price | | 40.0 | | 32.0 | | 48.0 |

| *(b) Sales budget in units* | X | Y | Z |
|---|---|---|---|
| Budgeted at standard price | 800,000 | 1,280,000 | 2,400,000 |
| Unit selling price | 40.0 | 32.0 | 48.0 |
| Sales budget in units | 20,000 | 40,000 | 50,000 |

| *(c) Production budget in units* | X | Y | Z |
|---|---|---|---|
| Needed for sales | 20,000 | 40,000 | 50,000 |
| For stock purposes | 5,000 | 10,000 | 10,000 |
| To produce | 25,000 | 50,000 | 60,000 |

*(d) Direct materials purchases budget*

| *Materials* | *1* | *2* | *3* | *4* |
|---|---|---|---|---|
| Product X | – | 100,000 | 300,000 | 480,000 |
| Product Y (kg) | 900,000 | 700,000 | 500,000 | |
| Product Z | 1,440,000 | | 360,000 | 1,080,000 |
| | 2,340,000 | 800,000 | 1,160,000 | 1,560,000 |
| Cost (£) | £234,000 | £120,000 | £290,000 | £78,000 |

**47.1**

| | | | £ |
|---|---|---|---|
| *(i)* Net variance: | Actual cost per unit 35 × £9 | | 315 |
| | Standard cost per unit 30 × £10 | | 300 |
| | Net variance (adverse) | | 15 |
| Made up of: | Favourable price variance £1 × 35 | | 35 |
| | Adverse usage variance 5 × £10 | | 50 |
| | Net variance (adverse) | | 15 |
| *(ii)* Net variance: | Actual cost per unit 54 × £16 | | 864 |
| | Standard cost per unit 60 × £15 | | 900 |
| | Net variance (favourable) | | 36 |
| Made up of: | Favourable usage variance 6 × £15 | | 90 |
| | Adverse price variance 54 × £1 | | 54 |
| | Net variance (favourable) | | 36 |
| *(iii)* Total variance: | Actual cost per unit 38 × £28 | | 1,064 |
| | Standard cost per unit 30 × £24 | | 720 |
| | Variance (adverse) | | 344 |
| Made up of: | Adverse price variance 30 × £4 | | 152 |
| | Adverse usage variance 8 × £24 | | 192 |
| | Total variance (adverse) | | 344 |
| *(iv)* Total variance: | Actual cost per unit 28 × £18 | | 504 |
| | Standard cost per unit 31 × £20 | | 620 |
| | Total variance (favourable) | | 116 |
| Made up of: | Favourable price variance 28 × £2 | | 56 |
| | Favourable usage variance 3 × £20 | | 60 |
| | | | 116 |
| *(v)* Total variance: | Actual cost per unit 310 × £5 | | 1,550 |
| | Standard cost per unit 280 × £4 | | 1,120 |
| | Total variance (adverse) | | 430 |
| Made up of: | Adverse price variance 310 × £1 | | 310 |
| | Adverse usage variance 30 × £4 | | 120 |
| | | | 430 |
| *(vi)* Total variance: | Actual cost per unit 4,950 × £66 | | 326,700 |
| | Standard cost per unit 5,000 × £75 | | 375,000 |
| | Total variance (favourable) | | 48,300 |
| Made up of: | Favourable price variance £9 × 4,950 | | 44,550 |
| | Favourable usage variance 50 × £75 | | 3,750 |
| | | | 48,300 |

**47.3**

| | | | £ |
|---|---|---|---|
| *(i)* | Actual cost per unit | 432 × £6 | 2,592 |
| | Standard cost per unit | 440 × £6 | 2,640 |
| | Favourable labour efficiency variance | | 48 |
| *(ii)* | Actual cost per unit | 230 × £5.8 | 1,334 |
| | Standard cost per unit | 230 × £5.6 | 1,288 |
| | Adverse wage rate variance | | 46 |
| *(iii)* | Actual cost per unit | 480 × £5.7 | 2,736 |
| | Standard cost per unit | 400 × £5.7 | 2,280 |
| | Adverse labour efficiency variance | | 456 |
| *(iv)* | Actual cost per unit | 206 × £7 | 1,442 |
| | Standard cost per unit | 280 × £7 | 1,960 |
| | Favourable labour efficiency variance | | 518 |
| *(v)* | Actual cost per unit | 136 × £5.1 | 693.6 |
| | Standard cost per unit | 136 × £5.7 | 775.2 |
| | Favourable wage rate variance | | 81.6 |
| *(vi)* | Actual cost per unit | 68 × £5.6 | 380.8 |
| | Standard cost per unit | 60 × £5.6 | 336.0 |
| | Adverse labour efficiency variance | | 44.8 |
| *(vii)* | Actual cost per unit | 154 × £5.5 | 847 |
| | Standard cost per unit | 140 × £5.5 | 770 |
| | Adverse labour efficiency variance | | 77 |
| *(viii)* | Actual cost per unit | 200 × £6.1 | 1,220 |
| | Standard cost per unit | 200 × £5.8 | 1,160 |
| | Adverse wage rate variance | | 60 |

**47.5**

*(a)* *See* text.

*(b)* Standard hours produced in March

| | |
|---|---|
| Dishwashers 150 × 10 | 1,500 |
| Washing machines 100 × 12 | 1,200 |
| Refrigerators 90 × 14 | 1,260 |
| Total standard hours | 3,960 |

*(c)* *(i)* Standard hours × Standard hourly rate

| | |
|---|---|
| 3,960 × £4 | 15,840 |
| Actual wages | 18,450 |
| Total direct labour variance | 2,610 (Adverse) |

*(ii)*

| | |
|---|---|
| Standard pay 4,100 × £4 | 16,400 |
| Actual pay | 18,450 |
| Direct labour rate variance | 2,050 (Adverse) |

*(iii)* Direct labour efficiency variance
Standard hours − Actual hours × Standard rate
3,960 − 4,100 × £4 = 560 (Adverse)

*(d)* Labour rate variance:
1 Higher grade labour used than necessary.
2 Job running behind time so extra people brought in to help.

Direct labour efficiency variance:
1 Using unsuitable machinery.
2 Workers slowing up work so as to get overtime rates paid.

**47.7**

*(a)* *Profit Statement for the month of July 2018*

| | *Budgeted* | | *Actual* | |
|---|---|---|---|---|
| Revenue | | 1,000,000 | | 1,071,200 |
| *Less Manufacturing costs* | | | | |
| Direct materials | 200,000 | | 201,285 | |
| Direct labour | 313,625 | | 337,500 | |
| Variable overheads | 141,400 | | 143,000 | |
| Fixed overheads | 75,000 | 730,025 | 71,000 | 752,785 |
| Gross profit | | 269,975 | | 318,415 |
| *Less* Variable sales o/h | 64,400 | | 69,500 | |
| Admin. costs | 150,000 | 214,400 | 148,650 | 218,150 |
| | | 55,575 | | 100,265 |

*(b)* *(i)* Materials price variance
= (Standard price − Actual price per unit) × Quantity purchased
= 10.00 − 10.65 = 0.65 × 18,900 = 12,285 Adverse

Material usage = (Standard quantity − Actual quantity used)
× Standard price = (20,000 − 18,900) × 10 = 11,000 Favourable

| *Summary*: | | | |
|---|---|---|---|
| | Materials price variance | 12,285 | (A) |
| | Materials usage variance | 11,000 | (F) |
| | Materials cost variance | 1,285 | (A) |

*(ii)* Labour rate variance
= (Standard rate per hour − Actual wage rate) × Actual hours worked
= (6.50 − 6.75) × 50,000 = 12,500 (A)

Labour efficiency variance
= (Standard labour hours − Actual hours) × Standard rate per hour
= (48,250 − 50,000) × 6.50 = 11,375 (A)

| *Summary*: | | | |
|---|---|---|---|
| | Labour rate variance | 12,500 | (A) |
| | Labour efficiency variance | 11,375 | (A) |
| | Labour cost variance | 23,875 | (A) |

*(c)* In each case find out why the variance has occurred. Then it must be established whether the variances were outside the control of anyone in the firm or whether they were caused by the actions, or lack of action, by people in the organisation. Any necessary corrective action can then be taken.

**48.1**

| | | |
|---|---|---|
| (*a*) | Actual overhead | 8,400 |
| | Overhead applied to production × £6 | 9,000 |
| | Favourable variable overhead expenditure variance | 600 |
| (*b*) | Actual overhead | 61,000 |
| | Overhead applied to production 12,000 × £5 | 60,000 |
| | Adverse variable overhead expenditure variance | 1,000 |
| (*c*) | Actual fixed overhead | 9,400 |
| | Budgeted fixed overhead | 9,750 |
| | Favourable fixed overhead expenditure variance | 350 |
| (*d*) | Actual fixed overhead | 16,400 |
| | Budgeted fixed overhead | 16,320 |
| | Adverse fixed overhead expenditure variance | 80 |
| (*e*) | Actual hours × Standard rate (18,100 × £4) | 72,400 |
| | Budgeted hours × Standard rate (19,000 × £4) | 76,000 |
| | Favourable variable overhead efficiency variance | 3,600 |
| (*f*) | Actual hours × Standard rate (26,000 × £6) | 156,000 |
| | Budgeted hours (11,320 × 2 = 22,640). Standard rate (22,640 × £6) | 135,840 |
| | Adverse variable overhead efficiency variance | 20,160 |

**48.3**

The standard variable overhead rate is:

$$\frac{£120,000}{60,000} = £2 \text{ per direct labour hour and } £2.4 \text{ per unit}$$

The standard fixed overhead rate is:

$$\frac{£48,000}{60,000} = £0.8 \text{ per direct labour hour and } £0.96 \text{ per unit}$$

The variances are:

*Variable overhead*

| | | | |
|---|---|---|---|
| (*i*) *Expenditure variance* | | | |
| Actual overhead | | | 128,000 |
| Overhead applied to production 59,000 × £2 | | | 118,000 |
| Adverse expenditure variance | | | 10,000 |
| (*ii*) *Efficiency variance* | | | |
| Actual hours × standard rate 59,000 × £2 | | | 118,000 |
| Budgeted hours × standard rate 52,000 units which should be produced in 52,000 × 1.2 hours = 62,400 hours × £2 | | | 124,800 |
| Favourable efficiency variance | | | 6,800 |

*Fixed overhead*

| | |
|---|---|
| (*i*) *Efficiency variance* | |
| Actual units produced × Std rate 52,000 × 1.2 hrs per unit × £0.8 | 49,920 |
| Actual labour hours × Standard rate 59,000 × £0.8 | 47,200 |
| Favourable fixed overhead efficiency variance | 2,720 |
| (*ii*) *Expenditure variance* | |
| Actual fixed overhead | 46,000 |
| Budgeted fixed overhead | 48,000 |
| Favourable fixed overhead expenditure variance | 2,000 |
| (*iii*) *Capacity variance* | |
| Actual hours × Standard rate 59,000 × £0.8 | 47,200 |
| Budgeted hours × Standard rate 60,000 × £0.8 | 48,000 |
| Adverse fixed overhead capacity variance | 800 |
| | 3,920 |

The variances can be explained further:

*Variable overhead*

| | |
|---|---|
| Actual overhead | 128,000 |
| Budgeted overhead for actual production 52,000 units × £2.4 | 124,800 |
| Net adverse variance (made up of favourable efficiency variance £6,800 *less* adverse expenditure variance 10,000) | 3,200 |

*Fixed overhead*

| | |
|---|---|
| Actual overhead | 46,000 |
| Overhead based on units of production 52,000 × £0.96 | 49,920 |
| Net favourable variance (made up of favourable efficiency variance £2,720 *plus* favourable expenditure variance £2,000 *less* adverse capacity variance £800) | 3,920 |

**48.5**

| | | £ |
|---|---|---|
| Actual units sold 168,000 × Budget price | £2.50 = | 420,000 |
| 168,000 × Actual price | £2.40 = | 403,200 |
| Adverse price variance | £0.10 | 16,800 |

| | £ |
|---|---|
| Actual units sold 168,000 × Budget gross profit £0.30 = | 50,400 |
| Budgets units sold 140,000 × Budget gross profit £0.30 = | 42,000 |
| Favourable volume variance | 8,400 |

**48.7**

| | *Actual units sold* | *Budget price* £ | *Actual price* £ | *Unit price variance* £ | *Total price variance* £ |
|---|---|---|---|---|---|
| A | 1,224 | 6 | 8.20 | +2.20 | +2,692.8 |
| B | 2,160 | 9 | 11.60 | +2.60 | +5,616.0 |
| C | 216 | 8 | 10.90 | +2.90 | +626.4 |
| | 3,600 | | Total price variance | | +8,935.2 |

| | *Actual units sold* | *Actual units in budget (%)* | *Budget sales* | *Variance in units* | *Budget gross profit per unit* £ | *Total variance* £ |
|---|---|---|---|---|---|---|
| A | 1,224 | 900 | 1,000 | −100 | 2.00 | −200 |
| B | 2,160 | 1,800 | 2,000 | −200 | 2.50 | −500 |
| C | 216 | 900 | 1,000 | −100 | 2.20 | −220 |
| | 3,600 | 3,600 | 4,000 | −400 | | −920 |

| | *Actual units in budget (%)* | *Actual units sold* | *Variance in units* | *Budget gross profit per unit £* | *Total variance £* |
|---|---|---|---|---|---|
| A | 900 | 1,224 | +324 | 2.00 | +648 |
| B | 1,800 | 2,160 | +360 | 2.50 | +900 |
| C | 900 | 216 | −684 | 2.20 | −1,504.80 |
| | 3,600 | 3,600 | – | | +43.2 |

| *Summary of sales variance* | |
|---|---|
| Price variance favourable | 8,935.2 |
| Volume variance adverse | 920.0 |
| Mix variance favourable | 43.2 |
| Net favourable variance | 8,058.4 |

**48.9**

(*a*) *See* text, Section 47.1.

(*b*)

(*i*) **Singleton Ltd**

*Manufacturing Account for the year ending 31 August 2016*

| | *Actual* £ | *Budget* £ | *Variance* £ |
|---|---|---|---|
| Raw material consumed | 90,000 | 80,000 | (10,000) |
| Direct labour wages | 115,600 | 120,000 | 4,400 |
| Direct expenses | 6,000 | 5,800 | (200) |
| Prime cost | 211,600 | 205,800 | (5,800) |
| *Factory overhead expenses:* | | | |
| Factory rent | 10,000 | 10,000 | – |
| Factory maintenance | 6,100 | 6,700 | 600 |
| Heating and lighting | 3,900 | 2,900 | (1,000) |
| Depreciation | 10,500 | 8,900 | (1,600) |
| Wages, maintenance labour | 24,000 | 18,000 | (6,000) |
| Other factory overheads | 10,000 | 12,700 | 2,700 |
| Production cost of goods completed | 276,100 | 265,000 | (11,100) |

(*ii*) *Trading Account part of the Statement of Profit or Loss for the year ending 31 August 2016*

| | £ | £ |
|---|---|---|
| Revenue | | 405,000 |
| Inventory of finished goods 1 Sep 15 | 28,900 | |
| Production cost | 276,100 | |
| | 305,000 | |
| *Less* Inventory of finished goods 31 Aug 16 | 35,000 | |
| Cost of sales | | 270,000 |
| Gross profit | | 135,000 |

(*c*) *See* text.

*Note to exercises on breakeven analysis:*

The general idea of the questions is to get you to draw up the schedules of costs and revenues and then to draw them carefully on graph paper. It will be a waste of time if you do not use graph paper. It illustrates that accounting data can be represented in diagram form for some users in a more effective way than just using figures. It also puts over the idea that businesses exist to make a profit, and that until sufficient volume is achieved then the business will incur losses. The impact of fixed costs can be revealed quite sharply by this sort of analysis.

**49.1**

(*i*)

| No. of units | *Fixed cost* | *Variable cost* | *Total cost* | *Revenue* | *Profit* | *Loss* |
|---|---|---|---|---|---|---|
| 0 | 8,000 | – | 8,000 | – | – | 8,000 |
| 1,000 | 8,000 | 4,000 | 12,000 | 6,000 | | 6,000 |
| 2,000 | 8,000 | 8,000 | 16,000 | 12,000 | | 4,000 |
| 3,000 | 8,000 | 12,000 | 20,000 | 18,000 | | 2,000 |
| 4,000 | 8,000 | 16,000 | 24,000 | 24,000 | nil | nil |
| 5,000 | 8,000 | 20,000 | 28,000 | 30,000 | 2,000 | |
| 6,000 | 8,000 | 24,000 | 32,000 | 36,000 | 4,000 | |
| 7,000 | 8,000 | 28,000 | 36,000 | 42,000 | 6,000 | |
| 8,000 | 8,000 | 32,000 | 40,000 | 48,000 | 8,000 | |
| 9,000 | 8,000 | 36,000 | 44,000 | 54,000 | 10,000 | |
| 10,000 | 8,000 | 40,000 | 48,000 | 60,000 | 12,000 | |

(*ii*) Similar in style to Exhibit 49.2 in the chapter.

**49.2**

(*a*) (*i*) £24,000 (*ii*) £36,000 (*iii*) £44,000 (*iv*) £30,000
(*b*) (*i*) £18,000 (*ii*) £48,000 (*iii*) £33,000.

**49.4**

(*a*) Loss £2,000 (*ii*) Profit £12,000 (*iii*) Nil (*iv*) Profit £6,000 (*v*) Profit £9,000.

**49.6**

(*a*) $\dfrac{70{,}000}{(14 - 6)} = 8{,}750$ units ∴ profit is made for the first time when 8,751 units have been sold.

(*b*) 8,750 units at £14 *each* = £122,500.

**49.7**

(*a*)

(*i*) $\text{Breakeven point} = \dfrac{\text{Total fixed costs}}{\text{Selling price per unit} - \text{Variable cost per unit}}$

For 2016 $= \dfrac{250{,}000}{130 - 110} = 12{,}500$ units

$=$ sales of 12,500 units × £130 = £1,625,000 sales

For 2017 $= \dfrac{275{,}000}{129 - 118.5} =$ sales of 26,190 units × £129

$=$ £3,378,510 sales

For 2018 $= \dfrac{275{,}000}{128.5 - 122} =$ sales of 42,308 units × £128.5 = £5,436,578 sales

**49.7** *(cont'd)*

*(ii)*

### Polemic Ltd

*Actual & Forecast Statements of Profit or Loss for years ending 30 September (£000)*

| | *Actual 2016* | | *Forecast 2017* | | *Forecast 2018* | |
|---|---|---|---|---|---|---|
| Revenue | | 6,500 | | 6,708 | | 6,810.5 |
| Direct materials | 2,500 | | 2,860 | | 2,915 | |
| Direct labour | 1,500 | | 1,638 | | 1,749 | |
| Variable production | 500 | | 572 | | 636 | |
| Direct expenses | 250 | | 260 | | 318 | |
| Variable sales overhead | 750 | 5,500 | 832 | 6,162 | 848 | 6,466 |
| Contribution | | 1,000 | | 546 | | 344.5 |
| *Fixed costs* | | | | | | |
| Production | 50 | | 55 | | 55 | |
| Overhead | 200 | 250 | 220 | 275 | 220 | 275 |
| | | 750 | | 271 | | 69.5 |

*(b)* Should best be on graph paper. General idea follows:

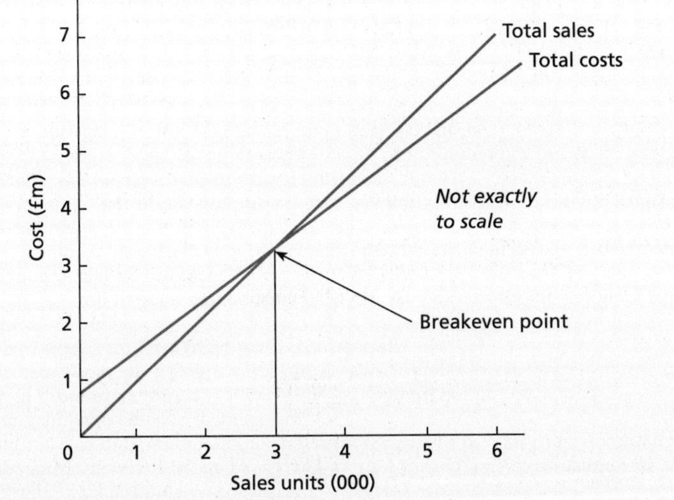


*(c)* The management of Polemic should be explaining to the union that their demand is unreasonable. As it is, profits have fallen dramatically and the break-even point in 2018 will be over three times higher than in 2016.

It is therefore almost impossible for the company to raise prices still further and maintain their level of sales. To try to do so would almost certainly mean a fall in demand and a shedding of a large part of the workforce.

*(d)* *See* text.

**49.9**

A

### Hampshire plc

*Profit Statement for first and second quarters*

| | *First quarter* | | *Second quarter* | |
|---|---|---|---|---|
| Revenue | | 126,000 | | 143,640 |
| Materials | 32,850 | | 39,420 | |
| Labour | 18,900 | | 22,680 | |
| Variable factory o/h | 12,600 | | 15,120 | |
| Variable selling costs | 7,650 | 72,000 | 9,180 | 86,400 |
| Contribution | | 54,000 | | 57,240 |
| Fixed costs: | | | | |
| Factory overhead | 21,375 | | 21,375 | |
| Selling and admin. | 16,125 | 37,500 | 16,125 | 37,500 |
| Net profit | | 16,500 | | 19,740 |

Contribution per unit $\frac{54,000}{9,000} = 6.00$ $\frac{57,240}{10,800} = 5.30$

B Draw on graph paper. Breakeven points are at:

$$\text{First quarter} = \frac{37,500}{14.00 - 8.00} = 6,250 \text{ units}$$

$$\text{Second quarter} = \frac{37,500}{13.30 - 8.00} = 7,075 \text{ units}$$

Margins of safety above these points.

C Profit statements incorporating suggestions:

| | *(i)* | *(ii)* | *(iii)* | *(iv)* | *(v)* |
|---|---|---|---|---|---|
| No. of units sold | 11,880 | 11,556 | 12,960 | 10,800 | 10,800 |
| Revenue (W1) | 158,004 | 158,317 | 155,131 | 143,640 | 143,640 |
| Materials | 46,926 | 43,913 | 47,304 | 39,420 | |
| Labour | 24,948 | 27,734 | 27,216 | 22,680 | *see* (W2) |
| Variable factory o/h | 16,632 | 16,178 | 18,144 | 15,120 | 87,900 |
| Variable selling o/h | 10,098 | 9,823 | 11,016 | 11,340 | |
| Total variable costs | 98,604 | 97,648 | 103,680 | 88,560 | 87,900 |
| Contribution | 59,400 | 60,669 | 51,451 | 55,080 | 55,740 |
| *Fixed costs* | | | | | |
| Factory | 21,375 | 21,375 | 21,375 | 21,375 | *see* (W3) |
| Selling, etc. | 16,125 | 16,125 | 16,125 | 12,025 | 35,000 |
| | 37,500 | 37,500 | 37,500 | 33,400 | 35,000 |
| Net profit | 21,900 | 23,169 | 13,951 | 21,680 | 20,740 |
| Redundancy | | | | | 12,000 |

*Workings:*

(W1) Selling price per unit *(i)* 13.30 *(ii)* 13.70 *(iii)* 11.97 *(iv)* 13.30 *(v)* 13.30.

(W2) Per accounts of second quarter in A 86,400 + extra costs 5p per component, 30,000 × 0.05 = 1,500. Total 87,900.
(W3) Fixed costs 37,500 − saving 2,500 = 35,000. Assumed that the 20% of the firm's fixed costs would still continue as they would have to be paid anyway. Question not too clear on this point.

D Briefly:
(*i*) Would increase profit by 21,900 − 19,740 = 2,160. Seems to be a sensible opportunity which should be considered.
(*ii*) Apparently increases profit by 23,169 − 19,740 = 3,429. No mention as to what the cost of maintaining the guarantee is likely to be. Until this is known it is impossible to come to a conclusion.
(*iii*) Fall in profit of 19,740 − 13,951 = 5,789. Should not be considered.
(*iv*) Increases profit by 21,680 − 19,740 = 1,940. Have to renegotiate terms of employment with sales staff. Worth considering.
(*v*) Firm
 (*a*) If we stop making components how can we be certain that suppliers will not later raise prices?
 (*b*) Would we have to keep larger stocks of components in case of breakdown of supply?
 (*c*) Possible that newly established firm has got its prices wrong and will be unable to maintain at this price for long.
 (*d*) Effect on morale of other employees. Local community: write generally about effects of unemployment and knock-on effects.

E *See* text, Section 49.4.

**49.11**
(*a*)

**Magwitch Ltd**
*Summarised Statement of Profit or Loss for the year ending 31 May 2018*

| | |
|---|---|
| Sales volume: units | 20,000 |
| | £ |
| Revenue £1.50 + 10% = 1.65 per unit | 33,000 |
| Variable costs (20 − 10) × 0.50 + 10% = 55p per unit | 11,000 |
| Contribution | 22,000 |
| Fixed costs 0.50 + 10% = 55p per unit | 11,000 |
| Profit | 11,000 |

(*b*)

**Compeyson plc**
*Statement of Financial Position as at 31 May 2018*

| | |
|---|---|
| Non-current assets (93 + 160) | 253 |
| Current assets (65 + 340 − 24 *see* W2) | 381 |
| | 634 |
| Current liabilities (26 + 110) | (136) |
| | 498 |
| Share capital (200 + 60 *see* W2) | 260 |
| Share premium (60 × 0.80) | 48 |
| Reserves | 190 |
| | 498 |

*Workings*:

| | | |
|---|---|---|
| (W1) Purchase price 12 × 11 = | | 132 |
| Net assets taken over | 71 | |
| + revalued property | 61 | 132 |
| Goodwill | | nil |
| (W2) Method of payment of purchase price | | |
| Shares 40 × 3/2 = 60 × 1.80 | 108 | |
| Cash (balance) | 24 | 132 |

(c) Shares 6,000 × 3/2 = 9,000 shares
Cash 6,000/40,000 × 24,000 = £3,600

**50.1**

| | *2017* | | *2018* |
|---|---|---|---|
| Equipment purchased | 34,000 | | |
| Sale of old equipment | | | (8,500) |
| Installation of equipment completed and paid | 6,800 | | |
| Costs incurred in commissioning equipment | 13,600 | | 4,000 |
| Rent on premises up to completion date | 20,400 | (6 months) | 10,200 |
| Training costs | | | 5,100 |
| Working capital | | | 27,200 |
| Net cash outlay | 74,800 | | 38,000 |

**50.2**

| | | | |
|---|---|---|---|
| Capital cost 2017 | | 74,800 | |
| 2017 | 25% WDA | 18,700 | @ 30% tax £5,610 received 2018 |
| | balance c/d | 56,100 | |
| New expenditure | | 19,300 | excluding scrap value and |
| | | 75,400 | additional working capital |
| 2018 | 25% WDA | 18,850 | @ 30% tax £5,655 received 2019 |
| | balance c/d | 56,550 | |
| 2019 | 25% WDA | 14,138 | @ 30% tax £4,241 received 2020 |
| | balance c/d | 42,412 | |
| 2020 | 25% WDA | 10,603 | @ 30% tax £3,181 received 2021 |
| | balance c/d | 31,809 | |

This will continue over the life of the equipment. In 2019 the cash received from the sale of old equipment will be taxed at 30%, resulting in a tax outflow of £2,550.

| | *2017* | *2018* | *2019* | *2020* | |
|---|---|---|---|---|---|
| Capital cash flow | (74,800) | (10,800) | | | |
| Tax relief | | 5,610 | 5,655 | 4,241 | *etc.* |
| Tax on sale | | | (2,550) | | |
| Net cash flow | (74,800) | (5,190) | 3,105 | 4,241 | *etc.* |

**50.3**

| | *Net cash flow* | *Discount factor 5%* | *Present value* |
|---|---|---|---|
| 2017 | (74,800) | 0.952 | (71,210) |
| 2018 | (5,190) | 0.907 | (4,676) |
| 2019 | 3,105 | 0.864 | 2,683 |
| 2020 | 4,241 | 0.823 | 3,490 |
| | | NPV at start | 69,713 |

**50.7**

| *Period* | *Amount* | *Balance* | |
|---|---|---|---|
| 0 | (20,000) | (20,000) | |
| 1 | 15,000 | (5,000) | |
| 2 | 8,000 | – | payback at 1 plus 5,000/8,000 years = 1.625 years |
| 3 | 4,000 | – | |
| 4 | 3,000 | – | |

**50.8**

| *Period* | *Amount* | *Discount factor 5%* | *Present value* |
|---|---|---|---|
| 0 | (20,000) | 1.000 | (20,000) |
| 1 | 15,000 | 0.952 | 14,280 |
| 2 | 8,000 | 0.907 | 7,256 |
| 3 | 4,000 | 0.864 | 3,456 |
| 4 | 3,000 | 0.823 | 2,469 |
| Overall net present value of cash flows | | | 7,461 |

**50.9**

| *Period* | *Amount* | *Discount factor 28%* | *Present value* | *Discount factor 24%* | *Present value* |
|---|---|---|---|---|---|
| 0 | (20,000) | 1.000 | (20,000) | 1.000 | (20,000) |
| 1 | 15,000 | 0.781 | 11,719 | 0.806 | 12,097 |
| 2 | 8,000 | 0.610 | 4,883 | 0.650 | 5,203 |
| 3 | 4,000 | 0.477 | 1,907 | 0.524 | 2,098 |
| 4 | 3,000 | 0.373 | 1,118 | 0.423 | 1,269 |
| | | | (374) | | 667 |

| | |
|---|---|
| 24% discount rate gives NPV of | 667 |
| 28% discount rate gives negative NPV of | 374 |
| | 1,041 |

The IRR is $\frac{667}{1041} \times 4\% = 2.56\% + 24\% = 26.56\%$.

**50.10**

From Table 4 in Appendix 1, the present value of an annuity of £1 for four years at 5% is 3.546. The NPV according to Question 46.8 is £7,461, therefore the annualised amount = 7,461/3.546 = 2,104.06.

**50.17**

| | *Net present value (6%)* |
|---|---|
| Machine X project | £15,240 |
| Machine Y project | £72,400 |

The Machine Y project should be selected.

**50.18**

| | *Internal rate of return* |
|---|---|
| Machine X project | 19.22% |
| Machine Y project | 26.39% |

The Machine Y project would be preferred.

**50.21**

From Table 4 in Appendix 1, the present value of an annuity of £1 for four years at 8% is 3.312. Therefore the annualised amount = £4,200/3.312 = £1,268.12.

**50.23**

Cost of machine £50,000 × (1 − 0.3) = 35,000
Cost of leasing £15,180 × (1 − 0.3) = 10,626

Present value for four years $= \frac{35,000}{10,626} = 3.294$

which, interpolating between the values for 8% and 9% in Table 4 of Appendix 1, is 8.25%.

**50.24**

*(a) (i)*

| *BN* | *0* | *1* | *2* | *3* | *4* | *5* |
|---|---|---|---|---|---|---|
| *Roadhog* | | | | | | |
| Cash inflow | | 12,500 | 15,000 | 20,000 | 20,000 | 20,000 |
| Cash outflow | | | | | | |
| fixed | | 2,000 | 2,000 | 2,200 | 2,400 | 2,400 |
| variable | | 3,000 | 3,600 | 4,800 | 4,800 | 4,800 |
| Operating cash flow | | 7,500 | 9,400 | 13,000 | 12,800 | 12,800 |
| Capital | 40,000 | | | | | 8,000 |
| | 40,000 | 7,500 | 9,400 | 13,000 | 12,800 | 20,800 |
| | 1.00 | 0.909 | 0.826 | 0.751 | 0.683 | 0.621 |
| | 40,000 | 6,817 | 7,764 | 9,763 | 8,742 | 12,916 |

NPV = 6,002 positive

| *FX Sprinter* | *0* | *1* | *2* | *3* | *4* | *5* |
|---|---|---|---|---|---|---|
| Cash inflow | | 12,500 | 15,000 | 20,000 | 20,000 | 20,000 |
| Cash outflow | | | | | | |
| fixed | | 1,800 | 1,800 | 1,800 | 2,000 | 2,200 |
| variable | | 4,000 | 4,800 | 6,400 | 6,400 | 6,400 |
| Operating cash flow | | 6,700 | 8,400 | 11,800 | 11,600 | 11,400 |
| Capital | 45,000 | | | | | 9,000 |
| | 45,000 | 6,700 | 8,400 | 11,800 | 11,600 | 20,400 |
| | 1.00 | 0.909 | 0.826 | 0.751 | 0.683 | 0.621 |
| | 45,000 | 6,090 | 6,938 | 8,862 | 7,923 | 12,668 |

NPV = 2,519 negative

| *VR Rocket* | *0* | *1* | *2* | *3* | *4* | *5* |
|---|---|---|---|---|---|---|
| Cash inflow | | 12,500 | 15,000 | 20,000 | 20,000 | 20,000 |
| Cash outflow | | | | | | |
| fixed | | 1,500 | 1,500 | 1,400 | 1,400 | 1,400 |
| variable | | 3,500 | 4,200 | 5,600 | 5,600 | 5,600 |
| Operating cash flow | | 7,500 | 9,300 | 13,000 | 13,000 | 13,000 |
| Capital | 50,000 | | | | | 14,000 |
| | 50,000 | 7,500 | 9,300 | 13,000 | 13,000 | 27,000 |
| | 1.00 | 0.909 | 0.826 | 0.751 | 0.683 | 0.621 |
| | 50,000 | 6,817 | 7,682 | 9,763 | 8,879 | 16,767 |

NPV = 92 negative

(*ii*) To the Directors of Road Wheelers Ltd
The NPV anticipated for the three vehicles is as follows:

| | | |
|---|---|---|
| BN Roadhog | £6,002 | Positive |
| FX Sprinter | £2,519 | Negative |
| VR Rocket | £ 92 | Negative |

On the basis of NPV assessment using a discount rate of 10% the BN Roadhog appears to be the best option.

The payback position on the three vehicles is as follows:

| | | |
|---|---|---|
| BN Roadhog | 3 years | 9.3 months |
| FX Sprinter | 4 years | 3.8 months |
| VR Rocket | 4 years | 3.2 months |

This indicates that the BX Roadhog recovers the cash outlay faster than the other two options which is in its favour.

Since the capital outlay on the BX Roadhog is also significantly lower than the other options this indicates a lower risk and will enhance the ROC on the statement of financial position figures.

The BN Roadhog appears to be the best choice.

(*b*) The problems in evaluating capital projects are essentially related to the estimates involved in forecasting the revenues and costs associated with the project. In this evaluation the relative performance of the three alternatives may be more reliable than overall estimates of the environment. In some situations important factors in the decision may not be readily quantified especially in areas of new technology where many factors are unknown.

The techniques of evaluating the cash flow data are well understood but care must be taken that an appropriate 'cost of capital' is chosen and that risk is taken into account.

**50.26**

(*a*) *Revised Operating Budget*

| *Ship A* | *2017* | *2018* | *2019* | *2020* | *2021* |
|---|---|---|---|---|---|
| Estimated revenue receipts | 5 | 7 | 9 | 11 | 13 |
| Extra revenue 10% | 0.5 | 0.7 | 0.9 | 1.1 | 1.3 |
| | 5.5 | 7.7 | 9.9 | 12.1 | 14.3 |
| Operating payments | 4.0 | 5.0 | 6.5 | 7.5 | 9.0 |
| Net cash flow Ship A | 1.5 | 2.7 | 3.4 | 4.6 | 5.3 |

| *Ship B* | 2017 | 2018 | 2019 | 2020 | 2021 |
|---|---|---|---|---|---|
| Estimated revenue receipts: | | | | | |
| Private | 2.5 | 3.5 | 5.0 | 6.5 | 7.5 |
| Commercial | 3.45 | 4.6 | 5.85 | 6.5 | 7.8 |
| | 5.95 | 8.1 | 10.85 | 13.0 | 15.3 |
| Operating payments | 4.8 | 6.0 | 7.9 | 9.0 | 10.8 |
| Net cash flow Ship B | 1.15 | 2.1 | 2.95 | 4.0 | 4.5 |

(*b*)

| | | *Ship A* | *Factor 15%* | | *Ship B* | *Factor 15%* | |
|---|---|---|---|---|---|---|---|
| *Cash flows* | 0 | (10.0) | 1.0 | (10.0) | (14.1) | 1.0 | (14.0) |
| | 2018 | 1.5 | 0.870 | 1.3 | 1.15 | 0.87 | 1.0 |
| | 2019 | 2.7 | 0.756 | 2.0 | 2.1 | 0.756 | 1.6 |
| | 2020 | 3.4 | 0.658 | 2.2 | 2.95 | 0.658 | 1.9 |
| | 2021 | 4.6 | 0.572 | 2.6 | 4.0 | 0.572 | 2.3 |
| | 2022 | 5.3 | 0.497 | 2.6 | 4.5 | 0.497 | 2.2 |
| | | NPV | | 0.7 | | | 5.0 |
| | | 7.5 | 0.497 | 3.7 | 10.5 | 0.497 | 5.2 |
| Assumed value of ship on market $^{15}/_{20}$ × *cost* | | | | 4.4 | | | 0.2 |

*Note*: The calculation has been done with a zero assumption about cash value of ships at the end of Year 5 and then with an assumed value equal to the unexplained cost value based on a 20-year life.

(*c*) The evaluation assumes an interest rate of 15% and evaluates cash flows over the first five years of the ships' lives. If the assumption is that at the end of five years the ships will have no value then ship A has a positive NPV of £0.7m while B has a negative NPV of £5.0m. However, it is unlikely that the ships would be valueless at the end of year 5 and if an assumption is made to take 15/20 of the cost as the realisable value then both NPVs become positive at £4.4m and £0.2m respectively.

From this evaluation ship A looks to give a better return. It is worth noting, however, that ship B does have much higher capacity. If operating revenues were to expand more than forecast over the five years and thereafter, this ship might provide much higher returns. This operating forecast and the likely market values of the two vessels should therefore be closely examined.

**51.1**
*See* text.

**51.2**
*See* text.

**51.3**
*See* text.

**51.4**
*See* text.

appendix 3

# Glossary

**Abnormal losses** (Chapter 38): Losses arising in the production process that should have been avoided.

**Absorption costing** (Chapter 37): The method of allocating all indirect manufacturing costs to products. (All fixed costs are allocated to cost units.)

**Accruals-based earnings management** (Chapter 28): Changing accounting numbers to achieve the desired financial position.

**Activity-based costing** (Chapter 37): The process of using cost drivers as the basis for overhead absorption.

**Adverse variance** (Chapter 43): A difference arising that is apparently 'bad' from the perspective of the organisation. For example, when the total actual materials cost exceeds the total standard cost due to more materials having been used than anticipated. Whether it is indeed 'bad' will be revealed only when the cause of the variance is identified. It may, for example, have arisen as a result of an unexpected rise in demand for the product being produced.

**Annuity** (Chapter 46): An income-generating investment whereby, in return for the payment of a single lump sum, the annuitant receives regular amounts of income over a predefined period.

**Articles of Association** (Chapter 4): The document that arranges the internal relationships, for example, between members of the company, and the duties of directors.

**Associate** (Chapter 26): A company or other entity which is not a subsidiary of the investing group or company but in which the investing group or company has a long-term interest and over which it exercises significant influence.

**Attainable standards** (Chapter 42): Standards that can be achieved in normal conditions. They take into account normal losses, and normal levels of downtime and waste.

**Balance sheet** (Chapter 13): A summary of the financial position of an entity at a point in time. (Now known as 'statement of financial position'.)

**Balanced scorecard** (Chapter 48): A technique that assesses performance across a balanced set of four perspectives – customers, internal processes, organisational learning and growth, and financial.

**Big bath** (Chapter 28): Manipulating a company's earnings to make poor results look even worse. It is often implemented in a bad year to artificially enhance the next year's earnings.

**Bonding cost** (Chapter 29): The cost to a principal of aligning the interests of an agent to that of the principal.

**Bonus shares** (Chapter 10): Shares issued to existing shareholders free of charge. (Also known as scrip issues.)

**Breakeven point** (Chapter 45): The level of activity at which total revenues equal total costs.

**Budget** (Chapter 39): A plan quantified in monetary terms in advance of a defined time period and usually showing planned income and expenditure and the capital employed to achieve a given objective.

**Business-to-business (B2B)** (Chapter 50): Businesses purchase from other businesses and/or sell their goods and services to other businesses.

**Business-to-consumer (B2C)** (Chapter 50): Businesses sell to consumers.

**By-product** (Chapter 38): Product of minor sales value that results from the production of a main product.

**Capital redemption reserve** (Chapter 6): A 'non-distributable' reserve created when shares are redeemed or purchased other than from the proceeds of a fresh issue of shares.

**Capital reserve** (Chapter 9): A reserve which is a balance of profit retained that can never be used for the payment of cash dividends. Examples include a capital redemption reserve and a share premium account.

**Cash-based accounting** (Chapter 34): A receipts-and-payments-based accounting system.

**Consolidated accounting** (Chapter 16): This term means bringing together into a single statement of financial position and profit and loss account the separate financial statements of a group of companies. Hence they are known as group financial statements.

**Contribution** (Chapter 37): The difference between sales income and marginal cost. (It can also be defined as sales income minus variable cost, which would virtually always produce the same answer.)

**Corporate governance** (Chapter 33): The exercise of power over and responsibility for corporate entities.

**Corporation tax** (Chapter 8): A form of direct taxation levied on the profits of companies. The rate is determined each year in the Finance Act.

**Cost centre** (Chapter 36): A production or service location, function, activity, or item of equipment whose costs may be attributed to cost units.

**Cost of control** (Chapter 17): An alternative expression for goodwill.

**Cost unit** (Chapter 36): A unit of product or service in relation to which costs are ascertained.

**Debt covenant** (Chapter 28): An agreement between a bank and a borrower whereby the borrower must not breach certain conditions, such as a financial ratio that must be maintained above a certain level. The covenant protects the interests of the bank. The borrower benefits by (a) receiving the loan and, (b) doing so at a lower interest rate than would otherwise be possible.

**Deferred taxation** (Chapter 8): Timing differences arise between the accounting treatment of events and their taxation results. Deferred taxation accounting adjusts the differences so that the accounts are not misleading.

**Earnings management** (Chapter 28): The use of accounting techniques to deliberately manipulate the company's earnings so that the figures match a predetermined target.

**Economic order quantity (EOQ)** (Chapter 39): A mathematical method of calculating the amount of inventory that should be ordered at a time and how frequently to order it, so that the overall total of the costs of holding the inventory and the costs of ordering the inventory can be minimised.

**Electronic commerce (e-commerce)** (Chapter 50): The use of electronic telecommunication technology to conduct business transactions over the Internet.

**Enterprise resource planning (ERP) system** (Chapter 49): A suite of software modules, each of which relates to a function of the organisation, such as order processing, production, creditor control, debtor control, payroll, marketing, and human resources.

**Equity accounting** (Chapter 26): A method of accounting for associated undertakings that brings into the consolidated profit and loss account the investor's share of the associated undertaking's results and that records the investment in the consolidated statement of financial position as the investor's share of the associated undertaking's net assets including any goodwill arising to the extent that it has not previously been written off.

**Fair value** (Chapter 11): The price that would be received to sell an asset or paid to transfer a liability in an orderly transaction between market participants at the measurement date.

**Favourable variance** (Chapter 43): A difference arising that is apparently 'good' from the perspective of the organisation. For example, when the total actual labour cost is less than the total standard cost because fewer hours were worked than expected. Whether it is indeed 'good' will be revealed only when the cause of the variance is identified – it may be that fewer hours were worked because demand for the product fell unexpectedly.

**Finance lease** (Chapter 2): This is an agreement whereby the lessee enjoys substantially all the risks and rewards associated with ownership of an asset other than legal title.

**Flexible budget** (Chapter 41): A budget which, by recognising the difference in behaviour between fixed and variable costs in relation to fluctuations in output, turnover or other factors, is designed to change appropriately with such fluctuations.

**Forensic accounting** (Chapter 51): The use of professional accounting skills in matters involving potential or actual civil or criminal litigation, including, but not limited to, generally acceptable accounting and audit principles; the determination of lost profits, income, assets, or damages; evaluation of internal controls; fraud; and any other matter involving accounting expertise in the legal system.

**Heuristic** (Chapter 29): A 'rule of thumb'. A shortcut to taking a decision that omits some of the information that could be used and so omits some of the steps that could be taken in arriving at a conclusion.

**Hire purchase agreements** (Chapter 2): These are legal agreements by which an organisation can obtain the use of an asset in exchange for payment by instalment.

**Holding company** (Chapter 16): The outdated term for what is now known as a 'parent'.

**Ideal standards** (Chapter 42): Standards that are based upon the premise that everything operates at the maximum level of efficiency. They take no account of normal losses, or of normal levels of downtime and waste.

**Income smoothing** (Chapter 28): The use of accounting techniques to level out net income fluctuations from one period to the next.

**Irrelevant costs** (Chapter 47): Those costs of the future that will not be affected by a decision.

**Job costing** (Chapter 38): A costing system that is applied when goods or services are produced in discrete jobs, either one item at a time, or in batches.

**Joint arrangement** (Chapter 26): Either a joint operation or a joint venture in which two or more parties have joint control.

**Joint operation** (Chapter 26): A joint arrangement whereby the parties that have joint control of the arrangement have rights to the assets, and obligations for the liabilities, relating to the arrangement.

**Joint products** (Chapter 38): Two or more products, each of which has significant sales value, created in the same production process.

**Joint venture** (Chapter 26): A joint arrangement whereby the parties that have joint control of the arrangement have rights to the net assets of the arrangement.

**Limited company** (Chapter 4): A form of organisation established under the Companies Acts as a separate legal entity, and required to comply with the provisions of the Acts. The members of the company, known as shareholders, are liable only to pay the full price of the shares, not for any further amount, i.e. their liability is limited.

**Limiting factor** (Chapter 37): Anything that limits activity. Typically, this would be the shortage of supply of something required in production, for example machine hours, labour hours, raw materials, etc. However, it could also be something that prevents production occurring, for example a lack of storage for finished goods, or a lack of a market for the products.

**Loan note** (Chapter 5): A bond or document acknowledging a loan to a company, normally under the company's seal and carrying a fixed rate of interest. (Also known as debenture.)

**Margin of safety** (Chapter 45): The gap between the level of activity at the breakeven point and the actual level of activity.

**Marginal costing** (Chapter 37): An approach to costing that takes account of the variable cost of products rather than the full production cost. It is particularly useful when considering utilisation of spare capacity.

**Master budget** (Chapter 41): The overall summary budget encompassing all the individual budgets.

**Memorandum of Association** (Chapter 4): The document that discloses the conditions governing a company's relationship with the outside world.

**Minority interest** (Chapter 17): Shareholder in subsidiary other than the parent or other group entities. (Now known as 'non-controlling interest'.)

**Monitoring cost** (Chapter 29): The cost to a principal of ensuring an agent behaves in line with the interests of the principal.

**Net present value (NPV)** (Chapter 46): The sum of the present values of a series of cash flows.

**Non-controlling interest** (Chapter 17): Shareholder in subsidiaries other than the parent or other group entities. (Previously known as 'minority interest'.)

**Normal losses** (Chapter 38): Losses arising in the production process that could not be avoided.

**Normative theories** (Chapter 29): Theories based on observation or analysis that indicate what *should* be done.

**Operating lease** (Chapter 2): An agreement whereby the lessor retains the risks and rewards associated with ownership and normally assumes responsibility for repairs, maintenance and insurance.

**Parent** (Chapter 16): An undertaking which controls the affairs of another undertaking.

**Positive theory** (Chapter 29): A theory or hypothesis that (*ex ante*) provides valid and meaningful predictions about phenomena not yet observed and (expost) can be used to describe and explain what has happened. Positive theories describe, explain and predict responses to specific stimuli.

**Pre-incorporation profit or loss** (Chapter 7): A profit or loss which arises immediately before a limited company is legally incorporated. Any such profit will be treated as capital profit not for distribution while, for sake of prudence, any such loss will be set against post-incorporation profits.

**Present value** (Chapter 46): The amount that a future cash flow is worth in terms of today's money.

**Process costing** (Chapter 38): A costing system that is applied when goods or services are produced in a continuous flow.

**Provision** (Chapter 9): An amount written off or retained by way of providing for depreciation, renewals or diminution in value of assets, or retained by way of providing for any known liability of which the amount cannot be determined with 'substantial accuracy'.

**Public sector** (Chapter 34): All organisations which are not privately owned or operated.

**Real earnings management** (Chapter 28): Manipulating transactions before they are entered into the accounting system so as to achieve the desired financial position.

**Regulatory capture** (Chapter 29): A situation where the people or organisations the legislation is intended to control become the regulators. That is, they have achieved a dominant influence over the content of the regulations that are issued.

**Relevant costs** (Chapter 47): Those costs of the future that will be affected by a decision.

**Residual cost** (Chapter 29): The costs of agency that cannot be eliminated.

**Resource accounting** (Chapter 34): An accounting system based on normal commercial practice, including accruals and movements in cash flows.

**Revenue reserve** (Chapter 9): A balance of profits retained available to pay cash dividends including an amount voluntarily transferred from the profit and loss appropriation account by debiting it, reducing the amount of profits left for cash dividend purposes, and crediting a named reserve account, such as a general reserve.

**Rights issue** (Chapter 5): An issue of shares to existing shareholders.

**Share discount** (Chapter 5): Where a share was issued at a price below its par, or nominal value, the shortfall was known as a discount. However, it is no longer permitted to issue shares at a discount.

**Share premium** (Chapter 5): Where a share is issued at a price above its par, or nominal value, the excess is known as a premium.

**Shares at no par value** (Chapter 5): Shares which do not have a fixed par, or nominal value.

**Sinking fund** (Chapter 6): An external fund set up to meet some future liability such as the redemption of loan notes. Cash is paid into the fund at regular intervals to accumulate with compound interest to the required future sum.

**Standard costing** (Chapter 42): A control technique that compares standard costs and standard revenues with actual costs and actual revenues in order to determine differences (variances) that may then be investigated.

**Standard costs** (Chapter 42): An estimate of what costs should be.

**Statement of financial position** (Chapter 13): A summary of the financial position of an entity at a point in time. (Previously known as 'balance sheet'.)

**Structured entity** (Chapter 26): An entity that has been designed so that voting or similar rights are not the dominant factor in deciding who controls the entity, such as when any voting rights relate to administrative tasks only and the relevant activities are directed by means of contractual arrangements.

**Subsidiary** (Chapter 16): An undertaking which is controlled by another undertaking or where that other undertaking exercises a dominating influence over it.

**Subsidiary company** (Chapter 16): The outdated term for what is now known as a 'subsidiary'.

**Sunk cost** (Chapter 47): A cost which has already occurred and cannot, therefore, be avoided whatever decision is taken. It should be ignored when taking a decision.

**Supply chain** (Chapter 49): Everything within the two end-points of the continuous sequence running from demand forecasting through to receipt of payment from customers.

**Supply chain management** (Chapter 49): The system of control over the information and/or item flows both within and outwith the organisation that make up the supply chain.

**Variance analysis** (Chapter 43): A means of assessing the difference between a predetermined cost/income and the actual cost/income.

**Variances** (Chapter 42): The differences between budget and actual.

**Work certified** (Chapter 3): The value of work in progress on a contract as certified by, for example, an architect or an engineer.

# Index

Glossary items appear in bold